The Marketing Book

The Marketing Book is everything you need to know, but were afraid to ask about marketing. Divided into 25 chapters, each written by an expert in their field, it's a crash course in marketing theory and practice. From planning, strategy and research through to getting the marketing mix right, branding, promotions and even marketing for small to medium-sized enterprises.

This classic reference from renowned professors, Michael Baker and Susan Hart, was designed for student use, especially for professionals taking their CIM qualifications. Nevertheless, it is also invaluable for practitioners due to its modular approach. Each chapter is set out in a clear and concise way with plenty of diagrams and examples, so that you don't have to dig for the information you need. Much of this long-awaited seventh edition contains brand new chapters, and a new selection of experts brings you bang up to date with the latest in marketing thought. Also included are brand new content in direct, data and digital marketing, and social marketing.

If you're a marketing student or practitioner with a question, this book should be the first place you look.

Michael J. Baker is Emeritus Professor of Marketing at the University of Strathclyde, UK. He founded the Department of Marketing in 1971.

Susan Hart will be Dean of Durham University Business School from July 2016; prior to this she was Dean and Associate Deputy Principal at the University of Strathclyde, UK.

'This is an essential starting point for any student wanting the most comprehensive survey of marketing theory and practice available today. You cannot beat it.'

Mark Tadajewski, *Durham University, UK*

'This is the go-to book of the marketing discipline – comprehensive, thought-provoking and utterly dependable. Its contribution reaches way beyond the business school. As a social marketer, I have worked for many years with colleagues in public health and often think how much they could learn from it. I have in mind not just the finer points of sustained behaviour change which marketers have mastered with such skill and which this text elucidates so well, but also the invaluable insights it provides into the methods of their competitors – what Margaret Chan, Director-General of WHO, calls "Big Tobacco, Big Food, Big Soda, and Big Alcohol" and whose powerful business interests, she reminds us, have to be combatted if public health is to prevail. *The Marketing Book* is the ideal user-manual for this vital work.'

Gerard Hastings, *The Institute for Social Marketing, University of Stirling, UK*

'Marketing has seen huge changes over the last 20 years with the opportunity from new digital media and technologies which have been enthusiastically adopted by consumers and businesses alike. Yet, the fundamentals of successful marketing remain the same and, for me, *The Marketing Book*, is the best single source to rapidly learn and return to for the core principles of applied marketing strategy from the leading specialists in the UK.'

Dave Chaffey, *Digital Marketing Strategist,*
Publisher of the digital marketing education site
www.SmartInsights.com and co-author of Emarketing Excellence:
Planning and Optimizing your Digital Marketing *(also by Routledge)*

The Marketing Book

Seventh edition

Edited by Michael J. Baker and Susan Hart

Routledge
Taylor & Francis Group

LONDON AND NEW YORK

First published 1987 by Butterworth-Heinemann, an imprint of Elsevier
This edition published 2016
by Routledge
2 Park Square, Milton Park, Abingdon, Oxon OX14 4RN

and by Routledge
711 Third Avenue, New York, NY 10017

Routledge is an imprint of the Taylor & Francis Group, an informa business

British Library Cataloguing in Publication Data
A catalogue record for this book is available from the British Library

Library of Congress Cataloging in Publication Data
Names: Baker, Michael John, editor. | Hart, Susan J., editor.
Title: The marketing book / edited by Michael J. Baker and Susan Hart.
Description: 7th edition. | Abingdon, Oxon ; New York, NY : Routledge, 2015. |
    Includes bibliographical references and index.
Identifiers: LCCN 2015039752 | ISBN 9780415703765 (hardback) |
    ISBN 9780415703772 (pbk.) | ISBN 9781315890005 (ebook)
Subjects: LCSH: Marketing.
Classification: LCC HF5415 .M297455 2015 | DDC 658.8—dc23
LC record available at http://lccn.loc.gov/2015039752

ISBN: 978-0-415-70376-5 (hbk)
ISBN: 978-0-415-70377-2 (pbk)
ISBN: 978-1-315-89000-5 (ebk)

Typeset in Bembo
by Swales & Willis Ltd, Exeter, Devon, UK
Printed and bound in Great Britain by
Ashford Colour Press Ltd, Gosport, Hampshire

MIX
Paper from
responsible sources
FSC® C011748
www.fsc.org

Contents

Figures

Tables

Contributors

Adrian Payne is a Professor of Marketing at the Australian School of Business at the University of New South Wales, Australia and Visiting Professor at Cranfield School of Management, Cranfield University in the UK. His main research interests are CRM, customer retention and relationship marketing. His publications have appeared in numerous journal including the *Journal of Marketing, Journal of the Academy of Marketing Science, Journal of Business Research, British Journal of Management, Industrial Marketing Management, Journal of International Business Studies, European Journal of Marketing, Long Range Planning* and *Human Relations and Marketing Theory*. He is the winner of the 2014 *Sheth Foundation/Journal of Marketing Award* for his joint article: 'A strategic framework for customer relationship management', an award recognising the best article published in the *Journal of Marketing* that has made long-term contributions to the field of marketing. He is the author or co-author of 15 books on marketing.

Adrian Sargeant is Professor of Fundraising at Plymouth University and Director of the Centre for Sustainable Philanthropy. He was formerly the first Hartsook Chair in Fundraising at the Lilly Family School of Philanthropy at Indiana University. He also holds visiting appointments at Avila University and the Australian Centre for Philanthropy and Nonprofit Studies, Queensland University of Technology. He has received many awards for his services to the profession, notably being named on the prestigious Nonprofit Times Power and Influence List in the United States in 2010. In the UK, he received a Civil Society Award for his outstanding contribution to fundraising.

He is a prolific author and educator. He has published over 10 books and around 150 peer reviewed academic publications in the domain of individual giving, fundraising and nonprofit marketing. Most recently, he has designed new qualification frameworks for fundraising professional bodies across the world. In the UK, for example, he designed the new Certificate/Diploma in Fundraising courses that are now offered by the Institute of Fundraising. He is doing similar work in the United States working with the Association of Fundraising Professions and has recently been commissioned to design a new higher-level qualification that will be shared internationally. The new Advanced Diploma in Fundraising will launch in the Spring of 2016.

Andrea Prothero is associate professor at University College Dublin, Ireland. Prior to moving to Ireland in 1999, Andy lectured at universities in Wales and Scotland and also spent a sabbatical period at Arizona State University in 2002. Her research broadly explores the area of marketing in society. Specific research projects have focused on, for example, advertising to children, motherhood and consumption, sustainability marketing and sustainable consumption. She has published widely in these areas. Andy currently serves as Associate Editor for the *Journal of Macromarketing* and the *Journal of Marketing Management*.

David F. Birks, BA, MSc (Management), MSc (Statistics), PhD. David is Professor of Marketing at the University of Winchester. He is Dean of the Faculty of Business, Law and Sport and Director of Winchester Business School. Prior to working at Winchester, David worked at the Universities of Southampton, Bath and Strathclyde. He has over 30 years experience in universities, primarily working on postgraduate research, marketing, management and design programmes. David is co-author of Europe's leading marketing research text: Malhotra, N. K., Birks, D. F. and Wills, P. *Marketing Research, An Applied Orientation*, fourth European edition, Pearson, 2012. David has continued to practise marketing research throughout his university career, managing projects in financial institutions, retailers, local authorities and charities.

David Smith, Senior Director, Simon-Kucher & Partners. Since joining Simon-Kucher & Partners in 2007, David has worked for both the London and San Francisco offices, and has conducted projects across the UK, Europe and the USA. David is a regular conference speaker and active blogger on pricing topics. He has a wide range of experience in marketing, strategy, sales and pricing, having worked with clients in various sectors both B2B and B2C. Prior to joining Simon-Kucher & Partners, David studied economics at the University of Warwick.

Francesca Dall'Olmo Riley is Professor of Brand Management at Kingston University Business School, UK. She has published her branding research in international journals, including the *Journal of Business Research*, the *International Journal of Research in Marketing*, the *Journal of Advertising Research* and the *Journal of Marketing Management*. Francesca is Associate Editor of the *Journal of Marketing Management* and sits on the Advisory Board of the *Journal of Customer Behaviour* and on the Editorial Review Board of the *Journal of Product & Brand Management*. She chairs the Academy of Marketing Special Interest Group in empirical replications and generalisations in marketing science. Prior to academia, Francesca worked in marketing management and direct marketing for several years in Italy, the USA and the UK.

Gill Hogg is Pro Vice Chancellor (External Relations) at Heriot-Watt University. She joined Heriot-Watt from Strathclyde Business School where she was Head of the Department of Marketing, and before taking up the PVC role, was Head of School of Management and Languages at Heriot-Watt from 2007–2013. Her research interests are in consumer behaviour, particularly in relation to services and work-life balance issues. Current responsibilities include coordinating the work of Heriot-Watt's campuses including Orkney, Dubai and Malaysia; embedding the Athena Swan Charter throughout the University and leading the establishment of the Scottish Confucius Institute for Business and Communication.

Ian MacQuillin is the founder and director of Rogare, the fundraising think tank at Plymouth University's Centre for Sustainable Philanthropy, where he is currently leading on a project to develop a new theory of fundraising ethics. He is a lecturer in fundraising and marketing, and is researching the fundamental drivers of stakeholder objections to fundraising for his doctoral study. He also edits the Critical Fundraising blog.

Jim Hamill has over 35 years International Management experience, Jim is widely recognised as a leading expert on international business/marketing, digital disruption, social media and digital business strategy. He has successfully delivered on a broad range of consultancy assignments around the world, with clients ranging from SMEs to multinational organisations such as the World Bank, United Nations Centre on Transnational Corporations, Economist Intelligence Unit, International Labor Office, Russian Foundation for SME Development, Malta Tourism Authority, the European

Union, Scottish Enterprise, Visit Scotland, National Trust, Glasgow City Council, First Group and many others.

Jim has held Visiting Professorships or delivered Senior Executive Programmes in the US, Singapore, Hong-Kong, Malaysia, China, Norway, Italy, Lithuania, Latvia, France, Iceland, Malta, Russia, the UAE and Oman. Author of several books and numerous papers, he is Owner and Director of Energise 2-0, a leading digital business and social media consultancy, based in Glasgow but operating globally. He is also Director of Future Digital Leaders, creating business leaders 'fit for purpose' in an era characterised by turbulent digital change and digital Darwinism. With 4,500 Twitter followers and blog page views exceeding 10,000 per month, Jim is internationally recognised as a leader in his field. He has received over 300 LinkedIn endorsements for his work in business strategy, marketing, digital business and social media.

In 2010, Jim was voted the 'Most Innovative Lecturer of the Year' by students at the University of Strathclyde for successfully redesigning the student learning experience around the use of social technologies. He is passionate about the role new technology can play in enhancing learning. When not working (which is very seldom), Jim's main hobbies are spending time with his grandson Liam, music and football (watching, no longer playing ☺).

Kate L. Daunt, PhD, is a Senior Lecturer in Marketing and Strategy at Cardiff University and is the Deputy Director of Cardiff Business School's PhD Programme. Kate is an Associate Editor at the *Journal of Services Marketing* and serves as an editorial board member at the *Journal of Service Research* and *Journal of Business Research*. Kate's main research interests include misbehaviour during service, service failure, strategy implementation and servicescape design. Kate's work has been published in multiple peer-reviewed journals including the *Journal of Service Research*, *Journal of Retailing*, *European Journal of Marketing*, *Journal of Business Research*, *Journal of Services Marketing* and *Journal of Marketing Management*.

Ken Peattie is Professor of Marketing and Strategy at Cardiff Business School and for over 11 years was also Director of the ESRC funded BRASS Research Centre, which specialised in research into business sustainability and corporate social responsibility. He is currently Co-Director of Cardiff University's Sustainable Places Research Institute. His research interests focus on the impact of sustainability concerns on marketing and corporate strategy making; social marketing for sustainable lifestyles and social enterprise. He has published three books and numerous book chapters and journal papers on these topics including contributions to *California Management Review, Journal of Business Research, Journal of Marketing Management,* and Public Policy and Marketing. His most recent book, co-authored with Professor Frank-Martin Belz, entitled Sustainability Marketing: A Global Perspective, won the 2011 German Academic Association for Business Research 'Business Book of the Year' award.

Leigh Sparks is Professor of Retail Studies and Head of the Stirling Graduate School at the University of Stirling. He was a geography undergraduate at the University of Cambridge and completed his PhD (on retail employment) at the University of Wales. The Institute for Retail Studies at the University of Stirling was established in 1983 and is acknowledged as one of the world's leading research and educational centres into retail studies. It provides undergraduate, postgraduate and management development programmes as well as undertaking academic and applied research for a range of client bodies, including governments, research agencies and private companies. Leigh has been professor at Stirling since 1992. Leigh was a Visiting Professor at Florida State University, Tallahassee from July 2000 to July 2001 and Visiting Professor at the

University of Tennessee, Knoxville from June to December 2006. He is Editor of the leading European retail journal *The International Review of Retail, Distribution and Consumer Research* and on the editorial boards of a number of other major marketing and management journals. He is well known for his research into aspects of retailing. This is undertaken for personal curiosity, on behalf of public and private clients and for the research councils and other funding bodies, as well as for major retailers. He has authored and edited a number of books, has published over 125 refereed journal articles as well as many practitioner, trade and newspaper pieces and runs a Scottish retailing blog (www.stirlingretail.com). In 2002–2004, he was the only academic member of the UK Department of Trade and Industry's Retail Strategy Group. Leigh is Chair of the Scotland's Towns Partnership, a board member and director of IDS Scotland Ltd, the company set up by Scottish Government to oversee Scottish Business Improvement Districts (2009 to date), and of the Centre for Scottish Public Policy (2012 to date). Leigh was a member of the External Advisory Group on the Scottish Government's Town Centre Review (2012–2013) and on the Expert Advisory Group advising the Scottish Government on the lessons to be learned from the Horsemeat Scandal (2013).

Len Tiu Wright is Professor of Marketing and heads the research group in Marketing, Branding and Innovation (GAMBI: http://www.hud.ac.uk/gambi) at the University of Huddersfield, UK. She was formerly Research Professor and Professor of Marketing at De Montfort University, Leicester and Visiting Professor at the University of Keele. Her full-time appointments include those at the universities of Keele, Birmingham and Loughborough. She has given guest lectures at universities and professional bodies in the UK and overseas as well as keynote addresses at conferences. Additionally, she has consultancy and industrial experience and has researched in the Far East, Europe and North America. Her writings have appeared in books, in American and European academic journals and at major conferences where some have gained best paper awards. She has organised workshops and conferences at universities and at IBM in Warwick, UK. She is on the editorial boards of a number of marketing journals, has carried out reviews of papers and special issues for leading marketing journals and is Founding Editor of *Qualitative Market Research*, an Emerald journal. She is currently Editor-in-Chief of *CogentOA Business & Management* series.

Lisa O'Malley is Head of Department of Management & Marketing at the Kemmy Business School, University of Limerick. She is interested in marketing theory and has been involved in teaching and research in the area for more than 20 years. Lisa has published widely on marketing and consumption and her work has appeared in *Marketing Theory, Journal of Marketing Management, Journal of Macromarketing, Consumption, Markets & Culture, Industrial Marketing Management, Journal of Business Research, European Journal of Marketing* and the *Service Industries Journal*.

Lloyd C. Harris is the Head of the Marketing Department and Professor of Marketing at Birmingham Business School, Birmingham University. After working in retail and service organisations, he received his PhD in marketing from Cardiff University and his DSc from Warwick University. His research results have been disseminated via a range of marketing, strategy, H.R.M. and general management journals. He has published widely in these fields and has published over 100 pieces. He is particularly proud of papers that have been published in the *Journal of Retailing, Journal of the Academy of Marketing Science, Journal of Management Studies, Human Resource Management, Organization Studies* and the *Annuls of Tourism Research*. He has consulted and run programmes for many leading private and public organisations, especially focusing on retailing and service organisations.

Lyndon Simkin is Executive Director of the Centre of Business in Society at Coventry University, before which he was Professor of Strategic Marketing at Henley Business School, University of Reading. Lyndon is Associate Editor of the *Journal of Marketing Management*, a member of the Academy of Marketing's Research Committee, and co-chair for the Academy's special interest groups in CRM and market segmentation/marketing strategy. He has published widely in most marketing journals and authored many books, including *The Dark Side of CRM*; *Marketing: Concepts and Strategies*; *Marketing Planning* and *Market Segmentation Success*, with an emphasis on B2B marketing strategy. Lyndon is a consultant to a diverse selection of organisations and a coach to several CEOs and leadership teams.

Malcolm McDonald, MA(Oxon), MSc, PhD, DLitt, DSc. Malcolm is an Emeritus Professor at Cranfield and a Visiting Professor at Henley, Warwick, Aston and Bradford Business Schools. Until 2003, Malcolm was Professor of Marketing and Deputy Director of Cranfield University School of Management, with special responsibility for e-Business. He is a graduate in English Language and Literature from Oxford University, in Business Studies from Bradford University Management Centre, and has a PhD from Cranfield University. He also has a Doctorate from Bradford University and from the Plekhanov University of Economics in Moscow. He has extensive industrial experience, including a number of years as Marketing and Sales Director of Canada Dry. Until the end of 2012, he spent seven years as Chairman of Brand Finance plc.

He spends much of his time working with the operating boards of the world's biggest multinational companies, such as IBM, Xerox, BP and the like, in most countries in the world, including Japan, USA, Europe, South America, ASEAN and Australasia.

He has written 46 books, including the best seller *Marketing Plans; How to Prepare Them; How to Use Them*, which has sold over half a million copies worldwide. Hundreds of his papers have been published. Apart from market segmentation, his current interests centre around the measurement of the financial impact of marketing expenditure and global best practice key account management. In 2006 he was listed in the UK's Top Ten Business Consultants by *The Times*.

Maria Lichrou is a lecturer in marketing at the Kemmy Business School, University of Limerick, where she teaches marketing theory to postgraduate students. As part of the course, she regularly engages in stimulating and – often – challenging conversations about the role of theory in marketing with students and colleagues. These have largely inspired her perspective on marketing theory. Her research interests centre on the marketing and consumption of place, drawing on the perspectives of critical marketing and consumer culture. Her research has examined the role of lived experiences, cultural meanings and myth-making in the branding of places, and the role of stakeholder narratives in inclusive place marketing. Her work has been published in the *Journal of Strategic Marketing*, the *Journal of Marketing Management*, *Place Branding and Public Diplomacy* and *Tourism and Hospitality Planning & Development*.

Mark Billige is Managing Partner of the UK practice of Simon-Kucher & Partners, having been with the firm since 2006. He is a chartered management accountant (ACMA) and has a BA (Hons) in Management from the University of Nottingham. Mark has 15 years' experience in the field of pricing and financial management, specialising in the development of marketing and pricing growth strategies, discount optimisation, sales force management and negotiation strategy. He is a regular speaker and chairman at conferences and business schools as well as a contributor on national broadcast media on the subject of pricing strategy. Mark's focus is primarily on network businesses and B2B services, and he also consults and advises for numerous private equity firms across their portfolio businesses.

Mark Gabbott graduated from the University of Essex with a BA(Hons) in Economics followed by an MSc in Technology Management from Imperial College, University of London. After working in government for six years in consumer policy and protection, he completed a PhD in Marketing and was Lecturer and then Senior Lecturer at the University of Stirling, researching and teaching in the areas of electronic and direct marketing, services marketing, consumer behaviour and consumer policy. Mark joined Monash University in 1997 as Professor of Marketing and became Head of Department and subsequently Deputy Dean of the Faculty of Business and Economics at Monash in 2006. In 2008, Mark was appointed Executive Dean of the Faculty of Business and Economics at Macquarie University, Sydney.

Mark's current research interests are in services marketing, customer relationship management, internet marketing, consumer behaviour and customer value. Mark has published 4 books and over 50 book chapters and journal articles. His research has been published in a variety of international academic journals including the *Journal of Services Research*, *Journal of Public Policy and Marketing*, *European Journal of Marketing* and the *Journal of Marketing Management*. Mark currently sits on the editorial boards of three international marketing journals.

He is a member of the European Marketing Academy, The UK Academy of Marketing, is past Chair of the American Marketing Association Services Interest Group, and is past President and Fellow of the Australian New Zealand Marketing Academy.

Michael J. Baker is Emeritus Professor of Marketing at the University of Strathclyde where he founded the Department of Marketing in 1971. He is the author/editor of more than 50 books including *Marketing Strategy and Management* (Palgrave, fifth edition, 2014) and *Marketing Theory* with Michael Saren (Sage, third edition, 2016).

Pennie Frow is Associate Professor of Marketing and Director of the Master of Marketing Program at the University of Sydney Business School, Australia. Before joining academia, she was Chief Marketing Officer of the largest conservation charity in Europe. Her main research interests are managing customer relationships, customer retention, co-creation and developing a customer-oriented culture. Her publications have appeared in many journals including the *Journal of Marketing*, *Journal of the Academy of Marketing Science*, *Industrial Marketing Management*, *Journal of Business Research* and *Journal of Marketing Management*. She is also co-author of two books: *Strategic Customer Management*, Cambridge University Press, 2013 and *Marketing Plans for Services*, Wiley, 2011 and many case studies. She is the winner of the 2014 Sheth Foundation/Journal of Marketing Award for her joint article: 'A strategic framework for customer relationship management', an award recognising the best article published in the *Journal of Marketing* that has made long-term contributions to the field of marketing.

Rachel Ashman is a lecturer in Marketing and early career researcher at the University of Liverpool, UK. She holds a BSc (Hons) in Fashion and Textile Retailing, and a PhD in Digital Consumption from the University of Manchester, UK. Her research interests include fashion retailing, digital marketing and cultural aspects of consumption, which have resulted in journal publications and awards for teaching. And, although she does not like to brag, she is also a fabulous baker, a culinary genius, an inspirational yoga teacher, a quiltmaking machine, a website designer and a proud vegan.

Rebekah Russell-Bennett is a Professor of Marketing at the QUT Business School, Queensland University of Technology, Australia and has extensive experience in the use of games/mobile technology and services marketing to facilitate behaviour change. Rebekah has collaborated with Brisbane City Council on a AUD6.5m digital social marketing program to change energy use in low-income earners, Queensland Catholic Education Commission to develop the GO:KA social marketing alcohol schools program, the Australian Red Cross Blood Service to identify key service factors that create barriers to redonation, the Australian Breastfeeding Association to develop MumBubConnect (world's first two-way automated SMS support service) and Queensland Health in improving the service experience for cancer screening. Rebekah is also the immediate past-President of the Australian Association for Social Marketing. Rebekah holds a PhD in Services Marketing, has over 150 peer-reviewed publications and is the co-editor of the *Journal of Services Marketing*.

Robin Wensley is Emeritus Professor of Policy and Marketing at Warwick University and Professor of Strategic Marketing at the Open University. He was Director the ESRC/EPSRC funded AIM Research initiative from 2004 to 2011 and Deputy Dean at Warwick Business School from 2000 to 2004. He was Chair of the School from 1989 to 1994 and Chair of the Faculty of Social Studies from 1997 to 1999. He was previously with RHM Foods, Tube Investments and London Business School, and was Visiting Professor twice at UCLA and once at the University of Florida. He was a Council member of the ESRC from 2000 to 2003, having been a member of the Research Grants Board from 1991 to 1995. He was also Chair of the Council of the Tavistock Institute of Human Relations from 1998 to 2003. His research interests include the long-term evolution of competitive markets and structures, the process of strategic decision making, the nature of sustainable advantages and issues of choice in public policy, and he has published a number of books, most recently *Effective Management in Practice: Analytical Insights and Critical Questions*, and articles in the *Harvard Business Review*, the *Journal of Marketing* and the *Strategic Management Journal* and has worked closely with other academics both in Europe and the USA. He was joint editor of the *Journal of Management Studies* from 1998 to 2002. In 2012, he was recipient of the British Academy of Management's Richard Whipp Lifetime Achievement Award and he has twice won the annual Alpha Kappa Psi Award for the most influential article in the US *Journal of Marketing*, as well as the *Journal of Marketing Management* Millennium Article award.

Rose Wright, BSc (Hons), MCOptom, is a member of a Research and Development Team at Sandwell and West Birmingham NHS Trust. She participates in the recruitment, data collection and analysis of a diverse range of commercial and clinical studies. Her spectrum of work is mainly centred around those with disabilities, particularly sight impairment. She is the owner of Vision Rose Ltd, a social enterprise funded by a small grant from the European Union intended to revolutionise care for those with low vision needs and to create innovative solutions to overcome visual challenges.

Spiros Gounaris has been a member of staff in the Department of Marketing of the University of Strathclyde since 2012. Before 2012, he was Associate Professor of Marketing in the Department of Marketing & Communication at the Athens University of Economics & Business since 1997, when he started his academic career.

His research interests pivot around the marketing of services, internal marketing, tourism marketing, sales management and key account management, retail marketing, pricing, relationship marketing and market orientation development.

He has been a Member of the European Marketing Academy since 1993, a Founding Member of the Greek Marketing Academy, member of the European Marketing Confederation Academic Board, while seating on the editorial board of the *Industrial Marketing Management Journal* and the *Journal of Service Research*.

His work has appeared in various prestigious international journals including *Industrial Marketing Management*, *Journal of Business Research*, *European Journal of Marketing*, *Journal of Business and Industrial Marketing*, *Journal of Services Marketing* and *Journal of Product Innovation Management*. He has received the Highest Quality Rating Award from ANBAR and best paper award from the *Journal of Business and Industrial Marketing*. He has also published two books in Greek, *Services Marketing*, the third edition of which has only recently been released, and *Key Account Management*. He is also actively involved in delivering consulting and tailor-made executive training programmes, having worked with both multinationals (including Iberdrola Group, Silver & Barite, Rilken, Dell Computers, Roche, Body Shop (GR), Vodafone (GR), Habitat (GR), Toyota (GR), Credi Com and many more) and leading Greek companies (including, among others, Intertrust Insurance, Hellenic Organization of Telecommunications, EFG Eurobank, Commercial Bank of Greece, Cyprus Telecommunication Authority, ALCON) from various sectors, sharing his knowledge and expertise in the fields of customer service, key account management, marketing research, strategic marketing, B2B marketing, negotiations and marketing leadership. As principal investigator he has also completed a number of projects including Understanding End-Users Behavior in the Cement Industry (Italcementi Group), Decoding Demand for Traditional Products and Artifacts, (the Cyclades Organization for Economic Development), Employee Satisfaction and Company Performance in the Hotel Industry, (the Municipality of Rhodes) and Decoding and Use of CRM systems by Greek B2B Manufacturers (Entersoft S.A.).

Stephen Brown is Professor of Marketing Research at Ulster University, Northern Ireland. He has written widely. He has written lots of other words as well, but none so deep as widely.

Steve Baron is Professor of Marketing at the University of Liverpool Management School. He is an Honorary Fellow of the Academy of Marketing and co-editor of the *Journal of Services Marketing*. He is co-author of textbooks on services marketing and relationship marketing and has published research in several journals, including *Journal of Service Research*, *Industrial Marketing Management*, *European Journal of Marketing* and *Journal of Business Research*.

Susan Hart From July 2016 Susan Hart is Dean of Durham University Business School, prior to which she was Dean and Associate Deputy Principal at the University of Strathclyde Business School and Executive Lead for Internationalisation across the University. She led the Business School's development of nine international centres and established the internationalisation strategy for the University, including its strategic partnerships, internationalisation of curricula, student experience, recruitment and alumni development. Prior to these executive appointments, she was Professor of Marketing and Head of Department at Strathclyde (2002–2004) and Vice Dean for Research. Previous posts held were Professor of Marketing and Head of Department at the University of Stirling from 1995–1998, and Professor of Marketing at Heriot Watt University from 1993–1995. In addition, Susan has worked for a variety of private sector companies, ranging from multinational to small manufacturers in consumer and industrial enterprises. Professor Hart is an elected Fellow of the Royal Society of Edinburgh, a Fellow of the Chartered Institute of Marketing, a Fellow of the Leadership Trust and an elected member of the International Board of Directors of AACSB, Executive Committee and Committee on Issues in Management Education; European Advisory Committee; EFMD Awarding Body and is an Accreditation Panel member for AACSB and EQUIS. She served as a Director of the RSNO between 2006 and 2012 and is currently a Board member of Yorkhill Children's Charity.

Professor Hart's research areas of interest include innovation and product-service development, marketing and competitive success, and marketing performance measurement. She has been awarded research grants by The Leverhulme Trust, Economic and Social Research Council, Science and Engineering Research Council, Design Council Scotland and the Chartered Institute of Management Accountants, Scottish Enterprise.

Journal articles have appeared in the *Journal of Product Innovation Management* and *Industrial Marketing Management* and two recent books include *Product Strategy and Management* and *The Marketing Book*. Professor Susan Hart was Editor of the *Journal of Marketing Management* for ten years (2001–2011).

Toni Hilton is Professor of Marketing and Dean of the Glasgow School for Business and Society. She has worked in higher education for over two decades and has held senior academic management positions at universities in New Zealand as well as in the UK. Toni read law at university and pursued a career in sales and marketing before joining academia. Toni now specialises in services marketing and the management of service, with a particular interest in the marketing of professional services and not-for-profit marketing. She has published in the *Journal of Marketing Management, Marketing Theory, Journal of Services Marketing, Journal of Customer Behaviour*, the *International Journal of the Legal Profession* and *Non-profit and Voluntary Sector Quarterly*. Toni also maintains an active interest in the development of the marketing curriculum and is a co-author of *Services Marketing: Text and Cases*.

Part I

Organisation and planning

1 What is marketing?

Michael J. Baker

The enigma of marketing is that it is one of mankind's oldest practices, but the most recent of the business disciplines.
(Baker 1976)

Marketing is also an enigma in the sense that while some people see it as a force for good, others see it as a force for evil. As with most things, the reality is that it may be either or both depending upon the uses to which people put marketing ideas and practices.

There are many misconceptions about marketing so we will only deal with 4, which we have encountered most frequently in more than 50 years' experience as both practitioner and academic. These misconceptions are:

1 marketing is a modern or 'new' approach to business;
2 that it is essentially a functional activity;
3 that it is concerned principally with advertising and high-pressure selling;
4 and that this is largely irrelevant.

The first misconception is that marketing first developed in the US in the early to mid-twentieth century. A useful benchmark for judging whether a subject or practice is of sufficient substance to justify formal study is to establish when it first began to be taught in leading universities. Using this criterion, we know that the first chair of marketing was established at the Wharton Business School in the 1880s and, by the turn of the century, the subject was being offered in most leading American universities. However, the subject taught then was very different from the modern marketing concept, which began to emerge in the aftermath of the Second World War and is the foundation of what is known today as the marketing management school of thought.

So marketing is a relatively new academic discipline with strong roots in America. The problem is that, as a **practice**, marketing has existed since time immemorial and so is very old indeed. As we shall see, it would not be extravagant to claim that modern civilisation owes its origins to the discovery that task specialisation and exchange (marketing) increases productivity and enhances both the standard of living and the quality of life. History also suggests that successful entrepreneurs and businesses have always understood the principles of effective marketing even if they did not describe their practices in quite the same language as we use today.

Prior to the industrial revolution, buyers and sellers enjoyed close contact with one another with the result that sellers often knew precisely what their individual customers wanted and did their best to satisfy them. Industrialisation and the development of the factory system were to change all that as they created both a physical and psychological distance between the producer and the consumer. As a result, it became necessary to develop new techniques to track the precise nature of consumer demand, to let consumers know about the availability of goods and services and to ensure the widest possible distribution to reach as many potential customers as possible. Early industrialists, like Josiah Wedgwood, were extremely successful at this and pioneered many techniques in the eighteenth century, such as market segmentation, branding, celebrity advertising, sales promotion, etc. long before any business schools came into existence. And so, the reality is that marketing is the oldest of the business practices, but among the newest, if not the newest, of the business disciplines.

The question as to whether marketing is a philosophy or function, frequently expressed in terms of statements along the lines, 'Marketing is a concept or way of thinking about the way organisations should interact with their customers', compared with the bald statement, 'Marketing is a practice', has already been partially answered a moment ago when it was claimed that marketing is probably the oldest of business practices but among the newest, if not the newest, of the business disciplines.

As taught in business schools, marketing is presented as a body of knowledge derived from observation of experience and theorisation about cause and effect in commercial exchange processes. Persons familiar with this body of knowledge should then be able to diagnose the interaction between sellers and buyers in the market place and propose future strategies for enhancing and improving these interactions by means of strategic marketing planning. Clearly, the emphasis is very much upon theory as a basis for successful practice.

However, many practitioners dismiss the relevance of theory and argue that marketing is a skill acquired through practice. And, in support of this view, there is plenty of evidence that academic research into marketing has very little direct impact upon successful practice.

But just as marketing is both old and new, so it is also about learning from experience, as well as capturing the nature of that experience, and careful research and analysis in order to better inform future decision-making. Where the mismatch occurs, if it does, is that theorising results in what at the Harvard Business School we used to call *currently useful generalisations*. But these can rarely provide precise answers to explicit questions of the kind that practising marketing managers are grappling with. It is because marketing problems are usually highly specific in an often unique context that useful generalisation cannot provide an exact answer. On the other hand, as we shall see, theories very often provide an analytical framework with which we can diagnose our problem, so that we can then draw on our practical knowledge and experience to solve it.

The third and fourth misconceptions are closely related. Many regard marketing as an unnecessary extra or 'trapping', which is really irrelevant as conveyed by the opinion that, 'Organisations got on fine before anyone mentioned marketing'.

Such misunderstanding about marketing is because, like an iceberg, the most visible part represents only a very small proportion of the total marketing effort. Information about products for sale is everywhere – on display in retail outlets, through advertising on television and radio, in print and in posters and, increasingly, in social media. But, as research shows, it is only when we experience an unfilled need or want that we catch sight of the tip of the iceberg and become aware of sellers who claim to have the answer to our need. To be in that happy position they will have to have identified a marketing opportunity and designed a product or service to satisfy it. They will then have to have acquired the plant, equipment, labour, supplies and all the other resources required to create a product and, apart from things that are made to order, they will then have to make and stock the product before letting it be known that it is available for sale – the tip of the iceberg! This is illustrated in Figure 1.1.

Figure 1.1 The marketing iceberg

The reality is summarised in the quotation, 'Marketing is essential to the long-term success of the organisation', which is from Peter Drucker (1954), probably the most influential of all the management gurus, which is making the point that if you don't get the product right, then all the costs that you have incurred would have been wasted and no amount of advertising and promotion will be able to put that right. Yes, advertising and promotion are important, but never as influential as some people make them out to be. It is much easier and cheaper to change a product than to change people's minds about it.

It is beyond doubt that modern civilisation owes its existence to the practice of marketing. Even in the subsistence economies of prehistory, when life was 'nasty, brutish and short', marketing offered a better standard of living than could be achieved through attempts at self-sufficiency. Long before the discovery of agriculture, or the domestication of animals, gender encouraged role specialisation with males responsible for hunting and security, and females for gathering and child rearing. However, the real breakthrough in human development occurred when specialisation extended to the performance of the many tasks necessary for survival. The benefit of task specialisation is that it increases output or productivity, so there is more of everything to go around. But, for this to happen, the specialist must be able to exchange what they have to offer for goods and services provided by others. The gains from task specialisation will soon be dissipated if we have to spend a lot of time trying to make contact with persons who have a coincidence of wants – we each have something the other needs, so we can negotiate an exchange. Obviously, we need a central place where anyone with something to exchange can meet up with other like-minded individuals, and this place is the market.

Over time, increased specialisation encouraged permanent settlement in locations with natural advantages and trade between them. To manage this trade, the medium of exchange (money) had to be created, as had writing and accounting to keep a record of stocks and transactions. This occurred in Phoenicia around 4000 BC. In time, the search for greater variety and choice

prompted trade between nations, exploration and wars. However, the great breakthrough in economic growth came in the eighteenth century with the Industrial Revolution in Great Britain.

The origins of 'modern' marketing

The Industrial Revolution, which gave birth to modern society and the practice of marketing as
we know it today, was the consequence of three major developments:

1   the application of science and technology to production and distribution;
2   the division of labour;
3   entrepreneurial management.

The division of labour was described eloquently by Adam Smith in his *Wealth of Nations* (1970
[1776]). Smith's description of the development of a primitive production line for the manufacture
of pins identified at least ten different tasks:

> One man draws out the wire, another straightens it, a third cuts it, a fourth points it, a fifth
> grinds it at the top for receiving the head; the head requires two or three distinct operations;
> to put it on is a peculiar business; to whiten the pins is another; it is even a trade by itself to
> put them into the paper.

Two points are of particular significance in this step forward. First, organisation is required to bring
together the men, provide a workplace and source raw materials. Second, the enormous increase
in output reduces the price of the product, necessitates the development of channels of distribution
to make it available to those with a demand for it, and leads to the exploitation of a much larger
market. It also means that the 'factory' tends to produce standardised products and no longer makes
to the order of individual customers.

While international trade has also existed since time immemorial, the development of manufacturing industry greatly accelerated its growth. Mass production demanded ever-increasing quantities
of raw materials, and overseas colonies and plantations were soon established in less-developed
countries to supply these. In turn, employment generated income and income transformed a latent
demand for manufactured goods into expanding export markets.

To begin with, manufacturing was concentrated in Europe and North America, where there
was a skilled workforce and the necessary infrastructure to support it, with the rest of the world
concentrating on mineral extraction and the supply of raw materials for conversion into manufactured goods. This distinction between advanced industrialised economies and the less-developed
primary producers was to continue well into the twentieth century and accounts for what has
become known as the 'three eras' conceptualisation.

Robert Keith (1960) first proposed the idea of three eras in the evolution of the marketing
concept based on his analysis of the evolution of the Pillsbury Company in the US. Pillsbury was,
and is, a manufacturer of bakery products, a category of which are generically termed 'fast moving
consumer goods' or FMCG. In the mid-nineteenth century its emphasis was on increasing supply
and reducing costs, which are the primary characteristics of a **production orientation**. As new
companies entered the market and competition intensified, more emphasis was given to selling
differentiated products, but this differentiation was based on what the firm could make using its
existing technology and assets. So, the distinguishing features of the **sales orientation** is, 'selling
what we can make'.

As a result of rapid economic growth, the potential for excess supply developed and it became clear that selling *harder* needed to be replaced by selling *smarter*. Selling smarter means that, before committing yourself to the sale of a new product in the hope of maintaining competitiveness, you need first to establish what it is the customer wants. In the days of craft industry, this was relatively simple – the potential customer discusses their wants with you, and you produce what they specified. But, with industrialisation and the concentration of production in factories, this contact was broken. So long as demand exceeds supply, customers cannot afford to be too choosy and have to buy what is available. However, as variety and choice increase, customers will prefer those sellers whose offering most closely matches their needs – usually those who are closest to the customer – and others will go out of business for lack of custom. In order to restore and maintain competitiveness, a new strategy is called for, which is based on determining what the customer wants and then *making what we can sell*. It is this that we call a **marketing orientation**.

It is generally agreed that the need for a new marketing orientation occurred in the 1950s, and the first person to describe and analyse this was Harvard Business School professor, Ted Levitt. In an article called 'Marketing myopia', published in the *Harvard Business Review* in 1960, Levitt opened by stating, 'Every major industry was once a growth industry', but he then went on to point out that many such industries were in a state of stagnation or decline. The reason for this stagnation, he claims, was due to, 'a failure of management'.

Simply put, Levitt's thesis is that new industries come into existence, because innovators and entrepreneurs discover new and better ways of meeting people's needs. As this becomes known, customers gradually switch their allegiance from the old to the new, and the old industry declines while a new one grows to take its place. Thus, like biological organisms, every product and every industry has a life cycle. In my view, this insight is both an original and powerful idea, the appreciation of which is vital to the avoidance of failures of management due to myopia.

As to what causes myopia, Levitt's diagnosis was that it was largely due to the fact that management was focused on the product it sold to the neglect of the customers to whom it was selling. To illustrate his point, Levitt enquired why the American railroad system was on the verge of collapse in the 1950s when in 1900 its stock was considered the bluest of blue-chip investments on the American stock exchange. His answer was that those responsible for the railroad business had failed to address the most basic question of all, 'What business are we in?' If the answer is that we are in the railroad business, then this will remain our focus and all our efforts will be concentrated on making railroads better. But, if we define the business we are in in terms of the basic need that we serve, then the answer would be, 'We are in the transportation business' and, if we see this as our mission, then we will constantly seek new and better ways of providing transportation. In 1900 the internal combustion engine was at a very early stage of development and not considered to be any threat to the railroads. In reality, the horseless carriage was a much better solution to local transportation needs that were not served by trains running between fixed points. Over time, cars and lorries replaced horse-drawn vehicles and encouraged the development of a road network. It is interesting to speculate what would have happened if those responsible for running the railroads had welcomed the development of cars and lorries and incorporated them into an integrated transportation system, rather than ignoring them and later discovering that they were their main competitors! A marketing orientation would have avoided this failure.

Defining marketing

It has been said that there are as many definitions of marketing as there are people willing to make one! For our purposes, we will have to be content with only a small selection that reflect some of the key ideas that define marketing and the way that these have changed over time.

There's probably no better place to start than with Peter Drucker, who is widely recognised as one of the most influential management thinkers. In 1954 he wrote:

> Marketing is not only much broader than selling, it is not a specialised activity at all. It encompasses the entire business. It is the whole business seen from the point of view of its final result, that is, from the customer's point of view. Concern and responsibility for marketing must therefore permeate all areas of the enterprise . . . Marketing is the distinguishing, the unique function of the business.

In 1972 Philip Kotler, author of the world's bestselling marketing textbook and generally regarded as the father of the marketing management school of thought, observed, 'Marketing is the set of human activities directed at facilitating and consummating exchanges'.

In 1976, as one of the first professors of marketing in the UK, I proposed the definition, which I still believe captures the essential essence of marketing in the most economic way, namely, 'Marketing is concerned with the creation and maintenance of mutually satisfying exchange relationships'. In 1983 Ted Levitt also suggested a succinct definition when he said, 'The purpose of the business is to create and keep a customer'.

The latter two definitions both anticipate the most recent attempt to capture the role and nature of marketing, as proposed by American academics, Vargo and Lusch, in what they call a new 'service-dominant logic' in which they argue that value is created through interaction between buyer and seller, i.e. co-created, and consists of a combination of both physical (product) attributes and service activities.

Finally, the definitions proposed by the two major professional marketing bodies are as follows:

> Marketing is the activity, set of institutions, and processes for creating, communicating, delivering, and exchanging offerings that have value for customers, clients, partners, and society at large.
>
> (Approved October 2007 AMA Board of Directors)

> Marketing is the management process responsible for identifying, anticipating and satisfying customer requirements profitably.
>
> (Chartered Institute of Marketing)

Based upon an analysis of more than 50 definitions of marketing in the 1970s, Keith Crosier (1975) suggested that they could all be accommodated within one of three approaches.

The view of marketing as a **process** dominated thinking in the late nineteenth century through to about 1930. It was strongly associated with the land grant universities in the USA, with a concern for the selling and distribution of primary agricultural products, along with the new business schools, mainly endowed by wealthy industrialists who had a strong interest in industrial products, and what we now call business-to-business marketing or B2B. Individual consumers were of limited interest, and economic concepts of competition and market forces commanded most attention.

As we have seen, the production era reflected a situation when the nature of basic demand was fairly obvious, and the challenge was to create a supply to satisfy this. As supply began to catch up with basic demand, producers had to sell more aggressively, and we moved into the sales era with an emphasis upon demand stimulation through advertising and personal selling. However, this only provided temporary relief as firms came to realise that they needed a much better understanding of the final consumer's needs if they were to succeed in an increasingly competitive marketplace.

Therefore, the marketing era was born as the theory of perfect or monopolistic competition began to give way to the theory of imperfect competition. Fundamentally, this meant dropping the assumption that consumers are homogeneous and accepting the fact that they are heterogeneous with different needs and a willingness to pay for differentiated products that match such needs better. In turn, this recognition directed attention towards the behavioural sciences, and particularly psychology and sociology, as marketing became to be seen as a business **philosophy** founded on the notion of consumer sovereignty.

Acceptance of this idea required a radical rethinking of the firm's basic strategy from one focused on production and selling, i.e. the firm itself, to one focused on the market and customers. In other words, the firm's primary orientation was to be marketing, which, from being a support **function**, now moved to centre stage and became the dominant managerial orientation, giving rise to the marketing management school of thought.

Since then, our understanding of marketing has continued to evolve as reflected in my own definition that seeks to integrate and synthesise the three approaches and sees marketing as concerned with mutually satisfying exchange relationships that require the coordination of all three approaches.

The marketing management school of thought

The marketing management school of thought dominated the teaching and practice of marketing for around 30 years from 1960 to 1990 and was epitomised by the writings of Eugene McCarthy and Philip Kotler. It was McCarthy (1966) who introduced the four Ps of marketing – products, price, place and promotion – which provided structure to most textbooks and courses and is still evident today.

McCarthy's four Ps is a simplified version of a more complex model conceived by Professor Neil Borden (1964) of the Harvard Business School. As stated by him, the marketing mix is:

A schematic plan to guide analysis of marketing problems through utilisation of (a) a list of the important forces emanating from the market which bear upon the marketing operations of an enterprise; (b) a list of the elements (procedures and policies) of marketing programs.

The marketing mix refers to the apportionment of effort, the designing, and the integration of the elements of marketing into a program or 'mix' which on the basis of appraisal of the market forces, would best achieve the objectives of an enterprise at a given time.

However, Borden's (1964) list comprised 12 different elements and so lacked the simplicity and memorability of McCarthy's much simplified model, as a result of which the latter has dominated the marketing curriculum for 50 years or more.

Inevitably, its popularity has encouraged other authors to propose alternative models for which they can claim ownership. SIVA is such a model, standing for: solution, information, access and value. Unfortunately, these four attributes do not match across the original four Ps, neither is SIVA quite such a memorable mnemonic. Further, with the growth of services, it has been found necessary to add at least another three Ps to the original four.

The first of the additional Ps is *people*, which recognises the fact that exchange involves human interactions between buyer and seller. Where there is only limited interaction, the exchange is often referred to as a transaction, but, when it involves significant involvement between both buyer and seller, the process develops into a relationship. In the case of physical products, the nature of these relationships may well become the dominant factor in deciding the outcome and, similarly, where we think the exchange is a service, then it is the people who provide the service who provide that physical evidence.

However, the point remains that the role of the marketing manager is seen to be the creation of a unique recipe through the manipulation and integration of the mix elements. In turn, this process is reflected in the subtitle of Philip Kotler's (1972) eponymous *Marketing Management*, the subtitle of which is, 'analysis, planning, implementation and control'. Hence, the APIC model of marketing, which, as we shall see, was to evolve into the relationship marketing concept in the 1990s.

However, before looking at the emergence of 'relationship marketing', we would like to address the frequently voiced criticism that marketing is a triumph of style over substance.

Style versus substance

Initially, suppliers concentrated upon producing standardised or homogeneous products at the lowest cost to enable them to reach the widest possible market. As the demand for low cost and undifferentiated products began to become saturated, producers increasingly came to appreciate that many of their customers with high disposable incomes would be willing to pay more for a version of the product that offered more features and benefits. Of course, this has always been the case, but, if you consider 'growth' to involve selling more and increasing your gross revenue, then you will try to get your costs down as low as possible in order to appeal to the largest possible market. In pursuing this strategy, it is accepted that the maximum economies of scale that enable you to reduce costs will be associated with standardisation. Standardised products are often known as commodities and, as the operation of the commodity market shows, the lowest cost producer will attract the most buyers until they have sold all of their available supply, at which point the market price will rise.

However, where the intending buyer is able to pay more than the prevailing market price, they may be willing to do so if offered a product that offers added value. To do so we will have to shop around – hence shopping goods –and will compare the claims of competing sellers. And, if you believe that free range eggs or organic food will give you greater satisfaction, you will be prepared to pay more to get it. Now eggs from battery hens and free range eggs possess the same basic attributes and so may be easily substituted for one another in preparing egg-based dishes – so much so that in a blind taste test you probably couldn't tell the difference between them. In other words, the value-added is a subjective belief that one method of egg production is superior to another and, if you think this, you will shop around to buy the kind of egg that gives you greater satisfaction in return for the price paid.

The influence of our selective perception on our buying behaviour may be such that certain goods and services take on a special meaning for us – what are called speciality goods – with the result that we will go to considerable lengths to obtain supplies of them – and may well pay a great deal more to secure this preferred object. At one level gin- or cola-flavoured carbonated beverages are commodities and, if sold in identical packages simply labelled gin or cola the rational buying decision would be to buy supplies at the lowest price. But if I offer you a coloured bottle labelled 'Baker's Best' and ask you for 20 per cent more on the price you may well believe that the higher price reflects higher quality and buy mine rather than the lowest cost offering. And if over time you come to believe that Baker's is genuinely the very best available, you may refuse to buy substitutes and pay an even higher price, which suggests that ultimately it is style or presentation that determines our buying behaviour.

Understanding buyer behaviour

The fact that people attach different importance to products is that it reflects their own personal preferences. When I experience a basic need, such as hunger or thirst, I begin to think of objects with attributes that will satisfy this need. One has only to pay a visit to their local supermarket to find that they probably have 15,000 to 20,000 objects that would do so. If I am indifferent to the differences between potatoes, genetically modified potatoes, fair trade potatoes, organic potatoes, etc., then I will select the lowest price available. However, if I think that there are meaningful differences between potatoes, then initially I may have to think quite hard about how to decide between those on offer. I may also have to choose between the different features that enable me to differentiate what is available. Only when I have consumed the potatoes will I know whether they satisfy my need and deliver the desired benefits. If they do, then I will save a lot of time when I next go shopping if I repeat purchase the same thing. Otherwise, I'll have to go through the same choice selection and find an alternative.

For low value products the easiest way to determine whether they will meet your need is to buy and consume them. For more expensive goods and/or durable products like cars or washing machines that will last for a long time, trial and error is not a sensible option and you will put more effort into gathering and evaluating information before making a purchase decision. In both instances, the challenge for the seller is to establish what are considered to be the essential attributes of a product category, i.e. the thing you are considering buying. What importance is attached to features that differentiate between products with the same attributes, and how do prospective customers describe the benefits that they are looking for in their ideal product?

To answer these questions firms invest heavily in marketing research so that they can classify potential customers in terms of their activities, interests and opinions. Once they have secured this data they can use it to allocate people into different categories, each of which may be expected to respond differently to a different marketing mix.

Once the firm has collected sufficient data to enable it to profile the potential market it will be able to develop a marketing plan, which will make best use of the skills and resources it has to offer. This will be achieved through a process known as segmentation, targeting and positioning.

In essence, positioning means the achievement of a unique place in a competitive market for a particular product such that some worthwhile subgroup of consumers or segment perceives it to be different in some meaningful and important respect from all other competitors. In order to determine the position of a product – whether one's own or a competitor's – the first step must be to establish what are the key criteria or attributes, which consumers use to judge performance and distinguish between the competitive offerings available to them. Once these key attributes have been defined, a survey may be undertaken to find out how consumers perceive each of the different brands in terms of the relevant criteria using AIO (attitudes, interests and opinions) research.

By combining this information one can develop what is called a perceptual map of a market and decide where and how to position oneself against competition. Once this position has been chosen, it becomes possible to identify what features and benefits may be used to differentiate one's own product in the mind of the buyer. As we have seen, to do this the marketer must develop a unique marketing mix based on the ingredients available. As with cooking, one can develop numerous recipes from the same ingredients but, in the final analysis, it is the way you do this – the implementation – that determines how successful you are.

Generations of marketing managers have been brought up on the Kotlerian view of marketing management as a process comprising the sequence analysis, planning, implementation and control, hence, the APIC model of marketing. On closer examination, however, it is clear that the APIC model does not necessarily reflect the marketing concept. In a nutshell, marketing management is about what we need to do **to** customers to get them to buy our goods – in other words, bending demand to absorb the available supply. By contrast, the marketing concept and market orientation are about what firms need to do **for** customers that will secure their patronage, goodwill, trust, commitment and, ultimately, their loyalty.

Substance over style?

During the 1980s criticisms began to emerge about the practice of marketing, prompting the consultants McKinsey and Co to describe it in 1993 as suffering a 'mid-life crisis' (Brady and Davis 1993). From being the driving force behind competitive strategy, much marketing was seen to have lost its edge with one firm's marketing activities cancelling out another's. It is also important to note that the marketing management school of thought was applied primarily to the marketing of consumer goods, or B2C marketing. In the case of what was originally known as industrial marketing, and is now called business-to-business or B2B marketing, a different emphasis prevailed with the stress upon interaction between buyer and seller and the development of networks. In turn, this focused attention upon the relationship between buyer and seller.

The late 1970s and early 1980s also witnessed a new concern for what was identified as 'macro marketing', with an emphasis upon the overall impact of marketing practices on social and human welfare – as with the discipline of economics with a distinction between microeconomics focused on competition between firms and industries, and macroeconomics that concentrated on the policy implications of economic activity for national and international progress and success. This distinction was less marked in the marketing discipline possibly because environmental considerations were factored into the organisation's analysis when formulating its marketing strategy. However, today, concerns for sustainability, the impact of climate change and awareness that one-third of the world's population lives below the poverty line have resulted in these macromarketing issues assuming a more visible and important role in marketing practice.

The debate about which approach best represented the implementation of the marketing concept was crystallised by the collapse of the Berlin Wall and the communist regime that had led to its erection in the first place. This event called for a complete rethink about models of economic organisation. Following the end of the Second World War, thinking about the most effective form of economic organisation had polarised opinion by focusing upon centrally controlled command economies, as practised in Russia and its allies, and the emphasis on free-market capitalism, as practised in the US and other free economies. With the demise of communism it became clear that the so-called Anglo-Saxon model practised in the US and the UK that encouraged firms to compete with one another aggressively – what Milton Friedman referred to as capitalism red in tooth and claw – was not always to the best advantage of consumers. Many agreed with John Kenneth Galbraith (1958) of the need for countervailing power to curb the excesses of big business, which, in turn, presumed some form of regulation of the marketplace. In fact, a political model of a regulated free-market economy had emerged in Austria in the mid-nineteenth century and had become known as the Germanic Alpine model, as it was widely adopted in that geographical area. As the collapse of the banking system in 2008 in countries subscribing to the Anglo-Saxon model and the subsequent recession have made clear, this was essentially a consequence of a lack of regulation, and we may anticipate an increase of this in future as the state seeks to control the excesses of big business and their marketing practices.

Of course, too much regulation can be a bad thing as it stifles competition and innovation. Far better that organisations put their own houses in order, and there is evidence of this in the growing emphasis given to relationship marketing. The key difference between marketing management and relationship marketing is that the former is a functional approach to physically managing the mix elements, while the latter promotes the view that the successful organisation needs to bend all its efforts to the satisfaction of its customers – a cultural or philosophical view derived from the marketing concept, which is what I had in mind when I first proposed my own definition of marketing in 1976.

Many firms now claim that they have adopted the relationship marketing approach and are implementing it through a system of customer relationship management (CRM). In deciding whether to accept the claim that this is a move away from the marketing management approach, one needs to examine closely what are the defining elements of most CRM schemes. But, if you do so, it is likely that you will find CRM practices are a more sophisticated means of manipulating knowledge about consumers to get them to buy what you have to sell, which, as we have seen, is quite different from the marketing concept's belief that we start with the customer's needs and wants and then create products and services to satisfy them.

People who subscribe to the latter view would argue that if you seek to manage a relationship you are likely to destroy it, as 'relationship' implies that the partners will work together to achieve a common objective. Accordingly, relationships are seen to involve the co-creation of value through the interaction between producer and consumer, and it is this perspective that has led to the most recent shift in thinking about marketing to what is known as the 'service-dominant logic (SDL)'. The notion of SDL was first proposed by Vargo and Lusch in 2004 when they argued that 'marketing, has moved from a goods-dominant view, in which tangible output and discrete transactions were central, to a service-dominant view, in which intangibility, exchange processes, and relationships are central'. These propositions are still the subject of wide debate and beyond the scope of an introductory overview designed to introduce expert contributions on a wide diversity of marketing topics, many of which have become distinctive subfields in their own right. As will become clear, the SDL paradigm reflects the continuing evolution of ideas about the nature and practice of marketing and the current state of play.

The notion that marketing is concerned with the relationship between an organisation and its customers suggests that this relationship should not be confined solely to those who work in the marketing department or a marketing function. In other words, marketing is 'everybody's' business.

There is an intrinsic danger in accepting such a proposition because when something becomes everybody's business, it may well become nobody's business on the grounds that everyone assumes that someone else is taking care of it. To overcome this danger a conscious effort must be made to avoid it.

First, everyone needs to understand the nature of the marketing concept and the fact that this is a way of thinking about how an organisation will conduct its business, which, clearly, will involve all members of that organisation. To begin with then, everyone must subscribe to the view that the overall success of the organisation depends upon everyone within it working towards that goal. Achieving this is not an easy task. I have worked with many organisations in which persons in a designated marketing function believe that they are somehow more important than are other members of their organisation, possibly because they are the point of contact between the organisation and its customers. This attitude can alienate other members of an organisation and become dysfunctional, especially where professional marketers perceive telephone operators, receptionists and other contact personnel as less important and subordinate to them. Given that such people are often the first point of contact between a prospective or existing customer and the organisation, it is imperative that they understand the importance of their role in developing relationships. It follows that every member of an organisation needs to understand what is meant by a marketing culture and their part in creating this.

To achieve this calls for internal marketing, the purpose of which has been defined as having motivated customer conscious employees and involves management in seeing those employees as 'customers' who need to be informed and educated about the meaning of a marketing orientation, the creation of customer value and its delivery.

During 2013/2014, I was fully involved in preparing a radically revised new edition of my textbook *Marketing Strategy and Management*, first published in 1985, in parallel with revising this chapter and a similar one, which acts as the introduction to *Marketing Theory*. In the final Chapter 25, 'Transformational marketing', I attempt a summary of my perception of how the discipline of marketing has evolved over the past 60 years or so. After careful consideration, I decided that I really did not wish to modify the conclusion of this chapter which, with some modification, is repeated here. In doing so I am conscious that some purists might consider this to be self- plagiarism for which my defence is to cite Pamela Samuelson's (1994) justification that 'I said it so well the first time that it makes no sense to say it differently a second time'. I also hope that this self-reference will encourage you to consult the chapter, which also contains my personal views on how the marketing discipline may develop in future.

Six decades of change

Since the articulation of the modern marketing concept around 1950 we have experienced a period of rapid and accelerating change – technological, social and economic – that have had a major impact on the competitive environment. Simplistically, we may identify these decades as:

- 1950s post-war reconstruction;
- 1960s materialism/consumerism;
- 1970s newly industrialising countries;
- 1980s globalisation;
- 1990s emerging economies and sustainability;
- 2000s the internet and social media.

In response to these changes we have seen a considerable growth of interest in the importance of interaction and networks giving rise to an emphasis upon relationship marketing. In turn, this has highlighted the importance of corporate social responsibility and the view that marketing is 'everybody's business' with a consequential focus on internal marketing, while the impact of information and communications technology (ICT) and, particularly, the internet, has promoted the view that we are seeing the emergence of a 'new economy'. Associated with these changes has been a search for a new 'business model' with an accent on value and its co-creation through the exchange process.

In parallel with these developments there has also been a growing recognition that while marketing has been blamed as a practice that promotes materialism and excessive consumption, potentially it is a discipline that offers the best prospect for encouraging conservation and sustainability. After all, if marketing tools and techniques have the ability to shape attitudes and modify behaviour there is no reason why they cannot be deployed for this purpose by means of what has come to be known as 'transformational marketing'. Simplistically, many see this as just adopting the tools and practices refined by practitioners belonging to the marketing management school of thought, which still tends to dominate the marketing curriculum and education. I hope sincerely that this is a forlorn hope. If marketing is to become 'transformational', much more radical measures are called for. It is also highly unlikely that marketing alone could have the desired effect, as any new business model must involve the contributions of other business disciplines in a truly interdisciplinary approach.

As has been made clear when discussing the notion of 'orientation', different organisations may have quite different orientations – production, sales, financial, etc. – one of which tends to dominate and drives the organisational culture – the way we do things around here. Given that the implementation of a strategy requires the coordination of inputs from all the business disciplines, which are usually organised into divisions or departments with a disciplinary bias, the distinction between 'interdisciplinary' and 'multidisciplinary' is not trivial. In a multidisciplinary environment, each of the different disciplines tends to interpret the environment and the problems to be solved from the perspective of that discipline and, inevitably, tends to persuade others to 'see it my way'. By contrast, an interdisciplinary approach seeks to combine potentially different perspectives into a single agreed and coordinated solution, which combines and builds upon the contribution of them all. This difference has been made explicit in our emphasis upon the distinction between marketing as a philosophy that starts with the customer and attempts to maximise their satisfaction, and marketing as a function that is focused on efficient and effective practice. But, the need to constantly affirm this difference suggests that a more successful approach would be to avoid incorporating 'marketing' into the name of a new business model and settle for something less controversial. As one thing that all the proponents of such a model appear to agree upon is that it should be focused on human welfare and well-being, then social business appears to strike a balance between the various alternatives and a worthy objective of what we might call 'transformational marketing'.

Transformational marketing and social business

While there are numerous dedicated publications that address aspects of social business from a disciplinary perspective, in 2010 there appeared to be few if any taking a multidisciplinary approach, and it was suggested to me that having founded other journals I might like to attempt another one to fill this gap. Details of the outcome can be found on the website socialbusinessperiodical.com with the inaugural issue appearing in Spring 2011. To populate this (and subsequent issues), approaches were made to persons with expertise and established reputations including Professor Ken Peattie, who is Director of the ESRC Research Centre for Business Relationships, Accountability, Sustainability and Society (BRASS) at Cardiff University, whom I asked to write a commentary on a paper that he had published in 2001 in *The Marketing Review*.

In his paper (Peattie 2011), 'Towards sustainability: Achieving marketing transformation – a retrospective comment', Peattie had the following to say about the need to rethink marketing if it was to have a transformative effect:

> The notion that our marketing thinking may also be increasingly unsustainable is an idea that has also gained currency from within the mainstream. *In Search of a New Logic of Marketing* by Christian Grönroos (2007) describes marketing as an area of business thought and practice that has failed to evolve. He feels that a marketing executive time-travelling forward from fifty years ago would fit quite comfortably into a contemporary marketing department, given a little coaching on the technology involved. To Grönroos marketing is in danger of becoming an increasingly costly function whose strategic role and credibility within business is eroding because it has become unable to break out of its existing ways of thinking: '*The productivity of marketing cannot be improved within the existing frameworks and structures. As long as marketing's major responsibility is customer acquisition and promise-making, the costs of marketing will continue to grow, and its effectiveness will continue to go down . . . The development of brand management and adopting*

a branding terminology in marketing is only more of the same, in some situations making conventional marketing more effective perhaps, but offering no innovative new avenues for customer management. Marketing as a discipline is in crisis. And marketing as a business practice responsible for customer management is losing credibility'.

(Peattie 2011: 16)

Grönroos proposes an alternative vision of marketing that is centred around marketing as a process of managing relationships with customers, rather than of facilitating exchanges with them. In doing this, it shifts the focus away from the marketing of products to customers and instead emphasises the need to deliver value to customers. What is particularly interesting is the extent to which Grönroos's analysis of the shortcomings of conventional marketing from a relationship management perspective fit with critiques of conventional marketing from a socio-environmental perspective. This perhaps provides a clue as to how the transformation to sustainability based marketing might be achieved in both marketing practice and scholarship. In the book *Sustainability Marketing – A Global Perspective* (Belz and Peattie 2009) they propose that the evolution from the managerialist *modern marketing* that has dominated the mainstream for the past 50 years can be achieved by integrating two emerging schools of thought: first, the transition from transactions to relationships perspective (Vargo and Lusch 2004); second, increasing the scope of marketing from a narrow and short-term focus on the wants of current consumers to a much broader consideration of stakeholders that includes non-consumers, the environment and future generations of consumers. The result would be marketing based on relationships delivering sustainable value to consumers and society.

If that integration can be achieved, then the prospects for achieving a transformation in our marketing practices and thinking, and in the sustainability of our production and consumption systems, will be much improved. To do it, we will need more scholars working in these areas, and more channels through which their research can reach an audience and make a difference. For that reason, I strongly welcome the emergence of *Social Business* and look forward to it driving the field forward over the next ten years.

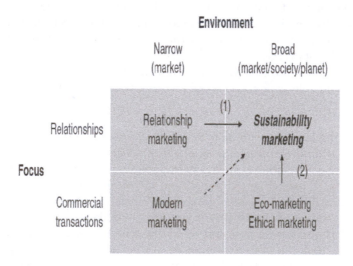

Figure 1.2 The emergence of sustainability marketing

Source: Belz and Peattie 2009: 18.

What Peattie calls 'sustainability marketing' and I identify as 'social business' were both identified by leading American scholars, Ravi Achrol and Philip Kotler (2012), in a paper entitled 'Frontiers of the marketing paradigm in the third millennium' in which they proposed 'a three-tiered explanation of the emerging field of marketing – its sub phenomena (consumer experiences and sensory systems), its phenomena (marketing networks), and its super phenomena (sustainability and development)'.

To begin with, it is stressed that the focus is upon the future and the emerging paradigms of marketing. However, to do so, it is necessary to summarise perceived assumptions of both the received and emergent marketing paradigms as interpreted by the authors, and these have been summarised in Table 1.1. Effectively, their analysis leads them to suggest a three tiered framework comprising consumption experiences, marketing networks and sustainability.

The first three assumptions all relate to aspects of what are described as 'sub phenomena' relating to consumer behaviour. These are elaborated on as covering: marketing and the human senses; neurophysiology and marketing; and marketing and nanotechnology. The next four assumptions define what are described as 'phenomena' and deal with 'mid-range theories that have predictive power' and are concerned with relational concepts that are bringing '*production and consumption* closer together'. The topics explored here include: the evolution of production and innovation networks; distributed production-consumption networks; and consumption networks. And, finally, four assumptions identified as 'super phenomena' of which two, *sustainability and poverty*, are selected for detailed discussion. Topics covered include the sustainable marketing concept and base of the pyramid marketing.

Table 1.1 Key issues and assumptions underpinning the current and future marketing paradigm

Paradigm Statusi / Issue	Current	Future
A SUB-PHENOMENAL: **CONSUMER BEHAVIOUR**		
1 Experience	Need satisfaction	Sense-making
2 Disciplinary focus	Cognitive psychology	Neurophysiology
3 Sensory focus	Objective	Subjective
B PHENOMENAL: **RELATIONAL CONCEPTS**		
4 Supply orientation	Mass production	Co-creation. One-to-One
5 Dominant technology	Computer based	Bio and nanotechnology
6 Managerial orientation	Internally focused	Externally directed
7 Source of competitive advantage	Distinctive competence	Leadership in production and consumption networks
C SUPER PHENOMENAL		
8 Strategic management priorities	Growth emphasis on customers with discretionary purchasing power, anthropocentric	Circular economy and sustainability, bio-centric
9 Unit of analysis	Buyer-seller	Society
10 Strategic emphasis	Corporate social responsibility	Human welfare
11 Public policy	Laissez-faire	Regulated social business

Source: Adapted from Achrol, R. S. and Kotler, P. (2012), 'Frontiers of the marketing paradigm in the third millennium', *Journal of the Academy of Marketing Science*, 40: 35–52.

As suggested in this review, and confirmed and endorsed by numerous authors and theorists, the marketing paradigm has evolved from a focus on marketing as a *function*, through marketing as a *managerial practice* to marketing as *exchange*. While credit for this evolution is largely attributed to the work of American scholars, it is felt that this largely overlooks the contributions of numerous European and other scholars whose work, chronologically, preceded recognition of marketing as mutual exchange that I summarised was based upon the 'creation and maintenance of mutually satisfying exchange relationships' (Baker 1976). Founded in Europe at about the same time, the Industrial Marketing and Purchasing (IMP) Group focused upon the interaction between parties to an exchange and the relationships in the networks formed between them. In parallel, the role of service and services were given explicit recognition. It is significant that apart from Gummesson (1998) none of this research is cited by the authors. On these grounds we consider it wrong to attribute the view that we are now 'at the threshold of the *network* paradigm' to an earlier paper by the authors in 1999.

In making this observation, I fully acknowledge that both authors, and especially Philip Kotler, have made very important contributions to the evolution of marketing thought and theory. Indeed, many developments like the transfer of the marketing concept to a non-commercial context (social marketing) are founded on insights first promoted by Kotler and Kotler and Levy. Nonetheless, the failure to consider the publication of research findings in non-American journals constitutes a form of 'research myopia' that I referred to directly in an address to the American Marketing Association's Winter Educators (1994) meeting. To avoid a similar oversight. it is important that one does not confine one's research solely to papers published in leading American journals.

This advice is confirmed by Volume 6 in the *Legends in Marketing* series edited by Roderick Brodie (2013), which is concerned with marketing theory and chronicles the published work of Finnish scholar, Christian Gronroos. The volume contains thirteen papers written by Gronroos together with commentaries by Brodie and four other contributors including myself. In the absence of any contact between me and Richard Brookes and Victoria Little, who contributed chapter 14 'What-really-is marketing?', it was reassuring to find a high level of agreement in our answers to the question that is the subject of this chapter. Brookes and Little identify three overriding themes in Gronroos's work:

1   critique of the mainstream (AMA) approach;
2   a customer management/marketing practice perspective;
3   a business marketing, service, and relationship lens.

Their commentary concludes with an observation which is an appropriate introduction to this book:

> However, clearly, we are still looking for the answers to that basic question: '*What-really-is marketing?*' We have seen that it can be a philosophy, a toolkit, process, a set of practices and, in large organisations, a dedicated but somewhat constrained function. Christian has long argued that perhaps we need a new word for what has been labelled marketing. It would need to be a word which connotes what the combined part-time and full-time 'marketers' really do to gain, keep, and grow their customers.

Summary

Our attempt to provide at least some answers to the question, 'What is marketing?' has indicated that the answer has evolved and changed over time. As it has adapted to changing circumstances, so it has found it necessary to embrace and incorporate insights and ideas from other disciplines.

Initially, the focus was seen as solving the central economic problem of maximising satisfaction through the utilisation of scarce resources. Originally, economists thought that this would be achieved through maximising efficiency and producing the largest possible supply at the lowest possible cost. However, to do so required the heroic assumption that demand for a product was homogeneous, so that the same product would satisfy everybody, i.e. the greatest good of the greatest number. But, as technological innovation made it possible to increase both the quantity and variety of goods available for consumption, it became accepted that demand is not homogeneous, and overall satisfaction could be increased through the provision of differentiated products designed to serve the same use and need. In order to understand how to do this, it became necessary to extend the principles of marketing to incorporate ideas from a number of other disciplines, such as anthropology, geography, psychology and sociology and integrate these into a more broadly based explanation of marketing. It is for this reason that we regard marketing as a synthetic discipline in the sense that it seeks to synthesise knowledge and ideas derived from other disciplines into an integrated and systematic way of thinking about exchange processes. What distinguishes modern marketing from earlier practice is that it has converted from a craft to a profession in exactly the same way as architecture, engineering and medicine, all of which are synthetic disciplines. Marketing is not just an abstract way of thinking about exchange, it is a model for efficient and effective practice.

And so, in looking to the future, it has become apparent that marketing ideas and practice can be deployed in many other contexts beyond that of business or commercial exchange where they originated. Marketing has the capability of transforming all kinds of exchange relationship, whether for-profit or not-for-profit, as well as in promoting social welfare and sustainability. As American marketing scholar, Jagdish Sheth, has pointed out, as a result of our past success in improving the quality of life we have to recognise that, for the first time ever, there are five generations living in an economy. Furthermore, we need to think through the implications of an ageing population and its impact on lifestyle and consumption. To these we would add environmental or 'green' issues, concerns for social responsibility and ethical corporate behaviour, together with the challenge of emerging economies.

If marketers are to meet and resolve these challenges, then they need to be customer focused, build long-term relationships with customers, and think of their lifetime value as opposed to their short-term profitability. In other words, observe the golden rule – do unto others as you would be done by – and create and maintain mutually satisfactory exchange relationships. In the following chapters you will find a diversity of views as to how this ambition may be fulfilled.

References

Achrol, R. S. and Kotler, P. (2012), 'Frontiers of the marketing paradigm in the third millennium', *Journal of the Academy of Marketing Science*, 40: 35–52.

Baker, M. J. (ed.) (1976), *Marketing: Theory and Practice*, London: Macmillan.

Baker, M. J. (2014), *Marketing Strategy and Management*, fifth edition, Basingstoke, UK: Palgrave.

Belz, F.-M. and Peattie, K. (2009), *Sustainability Marketing – A Global Perspective*, Chichester, UK: Wiley, p. 18.

Borden, N. (1964), 'The concept of the marketing mix', *Journal of Advertising Research*, 4(2): 2–7.

Brady, J. and Davis, I. (1993), 'Marketing's mid-life crisis', *The McKinsey Quarterly*, 2(2): 17–28.

Crosier, K. (1975), 'What exactly is marketing?', *Quarterly Review of Marketing*, 1(2).

Drucker, P. F. (1954), *The Practice of Management,* New York: Harper & Row.

Galbraith, J. K. (1958), *American Capitalism: The Concept of Countervailing Power*, Boston, MA: Houghton Mifflin.

Gummerson, E. (1998), 'Implementation requires a relationship marketing paradigm', *Journal of the Academy of Marketing Science*, 26(3): 242–249.

Keith, R. J. (1960), 'The marketing revolution', *Journal of Marketing* 24(3): 35–38.

Kotler, P. (1972), *Marketing Management: Analysis, Planning, Implementation and Control*, second edition, Englewood Cliffs, NJ: Prentice-Hall.

Levitt, T. (1960), 'Marketing myopia', *Harvard Business Review*, July/August: 45–56.

Levitt, T. (1983), *The Marketing Imagination,* New York: Free Press.

McCarthy, E. J. (1966), *Basic Marketing,* Homewood, IL: Irwin.

Peattie, K. (2011), 'Towards sustainability: Achieving marketing transformation – a retrospective comment', *Social Business*, 1(1): 85–104.

Smith, A. [(1970) 1776], *The Wealth of Nations,* Skinner, A. (ed.), Harmondsworth, UK: Pelican Books.

Vargo, S. L. and Lusch, R. F. (2004), 'Evolving to a new dominant logic of marketing', *Journal of Marketing*, 68(1): 1–17.

2 Postmodern marketing

Dead and buried or alive and kicking?

Stephen Brown

Be sure your sin will find you out.

(Numbers 32: 23)

Backstory

What goes around comes around. Or so they say. It does in my case, that's for sure. The best part of a decade ago I wrote a root and branch critique of service-dominant logic (SDL) (Vargo and Lusch 2004). At the time, SDL was being talked up as the biggest thing to hit marketing since the proverbial sliced loaf (or Kotler's indigestible textbooks at least). SDL was a whole new way of thinking. SDL was opening up vast intellectual territories hitherto untapped and ripe for exploration. SDL was nothing less than a paradigm shift – hold the front page and nobody leave the room! – though the authors were careful not to employ that particular P word, because marketing already has more Ps than you can shake a pod at.

Anyway, I penned a cheap and nasty critique of this much-lauded notion, marketing's latest next big thing (Brown 2007). I noted that the basic idea was not new, since service's pre-eminence had been highlighted many years before by Ted Levitt. I pointed out that the authors' terminology was contradictory, confusing and historically inaccurate forbye. I took issue with their insinuation that marketing practitioners would be the ultimate beneficiaries of their breakthrough. I doubted, furthermore, if any real world managers would read their badly written, jargon-filled, self-aggrandising farrago of flatulent nonsense, which was unlikely to survive an encounter with empirical evidence. I said some nice things too. Honest I did. But, I cut them out prior to publication, because Vargo and Lusch needed to be taken down a peg or three.

My paper was duly published, to ominous silence. I had misjudged the temper of the times. Marketing academia was gagging for SDL. The idea took off like Beanie Babies back in the day, like Michael Jordan in his Air-shod ascendency, like Virgin Galactic's gonna do sometime soon, or so they say (once the accompanying squadron of pigs is in place, presumably). Articles appertaining to SDL cascaded from the ivory towers. SDL anthologies were rushed off the presses. Workshops, seminars, dedicated conferences and special issues of learned journals sprouted like hens' teeth. Main chance-minded scholars leapt on the SDL bandwagon, which had become a brand in all but name (Cova *et al.* 2009). My critique, meanwhile, languished between the pages of an eminent journal with nary a download or citation.

I'm not bitter.

A leading British academic, who must remain nameless for fear of reprisals against his entirely innocent family, eventually took pity on me. He sent me an email about my ill-judged article. A five-word email, to be precise. What goes around comes around, it said. I wasn't quite sure what he was getting at to begin with. But then I've never been the sharpest tool in the scholarly shed, nor the most diplomatic. Then it dawned on me. My esteemed correspondent – Robin of Wensley, for it was he, forsooth – was referring to the fact that I myself once occupied the SDL slot in marketing discourse. Ten years before SDL hit the streets, I was singing the praises of a paradigm-shifting, practitioner-alienating, terminologically-confusing, nothing-if-not-contradictory, historically-anachronistic next big thing. A next big thing called 'postmodernism'. I wasn't a one man band, admittedly. I wasn't even the conductor of the cacophonous post-modern choir. But I was probably PoMo's most vehement, vindictive, vainglorious proponent (though I prefer the v-word 'valiant').

SDL, in short, was my comeuppance, my noisome nemesis, my Oedipal academic offspring of sorts. Or, to put it another way: the worm turns, Stephen, the worm turns. With knobs on.

Further backstory

People sometimes ask me, 'Whatever happened to postmodernism?' Well, okay, that's not entirely true. I made it up for rhetorical purposes. No one asks me anything. After my intemperate article on SDL, I've been banished to the intellectual equivalent of Elba. Like a neo-Napoleon, I strut around in a tricorn hat with my hand artfully inserted in a watered silk waistcoat, waiting for the call that never comes . . .

In case you're wondering, the only reason I'm writing this is because Susan Hart has got me mixed up with the legendary Stephen Brown of services marketing fame. That's our little secret, BTW, so if she ever asks what you thought of *The Marketing Book* tell her that the chapter about SDL by Stephen Brown was worth the price of purchase alone.[1]

Sorry, where was I? Oh yes, whatever happened to postmodernism? Hmmmm. In order to answer that one, we need to go all the way back to the beginning, where an apt irony awaits us. Namely, that the 'postmodern' age was identified at the precise moment when 'modern' market-ing first appeared. More ironic still is that the person who coined the term 'postmodern' was one of the principal architects of 'modern' marketing. In 1957 the peerless Peter Drucker – whose famous statement, 'marketing is the distinguishing, the unique function of business' (Drucker, 1954: 35) is often taken to be the degree zero of our discipline – wrote a speculative work of futurism, *Landmarks of Tomorrow*. This comprised 'a report on the new "post-modern" world', where innovation is industrialised, big government is abandoned and Western culture bestrides the globe. Although Drucker is not renowned for phraseological prowess, his terminology took off as the principles and practices of postmodernism spread rapidly. Art, architecture, literature, theatre, poetry, opera, dance, the cinema – the entire cultural spectrum, in short – underwent a PoMo transformation, as did the humanities and social sciences, management and marketing among them (Calás and Smircich 1997). As the neo-Marxist economists, Hardt and Negri (2000: 151), noted in *Empire*, a monumental overview of late-capitalist culture, 'marketing has perhaps the clearest rela-tion to postmodernist theories, and one could even say that the capitalist marketing strategies have long been postmodernist *avant la lettre*'.

Marketing's postmodern disposition may have been evident to outside observers, but our discipline's esteemed establishment didn't see things that way. The first generation of PoMo marketers – Morris Holbrook, Russell Belk, John Sherry, Beth Hirschman, Melanie Wallendorf and so forth – were promptly dismissed as propagators of weird science (Sherry 1991). The second wave of proponents, such as Alladi Venkatesh, Dominique Bouchet, Bernard Cova, Fuat Firat, Richard Elliott *et al.*, were widely regarded as even weirder, if less threatening, than their trail-blazing forebears (Askegaard and Scott 2013). By the mid-1990s, nevertheless, postmodern marketing was a recognised academic entity, albeit a bit of a whipping boy for the quantitatively and managerially inclined mainstream. Nigel Piercy (1997) in particular took great pleasure in trashing marketing's trash-talking renegades, which only added to PoMo's insidious allure.

But what was it that attracted them and alienated the academic establishment? In order to answer that question we need to backtrack a tad and note that the multifaceted postmodern condition comprised three key components: *postmodernism*, an anti-elitist movement in the arts and popular culture; *postmodernity*, the socio-economic transformations that accompanied the demise of heavy industry and concomitant rise of today's information economy; and *postmodernisation*, a significant philosophical shift, which elevated the rule-less rules of Relativism above the perennial quest for scientific Truth (Appignanesi and Garratt 1995; Ward 1997; Best and Kellner 2001; Butler 2002). In addition to its three main components, moreover, PoMo was characterised by a relentlessly irreverent, ceaselessly subversive, couldn't care less attitude, coupled with an absolute refusal to defer to those holding the levers of power (while reflexively revelling in the ridiculousness of such a stance). As Apple (1984: 39) observed at the time, the postmodern moment is suffused with a, 'mixture of worldweariness and cleverness, an attempt to make you think that I'm half-kidding, though you're not quite sure about what'.

That was then

Regarded in retrospect, it's clear that PoMo's impertinent attitude was what especially irked marketing's great and good. Its nonchalant, affectless, shoulder-shrugging sensibility got up some people's noses, as did postmodernism's refusal to be pinned down to any definitive position or point of view. When invited to explain what it is, postmodernists replied that it isn't. When asked what it stands for, postmodernists said they preferred to sit down. When challenged to define the construct, PoMo's mafia maintained that it makes you an offer you can't understand (Brown 1995). Most postmodernists, moreover, went out of their way to deny that they were postmodernists, as did the intellectual leaders of the postmodern pack – Baudrillard, Derrida, Lacan and the like. Little wonder so many scholars responded negatively to its premises, whatever they were . . .

It's equally clear, in retrospect, that what attracted some people to postmodern marketing – and alienated so many others – was this very lack of specificity. For mainstream researchers, postmodernism's refusal to define itself formally or accept the right and proper rules of rigour, reliability, reproducibility and relevance, was a signifier of scholarly depravity. For those who rallied to the postmodern flag, it offered freedom of expression, freedom to communicate their ideas in unconventional academic forms, freedom to spurn the narrow-minded managerialism of most business schools, freedom to connect and converse with anti-establishment-minded thinkers in distal disciplines and, above all, freedom from marketing's increasingly ossified, practically fossilised principles and practices (see Gummesson 2001; Sheth and Sisodia 2006). Card-carrying postmodernists could be what they wanted to be, do what they wanted to do and say what they wanted to say in whatever weird and wonderful way they wanted to say it. PoMo meant liberty:

> Postmodern is the name for a renaissance moment in our subject's history . . . an exciting moment in which the filters that determined which theories were relevant became overwhelmed by the flow of radical theories that displaced previous assumptions, temporarily invigorating everything and licensing creative expositions that expressed alternatives. The name that we give to this

moment of the radical invigoration, the adrenaline of the new, and the sense of displacement coupled with disorientation, as old certainties give way, is postmodernism.

(Cova *et al.* 2013: 214–215)

More than that, though, the postmodern impulse was paralleled by developments in wider consumer society. PoMo wasn't just an ivory tower affectation. In what proved to be the high water mark of postmodern marketing, Firat and Venkatesh (1995) deconstructed and described the remarkable reenchantment of consumption that 'liberatory postmodernism' unleashes. PoMo, they proclaimed, is made up of five clearly discernible tendencies in contemporary consumer society: *hyperreality*, *fragmentation*, *reversed production and consumption*, *decentred subjects*, and the *juxtaposition of opposites*.

(Excuse me for a moment while I cut and paste my previous summary of their argument. But before you threaten me with Turnitin, I feel obliged to point out that self-plagiarism is one of the defining features of postmodernism. Okay, I just made that up. But hey ho, let's go . . . .)

Hyperreality

Exemplified by the virtual worlds of cyberspace and the pseudo worlds of theme parks, hotels and heritage centres, hyperreality involves the creation of marketing environments that are 'more real than real'. The distinction between reality and fantasy is momentarily blurred, as in the back lot tour of 'working' movie studios in Universal City, Los Angeles (Wolf 1999). In certain respects, indeed, hyperreality is *superior* to everyday mundane reality, since the unpleasant side of 'authentic' consumption experiences – anti-tourist terrorism in Egypt, muggings in New York, dysentery in Delhi – magically disappears when such destinations are recreated in Las Vegas, Busch Gardens, Walt Disney World or the manifold variations on the theme park theme. Ironically, however, the perceived superiority of the fake is predicated upon an (often) unwarranted stereotype of reality, and the reality of the fake, e.g. the queues in Disneyland may be much worse than anything the average visitor would actually experience in Egypt, New York, Delhi or wherever. But such is the cultural logic of postmodern marketing.

Fragmentation

Consumption in postmodernity is unfailingly fast, furious, frenetic, frenzied, fleeting, hyperactive. It is akin to zapping from channel to channel, or flicking through the pages of the glossies, in search of something worth watching, reading or buying. Shopping on speed. This disjointedness is partly attributable to the activities of marketers with their ceaseless proliferation of brands, ever-burgeoning channels of distribution, increasingly condensed commercial breaks and apparent preparedness to make use of every available surface as advertising space (sidewalks, urinals, foodstuffs, orbiting satellites, human flesh, fifties sitcoms and so forth). It is also due to the disconnected postmodern lifestyles, behaviours, moods, whims and vagaries of contemporary consumers (Falk and Campbell 1997). A product of profusion with a profusion of products, the prototypical 'postmodern consumer' performs a host of roles – wife and mother, career woman, sports enthusiast, fashion victim, DIY enthusiast, culture vulture, hapless holidaymaker, websurfing internet avatar and many more – each with its requisite brand name array. These identities or selves, furthermore, are neither sequential nor stable, but fluid, mutable and, not least, negotiable. Pick 'n' mix personae are proliferating. Off-the-shelf selves are available in every conceivable size, style, colour, fit and price point. Made-to-measure selves cost extra.

Reversed production and consumption

This fragmented, hyperrealised, postmodern consumer, it must also be stressed, is not the unwitting dupe of legend, who responds rat-like to environmental stimuli of Skinnerian caprice. Neither is the postmodern consumer transfixed, rabbit-like, in the headlights of multinational capital. Neither, for that matter, is he or she likely to be seduced by the sexual textual embeds of subliminal advertisers, though (s)he might pretend to be. On the contrary, the very idea that consumers have something 'done' to them by marketers and advertisers no longer passes muster. Postmodern consumers, in fact, do things with advertising; they are active in the production of meaning, of marketing, of consumption. As Firat and Venkatesh (1995) rightly observe:

> It is not to brands that consumers will be loyal, but to images and symbols, especially to images and symbols that *they* produce while they consume. Because symbols keep shifting, consumer loyalties cannot be fixed. In such a case a modernist might argue that the consumers are fickle – which perhaps says more about the modernist intolerance of uncertainty – while the postmodernist interpretation would be that consumers respond strategically by making themselves unpredictable. The consumer finds his/her liberatory potential in subverting the market rather than being seduced by it.
>
> (Firat and Venkatesh 1995: 251)

Decentred subjects

This idea of a multiphrenic, fragmented, knowing consumer is further developed in Firat and Venkatesh's notion of decentred subjectivity. The centredness that is characteristic of modernity, where individuals are unambiguously defined by their occupation, social class, demographics, postcode, personalities and so on, has been ripped asunder in postmodernity. Traditional segmentation criteria *may* be applied to such people and marketing strategies formulated, but it is increasingly accepted that these fleetingly capture, or freeze-frame at most, a constantly moving target market. Even the much-vaunted 'markets of one', in which marketing technologies are supposedly adapted to the specific needs of individual consumers, is doomed to fail in postmodernity, since each consumer comprises a multiplicity of shopping homunculi, so to speak. The harder marketers try to pin down the decentred consuming subject, the less successful they'll be (Grant 1999). Today's consumers are always just beyond the reach of marketing scientists, marketing strategists, marketing tacticians, marketing technologists, marketing taxonomists and all the rest. In the words of leading marketing authority, Alan Mitchell (2001):

> There is nothing wrong with trying to be scientific about marketing; in trying to understand cause and effect. And stimulus-response marketing has chalked up many successes. Nevertheless, it now faces rapidly diminishing returns. Consumers are becoming 'marketing literate'. They know they are being stimulated and are developing a resistance to these stimuli, even learning to turn the tables. Consumers increasingly refuse to buy at full price, for example, knowing that a sale is just around the corner. They have fun 'deconstructing' advertisements. The observed has started playing games with the observer. Buyers are starting to use the system for their own purposes, just as marketers attempted to use it for theirs.
>
> (Mitchell 2001: 60)

Juxtaposition of opposites

Although it is well-nigh impossible to 'target' or 'capture' the inscrutable, amorphous, unpin-downable entity that is the postmodern consumer, it is still possible to engage with, appeal to or successfully attract them. The key to this quasi-conversation is not ever more precise segmentation and positioning, rather the exact opposite. An open, untargeted, ill-defined, ambiguous approach, which leaves scope for imaginative consumer participation (e.g. ironic advertising treatments where the purpose, pitch or indeed 'product' is unclear), is typical of postmodern marketing (Brown 2006). This sense of fluidity and porosity is achieved by pastiche, by bricolage, by radical juxtaposition, by the mixing and matching of opposites, by combinations of contradictory styles, motifs and allusions, whether it be in the shimmering surfaces of pseudo rococo postmodern buildings or the ceaseless cavalcade of contrasting images that are regularly encountered in commercial breaks, shop windows or roadside billboards. Occasionally, these succeed in exceeding the sum of their parts and combine to produce a sublime whole, an ephemeral spectacular, a fleeting moment of postmodern transcendence, as in *Riverdance*, *Shrek* or Celine Dion at Caesar's Palace. Well, okay, maybe not.[2]

This is now

A couple of decades after the event, it's evident that Firat and Venkatesh's analysis was pretty much on the money. Many of the emergent traits they identified have since taken flight and fused into a massive PoMo mashup. *Hyperreality* is rampant in immersive and themed spaces, not to mention computer gaming, investment banking and the movies, where comic book-based blockbusters in glorious 3D are dominating the multiplexes and fully immersive showings of classic feature films like *Back to the Future* are becoming increasingly popular (Bradshaw 2014). *Fragmentation* is one of the defining features of the twenty-first century, thanks to an explosion of ever more micro-media – blogs, vlogs, podcasts, tweets, YouTube, Netflix, Facebook, Facetime, Skype and suchlike (Jenkins *et al.* 2013). *Reversed production and consumption* – aka crowdsourcing – is perhaps the preeminent management buzzword of our time, as is customer co-creation, another name for much the same thing, albeit some cynics see it as cyber slave labour (Morozov 2014). *Decentring* is equally evident, though it's no longer confined to consumer subjectivity.[3] It is discernible in the rise of offshoring, outsourcing, online shopping, social networking, computer dating and cloud computing, where our stuff – music, movies, books, learned articles – is stored somewhere in the ether and nobody seems to mind (Davenport 2014). Management, moreover, is a conceptual congeries of *juxtaposed opposites*, a paradoxical place where less is more (Robertson and Breen 2014), more is less (Schwartz 2007), winners are losers (Harford 2011), outsiders are insiders (Thorndike 2012), information technology is both master and slave (Carr 2010), innovations are renovations with good public relations (*Economist* 2014) and successful marketers cede control to creative consumers (Fournier and Avery 2011).

Firat and Venkatesh's analysis may have been prescient, but the brand name they embraced was less cannily chosen. Postmodernism had always been controversial, of course (Cova *et al.* 2012). The ire it attracted from antagonistic intellectuals, such as David Harvey, Terry Eagleton, Alex Callinicos, Raymond Tallis, Shelby Hunt and the O'Shaughnessys among others, was part of its subversive appeal, the illicit thrill that attracted younger scholars chafing under the stultifying orthodoxies of marketing science. Postmodernism, however, was losing its lustre in contiguous academic disciplines, even as it was gaining traction in marketing, thanks to an adroit rebranding exercise by Arnould and Thompson (2005), who renamed it Consumer Culture Theory (CCT) and assured the mainstream that postmodernists were committed to rigorous qualitative research, as well as the betterment of marketing management (Cova *et al.* 2009).

Indeed, in a brilliantly ironic twist that bears comparison with Drucker's initial nominative announcement, postmodern marketing was being mainstreamed at the precise moment when PoMo imploded in philosophy, its seemingly impregnable citadel in the social sciences. Written by Alan Kirby (2006), postmodernism's obituary was published in *Philosophy Now*, a mass circulation glossy magazine for deep thinkers who like a little *Hello* with their Hegel. In a coruscating critique, Kirby (2006) contended that far from being alive and kicking, as the liberal arts elite continued to assume, postmodernist culture was dead and buried and pushing up deconstructed daisies:

> Just look out into the cultural marketplace, buy novels published in the last five years, watch a twenty-first century film, listen to the latest music – above all just sit and watch television for a week – and you will hardly catch a glimpse of postmodernism. The people who produce the cultural material which academics and non-academics read, watch and listen to, have simply given up on postmodernism.

Kirby's elegy proved premature, mind you. Like the Lazarus of thought, PoMo has since risen from the sepulchre, albeit under the unappealing appellation 'post-postmodernism' (Nealon 2012). The latter, for sure, is just one among many terms used to describe the condition of contemporary culture now that postmodernity is history.[4] Its competitors include *hypermodernism*, Lipovetsky's (2005) claim that we live in an era where consumption is all-consuming in almost every sphere of social life; *auto-modernity*, Samuels' (2008) suggestion that universal access to information excess is creating a condition where technological automation and personal autonomy successfully co-exist; *digi-modernism*, Kirby's (2009) contention that popular culture is being radically transformed by the explosive growth of social networking, computer gaming, reality television and CGI-3D cinema; *metamodernism*, Vermeulen and van den Akker's (2010) mooted mode of neo-romantic discourse – already popular among architects, artists and movie-makers – that oscillates between modernist enthusiasm and postmodernist irony; and *altermodernism*, Bourriaud's (2009) bold hypothesis that the void beyond the postmodern is akin to a cultural constellation, a conceptual archipelago, where multitudes of alternative aesthetic possibilities prevail. The market leader, nevertheless, is post-postmodernism (Fjellestad and Engberg 2013).

What about tomorrow?

So, where does this leave marketing? Having cast off our postmodern callipers for the conceptual crutch called CCT, is it wise to shackle ourselves to post-postmodernism? The case for doing so has been made by Cova *et al.* (2013). After summarising the manifold benefits that PoMo brought to marketing thought, not least casting off the pseudo scientific straightjacket, Cova *et al.* (2013: 213) conclude that post-postmodernism has much to offer our field. Specifically, it helps locate marketing phenomena in 'their wider social, cultural and historical contexts to expose embedded power relationships and ideologies'.

There's a much more elemental selling point, however. Namely, that for all its undoubted shortcomings, affectations and idiocies (O'Shaughnessy and O'Shaughnessy 2002), postmodernism remains a universal language of sorts. It is spoken by academics across the entire spectrum of the social sciences and the humanities, and the physical sciences on occasion. The CCT rebrand has rendered PoMo acceptable to marketing's mainstream, but it has come at the cost of conversing with the wider academic community. CCT speaks to a very small constituency and even if mainstream marketing were included in that constituency, it's still miniscule compared to the distant reach of postmodern discourse. True, CCT's champions maintain that their fiefdom is open to all (Arnould and Thompson 2007). But the sad reality is that CCT articles are rarely cited by researchers in contiguous disciplines, let alone those on the far shores of the academic archipelago. Postmodern marketing publications, by contrast, were rather less ghettoised back in the day and, while they never stopped radical sociologists or rabid anthropologists in their anti-capitalist tracks, it is noteworthy that Hardt and Negri's (2000) *Empire* – the bible of neo-Marxian economics – not only mentions the work of postmodern marketers but does so with approval.

Speaking personally, I'm very much in favour of Cova *et al.*'s recommendations. But their putative paradigm shift is unlikely to happen. The ridicule that any such reversion would invite – make up your minds, people! – means that marketing's postmodernists will continue to nail their colours to the CCT mast rather than be regarded as intellectual dilettantes. CCT is in the throes of formalising itself, furthermore, complete with executive committees, annual conferences, membership fees and dedicated journals. The die has been cast and, like Napoleon at Waterloo, post-postmodernism is unlikely to withstand the hard pounding.[5] PoPoMo may triumph elsewhere, but marketing is already retreating into its scholarly shell, dreaming dreams of SDL and imminent scientific breakthroughs.

Few marketers, then, are likely to rally to the post-postmodern flag, or fight the good fight under its auspices. Yet, akin to Tom Brown's body which lies a-mouldering in the grave, PoMo's soul goes marching on. Three aspects of the postmodern condition are still apparent in marketing and seem set to stick around for some considerable time. They are its *aesthetic emphasis*, its *backward leanings* and its *critical concerns*.

Aesthetic emphasis

In a classic overview of the postmodern condition, Featherstone (1991) claimed that its principal distinguishing feature was the 'aestheticisation of everyday life'. And, while other commentators on the construct had their own personal hobbyhorses – Cova (1996) considered 'co-creation' the kingpin, O'Donohoe (1997) made the case for 'intertextuality', Sherry (1998) sang the praises of 'space and place' – most would agree that aestheticisation is still going strong. The experiential school of thought within marketing, which finds expression in fabulous flagship stores, extravagantly themed restaurants, marvellous brand museums and more (Lindgreen *et al.* 2009), are testament to the aestheticisation impulse, as are exquisitely designed, beautiful to behold and even better to handle products like the iPhone and its manifold organoleptic analogues. Then there's the wondrous Potty Palooza:

Charmin's twenty-seven-room de-luxe traveling bathroom facility. Painted sky-blue with fluffy white clouds, complete with flushing porcelain toilets, hardwood floors and air conditioning, Potty Palooza gets little competition from the ranks of rented porta-potties lined up outside the concerts, sporting events, and festivals it frequents.

Since its debut in 2002, the Palooza truck has been on the road for as much as eleven months a year, visiting twenty-six to thirty events annually, from the Super Bowl to the Arizona Hot-Air Balloon Festival. In light of its success, Procter & Gamble has added a smaller, twelve-stall truck (Potty Palooza number 2) and developed similar traveling shows for Crest Toothpaste and the Gillette Fusion Razor.

'Guests' at Potty Palooza are offered a menu of toilet paper options that go beyond the standard white roll, with features that appeal to customers' sense of smell and touch – a multisensory experience. A selection of offerings from years past includes Charmin Ultra (the brand's premium offering, upgraded in 2000 and standard on the tour), Charmin Plus (with chamomile), Charmin Aloe and E, and Charmin Scents – with perfumes like Wildflower Fresh and Shower Fresh built into the roll. All told, Charmin's five million annual guests use some ten thousand cushioned rolls, enough to necessitate a separate supply truck in the Potty Palooza caravan.

(Conley 2008: 69–71)

Charmin's restroom reboot is more than the acme of experiential excrementalism, it is a metaphor for marketing thought. Aestheticisation is no less evident in the academy. It is evident in the latter-day uptick in analyses of arts marketing and the cultural industries more generally. It is evident in the blogrolls and social media presence of prominent members of the professoriat such as Robert Kozinets, Christopher Hackley and Grant McCracken. It is evident in the articles learned academics write, which are becoming less unreadable than heretofore. Conventional modes of academic discourse – flat, factual, impersonal, passive voiced, ostentatiously unembellished, exaggeratedly scientific – are being supplemented with works of poetry, drama, photography, videography, musical performances and multi-volume blockbuster novels in a variety of genres (Schroeder 2014). Our journals are jangling with exercises in experimental writing involving exaggeration, alliteration and flights of rhetorical fancy, often employing the once unthinkable first person singular or directly addressing the readership. I ask you!

True, such exercises are deplored by many mainstream marketing scholars, who purport to be appalled by egregious acts of literary self-indulgence. It is arguable, moreover, that the novels, plays, paintings, videographies, etc. are not only embarrassingly amateurish but rather less insightful than the marketing-related ruminations of 'proper' poets, playwrights, novelists and non-fiction writers with the common touch. Consider the following reflections on IKEA and the personalities of British biscuit brands (Table 2.1), which put academia's creative output to shame:

IKEA fucks with your head. All you want is some furniture: why do they want your sanity in return? The layout alone makes you feel like a lab rat. The stores are like psychoactive jigsaw puzzles with moving pieces, designed by a sick Swedish physicist with access to extra dimensions. They have what look like short cuts between adjoining sections, allowing you to pop through a little walkway from one part of the store to another. But where you end up won't be where you were trying to get to, even if the store map said it would be. Worse, if you decide you were better off where you were, and pop back through the hole, you won't end up where you started, but in a different section again. Sometimes on a different floor altogether. In a different branch of IKEA.

(Lowe and McArthur 2006)

Yet for all their creative shortcomings, the videos of Russell Belk, the poems of Sidney Levy, the short stories of John Schouten, the *Strictly Come Branding* dance routines of Stephen Brown – don't ask! – illustrate that there's more than one way to skin a scholarly cat. Woodward and Holbrook's (2013) learned dialogue; Quinn and Patterson's (2013) two-hander on everyday rituals; and Chris Hackley's (2013) wry ruminations on the customer service experiences appertaining to his BMW are helping 'break the cake of custom' (Levitt 1991: 57) that encrusts marketing scholarship.

This aesthetic emphasis is an admirable endeavour. Long may it continue.

Table 2.1 Half man, half biscuit

'It's the prince of biscuits really, isn't it? The custard cream.'

Oliver Sweeny, aesthete, gourmand, bon viveur, had assumed his mid-morning tea-break position – sprawled in his chair, feet on the desk, mug in fist . . .

'Isn't that the Garibaldi?' I asked.

'No, no, no.' He glared at me. 'You're getting mixed up with the, er . . . with Machiavelli. No, none of your foreign muck here . . . '

He paused while his inky fingers stabbed again at the packaging.

'No, there's no doubt, the custard cream has it all: fine texture, nice filling, not too sweet, holds together in a tight spot, but at the same time not afraid to show its feminine side.'

'Sounds more like my uncle Toby,' I said. 'By the way, what's your position on the Jacobs' Mikado?'

'Ah, now.' Oliver set down his mug and clasped his hands together under his fleshy chin, making a steeple of his index fingers. 'Essentially a satirist. Walks the line between biscuit and sex toy.'

'Yes, I've always considered it a bit of a tease myself.'

I was warming to the topic.

'Give me the firm handshake of a chocolate digestive any day.'

'Or the iron fist of the gingernut.'

We ate and sipped in meditative silence. We were in no hurry. Large expanses of our working day often passed in this way.

'I have to say,' Oliver continued. 'I'm quite partial to a Hobnob, although they can be a bit hairy without a cup of tea.'

'Aren't they just digestives with a bit of rope mixed in?'

'Well, they have a certain rustic charm . . . I'm not sure about *rope*.'

'No, no, Gypsy Creams have rustic charm – you can see it in the adverts – Hobnobs are just agricultural . . . like being taken roughly by a farmhand with eyebrows on his cheeks. They should have put a bit of chocolate on them.'

'Actually, I believe they *have* brought out a chocolate version.'

'Oh yes?'

'You know two items whose credentials I view with suspicion? The Jaffa Cake and the Wagon Wheel, and here's why . . . '

Source: Smith (2012: 7–9).

Backward leaning

Alongside aesthetics, the living legacy of postmodernism includes an incongruous yearning for yesteryear. As Fjellestad and Engberg (2013) rightly observe:

> Today's discourses are saturated with terms of re-making. Thus we remix, reconfigure, remediate, recombine, reorganise, reengage, relocate, recontextualise, reassess, reposition, remythologise, reconstruct, revoke, reconstitute, recollect, recast, rebrand, reframe, remap, revisit, repurpose, remobilise, rethink, reinterrogate, rearticulate, reconceptualise, recompose, reevaluate, redirect, rerun, renew, reconsider, reshape, refashion.
>
> (Fjellestad and Engberg 2013: 4)

Few marketers, I suspect, would argue with Fjellestad and Engberg's summary. On the contrary, they might be tempted to ask what took them so long to catch on. A decade before their insightful reflections, Brown *et al.* (2003) identified a nascent trend termed retrobranding. Taking the then resurgent *Star Wars* franchise and the relaunched Volkswagen Bug as indicative exemplars, they contended that the rise of retromarketing was more than a passing fad. It was a long-term trend attributable to the ageing of the Baby Boom generation (with the attendant increase in personal and communal nostalgia). It was a consequence of increasingly turbulent economic, political and technological conditions (since troubled times increase consumers' desire for 'the good old days'). It was likewise due, they determined, to plain and simple corporate imperatives, where it is cheaper and less risky to re-release bygone brands than build them up (then break them through) from scratch.

A decade on from Brown *et al*.'s initial article, it's clear that we live in a retrospective epoch (Kozinets 2013). Not only have the Volkswagen Bug and *Star Wars* saga been subject to a second round of revival respectively – the first episode of *Star Wars*' new trilogy (starring Harrison Ford, Mark Hamill and Carrie Fisher) is scheduled for release in 2015 and the neo-retro VW (aka the new New Beetle) was successfully relaunched with a more masculine shape in 2012 – but nostalgia mining has moved from the margins to the mainstream. Every major car manufacturer now includes one or more retro autos in its range; every other blockbuster movie is a sequel or prequel or remake or reboot of a pre-existing property; every ageing rock band is re-releasing an enhanced version of its greatest hit and going on tour to play their cobwebbed album tracks in sequence; every big-name sports brand is selling a selection of heritage sneakers, such as the once futuristic now anachronistic Nike Air Max; every legendary fashion label is rifling through its archive for forthcoming collections or taking its cue from retro television series like *Mad Men*, *Downton Abbey* or *Boardwalk Empire*; every fast moving consumer good with a long-tailed marketing legacy is either disinterring its former logo, or resurrecting long-dead slogans, or rebirthing half-forgotten mascots, or rebroadcasting choice selections of monochrome television ads or reappearing in its youthful packaging, fresh faced and innocent (Lowenthal 2014).

And it's not only customer-facing corporations who are wrestling with retro. Marketing scholars too are taking renewed interest in golden-oldie issues. The study of consumer nostalgia has burgeoned in the aftermath of Holbrook's (1993) scale-development endeavours (Zhou *et al*. 2012). Heritage-heavy branded experiences like Walt Disney World (Bettany and Belk 2011), American Girl Place (Diamond *et al*. 2009), Colorado's stock show (Peñaloza 2001) and the Burning Man festival – for aptly named 'modern primitives' (Kozinets 2003: 200) – have been studied in detail. Consumers' embrace of immemorial, myth-informed archetypes for personal identity purposes has come under close scrutiny (Thompson 2004). The genealogies of past-powered icons, such as Coca-Cola, Harley Davidson and Jack Daniel's, have been painstakingly unpacked (Holt 2004, 2005) and all sorts of 'retroscapes', from theme restaurants to festival malls, have been mapped, modelled, and admired by the museologists of modern marketing (Sherry 2003). History has never been hotter.

Critical concerns

In one of the most accessible overviews of postmodern social science, Rosenau (1992) makes a crucial distinction between *sceptical* and *affirmative* traditions. The former is the intellectual equivalent of a Gallic shrug. It is typified, according to Foxall *et al*. (1998: 240), by 'irony, parody, playfulness, irreverence, insolence, couldn't care less cynicism, tongue-in-cheek insouciance, and absolute unwillingness to accept the accepted'. It doesn't provide an alternative to established marketing concepts. It simply informs us that they are inadequate, as are all attempts to conceptualise marketing theory and practice. *Ça va?*

The affirmative wing of postmodernism is the wing that's really taken flight in latter-day marketing scholarship. Do-gooding marketing thinkers don't have much time for the sceptics' sniggering self-indulgence. Instead, they aim to expose the iniquities of Western capitalism, fight for the rights of oppressed minorities and overthrow the hegemonic nexus of string-pulling, back-scratching, trough-truffling, tax-dodging, Davos-attending, pocket-lining, power-broking corporate fat cats. Provided, that is, they're allowed regular fair trade coffee breaks in the faculty refractory, receive hefty annual increments to their ample professorial salaries, and given generous travel budgets-cum-research grants to read up on, and fly off to, hot spots in the developing world that desperately need their theoretically-informed, Horkheimer-quoting, Badoit-bolstered, Žižek-citing insights. They're a marketing version of Harry Potter's high-minded yet fortuitously photogenic Professor Gilderoy Lockhart, whose simpering ambition is to save the world and market his own range of haircare potions.

Like Lockhart, marketing's critical theorists are our defence against the dark arts, except that they're neither so hirsute nor as handsome. And just as the gilded Gilderoy was never averse to self-promotion, our critical contingent is assiduously advancing its cause (see Scott 2007; Tadajewski 2010; Ellis *et al.* 2011). Textbooks, anthologies, conferences, seminar series and special issues of assorted journals have been published, assembled, organised, underwritten and edited respectively. For thinkers who condemn the iniquities of marketing thinking, they are pretty good at marketing their version of marketing thought, even if it means pulling down the postmodern platform that supported them:

> While we agree that postmodernism has presented a challenge to mainstream marketing thought, it overstates the degree to which all persons in this world have been beneficiaries of the changing nature of capitalism . . . The apparent postmodernisation of the Western world is predicated on the maintenance of a subaltern population who produce those beautifully marketed goods that we can purchase at relatively low prices . . . This seriously calls into question much postmodern marketing research.
>
> (Tadajewski and Brownlie 2008: 304–305)

Sceptics might be tempted to point out that subaltern copyeditors and fact-checkers also contribute to the authors' virtuous, voluminous and vastly expensive critiques, which are priced far above the means of the downtrodden, often illiterate, masses. But hey . . .

None of this means that marketing is above criticism. Marketing is a dark and dirty business. Indeed it's doubly dark insofar as it purports to have consumers' best interests at heart even as it squanders natural resources, despoils the environment, exploits low-paid workers in far-flung sweatshops and takes commercial advantage of human frailties like vanity, gluttony and sloth. It inculcates an avaricious, gimme-gimme-gimme, more-more-more, me-me-me mindset of gotta-get-it instant gratification that's given rise to the obesity crisis, the binge drinking crisis, the body dysmorphia crisis, the shopping addiction crisis and countless other crises that assail contemporary Western society. The, 'great grinding marketing machine' (Wallace 2004: 25) has a lot to answer for.

Happily, marketing has plenty of hypocritical theorists to help discipline our discipline and keep ethical malefactors on the straight and narrow. Hackley (2009) informs us that there are four areas where critical theory contributes to the betterment of things: *functional critique*, ensuring our techniques are fit for purpose; *intellectual critique*, determining whether our concepts make sense; *ethical critique*, evaluating our ideas' impact on the wider world; and *political critique*, asking if the beneficiaries of our intellectual largesse deserve such learned benefactions. Cova *et al.* (2013) maintain that the many and varied forms of neo-Marxism, which have emerged, hydra-like, from the ashes of capitalism's great financial crisis, are just the ticket for left-leaning, right-on tenured radicals in business schools and management departments. Thank goodness Tadajewski *et al.* (2014) are also on hand to discipline the disciplinarians of our discipline. In their self-appointed role as academia's internal affairs department, they have taken the critical thinkers in CCT to task for their intellectual failings, ideological blinkers, historical amnesia and all-American exceptionalism.

Whatever.

Now, no one doubts that the critical marketing crew is well meaning. They have their hearts in the right place: on their sleeves, needless to say. The causes they champion need championing and the changes they advocate are admirable for the most part. But they make their case in such a conceited, holier-than-thou, mother-knows best manner, that they only succeed in alienating those who would otherwise support them. They don't raise consciousness with their conscious-ness-raising critiques. They merely convince the unconverted that they're cranks, a collection of idealistic daydreamers who seem to believe that their lengthy, earnest, jargon-riddled articles about Occupy are going to bring big, bad Western capitalism to its knees. Whatever happened to Occupy, by the way?

Over and out

Twenty years ago, PoMo was the intellectual grit in marketing's managerialist oyster. Today, it's part of the academic furniture. Its once-radical ideas have been absorbed, institutionalised, domesticated, defanged. So sanitised has 'postmodern' become that the word is a synonym for 'contemporary'. That is to say, people despair of our 'postmodern' world the way they once despaired of its 'modern' equivalent. PoMo is a phatic term of mild disapproval that pertains to our amoral, exploitative, unpre-dictable, incomprehensible, socially mediated, genetically modified, disruptively innovative, creatively destructive, blog eat blog, lolcat loving, speed dating, overheating, overeating, greenhouse gassed times. It's usually accompanied by a heavy sigh and rueful shake of the head.

When all is said and done, postmodern marketing is neither alive and kicking nor dead and buried. It is somewhere between the two, alive yet buried, dead yet kicking spasmodically. In cer-tain respects, PoMo is the undead of marketing discourse, an academic counterpart of the zombie brands, vampire brands, Frankenbrands and doppelgänger brands that stalk our streets and super-markets and shopping centres and online cyberspaces (Walker 2008). Brands that go bump in the night. Don't look now, but the ghost of PoMo's behind you!

Further reading

Modesty forbids, you understand, but you might find the following of interest:

Brown, S. (1995), *Postmodern Marketing*, London: Routledge. Summarises the major strands of postmodern thought, coupled with a critique of 'modern' marketing theory.

Brown, S. (1998), *Postmodern Marketing Two: Telling Tales*, London: International Thomson. Extends the first book by arguing that art, aesthetics, storytelling *et al.* offer a possible way forward for twenty-first-century marketing scholarship.

Brown, S. (2001), *Marketing – The Retro Revolution*, London: Sage. Rummages through the dustbin of marketing history and comes up with an alternative to the 'modern' marketing paradigm.

Notes

1   Not that you actually paid for it, of course. You ordered an inspection copy, like everybody else, and forgot to return it when requested, like everybody else. Hey, what are they gonna do, hunt you down like a dog for the sake of a freebie? A freebie, furthermore, that you might conceivably list as 'required' reading (no chance) or 'recommended' reading (perhaps a chapter or two) or 'additional' reading (a library copy, in other words).

2   As I write these words (okay, okay, cut and paste them – gimme a break, why don't ya?!), *Riverdance* is still going strong on its everlasting farewell tour, *Shrek* is a wildly popular West End musical and Celine Dion continues to pack them in like nobody's business.

3   They were wrong about the 'market of one'. Technological advances, courtesy of Big Data's fiendish algorithms, mean that the Googles, Amazons and Tescos of this world have a pretty good handle on our shopping behaviours, intentions, etc.

4   Interestingly, the word 'post-postmodern' appeared in marketing discourse *before* the CCT reboot (Holt 2002). But it never caught on. Timing's everything, in academia, as elsewhere.

5   Yes, I know it was Wellington, not Napoleon, who suffered the 'hard pounding' at Waterloo. Postmodernists aren't renowned for their attention to historical detail (which may not worry you, but, by God, it frightens me).

References

Appignanesi, R. and Garratt, C. (1995), *Postmodernism for Beginners*, Cambridge, UK: Icon.

Apple, M. (1984), *Free Agents*, New York: Harper & Row, reprinted in McHale, B. (1992), *Constructing Postmodernism*, London: Routledge, pp. 38–41.

Arnould, E. J. and Thompson, C. J. (2005), 'Consumer culture theory (CCT): Twenty years of research', *Journal of Consumer Research*, 31(March): 868–882.

Arnould, E. J. and Thompson, C. J. (2007) 'Consumer culture theory (and we really mean theoretics): Dilemmas and opportunities posed by an academic branding strategy', in Belk, R. W. and Sherry, J. F. Jr, (eds) *Research in Consumer Behavior, Vol. 11: Consumer Culture Theory*, Oxford, UK: JAI Press, pp. 3–22.

Askegaard, S. and Scott, L. M. (2013), 'Consumer culture theory: The ironies of history', *Marketing Theory*, 13(2): 139–147.

Best, S. and D. Kellner (2001), *The Postmodern Adventure*, New York: Guildford.

Bettany, S. and Belk, R. W. (2011), 'Disney discourses of self and other: Animality, primitivity, modernity, and postmodernity', *Consumption Markets & Culture*, 14(2): 163–176.

Bourriaud, N. (2009), 'Altermodern', in N. Bourriaud (ed.) *Altermodern: Tate Triennial*, London: Tate Publishing, pp. 11–24.

Bradshaw, P. (2014), 'Secret cinema, Back to the Future', *The Guardian*, July 31, www.theguardian.com (accessed 10 October 2014).

Brown, S. (1995), *Postmodern Marketing*, London: Routledge.

Brown, S. (2006), 'Ambi-brand culture: On a wing and a swear with Ryanair', in Schroeder, J. E. and Salzer-Mörling, M. (eds) *Brand Culture*, London: Routledge, pp. 50–66.

Brown, S. (2007), 'Are we nearly there yet? On the retro-dominant logic of marketing', *Marketing Theory*, 7(3): 291–300.

Brown, S., Kozinets, R. V. and Sherry, J. F. (2003), 'Teaching old brands new tricks: Retro branding and the revival of brand meaning', *Journal of Marketing*, 67(July): 19–33.

Butler, C. (2002), *Postmodernism: A Very Short Introduction*, Oxford: Oxford University Press.

Calás, M. B. and Smircich, L. (1997) (eds), *Postmodern Management Theory*, Aldershot, UK: Dartmouth/Ashgate.

Carr, N. (2010), *The Shallows: How the Internet is Changing the Way We Read, Think and Remember*, London: Atlantic.

Conley, L. (2008), *Obsessive Branding Disorder: The Illusion of Business and the Business of Illusion*, New York: Public Affairs.

Cova, B. (1996), 'What postmodernism means to marketing managers', *European Management Journal*, 14(5): 494–499.

Cova, B., Ford, D. and Salle, R. (2009) 'Academic brands and their impact on scientific endeavour: The case of business market research and researchers', *Industrial Marketing Management*, 38(6): 570–576.

Cova, B., Prévot, F. and Spencer, R. (2012) 'Ahoy all postmodern navigators! Conceptual havens in a stormy ocean', *Industrial Marketing Management*, 41(2): 365–367.

Cova, B., Maclaran, P. and Bradshaw, A. (2013) 'Rethinking consumer culture theory from the postmodern to the communist horizon', *Marketing Theory*, 13(2): 213–225.

Davenport, T. H. (2014), *Big Data at Work*, Boston: Harvard Business Review Press.

Diamond, N., Sherry, J. F., Muñiz, A. M., McGrath, M. A., Kozinets, R. V. and Borghini, S. (2009), 'American Girl and the brand gestalt: Closing the loop on sociocultural branding research', *Journal of Marketing*, 73(May): 118–134.

Drucker, P. (1954), *The Practice of Management*, New York: Harper & Row.

Drucker, P. (1957), *Landmarks of Tomorrow: A Report on the New 'Post-Modern' World*, New York: Harper & Row.

Economist (2014), 'Second wind: Some traditional businesses are surviving in an age of disruptive innovation', *The Economist*, June 14, p. 76.

Ellis, N., Fitchett, J., Higgins, M., Jack, G., Lim, M., Saren, M. and Tadajewski, M. (2011), *Marketing: A Critical Textbook*, London: Sage.

Falk, P. and Campbell, C. (eds) (1997), *The Shopping Experience*, London: Sage.

Featherstone, M. (1991), *Consumer Culture and Postmodernism*, London: Sage.

Firat, A. F. and Venkatesh, A. (1995), 'Liberatory postmodernism and the reenchantment of consumption', *Journal of Consumer Research*, 22(December): 239–267.

Fjellestad, D. and Engberg, M. (2013), 'Toward a concept of post-postmodernism or Lady Gaga's reconfigurations of Madonna', *Reconstruction*, 12(4), www.reconstruction.eserver.org (accessed 27 June 2013).

Fournier, S. and Avery, J. (2011), 'The uninvited brand', *Business Horizons*, 54(2): 193–207.

Foxall, G. F., Goldsmith, R. E. and Brown, S. (1998), *Consumer Psychology for Marketing*, London: International Thomson.

Grant, J. (1999), *The New Marketing Manifesto*, London: Orion.

Gummesson, E. (2001), 'Are current research approaches in marketing leading us astray?' *Marketing Theory*, 1(1): 27–48.

Hackley, C. (2009), *Marketing: A Critical Introduction*, London: Sage.

Hackley, C. (2013), *Marketing in Context: Setting the Scene*, Basingstoke, UK: Palgrave Macmillan.

Hardt, M. and Negri, A. (2000), *Empire*, Cambridge, MA: Harvard University Press.

Harford, T. (2011), *Adapt: Why Success Always Starts With Failure*, London: Little, Brown.

Holbrook, M. B. (1993), 'Nostalgia and consumption preferences: Some emerging patterns of consumer tastes', *Journal of Consumer Research*, 20(September): 245–256.

Holt, D. B. (2002), 'Why do brands cause trouble? A dialectical theory of consumer culture and branding', *Journal of Consumer Research* 29(June): 70–90.

Holt, D. B. (2004), *How Brands Become Icons: The Principles of Cultural Branding*, Boston, MA: Harvard Business School Press.

Holt, D. B. (2005), 'How societies desire brands: Using cultural theory to explain brand symbolism', in Ratneshwar, S. and Mick, D. G. (eds) *Inside Consumption*, London: Routledge, pp. 273–291.

Jenkins, H., Ford, S. and Green, J. (2013), *Spreadable Media: Creating Value and Meaning in a Networked Culture*, New York: New York University Press.

Kirby, A. (2006), 'The death of postmodernism and beyond', *Philosophy Now*, 58 (November/December), n.p.n., www.philosophynow.org (accessed 1 September 2013).

Kirby, A. (2009), *Digimodernism: How New Technologies Dismantle the Postmodern and Reconfigure Our Culture*, New York: Continuum.

Kozinets, R. V. (2003), 'The moment of infinite fire', in Brown, S. and Sherry, J. F. (eds) *Time, Space and the Market: Retroscapes Rising*, Armonk, NY: M.E. Sharpe, pp. 199–216.

Kozinets, R. V. (2013), 'Retrobrands and retromarketing', in Jenkins, H., Ford, S. and Green, J. (eds) *Spreadable Media: Creating Value and Meaning in a Networked Culture* (web enhanced version), New York: New York University Press, http://spreadablemedia.org/essays/kozinets/#.VnQxR6SzWpo (accessed 19 December 2013).

Levitt, T. (1991), *Thinking About Management*, New York: Free Press.

Lindgreen, A., Vanhamme, J. and Beverland, M. B. (2009), *Memorable Customer Experiences: A Research Anthology*, Farnham, UK: Gower.

Lipovetsky, G. (2005), *Hypermodern Times*, Cambridge, UK: Polity.

Lowenthal, D. (2014), *The Past is a Foreign Country: Revisited*, Cambridge, UK: Cambridge University Press.

Lowe, S. and McArthur, A. (2006), *Is it Just Me or is Everything Shit?* London: Time Warner.

Mitchell, A. (2001), *Right Side Up: Building Brands in the Age of the Organised Consumer*, London: HarperCollins.

Morozov, E. (2014), *To Save Everything Click Here*, London: Penguin.

Nealon, J. T. (2012), *Post-Postmodernism: Or, the Cultural Logic of Just-in-Time Capitalism*, Stanford, CA: Stanford University Press.

O'Donohoe, S. (1997), 'Raiding the pantry: Advertising intertextuality and the young adult audience', *European Journal of Marketing*, 31(3/4): 234–253.

O'Shaughnessy, J. and O'Shaughnessy, N. J. (2002), 'Postmodernism and marketing: Separating the wheat from the chaff', *Journal of Macromarketing*, 22(1): 109–135.

Peñaloza, L. (2001), 'Consuming the American West: Cultural meaning and memory at a stock show and rodeo', *Journal of Consumer Research*, 28(December): 369–398.

Piercy, N. (1997), *Market-Led Strategic Change*, Oxford, UK: Butterworth-Heinemann.

Quinn, L. and Patterson, A. (2013), 'Storying marketing research: The twisted tale of a consumer profiled', *Journal of Marketing Management*, 29(5/6): 720–733.

Robertson, D. and Breen, B. (2014), *Brick by Brick: How Lego Rewrote the Rules of Innovation and Conquered the Global Toy Industry*, New York: Random House.

Rosenau, P. M. (1992), *Postmodernism and the Social Sciences: Insights, Inroads, and Intrusions*, Princeton, NJ: Princeton University Press.

Samuels, R. (2008), 'Auto-modernity after postmodernism: Autonomy and automation in culture, technology, and education', in McPherson, T. (ed.) *Digital Youth, Innovation, and the Unexpected*, Cambridge, MA: MIT Press, pp. 219–240.

Schroeder, J. (2014), 'Editorial', *Consumption Markets and Culture*, 17(6): 485–489.

Schwartz, B. (2007), *The Paradox of Choice: Why More is Less*, New York: HarperCollins.

Scott, L. M. (2007), 'Critical research in marketing: An armchair report', in Saren, M., Maclaren, P., Goulding, C., Elliott, R., Shankar, A. and Catterall, M. (eds) *Critical Marketing: Defining the Field*, Oxford, UK: Butterworth-Heinemann, pp. 4–17.

Sherry, J. F. (1991), 'Postmodern alternatives: The interpretive turn in consumer research', in Robertson, T. S. and Kassarjian, H. H. (eds) *Handbook of Consumer Research*, Englewood Cliffs, NJ: Prentice-Hall, pp. 548–591.

Sherry, J. F. (ed.) (1998), *Servicescapes: The Concept of Place in Contemporary Markets*, Chicago, IL: NTC Books.

Sherry, J. F. (2003), 'What's past is prologue: Retroscapes in retrospect', in Brown, S. and Sherry, J. F. (eds) *Time, Space, and the Market: Retroscapes Rising*, Armonk, NY: M.E. Sharpe, pp. 313–320.

Sheth, J. and Sisodia, R. (2006), *Does Marketing Need Reform?: Fresh Perspectives on the Future*, Armonk, NY: M.E. Sharpe.

Smith, K. (2012) *Jammy Dodger: A Novel*, Dingwall, UK: Sandstone Press.

Tadajewski, M. (2010), 'Towards a history of critical marketing studies', *Journal of Marketing Management*, 26(9/10): 773–824.

Tadajewski, M. and Brownlie, D. (2008), 'Past postmodernism', in Tadajewski, M. and Brownlie, D. (eds) *Critical Marketing: Issues in Contemporary Marketing*, Chichester, UK: Wiley, pp. 301–310.

Tadajewski, M., Chelekis, J., DeBerry-Spence, B., Figueiredo, B., Kravets, O., Nuttavuthisit, K., Peñalosa, L. and Moisander, J. (2014), 'The discourses of marketing and development: towards critical transformative marketing research', *Journal of Marketing Management*, 30(17/18): 1728–1771.

Thompson, C. J. (2004), 'Marketplace mythology and discourses of power', *Journal of Consumer Research*, 31(June): 162–180.

Thorndike, W. N. (2012), *Outsiders: Eight Unconventional CEOs and their Radically Rational Blueprint for Success*, Boston, MA: Harvard Business Review Press.

Vargo, S. L. and Lusch, R. F. (2004), 'Evolving to a new dominant logic for marketing', *Journal of Marketing*, 68(1): 1–17.

Vermeulen, T. and van den Akker, R. (2010), 'Notes on metamodernism', *Journal of Aesthetics and Culture*, 2: 1–14.

Walker, R. (2008), 'Can a dead brand live again?' *New York Times*, May 18, www.nytimes.com (accessed 18 June 2008).

Wallace, D. F. (2004), *Oblivion: Stories*, London: Abacus.

Ward, G. (1997), *Teach Yourself Postmodernism*, London: Hodder Headline.

Wolf, M. J. (1999), *The Entertainment Economy*, London: Penguin.

Woodward, M. N. and Holbrook, M. B. (2013), 'Dialogue on some concepts, definitions and issues pertaining to "consumption experiences"', *Marketing Theory*, 13(3): 323–344.

Zhou, X., Wildschut, T., Sedikides, C., Shi, K. and Feng, C. (2012), 'Nostalgia: The gift that keeps on giving', *Journal of Consumer Research*, 39(June): 39–50.

3 Marketing theory

Lisa O'Malley and Maria Lichrou

Introduction

Marketing is everywhere around us. It is perhaps the most visible aspect of business and even if not everyone has had the experience of *being* a marketer, there are very few people in the world who have not been exposed to marketing activities in their capacity as customers. As a result, a common mistake made by students who are new to marketing is to believe that they already pretty much know everything there is to know about marketing (Celly 2007). Exacerbating this, for many third-level institutions introductory marketing courses are largely based on teaching a toolbox-based approach (O'Malley and Patterson 1998; Catterall *et al.* 2002; Hill and McGinnis 2007) with assessment often involving short or multiple choice questioning. As a result, a great number of students do not connect with marketing theory in any meaningful way, and deep learning and engagement are certainly not fostered (Celly 2007).

Why is this important for you? Well, that all depends on why you are studying marketing. If, like many people, you believe that the purpose of marketing education is to prepare students for the world of work (Hill and McGinnis 2007), then you need to be confident that what you learn now, and how you learn, will prepare you well for your future. However, it is not always easy to know if what you learn now will be sufficient for the work you will later be required to do. What we do know is that marketing managers of the future will have to deal with extraordinary levels of disruption and change – much more than marketers of any previous generation. They will have to deal with rapidly changing technology and shorter product lifecycles (Christensen and Overdorf 2001; Gilbert and Bower 2002; Hill and McGinnis 2007). They will operate in a complex, dynamic global marketplace in which consumers' continue to demand increasingly new, different and more meaningful experiences (Pine and Gilmore 2011). Knowledge of the past is unlikely to be sufficient to deal with complex new issues as they arise in the future (Hill and McGinnis 2007). Therefore, future marketing managers will need to be able to evaluate whether extant marketing theories remain useful, whether they can be adapted or whether completely new theories are required. In order to negotiate the complex marketplace and make informed practical decisions, these managers will need to be effective learners and thinkers in action. An essential *meta skill* in this regard is the ability to think – in critical, creative and reflexive ways – and this is foundational to becoming an effective practitioner in whatever capacity you choose to work (Schon 1983; Catterall *et al.* 2002; Cunliffe 2004; Paul and Elder 2004; Hill and McGinnis 2007; Hill *et al.* 2007). The ability to *think about* theory therefore becomes more important than the content of the theory itself – because *thinking about* is a transferrable meta skill that you can take from education to the world of work. Mastering this skill is essential to becoming an effective marketing practitioner.

This chapter first reviews the nature and purpose of theory as a tool of thought that enables the development of reflexive practitioners. We then introduce you to the rich and diverse landscape of marketing theory, and we revisit seminal debates that shaped marketing thought and practice. In doing so, we hope to highlight the transformative potential of marketing theory; learning from the past can lead to better future marketing thought and practice (Witkowski 1989).

Understanding the nature and purpose of theory

Theory is a tool of thought, which helps us to make sense of the world we live and work in. It is, however, difficult to define what theory is, because theory can represent many positions on a continuum ranging from speculation at one end, through to well-developed arguments, and eventually, to principles based on scientific evidence. Thus, 'depending on how one defines the term "theory", marketing could either be theory rich or theory poor' (Burton 2005: 9). Exacerbating this problem, there are debates in marketing (and elsewhere) regarding what a theory should be, and how it should be tested. This is because all knowledge is socially constructed and is the result of negotiated, accepted views within a field (Goffman 1959; Berger and Luckmann 1967; Garfinkel 1967). While particular viewpoints can prevail at different points in time, they are occasionally challenged, and this becomes the basis for debate within a discipline. What comes to be accepted as knowledge is often the result of existing power structures within a discipline through which some views become accepted while others are marginalised.

> This perspective argues that a 'fact' is not a 'fact' in the sense that it is a product of structures of power, and hence lacks neutrality (Foucault 1980). In this perspective, any fact can be thought of as nothing more than a conclusion with political implications. It is a fact, because it has been deemed to be the accepted conclusion.
>
> (Hill *et al.* 2007: 344)

This can be illustrated through a relatively simple example. From ancient times, the Babylonians, ancient Egyptians, early Hebrews and most Greeks believed the world to be flat. Although the 'flat earth' was accepted as truth for quite some time, in late medieval and early modern times a number of prominent individuals believed this to be untrue and, for a variety of reasons, subscribed to a 'round earth' theory. These included Roger Bacon, Copernicus, Galileo, Columbus and Magellan. While retrospectively it is sometimes easy to see which theory was correct (the world is now generally accepted as being round!), it is useful to consider what it meant to people living in the world when the dominant belief (theory) was that the world was flat.

When Columbus set off for the New World, many people believed that his ship would fall off the edge of the planet, that his men were doomed and that, ultimately, his journey was futile. They believed this because they knew the world to be flat. But Columbus believed that the world was most likely round because of alternative 'round world' theories proposed by a number of scientists over the previous four or five hundred years, which he found to be quite compelling. In acting upon this theory, and sailing his ship in a new direction, not only did Columbus prove that the world was round but he also, allegedly, discovered America. There are a number of important ideas that we can explore through this story.

- People act in accordance with the theories that are accepted as true. Rather than being distant and divorced from practice, theory influences our decisions every single day. So, in our example above, because the sailors believed the world to be flat they did not want to sail to the edge of the world lest they fall off! Because Columbus believed differently (subscribed to a different theory) he behaved differently.

- People do not necessarily think about or acknowledge theory as being a 'theory'. Often, they simply believe these to be truths or facts. This explains how knowledge is socially constructed – in other words, what we accept as truth or facts is often the outcome of dominant beliefs that prevail at a particular time. What we know may change, however, when dominant beliefs are incontrovertibly challenged. In demonstrating the world to be round rather than flat, theories that had previously been ignored were embraced and theories of a flat world were ultimately debunked.

While it is relatively easy to look back at this debate and identify whose theories were correct and whose were incorrect, it is not always easy to be so clear-cut when competing theories exist at a particular moment in time. This becomes even more problematic when considering theories that describe social (behaviour of people) rather than natural (shape of the earth) phenomena. This becomes particularly important when we consider theory in marketing. As we will see later in the chapter, marketing scholars (and practitioners alike) often have different views of theory depending on their philosophical orientation (Maclaran and Stevens 2008). In other words, they often ascribe to different *paradigms*.

The term paradigm, introduced by Thomas Kuhn (1962), can be broadly defined as a set of assumptions and principles that are accepted and shared among the members of a scientific community. A paradigm is important, because it embodies 'the commonality of perspective which binds the work of a group of theorists together in such a way that they can be usefully regarded as approaching social theory within the bounds of the same problematic' (Burrell and Morgan 1992 [1979]: 23). Furthermore, many scholars have drawn on Kuhn's initial notion of *incommensurability*, which suggests that proponents of different paradigms 'are unable to communicate, and that there is no recourse to neutral experience or objective standards to adjudicate between theories' (Sankey 1993: 760). Even though Kuhn's treatment of the concept has changed into weaker definitions of incommensurability (Sankey 1993; Tadajewski 2008), 'his arguments about different communities exhibiting sometimes marked differences of interpretation still resonate' with current marketing scholars (Tadajewski 2014: 316).

Paradigms are important, because they largely influence those assumptions, concepts and frameworks we take for granted. In reviewing important debates within marketing, we can develop our own appreciation of how our current understanding of marketing may have been shaped by particular paradigms, as well as new ways of thinking and doing marketing. Otherwise, we are likely to uncritically conform to others' thinking (Paul and Elder 2004).

Becoming reflexive practitioners

If we consider that marketing education is simply about equipping practitioners with the necessary models and techniques to produce useful knowledge for them, then the focus is on transferring technical skills and competences from expert (academic) to novice (student/practitioner); then education is a relatively simple process. Moreover, if we assume that organisations are independent of other organisations and other stakeholders, then those decisions can be considered in isolation (cf. Ford and Mouzas 2013). This leads to the rather simplistic assumption that all we will need to do is apply the correct tools, or plug the right model into a given situation (Hill *et al.* 2007). This technocratic approach to marketing education has been criticised for failing to produce the kinds of marketing graduates that industry needs (Catterall *et al.* 2002; Burton 2005). Essentially, these are, 'managers who are able to recognise, be sensitive to and have the confidence and ability to cope with a multiplicity of very different and often contradictory discourses' (Catterall *et al.* 1999: 352). As such, industry values marketing graduates who have *meta skills* that enable them to manage themselves, solve problems and be adaptable (Finch *et al.* 2012). This means moving beyond the technical skills that business schools are so adept at developing, and accepting that as managers of the future we will need to be responsible and accountable for our actions (Cunliffe 2004). Future marketers will need to formulate solutions to the messy problems they are presented with, and be able to articulate and defend their solutions.

> In real-world practice, problems do not present themselves to the practitioner as givens. They must be constructed from the materials of problematic situations which are puzzling, troubling and uncertain. Therefore, an ability to think through problems as they arise is the hallmark of an effective practitioner.
>
> (Schon 1983: 40)

Becoming an effective practitioner involves fostering reasoned intellectual development, through critical and creative thinking, as well as explicitly enhancing our emotional intelligence so we can consider moral and ethical problems as they arise.

> This can be seen as a sort of growth, in the old and clichéd sense that 'education broadens the mind', but it has a very real meaning. Being able to look at the world from a number of different and possibly incompatible points of view is a matter of learning to think against oneself and open oneself out.
>
> (Craib 1992: 257)

Intellectual development is essential for students across all disciplines (Yang *et al.* 2008) and no less so for marketing students, who will be required to operate within a global marketplace that is both dynamic and complex. It is important, therefore, to be able to learn effectively in new situations. Developing an appropriate language that helps us think about our own thinking and the thinking of others is essential in this regard. We should be able to move beyond our own individual viewpoints, question assumptions, ideologies and beliefs, empathise with different perspectives, and consider and respond to issues emotionally as well as cognitively (Catterall *et al.* 1999). Engaging with theory and theoretical debates in marketing offers us an exciting opportunity to develop that language, to enhance our intellectual abilities. It requires us to deal with diverse ideas, concepts, frameworks and theories, to choose between competing positions, and allows us to articulate and defend our own points of view. Essentially, this involves developing our abilities to think in critical, creative and reflexive ways (Figure 3.1).

- *Critical thinking* involves evaluating ideas (including those of others and one's own) and identifying the best ones. It involves developing an ability to separate facts from opinion, analyse arguments, recognise errors in reasoning and make ethical judgements (Ruggiero 2003). In order to think critically, we need to have a reasonable grasp of the systems of thought within our discipline and, therefore, engaging with marketing theory is important.
- *Creative thinking* involves being open to new and different things, allowing us to see new patterns or develop new ideas. This often demands that we think outside the established systems and conventions within our discipline. Creativity requires boldness and confidence, an ability to take intellectual risks, and to be able to recognise and overcome constraints.

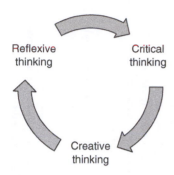

Figure 3.1 The virtuous cycle of critical, creative and reflexive thinking

- *Reflexive thinking* demands a consideration of why things are the way they are. It involves questioning our own assumptions as well as the assumptions, theories and frameworks that prevail within a discipline. Thus, reflexive thinking encourages us to think about 'where/who we are and where/who we would like to be' (Cunliffe 2004: 411), both as individuals and as members of the marketing community.

Engaging critically, creatively and reflexively with marketing theory will provide us with the 'ability to understand and use words and language to defend [ourselves] and the marketing world in which we live' (Celly 2007: 150). We can read the history of marketing as the negotiation of diverse ideas, theories and concepts (for example micro or macro, academic or applied, individual or societal). Some ideas that were once the subjects of debate have now become taken for granted. In reviewing these debates, we should endeavour to not uncritically conform to the thinking of others (Paul and Elder 2004), but to actively develop our own thinking.

Theories of marketing and theories in marketing

Theory development is essential for a discipline's knowledge creation and academic status (Maclaran *et al.* 2009). There are differing views about what theory is, or should be, within any discipline. In marketing, Burton (2005) makes a helpful distinction between *theories of marketing* and *theories in marketing*. A theory of marketing attempts to explain all the behaviours of actors in the marketplace and provides an overarching definition of what marketing is. This has proven to be an incredibly ambitious endeavour and has inevitably been fraught with difficulties (Hill and McGinnis 2007). While there is some agreement that exchange could be a central, organising principle (Bagozzi 1975), it has not been uncontroversial.

Rather than focusing on the challenges of developing the elusive theory of marketing, it may be helpful to consider the extent to which theories in marketing have developed. To a great extent, this has been a bottom-up rather than a top-down approach to theory building (Burton 2005). By working within very particular marketing specialisms and focusing on specific instances of phenomena, theory development has proven more fruitful. Indeed, marketing's 'intellectual path to the present day is marked by contributions from numerous academics, practitioners, and those who operated between these domains who approached their endeavours by drawing from the best and widest perspectives of their time' (Tadajewski and Jones 2014: 1271).

There have been different attempts to classify the main schools of marketing theory (for example, Carman 1980; Fisk and Meyers 1982; Sheth *et al.* 1988; Shaw and Jones 2005). Building on

Table 3.1 Marketing schools of thought

	Question(s) addressed	Level or focus of analysis	Key concepts and theories
Marketing functions school	What activities (i.e. functions) comprise marketing?	*Macro*: middlemen who perform marketing functions	Value added by marketing activities
Marketing commodities school	How are different types of goods classified and related to different types of marketing functions?	*Macro*: trade flows; distinctive characteristic of goods	Classification of goods into: industrial and consumer; convenience, shopping and speciality; products and services; search and experience goods
Marketing institutions school	Who performs marketing functions on commodities?	*Macro*: retailers; wholesalers; middlemen; channels of distribution	Channels of distribution: market gaps and flows; parallel systems depots; transactions and transvections; sorts and transformations; postponement and speculation; conflict and cooperation; power and dependence
Marketing management school	How should managers market products and services to customers?	*Micro*: business firm as seller/ supplier; any individual or organisation as supplier	Marketing mix; marketing concept; segmentation, targeting and positioning
Marketing systems school	What is a marketing system? Why does it exist? How does a marketing system work? Who, where and when, performs marketing work?	*Micro*: firms and households *Macro*: channels of distribution and aggregate marketing systems	Interrelationships between parts and whole; unity of thought; micro and macro marketing; societal impact
Consumer behaviour school	How and why do customers and consumers buy? How do consumers think, feel and act? How can people be persuaded?	*Micro*: organisational buyer behaviour; consumer behaviour; individual and household consumption	Motivation; needs and wants; learning; personality; attitudes; hierarchy of effects; information processing; symbolism and signs; opinion leadership; social class, culture and sub-cultures
Macro-marketing school	How do marketing systems impact society and vice versa?	*Macro*: industries; channels; consumer movements; public policy; economic development	Standard of living; quality of life; marketing systems; aggregate marketing performance
Exchange school	What are the forms of exchange? Who are the parties to exchange? Why do they engage in exchange?	*Macro*: aggregations of buyers and sellers *Micro*: firms and households; any two parties or persons	Transactions: social, economic and market exchange; generic exchange
Marketing history school	When did marketing practices, ideas, theories and schools of thought emerge and evolve?	*Macro and micro*: marketing thought and practice	History of marketing practice; history of marketing thought

Source: Adapted from Shaw and Jones (2005).

Sheth *et al.*'s (1988) discussion of marketing theory schools, Shaw and Jones (2005) identify a number of distinct schools of marketing thought and map their origins, development and interrelations, providing a panoramic view of marketing thought schools (Table 3.1). They define a school of thought as having a substantial body of knowledge, developed by a number of scholars, describing at least one aspect of what, why, where, when, how and who performs marketing activities. Their classification reveals the broad and diverse landscape of marketing theory.

Despite articulating ten distinctive schools of marketing thought, the *marketing management* school is often represented as the only school of thought, with other perspectives less represented in marketing textbooks. This is because the majority of textbooks available for students are marketing management texts. Moreover, because the marketing management school is so significant within the discipline, marketing theory is generally evaluated in terms of the goals, questions and orientation of this school. As a result, a great deal of marketing knowledge has been overlooked (Wilkie and Moore 2003), primarily because it has not been considered relevant to marketing practice (e.g. Levy 2002). Holbrook (1995) questions whether this is appropriate within an academic discipline and uses a metaphor to argue that the preoccupation with pleasing marketing practitioners is akin to dogs obediently obeying their master. It is also worth considering whether this limits marketing students' exposure to critical and creative thinking within the wider discipline.

Marketing academics: Cats or dogs

Morris Holbrook argues that the almost exclusive focus of the discipline on marketing management has created marketing academics who are more akin to dogs (obedient, unquestioning) rather than cats (curious, independent). He questions whether this is an appropriate role for marketing academics within contemporary universities:

> Dogs are obedient, anxious to please their masters, willing to perform tricks in order to earn the reward of praise, and only too happy to go fetch the newspaper or to point toward various objects of interest. By contrast, cats are individualistic, mostly anxious to please themselves, willing to do only what suits their own natures, and inclined to sleep peacefully curled up in the corner rather than catering to the whims of the lords and ladies of the manor. Applied research of the managerially relevant variety lends itself to the canine temperaments of marketing researchers anxious to go fetch like a Golden Retriever or to point like an Irish Setter. By contrast, truly individual scientists and scholars – lovers of academic freedom – tend to be feline in their inclinations and refuse to fetch obediently the data that managers want or to point helpfully toward information of relevance to marketing decisions (Holbrook 1995: 646).

Given our brief review, it is obvious that the discipline of marketing includes a whole range of theories, that some of these theories support each other, and that many of them offer competing explanations about marketing phenomena. If theory is simply an effort to explain a phenomenon, it might appear that we can simply choose between these alternative explanations (theories) relatively easily. However, because these theories are influenced by diverse disciplines (economics, psychology, sociology, management, strategy, anthropology, cultural studies and education) they represent alternative worldviews. As a result, they are not easily comparable, and how competing theories should be evaluated is itself the subject of considerable debate.

Seminal debates in marketing thought

The development of marketing as an academic field was shaped by influential debates within the discipline, which began in the 1940s. These ongoing debates concern the status of marketing as an academic discipline, the nature of marketing knowledge and marketing's territorial boundaries. Revisiting seminal debates offers opportunities for developing marketing thought and practice. It is a source of important historical knowledge, which has much to contribute 'to the developing managerial skills and judgement of marketing students' (Witkowski 1989: 55), because it helps us learn from the lessons of the past and avoid naïve viewpoints and statements (Witkowski 1989).

Is marketing an art or a science?

Marketing has long pursued the status of a science. Kerin (1996) maps the 60-year *pursuit* of the *scientific ideal* in the *Journal of Marketing*. He classifies it in six stages: marketing as applied economics, marketing as a managerial activity, marketing as a quantitative science, marketing as a behavioural science, marketing as a decision science and marketing as an integrative science. In the 1920s and 1930s (e.g. Cherington 1937; Coutant 1937) marketing scholars were interested in 'securing the legitimacy of their intellectual and practical activities' (Tadajewski 2014: 308). In the 1940s, Converse's (1945) survey, sparked a debate that spanned many decades regarding whether marketing was a science or an art (Hutchinson 1952; Pinson *et al.* 1972; Demirdjian 1976; Hunt 1976; Brown 1996). The meanings of 'theory' and 'science' became the focus of discussions (Bartels 1951). Depending on their understanding of the nature of theory and science and on whether they focused on the development of a theory *of* marketing or the use of a range of theories *in* marketing, authors supported that marketing was either a science or an art.

For some authors, the scientific status of marketing depended on the development of systematic knowledge and general principles (e.g. Bartels 1944) fashioned in the model of natural sciences. These authors emphasised the development of 'the general or abstract principles underlying the body of facts which comprise this field' (Alderson and Cox 1948: 137; cf. Bartels 1944). If marketing were to qualify as a science, it would have to meet stringent requirements. These are summarised in the following definition of science:

> [a] classified and systematized body of knowledge . . . organized around one or more central theories and a number of general principles . . . usually expressed in quantitative terms . . . knowledge which permits the prediction and, under some circumstances, the control of future events.
>
> (Buzzell 1963: 33)

Definitions of the nature of science were thus debated in favour of marketing's scientific status (Hunt 1976). However, other authors, most notably Vaile (1949) and Hutchinson (1952), expressed concerns about whether marketing should be considered a science, questioning the very idea of establishing a science called marketing (Brown 1996). For these authors, marketing involves the application of scientific principles, but it is not a science, because problem solving in marketing lies largely on managers' judgement rather than on scientific principles (Stainton 1952). Thus, similarly to engineering and medicine, they understood marketing to be a *practice*. Their focus was less on the kind of theory marketing should have, but on how the practice of marketing requires the application of many different theories.

There is a real reason, however, why the field of marketing has been slow to develop an unique body of theory. It is a simple one: marketing is not a science. It is rather an art or a practice and, as such, much more closely resembles engineering, medicine and architecture than it does physics, chemistry or biology. The medical profession sets us an excellent example, if we would but follow it; its members are called 'practitioners' and not scientists. It is the work of physicians, as it is of any practitioner, to apply the findings of many sciences to the solution of problems.

(Stainton 1952: 89–90)

Other scholars supported the interplay between science and art (Taylor 1965); marketing could thus be seen as both a science and an art. Even though it had its critics, the managerial perspective was widely adopted within the discipline, evidenced by the dominance of the marketing management school. The pursuit of scientific status was also legitimised; however, it took a different form. Throughout the 1980s and 1990s scholars debated the appropriate philosophy of science for marketing (Brown 1996). Thus, despite being unresolved, the art or science debate had a lasting influence on how the discipline developed.

What is the appropriate philosophy of science for marketing?

The pursuit of *marketing as science* had another implication for the discipline. A particular view of science, namely a branch of positivism known as logical empiricism, became the dominant paradigm in marketing research (Deshpande 1983). In line with the notion of theories becoming accepted as truth or facts discussed earlier, positivism was largely unchallenged in the discipline, because it fitted our perceptions of the characteristics of an ideal scientist: objective, rational, value free and open-minded (Tadajewski 2008). The debate was initiated by scholars who questioned the premises of logical empiricism (and most generally positivism) as the dominant paradigm in marketing (e.g. Anderson 1983, 1986; Peter and Olson 1983; Arndt 1985; Hirschman 1986; Hudson and Ozanne 1988; Hirschman and Holbrook 1992). This, in turn, was contested by proponents of positivism (Hunt 1976, 1990, 1991, 1992, 1993, 2003). The debate continued throughout the 1980s and 1990s and is still evident in current academic work (e.g. Tadajewski 2008, 2014).

Broadly, the debate involved the opposing views between those scholars who ascribed to a positivistic view of science, often associated with the development of the natural sciences, and those who proposed more relativistic views of science, largely inspired by the interpretive turn in the social sciences. This brought to the fore a more humanistic approach to marketing inquiry, quite distinct from the methods used by physical scientists (Hirschman 1986). This is reflected in Peter and Olson's (1983) outline of the differences between positivist and relativist views of science. These can be summarised as follows (Peter and Olson 1983: 119, emphasis added):

- From a positivist/empiricist point of view: *science discovers the true nature of reality*; only the logic of justification is needed to understand science; science can be understood without considering cultural, social, political and economic factors; science is objective; scientific knowledge is absolute and cumulative; science is capable of discovering universal laws that govern the external world; science produces theories that come closer and closer to absolute truth; science is rational since it follows formal rules of logic; there are specific rules for doing science validly (e.g. falsification); scientists subject their theories to potential falsification through rigorous empirical testing; measurement procedures do not influence what is measured; data provide objective, independent benchmarks for testing theories.

- From a relativist/constructivist point of view: *science creates many realities*; the processes by which theories are created, justified and diffused throughout a research community are needed to understand science; science is a social process and cannot be understood without considering cultural, social, political and economic factors; science is subjective; scientific knowledge is relative to a particular context and period of time in history; science creates ideas that are context-dependent, i.e. relative to a frame of reference; truth is a subjective evaluation that cannot be properly inferred outside of the context provided by the theory; science is rational to the degree that it seeks to improve individual and societal well-being by following whatever means are useful for doing so; there are many ways of doing science validly that are appropriate in different situations; scientists seek supportive, confirmatory evidence in order to market their theories; nothing can be measured without changing it; data are created and interpreted by scientists in terms of a variety of theories, and thus are theory laden.

As we can see, these perspectives vary in terms of *ontology* (the nature of reality and the nature of social beings), *epistemology* (what constitutes valuable knowledge for a discipline) and *axiology* (the overriding goal of research) (Hudson and Ozanne 1988). From a relativist/constructionist point of view, objective, value free research is not possible, because as marketing researchers we are inevitably part of the reality we seek to examine. Researcher and phenomenon are thus mutually interactive, and the researcher unavoidably influences 'the choice of *phenomenon*, choice of *method*, choice of *data* and choice of *findings*' (Hirschman 1986: 238 original emphasis). On the other hand, from a positivist point of view, the pursuit of objectivity is a moral imperative (Hunt 1993) and value free research is possible:

> [t]o the extent that there are theories that have long-run success in explaining phenomena, predicting phenomena, or assisting in the solution of pragmatic problems in society, we are warranted in believing that something like the postulated entities and their structure of relationships exist, that is, they truly represent or correspond to some reality external to the theorist.
>
> (Hunt 1990: 11)

Even though this debate reached a stage that became repetitive and confusing, especially due to the proliferation of complex philosophical terms (Kavanagh 1994), it has contributed much to the marketing discipline in that it '(a) uncovered alternative epistemologies and methodologies, (b) provided reasoned arguments for and against specific epistemological positions, and (c) dispelled some of the ill-informed rhetoric by clarifying much of the philosophical terminology' (Kavanagh 1994: 27). Positivism has remained the dominant paradigm in marketing, but the debate opened up the space for the development of alternative paradigms in research and theory within marketing (Brown 1996; Shankar and Patterson 2001).

What is the domain of marketing?

What is the appropriate focus for marketing? The debate flourished in the period from the 1960s to the 1980s and it was tied very closely to the art or science debate. And, of course, because a science has boundaries, marketing also needed to have boundaries. One way to decide upon the domain is to first identify its *central concept* − then anywhere that concept is relevant would fall within the domain of the discipline. In marketing, exchange was identified as the core construct or central organising principle for marketing. In this light, the subject matter of marketing is based on the 'processes involved in the creation and resolution of exchange' and 'these processes depend on, and cannot be separated from, the fundamental character of human and organisational needs' (Bagozzi 1975: 36). Bagozzi's work thus prompted a reconsideration of the accepted domain of marketing, from 'the performance of business activities that direct the flow of goods and services from producer to consumer or user' (Alexander 1964) to a much broader domain, 'encompassing all activities involving exchange and the cause and effect phenomena associated with it (Bagozzi 1975: 32). Marketing was now seen as an important aspect of not only economic but all human behaviour (Enis 1973). As such, Bagozzi (1975: 38) argued that 'the problems of marketing are universal'. He also noted that most exchanges are mixed, involving both utilitarian and symbolic dimensions. Symbolic exchange refers to the mutual transfer of psychological, social and other intangible entities between two or more parties. However, it is important to note marketing understands human behaviour in a *particular way*; it implies that all human relationships 'are concerned with exchange, bargaining, influence and negotiation' (Morgan 1992: 143).

Kotler and Levy (1969) proposed that marketing concepts could be applied to non-business organisations through the use of generic product definitions, target group definitions and consumer behaviour analysis. Their paper sparked contrasting views from a number of scholars. Enis (1973: 61) welcomed the idea that 'concepts and techniques that bear the marketing label can be useful in understanding phenomena beyond the traditional boundaries of the marketing discipline', as this was essential for the development of the discipline. He argued, however, that a *deepening* of the concept should also take place so that the nature of the product exchanged (economic goods and services) could be broadened to anything of value; the objective of the exchange (profit) could be broadened to any type of payoff; and the target audience of the exchange (customers) could be broadened to any 'public' that relates to an organisation (Enis 1973: 59).

Others raised concerns against broadening. For example, Luck (1969: 54) argued that the focus of marketing should be the *market transaction*, because it 'is concerned with markets, of course, and markets must be characterized by buying–and–selling'. For others, the problem of broadening was that it extended the marketing domain too far: 'If marketing embraces all kinds of exchanges, then everyone is a "marketer" because virtually everyone engages in some social exchanges' (Graham 1993: 9). The broadened concept of marketing would have important implications for the discipline by directing attention away from important issues – within the traditional domain – that were in need of research and knowledge development towards non-business interests (Bartels 1974).

> Without a clear delineation of marketing's boundaries, the discipline will develop without direction and without guidance. Such aimless wandering is likely to result in the discipline becoming extremely fragmented with fringe topics that have questionable marketing relevance. The discipline cannot be all things to all people; a clear focus is essential toward the development of professionalism in any discipline, and marketing is no exception.
>
> (Martin 1985: 9–10)

In an effort to resolve the ongoing debate about what should be included and what not within the domain of marketing, Hunt (1976) developed a schema, which encapsulated the total domain of marketing (Table 3.2). Hunt himself argued that another advantage of the model is that it was 'inclusive and healing' rather than 'exclusive and divisive' (Arndt 1982). His schema was based on three dichotomies (Hunt 1978): profit and non-profit sectors, micro and macro foci, and positive and normative approaches. This effectively contributed to the argument for broadening the domain of marketing. As Kotler and Levy had predicted in 1969, the choice for all organisations became not whether to engage in marketing but how well to perform marketing.

Table 3.2 The domain of marketing

		Positive	Normative
Profit	**Micro**	1 Problems, issues, theories and research concerning marketing activities performed by firms and individual consumer behaviour. For example, how firms determine the marketing mix; case studies of marketing practices; how consumers make buying decisions.	2 Problems, issues, normative models and research concerning how firms *should* perform marketing activities. For example, how should firms make marketing mix decisions; make international marketing decisions; organise, control and plan their marketing efforts; manage retailers and wholesalers; implement the marketing concept?
	Macro	3 Problems, issues, theories and research concerning aggregate marketing activities and their societal implications. For example, aggregate consumption patterns; marketing commodities; channels of distribution; legal aspects of marketing; the role of marketing in economic development.	4 Problems, issues, normative models and research concerning how marketing systems and aggregate marketing activities can be made more efficient and effective. For example, the role of distribution costs; whether marketing systems and practices are socially desirable; whether consumer sovereignty is socially desirable; what kind of laws regulating marketing are optimal.
Non – profit	**Micro**	5 Problems, issues, theories and research concerning marketing activities performed by non-profit organisations (social marketing) and consumer behaviour in non-profit contexts. For example, consumers' purchasing of public goods; how non-profit organisations determine the marketing mix; studies of public goods marketing.	6 Problems, issues, normative models and research concerning how organisations *should* perform social marketing activities. For example, how should non-profit organisations make marketing mix decisions; make international marketing decisions; organise, control and plan their marketing efforts?
	Macro	7 Problems, issues, theories and research concerning aggregate marketing activities in non-profit contexts. For example, the institutional framework of public goods; does television advertising influence elections; does public service advertising influence behaviour?	8 Problems, issues, normative models and research concerning the social desirability of social marketing. For example, whether society should allow politicians to be 'sold' like toothpaste; whether demand for public goods should be stimulated; whether the army should be allowed to advertise for recruits.

Source: Adapted from Hunt (1976).

While this schema proved useful, for Foxall (1989) there is an important distinction between marketing as a common, human, economic activity and marketing oriented management, which takes place under particular circumstances in which the 'customer' has discretion over spending and can choose whether and which products or services to buy. However, he argued that, in conditions of scarcity and when demand exceeds supply, in other words, when the 'customer' has no discretion, marketing oriented management is less appropriate. This is the case with certain public services, such as the revenue service, 'where the "customer" has no discretion because he has no choice of supply; cannot withdraw his taxes; nor is he able to resist the legally-enforced ministrations of social workers' (Foxall 1989: 19).

Regardless of its critics, the broadened concept of marketing has largely been accepted within the discipline. The expanded marketing domain means that marketers are now faced with the need to understand and respond to a range of social and economic contexts beyond the traditional context of market transactions. However, while the concept has been broadened to non-business contexts, the dominant school on which we draw remained that of marketing management, or in Tucker's (1974) words, the 'channel captain' view. However, for marketers to fully embrace the range of social and economic contexts they now face demands a broadened orientation to encompass the well-being of consumers and society at large (Tucker 1974). 'The interest must lie in understanding and explaining the phenomenon itself, rather than understanding it from the perspective of only one of the participants' (Anderson 1983: 28). A first step in this, we argue, is a critical, creative and reflexive engagement with the rich landscape of marketing theory and its seminal debates.

Conclusion

So why is marketing theory important? We have shown that in marketing, as in other disciplines, there are different schools of thought. Engaging with theory is not merely a matter of aligning with one school or another, but rather to interrogate these perspectives and understand how they have shaped the body of knowledge that constitutes marketing today. Developing a 'theory of marketing' has proven too challenging because of the fundamental disagreement regarding the nature of the discipline (science or art), the basis for producing and evaluating knowledge in the discipline (epistemology) and the context in which marketing knowledge can be applied (domain). Despite such controversies, theory development has proven more fruitful when adopting a bottom–up approach within particular specialisms and involving a focus on specific instances of phenomena.

These debates allow us to consider how certain theories have come to be accepted in the marketing discipline and how others have attracted less attention. These debates are not simply historical or the concerns of those living in the 'ivory tower' of academia. Rather, marketing managers need to engage with these issues on a very practical level as they go about their work. In dealing with the domain of marketing, practitioners must consider whether marketing a bar of soap or a car is the same as marketing a political party or a university. In considering how best to generate insights about customers and other marketplace actors, they are dealing with epistemology – essentially what constitutes valuable knowledge for them. Moreover, because marketing practice involves much more than simply identifying the 'correct' theory for a given problem, decision-making demands considerable managerial judgement. Therefore, managers need theory to help them *think through* the everyday problems they face. Thus, there will always be a need for pure research that challenges and extends current thinking about how things are, should or could be. To use Holbrook's (1995) analogy, we should attempt to be curious (like a cat) and to make decisions based on what we truly believe, rather than to be unquestioningly obedient to our masters.

Further reading

Baker, M. J. and Saren, M. (eds) (2010), *Marketing Theory: A Student Text*, London: Sage.

Ellis, N., Fitchett, J., Higgins, M., Jack, G., Lim, M., Saren, M. and Tadajewski, M. (2010), *Marketing: A Critical Textbook*, London: Sage.

Maclaran, P., Saren, M., Stern, B. and Tadajewski, M. (eds) (2009), *The SAGE Handbook of Marketing Theory*, London: Sage.

Saren, M. (2010), 'Overview of marketing theory', in Baker, M. J. and Saren, M. (eds) *Marketing Theory: A Student Text*, London: Sage, pp. 26–50.

Tadajewski, M. and Brownlie, D. T. (eds) (2008), *Critical Marketing: Contemporary Issues in Marketing*, Chichester, UK: Wiley.

References

Alderson, W. and Cox, R. (1948), 'Towards a theory of marketing', *Journal of Marketing*, 13(October): 37–152.

Alexander, R. S. (1964), *Marketing Definitions*, Chicago, IL: American Marketing Association.

Anderson, P. F. (1983), 'Marketing, scientific progress, and scientific method', *The Journal of Marketing*, 47: 18–31.

Anderson, P. F. (1986), 'On method in consumer research: A critical relativist perspective', *Journal of Consumer Research*, 13(September): 155–173.

Arndt, J. (1982), 'The conceptual domain of marketing: Evaluation of Shelby Hunt's three dichotomies model', *European Journal of Marketing*, 16(1): 27–35.

Arndt, J. (1985), 'On making marketing science more scientific: Role of orientations, paradigms, metaphors, and puzzle solving', *The Journal of Marketing*, 49(3): 11–23.

Bagozzi, R. P. (1975), 'Marketing as exchange', *The Journal of Marketing*, 39(4): 32–39.

Bartels, R. D. (1944), 'Marketing principles', *The Journal of Marketing*, 9(October): 151–157.

Bartels, R. D. (1951), 'Can marketing be a science?', *The Journal of Marketing*, 15(January): 319–328.

Bartels, R. D. (1974), 'The identity crisis in marketing', *The Journal of Marketing*, 38(October): 73–76.

Berger, P. L., and Luckmann, T. (1967), *The Social Construction of Reality: A Treatise on the Sociology of Knowledge*. Garden City, NY: Doubleday.

Brown, S. (1996), 'Art or science?: Fifty years of marketing debate', *Journal of Marketing Management*, 12(4): 243–267.

Burrell, G. and Morgan, G. (1992 [1979]), *Sociological Paradigms and Organisational Analysis*, Oxford, UK: Ashgate.

Burton, D. (2005), 'Marketing theory matters', *British Journal of Management*, 16(1): 5–18.

Buzzell, R. D. (1963), 'Is marketing a science?', *Harvard Business Review*, 41(1): 32–40.

Carman, J. M. (1980), 'Paradigms for marketing theory', in *Research in Marketing*, Greenwich, CT: JAI Press, pp. 1–36.

Catterall, M., Maclaran, P. and Stevens, L. (1999), 'Critical marketing in the classroom: Possibilities and challenges', *Marketing Intelligence and Planning*, 17(7): 344–353.

Catterall, M., Maclaran, P. and Stevens, L. (2002), 'Critical reflection in the marketing curriculum', *Journal of Marketing Education*, 24(3): 184–192.

Celly, K. (2007), Fostering critical thinking in business courses: Pedagogical innovations and strategies, *The Business Review Cambridge*, 8(1): 148–154.

Cherington, P. T. (1937), 'Marketing marketing', *The Journal of Marketing*, 1(3): 223–225.

Christensen, C. M. and Overdorf, M. (2001), 'Meeting the challenge of disruptive change', *Harvard Business Review on Innovation*, Cambridge, MA: Harvard Business School Press, pp. 103–152.

Converse, P. D. (1945), The development of the science of marketing: An exploratory survey, *The Journal of Marketing*, 10(1)14–23.

Coutant, F. R. (1937), 'Scientific marketing makes progress', *The Journal of Marketing*, 1(3): 226–230.

Craib, I. (1992), *Modern Social Theory*, second edition, London: Palgrave Macmillan.

Cunliffe, A. L. (2004), 'On becoming a critically reflexive practitioner', *Journal of Management Education*, 28(4): 407–426.

Demirdjian, Z. S. (1976), 'Marketing as a pluralistic discipline: The forestalling of an identity crisis', *Journal of the Academy of Marketing Science*, 4(4): 672–681.

Deshpande, R. (1983), '"Paradigms lost": On theory and method in research in marketing', *The Journal of Marketing*, 47(4): 101–110.

Enis, B. M. (1973), 'Deepening the concept of marketing', *The Journal of Marketing*, 37(4): 57–62.

Finch, D., Nadeau, J. and O'Reilly, N. (2012), 'The future of marketing education: A practitioner's perspective', *Journal of Marketing Education*, 35(1): 54–67.

Fisk, G. and Meyers, P. (1982), 'Macromarketer's guide to paradigm development' in Bush, R. F. and Shelby Hunt, S. (eds) *Marketing Theory: Philosophy of Science Perspectives*, Chicago, IL: American Marketing Association, pp. 281–285.

Ford, D. and Mouzas, S. (2013), 'The theory and practice of business networking', *Industrial Marketing Management*, 42(3): 433–442.

Foxall, G. (1989), 'Marketing's domain', *European Journal of Marketing*, 23(8): 7–22.

Garfinkel, H. (1967), *Studies in Ethnomethodology*, Englewood Cliffs, NJ: Prentice-Hall.

Gilbert, C. and Bower, J. L. (2002), 'Disruptive change: When trying harder is part of the problem', *Harvard Business Review*, 80(5): 94–101.

Goffman, E. (1959), *The Presentation of Self in Everyday Life*, Garden City, NY: Doubleday.

Graham, P. (1993), 'Marketing's domain: A critical review of the development of the marketing concept', *Marketing Bulletin*, 4(1): 1–11, available at http://faculty.mu.edu.sa/public/uploads/1358096368.7852MB_V4_A1_Graham.pdf (accessed 4 January 2016).

Hill, M. E. and McGinnis, J. (2007), 'The curiosity in marketing thinking', *Journal of Marketing Education*, 29(1): 52–62.

Hill, M. E., McGinnis, J. and Cromartie, J. (2007), 'The obstacles to marketing thinking', *Marketing Intelligence and Planning*, 25(3): 241–251.

Hirschman, E. C. (1986), Humanistic inquiry in marketing research: Philosophy, method, and criteria. *Journal of Marketing Research*, 23(3): 237–249.

Hirschman, E. C. and Holbrook, M. B. (1992), *Postmodern Consumer Research: The Study of Consumption As Text*, volume 1, London: Sage.

Holbrook, M. B. (1995), 'The four faces of commodification in the development of marketing knowledge', *Journal of Marketing Management*, 11(7): 641–654.

Hudson, L. A. and Ozanne, J. L. (1988), 'Alternative ways of seeking knowledge in consumer research', *Journal of Consumer Research*, 14(1): 508–521.

Hunt, S. D. (1976), 'The nature and scope of marketing', *The Journal of Marketing*, 40(3): 17–28.

Hunt, S. D. (1978), 'A general paradigm of marketing: In support of the "3-dichotomies model"', *The Journal of Marketing*, 40(2): 107–110.

Hunt, S. D. (1990), 'Truth in marketing theory and research', *The Journal of Marketing*, 54(3): 1–15.

Hunt, S. D. (1991), 'Positivism and paradigm dominance in consumer research: Toward critical pluralism and rapprochement', *Journal of Consumer Research*, 18(June): 32–44.

Hunt, S. D. (1992), 'For reason and realism in marketing', *Journal of Marketing*, 56(April): 89–102.

Hunt, S. D. (1993), 'Objectivity in marketing theory and research', *The Journal of Marketing*, 57(2): 76–91.

Hunt, S. D. (2003), *Controversy in Marketing Theory: For Reason, Realism, Truth and Objectivity*, Armonk, NY: M.E. Sharpe.

Hutchinson, K. D. (1952), 'Marketing as a science: An appraisal', *Journal of Marketing*, 16(January): 286–293.

Kavanagh, D. (1994), 'Hunt versus Anderson: Round 16', *European Journal of Marketing*, 28(3): 26–41.

Kerin, R. A. (1996), 'In pursuit of an ideal: The editorial and literary history of the Journal of Marketing', *Journal of Marketing*, 60(1): 1–13.

Kotler, P. and Levy, S. J. (1969), 'Broadening the concept of marketing', *The Journal of Marketing*, 33(1): 10–15.

Kuhn, T. S. (1962), *The Structure of Scientific Revolutions*, Chicago, IL: University of Chicago Press.

Levy, S. J. (2002), 'Revisiting the marketing domain', *European Journal of Marketing*, 36(3): 299–304.

Luck, D. J. (1969), 'Broadening the concept of marketing too far', *The Journal of Marketing*, 33(3): 53–55.

Maclaran, P. and Stevens, L. (2008), 'Thinking through theory: Materialising the oppositional imagination', in Tadajewski, M. and Brownlie, D. (eds) *Critical Marketing: Issues in Contemporary Marketing*, Chichester, UK: Wiley, pp. 345–361.

Maclaran, P., Saren, M., Stern, B. and Tadajewski, M. (2009), 'Introduction', in Maclaran, P., Saren, M., Stern, B. and Tadajewski, M. (eds) *The SAGE Handbook of Marketing Theory*, London: Sage, pp. 1–24.

Martin, C. L. (1985), 'Delineating the boundaries of marketing', *European Journal of Marketing*, 19(4): 5–12.

Morgan, G. (1992), 'Marketing discourse and practice: Towards a critical analysis', in Alvesson M. and Willmott, H. (eds) *Critical Management Studies*, London: Sage, pp. 136–158.

O'Malley, L. and Patterson, M. (1998), 'Vanishing point: The mix management paradigm re-viewed', *Journal of Marketing Management*, 14(8): 829–851.

Paul, R. and Elder, L. (2004), *Critical and Creative Thinking*, Dillon Beach, CA: The Foundation for Critical Thinking.

Peter, J. P. and Olson, J. C. (1983), 'Is science marketing?', *The Journal of Marketing*, 47(Fall): 111–125.

Pine, B. J. and Gilmore, J. H. (2011), *The Experience Economy*, Boston, MA: Harvard Business Press.

Pinson, C. R., Angelmar, R. and Roberto, E. L. (1972), 'An evaluation of the general theory of marketing', *The Journal of Marketing*, 36(3): 66–69.

Ruggiero, V. R. (2003), *Making Your Mind Matter: Strategies for Increasing Practical Intelligence*, Lanham, MD: Rowman and Littlefield Publishers.

Sankey, H. (1993), 'Kuhn's changing concept of incommensurability', *The British Journal for the Philosophy of Science*, 44(4): 759–774.

Schon, D. A. (1983), *The Reflexive Practitioner: How Professionals Think in Action*, New York: Basic Books.

Shankar, A., and Patterson, M. (2001), 'Interpreting the past, writing the future', *Journal of Marketing Management*, 17(5/6): 481–501.

Shaw, E. H. and Jones, D. B. (2005), 'A history of schools of marketing thought', *Marketing Theory*, 5(3): 239–281.

Sheth, J. N., Gardner, D. M. and Garrett, D. E. (1988), *Marketing Theory: Evolution and Evaluation*, vol. 1, New York: Wiley.

Stainton, R. S. (1952), 'Science in marketing', *The Journal of Marketing*, 17(1): 64–65.

Tadajewski, M. (2008), 'Incommensurable paradigms, cognitive bias and the politics of marketing theory', *Marketing Theory*, 8(3): 273–297.

Tadajewski, M. (2014), 'Paradigm debates and marketing theory, thought and practice', *Journal of Historical Research in Marketing*, 6(3): 303–330.

Tadajewski, M. and Jones, D. B. (2014), 'Historical research in marketing theory and practice: A review essay', *Journal of Marketing Management*, 30(11/12), 1239–1291.

Taylor, W. J. (1965), 'Is marketing a science? Revisited', *The Journal of Marketing*, 29(July): 49–53.

Tucker, W. T. (1974), 'Future directions in marketing theory', *The Journal of Marketing*, 38(2): 30–35.

Vaile, R. S. (1949), 'Towards a theory of marketing: A comment', *Journal of Marketing*, 14(April): 520–522.

Wilkie, W. L. and Moore, E. S. (2003), 'Scholarly research in marketing: Exploring the "4 eras" of thought development', *Journal of Public Policy and Marketing*, 22(2): 116–146.

Witkowski, T. H. (1989), 'History's place in the marketing curriculum', *Journal of Marketing Education*, 11(2): 54–57.

Yang, H., Kang, H. and Mason, R. (2008), 'An exploratory study on meta skills in software development teams: Antecedent cooperation skills and personality for shared mental models', *European Journal of Information Systems*, 17(1): 47–61.

4   The basics of marketing strategy

Robin Wensley

Marketing strategy sometimes claims to provide an answer to one of the most difficult questions in our understanding of competitive markets: how to recognize and achieve an economic advantage that endures. In attempting to do so, marketing strategy, as with the field of strategy itself, has had to address the continual dialectic between analysis and action or, in more common managerial terms, between strategy formulation and strategic implementation. At the same time, it has also had to address a perhaps more fundamental question, 'How far at least from a demand or market perspective can we ever develop general rules for achieving enduring economic advantage?'.

Strategy: from formulation to implementation

From the late 1960s to the mid-1980s at least, management strategy seemed to be inevitably linked to issues of product–market selection and hence to marketing strategy. Perhaps ironically this was not primarily or mainly as a result of the contribution of marketing scholars or indeed practitioners. The most significant initial contributors, such as Bruce Henderson (1980) and Michael Porter (1979, 1985), were both to be found at or closely linked to the Harvard Business School, but were really informed more by particular aspects of economic analysis: neo-marginal economics[1] and industrial organizational (IO) economics, respectively. However, in various institutions the marketing academics were not slow to recognize what was going on and also to see that the centrality of product–market choice linked well with the importance attached to marketing. This expansion of the teaching domain had a much less significant impact on the research agenda and activity within marketing itself, where the focus continued to underplay the emerging importance of the competitive dimension (Day and Wensley 1983). Hence, the relatively atheoretical development continued into the process of codification of this new area, most obviously in the first key text by Abell and Hammond (1979), which was based on a, by then, well-established second year MBA option at Harvard.[2]

In retrospect, this period was the high point for the uncontested impact of competitive market-related analysis on strategic management practice. With the advantage of hindsight, it is clear that a serious alternative perspective was also developing, most obviously signalled by Peters and Waterman (1982), which was to have a very substantial impact on what was taught in strategic management courses and marketed by consultancies. It was also a significant book in the sense that, although not widely recognized as so doing, it also attempted to integrate at least to some degree earlier work by other relevant academics such as Mintzberg (1973), Pettigrew (1973) and Weick (1976).

As the 1980s progressed, it was inevitable that at least to some degree each side recognized the other as a key protagonist. Perhaps one of the most noteworthy comments is that in which Robert Waterman challenged the value of a Michael Porter-based analysis of competition.

Waterman (1988) argued that the Porter approach does not work, because 'people get stuck in trying to carry out his ideas'[3] for three reasons: the lack of a single competitor, the actual nature of interfirm co-operation as well as competition and, finally, the fact that competitors were neither 'dumb nor superhuman'.[4]

Equally, the economists did not take such attacks lying down: Kay (1993) attempted to wrest back the intellectual dominance in matters of corporate strategy, and Porter (1990) extended his domain to the nation-state itself. The story, of course, has also become complicated in other ways, many of which are outside the scope of this chapter. In terms of key perspectives, Tom Peters has become more and more polemical about the nature of success,[5] C. K. Prahalad has refined his original notion of dominant logic to reflect in general terms the importance of transferable capabilities and technological interdependencies in the development of strategic advantage,[6] whilst Gary Hamel who started his work with C. K. Prahalad on *Strategic Intent* (1989) has moved on to espousing radical and revolutionary change (Hamel 2000) and, of course, Peter Senge (1992) reiterated the importance of information structures and Hammer and Champy (1993) introduced a 'new' approach labelled business process analysis.

In terms of the disciplinary debate, what was originally broadly a debate between economists and sociologists, now also involves psychologists, social anthropologists and, if they are a distinct discipline, systems theorists.

However, the key change in emphasis has been the one from analysis to process, from formulation to implementation. Perhaps the single most important contributor to this change has been Henry Mintzberg, who has developed over the period an extensive critique of what he calls the 'Design School' in strategic management, culminating in his 1994 book. In this he even challenges the notion of planning in strategy:

> Thus we arrive at the planning school's grand fallacy: Because analysis is not synthesis, strategic planning is not strategy formation. Analysis may precede and support synthesis, by defining the parts that can be combined into wholes. Analysis may follow and elaborate synthesis, by decomposing and formalizing its consequences. But analysis cannot substitute for synthesis. No amount of elaboration will ever enable formal procedures to forecast discontinuities, to inform managers who are detached from their operations, to create novel strategies. Ultimately the term 'strategic planning' has proved to be an oxymoron.
>
> (Mintzberg 1994: 321)

Since then, he has extended his critique to the whole domain of management teaching, particularly MBAs, rather than just strategic planning (Mintzberg 2004).[7] Overall, whilst his approach and indeed critique of strategy analysis is itself rather polemical[8] and overstated, there is little doubt that he is broadly correct in that the general emphasis in strategic management has shifted significantly towards implementation and away from formulation and planning.

The nature of the competitive market environment

As our analysis of marketing strategy has developed since the 1980s, so our representation of the marketing context has also changed. In the mid-1980s the marketing context was presented with what would now seem to be a number of major omissions. In particular, there was little recognition of competitors, and distribution was clearly seen as a solely logistical function. On top of this, customers were very much represented as 'at a distance', in that advertising and market research were the intermediary activities between the firm and its customers.

More recently, marketing has recognized much more explicitly this further range of issues, including the key role of competition and the importance of a longer-term so-called relationship perspective, particularly in the context of customers. On top of this, various entities in the distribution chain are now clearly seen as very active intermediaries rather than just passive logistics agents.

However, the development of this more complex dynamic representation of the competitive market, which can be seen broadly in the marketing strategy triangle of the 3Cs – customers, competitors and channels – also implies a more fluid and complex context for systematic modelling purposes.

Customers, competitors and channels

The early, more static, model of the nature of the competitive market, which informed many of the still current and useful tools of analysis, was both positional and non-interactive. It was assumed that the market backcloth, often referred to as the product–market space, remained relatively stable and static so that at least in terms of first order effects, strategies could be defined in positional terms. Similarly, the general perspective, strongly reinforced by the earlier representations, was that actions by the firm would generally not create equivalent reactions from the relatively passive 'consumers'. This perspective on the nature of marketing, which might be fairly labelled the 'patient' perspective (Wensley 1990), is to be found rather widely in marketing texts and commentaries despite the continued espousal of slogans such as, 'the customer is king (or queen)'.

With the adoption of the more interactive and dynamic perspective implied in the 3Cs approach, the nature of market-based strategy becomes much more complex. At the same time, we must be wary of the temptation to continue to apply the old tools and concepts without considering critically whether they are appropriate in new situations. They represent in general a special or limiting case that quite often requires us to distort the nature of the environment that we are attempting to characterize. The key question as to how far this distortion is, as our legal colleagues would say, material, is another yet frequently unresolved matter. This notion of materiality is really linked to the impact on actions rather than just understanding and to the degree to which particular forms of marketing strategy analysis encourage actions that are either sub-optimal or indeed dysfunctional.

Lacking further experimental or research evidence on this question, this chapter is mainly written around the assumption that, in using these simplifying approaches, we need to recognize that: (1) the degree to which they actually explain the outcomes of interest will be limited, particularly when we focus on individual competitive performance; and (2) there are often ways in which the underlying assumptions can cause unintentional biases.

The evolution of analysis, interpretation and modelling in marketing strategy from customers to competitors to channels

Given that the underlying representation of the competitive market environment has changed, so, not surprisingly, have our processes of analysis, interpretation and modelling. Initially, the key focus was on customer-based positioning studies in a particular product–market space. Such work remains a key component in the analysis of much market research data, but from the marketing strategy perspective, we need to recognize that the dimensionality of the analytical space has often been rather low, indeed in some situations little more than a single price dimension, which has been seen as highly correlated with an equivalent quality dimension.[9]

The increased emphasis on the analysis of competitors has also required us to make certain compromises. One, of course, relates to the balance between what might be termed public information, legitimate inference and private information, respectively. The other to the fact that our colleagues in business strategy now give emphasis to two rather different perspectives on the nature of competitive firms, one essentially based on similarities (strategic groups: McGee and Thomas 1986) the other on differences (resource-based perspective: Wernerfelt 1984, 1995a).[10] Sound competitor analysis should at least enable us to avoid making inconsistent assumptions, particularly in the context of public data, like, for instance, assuming that we will be able to exploit an opportunity, which is known to all, without a significant amount of competitive reaction.

Finally, there is the question of channels, or in more general terms, supply chains. The issue of retailers in particular as independent and significant economic intermediaries, rather than just logistical channels to the final consumer, has been an important consideration in consumer marketing, at least since the 1970s. Similarly, in industrial markets the issue of the supply chain and the central importance of some form of organization and co-ordination of the various independent entities within the chain have been seen as increasingly important strategic issues. Both these developments have meant that any strategic marketing analysis needs to find ways to evaluate the likely impact of such independent strategies pursued by intermediaries, although in many cases our tools and techniques for doing this remain rather limited and often rely on no more than an attempt to speculate on what might be their preferred strategic action.[11]

The codification of marketing strategy analysis in terms of three strategies, four boxes and five forces

What can now be regarded as 'traditional' marketing strategy analysis was developed primarily in the 1970s. It was codified in various ways, including the strategic triangle developed by Ohmae (1982), but perhaps more memorably, the most significant elements in the analysis can be defined in terms of the three generic strategies, the four boxes (or perhaps more appropriately strategic contexts) and the five forces.

These particular frameworks also represent the substantial debt that marketing strategy owes to economic analysis. The three strategies and five forces are taken directly from Michael Porter's (1980) influential work, which derived from his earlier work in IO economics. The four contexts were initially popularized by the Boston Consulting Group (BCG) under Bruce Henderson, again strongly influenced by micro-economic analysis. Whilst each of these approaches became a significant component in much marketing strategy teaching (see Morrison and Wensley 1991), we also need to recognize some of the key considerations and assumptions that need to be considered in any critical application.

The three strategies

It could reasonably be argued that Porter really reintroduced the standard economic notion of scale to the distinction between cost and differentiation to arrive at the three generic strategies of focus, cost and differentiation. Indeed, in his later formulation of the three strategies they really became four in that he suggested, rightly, that the choice between an emphasis on competition via cost or differentiation could be made at various scales of operation.

With further consideration, it is clear that both of these dimensions are themselves not only continuous but also likely to be the aggregate of a number of relatively independent elements or dimensions. Hence, scale is in many contexts not just a single measure of volume of finished output but also of relative volumes of sub-assemblies and activities that may well be shared. Even more so in the case of 'differentiation', where we can expect that there are various different ways in which any supplier attempts to differentiate their offerings. On top of this, a number of other commentators, most particularly John Kay (1993), have noted that not only may the cost–differentiation scale be continuous rather than dichotomous but it also might not be seen as a real dimension at all. At some point, this could become a semantic squabble, but there clearly is an important point that many successful strategies are built around a notion of good value for money rather than a pure emphasis on cost or differentiation at any price. Michael Porter (1980) might describe this as a 'middle' strategy, but rather crucially, he has consistently claimed that there is a severe danger of getting 'caught in the middle'. In fact it might be reasonable to assume that in many cases, being in the middle is the best place to be: after all, Porter never presented significant systematic evidence to support his own assertion (cf. Wensley 1994) and more recent work has suggested that such systematic empirical evidence is indeed lacking (Campbell-Hunt 2000).

The four contexts

The four boxes (contexts) relate to the market share/market growth matrix originally developed by BCG under Bruce Henderson. Although there have inevitably been a whole range of different matrix frameworks, which have emerged since the early days, the BCG one remains an outstanding exemplar not only because of its widespread popularity and impact – more recently even university vice-chancellors have been heard to use terms such as 'cash cow' – but because there was an underlying basic economic logic in its development. Other similar frameworks often adopted the rather tautologous proposition that one should invest in domains, which were both attractive and where one had comparative advantage!

The market growth/market share matrix, however, still involved a set of key assumptions that were certainly contestable. In particular, alongside the relatively uncontroversial one that, in general, over time, the growth rate in markets tends to decline, there were the assumptions that it was in some sense both easier to gain market share in higher growth rate markets and also that the returns to such gains were likely to be of longer duration.

This issue which can be seen as assumptions about first the cost and then the benefit of investment in market share, has been discussed and debated widely in marketing literature over the last 25 years (see Jacobson and Aaker 1985; Jacobson 1994). The general conclusions would appear to be that:

a   Market share as an investment is not, on average, under-priced, and may just as well be over-priced.
b   The cost of gaining market share is less related to the market growth rate and much more to the relationship between actual growth rates and competitors' expectations.
c   Much of the benefit attributed to market share is probably better interpreted as the result of competitive advantages generated by more specific resources and choices in marketing activities or other corporate areas.

On this basis, it would seem that the bias implied in the BCG matrix towards investment in market share at the early stages of market growth is not really justified, particularly when one takes into account that at this stage in market development many investments are likely to be somewhat more risky as well.[12] However, companies can benefit from a focus on market share position when it encourages them to place greater emphasis on the marketing fundamentals for a particular business.

More generally, the matrix as an analytical device suffers from some of the problems, which we illustrated for the three strategies approach: an analysis, which is essentially based on extreme points when, in practice, many of the portfolio choices are actually around the centre of the diagram. This implies that any discrimination between business units needs to be based on much more specific analysis rather than broad general characteristics.

The five forces

The five forces analysis was originally introduced by Michael Porter (1980) to emphasize the extent to which the overall basis of competition was much wider than just the rivalries between established competitors in a particular market. Whilst not exactly novel as an insight, particularly to suggest that firms also face competition from new entrants and substitutes, it was presented in a very effective manner and served to emphasize not only the specific and increasing importance of competition as we discussed but also the extent to which competition should be seen as a much wider activity within the value chain as Porter termed it.

Porter (1980) used the term value chain when in essence he was concentrating more on the chain of actual costs.[13] Whilst ex post from an economic point of view there is little difference between value and cost, it is indeed the process of both competition and collaboration between various firms and intermediaries that finally results in the attribution of value throughout the relevant network. In this sense, as others have recognized, a supply chain is an intermediate organization form where there is a higher degree of co-operation between the firms within the chain and a greater degree of competition between the firms within different chains. In this context, Porter's analysis has tended to focus much more clearly on the issue of competition rather than co-operation. Indeed, at least in its representational form, it has tended to go further than this and focus attention on the nature of the competitive pressures on the firm itself rather than interaction between the firm and other organizations in the marketplace.[14]

The search for generic rules for success amidst diversity

As we have suggested above, the codification of marketing strategy was based on three essential schemata. Whilst it was based on some valid theoretical concepts, this did not really provide a systematic approach to the central issue of the nature of sustained economic performance in the competitive marketplace. Although such an objective was clearly recognized in the so-called search for sustainable competitive advantage (Day and Wensley 1988), there remained some central concerns as to whether such a notion was realistic given the dynamic and uncertain nature of the competitive marketplace (Dickinson 1992).

Indeed, not only is it dynamic and uncertain but it is also diverse: firms are heterogeneous and so is the nature of demand. A useful way of looking at demand side heterogeneity is from the user perspective directly. Arguably, from its relatively early origins, marketing, or at least the more functional focused study of marketing management, has been concerned with managerial effective ways of responding to this heterogeneity, particularly in terms of market segmentation. Indeed, it would be reasonable to suggest that without a substantial level of demand heterogeneity, there would be little need for marketing approaches as they are found in most of our textbooks. Whilst there remains a substantial debate about the degree to which this market-based heterogeneity is indeed 'manageable' from a marketing perspective (cf. Saunders 1995; Wensley 1995), to which we will return later in this chapter, our concern at the moment is merely to recognize the substantial degree of heterogeneity and consider the degree to which such diversity on both the supply and demand side facilitates or negates the possibility of developing robust 'rules for success'.

To address this question, we need to consider the most useful way of characterizing the competitive market process. This is clearly a substantial topic in its own right with proponents of various analogies or metaphors along a spectrum, including game theory, sports games and military strategy.

To illustrate this issue, let us consider the field of ecology[15] where we observe wide diversity in terms of both species and habitat. There are two critical aspects that must inform any attempt to transfer this analogy into the field of strategy. The first is the interactive relationship between any species and its habitat, nicely encapsulated in the title of the book by Levins and Leowontin (1985): *The Dialectical Biologist*. Particularly in the context of strategy it is important to recognize that the habitat (for which read market domain) evolves and develops at least as fast as the species (for which, rather more problematically, read the individual firm).[16]

The second aspect addresses directly our question of 'rules for success'. How far can we identify particularly through the historical record, whether there are any reliable rules for success for particular species' characteristics? Of course, it is very difficult to address this question without being strongly influenced by hindsight, and most specific observations can be seen as contentious.[17]

It would seem that we should at least be very cautious in searching for rules for success amidst a world of interactive diversity. Hence, we should hardly be surprised that marketing strategy analysis does not provide for consistent and sustainable individual success in the competitive marketplace. However, we do have a set of theoretical frameworks and practical tools that at least allow us to represent some of the key dynamics of both customer and competitive behaviour in a way that ensures we avoid errors of inconsistency or simple naïveté.

As we have discussed above, most analysis in marketing strategy is informed by what are essentially economic frameworks and so tend to focus attention on situations in which both the competitive structure of the market and the nature of consumer preferences are relatively well established. As we move our attention to more novel situations, these structures tend to be at best indeterminate and therefore the analytical frameworks are less appropriate. We encounter the first of many ironies in the nature of marketing strategy analysis. It is often least applicable in the very situations in which there is a real opportunity for a new source of economic advantage based on a restructuring of either or both the competitive environment and consumer preferences.[18]

Models of competition: game theory versus evolutionary ecology

To develop a formal approach to the modelling of competitive behaviour we need to define:

1 the nature of the arena in which the competitive activity takes place;
2 the structure or rules that govern the behaviour of the participants;
3 the options available in terms of competitor behaviour (when these consist of a sequence of actions through time, or over a number of 'plays', then they are often referred to in game theory as strategies).

In this section, however, we particularly wish to contrast game theory approaches, which in many ways link directly to the economic analysis to which we have already referred, and analogies from evolutionary biology, which raise difficult questions about the inherent feasibility of any systematic model building at the level of the individual firm.

Game theory models of competition

A game theory model[19] is characterized by a set of rules, which describe: (1) the number of firms competing against each other; (2) the set of actions that each firm can take at each point in time; (3) the profits that each firm will realize for each set of competitive actions; (4) the time pattern of actions – whether they occur simultaneously or one firm moves first; and (5) the nature of information about competitive activity – who knows what and when. The notion of rationality also plays a particularly important role in models of competitive behaviour. Rationality implies a link between actions and intentions, but not common intentions between competitors. Models describing competitive activity are designed to understand the behaviour of 'free' economic agents. Thus, these models start with an assumption of 'weak' rationality – the agents will take actions that are consistent with their longer-term objectives. The models also assume a stronger form of rationality – the intentions of the agents can be expressed in terms of a number of economic measures of outcome states such as profit, sales, growth or market share objectives.

Do the results of game theory model indicate how firms should act in competitive situations? Do the models describe the evolution of competitive interactions in the real world? These questions have spawned a lively debate amongst management scientists concerning the usefulness of game theory models. Kadane and Larkey (1982) suggest that game theory models are conditionally normative and conditionally descriptive. The results do indicate how firms should behave given a set of assumptions about the alternatives, the payoffs and the properties of an 'optimal' solution (the equilibrium). Similarly, game theory results describe the evolution of competitive strategy, but only given a specific set of assumptions.

The seemingly unrealistic and simplistic nature of the competitive reactions incorporated in game theory models and the nature of the equilibrium concept led some marketers to question the managerial relevance of these models (Dolan 1981). However, all models involve simplifying assumptions, and game theory models,[20] whilst often highly structured, underpin most attempts to apply economic analysis to issues of competition amongst a limited number of firms. Indeed, as Goeree and Holt (2001) observe, 'Game theory has finally gained the central role . . . in some areas of economics (e.g. IO) virtually all recent developments are applications of game theory' (Goeree and Holt 2001: 1402).

As discussed above, IO economics provides one way of extending basic game theory approaches by examining the nature of competitive behaviour when assumptions about homogeneous firms and customers are relaxed. IO economists, especially Richard Caves (1980) and Michael Porter (1981), directed the development of IO theory to strategic management issues. The concepts of strategic groups and mobility barriers were key elements in this new IO perspective (Caves and Porter 1977). As Richard Caves indicates:

> the concepts of strategic groups and mobility barriers do not add up to a tight formal model. Rather, they serve to organize predictions that come from tight models and assist in confronting them with empirical evidence – a dynamized add-on to the traditional structure–conduct–performance paradigm.
>
> (Caves 1984)

Evolutionary ecological analogies

Evolutionary ecology has also emerged as a popular analogy for understanding the types of market-based strategies pursued by companies (Coyle 1986; Lambkin and Day 1989; Summut-Bonnici and Wensley 2002). These analogies have been previously used to describe both the nature of the competitive process itself (Henderson 1983) as well as the notion of 'niche' strategy (Hofer and Schendel 1977). Organizational theorists and sociologists have adopted an ecological model, describing the growth of a species in an ecology, to describe the types of firms in an environment.

r- and k-strategies

From an ecological perspective, there is an upper limit on the population of a species in a resource environment. When the population of a species is small, the effects of the carrying capacity are minimal and the growth is an exponential function of the natural growth rate. The carrying capacity only becomes important when the population size is relatively large compared to the carrying capacity. The parameters of the standard growth model have been used to describe two alternatives strategies: r-strategies and k-strategies. R-strategists enter a new resource space (product–market space) at an early stage when few other organizations are present, whilst k-strategists join later when there are a larger number of organizations in the environment. Once a particular type of organization establishes itself in an environment, it resists change for various reasons. The number of firms in an environment at one point in time, referred to as the population density, is a proxy for the intensity of competition.

Based on this perspective, the initial entrants into an environment are usually r-strategist-small, new firms that are quick to move and not constrained by the inherent inertia confronting firms established in other environments. Whilst r-strategists are flexible, they are also inefficient due to their lack of experience. After several r-strategists have entered a new environment, established organizations, k-strategists, overcome their inertia, enter the environment and exploit their advantage of greater efficiency based on extensive experience. The characteristics of the environment and particularly the viable niches that emerge determine whether these successive entrants can coexist.

A niche is defined as the specific combination of resources that is needed to support a species or type of organization. Niche width indicates whether this combination of resource is available over a broad range of the resource source space or whether it is only available in a narrow range of the space. A generalist is able to operate in a broad range whilst a specialist is restricted to a narrow range. The nature of a particular environment favours either generalists or specialists.

Environments are described by two dimensions: variability and frequency of environmental change. In a highly variable environment, changes are dramatic, and fundamentally different strategic responses are required for survival. In contrast, strategic alterations are not required to cope with an environment of low variability. A specialist strategy in which high performance occurs in a narrow portion of the environment is surprisingly more appropriate when environmental changes are dramatic and frequent. Under these conditions, it is unlikely that a generalist would have sufficient flexibility to cope with the wide range of environmental conditions it would face, whilst the specialist can at least outperform it in a specific environment.[21] A generalist strategist is most appropriate in an environment characterized by infrequent, minor changes, because this environment allows the generalist to exploit its large-scale efficiencies.

Comparing the key elements in different models of competition[22]

The strategic groups and mobility barriers in the IO economics approach recognize the critical asymmetries between competing firms. It identifies three methods by which firms can isolate themselves from competition: (1) differentiation; (2) cost efficiency; and (3) collusion. The developments within the IO paradigm have therefore tended to usefully focus on the nature and significance of various mechanisms for isolating the firm from its competition. The evolutionary ecological analogy, on the other hand, focuses on the notion of scope with the general distinction between specialists and generalists. The ecological approach also raises interesting questions about the form, level and type of 'organization' that we are considering. In particular, we need to recognize most markets as forms of organization in their own right, as those who have argued the 'markets-as-networks' approach have done and question how far we can justify an exclusive focus on the firm as the key organization unit. Finally, the analogy raises more directly the concern about the interaction between various different units (species) and their evolving habitat. The marketplace, like the habitat, can become relatively unstable and so both affect and be affected by the strategies of the individual firms.

Any analogy is far from perfect, as we would expect. The limitations are as critical as the issues that are raised, because they give us some sense of the bounds within which the analogy itself is likely to be useful. Extending it outside these bounds is likely to be counter-productive and misleading.

The IO approach in practice tends to neglect the interaction between cost and quality. We have already suggested that whilst the notion 'focus' within this analogy is an attempt to recognize this problem; it is only partially successful, because it subsumes a characteristic of any successful competitive strategy into one generic category. We must further consider the extent to which we can distinguish reasonably reliably between the various forms of mixed strategies over time and the extent to which the strategic groups themselves remain stable.

The limitations of analogies from evolutionary ecology are more in terms of the questions that are not answered than those where the answers are misleading. The nature of 'competition' is both unclear and complex, there is confusion as to the level and appropriate unit of analysis, and the notion of 'niche', which has become so current in much strategy writing, overlooks the fact that by definition every species has one anyway.

Characterizing marketing strategy in terms of evolving differentiation in time and space

Central to any notion of competition from a marketing strategy viewpoint is the issue of differentiation in time and space. In a 'real' market: (1) demand is heterogeneous; (2) suppliers are differentiated; and (3) there are processes of feedback and change through time. Clearly, these three elements interact significantly, yet in most cases we find that to reduce the complexity in our analysis and understanding we treat each item relatively independently. For instance, in most current treatments of these issues in marketing strategy we would use some form of market segmentation schema to map heterogeneous demand, some notion of the resource-based view of the firm to reflect the differentiation amongst suppliers and some model of market evolution such as the product lifecycle to reflect the nature of the time dynamic.

Such an approach has two major limitations that may act to remove any benefit from the undoubted reduction of analytical complexity by looking at three sub-systems rather the whole system. First, it assumes implicitly that this decomposition is reasonably first order correct: that the impact of the individual elements is more important than their interaction terms. To examine this assumption critically, we need some alternative form of analysis and representation, such as modelling the phenomena of interest as the co-evolution of firms and customers in a dynamic phase space, which allows for the fact that time and space interact. Second, it assumes that the ways of representing the individual elements that we use, in particular market segmentation and product lifecycle concepts, are in fact robust, but partial representations of the underlying phenomena. In terms of the adequacy of each element in its own terms, we need to look more closely at the ways in which individual improvements may be achieved. Finally, we might wish to consider whether it would be better to model partial interactions, say, between two elements only rather than the complete system.

Differentiation in space: issues of market segmentation

The analysis of spatial competition has, of course, a long history back at least to the classical Hotelling (1929) model of linear competition such as that faced by the two ice-cream sellers on the seafront. The basic Hotelling model, however, did capture the two critical issues in spatial competition: the notion of a space dimension that separated the various competitive suppliers as, well as the fact that these suppliers themselves would have some degree of mobility. In traditional economic terms Hotelling was interested in establishing the equilibrium solution under these two considerations, whereas in marketing we are often more concerned with the impact and likelihood of particular spatial moves, although some notion of the stable long-term equilibrium, if it exists, is obviously important. The Hotelling model provides us with the basic structure of spatial competition: a definition of the space domain, some model of the relationship between the positioning of the relevant suppliers within this space and their relative demands.

In marketing, the competitive space is generally characterized in terms of market segmentation. Of course, market segmentation has received considerable attention in both marketing research and practice, but there remain some critical problems. In particular:

1   We have evidence that the cross-elasticities with respect to different marketing mix elements are likely to be not only of different orders but actually imply different structures of relationship between individual product offerings.
2   Competitive behaviour patterns, which after all in a strict sense, determine the nature of the experiment from which the elasticities can be derived, seem to be, to use a term coined by Leeflang and Wittick (1993), 'out of balance' with the cross-elasticity data itself.

The topic of market segmentation is covered in much greater depth elsewhere in this book, but for the purposes of this chapter we wish to concentrate on the specific question as to how far segmentation provides us with an appropriate definition of the space within which competition evolves. In this sense, the key questions are, as we discussed above, about the dimensionality of the space concerned, the stability of the demand function and the degree of mobility for individual firms (or more correctly individual offerings) in terms of repositioning. These are in practice very difficult questions to deal with for two critical reasons:

1   The nature of the choice process is such that for many offerings, individual consumers chose from a portfolio of items rather than merely make exclusive choices, and, hence, in principle it is difficult to isolate the impact of one offering from the others in the portfolio.
2   The dimensions of the choice space are often inferred from the responses to current offerings, and therefore it is difficult to distinguish between the effects of current offerings and some notion of an underlying set of preference structures.

Segmentation and positioning

In principle, we can describe the nature of spatial competition in a market either in demand terms or in supply terms. Market segmentation represents the demand perspective on structure, whilst competitive positioning represents the supply perspective.

Market segmentation takes as its starting point assumptions about the differing requirements that individual customers have with respect to bundles of benefits in particular use situations. Most obviously in this context, it is an 'ideal' approach in that it is effectively assumed that each customer can specify their own ideal benefit bundle, and their purchase choice in the relevant use situation is based on proximity to this ideal point. In consumer psychology this is equivalent to an assumption that individuals have strong and stable preferences.

The competitive positioning approach uses consumer judgements, normally on an aggregate basis, on the similarities and differences between specific competitive offerings. In principle, this provides an analytical output roughly equivalent to the spatial distribution in the Hotelling model. Such an analysis can also be used to provide an estimate of the dimensionality of the discriminant space, but in many situations, for ease of presentation, the results are presented in a constrained 2D format. Equally, benefit segmentation studies can be used along with techniques such as factor analysis to try and arrive at an estimate of the dimensionality of the demand side.

We can be reasonably certain that the attitude space for customers in any particular market is generally, say, $N > 3$: factor analytical studies might suggest at least four or five in general and that of competitive offerings is of at least a similar order. Indeed, in the latter case if we considered the RBV of the firm very seriously, we might go for a dimensionality as high as the number of competitors.[23]

Of more interest from a strategy point of view is how we represent what happens in terms of actual purchase behaviour in a competitive market through time. Although there is relatively little high-quality empirical and indeed theoretical work in this area, so far there are intriguing results to suggest that the dimensionality of the market space for this purpose can be much reduced, although we may still then have problems with some second order effects in terms of market evolution. There have been a number of attempts to apply segmentation analysis to behavioural data with much less information as to attitudes or intention. In one of the more detailed of such studies, Chintagunta (1994) suggested that the dimensionality of the revealed competitive space was two-dimensional, but even this might really be an overestimation.[24] In his own interpretation of the results, he focuses on the degree to which the data analysis reveals interesting differences in terms of brand position revealed by individual purchase patterns through time.

In terms of second order anomalies, we can also consider some of the issues raised by so-called 'compromise effect' in choice situations where the choice between two alternatives depends on other, less attractive, alternatives. In an intriguing paper, Wernerfelt (1995b) argues that this effect can be systematically explained by the notion that consumers draw inferences about their own personal valuations from the portfolio of offerings. However, it may be that a compromise effect could also be seen as the result of mapping an $N > 1$ attribute and preference space on to an $N = 1$ set of purchase decisions.[25]

A simple model of spatial competition might therefore be one in which a considerable amount of competition can be seen along a single dimension, in circumstances in which multiple offerings are possible, and where there is no reason to believe a priori that individual offerings will be grouped either by common brand or specification, with a fixed entry cost for each item and a distribution of demand, which is multi-modal. To this extent it may actually be true that the very simplifications that many criticize in the Porter (1980) 'three generic strategies' approach may be reasonably appropriate in building a first order model of competitive market evolution (see Campbell-Hunt 2000). In the short run, following the notion of 'clout' and 'vulnerability' (Cooper and Nakanishi 1988), we might also expect changes in position in this competitive dimension could be a function of a whole range of what might often be seen as tactical as well as strategic marketing actions.

Cooper extended his own approach to understanding market structures by marrying two different data types – switching probabilities and attribute ratings (Cooper and Inoue 1996). Despite the fact that the models developed appear to perform well against the appropriate statistical test, there remain basic issues, which link to the time dynamic evolution of the market or demand space. When the model is applied to the well-established dataset on car purchase switching behaviour (Harshman *et al.* 1982), it is clear that it provides an interesting and informative analysis of the ways in which various customer 'segments' have evolved over time both in terms of their size and attribute preferences. However, given the nature of the data and the form of analysis, the dynamic process whereby customer desires change in response to both new competitive offerings and other endogenous and exogenous factors can only be seen in terms of changes in attributes and specific switching decisions. We must now consider, however, particularly in the context of understanding the time-based nature of market strategies, how we might incorporate in more detail a longer-term time dimension with a stronger customer focus.

Differentiation in time: beyond the PLC – characterizing the nature of competitive market evolution

'Few management concepts have been so widely accepted or thoroughly criticized as the product life cycle' (Lambkin and Day 1989: 4).

The product life cycle has the advantage that it does represent the simplest form of path development for any product (introduction, growth, maturity, decline), but as has been widely recognized, this remains a highly stylized representation of the product sales pattern for most products during their lifetime. Whilst it is reasonably clear that it is difficult if not impossible to propose a better single generic time pattern, any such pattern is subject to considerable distortion as a result of interactions with changes in technology as well as both customer and competitor behaviour.

Lambkin and Day (1989) suggested that an understanding of the process of product–market evolution required a more explicit distinction between issues of the demand system, the supply system and the resource environment. However, they chose to emphasize the nature of the demand evolution primarily in terms of diffusion processes. This approach tends to underestimate the extent to which demand side evolution is as much about the way(s) in which the structure of the demand space is changing, as the more aggregate issue of the total demand itself. Lambkin and Day (1989) treat these two issues at different levels of analysis with 'segmentation' as an issue in market evolution, which is defined as the resource environment within which the process of the product life cycle takes place.

Beyond this, more recent research on the process of market evolution, partly building on some of the ideas developed by Lambkin and Day (1989), has attempted to incorporate some insights from, amongst other areas, evolutionary ecology. In particular, work on the extensive disk-drive database, which gives quarterly data on all disk-drive manufacturers, has allowed Christensen (1997) and Freeman (1997) to look at the ways in which at the early stages in market development, the existence of competitive offerings seems to encourage market growth whereas at later stages the likelihood of firm exit increases with firm density. Other computer-related industries have also provided the opportunity for empirical work on some of the issues relating to both the impact of standardization and modularization and the nature of generation effects (Sanchez 1995), although in the latter case it must be admitted that the effects themselves can sometimes be seen as a result of marketing actions in their own right.[26]

The nature of research in marketing strategy: fallacies of free lunches and the nature of answerable research questions

Distinguishing between information about means, variances and outliers

As we indicated at the start of this chapter, much research in marketing strategy has attempted to address what is in some senses an impossible question, 'What is the basic generalizable nature of a successful competitive marketing strategy?'. Such a question presumes the equivalent of a free lunch: we research to find the equivalent of a universal money machine. Before we explore this issue further, we need to establish a few basic principles. The competitive process is such that:

1   Average performance can only produce average results, which in the general nature of a competitive system means that success is related to above average and sometimes even outlier levels of performance.
2   We can expect our competitors to be able on average to interpret any public data to reveal profitable opportunities as well as we can. In more direct terms it means that on average competitors are as clever or as stupid as we are. A combination of public information and the impact of such basic rational expectations approaches, therefore, means that the route to success cannot lie in simply exploiting public information in an effective manner, although such a strategy may enable a firm to improve its own performance.
3   The basis of individual firm or unit performance is a complex mix of both firm, competitor and market factors. Therefore, we can expect that any attempt to explain performance will be subject to considerable error given that it is difficult if not impossible to identify an adequate range of variables, which cover both the specifics of the firm's own situation and the details of the market and competitor behaviour.

For these reasons research in marketing strategy, as in the strategy field as a whole, has almost always tended to be in one of the two categories:

1   Quantitative database analysis that has relied on statistical and econometric approaches to produce results, which indicate certain independent variables that on average correlate with performance. As McCloskey and Ziliak (1996) indicated more generally in econometric work, there is a danger that we often confuse statistical significance for what they term economic significance. From a managerial perspective, this notion of economic significance can be broken down into two elements: first, the extent to which the relationship identified actually relates to a significant proportion of the variation in the dependent variable, and second, the extent to which, even if it does this, regularity actually enables one to produce a clear prescription for managerial action.[27]
2   Case study-based research on selected firms, often based on the notion of some form of outliers, such as those that perform particularly well. Here the problems are the extent to which the story that is told about the particular nature of the success concerned can be used to guide action in other organizations. In practice, this often results in managerial prescriptions that are rather tautological and at the same time not adequately discriminating.

Market share and return on investment (ROI): the 10 per cent rule in practice

One of the most famous results from the Profit Impact of Market Strategy (PIMS) database was that first reported by Bob Buzzell, Brad Gale and Ralph Sultan in the *Harvard Business Review* in 1975 under the title 'Market share: A key to profitability'. They reported on the relationship between ROI and market share on a cross-sectional basis within the then current PIMS database. Although over the years estimates of the R^2 of this relationship have varied, it generally shows a value around 10 per cent up to a maximum of 15 per cent. We can start by simulating the original data that were used. Figure 4.1 is a scatter plot of 500 data points (notional observations) where the relationship between the two implied variables is actually the equivalent of an R^2 of 0.12 or 12 per cent.[28]

In their original article, Buzzell *et al.* (1975) 'removed' much of the variation by calculating cohort means. We can do the same and also use more typical, modern computer-generated graphics to represent the results (Figure 4.2). The cohort mean approach, although now not commonly used in strategy research of this sort, will show, as above, some deviations from the straight-line trend at sample sizes such as 500. However, as samples get even larger the deviations become, on average, even smaller; indeed, some textbook representations of the results go as far as merely illustrating the trend with no deviations at all. Hence, in the process of producing a clearer message from the data we have nearly eliminated 90 per cent of the variability in our performance variable.

How does one explain the 'unexplained' 90 per cent?

If we return to the scatter diagram in Figure 4.1 and treat it as if it represented the current performance of 500 business units within a single corporate portfolio in terms of the relationship between ROI and market share, then we can see some of the problems that arise when we try and make

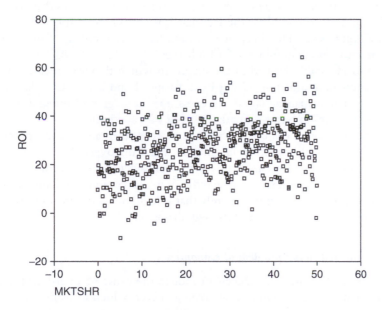

Figure 4.1 A scatter plot of 500 notional observations

Note: Copyrighted material, Taylor & Francis.

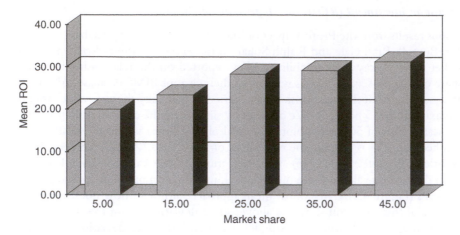

Figure 4.2 A chart of the cohort means

Note: Copyrighted material, Taylor & Francis.

managerial evaluations. The first set of problems relates to the nature of the data itself and the way in which the axes are measured. In most analysis of this sort, and in the PIMS data as we discussed above, the data are essentially cross-sectional, that is, they are either annual or averaged out over a longer, fixed period. It therefore excludes any lead or lag effects and also compensates for particular one-off effects only to the extent that they are already discounted from the input data that are normally based on management accounts. The nature of the axes in a standard market share/ROI analysis is a problem in that they are both ratios. There are very considerable advantages that accrue from using ratios in this situation: most obviously is the fact that it is possible to plot on the same graph units of very different absolute sizes. However, we do then have the problem of measurements' errors in both the numerator and denominator for both axes.

Finally, the basic data are also inevitably limited in the extent to which they can measure the specifics of any particular business unit situation. Using basic financial and accounting data we cannot take into account issues such as managerial effectiveness nor the degree of integration to achieve scale economies and efficiencies in terms of marketing and other activities.

However, we must also put this overall critique of 'market share/return' analysis in context. We should not underestimate the original impact of the 'market share' discovery. Even if it only 'explains' around 10 per cent of financial performance, this is still a considerable achievement. The problem is that, as we have seen, even at this level we face difficult interpretation problems. In the end, we can perhaps conclude its greatest impact was merely that it legitimized debate and discussion about key competitive market assumptions in any strategy dialogue.

Getting to management action: the additional problem of economics

Even if we can identify the source of a particular success or indeed the cause of a particular failure, it is a big jump to assume that suitable action can be taken at a cost, which is justified by the subsequent benefits.

We therefore need to overlay our notion of practical significance with one of economic significance: a factor or set of factors, which explain a significant proportion of success and can also be used as a decision rule for subsequent successful management action. To return to the market share/ROI relationship, even if we conclude that there is a significant correlation between market share and profitability we have to make two further assumptions to justify an economic rule of 'investing' in market share. First, we have to move from the more general notion of 'correlation' or 'explanation' to the much more specific one of 'causation', and second, we have to assume whatever its benefits that market share is somehow under-priced. If our first assumption is correct then broadly it can only be under-priced if either our competitors, both current and potential, have a different view or, for some unspecified reason, happen to value the asset (market share) significantly lower than we do. In fact, in specific situations this latter assumption may be rather less unlikely than it at first appears: our competitors could indeed value the benefits differently given their differing portfolio of assets and market positions, but it all depends on the specifics and the details of the individual situation rather than the general.

In the end, it is likely that the continued search for general rules for strategic success via statistical analysis and large databases will prove illusory even given the current claims made about the impact of so-called 'big data'. This does not make the research effort worthless, rather we merely have to be realistic about what can and cannot be achieved. After all, the in-depth case study narrative approach[29] often results in another type of economic rule: the truth that is virtually impossible to apply. Perhaps the best example is to be found in Peters and Waterman's (1982) original work. Amongst many memorable criteria for success to be found in *In Search of Excellence* was that undeniable one: the achievement of simultaneous 'loose–tight' linkages. To those who thought that this might seem contradictory, Peters and Waterman provided the helpful observation that 'These are the apparent contradictions that turn out in practice not to be contradictions at all' (Peters and Waterman 1982: 320).

More recently in marketing strategy, as in strategy as a whole, there has been a move away from analysis based on real substantive recommendations for management action, towards a concern more for processes, people and purposes rather than structure, strategies and systems.[30] Whilst this shift can be seen as a reasonable response to our lack of substantive generalizable knowledge about the nature of successful marketing strategies in a competitive marketplace, as we have discussed above, it should also be seen as one that itself has rather limited evidence to support it. In marketing strategy in particular, two areas can be identified where this trend has been very evident and we will look critically at both of these: the shift towards a focus on networks and relationship marketing and the increased emphasis on marketing processes within the firm.

Markets as networks

It is clear, as Easton (1990) has indicated, that actual relationships between one firm and another must be seen on a spectrum between outright competition at one end and collusion at the other. At the very least, such a self-evident observation raises the issue of the firm (or business unit) as the basic, and often only, unit of analysis. In certain circumstances we might more appropriately consider an informal coalition of such firms as the key unit:

> Earlier, the border of the company was seen as the dividing line between co-operation and conflict – co-operation within the company and conflict in relation to all external units. The corresponding means for co-ordination are hierarchy and the market mechanism. The existence of relationships makes this picture much more diffuse. There are great opportunities for co-operation with a lot of external units forming, for example, coalitions. Thus, it is often more fruitful to see the company as a part of a network instead of a free and independent actor in an atomistic market.
>
> (Hakansson 1987: 13)

However, the recognition that there is a network of relationships is merely the first step. Approaches need to be developed for the analysis of the network. For instance, Hakansson has suggested that the key elements of any network are actors, activities and resources. He also suggests that the overall network is bound together by a number of forces, including functional interdependence, as well as power, knowledge and time-related structure.

There is a danger in confusing a detailed descriptive model with a simple but robust predictive one, let alone one that aids the diagnostic process. The basic micro-economic framework, which underlies the 'competitive advantage' approach, central to much marketing strategy analysis, should not be seen as an adequate description of the analytical and processual complexities in specific situations. It is a framework for predicting the key impacts of a series of market-mediated transactions: at the very least outcomes are the joint effect of decisions themselves and the selection process. In this sense the only valid criticisms of the application of such a model is either that the needs of the situation are not met by the inherent nature of the model, or that the model fails to perform within its own terms.

Relationship marketing

Beyond this there has been a broader attempt to introduce what has become known as relationship marketing. Whilst the relationship perspective rightly moves our attention away from individual transactions towards patterns of interaction over longer-time periods, it often seems to assume that the motivations of each party are symmetric. In practice, in both consumer (Fournier *et al.* 1998) and industrial markets (Faria and Wensley 2002), this may prove to be a very problematic assumption.

Equally, we may wonder how far the newfound concern for relationship marketing is indeed new at all. The recognition that customers faced switching costs and that therefore the retention of existing customers was clearly an effective economic strategy, is certainly not new. One can therefore sympathize with Baker when he commented on the book by Regis McKenna (1992) entitled *Relationship Marketing*:

> For example, the propositions that companies need to understand the industry infrastructure and/or that working closely with customers is likely to improve product development success rates have been known and accepted [for] many years now, and are embedded in the curricula of most business schools.

> (Baker 1993)

Mattsson (1997) has considered much more critically the relationship between the underlying approaches in the 'markets-as-networks' and relationship marketing perspectives. He rightly observed that much of the problem lay in the various different approaches claiming to represent relationship marketing:

> My conclusion is that if we take the limited view of relationship marketing, we come close to the first extreme position stated in the beginning of this article: relationship marketing and the network perspective have very little in common. Some relationship marketing aspects are even contradictory to basic views in the network perspective. Relationship marketing in its limited interpretation is just a marketing strategy aimed to increase customer loyalty, customer satisfaction and customer retention. Relationship marketing is aided by modern information technology that makes it possible to individualize communication with customers in a mass market. In that sense relationship marketing is just a basic application of the marketing management thinking.

However, let us consider the extended view that relationship marketing means true interaction between the parties over time, a relatively high mutual dependency between seller and buyer and a major concern for how individual relationships are interconnected in nets and networks. Then we will come much closer to my second initial position that relationship marketing and the network perspective have much to gain from more research interaction and mutual awareness than what is presently the case. Relationship marketing research would benefit from the following aspects of network perspective research: more focus on embeddedness of actors and relationships, more consideration of the buyers [sic] point of view, more descriptive studies on interaction and relationships over time, more concern at the meso and macro levels in the governance structure, more use of longitudinal research methods, including case studies. Obviously, both relationship marketing and the network perspective must become increasingly aware of, and contribute to, research developments in a broader social science framework where the focus is on the function of relationships between economic actors.

More recently, Vargo and Lusch (2004) developed the argument further on the assumption of a dominant trend from the marketing of goods to the provision of services, in developing what they termed a service-dominant logic (SDL) framework. They argued that inter alia all economies are service economies, that the customer is always a co-producer and that the enterprise can only make value propositions.[31] In a sense, however, to describe, as they do, the trend as being from goods-dominant to service-dominant perspectives over a period of around 100 years, is to describe a genuine shift in perspective, albeit a less clear shift in the underlying realities.

The whole development might remind one rather more of M. Jourdain in Moliere's *Le Bourgeois Gentilhomme* who discovers that he has been effortlessly speaking prose all his life. The proposed move towards a more relational and service-based perspective reflects more a changing view of the nature of the customer: from consumer to co-producer than the fact that those who used to be characterized as consumers are now in some objective way more co-producers.[32]

We would do well to remember that memorable expression of Ivan Illich (1981), 'shadow work' to describe real work, which we do not see because of the nature of our measurement or value systems. Arnould (2006) notes the clear potential link between the approach advocated by Vargo and Lusch and consumer culture theory, but also notes that these aspects are less well developed in their initial presentation. Moreover, Schembri (2006) suggests that the approach adopted still remains somewhat rooted in the more traditional goods centred logic, and needs to engage more with approaches focused around the nature of the customer experience.

With the more recent development of the SDL framework, it has become clear that there are significant overlapping domains of interest between SDL coming primarily from marketing, service systems approaches coming out of operations management and co-production coming primarily from knowledge development and innovation. Will this mean the development of a wider trans-disciplinary set of perspectives for marketing and hence also for marketing strategy? At this stage it is difficult to know, but it seems clear that to address the central questions in marketing strategy we will also need to be able to incorporate some appropriate framework of value (see, for instance, Gummerus 2013).

Each of what we might call these four traditions has itself quite a long history:

1   The foundation article on SDL by Vargo and Lusch (2004) reflects, as particularly Bob Lusch (2006) recognizes, some of the critical ideas of Wroe Alderson's writings in the 1950s and 1960s such as Alderson's distinction between a transaction perspective and a 'transvection' one (see Alderson 2006).

2   The phrase service system was used in a book title by Riordan (1962), which focused on queuing theory and illustrated the application of analytical principles derived from the management science approach.
3   The term 'co-production' in public services was originally coined in the late 1970s by Elinor Ostrom and colleagues at Indiana University to explain why neighbourhood crime rates went up in Chicago when the city's police officers retreated from the beat into cars. In a different context, Alvin Toffler (1980) coined the term 'prosumer' when he predicted that the role of producers and consumers would begin to blur and merge.
4   Holbrook (1999) was the first to link axiology and marketing when exploring customer-perceived value. He argued that axiology and value theory (see Frondizi 1971) had links to marketing and consumer behaviour research, because axiology is concerned with the internal systems used by individuals to value items.

Overall, therefore, SDL represents a significant attempt to provide a conceptual framework, which incorporates to a lesser or greater extent at least four distinct analytical strands. Not surprisingly, the overall approach is both eclectic and somewhat indeterminate, if not also evolving itself. In the context of strategic marketing, it seems unlikely that it will provide specific 'rules' for the analysis of competitive market success: it is more likely to encourage a focus on aspects of the marketing process, which derive from one or more of the four strands As an example, Steve Vargo and Bob Lusch (2014) explore how value creation, both its nature and scope, can be better and more accurately understood by inverting various characteristics of goods-dominant logic.

It may well be that the relationship marketing movement as well as further developments within SDL will in the end have a rather similar impact on marketing as the market share one did in the 1970s and early 1980s. As such, the renewed emphasis on the nature of the customer relationship, which is self-evidently important in industrial markets, will encourage retail marketers to take their customers more seriously, even to regard them as intelligent and rational agents. To do so, however, would also mean recognizing severe scepticism about some of the various developments in relationship marketing, such as 'loyalty' cards and one-to-one targeting.[33]

However, it may also be true that the relationship and network perspective will, in the longer run, change our perception of the critical strategic questions faced by firms as they and their 'markets' evolve and develop. Easton *et al.* (1993), for instance, suggest that the notion of competition and markets is really only appropriate at specific stages in the lifecycle of the firm or business unit. Indeed, their approach could be taken further to suggest that at the time when there is significant indeterminacy in terms of competitor and customer choice, this way of characterizing strategic choice is, of itself, of limited either theoretical or practical value. Almost by definition, the product technology and market structure needs to be relatively stable for such strategic choices to be formulated, yet, by this stage, the feasible choice set itself may be very restricted.[34]

Emergent or enacted environments

The notion of emergent phenomena has itself emerged as a key concept in organizational strategy. Much of the credit for this must go to Mintzberg (1994), but ironically, his analysis of the concept itself has been perhaps rather more limited than it could have been. Indeed, in his more recent work, he has tended to define the nature of emergent phenomena in a rather idiosyncratic manner:

> Much as planners can study and interpret patterns in the organization's own behavior to identify its emergent strategies, so too can they study and interpret patterns in the external

environment to identify possible opportunities and threats (including as already noted, the patterns of competitors [sic] actions in order to identify their strategies).

(Mintzberg 1994: 375)

This implies that emergent phenomena are such that they can ex post be related to intentions or actions through time of the individual actors.[35] However, a more common use of the term emergence incorporates some notion of interpretation at different levels of aggregation.[36] After all, for instance, as a number of authors have previously commented, markets themselves are emergent phenomena. It was originally Adam Smith's insight that each actor in a market following their own interest could under certain conditions create an overall situation of welfare maximization: in this sense the invisible hand was much more effective than any attempts at local or even global optimization.

Others have paid much greater attention to the nature of emergent properties, but we also need to recognize a further distinction between what have been termed emergent and enacted environments. In a number of relevant areas, such as information systems, there is no overall agreement on the nature of the differences (see Mingers 1995). In the absolute, an emergent environment is one in which there is a set of rules, but the specific outcome state is undetermined or at least the only way in which an outcome state can be predicted is by a process of simulation. An enacted environment is one in which the nature of the environment is itself defined by the cognitive patterns of the constituents.

This distinction is particularly important when we consider the possibility of 'markets-as-networks' as a perspective to understand the nature of competitive market phenomena. If we understand the nature of the phenomena we are trying to understand as essentially emergent, then there remains considerable value in attempting to model the relevant structure of rules or relationships that characterize the environment.[37] If on the other hand, we are more inclined to an enactive view of the relationship between organizations and their environment, we need to consider the degree to which the structure of the network is not more than a surface phenomenon, itself resulting from other deeper processes. In this analysis we need to consider the phenomenon that Giddens (1979) identifies in terms of 'structuration'. Here, agents and organizations are simultaneously both creators of structures, but also have their action constrained by these structures.

However, even if we are willing to give a relatively privileged ontological status to the detailed network structure in a particular context,[38] we may still face insurmountable problems in developing high-level regularities from a more detailed analysis. As Cohen and Stewart (1995) assert:

> We've argued that emergence is the rule rather than the exception, and that there are at least two distinct ways for high-level rules to emerge from low-level rules – simplexity and complicity.[39] Can we write down the equations for emergence? The short answer is no . . . Essentially what is needed is a mathematical justification for the belief that simple high-level rules not only can, but usually do, emerge from complex interactions of low-level rules. By 'emerge' we mean that a detailed derivation of the high-level rules from the low-level ones would be so complicated that it could never be written down in full let alone understood.

(Cohen and Stewart 1995: 436)

It seems that whilst Cohen and Stewart (1995) warn convincingly about the dangers of drowning in the detail of low-level rules, they give only limited useful advice as to the practical nature of the alternatives. There continues to be a spate of interest in mathematical approaches under the general title of 'Complexity'. In the context of the economics of forms of market organization, perhaps the most obvious is that due to Kaufmann (1995):[40]

Organizations around the globe were becoming less hierarchical, flatter, more decentralized, and were doing so in the hopes of increased flexibility and overall competitive advantage. Was there much coherent theory about how to decentralize, I wondered. For I was just in the process of finding surprising new phenomena, that hinted at the possibility of a deeper understanding of how and why flatter, more decentralized organizations – business, political or otherwise – might actually be more flexible and carry an overall competitive advantage.

(Kaufmann 1995: 245–246)

Kaufmann goes on to discuss the logic of what he calls a 'patch' structure in which at various levels the form of organization involves a series of relatively autonomous sub-units, which under certain conditions are more effective at achieving a system-wide performance maxima compared with the more extreme options, which he terms rather controversially, the fully integrated 'Stalinist' system, or the fully autonomous 'Italian leftist' system![41]

However, despite the fact that some of these general notions have been seen in the mainstream of strategic management thought for some considerable time (see Stacey 1995), we should remain cautious. Horgan (1997) suggests that we should be cautious of the likely advances to be made in the field that he has dubbed 'chaoplexity':

So far, chaoplexologists have created some potent metaphors, the butterfly effect, fractals, artificial life, the edge of chaos, self-organized criticality. But they had not told us anything about the world that is both concrete and truly surprising, either in a negative, or in a positive sense. They have slightly extended the borders of our knowledge in certain areas, and they have more sharply delineated the boundaries of knowledge elsewhere.

(Horgan 1997: 226)

Marketing processes

Not surprisingly, the 1990s saw a renewed interest in the marketing process, particularly in the nature of the processes that support the development of a marketing orientation. This approach had been encouraged by the renewed attempts to model the nature of marketing orientation due to both Narver and Slater (1990) and Kohli and Jaworski (1990). In essence the shift is one that Simon (1979) recognized in his original distinction between substantive and procedural rationality in which he suggested that an appropriate response to the problem of bounded rationality was to focus attention more on the appropriate process for arriving at a particular choice, rather than developing a general analytical approach to make that choice in any particular situation.

Much empirical research, in particular that based on key informant surveys, has been undertaken to establish the extent to which various operational measures of marketing orientation are correlated with commercial success. On top of this, there has been work to establish some of the possible antecedents for such orientation, including measures related to the accumulation and organizational dispersion of market research data. The results remain somewhat contradictory, but it seems likely that some level of association will finally emerge, although whether it will achieve the minimum 10 per cent target, which we considered earlier, is rather another question.

It is also important to note that the two approaches to measuring market orientation focused on substantially different approaches; one essentially related to a more organizational 'cultural' or attitude measure and the other to an information processing perspective around market-based data. Hult *et al.* (2005) reported on a study still based primarily on survey data, which not only incorporated both of these measures but also attempted to overcome one of the common criticisms of much of the other empirical work, in that they used an independent and leading performance measure.[42]

On top of this, we need to address more fundamental questions about the underlying logic of procedural rationality in this context. As we have suggested above, it is reasonable to argue that some consideration in any marketing context of each element in the 3Cs (customers, competitors and channels) must surely be seen as sensible. How far such a process should be routinized within a particular planning or decision-making schema, is another matter. Much of the writing in the area of marketing orientation suggests that the appropriate mechanisms and procedures are unproblematic, yet everyday experience in organizations suggests that achieving effective response to the market is difficult and indeed may not be susceptible to programmed responses and practices.[43]

The new analytics: resource advantage, co-evolution and agent-based modelling

Earlier on in this chapter we identified a number of key characteristics of a competitive market, which determine the effectiveness of any specific strategic analysis, in particular the heterogeneity of demand, the interaction between customer choices and producer offerings and the degree to which both producers and customers are active agents in this process. More recently, various new analytical approaches have given us updated and different ways to address these central issues.

First, Hunt (2000a) has argued that the, by now, more traditional RBV of the firm is so dominated by a supply side perspective that a more comprehensive theoretical approach, which he labels 'resource advantage', is required.

There are some concerns, however, as to whether Hunt's framework actually provides the most effective way of incorporating heterogeneity of demand (Wensley 2002), particularly in the context of the evolution of market structure. For instance, one of most established issues in the nature of a market structure is what Wroe Alderson (2006) referred to as the sequential processes of 'sorting' between supplier offerings in order to 'match' specific portfolios to customer demands. Yet Hunt himself observes that so far he is unclear as to how this might be incorporated within his framework (Hunt 2000b). Others, such as Zander and Zander (2005) have gone back to the earlier work of Edith Penrose (1959), often seen as the key precursor to the RBV approach, to argue that the demand perspective is better incorporated within her notion of the 'inside track', which is embodied in market intelligence resulting from longer-term organizational relationships.

At best, therefore, it remains an open question as to how far the developments proposed by Hunt will help us to further understand not only a static view of market demand but even more a dynamic and evolving one, although it does provide a very useful perspective on the nature of strategic choices for the individual firm or business unit. There are three alternative approaches, which might also yield useful results.

First, is to focus more on the ability of firms to adapt to an evolving and changing market. This resonates with developments in the field of strategic management in what are termed 'dynamic capabilities' (Teece *et al.* 1997; Winter 2003). Whilst previously, Day (1994) has suggested that an analogous approach to understanding the nature of market-based firms can prove useful, the overall study of such dynamic capabilities has, unfortunately, proved so far to be 'riddled with inconsistencies, overlapping definitions and outright contradictions' (Zahra *et al.* 2006).

Second, there have also been interesting developments in empirical studies of co-evolution, but, again, unfortunately, most of these so far have focused solely on the competitive and co-operative processes between organizations, as Lewin and Volberda (1999) note:

However, studies of simultaneous evolution or co-evolution of organizations and their environments are still rare. We define co-evolution as the joint outcome of managerial intentionality, environment and institutional effects. Co-evolution assumes that change may occur in all interacting populations of organizations. Change can be driven by direct interactions and feedback from the rest of the system. In other words, change can be recursive and need not be an outcome of either managerial adaptation or environmental selection but rather the joint outcome of managerial intentionality and environmental effects.

As an exception, they also note the Galunic and Eisenhardt (1996) study on selection and adaptation at the intra-corporate level of analysis, which used charter changes to align and realign the competencies of various divisions with co-evolving markets and opportunities. However, the model adopted for the process of market evolution remained a simple three-stage lifecycle one: start-up, growth and maturity. They found that, broadly speaking, the process of charter changes, which equate with the agreed domain of any division's activity, could be seen as one that was based on selecting the successes from a portfolio of start-ups, then reinforcing focus and finally requiring disposals as the particular market opportunity went through the three stages. More recently, Eisenhardt has developed empirically and theoretically with others this particular perspective on the process of market 'creation' by looking at the development of organization boundaries (Santos and Eisenhardt 2005) and the nature of market structure (Davis *et al.* 2006).

From a market strategy perspective, however, it is noteworthy that even those few studies, which attempt to model the nature of market evolution specifically, rather than treat it more as a backcloth upon which other sociological and economic processes take place, tend to represent the actual process in very limited ways. Only in the resource partitioning approach (Carroll and Swaminathan 1992) do we perhaps see the direct opportunities for a more complex model of market development, which represents both its continuity – in the sense that one reasonably expects cycles of competitive imitation followed by the emergence of new forms and market positions for competition – and its indeterminacy, in that various new 'realized niches' could emerge. Even here, however the implicit emphasis is on the individual firms as the motivating force rather than the collective of customers in the various markets.

Third, advances in agent-based modelling promise new ways of simulating more complex interactive processes of spatial competition (Ishibuchi *et al.* 2001; Tesfatsion 2001). Agent-based modelling essentially depends on allowing a simulation to evolve with individual 'agents' making choices within an undetermining, but defined rule structure. It may well provide us with a better understanding of the patterns of market-based evolution and the nature of some of the key contingencies. However, again, it is proving difficult to adequately reflect the evolving behaviour of customers in the marketplace. Chang and Harrington (2003) did included a process of consumer search in their model, but their focus remained on the potential advantages of centralization for what were in effect multi-unit retailers.

Conclusions: the limits of relevance and the problems of application

The study and application of marketing strategy therefore reflects a basic dilemma. The key demand in terms of application is to address the causes of individual firm or unit success in the competitive marketplace, yet we can be reasonably confident from a theoretical perspective that such knowledge is not systematically available, because of the nature of the competitive process itself. In this way, the academic study of marketing strategy remains open to the challenge that it is not relevant to marketing practice. Yet to represent the problem solely in this way is to privilege one particular notion of the nature and use of academic research in marketing, as well as the relationship between research and practice.[44] Recognizing the limits to our knowledge in marketing strategy may also help in a constructive way to define what can and cannot be achieved by more investigation and research.

There are a number of areas in which we can both improve our level of knowledge and provide some guidance and assistance in the development of strategy. First, we can identify some of the generic patterns in the process of market evolution that give some guidance as to how we might think about and frame appropriate questions to be asked in the development of marketing strategy. Such questions would be added to those we are used to using in any marketing management context, such as the nature of the (economic) value added to the customer based on market research evidence and analysis. It has been suggested in strategy that such additional questions are most usefully framed around questions of imitation and sustainability, but, rather as Dickinson (1992) argues,[45] this really assumes sustainability is a serious option. It may be more appropriate to frame such additional questions around the more general patterns of market evolution: standardization, maturity of technology and stability of current networks rather than attempt to address the unanswerable question of sustainability directly.

When it comes to the generics of success, we face an even greater problem. By definition, any approach, which really depends on analysis of means or averages leaves us with a further dilemma: not only does any relative 'usable' explanation just provide us with a very partial picture where there are many unexplained rather than explained outcomes but also the very notion of a publicly available 'rule for success' in a competitive market is itself contradictory, except in the context of a possible temporary advantage.[46] We can try and resolve the problem by looking at the behaviour of what might be called successful outliers, but here we face a severe issue of interpretation. As we have seen, and as we might expect the sources of such success are themselves ambiguous and often tautological: we end up often really asserting either that to achieve success one needs to be successful or that the route to success is some ill-defined combination of innovation, effectiveness and good organization.

It may well be that the best we can do with such analysis is to map out the ways in which the variances of performance change in different market contexts. Just like our finance colleagues, we can do little more than identify the conditions under which variances in performance are likely to be greater and therefore through economic logic the average performance will increase to compensate for the higher risks.

Finally, we may need to recognize that the comfortable distinction between marketing management, which has often been framed in terms of the more tactical side of marketing, and marketing strategy, is not really sustainable. At one level, all marketing actions are strategic: we have little knowledge as to how specific, even brand choices at the detailed level impact or not on the broad development of a particular market, so we are hardly in a position to label some choices as strategic in this sense and others as not. At another level, the knowledge that we already have and are likely to develop in the context of the longer-term evolutionary patterns for competitive markets will not really enable us to also engage directly with marketing managerial actions and choices at the level of the firm: the units of both analysis and description are likely to be different. In our search for a middle way, which can inform individual practice, it may well be that some of the thinking tools and analogies that we have already developed will prove useful, but very much as a means to an end rather than solutions in their own right.

Notes

1 Labelling the intellectual pedigree for Bruce Henderson and the Boston Consulting Group is rather more difficult than for Michael Porter. This is partly because much of the approach developed out of consulting practice (cf. Morrison and Wensley 1991) in the context of a broad rather than focused notion of economic analysis. Some of the intellectual pedigree for the approach can be found in Henderson and Quant (1958), but some basic ideas such as dynamic economies of scale have a much longer pedigree (see, for instance, Jones (1926)).

2 The book itself is clearly influenced by the work related to the PIMS project, as well as work in management consultancies such as McKinsey, ADL and, perhaps most importantly, Boston Consulting Group, whose founder, Bruce Henderson had close links with Derek Abell. The MBA course itself started in 1975 with a broad notion of 'filling the gap' between what was seen then as the marketing domain and the much broader area of business policy, so encompassing issues relating to R&D, distribution and competitive costs. The course itself was a second year elective and rapidly expanded to four sections with a major commitment on development and case writing in 1976 and 1977. For a more historical analysis of the ways in which the case method has been used to incorporate new issues in management whilst avoiding some central concerns about the nature of power and influence, see Contardo and Wensley (2004).

3 It is noteworthy that the very representation of the five forces diagram for instance is one, which emphasizes that the firm is under pressure from all sides.

4 This is a particular and rather colourful way of representing the notion of 'rational expectations' (Muth 1961; Simon 1979) in economics to which we will return later in this chapter.

5 Indeed, to the extent of arguing in one interview that innovative behaviour now depends on ignoring rather than exploiting market evidence.

6 For instance, see Prahalad and Bettis (1986, 1989) and Prahalad and Hamel (1990).

7 As often, his approach has also been subject to critique and challenge (see Shepherd 2005).

8 In fact Mintzberg himself goes on to argue three roles for 'corporate planning': (1) a more refined approach in traditional contexts; (2) a focus on techniques, which emphasize the uncertain and emergent nature of strategic phenomena; and/or (3) a more creative and intuitive form of strategic planning (see Wensley 1996).

9 There are undoubtedly good reasons for adopting such a low dimensionality approach in the name of either stability, which is clearly a critical issue if strategic choices are going to be made in this context, and/or a hierarchy of effects in which strategic choices at this level dominate later more complex choices in a higher dimension perceptual space. But, it is often doubtful whether either or both of these rationales are based on firm empirical evidence in many situations.

10 More recently, it would seem that the differences approach in the form of the RBV is in the ascendancy.

11 It should also be noted that the very complexities of modelling and interpreting competitive and intermediary response have led some marketing scholars to suggest that it would be better to focus on so-called monopoly models and ignore issues of competitive reaction (Shugan 2002).

12 We do, however, need to be clear between the simple trade-off between risk and return and the undoubted fact that in more risky situations, it may be more advisable to make optional investments, i.e. to look at what are termed 'real options' (see Dixit and Pindyck 1995; Adner and Levinthal 2004a, 2004b).

13 More recent commentators, such as McGee (2002), maintain a distinction between the value chain, which represents those activities undertaken by a firm, and the supply chain, of which the value chain is a subset, which refers to all the activities leading up to the final product for the consumer.

14 In particular, others have emphasized the importance of co-operative as well as competitive behaviour, particularly in terms of knowledge flows (see Cooke 2002) and strategic alliances (Todeva and Knoke 2005).

15 This links to an interest in co-evolutionary processes, but much of the strategy-related writing in this area has focused on interactions between organizations rather than between organizations and users (see Volberda and Lewin 2003).

16 For a much more developed discussion of the application of such notions as species to competitive strategy at the firm level, see McKelvey (1982).

17 Stephen Jay Gould (1987, 1990) has perhaps most directly considered this issue in his various writings, in particular the analysis of the Burgess Shale, and come to the uncompromising conclusion that it is difficult, if not impossible, to recognize any species' features or characteristics that provided a reliable ex ante rule for success.

18 However, some detailed work on customer perceptions of market structure actually suggests that in even relatively stable contexts such as autos and motorcycles, the structures may be quite dynamic (Rosa et al. 1999; Rosa and Porac 2002).

19 A wider and comprehensive review of the application of game theory to marketing situations can be found in Moorthy (1985). For a more recent but broader and rather patchy review, see Chatterjee and Samuelson (2001).

20 A good coverage of game theory approaches is to be found in Kreps (1990), but as indeed Goeree and Holt (2001) note, there remain some significant problems with the predictive power of game theory models when they are compared with actual behaviour, most obviously in asymmetric pay-off situations, which raises questions about the underlying notion of rationality.

21 For a more detailed discussion of this analysis see Lambkin and Day (1989), as well as an introduction to more complex strategy options involving polymorphism and portfolios. Achrol (1991) also develops this approach further with some useful examples. In strategy language, we recognize that the ability to adapt in a more rapidly changing or turbulent environment is down to being a 'learning organization', or having so-called 'dynamic capabilities' (Teece *et al.* 1997).

22 In this analysis we have left out two other generic types of competitive analogy that are commonly used: sports games and military conflict. Whilst in general these can both be illuminating and informative, they represent in many ways intermediate categories between game theory and evolutionary ecology.

23 The RBV approach focuses particularly on the nature of idiosyncratic and difficult to imitate resources in each individual firm. For a thorough presentation and analysis of the RBV approach, see Barney and Clark (2007).

24 In fact, on closer inspection, it is clear that we can achieve a high level of discrimination with the one-dimensional map where there are two distinct groupings, and one intermediate brand and one 'outlier' brand. It is significant that these groupings are neither brand nor pack-sized based, but a mixture. In fact, the only result in moving from the one-dimensional to the two-dimensional analysis is that one brand has become less discriminated. Hence, it would appear that we could rather surprisingly reduce the effective competitive space to a single dimension with the possibility of only some second order anomalies.

25 The classical Victorian monograph *Flatland* (Abbot 1992) provided an early illustration of many perceptual problems of moving between spaces of different dimensions.

26 Much of the market shift towards standardization as it evolves can be seen as analogous to more recent work on the mathematics of chaos and particular questions of the nature of boundaries between domains of chaos and those of order, often labelled the phenomena of complexity (Cohen and Stewart 1995). Whether we can use such models to provide a better understanding of the nature of market evolution beyond the basic analogy remains an important question for empirical research.

There have been more recent attempts to apply spatial competition models, which demonstrate some level of chaotic or complexity characteristics either to competitive behaviour in a retailing context (Krider and Weinberg 1997), or to multi-brand category competition (Rungie 1998) or competition between audit service providers (Chan *et al.* 1999). Whilst these approaches suggested that such models might be able to give us significant new insights as to the nature of competitive market evolution, there has been little further progress.

27 As they recognize, this is not an issue of statistical significance of individual coefficients. For samples of only 50, we can roughly speaking achieve a significant result using the 'normal' $p < 0.05$ criterion, and yet only have about 5 per cent of the variability 'explained'. For a further and broader discussion on both the issues of statistical reliability and research inference in management research, see Starbuck (2004).

28 Because of the statistical nature of the data distribution in the PIMS database: the fact that it is not strictly normal, it is only possible to simulate a dataset, which has either the right range or the right slope within the correct proportion of variance explained. This simulation is based on the right range of values, so that the extreme points are estimated correctly as a result however the actual slope is underestimated (see Roberts 1997; Wensley 1997a, 1997b).

29 Perhaps the best example of both the value but also the risks of relying on an in-depth case study lies in the continuing debates about the interpretation of the story of Honda and their entry into the American motorcycle market (Mintzberg 1996; Goold 1996; Rumelt 1996; Mair 1999).

30 Bartlett and Ghoshal (1995) in their influential *Harvard Business Review* article played a key role in this change.

31 For a generally constructive and useful set of commentaries on the Vargo and Lusch approach, see the special issue of *Marketing Theory* (Aitken *et al.* 2006).

32 And in this sense, another long-running debate in marketing (Wensley 1990).

33 And also, perhaps, a more critical look at the overall and very central issue of branding. For instance, some commentators see the new service logic as consistent with many aspects of a traditional view on branding (Brodie *et al.* 2006).

34 The argument is, of course, rather more complicated than this and relates to the previous debate between Child (1972) and Aldrich (1979) on the more general issue of strategic choice, as well as to some degree the wide field of actor-network theory (Latour 2005).

35 In many ways, issues of intention and anticipation are both central to any analysis of strategic behaviour, but are also complex and multi-faceted (see Wensley 2003).

36 For a broader discussion of emergence, see Johnson (2002).

37 Actually, even this statement incorporates another critical assumption. As Mingers notes in commenting on assumptions about the nature of social systems and the degree to which they can be seen as self-producing (autopoietic), even those who develop such an analysis define the nature of the organizations and their environment in unexpected ways:

> Luhmann . . . in conceptualizing societies as autopoietic . . . [sees them] as constituted not by people but by communications. Societies and their component subsystems are networks of communicative events, each communication being triggered by a previous one and leading in turn to another . . . People are not part of society but part of its environment.
>
> (Mingers 1995: 211)

38 A position that others such as Margaret Archer would indeed challenge (Archer 1995).

39 Cohen and Stewart use specific meanings for both 'simplexity' and 'complicity', which roughly describe phenomena where, in the former case, similar low-level rules create high-level similar structures, whereas in the latter case, 'totally different rules converge to produce similar features and so exhibit the same large-scale structural patterns' (Cohen and Stewart 1995: 414). As they emphasize, in the case of complicity, one of the critical effects is the way in which, 'this kind of system . . . *enlarges the space of the possible*' (original emphasis).

40 With a fine, if totally unintentional sense of irony, the chapter in Kaufman's (1995) book, which addresses these questions, has the same title as the infamous Peters and Waterman classic *In Search of Excellence*. Interestingly, however, Kaufman (1995) is drawing a distinction between the 'lesser' criteria of 'excellence' compared with 'optimality'!

41 One can see analogies between this argument and Herb Simon's (1969) explanation of the robustness of modular systems of assembly.

42 Admittedly, the performance measure was only leading by one year, but this was clearly an improvement on most cross-sectional studies, which even when they try and incorporate time effects, have to rely on informant recall.

43 Indeed, the issue of the actual nature of organizational routines themselves remains contentious (Feldman 2000).

44 The issue of the relationship between theory and practice, and the notion of relevance as the intermediary construct between the two is, of course, itself both problematic in general (Brownlie 1998) as well as open to a range of further critical questions. This is particularly so with respect to the institutional structures that have been developed and sustained on the assumption of the divide itself (Wensley 1997c, 2007) and therefore at some level represent interest in maintaining the divide, but in the name of bridging it!

45 Of course, such a view about sustainability is also very much in tune with both Schumpeterian views about the nature of economic innovation and the general Austrian view about the nature of the economic system (Wensley 1982; Jacobson 1992).

46 Indeed it would appear that in very rapid response markets, such as currency markets, this temporal advantage is itself measured only in seconds: it is reasonable to assume it is somewhat longer in product and service markets!

References

Abbot, E. A. (1992), *Flatland: A Romance of Many Dimensions*, Mineola, NY: Dover Publications, first published by Seeley and Co Ltd, London 1884.

Abell, D. and Hammond, J. (1979), *Strategic Marketing Planning: Problems and Analytical Approaches*, Englewood Cliffs, NJ: Prentice-Hall.

Achrol, R. S. (1991), 'Evolution of the marketing organisation: new forms for turbulent environments', *Journal of Marketing*, 55(4): 77–93.

Adner, R. and Levinthal, D. A. (2004a), 'What is not a real option: Considering boundaries for the application of real options to business strategy', *Academy of Management Review*, 29(1): 74–85.

Adner, R. and Levinthal, D. A. (2004b), 'Reply: Real options and real tradeoffs', *Academy of Management Review*, 29(1): 120–126.

Aitken, R., Ballantyne, D., Osborne, P. and Williams, J. (2006), 'Introduction to the special issue on the service-dominant logic of marketing: Insights from The Otago Forum', *Marketing Theory*, 6(3): 275–280.

Alderson, W. (2006), 'Transactions and transvections', in Wooliscroft, B., Tamilia, R. D. and Shapiro, S. J. (eds) *A Twenty-First Century Guide to Aldersonian Marketing Thought*, New York: Springer, pp. 229–249.

Aldrich, H. E. (1979), *Organizations and Environments*, Englewood Cliffs, NJ: Prentice-Hall.

Archer, M. (1995), *Realist Social Theory: The Morphogenetic Approach*, Cambridge, UK: Cambridge University Press.

Arnould, E. J. (2006), 'Service-dominant logic and consumer culture theory: Natural allies in an emerging paradigm', *Marketing Theory*, 6: 293–297.

Baker, M. (1993), 'Book review', *Journal of Marketing Management*, 9: 97–98.

Barney, J. and Clark, D. (2007), *Resouce-Based Theory: Resources, Capabilities, and Sustained Competitive Advantage*, Oxford, UK Oxford University Press.

Bartlett, C. A. and Ghoshal, S. (1995), 'Changing the role of top management: beyond systems to people', *Harvard Business Review*, 73(3): 132–142.

Brodie, R. J., Glynn, M. S. and Little, V. (2006), 'The service brand and the service-dominant logic: Missing fundamental premise or the need for stronger theory?', *Marketing Theory*, 6(3): 363–379.

Brownlie, D. (1998), 'Marketing disequilibrium: On redress and restoration', in Brownlie, D., Saren, M., Wensley, R. and Whittington, R. (eds) *Rethinking Marketing*, London: Sage.

Buzzell, R. D., Gale, B. T. and Sultan, R. G. M. (1975), 'Market share: A key to profitability', *Harvard Business Review*, 53: 97–106.

Campbell-Hunt, C. (2000), 'What have we learned about generic competitive strategy: A meta-analysis', *Strategic Management Journal*, 21(2): 127–154.

Carroll, G. R. and Swaminathan, A. (1992), 'The organizational ecology of strategic groups in the American brewing industry from 1975 to 1990', *Industrial and Corporate Change*, 1: 65–97.

Caves, R. E. (1980), 'Industrial organization, corporate strategy and structure', *Journal of Economic Literature*, 18: 64–92.

Caves, R. E. (1984), 'Economic analysis and the quest for competitive advantage', *American Economic Review*, 74(2): 127–132.

Caves, R. E. and Porter, M. E. (1977), 'From entry barriers to mobility barriers: Conjectural decisions and contrived deterrence to new competition', *Quarterly Journal of Economics*, 91(2): 241–262.

Chan, D. K. (1999), '"Low-balling" and efficiency in a two-period specialization model of auditing competition', *Contemporary Accounting Research*, 16(4): 609–642.

Chang, M.-H. and Harrington, J. E. Jr. (2003), 'Multi-market competition, consumer search, and the organizational structure of multi-unit firms', *Management Science*, 49(4): 541–552.

Chatterjee, K. and Samuelson, W. F. (2001), *Game Theory and Business Applications*, Norwell, MA: Kluwer Academic Publishers.

Child, J. (1972), 'Organisational structure, environment and performance: The role of strategic choice', *Sociology*, 6: 1–22.

Chintagunta, P. (1994), 'Heterogeneous logit model implications for brand positioning', *Journal of Marketing Research*, 31: 304–311.

Christensen, C. M. (1997), *The Innovator's Dilemma*, Boston, MA: Harvard Business School Press.

Cohen, J. and Stewart, I. (1995), *The Collapse of Chaos*, London: Penguin Books.

Contardo, I. and Wensley, R. (2004), 'The Harvard Business School Story: Avoiding knowledge by being relevant', *Organization*, 11(2): 211–231.

Cooke, P. (2002), *Knowledge Economics: Clusters, Learning and Co-operative Advantage*, London: Routledge.

Cooper, L. G. and Inoue, A. (1996), 'Building market structures from consumer preferences', *Journal of Marketing Research*, XXXIII: 293–306.

Cooper, L. and Nakanishi, M. (1988), *Market Share Analysis: Evaluating Competitive Marketing Effectiveness*, Boston, MA: Kluwer Academic Press.

Coyle, M. L. (1986), *Competition in Developing Markets: The Impact of Order of Entry*, the Faculty of Management Studies Paper, University of Toronto, June.

Davis, J. P., Eisenhardt, K. M. and Bingham, C. B. (2006), *Complexity Theory, Market Dynamism, and the Strategy of Simple Rules*, Working Paper, Stanford University, available at http://www.stanford.edu/~jpdavis/complexity.pdf, accessed 12 October 2006.

Day, G. S. (1994), 'The capabilities of market-driven organizations', *Journal of Marketing*, 58(4): 37–52.

Day, G. S. and Wensley, R. (1983), 'Marketing theory with a strategic orientation', *Journal of Marketing*, 47(Fall): 79–89.

Day, G. S. and Wensley, R. (1988), 'Assessing advantage: A framework for diagnosing competitive superiority', *Journal of Marketing*, 52(2): 1–20.

Dickinson, P. R. (1992), 'Toward a general theory of competitive rationality', *Journal of Marketing*, 56(1): 68–83.

Dixit, A. K. and Pindyck, R. S. (1995), 'The options approach to capital investment', *Harvard Business Review*, 73(3): 105–115.

Dolan, R. J. (1981), 'Models of competition: A review of theory and empirical findings, in Enis, B. M. and Roering, K. J. (eds) *Review of Marketing*, Chicago, IL: American Marketing Association, pp. 224–234.

Easton, G. (1990), 'Relationship between competitors', in Day, G. S., Weitz, B. and Wensley, R. (eds) *The Interface of Marketing and Strategy*, Greenwich, CT: JAI Press.

Easton, G., Burell, G., Rothschild, R. and Shearman, C. (1993), *Managers and Competition*, Oxford, UK: Blackwell.

Faria, A. and Wensley, R. (2002), 'In search of "inter-firm management" in supply chains: Recognising contradictions of language and power by listening', *Journal of Business Research*, 55(7): 603–610.

Feldman, M. S. (2000), 'Organizational routines as a source of continuous change', *Organizational Science*, 11(6): 611–629.

Fournier, S., Dobscha, S. and Mick, D. G. (1998), 'Preventing the premature death of relationship marketing', *Harvard Business Review*, January/February: 42–50.

Freeman, J. (1997), 'Dynamics of market evolution', *European Marketing Academy. Proceedings of the 26th Annual Conference*, May, Warwick University: Warwick.

Frondizi, R. (1971), *What Is Value?: An Introduction to Axiology*, second edition, Chicago, IL: Open Court Pub Co.

Galunic, D. C. and Eisenhardt, K. M. (1996), 'The evolution of intracorporate domains: Divisional charter losses in high-technology, multidivisional corporations', *Organization Science*, 7(3): 255–282.

Giddens, A. (1979), *Central Problems in Social Theory: Action, Structure and Contradiction in Social Analysis*, London: Macmillan.

Goeree, J. K. and Holt, C. A. (2001), 'Ten little treasures of game theory and ten intuitive contradictions', *The American Economic Review*, 91(5): 1402–1422.

Goold, M. (1996), 'Learning, planning and strategy: Extra time', *California Management Review*, 38(4): 100–102.

Gould, S. J. (1987), *Time's Arrow, Time's Cycle: Myth and Metaphor in the Discovery of Geological Time*, Cambridge, MA: Harvard University Press.

Gould S. J. (1990), *Wonderful Life: The Burgess Shale and the Nature of History*, London: Hutchinson Radius.

Gummerus, J. (2013), 'Value creation processes and value outcomes in marketing theory: Strangers or siblings?', *Marketing Theory*, 13(1): 19–46.

Hakansson, H. (1987), *Industrial Technological Development: A Network Approach*, London: Croom Helm.

Hamel, G. (2000), *Leading the Revolution*, Harvard, MA: Harvard Business School Press.

Hamel, G. and Prahalad, C. K. (1989), *Strategic Intent*, Harvard, MA: Harvard Business School Press, Harvard Business Review, May–June.

Hammer, M. and Champy, J. (1993), *Reengineering the Corporation: A Manifesto for Business Revolution*, London: Brealey.

Harshman, R. A., Green, P. E., Wind, Y. and Lundy, M. E. (1982), 'A model for the analysis of asymmetric data in marketing research', *Marketing Science*, 1(Spring): 205–242.

Henderson, B. D. (1980), *Strategic and Natural Competition*, BCG Perspectives, p. 231.

Henderson, B. D. (1983), 'The anatomy of competition', *Journal of Marketing*, 47(Spring): 7–11.

Henderson, J. M. and Quant, R. E. (1958), *Microeconomic Theory: A Mathematical Approach*, New York: McGraw-Hill.

Hofer, C. W. and Schendel, D. (1977), *Strategy Formulation: Analytical Concepts*, St Paul, MN: West Publishing.

Holbrook, M. B. (1999), 'Introduction to consumer value', in Holbrook, M. B. (ed.) *Consumer Value: A Framework for Analysis and Research*, London: Routledge, pp. 1–28.

Horgan, J. (1997), *The End of Science*, New York: Broadway Books.

Hotelling, H. (1929), 'Stability in competition', *Economic Journal* 39(153): 41–57.

Hult, G. T. M., Ketchen, D. J. Jr. and Slater, S. F. (2005), 'Market orientation and performance: An integration of disparate approaches', *Strategic Management Journal*, 26(12): 1173–1181.

Hunt, S. D. (2000a), *A General Theory of Competition: Resources, Competences, Productivity and Economic Growth*, Thousand Oaks, CA: Sage Publishing.

Hunt, S. D. (2000b), 'A general theory of competition: Too eclectic or not eclectic enough? Too Incremental or not incremental enough? Too neoclassical or not neoclassical enough?', *Journal of Macromarketing*, 20(1): 77–81.

Illich, I. (1981), *Shadow Work*, London: Marion Boyars.

Ishibuchi H., Ryoji S. and Tomoharu N. (2001), 'Evolution of unplanned coordination in a market selection game', *IEEE Transactions on Evolutionary Computation*, 5(5): 524–534.

Jacobson, R. (1992), 'The "Austrian" School of Strategy', *Academy of Management Review*, October: 782–807.

Jacobson, R. (1994), *The Cost of the Market Share Quest*, Working Paper, University of Washington, Seattle.

Jacobson, R. and Aaker, D. (1985), 'Is market share all that it's cracked up to be?', *Journal of Marketing*, 49(4): 11–22.

Johnson, S. (2002), *Emergence: The Connected Lives of Ants, Brains, Cities and Software*, London: Penguin.

Jones, H. J. (1926), *The Economics of Private Enterprise*, London: Pitman and Sons.

Kadane, J. B. and Larkey, P. D. (1982), 'Subjective probability and the theory of games', *Management Science*, 28(2): 113–120.

Kaufmann, S. (1995), *At Home in the Universe*, New York: Oxford University Press.

Kay, J. (1993), *Foundations of Corporate Success*, Oxford, UK: Oxford University Press.

Kohli, A. K. and Jaworski, B. J. (1990), 'Market orientation: the construct, research propositions and managerial implications', *Journal of Marketing*, 54(2): 1–18.

Kreps, D. (1990), *Game Theory and Economic Modelling*, Oxford, UK: Oxford University Press.

Krider, R. E. and Weinberg, C. B. (1997), 'Spatial competition and bounded rationality: Retailing at the edge of chaos', *Geographical Analysis*, 29(1): 17–34.

Lambkin, M. and Day, G. (1989), 'Evolutionary processes in competitive markets: Beyond the product life cycle', *Journal of Marketing*, 53(3): 4–20.

Latour, B. (2005), *Reassembling the Social: An Introduction to Actor-network-theory*, Oxford, UK: Oxford University Press.

Leeflang: S. H. and Wittick, D. (1993), 'Diagnosing competition: Developments and findings', in Laurent, G., Lillien, G. L. and Pras, B. (eds) *Research Traditions in Marketing*, Norwell, MA: Kluwer Academic.

Levins, R. and Leowontin, R. (1985), *The Dialectical Biologist*, Cambridge, MA: Harvard University Press.

Lewin, A. Y. and Volberda, H. W. (1999), 'Prolegomena on coevolution: A framework for research on strategy and new organizational forms', *Organizational Science*, 10(5): 519–534.

Lusch, R. F. (2006), 'Alderson, sessions and the 1950s manager', in Wooliscroft, B., Tamilia, R. D. and Shapiro, S. J. (eds) *A Twenty-First Century Guide to Aldersonian Marketing Thought*, New York: Springer, pp. 275–281.

Mair, A. (1999), 'The business of knowledge: Honda and the strategy industry', *Journal of Management Studies*, 36(1): 25–44.

Mattsson, L.-G. (1997), '"Relationship marketing" and the "markets-as-networks approach": A comparative analysis of two evolving streams of research', *Journal of Marketing Management*, 13(5): 447–461.

McCloskey, D. N. and Ziliak, S. T. (1996), 'The standard error of regressions', *Journal of Economic Literature*, 34(March): 97–114.

McGee, J. (2002), 'Strategy as knowledge', in Cummings, S. and Wilson, D. (eds) *Images of Strategy*, Oxford, UK: Blackwells.

McGee, J. and Thomas, H. (1986), 'Strategic groups: Theory, research and taxonomy', *Strategic Management Journal*, 7(2): 141–160.

McKelvey, B. (1982), *Organisational Systematics: Taxonomy, Evolution, Classification*, Berkeley, CA: University of California Press.

McKenna, R. (1992), *Relationship Marketing*, London: Century Business.

Mingers, J. (1995), *Self-Producing Systems*, New York: Plenum Press.

Mintzberg, H. (1973), *The Nature of Managerial Work*, New York: Harper and Row.

Mintzberg, H. (1994), *The Rise and Fall of Strategic Planning*, Englewood Cliffs, NJ: Prentice-Hall.

Mintzberg, H. (1996), 'CMR forum: The Honda effect revisited', *California Management Review*, 38(4): 78–79.

Mintzberg, H. (2004), *Managers not MBAs*, San Francisco, CA: Berrett Koehler Publishers, Inc.

Moorthy, J. S. (1985), 'Using game theory to model competition', *Journal of Marketing Research*, 22(August): 262–282.

Morrison, A. and Wensley, R. (1991), 'A short history of the growth/share matrix: Boxed up or boxed in?', *Journal of Marketing Management*, 7(2): 105–129.

Muth, J. F. (1961), 'Rational expectations and the theory of price movements', *Econometrica*, 29(3): 315–335.

Narver, J. C. and Slater, S. F. (1990), 'The effect of market orientation on business profitability', *Journal of Marketing*, 54(4): 20–35.

Ohmae, K. (1982), *The Mind of the Strategist*, London: McGraw-Hill.

Penrose, E. T. (1959), *The Theory of the Growth of the Firm*, Oxford, UK: Blackwell.

Peters, T. J. and Waterman, R. H. (1982), *In Search of Excellence*, New York: Harper and Row.

Pettigrew, A. M. (1973), *The Politics of Organisational Decision Making*, London: Tavistock.

Porter, M. E. (1979), 'The structure within industries and companies' performance', *Review of Economics and Statistics*, 61: 214–227.

Porter, M. E. (1980), *Competitive Strategy: Techniques for Analyzing Industries and Competitors*, New York: Free Press.

Porter, M. E. (1981), 'The contribution of industrial organization to strategic management', *Academy of Management Review*, 6(4): 609–620.

Porter, M. E. (1985), *Competitive Advantage*, New York: Free Press.

Porter, M. E. (1990), *The Competitive Advantage of Nations*, New York: Free Press.

Prahalad, C. K. and Bettis, R. A. (1986), 'The dominant logic: A new linkage between diversity and performance', *Strategic Management Journal*, 7(6): 485–501.

Prahalad, C. K. and Bettis, R. A. (1989), 'The dominant logic: A new linkage between diversity and performance', *Strategic Management Journal*, 10(6): 523–552.

Prahalad, C. K. and Hamel, G. (1990), 'The core competence of the corporation', *Harvard Business Review*, May/June: 79–91.

Riordan, J. (1962), *Stochastic Service Systems*, New York: Wiley.

Roberts, K. (1997), 'Explaining success: Hard work not illusion', *Business Strategy Review*, 8(2): 75–77.

Rosa, J. A. and Porac, J. F. (2002), 'Categorization bases and their influence on product category knowledge structurer', *Psychology and Marketing*, 19(6): 503–531.

Rosa, J. A., Porac, J. F., Runser-Spanjol, J. and Saxon, M. S. (1999), 'Socio cognitive dynamics in a product market', *Journal of Marketing*, 63(4): 64–77.

Rumelt, R. P. (1996), 'The many faces of Honda', *Californian Management Review*, 38(4): 103–111.

Rungie, C. (1998), *Measuring the Impact of Horizontal Differentiation on Market Share*, Working Paper, Marketing Science Centre, University of South Australia, November.

Sanchez, R. (1995), 'Strategic flexibility in product competition', *Strategic Management* Journal 16(Special Issue): 135–159.

Santos, F. M. and Eisenhardt, K. M. (2005), 'Organizational boundaries and theories of organization', *Organization Science*, 16(5): 491–508.

Saunders, J. (1995), 'Invited response to Wensley', *British Journal of Management*, 6(Special Issue).

Schembri, S. (2006), 'Rationalizing service logic, or understanding services as experience?', *Marketing Theory*, 6(3): 381–392.

Senge, P. (1992), *The Fifth Discipline: The Art and Practice of the Learning Organization*, London: Century Business.

Shepherd, J. (ed.) (2005), 'Special book review: Henry Mintzberg: Managers not MBAs', *Organisation Studies*, 26(7): 1089–1109.

Shugan, S. M. (2002), 'Editorial: Marketing science, models, monopoly models, and why we need them', *Marketing Science*, 21(3): 223–228.

Simon, H. A. (1969), *The Sciences of the Artificial*, Cambridge, MA: MIT Press.

Simon, H. A. (1979), 'Rational decision making in business organizations', *American Economic Review*, September.

Stacey, R. D. (1995), 'The science of complexity: an alternative perspective for strategic change processes', *Strategic Management Journal*, 16(6): 477–495.

Starbuck, W. H. (2004), 'Vita contemplativa: Why I stopped trying to understand the real world', *Organization Studies*, 25(7): 1233–1254.

Summut-Bonnici, T. and Wensley, R. (2002), 'Darwinism, probability and complexity: Market-based organizational transformation and change explained through the theories of evolution', *International Journal of Management Reviews*, 4(3): 291–315.

Teece, D. J., Pisano, G. and Shuen, A. (1997), 'Dynamic capabilities and strategic management', *Strategic Management Journal*, 18(7): 509–533.

Tesfatsion, L. (2001), 'Guest editorial: Agent-based modelling of evolutionary economic systems', *IEEE Transactions on Evolutionary Computation*, 5(5): 437–441.

Todeva, E. and Knoke, D. (2005), 'Strategic alliances and models of collaboration', *Management Decision*, 43(1): 123–148.

Toffler, A. (1980), *The Third Wave: The Classic Study of Tomorrow*, New York: Bantam.

Vargo, S. L. and Lusch, R. F. (2004), 'Evolving to a new dominant logic for marketing', *Journal of Marketing*, 68(1): 1–17.

Vargo, S. L. and Lusch, R. F. (2014), 'Inversions of service-dominant logic', *Marketing Theory*, 14(3): 239–248.

Volberda, H. W. and Lewin, A. Y. (2003), 'Coevolutionary dynamics within and between firms: From evolution to co-evolution', *Journal of Management Studies*, 40(8): 2111–2136.

Waterman, R. H. (1988), *The Renewal Factor*, London: Bantam Books.

Weick, K. E. (1976), 'Educational organizations as loosely coupled systems', *Administrative Science Quarterly*, 21(1): 1–19.

Wensley, R. (1982), 'PIMS and BCG: New horizon or false dawn', *Strategic Management Journal*, 3: 147–153.

Wensley, R. (1990), '"The voice of the consumer?" Speculations on the limits to the marketing analogy', *European Journal of Marketing*, 24(7): 49–60.

Wensley, R. (1994), 'Strategic marketing: A review', in Baker, M. (ed.) *The Marketing Book*, London: Butterworth-Heinemann, pp. 33–53.

Wensley, R. (1995), 'A critical review of research in marketing', *British Journal of Management*, 6(Special Issue): S63–S82.

Wensley, R. (1996), 'Book review: Henry Mintzberg and Kevin Kelly', *BAM Newsletter*, Spring, pp. 4–7.

Wensley, R. (1997a), 'Explaining success: The rule of ten percent and the example of market share', *Business Strategy Review*, 8(1): 63–70.

Wensley, R. (1997b), 'Rejoinder to "hard work, not illusions"', *Business Strategy Review*, 8(2): 77.

Wensley, R. (1997c), *Two Marketing Cultures in Search of the Chimera of Relevance*, keynote address at joint AMA and AM seminar 'Marketing without Borders', Manchester, July.

Wensley, R. (2002), 'Marketing for the new century', *Journal of Marketing Management*, 18(1): 229–238.

Wensley, R. (2003), 'Strategy as intention and anticipation', in Wilson, D. and Cummings, S. (eds) *Images of Strategy*, Oxford, UK: Blackwell.

Wensley, R. (2007), 'Beyond rigour and relevance: The underlying nature of both business schools and management research', WP No. 051-January-2007, London: AIM.

Wernerfelt, B. (1984), 'A resource-based view of the firm', *Strategic Management Journal*, 5(2): 171–180.

Wernerfelt, B. (1995a), 'The resource-based view of the firm: Ten years after', *Strategic Management Journal*, 16(3): 171–174.

Wernerfelt, B. (1995b), 'A rational reconstruction of the compromise effect', *Journal of Consumer Research*, 21(4): 627–633.

Winter, S. G. (2003), 'Understanding dynamic capabilities', *Strategic Management Journal*, 24(10): 991–995.

Zahra, S. A., Sapienza, H. J. and Davidsson, P. (2006), 'Entrepreneurship and dynamic capabilities: A review, model and research agenda', *Journal of Management Studies*, 43(4): 917–955.

Zander, I. and Zander, U. (2005), 'The inside track: On the important (but neglected) role of customers in the resource-based view of strategy and firm growth', *Journal of Management Studies*, 42(8): 1519–1548.

5 Strategic marketing planning

Theory and practice

Malcolm McDonald

In order to explore the complexities of developing a strategic marketing plan, this chapter is written in two parts.

The first part describes the strategic marketing planning process itself and the key steps within it. It spells out the output of the process – the strategic plan and its contents. It deals with implementation issues and barriers to marketing planning. Finally, it summarizes the first part by setting out ten guidelines to ensure that the process and output are customer focused and considers the strategic dimension of all the relationships the organization has with its business environment.

The second part provides a brief overview of a process for assessing whether the strategic marketing plan creates or destroys shareholder value, having taken account of the risks associated with the plan, the time value of money and the cost of capital. It also outlines other metrics for measuring the effectiveness of the marketing strategy.

PART 1: THE STRATEGIC MARKETING PLANNING PROCESS

Introduction

Research into the efficacy of formalized marketing planning (Thompson 1962; Leighton 1966; Kollatt *et al.* 1972; Ansoff 1977; Greenley 1984; McDonald 1984; Piercy 1997; Smith 2003) has shown that marketing planning can make a significant contribution to commercial success. The main effects within organizations are:

- the systematic identification of emerging opportunities and threats;
- preparedness to meet change;
- the specification of sustainable-competitive advantage;
- improved communication among executives;
- reduction of conflicts between individuals and departments;
- the involvement of all levels of management in the planning process;
- more appropriate allocation of scarce resources;
- consistency of approach across the organization;
- a more market-focused orientation across the organization.

However, although it can bring many benefits, a strategic marketing plan is mainly concerned with competitive advantage – that is to say, establishing, building, defending and maintaining it. In order to be realistic, it must take into account the organization's existing competitive position, where it wants to be in the future, its capabilities and the competitive environment it faces. This means that the marketing planner must learn to use the various available processes and techniques, which help to make sense of external trends, and to understand the organization's traditional ways of responding to these.

However, this poses the problem of which are the most relevant and useful tools and techniques, for each has strengths and weaknesses and no individual concept or technique can satisfactorily describe and illuminate the whole picture. As with a jigsaw puzzle, a sense of unity only emerges as the various pieces are connected together.

The links between strategy and performance have been the subject of detailed statistical analysis by the Strategic Planning Institute. The PIMS (profit impact of market strategy) project identified six major links from 2,600 businesses, (Buzzell and Gale 1987). From this analysis, principles have been derived for the selection of different strategies according to industry type, market conditions and the competitive position of the company.

However, not all observers are prepared to take these conclusions at face value. Like strategy consultants, Lubatkin and Pitts (1985), who believe that all businesses are unique, they are suspicious that something as critical as competitive advantage can be the outcome of a few specific formulae. For them, the PIMS perspective is too mechanistic and glosses over the complex managerial and organizational problems, which beset most businesses. What is agreed, however, is that strategic marketing planning presents a useful process by which an organization formulates its strategies, *providing it is adapted* to the organization and its environment.

Positioning marketing planning within marketing

Smith's PhD thesis (2003) proved a direct link between organizational success and marketing strategies that conform to what previous scholars have agreed constitutes strategy quality, which was shown to be independent of variables such as size, sector, market conditions and so on. This thesis linked superior performance to strategies with the following qualities:

1 homogenous market segment definition;
2 segment specific propositions;
3 strategy uniqueness;
4 strength leverage and weakness minimization;
5 creation of internal and external synergies;
6 provision of tactical guidance;
7 alignment to objectives;
8 alignment to market trends;
9 appropriate resourcing;
10 clear basis of competition.

Let us first position strategic marketing planning firmly within the context of marketing itself. As can be deduced from Chapter 1, marketing is a process for:

- defining markets;
- quantifying the needs of the customer groups (segments) within these markets;
- determining the value propositions to meet these needs;
- communicating these value propositions to all those people in the organization responsible for delivering them and getting their buy-in to their role;

- playing an appropriate part in delivering these value propositions to the chosen market segments;
- monitoring the value actually delivered.

For this process to be effective, we have also seen that organizations need to be consumer/customer-driven. A map of this process is shown in Figure 5.1. This process is clearly cyclical, in that monitoring the value delivered will update the organization's understanding of the value that is required by its customers. The cycle is predominantly an annual one, with a marketing plan documenting the output from the 'understand value' and 'determine value proposition' processes, but equally changes throughout the year may involve fast iterations around the cycle to respond to particular opportunities or problems.

It is well known that not all of the value proposition delivering processes will be under the control of the marketing department, whose role varies considerably between organizations. The marketing department is likely to be responsible for the first two processes, 'Understand value' and 'Determine value proposition', although even these need to involve numerous functions, albeit co-ordinated by specialist marketing personnel. The 'Deliver value' process is the role of the whole company, including, for example, product development, manufacturing, purchasing, sales promotion, direct mail, distribution, sales and customer service. The marketing department will also be responsible for monitoring the effectiveness of the value delivered.

The various choices made during this marketing process are constrained and informed not just by the outside world but also by the organization's asset base. Whereas an efficient new factory with much spare capacity might underpin a growth strategy in a particular market, a factory running at full capacity would cause more reflection on whether price should be used to control demand, unless the potential demand warranted further capital investment. As well as physical assets, choices may be influenced by financial, human resources, brand and information technology assets, to name just a few.

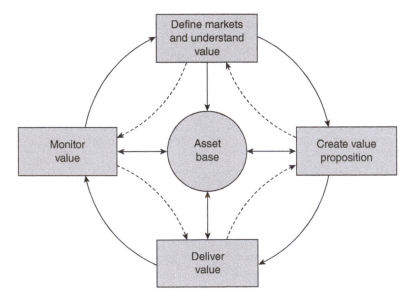

Figure 5.1 Map of the marketing process

Thus, it can be seen that the first two boxes are concerned with strategic marketing planning processes (in other words, developing market strategies), while the third and fourth boxes are concerned with the actual delivery in the market of what was planned and then measuring the effect.

Input to this process will commonly include:

- the corporate mission and objectives, which will determine which particular markets are of interest;
- external data such as market research;
- internal data which flow from ongoing operations.

Also, it is necessary to define the markets the organization is in, or wishes to be in, and how these divide into segments of customers with similar needs. The importance of doing this correctly was emphasized earlier in the reference to Smith's (2003) PhD. The choice of markets will be influenced by the corporate objectives as well as the asset base. Information will be collected about the markets, such as the market's size and growth, with estimates for the future.

The map is inherently cross-functional. 'Deliver value proposition', for example, involves every aspect of the organization, from new product development through inbound logistics and production to outbound logistics and customer service.

The map represents best practice, not common practice. Many aspects of the map are not explicitly addressed by well-embedded processes, even in sophisticated companies. Also, the map is changing. One-to-one communications and principles of relationship marketing demand a radically different sales process from that traditionally practised. Hence, exploiting new media such as the internet requires a substantial shift in thinking, not just changes to IT and hard processes. An example is illuminating. Marketing managers at one company related to us their early experience with a website, which was enabling them to reach new customers considerably more cost-effectively than their traditional sales force. When the website was first launched, potential customers were finding the company on the web, deciding the products were appropriate on the basis of the website, and sending an e-mail to ask to buy. So far, so good. But stuck in a traditional model of the sales process, the company would allocate the 'lead' to a salesperson, who would phone up and make an appointment perhaps three weeks' hence. The customer would by now probably have moved on to another online supplier who could sell the product today, but those that remained were subjected to a sales pitch, which was totally unnecessary, the customer having already decided to buy. Those that were not put off would proceed to be registered as able to buy over the web, but the company had lost the opportunity to improve its margins by using the sales force more judiciously. In time, the company realised its mistake: unlike those prospects, which the company identified and contacted who might indeed need 'selling' to, many new web customers were initiating the dialogue themselves and simply required the company to respond effectively and rapidly. The sales force was increasingly freed up to concentrate on major clients and relationship building.

Figure 5.2 shows where marketing planning fits in with other corporate strategies. From this, it will be seen that the only real corporate objective in capital markets is to make profit, because unless it does, they will not be able to fulfil their obligations to all other stakeholders. For anyone who disagrees, it should be remembered that the likes of ICI had admirable corporate social responsibility strategies, but because they didn't make sufficient profits by satisfying customer needs, there are today thousands of acres of empty chemical plants, destroyed communities and the like. There is no argument, of course, that shareholders and other stakeholders are inextricably linked in long-term successful companies like Johnson and Johnson, but let's not forget that companies like this also create shareholder value by meeting the needs of customers better than their competitors.

1 corporate objective (what): profit;
2 corporate strategies (how):

- facilities (i.e. operations, R&D, IT, distribution, etc.);
- people (personnel);
- money (finance);
- products and markets (marketing);
- other (CSR, image, etc.).

Figure 5.2 Corporate objectives and strategies

It will also be seen that marketing strategies are about what to sell and who to sell it to. In the best companies in the world, this part of the jigsaw is done first – founded of course on their asset base. Once agreed, all other corporate strategies can then be developed to deliver the promised customer value. Finally, in many companies, the total process is summarized in a corporate or business plan. It is difficult, however, to envisage how a corporate plan can be put together in the absence of a customer-based plan.

Having put marketing planning into the context of marketing and other corporate functions, we can now turn specifically to the marketing planning process, how it should be done and what the barriers are to doing it effectively. We are referring, of course, specifically to the second box in Figure 5.1.

The marketing planning process

Most managers accept that some kind of procedure for marketing planning is necessary. Accordingly, they need a system, which will help them to think in a structured way and also

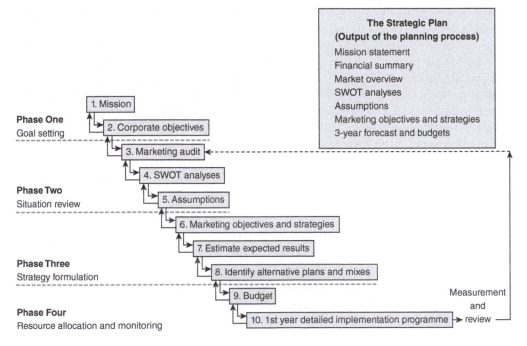

Figure 5.3 The ten steps of the strategic marketing planning process

make explicit their intuitive economic models of the business. Unfortunately, very few companies have planning systems, which possess these characteristics. However, those that do tend to follow a similar pattern of steps.

Figure 5.3 illustrates the several stages that have to be gone through in order to arrive at a marketing plan. This illustrates the difference between the *process* of marketing planning and the actual plan itself, which is the *output* of the process. This is discussed later in this chapter.

Each of the process stages illustrated in Figure 5.3 will be discussed in more detail in this chapter. The dotted lines joining up stages 5–8 are meant to indicate the reality of the planning process, in that it is likely each of these steps will have to be gone through more than once before final programmes can be written.

How formal should this process be?

Although research has shown these marketing planning steps to be universally applicable, the degree to which each of the separate steps in the diagram needs to be formalized depends to a large extent on the size and nature of the company. For example, an undiversified company generally uses fewer formalized procedures, since top management tends to have greater functional knowledge and expertise than subordinates, and because the lack of diversity of operations enables direct control to be exercised over most of the key determinants of success. Thus, situation reviews, the setting of marketing objectives and so on are not always made explicit in writing, although these steps have to be gone through.

In contrast, in a diversified company, it is usually not possible for top management to have greater functional knowledge and expertise than subordinate management, hence planning tends to be more formalized in order to provide a consistent discipline for those who have to make the decisions throughout the organization. Either way, there is now a substantial body of evidence to show that formalized planning procedures generally result in greater profitability and stability in the long term and also help to reduce friction and operational difficulties within organizations.

Bailey *et al.*'s (2000) typology of the different styles of planning went some way to throwing light on the actual degree of formalization of marketing planning processes, although Smith's 2003 thesis reduced these to three – visionary processes, rational processes and incremental processes, with most successful companies using some combination of all three.

Where marketing planning has failed, it has generally been because companies have placed too much emphasis on the procedures themselves and the resulting forecasts, rather than on generating information useful to and consumable by management. But more about reasons for failure later. For now, let us look at the marketing planning process in more detail, starting with the mission statement.

Step 1 Mission statement

Figure 5.3 shows that a strategic marketing plan should begin with a mission or purpose statement. This is perhaps the most difficult aspect of marketing planning for managers to master, because it is largely philosophical and qualitative in nature. Many organizations find their different departments, and sometimes even different groups in the same department, pulling in different directions, often with disastrous results, simply because the organization hasn't defined the boundaries of the business and the way it wishes to do business.

There are two levels of mission. One is a *corporate* mission statement; the other is a lower level, or *purpose* statement. But there is yet another level, as shown in the following summary:

- **Type 1** 'Motherhood' – usually found inside annual reports designed to 'stroke' shareholders. Otherwise of no practical use.
- **Type 2** The real thing. A meaningful statement, unique to the organization concerned, which 'impacts' on the behaviour of the executives at all levels.
- **Type 3** This is a 'purpose' statement (or lower level mission statement). It is appropriate at the strategic business unit, departmental or product group level of the organization.

The following is an example of a meaningless, vapid, motherhood-type mission statement, which most companies seem to have. They achieve nothing and it is difficult to understand why these pointless statements are so popular. Employees mock them and they rarely say anything likely to give direction to the organization. We have entitled this example 'The generic mission statement' and they are to be avoided.

The generic mission statement

Our organization's primary mission is to protect and increase the value of its owners' investments while efficiently and fairly serving the needs of its customers.

[. . . insert organization name . . .] seeks to accomplish this in a manner that contributes to the development and growth of its employees, and to the goals of countries and communities in which it operates.

The following should appear in a mission or purpose statement, which should normally run to no more than one page:

1 *Role or contribution* – profit (specify), service or opportunity seeker;
2 *Business definition* – define the business, preferably in terms of the *benefits* you provide or the *needs* you satisfy, rather than in terms of what you make;
3 *Distinctive competences* – these are the essential skills/capabilities resources that underpin whatever success has been achieved to date. Competence can consist of one particular item or the possession of a number of skills compared with competitors. If, however, you could equally well put a competitor's name to these distinctive competences, then they are not distinctive competences;
4 *Indications for the future* – what the firm *will* do; what the firm *might* do; what the firm will never do.

Step 2 Setting corporate objectives

As shown in Figure 5.2 above, corporate objectives usually contain at least the following elements:

1 the desired level of profitability;
2 business boundaries:

- what kind of products will be sold to what kinds of markets (marketing);
- what kinds of facilities will be developed (operations, R&D, information systems, distribution, etc;

- the size and character of the labour force (personnel);
- funding (finance);

3   other corporate objectives, such as social responsibility, corporate image, stock market image, employer image, etc.

Such a corporate plan, containing projected profit and loss accounts and balance sheets, being the result of the process described above, is more likely to provide long-term stability for a company than plans based on a more intuitive process and containing forecasts, which tend to be little more than extrapolations of previous trends. This process is further summarized in Figure 5.4.

Step 3 The marketing audit

Any plan will only be as good as the information on which it is based, and the marketing audit is the means by which information for planning is organized. There is no reason why marketing cannot be audited in the same way as accounts, in spite of its more innovative, subjective nature. A marketing audit is a systematic appraisal of all the external and internal factors that have affected a company's commercial performance over a defined period.

Given the growing turbulence of the business environment and the shorter product life cycles that have resulted, no one would deny the need to stop at least once a year at a particular point in the planning cycle to try to form a reasoned view of how all the many external and internal factors have influenced performance.

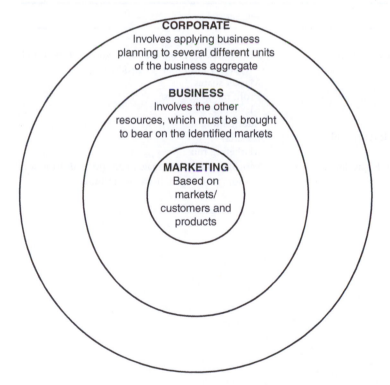

Figure 5.4 Marketing planning in the context of business and corporate planning

Sometimes, of course, a company will conduct a marketing audit because it is in financial trouble. At times like these, management often attempts to treat the wrong symptoms, most frequently by reorganizing the company. However, such measures are unlikely to be effective if there are more fundamental problems that have not been identified. Of course, if the company survived for long enough, it might eventually solve its problems through a process of elimination. Essentially, though, the argument is that the problems have first to be properly defined. The audit is a means of helping to define them.

Two kinds of variable

Any company carrying out an audit will be faced with two kinds of variable. There is the kind over which the company has no direct control, for example, economic and market factors. Second, there are those over which the company has complete control, the operational variables, which are usually the firm's internal resources. This division suggests that the best way to structure an audit is in two parts: external and internal. Table 5.1 shows areas that should be investigated under both headings. Each should be examined with a view to building up an information base relevant to the company's performance.

Many people mistakenly believe that the marketing audit should be some kind of final attempt to define a company's marketing problems, or, at best, something done by an independent body from time to time to ensure that a company is on the right track. However, many highly successful

Table 5.1 Conducting an audit

External audit	Internal audit
Business and economic environment	Own company
Economic political, fiscal, legal, social, cultural	Sales (total, by geographical location, by industrial type, by customer, by product
Technological	Market shares
Intra-company	Profit margins, costs
	Marketing
The market	information
Total market, size, growth and trends (value volume)	research
Market	Marketing mix
characteristics, developments and tends; products, prices, physical distribution, channels, customers, consumers, communication, industry practices	variables: product management, price, distribution, promotion, operations and resources
	Key strengths and weaknesses
Competition	
Major competitors	
Size	
Market share coverage	
Market standing and reputation	
Production capabilities	
Distribution policies	
Marketing methods	
Extent of diversification	
Personnel issues	
International links	
Profitability	

companies, as well as using normal information and control procedures and marketing research throughout the year, start their planning cycle each year with a formal, audit-type process of everything that has had an important influence on marketing activities. Certainly, in many leading consumer goods companies, the annual self-audit approach is a tried and tested discipline.

Objections to line managers doing their own audits usually centre on the problem of time and objectivity. In practice, a disciplined approach and thorough training will help. But the discipline must be applied from the highest to the lowest levels of management if the tunnel vision that often results from a lack of critical appraisal is to be avoided.

Where relevant, the marketing audit should contain life cycles for major products and for market segments, for which the future shape will be predicted using the audit information. Also, major products and markets should be plotted on some kind of matrix to show their current competitive position.

Some companies consume valuable resources carrying out audits that produce very little in the way of results. The audit is simply a database and the task remains of turning it into intelligence, that is, information essential to decision making.

The next question is, 'What happens to the results of the audit?'. This step, which appears prominently in the actual strategic marketing plan, should spell out clearly:

- what the market is;
- how it works;
- what the key decision making points are;
- what the segments are.

Market definition is fundamental to success and must be made in terms of need sets rather than in product/service terms. Thus, Gestetner failed by defining its markets as 'duplicators' and IBM

Table 5.2 Some market definitions (personal market)

Market	Need (on-line)
Emergency Cash ('Rainy Day')	Cash to cover an undesired and unexpected event often the loss of/damage to property).
Future Event Planning	Schemes to protect and grow money which are for anticipated and unanticipated cash calling events (eg. Car replacement/repairs, education, weddings, funerals, health care)
Asset Purchase	Cash to buy assets they require (eg. Car purchase, house purchase, once-in-a-lifetime holiday).
Welfare Contingency	The ability to maintain a desired standard of living (for self and/or dependants) in times of unplanned cessation of salary.
Retirement Income	The ability to maintain a desired standard of living (for self and/or dependants once the salary cheques have ceased.
Wealth Care and Building	The care and growth of assets (with various risk levels and liquidity levels).
Day-to-Day Money Management	Ability to store and readily access cash for day-to-day requirements.
Personal Financial Protection and Security from Motor Vehicle Incidents	Currently known as car insurance.

almost failed by defining its market as 'main frames'. A more recent example is Kodak, who thought they were in the camera market. Accordingly, a pension is a product, not a market, as many other products can satisfy the same or similar needs. Table 5.2 lists hypothetical markets in the financial services sector.

Figures 5.5 and 5.6 show the market for marketing books in the UK. The first shows the market 'mapped' solely as marketing books. The second shows the market mapped in terms of the broader market definition of knowledge promulgation, from which it can be seen that new competitors and distribution channels come into play. Thinking and planning like this certainly had a dramatic effect on the marketing strategy of the major publisher involved.

Figure 5.7 is a generic market map, which shows how a market works from suppliers to users and, like a balance sheet, it must 'balance', in the sense that if five million radiators are made or imported, five million radiators must be distributed, five million radiators must be installed and the decision about which radiators are to be installed must be made by someone. It is the purpose of the market map to spell all this out quantitatively.

It is at key decision points that market segmentation should take place. A segment is a group of customers or consumers that share the same (or approximately the same) needs. This step is crucial, for it is upon the key segments from the market map that SWOT analyses should be completed. For a detailed step-by-step process for carrying out needs-based market segmentation, see McDonald (2012).

Step 4 SWOT analyses

The only remaining question is what happens to the results of the audit? Some companies consume valuable resources carrying out audits that bring very little by way of actionable results.

Indeed, there is always the danger that, at the audit stage, insufficient attention is paid to the need to concentrate on analysis that determines which trends and developments will actually affect the company. While the checklist demonstrates the completeness of logic and analysis, the people carrying out the audit should discipline themselves to omit from their audits all the information that is not central to the company's marketing problems. Thus, inclusion of research reports, or over-detailed sales performance histories by product, which lead to no logical actions whatsoever, only serve to rob the audit of focus and reduce its relevance.

Since the objective of the audit is to indicate what a company's marketing objectives and strategies should be, it follows that it would be helpful if some format could be found for organizing the major findings. One useful way of doing this is in the form of a number of SWOT analyses.

A SWOT analysis is a summary of the audit under the headings internal strengths and weaknesses as they relate to external opportunities and threats. A SWOT should be conducted for each segment that is considered to be important in the company's future. These SWOT analyses should, if possible, contain just a few paragraphs of commentary focusing on *key* factors only. They should highlight internal *differential* strengths and weaknesses *vis-á-vis* competitors and *key* external opportunities and threats. A summary of reasons for good or bad performance should be included. They should be interesting to read, contain concise statements, include only relevant and important data, and give greater emphasis to creative analysis. A completed example is given in Table 5.3.

To summarize, carrying out a regular and thorough marketing audit in a structured manner and focusing it into SWOT analyses will go a long way towards giving a company a knowledge of the business, trends in the market and where value is added by competitors, as the basis for setting objectives and strategies.

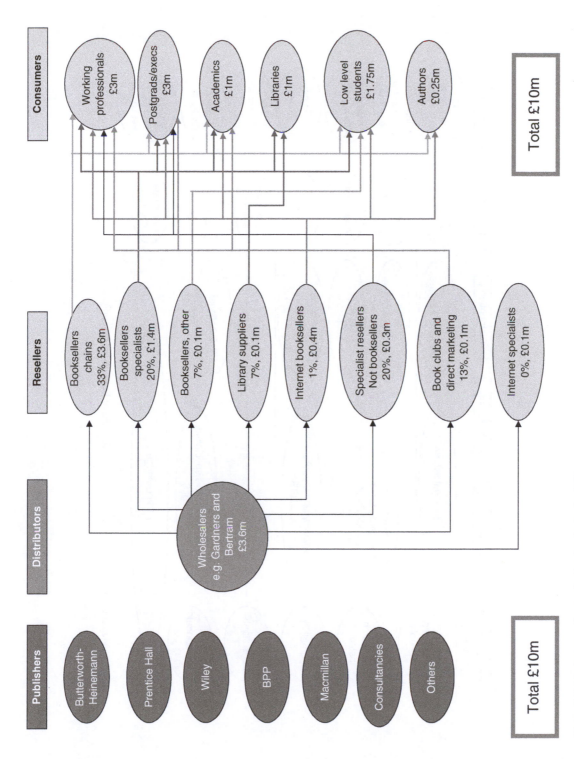

Figure 5.5 Market map for marketing books in the UK

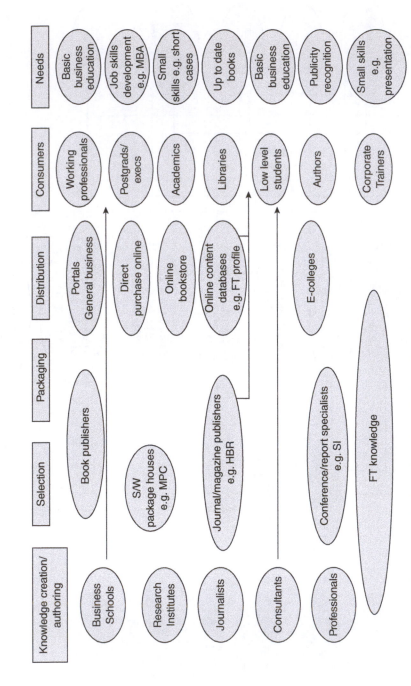

Figure 5.6 Map for marketing books in the wider definition of knowledge promulgation

. . . including the number of each customer type

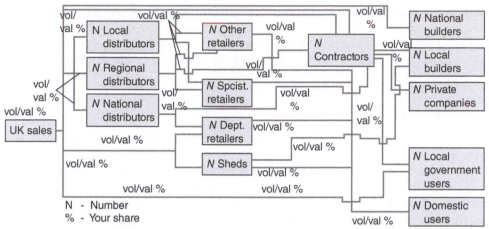

NB. Sketch out complex junctions separately. Alternatively, build an outline map, applying details at the junctions to be segmented.

Figure 5.7 A generic map

Step 5 Assumptions

Let us now return to the preparation of the marketing plan. If we refer again to the marketing planning process and having completed our marketing audit and SWOT analyses, assumptions now have to be written.

There are certain key determinants of success in all companies about which assumptions have to be made before the planning process can proceed. It is really a question of standardizing the planning environment. For example, it would be no good receiving plans from two product managers, one of whom believed the market was going to increase by 10 per cent, while the other believed the market was going to decline by 10 per cent. Examples of assumptions might be:

Table 5.3 An example of a SWOT analysis

Critical success factors (What are the few key things that any competition has to do right to succeed?)	Weighting (How important is each of these CSFs? Score out of 100)		Strengths/weaknesses analysis (Score yourself and each of your main competitors out of 10 on each of the CSFs, then multiply the score by the weight)			
			You	*Comp A*	*Comp B*	*Comp C*
1 Product	20		9 = 1.8	6 = 1.2	5 = 1.0	4 = 0.8
2 Price	10		8 = 0.8	5 = 0.5	6 = 0.6	10 = 0.1
3 Service	50		5 = 2.5	9 = 4.5	7 = 3.5	6 = 3.0
4 Image	20		8 = 1.6	8 = 1.6	5 = 1.0	3 = 0.6
These should normally be viewed from the customer's point of view	Total 100	Total score × weight	6.7	7.8	6.1	5.5

With respect to the company's industrial climate, it is assumed that:

1   Industrial overcapacity will increase from 105 per cent to 115 per cent as new industrial plants come into operation.
2   Price competition will force price levels down by 10 per cent across the board.
3   A new product in the field of x will be introduced by our major competitor before the end of the second quarter.

Step 6 Marketing objectives and strategies

The next step in marketing planning is the writing of marketing objectives and strategies, the key the whole process.

An *objective* is what you want to achieve. A *strategy* is how you plan to achieve your objectives. Thus, there can be objectives and strategies at all levels in marketing. For example, there can be advertising objectives and strategies, and pricing objectives and strategies. However, the important point to remember about marketing objectives is that they are about *products* and *markets* only. Common sense will confirm that it is only by selling something to someone that the company's financial goals can be achieved, and that advertising, pricing, service levels and so on are the means (or strategies) by which we might succeed in doing this. Thus, pricing objectives, sales promotion objectives, advertising objectives and the like should not be confused with marketing objectives. Marketing objectives are simply about one, or more, of the following:

- existing products for existing markets;
- new products for existing markets;
- existing products for new markets;
- new products for new markets.

They should be capable of measurement otherwise, they are not objectives. Directional terms such as 'maximize', 'minimize', penetrate', 'increase', etc. are only acceptable if quantitative measurement can be attached to them. Measurement should be in terms of some, or all, of the following: sales volume; sales value; market share; profit; percentage penetration of outlets (for example, to have 30 per cent of all retail outlets stocking our product by year 3).

Marketing strategies are the means by which marketing objectives will be achieved and generally are concerned with the four Ps, as follows:

- product – the general policies for product deletions, modifications, additions, design, branding, positioning, packaging, etc;
- price – the general pricing policies to be followed by product groups in market segments;
- place – the general policies for channels and customer service levels;
- promotion – the general policies for communicating with customers under the relevant headings, such as advertising, sales force, sales promotion, public relations, exhibitions, direct mail, etc.

Steps 7 and 8 Estimate expected results and identify alternative plans and mixes

Having completed this major planning task, it is normal at this stage to employ judgement, analogous experience, field tests and so on, to test out the feasibility of the objectives and strategies in terms of market share, costs, profits, etc. It is also normally at this stage that alternative plans and mixes are considered, if necessary.

Step 9 The budget

In a strategic marketing plan, these strategies would normally be costed out approximately and, if not practicable, alternative strategies would be proposed and costed until a satisfactory solution could be reached. This would then become the budget. In most cases, there would be a budget for the full three years of the strategic marketing plan, but there would also be a very detailed budget for the first year of the plan, which would be included in the one-year operational plan.

It will be obvious from all of this that the setting of budgets not only becomes much easier but the resulting budgets are more likely to be realistic and related to what the *whole* company wants to achieve, rather than just one functional department. The problem of designing a dynamic system for budget setting, rather than the 'tablets of stone' approach, which is more common, is a major challenge to the marketing and financial directors of all companies. The most satisfactory approach would be for a marketing director to justify all marketing expenditure from a zero base each year against the tasks they wish to accomplish. A little thought will confirm that this is exactly the approach recommended in this chapter. If these procedures are followed, a hierarchy of objectives is built up in such a way that every item of budgeted expenditure can be related directly back to the initial corporate financial objectives. For example, if sales promotion is a major means of achieving an objective in a particular market, then when sales promotional items appear in the programme, each one has a specific purpose, which can be related back to a major objective. Doing it this way not only ensures that every item of expenditure is fully accounted for as part of a rational, objective and task approach but also that when changes have to be made during the period to which the plan relates, these changes can be made in such a way that the least damage is caused to the company's long-term objectives.

The incremental marketing expense can be considered to be all costs that are incurred after the product leaves the factory, *other than* costs involved in physical distribution, the costs of which usually represent a discrete subset. There is, of course, no textbook answer to problems relating to questions such as whether packaging should be a marketing or a production expense, and whether some distribution costs could be considered to be marketing costs. For example, insistence on high service levels results in high inventory carrying costs. Only common sense will reveal workable solutions to issues such as these.

Under *price*, however, any form of discounting that reduces the expected gross income, such as promotional discounts, quantity discounts, royalty rebates and so on, as well as sales commission and unpaid invoices, should be given the most careful attention as incremental marketing expenses. Most obvious incremental marketing expenses will occur, however, under the heading promotion, in the form of advertising, sales salaries and expenses, sales promotional expenditure, direct mail costs and so on. The important point about the measurable effects of marketing activity is that anticipated levels should be the result of the most careful analysis of what is required to take the company towards its goals, while the most careful attention should be paid to gathering all items of expenditure under appropriate headings. The healthiest way of treating these issues is a zero-based budgeting approach.

Step 10 First year detailed implementation programme

In a one-year tactical plan, the general marketing strategies would be developed into specific sub-objectives, each supported by more detailed strategy and action statements.

- A company organized according to functions might have an advertising plan, a sales promotion plan a pricing plan, etc.

- A product-based company might have a product plan, with objectives, strategies and tactics for price, place and promotion as necessary.
- A market or geographically based company might have a marketing plan, with objectives, strategies and tactics for the four Ps as necessary.
- A company with a few major customers might have customer plans.

Any combination of the above might be suitable, depending on the circumstances. A written strategic marketing plan is the back drop against which operational decisions are taken. Consequently, too much detail should be avoided. Its major function is to determine where the company is, where it wants to go and how it can get there. It should be distributed on a 'need to know' basis only. It should be used as an aid to effective management. It cannot be a substitute for it.

What should appear in a strategic marketing plan?

Table 5.4 summarizes the components of the strategic marketing plan.

Too much detail should be avoided. Its major function is to determine where the company is, where it wants to go and how it can get there. It lies at the heart of a company's revenue-generating activities. This strategic marketing plan should be distributed only to those who need it, but it can only be an aid to effective management. It cannot be a substitute for it.

It will be obvious from Table 5.4 that not only does budget setting become much easier and more realistic but the resulting budgets are more likely to reflect what the whole company wants to achieve, rather than just one department.

Marketing planning systems design and implementation

While the actual process of marketing planning is simple in outline, a number of contextual issues have to be considered that make marketing planning one of the most baffling of all management problems. The following are some of those issues:

- When should it be done, how often, by whom and how?
- Is it different in a large and a small company? Is it different in a diversified and an undiversified company?
- What is the role of the chief executive?
- What is the role of the planning department?
- Should marketing planning be top-down or bottom-up?
- What is the relationship between operational (one-year) and strategic (longer-term) planning?

Requisite strategic marketing planning

Many companies with financial difficulties have recognized the need for a more structured approach to planning their marketing and have opted for the kind of standardized, formalized procedures written about so much in textbooks. Yet, these rarely bring any benefits and often bring marketing planning itself into disrepute. It is quite clear that any attempt at the introduction of formalized marketing planning requires a change in a company's approach to managing its business. It is also clear that unless a company recognizes these implications, and plans to seek ways of coping with

Table 5.4 What should appear in a strategic marketing plan?

The Contents of a Strategic Marketing Plan (<20 pages)

- Mission or Purpose Statement
- Financial Summary

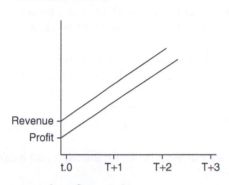

Key (revenue and profit growth)
- from productivity;
- by product for market for existing products from existing markets;
- from new products in existing markets;
- from existing products in new markets;
- from new products in new markets.

Plus a few words of commentary.

Market overview/summary
- market definition;
- market map showing vol/rev flows from supplier through to end user, with major decision points highlighted;
- where appropriate, provide a future market map;
- include commentary/conclusions/implications for the company;
- at major decision points, include key segments.

SWOT analyses on key segments
- include pictorial representations of the SWOTs, such as bar charts;
- highlight major conclusions/issues to be addressed.

Portfolio summaries of the SWOTs
Include directional policy matrix (DPM) summaries of:

- the attractiveness of the segments over the next 3 to 5 years;
- the current relative competitive position of your company in each segment;
- the planned competitive position of each segment over the next 3 to 5 years.

Marketing objectives and strategies for the next 3–5 years
- include objectives (volume, value, market share, profit, as appropriate) for the next 3 to 5 years for each segment as represented by the planned position of each circle on the DPM;
- include strategies (the 4 Ps) with costs for each objective.

Consolidated budget for the next 3 to 5 years
This will be a consolidation of all the revenues, costs and profits for the next 3 to 5 years and should accord with the financial summary provided earlier.

them, formalized strategic planning will be ineffective. Research (McDonald 1982) has shown that the implications are principally as follows:

1   Any closed-loop planning system (but especially one that is essentially a forecasting and budgeting system) will lead to dull and ineffective marketing. Therefore, there has to be some mechanism for preventing inertia from setting in through the over-bureaucratization of the system.
2   Planning undertaken at the functional level of marketing, in the absence of a means of integration with other functional areas of the business at general management level, will be largely ineffective.
3   The separation of responsibility for operational and strategic planning will lead to a divergence of the short-term thrust of a business at the operational level from the long-term objectives of the enterprise as a whole. This will encourage preoccupation with short-term results at operational level, which normally makes the firm less effective in the longer term.
4   Unless the chief executive understands and takes an active role in strategic marketing planning, it will never be an effective system.
5   A period of up to three years is necessary (especially in large firms) for the successful introduction of an effective strategic marketing planning system.

The same PhD (McDonald 1982) also found that the principal barriers to implementing marketing planning are those listed in Table 5.5.

Let us be dogmatic about requisite planning levels. First, in a large diversified group, irrespective of such organizational issues, anything other than a systematic approach approximating to a formalized marketing planning system is unlikely to enable the necessary control to be exercised over the corporate identity. Second, unnecessary planning, or over planning, could easily result from an inadequate or indiscriminate consideration of the real planning needs at the different levels in the hierarchical chain. Third, as size and diversity grow, so the degree of formalization of the marketing planning process must also increase. This can be simplified in the form of a matrix, Figure 5.8.

Table 5.5 Barriers to the integration of strategic marketing planning

---

1   weak support from the chief executive and top management;
2   lack of a plan for planning;
3   lack of line management support due to any of the following, either singly or in combination:

- hostility;
- lack of skills;
- lack of information;
- lack of resources;
- inadequate organizational structure.

4   confusion over planning terms;
5   numbers in lieu of written objectives and strategies;
6   too much detail, too far ahead;
7   once-a-year ritual;
8   separation of operational planning from strategic planning;
9   failure to integrate marketing planning into total corporate planning system;
10   delegation of planning to a planner.

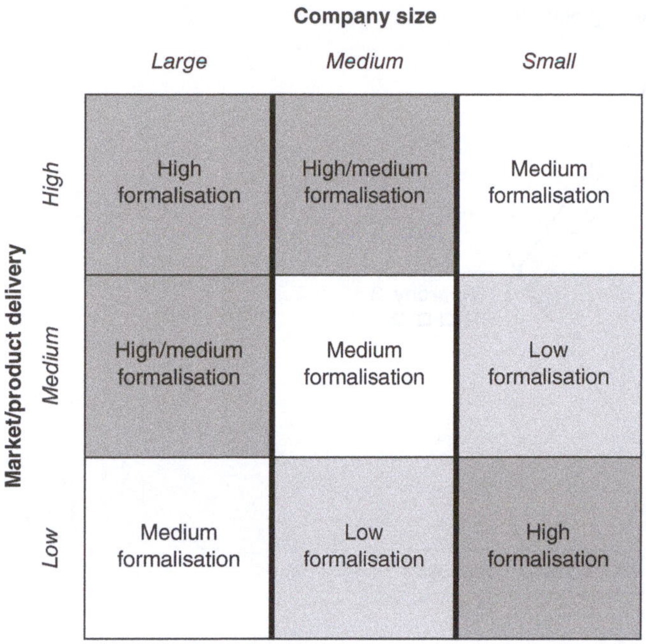

Company size

	Large	Medium	Small
High	High formalisation	High/medium formalisation	Medium formalisation
Medium	High/medium formalisation	Medium formalisation	Low formalisation
Low	Medium formalisation	Low formalisation	High formalisation

(left axis: Market/product delivery)

Figure 5.8 Planning formalisation

It has been found that the degree of formalization increases with the evolving size and diversity of operations (see Figure 5.8). However, while the degree of formalization will change, the need for an effective marketing planning system does not. The problems that companies suffer are a function of either the degree to which they have a requisite marketing planning system or the degree to which the formalization of their system grows with the situational complexities attendant upon the size and diversity of operations.

Figure 5.9 shows four key outcomes that marketing planning can evoke. It can be seen that systems 1, 3 and 4 (i.e. where the individual is totally subordinate to a formalized system, or where there is neither system nor creativity) are less successful than system 2, in which the individual is allowed to be entrepreneurial within a total system. System 2, therefore, will be an effective marketing planning system, but one in which the degree of formalization will be a function of company size and diversity.

One of the most encouraging findings to emerge from research is that the theory of marketing planning is universally applicable. While the planning task is less complicated in small, undiversified companies and there is less need for formalized procedures than in large, diversified companies, the fact is that exactly the same framework should be used in all circumstances, and that this approach brings similar benefits to all.

How far ahead should we plan?

It is clear that one- and three-year planning periods are by far the most common. Lead time for the initiation of major new product innovations, the length of time necessary to recover capital investment costs, the continuing availability of customers and raw materials, and the size and usefulness of existing plant and buildings are the most frequently mentioned reasons for having a three-year planning horizon.

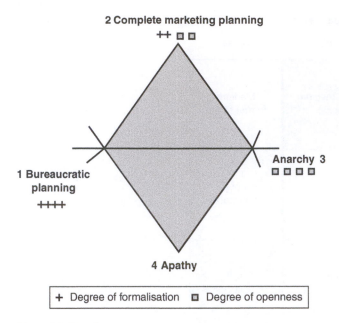

Figure 5.9 Four key outcomes

Many companies, however, do not give sufficient thought to what represents a sensible planning horizon for their particular circumstances. A five-year time span is clearly too long for some companies, particularly those with highly versatile machinery operating in volatile fashion-conscious markets. The effect of this is to rob strategic plans of reality.

The conclusion to be reached is that there is a natural point of focus into the future beyond which it is pointless to look. This point of focus is a function of the relative size of a company. Small companies, because of their size and the way they are managed, tend to be comparatively flexible in the way in which they can react to environmental turbulence in the short term. Large companies, on the other hand, need a much longer lead time in which to make changes in direction. Consequently, they tend to need to look further into the future and to use formalized systems for this purpose, so that managers throughout the organization have a common means of communication.

How the marketing planning process works

As a basic principle, strategic marketing planning should take place as near to the marketplace as possible in the first instance, but such plans should then be reviewed at higher levels within an organization to see what issues may have been overlooked.

It has been suggested that each manager in the organization should complete an audit and SWOT analysis on their own area of responsibility. The only way that this can work in practice is by means of a hierarchy of audits. The principle is simply demonstrated in Figure 5.10. This illustrates the principle of auditing at different levels within an organization. The marketing audit format will be universally applicable. It is only the detail that varies from level to level and from company to company within the same group.

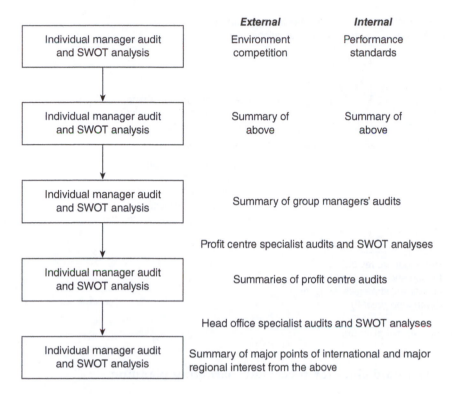

	External	**Internal**
Individual manager audit and SWOT analysis	Environment competition	Performance standards
Individual manager audit and SWOT analysis	Summary of above	Summary of above
Individual manager audit and SWOT analysis	Summary of group managers' audits	
	Profit centre specialist audits and SWOT analyses	
Individual manager audit and SWOT analysis	Summaries of profit centre audits	
	Head office specialist audits and SWOT analyses	
Individual manager audit and SWOT analysis	Summary of major points of international and major regional interest from the above	

Figure 5.10 Hierarchy of audits

Figure 5.11 illustrates the total corporate strategic and planning process. This time, however, a time element is added, and the relationship between strategic planning briefings, long-term corporate plans and short-term operational plans is clarified. It is important to note that there are two 'open-loop' points on this diagram. These are the key times in the planning process when a subordinate's views and findings should be subjected to the closest examination by their superior. It is by taking these opportunities that marketing planning can be transformed into the critical and creative process it is supposed to be, rather than the dull, repetitive ritual it so often turns out to be.

Since in anything but the smallest of undiversified companies it is not possible for top management to set detailed objectives for operating units, it is suggested that at this stage in the planning process strategic guidelines should be issued. One way of doing this is in the form of a strategic planning letter. Another is by means of a personal briefing by the chief executive at 'kick-off' meetings. As in the case of the audit, these guidelines would proceed from the broad to the specific and would become more detailed as they progressed through the company towards operating units. These guidelines would be under the headings of financial, manpower and organization, operations and, of course, marketing.

Under marketing, for example, at the highest level in a large group, top management may ask for particular attention to be paid to issues such as the technical impact of microprocessors on electromechanical component equipment, leadership and innovation strategies, vulnerability to attack from the flood of Japanese, Korean and emerging market products, and so on. At operating company level, it is possible to be more explicit about target markets, product development and the like.

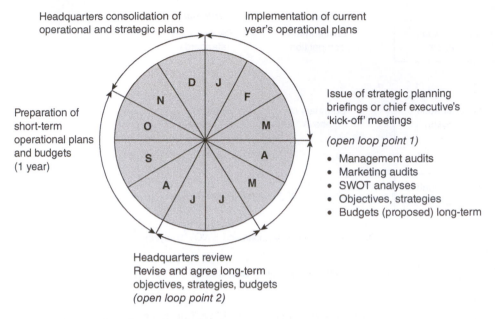

Headquarters consolidation of
operational and strategic plans

Implementation of current
year's operational plans

Issue of strategic planning
briefings or chief executive's
'kick-off' meetings

(open loop point 1)

Preparation of
short-term
operational plans
and budgets
(1 year)

- Management audits
- Marketing audits
- SWOT analyses
- Objectives, strategies
- Budgets (proposed) long-term

Headquarters review
Revise and agree long-term
objectives, strategies, budgets
(open loop point 2)

Figure 5.11 Strategic and operational planning

Part 1 conclusions. Ten guidelines for successful marketing planning

1 Understand that marketing is the driver of strategy in the boardroom.

 a it is NOT promotion;
 b everything an organization does from R&D through to delivery adapts to and converges on the business value proposition that is projected to the customer.

2 Understand your market and how it works.

 a define the market in terms of needs, not products;
 b map how it works from end to end, showing product/service flows in total and your shares;
 c understand how it is changing;
 d identify major decision makers.

3 Carry out proper, needs-based segmentation on decision makers.

 a do not confuse needs-based segmentation with descriptors such as socioeconomics, demographics, geodemograhics and psychographics;
 b list what is bought (including applications, where and when);
 c list who buys;
 d list why they buy;
 e group those with similar needs; these are market segments.

4 Understand your own strengths and weaknesses.

 a for each segment, list their needs and the relative importance of each (weights);
 b score out of ten how you and each of your major competitors meet these needs;

  c list the external opportunities for each segment;
  d list the major issues that need to be addressed for each segment.

5 Understand your portfolio of segments.

  a classify on a four box matrix each segment according to its potential for growth in your profits over the planning period (the vertical axis);
  b classify each segment according to your relative strengths in each (the horizontal axis);
  c this will position each segment as follows:

     i   less attractive segments where you have strengths (1);
     ii more attractive segments where you have strengths (2);
     iii more attractive markets where you have few strengths (3);
     iv less attractive markets where you have few strengths (4).

6 Set realistic objectives and strategies for each segment to grow your sales and profits.

  a set clear priorities and stick to them – you cannot be all things to all customers;
  b for quadrant 1, manage for sustained earnings;
  c for quadrant 2, manage for growth in revenue and profits;
  d for quadrant 3, select the most promising segments and invest for improving your competitive position – do NOT try to maximize your profits in these segments;
  e for quadrant 4, manage for cash and minimize costs.

7 Focus and play to win in a few segments only.

  a develop a winning offer for each;
  b quantify the value proposition (creating advantage, not just avoiding disadvantage);
  c become the best in your chosen segments.

8 Calculate whether your objectives and strategies will create shareholder value.

  a carry out risk assessment on each strategy in each segment;
  b calculate risk-adjusted net free cash flows for each segment over the planning period;
  c allocate the relative capital employed multiplied by the cost of capital for each segment;
  d an overall surplus means that the plan is creating shareholder value.

9 Justify financially investments in marketing.

  a measure the indirect impact on sales and profits of all marketing expenditure;
  b measure the impact of promotional expenditure using econometric models;
  c measure and report to the board that your risk-adjusted marketing strategy creates shareholder value.

10 Be professional and ethical.

  a develop professional marketing skills;
  b if possible, get qualified like other professions;
  c be innovative and open-minded;
  d be ethical at all times and consider the impact of your actions on all stakeholders.

In concluding this section, we must stress that there can be no such thing as an off-the-peg marketing planning system, and anyone who offers one must be viewed with great suspicion. In the end, strategic marketing planning success comes from an endless willingness to learn and to adapt the system to the people and the circumstances of the firm. It also comes from a deep understanding about the nature of marketing planning, which is something that, in the final analysis, cannot be taught.

However, strategic marketing planning demands that the organization recognizes the challenges that face it and their effect on its potential for future success. It must learn to focus on customers and their needs at all times and explore every avenue, which may provide it with a differential advantage over its competitors.

Lest readers should think that the ten factors for success are a figment of the imagination, there is much recent research to suggest otherwise. The four ingredients listed in Figure 5.12 are common to all commercially successful organizations, irrespective of their national origin. From this is can be seen that the core product or service on offer has to be excellent. Second, operations have to be efficient and, preferably, state-of-the-art. Third, the research stresses the need for creativity in leadership and personnel – something frequently discouraged by excessive bureaucracy in large organizations. Finally, excellent companies enjoy professional marketing. This means that the organization continually monitors the environment, the market, competitors and their own performance against customer-driven standards.

PART 2: DO MARKETING PLANS CONTRIBUTE TO PROFITABILITY?

Marketing metrics, or accountability, is one of the biggest challenges facing the marketing community today. It is a major theme of research at the Australian Marketing Institute, the Worshipful Company of Marketors, the British Chartered Institute of Marketing, the Chief Marketing Officer, Council of America and at Cranfield School of Management, to name but a few.

The reason is not hard to find, given the pressure that so many Western European and American companies are under, because of maturing markets. Certainly, if any chief executive officer were to ask their marketing officer what shareholders had received from the millions spent on advertising, and the answer was 'a change in attitude or an improvement in awareness', they would be justified in replacing them with someone who could be more accountable and responsible. So, in a chapter on marketing planning, it would be remiss not to address this topic.

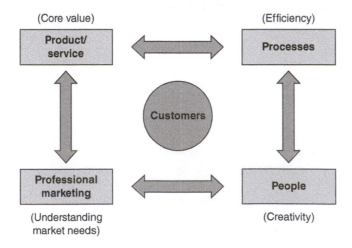

Figure 5.12 Factors for success

Three distinct levels for measuring marketing effectiveness

When the author was marketing director of a fast-moving consumer goods (FMCG) company 30 years ago, there were many well tried and tested models for measuring the effectiveness of marketing promotional expenditure. Indeed, some of these were quite sophisticated and included mathematical models for promotional campaigns, for advertising threshold and wear out levels and the like.

Indeed, it would be surprising if marketing as a discipline did not have its own quantitative models for the massive expenditure of FMCG companies. Over time, these models have been transferred to business-to-business and service companies, with the result that, today, any organization spending substantial sums of shareholders' money on promotion should be ashamed of themselves if those responsible could not account for the effectiveness of such expenditure.

At this level, however, accountability can only be measured in terms of the kinds of effects that promotional expenditure can achieve, such as awareness, or attitude change, both of which can be measured quantitatively.

But to assert that such expenditure can be measured directly in terms of sales or profits is intellectually indefensible when there are so many other variables that affect sales, such as product efficacy, packaging, price, the sales force, competitors and countless other variables which, like advertising, have an intermediate impact on sales and profits.

So, the problem with marketing accountability has never been with how to measure the effectiveness of promotional expenditure –we have had this for many years. No, the problem occurs because marketing is not just a promotional activity. As was illustrated in Figure 5.1 earlier in this chapter, in world class organizations where the customer is at the centre of the business model, marketing as a discipline is responsible for defining and understanding markets, for segmenting these markets, for developing value propositions to meet the researched needs of the customers in the segments, for getting buy-in from all those in the organization responsible for delivering this value, for playing their own part in delivering this value and for monitoring whether the promised value is being delivered.

Indeed, this definition of marketing as a function for strategy development, as well as for tactical sales delivery, when represented as a map, can be used to clarify the whole problem of how to measure marketing effectiveness (see Figure 5.13).

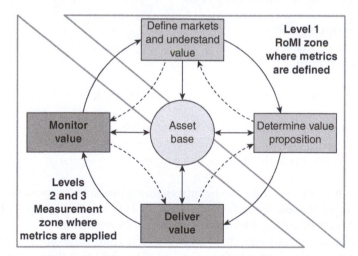

Figure 5.13 Map of the marketing domain with metrics superimposed

From this map, it can be seen that there are three levels of measurement, or metrics:

1   Level 1: creating shareholder value;
2   Level 2: marketing due diligence;
3   Level 3: promotional effectiveness.

Level 1: creating shareholder value

Level 1 is the most vital of all three, because this is what determines whether or not the marketing strategies for the longer term (usually three to five years) destroy or create shareholder value added. In capital markets, success is measured in terms of shareholder value added, having taken account of the risks associated with the strategies set out in the strategic marketing plan, the time value of money and the cost of capital. This is a totally different measurement from outmoded accounting notions of profit.

It is justified to use the strategic marketing plan for assessing whether shareholder value is being created or destroyed because, as Sean Kelly agrees:

> The Customer is simply the fulcrum of the business and everything from production to supply chain, to finance, risk management, personnel management and product development, all adapt to and converge on the business value proposition that is projected to the customer.
>
> (Kelly 2005)

Thus, corporate assets and their associated competences are only relevant if customer markets value them sufficiently highly that they lead to sustainable competitive advantage, or shareholder value added. This is our justification for evaluating the strategic plan for what is to be sold, to whom and with what projected effect on profits as a route to establishing whether shareholder value will be created or destroyed.

Once the hype and jargon is cleared away, all marketing plans say the same thing, 'We're going to do these things in this market and make this much profit'. Digging deeper, we can discern three fundamental assertions that lie at the root of all marketing plans:

1   the market we are going for is this big;
2   our strategy will achieve this much share;
3   that share will result in this much profit.

It is these three assertions that give rise to the three components of business risk:

1   Market risk: the risk that the market is not as big as you think it will be.
2   Share risk: the risk that your strategy will not deliver the share it promises.
3   Profit risk: the risk that you will not make the margins you promised.

It is comparatively easy to envisage how each of these can be broken down into sub-components of risk, which can be assessed using the basic tools of marketing, such as Ansoff's matrix (Figure 5.14), product life cycle analysis, market segmentation robustness, offer specificity and so on.

Cumulatively, these three component risks add up to business risk. If all three are certain, then there is no risk and the plan will deliver what it promises. To the extent that there is some uncertainty in one or more areas, the plan is risky and the promised returns must be higher to compensate for the risk. If we could objectively assess business risk by using data in a specific and systematic way, it would help us to create shareholder value in two ways. First, it would allow us to identify the main areas of risk in our strategy and act to reduce that risk. Second, it would give us a tool to sell our strategy to investors, demonstrating in detail that our plan is well thought out and creates shareholder value. The challenge lies in accurately assessing each of those three areas of risk.

The process for doing this has been labelled 'marketing due diligence' based on years of research at Cranfield School of Management. In short, marketing due diligence is a process that assesses the probability of a marketing plan delivering its promises. It then adjusts the promised profit to reflect that probability and calculates if, for the firm's cost of capital, the plan would create or destroy shareholder value.

Level 2: marketing due diligence

There is another level, however, that few academics or practitioners have addressed to date. We shall describe it briefly here, although once the process of marketing due diligence has been applied to the long-range marketing strategy, it remains central to the issue of marketing metrics and marketing effectiveness. Further, however, let us destroy once and for all one of the great myths of measurement – marketing return on investment. This implies 'return' divided by 'investment' and, for marketing expenditure such as promotional spend, it is an intellectually puerile notion. It's a bit like demanding a financial justification for the wings of an aircraft! Also, as McGovern *et al.* (2004) say:

> Measuring marketing performance isn't like measuring factory output – a fact that many non-marketing executives don't grasp. In the controlled environment of a manufacturing plant, it's simple to account for what goes in one end and what comes out the other and then determine productivity.

> But the output of marketing can be measured only long after it has left the plant.

Neither is the budget and all the energy employed in measuring it a proxy for measuring marketing effectiveness. Indeed, as Simon Caulkin (2005) says:

> 90% of USA and European firms think budgets are cumbersome and unreliable, providing neither predictability nor control.

- They are backward-looking and inflexible. Instead of focussing managers' time on the customers, the real source of income, they focus their attention on satisfying the boss, ie. the budget becomes the purpose.
- Cheating is endemic in all budget regimes. The result is fear, inefficiency, sub optimisation and waste.
- In companies like Enron, the pressure to make the numbers was so great that managers didn't just doctor a few numbers, they broke the law.
- People with targets and jobs dependent on meeting them will probably meet the targets, even if they have to destroy the enterprise to do it.

So, once the marketing due diligence is completed, we can turn our attention to what needs to be measured in the one-year plan.

Figure 5.14 shows the Ansoff matrix. Each cell consists of products for markets or segments. Each of these will have been included in the one-year marketing plan, and for each one objectives will have been set for volume, value and profit. Strategies will also have been set for each objective. It will be recalled that these strategies are the CSFs that were included in the SWOT analysis, weighted according to their relative importance to the customer in each segment (see Figure 5.15).

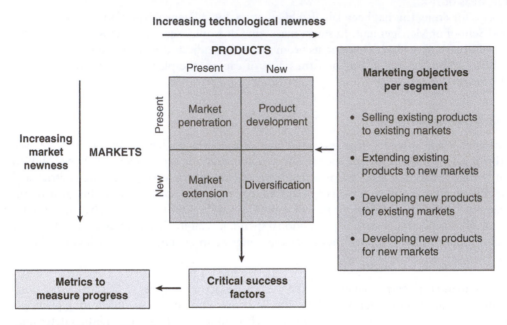

Figure 5.14 The Ansoff matrix

Critical success factors	Weighting factor	Your organisation	Competitor A	Competitor B	Competitor C
CSF 1					
CSF 2		• Strategies to improve competitive position/achieve objectives over time (4Ps) • Metrics (each CSF) to measure performance over time in achieving goals			
CSF 3					
CSF 4					
Total weighted score (score x weight)	100				

Figure 5.15 Critical success factors: in each segment, defined by the segment

It is unlikely that the marketing function will be directly responsible for what needs to be done to improve a CSF. For example, issues like product efficacy, after sales service, channel management and, sometimes, even price and the sales force, are often controlled by other functions, so marketing needs to get buy-in from these functions to the need to improve the CSF scores.

There will be other responses that will need to be measured such as productivity factors and hygiene factors, but to keep it simple, we have only shown customer-based CSFs here in Figure 5.16. Figure 5.16 shows another level of detail, i.e. the actions that have to be taken, by whom and at what cost.

Figure 5.17 shows how these actions multiply for each box of the Ansoff matrix.

Thus, it can be seen how the expenditure on marketing and other functional actions to improve CSFs can be linked to marketing objectives and, ultimately, to profitability, and it becomes clear exactly what must be measured and why. It also obviates the absurd assumption that a particular marketing action can be linked directly to profitability. It can only be linked to other weighted CSFs, which, if improved, should lead to the achievement of volumes, value and, ultimately, profits.

We stress, however, that the corporate revenue and profits shown in the right of Figures 5.16 and 5.17 are not the same as shareholder value added, which takes account of the risks involved in the strategies, the time value of money and the cost of capital.

Figure 5.18 summarizes all of this in one flow chart, which clearly spells out the difference between 'lag indicators' and 'lead indicators'. Lead indicators are the actions taken and the associated expenditure that is incurred. These include, of course, promotional expenditure, which will be addressed later in this chapter. Lag indicators are the *outcomes* of these actions and expenditures and need to be carefully monitored and measured. Thus, retention by segment, loss by segment, new customers, new product sales, channel performance and the like are *outcomes*, but these need to be linked back to the appropriate *inputs*.

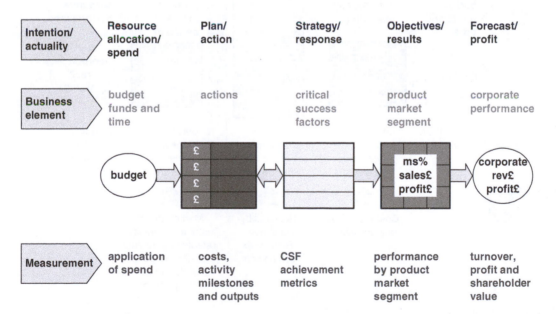

Figure 5.16 Customer-based CSFs

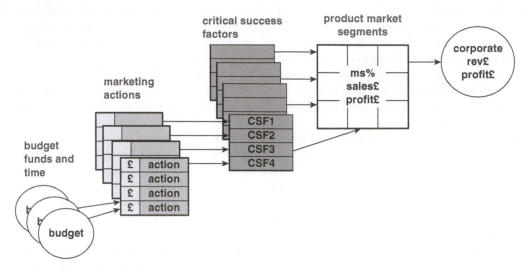

Figure 5.17 Actions and costs

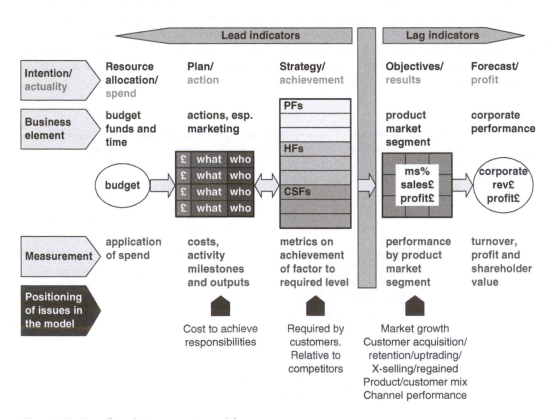

Figure 5.18 Overall marketing metrics model

Level 3: promotional effectiveness

Level 3 is the fundamental and crucial level of promotional measurement. Nonetheless, with the advent of different promotional methods and channels, combined with an empowered and more sophisticated consumer, the problems of measuring promotional effectiveness have increased considerably. Consequently, this remains one of the major challenges facing the marketing community today.

For example, in FMCG, supermarket buyers expect and demand a threshold level of promotional expenditure in order to be considered for listing. Indeed, in most commercial situations, there is a threshold level of expenditure that has to be made in order just to maintain the status quo, i.e. keep up the product or service in consumer consciousness to encourage them to continue buying. The author refers to this as 'maintenance' expenditure.

In most situations, however, not to maintain existing levels of promotion over time results in volume, price and margin pressure, market share losses and a subsequent declining share price. There is some evidence from the Institute of Practitioners in Advertising's (IPA's) analysis of almost 900 promotional campaigns, presented in a report (Golding 2010). Figure 5.19 shows that, in one experimental scenario, the promotional budget was cut to zero for a year, then returned to normal, while in another, the budget was cut by 50 per cent. Sales recovery to pre-cut levels took five years and three years respectively, with cumulative negative impacts on net profits of £1.7 million and £0.8 million.

It is important to make one final point about measuring the effectiveness of promotional expenditure in taking account of 'maintenance' expenditure. This point relates to the tried and tested method of measuring the financial impact of promotional expenditure – net present value (NPV).

As can be seen from the following, by not taking account of the expenditure to maintain current sales and by including total promotional expenditure in the NPV calculations, a totally false result ensues. However, by taking account of maintenance expenditure, a much better result emerges.

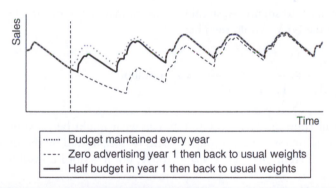

Long term case history

	Budget saved	Sales foregone	Profit on foregone sales	Impact on bottom line	Time to recover
Zero budget year 1	£1.8m	£8.6m	£3.5m	£1.7m	5 years
Half budget year 1	£0.9m	£4.3m	£1.7m	£0.8m	3 years

ROI defined as the incremental revenue generated from advertising per unit of spend   Data2Decisions

Figure 5.19 ROI. Long-term case history

Present value (PV)

Discounting a future stream of revenue into a 'present value' assumes that a rational investor would be indifferent to having a dollar today, or to receiving in some future year a dollar plus the interest that could have been earned by investing that dollar for those years.

Thus, it makes sense to assess investments by dividing the money to be received in future years by $(1 + r)$, where r is the discount rate (the annual return from investing that money) and n is the number of years during which the investment could be earning that return. PV, or NPV or discounted cash flow is denoted as:

$$PV = \frac{\Sigma C_t}{(1 + r)^n}$$

where Σ is the sum of the cash flows in years t (1, 2, 3, 4, etc.).

This summation of the cash flows is then divided by $(1 + r)^n$ where r is the discount rate and n is the number of years the investment could be earning that return. Hence, for a net free cash flow of $2 million a year over 4 years and a cost of capital of 10%, the NPV is:

$$\frac{2}{(1.1)} + \frac{2}{(1.1)^2} + \frac{2}{(1.1)^3} + \frac{2}{(1.1)^4} = \$6.4 \text{ million}$$

Minus an initial investment of, say, $5 million, the NPV of this investment is $1.4 million. However, a promotional investment of, say, $7 million, using the above figure, would produce a loss of $0.6 million.

If, however, a company needs to spend say $6 million just to maintain current sales, the investment is only $1 million and the NPV would then be:

$$-\$1 million + \frac{2}{(1.1)} + \frac{2}{(1.1)^2} + \frac{2}{(1.1)^3} + \frac{2}{(1.1)^4} = \$5.4 \text{ million}$$

The research issue facing our community is how to estimate what might be classified as 'maintenance' promotion and what as 'investment' promotion. This is complicated by the different forms of promotion and the many different channels available today, but it is not impossible.

Part 2 conclusions

Compliant marketing plans, in the sense of being theoretically sound, which do not make a measurable contribution to achieving an organization's objectives, are really not worth all the effort in putting them together. This section outlined three levels of marketing measurement, the most important of which is whether the plan achieves shareholder value, having taken account of the risks associated with the strategies outlined in the plan, the time value of money and the cost of capital.

Summary

Strategic marketing planning, when sensibly institutionalized and driven by an organization's top management, can make a significant contribution to the creation of sustainable competitive advantage. It is, however, important to distinguish between the process of marketing planning and the output. Indeed, much of the benefit will accrue from the process of analysis and debate among relevant managers and directors than from the written document itself.

Ten guidelines were provided, which have been shown to be significant contributors to determining an organization's effectiveness.

Finally, some processes were outlined for measuring the effectiveness of marketing planning, because clearly, a theoretically compliant plan that doesn't contribute measurably to an organization's objectives cannot be worth the effort.

Further reading

Brown, S. (1996), 'Art or science?: Fifty years of marketing debate', *Journal of Marketing Management*, 12: 243–267. This fascinating and highly readable paper discusses the eternal debate about whether marketing is more art than science. It is recommended here because readers should never lose sight of the need for strategic marketing plans and for the process that produces them to be creative as well as diagnostic.

Leppard, J. and McDonald, M. (1987), 'A reappraisal of the role of marketing planning', *Journal of Marketing Management*, 3(2): 18–26. This paper throws quite a considerable amount of light onto why marketing planning is rarely done. It examines the organization's context in which marketing planning takes place and gives a fascinating insight into how corporate culture and politics often prevent the marketing concept from taking hold.

McDonald, M. (1996), 'Strategic marketing planning: Theory; practice; and research agendas', *Journal of Marketing Management*, 12(1/3): 4–27. This paper summarizes the whole domain of marketing planning, from its early days to the current debate taking place about its contribution. It also explores forms of marketing planning other than the more rational/scientific one described in this chapter.

McDonald, M. (1999), *Marketing Plans: How to Prepare Them; How to Use Them*, seventh edition, Chichester, UK: Wiley. This book is the standard text on marketing planning in universities and organizations around the world. It is practical, as well as being based on sound theoretical concepts.

References

Ansoff, H. I. (1977), 'The state and practice of planning systems', *Sloan Management Review*, 18(2): 1–24. (Article on planning systems by a leading writer on strategy.)

Bailey, A., Johnson, G. and Daniels, K. (2000), 'Validation of a multi-dimensional measure of strategic development process', *British Journal of Management*, 11(22): 151–162.

Burns, P. (1994) *Growth in the 1990s: Winner and losers*, Special Report 12, 31 European Enterprise Centre, Cranfield School of Management, UK.

Buzzell, R. D. and Gale, B. T. (1987) *The PIMS Principles: Linking Strategy to Performance*, Free Press, New York.

Caulkin, S. (2005), 'Escape from the budget straightjackets,' *Management Today*, January: 47–49.

Golding, D. (ed.) (2010), *Advertising Works 19. Proving the Payback on Marketing Investment*, London: IPA.

Greenley, G. (1984), 'An exposition into empirical research into marketing planning', *Journal of Marketing Management*, 3(1): 83–102. (This paper reviews all recent empirical research into the process of marketing planning, conclusion that it remains one of the most difficult domains in the whole field of marketing.)

Kelly, S. (2005), *Customer Intelligence*, Chichester, UK: Wiley.

Kollatt, D. J., Blackwell, R. D. and Robeson, J. F. (1972), *Strategic Marketing*, New York: Holt, Rinehart & Winston. (Standard textbook on strategic marketing, including sections on planning.)

Lubatkin, M. and Pitts, M. (1985) The PIMS and the policy perspective: A rebuttal, *Journal of Business Strategy*, Summer, 85–92.

Leighton, D. S. R. (1966), *International Marketing: Text and Cases*, New York: McGraw-Hill. (This textbook includes a useful section on planning in international marketing.)

Lubatkin, M. and Pitts, M. (1985), 'The PIMS and the policy perspective: A rebuttal', *Journal of Business Strategy*, Summer, 85–92.

McDonald, M. (1982), The Theory and Practice of Industrial Marketing Planning, PhD thesis, Cranfield, UK: Cranfield Institute of Technology.

McDonald, M. (1984), The Theory and Practice of Marketing Planning for Industrial Goods in International Markets, PhD thesis, Cranfield, UK: Cranfield Institute of Technology. (This thesis investigated marketing planning with special reference to industrial goods.)

McDonald, M. (1994) 'Marketing at the crossroads. A comment', *Marketing Intelligence and Planning*, 12(1): 42–45.

McDonald, M. (2012), *Market Segmentation: How to Do It; How to Profit from It*, Chichester, UK: Wiley.

McGovern, G. J., Court, D., Quelch, J. A. and Crawford, B. (2004), 'Bringing customers into the boardroom', *Harvard Business Review*, 82(11): 70–80.

Piercy, N. F. (1997), *Market-Led Strategic Change: Transforming the Process of Going to Market*, third edition, Oxford, UK: Butterworth-Heinemann.

Smith, B. D. (2003), The Effectiveness of Marketing Strategy Making in Medical Markets, PhD thesis, Cranfield, UK: Cranfield Institute of Technology.

Thompson, S. (1962), *How Companies Plan*, AMA Research Study no. 54, Chicago, IL: AMA. (Report on research study conducted on behalf of the American Marketing Association.)

6 Implementing strategic change

Lloyd C. Harris and Kate L. Daunt

Introduction

Reflecting on a particularly intense and erudite discussion of meta-theory and postmodernism (involving lots of big words like 'phenomenology' and clever-sounding words like 'ontology'), Kate and I agreed that getting stuff changed in business schools is about as easy as persuading professors to stop showing off, using long and clever-sounding words. If you feel particularly bored with life and you can bear talking to any professor ask them, 'what needs to change around here'? A good three hours later the professor will be detailing the precise shade of purple that the corridors *should* be painted. At this point run (don't worry – they won't be offended – most won't even notice that you've left). The issue, as ever, is not that people don't see the need for change it's just . . . well, everybody seems to disagree about what should be changed, when it should happen, who should do it, why it needs to be done, whether tea or coffee is needed, when things should start, whose fault it is, who can we blame, who should pay for it, who should bring the biscuits and well . . . everything else. Throughout this chapter (undoubtedly using irritating jargonese and pretentious terms – all of which are Kate's fault), we shall try to elucidate (see!) the problem of 'getting stuff done' or what Kate (and everyone else aside from Lloyd) calls 'implementing strategic change'.

On reflection, if we look back at past academic research a whole tribe of scholars have squabbled, pontificated and generally whined about the need for a better understanding of the development and implementation of strategic marketing planning. During this time, planning theory has evolved from what we used to call 'long-range planning' to 'strategic planning' to the present 'hybrid' of strategic marketing planning. The results of scholarly interest have been twofold; first, the development of innumerable and increasingly sophisticated planning models; and second, various analyses of the difficulties of implementation. However, despite this level of academic attention, studies of practice continually find that very few strategic marketing plans are actually implemented successfully (the most common statistic cited being that fewer than 15 per cent of plans are actually implemented – see Hoskin and Wood (1993) – although in our experience the figure is probably much lower). Somehow our grand plans and carefully crafted strategies are being wasted. In short – stuff isn't happening and folks are running around like headless chickens and getting their metaphorical asses whooped (apologies for the mixed chicken-related metaphor here) by other folks who have actually got their stuff together!

By the end of this chapter we aim to have illuminated some of these problems and presented some suggestions for overcoming them. The first part of the chapter looks at why and how change gets resisted. This includes looking at why implementation so commonly goes wrong and what obstacles prevent us from achieving our aims and how this generates unintended change outcomes (or in other words why, how and what goes wrong). These insights lead us towards the argument that, ~~paradoxically~~ funnily enough, the development of an externally-oriented market focus, hinges on the astute management of internal-organizational dynamics (or what could also be called 'getting our people to listen, agree and then do stuff'). After this we talk through four main strategies for implementing strategic change; each with sub-tactics that we think could be useful.

The starting point

Most people when asked for directions will *think* (and the intellectually challenged actually *say*), 'I wouldn't start from here'. Such is the case with implementation. If you *begin* with implementation you might as well give up, go home and blame the cat. The thing is that implementation involves implementing something (normally a plan of some description). If you only consider implementation when you have something to implement, as opposed to also when you're formulating something to implement, you are likely to end up frustrated and kicking the aforementioned cat (our lawyers undoubtedly advising that such feline-related violence is not endorsed). This problem is what academics call the formulation-implementation dichotomy (or in more digestible terms, 'thinking about how you're going to do something while you're planning what to do' – what my young daughter, Tabitha, calls 'thinking ahead'). Cespedes and Piercy (1996) were among the first to highlight this issue, arguing that many of the problems that we encounter during implementation occur, because so-called 'conventional' models of marketing planning typically present formulation and implementation as separate (albeit sequential) stages of planning. This is argued to lead a ~~plethora myriad~~ lot of potential difficulties that significantly reduce the probability that a given plan will actual happen. Problems include:

- Coming up with plans that are divorced from reality and ignore the idiosyncratic implementation skills and capabilities of the organization.
- The development of strategies and plans that are incapable of being implemented because we don't have the resources to do them.
- The risk that planning formulation becomes myopically detached from the complex realities and contingencies of the context (that is, the planners play a lot of golf, attend numerous 'workshops' and write plans that might work on Mars but not right here)!
- The massive underestimation of the importance of the internal political and cultural infrastructure of the organization (or, in other words, all the things that can stop change happening)!

Overall, while many writers have pondered the difficulties that occur within planning processes, a surprisingly small number of studies have recognized that formulation and implementation are interrelated, inseparable and at times indistinguishable. One of the most persuasive studies can be found in the work of Judson (1996) who discusses ten major potential problems in implementing marketing strategy and concludes that the first nine potential problems can be perceived as the 'upstream' flaws in the planning process, which cause the final 'downstream' implementation problem (it can be argued that the reverse is also true). Now I know that for the average student this was written way back in the mists of time (the last century being virtually black and white), however, I would note that if something that is right, is still right no matter when it was written (or possibly nobody has been able to do better since then)! These ten problems are presented in Figure 6.1.

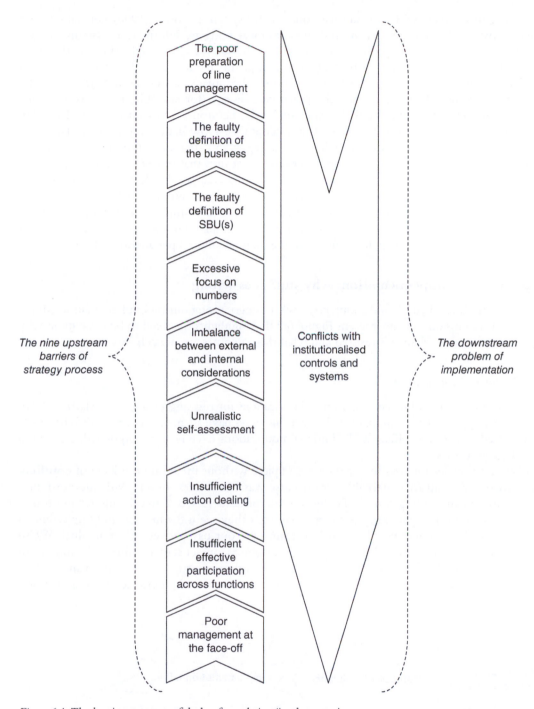

The poor
preparation
of line
management

The faulty
definition of
the business

The faulty
definition of
SBU(s)

Excessive
focus on
numbers

Imbalance
between external
and internal
considerations

Conflicts with
institutionalised
controls and
systems

Unrealistic
self-assessment

Insufficient
action dealing

Insufficient
effective
participation
across functions

Poor
management at
the face-off

*The nine upstream
barriers of
strategy process*

*The downstream
problem of
implementation*

Figure 6.1 The barriers to successful plan formulation/implementation

Source: A diagrammatic representation of the list presented in Judson 1996: 14–41.

Referring to conflicts with institutional controls and systems, Judson (1996) concentrates on conflicts between the developed plan and organizational budgets, information systems, reward structures and procedures of control. In our experience, Judson is right to highlight how the existing systemic architecture of a firm acts as a brake on implementation efforts. However, we would argue that merely 'fixing' these internal artefacts does rather smack of treating the symptoms of a problem rather than attempting to cure the underlying disease (for example, if we do not really believe that our reward systems should be based on levels of customer satisfaction rather than sales, how likely is it that managers will enthusiastically adopt this? How many employees will circumvent this change? How many managers will simply disregard this after a few months?). Our view is that the systems and structures of a firm are creations of that firm that reflect its underlying culture attitudes and beliefs. Thus, if we are to achieve long-lasting change, should not our efforts focus on *either* generating plans that are consistent with our intra-firm cultural beliefs (that is, plans in which we believe), *or* driving our culture so that the strategically imperative becomes culturally acceptable? In this way, it seems logical that we accept that implementation hinges on developing a realistic and coherent plan, which is tailored to the internal cultural peculiarities of the firm.

The problems of implementation: why stuff goes wrong

Go to any textbook and you'll find a long list of what can go wrong during implementation efforts. To guide our discussion, we first present Figure 6.2 that highlights the need to be clear about why change is resisted, how change is resisted and what the outcomes are of such issues.

Rationales for resisting change

An earlier study by Lloyd looked at common justifications for resisting change (see Harris 2002a). However, as is typical of academics, over the years his views have adapted (in other words he's realized he missed something – Kate) and additional justifications have been incorporated. Figure 6.3 depicts these rationales.

No list of rationales for resisting change is complete without including the issue of **conflicting pressures**. An old (if remarkable clean) curse was to threaten others with the possibility that they 'live in interesting times'. Today, outside of academia, we live in interesting times. We're told that customers are kings – yet as sovereigns they seem damn rude and unpleasant to us republicans. We're encouraged to work in teams, yet our pay packets are individual. We're told to put our customer first and yet we pay our customer-contact staff as close to the minimum wage as we can. We're harangued by well-meaning enthusiasts to, 'care for the planet' while our shareholders (whose money we're playing free and easy with) demand more and more.

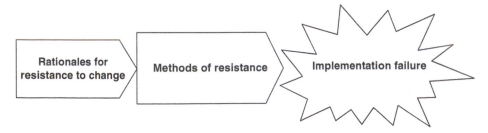

Figure 6.2 The rationales, methods and outcomes of resistance to change

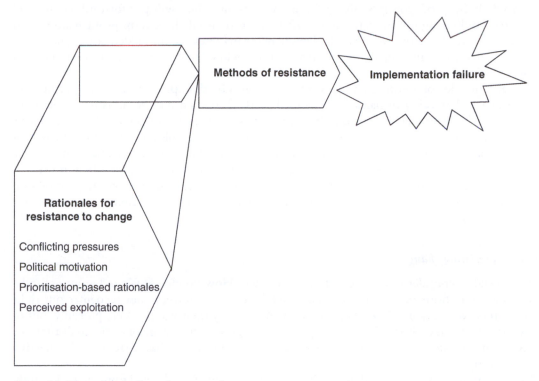

Figure 6.3 The rationales for resistance to change

Inherently our jobs, roles and lives are riddled with conflicting paradox. Under such pressures, is it surprising that employees attempt to simplify and control their world by feverishly clinging to the rock of the past? I think not.

Invariably, organizations are riven with political bickering and factions. Consequently, the second rationale for resisting change, is **politically motivated resistance**. Employees are (largely) rational beings who defend their positions and egos accordingly (unless they're academics, in which case when their egos are so large that mindless vociferous attack is standard). Normally, where a change is perceived *negatively* to affect the status or authority of a manager's or executive's 'home' department, resistance is logically advocated, whereas when change affects comparative power *positively*, change is encouraged and actively supported. While this all seems rather petty, so much of our working dynamics are petty! 'Organizational politics' sounds grandiose and noble, but ultimately it is about little people with big egos protecting their little world and flexing their little muscles. Real organizational politics is about petty jealousies, nasty egotists and narrow-minded bureaucrats – not glamorous but mean-spirited and unpleasant.

Such maliciousness is balanced by organizational members who genuinely and sincerely care about the good of the firm. These idealists often have **prioritization-based** rationales for resisting change on the grounds that other more pressing objectives should be given a higher priority, at least in the short term. This view is common at the (fresh-faced, innocent) lower management levels and among frontline staff. Here change can be resisted for a remarkably diverse number of reasons. Typical are arguments that claim that the espoused market-oriented change programme will cause operational inefficiencies and impede customer service (in other words, generally cause a whole heap of work). Similarly, bean counters and alike will put forward 'economic' reasons to avoid changing the status quo – often citing reduced short-term profit margins and other such financial horrors. While such views may (or may not) be misguided, a key characteristic here is that such individuals resist change as they believe that to do so is in the interest of the organization.

A final rationale for resisting change centres on **perceived exploitation**. This justification for opposing and resisting management-espoused market-oriented change initiatives centres on beliefs that such changes entail unreasonable, subjugating or emasculating demands. As such, this rationale is primarily found among frontline, customer-contact employees whose experience of the market-oriented change programmes can often be far from wholly positive. That is, frequently market-oriented change initiatives, to varying degrees, lead to an escalation of the labour process of frontline staff (see Gabriel 1999). Such changes can include increased expectations, responsibilities, stress, hours of work and higher standards of customer service. Under such circumstances, are you surprised that change is resisted?

Methods of resisting change

Next we need to consider *how* change efforts are resisted. How do individuals and groups of individuals resist our efforts to implement change? Surely, these employees must recognize our right to dictate their working lives? Do they not know that we pay their wages? Well, probably, but in my experience it makes little difference; employees can adopt a wide range of tactics to disrupt our efforts. Figure 6.4 depicts two main forms of resistance – individual-based tactics and collective efforts of groups.

All of the individual tactics used by employees to resist change are derived from an earlier study of employee behaviour (Harris 1996). First, managers and employees can **deflect the process** of implementation. This ploy hinges on deflecting the process of planning away from its original goals. In one company we looked at, a senior executive of the firm managed to derail a huge effort towards market-oriented culture change through forcing the change agents to focus on the financial issues of the change, effectively turning the planned change into a revised budgeting system!

Really sneaky tactics of resistance can centre on simply **moving the goal posts** a sufficient number of times. A popular gambit here is to impede change through supplying a continuing (and if possible a constant) barrage of alternative short-term goals. A good idea here is to identify areas of the company, which you know (ever twitchy) senior executives or (even better) owners consider to be crucial to company success (in other words, their favoured hobby horses). This is comparatively easily achieved if you listen to the last few speeches given at the last annual company get together. At some point some old buzzard will have stood up and talked for rather too long about the 'future' and at this point thrown in a few fashionable management buzzwords and drifted off to ramble on about their personal hobby horse. Once you are in possession of this, it is relatively simply to either move the goal post yourself (or encourage others to do so) through numerous alternative suggestions for company 'crucial' short-term company targets.

Should plans look as if they might actually succeed, a good tactic is to make **resources scarce**. Through the creation or identification of 'more pressing' short-term goals, you should be able to stop members of your department participating in planning efforts through the allocation or promotion of 'important' projects. A good ruse (particularly during the current downturn) is to limit financial resources. In another company we looked at a vociferous senior executive that we (rather melodramatically) called 'the anti-planner' held partial responsibility for organizational internal finance allocation. Thus, attempts at planning found severe limitations put on their ability to, for

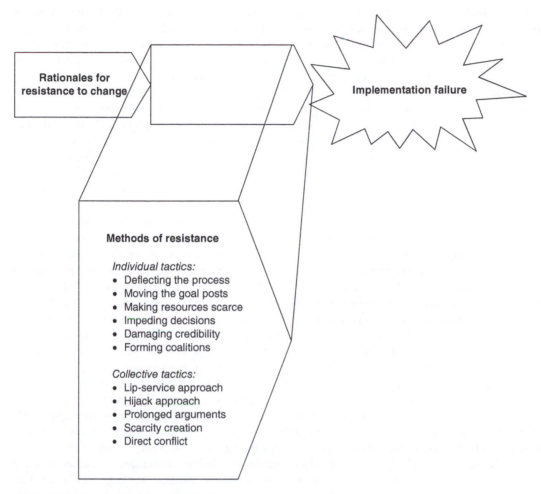

Figure 6.4 The methods change resistance

example, commission external market research, significantly reducing their ability to outline strategic options. Similarly, constraints were put on off-the-job training, hampering efforts to educate and enthuse employees about the planned changes and generally dampening the whole effort!

Equally, individuals can slow down change via **impeding decisions**. Anybody who works (ha!) in a university will recognize the decision impediment via *death by committee*. This tactic is designed to attempt to delay decisions through allocating the responsibility of a decision to a special committee. Preferably, this special committee or working group or cross-functional team (use the one that sounds the best) will meet in many months' time and agree to dedicate considerable effort in analysing the issues. If 'away days' in country hotels can be arranged this will happen and many working lunches will have to be taken. Eventually the hope is that a tentative suggestion that further research is needed will eventually be made (hopefully a good six months *after* the whole issue was important).

We also think that individuals resist change through **damaging the credibility** of key change-related personnel. This is most easily accomplished via the judicious use of rumour and innuendo to generate doubt in the minds of supporters and provide a focus for distrust. Without wishing to be negative about people in general, it really is surprising what people choose to believe. In mitigation, we are conditioned from an early age to trust each other and generally to believe what others tell us. Our parents lie to us about the Tooth Fairy and Father Christmas – but wasn't it Gregory House who said 'everybody lies'? Thus, when a senior and well-respected colleague mentions over a cup of coffee that Jones-in-accounts is really a 147-year-old, pigeon-fancier, eccentric millionaire with six toes, our first reaction is to accept this (albeit sceptically, 'I mean how do *you* know s/he's got six toes – I'd heard it was seven'). As a ruse to impede the implementation of change, this can be very effective. A huge amount of effort will need to be dedicated to counteracting rumours (with varying grains of truth) about our plans. Typically these rumours will focus on fears: concerns about job losses, delayering, relocations, loss of privileges, the list is endless. The idea is to find out what colleagues care about (ranging from redundancy to the make of company cars) and make them worried that change will take all of it away!

Individual tactics become collective with the resistance of change through **forming coalitions**. Given that those advocating change have often persuaded others of the importance of their support, those resisting change should also take the time to consider who in the firm is likely not to support this view and (more importantly) which individuals or groups does the change need to succeed. This analysis is likely to lead to the identification of two or three departments whose support is crucial. Thereafter, it is a relatively simply process of forming coalitions against this change using a variety of means: education, collaboration, coercion, political manoeuvring (the choice is really context-specific). The goal is to form a partnership of those who agree or who are willing to be seen to agree with your views. This alliance can persuade itself that their actions are for the good of the firm and then happily obstruct any implemented changes without feeling guilty (after all, 'it's not just me that thinks this, look at Jones-in-accounts he . . . err . . . she agrees with me').

Team or collective approaches to resisting change can involve numerous different tactics. Figure 6.4 depicts five approaches, originally discussed in Harris (2002a). The first is the **lip-service approach** to impede change, which entails the overt and public acceptance and oral agreement with the initiative, matched by the intentional obstruction of change by inactivity. In short, contributors acquiesce and publicly support the change, but collectively continue to behave in whatever manner they see fit. This approach may be viewed as a form of instrumental compliance (see Legge 1994) in that, in recognising the legitimate authority of the hierarchy and the benefits of continued employment, employees overtly, orally conform, but covertly resist change. In some respects, this can be viewed as a collective approach to impede decision-making in a non-confrontational manner.

Hijacking approaches to resisting a market-oriented culture change programme involve the intentional attempt to derail, refocus, reorient or subvert the content, processes or objectives of the initiative originally conceived. That is, opponents of the programme endeavour to transform the espoused change into something more 'acceptable' to their function, or simply something more personally palatable. In this sense, 'hijacking' can be viewed as a team effort by individuals employing the process deflection tactic. Typically, top managers endeavouring to resist market-oriented culture change use this approach to derail the initiative at an early stage, by transforming the espoused change into a less 'adventurous' change or through the strict adherence to a particular 'tenet' (see Narver *et al.* 1998) of change as a rationale for ignoring others.

Another strategy (much favoured by boorish pedants) is the obstruction of implementation through **prolonged** (and preferably tedious) **argument**. This involves the tenacious use of protracted and pedantic arguments *upon all possible occasions* to erode enthusiasm, support or agreement with the espoused change. In many ways, this collaborative effort involves aspects of the individual tactics of first, the tenacious deflection, the process of change, aligned with, second, efforts to damage the creditability of the change. This should be viewed as more active than the lip-service approach since the argumentative approach involves actively seeking opportunities to attack, deride or otherwise disparage the change programme, while boring everyone to tears of frustration. Although such actions may be viewed by top management and their supporters as dysfunctional (see Griffin *et al.* 1998) or 'counterproductive' (see Kolz 1999), those employing this strategy consider their motives logical, justifiable and largely a by-product of contemporary organizational politics (see Buchanan and Badham 1999).

Similar to the individual tactic of making resources scare, groups can use collective efforts of **scarcity creation**, in effect to undermine the change effort. Whereas individuals often employ similar tactics, joint efforts to create scarcity of needed resources, is far more effective. All attempts to implement change require resources in the form of management time, finance, information, personnel and even office space. Consequently, through diverting, consuming or restricting access to particular resources, the effectiveness of market-oriented change may be severely restricted. The calculated nature of this approach to undermine espoused change constitutes purposeful behaviour of a more confrontational form. In this sense, the intentional creation of scarcity in vital resources represents an approach that is political in nature (see Harris 1998), but which also demonstrates sensitivity to the capabilities and resources required during market-oriented change (see Day 1999).

Management of change can also be derailed via a final and most actively confrontational approach to obstructing change focuses – **direct conflict**. Direct conflict is more common during the earlier phases of change, although top managers frequently remain stalwarts of this approach long after the early phases. Such resistance to change reflects extremely pronounced personal opposition to change as well as strongly entrenched cultural values that remain orthogonal to the espoused initiative (see Harris 1998), despite prolonged efforts of persuasion, education and communication. Middle-to-top managers adopting a conflictual strategy commonly evoke authority or resource-based justifications for their views. Those continuing a strategy of direct conflict at a junior level are either tacitly supported by direct superordinates or ignored as eccentrics. At senior levels, refusing to cooperate with change and constantly challenging the initiative is typically viewed as anachronistic behaviour that, ultimately, will eventually abate.

Implementation failure: the outcomes of resisted change efforts

A discussion of past planned changes with executives quickly reveals that it is common for most of them to refer to such efforts in quite black and white terms. Changes either happen or they don't and are quietly forgotten about until somebody writes a cliché-filled memo explaining that such matters have been put on the back burner until an appropriate strategic window of opportunity arises (management-gibberish for it didn't work, we're quite embarrassed we even thought of it, so let's all forget about it, after all I'm the person doing your annual review next week). However, if we approach a critical perspective on change it is apparent that change rarely happens in this black and white way. Organizations can be incredibly complex and this complexity means that resistance to efforts to change more typically lead to implementation failure that is not complete failure, but certainly fails to achieve all the set objectives. In other words, implementation frequently leads to unanticipated consequences – of which eight are common (see Harris and Ogbonna 2002) (Figure 6.5).

Lamentably, many plans are doomed to failure not necessarily because they are poor plans but because past change efforts have sapped all enthusiasm for change, leaving the victims as zombie-like automatons who every twelve months work their way through whatever plan is placed in front of them. In other words, initiatives become **ritualized**. While the implementation programmes

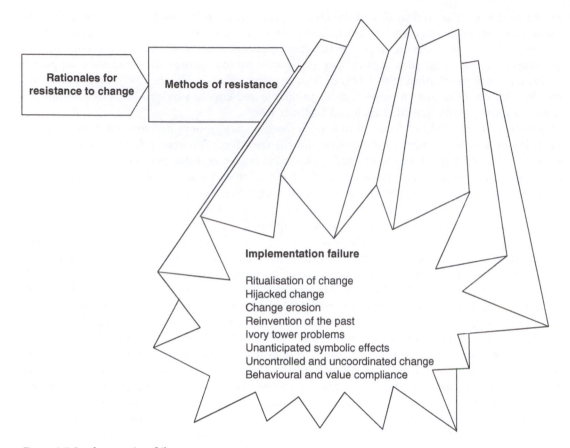

Figure 6.5 Implementation failure

vary tremendously in application, more sophisticated intervention efforts recognize that successful change efforts require ongoing interventions. A consequence of the recognition that frequent
interventions are needed is the development of long-term plans for change, which when accounted
for on the standard annual basis, become rituals which typically occur but once per year. The difficulty here is that organizations need to balance conflicting demands. On the one hand, successful
change typically requires multiple and ongoing interventions. However, on the other, the more
routinized the interventions become, the greater the likelihood that espoused changes will be
ignored or that lip-service will be paid.

Linked to ritual (mindless) planning-implementation efforts is the possibility that the original
aims and process become **hijacked** and the course of change diverted. Although those attempting
to implement change expect to manage or manipulate the culture of their company, an unintended
consequence of their actions is the generation of an opportunity for others to hijack this process
for their own (often orthogonal – Machiavellian) reasons. Nearly all of change initiatives studied
begin with clear and unsullied aims and objectives. Indeed, the setting of change targets is most
commonly undertaken by senior management (preferably during a 'strategy away-day' – often
called 'golf' by the uninitiated) and sometimes specialist culture change teams (that is, management consultants who get paid a heap of cash to document the 'bleeding obvious' – henceforth

'strategic aims'). However, often during the planning process, these objectives become adulterated by 'non-specialists' (read – 'people who know what they are talking about') or hijacked by individuals, departments or outlets for their own purposes (power hungry-types who prefer to do things their way). The impact of such interference is either the subversion of the process or the camouflaging of the process, so that change programmes degenerate into cost cutting, customer service or de-layering initiatives.

While most change efforts have laudable aims, almost inevitably implementation frequently suffers from **change erosion** (see Harrison and Carrol 1991). That is, the extent to which the espoused ideals are eroded by subsequent events. While the over ritualization of change (often into a once-a-year, almost, ceremonial event) is potentially damaging, it is also the case that attention to the perpetuation of change was an important issue. In many cases, programmes for change will change what many employees do and also what some employees think. However, the continuance of such behaviours and the reinforcement of espoused beliefs tends not to happen over the long term. In the short term people can be enthused by proposed changes and change their behaviours and attitudes accordingly. However, while managements will take steps to sustain such changes, those against change will also tenaciously resist and dampen enthusiasm, which, combined with staff turnover effects, can quickly lead to an erosion of the change, sometimes into something entirely different from that which was originally intended.

In many change programmes, the change effort is subverted by a form of **reinvention**. Cultural or change reinvention is used to denote instances when a change effort results in the espousal of attitudes and behaviours, which while appearing 'new' merely camouflage the continued adherence to the old (and often more comfortable) culture. In other words, the change programme either intentionally or unintentionally repackages the 'old' culture under a veneer of the 'new'. Typically, old emphases on sales orientations become thinly veiled under the guise of service quality programmes, while customer loyalty schemes are camouflaged as relationship building programmes. This unintended consequence is especially prevalent at the outlet level where the change is closest to the demands of the customer interface, but furthest from the control of culture change agents.

Limited implementation can also occur due to what could be labelled **ivory tower** effects. While cultural reinvention largely centres on the reinterpretations of outlet-level employees, unintended consequences also emerge where planners design changes without sufficient awareness of the diversity of views throughout the organization. A key issue here is 'unitary' thinking – basically a pretentious way of saying the managers and executives tend to think about single things – they assume that there is a single culture, a single view, a single one-best-way (often their own). This is at best unwise and at worst as dumb as daytime television. Organizations are mosaics of subculture with vast numbers of concurrent and sometime competing dialogues (and monologues). Assuming that everyone thinks and acts the same way is likely to be met with derision, but ivory tower planners are often ignorant of a series of 'realities' ranging from motivation and commitment levels through to practices and procedures. Given such limitations, it is not surprising that the unrealistic plans developed are resisted by individuals and groups who (often, rightly) seize on the flaws to deride and derail the changes.

Losing implementation efforts also frequently fails to pay sufficient attention to **symbolism during change**. Dandridge *et al.* (1980: 77) define symbols as 'those aspects of an organization that its members use to reveal or make comprehendible the unconscious feeling, images, and values that are inherent in that organization'. We often talk of changing the behaviours and attitudes of employees, but rarely acknowledge the importance of symbolic meaning. Nevertheless, such organizational myths and symbolic actions during change can have a profound effect on the change process. In particular, small actions and decisions, which are inconsistent with the espoused change, can take on symbolic meaning and be quickly disseminated through the grapevine. Although such symbols and symbolic impacts are obviously organizational-specific, the symbols often focus on inconsistent management actions, customer service issues and reward systems.

Yearly-based change efforts frequently become ritualized. However, less structured efforts can degenerate into **uncontrolled and uncoordinated change** efforts. Although in the majority of instances firms will control change by using a central agency or group, in some cases, unintended effects will be strongly linked to the lack of centralized control. Without control and coordination, planned changes are unlikely to be implemented as conceived. Things will be interpreted in different ways, systems will be tailored to local idiosyncrasies, objectives will be given differing priorities, in other words things may change, but not in the way planned. This isn't necessarily a bad thing. Often, things can be implemented more effectively. However, if this isn't coordinated and fed back into the system, efficiencies are lost and consistency eroded.

Equally problematic are implementation efforts that merely generate **behavioural compliance**. Emmanuel Ogbonna (1993) argues that many change interventions fail in their objective of value change, but *do* influence the behaviours of organizational members. That is, the change effort alters what people *do*, but fails to change what people *think*. This is dangerous for a variety of reasons, not least being that compliance only tends to occur when people are watching and, when the managerial eye turns elsewhere, employees will quickly revert to their old behaviours. So, all too frequently, while our plans detail the long-term aims of changing the values, beliefs and opinions, all too often the implementation of such programmes degenerates into a farce where employees adhere to our behavioural rules (at least when we're watching), but blithely ignore the efforts to win their hearts and minds and change their cultural beliefs.

Getting stuff done: strategies and tactics to reduce implementation failure

Many existing studies and texts discuss what factors lead to successful implementation. Indeed, in a review of these texts, the reader can very quickly spot the simple bullet-point list that details exactly what should be in place for a successful implementation effort. Typically, these lists look something like this:

- Make sure that you have sufficient resources available throughout the entire planning effort ('well, duh!', as my eldest daughter Amelia would say).
- Strategic implementation effort should be led by an executive with good leadership skills (if needing good leadership skills was an entry requirement to executive status, how many executives in your company would pass?).
- All employees should be enthusiastic supporters of the planned changed (we should all floss every day too).
- Consideration should have been paid to issues of communication and coordination (as opposed to keeping your plans secret and locking them away . . .)
- The developed plan should recognize and deal with any issues of existing structure (well obviously!).
- The existing culture of the firm should be taken into account and any changes be well supported (well, if it were that easy . . .).
- The feedback systems for implementation should be rigorous and robust (that is, our accounting department really wants to take control).

Alright! Alright! We may have added one or two comments. However, for most people, on first inspection, these factors seem both rational and deceptively, intuitively logical. While such lists tend to give us warm feelings and satisfy our need for a gratifying checklist against which we can evaluate our efforts, other than as a comfort blanket, such lists are not really much use (read – 'are no use at all, but sell management books to the gullible').

In Harris (2002b), Lloyd looked at the various types of approaches that different managements adopted during their implementation efforts. This found that four main emphases were stressed during change.

- First, **strategic marketing approaches** processes focusing on the initiation and/or maintenance of reciprocal, mutually beneficial long-term relationships with customers in order to enhance comparative customer orientation and improve responsiveness to buyer needs, wants and demands.
- Second, in some firms, implementing change was found to centre on **political approaches** designed to persuade, cajole or coerce adherence to espoused change.
- Third, were **human resources/management approaches** designed to change the behavioural and emotional display of (largely) frontline staff to those display prescriptions espoused by management.
- Finally, were **culture-oriented approaches** with an emphasis on 'hearts and minds' during change, which were found where the focus is on the need fundamentally to change the existing attitudes and beliefs of employees to those values espoused by management.

Leveraging these four strategic approaches or foci provides us with some insights into the approaches managements can adopt and the emphases on which they focus. In some regards, this forms a categorization of the overall strategies for implementing change. However, what about the nuts and bolts nitty-gritty tactics of change? For this, we need insights into *how* changes are implemented at the coalface. Unfortunately, the issues here are not simple. To my mind, there isn't a magic wand, a checklist, an agenda that can be adopted and everything will suddenly happen (or, at least, if there is one, nobody's told me yet). In contrast, there are levers and tools that should be considered and can be employed, depending on the contingencies of the change. In other words, there is no 'quick-fix', but there are tools and tactics that *can* help at different times. Within each general strategy/approach there are numerous different tactics that could be employed. Figure 6.6 lists particularly useful tactics for each general approach, and the remainder of the chapter is dedicated to their discussion. No approach is better than another and adopting a single approach is no better or worse than adopting multiple approaches and tactics. The idea is that each context is idiosyncratic and therefore requires an individually-tailored approach – think of Figure 6.6 as either a smorgasbord or a pick-n-mix (depending on your personal preference)!

Strategic marketing

Lots of different strategic marketing tools and techniques could aid an implementation effort. Figure 6.6 presents three strategic marketing tactics to drive change. Specifically, these are tactics addressing ownership, communications and internal marketing.

Establishing and exploiting ownership

Calls to change commonly begin with a charismatic leader highlighting key strategic issues. Although we fully accept that leadership can aid the implementation of change (indeed, leadership

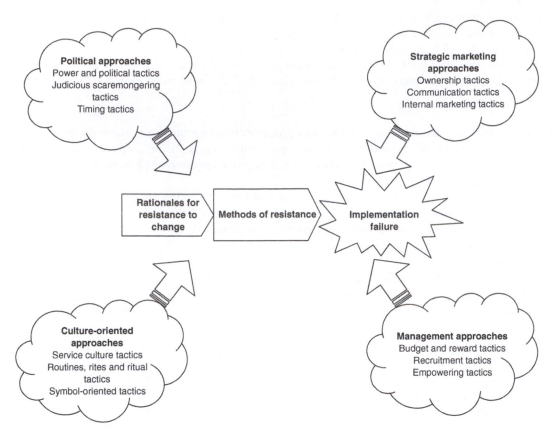

Figure 6.6 Strategies and tactics to reduce resistance to change and implementation failure

could well be another HR-related lever for change), given the choice between a good (or even fair) leader and a whole load of folks believing in the change and feeling a sense of ownership over what is happening, we'd always plump for ownership (somewhat spuriously since the generation of ownership should also lead to the identification of leaders). Different disciplines define 'ownership' in differing ways. For us, ownership refers to the extent to which those implementing a plan feel a sense of propriety over the plan – they feel like they are responsible for part or all of the plan. In this regard, a sense of ownership is considered a necessary precursor to a genuine sense of commitment by those who execute plans.

Harking back to the formulation-implementation dichotomy discussed earlier, one way to facilitate the simultaneous consideration of formulation and implementation issues is through broadening the base of involvement and ensuring that for each strategy, tactic, operational or action plan support already exists and an individual or group is ready and willing to champion or lead the process – not because we think that they should (although it helps) but because *they believe in what needs to be done and feel a sense of propriety over the change*. It is almost impossible to generate widespread ownership after a plan has been developed. It is *theoretically* possible that a developed plan will be so perfect that it will be universally approved throughout a firm and enthusiastically adopted by everyone – yes senior management can really be this dim! However, more realistically, widespread ownership will not happen by chance or luck, but requires careful design and management from the very start of the process.

Invariably, executives and senior managers are terrified of such notions. As a rule, the higher the manager the greater their love of anything that is analytically sophisticated (huge preferences being shown to complex graphics during presentations with lots and lots of big equations and sums preferably supplied by a pale, twitchy-look presenter who uses lots of mathematical notation that sounds really, really clever and nobody really understands – 'after all if we don't understand it and we're *really* clever then it must be brilliant'). Establishing ownership makes managers uneasy for a number of reasons. Most notably, since it is based on participation (which involves testing ideas with those who will actually do them), managers get jittery about security (after all, all our competitors really, really want to know what's going to happen to the pensions department) and loss of control (the problem here is that managers want to manage and tend to feel that participative decision-making lessens their worth – it does, but don't tell them). Nevertheless, despite their misgivings, managers need to be ~~educated and cajoled~~ forced into managing participation and generating ownership properly (that is not just paying lip-service). A few early successes here can make a big difference and serve as a symbolic illustration of the power of ownership.

Forms of managing the participation process are almost innumerable. A very effective way is for a core group of initial planners either to request input from particular groups as the process progresses and/or for the core group to divide issues among themselves, task each member with identifying others needed in implementation and drawing such people into the group by testing ideas via informal discussions or more formal means of data collection (for example, surveys). Care should be taken to ensure that those participating represent a wide range of interests. If the aims are to reduce future resistance and increase the probability of implementation, we should include those with a vested interest, the culture carriers, the politically powerful as well as those functional groups or hierarchical levels who will be tasked with actually doing the work and (hopefully) taking leadership of each change.

Effective communication

Scores of varying quality management texts drone on at length about the purpose and utility of communication programmes in leveraging change, often casually mentioning the need for systematic communications (largely on the basis that everyone will need to be told about the plan to garner their support). This makes us spit blood for a number of reasons. First, communication is supposed to be two-way – a dialogue wherein both parties exchange views *and* listen. I've nothing against autocratic management and am very fond of some dictator-like managers (in academia you meet so many . . .). However, (and this is supposed to signify very loud shouting) – **NOT DURING THIS PART OF PLANNING FORMULATION/IMPLEMENTATION!** Second, if the planning process has reached this stage without *already* communicating with those who will be tasked with implementing the plan, it is doomed to failure (see earlier).

Planning communications are fundamental to our efforts to consider both formulation and implementation. Without such an iterative process, developed plans are significantly less likely to be executed in a meaningful way. In this regard, it can be argued that, typically, planners misjudge: (1) the need for communicating the necessity for change; (2) the need for communication to educate, illuminate and cajole support from others; and, arguably the most important (3) the need to facilitate the generation or plan ownership by those at the sharp end of change.

Obviously given the idiosyncratic nature of most implementations, it is impossible to provide a quick-fix, one-size-fits-all guide to effective communication (if you want one – start again at the beginning of the chapter – if you have already done this and reached here again with the same need, pass this text onto somebody else – it isn't for you – try the latest Jeffery Archer). This said, there are some issues that should be considered in most, but not all cases. The first is the need for an ongoing programme of communication. As stated above, effective communication is needed from the very earliest stages of planning (to ensure that plans are implementable). However, at the other extreme, a communication programme is also needed long after the change has been implemented – for reasons for control. The means of communication should also be considered carefully. Although impersonal media have their uses, too much generalized, superficial information is likely to generate mistrust and erode ownership. Conversely, too much individualized information may cause overload and reinvention. In this sense, implementers need to tailor their communications according to the complexity of mundaneness of the change. Finally, there is often the need to allocate the responsibility for communication to an individual. This is far from an easy, enjoyable or even exciting role. Indeed, this places somebody at the forefront of conflicts and disagreements. Consequently, many firms give this to somebody nobody likes, with little power, dandruff, six toes, body odour and frequently pretty lousy communication skills. This is not ideal. Preferably, a senior manager and executive with broad experience, social sensitivity and (if possible) personal charisma is really the individual who should be targeted.

Internal marketing

The tactic that has the potential to be the most effective during implementation (and thus the tactic that is most often poorly done) is that of internal marketing. Seductively simple in nature, internal marketing has huge potential to aid our implementation efforts, but all too frequently is poorly done by folks who think intuitively logical equates to easy (it doesn't – internal marketing is soft and squishy, but damn hard to do well). Ahmed and Rafiq (2002) argue that while there are numerous models of internal marketing, most can be considered to be grounded in the work of two original pieces. First, there are models which are largely based on the work of Leonard Berry (1981). This way of thinking about internal marketing centres on the assumption that if employees are treated as customers, this good treatment will increase employee satisfaction and thence their service mindedness. To do this means that we need to think of the tasks employees undertake as internal products, while considering the needs, wants and demands of our internal customers (employees). This contrasts with the second way of thinking about internal marketing traceable back to the work of Christian Grönroos (1985). This view argues that if service employees are to be genuinely customer conscious, the recruitment procedures, reward systems and management style of firms need to be supportive of allowing customer-contact employees discretion during service encounters to capitalize on opportunities. This focus on interactive exchange is argued to lead to better perceived service quality and ultimately higher sales and profits.

These differing views have merit and, although internal marketing has been argued to be different things by different people, the position that forwards internal marketing as the implementation for strategic marketing plans seems, by far, the most conceptually sound and (more importantly) pragmatic. Nigel Piercy and Neil Morgan, back in 1990, first presented this perspective through arguing that efforts to formulate marketing programmes for *external* customers should be developed alongside programmes designed for *internal* customers. A good way of presenting this position is shown in Figure 6.7.

Each side of marketing is important – the idea is that programmes of external marketing are critically evaluated for necessary changes, and internal marketing activities are put in place to maximize the probability of successful implementation It is also suggested that internal marketing programmes supply grounded insights back into the process of planning.

Figure 6.7 An internal marketing perspective

Source: Adapted from Piercy and Morgan (1990).

Dangerously, most marketers feel uncomfortable dealing with intra-organizational issues (after all, that's why we have ~~personnel~~ – stop it! – HR departments). Historically, the perspective of strategic marketers has been (understandably) on the external marketplace. Indeed, much of our training and most of our marketing education relentlessly expounds the virtues of outside-in perspectives, market focus and customer orientation, while warning us of marketing myopia and other such perilous predilections. While this has merit to a point, the consistently high levels of failed implementation do rather leave one with the impression that maybe, just maybe, marketers have become too hyperopically focused on extra-firm activities and grown scared of internal analysis and retrospection (it is after all easiest to stick with what we feel most comfortable with). Internal marketing requires us to turn our market-focused eye (at least briefly) away from external customers and to employ our marketing tools and techniques on those inside the organization. If we follow Piercy and Morgan's (1990) suggestions, we can even package the programmes in similar ways and using terminology with which we're comfortable (product, place, etc.). In the final analysis, nobody would argue that strategic marketers need to stop being focused on market needs and acting as the voice of the customer inside the firm. However, there is a case to argue that marketers should stop themselves being oriented towards a merely external context and struggle to position themselves, Janus-esque, with a dual internal *and* external perspective.

Political plays

Another series of implementation tactics can be loosely grouped as politically oriented. Returning to Figure 6.6 above, this presents three political tactics to drive change: tactics addressing power and politics, scaremongering and timing.

Power and politics

Real-life power can be defined as the latent ability of an individual or group to cause others to do things that otherwise they might not have done. This differs from organizational politics that centres on activities to increase power and pursue goals favourable to the individual or group. In this way, the acquisition and employment of power via internal political manoeuvring constitutes a valuable mechanism for leveraging implementation. For 30 years or more, Nigel Piercy (1989, 2008) has cleverly argued that the implementation of market-led strategic change can be achieved through the successful analysis and management of the corporate political environment. He argues that corporate culture is best understood as a political phenomenon and that an organization's culture can be operationalized through power and politics (that is, structure, information and process). Thus, he contends that the implementation of market-oriented strategy is dependent upon the management of internal power and politics as symbols of culture.

Management texts replete with lists of the sources of power within organizations are well documented. Of particular interest to implementers are power derived from formal authority (also known as legitimate authority), information control, indispensability, control over rewards (including everything from career progression to remuneration to who decides the size of expense accounts), referent power, expertise and success (power accruing to winners). Each of these is a source of power that can be pursued, gained and subsequently employed via politics to achieve our ends. This process necessarily involves an analysis of existing power structures and often illuminates the real powers in the organization.

All this power needs to be used via the dirty world of organizational politics. Personally and professionally, we have always favoured Machiavelli's three principles (although Lloyd has always struggled with the third – Kate).

- First, establish whether you are sufficiently strong to stand alone or need the help of others.
- Second, achieve successes to keep those around you uncertain and occupied.
- Third, cherish those with power, but also ensure that the rabble do not hate you.

These principles of politics give rise to innumerable political mechanisms to facilitate change. In a study, Harris and Ogbonna (2006) looked at the tactics that can be applied for personal gain, and we have adapted them below to encompass individual and group gain. These tactics highlight how political manoeuvring can be used to construct power bases, overcome resistance and accomplish compliance.

- *Obligation creation and exploitation*: a focus on purposefully forming, maintaining and taking advantage of perceived indebtedness.
- *Personal-status enhancement*: the approach of intentionally improving the perceived standing or position of an individual, group or function relative to others.
- *Information acquisition and control*: the careful collection of pertinent and advantageous information and its judicious control to the perceived benefit of an individual, group or function.
- *Similarity exploitation*: a focus on deliberately taking advantage of similarities with others (almost exclusively influential superordinates) for the purpose of gain.
- *Proactive vertical alignment*: the deliberate search, identification, pursuit and development of close personal relationships with individuals in positions of authority or influence to enhance individual, group or function gain.

These five tactics provide a starting point from which those seeking change can leverage their position to the point where implementation is not only politically desirable but also an advantageous political mechanism.

Judicious scaremongering

Deliberate, judicious scaremongering can be viewed as the *riposte* of planners to the efforts of anti-planners (or indeed anyone else) to damage the credibility of change. This tactic for implementation is strongly political in nature and involves an individual or group, overtly or surreptitiously promoting a series of future scenarios all of which are negative for the organization, groups or even particular individuals. However, this approach is also cleverly cultural in origin in that it focuses on the controlled creation/publication of cultural *crises*.

It has previously been argued that most changes grind against the existing culture and climate of a firm. However, Martin (2002) builds on earlier work persuasively to note that cultures are especially susceptible to manipulation (even at the highest cognitive levels) during periods of crises (ranging from leadership turnover to financial crisis – particularly useful given the current economic climate). The logic for creating/stressing crises is that (with appropriate and well-timed action) either the desired change will become highlighted as a solution (or part-solution) to the crisis, a previously unacceptable change will become more palatable (and thus less resisted) or planners can suggest desired changes as potential resolutions to the looming predicament. Innumerable crises can be used in this way including, the prospective loss of major clients, plummeting customer satisfaction/loyalty levels (interestingly, the statistics for which should be generated and controlled by marketers), the probable loss of senior personnel, fears of sector-wide structural changes and the establishment or the expansion or failure of major competitors.

Timing considerations

Linked to judicious scaremongering and other political ploys to create crises is the issue of timing during implementation efforts. While our goals and objectives are (hopefully) long-term, the implementation of change is, more commonly, about the here-and-now. Assume that we are at the stage where we have generated implementable plans and that the organization is enthused about the planned change. At this juncture, consideration should be given to the symbolic and practical impact of visible successes. Ultimately, the aim is to implement all of the planned changes. However, during the early stages of change, attention should be paid to the need for achieving quick and noticeable successes.

Lots of early successes can create a tsunami (what us oldies call a 'tidal wave') effect and drive later changes through more easily. So, to maintain enthusiasm and counter resistance, it is really important that conspicuous accomplishments are not only made but that the results are also disseminated across the organization. This should not rely on luck, but should be the result of careful planning and timing – although luck is good too! The aim here is *explicitly* to demonstrate that the planned changes are: (1) achievable (thus raising the credibility of the plan and the moral authority of those involved in the change); (2) beneficial to the firm and (where possible) employees; and (3) are directly linked to the implemented changes (adding to the perceived value of the change programme). Such changes should be designed to provide symbols of the aims of change, generate focus and aid in the process of garnering commitment and gaining momentum.

Obviously, timing considerations should also encompass tactical issues regarding the scheduling or initiation of change. Marketers have long since recognized that there are some changes that, while desirable, are at certain times not politically expedient. Nigel Piercy and Ken Peattie back in (1988) refer to a number of tactics of implementation that involve judicious timing (one being waiting for eventual cultural change, another being the application of political 'grease' as a precursor to change). In Harris (2000) evidence is also found that, for some firms, a wait-and-see or *laissez-faire* approach can be sensible for some elements of change. That is, rather than attempting to force change, where change is unlikely, pro-planning individuals wait for an appropriate moment to suggest the need for the desired change. This ploy was often in anticipation that future events would supply a propitious time (such as the loss of a major client) for such a proposal. It is important that this tactic is not confused with not responding to change. A decision or course of 'action', which centres on simply ignoring the pressures for change is clearly unwise and likely to meet with failure. In contrast, the *laissez-faire* tactical response involves a conscious decision by an individual or group that responding to the pressure for change is inappropriate *at that current time* since the attempt at change would be *more* damaging. Hence, firms adopting a *laissez-faire* response frequently argued that change in the near future was needed, but at present, environmental or organizational contingencies were not propitious.

Management resource

Success implementation pivots on managing people. Returning once again to Figure 6.6 we can see three management tactics to drive change: tactics addressing budgeting and reward, recruitment and empowerment.

Budgeting and reward systems

A consistent argument throughout this chapter has been that for plans to be implemented successfully, then congruence is needed within the existing context of the firm (note congruence does not necessarily denote subservience). Budgets and reward systems are particularly important artefacts of culture that can form monumental obstacles to change. Judson (1996: 183) addresses this topic and eloquently contends that budgets are often insufficiently considered during the development of plans, leading to post-formulation conflict where, 'in most organizations, the budget is a more deeply entrenched and respected than strategic and operational planning. Thus it is the budget that prevails and the plan that suffers'. Consequently, Judson (1996) argues that firms should adopt the radical idea of basing budgets on strategy. This may sound obvious to students of marketing strategy, who will assume that corporations who bother to plan for their future will budget accordingly. However, despite much screaming and shouting, even today, this is often almost always the opposite of the case! A strategy-based budgeting system entails setting a minimum baseline budget for each function/department followed by a process of costs and returns analysis for each action programme supporting the strategy and operating plans. Thereafter, for each strategy (and action programme), expenses and revenues are totalled for each department and layered on top of the baseline. This process should assist greatly in ensuring that functions have the resources needed for change and thus for getting change to happen.

Reward systems are also highlighted by Judson (1996) as important mechanisms in facilitating the implementation of strategic change. Regrettably, strategic marketers, typically, think that 'reward systems' are entirely systems of financial compensation. Monetary rewards are important, but should be considered merely an element of reward. There are far fewer forms of direct compensation (salaries, bonuses, stock options, profit sharing, etc.) than forms of intrinsic rewards (job enrichment, redesign, etc.), let alone indirect forms of compensation (largely preferred treatments). These forms or rewards are a potentially abundant source of rewards for those involved in planning and implementing change and, as such, form a powerful lever of bribes, enticements, sweeteners and incentives for encouraging (and thus managing) the implementation of change. We appreciate here that we're stepping on the toes of the HR ~~Dictators~~ Department. However, given the mess they've made of bank bonuses, executive pay, etc. – surely the marketing department can't be worse at it than they are?

Recruitment/HR interface

Early in his career, Lloyd once attended a conference where a senior professor was bemoaning the problems of implementing change, noting that getting change to happen really all goes wrong, because 'implementing changes involves people'. This, seemingly trite, insight is not as superficial as you would think. One would hope that those in strategic marketing functions are astute observers and managers of human nature (after all our job is largely to be focused on customers). Unfortunately, our experience of, all too many, planning groups is that this is far from the case (in fact, most are socially inadequate, twitchy types who really should get out more). These observations and arguments have led a whole bunch of commentators to contend that the marketing/ HR interface is crucial to successful implementation efforts (a great example of a well-written and interesting text being that of Piercy 1998).

Chimhanzi (2004) provides an academic study of the marketing-HR interface and argues that marketers need to focus on HR issues. Unfortunately, while there are a plethora of studies looking into the interaction of marketing with R&D, manufacturing, engineering and sales (see Chimhanzi 2004), very few studies have concentrated on the marketing/HR relationship. Although many reasons have been cited for this gap, personally I think it is because (deep down) we are resentful that personnel departments got all snotty on us and started calling themselves human resource directorates (I have suggested previously that to redress this imbalance, we rebrand ourselves as the strategic marketing overlords – this has yet to meet universal acceptance). More realistically, if we accept that marketing's interaction with HR can assist in levering change, attention must be paid to this interface. Jackie Chimhanzi (2004) looks at just this issue. She theorizes that the extent of formal and informal connectedness, communication and conflict are linked with marketing strategy implementation effectiveness. While the empirical results were a little confused, the central argument appears valid; if we can improve this interface, then our skills are likely to improve and our HR systems and procedures are likely to assist our efforts to change rather than hinder them. As such, HR systems can provide a useful and powerful mechanism to leverage change. The HR function in most firms forms a key channel of communication and education. New candidates can be screened for desired skills or espoused attitudes. Induction processes acculturize new employees into the espoused way of thinking and doing things. Training processes can be realigned or refocused to concentrate on the change objectives (ranging from encouraging a customer orientation to training customer-contact employees in how to be responsive to deviant consumer behaviour). Appraisal and mentoring systems can be used to gauge employee achievements and satisfaction. The opportunities are endless, but are all contingent on ensuring that the ~~personnel~~ HR function engages and collaborates with the implementation process. It is worth noting that the engagement of HR is significantly enhanced if this involvement and cooperation begins right at the very start of the planning process. In this sense, the utility of the HR interface in generating change is linked to the extent to which such issues are considered during the concurrent processes of plan formulation and implementation.

Enriching and empowering employees

Overwhelmingly, it is acknowledged that the way in which firms treat their employees is the same manner in which employees will treat customers in return. Therefore, satisfied, enthusiastic and empowered employees are crucial to the success of strategy implementation. After all, these are the guys on the frontline who have to 'do' all of the fancy plans envisaged in the board room, while simultaneously serving moody customers and keeping out of the firing line of their harassed line manager who is under pressure to perform from their own manager (and thus the hierarchy continues). Jackson and Sirianni (2009) argue that employees cannot enthuse about meeting the needs of customers if their own needs are not first being met by the organization. Thus, investment in frontline employee development is money well spent. Employee empowerment involves moving (at least some) decision-making and power down the organizational hierarchy, so that those working on the frontline of organizations are able to act in a more autonomous fashion and perform their jobs effectively. When done in a genuine manner (as opposed to only allowing employees to organize their own lunch breaks), employee empowerment results in increased levels of employee performance and satisfaction and reduces levels of employee stress and burnout. The double whammy outlined by the service profit chain (Heskett *et al.* 1994) is that such positive employee effects relay to customers, and greater levels of customer satisfaction and loyalty are experienced. In identifying a number of components of employee development, Jackson and Sirianni (2009) highlight six action points, of particular interest of which are mentoring, job enrichment, job rotation and training programmes.

Obviously, mentoring involves a more experienced person taking a less experienced person under their wing with the aim of supporting that individual. However, rather than simply elbowing two people together based on the number of years served, the most successful mentoring relationships are based on mutuality. That is, the mentor and mentee have personal traits and goals in common and both benefit from the mentor-mentee relationships. Thus, while it is beneficial to have a formal mentoring programme in place, how mentor and mentee relationships are best formed and performed is a worthy area for consideration. Having a mentor programme in place alone does not guarantee enriched or empowered employees.

Likewise, job enrichment is described by Jackson and Sirianni (2009: 285) as occurring when 'managers give their employees increases in job responsibilities and variety of tasks in order to provide challenges and motivation'. While this sounds much like the activities enacted by the keepers at Monkey World (including providing the apes with blankets and tasks to retrieve food from hard to reach places – much like a scene from a staff room with a vending machine), the aim of such endeavours is to increase employees' levels of empowerment. Thus, enriching employees' jobs reduces the monotony of day-to-day life and creates happier employees (and customers).

Built in job rotation enables employees to experience various jobs within the organization. Not only does this create an opportunity for employees to gain new skills and knowledge of the broader functions of the firm but when all levels of the hierarchy engage with the scheme, it can result in powerful outcomes. Too often, employees on the frontline feel that those making corporate decisions in fancy glass offices know nothing of their daily trials on the frontline. Too often, managers in fancy offices think that those on the frontline have it easy. Bringing these two worlds together by managers spending time working on the frontline allows managers to see what is really going on and indicates to those on the frontline that management care and understand their plight. Separation fosters hostility, mutual understanding fosters a healthy working environment (or so we are told).

Ultimately, we should also consider training programmes, as an obvious, but essential lever. There is nothing more frustrating from the customer's perspective of interacting with an employee who does not know what they are doing. There is also nothing more demoralizing and demotivating from an employee's perspective as performing tasks or roles without having the foggiest idea what they are doing. Training helps employees to grow (metaphorically, not in height) and aids in the provision of high service quality (which keeps customers happy). Thus, the key theme from our discussion on enriching and empowering employees is that investing in your employees is investing in the success of your firm.

Culture-oriented tactics

The three culture-oriented tactics to drive change in Figure 6.6 are tactics addressing service culture, routines and symbolism.

Developing a (more) service-oriented culture

Quintessentially, putting customers (both internal and external) at the core of any business is a key factor to success. It's generally accepted that firms who embody market-oriented cultures are more successful than organizations that are rigid and internally focused. However, as is discussed above, cultural change is difficult and Harris and Ogbonna (2000) document seven different ways in which employees respond to market-oriented culture change programmes. Their findings range from employees refusal to accept change (and thus withdraw and/or actively campaign against the change), to confusion, to feigned acceptance (doing one thing, but thinking another), to genuine acceptance and compliance with the cultural change initiatives. Moving beyond the development of a market-oriented culture and in light of the dominance of the service economy in many developing and developed nations, Bitner and Brown (2008) introduce 'the service imperative'.

With great insight, Bitner and Brown (2008) argue that organizations must find ways in which to be competitive in a service-dominated world. At the heart of the service imperative is the need for firms to embed service research and service innovation within their organizational cultures (that is stopping thinking about products as being the main assets of firms and switch attention to service). The authors highlight various ways in which firms can compete through service, indicating the need for service to be ingrained in organizational culture. First, is providing customers with exemplary customer service. This goes beyond service with a smile – companies who truly master this (and arguably there are only a few), base the very core of their business on going all out for customers and providing customer service in unique ways. It's not what they do, it's who they are (and all that jazz). Second, it is argued that success can be achieved for firms who are truly at the forefront of new service innovations in their industry. Such innovations do not occur solely because of the efforts of the research and design team, but rather, all employees, no matter what their role contribute to the identification of service gaps. Innovations do not necessarily need to be a totally new invention, but rather can be new to the industry or context. However, they should be centred on customers' needs and wants. For example, Amazon revolutionized online shopping with their easy to navigate shopping basket (and in doing so spawned a whole new generation of shopaholics).

Going forward, Bitner and Brown (2008) also discuss services as revenue-producing offerings in non-service industries. Here, they recognize that many firms in manufacturing and other non-service industries have in recent years introduced value-added services that by themselves produce revenues (as opposed to just regurgitating the same old product in a new colour, flavour or design). In a service-dominated world an integrated marketing mix containing both product and service offerings is argued to constitute the way forward. The authors document firms, including IBM, who have experienced tremendous growth via the adoption of this strategy. However, in order to be successful, an understanding of the customer and their current and latent needs must underpin the organization and its cultural manifestations. Next, focusing specifically on the issue of culture itself, it is argued that a service culture must be one that differentiates. This isn't just in the mind of the customer, but importantly it should differentiate itself in the mindset of the workforce. In doing so, the firm attracts the best calibre of employee, because it's a place where people want to work – why do you think that Google is so successful?! This goes back to the service profit chain (Heskett *et al.* 1994) in creating a culture within which the best and brightest employees want to work and the finest services are developed, which in turn promotes customer satisfaction and loyalty.

Evidently, firms can also compete in the service-dominant world via technology-delivered and technology-enabled services. Here, by embracing new technological developments, firms can now serve customers who were previously unreachable and employ previously untenable business models. For example, the internet has revolutionized how folk purchase holidays and the kinds of vacations that they take. No longer must one sit through an hour of the clack-clack of a travel agent smeared in bronzer trying to find you the best 'deal', but now you are free to build your travels to suit what you want and when you want it with the help of sites such as Expedia. In some cases, technological innovations enable firms to shift service production to their customers through self-service technologies (as customers we seem to love this; take self-service checkouts at supermarkets, we blindly queue to serve ourselves for no financial gain, but rather take some form of enjoyment in playing shop by zapping the barcode across the flickering red light and waiting for the all-important 'beep'). Thus, fostering a strong service culture is argued to be essential to organizational success in a future dominated by the production and consumption of services.

Changing routines, rites and rituals

The routines, rites and rituals of a firm are akin to organizational-specific behavioural habits that reflect 'what we do around here'. These behavioural routines are incredibly ingrained in most organizations and act as key barriers to change as managers grow ever more committed to the comfort of the *status quo* (see Geletkanycz 1997). The behavioural patterns of employees at work serve a number of different functions. However, most importantly, such behaviours are manifestations of influence and status (see Ott 1997) and, as such, are powerful levers for change. Not only does changing how people behave during work alter the, 'way we do things around here' but some commentators believe that, over time, what we do affects what we think. For example, the implementation of recycling and waste reduction programmes in the workplace increases employee awareness of green issues and results in employees having stronger positive attitudes (and behaviours) towards green habits both inside and outside of the workplace.

Simply because employees are doing what management espouse (at least while they are looking), it doesn't mean that their attitudes have changed (the world is full of people who say one thing and think another). However, a number of scholars have argued that enforced or compulsory changes to behaviours can act as a physical impetus to trigger reflective questioning of existing beliefs, values and even basic assumptions (see Hatch 1993). Humans are creatures of habit and traditionally dislike change. However, once the benefits of change are experienced, individuals' can be quick to engage in the creation of yet further change. For example, a well-known restaurant implemented a new customer feedback system. The employees initially hated it believing that 'big brother' was further encroaching on their working lives. However, once the benefits of the scheme were realized (increased employee perks, rewards and recognition), employees engaged with the scheme and developed improvements and developments to the scheme that were subsequently implemented. While planners typically prefer to think about so-called 'high-level' strategy and leave the petty *minutiae* to subsequent stages of implementation, the folly of such a position has previously been highlighted during the discussion of the formulation–implementation dichotomy.

Ultimately, planning should uncover the key success factors and aims of change; planners should also encompass operational issues, which will involve alterations to the routines, rites, rituals and ceremonies of employees (i.e. what is done at the frontline). It is at this level that a strategy is operationalized into changes that affect how things are done. So, two issues are imperative here.

First, those at operational levels (or certainly intimate knowledge of this level) should be involved in the planning process to ground changes in organizational reality and identify the behavioural patterns that require changing (in simple terms, the planner needs to know the 'real' organization, not just what is written in the annual company report). Second, once changes are identified, individuals need to be given the responsibility of not only ensuring that the changes occur but also that the changes are maintained (i.e. it's no good making recommendations of change in a written report alone, individuals need to take ownership of the change and monitor such efforts to ensure that the plans become part of the daily business). Hence, the success of such changes are, in part, contingent on concurrent control and surveillance systems to monitor performance.

Attention to symbols and symbolic meaning

Purist marketers will be uncomfortable reading about symbols (which to most marketers are the only musical instruments they were allowed to play in the school orchestra or something in the television series *Lost*). However, symbols are important – more important than you think. Symbols can be thought of as artefacts, events or actions that connote meanings greater than their intrinsic content. That is, they are imbibed with subjective meaning, which, in an organizational context, becomes shared as a natural outcome of human social interaction. Such issues are important since symbols constitute an important means through which we form our beliefs, attitudes and even our basic assumptions about our working lives. Thus, from a symbolic perspective, Smircich and Morgan (1982) argue that, 'the key challenge for a leader is to manage meaning in such a way that individuals orient themselves to the achievement of desirable ends'. In this regard, symbols and the management of symbolic meaning form an important lever through which change can be implemented.

Most marketers ignore symbols, but Turner and Spencer (1997) examine just this issue. They argue that while symbolic meaning can be found in a plethora of forms, language, stories, ceremonies and physical symbols were those that could most easily be employed to facilitate change. In terms of language, the terminology and tone used by planners and change agents sends out important and multi-layered signals about a desired change and can have a key impact on subsequent interpretations of change efforts. For example, many professional service providers go to extreme lengths to avoid the term 'customers' (they have 'clients', 'patrons' or 'patients'). Imagine the symbolic impact of a CEO of a hospital banning the word 'patient' and replacing it with 'customer'. Second, language is not limited to the spoken word. The language of an espoused vision or mission should be designed to epitomize the values and aspirations of an organization (and therefore should have a 'yeah' rather than a 'yuck' factor). Stories are also a powerful lever for change. Theoretically based on true events (but more often devised by astute managers), stories convey meaning and can serve as illustrations of the espoused values of a firm. Thus, shrewd storytelling via newsletters, bulletin boards or emails can be used to highlight and bring to life espoused corporate values. Here, a 'real-life' event that readers can relate to or that they may have experienced is used to illustrate a deeper meaning or issue.

Yearly, monthly or even weekly organizational ceremonies are conscious celebrations of the beliefs and values inherent in a culture. As such, these events are ideal for communicating and reinforcing values and generating shared meaning. Big events (annual company meetings or regional conferences) and small events (training sessions and induction) alike can be utilized to inspire or reinforce championed organizational virtues. Finally, physical symbols can also be used to trigger change. For example, during the recent times of economic hardship one company that we studied made a point of ensuring that all employees, regardless of status or pay grade, drove the same model and make of car and had the same office furnishings, thus symbolizing that they were all in it together and that no one was more important to the overall functioning of the firm than anyone else.

Summary and conclusions

No single chapter or text can cover all of the issues involved in implementation. Implementing strategic change is simply too complicated, too messy and too damn easy to get wrong. However, in this chapter we have tried to provide a good, practical overview of some of the core issues.

Our chapter began with a series of observations and theories that developed the case that implementing strategic change is difficult and, all too frequently, prone to failure. First, to explore these issues, we emphasized that the wrongful separation of plan formulation and implementation is a common cause of complications experienced during implementation. Accordingly, the arguments of a number of commentators were synthesized and the formulation–implementation dichotomy highlighted as a serious cause of difficulties. Subsequently, in order to elucidate the main issues involved in implementing strategic change, we examined two broad issues. First, we focused on why and how attempts to implement change go wrong. Rather than assume that resistance to change is irrational, a range of rationales for resisting change was explored. This process revealed that many individuals resist change for reasons that are logical and understandable from their own perspective. This led to a discussion of how both individuals and groups react behaviourally to change initiatives and consciously or unconsciously resist the efforts of planners. Finally, the outcomes of such efforts were examined and the range of unexpected or unanticipated outcomes of change highlighted. The second half of the chapter concentrated on identifying suggested levers for change. In this sense, the latter half of the chapter is an effort to supply marketers with tools to overcome or bypass the problems raised in the first half.

So, in conclusion, this chapter has attempted to identify and underscore both *how* and *why* change goes wrong. As a discipline, we concentrate too much on the functional – what goes right, what should be the best way, etc. This is okay and understandable. However, this focus is often detrimental to generating a genuine understanding of why we get things wrong, why our beautiful plans are rejected and our carefully computer-modelled changes are met with derision. If we are truly interested in success, we must first delve into the less glamorous, less prestigious and definitely less comfortable world of failure.

Efforts to improve our implementation efforts are focused in the latter half of this chapter, which forwards a series of levers for implementing change as well as a potential package for many of them. However, it must be stressed that these are only suggestions. There are no quick-fix, universally-applicable solutions. Each change is limited by context, and each context is individual and idiosyncratic. Hence, levers for change *must* be tailored and customized for each bespoke eventuality.

Further reading

Ahmed, P. K. and Raqiq, M. (2002), *Internal Marketing: Tools and Concepts for Customer-Focused Management*, Oxford, UK: Butterworth-Heinemann. An interesting text that focuses on the concept of internal marketing. To my mind the first three chapters are the most conceptually illuminating, although there are also a number of case studies that are insightful. The authors go into detail about both of the perspectives on internal marketing mentioned in the text and supply a hybrid version that seems logical, albeit, rather complex.

Harris, L. C. (2000), 'Getting professionals to plan: Pressures, obstacles and tactical responses', *Long Range Planning*, 33(6): 849–877. This is a study of the difficulties of getting planning started in the context of professional services firms. It provides some useful insights into the pressures, barriers and approaches that can be adopted to make planning happen.

Harris, L. C. (2002), 'Sabotaging market-orientated culture change: An exploration of resistance justifications and approaches', *Journal of Marketing Theory and Practice*, 10(3): 58–75. This is a qualitative study of how and why managers in firms attempt to resist efforts to develop a market-oriented culture. The literature review provides a useful introduction to market orientation and also deals with issues of cultural manipulation.

Harris, L. C. and Ogbonna, E. (2000), 'The responses of front-line employees to market oriented culture change', *European Journal of Marketing*, 34(3/4): 318–340. This is a qualitative study of how customer-contact employees react to efforts to change their ways of thinking about work and their ways of doing work. Plotting willingness to change and pre-existing subcultural strength on axes, nine reactions to change are described. A useful way of thinking about the probable responses of employees to change efforts.

Harris, L. C. and Ogbonna, E. (2006), 'The initiation of strategic planning: An empirical investigation of antecedent factors', *Journal of Business Research*, 59(1): 100–111. This builds on two earlier qualitative studies, both in the *Journal of Strategic Marketing* in 1996. This later study presents the results of a survey into the barriers to getting planning started. While this isn't directly about the implementation of change, it seems to me that firms often have equal difficulties in starting the process.

Hatch, M. J. (1993), 'The dynamics of organizational culture', *Academy of Management Review*, 18(4): 657–693. Although this article is a little dated, the perspective forwarded remains fresh and deeply illuminating. Much of this chapter has alluded directly or indirectly to the concept of organizational culture. In this paper, the components and dynamics of culture are identified and elucidated by one of the world's leading culture experts.

Judson, A. S. (1996), *Making Strategy Happen: Transforming Plans into Reality*, Oxford, UK: Blackwell. A very good text with many practical insights into the formulation/implementation issue. The first four chapters are dedicated to explaining why plans fail and the remainder of the text details a series of suggestions for how successful and implementable plans can be generated.

Piercy, N. F. (2008), *Market-Led Strategic Change: Transforming the Process of Going to Market*, Oxford, UK: Butterworth-Heinemann. This fourth edition of *MLSC* is an incredibly useful text that provides practitioners and students of marketing with useful and illuminating insights into the practical dynamics of getting marketing to happen. This and earlier editions certainly shaped my perspective on what strategic marketing is and should be and definitely were important in shaping my early writing on planning initiation that is clearly grounded in this tradition.

Turner, G. B. and Spencer, B. (1997), 'Understanding the marketing concept as organizational culture', *European Journal of Marketing*, 31(2): 110–121. This is a conceptual examination of how we can understand the concept of marketing as a multi-faceted organizational culture. Adopting an organizational symbolism perspective, this paper provides practical insights into how managers can use symbols to leverage change.

References

Ahmed, P. K. and Rafiq, M. (2002), *Internal Marketing: Tools and Concepts for Customer-Focused Management*, Oxford, UK: Butterworth-Heinemann.

Berry, L. L. (1981), 'The employee as customer', *Journal of Retailing Banking*, 3: 25–28.

Bitner, M. J. and Brown, S. W. (2008), 'The service imperative', *Business Horizons*, 51(1): 39–46.

Buchanan, D. A. and Badham, R. (1999), *Power, Politics, and Organizational Change: Winning the Turf Game*, London: Sage Publications.

Cespedes, F. V. and Piercy, N. F. (1996), 'Implementing marketing strategy', *Journal of Marketing Management*, 12(1): 135–160.

Chimhanzi, J. (2004), 'The impact of marketing/HR interactions on marketing strategy implementation', *European Journal of Marketing*, 38(1/2): 73–98.

Dandridge, T. C., Mitroff, I. and Joyce, W. F. (1980), 'Organizational symbolism: A topic to expand organizational analysis', *Academy of Management Review*, 5(1): 77–82.

Day, G. S. (1999), *The Market Driven Organization: Understanding, Attracting and Keeping Valuable Customers*, New York: The Free Press.

Gabriel, Y. (1999), 'Beyond happy families: A critical reevaluation of the control-resistance-identity triangle', *Human Relations*, 52(2): 179–203.

Geletkanycz, M. A. (1997), 'The salience of "culture's consequences": The effects of cultural values on top executive commitment to the status quo', *Strategic Management Journal*, 18(8): 615–634.

Griffin, R. W., O'Leary-Kelly, A. and Collins, J. (1998), 'Dysfunctional work behaviors in organizations', in Cooper, C. L. and Rousseau, D. M. (eds) *Trends in Organizational Behavior*, volume 5, New York: John Wiley, pp. 66–82.

Grönroos, C. (1985), 'Internal marketing: Theory and practice', *American Marketing Association's Services Conference Proceedings*, pp. 41–47.

Harris, L. C. (1996), 'The impediments to initiating planning', *Journal of Strategic Marketing*, 4(2): 129–142.

Harris, L. C. (1998), 'Cultural domination: The key to a market oriented culture?', *European Journal of Marketing*, 32(3/4): 354–373.

Harris, L. C. (2000), 'Getting professionals to plan: Pressures, obstacles and tactical responses', *Long Range Planning*, 33(6): 849–877.

Harris, L. C. (2002a), 'Sabotaging market-orientated culture change: An exploration of resistance justifications and approaches', *Journal of Marketing Theory and Practice*, 10(3): 58–75.

Harris, L. C. (2002b), 'Developing market orientation: An exploration of management approaches', *Journal of Marketing Management*, 18(7/8): 603–632.

Harris, L. C. and Ogbonna, E. (2000), 'The responses of front-line employees to market-oriented culture change', *European Journal of Marketing*, 34(3/4): 318–340.

Harris, L. C. and Ogbonna, E. (2002), 'The unintended consequences of culture interventions: A study of unexpected outcomes', *British Journal of Management*, 13(1): 31–50.

Harris, L. C. and Ogbonna, E. (2006), 'Approaches to career success: An exploration of covert, clandestine, and concealed strategies', *Human Resource Management*, 45(1): 43–66.

Harrison, J. R. and Carrol, G. R. (1991), 'Keeping the faith: A model of cultural transmission in formal organizations', *Administrative Science Quarterly*, 36(3): 552–582.

Hatch, M. J. (1993), 'The dynamics of organizational culture', *Academy of Management Review*, 18(4): 657–693.

Heskett, J. L., Jones, T. O., Loveman, G. W., Earl Sasser, W. and Schlesinger, L. A. (1994), 'Putting the service-profit chain to work', *Harvard Business Review*, 72(2): 164–174.

Hoskin, R. and Wood, S. (1993), 'Overcoming strategic planning disconnects', *Journal for Quality and Participation*, 16(4): 50–58.

Jackson, D. W. Jr. and Sirianni, N. J. (2009), 'Building the bottom line by developing the frontline: Career development for service employees', *Business Horizons*, 52(3): 279–287.

Judson, A. S. (1996), *Making Strategy Happening: Transforming Plans into Reality*, Oxford, UK: Blackwell.

Kolz, A. R. (1999), 'Personality predictors of retail employee theft and counterproductive behavior', *Journal of Professional Services Marketing*, 19(2): 107–114.

Legge, K. (1994), 'Managing culture: Fact or fiction', in Sisson, K. (ed.) *Personnel Management: A Comprehensive Guide to Theory and Practice in Britain*, Oxford, UK: Blackwell, pp. 397–433.

Martin, J. (2002), *Organizational Culture: Mapping the Terrain*, London: Sage.

Narver, J. C., Slater, S. F. and Tietje, B. (1998), 'Creating a market orientation', *Journal of Market Focused Management*, 2(3): 241–255.

Ogbonna, E. (1993), 'Managing organizational culture: Fantasy or reality?', *Human Resource Management Journal*, 3(2): 42–54.

Ott, J. S. (1997), *The Organizational Culture Perspective*, Chicago, IL: Dorsey Press.

Piercy, N. F. (1989), 'Marketing concepts and actions: Implementing market-led strategic change', *European Journal of Marketing*, 24(2): 24–42.

Piercy, N. F. (1998), 'Marketing implementation: The implications of marketing paradigm weakness for the strategy execution process', *Journal of the Academy of Marketing Science*, 26(3): 222–236.

Piercy, N. F. (2008), *Market-Led Strategic Change: Transforming the Process of Going to Market*, Oxford, UK: Butterworth-Heinemann.

Piercy, N. F. and Peattie, K. J. (1988), 'Matching marketing strategies to corporate culture: The parcel and the wall', *Journal of General Management*, 13(4): 33–44.

Piercy, N. F. and Morgan, N. (1990), 'Internal marketing strategy: Leverage for managing marketing-led strategic change', *Irish Marketing Review*, 4(3): 11–38.

Smircich, L. and Morgan, G. (1982), 'Leadership: The management of meaning', *The Journal of Applied Behavioral Science*, 18(3): 257–273.

Turner, G. B. and Spencer, B. (1997), 'Understanding the marketing concept as organizational culture', *European Journal of Marketing*, 31(2): 110–121.

Part II
The framework of marketing

7 Consumer behaviour

Mark Gabbott and Gill Hogg

As long ago as 1776 Adam Smith in his *Wealth of Nations* recognized the vital importance of consumers to market economies, famously stating that 'consumption is the sole end and purpose of all production' (Smith 1776: 719). We all consume and therefore understanding how and why consumers make choices, what motivates these decisions and how they are implemented, is central to marketing. Without consumers exercising choice, there would be no markets; there would no need for marketing. The study of consumer behaviour guides our understanding of how consumers will react to a new product offering, a new advertising campaign, the introduction, or withdrawal, of a service. Consumer behaviour informs the way governments and policy makers act, for example, to decide the format and provision of food labelling, the introduction of restrictions on gambling, the design and execution of road safety campaigns or the delivery of improved health care. It underpins the design of consumption spaces, for example, shopping centres, restaurants even web pages on the internet; it is central to cultural events, the entertainment industry and most importantly the democratic process. There is no part of twenty-first century life that does not rely on an understanding of people, and how and why they consume. An understanding of consumer behaviour, therefore, is central to marketing.

By way of definition, consumer behaviour is the study of individuals, groups or organizations and the processes they use to select, secure, use and dispose of goods, services, experiences and ideas, which are associated with the satisfaction of their needs. It also includes consideration of the impact of these processes upon consumers, organizations and society in general. It is very difficult to succinctly describe consumer behaviour, as it comprises a multitude of different sub-components, which, depending upon how you configure them, can provide quite contrasting understandings. The economic behaviourist has a very different explanation of how consumers operate in the economy when compared to a psychologist, sociologist or anthropologist. Yet, these perspectives are all valid interpretations of what is known about consumers. Much like natural science, the study of consumer behaviour has been the subject of constant revision, with early assumptions and understandings being challenged by a series of crises of falsification (a process observed by Kuhn 1962). Simply, what we thought we knew did not match with what we observed and, as a result, we needed new explanations.

The problem is how to reflect what is known about consumer behaviour without adopting a particular theoretical stance through selection or exclusion. In order to attempt to maintain objectivity, this chapter will be structured around three perspectives or paradigms, each providing its own illumination on consumption behaviour. The first is a focus upon the individual and the internal psychological processes associated with consumption. The second approach seeks to understand consumption by viewing the individual not as an isolated decision-maker, but as a social being subject to influence from others. Finally, the third perspective sees consumers as reactive to context and consumption environments. We will consider each perspective separately, but as each one is an important part of understanding and appreciating the complexity of consumer behaviour, each approach should also be viewed as acting in concert.

Before considering each of these paradigms, it is worth a brief digression to consider the history of consumer behaviour as a way of introducing some of the main ideas and explaining how they fit into these three perspectives.

Historical roots of the discipline

There is a tendency to attribute the rise of the so-called consumer society as a twentieth-century phenomenon, fuelled by the mass production of goods and the rise in affluence that allowed consumers to consume not from necessity, but through choice. In tracing the history of consumption, however, McCracken (1988) traces the politics of consumption back to the court of Elizabeth I. Elizabeth insisted her nobles attend court and indeed took her court to them as she toured her realm. In order to stand out at court and to find favour with the Queen and be the recipient of royal largesse, the aristocracy needed to find ways to stand out, to be noticed. This fundamentally changed the nature of demand, particularly with regard to clothing and household goods; an indication of social status based not on heritage and patina, but fashion, a demand for the 'new' that indicted wealth and prosperity. Consumption became part of the politics of power and the dawn of the material culture.

Another important change in the nature of the consumer society was driven by the economics, rather than politics, of the eighteenth century. The industrial revolution, with an explosion of mass production, required mass consumption. This is the emergence of advertising and mass marketing, an acknowledgement that fashion and social status are bound together by the creation of demand for goods not only for their utility value but for the message they send (Corrigan 1998). The rise of the consumer society and the professionalization of marketing emphasized the need to develop an increasingly sophisticated understanding of consumers. Hence, we turn to the origins of contemporary consumer research.

Academic research in consumer behaviour prior to 1945 was based upon a philosophy, which is consistent with market-based economics. In accepting neo-classical economic models, individuals were assumed to be calculating, rational and self-motivated. More specifically, the assumptions about consumers within the neo-classical tradition were focused upon three key drivers of behaviour (see Ackerman 1997):

1   asocial individualism: consumers' desires and preferences were not affected by social or economic institutions, interactions with others or the observation of others' consumption;
2   insatiability: that a consumer has a multiplicity of insatiable material desires, the more 'goods' we consume the more satisfied we are and that provides the innate motivation to consume;
3   commodity orientation: consumer preferences consist of well-informed desires for specific goods and services, they have perfect knowledge of all that is available to them.

Clearly, these assumptions were not tenable in any real sense, but it was not until post-1945 that a number of influential authors started to challenge the assumptions directly, most notably Duesenberry (1949), Leibenstein (1950) and Galbraith (1958). Their economic commentary recognized that consumers were not asocial, but that social factors had a marked impact upon their consumption decisions. This thread of thinking added to the already substantial criticism of insatiability put forward by Marshall (1920) and Keynes (1930). Work was already underway to question the commodity orientation, which started to gain ground through the extensive work of Lancaster (1966). This debate in economics is still continuing today as behavioural and radical economists attempt to incorporate more realistic depictions of human behaviour within an economic paradigm (see, for example, Freakonomics 2005; Super Freakonomics 2009; Think Like a Freak 2014).

A second developmental thread was occurring in the psychology discipline, as the work of Freud indicated that human behaviour was highly dependent upon repressed desires and unconscious wishes. In a sense, overt behaviours were a function of hidden and subconscious drives. The publication of *The Interpretation of Dreams* (Freud 1899), *Totem and Taboo* (Freud 1913) and *The Ego and The Id* (Freud 1923) were markers for a psychoanalytic stream of research, which eventually found application to consumption by Dichter (1964) in his study on consumer motivation. To this work was added the emergent understandings of personality originated by Allport (1937), which examined differences between individual behaviour suggesting the existence of different personality types and inconsistent behavioural responses to the same stimuli. Other notable events during this period include the publication by Maslow (1943) on human needs, the emergence of humanist psychology in the early 1900s (see Watson 1913; Pavlov 1927) followed by Skinner (1938), which examined how cognition and learning were structured. Haire's study (1950) of responses to new products also marked a significant shift towards the application of psychology to the domain of consumption.

Putting these two threads together, we can see that the economic view, which was decidedly 'in'human, was significantly extended by psychologists who began to illustrate some underlying human motives and by emergent social psychologists who were beginning to see the significance of context. The importance for marketers of the emergence of this new thinking about human behaviour should not be underestimated. Consumer behaviour as a discipline emerged at this time, a time when current economic understandings about consumption and consumer behaviour were going through a period of re-examination. The new 'marketing concept' required organizations to understand their customers, preferably be able to predict how they would behave and more importantly identify unmet opportunities for new products. While neo-classical economics and the newer discipline of psychology were developing their understanding of human behaviour, marketing had an almost unique opportunity during the late 1950s and 1960s to craft a new cross-disciplinary approach, taking and adapting knowledge from very many different disciplines to help understand consumption behaviour.

If anything is distinctive about the study of consumer behaviour in marketing, it is this freedom from a single paradigm and an inclusive theoretical and methodological approach. This has been driven by an eclectic development and the willingness to re-examine assumptions in the light of actual customer behaviour. Perhaps more significant is that consumer behaviour in marketing has the benefit of being applied to a specific set of behaviours, which provides a basis for theory development. Having looked briefly at how the discipline emerged, the next section examines its early development.

Developing models of consumer choice

In 1961 the Ford Foundation commissioned a report on the study of marketing at US business schools (see Howard 1963). Two chapters of the foundation report summarized available research from economics and psychology, which was relevant to understanding consumer behaviour. This first codification did much to stimulate the development of marketing research, including the development of the product life cycle. More specifically, subsequent studies in conjunction with

General Foods and Nestlé provided some face validity for a generalized model of consumer behaviour based upon some recurring features of existing knowledge. In other words, a framework started to emerge that summarized how consumers arrived at a purchase. The format of this framework prompted a number of derived models, or grand theories to explain sequences, processes and relationships for individual purchase decision-making. Early works by Andreasen (1965), Nicosia (1966), Engel *et al.* (1968) and Howard and Sheth (1969) all had a common format. Simply, that the individual receives information from a variety of different sources, which is filtered through the five senses. The interpreted information influences internal processes, such as the formation of opinions, likings and attitudes, which, once activated by a need or want, prompts search and evaluation behaviour ultimately leading to a purchase.

The Engel model was perhaps the most elegant of these grand theories for three reasons. First, it identified the individual as the central control mechanism engaged in an almost constant process of problem solving. Second, this model is notable, because it included external influences on the problem-solving process (such as family, references groups, society and government). This was a key shift in how consumer behaviour was represented. Finally, the model was significant, because it provided for a feedback loop. This suggested that individuals learn from activity and experience, and these understandings are used again in subsequent problem solving.

While the intention was to provide a comprehensive exposition of how consumers behave, in actual fact these models proved difficult to use and embodied a view of consumers that was confining for many researchers (see, for example, Foxall 1980). Many of the relationships were untestable, and where testable produced conflicting results. Ultimately, their contribution was not so much a theory, but more a schematic representation, which served to order and categorize research and known elements of behaviour. For our purposes, though, the relevance of this early work was to focus attention on three key components:

1   the individual: their psychological processes, their underlying needs and drives, how they handle information, interpret communications, derive attitudes and beliefs, and make choices;
2   the social environment: social media, word of mouth communication, the influence of family and other consumers, marketing activity, regulations and suppliers;
3   the physical environment: we observe that people behave differently in different settings and experience and respond to their environments in different ways. This would suggest that physical surroundings may influence consumption.

While these three components are very obvious, they provide a good structure for the rest of this chapter, since each embodies a particular consumer behaviour paradigm. In the first case, focusing upon the individual allows us to examine the information processing view of consumer behaviour, so influential in the academic literature for the last 50 years. It also allows us to examine the consumer decision-making framework, which has been applied as part of this approach. The second theme focuses upon the social context of consumers and reflects a growing practitioner and academic view that consumer behaviour can only be understood by examining the social context of consumption. The final section on the market environment draws together a number of themes from the first two and looks at the impact of the market environment on behaviour. In this area we draw on the environmental psychology literature on consumer behaviour, as well as more (post) modern expositions on consumer behaviour, with its reliance upon decoding and re-interpreting what we experience in our everyday lives. While these are considered separately for ease of exposition, it should be clear that they are intimately connected to each other in fully understanding consumer behaviour.

Following the delineation of the comprehensive models of behaviour in the 1960s, a number of key underlying propositions were evident. The first was that psychological processes associated with individual consumption behaviour were goal directed. In other words, the behaviour that was observed was the outcome of some internal and unobservable psychological process focused upon achieving something. The Engel-Kollatt model also made it clear that the consumer's decision process was an entirely rational and goal directed one. In that sense, we could understand the behaviour we observed (purchase) as the outcome of a series of sequential steps, where the consumer made rational and conscious decisions to consume.

Several models were put forward to describe this process. Although there were variations in the precise construction, the main steps were considered to be the following: recognizing needs, information search, evaluation of alternatives, purchase and post-purchase evaluation. This series of sequential tasks is the core of consumer behaviour and, while the process was influenced by a range of internal, external and situational variables, the sequence of activity and the impact of such activity upon marketing communications is still recognized today. Because of the dominance of this model, it is worth spending some time examining the steps.

Need recognition

The first step is the recognition of needs and wants. To make a cursory distinction, needs are things you feel you cannot do without, but wants are more abstract desires for things, events or experiences. The process of recognition asserts that these needs and wants are continuously present, but remain at a low and tolerable level for us until some event causes them to become acute. For instance, your need for food to sustain you is a continuous need. However, it is likely to be irrelevant just after a meal. As time goes by, you will start noticing hunger and then you will be prompted to satisfy that hunger with food once again. There are also symbolic needs associated with how we perceive ourselves, such as the need to belong to a group, to display certain behaviours, or to have status or recognition. Finally, there may also be needs which are hedonic, in other words they reflect our desires, such as novelty, enjoyment, sensory pleasure and play. Needs are not always driven from latent to acute just by the physiological processes of the body, but are driven by feelings of loneliness, failure, excitement or celebration, reactions to communications, environments or imagination.

There is no way we can categorize or summarize all the various needs and wants that consumers have. However, we can point to a number of their characteristics:

1   Needs and wants exist in some sort of hierarchy, in other words some are more important to us than others, and their predominance reflects both psychological processes and situational circumstances.
2   Multiple needs and wants may be activated simultaneously, and any associated behaviour may satisfy none, some or all those activated.
3   Needs are dynamic and are never fully satisfied; they can become acute or latent at different times and in different circumstances.
4   Needs may often conflict with each other such that we must make trade-offs. For example, eating high calorie foods, because they taste so good, at the same time as wanting to lose weight.
5   Needs can be aroused as the result of both internal reflection and externally. An internal decision to 'sort out your life' after a setback can trigger needs as well as the smell of fresh bread or perfume, the viewing of an advertisement or reading a magazine.

There is some uncertainty as to how needs and wants operate, but for marketers the identification and stimulation of customer needs and wants and the associated presentation of satisfiers of those needs and wants are considered to be one of the core functions of marketing. The debate about whether needs can be created where they do not previously exist, is one which is unresolvable, as is the suggestion that individuals have no control over need activation and their subsequent behaviours. If you see food and start to feel hungry, is that because you were hungry anyway, but did not recognize it? Or, were you not hungry and the food made you hungry?

Information search and evaluation

Once need activation has occurred, the second step in the generalized model of consumer decision- making is to collect information. When considering needs above, we had implicitly assumed that a need could be readily associated with a satisfying behaviour; however, in many cases it cannot. How many times have you felt some drive to do something but not known exactly what? This may be because we recognize that our information about alternatives may be out of date, that we have not undertaken this type of purchase before, or we have specific requirements. There are generally two sources of information – those held internally by the individual in the form of memory and those which are external. In simple terms, memory not only is drawn upon to aid the current decision activity but can also provide a framework for how information is interpreted. If we walk into a building and it looks like a restaurant, then this frames the way we interpret information. We will wait to be seated, we will expect certain things of the environment, the service process and the people in that space. These will be different if we frame the space as a store, or a private house or an office.

Internal information is drawn from memory, and research has focused specifically upon how consumers recall product attributes, previous product evaluations, previous experiences and brand communications to derive understanding about the decision facing them. It may also help direct additional information search in the external environment. We know from psychology that the human brain processes huge volumes of information on a daily basis. It manages to select key bits of information to hold in the memory in order to associate bits of information together, and alters or updates information stored based on new information. In the context of the individual consumer, some purchase decisions will be relatively routinized, and the individual will rely upon habit and memory. Other decisions will be so new that the individual recognizes that they have no information directly relevant, and this will prompt extensive information search.

Clearly, the accumulation of information associated with a prospective purchase is made with the intention of optimizing the purchase decision. In consumer theory, the purchase decision is characterized as a choice between competing alternatives, a judgement based upon the information available as to which product or service is most likely to satisfy the aroused needs or wants. The mechanics of evaluation are presented as highly complex and as highly diverse, which, when you consider what we are trying to understand, is not a surprise. We do know that search and evaluation take place simultaneously and that some tasks require extensive evaluation and others almost none. Complex tasks are not immediately self-evident and certainly cannot be conclusively categorized by the type of product or service. Some consumers may find it difficult to evaluate different cars; others find that same task no problem at all. Some consumers can choose a newspaper or a chocolate bar without even noticing it, yet others will deliberate for some time. In general, we know that some evaluations are difficult and some are simple, but we do not know precisely which is to be purchased for any particular group of consumers. We also know that consumer learning allows for the configuring and adapting of evaluation rules, such as buying the most expensive, the one made in Europe or a particular brand. There is also some complexity represented by evaluating alternatives, which are substantially different (for instance comparing a holiday with a new TV). In this case, there are no common product attributes, but nevertheless the alternatives need to be evaluated comparatively on more abstract benefits.

Purchase and post-purchase evaluation

The actual purchase is the culmination of these previous phases, but it would appear that the process of purchase can also encapsulate more decision-making. There may be new products that have not been found before, the impact of service personnel, alternatives that were not considered, pricing and payment circumstances, different channels to use in acquisition, etc. The specialist consumer behaviour texts skim over purchase as something, which everyone knows about and there is not much to say, but increasingly, as services dominate the experiences associated with purchase, it becomes a major consideration for marketers. This is especially true when we consider the emotional, cognitive and physical resources needed to consummate a purchase. We will return to a consideration of the purchase environment later in this chapter.

It should be evident that the decision process does not end once a purchase has been made, since the consumer will continue to evaluate the product or service in use. This evaluation will feed into subsequent decisions. If the product is not satisfying, then it will not be considered again, or if the product becomes superseded, cannot be used due to the unavailability of peripherals or replenishment, its performance will be compromised. There are also some processes that the individual consumer uses to come to terms with their purchase. How many times have you checked the price of a product you have just purchased in different stores just to reassure yourself you got a good deal? How many product reviews have you read hoping that the product you purchased is highly rated? This is all part of the post-purchase evaluation. Clearly, the outcome of this phase of our generalized decision model will impact upon future purchases, loyalty and brand equity.

Depending upon how you break down the various stages in the decision model, you will have differing numbers of steps, but the elements will be roughly the same. This consumer decision-making framework, which emerged from the early literature and the comprehensive models, was an important step forward. It not only focused upon the individual as the key to consumer behaviour but it also served as an agenda for subsequent research. This was characterized with a focus upon the details of how consumers' psychological process operated, and it became known as the information processing approach, which dominated consumer behaviour research through the 1970s (see Bettman 1979).

The key assumptions of the information processing approach are that individual consumers engage in both active and conscious information processing when making choices, and second, that the rules (which dictate how the information is managed) can be modelled. Remember that we cannot actually observe this phenomenon, so the early modelling had to rely upon inference. In practice, consumers were asked to talk through what they were thinking during a decision-making event.

While these early studies proved instructive, it was the adoption of research from psychology that really started to put some weight behind an information processing view of the consumer. By understanding the ways in which information is stored, organized and retrieved, consumer behaviour researchers could examine how decisions and evaluations were conducted. Three cognitive operations were critical. First, how consumers managed to associate new information with what they already held (specifically the role of rehearsal in strengthening new associations). Second, how information is encoded so that it is stored and retrieved. Third, how information is structured so that data could be retrieved together.

Information processing was important, because it was predicted that the outcome of this information activity fed directly into individual consumer beliefs and attitudes about products. Beliefs are those things which consumers believe to be true or factually correct. For example, I might believe that Ariel is a well-known soap powder, or that Heinz products are available in every supermarket. By contrast, attitudes are evaluations of a product. For example, I think Ariel is too expensive, or I do not like the packaging of Heinz products. The importance from the information processing perspective is that our beliefs and attitudes combine to form intentions, which are then translated into purchases.

The elegance of the information processing approach was in the detailed modelling and extensive experimentation used to infer cognitive processes. But there were also two problems. The first was that while the processing models were elegant, they were all based upon individual experimentation. There were some significant problems caused by aggregation, where it became evident that individual consumers were not very alike. The second and probably more significant problem was that attitudes, intentions and actual behaviour seemed to have very little correlation. In other words, when it got to observable behaviour, the theory did not stack up. A contribution by Fishbein and Ajzen (1975) went some way towards retrieving this desperate situation by focusing not on attitudes towards a particular product or object, but shifting the focus by measuring attitude towards a behaviour. In other words, rather than looking for attitudes towards an object (product) as a means to predict behaviour, they measured attitude towards the behaviour in terms of the object (buying it). In the past, researchers had asked people what they thought about a product and then used these evaluations to predict purchase. The Fishbein approach asked consumers about their attitude towards buying a particular product on their next shopping trip. A development of this research incorporated a subjective norm component with attitude to determine behavioural intentions. The resulting Theory of Reasoned Action (1975, 1980) and the Theory of Planned Behaviour (1985) are still used as the basis for research today.

Before we leave the domain of the individual, we should also mention recent consumer behaviour research, a major thread of which is the focus upon experiential consumption by individuals. This suggests that individual consumer behaviour is motivated not by rational decisions but by emotions and experiences. In the last three decades, marketing researchers have started to study the emotions prompted by products and brands (Holbrook and Hirschman 1982). These studies have examined consumers' emotional responses to advertising (e.g. Derbaix 1995) and the role of emotions in customer satisfaction (e.g. Phillips and Baumgartner (2002); complaining (Stephens and Gwinner 1998); service failures (Zeelenberg and Pieters 1999); and attitudes (Dube *et al.* 2003). This thread of consumer research shows some promise in understanding the often volatile and unpredictable responses of consumers to marketing efforts. In the next section we leave the domain of the individual operating in isolation and turn to the social context of consumer behaviour.

Even the early comprehensive models of consumer behaviour recognized that consumers operate within a social context. Other people have a part to play in determining our needs and wants, providing us with information, helping us evaluate different offerings, directing our purchase behaviour and even determining how satisfied we are after a purchase. This section considers social influences, framed within two recognized social structures: family and social/reference groups. The third social influence is culture, which is a study in its own right.

Family

It has been argued that the family is the most important consumption unit in the economy, because the household is a cohesive and interdependent consumption unit in its own right, and many of the consumption behaviours by individuals are in fact concerned with household not individual consumption. There is a degree of confusion about the definitions of household and family, but we can distinguish them for the purpose of this discussion. A household comprises all the people who live within a single place, which can be a single person ranging to multiple persons, such as a shared house. Families are defined in this context as two or more cohabiting people connected by means of marriage, partnership, blood or legal relationship, but excluding financial relationships. If we take a traditionally structured nuclear family, we can determine consumption decisions taken by the individual members of that family, for example, by a parent, child or either partner. However, of more interest to this discussion are consumption decisions taken on behalf of the family by one party, decisions that are taken jointly by the family unit and the various decision roles adopted. The reason why this is of importance is that often the buyer of a product or service is not the ultimate consumer. Consider that within a family, men and women may undertake different roles and be responsible for different purchase decisions. Within some decisions, children or other family members may have a substantial influencing role, especially where the decision is collective, such as a family holiday.

We can also track the influence of different family members depending upon the stage of the decision. Kirchler (1981) tracked family decision-making using diaries and determined that individuals adopt different roles. The initiator starts the process by defining the problem, such as running out of tea, or the need for a new TV, and may suggest the type, style or brand. The influencer may approve or disapprove of the need or the choice and suggest alternative solutions. The decision-maker is the person who finally decides or, at least, determines the range of alternatives to be considered. The buyer is the one who goes to the shop and buys the product. The users are those who actually consume the product's benefits. For marketing, it is important to understand this process, as it allows more targeted communications and delivery decisions.

The early work by Sheth (1974) suggested that 'middle class' families took more joint (syncratic) decisions, while 'upper class' families took more individual decisions. 'Lower class' families had more strictly defined purchase roles. In other words, the purchase of particular products or services was the responsibility of a defined member of the family. Sheth also found that the stage of the family life cycle was also important in that young families took more joint decisions and took longer to make a decision. This research is somewhat undermined by the rapidly changing family structures evident today. The high divorce rate, blended and restructured families, children remaining at home longer and single and communal living arrangements have all made the simple family/household decision scenario more complex.

Social and reference groups

Outside the family, the individual consumer operates within a social environment dominated by groups of others. These social groups to which an individual consumer belongs impact the behaviour of its members through the determination of group norms, the development of group values and also the exchange of information. Group norms are the collective opinions about how people should behave in certain circumstances, for example a formal board meeting versus a meeting over a coffee. The group may enforce its norms through sanctions, such as overt disapproval or even rejection from the group. Clearly, some groups require more conformity than others, and the individual may have to trade conformity with individualism. For instance, the membership of a sporting club may impose certain expectations about what type of sports equipment you should purchase. It may require attendance at certain sporting events, the adoption of certain political or social views or the adoption of certain behaviours.

Group values are associated with group norms to the extent that they represent how the group views the world. A particular social group may have clear environmental values, clear lifestyle values or even child rearing values. These values may be the reason why an individual is attracted to them (such as membership of Amnesty International or Greenpeace), or they may be learned and adopted over time. The operation of group values and norms can have a significant influence upon purchase behaviour. You need only ask a member of generation Y what clothing brands are acceptable and why, and which are not, to get some idea of the impact of social groups in product selection.

Leibenstein (1950) identified two consumption effects emanating from social groups. The first was the 'bandwagon effect', which simply describes how, within a particular group, the more people who own a product the more pressure is exerted on non-owners to conform by purchasing. The second effect was called the 'Veblen effect' (1899) and describes how group members may purchase expensive or high status products to display their own wealth or success and achieve status within the group. This social influence on consumption is communicated and expressed in myriad different ways. It might be through a dominant member exerting authority, it might through modelling behaviour on other group members, it may involve sanctions (such as being laughed at) or rewards (such as more intense social connections). Social groups can be categorized according to their formality, with high formality groups exhibiting formalized structures and operations, such as societies or clubs. Social groups may vary according to their degree of attraction for the individual, which may range from very positive (aspiration or affiliation groups) to very negative (dissociative groups).

There is increasing attention being paid to the impact of word of mouth communication in marketing, not least because it provides a relatively believable source of information in today's information-rich environment. More significantly, though, is the impact of technology in providing consumers with greater access to each other and to an information source (internet, social media, etc.). As consumers become more connected to each other, the opportunity to engage in word of mouth communication also increases. New media takes word of mouth out of a geographical location and makes it international. TripAdvisor makes every traveller into a hotel critic; Twitter makes every consumer experience into a shared experience; the internet provides every patient with a diagnosis and health advice. Research clearly demonstrates that consumers place more credibility in peer-to-peer communication and are more likely to believe a fellow consumer than a marketer or even professional (Laing and Hogg 2008).

The predominant view of consumer behaviour is focused upon cognitive psychology. Specifically, before people buy, they engage in a cognitive process involving information held and information gained from the environment. This is either a complex or simple process depending upon the task. The outcome of this cognitive processing of information (choice/preference) then directs purchase behaviour. This view reflects the idea that the 'core' of decision-making is the individual's conscious deliberations. The consumer negotiates purchasing behaviour by carefully evaluating the pros and cons of every purchase.

An alternative view is that while consumers may exhibit elements of a rational approach to choice and consumption, they are highly influenced by their perception of both the physical and digital environment and the behaviour of others within these domains. Donovan *et al.* (1994) make the point that consumers' emotional responses to environments are directly related to their willingness to engage with it by spending time, money and effort. The design of an environment to enhance positive emotions increases the likelihood that consumers will be receptive. We will consider physical and digital environments separately.

Mehrabian and Russell (1974) were the first to focus upon an individual's emotional response to a physical environment, something referred to as environmental psychology. They categorized the range of emotional responses to a physical place as pleasure, arousal and dominance. Pleasure responses can be verbally described as feelings of happiness, satisfaction and contentment. Arousal responses are described as feeling stimulated, excited and wide-awake. Dominance responses are verbally described as feeling controlled and overwhelmed. It is possible to imagine different retail spaces that might high on one or more of these criteria. For a more complete discussion, see Dawson *et al.* (1990) and Foxall and Greenley (1999).

A competing view is that consumers often react mindlessly to certain environmental stimuli. This fact had caused a degree of difficulty for the information processing adherents, since it challenged the whole basis of rational consumption. While a partial solution was to point to 'instantaneous' evaluation and impulse behaviours, it did not accommodate the increasing evidence of an emotional and highly malleable set of experience-based effects. Cialdini (2001) provided powerful evidence through a range of experiments for a 'click-zoom' response. In other words, certain environmental cues elicited almost instant behaviour change in certain settings. This was supported by the work of Wheeler and Petty (2001), who suggest that perception of the social environment will automatically cause the consumer to behave consistently. The range of responses varies from simple mimicry such as facial expression, or physical disposition (see Chartrand and Bargh 1999; Johnston 2002) through to goal contagion (see Aarts *et al.* 2004), where consumers subconsciously adopt observed behaviours and their associated outcomes. The implications of this work are far reaching, as it suggests that consumers are highly susceptible to their perception and understanding of their immediate environment. This places environmental design, atmospherics and emotional responses at the very forefront of influencing a range of behaviours. In other words, it is not the purchase of specific bundles of product benefits, but the consumption of a purchase experience. North *et al.* (1997) found that playing French music in a supermarket increased the sales of French wine, while playing German music increased the sales of German wine. The theoretical basis of this work provides support for the wide range of research experiments on the effects of music, smell and temperature on buyer behaviour.

Perhaps one of the biggest changes to actual consumer behaviour has been the advent of the internet and the associated rise of digital consumption. We consider it here as a specific consumption environment, following Shih (1998). The digital environment has a range of characteristics that impact upon consumer behaviour. We will consider two. First, the impact of the digital environment upon individual information processing such as the density of information available, enhanced search and comparison facilities and the almost global sourcing opportunities (see, for example, Ratchford *et al.* 2007; Huang *et al.* 2009; Blazevic *et al.* 2013). Second, the impact upon the social context of consumption, specifically the increased connectivity between consumers and their ability to collaborate with, and learn from, each other (Hennig-Thurau *et al.* 2010).

The digital shopper is both highly educated and affluent and, as such, this group of consumers engages in extensive search and comparison. The sheer availability of information reduces the impact of geographic location, reduces search costs and allows for greater market accessibility (see Lal and Sarvary 1999). Comparison sites, aggregators and crawlers allow consumers to get instantaneous information about pricing, availability and access to a wide range of payment options. This reduction in search and transaction costs is making the digital environment highly attractive, while simultaneously making the restrictions of the physical environment more obvious. Ultimately, as markets become more transparent, consumer market power will increase.

A second related development has been the impact of the digital environment upon consumer-to-consumer connectivity. The ability of the internet to create and support communities of shared interest and to connect individuals, places individual consumption in a highly social context (see Heinonen 2011; Forbes and Vespoli 2013; Hajli 2014). This in turn impacts upon the creation of shared beliefs about products, services and brands and the development of truly collaborative forms of consumption (see Denegri-Knott and Molesworth 2013). One unforeseen impact of digital consumption has been the ability of firms to collect and aggregate more detailed behavioural data and, through personalization and data analytics, to provide increasingly personalized and adaptive consumption environments.

Postmodern approaches

We turn now to the final consideration in this chapter, which falls somewhere between the society and the environment, the idea of a postmodern perspective on consumer behaviour. The voluminous and insightful commentaries from Brown (1998), as well as the research by Belk (1988), McCracken (1990), Richins (1994) and Cova (1997), drew together a modern sociological stance on consumption. The Frankfurt School of Critical Theory, and particularly the work of Marcuse (1964) and Fromm (1976), was instrumental in developing a humanistic perspective on consumption behaviour. In simple terms, a consumer is characterized by what they consume. The individual 'self' constructs a reality through the acquisition of goods, services and experiences (see also Belk 2014). For the purposes of this chapter, observed consumer behaviour is dependent upon the model of 'self', which has, or is being, constructed by the individual.

According to Shove and Warde (2003), three clear developments led to the current explosion of interest in the philosophy of consumption. The first was the role of consumption behaviour in the process of social differentiation, with Bourdieu's (1984) analysis generating a wealth of activity around the relationship between social position and aspects of lifestyle and consumption. The second development was the concept of collective consumption, particularly institutional theory and the nature of social capital (Castells 1977 [1972]). The third development was the emergence of cultural studies and multi-disciplinary approaches to analysing the use and meanings of goods and artefacts in everyday life.

The observation that we now inhabit a social world where consumption has replaced work as people's central life interest (Moorhouse 1983; Offe 1985) is subjected to critical analysis, with Western consumer culture being criticized on a number of fronts. These include the exclusion of large sections of the population of the world from the benefits associated with consumption. Material prosperity seemingly fails to bring happiness or improved satisfaction; materialism compromises social and spiritual values and leads to isolationism and a scarcity mentality; mass culture is vulgar, degrading and panders to the lowest denominator, etc. However, perhaps the most current concern is the impact of our expanding levels of consumption upon our natural environment (e.g. Gabriel and Lang 2006). This criticism is largely associated with globalization and the increasing prevalence of consumer culture. This reflective stance from consumer behaviourists may yet cause the study of consumption to change its focus from improving or enhancing consumption to reducing and minimizing the impact of consumption.

Conclusion

Consumer behaviour is a particularly challenging field of study. Not only does it require consideration of a wide range of theoretical perspectives but, like any aspect of human behaviour, it is very difficult to deal in absolutes. That having been said, it is also one of the most interesting, dynamic, challenging and frustrating areas of study.

In their book, *The Unmanageable Consumer*, Gabriel and Lang (2006) describe contemporary consumers playing nine different roles: chooser, communicator, explorer, identity seeker, hedonist, victim, rebel, activist and citizen. Each of these roles presents particular challenges for the marketer attempting to understand how to predict how consumers are likely to interpret marketing messages. And yet an individual consumer may play all of these roles in any one consumption decision. Central to consumer behaviour is therefore an understanding of consumer value, both what the consumer values in any consumption decision and how their own values underpin their decisions. Little wonder then that as Gabriel and Lang (2006) point out, the history of consumption is full of dead ends (Gabriel and Lang 2006: 191). In attempting to understand consumer behaviour we must try to pull together the various underpinning threads and consider the complexity of understanding any human behaviour so bound up with our own identities. Marketing has a responsibility, however, to continue to develop this understanding, because without understanding consumers, no business will succeed in the longer term.

References

Aarts, H., Gollwitzer, P. and Hassin, R. (2004), 'Goal contagion: Perceiving is for pursuing', *Journal of Personality and Social Psychology*, 87(1): 23–37.

Ackerman, F. (1997), 'Consumed in theory: Alternative perspectives on the economics of consumption', *Journal of Economic Issues*, 31(3): 651–664.

Allport, G. W. (1937), *Personality: A Psychological Interpretation*, New York: Holt, Rinehart and Winston.

Andreassen, A. R. (1965), 'Attitudes and customer behaviour: A decision model, in Preston, L. E. (ed.) *New Research in Marketing*, University of California, Berkeley: Institute of Business and Economic Research.

Belk, R. (1988), 'Possessions and the extended self', *Journal of Consumer Research*, 15(September), 139–168.

Belk R. (2014), 'Digital consumption and the extended self', *Journal of Marketing Management* (serial online), 30(11/12): 1101–1118, available from Ipswich, MA: Business Source Premier, accessed 22 May 2015. http://www.

Bettman, J. R. (1979), *An Information Processing Theory of Consumer Behaviour*, Boston, MA: Addison-Wesley.

Blazevic, V., Hammedi, W., Carl W., *et al.* (2013), 'Beyond traditional word-of-mouth', *Journal of Service Management* (serial online), 24(3): 294–313, available from Ipswich, MA: Business Source Premier, accessed 22 May 2015. http://www.

Bourdieu, P. (1984), *Distinction: A Social Critique of the Judgement of Taste*, London: Routledge-Keegan Paul.

Brown, S. (1998), *Postmodern Marketing Two: Telling Tales*, London: Thomson Press.

Castells, M. (1977 [1972]), *The Urban Question: A Marxist Approach*, London: Edward Arnold.

Chartrand, T. L. and Bargh, J. A. (1999), 'The chameleon effect: The perception behaviour link and social interaction', *Journal of Personality and Social Psychology*, 76(6): 893–910.

Chuan-Fong (Eric) S., (1998), 'Conceptualizing consumer experiences in cyberspace', *European Journal of Marketing*, 32(7/8): 655–663.

Cialdini, R. B. (2001), *Influence: Science and Practice*, New York: Harper Collins.

Corrigan, P. (1998), *The Sociology of Consumption*, London: Sage.

Cova, B. (1997), 'Community and consumption: Toward a definition of the linking value of product or services', *European Journal of Marketing*, 31(3/4): 297–316.

Dawson, S., Bloch, P. and Ridgeway, N. (1990), 'Shopping motives, emotional states and retail outcomes', *Journal of Retailing*, 66(4): 408–428.

Denegri-Knott, J. and Molesworth, M. (2013), 'Redistributed consumer desire in digital virtual worlds of consumption', *Journal Of Marketing Management* (serial online), 29(13/14): 1561–1579, available from, Ipswich, MA: Business Source Premier, accessed 22 May 2015. http://www.

Derbaix, C. (1995), 'The impact of affective reactions on attitudes toward the advertisement and the brand: A step toward ecological validity', *Journal of Marketing Research*, 32(4): 470–480.

Dichter, E. (1964), *Handbook of Consumer Motivations: The Psychology of the World of Objects*, New York: McGraw-Hill.

Donovan, R., Rossiter, J., Marcoolyn, G. and Nesdale, A. (1994), 'Store atmosphere and purchase behaviour', *Journal of Retailing*, 70: 283–294.

Dube, L., Cervellon, M. C. and Han, J. (2003), 'Should consumer attitudes be reduced to their affective and cognitive bases? Validation of a hierarchical model', *International Journal of Research in Marketing*, 20(3): 259–272.

Duesenberry, J. S. (1949), *Income, Saving and the Theory of Consumer Behaviour*, Cambridge, MA: Harvard University Press.

Engel, J. F., Kollatt, D. J. and Blackwell, R. D. (1968), *Consumer Behaviour*, New York: Dryden Press.

Fishbein, M. and Ajzen, I. (1975), *Belief, Attitude, Intention and Behaviour: An Introduction to Theory and Research*, Boston, MA: Addison-Wesley.

Forbes, L. P. and Vespoli, E. M. (2013), 'Does social media influence consumer buying behaviour? An investigation of recommendations and purchases', *Journal of Business & Economics Research*, 11(2): 107–111.

Foxall, G. (1980), 'Marketing models of consumer behaviour: a critical review', *European Research*, 8: 195–206.

Foxall, G. and Greenley, G. (1999), 'Consumers' emotional responses to service environments', *Journal of Business Research*, 46: 149–158.

Freud, S. (1899), 'The interpretation of dreams', in Marinelli, L. and Andreas, M. A. (2003) *Dreaming by the Book: A History of Freud's 'The Interpretation of Dreams' and the Psychoanalytic Movement*, New York: Other Press.

Freud, S. (1913), *Totem and Taboo* (first published in German in 1913 as Totem und Tabu: Einige Übereinstimmungen im Seelenleben der Wilden und der Neurotiker).

Freud, S. (1923), *The Ego and The Id* (first published in German as Das Ich and Das Es).

Fromm, E. (1976), *To Have or To Be?*, London: Jonathan Cape.

Gabriel, Y. and Lang, T. (2006), *The Unmanageable Consumer: Contemporary Consumption and Its Fragmentation*, London: Sage.

Galbraith, J. K. (1958), *The Affluent Society*, Cambridge, UK: Riverside Press.

Haire, M. (1950), 'Projective techniques in marketing research', *Journal of Marketing*, XIV(5): 649–657.

Hajli, M. (2014), 'A study of the impact of social media on consumers', *International Journal Of Market Research* (serial online), 56(3): 387–404, available from Ipswich, MA: Business Source Premier, accessed 22 May 2015. http://www.

Heinonen, K. (2011), 'Consumer activity in social media: Managerial approaches to consumers' social media behaviour', *Journal of Consumer Behaviour*, 10(6): 356–364.

Hennig-Thurau, T., Malthouse, E., Skiera, B., *et al.* (2010), 'The impact of new media on customer relationships', *Journal Of Service Research* (serial online), 13(3): 311–330, available from Ipswich, MA: Business Source Premier, accessed 22 May 2015. http://www.

Holbrook, M. and Hirschman, E. (1982), 'The experiential aspects of consumption: Fantasies, feelings and fun', *Journal of Consumer Research*, 9(2): 132–139.

Howard, J. (1963), *Executive and Buyer Behaviour*, New York: Columbia University Press.

Howard, J. and Sheth, J. N. (1969), *Theory of Buyer Behaviour*, New York: John Wiley & Sons.

Huang, P., Lurie, N. and Mitra, S. (2009), 'Searching for experience on the web: An empirical examination of consumer behaviour for search and experience goods,' *Journal of Marketing* (serial online), 73(2): 55–69, available from Ipswich, MA: Business Source Premier, accessed 22 May 2015. http://www.

Johnston, L. (2002), 'Behavioural mimicry and stigmatization', *Social Cognition*, 20: 18–35.

Keynes, J. M. (1930), 'Economic possibilities for our grandchildren', in *Essays in Persuasion*, New York: W. W. Norton.

Kirchler, E. (1981), 'Diary reports on daily economic decisions of happy versus unhappy couples', *Journal of Economic Psychology*, 9: 327–357.

Kuhn, T. S. (1962), *The Structure of Scientific Revolutions*, Chicago, IL: Chicago University Press.

Laing, A. and Hogg, G. (2008), 'Re-conceptualising the professional service encounter: Information empowered consumers and service relationships', *Journal of Customer Behaviour*, 7(4): 333–346.

Lal, R. and Sarvary, M. (1999), 'When and how is the internet likely to decrease price competition?', *Marketing Science* (serial online), 18(4): 485–503, available from Ipswich, MA: Business Source Premier, accessed 22 May 2015. http://www.

Lancaster, K. (1966), 'Change and innovation in the technology of consumption', *American Economic Review*, 56(1): 14–23.

Leibenstein, H. (1950), 'Bandwagon, snob and Veblen effects in the theory of consumers' demands', *Quarterly Journal of Economics*, 64(2): 198–207.

Marcuse, H. (1964), *One Dimensional Man*, Boston, MA: Beacon.

Marshall, A. (1920), *Principles of Economics*, London: Macmillan.

Maslow, A. (1943), 'A theory of human motivation', *Psychological Review*, 50: 370–396.

McCracken, G. (1988),

McCracken, G. (1990), *Culture and Consumption*, Bloomington, IN: Indiana University Press.

Mehrabian, A. and Russell, J. A. (1974), *An Approach to Environmental Psychology*, Cambridge, MA: MIT Press.

Moorhouse, H. (1983), 'American automobiles and workers' dreams', *Sociological Review*, 31(3): 403–426.

Nicosia, F. M. (1966), *Consumer Decision Processes: Marketing and Advertising Implications*, Englewood Cliffs, NJ: Prentice-Hall.

North, A., Hargreaves, D. J. and McKendrick, J. (1997), 'In store music affects product choice', *Nature*, 390: 132.

Offe, C. (1985), 'The future of work', in Offe, C. (ed.) *Disorganised Capitalism*, Cambridge, UK: Polity Press.

Pavlov, I. P. (1927), *Conditioned Reflexes: An Investigation of the Physiological Activity of the Cerebral Cortex* (translated), London: Oxford University Press.

Phillips, D. and Baumgartner, H. (2002), 'The role of consumption emotions in the satisfaction response', *Journal of Economic Psychology*, 12(3): 243–252.

Ratchford, B., Talukdar, D. and Myung-Soo, L. (2007), 'The impact of the internet on consumers' use of information sources for automobiles: a re-inquiry', *Journal Of Consumer Research* (serial online), 4(1): 111–119, available from Ipswich, MA: Business Source Premier, accessed 22 May 2015. http://www.

Richins, M. (1994), 'Valuing things: The public and private meanings of possessions', *Journal of Consumer Research*, 21(December): 504–521.

Sheth, J. (1974), *A Theory of Family Buying Decisions, Models of Buyer Behaviour*, New York: Harper Row.

Shove, E. and Warde, A. (2003), *Inconspicuous Consumption: The Sociology of Consumption and the Environment*, Lancaster University, Lancaster, UK: Department of Sociology, available at http://www.comp.lancs.ac.uk/sociology/papers/Shove-Warde-Inconspicuous-Consumption.pdf, accessed 19 January 2007.

Skinner, B. F. (1938), *The Behaviour of Organisms: An Experimental Analysis*, New York: Appleton Century.

Smith, A. (1970 [1776]) *The Wealth of Nations*, Penguin.

Stephens, N. and Gwinner, K. (1998), 'Why don't some people complain? A cognitive-emotive process model of consumer complaint behaviour', *Journal of the Academy of Marketing Science*, 26(3): 172–189.

Veblen, T. (1899), *The Theory of the Leisure Class: An Economic Study of Institutions*, New York: Viking Press.

Watson, J. B. (1913), 'Psychology as the behaviourist views it', *Psychological Review*, 20: 158–177.

Wheeler, S. and Petty, R. (2001), 'The effects of stereotype activation on behaviour', *Psychological Bulletin*, 27(6): 797–826.

Zeelenberg, M. and Pieters, R (1999), 'Comparing service delivery to what might have been: Behavioural responses to regret and disappointment', *Journal of Services Research*, 2(1): 86–97.

8 Marketing research

David F. Birks

Introduction

If one were to look back at early editions of the *Journal of Marketing* from its launch in 1936, it would be clear to see the amount of attention devoted to marketing research methods. Committees were formed to address and publish guidance on how surveys, samples and interviews (plus many other methods and techniques) should be formulated and applied. It was clear that the new marketing profession and academic discipline wanted to establish how one might best encapsulate the essential characteristics of consumers who should be at the heart of an enterprise. This quest to gain greater insight into the attitudes and behaviour of consumers and what drives them to buy or not buy, continues to this day. From an academic perspective, the discipline of marketing research is in robust health; the quest to develop strong and relevant marketing theory is vibrant.

From an industry perspective that is the most contentious and thus the primary focus of this chapter: the discipline of marketing research is far from healthy. The quest remains to measure and understand consumers to support better decision-making, but this quest is not necessarily within the domain of what traditionally has been covered in textbooks and marketing degrees as 'market research' or 'marketing research'. There are now many different ways in which decision-makers can be supported, resulting in debates about the relevance, value and feasibility of marketing research. These debates are encapsulated in the following:

> With new streams of data that provide fresh types of insight becoming available, what role (if any) do traditional market-research techniques and skills have? What is the real 'value add' of the market researcher? If market researchers are not making sense of this world of data, who is?
>
> (Mitchell 2012)

From the tone of many commentators on changes affecting the manner in which marketing decision-makers are supported, by the time *The Marketing Book* is published in its eighth edition there may be no need for a chapter on marketing research. The purpose of this chapter is therefore to make the case for the integrity and value of marketing research. It will set out the nature, value and limitations of marketing research. The role and value of marketing research will be developed to set a context for the many different ways that decision-makers may be supported. The growth and impact of technological developments upon marketing research methods will be evaluated, especially how these developments impact upon the marketing research process. Technological developments have shaped the development of a whole body of social media research methods. Understanding the nature of 'new' research methods will help to illustrate the breadth of other streams of data that support decision-makers, but it will also show the distinctive contribution and value of marketing research.

Evaluating these streams of data helps to position the ethical challenges faced by marketing researchers and also the future skills demanded of the profession. The conclusions will make the case that there are distinctive values for organisations that invest in marketing research, that there is a future for the discipline and a case to continue this subject in the next edition of *The Marketing Book*.

What does marketing research encompass?

The term 'marketing research' is broad in meaning and application. This chapter should make apparent that marketing research relates to supporting decision-making using many well-established and new digital research methods, in an ethical manner.

Definition of marketing research

Perspectives of a definition of marketing research are generally founded on the definition approved by the American Marketing Association (AMA) (2004). For the purpose of this chapter, which will emphasise the need for information of the highest integrity in the support of decision-making, marketing research is defined as:

> **Marketing research** is the function that links the consumer, customer, and public to the marketer through information . . . information used to identify and define marketing opportunities and problems; generate, refine, and evaluate marketing actions; monitor marketing performance; and improve understanding of marketing as a process. Marketing research specifies the information required to address these issues, designs the method for collecting information, manages and implements the data collection process, analyses the results, and communicates the findings and their implications.

Several aspects of this definition are noteworthy. It stresses the role of 'linking' the marketer to the consumer, customer and public to help improve the whole process of marketing decision-making. It also broadly sets out a research process that enables researchers to offer support to help decision-makers formulate better decisions and/or decisions with lower risks.

There can be some confusion with the distinctions between marketing research and market research. These distinctions can arise from many research practitioners across Europe seeing their profession in different ways to the United States. The European Society for Opinion and Market Research (ESOMAR) (2007) defines market research as:

> **Market research** is the systematic gathering and interpretation of information about individuals or organisations using the statistical and analytical methods and techniques of the applied social sciences to gain insight or support decision-making. The identity of participants will not be revealed to the user of the information without explicit consent and no sales approach will be made to them as a direct result of their having provided information.

This definition still sees a focus upon the consumer to support decision-making, but does not explicitly refer to the broader context in which this works. It is worth noting the ethical dimension of this definition, i.e. in the protection of the identity of individuals who participate in research. This point will be developed later as the integrity earned by ethical researchers will do much for the sustainability of the marketing research discipline and profession. The final point of note is the use of the word 'insight'. For many years, marketing and market research professionals and functions have been termed or associated with 'consumer insight'. There has been much debate about what consumer insight means and how this may give a 'richer' understanding of consumers compared to traditional notions of market research. In many market research businesses and research functions within business, the term 'market research' has been replaced with 'consumer insight'. The use of the term 'insight' has become ubiquitous within the market research profession. The early adoption of the term focused on the interpretation of consumer behaviour and the subsequent lines of thought relevant to the development of innovation and providing added value to consumers. Definitions of consumer insight include:

> **Consumer insight** is: 'A penetrating discovery about consumer motivations, applied to unlock growth'. Consumer Insights are not static; they are dynamic as a result of the dynamics of the market in which marketers are active.
>
> (Renkema and Zwikker 2003)

> **Consumer insight** is derived from an understanding of the purchase decision process and usage behavior. Insight connects different sets of associations that lead to a thought or solution that was not apparent before.
>
> (Gordon 2002)

These notions of insight recognise that encapsulating the essential characteristics of consumers who should be at the heart of an enterprise are being delivered by a much broader and diverse array of data gathering techniques, sources of data, forms of analysis and data reporting, storytelling and visualisation. This breadth and diversity of new approaches may simply reflect a redefinition of the nature and scope of the practice of marketing research. It is worth noting that the arguments presented by many writers use the terms 'marketing research', 'market research' and 'consumer insight' interchangeably. Rather than unpacking the subtleties and nuances of how these definitions are used, progress through the chapter will be made using the AMA definition of marketing research. Working with the AMA definition, with its focus on generating information of integrity to support marketing decision-making, a broad context of research practice is set that can embrace and adopt new skills, methods and technologies.

Focusing upon 'marketing research' helps to encapsulate the profession of managing the process of measuring and understanding consumers in order to better support marketing decision-making, a profession that strives for the highest levels of integrity in applying sound research methods in an ethical manner. It is recognised that marketing research can include understanding the macro business operating environment, monitoring market trends, conducting competitive analyses, answering business questions, identifying business opportunities and assessing potential risks. Additional forms of analysing disparate data sources, developing creative connections in data to reveal insights and future thinking are demanded from researchers to help decision-makers better understand their customers, their marketplace(s) and the overall business environment. Researchers have to continually adapt and respond to the challenges faced by marketing decision-makers.

The role of marketing research

Understanding the nature and scope of marketing research can be illustrated using a basic 'exchange of values' marketing paradigm, as depicted in Figure 8.1. An essential assumption that underlies Figure 8.1 is that marketers wish to generate satisfied customers. In order to generate satisfied customers (existing and potential), an emphasis is placed on understanding customer experiences and the delivery of satisfaction. To understand customer experiences and to implement marketing strategies and plans aimed at delivering satisfying experiences, marketers need information about customers, competitors and other forces in the marketplace. This seems straightforward, but many factors within the operating environment of businesses have driven the speed of changes in consumer expectations and purchasing and media usage behaviour. Rapidly changing expectations and behaviour have increased the need for decision-makers to be able to access more accurate and timely information. As businesses have become national and international in scope, the need for information on larger and more distant markets has increased. As consumers have become more affluent, discerning and sophisticated, decision-makers need better information on how they will respond to new products and other new experiences. As competition has become more intense, decision-makers need information on the effectiveness of their marketing plans and actions. As the environment changes more rapidly, decision-makers need more timely information to cope with the impact of changes (Roberts and Adams 2010).

Marketers make decisions about what they see as potential opportunities and problems with their current and potential consumers. They go on to devise the most effective ways to realise these opportunities and overcome problems they have identified. They do this based on a 'vision' of the distinct characteristics of their target markets and customer groups. From this 'vision' they develop, implement and control marketing programmes. This 'vision' of markets and subsequent marketing decisions may be complicated by the interactive effects of an array of environmental forces that shape the nature and scope of target markets. These forces also affect the decision-makers' ability to deliver experiences that will satisfy their chosen target markets. Within this framework of decision-making, marketing research helps to set an environmental context of marketing variables that connect to customer groups. Marketing research helps remove some of the uncertainty faced by decision-makers by providing relevant information about an operating environment and how this connects to marketing variables, and consumers.

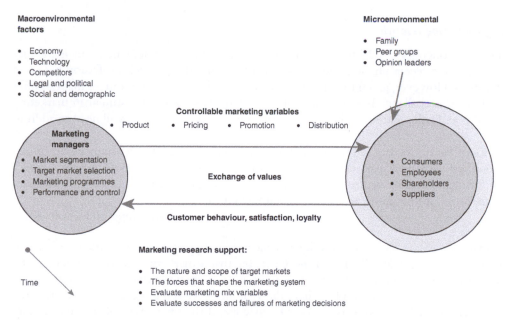

Figure 8.1 The role of marketing research within the marketing system

The role of the researcher in supporting the decision-makers can therefore be summarised as helping to measure and understand:

- the nature and scope of existing and potential customer groups;
- the nature and impact of forces that shape customer groups;
- the nature and impact of forces that shape the marketer's ability to satisfy targeted customer groups;
- individual and interactive variables that shape consumer experiences;
- factors that shaped past successes and failures in marketing decisions.

In undertaking these roles, researchers take responsibility for designing and crafting research of integrity and providing relevant information support. Delivering accurate, current, sufficient and relevant information is crucial to this role of supporting decision-makers to make better decisions.

Descriptions of the nature of 'researchers' and 'decision-makers' could be presented, but the clarity and distinction of these roles are blurring somewhat. Researchers have had to become more aware of decision-making; conversely, decision-makers have had to become more aware of the nature and value of evidence, given their dependence upon an eclectic array of data sources that can support their decision-making. There has been a shift in the nature and scope of marketing research, where increasingly the measurement and understanding of consumers is being undertaken not only on an ongoing basis but sometimes even on a 'real-time' basis. This 'real-time' capability contrasts with perhaps a traditional notion of research being in response to specific marketing opportunities or problems that may be investigated on an ad hoc basis. Technological developments and how managers, researchers and consumers interact with new technologies are changing how research is conducted and valued. Having a sense of a shifting perspective of what constitutes 'marketing research' is vital, as enterprises question their returns on 'crafting research of integrity and providing relevant information support'.

The value of marketing research

One of the key challenges faced by researchers is to justify the investment made in marketing research. This is not a recent phenomenon; it is a challenge that the research profession has faced from its inception. However, given the growth of an array of alternative data sources that can offer decision support, this challenge has become more prevalent. Return on investment in marketing research spend is and will continue to be a factor that all practising researchers will need to address:

> [t]he price of consumer data is trending downwards and parts of market research are becoming commoditised. This is in part driven by aggressive procurement processes, growing expectations for demonstrable return on investment and increasing macro-economic pressure. 'Consumer data' is now more abundant and automated.
>
> (Woodnutt and Owen 2010)

If decision-makers use researchers, even if the best theories and practice of the marketing research process are followed 'to the letter', there is no guarantee that a marketing decision supported by research will be successful. The acts of decision-making and conducting marketing research are distinctive activities, and there are examples where the vital link between these activities has resulted in failure. If decision-makers have gaps in their knowledge, if they perceive risk and uncertainty in their decision-making and cannot find support at hand, they can gain support from marketing research. However, many decision-makers can recount cases where the use of marketing research has resulted in failure, or where decisions based upon gut feeling or intuition have proved to be successful. Such cases present a challenge to researchers, especially in light of the competition faced by the profession from alternative data sources (ESOMAR 2010). Reflecting upon such cases should remind researchers to maintain a focus on offering real and valuable support to decision-makers. Understanding what real and valuable support means should underpin the whole array of creative data collection and analysis procedures available to the researcher.

Anita Roddick of The Body Shop once made the damning comment that 'market research is like looking in the rear view mirror of a speeding car' (Lury 2000). This may be a valid point if one sees the relationship of marketing and marketing research from the perspective illustrated by the respected research practitioner, Wendy Gordon (2000):

> Traditional marketers delegate responsibility to the processes of marketing research. They believe that you can ask people what they want and need in the future and then deliver it to them. It is a fallacy. Marketing research removes people from experiencing reality, where the signs of change bubble up in unexpected places. Sitting in comfort behind a one-way mirror, listening to a debrief from researchers describing the world 'out there' or reading statistical reports on markets and the 'aggregate consumer' is not real, it is sanitised and second-hand.

Anita Roddick's view of market research not being able to help with 'future thinking' or Wendy Gordon's view that it removes marketers from 'experiencing reality' give clear hints as to why decision-makers may use alternative data sources. These criticisms are not new, and it has to be acknowledged that there are cases where the use of marketing research has resulted in poor decision-making or even failed outcomes, especially in the areas of new product launches or communications campaigns. The clarity and distinction of what constitutes 'research' and 'decision-making' are key to these criticisms. Written over two decades ago, Lehmann (1994) argued that there are two key misconceptions of the role of marketing research. These still hold:

1 *Marketing research does not make decisions.* The role of marketing research is not to make decisions. Rather, research replaces hunches, impressions or a total lack of knowledge with information that can be trusted.
2 *Marketing research does not guarantee success.* Research, at best can improve the odds of making a correct decision. Anyone who expects to eliminate the possibility of failure by doing research is both unrealistic and likely to be disappointed. The real value of research can be seen over a long period where increasing the percentage of good decisions should be manifested in improved bottom-line performance and in the occasional revelation that arises from research.

The last point shows the long-term benefits of conducting marketing research, i.e. that the results of a study may help decision-makers with an immediate problem. But, by building their knowledge on sources and processes that can be trusted, decision-makers can also reap long-term benefits from marketing research. Given the array of readily available data sources, marketing research may not necessarily deliver the best value or guaranteed means to support decision-making. Over the long term, however, marketing research can be conceived to tackle the gaps in decision-makers' knowledge that other data sources cannot address. Over the long term, marketing research can be juxtaposed and interpreted in the context of other data sources, delivering insight and value that other data sources, taken on their own, cannot deliver.

Out of the array of research and information support approaches, there is no one guaranteed approach, research design or method that can create the perfect means to support decision-makers. If decision-makers complain that research is misleading or is only telling them what they already know, the researcher may argue that the fault lies with managers who pose the wrong questions or problem in the first place. If one takes the narrow view that the decision-maker poses the questions and the researcher finds the answers, there may be some validity in such an argument. It does not hold if one considers that the decision-maker and the researcher have a joint commitment to solve problems. In this joint commitment they have quite distinct, but complementary, creative skills that they can bring together to understand what problem they should be researching, how they conduct the research and how they interpret their findings.

The breadth of support available to marketing decision-makers

This section evaluates the array of data sources available to support marketing decision-making, the impact of technology upon the research process and the emergence and nature of social media research methods.

Data sources

To illustrate the variety of data sources available to support decision-makers, an example presented earlier of just one of the roles of marketing research will be used, 'Measure and understand the nature and scope of existing and potential customer groups'.

Traditionally, this would be seen as performing segmentation analyses and using these analyses to define and select target markets. It is not intended to work through the theory, practice or implementation of segmentation or target marketing. However, it is worth examining how different data sources can be linked and integrated to make segmentation and targeting work more effectively. Figure 8.2 sets out five basic methods of segmenting markets. Individually, each of these methods delivers different levels of insight to decision-makers. They also demand that different types of data be captured, with differing challenges in that capturing process. Figure 8.2 is somewhat deceiving in that it may imply the process of building stronger profiles of consumers is a linear process and that once one level is complete, one moves onto the next. The reality is that consumers may be constantly changing, and the building up of profiles of consumers is an iterative process and may never be complete. Building profiles of existing and potential customer groups will use constantly updated data to represent who these customers are, where they are located, what they 'do' and why they behave in that manner (and indeed could behave).

Figure 8.2 gives examples of where data may be obtained to help build up profiles of customers and markets. In the example of 'psychographics' or lifestyle measurements, data may be generated from customer relationship management (CRM) databases, web analytics or surveys. In the case of CRM data and web analytics, the purchasing or even browsing of particular types of products can indicate characteristics of a lifestyle. In a more direct manner, questions in a survey or qualitative study can help to build a profile of lifestyle behaviour. In its own right, 'lifestyle' can be a valid means of segmenting a market, perhaps positioning products and services to consumers who aspire to a particular lifestyle. However, being able to combine demographic measurements, broader behavioural characteristics and knowledge of where these consumers live, helps to build a 'picture' of consumers that facilitates more valid decision-making support. Figure 8.2 indicates that as one moves from demographic through to psychological characteristics the measurement, understanding and capturing process can become more difficult. Putting aside the differences in techniques

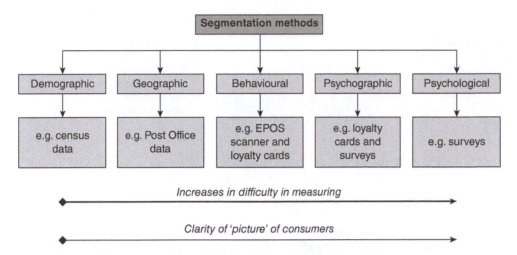

Figure 8.2 Methods of segmenting markets

to capture 'demography', 'behaviour' or 'psychology', what is being encapsulated becomes more difficult as one moves towards psychological variables. If one considers psychological variables that are vital to marketing and could be captured, examples such as satisfaction, loyalty, trust and quality are not as easy to capture as questions such as gender, age or where one lives.

Conversely, as measurements and understanding become more difficult to conduct, they add more richness to the 'picture' of customer and market profiles. To say that a target market is primarily female, aged between 25 and 40 and lives in a detached property with a mortgage starts to build a very basic 'picture' of target customers. To add details of their media behaviour, the array of products and services they buy, characteristics of their lifestyle and even something of their dreams and aspirations in life can help to build up a rich and, for decision-makers, a much more powerful 'picture' of target customers. Examining the variety of data sources that can be used in an interrelated manner to build market profiles, it is clear to see distinct contributions and value from externally generated secondary data founded in geodemographic information systems, transactional scanned data, loyalty card data, customer data in CRM systems, web analytics data, social media data, competitor intelligence and the use of traditional survey work and, indeed, other forms of quantitative and qualitative marketing research.

There is a clear interdependence amongst these different data sources and, for some commentators, many sources usurp the need for research, 'Marketing managers may need to reassess the role and usage of traditional market research as CRM duplicates much of it' (Lichtenstein *et al.* 2008).

With the technology and analytical methods needed to integrate these sources, richer more creative consumer insights can be generated. The main approaches to generating consumer insight can be summarised in Figure 8.3. Though each of the four segments is presented as distinct approaches, and there are organisations that deliver these distinct specialisations, there is much overlap in how they work.

This overlap is especially prevalent in the development and use of social media research. Practitioners in CRM, web analytics and business intelligence, as well as marketing research, see the development of their disciplines tightly interwoven with developments in social media research. Social media research has the potential to add many psychological characteristics of consumers and, as such, has much to add to the other three broad approaches to gaining customer insight, as laid

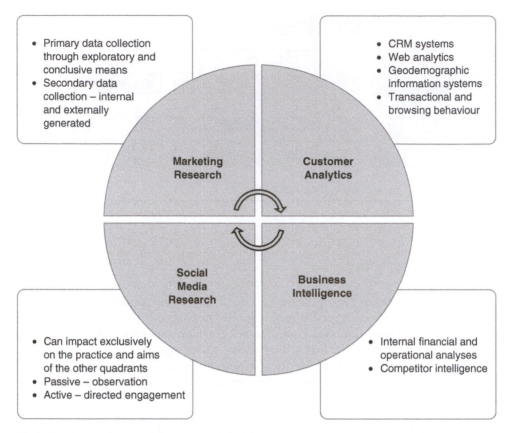

Figure 8.3 Approaches to gaining consumer insight

out in Figure 8.3. The explosion of data generated through social media and communications technology, and the manner in which individuals are engaging and articulating or even curating their lives online, could well lead to far more integration between these approaches. Organisations that adapt to the new scales of available data and the challenges of integrating disparate sources of data will thrive. Adapting organisations will create a single enterprise view of their business, not to replace the traditional single customer view but to augment it. This will allow them to access huge volumes of data, producing intricate analytics and targeted marketing that has both mass economies of scale and single customer precision (Maex 2009).

The impact of a continuing digitisation of so many dimensions of everyday life means that more individual-level data about consumer behaviour are available for marketers to respond to (Hayward 2009). Marketing research, like any of the other approaches in Figure 8.3, has to recognise that it contributes part of a wider understanding required to formulate effective and successful business and marketing strategies. Relying on marketing research as a sole data source, or arguing that it is the most valid data source, could lead to a very one-dimensional view of consumers and the full richness of the worlds they live in. Researchers need to recognise that marketing research exists within a context of other data sources that sometimes may be shallow, unrepresentative or unethical, but are being used by decision-makers. Within this context, marketing research has a distinctive role to play in a single enterprise view of a business, adding value and distinction through being able to:

1   focus upon filling in knowledge gaps of both existing and potential customers;
2   use quantitative and qualitative approaches to tap into a rich array of consumer attitudes, emotions and aspirations;
3   tap into the rich array of sensory and experiential characteristics of consumers;
4   draw on a well-established and a robust theoretical base in measuring and understanding consumers;
5   draw on well-established and a robust theoretical base in drawing inferences, being 'representative' and generalising target populations;
6   demonstrate integrity with research participants by being socially responsible through a long established, proactive and open code of conduct.

Researchers, who may conduct studies to meet specific objectives and just deliver the results of the research, may become a rarity. They will be employed for their technical abilities to respond to a fixed brief to gather, analyse and present data. By not engaging in a broader context of data sources, such researchers are defining the nature and scope of their work in a most narrow sense. They could be designing and delivering relatively weak research by not tapping into the array of data that can give valuable focus to the nature of their research questions, research approach and interpretation of findings. In order to utilise a breadth of disparate data, researchers need to equip themselves with more information gathering skills and techniques than they have been tradition-ally trained to do. In order to thrive, researchers need to become 'data curators' by embracing and integrating new information sources, 'We must ensure that we are the "aggregators" not just the aggregated' (Woodnutt and Owen 2010).

The marketing research process and the impact of technology

Marketing research can offer means to support decision-makers in ways that other data approaches alone cannot. It can also have great value when properly integrated with customer data captured through other approaches. In order to realise the value of research, a clear focus of what should be researched and the process of effectively addressing research questions should be planned. When decision-makers and researchers come together to creatively address research questions and their solutions, they are working through the marketing research process. The following stages essentially set out that marketing research process:

- define research problem(s);
- develop research approach(es);
- develop research design(s);
- design data collection methods;
- establish data integrity and conduct analyses;
- report and present findings.

This process is founded upon an understanding of the marketing decision(s) needing support. From this understanding, research aims and objectives are defined. To fulfill defined aims and objec-tives, an approach to conducting the research is established. Next, relevant information sources are identified and a range of data collection methods are evaluated for their appropriateness, forming a research design. The data are collected using the most appropriate method(s); they are analysed and interpreted and inferences are drawn. Finally, the findings, implications and recommendations are provided in a format that allows the information to be used for marketing decision-making and to be acted upon directly.

The marketing research process is a valuable and well-established means to ensure than research is well-planned and addresses the questions faced by decision-makers. The process seems linear, logical and straightforward. The reality of negotiating and planning such a process is not always that simple and, as such, many marketing research books spend much time in unpacking and describing the process.

Rather than adding another version that describes this process, we evaluate how technological developments are affecting the sense of how 'decision-makers and researchers come together to creatively address research questions and their solutions'. The biggest factor in shaping the scope, advances and future of marketing research has been, and still is, the impact of new technology. Technological developments have been impacting upon the nature and practice of marketing research for decades. Prior even to the earliest days of market research, the science of population-based statistics was driven forward by a series of technical innovations in collecting and processing data. The punched card designed for census data in the United States at the end of the nineteenth century and the creation of computational machines in the early twentieth century for handling this codified data, are considered by many not just to have given rise to the market research industry but the computer industry too. Without electronic data storage, data processing and modern data communications, most marketing research conducted today simply could not happen. However, technology has done much more for marketing research than allow it to meet clients' constant demands for faster turnaround and reduced cost. Technology has allowed, and continues to allow, research to innovate in its practices and find new ways to collect and treat data, as well as provide new and often better ways to solve research problems (Macer 2009).

In recent years, the sheer pace and impact of technology has massively changed what happens in the marketing research process. More powerful computers and software developments have facilitated progress in the capture, storage and analysis of research data. The manner in which individuals have integrated technology into their lives, especially through mobile devices, has radically altered the relationship between researchers and consumers. The rapid expansion of communication technology in the past ten years has created possibilities that early researchers would have regarded as science fiction. Recent advances in computing and communication technology have made it possible to collect market research data and deliver analysis that was impossible only a few years ago (Phillips 2013). The internet and social media have radically transformed the manner in which researchers connect across the world and the manner in which participants can be questioned and observed. New technologies have facilitated an explosion of rich and diverse quantitative and qualitative data in and around organisations. This has seen the emergence of several new means of supporting marketing decision-makers that appear to compete with marketing research in the forms of social media data, customer database analysis, web analytics and competitor intelligence. Marketing research users can be drowned in data, and new technologies have a pivotal role in enabling the engagement and interaction of users with all of this data (Birks and Macer 2009).

Though there are many valuable benefits and opportunities that researchers can derive from technology developments, Valle (2013) summarises one of the key challenges faced by marketing researchers:

> Industry 'outsiders' have taken research into their own hands and have bypassed the professional research function. And business leaders have become more demanding in their expectations of what market research should be able to do. All of this has cast a pall of fear and concern about where the industry is headed and whether the insights function will be taken over by non-researchers who do not appreciate the craft of research and the importance of research quality.

Valle is but one of many practitioners and writers in the research profession who question how marketing researchers can survive in an age of increasing competition from other information providers. Can they cope with the threats of growth in in-house research, new entrants to the profession that adopt new technologies and techniques, especially in the use of social media? Can marketing researchers fend off the challenge from the armies of consultants and avoid research being seen as a commodity (ESOMAR 2010)? The challenges of bringing fresh perspectives to business problems can be seen in how recent changes have impacted upon the research process.

To put these challenges into context, the marketing research process is re-presented. Alongside each stage, a short evaluation of the impact of technological developments will be presented. These developments can be seen as threats or opportunities to marketing research.

- **Define research problem(s)**. The tasks involved in problem definition consist of discussions with decision-makers, qualitative interviews with industry experts and other knowledgeable individuals, and analysis of readily available secondary data. These tasks help the researcher to understand the background of the problem by analysing the environmental context. The key challenges faced by researchers lie in how they gain access to key individuals and relevant data. This access challenge has to be completed in shortening time periods. Technology is enabling researchers to reach key individuals and data in more rapid and creative manners. Technology has also opened up a huge wealth of internal and externally generated secondary data and intelligence that can help in bringing focus to the definition of research problems.
- **Developing approach(es)**. Once a decision-maker(s) and researcher(s) have clarified the research problem they face, it has to be decided how to approach the research problem. How they collectively perceive the research problem affects the paradigm they will adopt in either an implicit or an explicit manner. Their adopted paradigm is built upon a set of assumptions. These assumptions consist of 'agreed-upon' knowledge, criteria of judgement, problem fields and ways to address such problems. With new techniques that encapsulate consumer behaviour and attitudes through tracking, observing and listening, 'agreed-upon' assumptions can be more challenging. The growth of new research techniques takes paradigm debates beyond traditional 'qualitative vs. quantitative' debates. With new research approaches come new ethical challenges, especially around protecting the identity of participants.
- **Develop research design(s)**. Exploratory research is characterised by flexibility and versatility with respect to the use of different methods. Researchers have to be alert to new ideas and insights as they proceed. Conclusive research is used to describe specific phenomena, to test specific hypotheses and to examine specific relationships. Conclusive research is typically more formal and structured than exploratory research; it is based on large, representative samples. In both the development of exploratory and conclusive research design, technology developments offer richer opportunities to understand and/or measure consumers. Researchers are able to formulate designs that are 'reward driven', to ensure that participants can be accessed and to ensure they engage with the research process. The creativity and ingenuity of the researcher plays a major role in using technology to develop research designs that are meaningful and relevant to participants.
- **Design data collection methods**. Online research methods, including social media research methods, are delivering more opportunities for researchers to be creative in crafting research methods that are relevant to different types of participant and in different contexts and modes of engagement. These opportunities are not just traditional research methods that can be facilitated online but entirely new methods. Digital applications are enabling marketing research methods to be more engaging, making the process of questioning, debate and sharing views more natural. These developments mean that researchers have to more seriously address how

participants view chosen research methods. This viewpoint should encompass the issues to be questioned or observed and the context in which research is conducted.

- **Establish data integrity and conduct analyses**. Data integrity includes the editing, coding, transcription and verification of data. This is essentially the same process for any type of data, secondary or primary, qualitative or quantitative. Considerations of data analysis do not occur after data have been collected: such considerations are an integral part of a research approach, research design and data collection methods. Data analyses should be founded upon a strategy. The researcher should build a strategy that addresses the set research problem(s), bringing together all stages of the research process, the known characteristics of the data, the nature of analysis techniques and the appropriate software to perform analyses. Technological developments have delivered great benefits in the means of collecting and storing data, and the ability to check the integrity of data. Processing speeds and capabilities of handling of large quantities and disparate data continue to improve. The fusion of like data sources and disparate types of data, such as numeric, narrative and visuals, are allowing researchers to connect and juxtapose data and interpret findings in contexts relevant to the needs of decision-makers.

- **Report and present findings**. Given the ability to search electronically and tailor reports online, research findings are becoming more 'pull' oriented, as opposed to the 'push' orientation of a printed report. The 'pull' orientation means that decision-makers and other research users can conduct analyses to suit their needs, sometimes working with raw data. Beyond the researcher's presentation of the focus and findings of a study, many interactive reporting formats enable users to create their own unique reports. Using database-driven technology and reporting software, it is possible to have a completely interactive experience that allows data interrogation through the specification of questions, filters, cross-tabulations and applied weighting (Macer 2006). Researchers increasingly need storytelling skills that inspire action (Lewis 2012). Delivering stories can be supported by the use of digital dashboards and data visualisation software. These formats enable much flexibility in terms of presenting both quantitative and qualitative data and how research findings are received and used. 'The days are gone when senior managers are prepared to sit through a presentation of 200 slides; nowadays, market researchers must make clear recommendations that address the specific business question at hand' (Hein 2012).

The development and use of technology continues to drive changes in the way that research is planned, executed and delivered to decision-makers. It is not just the development of new hardware or devices, or new software and apps that are driving changes in the stages of the research process. The changes in how individuals as consumers, researchers and managers are using and integrating technology into their lives are producing profound effects upon the nature and scope of marketing research.

Social media research

Perhaps the most important impact upon the nature of marketing research has been the development of social media. Social media networks encompass a great breadth of means by which individuals can enjoy and engage in discussions, chat, webcasts, photos, videos, podcasts, animation, surveys, games and virtual worlds. Individuals interact with and use social media in many different ways and contexts. For example, participants form online communities by combining one-to-one (e.g. email and instant messaging), one-to-many (web pages and blogs), and many to many (wikis) communication modes.

Many researchers have recognised that the user-generated content of social media make them very relevant as a domain for conducting new forms of marketing research. In response to these opportunities, many traditional research methods have been adapted and new methods have been developed. These new methods may be seen as a supplement to 'traditional' forms of marketing research. Engaging with individuals and communities in all the manners that individuals engage with social media has opened up new avenues for understanding, explaining and predicting the behaviour of consumers. Social media can be used in a variety of problem identification and problem solving marketing research applications, including segmentation, idea generation, concept testing, product development, brand launches, pricing and integrated marketing communications.

The term used in the marketing research profession to describe the development of social media research was 'Research 2.0' or 'NewMR'. Research 2.0 grew out of the development of Web 2.0, a term first coined by O'Reilly (2005) to describe two interrelated phenomena. The first phenomenon was the growth in websites where users could contribute content to the website, often referred to as user-generated content. The second phenomenon that was embraced under the term Web 2.0 was the creation of a wide range of tools that made using the web much easier and more rewarding. In the world of marketing research, the term 'Research 2.0' came into being in 2006, to reflect a shift away from the old 'command and control' paradigm of marketing research, towards a more collaborative approach.

'Command and control' is a term used to summarise what many researchers saw as the limitations of traditional marketing research, especially in the use of surveys. Characteristics of this perspective would include where researchers frame the questions from their own social and cultural perspective and may omit certain topics that participants find important. It would also include the use of the term 'subject' or 'respondent' to describe individuals measured, as in the physical sciences. The term 'respondent' could be seen to denote an individual who simply responds to questions 'commanded' by the researcher. The structure, process and research process can be seen as 'controlled' by the researcher, i.e. controlled as in the physical sciences. Within this context, many researchers argued that the marketing research profession was 'stuck in the 1990s' in that it was using the web merely to conduct the same research online as it would have done offline. It was argued that by not taking full advantage of Web 2.0 capabilities, the marketing research profession was relying on research methods that only scratched the surface of what consumers really thought and felt. Research 2.0 became a movement that embraced tapping into consumer-generated web data. The benefits of embracing Research 2.0 were seen as:

- *spontaneous* – enabling access to natural, spontaneous conversations, to consumer agendas, ways of thinking and the subtleties of their language (which could include visual stills, videos, music, poetry, games and other art forms);
- *heartfelt* – more emotionally rich responses facilitated by the anonymity of the internet;
- *cutting edge* – enabling access to more leading-edge and involved consumers: those who wish to articulate views (positive and negative) about brands, products, services, experiences;
- *immediate* – enabling feedback in real time as events unfold, rather than when their impact begins to be felt in the marketplace.

Research 2.0 was the catalyst to the emergence of new research methods and a critical reflection of how traditional marketing research methods are planned and implemented. It marked the recognition of a shift in respect to the experiences of individuals that researchers wish to measure and understand. This was a move from respondents being 'commanded and controlled' to a more collaborative relationship with participants, researchers and brands in sharing a research experience. Social media research has not replaced traditional marketing research; each approach has its own distinctive strengths and challenges and can best be seen as supportive and supplemental. It must be recognised, however, that participant experiences of social media research are shaping the expectations of research participants in terms of how rewarding and engaging research should be. Table 8.1 summarises the distinctive strengths and challenges of traditional marketing research and social research methods.

Of particular note in Table 8.1 is the great body of theory and cases over decades that have supported the development of traditional research methods, not just in marketing research but also across the social sciences. In contrast, many new and emerging cases illustrate the successful use of social media research. However, the underpinning theories that address the challenges of sampling, data collection and analytical techniques are still emerging. The same can be said of the ethical challenges in conducting traditional marketing research. Professional research associations such as ESOMAR and the Market Research Society have taken care to develop and apply codes of practice in order to differentiate bona fide research activities from other data gathering and marketing ventures. Social media research has created a number of ethical challenges. Responses to those challenges are also still emerging. Finally, it is worth noting that even though huge amounts of data may be gathered with sometimes far more individuals represented in comparison to sample surveys, social media research is qualitative in nature. It is primarily exploratory, embracing and synthesising multifarious forms of data. Social media research is organic in terms of how issues and questions emerge and are addressed.

Table 8.1 The relative strengths and challenges of traditional marketing research and social media research methods

	Strengths	*Challenges*
Traditional marketing research	• Robust theoretical underpinnings to sampling, research methods and data analyses • Robust development of ethical codes of practice, especially protecting participant anonymity • Breadth of quantitative and qualitative research methods to measure and understand participants • Can focus upon specific existing and potential consumers to capture behaviour, attitudes, emotions, aspirations and sensory experiences	• Gaining access to participants – declining response rates • Complaints of boring research experiences. This sets challenges to design engaging research processes • Debates on the quality of samples used in survey work – especially in the use of access panels • The costs and time taken to conduct research of quality – relative to other forms of data that may support decision-makers
Research 2.0 social media research	• Can reach notoriously difficult to access target participants • Engaging experiences, technology and context can be suited to participants • Participants can express themselves in ways that they are comfortable with • Speed of capturing a great amount of disparate data	• Newly developed methods with little theoretical underpinning • Representativeness – can count incidences of behaviour, but primarily qualitative • Ethical challenges – participant identities and forms of expression • Conversely an inability to target specific types of participants (through non-engagement with social media) and/or specific topics

Being passive or active in social media research

Social media research methods can be broadly classified as passive and active. 'Passive' social media research can be seen as an approach akin to observing what is being discussed and displayed in social media. Another term for passive research that is perhaps more commonly used to represent passive social media research is 'listening'.

Listening involves the evaluation of naturally occurring conversations, behaviours, and signals. The information that is elicited may or may not be guided by other participant interactions, but it brings a sense of consumers' lives. Continually, millions of consumers across the globe talk online about all aspects of their lives, lifestyles and aspirations. This wealth of naturally occurring consumer expression offers the opportunity to understand consumers on their terms, using their language and logic. Through 'conversational webs' of blogs, forums, social networks, Twitter, communities and wikis, consumers are talking with one another about their problems, experiences, likes and dislikes, life in general, and their feelings and experiences of brands. By tuning in to relevant conversations (i.e. by listening), it is argued that more can be learned about consumer attitudes and needs than through traditional 'questioning' methods alone. By listening, researchers may be able to learn more about consumers and prospects by understanding the natural, rich, unfiltered word of mouth around products and service experiences.

'Active' social media research can be seen as an approach akin to both observing and engaging in what is being discussed and displayed in social media. Rather than standing back, observing and listening, researchers can join communities and may choose to direct specific questions or tasks to participants. The main advantage of this approach is that researchers can direct participants and communities to address issues and questions that they deem to be important. They can also establish quality standards in how data is collected in much the same way that many qualitative researchers work. The main disadvantage is that specific research issues and questions driven by researchers may not be of interest to participants or communities. Great care has to be taken to protect the values of brands that may be seen as alien to the agendas of particular communities.

Social media research methods

There is a growing body of passive and active social media research methods. It is not possible in a chapter to represent fully contemporary technological developments that individuals use to engage with social media. Further, it is not possible to illustrate fully how these developments have been adapted to encapsulate the essential characteristics of consumers. It is worth noting, however, that these developments continue apace and many of the individuals and companies engaged in encapsulating the essential characteristics of consumers do not come from traditional marketing research backgrounds. Rather than list and describe a body of emerging methods, the focus here is upon methods that have been seen by decision-makers as delivering value. These represent a growing base of case material that describes how different methods are applied and what benefits and challenges are inherent in a selected method. The methods chosen can broadly be categorised as research that utilises blogging, communities and crowdsourcing.

Blogging

Blogging as a research term can represent both passive and active forms of social media research. The use and value of the blog in an active and passive sense can largely be attributed to the great diversity of ways that blogs may be created and presented. The 'blog' can be presented as a piece of writing both short, e.g. Twitter feeds, and longer forms of writing, poetry, drawings, still visuals, moving images, music or any combination of these. The blogger may take time to research, edit and articulate their views. They may also produce a blog extremely quickly as a representation of opinions and feelings as they experience them or respond to other blogs. The term used to represent passive research using blogs is 'blog and buzz mining'. Such an approach provides the means to observe, track or initiate views in research communities, social networks and anywhere else that people post comments, visuals, music and other forms of art on the internet. Individual researchers can undertake blog or buzz mining. This can be done by searching the internet for conversations and postings in an array of blogs that could include Twitter and comments about news stories. Individual researchers do this with a specific set of research objectives to guide their search. Regardless of how many postings researchers gather or how quantitative specific elements of blog analysis may be, e.g. statistics from Twitter analyses, it should be remembered that blog and buzz mining is exploratory and qualitative in nature. The researcher is looking for the juxtaposition of different ideas and forms of expression, emerging patterns and 'nuggets' of expression that articulate feelings or opinions really well. In addition to the individual researcher addressing specific research objectives, decision-makers may turn to specialist research companies that work in blog and buzz mining.

Blog and buzz mining can help to reveal how a series of events unfolds and what may be shaping those events. A sense of the impact of specific developments in the marketplace, such as the launch of a new product by a competitor, can be monitored. Rapid feedback on the impact of decisions, such as the use of a new celebrity to endorse a brand, can be gathered. As a result, questions can be addressed of what is occurring now for decision-makers and what could be happening through the emergence of specific trends. These questions can be addressed without having to recruit, engage or reward participants. Whilst blog and buzz mining can save the time and costs associated with interacting with participants, these resource savings cover a major drawback. Researchers may identify particularly interesting participants whose ideas, experiences and forms of articulation are seen as being really valuable. Particular issues, points of debate and novel ideas may emerge, but may be lost if the researcher is unable to interject. Thus, there may be individuals and issues that the researcher may wish to question in more depth. The means of response may continue in a blog format and may also be in the public domain.

When researchers direct questions to develop blogs, they are conducting active social media research. The term used to represent active research using blogs is 'participatory blogging'. Participatory blogging occurs when researchers interact with individuals in communities and social networks. Individual participants can be targeted and given blogging tasks that relate to specific research objectives. Of particular note is what may be deemed as a 'blog'. There can be a clear use of narrative and visuals combined to articulate what participants are doing, what they would like to do and how they feel: their emotional engagement. Participants can be given tasks that are more engaging than answering direct questions. The outcome of the blogs can feed into traditional forms of marketing research, helping to develop and validate the views expressed in the blogs. A blogging exercise can be engaging and enjoyable for participants and the outcomes of great value for decision-makers. Researchers can address issues specifically to suit the motivations and characteristics of individual participants. In turn, participants can choose the timing and context of engagement with the blogging task set.

Communities

Many blogs are delivered, enjoyed and commented upon in a community setting. Communities are spaces where individuals co-exist and share many interests and aspirations. Individuals may share their community in harmony, but for some an element of dissent or debate is an essential character-istic of their membership. In virtual or online communities members generally have the option to easily join or leave a community, depending upon how well it serves their priorities and interests.

An example of an online community is the parents' website Mumsnet www.mumsnet.com. The community that uses Mumsnet can view and share a huge breadth of issues, likes, dislikes and concerns that relate to the myriad challenges and joys of bringing up children and being a parent. From a researcher's perspective, there is a huge amount to learn about parents in a passive manner. Individuals within the community may strongly relate to the issues presented and discussed, they could be emotionally charged, supportive and really open. Where there exists a specific prob-lem or challenge (e.g. in the parenting context of coping with a child who is copying unsavoury characteristics of their favourite television character), interested community members can come together to co-create possible solutions or future directions. These forms of expression are what many researchers want from participants in their studies. As such, many brands and researchers try to establish communities. These communities are termed Market Research Online Communities or MROCs.

MROCs may be devoted to a particular group of individuals, selected countries and/or particular issues. However, given the investment needed to build, maintain and reward a community, many MROCs are built around specific sponsoring brands. A dedicated brand MROC can enable a com-pany to recruit a panel of 'consumer-advisers'. A company and their researchers can engage with members using a variety of quantitative and qualitative techniques, often unfolding over a period of months. A brand MROC establishes a channel that decision-makers and designers working for a brand can use to communicate with participants and engage in projects ranging from measuring attitudes, exploration and ethnography, to concept and product development and testing.

Brand MROCs can be seen as a means to address specific research objectives. However, a fundamental difference of the brand MROC compared to other research approaches is the extent to which they feature brand engagement. They actively seek to invite participants to immerse themselves in the world of the brand. This can mean that the aim of a MROC is to develop a relationship with participants to a stage where they become 'critical friends' to the brand, offer-ing continuing 'honest' feedback. There are three purposes fulfilled in a MROC, but a specific purpose may be seen as the main driver. The first would be to create *brand ambassadors*, i.e. by nurturing participants who are seen as thought leaders. With a deep understanding of the values and personality of a brand, plus an emotional commitment to the brand, these participants could be highly persuasive to an array of target markets. The second would be to create a *brand analyst*, i.e. by nurturing participants who would test particular concepts and designs. Again, with a deep understanding of the brand, the 'fit' of a new idea to the values of a brand could be tested. This form of testing could be in the use: of words, e.g. a new product description; of images, e.g. the use of new celebrity endorsement; or of design, e.g. the look, form and function of a new product. The third would be to create *consumer insight*, i.e. by eliciting characteristics of participants' behav-iour, attitudes and emotions. Measuring and understanding characteristics of participants could work using a breadth of traditional research methods, allowing participants to reflect and express themselves in a variety of manners.

The key advantages of the use of social media research in the context of communities are worth noting:

- **Community** – An MROC can help participants articulate issues that are dear to them, in con-texts and forms they are comfortable with (visual, narrative, music, etc.). The context of discussion in an MROC enables topics to be listened to, developed and challenged over periods of time.

- **Engaging** – New topics can be introduced to MROCs. These topics can be set by what the researcher sees as being vital to support marketing decision(s) and/or what is discerned as being interesting and relevant to the community.
- **Rewards** – In MROCs participants explicitly know they are addressing issues around an enterprise or brand. As such, they expect to be rewarded with tangible incentives for taking part. There are intangible rewards that lie in the control that participants have in engaging with the community. They can choose if, how and when to respond, and as such they have to be given tasks that they find interesting. They have to be treated with respect.
- **Mixed methods** – Surveys can be administered in an MROC. The focus of the questions set in the survey could emerge from qualitative discussions and/or the posting of images or any art/design representations.
- **Timing and costs** – Traditional marketing research methods could be used to generate the knowledge and insight generated in the community, but in comparative terms an MROC can generate a huge breadth of decision support quickly and cheaply.

The key challenge MROCs face in working with communities is one of building relationships with participants and maintaining integrity. Many communities may be naturally wary of 'outsiders' who may hold questionable values, who observe them, and sometimes aim to shape community agendas. There are examples of researchers locating and engaging with founders or influential 'elders' within communities. Such engagements can build researcher integrity and facilitate more natural conversations. For researchers to properly connect with communities and properly realise their inherent powers of expression, well-planned and targeted communications are vital. The community is clearly a context in which to conduct research where the previously described stance of 'command and control' would be doomed to fail.

Crowdsourcing

Crowdsourcing is the act of taking a job traditionally performed by a designated agent (usually an employee) and outsourcing it to an undefined, generally large group of people in the form of an open call. Crowdsourcing has been applied in many areas to perform services, design products and solve problems. In terms of conducting research, crowdsourcing enables ideas to be elicited and potential insights and actionable solutions based on those insights to be tested and developed. The process of crowdsourcing is a means to draw together the creative thinking and talents of a wide body of individuals. Through the use of online communities, a great breadth and diversity of thinking and talents can be drawn together to generate ideas and actionable solutions.

Perhaps the best known example of community crowdsourcing is Wikipedia (http://www.wikipedia.org). The encyclopedia was created and is maintained by participants who freely engage in volunteering their ideas. Wikipedia is not just an example of a crowd creating a body of information that competes with conventional commercial encyclopedias. It is also an example of a community taking ownership of a project by working to ensure the validity of information and that the process of validation is within a code of conduct.

In the context of conducting marketing research, crowdsourcing constitutes an active social media research method. Its impact is realised by researchers contacting and engaging self-selecting participants through different online communities, primarily through social media. If these individuals can be inspired by a particular research challenge that they see as being credible, they may spread the word to other individuals within their communities using, for example, Facebook or Twitter. As was discussed in the context of communities, well-planned and targeted communications are vital to inspire individuals to want to become part of the crowd and to fully engage in the tasks set for the crowd. Once individuals are drawn into the crowd and become participants, the researcher can achieve the following benefits:

- **Co-creation** is a process by which a group of participants collaborate to evaluate the challenges and opportunities inherent in a research task. They can go on to design solutions to those challenges. This group can be really diverse and bring together many different forms of thinking and expression. The nature of debate within this group can develop new, unexpected agendas that can draw in the energy and thinking of new participants. The nature of debate, forms of expression and quality of debate can create a most engaging co-creation experience for participants.
- **Brainstorming** has been used for several decades, especially in the context of marketing research. Whether formal or informal, the process is the same: participants think of as many ideas as they can and express them; leave the evaluation until later; build on and combine others' ideas; be as imaginative as possible, the wilder the ideas the better. When it works well, ideas flow freely from an interplay that may never have occurred if the group had not brainstormed together.
- **In-depth** understanding of issues. Particular ideas and solutions may be explored in depth. The exploration may occur naturally, as different participants are drawn in to explain and illustrate ideas, to present better arguments and to question the ideas and arguments of other participants. Moderators can be used (and may be vital to the success of crowdsourcing in managing debate and contention) to drill down into the source and nature of ideas. Participants can express and illustrate their ideas through a variety of media including writing, still and moving images or even music.
- **Evaluate** emerging insights and proposed actions. Researchers can build analyses and interpretations of themes that are discussed in a crowd. They can present what they see as the meaning of themes and even what may be seen as an optimum solution to a particular challenge. The popularity of particular solutions may be tested through simple polls through to detailed articulations of what is liked/disliked, will work/not work.

Ethics and the future of marketing research

The growth of alternative means to support marketing decision-makers, especially researching online and in the sphere of social media research, has created many ethical challenges. Many of these challenges are not new for researchers, but new technologies have created sometimes conflicting expectations in decision-makers and participants of the value and integrity of marketing research. How researchers address ethical challenges will shape perceptions of their future role and value.

Marketing research often involves contact with participants and a wider public, usually by way of data collection, dissemination of research findings, and marketing activities such as advertising and PR campaigns based upon research findings. There is the potential to abuse or misuse marketing research by taking advantage of these individuals. If participants feel that they or their views are being abused or misrepresented, they will either not take part in future studies or may do so without honesty or full engagement in the issues being researched. They may also lobby politicians to protect them from what they see as intrusions into their privacy and liberties. In short, unethical research practices can severely impair the quality of the research process, undermine the validity of research findings and ultimately inflict serious damage upon the body of professional researchers. There are many instances where it is difficult to distinguish between genuine marketing research and telemarketing, or direct marketing practices where surveys are used to gain access to participants to deliver a sales pitch. When participants become confused by the legitimacy of survey practices, there can be severe repercussions for the marketing research profession through legislation designed to protect the privacy of citizens.

The Market Research Society distinguishes marketing research from other competitive forms of data gathering, primarily through the issue of the anonymity of participants. It stresses that in marketing research, the identity of the provider of information is not disclosed. It makes a clear distinction between marketing research and direct marketing where the names and addresses of the people contacted are to be used for individual selling, promotional, fundraising or other non-research purposes. The distinction between marketing research and the database as a research tool is ultimately not so clear. There is a growing amount of support given to marketing decision-makers from database analyses and Research 2.0 activities, which are not 'participant specific'. It is possible to perform database analyses with the same level of professional standards as is applied in the marketing research profession, but social media research techniques are not so clear. In celebrating 60 years since they first adopted a self-regulatory code in November 1954, the Market Research Society (2014) has formulated a new code of conduct. This code is designed to help guide researchers through the challenges posed by alternative forms of data, including social media research.

The Market Research Society has ten principles that encapsulate the scientific aim and character of marketing research, as well as its special responsibility towards participants, clients and the public. The ten principles that have now been incorporated into the Market Research Society's code of conduct require that researchers shall:

1 ensure that participation in their activities is based on voluntary informed consent;
2 be straightforward and honest in all their professional and business relationships;
3 be transparent as to the subject and purpose of data collection;
4 respect the confidentiality of information collected in their professional activities;
5 respect the rights and well-being of all individuals;
6 ensure that participants are not harmed or adversely affected by their professional activities;
7 balance the needs of individuals and clients and their professional activities;
8 exercise independent professional judgement in the design, conduct and reporting of their professional activities;
9 ensure that their professional activities are conducted by persons with appropriate training, qualifications and experience;
10 protect the reputation and integrity of the profession.

These principles say much of what it is to 'be' a marketing researcher, but researchers cannot remain isolated from other forms of decision support and how decision-makers may use and value that support. There are many instances where database analyses generated from store data, loyalty card and web analytics can add clarity and focus to marketing research activities. In addition, the use of online interactions and social media has shown that people are far more willing to self-disclose and to trade information about themselves. Protecting the identity of participants and the integrity of marketing research is far more challenging in a world of social media research. Cooke (2008) summed up the challenge of 'what happens to the principles of knowledge and control when it comes to consumer data on the internet?' by contending, 'If we can collect vast amounts of data passively without the individual being aware of the data trail they are leaving, does that give researchers the right to use it for other purposes?'. Some researchers would answer with a resounding 'yes', and see chat rooms, forums and blogs as the ideal setting to conduct unbiased ethnography by 'lurking' at the sites of interest without announcing their presence. One view within the research community seems to be that postings and blogs are 'published material'. However, bloggers and networkers might not see it in the same way. Teenagers often rue what they have written on Facebook or Twitter when they realise employers and university admissions tutors are able to view their 'published' outpourings. These dilemmas have yet to be resolved within the marketing research profession, but it has been argued that in order to abide by the spirit of the marketing research code of conduct, researchers should be able to answer in the affirmative to the following questions, 'Are my research intentions transparent?', 'Has the participant given informed consent?', 'Can I verify the age of my participant?', 'Can I verify that I have parental permission of under-16s?'.

Skills demanded of marketing researchers

An emerging generation of researchers will be expected to continue to master the skills of adapting and developing research methods and techniques from a breadth of social sciences. The challenges of writing engaging questionnaires, observing consumers, capturing consumer experiences and the context of their consumption, deciding what constitutes a meaningful sample, and making sense of data have to be understood and applied. Decision-makers are increasingly demanding a far more integrated approach to analysing, understanding and interpreting often contradictory and imperfect sources of evidence. There is a mounting need for decision-makers and researchers to work in an eclectic and holistic way with qualitative and quantitative data. Increasingly, researchers will have to analyse multiple and often imperfect datasets. In terms of engaging with decision-makers, the future researcher will be more than a project manager developing methods, coordinating fieldwork, analysing research material and finally compelling visual stories to engage decision-makers with research findings. The future researcher will be more of a creative consultant, working together with designer colleagues to produce videos or interactive presentations, but also skilled themselves in visualising results with the help of design software or interactive applications. Research will become more encompassing, holistic and multifaceted. To achieve all of this, researchers will need new holistic analytic frameworks to be able to make sense of the data and to present this to decision-makers in a coherent, confident and effective manner.

> In a world of so many data sources, where market research is 'just one part of a jigsaw', the big political question is: who owns the job of integration? It's a question market research, and researchers, still have to answer.
>
> (Mitchell 2012)

Mitchell's (2012) view that market researchers are not necessarily in a position to integrate data sources within organisations could readily be applied to direct marketing, CRM, social media and web-based intelligence gathering professionals. The research profession continues to have great opportunities to add value to research. Researchers can move up the value chain to offer more advice and insight, thus improving their stature and ultimately their profitability. They can help decision-makers to make sense of a variety of data sources, rather than walking away from a project when a research study is complete. Moving towards a business model that is driven by researchers offering actionable consumer insight means that researchers and the marketing research profession of the future will be required to:

- think conceptually – by developing 'conceptual' thinkers, i.e. researchers who feel comfortable working with higher order business concepts and talking the language of senior decision-makers. These individuals must understand the relationship between information and key business concepts. They must go beyond their technical and skill-based knowledge and offer strategic and tactical advice for business advantage based on detailed consumer and market knowledge;
- communicate in the way that those who commission research think – by knowing how to communicate in the way senior people think, i.e. researchers presenting findings as a compelling narrative, not as disparate blocks of information;
- interpret findings in terms of the whole picture – by thinking holistically about 'evidence', i.e. researchers with the skills to work in a 'holistic' way with all available customer evidence, recognising the need to interpret often imperfect marketing information. They must draw knowledge from a host of different sources including qualitative and quantitative techniques, a variety of forms of observation, CRM systems, financial and customer profile information. These individuals will have to draw heavily upon the use of analytical models that represent the way customers think and behave;
- integrate findings with others that support marketing decision-makers – by working in a multidisciplinary way with related marketing services companies, with researchers working alongside branding and design and other marketing specialisms to gain a wider market understanding. This makes sure that everything is tailored to business solutions and is not just the result of rigid prescriptive research designs. This bottom-up, multidisciplinary approach provides flexibility and differentiates 'strategic marketing intelligence' from the 'top-down' approach of full-blown management consultants. This will also mean the cultivating of a more creative environment with a more 'hands-off' management style, rather than a prescriptive techniques-driven approach.

In 2011 the Cambiar Future of Research Study looked ahead to 2020 and also explored the barriers and enablers for the success of the research profession, drawing on perspectives from both corporate researchers and senior research agency executives. The study concluded that market research will need more than ever to synthesise and make sense of all information sources within organisations and that research agencies will evolve into integrated insight-consulting companies. Research will be more about listening to consumers and customers through social media and using new techniques that have yet to be invented; mining information (aka big data), rather than initiating a research project. Corporate researchers and research companies will need each other to be successful. Corporate researchers will increasingly become consultants and storytellers who provoke action and are fuelled by synthesising knowledge from a 'river of information'. Research companies will need to become integrated 'insight for impact' consultants that form business impact partnerships with their clients (Lewis 2012).

Conclusions

Marketing research as a discipline and profession has always addressed the best ways to encapsulate the essential characteristics of consumers who should be at the heart of an enterprise. In the quest to measure and understand consumers, it is clear that marketing research is not the only means to support marketing decision-making. There are many disparate sources of marketing data gathered through approaches that may seem indefensible to researchers that decision-makers use and value. There are many pressures on the marketing research profession to deliver consumer insights that are relevant to decision-makers, but delivered more quickly and cheaply than have hitherto been possible. Technological developments continue to change the nature, scope and value of marketing research. These developments can be seen as a threat to 'traditional' means of conducting marketing research, with research being perceived as a commodity. Conversely, these developments can be seen as a great opportunity to augment the future thinking, creative and responsible qualities of researchers. Researchers can take the stance of being 'data curators' for enterprises. Being a 'data-curator' means being able to use the insights gained from other means of encapsulating consumers. These insights can help to drive and formulate research projects of greater focus, relevance and value. These insights can also help to contextualise research findings and add impact to interpretations derived from research. In all, researchers have great opportunities to demonstrate their value to decision-makers through the integrity of how they encapsulate and represent current and potential customers. This integrity comes from the quality of evidence they can provide and the ethical stance that can protect participants, decision-makers and their brand relationships. Marketing researchers who work proactively, creatively and ethically with decision-makers, who understand what constitutes 'quality data', who embrace opportunities inherent in new technologies and social media, who see the rich and creative opportunities that lie in alternative ways consumers may be measured and understood, will be in great demand. Such researchers and the profession they embody will justly deserve to be represented in the next edition of *The Marketing Book*.

References

AMA (2004), available at https://www.ama.org/AboutAMA/Pages/Definition-of-Marketing.aspx, accessed 1 September 2014.

Birks, D. F. and Macer, T. (eds) (2009), *Marketing Research: Critical Perspectives on Business and Management*, Abingdon, UK: Taylor & Francis, p. 2.

Cambiar (2011), *Future of Research Study*, available at http://media.wix.com/ugd/e94d21_4c3572dbbc784a81bbb8 7f6ae38b5636.pdf, accessed 21 December 2015.

Cooke, M. (2008), 'Guest editorial: The new world of web 2', *International Journal of Market Research*, 50(8): 570–572.

ESOMAR (2007), *ICC/ESOMAR International Code on Market and Social Research*, p. 5, available at https://www. esomar.org/uploads/public/knowledge-and-standards/codes-and-guidelines/ESOMAR_ICC-ESOMAR_ Code_English.pdf, accessed 21 December 2015.

ESOMAR (2010), 'Global Market Research', ESOMAR Industry Report, p. 48, available at https://www. esomar.org/uploads/industry/reports/global-market-research-2010/ESOMAR_GMR2010_Cover-Contents-FirstChapter.pdf, accessed 21 December 2015.

Gordon, W. (2000), 'Be creative to innovate', *Research*, December, hard copy only.

Gordon, W. (2002), 'I'll have one small insight and two large ones please', *Admap*, 434(December): 19–21.

Hayward, M. (2009), 'Connecting the dots: Joined up insight finally becomes possible', *International Journal of Market Research*, 51(2): 269–271.

Hein, T. (2012), *A Bright Future for Market Research*, available at http://www.marketresearchworld.net/content/ view/5037/77/, accessed 1 September 2014.

Lehmann, D. R. (1994), *Market Research and Analysis*, third edition, Homewood, IL: Irwin, p. 14.

Lewis, I. (2012), 'The future of market research', *International Journal of Market Research*, 54(1): 11–13.

Lichtenstein, S., Bednall, D. H. B. and Adam, S. (2008), 'Marketing research and customer analytics: Interfunctional knowledge integration', *International Journal of Technology Marketing*, 3(1): 81–96.

Lury, G. (2000), 'Market research cannot cover for the "vision thing"', *Marketing*, November, p. 34.

Macer, T. (2006), 'On your marks, get set . . . ', *Research in Business*, May, 7–8, no longer published.

Macer, T. (ed.) (2009), *Technology Futures: Perspectives on How Technology Will Transform the Market Research of Tomorrow*, Market Research Society, Annual Conference, available at http://www.research-live.com/ Journals/1/Files/2010/4/21/Research%202009.pdf, accessed 21 December 2015.

Maex, D. (2009), *The New Landscape of Marketing Analytics*, Ogilvy Insight: Intellectual Capital from Ogilvy, available at https://assets.ogilvy.com/truffles_email/math_marketing/Math_Marketing_August_2009_O_M_version.pdf, accessed 21 December 2015.

Market Research Society (2014), *Code of Conduct 60: Celebrating Sixty Years of Successful Self-Regulation*, September, available at https://www.mrs.org.uk/pdf/mrs%20code%20of%20conduct%202014.pdf, accessed 1 September 2014.

Mitchell, A. (2012), 'Make or break for market research', *Marketing*, 13 June: 30–32.

O'Reilly, T. (2005), 'What is Web 2.0?', 30 September, available at http://www.oreillynet.com/pub/a/oreilly/tim/news/2005/09/30/what-is-web-20.html, accessed 1 September 2014.

Phillips, A. (2013), 'A marginalised future for market research?', *International Journal of Market Research*, 53(6): 735–736.

Roberts, D. and Adams, R. (2010), 'Agenda development for marketing research: The user's voice', *International Journal of Market Research*, 52(3): 339–363.

Renkema, R. and Zwikker, C. (2003), 'Development of a new brand concept: Means-end approach applied to consumer insight', *ESOMAR: Consumer Insights Conference*, Madrid, April, available at https://www.esomar.org/web/research_papers/Qualitative_162_Development-of-a-new-brand-concept-br-Means-end-approach-applied-to-consumer-insight.php, accessed 5 January 2016.

Valle, M. (2013), 'Re-discovering market research: Seizing opportunity and innovation', *Marketing Insights*, Winter: 12–13, available at https://www.ama.org/publications/MarketingInsights/Pages/behavioral-economics-big-data-innovation.aspx, accessed 5 January 2016.

Woodnutt, T. and Owen, R. (2010), 'The research industry needs to embrace radical change in order to thrive and survive in the digital era', *Market Research Society, Annual Conference*, available at www.warc.com, accessed 5 January 2016.

9 Qualitative research

Len Tiu Wright and Rose Wright

Introduction

This chapter concentrates on the importance of qualitative research in marketing. It is not in the remit of this chapter to cover the numerous typologies and specialisms of qualitative research used in the social sciences. The chapter's orientation is directed at where some of the traditions and applications inherent in qualitative research are suited to marketing. Figures to support the growth of the international market research industry are provided. The scope of qualitative research covers its enduring quality from theoretical underpinnings and the differences between qualitative and quantitative approaches to data collection methods and what validity, reliability and triangulation mean. Qualitative research and reflections draw on existing traditional types of inquiry, namely autobiography, biography, ethnography, grounded theory, phenomenology and the case study. Examples of qualitative research in the broader realms of applications range from discussions of applications using mobile handheld devices and computer-assisted qualitative data analysis to web mining and sentiment analysis. The chapter concludes with an awareness of the nature, risks and importance attributed to qualitative research in marketing.

There has been a long tradition in the social sciences of observing, studying and recording what it is that people do and how they live. Qualitative research is rooted firmly in this tradition, drawing from the various social science disciplines, such as those of anthropology, education, history, politics, linguistics, psychology, sociology and the practices of business, management and marketing to inform each brand of study. It is represented and interpreted by many, such as academics, filmmakers, essayists, writers and social critics (Denzin and Lincoln 2013) and informed through an approach that consists of being naturalistic, humanistic, holistic and speculative (Mariampolski 2001: 7–9). Hence, qualitative research has been described as both art and science, as it cuts across different fields and subject matter. In the study of marketing, qualitative research lends itself to investigating and interpreting the interactions, relationships and networks of people in their exchange processes. As Czinkota and Ronkainnen (2013: 21) put it, there are the relationships between customers and the 'consequences of the marketing effort for other parties, such as suppliers, distributors, investors or family members who can play the role of both clients and partners'.

Since humans are as subject to received wisdom as they are to infinite thirst for knowledge and imaginary leaps of faith, so qualitative researchers are unbounded by conventional wisdom in seeking new interpretations and challenges to advance knowledge in the human race. While this gives qualitative research its unique and timeless quality, it has to be said that there is a caveat to qualitative research. It is to be expected that there are differences in the abilities of the people conducting qualitative research, as there are variations in the quality of the material being researched. There are individual value judgements garnered from interpretations in the field, and these can give rise to consensus supported by others or to differences leading to reported controversies, examples of which are discussed under the subheading of ethnography. This is one of the reasons why international research agencies send experienced moderators to train indigenous researchers in the field, so that their conduct of focus groups could be carried out at a level that is comparable and equivalent, therefore of an expected international quality standard. Training courses for moderators are also provided by the Association for Qualitative Research (AQR 2014) in the UK.

What is important to recognise is that there is much good qualitative research being carried out. The growth in market research industry revenue, which incorporates both qualitative and quantitative research activities, attests to this. When Neil Borden introduced the term 'the marketing mix' in his seminal publication (Borden 1964) he included market research as one of the twelve components of the mix. Since then the market research industry has grown to be a large and important industry in its own right, as evidenced by the European Society for Opinion and Marketing Research (ESOMAR) publications of annual reports on turnover and spend in the market research industry. In 1997 ESOMAR put the size of the world research market at more than €10.4 billion or approximately US$13.3 billion. ESOMAR listed among 'the top ten research groups world wide' those companies that were also among the top ten in the EU. The EU (41 per cent) and the United States (37 per cent) accounted for the largest shares of world turnover for qualitative research (ESOMAR 1998). In 2010 total market research revenues for the 78 countries in ESOMAR's industry report rose to US$31.2 billion, up from the previous year (ESOMAR 2011). Investments in central and eastern European countries helped to put these within the top five research growth markets in Europe. The Asia Pacific and African regions had growth in research revenues, while, in contrast, the Middle East with its varied areas of instability, showed decline. North America, after two consecutive years of decline, increased research revenues from 3.1 per cent to US$9.9 billion, while Latin America recorded a fast 13.9 per cent growth rate taking it to US$1.8 billion. There is recorded growth in the UK market research industry, given in the Market Research Society (MRS) Research and Insight Industry League Table (UK) 2012, produced by MRS (2013). This puts the market size at over £2.2 billion or approximately over US$2.8 billion.

There are a number of reasons why qualitative research in marketing thrives. The increasing sophistication in analytics and big data provide opportunities for qualitative researchers who can process information directly from sources, be they human or virtual, with the speed of qualitative data processing. Moreover, all kinds of organisations and their consultants conduct qualitative investigations in many and different fields, such as for academia, charities, media, public relations and government departments, which conduct qualitative research to find out the attitudes or opinions, behaviour and motivations of targeted groups and individuals. In the twenty-first century the creation of new industries and markets, and goods and services replacing many old products from manufacturing and old service industries have led to new types of consumption and user behaviour, such as with new products and services in the modern electronics, telecommunications and entertainment sectors. There are proponents of more qualitative research to enable greater 'nuance based audience definitions' away from static measurement, as in an Indian example by Nye and as quoted by Mackenzie (2005: 8). The increasing number of universities and practitioner institutions worldwide teaching qualitative research as part of marketing and market research courses can be seen in trawling through their specific websites. In the academic and practitioner spheres there are informative and instructive books on qualitative research, examples of which are included in 'References' and 'Further readings' at the end of this chapter.

Definition and traditions of qualitative research

Qualitative research is an overall term to describe the work researchers do in formulating their interpretations of the subjects of their studies and giving representations of these interpretations in order to add to a body of knowledge. Perhaps qualitative research needs to carry a health warning. A variety of explanations for the theoretical understanding of qualitative research is given in this section.

Within the humanities, the sociological and educational perspectives are expounded by Denzin and Lincoln (2011) who defined qualitative research as 'a field of inquiry in its own right' being a 'complex, interconnected family of terms, concepts and assumptions' associated with, 'methods connected to cultural and interpretive studies'. The authors describe qualitative research within a North American tradition representing eight phases in:

> [t]he traditional (1900–1950); the modernist/golden age (1950–1970); blurred genres (1970–1986); the crisis of representation (1986–1990); the postmodern (1990–1995); postexperimental inquiry of experimental and new ethnographies (1995–2000), the methodologically contested present (2000–2010); and the fractured future (2010) and onwards.

For explanations of these terms see Denzin and Lincoln (2011: 3).

Ontology

The sense of tradition, place, time and 'of being' are echoed in qualitative research. The deep philosophical position of ontology is the concern with the nature of being or existence, as envisioned by Descartes's phrase *cogito ergo sum* (I think, therefore, I am) and which has been present in one form or another within the principles about life and morals, as taught by philosophers through the earlier ages, e.g. Aristotle (384 BC) and Confucius (551 BC). Byrne (2001: 372) described qualitative research as 'contextually laden, subjective, and richly detailed'. These include details about people as subjects in qualitative studies: what they wear; their mannerisms and their proximity to others; what they say with inflections of tone and volume; what they show by body movements, mannerisms or in their stillness; what they see/do not see and appreciate/do not appreciate about the contents within physical settings and the contexts of an occasion within each setting; which all convey rich data to qualitative researchers. The procedural nature for valuable or good qualitative research can be established in following the rule of epistemology.

Epistemology

Epistemology is the study or the theory of the nature, methods and limits of experience, belief and knowledge. Since epistemology primarily addresses the questions, 'What is knowledge and how is knowledge acquired?' there are inevitable debates arising from these. What people think they understand as knowledge depends on the perspectives or the beliefs they hold and how able they are to analyse and explain the nature of such knowledge. A researcher needs to state that an inductive reasoning process based on observation and experience has taken place and how, by following this logical line of reasoning, other researchers can judge its credibility. 'Analytic logic' and its 'interpretive authority' (Morse 1997: 121) require making clear what the researcher's reasoning is, from, 'the inevitable forestructure to the interpretations and knowledge claims made on the basis of what was learned in the research'. Interpretive authority stems from the requirement that researchers should make statements founded upon observations, which are not prejudicial, but objective. Therefore, qualitative researches are considered 'good or excellent' when they can be justified on these grounds.

Realism and interpretivist traditions

There is a richness in qualitative studies in throwing much light on the way respondents think, feel and behave. Qualitative researchers, according to Silverman (2005: 9), look for details in the, 'precise particulars of such matters as people's understandings and interactions . . . a non-positivist model of reality'. Realism and the interpretivist traditions are generally held up as alternative approaches to positivism (see next section). Philosophical realism is a belief that reality exists independent of observers, while critical realism extends this to the proposition that while some of what we see and sense around us relating to external objects and events can be taken to be accurate representations, there are other sense-data, which may not be accurately portrayed. We see plentiful examples of this in marketing. One example is the the gulf between the advertising agencies and public relations people with the consuming public caught in the middle, see Bell (2005):

> The truth is the ad industry thinks that PR men are idiots, a waste of time, good at lunch and not much else . . . PR men think that ad men are grossly overpaid, whilst producing far too much rubbish and that for an industry that reaps billions of dollars its vast output has no effect on anything.
>
> (Bell 2005: 21)

It is not surprising that in critical and postmodern marketing writings there is a sense of limitations about marketing theory. However, while both critical marketers and postmodernists have raised awareness of shortcomings in their critiques of marketing, there has been very little that is of relevance in terms of their establishing any alternative new marketing theories or new methods for their applications.

The generalised nature of the interpretivist approach to qualitative research has usually been contrasted to positivism (see the next section), because the interpretive researcher looks for hidden meanings beyond the external façades of people, in their dealings with their peer and reference groups, e.g. contemporaries and family members, or in society as a whole. Body language, movements, looks, speech or inflections of voice, verbal anecdotes, jokes and story telling all contain subtle meanings that need to be explored. At the sub-conscious level individuals interacting with others have hidden intentions and meanings that may mean more on interpretivist examination than realism, i.e. the realist perspective of what is seen represented in the world.

Discourse analysis for studying language, verbal and textual, also looks for layers of meaning and reference points, e.g. how many times a key word or phrase was used and what meaning these same key words tell us of the writer/speaker and the characters they use. Qualitative researchers apply other methods such as a technique in using personal photographs (Holbrook 1995) and films use by Bank (1995). As Black (2006) puts it, 'how can words fully express the meaning inherent in our observations, personal interviews and pictures when so much of it is subtle, hidden and contextually bound?'. Interpretivists see their strength as being able to go beyond the surface complexities to uncover hidden layers, e.g. in marketing these might be the deeper meanings of consumption situations to certain people.

Qualitative research, according to Bill Schlackman (1999), started out as motivational research with its roots in psychology and owed credit for its initial popularisation to Dr Ernest Dichter in the US. Schlackman, who has been widely credited with introducing qualitative research in the UK in the 1960s had seen motivational research lose its title to become 'qualitative research', which he thought was a more accurate description. In Britain, as on the Continent, much pioneering work came from social reformers and early consumer groups, which undertook limited social and market studies in efforts to persuade their governments, influential ruling classes and business corporations that there were cases for reform. Social class divisions, with their impact on poverty among the working classes, limited provision of education, poor living conditions and low welfare standards, were items for reform on their agendas. Governments, in expanding their public sector commitments, set up more national corporations such as those overseeing broadcasting and public transport. After the Second World War, the expanding public and private sectors provided much work for market research agencies.

Theory and practice

Qualitative researchers can come from any discipline, from the social sciences and other more mathematical fields, as represented in the persona of Bronislaw Malinowski who had a background in mathematics and who applied scientific logic to the traditional field of ethnography. He disagreed with the traditional view of ethnography that was reliant on believing what people said they did. His view was that ethnography should be about observing what others did. This view of researcher immersion by seeing what people were doing and then reporting on their lives and activities was also found in the work by Tom Harrison. *Mass Observation* was started in the 1930s when Harrison led a group of young researchers to study the cultures of working men and women in the north of England (BBC Four 2007). It was the start of a social phenomenon when market research uncovered the attitudes and behaviour of working classes at a time when politicians were becoming aware of consumer research as a growing force for change. *Mass Observation* became one vehicle by which government agencies listened to their publics, helping to establish it as one of the best known in market research.

Qualitative research associations are at the forefront of pushing the discipline in the US and Europe. They include qualitative consultants from all kinds of social science backgrounds. The UK professional body for qualitative researchers, the AQR, holds annual conferences and opportunities for networking for its members. Such bodies are normally practitioner dominated, as is MRS in the UK. Annual conferences for academics, such as those run by the Association for Consumer Research in the US, the Academy of Marketing in the UK, the European Marketing Academy and the American Marketing Association all include tracks for papers that have qualitative content. The Worldwide Biennial Conference on Qualitative Research (WBCQR) is a joint venture between the two leading associations representing the discipline, the AQR in the UK and the Qualitative Research Consultants Association (QRCA) based in the US. Its aim is to create a forum to showcase best thinking and practices, to reflect all aspects of qualitative research from the perspectives of those who commission, design, execute and apply the findings of research studies. The WBCQR also creates numerous opportunities for networking with the discipline's leaders, as well as with prospective clients and business partners, by scheduling diverse types of sessions and sponsoring a social programme that takes advantage of the diverse international locations for its conferences.

A wide ranging and inclusive list of the versatility of the qualitative researcher's toolkit is offered by Gummesson (2007). His choice of:

interactive research . . . includes case study research (recognizing complexity, context and ambiguity); grounded theory (letting reality tell its story on its own terms); anthropology/ethnography (the importance of being there); action research (making it happen and reflecting); narrative research (making reality come alive) . . . network theory (addressing complexity, context and dynamism) including recent developments in natural sciences.

These are among the most commonly used theoretical research paradigms, as stated by Creswell (1998: 11) and in part by Richards and Morse (2007: 12), namely autobiography, biography, ethnography, grounded theory, phenomenology and the case study.

Autobiography and biography

The intellectual strands of autobiographical and biographical writings have their roots in many disciplines. There have been in existence through the decades extensive numbers of autobiographies and biographies, too numerous to mention here. Some provide highly interesting content such as those written by and about past American presidents. Some writers are stimulated to compile biographies of other people even when these people are alive and might not have consented to the work being done or have divorced themselves from it. Some are written out of interest, yet many are done to tap into the markets where there exist potential readerships and, hence, profits to the publishers marketing the books. An autobiography is a life story of a person written by the same person. A politician's memoirs followed by a full autobiography of themselves can invoke feelings of anticipation or distaste, depending on one's view of their abilities while holding public office. In the 1980s one such politician, the then UK Prime Minster, Mrs Thatcher, had a re-run of her memoirs in 2006 adapted for television audiences. Such anticipation or distaste has also followed biographical studies, written by others, of various people, e.g. biographies of Princess Diana are annually sold years after her death with the excuse of satisfying consumer demand. There are radio interviews and dedicated internet websites for the rich and famous, including infamous ones, which sought to provide insights for the consuming public. For qualitative researchers both autobiographies and biographies provide rich sources of secondary, historical, anthropological and ethnographic data, The fascination with past famous figures by modern writers and the consumers who buy their writings has helped to keep a whole genre of film and book suppliers in strong marketing and subsequent good financial health.

Phenomenology

This is a method largely developed by Edmund Husserl (1859–1938). The first step of phenomenological reduction is to suspend all preconceptions about experience. The phenomenologist describes the invariant essences of objects rather than the consideration of their objective states. Transcendental phenomenology is based on insights from the exploration of how knowledge comes into being. It is interpretive, based on intentionality and vivid attention to description. Existential phenomenology regards human reality as a reciprocal relationship between the researcher and the phenomenon of all the existence of thoughts, moods and actions, i.e. a lived experience. Hermeneutical phenomenology includes the arts, myths, religion and symbols in cultures. Linguistical phenomenology finds meanings residing within the language binding to historical and cultural contexts. Marketing studies of people's lived experiences have led to the creation of advertising campaigns around the 'desirability' of product brands. For example, work carried out by a small group of qualitative marketing researchers led by Henry and Caldwell from Sydney

University featured various phenomena concerning specific groups, in-group behaviour and out-group behaviour carried out with observation and in-depth interviewing techniques. These included following the respondents around and filming the events of heavy rock music groups (to investigate the influence of music on consumption life styles and vice versa) and the Cliff Richard Fan Club in Melbourne (looking at fandom or fan worship of a pop star). Recognition of such qualitative in-depth marketing studies came with a European film award in 2006 for 'Living Doll' (title of a Cliff Richard's song), which was based around the topic of fandom or fan worship of specific celebrities. For more phenomenological research methods and examples, see also Finlay (2009) and Küpers (2005).

Grounded theory

This starts from the intention to generate, or to discover, a theory by studying how people interact in response to a particular phenomenon. Theoretical propositions are developed from interview data and field research (Goulding 2005). Grounded theory is often about looking at how people react in a visual way and the signs or cues in their individual and group behaviour. It is about defining and refining categories and revisiting the questions arising from the research repeatedly until specific, tenable propositions arise. These propositions or theories are then developed for further research. By not presupposing prior concepts, which might impose assumptions, a researcher could then be freer to being sensitive to field data as they occur. Glaser and Strauss (1967) popularised the concept of grounded theory. In their research on dying and death, they developed categories to reflect their data, added more cases to saturate and compare. Furthermore, they developed such categories in analytic frameworks that could be appropriate for other external users. However, there can be confusion about the variations in the way grounded theory is used, because what originates from individual researchers are their 'varied' research experiences and skills and their differences in extensive/not extensive understanding of the context-laden aspects of a particular situation. These could affect their interpretations of the many clues in the field. Qualitative researchers, therefore, need to take care in collecting, categorising, comparing and recording their data (El-Hussein *et al.* 2014). A benefit of the grounded theory approach is in researching areas of sensitivity, e.g. in researching cases of people suffering from disease-related illnesses. As another example when it is difficult to research overseas markets when Western theories about female emancipation and effects on female lifestyles will not fit with overseas native/indigenous societies' treatment of the issue, then a grounded theorist perspective could be justifiable as a research approach over other types. For grounded theorists, the theoretical basis for the coding of data and the methods for coding also lend themselves to computer software analysis. This is explored further in the section 'Using computers in qualitative research'.

Ethnography

Ethnography is the description or interpretation of the observable and learned patterns of behaviour in a social group or setting. The researchers will immerse themselves in a variety of ways into the culture of the group to be studied (Hammersley and Atkinson 2007). For example, they might live with the community, experiencing their day-to-day lives and/or pursuing one-to-one interviews with members of the group. By doing this, researchers experience at first hand how the subjects of the study are living, working and behaving, while taking notes and observing or being a participant (researcher immersion) in the community. Mariampolski (2005) discussed ethnography as a guide for marketers in understanding consumers (consumer immersion).

Some historical ethnographers' studies are open to controversy, e.g. the evidence presented by Margaret Mead in her book *Coming of Age in Samoa* and Derek Freeman's dispute of her theories in his book *Coming of Age in Samoa: Making and Unmaking of a Myth*. Mead gave her account as evidence that Samoan teenagers were not prone to the pain and stress of growing up compared to American teenagers. Freeman publicised different evidence disproving her theories in his book and in subsequent writings. The moral of this story is that the scientific basis about racial difference rests on shaky ground. Early ethnographers went from the West to remote island or village communities to justify observed differences in race. Marketing studies found that 'within group' differences of genetic variations within the same race groups and those found between 'out groups' representing different races do not need to get in the way of branding. The successes of global brands with one global message and brand image are a part of our modern history, e.g. Coca-Cola, IBM, Sony. The global brand is sold to the human race, which would consume or use the product in the way it was marketed by the company, whatever anyone's race.

International marketing and market segmentation studies concerning geodemographics and psychographic/lifestyle with the targeted segments/consumer groups concentrate on attitude and usage data and generally do not focus on the challenges of 'race'. So much of what we consume is international in one way or another, as grown in Africa, made in Indonesia, mass produced in China and used in similar ways from the industrialised Western countries to newly developing economies. For example, teas and coffees from PG Tips, toothpaste and detergents from Procter & Gamble, and Nike and Reebok clothing and shoes are sold to markets all over the world.

Case study

Marketing studies add to a huge caseload, as published by many academic writers and institutions. A case study about an event, an activity or individuals builds a scenario (e.g. Yin 2014) with contrasting individual perspectives and for businesses, there would be managerial implications. Qualitative research contributes to case studies by finding out detailed and intimate information about people using multiple perspectives to build up a picture of individuals and their contributions to a particular situation.

The case study is a theoretical or simulated way of presenting information to others by telling an account, a narrative or story involving various people and their roles. Creswell (1998: 61) explained case research as an 'exploration of a "bounded system" or a case (or multiple cases) over time through detailed, in-depth data collection involving multiple sources of information rich in context'. In marketing teaching and research, the case study has a specific role for the instructor of the case and the students set to work on the problems of the case. It is the educational value of teaching the case study that keeps a research study alive for years to come.

Validity and reliability

Confusion about what is validity and reliability and the interchangeability of these terms in popular use usually result from misunderstandings over how to justify the small sample sizes and choices of method. In qualitative research, it is important to recognise that there is 'no one size to fit all'. Take, for example, the thick descriptions envisaged by ethnographers who craft their own reports from verbatim accounts of their data, or grounded theorists who use selective criteria for their coding in field research. The bases for inductive reasoning and making judgements are based on observations and experiences that involve statements, which have different levels of validity. It is important to distinguish between prejudicial and objective statements, while the latter are more acceptable if they are based on many observations and supported by general opinion from other researchers and experts in the field: a process of consultative validity. Validity of results in marketing describes how the information and recommendations from qualitative studies are considered defensible or logically sound and are of use to the clients paying for the studies about their markets. Validity is a truth or belief. While Table 9.1 is not intended to show all the different types of validity, it nevertheless represents common types of validity found in qualitative research.

When qualitative studies use small samples, as in marketing, it can be hard sometimes to justify the reliability of the researches undertaken. So long as there is some relationship to one or more types of validity and, provided the processes of research and results can be extrapolated to other groups, then reliability can be justified.

Reliability presupposes that the particular theoretical approach to inform a given method has taken place and that the findings uncovered by such a method can be duplicated if the study was repeated with other groups. In doctoral research, 'the contribution to knowledge' is ingrained in the expectation that there will be some originality in the work. This could be new theories, new methods or new findings. In general, most research studies tend to add a little to existing knowledge rather than the big breakthroughs in innovations. For instances of understanding qualitative research and reality traps, see Kapoulas and Miljana (2012). In academia, examiners of doctoral qualitative theses need to see whether such works stand up to scrutiny if applied in more than one study. Reliability adds consistency of approach with an external dimension whether or not a researcher's study is revisited by the same researcher or other external researchers assigning the same principles or categories and getting similar or fairly similar types of results. Of course, one has to bear in mind that 'revisions' are a normal part and parcel of research work in adapting to change.

Triangulation

The origin of triangulation is as a mathematical concept relating to the measurement of the elements for determining the network of triangles or trigonometric operation for finding a position from two fixed points, a known distance apart (Longman Dictionary 2014). The expression of 'a love triangle' is used subjectively by storytellers when describing the entanglements of three people emotionally involved with each other (A loves B, B loves C and C loves A). Sequential triangulation reflects the strong links between qualitative and quantitative research. For example, in health studies research it is necessary before a new drug is marketed for a pharmaceutical company to conduct field trials with doctors, nurses and patients to gather observations and measurements in order to determine whether the intervention of the drug for a particular treatment is justifiable or not. Given this context, the application of triangulation from these sources becomes another form of validating the credibility of both qualitative and quantitative studies.

Table 9.1 Example of types of validity

Theoretical validity – where research procedures can be justified, through reference to prior established theoretical perspectives, or where original work has led to new theories being established.

Instrumental validity – when the procedural method generated matches with the data generated.

Consultative validity – when others knowledgeable in the field are consulted and have given their feedback in terms of validating what is done.

Internal validity – where there is coherence in the fit between data and results.

External validity – where the results produced match the kinds of information accepted by others.

Source: Adapted from Sykes in Wright *et al.* (2000).

In qualitative research the word *triangulation* takes on a separate meaning from the mathematical one, to refer to a combination of several methods, such as observation and interviews in researching the same phenomenon. It is also another way of proving reliability. For example, in marketing studies multiple points of view can be gathered about a particular type of marketing theory, method and product or service concept. A simplified version would be to ask three observers selected for their different types of expertise or background about a particular phenomenon to determine how far their three statements coalesce for now. In revisiting this at a later stage, the judgement about reliability would be whether this position would still hold. The degree of agreement can then be assessed. In marketing studies, determining the extent of competition and market risk can be difficult. The resultant conclusion of this process becomes a compromise in using multiple frames of reference sourced from expert views, consumer responses and backed up by secondary data sources. The skill of the qualitative researcher in using triangulation is in balancing multiple perspectives in the research design and multiple realities from the research data, thereby reducing the risks of or avoiding biases and prejudices.

Differences in research traditions: qualitative and quantitative approaches

The variety of qualitative approaches, as discussed in the previous section, remains in stark contrast to quantitative research. The theoretical paradigm of positivism is a label generally applied to quantitative research. The theoretical stance of *positivism*, postulated by Auguste Comte in 1856, stated that the only authentic knowledge is scientific knowledge, which comes from positive affirmation of theories tested through strict scientific methods of investigation. This is a view propounded by technocrats and others in scientific and mathematical circles who regard scientific progress as the means of gathering knowledge applicable to standing up to the rigours of validity and reliability in research design and outcomes.

The structured approach of closed ended questioning and multiple numbers of questions allow quantitative researchers to send questionnaires via the post, telephone and computer to hundreds and thousands of people simultaneously in order to conduct large-scale surveys. The quantitative research approach has the comfort of numbers giving the advantage of reliability in producing statistical evidence for such surveys. The biggest examples of such surveys are by national governments conducting censuses to help their planning and forecasting, and international agencies collecting information on matters of global concern, such as on world health and environmental issues in order to mobilise support from world leaders and the public. The data gathered are subjected to mathematical analysis and modelling to explain national and global phenomena by showing their key constructs, their inter-relationships and their relative strengths within these inter-relationships. So decisions can be based on statistically proven facts with known margins of error.

Critics of qualitative research point to the problem of replicating qualitative studies, given the labour intensive nature of its inquiry and therefore the relatively small sample sizes involved, in comparison to quantitative work. However, there remain weaknesses in the quantitative approach when questions and answers are limited to tight designs and controlled by predetermined constructs. Quantitative research has been criticised for, 'scraping the surface of peoples' attitudes and feelings'. The complexity of the human soul is 'lost' through the counting of numbers, giving rise to the failure to follow unexpected clues or to research a topic in greater detail through deeper probing and understanding of respondents' motivations and behaviour during a research investigation. Our mental faculties allow us to use our five senses of sight, smell, taste, touch and hearing, as well as what those who 'sense' the paranormal might think of as our sixth sense. Respondents differ in how they are able to feel/not feel about what is put before them, what they like/dislike and whether they treat researchers with rudeness or charm. So many factors and influences affect people in their everyday lives that when qualitative researchers set out to understand the complexities surrounding the underlying causes of behaviour, qualitative inquiry in such cases could be more appropriate than quantitative research methods. Stake (2010) explained the importance of the researcher getting personal to gain valued insights into the respondent's own situational, experiential and interpretive conditions.

It makes sense to utilise both the qualitative and quantitative approaches to solve marketing or social problems. Both have strengths in their inductive and deductive approaches and, when used together, can work well in reducing risks and complementing each other's strengths. Mixed qualitative and quantitative methods are used in profit and not-for-profit sectors when there are resources to accommodate both. Exploratory research is a well-known mode of qualitative research that is adaptable and versatile to help get the right questions asked in the initial stage of a research study. It is commonly used as a precursor to conducting large and expensive quantitative surveys. At the end of a quantitative survey, there is broadly sequential triangulation from qualitative to quantitative based upon qualitatively derived measures, interventions and relationships that will enable managers to have three types of valid bases upon which to fine tune their go/no go decisions about marketing data. The final decisions that client managers take are inevitably qualitative.

Using computers in qualitative research

Using computers has helped to narrow the division between qualitative and quantitative approaches. The computer is a great equaliser. It is inanimate and yet both parties can point to their software use to legitimise the procedures in analysing data. The manual processes of content analysis of texts transferred to the setting of the computer with the added sophistication of coding and structure, the speed of multiple data entries and linking of data has revolutionised the ways in which qualitative researchers can now work. Larger numbers of interviews and data can be added, coded, categorised, stored and revisited, etc. It is the case now that computers with higher specifications, i.e. faster speed of processor and greater capacities of hard drive and memory are cheaper relative to five years ago, so that more people can afford to turn to computers for qualitative data analysis.

Software for qualitative research offers detailed exploration, coding and analysis of textual and other non-numerical data with the acronym of 'Computer Assisted Qualitative Data Analysis Software' (CAQDAS). More commonly referred to simply as 'QDA software' or 'qualitative software' it was, historically, more widespread in social research studies (Seidel and Clark 1984). As improvements in technology came along, so did the updates to the software to make it more responsive and to incorporate new features, e.g. for videoing, editing, recording and analysing as in NVivo 10 (QSR International 2014). There are institutions and agencies, which provide introductory, intermediate and advanced courses for ATLAS.ti, NVivo, Qualrus and MAXqda. For clear and step-by-step explanations about CAQDAS, see Searle's work on 'Using computers to analyse qualitative data' (Silverman 2005). Courses and conferences are run by the CAQDAS Networking Project at Surrey University (2014), a leader in the field. In practice, users can view the applications of software in terms of a computer-assisted strategy to expedite and generally enhance the qualitative research process by viewing online videos (e.g. Gibbs 2014) and reading books (Lewins and Silver 2007; Richards 2012).

There are, of course, limitations with any method including the use of the computer, which distances the researcher from the data prompting them to follow an established pattern of behaviour instead of noticing the little nuances in the data itself. Some authors have pointed to the risks of using CAQDAS in creating too many codes (Roberts and Wilson 2002), or confusing coding with analysis (Coffey *et al*. 1996) or creating bias towards grounded theory (Lonkila 1995). However, it can be said that the computer has its many uses, such as its renowned ability to handle data search and large data sets, hypotheses testing and generating information for clients of research in professional looking, presentational formats. A computer-assisted strategy is an additional way to add rigour to data handling and evaluation by qualitative researchers.

In the market research industry CAQDAS packages were reportedly rarely used in the 1990s (Nancarrow *et al*. 1996) and now with IT literacy and training courses there are more uses for computer packages including CAQDAS and NVivo). Back then and now, clients often want quick results for their money, and turnaround time for qualitative studies in markets can be very short. If computer coding cannot take place, i.e. someone has to do the laborious work of inputting data, and when speed is of the essence, then the tried and trusted way of transcribing data is used. If even this method is not fast enough or too expensive, there are other methods, such as videoing or tape recording or online interviewing and web forum discussions. A focus group discussion in a room that has a one-way mirror system, where the market researcher and the client can view the proceedings without the members of the focus group being able to see them, is still a quick and efficient method to get fast turnaround of results. Web forum discussions, interviews on Skype and online messaging are other ways to get quick results for small qualitative research agencies without much resource.

Adding value through qualitative research

From the marketing perspective, the view of the practitioner is aptly described by Keegan (2009) and Goodyear (2000). As Goodyear (2000: 374–375) indicated, the focus of qualitative researchers is representing the consumer and their world 'as accurately as possible for decision-makers in marketing or social policy'. When one considers the job of the qualitative researcher as acting as an interpreter between the consumer and the client by interacting and talking with the consumer, the qualitative researcher is able to add value by making detailed and at times more intimate discoveries about the consumer. The researcher interprets these in a manner suitable for answering the client's marketing questions. As Goodyear stated, within the world of advertising this is colloquially known as, 'bringing the consumer into the agency'. Here, the particular value of qualitative research is to add value to creative development in advertising or in general to developing marketing communications. This is because by understanding the specifics of consumer likes and dislikes about brands, advertising, companies, media and film celebrities, etc., suppliers gain knowledge about the general marketing environments in which consumers spend their money. Qualitative inquiry extends to getting people to imagine what they would do given past, present and future scenarios. Intricate demands are placed on researchers to be good at writing and communicating, to be able to disseminate findings and to have strategies in place to make recommendations.

Many companies, particularly larger ones, through their researches and interactions with their consumers and business customers already have big resources of information to draw upon, especially when supplemented with updated field research or secondary data. In this situation, they do not need to reinvent the wheel. In these departments qualitative researchers work within the remits of their organisation's resources and parameters, such as gathering and evaluating feedback from consumers, retailers and distributors about new product launches.

Individual interviews and focus group discussions with consumers are the qualitative marketers' tried and tested means of elucidating information about consumer habits and preferences with regard to current shopping for goods and services, or in contributing ideas for new product development and new marketing promotions.

Data collection methods

Codes of practice from associations, such as the American Marketing Association (AMA), ESOMAR and MRS in the UK, give guidance about good practices in establishing rapport with respondents, not breaching confidentiality and avoiding infringement of data protection laws. Malhotra *et al.* (2013: 7) referred to integrity and trust as important and not just robustness in data collection and analysis as, 'such insights should lead to fresh perspectives to business problems and/or a competitively advantaged solution'.

Unlike quantitative research, which collects data for statistical analysis, the data gathered in qualitative research ranges from the unstructured to the semi-structured kind. In the unstructured form, the qualitative research approach can rely on innumerable tangible and intangible forms of self-expression by respondents. For example, qualitative researchers can get respondents to see, smell and touch tangible artefacts or other physical objects and pictures in order to let the respondents describe how they feel about them. Alternatively, they can challenge the respondents to imagine in an intangible way what it feels like to be in a particular situation or to lose a favourite brand. Both forms of inquiry allow respondents to describe their feelings and emotions. To capture these moments, researchers often rely on one or more of note-taking, tape recording, camera surveillance and the computer to capture the data. Such data include similarities and peculiarities of respondents' facial expressions, behaviour and their verbal answers. The semi-structured kind normally involves a questionnaire as the research instrument where respondents are asked to tick boxes for their preferences and to rate or rank a product, service or corporate entity usually in terms of whether the respondents think favourably or not favourably of these. It gives flexibility where numbers are required for coding either manually or electronically by qualitative software. The semi-structured questionnaire has spaces for comments with each main question where respondents are encouraged not only to give factual answers but also to dig deeper into their consciousness and to project their feelings, e.g. marketing managers when interviewed could be asked about their marketing decisions and the impact they think these might have had on others involved, such as competitors, distributors and consumers.

Qualitative research can be undertaken to check that the appropriate questions are asked through an initial exploration of the market to product launch into a new market. When marketing managers are seeking answers to marketing problems and investigating opportunities, the qualitative approach has much to contribute. Mistakes are costly and there are not only financial risks inherent in new developments of products and services. There is also the risk of market share loss in alienating consumers, as Coca-Cola found in the 1980s with its unpopular variation of its long-established recipe for its product and in the 1990s when its new range of carbonated water was introduced into the market.

Test decisions for new product and service introductions are informed from qualitative feedback of users and experts in many markets investigated. There are numerous goods and services investigated, such as those in fast moving and durable consumer markets to commercial and public services, utilities and industrial machinery and robotics.

The flexibility of qualitative research with its small samples means that observing and asking questions of respondents can take place anywhere on a one-to-one or small group basis. A typical small focus group can be around 6 to 10 or 8 to 12 individuals, depending on the extent of the topic and researcher preferences. The study can take place anywhere by interviewing respondents in their homes, on the street in shopping malls and in public places, including hiring halls to get respondents to try out or test new products. They can take place in business premises where researchers and their client managers can observe respondents' behaviour and interactions through specially adapted viewing facilities for studying respondents. Researchers can conduct mystery shopping where they visit stores to observe behaviour, without letting the subjects of their study know their identities. Researchers and respondents' interactions for research can be conducted via internet, audio and visual links using headsets and webcams.

Questionnaires types

The common prevalence of the use of the questionnaire method means that it is difficult for people to avoid participating in questionnaires about themselves, for example, in applications for financial services products such as mortgages and insurance policies, or to take part in direct marketing mail shots linked to sales promotions. Most people become familiar with the notion of questionnaires before they reach adulthood, having disclosed information on themselves in applications, for example, to study at educational establishments or membership of sports and travel clubs.

Consequently, there are many questionnaires put forth by organisations and individuals, which vary between two basic types. These take the form of being fully structured, with closed questions at one extreme, to being completely unstructured, with open-ended questions at the other. A compromise is the semi-structured questionnaire, which incorporates a mix of the two.

Unstructured questionnaire: Most of the questions are open-ended. The interviewer is free to change the order of asking questions and to explain them. The questionnaire may take the form of a checklist for discussion. The unstructured questionnaire is used in 'depth' interviews, group discussions and in non-domestic surveys. The interview can be respondent-led, particularly if the interview is with an expert in the field, so that the observations and expertise of the respondent can be taken account of.

Semi-structured questionnaire: This usually constitutes a mixture of closed or fixed-response questions, quick response ranking or rating scales for measuring attitudes, organisational and product attitudes and open-ended questions or spaces for respondents to fill in their comments. Semi-structured questionnaires are useful in enabling the interviewer to 'stage-manage' the interview by making sure that all questions are covered, with room for the interviewee (respondent) to add comments to the specific questions already asked.

Stimulus materials: These are used as aids in the data collection process. Various types of stimulus materials are used in marketing to prompt and to test respondents, whether in a group discussion or an extended face-to-face interview. The choice of material, including degree of finish, demands professional judgement based on experience and training in the behavioural sciences. Examples of stimulus materials are given in Table 9.2.

Table 9.2 Stimulus material

Concept boards – single boards showing visual or written ideas for a product, pack or advertised service.
Storyboards – key frames shown as in comic strips and commercials.
Animatics – key frames are drawn and filmed with sound tracks added.
Admatics – animatics that have their graphic images generated by the computer so that the finished version resembles a commercial.
Photomatics – animation for photographs is used instead of drawing key frames, to give a more realistic appearance.

Pushing boundaries in marketing

The global nature of the marketing industry needs to include the *entrepreneurial* or *organisational view*, with emphasis on resources and who does what with the resources; the *business view*, looking at development of strategy for the profitable achievement of organisational objectives; and the *consumer view*, which focuses on consumer needs and wants. In the UK both central government and local government authorities, e.g. Warwickshire's youth forums, have used qualitative research in focus groups to find out new public opinions on a broad range of government provisions from rubbish collections to new youth centres and issues of widespread concern, such as hospital waiting lists to crime reports. The Crime Survey for England and Wales (previously the British Crime Survey) is a case in point. Carried out by the British Market Research Bureau (BMRB) Ltd for the Home Office, the participants are chosen by random sampling and the questioning is undertaken in their homes. From January 2009, this survey for England and Wales has asked around 50,000 people aged 16 and over about crimes they experienced in the previous year. While the questionnaire is activated on the computer and taken for quantitative analysis, the qualitative element is present, because respondents qualitatively reflect on their personal circumstances to answer an average of an hour's questioning.

Qualitative research processes for domestic and international markets are continually evolving in uncovering and interpreting meanings behind people's thoughts, behaviours and motivations either through non-participant study or via participant interactions with the people they are studying, or by a mix of both. It lends itself to the analyses of attitudes, lifestyles and people's preferences for what they purchase and consume. The three most common data collection methods are observations, personal in-depth interviews and group discussions. Lees and Broderick (2007) pointed to the power of modern technology when they demonstrated the importance of eye-tracking technologies to observation research.

With the advent and pervasiveness of the internet, email and website provisions, qualitative data collection methods have extended to other forms of inquiry, such as comparisons of offline and online buying behaviour, online focus group interviewing and gathering feedback from internet chat rooms and individual 'blogs' containing personal statements linked to the web. The forcefulness of the effects of electronic word of mouth, blogging and social media networks are provided in thought provoking papers and workshops from delegates at UK and international marketing and market research conferences, such as the Academy of Marketing, AMA and the MRS.

Today's generation of young children and teenagers is exposed to the internet revolution and consequently are targets for more qualitative research. In the education sector, both primary and secondary school children are introduced to a connected world where computers, mobile phones and handheld video and voice sets are connected for downloading music, games, films and internet content. This provides a multi-media landscape where increasingly, 'multi-dimensional entertainment experiences' are introduced by suppliers looking to maximise their profits in selling such technological products and downloadable contents, such as the success of Facebook in attracting advertisers and YouTube in growing as an internet showcase for demonstrating skills, talent and performing arts.

Transformation of the global qualitative research landscape

The advent of the internet overcoming geographical distances and costs for researchers has radically changed the global landscape for qualitative researches, as organisations and individuals add online experiences to their traditional offline researches into markets or dedicate their services to online studies. Now, new developments in their different ways are transforming the qualitative landscape again, by offering opportunities in the ways people view and use information. For example, new developments in sophisticated handheld mobile devices and the advanced capabilities of computing systems to upload, analyse and store data, such as cloud computing and network applications, have revolutionised the ways for people to search and join in the sharing of their data. When these are freely available and highly accessible, as with those provided by search engines, social media networks, micro-blogging and video-sharing formats, e.g. Google, Facebook, Twitter and YouTube, there are seemingly endless possibilities for individuals to upload their new contributions in 'procreating' or by sharing with others, their own 'live' experiences and knowledge. In such contexts, behavioural experiences of individual consumers and organisational buyers, forged from time spent dwelling on such provisions and 'apps' usage from their devices, are continually altering perceptions for firms in devising their new products and services, and qualitative researchers in studying and reporting consumer and organisational phenomena.

Co-creation with other individuals and groups to contribute specialised competences in upstream and downstream ways are also facilitated. An example of co-creation is provided by Barrutia and Echebarria (2013) who analysed the network effect as a social marketing tool in a Basque region. They reported integrating a target market (municipalities) in the design of the complements necessary to achieve their aims with various stakeholders, including final users to allow for the flow of downstream and upstream perspectives. While the authors did a quantitative study, their literature review took in the work of Dann (2010) who developed a comprehensive definition of social marketing based on a qualitative research technique for text mining to uncover the core attributes. Dann's definition of social marketing (Dann 2010: 151) incorporates, 'adaptation and adoption of commercial marketing activities, institutions and processes as a means of inducing behavioural change in a targeted audience on a temporary or permanent basis to achieve a social goal'. There is value in qualitative research to add understanding of how social marketing campaigns and communications evolve and to contribute to marketing strategies that can achieve the desired effects.

The widespread nature and examples of IT provisions to accommodate the nature of 'big data', can also be found in the academic, consultancy and training sectors, where better storage, security and accessibility issues are linked to online materials, be they for offsite or on-campus and inhouse usage. However, there are occasions when both qualitative and quantitative researches take a backseat, as indicated by Professor Merlin Stone (2014) in the following boxed section:

Qualitative market research and the web: sentiment analysis and all that

Digital marketing has upset market research's apple cart in many ways, but the most important way is that it has virtually abolished the distinction between quantitative and qualitative data. This is because the information systems on which digital marketing runs (company's own websites, third-party/partner websites, social media websites, mobile telephone networks and – if I can claim them for digital marketing – contact centre systems including not just web chat but also call records, which can be subjected to text recognition and mining software) host massive flows of interactions between companies and customers. These flows can be analysed in many different ways, both qualitative and quantitative.

Two areas that have interested qualitative market researchers are sentiment analysis and opinion mining (Vinodhini and Chandrasekaran 2012; Rambocas and Gama 2013; Gunter *et al.* 2014). The two are not identical. Both involve analysing large amounts of text data (generally entered by customers). Sentiment analysis focuses on the attitudes, judgements, evaluations or emotional states of the customer, in particular whether it is positive or negative. Opinion mining focuses more on the 'facts' – what the customer is saying, about what (product event, for example) and which customer is saying it. Naturally, the two overlap in terms of marketing applications. Broadly, it involves a range of techniques in which automation is increasingly being used – keyword spotting, identification of grammatical relationships, lexical affinity and development of concept levels. Statistical methods (including data mining) are deployed to identify frequencies and associations. Human intervention is usually required to some extent.

Where sentiment analysis is concerned, humans are not perfect judges of the sentiment expressed by a set of words, or by a series of statements made over time (i.e. different raters of the words may not agree), so automated methods are not expected to achieve perfection – merely to get somewhere near human levels.

Assessing sentiment is not a simple translation task. Here are some reasons for difficulties: a word that is positive in one situation may be negative in another; opinions are expressed in different ways directly or indirectly, through sarcasm, etc.; small differences in words make big differences in meanings; customers can contradict themselves as reviews may contain positive and negative comments, often in one sentence; and reviews may refer to or make comparisons with other reviews or previous statements made by the reviewer.

Sentiment analysis and opinion mining can be used in many ways. Examples include to get input into product design; to identify whether particular marketing tactics are working, e.g. is the advertising appealing or new product just launched achieving its objectives in terms of how customers like it; is pricing too high or too low; which kinds of customers like the product most; and is the product easy enough to obtain and to use. Advantages include identifying whether a relationship is being managed well; whether there are problems with customer service; or if there are problems, why they exist.

For a manager of customer insight, aiming to extract from the data a whole range of useful data, the distinction between sentiment analysis, opinion mining and other ways in which data about customers' thoughts, feeling and attitudes can be inferred from data, is less important. In the world of digital marketing, a given set of data is valuable, because it may indicate anything from transactions to attitudes, and all the tools of analysis can be deployed on it. Just as importantly, the tools of integration can be used, so that data about a customer's opinion and sentiment can be matched with data about a customer's identity, personal characteristics and transactions. This makes it possible, for example, for the company to know whether sentiments or opinions are from customers who are valuable or not, or from customers who are likely to recommend or not.

What is clear is that when a company moves towards integration of different sources including text flows, which can be analysed for perceptions, opinions, needs and all other areas that qualitative market research traditionally explores, the company's use of pure qualitative market research may be at risk. If a gap in knowledge emerges, companies with such an integrated approach are more likely to ask their customer insight professionals rather than qualitative market researchers to identify whether a relevant stream of text/comment can be created (and then analysed), whether on the company's own sites or in social media or via scripts in contact centres.

Conclusion

Qualitative research has much to contribute as the discussion of the theoretical traditions and methods has shown. While there are differences in approaches between the various disciplines of the social sciences, it can be said that there is also much common ground between them, with shared terminologies and methodologies emanating from the implementation of qualitative research. It is an established field in its own right, contributing valued insights into personal, situational, experiential and interpretive conditions. As such, qualitative research is implemented on its own or within mixed methods to complement quantitative research in the marketing sphere.

Qualitative research is continually evolving and none more so than in the wake of reporting and creating new ways of doing these. Woodside (2010) discusses consumer storytelling and narratives in research about brands. As Stake (2010) explained, the researcher is also the research instrument in getting to a personal basis with individuals. Qualitative researchers, as collectors and users of marketing information, create diversity and challenges when they talk to and interact with individuals as potential customers for their clients within globally accessible social media networks. It is challenging to try to understand the myriad ways in which people think, to dig deep down into the underlying motivations of people linked to the diverse ways in which they communicate positively, negatively or not at all, whether verbally in speech and non-verbally through body language.

For marketers, qualitative research places importance on 'understanding' the respondent or the individual consumer and 'interpretation of his or her actions' in order to 'inform' an aspect of market need and consequence of societal change. The internet, world wide web and computing advances have helped to create new opportunities for generating, analysing and reporting such information. There are risks for organisations in providing the social and marketing infrastructures to 'grow' their goods and services, so qualitative research has a role in contributing valued insights. There are also potentially great rewards for companies involved in managing and marketing goods and services, because of satisfying the needs of their constituencies. There is a complex web of cultural and market differences plus international regulations and competition faced by marketing companies. Qualitative research has fuelled the growth of the market research industry domestically and internationally, with the marketplace constantly evolving and innovative firms pursuing new ways in using the web with technological devices to reach and target consumers, regardless of geographical distances. The power of qualitative research is supported by the long tradition of social science research and the extensive body of knowledge about the study of people.

Further reading

Holmes, D. and Marcus, G. (2005), 'Refunctioning ethnography: The challenge of an anthropology of the contemporary', in Denzin, N. and Lincoln, Y. *The Sage Handbook of Qualitative Research*, New York: Sage Publications, pp. 1099–1113.

Giorgi, A. (1997), 'The theory, practice and evaluation of the phenomenological methods as a qualitative research procedure', *Journal of Phenomenological Psychology*, 28: 235–281.

Glaser, B. and Strauss, A. (1967), *The Discovery of Grounded Theory: Strategies for Qualitative Research*, Chicago, IL: Aldine.

Moustakas, C. (1994), *Phenomenological Research Methods*, Thousand Oaks, CA: Sage Publications.

For regular coverage of issues and updated studies of qualitative research, see:

Qualitative Market Research: An International Journal, Emerald: UK.

References

AQR (2014), *Sweating the small stuff: the small but critical techniques that will help intermediate moderators take their performance from good to great*, November 6th, available at http://www.aqr.org.uk/calendar/info.shtml?event=TC15MSA, accessed 7 March 2016.

Barrutia, J. M. and Echebarria, C. (2013), 'Networks: A social marketing tool', *European Journal of Marketing,* 47(1/2): 324–343, available at https://scholar.google.com/citations?view_op=view_citation&hl=en&user=ND_BcD QAAAAJ&cstart=20&citation_for_view=ND_BcDQAAAAJ:pqnbT2bcN3wC, accessed 7 March 2016.

BBC Four (2007), *Tales From The Jungle: Bronislaw Malinowski*, 22 January, 9 p.m. to 10 p.m.

Bell, L. (2005), Industry Talk, *Research*, January, 21–23.

Black, I. (2006), 'Viewpoint: The presentation of interpretivist research', *Qualitative Market Research: An International Journal*, 9(4): 319–324.

Borden, N. (1964), 'The concept of the marketing mix', *Journal of Advertising Research*, 4: 2–7.

Byrne, M. (2001), 'Disseminating and presenting qualitative research findings', *AORN Journal*, 74(5): 371–372.

CAQDAS (2014), *Networking Project* at Surrey University, available at http://www.surrey.ac.uk/sociology/study/daycourses/events/2013–2014/140501-CAQDAS2014.htm, accessed 3 January 2013.

Creswell, J. (1998), *Qualitative Inquiry and Research Design*, London: Sage Publications, p. 11.

Czinkota, M. and Ronkainnen, I. (2013), *International Marketing*, tenth edition, London: Cengage Learning, p. 21.

Dann, S. (2010), Redefining social marketing with contemporary commercial marketing definitions, *Journal of Business Research*, 63(2), 147–153.

Denzin, N. and Lincoln, Y. (2013), *The Sage Handbook of Qualitative Research*, London: Sage Publications, p. 4.

El-Hussein, M. E., Hirst, S., Salyers, V. and Osuji, J. (2014), 'Using grounded theory as a method of inquiry: Advantages and disadvantages', *The Qualitative Report 2014*, 19(27): 1–15, How To Article 3, available at http://www.nova.edu.ssss/QR/QR19/el-hussein13.pdf, accessed 16 November 2015.

ESOMAR (1998), *ESOMAR Annual Study on the Market Research Industry 1997*.

ESOMAR (2011), *ESOMAR Annual Study on the Market Research Industry 2010*.

Finlay, L. (2009), 'Debating phenomenological research methods', *Phenomenology and Practice*, 3(1): 6–25.

Freeman, D. (1986), *Coming of Age in Samoa: Making and Unmaking of a Myth*, London: Penguin.

Gibbs, G (2014), https://www.youtube.com/user/GrahamRGibbs, accessed 1 January 2013.

Goodyear, M. (2000), 'Qualitative research', in Wright, L. T. and Crimp, M. *The Marketing Research Process*, fifth edition, London: FT Prentice Hall, pp. 374–375.

Goulding, C. (2005), 'Grounded theory, ethnology and phenomenology', *European Journal of Marketing*, 39(3/4): 294–309.

Gummesson, E. (2007), 'Access to reality: Observations on observational methods, commentary', *Qualitative Market Research: An International Journal*, 10(2): 130–134.

Gunter, B., Koteyko, N. and Atanasova, D. (2014), 'Sentiment analysis: A market-relevant and reliable measure of public feeling?', *International Journal of Market Research*, 56(2): 231–247.

Hammersley, M. and Atkinson, P. (2007), *Ethnography: Principles in Practice*, third edition, Abingdon, UK: Taylor & Francis.

Holbrook, M. B. (1995), *Consumer Research: Introspective Essays on the Study of Consumption*, London: Sage Publications.

Kapoulas, A. and Miljana, M. (2012), 'Understanding challenges of qualitative research: Rhetorical issues and reality traps', *Qualitative Market Research: An International Journal*, 15(4): 354–368.

Keegan, S. (2009), *Qualitative Research: Good Decision Making Through Understanding People, Cultures and Markets*, London: Kogan Page Ltd.

Küpers, W. (2005), 'Phenomenology of embodied implicit and narrative knowing', *Journal of Knowledge Management*, 9(6): 114–133.

Lees, N. and Broderick, A. (2007), 'Guest editorial: The past, present and future of observational research in marketing', *Qualitative Market Research: An International Journal*, 10(1): 121–129.

Lewins, A. and Silver, C. (2007), *Using Software in Qualitative Research: A Step-By-Step Guide*, London: Sage Publications.

Longman Dictionary of Contemporary English, (2014), sixth edition, Harlow, UK: Pearson Longman.

Lonkila, M. (1995), 'Grounded theory as an emerging paradigm for computer-assisted qualitative data analysis', in Kelle, U. (ed.) *Computer-Aided Qualitative Data Analysis: Theory, Methods and Practice*, London: Sage Publications.

Mackenzie, Y. (2005), BBC man takes issue with TV research in India, *Research*, January, p. 8.

Malhotra, N., Birks, D. and Wills, P. (2013), *The Essentials of Marketing Research*, Harlow, UK: Pearson Education Ltd, p. 7.

Mariampolski, H. (2001), *Qualitative Market Research*, New York: Sage Publications, pp. 7–9.

Mariampolski, H. (2005), *Ethnography for Marketers: A Guide to Consumer Immersion*, New York: Sage Publications.

Mead, M. (1928), *Coming of Age in Samoa*, New York: William Morrow.

MRS (2013), *MRS Research and Insight Industry League Table (UK) 2012*, available at https://www.mrs.org.uk/intelligence/industry_league_table, accessed 2 August 2014.

Morse, J. (1997), *Completing a Qualitative Project*, New York: Sage Publications, p. 121.

Nancarrow, C., Moskvin, A. and Shankar, A. (1996), 'Bridging the great divide: The transfer of techniques', *Marketing Intelligence and Planning*, 14(6): 27–37.

QSR International (2014), Available at http://www.qsrinternational.com/about-qsr_history.aspx, accessed 1 January 2013.

Rambocas, M. and Gama, J. (2013), *Marketing Research: The Role of Sentiment Analysis*, FEP Working Paper no 4989, Porto, Portugal: University of Porto, School of Economics and Management.

Richards, L. (2012), *Handling Qualitative Data: A Practical Guide*, London: Sage Publications.

Richards, L. and Morse, J. (2007), *User's Guide To Qualitative Methods*, New York: Sage Publications, p. 12.

Roberts, K. A. and Wilson, R. W. (2002), 'ICT and the research process: Issues around the compatibility of technology with qualitative data analysis', *Forum Qualitative Social Research*, 3(2), available at http://www.qualitative-research.net/fqs-texte/2–02/2–02robertswilson-e.htm, accessed.

Schlackman, B. (1999), 'The history of UK qualitative research, according to Bill Schlackman', *The AQRP Directory and Handbook of Qualitative Research 1989–1999*, St Neots, UK: AQR, p. 16.

Seidel, J. and Clark, J. (1984), 'The Ethnograph: A computer programme for the analysis of qualitative data', *Qualitative Sociology*, 7(1/2): 110–125.

Silverman, D. (2005), *Doing Qualitative Research*, London: Sage Publications.

Stake, R. (2010), *Qualitative Research: Studying How Things Work*, New York: The Guildford Press, Guildford Publications Inc.

Stone, M. (2014), available at http://www.merlin-stone.com/ for business and http://creative.merlin-stone.com/ for creative writing, accessed 3 September 2015.

Sykes, W. (2000), 'Different types of validity', in Wright, L. T. and Crimp, M. *The Marketing Research Process*, London: FT Prentice Hall.

Vinodhini, G. and Chandrasekaran, R. (2012), 'Sentiment analysis and opinion mining: A survey', *International Journal of Advanced Research in Computer Science and Software Engineering*, 2(6): 282–292.

Woodside, A. (2010), 'Brand-consumer storytelling theory and research: Introduction to a *Psychology and Marketing* special issue', *Psychology and Marketing*, 27(6): 531–540.

Yin, Y. K. (2014), *Case Study Research: Design and Methods*, fifth edition, New York: Sage Publications.

10 Quantitative methods in marketing

Steve Baron and Rachel Ashman

Introduction

The importance of quantitative skills for researchers in all the social sciences has long been recognised. Equally, concerns have been expressed that existing training frameworks in quantitative methods were not resulting in sufficient numbers of quantitatively able social scientists. A report issued in 2007 by the UK's Economic and Social Research Council (ESRC) identified the following issues:

- Social science students (in many countries) have become increasingly hostile towards pursuing more mathematical topics.
- The teaching of quantitative methods (often disliked by the majority of students) is generally carried out in isolation from the rest of the curriculum.
- Learning the concepts of probability (the early foundations of many quantitative methods programmes) can be counterintuitive, seen as irrelevant, and inherently difficult for students.
- Learning difficult skills that may not be employed in the degree programme, or afterwards, is seen by students as unimportant.

Rather than following the traditional routes and structures to presenting quantitative methods (often based on logics put forward by statisticians), we have attempted to structure this chapter based on the likely needs of marketing students at undergraduate and postgraduate level. It is hoped that, by so doing, we may address the points above. The needs we have categorised are concerned with 'reading' and 'doing'. We believe that readers/students will benefit from:

- being able to read and make sense of quantitative approaches put forward in marketing journal papers and some other books;
- being able to engage with the software packages that are used in quantitative research in marketing.

Additionally, we recognise that marketing students and scholars come from differing backgrounds and that these backgrounds colour their views of quantitative methods. The two authors of this chapter arrived at their interest in and passion for quantitative methods by completely different routes, as illustrated by the preliminaries to the sections on 'reading quantitative work' and 'doing quantitative marketing research'. How people interpret what they read, and how they use available software to aid analysis of their own data, is often driven by their own background and experiences. In particular, when researchers and students undertake their own quantitative studies, it becomes a personal experience that is reflected in the presentation style of the section on 'doing quantitative marketing research'. Throughout the chapter, the intention is to bring to life the real world of quantitative methods usage in marketing.

Reading quantitative work: aim and perspective

This section of the chapter has the aim of enabling students to make sense of, and appreciate, the strengths/weaknesses of published quantitative methods work in marketing. My name is Steve Baron, and I have been around a long time: in fact I studied mathematics and statistics in the late 1960s. I came to marketing much later in my life and was amazed by how much of marketing research involved the use of statistical analysis. Initially, although vaguely aware of market research procedures, I couldn't understand what would motivate marketers to engage in relatively complex statistical analysis. My own early training and experiences in statistical applications, where data collected, for example, on crop yields or blood pressures, were used in tests of experimental versus control groups in agriculture and medicine, seemed a million miles away from marketing attitude data obtained via Likert scales. The early training also included mathematical statistics in which the theories and assumptions behind the derivations of the most commonly used statistical measures and tests were of uppermost importance. This knowledge has not left me.

Since the 1960s, there have been developments in statistical methodologies favoured by marketers and other social scientists, for example, 'factor analysis' in the 1980s and 1990s, and 'structural equation modelling (SEM)' from the turn of the century to the present day. I, like many others I suspect, find it difficult to keep track of all the variations of statistical methods and tests that are currently employed by marketing researchers. Nevertheless, there are certain basic understandings, which are relevant to all situations, and they provide the focus of this section. In order to introduce the understandings, I've identified what I consider to be the key motivations for marketing researchers to use quantitative methods.

Motivations for taking a quantitative approach

Five of the most common motives for marketing researchers to adopt a quantitative approach are:

1   examining potential differences between populations;
2   exploring relationships and correlations;
3   identifying latent factors/data reduction;
4   developing scales and measures;
5   seeking 'goodness-of-fit'.

Each of these is now explained through examples selected from the marketing and consumer behaviour literature. In some cases, details from the examples have been simplified in order to aid explanation. The questions that are raised below, and the features highlighted in italics, will be addressed later.

Examining potential differences between populations

Quantitative methods are often used to test for differences between *populations* with respect to a variable of interest to marketers. Because the population data is unavailable or inaccessible, decisions have to be made based on *samples* taken from the populations. There are many instances of this aspect of motivation. Two examples are shown below to give a flavour.

Example 1

East *et al.* (2014) sought to investigate, as part of a larger study, how the impact (in terms of consumer decision-making) of positive and negative word-of-mouth varied by sex. The variable of interest is impact of word-of-mouth, and the populations consist of women and men in the Southeast of the UK. Clearly not all women and men in the Southeast of the UK could be surveyed. In the event, relevant questionnaires were completed by a sample of 2,800 residents of whom 61 per cent were women. The decision as to whether or not the impact of word-of-mouth varies between women and men has to be made based on sample information only. There will always be a risk of making the wrong decision (i.e. drawing the wrong conclusion). By applying *statistical significance tests*, such risks are minimised or acknowledged implicitly.

Example 2

Liu *et al.* (2013) chose to explore the similarities and differences in luxury shopping behaviours between online and in-store shoppers. Price-consciousness was one of the constructs being considered, and this is a variable of interest. The populations consist of online and in-store luxury buyers in the US. As before, the complete data from the populations is unattainable. Their conclusions were based on a sample of 91 online and 119 in-store luxury goods buyers. Appropriate *statistical significance tests* were used to test for differences in price-consciousness of luxury goods, between online and in-store luxury buyers, which acknowledge the issue of drawing conclusions based on the relatively small sample sizes.

Questions raised

- How can and should populations be defined?
- How are samples selected that are representative of the populations?
- What measures can and should be used?
- What is meant by a statistically significant difference?
- Is significance synonymous with importance?

For the researchers involved with the studies in Examples 1 and 2, there is the added complication of choosing and designing the appropriate statistical tests to use on their data from the many that are available.

Exploring relationships and correlations

There are many instances where marketing researchers wish to explore relationships between variables. Where they seek to simply demonstrate an association between variables, this is achieved through the calculation of a *correlation coefficient*. Where they seek to quantify the effect of one or more variables (labelled *independent* or *explanatory variables*) on another variable (the *dependent variable*) some form of (multiple) *regression analysis* is employed. The following two examples demonstrate this form of motivation.

Example 3

Levy (2014) examines the relationship between customers' usage levels of online banking and their loyalty to the bank, as part of a larger study on the quality of online banking services. Prior studies had suggested that there might be a negative relationship between usage levels of online banking and bank loyalty (i.e. the higher the usage level of online banking, the lower the loyalty to the bank, and vice versa). In order to put this to the test, Levy presented questions on usage of online banking services and bank loyalty (each requiring numerical answers) to a sample of 260 bank users in Israel. The resulting negative correlation coefficient offered further evidence for the postulated negative relationship. Furthermore, in the discussion, the author suggests that customers with high-level usage of online banking services feel less committed to the bank, based on a subsequent regression-based analysis that specifies bank loyalty as the dependent variable.

Example 4

Khare *et al.* (2013) explore relationships in the context of green marketing. Specifically, they examine the green purchase behaviour of Indian consumers (dependent variable) and the influence of a number of independent variables – self-esteem, normative and informational values, and social influence. A sample of 501 Indian shopping mall consumers filled in self-administered questionnaires relating to the study. Through the use of (stepwise) regression analysis, it was concluded that social influence, membership esteem and normative influence each have a (statistically) significant effect on green purchase behaviour and, between them, account for 34.4 per cent of Indian consumers' green product purchase.

Questions raised

- Is there a connection between correlation and cause and effect?
- Can regression analysis be used for predictions?
- What does statistical significance mean in this context?

Identifying latent variables/data reduction

In many marketing research studies, several variables have relevance to the topic being studied, often discovered through prior qualitative analysis. Some variables may have similarities to others. There may be too many variables involved for clear conclusions to be formed, or for managerially useful outcomes. In these cases, the motivation for the use of quantitative methods is *data reduction*; reducing the number of variables to a manageable size through the identification of *latent variables*. A latent variable is unobserved and represents a dimension that captures the meanings of several variables under one umbrella and is distinct from other latent variables. The technique usually employed is *factor analysis*.

Example 5

In a seminal study, Parasuraman *et al.* (1988) explored the concept of perceived service quality. Starting with 97 items (variables) seen as relevant to the construct of perceived service quality, the authors used data reduction techniques to identify the most important and relevant 22 items, through responses from 4 independent samples from different service sectors, each of 200 respondents. Subsequently, with the aid of factor analysis, the items were grouped into five dimensions – tangibles, reliability, responsiveness, assurance and empathy – which became known as the SERVQUAL dimensions of perceived service quality. Each dimension consists of four or five items. The five dimensions represent the latent variables, the labels of which were agreed by the authors as representing the combined meaning of the four or five items. For managers, this was a way of improving perceived service quality through focusing on the five SERVQUAL dimensions.

Example 6

Bennett *et al.* (2007) undertook a study of consumer motivations for participating in charity-affiliated sporting events. Prior research had identified 12 reasons for participation, each consisting of 3 to 5 items (variables), and so this research was more linked to confirming and adapting the reasons, rather than conducting totally exploratory research. A sample of 579 individuals completed a relevant questionnaire. In the event, through the application of factor analysis, the authors reduced the motives (latent variables) from 12 to 10, and further identified the 4 most dominant motives – personal involvement with the good cause(s) supported by an occasion, opportunities to lead a healthy lifestyle provided by the event, an individual's involvement with the sport in question and the desire to mix socially with other attendees.

Questions raised

* Given the large number of items (variables) involved, what size of sample is desirable?
* How can we justify that items/variables are being grouped into appropriate factors/dimensions?
* Are there guidelines on labelling latent variables?
* Can the data reduction methods be applied whether or not there has been prior research on the topic?

Developing scales and measures

Having derived the key dimensions of a construct such as perceived service quality, a natural step forward is to offer practical help in measuring the construct. The aim here is to offer a *reliable* and *valid* scale for the use in survey-based questionnaires, which yields helpful quantitative information. It should be a concise scale that is meaningful to a range of practical applications. Examples 7 and 8 below illustrate the process involved with the development of multiple-item scale measures – in each case, scales that have been adopted subsequently by numerous academics and practitioners.

Example 7

This is a continuation of the study in Example 5. Having identified the five dimensions of perceived service quality, each consisting of four or five items, the authors proceed to assess the reliability and validity of this multiple-item scale. Samples of service customers from four service sectors filled in questionnaires consisting of the scale items. The first test was of the internal consistency of items within each dimension. Based on the sample data, a statistic, *Cronbach alpha*, is calculated for the items in each dimension. If the alphas meet a recognised threshold, then this aspect of reliability is confirmed. A combined reliability measure is also required. Content validity is considered more subjectively: has the scale purification been done thoroughly? Do the items fully represent the domain of service quality? Based on the confirmation of reliability and validity, the multiple-item scale becomes a recommended method for collecting and summarising data on perceived service quality.

Example 8

In the late 1980s there was considerable interest in understanding the acceptance of information technology by potential users. Initially, the user groups studied were company employees. In the twenty-first century, given the increased access to the internet, technology acceptance by consumers became a hot topic. The paper by Davis (1989) was the first to derive measurement scales for predicting user acceptance of computers. Two dimensions – perceived usefulness and perceived ease of use – were identified and, after testing for reliability and validity in a similar manner to that of Example 7, 6-item scales were refined for each of the 2 dimensions, based on data collected from a sample of 152 computer users. The measurement scales were used and augmented by numerous practitioners and academic researchers wishing to facilitate information technology acceptance in diverse applications.

Questions raised

- What is the difference between reliability and validity?
- Can the suggested scales be modified to meet specific circumstances?
- Is there a recognised template/procedure for scale development?

Seeking 'goodness-of-fit'

Examples 7 and 8 demonstrate the potential practical implications associated with the identification of latent variables. For many academic scholars, the identification and confirmation of latent variables can be the forerunner of theoretical developments; developments of *models* that represent the relationships in the field of interest. In these cases, it is of importance to assess the fit between empirical data and the proposed model. This is done through the calculation of *goodness-of-fit* statistics. In Examples 9 and 10, establishing goodness-of-fit of a proposed model is a key motive of the research.

Example 9

Gironda and Korgaonkar (2014) studied customer motivations to use social networking sites (SNS). Drawing on prior planned behaviour theories, they developed a conceptual model to explain general SNS activity behaviour (which contained 11 variables, each with multiple items to represent them). After conducting the appropriate reliability and validity tests on the measurement scales, they used the data from an online survey of students from a southeast US university to also test the goodness-of-fit of their model. This is done by calculating statistics such as chi-square (χ^2), chi-square divided by degrees of freedom (χ^2/f), comparative fit index (CFI), non-normal fit index (NNFI) and root mean square error of approximation (RMSEA). There are guidelines (see later), which provide cut-offs and thresholds against which these statistics can be compared in order to conclude that the model is a good fit (which was the case in this example).

Example 10

Customer and employee misbehaviours during service encounters have been the subject of several service marketing research studies. Daunt and Harris (2014) put forward a model that connects perceived employee service deviance with the severity of customer misbehaviour based on equity, power and differential association theories. It involved four dimensions, each measured through three or four items. Based data collected from a sample of 380 UK customers of bars, hotels and restaurants, and after undertaking appropriate reliability tests with pilot samples, goodness-of-fit indices – χ^2, χ^2/f, CFI, NNFI and RMSEA – all fell within the recommended ranges, confirming the model fit.

Questions raised

- What are the cut-off and threshold values against which the fit indices are judged, and how fixed are they?
- Can more than one model provide a fit?
- What is done if the model does not provide a good fit?

Important common features and principles

The highlighted expressions and questions raised give rise to a number of general features and principles, which offer important guidelines in making proper sense of quantitative findings of marketing studies. They also provide some pointers as to the scope of the study and possible limitations of the findings. It can be so easy to be dazzled by the statistical sophistication and seeming precision of numerical findings, and so it is always worth adopting a questioning attitude to the overall study. The common features and principles to be discussed are:

- populations, sampling and sampling distributions;
- hypotheses and hypothesis testing;
- statistical significance;
- dependent and independent (explanatory) variables;
- reliability and validity;
- degrees of freedom;
- goodness-of-fit.

The categories are not mutually exclusive, but the headings reflect the order of issues raised earlier.

Populations, sampling and sampling distributions

In dictionaries, the word 'population' has several meanings, e.g. all the inhabitants of a particular place; the extent to which an area is or has been populated; a community of animals, plants or humans among whom members' interbreeding occurs (Oxford English Dictionary). In a quantitative methods context, there is a specific understanding of what is meant by a *statistical population*. The definition given by Easton and McColl, in their statistics glossary, conveys the commonly understood features of a statistical population: 'A population is any entire collection of people, animals, plants or things from which we may collect data. It is the entire group we are interested in, which we wish to describe or draw conclusions about'.

This definition can, and should, be borne in mind when reading marketing journal articles which employ quantitative methods. It is always worth asking oneself, 'What is (are) the population(s) being studied?' This 'entire collection' is extremely important to be clear about, as it determines the scope of relevance of a study's findings.

While there are potentially insightful findings from all the studies used in Examples 1 to 10, the reader must be clear as to the range of application of the findings based on the (implied) population(s) being studied. For example, the findings of Example 1 only relate to the populations of women and men in the Southeast of the UK, the findings of Example 3 only relate to the population of online banking service users in Israel, and the findings of Example 10 only relate to the population of UK bar, hotel and restaurant customers. All the studies may have implications for wider and larger populations, but the specific study limitations must be understood.

There are very rarely cases where the 'entire collection' is accessible for the purpose of collecting data. Thus, conclusions cannot normally be drawn about a statistical population with certainty. The normal procedure therefore is to select a sample from the population and make inferences about the population, in the full knowledge of the imprecision and uncertainty involved with such a process. The inferences that are/can be made rely on probabilities based on various properties of the sample and sampling processes. Rather like legal processes, statistical inferences work on a balance of probabilities. We cannot be absolutely certain that women and men differ in terms of the impact on them of word-of-mouth, but we should be able to derive the probabilities that this is, or is not the case.

But where do the probabilities come from? It is clear that measures (such as the mean number of instances of positive word-of-mouth in the previous six months) calculated from different samples, taken from the same population, would vary. Statisticians from an early age have explored such variations in the form of sampling distributions and are able to calculate probabilities based on the pattern of such distributions. There are assumptions behind these calculations, for example, that the sample has been randomly selected from the population, which are discussed later. In the meantime, it is worth scrutinising how a sample in a published article has been selected and how the data have been collected. Can the sample be deemed representative of the population from which it is taken?

Quite often, and this is understandable, samples are chosen, and sample data collected, because they are accessible. A particular issue of concern in this respect is the use of 'student samples' (see Example 9). Are they used because student samples can be reached easily through the classroom, or could they be seen to be representative of young adults generally? Similar concerns may be expressed when samples of people are selected via mall interviews (Example 4) or through other forms of convenience or snowball sampling. This is not to say that such studies do not have worth, but the classical sampling process – where a population has been clearly specified, and a random sample has been selected from the population – has not been carried out, because of practical and pragmatic reasons. However, most of the theory behind statistical measures and tests does assume that this classical sampling process has been undertaken. Then there is an issue as to how robust the tests are when the assumptions are violated.

Hypotheses and hypothesis testing

Underpinning most quantitative studies is the process of formulating and testing hypotheses. Through using the following scenario, key features of this process are introduced.

> Research via a passenger questionnaire was carried out at a large airport. One of the questions asked passengers (sitting in the boarding area) whether they had purchased any items from the duty-free shops. Another part of the questionnaire recorded the gender of the respondents.

The researchers were interested in testing whether there was any difference between males and females in the percentage who purchase items from the duty-free shops. The populations would consist of all male and female passengers who travel from the airport. The samples consist of the males and females interviewed by the researchers.

In classical hypothesis testing, two hypotheses should have been formulated *prior to* the data collection – the *null hypothesis* (H_0) and the *alternative hypothesis* (H_1). The null hypothesis postulates that there is *no difference* between males and females in the percentage who purchase items from the duty-free shop. The alternative hypothesis postulates that there is a difference between males and females in the percentage who purchase items from the duty-free shop. In many marketing research studies, only an alternative hypothesis is formally stated. However, it is key to always remember that behind every alternative hypothesis, is the important null hypothesis. There are two reasons:

- Classical scientific research is based on assuming that there is 'no difference' until sufficient evidence is supplied to warrant rejection of that assumption. It is very like the legal assumption of innocent until proven guilty.
- The evidence for rejecting, or not, a null hypothesis can be quantified in the form of a probability (known as the p statistic). The p statistic is a measure of the probability that the null hypothesis is true.

Going back to the scenario, suppose 100 males and 100 females were interviewed. We look at two possible outcomes resulting from the sample data:

1   *Outcome 1* – 45 males (45 per cent) and 55 females (55 per cent) made duty-free purchases. We find that p = 0.42 (see later for methods of calculating p). What does this mean, and what conclusions should we draw? The p statistic indicates that there is a probability of 0.42 that the null hypothesis is true, even though there is a sample difference of 10 per cent. This is based on knowledge that sampling differences of 10 per cent can arise simply through chance, given the variations that occur when different samples are taken from the populations under study. So, because the p statistic is quite high, we must conclude that there is insufficient evidence to reject H_0. Would you find someone guilty if there was a probability of 0.42 of them being innocent?

2   *Outcome 2* – 45 males (45 per cent) and 65 females (65 per cent) made duty-free purchases. We find that p = 0.03. This indicates that there is a probability of 0.03 that H_0 is true, given that the sample difference is 20 per cent. It is highly unlikely that this is a chance sampling difference (i.e. only 3 in a 100). Therefore, there is evidence to reject H_0 and accept H_1. In this case, we would conclude that the difference in the percentage of duty-free purchases between males and females is *statistically significant*, which brings us to the next section.

Statistical significance

Following on from the scenario above, elaboration is useful on three aspects:

1   There is inevitably some degree of subjectivity in drawing conclusions based on the value of the p statistic. Someone might ask, based on the legal analogy, whether the benefit of doubt should be given to H_0 when there is still a probability of 0.03 of it being true. Because of this, most researchers adopt a threshold, known as *the level of significance*, to present their results. So,

if $p < 0.05$, results are said to be statistically significant at the 0.05 level of significance. If $p < 0.01$, they are said to be statistically significant at the 0.01 level of significance, and so on. Researchers may often use a shorthand code for presenting their results:

a   n.s. means 'not statistically significant';
b   * means $p < 0.05$ i.e. statistically significant at the 0.05 level;
c   ** means $p < 0.01$ i.e. statistically significant at the 0.01 level;
d   *** means $p < 0.001$ i.e. statistically significant at the 0.001 level.

The reader then has the information on whether or not to reject the underlying null hypothesis.

2   It seems counterintuitive, but the rule is that *the lower the value of p, the more statistically significant is the result.* There has been a deliberate effort here to refer to 'statistical significance' as opposed to merely 'significance'. Statistical significance is not synonymous with importance (neither is a non-statistically significant result unimportant). In the given scenario, it can be as equally important to know that there is unlikely to be a difference between males and females in their duty-free purchase habits, as it is to know that there is a difference. Where journal paper authors carelessly use 'significant differences' rather than 'statistically significant differences', this should be borne in mind.

3   Thus far, the emphasis has been on statistical significance in the context of examining potential differences between populations. The same logic applies, however, in most of the quantitative marketing studies. For example, it is necessary to assess whether a correlation coefficient is statistically significant. A correlation coefficient is normally calculated to measure the linear association between two variables such as social influence and green purchase behaviour (Example 3). Like any other sample statistic, it is subject to sampling variations (the coefficient will vary between samples taken from the same population). In all cases, H_0 postulates that there is *no* correlation (linear association) between the two variables. A statistically significant result means that we would reject H_0 at the chosen level of significance. Again, it is important to recognise that a statistically significant correlation coefficient means only that it is unlikely to be zero! The same applies to regression coefficients in the context of multiple regression analyses (see p. 222). Always, the null hypothesis is that the regression coefficient is zero, and a statistically significant regression coefficient is one, which is unlikely to be zero.

Dependent and independent (explanatory) variables

Marketing researchers are often interested in how one set of variables, labelled dependent variables, may depend on another set of variables, labelled independent variables, or explanatory variables. For example, in Example 3 above, the research set out to determine how loyalty to a bank (dependent variable) might be determined by level of online banking services usage (independent variable). In Example 4 the research focused on green product purchase behaviour (dependent variable) and examined the effect of self-esteem, normative values, informational values and social influence (independent variables).

Cause and effect

It is very important to recognise that:

1   A correlation coefficient does not measure cause and effect. Positive or negative correlation coefficients (which can vary between $+1$ and -1) simply represent the strength of the

positive or negative linear associations between the variables. They do not identify which is the dependent and which is the independent variable. That has to be argued through non-statistical means. A negative correlation coefficient of −0.13* between bank loyalty and level of online banking services usage implies a statistically significant negative (linear) association between the two variables at the 0.05 level. Of itself, it says nothing about cause and effect. It could be that high levels of usage of online banking services result generally in lower bank loyalty. Equally, on the basis of the correlation coefficient only, it could be that high bank loyalty results in lower levels of online banking service usage.

2   The choice of dependent and independent variables is determined by non-statistical criteria, often argued through the application of prior theory and evaluations of prior literature. Thus, all statistical analyses that employ versions of multiple regression analyses require a prior justification for the model being used, and solid arguments as to the choice of dependent and independent variables. Once the model is stipulated, coefficients of the independent variables can be computed and tested for statistical significance, thereby providing confirmation, or otherwise, of the influence of the independent variables on the dependent variables.

Bivariate correlation and regression

When there are only two variables to consider, it is possible to provide a more visual and understandable explanation of many of the key features of correlation and regression. Data that are collected on the two variables, one of which (variable y) has been designated as the dependent variable, and the other (variable x) has been designated as the independent variable, can be represented on a scatter diagram. The scatter diagram gives a first indication of the association (or not) of the two variables. For example, Figures 10.1 and 10.2 show strong associations between x and y and they appear linear. Therefore, they would produce high values of the correlation coefficient (positive for Figure 10.1, a value close to +1; and negative for Figure 10.2, a value close to −1). Figure 10.3 shows no real association between x and y, and so would result in a correlation coefficient close to zero. Figure 10.4 shows a strong association between x and y, but it is not *linear,* and so the correlation coefficient would be close to zero.

Where, for example in Figures 10.1 and 10.2, there may be an indication of a strong correlation between x and y, the underlying relationship can be represented by a straight line of best fit to the points on the scatter diagram. The method employed to derive the line of best fit, in this bivariate context, is known as least squares (or ordinary least squares, (OLS)). The line is represented mathematically by the equation of a straight line, known as the linear regression equation:

$$Y = a + bx$$

where a and b are coefficients calculated using the method of least squares from the pairs of sample data on the variables x and y. The regression coefficient b is considered especially important as, being the slope of the regression line, it estimates the effect of the independent variable on the dependent variable. If b is found to be statistically significant, this means that the population regression coefficient is unlikely to be zero, i.e. the independent variable has some effect on the dependent variable. Equally, if b is found to be non-statistically significant, this indicates that the independent variable has no real effect on the dependent variable.

In the bivariate case, the correlation coefficient is usually denoted by the symbol r. As a bi-product of correlation and regression analysis, the square of the correlation coefficient, r^2, is known to estimate the proportion of variation in the dependent variable that can be accounted for by the linear influence of the independent variable (sometimes called the 'variance explained' of the dependent variable). For example, if r = −0.4, then this indicates that a proportion of 0.16 (i.e. 16 per cent) of the variation in y is explained by the linear influence of x.

In Figure 10.4 there does appear to be a relationship between variables x and y, but the relationship is non-linear. This will lead some researchers to explore non-linear regression procedures, often through transformations of the variables (e.g. transforming y to log y, and x to log x) which result in a linear relationship between the transformed variables. Where researchers adopt, for example, log-linear regression methods, this is the reason.

Multiple regression

Most marketing research publications go beyond bivariate correlation and regression to consider relationships between several variables. Clearly, once you move to more than two dimensions, it becomes impossible to display meaningful visualisations such as scatter diagrams. However,

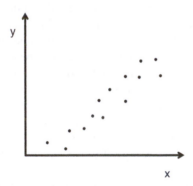

Figure 10.1 Positive association

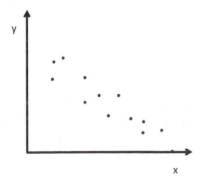

Figure 10.2 Negative association

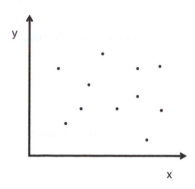

Figure 10.3 No association

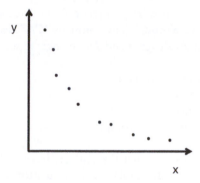

Figure 10.4 Non-linear association

mathematically, through matrix algebra, there is a logical extension from two to many dimensions, and much of the logic behind bivariate regression applies to multiple regression. The first natural extension is multiple regression, whereby the relationship between a dependent variable (Y) and n independent variables $(X_1, X_2 \ldots X_n)$ can be represented by the equation:

$$Y = a + b_1X_1 + b_2X_2 + \ldots + b_nX_n$$

The principal aim of studies employing multiple regression methods is to estimate the regression coefficients $(b_1, b_2 \ldots b_n)$, test them for statistical significance, and estimate the amount of variation in the dependent variable that can be explained by the linear influence of the independent variables. The estimation of the regression coefficients and the calculation of the corresponding p statistics is demonstrated in the section on 'doing the marketing research'. The overall multiple correlation coefficient is denoted by uppercase R for multiple regression studies. In these cases, the calculated $R^2 \times 100$ represents the percentage of variation in the dependent variable that is explained by the linear influence of the explanatory variables. In theory, the more independent variables that are included in the model, the greater the R^2 value. However, the key to meaningful findings is to identify only a few statistically significant independent variables, which generate a relatively high R^2 value.

Reliability and validity

Where statistical measures and scales provide both inputs and outputs to the research studies, the issues of reliability and validity of the measures are of great importance. These issues are discussed briefly here and in more detail later.

Reliability

Reliability represents the degree to which a proposed set of measures produces consistent results. Two aspects, at the very least, must be considered.

Internal consistency

Do the different items representing a construct (latent variable) produce similar results? Examples 5 and 7 above refer to the development of the SERVQUAL measure of perceived service quality. It consists of five constructs, referred to as dimensions, one of which is 'responsiveness'. To measure responsiveness, four items are put to respondents regarding service provided by company XYZ, each requiring answers on a seven-point Likert scale, with 1 = strongly disagree and 7 = strongly agree:

- XYZ does not tell customers exactly when services will be performed.
- You do not receive prompt service from XYZ's employees.
- Employees of XYZ are not always willing to help customers.
- Employees of XYZ are too busy to respond to customer requests promptly.

Do these items show internal consistency in measuring a construct that the authors have called responsiveness? There is a standard test for internal consistency. It involves the calculation of a statistic, known as Cronbach's alpha, or simply alpha, and comparing its value to a recommended threshold. It must exceed a certain minimum value, often stated as 0.6, but which varies according to source. In the SERVQUAL case, the alphas varied between 0.69 and 0.76 according to data collected in four different service sectors, and so internal consistency was confirmed. A similar conclusion was drawn for the other four dimensions of service quality.

Combined reliability

In addition to the internal consistency tests, it is necessary to test the reliability of the linear combinations of all of the constructs (dimensions). A formula suggested by Nunnally (1978) is computed for this purpose, and again the calculated statistic needs to be sufficiently high to confirm this aspect of reliability.

Many marketing researchers refer to the paper by Churchill (1979) when following these procedures. For readers wishing to know more about the subtleties of reliability (and validity which follows) it is recommended that they consult this seminal paper.

Validity

This refers to how well the scales measure what they are supposed to measure. Consistency may be demonstrated above, but what if the measure is consistently off-target? Could it be measuring something different from what is intended? There are many forms of assessing validity. Two of the most common features, 'face validity' and 'construct validity', are judged through feedback from stakeholders or experts familiar with the topic under consideration. This was the case with SERVQUAL, for example. Other aspects of validity, for example, 'convergent validity' (assessment of the extent to which the measurement scale correlates with other methods) and 'discriminant validity' (assessment of the distinct novelty of the measurement scale, see p. 266) involve calculations of test statistics as demonstrated in Churchill (1979). Measures may be reliable but not valid. What are required are measures that are both reliable and valid.

Degrees of freedom

Intuitively, all other things being equal, the larger the sample taken from a population, the more likely the sample characteristics are to reflect those of the parent population. The number of items in a sample, i.e. the sample size, is therefore an important consideration in any statistical analysis. It is also the case that when there are a large number of coefficients (or parameters) to estimate, then the larger the sample size the better. Having a relatively small sample size, in comparison to the number of coefficients to estimate, can result in drawing false conclusions based on the calculated statistics, such as correlation or regression coefficients. An extreme example will illustrate this point.

> Suppose we have a situation of only two pairs of observations on variables, x and y, and wish to estimate the coefficients (a and b) of the linear equation $y = a + bx$. The scatter diagram will be as in Figure 10.5 below:

> What we would have is a perfect (positive) correlation, as a straight line would exactly fit the two points. However, that would be totally misleading. The assumed, perfect linear association is a result of the lack of sample data, rather than from any underlying relationship between x and y. For example, variable x could be the midday temperature in Dubai and variable y could be the Financial Times Index, and this would indicate a perfect correlation if data only consisted of two day's information. The problem arises because the sample size is the same as the number of parameters to be estimated. This example may seem relatively obvious and trivial. However, in many marketing studies, there are very large numbers of variables, and correspondingly large numbers of parameters to estimate, and the sample size must therefore be sufficiently large before we can have confidence that the conclusions relate to the underlying relationships, rather than a lack of sample data.

The concept of degrees of freedom addresses this issue. Essentially, it is the difference between the sample size and the number of parameters to estimate and is incorporated into many of the most

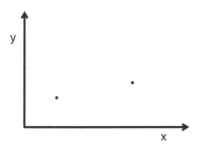

Figure 10.5 Linear equation

common statistical tests. However, it is still incumbent on the researcher to ensure there is a sufficiently large sample size. There are some guiding rules for choice of sample size. See later in the section on 'doing quantitative marketing research'.

Goodness-of-fit

Goodness-of-fit is a concept that has relevance in two main areas: assessing whether sample data can be regarded as arising from a particular population distribution; and assessing whether a theoretical model is a good fit to the sample data.

Sample data and population distributions

Much of the theory behind sampling distributions is based on an assumption that the sample is taken from a population that follows a normal distribution. Here, it should be noted that 'normal' does not mean usual or general, but refers to a very specific form of distribution – one with a precise mathematical formula. It has a bell-shaped appearance as in Figure 10.6.

Sample data variations can be represented by a histogram as in Figure 10.7.

Rather than rely on a purely visual judgement as to the fit (i.e. whether the sample data (histogram) has been taken from a normal distribution), a goodness-of-fit test is available using a χ^2 test of the null hypothesis that the sample data are consistent with the specified distribution. The χ^2 goodness-of-fit test can be applied to any theoretical population distribution, but it is particularly important with respect to the normal distribution as many statistical tests and techniques make the assumption that random sample(s) are taken from normal population(s), and this really should be verified.

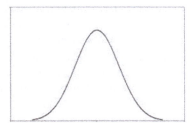

Figure 10.6 Population variable following a normal distribution

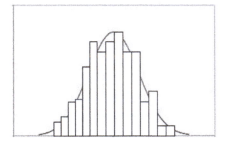

Figure 10.7 Sample data in the form of a histogram

Model goodness-of-fit

In Examples 9 and 10 it is theoretical models that are being empirically tested for goodness-of-fit. Here, the principle is the same, but a greater number of fit statistics need to be computed, and there is a greater element of subjectivity involved. There are guidelines available for judging the fit statistics, but no formal tests of statistical significance. The guidelines for common fit statistics are shown in Table 10.1.

Sometimes, however, the threshold guidelines are relaxed a little depending on circumstances, which is where the level of subjectivity arises.

Data types and common statistical tests

Data can be collected as various types. The two most common are known as:

- **Continuous data** – These are data that represent measurements on a continuous scale, such as the weight of crops, or the blood pressure of a person. Therefore, 'crop yield' and 'blood pressure' are example of continuous variables.
- **Categorical (discrete) data** – These are data that represent information about discrete characteristics. They are counted rather than measured. Thus 'occupation', 'marital status' and 'gender' are examples of categorical or discrete variables.

Most statistical tests have been derived on the assumption that data and variables are easily classified as either continuous or discrete. The following sections demonstrate the tests that are commonly used when continuous or discrete variables are the variables of interest. However, in marketing, it is not often the case that the variables are easily classified. As the earlier examples demonstrate, many marketing variables consist of answers on a five-, seven- or nine-point Likert-type scale. Should they be treated in the same way as continuous variables, or are they really more like discrete variables, given that only integer values can be assigned on a Likert scale? In most cases, the former is the case. Scale data are treated as if they are continuous data. This sometimes leads to a rather strange, over-precise presentation of results to several decimal places, when the input data are only integer estimates.

Statistical tests: continuous variables

Several of the early derived statistical tests were concerned with examining potential differences between populations, based on available continuous data from samples. For example, do different soil treatments result in different crop yields, as measured by weight? In these cases, tests were based on comparisons of *sample means*. Is the difference in the mean crop yield for those receiving soil treatment 1 statistically significant from the mean crop yield for those receiving soil treatment 2, or

Table 10.1 Threshold guidelines for common fit statistics

Fit statistic	Guidelines for good fit
χ^2/f	Between 1.0 and 5.0
CFI	≥ 0.95; the nearer to 1.0, the better the fit.
NNFI	≥ 0.95; the nearer to 1.0, the better the fit.
RMSEA	≤ 0.08; the nearer to zero, the better the fit

is it merely due to chance? Where there are only two populations (treatments), the *t-test* is appropriate to test for statistical significance. Where there are three or more populations (treatments), the *F-test*, using *ANOVA* (analysis of variance) is appropriate to test for statistical significance. While marketers are not often faced with the need to statistically test the significance between two or more sample means, the t-test and F-test (ANOVA) are also applicable to multiple regression and correlation studies, which lie at the heart of many marketing research studies. The t-test is used to test the statistical significance of each of the regression coefficients (remember it is a test of the null hypothesis that the coefficient is zero), and ANOVA, using the F-test, is applied to test whether the variation due to the regression (the total combination of the independent variables) is statistically significant. Where data are continuous and taken from normal distributions, the associated tests are labelled as parametric tests.

Statistical tests: discrete variables

A catalyst for deriving statistical tests involving discrete variables was the need to evaluate the effectiveness of cholera and typhoid vaccinations in World War 1. Was there a difference in contracting these diseases between those who had received or not received the vaccinations? The discrete variable was contracting a disease (either 'yes' or 'no') and the populations consisted of those who had and those who had not been vaccinated. The χ^2-test was derived for this purpose, i.e. testing whether the difference in *proportions*, which contracted or did not contract a disease, was statistically significant. This became known as the χ^2-test of independence. A form of the χ^2-test was also found to be the way to test for goodness-of-fit. In marketing research papers, the goodness-of-fit application of the χ^2-test is the mostly likely version to be encountered in published papers.

Where data are discrete (or ordinal), the associated tests are labelled as non-parametric tests.

In the section on 'doing quantitative marketing research', where the emphasis is on carrying out some statistical tests, it is very important that the type of data is understood in order to carry out the appropriate statistical tests.

Reading other people's work: what to look for

The aim of sections above is to enable students to make sense of quantitative work presented in marketing journals and books. Often students can be put off such articles simply because they appear to be highly mathematical and out-of-reach. The presumption here is that the main findings can be understood even by people with little or no formal statistics education. The steps below should help in this respect. On picking up a journal article:

1   First, try to assess whether or not the article is relevant to your own field of study. This can normally be done by reading only the abstract, keywords and possibly the conclusion. Sometimes, however, even the abstract is written in pseudo-mathematical/statistical jargon. In these cases, the discussions above should give you a real feel about what the article is about. It is highly likely that the motivation for carrying out the research will fit one of the categories outlined earlier.
2   Assuming that the article is relevant, it is a good idea to seek information on the population(s) being studied, so that the scope and limitations of the findings are known in advance. Where populations are not formally stated, you will be able to infer what they are from the description of the sample(s) used. It is wise to be cautious of studies, which use student samples. In these situations, you should expect the researchers to provide a justification as to why such a sample is appropriate.

3   Seek out the information on all aspects relating to the sample(s) – sample size, type of data collected, method of data collection (e.g. mall interview, online survey), and items used in a questionnaire-based survey. This should give you a feel for the quality of the input data.

4   Check the statistical techniques, which are being used and which are normally revealed in a section on methodology or methods. This may seem extremely complicated. For example, you may find that the research uses SEM with partial least squares (PLS). Don't let this be off-putting. There are standard templates that researchers follow (e.g. see Gefen *et al.* 2000), which ensure that appropriate techniques are applied to the type of data collected, measures satisfy reliability and validity criteria, assumptions (e.g. normality) are tested, and the proposed model has goodness-of-fit. All these notions have been addressed above. Furthermore, the article would normally pass through a rigorous peer review process before publication, so it is reasonably safe to assume that the statistical analysis has been done properly.

5   It is worth looking at how the findings (e.g. correlation coefficients, t-statistics, p-values) are presented. There can be a tendency for researchers to give a false sense of precision to their findings. Correlations and p-values can be given to three, four or even five decimal places, based on input data, which is much less precise (for example data that are integer estimates on a seven-point Likert scale). Where this occurs, it casts doubt on whether the researchers have a real feel for the data they are working with. Also, be careful to appreciate that some research-ers can miss out the adjective 'statistical' in the expression 'statistical significance', which can sometimes lead to a misleading impression that 'significant' findings are the important findings. Remember that a non-statistically significant finding can also yield important insights.

6   Where the research is largely about empirical fits to models, and the model has a good fit, it means that the statistical work carried out has provided additional evidence for the credibility of the model proposed by the researchers. It does not mean that it is the only model that could fit the data. Also, a piece of research that does not show a good model fit is unlikely to get published, even if the research was carried out rigorously. Researchers may use the flexibility of fit-statistic guidelines (Table 10.1) to ensure model fit has been achieved, suggesting, for example, that under certain circumstances, values of CFI ≥ 0.90 or RMSEA ≤ 0.90 are accept-able. In this case, it is rather like snipping the carpet and trimming the doorframe to ensure that the door fits. You must draw your own conclusions.

7   Finally, it is worth discerning what findings are new that have been discovered through the use of the quantitative analysis. This involves swapping the statistician's hat for a marketer's hat. What do the findings contribute to marketing theory and practice? Is it essentially a replication study? Is it a major or incremental step forward?

Doing quantitative marketing research

The second section of this chapter, whose mission is to demystify any lofty or inaccessible notions you have about quantitative market research, is all about actually doing quantitative data analysis and thus allowing this process to become real and achievable. My name is Rachel Ashman. I hold a PhD in fashion retailing, which employed a purely quantitative methodology, and I am now a lecturer of marketing. I teach market research among other things. I am not a naturally math-ematically minded, always carry a calculator and give me ten equations to solve for breakfast kind of researcher. What I have been successful in doing, though, is patiently and persistently arming myself with the tools I need to be a competent and confident statistician. If you feel that you are in the same boat as I am, then the skills you will need to succeed within this discipline are being able to read, research, plan and network effectively. You need to develop systematic thinking, patience, logic and above all, humility. In the next few sections I will show you (and actually show you, with pictures) what happens when you do some of the statistics often used in quantitative data analysis. I will also give you some handy hints and tips on how to organise yourself so that the process runs smoothly. The main aim of this section is to prevent any feelings of utter dismay, which may have arisen whenever you read a text labelled for 'non-mathematicians', which becomes filled with formulae, equations or calculations after page three. When reaching the end of this chapter you should feel that Steve and I have enabled you to see the statistical wood previously lost in a forest of mathematical trees. Consequently, the next sections included in this chapter are as follows:

1   the five P mantra for statistical survival;
2   approaches to organising and conducting data analysis;
3   examples of widely used statistical tests and their operation in SPSS and/or AMOS;
4   concluding thoughts, confidence building patter and further references.

From this point in the chapter we will be including some frequently used statistics and their working in the program SPSS. These are not by any means all the statistical procedures that you can carry out, and SPSS is not the only program you could use to carry out this work. But this can be used as a starting point to understand some of the things you could do using statistics and what that looks like in a statistics computer program. All the screen shots used in this chapter are from SPSS Version 20.

The five P mantra for statistical survival

After spending many wasted seconds, minutes, hours and sometimes even days feeling frustrated and confused about a statistics issue, I have developed a mantra. I wholeheartedly believe that this can help in having a smooth data analysis experience:

Proper Planning Prevents Poor Performance

This mantra sums up one of the fundamental characteristics of quantitative methods – that the design, creation and collection of the data are where most of the labour and time is spent. When these preliminary steps are properly undertaken, the data analysis, providing you understand how to do it, should be fairly fast and efficient. However, if you don't pay due attention to the crucial first stages, such as rigorously designing your questionnaire, having a plan of which analysis you want to undertake, pilot testing, creating a codebook, keeping your collected questionnaires properly organised and cleaning your data set – you will be in trouble (or just very lucky). To further clarify and introduce some of these steps, we will now breakdown the five P mantra for statistical survival.

Proper planning

As other chapters in this book will deal with research design in more detail, I won't labour the point, but planning before undertaking your quantitative data analysis will be instrumental in its success. The main activities relating to planning include designing a sensible questionnaire, which respondents will complete, checking this through pilot testing, and amending. You will also need to construct a detailed and clear codebook. If you don't fulfil the planning stage, the chances are that your poorly designed measuring instrument will only collect poor data, which then results in a poor set of data analysis.

Questionnaire design

You should develop a clear idea of what sort of data analysis you want to undertake before you design your questionnaire. Some statistical analyses have certain requirements from your data in terms of variable types and numbers of items so that they can be completed. These rules are plentiful, specific and should be researched in detail, but here are some of the main ones to look out for when undertaking questionnaire design:

- Quantitative data analysis generally works with closed questions, i.e. 'yes' or 'no', or number selection answers.
- In order to have a greater chance of reliable results you should use questions from previous and rigorously conducted research, rather than cherry picking questions from all over the place (or out of your head).
- Including some preliminary questioning, in terms of socio-demographics, can help you contextualise and set the scene of your sample. You can also split your data files by these to gain more nuanced statistical analysis.
- For confirmatory analysis or analysis using latent variables, each variable should have at least three items, which translate to three questions for each construct. I would use more than three items just in case of any issues with reliability and validity.

Pilot testing

Once you have created your questionnaire, pilot testing is a key and fundamental stage prior to your data collection. Pilot testing is taking the time to make sure your questionnaire is sound. Stages in this process include asking a supervisor or colleague to check your questionnaire and fill it in, before giving you some feedback. I recommend actually listening to this feedback and acting on the comments before you take your questionnaire and test it on your required sample. During this phase, you could conduct a small informal interview with them to find out insights for improvement. You then take your questionnaire and do a pilot test of your work on a slightly larger sample, having a look at the data and running some preliminary analysis to check that the results you are getting seem sensible (Lee and Lings 2008).

Code books

When you work with quantitative data, you have to translate all the data from your questionnaire, including the defining and labelling of each of your variables, and assigning a number to each of the responses you have elicited from respondents (Pallant 2007). The codebook is a document where all of these translations are written down and summarised so that you can keep track of all the coding between the questionnaires to the SPSS data file. When you work with numerical data, all of the names, numbers and questionnaire IDs can become very confusing very quickly, especially if you come back to work in a file after some time. Having a codebook to help you navigate these periods of confusion is vital. A codebook can also be very helpful for any colleagues or supervisors who you wish to take a look at your data analysis. The contents of the codebook should include all the variables in your questionnaire, the names you will give them in SPSS (these are abbreviated), and how the responses to these questions are coded and then inputted into the data file. An example of a codebook is given in Table 10.2 below.

Table 10.2 An example codebook

Variable	SPSS variable name	Coding instructions
Identification number	ID	Number assigned to each survey
What is your age?	Age	Age given
What is your gender?	Gender	1 = Female
		2 = Male
How many hours per day do you spend on the internet for leisure?	Internet for leisure	1 = 0
		2 = 1–2
		3 = 3–4
		4 = 5–6
		5 = 7–8
		6 = 9+
How often approximately do you go online to browse (not necessarily purchase) fashion items?	Fashion	5 = Daily
		4 = Weekly
		3 = Monthly
		2 = Every 3 months
		1 = Every 6 months
Outfit 1		
The likelihood of purchasing some or all of these products	Likelihood1	1 = Very low
		2 = Low
		3 = Quite low
		4 = Neutral
		5 = Quite high
		6 = High
		7 = Very high

Furthermore, it is also a good idea to code all of your questionnaires with an ID number as seen in the first row of Table 10.2. If your questionnaires are in paper format, you can put them all in a ring binder and give them ID numbers in one of the corners. If they are in electronic format, be sure that they are saved and numbered within a certain file. This way you can always confirm that your data input is correct, check missing values and re-examine any questionnaires for outlying responses (i.e. if a respondent answers '4' for everything in the entire questionnaire, this will most likely show up as an outlier and potentially affect the data's normality. It will therefore need to be checked and removed from the analysis).

These three stages including questionnaire design, pilot testing and creating a codebook are all vitally important to complete the 'proper planning' stage of The five P mantra for statistical survival.

Prevention

The next stage of this mantra is 'prevention'. This stage encompasses easy tasks that you can complete to ensure that you don't make unnecessary mistakes during your quantitative data analysis.

The use of the word 'prevention' here may seem somewhat dramatic, but arming yourself with the necessary materials before you begin your data analysis will help you to avoid confusion and error during your project. Furthermore, due to the somewhat inaccessible nature of the SPSS and AMOS interfaces, jumping in head first and 'giving it a go' without first paying your dues to the measures outlined here, could add up to a disorganised analysis and a demoralised researcher.

Surround yourself with literature

The first step towards 'prevention' is to surround yourself and read the correct literature (which you are already doing). This will stand you in good stead. You wouldn't go sky diving without a parachute, so don't begin your data analysis before having an idea of the interface you are using. While the results of not reading how to use SPSS will not be fatal, they are no less dramatic and catastrophic than tumbling through the open air (especially when numbers and symbols are flying all over the place without any apparent rhyme or reason).

Surround yourself with those 'in the know'

Error prevention also comes in the form of taking advice from someone who has previous experience of doing quantitative work. This could be a friend with some experience in industry or academia, a supervisor or online sources such as videos, forums or blogs. Oftentimes with statistical stumbling blocks, it is important to learn to ask the right questions about your analysis technique or data set. For example, when dealing with an issue about sample size, you may need to search for information on statistical power and power calculations to accurately find the answer to your questions.

Cleaning and checking your data

Another way to prevent your data analysis taking unnecessary downturns is to clean and check your data set and conduct tests of normality and outliers. You wouldn't begin cooking in a messy kitchen. You need to do the same with your data and start in a clean environment. Cleaning and checking your data will help you recognise, especially if you have entered your data manually, that you don't have any mistakes, missing values or additional data outside of your prescribed sample frame. Once you have established whether there are any mistakes, you can find and correct them to give you an uncompromised data set. To do this, you first need to find any errors by running a frequency analysis. To do this, follow the steps in Figures 10.8, 10.9, 10.10a and 10.10b. The data set contains a column representing the age of the respondent.

You can see that there are two missing ages in the data set and two which have been entered incorrectly as '3' and '4' (Figure 10.10b). You can go through and find the mistakes in your data by using the variable view and looking at how your variable was coded. After checking this and finding out the code for the data you wish to remove, you can go back to data view and use the sort function (by the chosen variable, see Figure 10.11) to see the cases all together, which you may wish to remove. You can then select these cases and delete them. Then return to the frequency analysis to double check that everything that you wanted to remove has gone (Figure 10.12). You need to do this before doing any preliminary analysis.

Multivariate normality

After checking and cleaning your data, testing for normality is a fundamental beginning step in nearly all multivariate analysis (Tabachnick and Fidell 2007). The term *normal* in statistics describes a bell-shaped symmetrical curve of results (when plotted on a graph, as shown earlier in Figure 10.6), which has the majority of scores in the middle, with less at the extremes (Pallant 2007). Normality is not a prerequisite for analysis, but your results will have an advantage if the variables have normal distributions (Tabachnick and Fidell 2007). Common tests for checking the normality of data are reviewing skewness and kurtosis values, which can be carried out by running 'explore' in 'descriptive statistics' and asking to see a histogram and a normality plot (Pallant 2007).

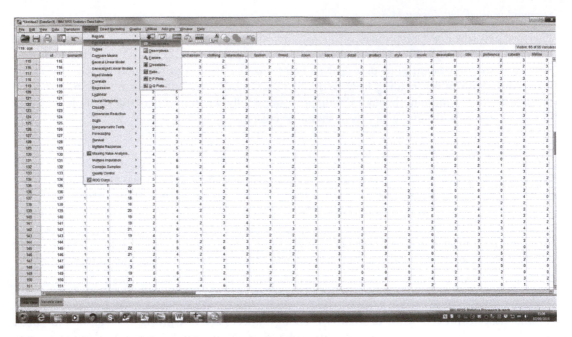

Figure 10.8 How to analyse descriptive statistics: frequency

Note: Go to 'analyse' and then 'descriptive statistics'. Then select 'frequencies'.

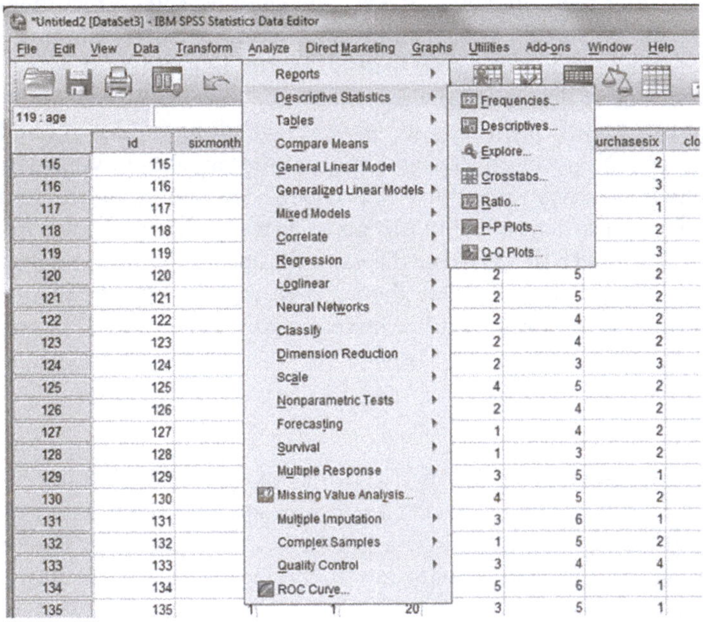

Figure 10.9 How to move the variables

Note: Move the variables you wish to analyse into the 'variables' column and click 'statistics'. Choose the frequency statistics you wish to see in the output, and press ok.

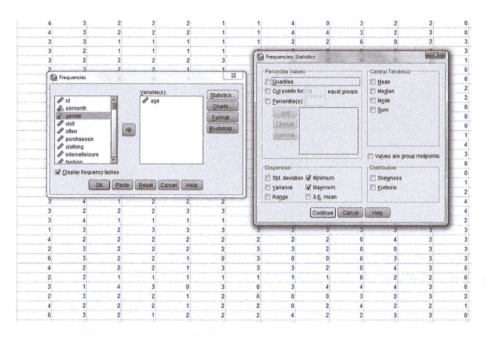

Figure 10.10a Output of the frequencies analysis

→ Frequencies

Statistics

age

N	Valid	314
	Missing	4

age

		Frequency	Percent	Valid Percent	Cumulative Percent
Valid	3	1	.3	.3	.3
	4	1	.3	.3	.6
	18	23	7.2	7.3	8.0
	19	61	19.2	19.4	27.4
	20	82	25.8	26.1	53.5
	21	73	23.0	23.2	76.8
	22	41	12.9	13.1	89.8
	23	13	4.1	4.1	93.9
	24	10	3.1	3.2	97.1
	25	5	1.6	1.6	98.7
	26	2	.6	.6	99.4
	28	1	.3	.3	99.7
	29	1	.3	.3	100.0
	Total	314	98.7	100.0	
Missing	System	4	1.3		
Total		318	100.0		

Figure 10.10b Using the variable view to correct errors

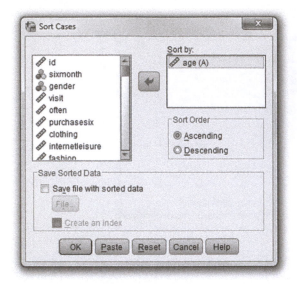

Figure 10.11 Using the sort function by variable 'age'

Note: Double checking a frequency analysis by sorting cases by the variable you are examining, in this case 'age'.

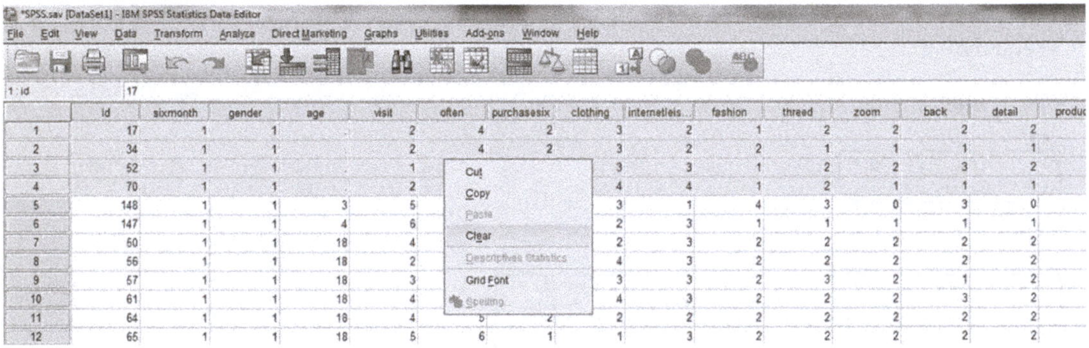

Figure 10.12 Using the sort function to clean your data

Note: SPSS then sorts your data by 'age', which will show up the missing values first and then the lower numbers. Simply select all the cases with errors and amend or clear.

You can see a diagram of what a normally distributed data sets looks like, as well as ones with skewness and kurtosis in Figure 10.13. Non-normality can be dealt with by transformations, additional sampling, bootstrapping, normalising scores or different methods of estimation (Schumacker and Lomax 2010). Skewness can impact the test of means, whereas kurtosis can impact tests of variances and covariances (Byrne 2010). When data has a normal distribution its skewness and kurtosis will have values of 0 (Tabachnick and Fidell 2007).

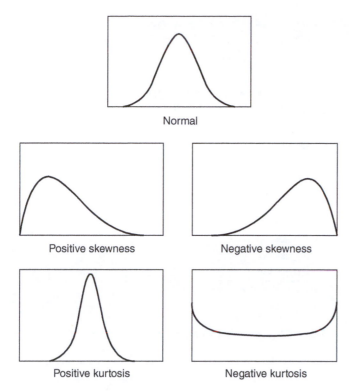

Figure 10.13 Normal distribution, distributions with skewness and distributions with kurtoses

Source: Tabachnick and Fidell (2007: 80).

However, it is worth noting that when a large sample is being used, skewness and kurtosis can be misrepresented. With a larger sample, a variable with statistically significant skewness may not depart far enough from normality to make a substantial impact on analysis (Tabachnick and Fidell 2007). Moreover, underestimates of variance related to positive kurtosis vanish with samples of 100 or more (Tabachnick and Fidell 2007). Therefore, with large samples, it is sensible to look at the shape of distribution instead, rather than purely at the results of formal tests of normality.

Outliers

In order to further check for normality, the data set must be examined for outliers. Anscombe and Tukey (1963: 146) define outliers as, 'observations that have such large residuals, in comparison with most of the others, as to suggest they ought to be treated specially'. Outliers are observations, which do not follow the pattern of the bulk of the data and can be detected using Mahalanobis distance (Rousseeuw *et al.* 1990). Mahalanobis distance is calculated by the patterns of variances and covariances amid the variables (Tabachnick and Fidell 2007). Tabachnick and Fidell (2007) suggest a very conservative p-value for a case to be an outlier as $p < .001$. In larger sample sizes, it is expected that this threshold should be increased. Some screen shots showing easy steps for detecting outliers are shown in Figures 10.14 to 10.17. The underlying data is on variables associated with fashion retail purchases.

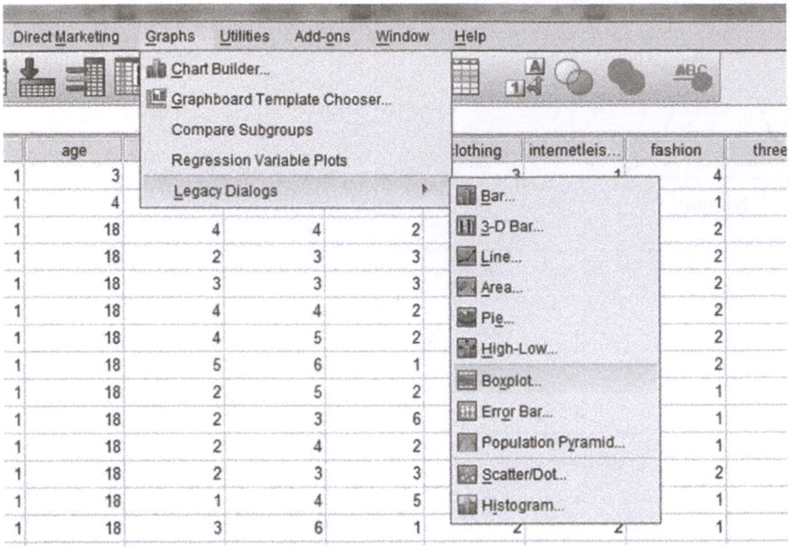

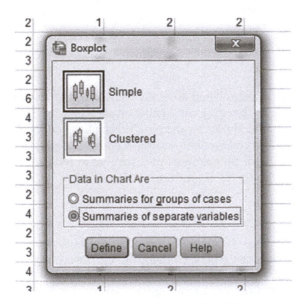

Figure 10.14 Locating your outliers

Note: To find your outliers, go to 'graphs', click 'legacy dialogs' and then choose 'boxplot'.

Figure 10.15 Locating your outliers continued

Note: Select 'boxplot' and click 'summaries of separate variables'.

This concludes the checking and cleaning section of the five P mantra. We can now move onto its last piece, that of poor performance.

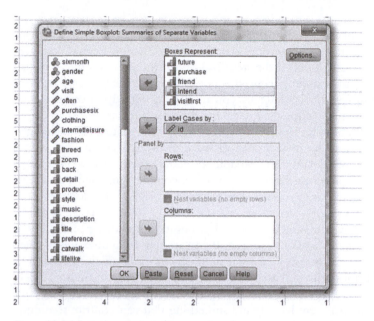

Figure 10.16 Locating your outliers continued

Note: Place the variables you wish to analyse in 'boxes represent' and then place your ID variable in 'label cases by'.

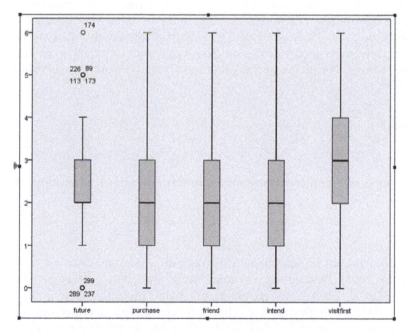

Figure 10.17 Removing your outliers

Notes: The boxplot will show you the distribution of your data and whether there are any outliers. Outliers are shown by the small dots outside of the lines. If there are a lot, you will need to double click on the circles to see them all. As you can see here, the variable 'future' has some outliers. To remove, go back to the data set and delete case by case.

Poor performance

Poor performance is the final piece of the five P mantra for statistical survival. As with any real-world piece of work, there are things that can go wrong. Statistics is no different. Even if you have a beautifully designed questionnaire, have fulfilled the steps laid out in the previous stages of this chapter, and generally feel that you are a good person, this does not necessarily mean that your results are going to be as expected or favourable. After all, you are dealing with data from real people who have numerous idiosyncratic peculiarities and changing thought patterns.

Phenomena also change over time. Simply consider how, for example, the internet has changed the way we shop and think about shopping in such a short space of time. Many people would have thought that typing their credit card details into a computer, sending them away to an anonymous person and waiting for receipt of goods for up to a week, a complete anathema ten years ago. Nowadays, people are shopping like crazy online. For example, in 2013 UK shoppers spent £91 billion online and are predicted to spend even more in 2014 (IMRG 2014). Change happens. Because of this, you must not shy away from any unexpected or negative results, especially if you have done all you can to create robust and rigorous research. If you are reporting unexpected findings, do not simply place the reasons for this on your own shoulders in the limitations section of your writing. Instead, you could explore the potential that these results provide in finding different contributions to the theory under test. If a hypothesis is rejected, this does not mean that your research is wrong and void. Indeed, you may have found something that can contribute unique and fresh perspectives to an existing academic discussion.

Unexpected results could also help you to think more creatively about your data analysis. During your analysis you could split your sample using the 'Data-Split File' command to look at whether there are any differences between other sample variables. For example, if you were conducting a study about consumers' use of video in the online environment, and you tested your sample for involvement with the internet, you could split your data by high and low involvement to see whether people with higher involvement used videos more than those with lower involvement. While statistical analysis has some rigidity, there are still ways to be creative within its rigorous framework. So don't give up!

Some statistical examples

Frequency distributions

Frequency distributions are counts of data pieces that build up to form numerical summations of your data.

Descriptive statistics

Descriptive research is popular and aims to describe its variables rather than uncover any relationship between them (Webb 2002). Descriptive research aims to accurately portray people, events or situations (Saunders *et al.* 2009) through pre-planned data collection, using large samples (Malhotra and Birks 2007). Descriptive research is concerned with determining the frequency with which something occurs (Churchill 2001). Data for descriptive research is usually uncovered in secondary sources and from surveys (Webb 2002). Uses of descriptive data may be for market size, sales turnovers and changes in market environments (Wright and Crimp 2000). However, problems can arise with descriptive research when it simply states an occurrence without any meaning attached to it (Saunders *et al.* 2009). Descriptive research projects are often conducted before explanatory research to define a certain area and are named descripto-explanatory studies (Saunders *et al.* 2009). Descriptive statistics can also be useful in ensuring that your data does not violate assumptions of skewness or kurtosis and that the mean and standard deviation are within the expected ranges. They can also provide a good preliminary overview of the characteristics of your sample. Descriptive statistics work differently for continuous and categorical variables. To explore your data set with categorical variables, use the frequencies tab in SPSS. In order to explore your data set with continuous variables, use the 'descriptives' function, as shown in Figures 10.18 and 10.19. Again, the underlying data relates to fashion retailing.

As you can see from Figure 10.20, you can use descriptive statistics to explore several variables in your data set at once. You can see whether there are any missing data. In this case, it looks like there is one piece of missing data on the questions, 'I have the feeling that I can physical grasp this item', and, 'For me, this item is very physically tangible'. You can also see whether there is a difference between means and standard deviations for the variables, which have all been measured on a seven-point Likert scale.

For skewness and kurtosis, Julia Pallant (2007: 56) provides some straightforward guidelines of how to interpret results:

- **perfectly normal distribution** – skewness and kurtosis value of 0;
- **positive skewness** – indicates a positive skew, i.e. scores clustered to the left at the low values;
- **negative skewness** – indicates a clustering of scores at the right side of the graph;
- **positive kurtosis** – indicates that the distribution is rather peaked, i.e. clustered in the centre with long and thin tails;
- **negative kurtosis** – indicates a distribution that is relatively flat, i.e. with too many cases in the extremes.

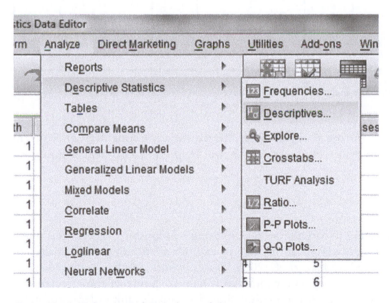

Figure 10.18 How to run descriptive statistics

Note: To run descriptive statistics click 'analyze' and then 'descriptives'.

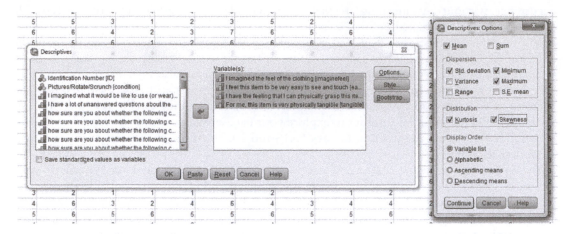

Figure 10.19 Selecting your statistics

Note: From there, move the variables you wish to examine into the 'variables column' and then click 'options'. Select the statistics you wish to look at.

Descriptive Statistics

	N	Minimum	Maximum	Mean	Std. Deviation	Skewness		Kurtosis	
	Statistic	Statistic	Statistic	Statistic	Statistic	Statistic	Std. Error	Statistic	Std. Error
I imagined the feel of the clothing	218	1	7	4.89	1.440	-.320	.165	-.599	.328
I feel this item to be very easy to see and touch	218	1	7	4.57	1.380	-.197	.165	-.447	.328
I have the feeling that I can physically grasp this item	218	1	7	4.38	1.571	-.282	.165	-.662	.328
For me, this item is very physically tangible	218	1	7	4.31	1.435	-.222	.165	-.337	.328
Valid N (listwise)	218								

Figure 10.20 The output from descriptive analysis

Once you have gained a feeling for the normality and characteristics of your data set, you can then go on to other statistical analysis techniques, which will help you to go deeper into your analysis.

Exploring relationships

Many of the techniques in marketing research focus on exploring relationships. There are a number of different statistical techniques, which can be used to explore relationships. The main aim of multivariate analysis, as stipulated by Hair *et al.* (2006), is to measure, explain and predict the degree of relationships between variants (combinations of variables). Some of these techniques include chi-square test for independence, Pearson correlation, Spearman's rank order correlation, multiple regression, factor analysis and SEM.

Chi-square test for independence

The chi-square (χ^2) test for independence (non-parametric) is used to test whether there is a relationship between two discrete constructs (or independent constructs) (Tabachnick and Fidell 2007). The chi-square test for independence tests whether two categorical constructs are related (Field 2009). In χ^2 analysis, the null hypothesis (a general statement, which indicates that there is no relationship between two phenomena) generates expected frequencies against which observed frequencies are tested. If the observed frequencies are similar to the expected frequencies then the value of the χ^2 is low and the null hypothesis is retained (the two constructs are independent of one another); however, if they are different then the χ^2 is high and the null hypothesis is rejected (the constructs are related to each other) (Tabachnick and Fidell 2007). The basic elegance of the chi-square test rests in the idea, 'of comparing the frequencies you detect in certain categories to the frequencies you might expect to get in those categories by chance' (Field 2009: 688). To carry out a chi-square test in SPSS, two categorical variables are needed with two or more categories. A research question that could be answered with a

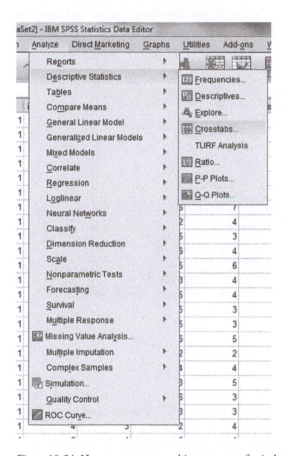

Figure 10.21 How to generate a chi-square test for independence

Note: From analyze choose 'descriptive statistics' and then 'crosstabs'.

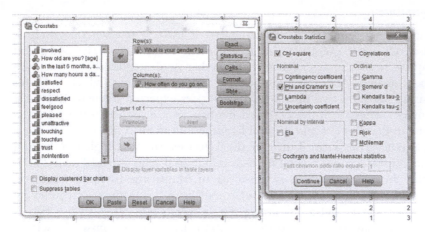

Figure 10.22 How to generate a chi-square test for independence continued

Note: Select your two categorical variables and place one in 'rows' and one in 'columns'. Choose 'statistics' and then select 'chi-square', 'phi and Cramer's V' and then 'continue'.

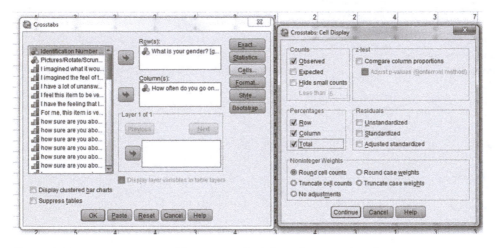

Figure 10.23 How to generate a chi-square test for independence continued

Choose 'cells' and select 'observed', 'row', 'column' and 'total' and then run the analysis.

chi-square test for independence would be, 'Is there an association between "gender" and "how often you buy clothing online"?' The stages in the Figures 10.21 to 10.23 show how to generate a chi-square test for independence.

Before interpreting your results, you should check the minimum expected cell frequency (seen underneath the 'chi-square tests' table) is higher than 5. The most important output table to look at when interpreting the chi-square test is the 'chi-square tests' table as shown in Figure 10.24.

Look for the 'Pearson chi-square row', unless both your variables have only two levels (then look at continuity correction). In this example, the value is .008 with a significance level (asymp. Sig column) of .92. As the significance value (i.e. p-value as explained in the earlier section) is over .05 our result is not statistically significant. In this case, there is no association between gender and frequency of buying clothing online.

Had this result been statistically significant, you could have calculated the effect size. To do this, you should take a look at the 'symmetric measures' table in the output. You need to look at the phi coefficient for variables with only two levels (.10 is small effect; .30 medium effect; .50 large effect) (Cohen 1988). If your variables have more than two levels you look at the 'Cramers V' value, although you must adjust your interpretation of this depending on the amount of degrees of freedom or levels in your variables (see Pallant 2007, or later for further guidance).

Pearson correlation

The Pearson correlation is a parametric standardised measure of the strength of a relationship between two variables (Field 2009). This can take any value from -1 (as one variable changes, the other changes in the opposite direction by the same amount), to $+1$ (as one variable changes the other changes in the same direction by the same amount) (Field 2009). This can provide information on the direction of the relationship, whether it be positive or negative (indicated by the '+' or '$-$') and the strength of association (the absolute value provides this) (Pallant 2007). A correlation coefficient of 0 indicates that there is no relationship between the two variables under study (Pallant 2007).

Chi-Square Tests

	Value	df	Asymp. Sig. (2-sided)
Pearson Chi-Square	21.434[a]	5	.001
Likelihood Ratio	17.788	5	.003
Linear-by-Linear Association	15.277	1	.000
N of Valid Cases	218		

a. 5 cells (41.7%) have expected count less than 5. The minimum expected count is .27.

Symmetric Measures

		Value	Approx. Sig.
Nominal by Nominal	Phi	.314	.001
	Cramer's V	.314	.001
N of Valid Cases		218	

Figure 10.24 Output from chi-square tests

Spearman's rank order correlation

Spearman's rank order correlation or 'rho' is the non-parametric version of the Pearson correlation and measures the amount of monotonic relationship between two ordinal variables (hence the non-parametric statistic) (Hardy and Bryman 2010). Spearman's rho works by using the comparison of the rank orderings of respondents within the two distributions (Hardy and Bryman 2010). This statistic performs the same function as Pearson's correlation and measures the strength of association between two variables. The output of this test is measured in significance, so if $p < .05$, then there is an association between variables, and if $p \geq .05$, then there is little association (Field 2009).

In SPSS both the Pearson correlation and Spearman's rank order correlation are generated through the same procedure, using two continuous variables or one continuous and one dichotomous variable. These are shown in the Figures 10.25 and 10.26, where we are using the research question, 'Does perceived risk when shopping online associate with a greater need to touch products?'

In interpreting the output from the correlations, have a look at the correlation coefficients between the variables chosen, the significance level and the number of cases. Be sure that you check the right correlation result: for Pearson your results can be found in the 'correlation' section and for Spearman's rank order, you can find this in the 'nonparametic correlations' section. When interpreting these results, a negative sign for the correlation coefficient means there is a negative correlation and a positive sign means there is a positive correlation. In this case there is a positive

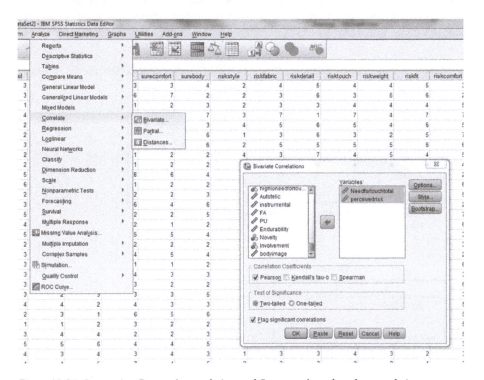

Figure 10.25 Generating Pearson's correlation and Spearman's rank order correlation

Note: Click on 'analyze', 'correlate' and the 'bivariate correlation'. Move the variables you wish to include in the analysis into the 'variables' column. Also check whether you wish to use Pearson correlation or Spearman's rank order correlation.

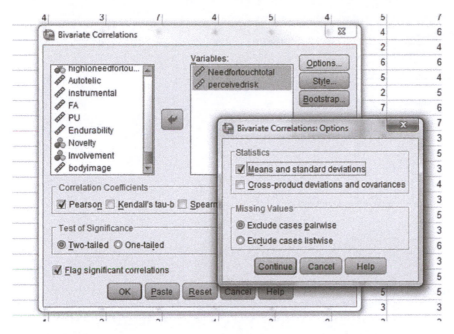

Figure 10.26 Generating Pearson's correlation and Spearman's rank order correlation continued

Note: Click on 'options' and select 'means and standard deviations' and 'exclude cases pairwise'.

correlation, which means that the more people need to touch products they buy, the more risk they feel when shopping online. The next thing you need to think about is how strong the correlation between the variables is. As mentioned before, correlations can range from −1 to +1, with −1 being no relationship and +1 being a perfect relationship. Cohen (1988) suggests guidelines for different relationship strengths (with a negative sign applied if there is a negative coefficient). A small relationship would have an effect size r =.10 to .29. A medium relationship would have an effect size r =.30 to .49 and a large relationship would have an effect size r =.50 to 1.0. In this case, we have effect sizes of .13 and .15, meaning this is a weak relationship, and we also see no significance here. The level of significance doesn't relate to the strength of the relationship, but rather suggests whether we should have confidence in the results (as explained earlier). If there was a statistically significant relationship here, it would be indicated by one or more asterisks '★'. You can also perform correlation analysis on lots of variables simultaneously, and present them all in a table (Figure 10.27).

Multiple regression

Regression is used to test hypotheses to discover causal relationships and can indicate the strength of these effects, as well as comparing the strength of effects across groups (Hardy and Bryman 2010). There are different types of regression analysis, including standard multiple regression, hierarchical regression, stepwise multiple regression and logistic regression. In this chapter we will focus on multiple regression, which measures the amount that one

Descriptive Statistics

	Mean	Std. Deviation	N
NeedForTouch	5.3753	1.06489	143
PerceivedRisk	3.8016	1.01954	143

Correlations

		NeedForTouch	PerceivedRisk
NeedForTouch	Pearson Correlation	1	.130
	Sig. (2-tailed)		.122
	N	143	143
PerceivedRisk	Pearson Correlation	.130	1
	Sig. (2-tailed)	.122	
	N	143	143

```
NONPAR CORR
 /VARIABLES=NeedForTouch PerceivedRisk
 /PRINT=SPEARMAN TWOTAIL NOSIG
 /MISSING=PAIRWISE.
```

Nonparametric Correlations

[DataSet5]

Correlations

			NeedForTouch	PerceivedRisk
Spearman's rho	NeedForTouch	Correlation Coefficient	1.000	.153
		Sig. (2-tailed)	.	.068
		N	143	143
	PerceivedRisk	Correlation Coefficient	.153	1.000
		Sig. (2-tailed)	.068	.
		N	143	143

Figure 10.27 Output from correlations

dependent construct is related to a set of independent constructs (Tabachnick and Fidell 2007). In multiple regression the emphasis is on the prediction of the dependent construct from the independent constructs (Tabachnick and Fidell 2007). The steps to perform a multiple regression are shown in Figures 10.28 to 10.33. Once again, the data set relates to research into fashion purchases.

Interpreting the output from multiple regression is somewhat more complicated than interpreting the output from previously described tests. The first thing you need to check for is multi-collinearity. This can be done by looking at the 'Correlations' table. Check that your independent variable shows a relationship with your dependent variable, above .3. Also be sure that the correlation between any independent variables is not too high, i.e. not above .7. From this example we can see that loyalty and trust are correlated at the right level (.519) (Figure 10.34a). If this is too high, the two variables may need to be composited. You can also check multi-collinearity by looking at the 'Coefficients' table at the values of 'Tolerance' and 'VIF' (variance inflation factor). The tolerance should be greater than .10 and the VIF should be less than 10 (Pallant 2007). In this example (see Figure 10.34b), we have .73 for tolerance and 1.368 for VIF, which does not suggest a case of multi-collinearity.

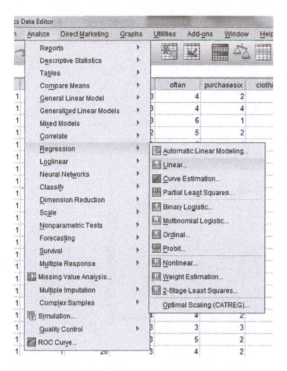

Figure 10.28 How to run a multiple regression

Note: To run a multiple regression choose 'analyze' and then 'regression' and then 'linear'.

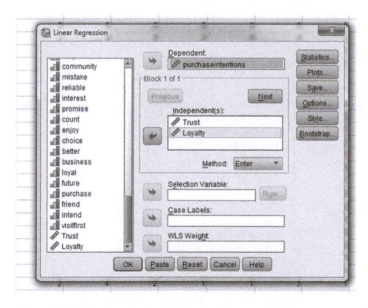

Figure 10.29 How to run a multiple regression continued

Note: Move the dependent continuous variable into the dependent section and the independent variables into the independent section.

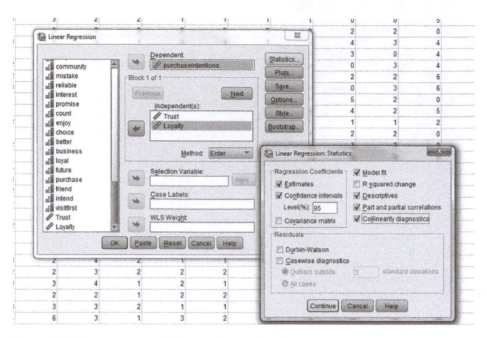

Figure 10.30 How to run a multiple regression continued

Note: Select 'statistics' and check 'estimates', 'confidence intervals', 'model fit', 'descriptives', 'part and partial correlations' and 'collinearity diagnostics'.

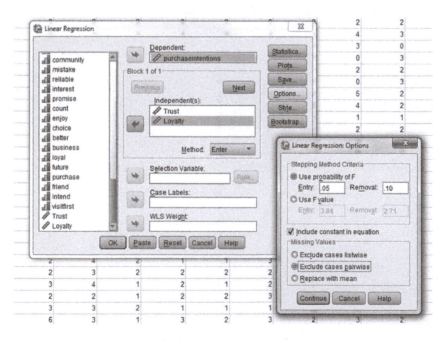

Figure 10.31 How to run a multiple regression continued

Note: Select 'options' and click 'exclude cases pairwise'.

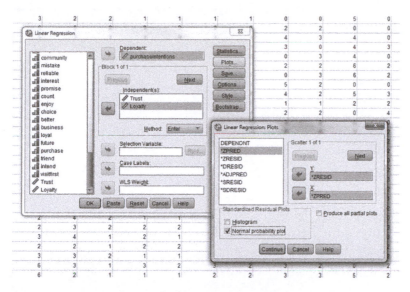

Figure 10.32 How to run a multiple regression continued

Note: Select 'plots' and move 'ZRESID' into the Y axis and then 'ZPRED' into the x axis. Check 'normal probability plot'.

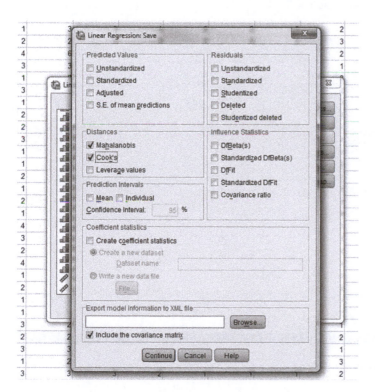

Figure 10.33 How to run a multiple regression continued

Note: Select 'save' and check 'Mahalanobis' and 'Cook's' in the distances column. Run the analysis.

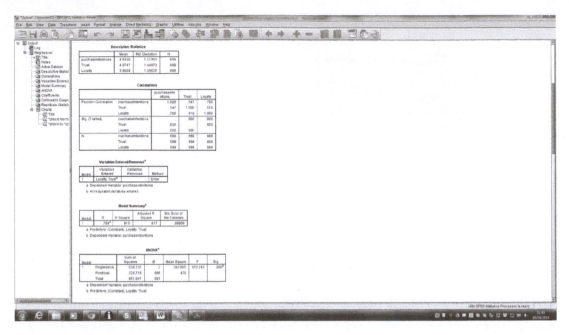

Figure 10.34a Output from multiple regression analysis

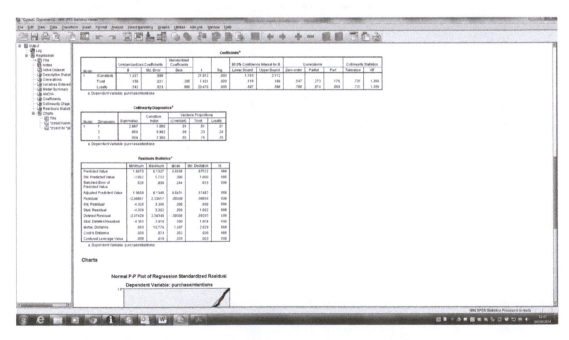

Figure 10.34b Output from multiple regression analysis

You should also check the normality of your data by reviewing the 'normal probability plot P-P' of the regression standardised residual and the scatterplot (Figure 10.35). For the 'normal probability plot' you are looking for a fairly straight diagonal line from the bottom left to the top right-hand corner of the graph. This confirms the normality of your data. For the scatterplot, you are looking for a rectangular shape with a concentration of data in the centre. This should be a fairly regular shape without one side moving higher than the other. If this is the case, it would suggest that there are some outliers within your data, which you need to deal with before proceeding with the analysis, as explained earlier. However, you should interpret this with caution, depending on the size of your sample. This example uses a very large sample size (n=688) and so the presence of some outliers is not surprising. For further information on how to deal with a case of violating assumptions see Pallant (2007) or later.

If this is all present and correct, you then move onto analysing the model. This can be done by viewing the 'model summary box' in the output in the heading 'R^2' to see how much variance within the dependent variable is explained by the independent variables. In this example (Figure 10.36) the R^2 was found to be .618 or 61.8 per cent. If you have a small sample size you may wish to refer instead to the 'adjusted R^2' value, which provides more accuracy with a smaller number of people. The 'ANOVA' table will then tell us whether the amount of variation explained by the linear regression is statistically significant. In this case it is, with Sig. =.000 or p < .0005. We then wish to know what effect the different independent variables have on the predicted dependent variable. You can find this information from the 'Coefficients' section in the output. Look at 'Beta' under 'Standardized Coefficients' and compare the contribution of the two independent variables. The largest coefficient here is loyalty (beta=.660), which makes the largest contribution to predicting purchase intentions. Trust has a lower beta coefficient of .205 in comparison. These contributions are both statistically significant. You can check this by looking under the 'Sig.' column. In this case we have both values at Sig. = .000. If the Sig. value were above .05, then the contribution would not be considered statistically significant.

You can also review the 'Part' correlation coefficients. If you square these values you get an idea of the contribution of the independent variable to the overall R^2. This tells you how much of the total variance in the dependent variable is explained by each independent variable. In this case, loyalty has a part coefficient of .564, which means that it explains 56.4 per cent of the variance in purchase intentions scores. For trust the part coefficient is .176, which means that it explains 17.6 per cent of the variance in purchase intentions scores.

This answers two questions, one pertaining to whether independent variables are predictors of dependent variables, and the other to what extent (how much variance) their unique contributions make.

Exploratory factor analysis (EFA)

EFA is a multivariate statistical technique, which is used to explore potential underlying factor sets from data without enforcing a premeditated structure on the outcome (Child 1990). Using the process of reduction and summarisation (Malhotra and Birks 2007), factor analysis explores whether the correlations between a set of observed variables come from their relationship to one or more latent constructs present in the data set (Field 2009). This technique is widely used and broadly applied in the social sciences (Costello and Osborne 2005). It is a complicated technique with few absolute guidelines and many choices (Costello and Osborne 2005). EFA is performed by observing the pattern of correlations between the observed variables (DeCoster 1998). Variables which are very highly correlated (this can be positive or negative) are probably influenced by the same factors (DeCoster 1998). EFA is usually undertaken in the earlier stages of research, helping condense variables and consequently constructing hypotheses (Tabachnick

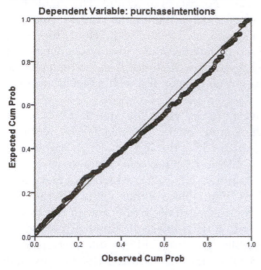

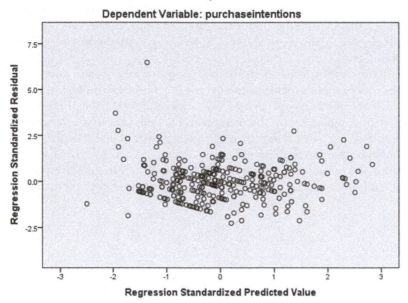

Figure 10.35 Output from multiple regression analysis

and Fidell 2007). Four main areas that need to be considered by the researcher when consider-ing EFA are: extraction, rotation, choosing the number of factors in a solution, and sample size (Costello and Osborne 2005). EFA does not use inferential statistics, but is performed by observ-ing the pattern of correlations between the observed variables (DeCoster 1998). EFA should be

Model Summary^b

Model	R	R Square	Adjusted R Square	Std. Error of the Estimate
1	.639^a	.408	.404	.67181

a. Predictors: (Constant), Loyalty, Trust

b. Dependent Variable: purchaseintentions

ANOVA^a

Model		Sum of Squares	df	Mean Square	F	Sig.
1	Regression	96.675	2	48.337	107.100	.000^b ,
	Residual	140.363	311	.451		
	Total	237.038	313			

a. Dependent Variable: purchaseintentions

b. Predictors: (Constant), Loyalty, Trust

Coefficients^a

Model		Unstandardized Coefficients		Standardized Coefficients	t	Sig.	95.0% Confidence Interval for B		Correlations			Collinearity Statistics	
		B	Std. Error	Beta			Lower Bound	Upper Bound	Zero-order	Partial	Part	Tolerance	VIF
1	(Constant)	.814	.119		6.865	.000	.580	1.047					
	Trust	.053	.048	.051	1.119	.264	-.040	.147	.232	.063	.049	.915	1.093
	Loyalty	.500	.037	.622	13.634	.000	.428	.572	.637	.612	.595	.915	1.093

a. Dependent Variable: purchaseintentions

Figure 10.36 Output from multiple regression analysis

used only to explore a data set and begin to see some boundaries (or factors), which can then be further tested using confirmatory methods (Costello and Osborne 2005). EFA cannot be used to test hypotheses and can tend towards error, even when the researcher possesses a large sample of normal data (Costello and Osborne 2005). EFA can be used as premeditation for confirmatory factor analysis, with the two complementing each other. The key statistics associated with EFA are shown in Table 10.3.

Suitability criteria for EFA

Data must be checked to ensure that it is factorable before EFA can be undertaken. Methods of checking this include determining the right sample size (Tabachnick and Fidell 2007), checking for communalities greater than .3, Bartlett's test of sphericity and the Kaiser-Meyer-Olkin (KMO) measure of sampling adequacy (Pallant 2007).

Sample size

Sample size in factor analysis is an issue highly debated by academics. Pallant (2007) suggests that the larger the sample size the better. Tabachnick and Fidell (2007) propose that samples of around 150 should be sufficient for factor analysis. Adequate sample size will be determined by the nature of the data (Costello and Osborne 2005). Hair *et al.* (2010) state that for factor analysis the sample must have more observations than variables and the minimum absolute sample size should be 50 observations. Others concede that it is not the sample size, which is important but the ratio of respondents to variables (Nunnally 1978). Both Nunnally (1978) and Hair *et al.* (2010) state that a ratio of ten respondents to one variable renders a data set suitable for factor analysis.

Table 10.3 Key statistics associated with exploratory factor analysis

Statistic	Description	Reference
Bartlett's test of sphericity	Test for the overall significance of all correlations within a correlation matrix	Hair *et al.* (2006)
Communality	The amount of variance a variable shares with all the other variables being considered	Malhotra and Birks (2007)
Correlation matrix	Table showing all inter-correlations among all variables	Hair *et al.* (2006)
Eigenvalue	Total amount of variance explained by each factor	Hair *et al.* (2006)
Factor loadings	Simple correlations between the variables and the factors	Malhotra and Birks (2007)
Factor matrix	Contains all the factor loadings of all the variables on the factors extracted, equivalent term for a structure matrix	Malhotra and Birks (2007); Field (2009)
Kaiser-Meyer-Olkin (KMO) measure of sampling adequacy	An index used to examine the appropriateness of factor analysis (whether a data set is factorable)	Malhotra and Birks (2007)
Scree plot	A graph which plots each factor in an analysis against its associated eigenvalue, which ultimately indicates the comparative importance of each factor	Field (2009)

Bartlett's test of sphericity and KMO's sampling adequacy

The KMO measure of sampling adequacy is an index used to review how factorable the data set is (Malhotra and Birks 2007). High values (between 0.5 and 1.0) indicate that factor analysis is suitable, whereas values below 0.5 imply that factor analysis may not be suitable (Malhotra and Birks 2007). Bartlett's test of sphericity is a very sensitive test of the hypothesis that the correlations in the correlation matrix are zero (Tabachnick and Fidell 2007). The value of this should be less than 0.5 for factor analysis to be undertaken (Pallant 2007).

Extraction

Stages in EFA include extraction, number of factors retained and rotation (Costello and Osborne 2005). Factor extraction includes minimising data into the smallest number of factors, which represent the interrelations within the data set, balancing the need to find a straightforward solution, while explaining as much variance in the data as possible (Pallant 2007). When using SPSS there are a number of extraction methods, including unweighted least squares, generalized least squares, maximum likelihood, principal axis factoring, alpha factoring and image factoring (Costello and Osborne 2005; Pallant 2007). Fabrigar *et al.* (1999) have argued that where data is normally distributed, maximum likelihood is the correct extraction method. However, if the data is not normally distributed then a principal factor method is suggested (Fabrigar *et al.* 1999).

Determining the number of factors

Following extraction, a decision must be made as to how many factors to retain for analysis. Generally, the more factors extracted, the better the fit and the more variance in the data is explained (Tabachnick and Fidell 2007). However, when high numbers of factors are extracted, the solution is less parsimonious (Tabachnick and Fidell 2007). Therefore, a trade-off must be made between these two criteria. There are a few indicators, which can make this decision easier, including looking at the eigenvalues, the scree-test and parallel analysis (Costello and Osborne 2005; Pallant 2007; Tabachnick and Fidell 2007). Eigenvalues represent variance and have been cited as among the least precise methods for determining the number of factors (Costello and Osborne 2005). The value of reported eigenvalues greater than one are generally accepted to indicate the number of factors needed for a solution (Pallant 2007). Overestimation when using eigenvalues to determine the number of factors is common as, generally, data must have fewer than 40 variables and a large sample size for an accurate estimate (Tabachnick and Fidell 2007). The scree-test is another (visual) method of determining the correct number of factors. It is negatively decreasing and plots eigenvalues against factors (Tabachnick and Fidell 2007). The researcher must look for a point where the positively retained factors turn into negatively retained factors, like moving from a cliff to a plain. Obviously, there is a subjective element to this analysis, although the results of a scree-test can be more obvious where sample size is large, communality values are high and each construct has several variables with high loadings (Tabachnick and Fidell 2007). Finally, parallel analysis concerns the comparison of the size of the eigenvalues with those obtained from a randomly generated data set of the same size (Pallant 2007). Only the eigenvalues, which are above the similar values from the random data set, are retained (Pallant 2007). This has been seen as a reliable method of determining the number of factors and is widely accepted in the fields of psychology and education (Pallant 2007).

Rotation

Rotation is the next stage in EFA. Rotation allows the researcher an easier interpretation of the variables and improves the scientific utility of the solution (Tabachnick and Fidell 2007). There are two main methods of rotation: oblique and orthogonal (Kim and Mueller 1978). A choice between these two methods is required, although it should be noted that with a good data set, different methods of rotation should yield similar results if the patterns of correlations within the data are clear (Tabachnick and Fidell 2007). The main difference between oblique and orthogonal rotation is that oblique rotation leaves factors correlated and the orthogonal rotation leaves the factors uncorrelated (Malhotra and Birks 2007). Oblique rotation is more complex than orthogonal, allowing orthogonal solutions to be more easily interpreted (Costello and Osborne 2005). However, within the social sciences, some correlation between factors is expected due to behaviours of people being rarely independent of external factors (Costello and Osborne 2005). Ford *et al.* (1986: 6) concur, denoting that, 'oblique rotation more accurately represents the complexity of the examined variables because constructs in the real world are rarely uncorrelated'. Direct oblimin is a type of oblique rotation, which simplifies factors by minimising the cross-products of loadings (Tabachnick and Fidell 2007).

Factor loadings

Tabachnick and Fidell (2007: 608) state that 'a factor is more easily interpreted when several observed variables correlate highly with it and those variables do not correlate with other factors'. This quote describes a desirable solution, but it is often the case that some variables will load onto more than one factor. Comrey and Lee (1992) have offered that loadings more than .71 are considered excellent; .63 are very good; .55 good; .45 fair; and .32 poor.

Confirmatory factor analysis (CFA)

CFA is a step on from EFA and allows a researcher to test how measured variables under test accurately represent the latent constructs under study (Hair *et al.* 2006). It is a deductive technique, which tests hypotheses regarding unmeasured sources of variability responsible for the commonality among a data set (Hoyle 2000). CFA can be used when there is some knowledge of the latency of the variables (Byrne 2010) and there is previous knowledge of theory. Relationships are specified by the researcher between the observed and latent constructs and then tested to determine their validity (Byrne 2010). A model made using CFA is termed a 'measurement model' (Byrne 2010). CFA is ultimately concerned with the validity of the measurement model, as no valid conclusions can exist if no prior valid measurement is made (Hair *et al.* 2006). There are three rules that are necessary to obtain identification of a confirmatory model, which are that every factor must have three observed variables, no observed variable must act as a part of more than one factor and that error terms are not correlated (Blunch 2008). Model fit statistics are used in order to evaluate whether a measurement model is a good representation of the data set. These fit statistics are calculated based on knowledge of the saturated model, independence model, sample size, degrees of freedom and the chi-square to output values of model fit, which range from 0 (no fit) to 1 (perfect fit) (Schumacker and Lomax 2010). Even though there are accepted thresholds for these fit statistics, the decision to accept or reject a model is ultimately based with the researcher.

CFA is a necessary step before attempting to construct a full latent (or structural) model. CFA can be used alone to test hypotheses, however, further inferences and understanding can stem from using it in tandem with full SEM (Hoyle 2000). It is important to check that the measurement of all the latent constructs in a study is psychometrically sound (Byrne 2010) before attempting to fit a full structural model. CFA deals with the relationships between measures of constructs, observed variables and the latent factors (Hoyle 2000). The structural model is only involved with the relationships between latent constructs (Hoyle 2000). Key statistics associated with CFA are shown in Table 10.4.

EFA and CFA

A graphical representation of the difference between EFA and CFA is shown in Figure 10.37. In the diagram, X1 to X6 represent the measured variables (i.e. questions within your questionnaire), F1 to F3 represent the latent constructs (i.e. factors which are groups of variables), and E1 to E6 represent error terms. EFA links measured variables and latent constructs together (see the left of the diagram), whereas CFA begins to specify which measured variables link with which latent constructs which are co-varied (see the right of the diagram).

Even though the two techniques are visually distinct from one another, both have advantages that can be utilised. With EFA, the researcher can confirm that the variables under test do represent the specified latent constructs. It does this by grouping variables. EFA can also help in identifying arbitrary variables or bad items, which should not be present in the analysis. However, what it can't do is indicate whether its solution hangs together with what is termed 'model fit'. It also doesn't confirm which factor a variable sits best within. CFA can be used to confirm the measurement model as a whole and its goodness-of-fit. It also helps to identify any other modifications (via modification indices), which need to be carried out before the researcher attempts a full latent (or structural) model.

Table 10.4 Key confirmatory factor analysis statistics

Statistic	Description	Reference
Identification	Whether on the basis of the sample data contained in the sample covariance matrix and the theoretical model implied by the population covariance matrix, a unique set of parameters can be found	Schumacker and Lomax (2010: 56–57)
Convergent validity	The amount to which indicators of a specific construct share a high proportion of variance in common	Hair *et al.* (2006)
Discriminant validity	How truly distinct one construct is from other constructs	Hair *et al.* (2006)
Measurement model	The part of a model which relates the measured variables to factors	Tabachnick and Fidell (2007)
Modification index	The amount that the model chi-square value would reduce by freezing any single particular path, which is not yet estimated	Hair *et al.* (2006)
Parameter	Numerical representation of a characteristic of a population	Hair *et al.* (2006)
Residuals	A value which represents the discrepancy between the hypothesised model (or individual variables) and the observed data	Byrne (2010)
Squared multiple correlations	A value that represents the amount, which a measured variables variance is explained by a latent factor	Hair *et al.* (2006)
Standardised residuals	The residuals of a model expressed in standard deviation units	Field (2009)

SEM

SEM is an advanced statistical modelling technique, which is based on general linear modelling (Hardy and Bryman 2010). SEM is 'a collection of statistical techniques that allow a set of relationships between one or more independent variables, either continuous or discrete, and one or more dependent constructs, either continuous or discrete to be examined' (Tabachnick and Fidell 2007: 676). SEM allows dependent constructs to act as predictor constructs within the same model (Hardy and Bryman 2010). It uses multivariate techniques to allow a set of relationships between independent constructs and dependent constructs, with these being directly measured or latent constructs (Hardy and Bryman 2010). When you combine EFA with multiple regression analysis, SEM is the result (Tabachnick and Fidell 2007). Byrne (2010) stipulates two aspects of SEM. First, that causal relationships are under study as represented by a series of regression equations, and second, that the structural relations are graphically modelled to show a clear conceptualisation of the theory under study.

A two-step approach to SEM is taken by first confirming the data fits with a measurement model, which is specified and measured during CFA. Once a measurement model is confirmed (which may take some modification), a full structural model can be specified and reliability can be rechecked. In order to be confident that the sample data is sufficient to produce an estimated population covariance matrix, an SEM needs to be over-identified or just-identified (Byrne 2010; Schumacker and Lomax 2010). The basic steps taken in SEM are given below (Schumacker and Lomax 2010):

1   model specification – the development of a theoretical model;
2   model identification – can a unique set of parameters be found from the sample data;

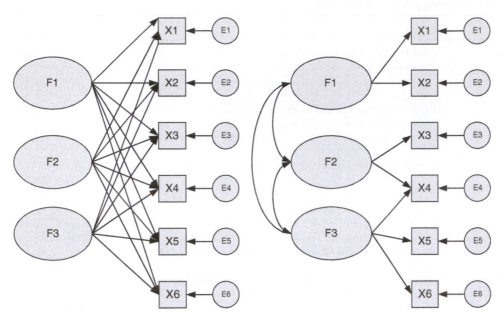

Figure 10.37 Exploratory and confirmatory factor analysis

Source: Blunch (2008).

3   model estimation – using a particular fitting function to minimise the difference between the implied matrix and the sample covariance matrix;
4   model testing – how well do the data fit the model;
5   model modification – modify and evaluate the new modified model.

Characteristics of SEM have been summed up by Kline (1998), who delineates that SEM is a priori and requires thought in terms of models; allows explicit representation of distinctions between observed and latent constructs; uses covariances; is flexible; needs a large sample size; and can test for statistical significance.

Explaining the step-by-step process of analysis for EFA, CFA and SEM is beyond the scope of this chapter, but hopefully this has served to dip your toe in to these more advanced methods.

Analysis of moment structures (AMOS)

AMOS deals with the analysis of mean or covariance structures (Byrne 2010). It is used as an add-on to SPSS and is used specifically for SEM, path analysis and CFA. There are three different AMOS interfaces, which can be used, including AMOS graphics, AMOS VB.NEW and AMOS C# (Byrne 2010). In the former, one works visually from a path diagram constructed by the researcher. In the latter two versions, the researcher works directly from equation statements. The choice of which program to use is based on the specification of models (whether you want to work graphically or from programming) (Byrne 2010). Of course, there are other packages you can use as well including R, M-Plus and LISREL. AMOS is mentioned here as it is quite widely used in the field of marketing.

Table 10.5 Summary of statistics used to explore relationships

Data analytical technique	Characteristics
Chi-square	Explores relationships between two constructs
Pearson correlation	Explores the strength and direction of relationship between two parametrically measured variables
Spearman's rank order correlation	Explores the strength and direction of relationship between two non-parametrically measured variables
Multiple regression	Explores relationships between a set of independent constructs on one dependent construct
Canonical correlation analysis	Explores relationships between two groups of constructs
Structural equation modelling	Explores relationships between one or more independent constructs and one or more dependent constructs and intervening constructs

Statistics to explore differences between groups: ANOVA

ANOVA begins to look at the differences between samples for the same phenomenon. It is a statistical method used to compare the means of two or more groups (Pallant 2007). Within ANOVA, you have two important terms – factors and levels. Factors are variables, e.g. gender, and levels are the differences within the factors. For example, with gender you have two levels, male and female. There are different types of ANOVA. One-way ANOVA is the most basic where you have one factor with at least two levels that are independent of each other (being manipulated). There is also a 'repeated measures' ANOVA, where you use one factor with at least two levels, and these levels are dependent (being measured). There is also a 'factorial' ANOVA, where you have two or more factors, each having at least two levels, which can be independent, dependent or mixed.

ANOVA has some assumptions, which need to be fulfilled. The first is normality, e.g. the distribution of sample means is normal. The second is that the errors between cases are independent of one another. The third is the absence of outliers. Any outliers need to be removed from the data set prior to analysis. The final assumption is homogeneity of variance. This means that the population of variances in different levels of each independent variable are equal. With ANOVA we are looking at the differences between groups, therefore, the null hypothesis in ANOVA is always that all levels being tested are equal to one another, with the alternative being that not all means are equal. When you have a difference in means with ANOVA, it is called a main effect. You can also run a test for an interaction effect when you have more than one factor. If we reject the null hypothesis with ANOVA, all we know is that there is a difference between the two groups somewhere. To find out where the difference lies, you can use post hoc tests. An example of how to perform a one-way ANOVA in SPSS is now demonstrated (see Figures 10.38 to 10.40).

Be sure to check in the descriptives table for the correct sample sizes in each group. Following this, check the significance value on Levene's test for homogenity of variance, which should be >.05 significance and is so in this case. The variance in scores is the same for each of the three groups. In the ANOVA column check the column marked Sig., which should be less than or equal to .05 for there to be statistically significant differences between the means scores on the dependent variable between the groups. In this example (Figure 10.41), the Sig value (.001) shows that there are statistically significant differences.

If you do see a statistically significant result, you then need to check the multiple comparisons table. This will tell you where the differences between the groups occurred. The column marked 'mean difference', where there are asterisks (*) will indicate which two groups are statistically

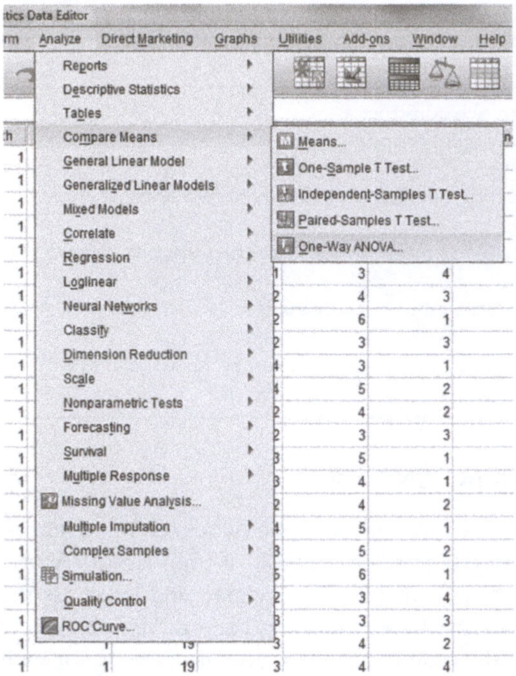

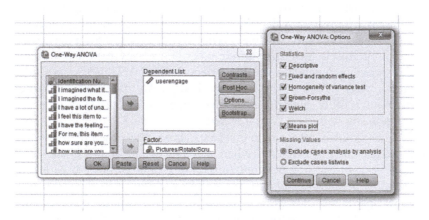

Figure 10.38 How to perform a one-way ANOVA

Note: Click on 'analyse' and then select 'one-way ANOVA'.

Figure 10.39 How to perform a one-way ANOVA continued

Notes: Place your continuous dependent variable in the 'Dependent List' box and then place your independent categorical variable in the 'Factor' box. Select 'Options' and click on 'Descriptive', 'Homogeneity of Variance Test', 'Brown-Forsythe', 'Welch' and 'Means Plot'. For missing values, select 'Exclude cases analysis by analysis'. This tells SPSS what to include in the output.

significantly different from one another. In this case (Figure 10.42) we can see that there are statistically significant differences between the 'pictures' and 'rotate' conditions, and between 'pictures' and 'scrunch', but not between 'rotate' and 'scrunch'.

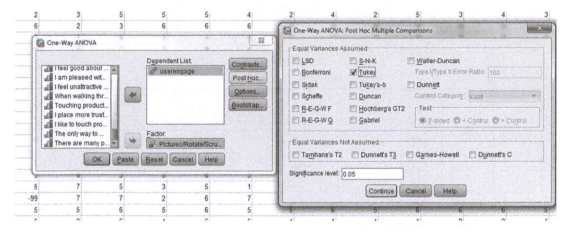

Figure 10.40 How to perform a one-way ANOVA continued

Note: Click on the 'Post-Hoc' button and select 'Tukey'. Click 'OK' and run the analysis.

The means plots table (Figure 10.43) shows us graphically where the differences lie. We can see here that the difference between pictures and the other two conditions is much larger than the difference between rotate and scrunch. You can also manually calculate how big your effect size is by dividing the sum of squares between groups by the total sum of squares (found in the ANOVA Table 9.41). A guide for effect sizes is .01 as a small effect; .06 as a medium effect; and .14 as a large effect (Cohen 1988). In this case we have an effect size (or ets squared) of .06, which is a medium-sized effect.

Necessary analysis to ensure statistically robust results

As you have probably gathered when reading this chapter, statistical analysis requires high quality data. You have to choose and perform analyses intelligently with the right kind of data, which has gone through many checks, to be sure that assumptions are not being violated. But, it doesn't stop there. You also need to perform reliability and validity analyses on your data to be sure that you gain statistically robust results. This section builds on ideas presented earlier and details some of the main types of reliability and validity, using real data to show how to present this in a correct and expected manner.

Reliability

Reliability, in terms of quantitative data, is explicitly about generating positive confirmation of results if the study were repeated. Malhotra and Birks (2007: 357) define reliability in terms of quantitative data as 'the extent to which a scale produces consistent results if repeated measurements are made on the characteristic'. Tull and Hawkins (1993) denote that reliability is the extent to which measures are free from random error, which produces inconsistency. There are many tests that can be done to establish whether the reliability of a data set is high or low, which include test-retest reliability, alternative-forms reliability, internal consistency reliability and coefficient alpha (Malhotra and Birks 2007). These techniques are summarised in Table 10.6.

The coefficient alpha is often used to assess reliability via internal consistency. The internal consistency of a scale is the amount by which the items in a scale work together, and whether they are

➜ Oneway

Descriptives

useregage

	N	Mean	Std. Deviation	Std. Error	95% Confidence Interval for Mean		Minimum	Maximum
					Lower Bound	Upper Bound		
Pictures	32	3.4000	.83318	.14729	3.0996	3.7004	1.70	4.80
Rotate	54	3.8685	.92733	.12619	3.6154	4.1216	1.80	5.70
Scrunch	57	4.0649	.67440	.08933	3.8860	4.2439	2.40	5.60
Total	143	3.8420	.84624	.07077	3.7021	3.9818	1.70	5.70

Test of Homogeneity of Variances

useregage

Levene Statistic	df1	df2	Sig.
2.545	2	140	.082

ANOVA

useregage

	Sum of Squares	df	Mean Square	F	Sig.
Between Groups	9.122	2	4.561	6.898	.001
Within Groups	92.566	140	.661		
Total	101.688	142			

Robust Tests of Equality of Means

useregage

	Statistic[a]	df1	df2	Sig.
Welch	7.393	2	76.680	.001
Brown-Forsythe	6.769	2	112.744	.002

a. Asymptotically F distributed.

Figure 10.41 Output for a one-way ANOVA

measuring the same thing (Pallant 2007). Internal reliability is used in connection with multiple indicator constructs, and determines whether they are all coherent and how affected they are by measurement error (Hardy and Bryman 2010). The Cronbach's alpha (α) coefficient is the most commonly used measure of internal consistency in marketing research (Pallant 2007; Hardy and Bryman 2010). This is equal to the average of all possible split–half reliability coefficients for a scale (Zeller and Carmines 1980: 56). The accepted threshold for the Cronbach's α value is .7 (Nunnally 1978). To test the Cronbach's alpha in SPSS you click 'analyze', 'scale' and then 'reliability analysis'. Further guidelines can be found in Pallant (2007 or later).

Post Hoc Tests

Multiple Comparisons

Dependent Variable: userengage

Tukey HSD

(I) Pictures/Rotate/Scrunch	(J) Pictures/Rotate/Scrunch	Mean Difference (I-J)	Std. Error	Sig.	95% Confidence Interval	
					Lower Bound	Upper Bound
Pictures	Rotate	-.46852*	.18140	.029	-.8982	-.0388
	Scrunch	-.66491*	.17962	.001	-1.0904	-.2394
Rotate	Pictures	.46852*	.18140	.029	.0388	.8982
	Scrunch	-.19639	.15442	.413	-.5622	.1694
Scrunch	Pictures	.66491*	.17962	.001	.2394	1.0904
	Rotate	.19639	.15442	.413	-.1694	.5622

*. The mean difference is significant at the 0.05 level.

Homogeneous Subsets

userengage

Tukey HSD[a,b]

Pictures/Rotate/Scrunch	N	Subset for alpha = 0.05	
		1	2
Pictures	32	3.4000	
Rotate	54		3.8685
Scrunch	57		4.0649
Sig.		1.000	.491

Means for groups in homogeneous subsets are displayed.

a. Uses Harmonic Mean Sample Size = 44.568.

b. The group sizes are unequal. The harmonic mean of the group sizes is used. Type I error levels are not guaranteed.

Figure 10.42 Output for a one-way ANOVA

Table 10.6 Reliability assessment tests

Reliability assessment tests	Description
Test–retest reliability	Respondents are administered identical sets of scale items at two different times, under as nearly equivalent conditions as possible.
Alternative-forms reliability	Requires two equivalent forms of the scale to be constructed and then the same respondents to be measured at two different times.
Internal consistency reliability	An approach for assessing the internal consistency of a set of items, where several items are summated in order to form a total score for the scale.
Coefficient alpha	A measure of the internal consistency reliability that is the average of all possible split-half coefficients resulting from different splittings of the scale items.

Source: Adapted from Malhotra and Birks (2007: 357–358).

Validity

Validity is a test of how accurately instrument measures to what it intends to measure (Field 2009), with construct validity being one facet of this. Construct validity is the degree to which a set of measured variables actually reflects the theoretical latent construct that the variables are designed to measure (Hair *et al.* 2006). Construct validity can be assessed by evaluating the discriminant validity and the convergent validity. These evaluation techniques will now be discussed.

userengage

Tukey HSD[a,b]

| Pictures/Rotate/Scrunch | N | Subset for alpha = 0.05 | |
		1	2
Pictures	32	3.4000	
Rotate	54		3.8685
Scrunch	57		4.0649
Sig.		1.000	.491

Means for groups in homogeneous subsets are displayed.

a. Uses Harmonic Mean Sample Size = 44.568.

b. The group sizes are unequal. The harmonic mean of the group sizes is used. Type I error levels are not guaranteed.

Means Plots

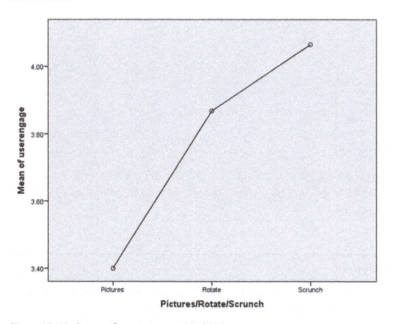

Figure 10.43 Output for a one-way ANOVA

Discriminant validity

Discriminant validity is the extent to which two associated concepts are distinct (Hair *et al.* 2006). Correlation values are used to examine discriminant validity, with them needing to be low in order to show the factors individuality from one another (Hair *et al.* 2006). Discriminant validity coefficients are correlations between measures of different constructs using the same instrument (Schumacker and Lomax 2010: 277–278). Discriminant validity is one part of broader ranging construct validity (Pallant 2007). In order to measure discriminant validity, the average variance extracted (AVE) calculation can be used (Fornell and Larcker 1981; Hair *et al.* 2006). This will be used in tandem with the standardised direct effects table retrieved from CFA and the factor correlation matrix obtained from EFA (using oblique rotation), as suggested in Fornell and Larcker (1981). The AVE can be calculated by dividing the sum of

Table 10.7 Factor loadings of final CFA measurement model (standardized direct effects)

	Purchase intention	Community	Multimedia	Trust	Product viewing
Purch1	.824				
Purch2	.842				
Purch3	.826				
Purch4	.760				
Commun1		.713			
Commun2		.830			
Commun3		.680			
Commun4		.731			
Commun5		.632			
Moving1			.885		
Moving2			.837		
Moving3			.727		
Trust1				.855	
Trust2				.841	
Trust3				.754	
Trust4				.730	
Static1					.739
Static2					.754
Static3					.560
Static4					.618

the squared factor loadings for that construct by the number of factors within that construct (Hair *et al.* 2006). In order to calculate the AVE values, the factor loadings are obtained from the standardised direct effects table found in the output from a CAF (see Table 10.7, derived from research on fashion retailing).

Discriminant validity is present if the AVE values for each construct are greater than the squared factor correlation values between constructs shown in the factor correlation matrix (Fornell and Larcker 1981) (see Table 10.8).

To claim discriminant validity, the AVE value (shown as the bold diagonal elements) must be greater than all other values in the corresponding columns (Hair *et al.* 2006). This shows that constructs are distinctly different from one another, and that they are uncorrelated. All cases within Table 10.8 are deemed valid.

Convergent validity

Convergent validity can be measured to assess the extent to which variables within a construct share a significant amount of variance in common (Hair *et al.* 2006). Convergent validity is part of construct validity, which involves testing a scale against theoretically derived hypotheses concerning latent constructs (Pallant 2007) and the accuracy of this measurement (Hair *et al.* 2006). There are three methods, which can be used to measure convergent validity, including the factor loadings, the AVE calculation and the reliability (Hair *et al.* 2006).

When analysing the factor loadings for convergent validity, it is recommended that a standardised score should be above .5 or higher (Hair *et al.* 2006). A standardised loading is looked at, because it explains the amount of variance in an item, which is explained by the latent factor

Table 10.8 Discriminant validity analysis results

	Purchase intention	Community	Multimedia	Trust	Product viewing	Guidance	Loyalty
Purchase Intention	**0.662**						
Community	0.050	**0.519**					
Moving Product	0.243	0.263	**0.671**				
Trust	0.516	0.199	0.233	**0.635**			
Static Product	0.290	0.134	0.182	0.275	**0.499**		

Notes

1 Diagonal elements in bold represent the AVE (average variance extracted) values;
2 Off-diagonal elements represent the squared factor correlations between factors.

Table 10.9 Convergent validity calculations

Factor	Variable	Standardised factor loading	Squared factor loading	Average variance extracted
Static Product	Static1	.739	0.546	45.4%
	Static2	.754	0.573	
	Static3	.560	0.314	
	Static4	.618	0.382	
Trust	Trust1	.855	0.731	63.5%
	Trust2	.841	0.707	
	Trust3	.754	0.569	
	Trust4	.730	0.533	
Moving Product	Moving1	.855	0.731	65.3%
	Moving2	.837	0.701	
	Moving3	.727	0.529	
Purchase Intention	Purch1	.824	0.679	66.2%
	Purch2	.842	0.709	
	Purch3	.826	0.682	
	Purch4	.760	0.578	
Community	Commun1	.713	0.508	51.3%
	Commun2	.830	0.689	
	Commun3	.680	0.462	
	Commun4	.731	0.508	
	Commun5	.632	0.399	

(Hair *et al.* 2006). The value should be .5 or higher so that the item is more explained by variance than it is error (Hair *et al.* 2006). From Table 10.9 we can see that the factor loadings are all above .5 and most are above .7. This suggests that there is evidence of convergent validity within the data.

Moreover, the percentage of AVE among a set of constructs can provide an indication of convergent validity (Hair *et al.* 2006). As previously mentioned, the AVE is the sum of the squared multiple correlations divided by the number of items within a construct (Hair *et al.* 2006). AVE calculations above .5 (or 50 per cent) are seen as adequately converged (Hair *et al.* 2006). Table 10.9 suggests adequately converged constructs, with static product presentation just short of the threshold with a score of 45.4 per cent.

Discussion and conclusion

There is little doubt that current marketing research offerings often adopt quantitative methods. To keep in touch with marketing research, it is necessary to have a good awareness of the range of quantitative methods that are regularly being used, and which form the methodological basis of research papers published in marketing journals. Equally, there are many potential and established marketing scholars who do find the rather arcane nature of many expositions of quantitative methods in marketing articles a barrier to understanding. This is not helped by the many business statistics textbooks, which adopt a 'statisticians' logic' to teaching and learning, a provider perspective that determines what students should know (e.g. probability theory), rather than what is helpful to them.

We hope that we have been able to remove some of the barriers, by offering a different approach in this chapter. If our assumption that marketing scholars require help in 'reading' and/or 'doing' quantitative research is correct, this chapter represents a useful starting point and should lead to an urge to learn more. Although statistics and quantitative methods may seem 'dry' to some people, we know that the journey to master it can be both emotional and worthwhile.

References

Anscombe, F. J. and Tukey, J. W. (1963), 'Analysis of residuals', *Technometrics*, 5: 141–160.

Bennett, R., Mousley, W., Kitchin, P. and Ali-Choudhury, R. (2007), 'Motivations for participating in charity-affiliated sporting events', *Journal of Customer Behaviour*, 6(2): 155–178.

Blunch, N. J. (2008), *Introduction to Structural Equation Modelling Using SPSS and AMOS*, London: Sage Publications.

Byrne, B, M. (2010), *Structural Equation Modelling with AMOS: Basic Concepts, Applications, and Programming*, second edition, London: Routledge.

Child, D. (1990), *The Essentials of Factor Analysis*, second edition, London: Cassel Education Limited.

Churchill, G. A. Jr (1979), 'A paradigm for developing better measures of marketing constructs', *Journal of Marketing Research*, XVI: 64–73.

Churchill, G. A. Jr (2001), *Basic Marketing Research*, fourth edition, Mason, OH: South Western Thompson Learning.

Cohen, J. W. (1988), *Statistical Power Analysis for the Behavioural Sciences*, second edition, New York: Erlbaum.

Comrey, A. L. and Lee, H. B. (1992), *A First Course in Factor Analysis*, second edition, Hillsdale, NJ: Lawrence Erlbaum Associates.

Costello, A. B. and Osborne, J. W. (2005), 'Best practices in exploratory factor analysis: Four recommendations for getting the most from your analysis', *Practical Assessment, Research & Evaluation*, 10(7): 1–9.

Daunt, K. L. and Harris, L. C. (2014), 'Linking employee and customer misbehaviour: The moderating role of past misdemeanours', *Journal of Marketing Management*, 30(3/4): 221–244.

Davis, F. D. (1989), 'Perceived usefulness, perceive ease of use, and user acceptance of information technology', *MIS Quarterly*, September: 319–340.

DeCoster, J. (1998), *Overview of Factor Analysis*, available at http://www.stat-help.com/notes.html, accessed 8 November 2014.

East, R., Uncles, M. D. and Lomax, W. (2014), 'Hear nothing, do nothing: The role of word of mouth in the decision-making of older consumers', *Journal of Marketing Management*, 30(7/8): 786–801.

Fabrigar, L. R., Wegener, D. T., MacCallum, R. C. and Strahan, E. J. (1999, 'Evaluating the use of exploratory factor analysis in psychological research', *Psychological Methods*, 4 (3): 272–299.

Field, A. (2009), *Discovering Statistics Using SPSS*, third edition, London: Sage Publications.

Ford, J. K., MacCallum, R. C. and Tait, M. (1986), 'The application of exploratory factor analysis in applied psychology: A critical review and analysi', *Personnel Psychology*, 39: 291–314.

Fornell, C. and Larcker, D. F. (1981), 'Evaluating structural equation models with unobservable variables and measurement error', *Journal of Marketing Research*, 18(1): 39–50.

Gefen, D., Straub, D. W. and Boudreau, M-C. (2000), 'Structural equation modeling and regression: guidelines for research practice', *Communications of the Association for Information Systems*, 4(7): 1–77.

Gironda, J. T. and Korgaonkar, P. K. (2014), 'Understanding consumers' social networking site usage', *Journal of Marketing Management*, 30(5/6): 571–605.

Hair, J. F., Black, W. C., Babin, B. J. and Anderson, R. E. (2010), *Multivariate Data Analysis*, seventh edition, London: Prentice Hall.

Hair, J. F., Black, W. C., Babin, B. J., Anderson, R. E. and Tatham, R. L. (2006), *Multivariate Data Analysis*, sixth edition, Upper Saddle River, NJ: Pearson Prentice Hall.

Hardy, M. and Bryman, A. (2010), *The Handbook of Data Analysis*, London: Sage Publications Ltd.

Hoyle, R. H. (2000), 'Confirmatory factor analysis', in Howard, E. A. and Brown, S. D. (eds) *Handbook of Applied Multivariate Statistics and Mathematical Modeling*, San Diego, CA: Academic Press Tinsley, pp. 465–497.

IMRG (2014), £91 billion Spent Online in 2013: IMRG Capgemini e-Retail Sales Index, available at http://www.uk.capgemini.com/news/uk-news/ps91-billion-spent-online-in-2013-imrg-capgemini-e-retail-sales-index, accessed 8 October 2014.

Khare, A., Mukerjee, S. and Goyal, T. (2013), 'Social influence and green marketing: An exploratory study on Indian consumers', *Journal of Customer Behaviour*, 12(4): 361–381.

Kim, J-O. and Mueller, C. W. (1978), *Introduction to Factor Analysis; What it is and How to do It*, Beverley Hills, CA: Sage Publications Ltd.

Kline, R. B. (1998), *Principles and Practice of Structural Equation Modelling*, New York: The Guildford Press.

Lee, N. and Lings, I. (2008), *Doing Business Research; A Guide to Theory and Practice*, London: Sage Publications Ltd.

Levy, S. (2014), 'Does usage level of online services matter to customers' bank loyalty?', *Journal of Services Marketing*, 28(4): 292–299.

Liu, X. C., Burns, A. and Hou, Y. (2013), 'Comparing online and in-store shopping behavior towards luxury goods', *International Journal of Retail & Distribution Management*, 41(11/12): 885–900.

Malhotra, N. K. and Birks, D. F. (2007), *Marketing Research; An Applied Approach*, third edition, London: Pearson Education.

Nunnally, J. C. (1978), *Psychometric theory*, second edition, New York: McGraw-Hill.

Pallant, J. (2007), *SPSS survival manual*, third edition, New York: Open University Press.

Parasuraman, A., Zeithaml, V. A. and Berry, L. L. (1988), 'SERVQUAL: A multiple-item scale for measuring consumer perceptions of service quality', *Journal of Retailing*, 64(1): 12–40.

Rousseeuw, P. J., Bert, C. and Zomeren, V. (1990), 'Unmasking multivariate outliers and leverage points', *Journal of The American Statistical Association*, 85(411): 633–651.

Saunders, M., Lewis, P. and Thornhill, A. (2009), *Research Methods for Business Students*, fifth edition, London: Pearson Education Limited.

Schumacker, R. E. and Lomax, R. G. (2010), *A Beginners Guide to Structural Equation Modelling*, third edition, London: Routledge.

Tabachnick, B. G. and Fidell, L. S. (2007), *Using Multivariate Statistics*, fifth edition, Boston, MA: Pearson International Education.

Tull, D. S. and Hawkins, D. I. (1993), *Marketing Research Measurement and Method*, sixth edition, New York: Macmillan Publishing.

Webb, J. R. (2002), *Understanding and Designing Marketing Research*, second edition, Cambridge, UK: Thomson Learning.

Wright, L. T. and Crimp, M. (2000), *The Marketing Research Process*, fifth edition, London: Pearson Education.

Zeller, R. A. and Carmines, E. G. (1980), *Measurement in the Social Sciences: The Link between Theory and Data*, Cambridge, UK: Cambridge University Press.

11 Segmentation

Lyndon Simkin

Introduction

Organisations operate with a set of selected target markets and product/service offerings. Each decides on its scope, field of activity and markets. Aston Martin manufactures cars, Waitrose operates supermarkets, Tilda produces rice, Red Bull manufactures a drink, Alba supplies audio products and Vodafone is a telecoms player. Except, none of these labels truly reflects what these businesses have opted to be. In practice, Aston Martin provides only high performance luxury cars; Waitrose operates upscale supermarkets retailing quality groceries; Tilda targets discerning consumers and scratch cooks with its premium rice; Red Bull manufactures performance energy drinks; value-focused Alba only supplies low-price audio equipment; and Vodafone is highly focused on mobile usage for web and phone. Each of these companies has defined its broad realm of interest and thereby its overall markets. Take a closer look and each of these businesses has more narrowly scoped a set of priority target markets within their broader marketplace. In so doing, they have consciously opted not to serve many consumers in the overall market and to instead address only specific segments.

Aston Martin provides an aspiration and eventually, after a long wait, a mode of transport to drivers who often possess several other vehicles and whose purchasing decision might have weighed up buying a luxury motor yacht or holiday island against adding a Vantage to their driveway. Waitrose is not chasing the customers of Asda, Morrisons, Aldi or Lidl, but seeks Tesco's *Finest* consumers and those shopping in Marks & Spencer. Tilda is happy to leave the less discerning rice buyer to purchase supermarket own label or a rival brand, so long as scratch cooks and foodies select its rices. Red Bull focuses on energy drinks for those with high energy lifestyles, rather than the thirsty consumers targeted by Coke or Pepsi. Alba does not seek to appeal to the end of the market drooling for the latest offering from Apple or Bose. Vodafone is not interested in all parts of the mobile telecoms market, instead focusing on business users, youths and family groups. In fact, if the target market strategy of any of these businesses is fully dissected, it becomes evident that each company has identified several sub-markets to attract and some markets to ignore. Why? Because they are practising market segmentation.

Market segmentation is the process by which customers in markets with some heterogeneity are grouped into smaller homogeneous segments of more 'similar' customers, who share similar needs, buying behaviour and characteristics. Therefore, a market segment is a group of individuals, groups or organisations sharing similar characteristics and buying behaviour that cause them to have relatively similar needs and purchasing behaviour. Segmentation is not a new concept: since the 1950s marketers have, in various guises, sought to break down a market into sub-groups of users, each sharing common needs, buying behaviour and marketing requirements. For most organisations, segmentation in some form or other is at the heart of their target market strategy. Not just in commercial markets but also in non-profit sectors. For instance, the recent uptake of social marketing in drives to alter behaviours regarding sustainability, personal debt, healthier eating, alcohol abuse and gambling, depends on the concept of market segmentation. With the advent of one-to-one marketing – enabled by growth in the web, digital marketing, customer relationship management (CRM) and analytics – segmentation was predicted to wane. In fact, the segmentation-led approach to target market strategy development has been rejuvenated in the past few years thanks to big data, smarter heuristics, computing power and the surge in analytics, as well as the more diverse set of stakeholders turning to segmentation to guide their strategy and customer engagement.

Ready access to data enables faster creation of a segmentation and the testing of propositions to take to market. 'Big data' has made the rethinking of target market segments and value propositions inevitable, desirable, faster and more flexible. The resulting information has presented companies with more topical and consumer-generated insights than ever before. The approach to segmentation today is much smarter and has stretched well away from the days of limited data explored only with cluster analysis. The coverage and wealth of the solutions are unimaginable when compared to the practices of a few years ago. Then, typically between only six and ten segments were forced into segmentation solutions, so that an organisation could cater for these macro segments operationally as well as understand them intellectually. Now there is the advent of what is commonly recognised as micro segmentation, where the complexity of business operations and customer management requires highly granular thinking.

CEOs, CFOs and COOs[1] are increasingly the sponsor of segmentation projects as well as the users of the resulting outputs, rather than CMOs or marketing directors. CEOs because recession has forced the re-engineering of value propositions and the need to look after core customers; CFOs because segmentation leads to better and more prudent allocation of resources – especially new product development and marketing – around the most important sub-sets of a market; and COOs because they need to look after key customers better and improve their satisfaction in service delivery. More and more it is recognised that with a new segmentation comes organisational realignment and change, so most business functions now have an interest in a segmentation project, not only the marketers.

Largely as a result of the digital era and the growth of analytics, directors and company leadership teams are becoming used to receiving more extensive market intelligence and quickly updated customer insight, so leading to faster responses to market changes, customer issues, competitor moves and their own performance. This refreshing of insight and a leadership team's reaction to this intelligence often result in there being more frequent modification of a target market strategy and segmentation decisions.

So many projects set up to consider multi-channel strategy and offerings, digital marketing, CRM, brand strategies, new product and service development, the rethinking of value propositions and so forth, now routinely commence with a segmentation piece in order to frame the ongoing work. Most organisations have deployed CRM systems and harnessed associated customer data. CRM first requires clarity in segment priorities. The insights from a CRM system help inform the segmentation agenda and steer how they engage with their important customers or prospects. The growth of CRM and its ensuing data have assisted the ongoing deployment of segmentation.

To ensure there is no ambiguity pertaining to what is meant by segmentation and its role in marketing strategy – indeed, in corporate strategy – this chapter commences with a short section restating a few of the basics of market segmentation and its benefits, before showcasing how one mobile phone player retained its leadership by adopting the principles of segmentation in a traditional segmentation project. The chapter progresses to explore each of the three phases of segmentation: the creation of market segments, the targeting decisions required to select a mix of segments to pursue and the role of brand positioning. Much is changing in the sphere of segmentation, so a brief review is included of research exploring these developments and the ways with which the onset of digital has impacted marketing strategy, market segmentation and target market selection.

The nature of segmentation

A *market* is defined as a group of people who, as consumers or as part of organisations, need and have the ability, willingness and authority to purchase products in a product class. In general use, the term *market* sometimes refers to the total population – or mass market – that buys products. However, the definition used here is more specific, referring to individuals seeking products in a specific product category. For example, students are part of the market for text books, as well as being markets for calculators, stationery, music, e-readers, laptops, smart phones, food, accommodation, travel, insurance and other products and services. Obviously, there are many different markets in any economy.

Markets can be divided into two categories: consumer markets or business markets. A *consumer market* consists of purchasers and/or individuals in their households who personally consume or benefit from the purchased products and who do not buy products primarily to make a profit from selling them on. Each of us belongs to numerous consumer markets for such products as housing, cars, appliances, furniture, clothing, food, financial services and leisure activities. A *business market* is sometimes referred to as an *organisational* or *business-to-business market* and consists of company individuals or groups that purchase a specific kind of product for one of three purposes: re-sale, direct use in producing other products or use in their organisation's general daily operations.

The varying characteristics, needs, wants and interests of consumers or business customers mean that there are few markets where a single product or service is satisfactory for all. The trend is away from a mass marketing approach. Markets in which all customers have different requirements are termed heterogeneous markets. For example, the market for wrist watches is quite diverse. Swatch designs relatively low-priced watches for the fashion-conscious customer. Rotary markets much more conservative and expensive designs for an older customer group. Polar produces technology-led time and measurement monitors for sports and health-focused consumers. In completely heterogeneous markets the only way to satisfy everyone is by offering tailor-made or bespoke products. This situation is more prevalent in some business-to-business markets. In any market, while it may not be feasible to offer every customer a tailor-made product, it is possible to aggregate customers into groups of consumers or businesses sharing similar product needs and buying behaviours. This creates market segments.

Market segmentation is the process by which customers in markets with some heterogeneity can be grouped into smaller, more similar or homogeneous segments. A *market segment*, therefore, is a group of individuals, groups or organisations sharing one or more similar characteristics and buying behaviour that cause them to have relatively similar needs and purchasing. Market segmentation involves identifying such groups, so that marketers are better able to develop product or service benefits that are appropriate just for them. They do this by designing products or services and brands to appeal to particular target segments, to be supported by an appropriate promotional campaign, relevant customer service and suitable pricing and place/distribution strategies. For example, clothing sold through Jack Wills is manufactured for youthful fashion-conscious consumers, typically older teens and students. This is reflected in the product styling, store design and locations, branding and marcomms, and the way in which Jack Wills' image is managed.

Once market segments have been identified, marketers decide which they intend to enter or serve. Many businesses choose to target a set of segments. No-one attempts to offer propositions to all segments within a particular market. Even mega-corporations such as Ford or Apple opt to ignore certain segments. A marketing programme covering all elements of the marketing mix can then be designed to suit the particular requirements of each segment targeted, as with the earlier examples of Aston Martin, Waitrose, Tilda, Red Bull, Alba and Vodafone. All organisations across all sectors practise segmentation, either explicitly or intuitively.

Segmentation provides businesses with a number of advantages that make it easier to develop and capitalise on the opportunities available to them.[2]

Customer analysis

Segmenting markets leads to a better understanding of customers' needs, wants and other characteristics to be achieved, providing topical insights and direction. The sharper focus that segmentation offers allows the personal, situational and behavioural factors that characterise customers in a particular segment to be considered. Questions about how, why and what customers buy can be addressed. By being closely in touch with segments, marketers can respond quickly to even slight changes in what target customers want and are more likely to develop ongoing relationships and build some brand loyalty. Undertaking segmentation forces an organisation to update its understanding of its customers' needs and buying behaviours, to look to consumers or business customers currently not engaging with the brand and to consider where next customers' desires will take them.

Competitor and PESTLE analysis

Most markets are characterised by intense competition. Within this hostile environment, companies need to understand the nature of the competition they face. Who are the main competitors? At which segments are these rivals targeting their products? What are they doing for customers in these target segments, particularly those segments in which they compete head on? What developments are there in terms of the external trading environment and how do these pose threats or opportunities? Answering these fundamental questions allows marketers to make decisions about the most appropriate segments to target and the kinds of competitive advantage to seek. When companies embark on segmentation, they are forced to update their knowledge of market trends and their competitive arena in order to make informed decisions about which segments to address and how. The process of creating and then targeting segments updates an organisation's appreciation of its opportunities, threats, competitive pressures, commercial imperatives and ability to differentiate. As such, there always are 'light-bulb' moments for leadership teams and senior executives as the segmentation project unfolds.

Effective resource allocation

All companies have limited resources; to target the whole of the market is usually unrealistic. In fact, it is hard to think of any company or brand that takes on a market in its entirety. The effectiveness of personnel, finances and material resources can be greatly improved when they are more narrowly focused on a particular segment of customers. It is evident during most segmentation projects that senior management, notably CFOs, COOs and CEOs, relish the clarity provided in terms of steering resource allocation and the spending of budgets. More often than not, the CFO or COO is a driving force within an organisation for conducting segmentation so as to focus resource deployment more prudently and narrow down the range of operations necessary as the target market strategy is rolled out.

Strategic marketing planning

Companies operating in a number of segments are unlikely to follow the same strategic plans in all of them. Dividing up markets into segments allows marketers and leadership teams to develop plans that give special consideration to the particular needs and requirements of customers in different segments and to combat more effectively competitors active in each segment. Segmentation requires a marketing plan in order to roll out effective engagement with those segments identified as target priorities. Marketing planning arguably requires the clarity in target market prioritisation resulting from segmentation, in order to focus available resources and create successful marketing programmes most likely to resonate with customers and fend off competitors.

Financial performance improvement

Few organisations are altruistic. Most seek strong financial returns from their marketing strategies. Segmentation is no different in that it must be seen to bring rewards in terms of return on investment, profitability, market share and volumes sold. Softer metrics, too, should benefit, such as increased brand awareness, higher levels of customer satisfaction, better customer retention, improved new customer ratios and other aspects, which are part of the fabric of marketing. Segmentation helps an organisation to develop fresh insights into customers, competitors, market trends and their own capabilities, so leading to a refreshed strategy more attuned to these market dynamics. Invariably, such topical thinking improves commercial performance. Targeting involves pulling back from some parts of the market in order to focus on the most attractive and beneficial segments. In so doing, resources are freed from underperforming segments, product areas, accounts and the tail of underperforming parts of the business is cut away. In those segments prioritised, propositions are rethought and tend to be more aligned to customers' expectations, customer engagement is enhanced and the organisation focuses better in terms of looking after these segments. Market share within these targeted segments rises and, once any marketing investments have been repaid, so does profitability. New segments are entered with much smarter propositions based on in depth understanding of the segments in question, improving the likelihood of successful engagement with intended customers. Barriers to competitors and longer-term customer relationships tend to result from segmentation, so supporting these increases in market share, sales volume and profitability.

Realigning and restructuring an organisation around newly defined target markets and segments is not pain-free. It is because of these benefits that organisations are willing to realign and alter their deployment of resources. The illustration below for the cellphone company reveals the typical scope of such changes in alignment, structure and allocation of resources, while describing the significant benefits, which resulted from adopting the new segmentation and target market strategy.

The stages of segmentation

There are three stages to carrying out market segmentation: segmentation, targeting and positioning,[3] along with some principles to which studies should adhere.

Segmenting the market

There are many ways in which consumers or business customers can be grouped and markets segmented. In different markets, the variables that are appropriate change. The key is to understand which are the most suitable for distinguishing between different product requirements and customer behaviours. For a long time, companies traditionally focused on only a few dimensions: socio-demographics, lifestyles, benefits sought, usage and attitude studies of consumers; or the customer's activity/sector, account size and firmographics in business markets. Big data, digital and new analytics are all steering changes to how companies conduct segmentation, as described later in this chapter.

Focusing only on customer needs or their demographics or their lifestyles and so forth is no longer deemed to be adequate. It is acknowledged that understanding as much as possible about consumers or business customers is desirable, as marketers who really 'know' their targets are more likely to design an appropriate marketing programme to attract and retain them.

Targeting strategy

Once segments have been identified, decisions about which and how many customer groups to target can be made. There are several options:

- Adopt an *undifferentiated approach*, focusing on the total market. Such a mass marketing approach is now very uncommon for it tends to be uncompetitive when challenged by rivals who have focused their propositions and customer engagement far more acutely.
- At the other end of the spectrum, an organisation could concentrate on only a *single segment* with one product/service and marketing programme. Specialisation and niching may result in leadership and segment domination, but most businesses prefer to spread their risk across several markets and segments.
- Offer one product/service and marketing programme, but across a number of segments. This is possible, but this approach risks failing to properly address the expectations of those in each separate segment being pursued and is likely to lose to far more focused and dedicated competing propositions tailored only at a single segment.
- Target a different product/service and marketing programme at each of a number of segments. Such *differentiated marketing* to a set of target market segments is the preferred option for most businesses, although it is costly. Segmentation divides the overall market into a set of market segments. The organisation then targets a selection of these, but each with a separate dedicated proposition and marketing mix.

Figure 11.1 shows the different generic targeting strategies.

With the arrival of digital, once target segments have been determined, an organisation has more flexibility than ever in tailoring propositions, customer handling and marketing communications to individuals within these priority segments. CRM tools enable much smarter handling of individual accounts than ever before, routinely capture information and develop profiles of the most desirable individual customers or accounts. Targeting propositions one-to-one within a particular segment is now very common, in effect differentiating the value derived from individuals within a target market segment on a one-to-one basis within an organisation's preferred segments.

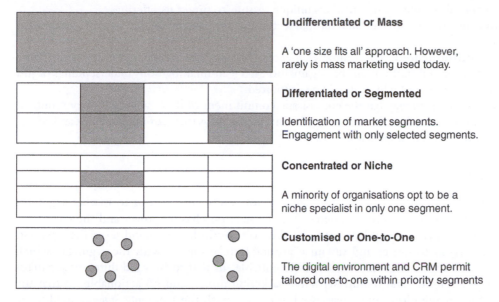

Undifferentiated or Mass

A 'one size fits all' approach. However, rarely is mass marketing used today.

Differentiated or Segmented

Identification of market segments. Engagement with only selected segments.

Concentrated or Niche

A minority of organisations opt to be a niche specialist in only one segment.

Customised or One-to-One

The digital environment and CRM permit tailored one-to-one within priority segments

Figure 11.1 Generic targeting strategies

Positioning the product or service

Companies must decide precisely how and where within the targeted segments to aim a product, service or brand. The needs, wants and perceptions of targeted customers must be translated into a tangible mix of product/service, personnel, price, promotion and place/distribution. Adopting an attractive and well-positioned proposition in line with targeted consumers' or business customers' expectations, creating an appropriate image and reputation, is the final phase of the traditional market segmentation process.

Airline Emirates has positioned itself around customer service and improving travellers' experience, while EasyJet focuses more on value for money and convenience. Bic pens are low-priced highly functional writing implements, while Mont Blanc pens write well, but their premium price positioning is centred on style, prestige and self-image. Positioning must be based on aspects of the brand and marketing mix, which realistically will appeal to consumers or business customers within the company's target market segments. In adopting a specific positioning – as is the case with each of the brands above – there is an inevitable exclusion of certain customer groups and a clear decision not to appeal to certain segments. It is important that an organisation first develops a clear strategy and understands the financial implications of its targeting strategy, before embarking on positioning activities. Positioning must be managed in conjunction with the overarching brand strategy and should be communicated to all agencies and creative partners involved in marketing communications. A well-positioned organisation[4] is:

- **Customer-centred**. The principal focus is on meeting the needs and wants of its target audiences. It tailors offerings and communications to those it wishes to influence.
- **Visionary**. A future for the organisation is articulated that offers a clear sense of where the organisation is going, what the 'new' enterprise will look like and what it will achieve when it meets with its offerings.

- **Differentiated**. It offers target markets unique reasons to prefer its offerings.
- **Sustainable**. Secure in feel and substance for the long term in the face of competitor reaction.
- **Easily communicated**. The central elements of strategy are simple and clear so that both target audiences and staff within the organisation have an unambiguous understanding of just what the strategy is and why it should be supported.
- **Motivating**. The strategy has the enthusiastic commitment of those who will carry it out.
- **Flexible**. Sufficiently broad to allow for diversity in the ways that staff implement it and adaptable to unforeseen contingencies.

Principles of robustness

To be fit for purpose and accepted, the segmentation study should lead to market segments which are: (i) measurable, in order to determine the size, purchasing power and the characteristics of the segment; (ii) accessible, so as to be able to realistically reach and serve the segment; (iii) substantial, so as to create and sustain a profitable relationship with the segment, which provides pay-back to the organisation; (iv) differentiable, in that to be valid different segments should behave differently and require separate marketing mixes; and (v) actionable, so that the resources of the organisation can be harnessed to engage with the segment. *Stability* used to be listed in this set of requisites, as segmentation change is disruptive for an organisation. However, the more immediate access to 'big data' and analytics, new communications options with targeted consumers and customers, including more two-way communication with customers, and faster moving competition, now means most segmentations are frequently and easily updated at low cost and in short timeframes.

The role of segmentation

To reaffirm the value of segmentation and its power in directing strategy, this section explores market segmentation in relation to a segmentation project conducted in the Eastern European telecommunications market for mobile phones. This example of a 'traditional' segmentation project provides a step-by-step view, from the inception of the project through to the selection of target segments and the roll out of marketing programmes. Insights into the practical reasons for carrying out segmentation are provided and the strategic benefits are revealed. The requirements for managing a segmentation project are highlighted. The performance benefits for this telecoms player were considerable, underpinning the value of segmentation-based strategy. This illustration of segmentation demonstrates well the traditional scope of segmentation in classic commercial markets, as companies seek to compete effectively, refresh their customer-facing propositions, strive to add value for their owners and investors, while exploring growth options in maturing markets.

A project targeting growth in the mobile phone market

The centrality of market segmentation to marketing strategy is well established, along with clearly developed academic views about the nature of the segmentation process. Practitioners are encouraged to handle market heterogeneity by using their understanding of customer needs, attitudes, perceptions, purchasing behaviour and influences, as the foundation for creating homogeneous segments. These segments foster marketing programmes, which are tailored to match customer needs. This illustration explores how a recent segmentation project was conducted in the Eastern European telecommunications market for mobile phones (cellphones).[5]

The project's aims

The company (referred to here as the 'teleco') operated in many countries. Either it was a domineering market leader in terms of market share, or the number one challenger. Unlike O2 or Vodafone, this operator traded under different brands in each country, often using several brands, each addressing different segments. Until this point there had been no real market segmentation: the teleco had simply categorised its customers either as business or private users, and in terms of whether they were on monthly tariffs/long-term contracts or 'pay-as-you-go' tariffs. This categorisation of customers was typical for most players in the cellphone industry around the world at this time.

The project's aims were to harness the power of market segmentation to shape the teleco's target market strategy, rethink its branding, achieve greater alignment with market trends and compete more effectively. The teleco intended to reorganise its sales, marketing and customer support personnel around the targeted segments. The sponsor was the teleco's CFO or Finance Director (FD). Throughout the segmentation project, a specially created team of managers and external consultants worked closely with the directors, to ensure the eventual solution adhered to the company's goals, which were:

1   to be the market leader or the number one challenger brand in each country;
2   to increase revenue per subscriber;
3   to grow customers' usage times per month;
4   to build the subscriber base;
5   to create a brand reputation for innovation, service delivery excellence and value.

Undertaking the segmentation project

A leading German marketing research organisation was selected to specify and implement a research project to identify market segments within four of the teleco's national markets (countries). The segmentation project combined qualitative and quantitative research methods. It took place over an eighteen-month period, from initial project scoping to the roll out of the final marketing plans, which had been designed for the key targeted segments. There were seven phases.

Phase i: preparation and scoping

During the preparatory phase, the current market structure was explored through an internal scoping workshop involving the organisation's senior leadership team, external industry experts and the research organisation. This workshop also identified the level of change desired within the organisation or anticipated as a result of the project, coverage of markets/businesses to include, key personnel to involve in the project, data requirements, anticipated timelines, deliverables and budgets.

(continued)

(continued)

Phase ii: exploratory qualitative marketing research

The researchers needed to delve into customers' behaviour and use of mobile phones. Exploratory focus groups were conducted in each country to learn more about mobile phone usage and the role of the phone in their lives, including customers' attitudes, motivations, stated behaviours, purchasing approaches, lifestyles and factors affecting their perceptions of currently available options. From these insights a questionnaire was prepared for use in the quantitative research phase.

Phase iii: the quantitative survey

A total of 10,000 consumer interviews were conducted (2,500 in each of the 4 countries) to provide data for a quantitative analysis of consumers' needs, required benefits, usage, lifestyles and attitudes towards mobile phones. Of these 2,500 interview targets, 1,000 were current users of the teleco's brand, with the remainder being users of competing brands and some non-users. This number provided a statistically valid sample on which to conduct the multivariate analyses and apply the necessary statistical significance tests for each country. The survey of corporate subscribers, involving a further 2,000 interviews, reflected the fact that the majority of the market in these countries is made up of private consumer subscribers. These corporate subscriber interviews were allocated in proportion to the size of the corporate subscriber base in each country. These business-to-business interviews covered the same usage, attitude, perception, lifestyle, functionality and profiling aspects as in the consumer interviews, but also examined the buying centre dynamics and corporate decision-making, billing and tariff issues that are pertinent to corporate subscribers.

Phase iv: multivariate analysis and identification of segments

A range of multivariate techniques, including factor and cluster analyses and structural equation modelling, was applied to the survey data to generate segments of homogeneous customers. Workshops with client personnel helped to test the intuitive logic of the emerging segments (see below for the eight segments). Once managers had approved these customer groupings, further 'deep-dive' focus groups were run within each identified segment to more accurately profile customer requirements and expectations, and to test the validity of the proposed segmentation.

Phase v: internal dissemination of the segmentation

Senior managers took part in reporting the segments throughout the organisation. This dissemination was customised to reflect managerial cultures and market conditions/challenges in each of the four countries. The intuitive logic of the eight segments encouraged rapid buy-in and staff support. Everyone viewing the segments found it straight forward to allocate themselves, family, friends and colleagues to a particular segment.

Phase vi: bringing the segments to life for marketing planning

Follow-up qualitative marketing research was used to test consumer and business customer views of the marketing propositions developed for the targeted segments and competitors' propositions. These insights informed the subsequent marketing planning and roll-out.

Phase vii: operationalisation of the segmentation

The final stage involved managing the adoption of these segments within the organisation and implementing the recommended segmentation solution. Various market analyses were used to steer the target market strategy and to determine which segments to pursue. These included reviewing existing performance, assessing internal capabilities, examining the competitive context and conducting a PESTLE review of market trends and the marketing environment. A SWOT analysis developed from the review of internal capabilities and market trends was used in conjunction with portfolio planning techniques[6] to determine the target segment selection and to inform the marketing plans, which were subsequently devised. Detailed competitive positioning strategies helped to steer the marketing programmes, which were developed. In order to operationalise these segmentations, a time-consuming and expensive process of mining the teleco's data warehouse was needed, so that existing customers could be profiled and then each allocated to the segments.

Segment evaluation

It is important to assess the quality of the emerging segmentation.[7] The marketing research company used a balanced set of evaluative criteria to validate the robustness of the segmentation solution. These combined quantitative/statistical measures with more qualitative/strategic criteria.

Statistical criteria	Qualitative and strategic criteria
Profiles: were the compositions of the apparently separate segments statistically different?	*Coherence*: were the segments plausible in relation to the base and descriptive variables used or were there contradictions?
Distribution of minima and maxima: were the emerging segments sufficiently different from each other or alternative ways for grouping these consumers?	*Vividness*: were the segments vivid? Did the segment solution provide a clear mental picture of the people within each segment?
Discriminance (F-value): how many variables had the power to discriminate segments?	*Differentiation*: did the consumers within each segment differ according to core dimensions, e.g. interest in cellphone services/applications, lifestyle and personality, general affinity towards technology, attitudes towards mobile phones, mobility, communication habits, etc?
Country distribution: could all segments be found in all countries and did they have a sufficient size to be viable?	
Robustness: could the segments be reproduced in further future runs or would the segment structure be different?	*Useful*: did the segments help with marketing? Could consumers within them easily be targeted with marketing programmes? Were the emerging segments adequately intuitively logical for managers to understand?

As with any quantitative analysis, statistical significance tests were needed to verify the robustness of the process and the ultimate segment solutions. Senior managers also recognised the need for recommendations, which were intuitively logical to those charged with implementing the segmentation. For example, managers needed to believe that existing

(continued)

(continued)

customers could readily be allocated to one of the emerging segments. The qualitative/strategic criteria were specifically devised to address this need. The segmentation solution that was eventually generated by the process was firmly rooted in customers' core needs and lifestyles, their mobile phone usage and attitudes towards their mobile world.

The emerging target segment strategy

Statistical analysis produced a statistically sound fourteen cluster solution: the respondents from the survey fell into fourteen homogeneous groups or market segments. However, the organisation had previously only operated with largely two broad 'categories' of (a) business users on contracts; and (b) consumers on pay-as-you-go tariffs. For the organisation to conceptually and operationally progress from two to fourteen customer groups was viewed as too major a transition to manage. The next statistical cut-off from the analysis, was the eight cluster solution. These eight remaining segments were statistically and intuitively robust and could be visualised readily by the managers tasked with implementing the segmentation strategy. The eight segments were also mutually exclusive, with each individual consumer or business customer clearly allocated to only one of the segments.

The eight segments' profiles

Talk 'n' texters – 'I just have a mobile phone because it is practical'.

- the conservative consumer, not immersed in technology but with a few practical needs that can be fulfilled by technical appliances. They rely on mobile phones for practical reasons only;
- interested in basic functions, especially SMS, but not attracted at all by more sophisticated or fun services, be it via mobile phone or the internet.

Talkative trendies – 'Talk around the clock'.

- the modern fun/fashion-oriented socialiser. This customer needs a mobile phone to keep in constant touch with the social scene and fulfil a strong need for communication;
- interested in all applications and services, particularly social media.

Aspiring to be accepted – 'Would like to have it, but is not really up to it'.

- wants to be part of the 'in-crowd', but is not there yet, and possibly never will be! These customers have a mobile phone, because they just want to show it off: they seek to have the same trendy handsets they believe are adopted by peer sets, which they aspire to join;
- show a special affinity towards photo, video and MP3 applications, and social media.

Laggards – 'Torn between conservative values and the modern world'.

- traditionalist views with low communication needs and basic technical usage;
- the Luddites or those late into the market;
- they hold specific aversions to mobile phones (SMS), but also view them as a practical-only device (e.g. for emergency calls only).

Gaming youths – 'Game oriented mobile world addict'.

- young and very technology-oriented people, belonging to the mobile generation, who need a mobile phone in order to maintain a fast-living fun life;
- games, games, games! Plus music and social media;
- these customers search for images and brands that help them keep track with the modern world.

Sophisticated careerists – 'Be successful with mobile technology'.

- career-oriented individualists with lots of contacts. Highly immersed in technology and very mobile;
- demanding value for money, but customer care and respect are very important to these customers;
- they need a mobile phone to organise their life and business, but they are not emotionally attached;
- self-choosers for work mobiles are included here.

Organisation paid – 'No choice – the corporation decides'.

- demanding value for money and customer care;
- network coverage, reliability and volume tariff discounts are the focus, along with data security;
- users have little influence on selection, so not particularly fashion or technology-led.

International business users – 'Frequent connected business travellers'.

- easy global roaming and smooth data transfer;
- some similarities with *Sophisticated careerists*, but with much greater emphasis on functionality and flexibility of at destination services;
- influenced by corporate choice of network and tariff plans.

The first five are consumer segments. The last two are business user segments. The *Sophisticated careerists* are mainly business users who self-select mobile network, handset and tariff option and behave as consumers rather than business users.

Note: In order to protect the commercial interests of the original client, the segment labels and descriptions, along with a few client-specific aspects of the data collection, segment analysis and subsequent data warehouse mining, have been disguised or amended.

These segment labels were deliberately attention-grabbing, to aid internal communication as the segmentation was rolled out. A further benefit was that these labels could readily be used to allocate mobile phone users to segments. No doubt you can do this for yourself, your friends, family members and colleagues . . . in which segment are you?

The marketers in the client teleco and those personnel responsible for product development, marketing campaigns and customer service, received a full range of information about each of the segments and their members. This included their technology affinity; mobility habits; communication habits; cellphone usage and attitudes; the relative importance of mobile services; any interest in special applications; spending and price sensitivity; information sources; internet usage and activities; reasons for operator/service provider choice; brand awareness and brand strength/attractiveness; satisfaction levels with a particular network; lifestyle/leisure activities; and demographics (age, gender, education, income). Summaries of the segment profiles and top-level marketing programme recommendations were also provided. The CFO produced detailed value stream analyses for each segment and assessments of ROI and profitability patterns.

Although the research suggested that all eight segments were present in each of the four countries, they varied considerably in terms of size and relative attractiveness. The project team agreed a set of eleven attractiveness criteria and used the directional policy matrix (DPM) portfolio planning approach to determine which segments should be prioritised by the organisation. Individual country management teams had flexibility in applying these attractiveness criteria, so each country was empowered to decide which segments to target. One country opted to address four of the eight segments. For another, the bulk of the

(continued)

(continued)

organisation's sales and marketing activity was focused on only two segments: in one segment a challenger brand was gaining market share, while the second segment showed the greatest growth prospects. In two countries, separate brands were devised to appeal to the distinctive behaviours and expectations in the different segments. In one country, the *Gaming youths* were offered a *Stay Connected . . . Play & Enjoy!* youth-oriented brand, while the *Talkative trendies* were targeted with the core brand in conjunction with *The Ultimate Network!* positioning. None of the countries chose to target all eight of the segments and no two countries shared identical target market strategies. This pragmatic approach enabled the teleco to respond to the contrasting market conditions and competitive contexts in each of the four countries. The CFO, as sponsor, was satisfied that the selections of segments to target reflected the strongest basis for financial performance growth, shareholder value and resource utilisation.

In the teleco illustration, having made their own targeting decisions, each country's management team developed marketing plans to tackle the chosen segments and to service the targeted customers. These marketing plans were informed by the detailed consumer insights provided by the segmentation study's marketing research, but also were steered by competitors' strategies/actions, changes to the regulatory environment, the financial value of customers, channel strategies and product developments. The result was that no two country management teams adopted a similar plan of action for engaging with the business customers or consumers in a particular market segment being addressed in more than one country. The resulting sales and marketing programmes were fine-tuned to reflect the unique conditions in each country, as well as the expectations of the chosen target market segments.

Over the next two years in all four countries, the new segmentation led to market share and revenue gains, and significant improvements to brand awareness and customer satisfaction in the targeted segments. Competitive advantage was derived from the fact that the teleco's rivals were far less strategic in their approach to target marketing or campaign development. Over the following two years, where the organisation was already market leader, challengers' shares were eroded and, where the teleco was the challenger brand, the company also achieved impressive market share gains. Directors and leadership teams were pleased with their first exposure to segmentation.

Segmentation is often utilised in this way. Segmentation has relevance across products and services in all markets, for consumers and business markets. However, motivations for undertaking such projects are changing, as are the available techniques. Many companies still emulate the approach described above and conduct segmentation as illustrated by this teleco player. But for others now practising segmentation, there are new and different reasons driving their adoption of the concept. Those seeking these strategic insights frequently are not traditional marketers. Analytics managers, FDs, operations personnel and leadership teams are just as likely to be the sponsors of segmentation work as marketing directors or sales teams. The available data and heuristics are significantly more varied and advanced compared with a few years ago, reducing the cost of conducting segmentation and reducing the time taken. The nature of customer insight research, as highlighted elsewhere in this book, has evolved to the point where a wealth of knowledge about consumers or business customers now informs segmentation.

The markets in which segmentation is deployed are far more diverse than ever before, particularly with the growth of social marketing, with targeted programmes to improve health and well-being by changing behaviours in a range of areas.[8] Behind every smoking cessation programme, healthier eating drive, debt management initiative, sustainable living strategy or welfare programme, is a segmentation study identifying who to target and how to position the messaging and interventions.[9] An example of segmentation within social marketing is provided below. Here, a UK government department examined the propensity for the UK public to be influenced within the Government's sustainability agenda, identifying segments revealing varying attitudes, behaviours and characteristics. The segment labels are DEFRA's.[10]

DEFRA's environmental segments

Greens

'I try to conserve whenever I can . . . a lot of people don't think like that'.

Greens are driven by their belief that environmental issues are critical. They are well-educated on green issues, positively connected to arguments, and do not see environmentally friendly people as eccentric.

Consumers with a conscience

'Going away is important . . . I'd find it hard to give up; well I wouldn't, so that [carbon off-setting] would make me feel better'.

Consumers with a conscience want to be *seen* to be green. They are motivated by environmental concern and seeking to avoid guilt about environmental damage. They are focused on consumption and making positive choices.

Wastage focused

'We now turn the thermostat down . . . This is to cut down the bill, but then you start to think about the environment as well'.

This group is driven by a desire to avoid waste of any kind. They have good knowledge about wastage and local pollution, although they lack awareness of other behaviours. Interestingly, this group believes it is ethically separated from greens.

Currently constrained

'I am on a restricted budget so I cannot afford organic food . . . When I earn more in the future I definitely will buy it'.

Currently constrained want to be green, they just do not think there is much they can do in their current circumstances. They have a focus on balance, pragmatism and realism.

Basic contributors

'Organic food – you pay twice the price and how can you be sure that it really is organic?'

(continued)

(continued)

This group is sceptical about the need for behaviour change. It tends to think about behaviour relative to that of others and they are driven by a desire to conform to social norms. They have a low knowledge of environmental issues and behaviours.

Long-term restricted

'I can't afford a car so I don't drive. I use the train instead'.

This group has a number of serious life priorities to address before they can begin to consciously consider their impact on the environment. Their everyday behaviours are often low impact for reasons other than environmental.

Disinterested

'Those Greenies, they're too concerned about the environment . . . they need to chill out, live a little'.

This group displays no interest or motivation to change their current behaviours to make their lifestyle more pro-environmental. They may be aware of climate change and other environmental issues, but this has not entered their current decision-making processes.

Conducting segmentation

Segmenting

Market segmentation is the process of dividing up a market into distinctive groups of consumers or business customers, each with specific needs, characteristics and behaviours, which require different value propositions. Perhaps the greatest challenge for marketing managers is to decide on the dimensions according to which the market should be segmented or sub-divided.

There are categories of variables listed within the marketing literature, including for consumer markets:

- geographic – country or world region, city or metropolis size, density or climate;
- demographic – age, gender, income, education, family, lifecycle, ethnicity or religion;
- psychographic – personal values and personality attributes, motives or lifestyle;
- behavioural – purchasing behaviour, usage rate or benefits sought.

In business markets, commonly cited variables for segmentation of corporate customers included the personal characteristics of those managers responsible for buying decisions; the nature of risk; situational factors, such as order size or urgency; the purchasing approach, such as buying centre structure, formality, competition; operating factors; and firmographics and their commercial sector of operation. Whether consumer of business segmentation, generally only a few of these dimensions would be explored and relied upon to create market segments, so that segmentation often was based on limited market insights and only partial understanding of consumers or business customers.

Today, the use of demographics with some psychographic and behavioural data is no longer deemed adequate by consumer marketers, and few business marketers would depend solely on categorising their customers' business sectors and firmographics. Until a few years ago, these would have been seen as robust approaches to segmentation, but not now. Instead, marketers develop multilayered understanding of the customers in a market. Computing power, new heuristics, data availability and knowledge of segmentation processes, mean that organisations tend to explore multiple segmentation bases and levels of data simultaneously, seeking to build extensive customer insight before considering which consumers or business customers to target.

Macro segments used to be identified through multivariate analyses, typically centred on cluster analysis and structural equation modelling. Once a few segments were identified as being the key to pursue, further deep-dive qualitative research examined these segments in more detail, often resulting in segment subdivision into micro segments. In the last few years, everything has changed. Management teams have far more data available or accessible with which to probe the behaviours, needs and characteristics of their customers, and the support of numerous consultants and data providers. The cost to acquire, time to analyse and ability to reflect on these data have all improved. Now commonplace is the creation of numerous micro segments and then engagement digitally with such customers, tailoring messages and individualising offers.

For example, segmentation of the mobile phone market involves developing an understanding of consumers, which goes way beyond knowing to which network they subscribe, their tariff and handset preferences and rudimentary demographic information. The segmentation project illustrated in this chapter involved the company probing how phones relate to people's behaviours, lifestyles, self-perceptions and aspirations, and the role of the phone in their lives. Instead of classifying customers into only corporate and private users, with some on contract and others opting for pay-as-you-go, a much more useful view of the market emerged enabling smarter customer engagement and retention plans to be formulated.

Today's analytics and ready access to data enabled the company to further break up the broad macro segments into what are known as micro segments. For example, within *Gaming youths*, there are differences between males and females; the latter being more sociable and chatty, requiring entertainment and social media applications, but not as many games as their male peers. Social media behaviour also varied within these *Gaming youths*, revealing micro segments of differing requirements. Previously, the required scale economies would have prohibited finessing propositions to this level, but with the advent of better CRM, digital interaction and smarter metrics, it is feasible to offer such tailoring. Some *Talkative trendies* prefer chatting one-to-one over the phone or via Skype, while other *Talkative trendies* prefer social media networking. Until recently, such tailoring to sub-divisions would not have been cost-effective or manageable, but in today's 'big data' and analytics-led digital environment, such subdivision into micro segments is feasible, quick, cheap and desirable.

Targeting

Target marketing strategies can be identified along a continuum from mass marketing or undifferentiated marketing strategies, where organisations do not differentiate among the segments in the market and try to serve the whole market with a single offer, to micro targeting on a one-to-one basis, where organisations tailor their offerings according to the needs and wants of each individual. The former results in poorly targeted propositions seeking to serve too many dissimilar customers, while the latter rarely is cost-effective. Instead, many organisations choose to operate somewhere in the middle of this continuum, based on their product category and market characteristics as well as their resources and capabilities. Therefore, the two widely used target marketing strategies are: (1) differentiated or segmented marketing; and (2) concentrated or niche marketing.[11] The vast majority of organisations turn to a differentiated strategy based around market segmentation. One-to-one tailoring then is focused at individuals within these priority target market segments.

Target marketing is essentially focusing the marketing efforts of the organisation on the customers that have been identified as the most profitable or valuable to attract and/or retain. Target marketing strategy involves identifying the most attractive market segments, learning their values, needs, wants, desires, practices, habits, likes and dislikes and focusing marketing efforts on satisfying these consumers or business customers in order to create and maintain profitable long-term relationships with them. Companies look at macro drivers from their marketing environment to map emerging threats and opportunities. They evaluate changing customer needs and behaviours, assess competitors' moves and evaluate financial pay-back and resourcing requirements before agreeing on which market segments to focus. In addition, other strategic tools may be used to evaluate the segments, such as variations of Ansoff's development matrix, the DPM, Dibb's competitive positions league table and Porter's Five Forces model.

Today, most organisations adopt a set of variables with which to monitor their performance and to judge the relative merits of each possible opportunity to pursue, as in the teleco illustration above. The DPM assists with this, enabling managers to select a mix of market, competitive, financial, technological and capability variables. The tool is very effective in helping to select which segments to pursue, as demonstrated in the teleco illustration.

The Teleco's selection of segments to target

Segment attractiveness variables	Business strength variables
• Willingness to spend on mobiles in the segment	• Network coverage and quality
• Interest in value-added services in the segment	• Service reliability
• Revenue/profitability (segment financial worth)	• Voice/data roaming
• Latent demand in the segment	• Appropriate tariffs
• Loyalty level in the segment	• Fair billing
• Size of the segment	• Value-added services
• Competitive intensity	• Sales network
• Likelihood of new entrants targeting the segment	• Strength of brand image
• Potential growth of the segment	• Quality of marketing staff and their outputs
• Current market share in the segment	• Customer orientation
• Interest in product development/web	

The mobile phone company's leadership identified these criteria for judging the relative merits of engaging with each segment. Each variable was weighted so that some were deemed more important than others. With these variables and their weightings, the company was able to plot a DPM, as shown below in Figure 11.2, in order to guide its selection of priority segments to address. Those plotted towards the upper left of the grid were most attractive, and the company's capabilities were well aligned to serve these. Other analyses assisted in the identification of which segments to prioritise, including an examination of marketing environment forces and trends, competitors' likely moves and the financial implications for the company of ignoring certain segments.

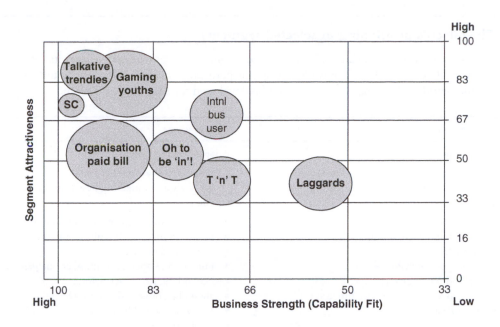

Figure 11.2 DPM grid revealing segment priorities

The DPM revealed very clear priorities in each country. In each country for which this segmentation project was engaged, the DPM plot revealed a different pattern. In no two countries was the identical set of target market segments selected.

Positioning

Positioning is the process of creating an image for a product or service in the minds of targeted customers. The selected positioning must resonate with these current or potential customers, differentiate the offering from competitors, be memorable and plausible and be sustainable. BMW's *the ultimate driving machine* is its positioning. In order to develop an effective positioning, it is necessary to possess marketing intelligence regarding customers, competitors and market trends.[12] Positioning describes the unique place that a product or organisation has in the mind of the customer relative to the competition.[13]

The teleco first selected the segments it would focus on. Having already explored customer expectations and perceptions in these segments, it turned to an evaluation of competitors' propositions and brand positionings. Its own positioning strategy for each segment had to reflect customer requirements, market trends, its own capabilities and credibility, but also seek to differentiate from the positionings adopted by its rivals. Having determined its positioning platform, as described in the illustration below, the teleco briefed its partners and marketing communications agencies to bring to life the agreed brand positionings.

The teleco's positioning in selected segments

The mobile phone company selected various segments to pursue in each of its territories. Unlike in the UK, licensing regulations permitted the use of various brands, so unique brand positioning strategies could be developed for each targeted segment.

Talkative trendies	*Gaming youths*
Adopted positioning:	Adopted positioning:
'Easy and quality comms . . . from simply **the** best mobile operator'.	'Fun for you everywhere you go . . . always something new from us to you'.
• we are everywhere for you;	• take what you want when you want it;
• best network;	• trend-setting apps, downloads and offers;
• hi-tech innovative company;	• living life digitally;
• trusted;	• number one operator – number one games;
• choice of the majority;	• networking like never before;
• prestigious company;	• always be connected – always be 'in';
• high investment in service provision;	• get the latest and be the first;
• most reliable.	• be entertained.

Gaming youths occasionally talk, but mainly download, listen/watch, play and chat digitally online. A positioning based on network quality and clarity around a tariff offering free minutes of talk-time would have little appeal to this segment, yet is exactly what is required to satisfy the *Talkative trendies*, who want the 'ultimate network'. The *Gaming youths* need social media, free game downloads, easy access to music and videos, and offers for music and clubbing events, linked to an online community.

Positioning the company's proposition in the mind of the customer means that it must be able to state what its product offer means to the customer and create an image deemed to have an affinity with those targeted consumers or business customers. This is achieved with the development of a value proposition. This is a statement that encapsulates the value offered to the customer. It is not an advertising strapline or advertising copy. Rather, it is a statement that enables all, internally and within third-party agencies (e.g. advertising, web, design or public relations agencies), to understand how the product is to be positioned in terms of value offering in the mind of the customer. Ultimately, the value proposition is used and translated by the organisation and its agencies to develop effective marketing programmes that communicate and have resonance with the target customers' needs.

The momentum for segmentation and drivers of change

Much has happened in the world of marketing in the last few years. Economic turmoil and the financial downsizing of many countries; associated changes in consumer values and behaviours; the emergence of big data, analytics and customer insight programmes; social media and more consumer-to-consumer communication; the ability to engage with customers one-to-one and on the move; and a move towards sustainable living and a growing CSR agenda are just some of the drivers for change, all of which have impacted on market segmentation. The leading drivers for change are radically altering the way in which segmentation is undertaken, for whom and in which markets.[14]

Market maturity inevitably leads companies and brands to seek additional or new user groups in order to achieve incremental growth and produce shareholder value, as with the example of the teleco player highlighted above. The digitally-inspired youth, ethnic markets, migrant workers and the ageing population are just some of the audiences companies have been keen to understand and engage, leading to re-engineered segmentations and target market strategies. Using topical consumer or business customer insights into their behaviours enables a company to refresh its go-to-market strategy, propositions and engagement practices. More and more businesses are recognising this to be the case, thereby embracing new-look segmentations.

Perhaps more pressingly, recession has forced companies to rethink their value propositions and competitive strategies, thereby requiring updated customer insights to enable reconfigured target market strategies. CEOs wanting to ride recession successfully, CFOs seeking budget savings and COOs wanting operational efficiencies and effectiveness, are as much behind new segmentation studies as CMOs and marketing directors.

The digital revolution provided the opportunity for the so-termed 'segment of one', with individualised and tailored marketing to specific customers and even individuals. However, a brand cannot tailor propositions to every single consumer in a market, as companies have been learning. There must still be an overarching target market strategy and agreement of priority segments into which to play out such bespoke messaging. Most organisations now have CRM systems and harness the associated customer data. These insights help inform their segmentation agenda and refine how they engage with their important customers or prospects. However, there is growing evidence that effective CRM depends on there first being a clear segmentation and awareness of priority audiences on which to focus CRM activity. The take-off of CRM undoubtedly renewed interest in segmentation.

Practitioners in the public and not-for-profit sectors have harnessed what has come to be termed social marketing (not to be confused with social networking), in order to develop and execute more shrewdly their targeting, campaigns and messaging. At the very heart of the concept of social marketing is the market segmentation process. The rise in the threat to security from global unrest, terrorism and crime has focused the minds of governments, security chiefs and their advisors. As a result, significant resources, intellectual capability, computing and data management, have been brought to bear on the problem. The core of this work is the importance of identifying and profiling threats, so mitigating risk. In practice, much of this security and surveillance work harnesses the tools developed for market segmentation and the profiling of different consumer behaviours.

'Big data' is a buzz term now being used daily. It stems from the wealth of interactive and almost instantaneous data permitted by harnessing social media and digital marketing. The resulting information has presented companies with more topical and consumer-generated information than ever before, providing customer engagement intelligence as was never previously possible. Many marketing teams, analytics directors and leadership teams feel overwhelmed by the sheer quantity and immediacy of such data. As a result, segmentation is both helping focus the analysis of these market and customer data and is being shaped by the resulting insights.

Related to digital marketing and big data, companies have recruited analytics and insight teams, often headed by senior personnel such as an insight manager or analytics director. Indeed, the situations vacant adverts for such personnel outweigh posts for brand and marketing managers. These teams, harnessing digital channels and social media, have endorsed the expectations among their peers and senior management teams for speedy topical insight, enabling well-honed product development, campaigns and retention strategies. A side benefit is that far more companies now possess the inhouse expertise necessary to help with segmentation analysis.

Largely as a result of the digital era and growth of analytics, directors and company leadership teams are becoming used to receiving extensive market intelligence and quickly updated customer insight, so leading to faster responses to market changes, customer issues, competitor moves and their own performance. This often results in modified target market strategy and segmentation decisions. The ability to revise a segmentation analysis and incorporate new insights has created a sense of expectancy in many leadership teams relating to rolling change and routine updates to segmentation recommendations and engagement programmes.

As a result of these trends and developments, market segmentation is now of more use than ever before, in a growing array of markets not just for-profit applications, at greater speed and cost-effectiveness than previously was possible.

Summary

Market segmentation is at the heart of the strategic marketing process and creating a marketing strategy. It is a process which seeks to identify sub-groups of consumers or business customers in a market, so that these customers can be better engaged and retained. Segmentation groups together consumers or business customers who are alike in terms of their needs, behaviours and characteristics, so that they can be treated as a homogeneous group for marketing purposes. The three stages of segmentation involve identifying the segments, selecting which of these to target, and determining an appropriate brand positioning for the segments targeted. This chapter has overviewed and illustrated each of these stages, as well as highlighted recent developments, which have altered the manner in which segmentation is undertaken and used.

Despite the advent of one-to-one marketing, segmentation is still pivotal in developing an understanding of a market and steering targeting strategy, providing the direction for proposition development, brand positioning, marketing programmes, one-to-one, customer retention and customer handling. Segmentation promotes market share growth, increases profitability and return on marketing investment and improves customer engagement.

The underlying motivations for embarking on segmentation are different today. Those seeking these strategic insights frequently are not traditional marketers. The available data and analytics are significantly more varied and advanced compared with a few years ago and the markets in which segmentation is deployed are much more diverse than ever before, particularly with the growth of social marketing's reach. Segmentation is routinely part of the fabric of an organisation's activities, underpinning other strategic initiatives and guiding business improvement. Segmentation is a fundamental concept in marketing and foundation for marketing strategy.

Notes

1 CFO = Chief Financial Officer or Finance Director; COO = Chief Operating Officer or Operations Director; CEO = Chief Executive Officer; CMO = Chief Marketing Officer or Marketing Director.
2 See Dibb, S. and Simkin, L. (2008), *Market Segmentation Success: Making It Happen!*, Routledge.
3 See Dibb, S. and Simkin, L. (2013), *Marketing Essentials*, Cengage.
4 Adapted from Andreasen, A. R. and Kotler, P. (2003), *Strategic Marketing for Non-Profit Organisations*, Prentice-Hall.

5   This case illustration was originally developed for the Academy of Marketing's conference case track. The identity of the client organisation is disguised for reasons of commercial confidentiality. An abridged version first appeared in *Marketing Theory*, edited by Michael Baker and Michael Saren, in a chapter exploring target segment strategy (Sage, 2010).

6   It is common to apply the directional policy matrix (DPM) in order to screen emerging segments to determine their relative attractiveness for full-on commercialisation, as explained in Dibb, S. and Simkin, L. (2008), *Market Segmentation Success: Making It Happen!*, Routledge.

7   See Dibb, S. and Simkin, L. (2010), 'Judging the quality of customer segments: Segmentation effectiveness', *Journal of Strategic Marketing*, 18(2): 113–131.

8   See Dibb, S. and Carrigan, M. (2013), 'Editorial: Social marketing transformed – Kotler, Polonsky and Hastings reflect on social marketing in a period of social change', Special Issue of the *European Journal of Marketing*, 47(9): 1376–1398.

9   See Dibb, S. (2014), 'Up, up and away: Social marketing breaks free', *Journal of Marketing Management*, available at http://dx.doi.org/10.1080/0267257X.2014.943264

10 Department for Environment, Food and Rural Affairs (DEFRA) (2006), 'The seven population segments' and 'Positioning of segments: Ability and willingness to act', in *An Environmental Behaviours Strategy for DEFRA: Scoping Report*, pp. 32–33, December.

11 See Dibb, S. *et al.* (2012), *Marketing: Concepts & Strategies*, Cengage, pp. 247–249, for an overview of its use in segmentation and pp. 368–371 for a step-by-step guide.

12 See Dibb, S. *et al.* (2012), *Marketing: Concepts & Strategies*, Cengage, pp. 251–255.

13 See Ries, A. and Trout, J. (2001), *Positioning: The Battle for Your Mind*, McGraw-Hill.

14 Simkin, L. (2013), 'To boardrooms and sustainability: The changing nature of segmentation', White Paper Series, the Henley Centre for Customer Management, University of Reading, November.

References

Agarwal, J., Malhotra, N. K. and Bolton, R. N. (2010), 'A cross-national and cross-cultural approach to global market segmentation: An application using consumers' perceived service quality', *Journal of International Marketing*, 18(3): 18–40.

Clarke, A. and Freytag, P. V. (2008), 'An intra- and inter-organisational perspective on industrial segmentation', *European Journal of Marketing*, 42(9/10): 1023–1038.

Cleveland, M., Papadopoulos, N. and Sprott, E. (2011), 'Identity, demographics, and consumer behaviours: International market segmentation across product categories', *International Marketing Review*, 28(3): 244–266.

Dibb, S. and Simkin, L. (2001), 'Market segmentation: Diagnosing and overcoming the segmentation barriers', *Industrial Marketing Management*, 30: 609–625.

Dibb, S. and Wensley, R. (2002), 'Segmentation analysis for industrial marketing: Problems of integrating customer requirements into operations strategy', *European Journal of Marketing*, 36 (1/2): 231–251.

Dibb, S. and Simkin, L. (2008), *Market Segmentation Success: Making It Happen!*; New York: The Haworth Press/Routledge.

Dibb, S. and Simkin, L. (2009), 'Implementation rules to bridge the theory/practice divide in market segmentation', *Journal of Marketing Management*, 25(3/4): 375–396.

Dibb, S. and Simkin, L. (2009), 'Bridging the segmentation theory/practice divide', *Journal of Marketing Management*, 25(3/4): 219–225.

Dibb, S. and Simkin, L. (2010), 'Judging the quality of customer segments: Segmentation effectiveness', *Journal of Strategic Marketing*, 18(2): 113–131.

Dolnicar, S. and Lazarevski, K. (2009), 'Methodological reasons for the theory/practice divide in market segmentation', *Journal of Marketing Management*, 25(3/4): 357–373.

Freytag, P. V. and Clarke, A. H. (2001), 'Business-to-business market segmentation', *Industrial Marketing Management*, 30(6): 473–486.

Gaston-Breton, C. and Marti'n Marti'n, O. (2011), 'International market selection and segmentation: A two-stage model', *International Marketing Review*, 28(3): 267–290.

Goller, S., Hogg, A. and Kalafatis, S. (2002), 'A new research agenda for business segmentation', *European Journal of Marketing*, 36(1/2): 252–271.

Hassan, S., Craft, S. and Kortam, W. (2003), 'Understanding the new bases for global market segmentation', *Journal of Consumer Marketing*, 20(5): 446–462.

Hooley, G., Saunders, J., Piercy, N. F. and Nicoulaud, B. (2004), *Marketing Strategy and Competitive Positioning*, Harlow, UK: Pearson/FT.

Hutt, M. D. and Speh, T. W. (2006), *Business Marketing Management: A Strategic View of Industrial and Organisational Markets*, Cincinnati, OH: South Western.

Keller, K. L. (2007), *Building, Measuring and Managing Brand Equity*, Englewood Cliffs, NJ: Pearson.

McDonald, M. and Dunbar, I. (2004), *Market Segmentation*, London: Palgrave Macmillan.

Palmer, R. A. and Millier, P. (2004), 'Segmentation: Identification, intuition, and implementation', *Industrial Marketing Management*, 33(8): 779–785.

Quinn, L., Hines, T. and Bennison, D. (2007), 'Making sense of market segmentation: A fashion retailing case', *European Journal of Marketing*, 41(5/6): 439–465.

Ries, A. and Trout, J. (2001), *Positioning: The Battle for Your Mind*, New York: McGraw-Hill.

Sausen, K., Tomczak, T. and Herrmann, A. (2005), 'Development of a taxonomy of strategic market segmentation: A framework for bridging the implementation gap between normative segmentation and business practice', *Journal of Strategic Marketing*, 13(3): 151–173.

Simkin, L. (2008), 'Achieving market segmentation from B2B sectorisation', *Journal of Business & Industrial Marketing*, 23(7): 464–474.

Simkin, L. and Dibb, S. (2011), 'Segmenting the energy market: Problems and successes', *Marketing Intelligence & Planning*, 29(6): 580–592.

Sismeiro, C., Mizik, N. and Bucklin, R. E. (2012), 'Modelling coexisting business scenarios with time-series panel data: A dynamics-based segmentation approach', *International Journal of Research in Marketing*, 29(2): 134–147.

Stone, M. and Foss, B. (2001), *Successful Customer Relationship Marketing: New Thinking, New Strategies, New Tools for Getting Closer to Your Customers*, London: Kogan Page.

Tonks, D. G. (2009), 'Validity and the design of market segments', *Journal of Marketing Management*, 25(3/4): 341–356.

Walsh, G., Hassan, L. M., Shiu, E., Andrews, J. C., Hastings, G. (2010), 'Segmentation in social marketing: Insights from the European Union's multi-country antismoking campaign', *European Journal of Marketing*, 44(7/8): 1140–1164.

Webber, H. (1998), *Divide and Conquer: Target your Customer through Market Segmentation*, Hoboken, NJ: Wiley.

Wedel, M. and Kamakura, W. (2000), *Market Segmentation: Conceptual and Methodological Foundations*, Boston, MA: Kluwer.

Weinstein, A. (2004), *Handbook of Market Segmentation: Strategic Targeting for Business and Technology Firms*, New York: The Haworth Press.

Weinstein, A. (2006), 'A strategic framework for defining and segmenting markets', *Journal of Strategic Marketing*, 14(2): 115–127.

Part III
Managing marketing in practice

12 The marketing mix[1]

Michael J. Baker

Introduction

In common with many other professions, the practice of marketing is often made complex and difficult due to the sheer diversity of the problems with which it is confronted. To a large degree this diversity is due to the fact that the principal actors in exchange processes are people, or organisations comprised of people, and so exhibit the dynamic and interactive behaviour associated with human beings. If human beings rarely became unwell, and then only from a small range of causes, we would have need for far fewer doctors than at present. Similarly, if disagreements between parties leading to litigation were limited in their origins, then we would have a need for far fewer lawyers. However, like marketing, these two professions have to deal with an enormous variety of factors, which might give rise to a need for medical care or litigation. Accordingly, professions have a need for diagnostic frameworks, which help them to isolate the most likely causes of the problem to be solved, so that these may become the focus of detailed examination.

In marketing, one such conceptual framework that is particularly useful in helping practitioners structure their thinking about marketing problems is that of the so-called 'marketing mix'. To devise a product or service, which will be seen as different in the eyes of prospective customers, to the point where they will prefer it to all competing substitutes, is obviously the ultimate objective of the marketer. In devising this unique selling proposition or bundle of benefits, the marketer has four basic ingredients that they can combine in an almost infinite number of ways to achieve different end results. These four basic ingredients are frequently referred to as the 4 'Ps' of marketing, following the classification first proposed by McCarthy (1978). These 4 'Ps' – product, price, place (or distribution) and promotion are the subject of separate treatment in later chapters. At this juncture our primary aim is to review how they may be combined to create a distinctive marketing mix. According to John O'Shaughnessy (1984):

> Product, price, promotion and distribution are factors that, within limits, are capable of being influenced or controlled. Marketing strategy can be viewed as reflecting a marketing mix of these four elements. Every market has its own logic whereby excellence on one element of the mix, whether product, price, promotion or distribution, is often a necessary condition for success . . . Knowing the key factor in the marketing mix is crucial in drawing up a marketing strategy since it means knowing what to emphasise.
>
> (O'Shaughnessy 1984: 54)

It is this emphasis upon 'controllable factors' that has endeared the mix concept to generations of practitioners so that it remains one of the best-known conceptual frameworks that is widely referred to and used in real-world marketing strategy and planning. However, as we shall see, the concept is not without its critics as innovations in marketing practice and, particularly, the emergence of the internet and social media, have introduced changes that are not under the direct control of the marketer (Dominici 2009).

The evolution of the marketing mix concept

Although marketers have always experimented with different combinations of product, price, place and promotion, it is only comparatively recently that serious attempts have been made to see if any particular combinations give better or worse results than others. Clearly, if this is the case, then such combinations are to be preferred or avoided as the case may be. One of the earliest studies of this kind was undertaken by the Harvard Business School Bureau of Business Research in 1929, which sought to determine if there were any common relationships to be found in the expenses on various marketing functions of a sample of food manufacturing companies.

Almost two decades later James Culliton (1948) set out to discover whether a bigger sample and more careful classification of companies would yield a different result from that found in the earlier study (in the 1929 study, no common figures had been found, which could be used for predictive purposes). Despite Culliton's more rigorous and larger-scale investigation, the results were the same, and it was this which led Culliton (1948) to describe the business executive as a 'decider', 'an artist', a 'mixer of ingredients who sometimes follows a recipe to the ingredients immediately available, and sometimes experiments with or invents ingredients no-one else has tried' (Culliton 1948). This description of a marketing executive as a mixer of ingredients appealed greatly to his fellow Harvard Professor, Neil Borden, who began to use the term 'marketing mix' to describe the results. Borden wrote that:

> Culliton's description . . . appealed to me as an apt and easily understandable phrase, far better than my previous references to the marketing man as an empiricist seeking in any situation, to devise a profitable 'pattern' or 'formula' of marketing operations from among the many procedures and policies that were open to him. If he was a 'mixer of ingredients', what he designed was a 'marketing mix'!
>
> (Borden 1964)

Given this idea of a marketing mix it follows that the next step is to identify and classify the various ingredients available to the marketer and the uses to which they may be put. In his original conceptualisation, Borden suggested the following list of market forces bearing upon the marketing mix:

1   consumer attitudes and habits:

    a   motivation of users;
    b   buying habits and attitudes;
    c   important trends bearing on living habits and attitudes.

2   trade attitudes and methods:

    a   motivation of trade;
    b   trade structure;
    c   trade practices and attitudes;
    d   trends in trade procedures, methods, attitudes.

3   competition:

  a   is competition on a price or non-price basis;
  b   what are the choices afforded consumers:

      o   in product;
      o   in price;
      o   in service.

  c   what is the relationship of supply to demand;
  d   what is your position in the market – size and strength relative to competitors; number of firms; degree of concentration;
  e   what indirect competition vs direct competition;
  f   competitors' plans – what new developments in products, pricing, or selling plans are impending;
  g   what moves will competition be likely to make to actions taken by your firm.

4   governmental controls:

  a   over product;
  b   over pricing;
  c   over competitive practices;
  d   over advertising and promotion.

Identification and listing of the ingredients of the marketing mix ranges from the very simple to the very complex. At one end of the spectrum there is Eugene McCarthy's (1978) 4 Ps of product, price, place and promotion while at the other there is the much longer listing of Borden (1975) himself, which is reproduced as Table 12.1.

At first glance Borden's list appears to be very comprehensive – much more so than the simple 4 Ps proposed by McCarthy. However, nearly all of the elements are the subject of separate chapters in this book containing much more detail, added to which there are several other topics that need to be taken into account and are described in additional chapters.

Nonetheless McCarthy's 4 Ps still enjoy considerable currency, although most observers would agree that at the very least they need to be extended to include consideration of people, which is the most basic, but probably most complex of the mix ingredients, as well as acknowledging the importance of research in determining both the nature of the ingredients to be used and the most appropriate recipe.

As Toni Hilton comments in her chapter (Chapter 19 in this book) on 'Services marketing', 'Booms and Bitner (1981) extended the "four Ps" (McCarthy 1960) of the marketing mix to include *people*, *process* and *physical evidence* to take account of four characteristics that differentiate services from products: *intangibility*, *inseparability*, *heterogeneity* and *perishability*'. In her chapter, she discusses the managerial implications of these characteristics as well as providing an alternative perspective that confirms my own view that:

> The extended marketing mix remains a useful way to analyse and manage the provision of services. People and the physical evidence comprise the *tangible* or *visible* elements of the service. Although less visible, the process is crucial to the service experience.

While the basic ingredients of the mix are valid in most situations there are environments in which they must be adapted to the specific needs of the marketplace. For a cosmetic manufacturer, packaging

Table 12.1 Elements of the marketing mix

1 Merchandising – product planning:

    (a) determination of product (or service to be sold – qualities, design, etc.) to whom, when, where and in what quantities;

    (b) determination of new product programme – research and development, merger;

    (c) determination of marketing research programme.

2 Pricing:

    (a) determination of level of prices;

    (b) determination of psychological aspects of price, e.g. odd or even;

    (c) determination of pricing policy; e.g. one price or varying price, use of price maintenance, etc;

    (d) determination of margins: freedom in setting.

3 Branding:

    (a) determination of brand policy, e.g. individual brand or family brand.

4 Channels of distribution:

    (a) determination of channels to use, direct sale to user, direct sale to retailers or users' sources of purchase, e.g. supply houses; sale through wholesalers

    (b) determination of degree of selectivity among dealers

    (c) devising of programmes to secure channel cooperation

5 Personal selling:

    (a) Determination of burden to be placed on personal selling and methods to be employed

        (1) For manufacturer's organisation

        (2) For wholesalers

        (3) For retailers

    (b) Organisation, selection, training and guidance of sales force at various levels of distribution

6 Advertising:

    (a) Determination of appropriate burden to be placed on advertising

    (b) Determination of copy policy

    (c) Determination of mix of advertising:
    to trade to consumers

    (d) Determination of media

7 Promotions:

    (a) Determination of burden to place on special selling plans or devices and formulation of promotions:

        (1) to trade

        (2) to consumers

8 Packaging:

    (a) Determination of importance of packaging and formulation of packages

9 Display:

    (a) Determination of importance and devising of procedures

10 Servicing:

    (a) Determination of importance of service and devising of procedures to meet consumer needs and desires

11 Physical handling – warehousing – transportation – stock policy

12 Fact-finding and analysis – marketing research

and advertising may be so important that they deserve classification as separate marketing activities, while storage may be so unimportant as not to deserve separate classification. Each marketer needs to decide their own classification of marketing activities, emphasising those important to the operation's success and possibly de-emphasising others.

Simon Majaro (1982) identified three factors, which help the marketer to make a decision as to whether a specific ingredient deserves a separate existence in the mix.

1   The level of expenditure spent on a given ingredient – every ingredient involving a significant expenditure would normally earn its separate identity. Basically, it is a question of resources allocated to each ingredient which matter. Thus, a firm that spends an insignificant amount of money on packaging would not bother to give this ingredient a separate existence, but will attach it to the product or the 'promotional' mix, whichever appears more appropriate in the circumstances.

2   The perceived level of elasticity and consumer responsiveness – where the marketer knows that a change in the level of expenditure (up or down) of a given ingredient will affect results, it must be treated as a separate tool in the mix. For example, if the marketer is able to alter the supply–demand relationship through price changes, this element deserves a separate place in the mix. On the other hand, for a firm enjoying a monopoly or where the price is fixed by government edict, the price will be less important or may be removed from the mix.

3   Allocation of the responsibilities – a well-defined and well-structured marketing mix reflects a clear-cut allocation of responsibilities. Thus, where the firm requires the services of a specialist to help develop or design new packaging, as in the case of cosmetics firms, it is perfectly proper to say that 'packaging' is an important and integral part of the mix and deserves a separate existence therein.

So while the ingredients of the mix described above are valid in most situations, the mix elements and their relative importance may differ from industry to industry, from company to company and quite often during the life of the product itself. Furthermore, the marketing mix must take full cognisance of the major environmental dimensions that prevail in the marketplace. This latter point adds a dynamic flavour to the marketing mix in so far as it has to be changed from time to time in response to new factors in the marketing scene.

Generally, in striving to maintain or improve their profit position, the marketer is an empiricist trying out changes in the several procedures and policies which make up what we call a 'marketing programme'. Success depends to a large extent on understanding the forces of the market, which bear upon any product or product line and skill in devising a 'mix' of marketing methods that conforms and adjusts to these forces in ways that produce a satisfactory net profit figure.

A study of the marketing programmes or mixes that have been evolved under this empirical approach shows a tremendous variation in their patterns. This variation is reflected in the operating statements of manufacturers, e.g. profit and loss account and balance sheets. As Culliton (1948) found among such statements, there is little uniformity even among manufacturers in the same industry. There are no common figures of expense that have much meaning as standards, as holds true for many retail and wholesale trades, where the methods of operation tend to greater uniformity. Instead, the ratios of sales devoted to the various functions of marketing are widely diverse. This diversity in methods and in expenditures by categories even within an industry is accounted for largely by the fact that products, the volume of sales, the market covered and the other facts that govern operations of each company tend to be unique and not conducive to uniformity with the operational methods of other companies, although there are tendencies towards uniformity among companies whose product lines are subject to the same market forces. As noted, in any category of expenses the percentage of sales spent may cover wide ranges. For instance, the advertising expense figure, which reflects the burden placed upon advertising in the marketing programme, will be found to vary among manufacturers from almost 0 per cent to over 50 per cent. Similarly, the percentages of sales devoted to personal selling will cover a wide range among different businesses.

To illustrate, proprietary medicine manufacturers often have no salesforce at all. Advertising is used to sell the product to consumers, and advertising literally 'pulls' the product through the channels of distribution. At the retail level little or no effort is made to secure selling support. In contrast, manufacturers of other types of products, e.g. heavy machinery, often put relatively little of the burden of marketing upon advertising and rely primarily on the 'push' of personal selling by either their own salesforce or the salesforce of distributors.

The part played in the marketing programme by the distributive trades varies markedly. Sometimes the trade plays a considerable part in the sales programme and the close support and co-operation of the trade is sought, as has generally been true with heavy appliances. In other instances the part played by the trade is not highly important and little effort is devoted to securing trade support, as is true among the proprietary medicine companies cited above. Likewise, the employment of sales promotional devices and of point of purchase effort in marketing programmes varies widely.

In the matter of pricing and pricing policy, wide variation is likely to be found. In some instances competition is carried out largely on price and margins are narrow. In other instances prices are set with wide margins and competition is carried out on non-price bases, such as product quality, services or advertising. In some instances resale prices are maintained; in others they are not. Similarly, it is possible to go on citing wide differences in the practices of branding, packaging and servicing that have been evolved.

In short, the elements of marketing programmes can be combined in many ways. Or, stated another way, the 'marketing mixes' for different types of products vary widely, and, even for the same class of product, competing companies may employ different mixes. In the course of time a company may change its marketing mix for a product, for in a dynamic world the marketer must adjust to the changing forces of the market. The goal of business in any instance is to find a mix that will prove profitable. To attain this end, the various elements have to be combined in a logically integrated programme to conform to market forces bearing on the individual product. To summarise, the concept of the marketing mix is a schematic plan to guide analysis of marketing problems through utilisation of:

- a list of the important forces emanating from the market, which bear upon the marketing operations of an enterprise;
- a list of the elements (procedures and policies) of marketing programmes.

Thus, the marketing mix refers to the apportionment of effort, the combination, the designing and the integration of the elements of marketing into a programme or 'mix' which, on the basis of an appraisal of the market forces, will best achieve the objectives of an enterprise at a given time.

Management of the marketing mix

In earlier editions of *The Marketing Book*, the late Professor Peter Doyle provided a clear exposition of the key issues involved in managing the marketing mix. As he pointed out:

There are two key decisions which are central to marketing management: the selection of target markets which determine where the firm will compete and the design of the marketing mix (product, price, promotion, and distribution method) which will determine its success in these markets.

Until now the emphasis has been upon defining the context within which exchange or marketing occurs; of the forces – economic, behavioural, technological, political and legal – which shape and influence the exchange process; and of procedures for analysing and interpreting all these factors as a basis for developing a coherent and viable strategy. But, as we have seen, strategy identifies future objectives to which the firm aspires and which are likely to be modified due to changing circumstances. Thus strategy charts a direction to be followed to achieve a destination that will probably be changed as we approach it. However, to ensure that we remain on course we will set a series of sub-objectives, which represent points along the way from where we are to where we want to be. Given the convention of reporting financial performance on an annual basis, it has also become conventional to set performance targets on an annual basis and develop short-term plans for their achievement. In turn, short-term (one-year plans) are usually a sub-set of a medium-term (three to five year) plan.

Short-term plans and, to a lesser extent, medium-term plans, are clearly the domain of operational management. It is this operational management, which is responsible for translating the strategy into plans and for devising marketing mixes for their realisation. Where a firm is practising undifferentiated or concentrated marketing, it will have only a single marketing mix, but where it is practising differentiated marketing, it will have several. Irrespective of whether it has one or several mixes the objective is the same – to develop and maintain a sustainable differential advantage (SDA). In order to do this it is necessary to undertake the kinds of analysis described in earlier chapters.

Simply analysing problems is not enough – as we have observed on several occasions it is a necessary, but not sufficient, condition for success. Marshalling evidence is a precondition for analysis, but it does not follow that all decision-makers will draw the same conclusion from a given data set (selective perception strikes again!). What matters is the quality of the plan devised by the manager based upon his analysis and the quality of the implementation. Central to all this is the understanding and deployment of the mix elements. Doyle (1999) provides a useful diagram to illustrate the nature of the matching process, which ensures that the marketing mix is consistent with the needs of customers in the target market.

Peter Doyle's discussion of the marketing mix in the fifth edition of *The Marketing Book* (Doyle 2002) was essentially a synopsis of the thinking developed in detail in his best-selling text book *Value-based Marketing: Marketing Strategies for Corporate Growth* (Doyle 2000). Following his death a new, second edition was published in 2008 with the factual content updated by a panel of his friends and remains essential reading for anyone concerned with strategic marketing planning. Similarly, Doyle's chapter in the fifth edition of this book (Doyle 2002) is well worth revisiting but, for our purposes here citation of his **Summary** will have to suffice:

1   The marketing mix is at the core of marketing. The marketing mix consists of the key decisions where marketing managers should exhibit their greatest expertise and professionalism. It has become common to summarize the elements of the marketing mix in the four Ps – product, price, promotion and place. Some writers have suggested adding a fifth P – people – to highlight the service element in marketing.

2   However, there is a crucial weakness in the way marketing authors and managers them-selves have approached the marketing mix. It has never been clear in marketing theory or practice what the objective is in determining the mix. Without a clear goal it is impossible to design an optimal marketing mix.

3   Marketing professionals have tended to assume the objective was to design a mix that meets purely marketing criteria – notably customer satisfaction or market share. But setting prices, communications budgets or designing products that maximize sales or customer satisfaction is a sure route to financial disaster, because it invariably results in negative cash flow and a failure to cover the cost of capital. Consumers will always perceive value in lower prices, more features and high customer support investments.

4   Equally fallacious is the view of many accountants that the marketing mix should be used to increase profits. This short-termism will usually produce immediate profit improve-ments but the cost, as many firms have discovered, is a long-term erosion in their market shares and the value investors place on the company.

5   In the private sector, the right marketing mix is the one that maximizes shareholder value. Shareholder value as an objective avoids the short-termism of the accountancy focus because it leads managers to take into account all future cash flows. Long-term performance is almost always a much more important determinant of shareholder value than the profits earned in the next few years. It also avoids the fallacy of the market-led approach by emphasizing that the purpose of the firm is not market share but to create long-term financial value.

6   While applying the shareholder value approach has, of course, many problems associated with forecasting future sales and cash flows (e.g. Day and Fahey, 1988, pp. [sic] 55–56; Doyle, 2000, pp. [sic] 64–66), it does provide a clear, rational direction for research and decision making.

7   Finally, shareholder value provides the vehicle for marketing professionals to have an increasing impact in the boardroom. In the past, senior managers have often discounted the recommendations of their marketing teams because the marketing mix and strategies for investment have lacked a rational goal. Marketers have not had the framework for translating marketing strategies into what counts for today's top executives – maximizing shareholder value. Value-based marketing provides the tools for optimizing the marketing mix.

(Doyle 2002)

Today, Doyle would no doubt have modified his emphasis on the owners or 'shareholders' to include all those involved in creating added value and so referred to the wider concept of stake-holder value.

Writing in the *Journal of Business Strategy*, Wise and Sirohi (2005) address the question of the best way to identify and implement the marketing mix. In their view the emphasis on growth and spending apparent in the annual reports of many leading companies has focused attention on marketing expenditures, 'perhaps the last significant elements on the income statement without explicit links to revenues and profits'. In turn, this requires marketers to identify and use appropri-ate metrics to ensure that the optimum mix is achieved. Accordingly:

Marketing budgets should be viewed as a portfolio of investments, each of which has a differ-ent growth potential and resource requirements. Proven ROI techniques can help marketers make the best tradeoffs by identifying the right data to track, the best metrics to use, and the right comparisons to make.

(Wise and Sirohi 2005)

Implicit in this recommendation is that one has a view of what marketing activities are associated with growth and how to establish the best combination (mix) of these activities.

Some criticisms of the marketing mix

While the marketing mix has become one of the best-known models in marketing, described in detail in every basic marketing text and widely used in practice, the concept is not without its critics. Writing in the *Companion Encyclopedia of Marketing*, Van Waterschoot (1999) identified a number of deficiencies in the concept, which may be summarised as:

1   It focuses on what marketers do *to* customers rather than *for* them.
2   It is externally directed and ignores the internal market.
3   It says nothing about interactions between the mix variables.
4   It takes a mechanistic view about markets.
5   It assumes a transactional exchange rather than a relationship.

In a nutshell, these five criticisms may all be seen to be dimensions of the same failing – a neglect of the people factor. It would seem appropriate, therefore, that we should extend and modify the 4 Ps model of marketing to include a fifth P – people. Putting people into marketing is essential for many reasons. Within the limits of a short chapter of this kind we may only consider three of the more important ones.

First, marketing is a professional practice – it is something which people do. While it is perfectly feasible to theorise about marketing in the abstract, like many other academic disciplines, the main reason people study the subject is to provide a basis for success, for practice. Like medicine, engineering and architecture, marketing is what we have described as a synthetic discipline. Not 'synthetic' in the pejorative sense of 'a poor substitute for the real thing', but synthetic in the sense defined by the Concise Oxford Dictionary as, 'the process or result of building up separate elements, especially ideas, into a connected whole, especially into a theory or system'. Thus, in marketing, we incorporate and integrate the best insight and ideas from core disciplines such as economics, psychology and sociology and synthesise them into implementable practices. Market segmentation, targeting and positioning are examples of how marketing reconciles the economist's assumptions of homogeneous demand with the psychologist's perception of every individual differing from every other in some degree, and provides a practical solution of creating choice at an affordable cost. Marketing is something done for people by people.

A second reason for putting people into the marketing mix is that increasingly it is the people who provide the basis of differentiation between competing suppliers on which buyers make their choices. Traditionally, differentiation between competing suppliers has tended to rest upon the creation of objective differences through technological innovation. Nowadays, such objective differences are rapidly eroded by competition (it is relatively easy to benchmark your competitors' product to see how they have improved it) or else overtaken by the ever quickening pace of new product development. It is this trend, which has led to the recognition that long-term competitive success depends on building relationships rather than seeing marketing management as responsible for ensuring that the seller gets the better of the buyer in a series of independent transactions, each of which must be profitable to the seller. In turn, this recognition has highlighted the importance of internal marketing and the fact that in an increasingly knowledge-based society, people (human capital) are the organisation's greatest asset.

Finally, a third reason for putting people into the marketing mix is because it is not only people who plan and devise marketing mixes: it is people who implement such plans. Further, a great deal of research into competitiveness in recent years has confirmed beyond doubt that in the final analysis it is the quality of implementation that distinguishes between success and failure. In *Marketing and Competitive Success* (Baker and Hart 1989), a rigorous survey into a matched sample of successful and less successful firms in six industries indicated that very few of the so-called critical success factors were present in successful firms and absent from unsuccessful firms, i.e. you could not infer they were related to improved performance. On reflection, the reasons are not hard to find.

To begin with, nobody wants to fail. Accordingly, management staff in less successful organisations are just as ambitious as their opposite members in successful firms in studying for professional qualifications, reading management books, attending seminars and seeking advice from experts. In other words **they know what to do**. It follows that if they are less successful, it is due to the quality of execution and, possibly, a little luck. The view conforms with Napoleon's expressed wish for lucky generals. Other things being equal, we must assume that the military commanders who become generals must both understand the principles of warfare and have demonstrated skill in their practice, or they would not have been promoted to command an army. In warfare, however, we have the extreme form of competition as a zero-sum game with a winner and a loser, so what determines the outcome? People! In the words of the song, 'It ain't what you do, it's the way that you do it'.

But, even with the addition of 'people', many still believe the mix concept has outlived its usefulness. A well-documented and certainly most readable criticism is to be found in an article by Lisa O'Malley and Maurice Patterson (1998), which appeared in the *Journal of Marketing Management*. Taking the view that theory development is an evolutionary process and one of displacement where new ideas supersede the old, O'Malley and Patterson utilise a road metaphor in the guise of a road movie to trace the origins and development of the marketing mix concept to support their view that it should now be left behind as we move towards more attractive destinations.

In tracing the evolution of marketing theory and practice it is pointed out that the 'mid-life crisis of marketing' identified by McKinsey & Company (Brady and Davis 1993) is not the first time that the discipline has reached a crossroads where it has had to determine the direction it has to take in the future. As noted by O'Malley and Patterson (1998), 'The philosophical position of early marketing scholars was heavily influenced by the historical approach to economics and was more concerned with pressing social issues than business practice'. The catalyst for shifting emphasis to the managerial implications of marketing 'can no doubt be attributed to an expansion of large scale enterprise, an increase in the number of affluent buyers (Benton, 1987) and widespread employment of marketing techniques in industrialised societies (Fullerton, 1988)'.

As we saw in Chapter 1, the marketing management approach evolved during the 1950s in the United States when the economic system was in danger of collapse as supply rapidly began to overtake demand. A similar imbalance had precipitated the Great Depression of the late 1920s and early 1930s and, as we have seen, an emphasis upon high pressure selling had been insufficient to overcome this imbalance. Clearly, a more sophisticated approach was called for which, in turn, resulted in a demand for marketing education and a change in focus to 'The extension, refinement and evaluation of marketing as an organisational or management technology rather than on macro level social issues, concerns, and problems (Benton 1987, p.240)'. As O'Malley and Patterson (1998) note, 'This shift in philosophical position is encapsulated in the mix management paradigm'.

Underlying criticism of the marketing mix mode, in our opinion, is the mistaken view that it was ever intended as a 'theory' of marketing rather than a currently useful generalisation (CUG) or helpful learning and teaching tool. Certainly, Borden (1964) in his original conceptualisation which, as we have seen, contains 12 variables, did not regard this as either a comprehensive or exhaustive list. It is equally certain than when McCarthy reduced the 12 mix elements to 4 – product, price, place and promotion – he, too, was more concerned with memorability than completeness.

Given that at least two generations of professional marketers have survived and indeed prospered believing in the marketing mix as a useful approach to the management of the marketing function, we should not now reject this approach on the grounds that its interpretation and implementation are flawed in terms of the philosophical intentions of the marketing concept itself. This point is highlighted by O'Malley and Patterson when they write:

> In terms of customer orientation, 'the marketing concept . . . calls for most of the effort to be spent on discovering the wants of a target audience and then creating goods and services to satisfy them (Kotler and Zaltman 1971, p5)'. However, far from being concerned with a customer's interests, the view implicit in the 4 Ps approach implies that the customer is somebody **to** whom something is done rather than somebody **for** whom something is done (Dickson and Blois, 1983). The managerial approach to marketing, therefore, concentrates on the seller, and subordinates the customer to a passive as opposed to a pivotal role (Grönroos, 1994). Rather than the function of marketing being dynamic and market oriented, it is instead a rather clinical, production oriented approach (Laylock, 1983; Grönroos, 1994).

As a result of the emphasis upon manipulation of the 4 Ps, the marketing management function became dominant resulting in the establishment of formal marketing departments. As we now know, this concentration of responsibility for marketing within a single department was a mistake as the essence of marketing was defined in Drucker's (1954) original statement that 'Concern and responsibility for marketing must permeate all areas of the enterprise'. This is certainly the view that prevails today and is reflected in the disestablishment of formal marketing departments, the growth of internal marketing and the recognition that all members of a successful business organisation need to be marketing oriented. Other failings associated with the marketing mix concept include:

1   the inherent assumption that the firm is independent of its environment (Andersson and Soderlund 1988);
2   the view that the seller is active and the buyer passive (Grönroos 1994);
3   the assumption that markets are homogeneous and amenable to the application of a standardised marketing mix;
4   the emphasis on marketing as a transaction which sees buyers and sellers as separate entities.

To accommodate these criticisms many authors have increased the number of Ps, as we have ourselves by suggesting the inclusion of people. Of course, by doing this they may just increase the complexity of the basic model and thereby reduce its memorability.

Fundamentally, however, the essential criticism of the marketing mix model by marketing scholars is that it is positivistic and prescriptive and so communicates an overly simplistic view of a complex reality. The fact that this chapter and several which have preceded it and will follow it contain discussions of alternative hypotheses and criticisms of prevailing models, should be sufficient to convince the reader that while the authors may have their own view as to how things are or ought to be, the reader is perfectly entitled to form an alternative viewpoint.

While debate on the application of the marketing mix model is to be welcomed, one should be careful not to discard it prematurely because of perceived weaknesses in it. In line with our own preferred definition of marketing as being concerned with, 'mutually satisfying exchange relationships' we must be careful not to tip the balance too much in favour of the buyer. The relationship between seller and buyer can only be mutually satisfying if both parties receive the benefit or satisfaction, which they looked for in entering into the relationship in the first place. In the case of the seller, this invariably means that income received exceeds the costs involved so that the selling organisation can survive, prosper and deliver benefits to the stakeholders who depend upon it. It follows that those responsible for the management of the selling organisation must have a clear view as to how they can manage the resources under their control to achieve this outcome. It further follows that they need to have a view on what to do when entering into relationships with customers. If we also take the view that customers know what they are doing when they enter into a relationship with a seller, then perhaps we can also assume that they are not as easily manipulated as critics of the marketing mix paradigm would have us believe. Thus, while we willingly accept that many of the conditions that prevailed when the marketing mix model was first formulated – mass marketing practised by large divisionalised, hierarchical and functional organisations – have declined in importance, marketing is still concerned with time, place and consumption utilities and these are still very much determined by product, price, place and promotion.

Although O'Malley and Patterson (1998) claim that 'The marketing mix is a myth', the reader will have to decide for themselves if this is the case (you should read the article in full before coming to any conclusions). For our part, we can only point out that since time immemorial people have believed in myths and this has and continues to have a significant impact on the way they lead their lives. Given that this book is as much about the practice of marketing as the theory which underpins it, the author's view is that the 4 Ps model is a useful simplifying device to enable marketing managers to impose some structure and direction on the tasks they must perform. It is in this belief that succeeding chapters deal with the key policies associated with the 4 Ps of product, price, place and promotion.

The debate continues

In July 2006 the *Journal of Marketing Management* contained a substantial article on the subject of the marketing mix by Efthymios Constantinides, together with a commentary on it by distinguished scholar Kristian Moller. Based on an extensive review of the literature (over 100 references) Constantinides, 'assessed the current standing of the 4Ps Marketing Mix framework as the dominant marketing management paradigm' and major criticisms of it emanating from five 'traditional' marketing areas – consumer, relationship, services, retail and industrial marketing as well as from the emerging field of electronic marketing. Based on this review the author identified a number of limitations and concluded that it is time to replace it with a more up-to-date analytical approach. In a nutshell, Moller disagrees! Clearly, both these articles should be read as they are among the more recent discussions of the topic. In the meantime, the following represents my own interpretation of the essence of their arguments.

Constantinides declares, 'the objective of the study is to present a realistic picture on the current standing of an old and ongoing debate about the merits of the 4P Marketing Mix as a present and future marketing management conceptual platform' (Constantinides 2006: 409). As limitations to his study the author acknowledges that his research is limited to the writings of academics and to the six spheres of activity identified earlier. The first limitation is mediated by the inclusion of normative prescriptions of the kind to be found in major textbooks, while the second could be easily addressed by extending the search/analysis to other sub-fields of marketing.

Since the articulation of the mix concept in 1964, Constantinides identifies several important landmarks in the evolution of marketing management theory:

- the 'broadening' of the marketing concept in the 1970s;
- the emphasis on transactions in the 1980s;
- the development of relationship marketing and TQM in the 1990s;
- the emergence of information and communication technologies (ICT) in the 2000s.

At the same period the consumer behaviour has also evolved (sic); one of the noticeable changes has been the gradual evolution from the mass consumer markets of the 60s (Wolf 1998) towards increasingly global, segmented, customised or even personalised markets of today (Kotler *et al.* 2001) where innovation, customisation, relationships building and networking have become issues of vital significance.

Taken together, these changes have led to the emergence of more-and-more specialised sub-fields of marketing, and it is proponents of these who are seen as most strident in their criticisms of the application of the 4Ps framework to their area of interest. Constantinides (2006) then proceeds to summarise major contributions to the debate originating in his six chosen sub-fields. (While some sources reviewed date back to the 1980s, the majority are post-1990.) Among the major reasons advanced for rejecting or possibly modifying the mix paradigm are the following:

1   The concept has an internal focus, i.e. it concentrates on what the firm should/needs to do. It is a production orientation rather than a customer orientation.
2   It lacks an appreciation of the need to interact with customers.
3   There is an absence of 'strategic' elements.
4   It is 'offensive' rather than collaborative in nature. This is a variant of 1 in that the focus on what the firm should do *to* the customer rather than *for* him.
5   It ignores the distinguishing features of services, especially the role of the individual delivering the service, the need for interaction (see 2), and the one-to-one nature of service marketing.
6   It neglects the importance of factors such as physical evidence, shopping experience and atmosphere, which are salient in retailing.

(These criticisms are very similar to those of Van Waterschoot cited earlier.) Despite these criticisms emanating from the 'traditional' sub-fields, it appears that in the newly emerging area of e-commerce, commentators are largely in favour of its use and application. Further, from the detail contained in the six tables (Constantinides 2006) in which the main contributions to each sub-field are documented, there seems to be a propensity for the critics recommending rejection of the 4Ps to propose its replacement with a new framework of their own that has the same intention and underlying framework – perhaps a case of a rose by another name? The challenge remains exercising control over actions intended to enhance competitiveness and profitability.

Based on their introduction and summary of *Rethinking Marketing: Developing a New Understanding of Markets* (Hakansson *et al.* 2004), Hakansson and Waluszewski (2005) then developed a paper in which they 'offer a critical analysis of existing marketing models, which mainly originate from the marketing mix (the 4Ps model), which in turn has a clear micro economic "allocation of resources" background'.

In their article the authors trace the origins of marketing mix model to Rasmussen (1955), McCarthy (1960) and Kotler (1967). Clearly, this differs somewhat from our own 'genealogy' outlined earlier and illustrates well the problems that still bedevil much of what passes for research in business and marketing. Basically this problem is an inadequate awareness of work being published in other places and, to a lesser degree, in other languages. (While English has become the main business language, there are still important contributions being made that are not published in this language.) Given that Rasmussen's book was published in 1955, it is unlikely that either McCarthy or Kotler were aware of it and so were following the Culliton/Borden conceptualisation described earlier. While the latter was presented as a simplifying framework to structure problems of resource allocation between various marketing activities to develop an effective marketing plan, the former appears to have been founded much more firmly in economic theory and it is this interpretation that Hakansson and Waluszewski (2005) analyse in their paper.

In essence, Hakansson and Waluszewski (2005) perceive that the original model is one of economic resource allocation based on the assumption 'that the relevant resources engaged in the exchange process, including the products, are homogeneous' (Hakansson and Waluszewski 2005: 111). Understandably, the 'fit' between this theoretical model and the real world experienced by marketing decision-makers is poor, and it is for this reason that many writers have recommended that the model be dropped. While acknowledging that the dynamic nature of marketing and the focus on interaction need to be factored in, Hakansson and Waluszewski (2005) consider that the 4 Ps model still has its merits. What is needed is a more explicit recognition of the heterogeneous nature of the mix elements and their interaction with each other when devising a unique marketing plan to address a unique problem in a dynamic environment.

So what does Kristian Moller have to say? To begin with, he acknowledges that since the 1990s marketing theorists have been engaged in a 'paradigm shift' from a transactional view of marketing to one founded on relationships. Nonetheless, in the process it is important that we recognise the contribution of notions like the marketing mix to the evolution of marketing theory. And, second, 'I think there is too little reflection on the theoretical foundations of the normative advice found in abundance in the textbooks'. Accordingly, while Constantinides's (2006) review is to be welcomed, it should not be allowed to pass without comment.

Moller's aim is 'to examine the Mix approach from a theoretical perspective; this involves uncovering the cognitive goals, theoretical driving forces, underlying assumptions, and the insights which the Mix offers to the marketing discipline' (Moller 2006: 439).

While acknowledging the scope of Constantinides (2006) review, Moller feels that he failed to dig down and explore its meta-theoretical underpinnings. In this sense it might be regarded as superficial (my word). Further, while examining the application of mix thinking in a number of different sub-fields is considered 'excellent' in that it explores a number of different contexts, Moller is concerned about the status of the six sub-fields (contexts) that are discussed. If these sub-fields are considered to be 'practical fields' then the analysis is acceptable. However, if Constantinides considers them to reflect sub-theories of topics like bank marketing, health care marketing, etc. then he is confusing practice with theory as the view that such sub-fields call for separate theories is outdated. In sum, 'I am afraid that Constantinides and many of the authors he cites, are misreading the Mix and consequently drawing misleading conclusions of the Mix as well' (Moller 2006: 441).

Moller's summary of the major criticisms contained in Constantinides's article are very similar to my own. His analysis and discussion of them is far more rigorous and documents clearly why most criticisms of the mix arise from an insufficient/incomplete understanding of the origins and foundations of the concept which, in turn, lead to the misleading conclusions referred to earlier.

A broadly based book of this kind is not the place to rehearse the detail of Moller's arguments and you should consult the original for these. However, the essence of Moller's comments is that one needs to consider the mix as an element in the thinking of the Managerial School of Marketing

(MSM) epitomised by Philip Kotler's (1967) seminal *Marketing Management: Analysis, Planning and Control*. In Kotler, and many others' view, the problem to be solved by the marketing manager is that of devising an optimal combination of product, place, price and promotion (as shorthand for all the tools and ingredients available) to achieve the organisation's objectives. As Moller observes:

> In sum, the deriving of an optimal marketing Mix involves solving a market segmentation problem, being able to carry out marketing positioning analysis, and finally being able to differentiate the Mix from the competitors' offers using the target customers (segment) preferences as criteria.
>
> (Moller 2006: 442)

With the current pre-occupation with relationship marketing and e-marketing, it is appropriate that one should question the applicability of theory and tools developed at an earlier time when a different emphasis prevailed. However, as a recognised authority on the subject of relationship marketing Moller's view that the MSM still provides the 'best approach and toolkit for those marketing management decision contexts where there exist a market of customers or a set of customer relationships, which can be characterised by market like exchange conditions' (Moller 2006: 445) carries considerable weight. It is certainly an opinion that I endorse and my personal views are as follows:

1   Practitioners like the 4Ps approach because, 'it does what it says on the tin'. It provides a relatively simple analytical framework that can be easily extended (remember Borden had 12 elements in his original conceptualisation) and adapted to address the specific problem under consideration.
2   Of course marketing management want to know what they can do to persuade potential customers to prefer them over the competition – that's what competition is all about.
3   It is naïve to the point of stupidity to assume that practitioners are not fully aware of the need to understand the potential customer as the starting point for creating an original solution or recipe that will appeal to them.
4   The whole point of the Mix approach is to remind the practitioner what tools are at their disposal to enable them to craft a differentiated marketing strategy. In order to do so it is self-evident that they need to gather intelligence about the macro-environment, competition and customer needs and wants. It is for this reason that discussions of the marketing mix are embedded within comprehensive treatments of the kind represented in this book.

While many criticisms of the mix have claimed that it is outdated and unsuited to the dynamics of modern markets, this is not the view taken by Carolyn Siegel (2005) in her textbook *Internet Marketing*. Indeed Module III of her book comprising four chapters is concerned with 'The internet marketing mix'. It opens with this introductory paragraph:

> The marketing mix or 4Ps of product, price, place (distribution), and promotion are known to anyone that has ever taken an introductory marketing class. Although many attempts have been made to replace or expand the Ps, they've endured as an effective method for organising the major tactical tools marketers can deploy in a competitive marketplace. Just as the 4Ps have an enduring place offline, their importance online is equally compelling. Many dot com failures can be attributed to weak or non-existent attention to the planning, implementation, and control of the marketing mix, and the essential details that mean the difference between profitability and bankruptcy.

Writing in 2009, Dominici identified what he calls 'digital business' as an evolution that required a 'greater need for differentiation of the mix'. In the abstract to his paper he comments:

> Throughout this evolutionary process, researchers have always been divided between the 'conservatives', who think the four Ps paradigm is able to adapt to the environmental changes by including new elements inside each 'P', and the 'revisionists', who affirm that the four Ps paradigms is obsolete and propose new paradigms.

Based on a literature review he seeks to clarify the implications of e-marketing and concludes that it may well give rise 'to a new widely accepted paradigm for marketing operations'.

Personally, we doubt this. In our view the evidence points to the increased awareness of sellers of the power of both the internet and social media and their efforts to exercise a degree of control over them in much the same way as they have traditionally done over the 4 Ps. To do otherwise would be to deny the relevance of the marketing management function.

Note

1 This chapter draws extensively on Baker (2006) and Baker (2014).

References

Andersson, P. and Soderlund, M. (1988), 'The network approach to marketing', *Irish Marketing Review*, 3: 63–68.

Baker, M. J. (2006), *Marketing*, seventh edition, Helensburgh, UK: Westburn Publishers Limited.

Baker, M. J. (2014), *Marketing Strategy and Management*, fifth edition, Basingstoke, UK: Palgrave.

Baker, M. J. and Hart, S. J. (1989), *Marketing and Competitive Success,* London: Philip Allan.

Booms, B. and Bitner, M. (1981), 'Marketing strategies and organisation structures for service firms', in Donnelly, J. and George, W. (eds) *Marketing of Services: Special Educators' Conference Proceedings*, Chicago, IL: American Marketing Association, pp. 46–51.

Borden, N. H. (1964), 'The concept of the marketing mix', *Journal of Advertsing Research*, 4: 2–7.

Borden, N. H. (1975), 'The concept of the marketing mix', in McCarthy, E. J. *et al.* (eds) *Readings in Basic Marketing*, Homewood, IL: Irwin, pp. 72–82.

Brady, J. and Davis, I. (1993) 'Marketing's mid-life crisis', *The McKinsey Quarterly*, 2(2): 17–28.

Constantinides, E. (2006), 'The marketing mix revisited: Towards the 21st century marketing', *Journal of Marketing Management*, 22(3/4): 407–438.

Culliton, J. W. (1948), *The Management of Marketing Costs*, Boston, MA: Division of Research, Graduate School of Business Administration, Harvard University.

Day, G. and Fahey, L. (1988), 'Valuing market strategies', *Journal of Marketing*, 52(3): 45–57.

Dominici, G. (2009), 'From marketing mix to e-marketing mix: A literature overview and classification', *International Journal of Business and Management*, 4(9): 17–24.

Doyle, P. (1999), 'Managing the marketing mix', in Baker, M. J. (ed.) *The Marketing Book*, fourth edition, Oxford, UK: Butterworth Heinemann.

Doyle, P. (2000), *Value-based Marketing: Marketing Strategies for Corporate Growth and Shareholder Value*, (second edition 2008), Chichester, UK: Wiley.

Doyle, P. (2002), 'Managing the marketing mix', in Baker, M. J. (ed.) *The Marketing Book*, fifth edition, Oxford, UK: Butterworth Heinemann.

Drucker, P. (1954), *The Practice of Management*, New York: Harper & Row.

Grönroos, C. (1994), 'From marketing mix to relationship marketing: Towards a paradigm shift in marketing', *Management Decision*, 32(2): 4–20.

Hakansson, H. and Waluszewski, A. (2005), 'Developing a new understanding of markets: Reinterpreting the 4Ps', *The Journal of Business and Industrial Marketing*, 20(2/3): 110–117.

Hakansson, H., Harrison, D. and Waluszewski, A. (eds) (2004), *Rethinking Marketing: Developing a New Understanding of Markets*, Chichester, UK: John Wiley.

Kotler, P. (1967), *Marketing Management*, first edition, Englewood Cliffs, NJ: Prentice-Hall.

Kotler, P., Armstrong, G., Saunders, J. and Wong, V. (2001), *Principles of Marketing*, third European edition, Harlow, UK: Prentice-Hall, Pearson Education Limited.

Majaro, S. (1982), *Marketing in Perspective*, London: George Allen & Unwin, pp. 20–21.

McCarthy E. J. (1978), *Basic Marketing: A Managerial Approach*, sixth edition, Homewood, IL: Irwin, pp. 7–8.

Moller, K. (2006), 'Comment on: "The marketing mix revisited: Towards the 21st century marketing"', *Journal of Marketing Management*, 22(3/4): 439–450.

O'Malley, L. and Patterson, M. (1998), 'Vanishing point: The mix management paradigm revisited', *Journal of Marketing Management*, 14(8): 829–852.

O'Shaughnessy, J. (1984), *Competitive Marketing: A Strategic Approach*, Winchester, MA: Allen & Unwin.

Rasmussen, A. (1955), *Pristeori eller Parameterteori*, Handelsjojskolen, Copenhagen: Forlag.

Siegel, C. F. (2005), *Internet Marketing*, second edition, Boston, MA: Houghton Mifflin Company.

Van Waterschoot, W. (1999), 'The marketing mix', in Baker, M. J. (ed.) *The IEBM Encyclopedia of Marketing*, London: International Thomson Business Press, pp. 319–330.

Wise, R. and Sirohi, N. (2005), 'Finding the best marketing mix', *The Journal of Business Strategy*, 26(6): 10–11.

Wolf, D. B. (1998), 'Developmental relationship marketing (connecting messages with mind: An empathetic marketing system)', *Journal of Consumer Marketing*, 15(5): 449–467.

13 New product development

Susan Hart

Introduction

International interdependence of markets, technological advances, competitive and consumer dynamics and increased intensity of and speed of communication require that organisations relearn and reconfigure the competences needed to review and reconstitute their products and services. Although the scope, pace and direction of change have dramatically increased since Levitt's (1960) treatise, which began: 'every declining industry was once a growth industry', the principle of competitive survival remains the same, necessitating the development of new products and services to replace current ones. Over the years, much research has reported success rates for product innovation as between 35 per cent and 75 per cent, with the very recent study reporting a more consistent average of 40 per cent (Castellion and Markham 2013). Although lower than some of the commonly cited failure rate figures of 80 per cent+, there is ample impetus to find ways to improve the success rate in new product development, given for example the fact that it takes $1billion to develop and launch a new car model from scratch (Talay *et al.* 2014).

In this chapter the activities, their sequence and organisation required to develop new products are discussed in the light of an extensive body of research into what distinguishes successful from unsuccessful new products. An enduring feature of this body of research is that although new conceptualisations of innovation processes have come (and some have gone), the centrality of process to new product success was confirmed in a meta-analytic study by Evanschitzky *et al.* (2012). The chapter starts by introducing the new product development (NPD) process model before going on to a general discussion of the usefulness of models in the NPD context, outlining the key practical considerations for their implementation. This leads to a discussion of processes that take place across firm boundaries, before a final consideration of the implications for organisational structures for NPD.

The process of developing new products

When we think of the products and services that are firmly embedded in our everyday business or personal lives, many seem to be such good ideas that their successes appear as inevitabilities. Take mobile music gadgets, from the Walkman to the MP3 and 4. Or music systems such as iTunes and Spotify. Might they have failed? What is the basic idea? Portable, personal audio entertainment. How else might the idea have been made real? And might this realisation have taken place less successfully than the products we now find so familiar and convenient? Alternative forms for personal audio entertainment include a bulkier headset, which contains the tape-playing mechanism and earphones; a small hand held player, complete with carrying handle, attached to earphones via a cord; a 'backpack' style player with earphones, player device attached to spectacles, sunglasses or forms of head gear. All of these ideas would have delivered to the idea of 'portable, personal audio entertainment', but could they have enjoyed the same success as the Walkman, Discman, Flashdrives, iPod, Spotify, to name but a few?

A second 'good idea' is the lightweight, low-pollution, low-cost, easily-parked town car. Now imagine one realisation of the idea: three-wheeled, battery-run (with 80km worth of charge only) and, for the British weather, an *optional* roof. This realisation is, of course, the widely-quoted failure, the C5. Yet the basic *idea* remains a good one. It is, however, important to work out how to translate ideas into realities that will work, especially when one considers the sums of money involved in the development of new products. (non seq The US car industry alone spends between $16 billion and $18 billion *annually* to develop and launch a new model (Talay *et al.* 2014).) More recent manifestations of such an idea have indeed been more successful, for example, Smart car, which enjoys sales in 36 countries – a total of 770,256 units sold between the launch in 1997 and 2006. Similarly, Renault's Twizy, another electric small, single seater car, has sold over 12,000 units since its launch in 2012.

Examples such as these serve to remind us that good ideas do not *automatically* translate into workable, appealing products. The idea has to be given a physical reality (in the case of products) or a deliverable reality (in the case of services), which performs the function of the idea and which potential customers find an attractive alternative to what is currently available to them and for which they are prepared to pay the asking price. This task requires NPD to be managed actively, working though a set of activities, which ensure that the eventual product is makeable, affordable, reliable and attractive to customers.

The activities carried out during the process of developing new products are well summarised in various NPD models. These are templates or maps, which can be used to describe and guide those activities required to bring a new product from an idea or opportunity, through to a successful market launch. NPD models take numerous forms, including those developed by Booz Allen Hamilton (1982), Cooper (1993), and Page and Schirr (2008). The process steps are somewhat similar, and research reports that firms do carry out key stages such as idea generation, screening, concept development and testing, business analysis, product development and testing, market testing and launch (Hart *et al.* 2003; Barczak *et al.* 2009). The Booz Allen Hamilton model is shown in Figure 13.1.

This model has been reformulated and shaped over several decades, with the influential derivative from Cooper (1990), known as the Stage–Gate™ Process, shown in Figure 13.2.

Whilst the study in the UK by Hart *et al.* (2003) reported 'variable recognition' of the different stage gates in the NPD process, more recently Markham and Lee (2013) report that 49.1 per cent of the 383 firms responding to the Product Development and Management Association's (PDMA) comparative performance study (Barczak *et al.* 2009) claimed to have a formal, cross-functional process for NPD. This contrasts with previous PDMA surveys, which showed that in 1994, 69 per cent of firms reported such a process. Despite the decrease in the overall reported usage of such models, Markham and Lee (2013) observed in their study that significantly more of the

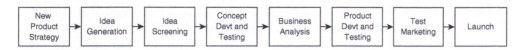

Figure 13.1 The Booz Allen Hamilton model of new product development

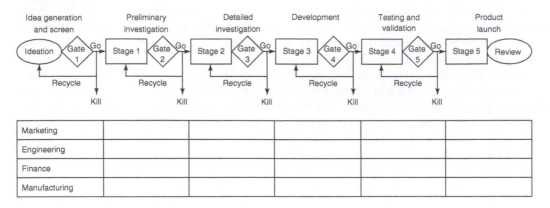

Figure 13.2 Stage-Gate™ NPD process

higher performing product developers (labelled *The Best*) used cross-functional models, whereas the remainder of the survey respondents (labelled *The Rest*) used the relay approach (department to department as each task is completed) to a greater extent. Despite the fact that the foundations of these models were laid down in the 1990s, researchers and practitioners alike tend to base their discussions and practices on a framework, which attempts to capture the really important capabilities concerned with directing and controlling the NPD process to ensure the efficient use of scarce resources. In other words, the development of capabilities often embedded within the frameworks of NPD models. These capabilities are described briefly below with respect to each of the key stages of the process models.

The stages of the NPD process

New product strategy

Sometimes called a product innovation charter or protocol, (Crawford 1984; Cooper 1993), a specific new product strategy explicitly places NPD at the heart of an organisation's priorities, and sets out how NPD will satisfy the competitive requirements of the company's overall strategy. A recent discussion paper by Dehoff and Neely (2004), placed on the Booz Allen Hamilton website (www.boozallen.com), noted that due to competing internal resources and priorities, the need to set priorities, clear barriers and instill focus were distinguishing features of good leadership that determined product innovation success. In the comparative performance assessment study (CPAS), Markham and Lee (2013) report that senior managers in the best performing firms support innovation significantly more than in the rest of the firms surveyed. This comes as no surprise given that senior management is responsible for the articulation and delivery of how an organisation will operate internally, and how it will approach the outside world. To be successful, NPD must be guided by, that is be derived from, the corporate goals of the company, and therefore there is a need to set clearly defined objectives for new product development projects. A new product strategy ensures that product innovations become a central facet of corporate strategies, that objectives are set and that the 'right' areas of business are developed. Thus, a critical success factor for NPD is the extent to which a specific strategy is set for guiding NPD efforts. The benchmarking study by Markham and Lee (2013) reported that there has been a drop in the proportion of firms overall that claim to deploy a specific new product strategy. In 2004 the benchmark study (Dehoff and

Neely 2004) had reported 74 per cent of firms as having a new product strategy, whereas in 2012 the figure had dropped to 60 per cent. Within this broad statistic, however, a significantly higher proportion (76 per cent) of the highest performing innovators still reported development of a new product strategy in comparison to only 54 per cent of the rest of the sample firms reported having new product strategies. These findings suggest that it is still important to have a new product strategy to articulate the direction and magnitude of the deployment of resources, but the drop in overall articulation of a new product strategy is still perplexing and raises the question as to whether this one study might be out of line with the general trends.

A different perspective is taken by a recent meta-analytic review (Evanschitzky *et al.* 2012) of new product success literature covering research studies spanning a 12-year period (1999–2011), which reported that amongst the most important predictors of success were new product strategy characteristics, such as market and technological synergy (familiarity with markets and technologies), dedicated human and company resources. An interesting addition to the dimensions of new product strategy was forwarded by Eling *et al.* (2013), where they reported that new product strategy should articulate the desired 'time to market' to ensure optimum profit impact of speed. Whilst it is often argued that NPD should be guided by a new product strategy, it is important that the strategy is not so prescriptive as to restrict, or stifle, the creativity necessary for NPD. Getting the balance right is not straightforward. The history of Canon's success is one classically described by Hamel and Prahalad (2005) where their strategic intent ('beat Xerox') was broken down into a series of product (and market) development tasks, including competitive study and technology licensing to gain experience, developing technology in-house and selective market entry to exploit the weakness of competition, before going on to develop completely new technological solutions in the form of disposable cartridges. This development in particular changed the rules of engagement in the photocopy market, reducing market prices by around 30 per cent, thereby making the threat from competitive imitation much less. The issue to note from this example is that with the overall target destination in mind, each of the steps towards the destination is given a purpose and a structure, thereby promoting the effective use of resources.

These examples show how the strategic focus given by top management is important for NPD success. Yet Beerens *et al.* (2004), in a report for Booz Allen Hamilton, found that many companies have difficulty in controlling their product development activities. Symptoms included ignorance of the NPD roles and responsibilities, frequent reprioritising of projects, the discovery of projects by top management previously unknown to them and a lack of robustness in the process and its management. In other words, a lack of strategic focus on product innovation. The ramifications of practices like these include working on projects that are unlikely to make money, overloading R&D people, not meeting schedules and increasing the chances of failure. Much of this resonates with a lack of top management involvement in product innovation strategy, a trend echoed in CPAS (Markham and Lee 2013), which reports a decrease in the proportion of companies with an executive responsible for NPD at the business unit from 75.6 per cent in 2004 to 62.6 per cent, with a slight decrease in the participation of corporate level NPD responsibility, from 66.8 per cent to 64.2 per cent in the same time frame. That said, the study also reports an increasing trend towards greater seniority in the mix of managers engaged in NPD strategy. Setting a clear direction for NPD not only provides guidelines for resource allocation but also sets up the key criteria against which all projects can be managed through to the market launch. The historic assault by Komatsu on Caterpillar through the 1970s and 1980s consisted of numerous strategies, amongst which features the frequent launch of new products developed to extend the product lines, future new products based on envisioning programmes and a period of matching increased product variety with efficiency gains. New product strategy is an effective 'stage', because it helps provide the standard against which a development project might be judged, particularly in the early phases. One key element of the protocol, product innovation charter or new product strategy for new product projects, relates to the extent of 'newness' to be pursued.

A majority of 'new' products and services are not entirely 'new'. The new product strategy specifies how innovative the firm intends to be in its NPD and how many new product projects should be resourced at any one time. In their study of NPD practices, Tzokas and Hart (2001) found that only 13 per cent of the new product innovations they studied were 'new to the world'. Similarly, research by Cooper *et al.* (2004) reported from the American Productivity and Quality Center study of best practices in product development, that new to the world products made up 10.2 per cent of the innovations they surveyed. So, how do companies decide how innovative they want to be and why is this important? The recent CPAS research (Markham and Lee 2013) included data on the extent to which companies' developments rated from incremental to radical, showed the less radical projects as *more* successful in terms of being delivered on time, on budget, together with meeting technical and market objectives. These findings are consistent with the relative ease of executing NPD where there is technical and market knowledge and therefore higher levels of predictability. More surprising perhaps, was the finding that incremental projects also contribute more to total profit than their more innovative counterparts do. Yet again, however, the 'best performing' innovators do gain significantly more profits from radical and more innovative products than they do for incremental improvements. These findings underline that it is not 'right' or 'wrong' to pursue an incremental or a radical strategy, but that there are decisions to be made with respect to developing a business and its financial success, which require the matching of aspiration, market demand and company capability. A related issue within the realm of NPD strategy relates to the number of new products developed simultaneously to achieve the goals of market success. According to Andrew and Sirkin (2003), many companies go down the route of generating many new product ideas, setting up new business ventures, floating venture capital funds to nurture corporate intrapreneurs in the belief that return on innovation investment will rise if only more ideas were forthcoming. This is a false assumption, leading to losses. The decisions regarding direction and resource allocation can mitigate poor rates of return in NPD. The seminal work of Booz Allen Hamilton in 1968 and in 1980 revealed the importance of this specification. In their 1968 study, an average of 58 new product ideas were required to produce one successful new product. By 1982, a new study showed this ratio had been reduced to seven to one. The reason forwarded for this change was the addition of a preliminary stage: the development of an explicit, new product strategy that identified the strategic business requirements new products should satisfy. Effective benchmarks were set up so that ideas and concepts were generated to meet strategic objectives. Of the companies studied, 77 per cent had initiated this procedure with remarkable success. Although written in the early 1980s, the lessons to be learned from the work of Booz Allen Hamilton are still relevant and, indeed, the most recent CPAS (Markham and Lee 2013) showed that 'the best' companies only began with 4.5 ideas to generate one new product success, whereas 'the rest' resourced 11.4 to obtain one success.

Whilst it is often argued that NPD should be guided by a new product strategy, it is important that the strategy is not so prescriptive as to restrict, or stifle, the creativity necessary for NPD. In addition to stating the level of newness, a new product strategy should encompass the balance between technology and marketing, the level and nature of new product differentiation and the desired levels of synergy and risk acceptance. Each of these is discussed below.

Technology and marketing

One of the most prevalent themes running throughout the contributions on setting new product strategy is the balance between technical and marketing emphasis. There is now broad acceptance that there should be a *fusion* between technology-led and market-led innovations at the strategic level, which is echoed throughout the studies reviewed by Evanschitzky *et al.* (2012). The examples of both Komatsu and Canon show how, at various times in their pursuits (efforts?) to topple the market leaders, both market and technology orientations have played their part. Similarly, problems can be found if one approach is allowed to dominate, despite competitive market and technological conditions. Classic examples include companies such as Kodak. Although dominant in analogue photography, Kodak was less able when making the change to digital camera technology. Nokia is another case in point, where there are sequential examples of reluctance to change from current to new design forms, such as the flip phone in the mid-2000s to the later delay to invest in touchscreen technology.

Product differentiation and advantage

New product literature has consistently referred to new product strategies, which emphasise the search for a differential advantage through the product itself. Once again, the most recent meta-review of literature confirms product as one of only two product-related factors (does 'product' not subsume the factors associated with it?) consistently associated with superior in-market performance (Evanschitzky *et al.* 2012). Product advantage is of course a subjective and multi-faceted term, but may be seen as comprising the following elements: technical superiority, product quality, product uniqueness and novelty, product attractiveness and high performance to cost ratio (Hultink and Hart 1998). In their attempt to rise to the competitive challenge of IT-based play products, the makers of iconic board games such as Scrabble and Monopoly, Hasbro, launched Hasbro Interactive. This new format began by converting Hasbro products to an interactive format and went on to develop video games bought on licence from TV shows, before finally investing in a new internet platform, games.com (Govindarajan and Trimble 2005).

Synergy

A further consideration for those developing new product strategies, identified in the literature, is the relationship between the NPD and existing activities, known as the synergy with existing activities. High levels of synergy are typically less risky, because a company will have more experience and expertise, although perhaps this contradicts the notion of pursuing product differentiation. With Hasbro, for example, the switch to interactive technology at first kept some synergies by sticking to the traditional games for which the company was known. Once the new interactive versions were successful, the company could then move to unfamiliar (less synergistic) games, before combining the completely new games with a new technological platform. Even then, there was a need for learning, as the corollary of less synergy is lack of knowledge. The Hasbro management team did not know whether it could turn other companies' video games into successes as it had done with its own games, neither did the team have any knowledge of how quickly video game players might switch to the internet (Govindarajan and Trimble 2005).

Risk acceptance

Finally, the creation of an internal orientation or climate, which accepts risk, is highlighted as a major role for the new product strategy. Although synergy might help avoid risk associated with lack of knowledge, the pursuit of product differentiation and advantage must entail acceptance that some projects will fail. An atmosphere that refuses to recognise this tends to stifle activity and the willingness to pursue something new. Again, the Hasbro example reveals some insights here. The original switch to an interactive platform took place back in 1997, and results for 1997/98 were strong. On the basis of early successes, the investment in the new platform was initiated, but results in both 1999 and 2000 were disappointing. Risk was accepted, but almost blindly, since according to Govindarajan and Trimble (2005), there was a reluctance to make predictions, or plan, based on the idea that both would be wrong anyway, and that first-to-market was the key to success. There was, therefore, a lack of planning and a lack of learning, which meant that little attempt was made to ditch the initiatives that were not succeeding and focus more resource on those that were doing well. A further example of the negative effects of not taking risks is the development of Nokia, where there was an admitted reluctance to take the risks necessary to keep up with, let alone lead, the new directions required to remain at the top of the mobile phone market internationally (Cheng 2014, accessed at www.CNET.com).

Once the general direction for NPD has been set, the process of developing new ideas, discussed below, can become more focused. From here on in, the NPD process is characterised by a set of 'development' activities, interpolated by a set of evaluative activities. Each of these development and evaluative activities is briefly described below.

Idea generation

Of the many 'discrete' processes in the staged view of NPD, perhaps that of generating ideas – and arguably their conceptual development – tends to attract more attention. Sometimes referred to as the beginning of the 'fuzzy front end', the identification and elaboration of ideas for new products into propositions that can be costed, tested and trialled, give cause for concern. Katz of Applied Marketing Science puts forward the view that the problem with most models is with their starting point of identifying or generating an idea (Katz 2011). Instead, he writes, there are two inter-locking sets of processes, which include discovery and definition, before going onto the phases of designing and evaluating the concept. Whilst this expanded view of the first phases of the NPD process brings a wide set of techniques, including the mining of market and consumer intelligence through ethnography and online communities, the pertinent issue is that any terminology describing these very early phases of NPD tend to assume that ideas have to be 'generated'. In many companies, this is not the case; they need, instead, to be managed. This involves identifying sources of ideas and developing means by which these sources can be activated. The aim of this stage in the process is to develop a bank of ideas that fall within the parameters set by 'new product strategy'.

Sources of new product ideas exist both within and outside the firm. Inside the company, technical departments such as R&D, design and engineering work on developing applications and technologies, which will be translated into new product ideas. Equally, commercial functions such as sales and marketing will be exposed to ideas from customers and competitors. Otherwise, many company employees may have useful ideas: service mechanics, customer relations, manu-facturing and warehouse employees who are continually exposed to 'product problems', which can be translated into new product ideas. Outside the company, competitors, customers, dis-tributors, inventors and universities are fertile repositories of information from which new product ideas come. The recent CPAS research (Markham and Lee 2013) reports that whilst only 30 per cent of firms use formal activities to generate ideas to fill gaps in the market, with a variety of informal and formal activities being used, the best companies engage significantly more in all activities aimed at understanding customer needs to identify and make early evaluations of new product ideas (Markham and Lee 2013).

Screening

Although the stages' boundaries are blurred and overlapping, as ideas emerge, the next task involves an initial assessment of the extent of demand for the emergent ideas and of the capability the company has to make the product. At this, the first of several evaluative stages, only a rough assessment can be made of an idea, which will not yet be expressed in terms of design, materials, features or price. Internal company opinion will be canvassed from R&D, sales, marketing, finance and production, to assess whether the idea has potential, is practical, would fit a market demand and could be produced by existing plant, and to estimate the payback period.

Recent research shows that these processes are mostly carried out using formal selection processes, with higher performing firms linking these formal processes to a budget to a greater extent than the rest of the sample (Markham and Lee 2013). The net result of this stage is a body of ideas, which are acceptable for further development.

Concept development and testing

Once screened, an idea is turned into a more clearly specified concept, and testing this concept begins to assess its fit with company capability and its fulfilment of customer expectations. Developing the concept from the idea requires that a decision be made on the content and form of the idea. Concept variations may be specified and then subjected to concept tests. Internally, the development team needs to know which varieties are most compatible with current production plant, which require plant acquisition and which require new supplies, and this needs to be matched externally to determine which versions are more attractive to customers. The latter involves direct customer research to identify the appeal of the product concept, or alternative concepts to the customer. Concept testing is worth spending time and effort on, collecting sufficient data to provide adequate information upon which the full business analysis will be made. Increasingly, concepts are presented via the internet. Over the past 20 years, as firms have become more global, more digital, more virtual, so too have concept development processes and techniques. Digital tools such as CAD packages, rapid prototyping technologies enabling many concept representations to be iterated and tested both within the developing organisations and with customer and other stakeholder groups, have been developed. These developments also facilitate the later stages of product development (see below).

Business analysis

At this stage, the major 'go–no go' decision will be made. The company needs to be sure that the venture is potentially worthwhile, as expenditure will increase dramatically after this stage. The analysis is based on the fullest information available to the company thus far. It encompasses:

1   a market analysis detailing potential total market, estimated market share within a specific time horizon, competing products, likely price, break-even volume, identification of early adopters and specific market segments;

2   an explicit statement of technical aspects, costs, production implications, supplier management and further R&D;

3   an explanation of how the project fits with corporate objectives.

The sources of information for this stage are both internal and external, incorporating any market or technical research carried out thus far. The output of this stage will be a development plan with a budget and initial marketing plan.

Product development and testing

Several tasks are related to this stage of development, where, in the case of physical products, prototypes will be produced to be evaluated in terms of functionality and market appeal. Until this point in the process, the product has only existed in theoretical form or mock-up. Whilst these can be effective in assessing in broad outline what the market reaction might be to the idea, look, feel and promise of a new product, only after the development can the product be used, felt, tasted and evaluated for the fulfilment of its conceptual promise. It is only when component parts are brought together in a functional form that the validity of the theoretical product can be definitively established. Second, it is the first physical step in the manufacturing chain. Whilst manufacturing considerations will have entered into previous deliberations, it is not until the prototype is developed that alterations to the specification or to manufacturing configurations can be designed and put into place. Third, the product has to be tested with potential customers to assess the overall impression of the test product. Some categories of product are more amenable to customer testing than others. Capital equipment, for example, is difficult to have assessed by potential customers in the same way as a chocolate bar can be taste-tested, or a dishwasher evaluated by an in-house trial. One evolving technique in industrial marketing, however, is called 'beta-testing', practised informally by many industrial product developers.

Test marketing

The penultimate phase in the development cycle, test marketing, consists of small-scale tests with customers. Until now, the idea, the concept and the product have been 'tested' or 'evaluated' in a somewhat artificial context. Although several of these evaluations may well have compared the new product to competitive offerings, other elements of the marketing mix have not been tested; neither has the likely marketing reaction by competitors. At this stage, the appeal of the product is tested amidst the mix of activities comprising the market launch: salesmanship, advertising, sales promotion, distributor incentives and public relations.

Test marketing is not always feasible, or desirable. Management must decide whether the costs of test marketing can be justified by the additional information that will be gathered. Further, not all products are suitable for a small-scale launch: cars, for example, have market testing completed before the launch, whilst other products, once launched on a small scale, cannot be withdrawn, as with personal insurance. Finally, the delay involved in getting a new product to market may be advantageous to the competition, who can use the opportunity to be 'first-to-market'. Competitors may also wait until a company's test market results are known and use the information to help their own launch, or can distort the test results using their own tactics. In addition, for some services, the relative cost of launching a new product is lower, because there are fewer tangible elements in which to invest, so a direct market entry (perhaps on a limited scale) is a viable alternative. Particularly in the fashion industry, a fabric, design, or cut will be launched directly into stores and, if popular, more designs using the same fabric, ideas and other features will be added.

Some of the problems faced as a result of test marketing have encouraged the development and use of computer-based market simulation models, which use basic models of consumer buying as inputs. Information on consumer awareness, trial and repeat purchases, collected via limited surveys or store data, are used to predict adoption of the new product.

The most recent CPAS research (Markham and Lee 2013) has grouped the tools and techniques used across the concept design and product development phases, reporting that most frequently used across these phases are 'voice of the customer' customer site visits and beta-testing, especially in the case of the more radical and innovative products. The better performing innovators used significantly more market research tools, including those mentioned above, as well as online communities, lead users, concept tests, online focus groups/surveys to name but a few. The most used engineering, R&D and design tools employed during these phases included critical path, PERT and GANNT and these again were used more by the higher performing innovators (Markham and Lee 2013).

Commercialisation or launch

This final stage of the initial development process is very costly. Decisions such as when to launch the product, where to launch it, how and to whom to launch it will be based on information collected throughout the development process. With regard to timing, important considerations include:

- seasonality of the product;
- whether the launch should fit any trade or commercial event;
- whether the new product is a replacement for the old one;
- whether it is advantageous to be first-to-market (much debate exists regarding this decision).

The factors upon which such decisions will be based depend upon the required lead-times for the product to reach all the distributive outlets and the relative power and influence of channel members. Whilst the possibilities of the internet make instant, international product launch possible in terms of the announcement of market entry, fulfilment still requires consideration being given to lead-times, distribution negotiations and market and supply chain familiarisation where the product is new to the market.

Launch strategy encompasses any advertising and trade promotions necessary. Space must be booked, copy and visual material prepared, both for the launch proper and for the pre-sales into the distribution pipeline. The sales force may require extra training in order to sell the new product effectively.

Attention has been given recently to those activities that are internally directed to support the new product – or particularly service – launch. For example, the research by Kuester *et al.* (2013) observed that across a sample of over 700 companies in both B2B and B2C industries, the internally directed launch activities had a direct effect on the success of the external product launch. These activities are directed at management and employees involved in organising the launch and contribute to fast market penetration of the new product by highlighting the complexities and proper incentivisation of the whole launch cycle and its intended outcome.

At this stage, the final target segments should not be a major decision for companies who have developed a product with the market in mind and who have executed the various testing stages. Attention should be more focused on identifying the likely early adopters of the product and on focusing communications on them. In industrial markets, early adopters tend to be innovators in their own markets.

Information roles in NPD

A recent study by Talke and Snelders (2013) looked at the different types of messages and their response in the adoption of new high-tech products. They found that adoption behaviour of consumers is positively affected by the inclusion of information on the personal and social consequences of using the new product, especially when such information is presented by using examples and figurative descriptions. Additionally, they found that when technical and financial information is conveyed using fact-based descriptions and specifications, there is also a positive and strong impact on adoption of the new product. This research and others in the same field underline the importance of using market research throughout the development and evaluation process to ensure that the right information will be presented in the right form to the intended market segment(s). The central concerns of the launch should be the development of a strong, unified message to promote to the market and to ensure that supply and delivery chains are stocked and equipped to fulfil demand and orders. Once accepted by the market, the company will elicit feedback to continue the improvement and redevelopment of the product.

This explanation of the NPD process has focused principally on the development phases of NPD. As noted earlier, common to all phased representations of the NPD process is the development of the new product through various stages and the evaluation of each new development – through corresponding evaluation gates.

Each evaluation set contained within a gate includes techniques that may be repeated as alternative design concepts of product configurations are developed. Such techniques are used to assess either the commercial or the technical feasibility of the developing product. The commercial techniques include beta-testing, perceptual mapping, conjoint analysis, QFD, Awareness-Trial-Repeat models, break-even analysis and sensitivity testing. In addition to these commercial evaluation techniques, technical evaluation sets include the assessment of design, production and functional feasibility and specifications. Each gate is therefore a combination of technical and commercial evaluation sets. Idea screening is the first of a series of evaluations, beginning when the collection of new product ideas is complete. This initial evaluation can never be very sophisticated. Idea screening, as defined above, is an initial assessment to weed out impractical ideas. As the development project proceeds, the data gathered on both technical and commercial possibilities become more voluminous, and because it relates less to something vague and abstract and more to something tangible and complete, the information has greater potential for increased reliability and validity (Cooper 1993). It follows that when a development project is undergoing market testing, the information revealed will be more complete than any previously revealed with respect to customer opinions, buying intentions, how the product performs when used, how it is manufactured and delivered and how it might be presented to its target market. This later evaluation can be more comprehensive than earlier phases of review, because of the quantity and quality of information that is (now) available.

Information

The role which information can play in facilitating an efficient NPD *process* and achieving *functional co-ordination* is implicit in the literature on success in NPD. The notion of reducing uncertainty as the main objective of the project development activities is reiterated throughout the literature. Project activities, 'can be considered as discrete information processing activities aimed at reducing uncertainty' (Moenaert and Souder 1990: 92). These activities include gathering and disseminating information and making decisions based upon this information, which must include evaluations of *both the market* and *technical aspects* of the development project. Indeed, it is ultimately this information, which is evaluated during the NPD process review through the 'gates'.

In order to reduce uncertainty, it is not sufficient that information be processed, it also has to be transferred between different functions (Moenaert and Souder 1990). At the same time, the efficient transfer of quality information between different functions encourages their co-ordination (Moenaert and Souder 1990). Information, therefore, is a base currency of the NPD process; evaluative information is crucial and must be efficiently disseminated to facilitate communication.

Research by Maltz (2000) has shown that the way in which information is communicated has a profound effect on its perceived quality and therefore use. Specifically, his study showed that, across functions involved in NPD, the frequency of communications needs to be above a threshold level before information is absorbed. Moreover, routine email, contributing as it does to the often unnecessary buzz and obscuring the substantive, is unlikely to be viewed as quality information. Scheduled telephone calls were shown to be of greater value, and impromptu face-to-face conversations are associated with higher levels of perceived information quality. A study by Harmancioglu *et al.* (2010) underlines the importance of collecting customer information, because of frequent changes in expectations, and a further investigation by Drechsler *et al.* (2013) concludes that the quality of marketing research and the capability of translating customer needs into technical specifications has a positive effect on the influence of marketing in NPD, which in turn improves innovation performance. Of course, over the years, there has been much commentary regarding the dampening effect on technological progress and radical innovation that accompanies an overreliance on market and customer information in the NPD process. It is something of a universal truth, however, that an overreliance on any one aspect in human endeavours is rarely commendable or effective and therefore, the point is rather absurd. Moreover, the meta-analytic study by Evanschitzky *et al.* (2012) confirms that both marketing and technological factors such as synergy and task proficiencies, as well as customer input, are recurrent associates of success in NPD.

Although it is clear that information management is central to NPD and that the models for NPD provide a framework for evaluation and control of information flows, there is considerable discussion regarding their utility, to which we now turn.

Usefulness of models

The usefulness of the process models, such as that by Booz Allen Hamilton, lies in the way in which they provide an indication of the magnitude of the project required in order to develop and launch a new product. NPD models are usually templates or maps, which can be used to describe and guide those activities required to bring a new product from an idea or opportunity, through to a successful market launch. Like all models, they attempt to capture the essence of the tasks required to complete a project. They are therefore general in their orientation and often criticised for not being applicable to specific situations. For example, it has been argued that the development of new services requires different stages and emphases when compared to product development, or that hi-tech product development does not follow the same steps as for fast-moving consumer goods, or that 'really new products' are a category of development all on their own.

Research by Ozdemir *et al.* (2008) found that developers of new services undertook each of the stages to a lesser extent than those developing new physical products. That said, it is also true that NPD models take numerous forms and have evolved in their level of prescription over the years. Early depictions of NPD models were rather blunt tools compared to those we have today. Often they described the NPD process by focusing on the departments or functions that hold responsibility for various tasks carried out. In a business-to-business, technology-based context, the ideas were often assumed to arise in the R&D department; design of the new product was carried out by the design department with the engineering function responsible for prototyping, followed by production who tended the manufacturing problems, in front of marketing, which planned and carried out the launch. These representations are rather outmoded. It is now accepted that the 'pass-the-parcel' or 'relay' approach to NPD from one department to the next is not only unnecessarily time-consuming but does nothing to foster ownership of, or strategic responsibility for, new products, and there is nothing in the way of market feedback, since marketing is presented with the product to market. These models have been largely abandoned by the literature, which examines NPD by major companies. The most recent CPAS study (Markham and Lee 2013) noted that flexibility in the way the process models are enacted was greater in the higher performing new product developers, who used overlapping stages, skipped stages and conditional decisions at various stages to a greater extent than did the rest of the sample. Moreover, although this study noted a weakening use of formalised process models by the entire sample that they studied, they still note that the best developers continue to use such models significantly more than the rest. As noted above, these processes consist of stages of activity, followed by review points, or gates, where the decision to continue (or not) with the development is made.

This approach clarifies the reality and importance of feedback loops, which although not impossible within the framework of the simpler activity-stage models, are usually not highlighted either. With the decision-stage models, each stage is viewed in terms of its potential output.

The models can provide a useful framework on which to build a complete picture of the development, particularly with regard to the potential advantage of the product viewed from the customers' perspectives. However, they do suffer from a number of criticisms.

NPD processes are idiosyncratic

The NPD process is idiosyncratic to each individual firm and to the new product project in question. Its shape and sequence depend on the type of new product being developed and its relationship with the firm's current activities (Cooper 1988; Hart and Ozdemir *et al.* 2008; Markham and Lee 2013). In addition to the need to adapt the process to individual instances, it should be stated that in real situations there is no clear beginning, middle and end to the NPD process. For example, from one idea, several product concept variants may be developed, each of which might be pursued. Also, as an idea crystallises, the developers may assess the nature of the market need more easily, and the technical and production costs become more readily identified and evaluated.

NPD processes go through many iterations

The iterative nature of the NPD process results from the fact that each stage or phase of development can produce numerous outputs, which implicate both previous development work and future development progress. Using the model provided by Booz Allen Hamilton, if a new product concept fails the concept test then there is no guidance as to what might happen next. In reality, a number of outcomes may result from a failed concept test, and these are described below and depicted in Figure 13.3.

A new idea

It is possible that although the original concept is faulty, a better one is found through the concept tests; it would then re-enter the development process at the screening stage.

A new customer

Alternatively, a new customer may be identified through the concept testing stage, since the objective of concept testing is to be alert to customer needs when formulating a new product. Any new customers would then feed into the idea generation and screening process.

Related strands of development

A further point in relation to the sequencing of product development tasks is the existence of related strands of development. These related strands of development refer to marketing, technical (design) and production tasks or decisions that occur as the process unwinds. Each strand of development gives rise to problems and opportunities within the other two. For example, if, at the product development stage, production people have a problem, which pushes production costs up, this could affect market potential. The marketing and technical assumptions need to be reworked in the light of this new information. A new design may be considered, or a new approach to the marketplace may be attempted. Whatever the nature of the final solution, it has to be based on the interplay between technical, marketing and manufacturing development issues, meaning that product development activity is iterative, not only between stages but also within stages. The crucial issue here is that the activity and decision-stage models do not adequately communicate the horizontal dimensions of the NPD process.

This shortcoming resulted first in the advancement of the idea of 'parallel processing', later 'process concurrency', which acknowledges the iterations between and within stages, categorising them along functional configurations. The idea of parallel processing is highly prescriptive. It advises that major functions should be involved from the early stages of the NPD process to its conclusion. This, it is claimed, allows problems to be detected and solved much earlier than in the classic task-by-task, function-by function models. In turn, the entire process is much speedier, which is now recognised to be an important element in new product success. It should be mentioned that a substantial amount of what has been written about the concept of parallel processing is in the engineering domain.

Although greater integration through parallel processing has been attempted by various technical disciplines, for example, manufacturing and engineering, the market perspective still appears to be 'tacked on' in the technical and engineering literature. True multi-disciplinary

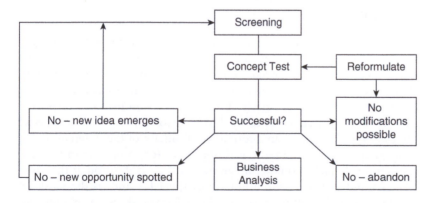

Figure 13.3 Iteration in the NPD process

integration, embracing technical and commercial functions, is seen as crucial to the outcome of new products and will be considered later in this chapter. Examination of different projects at Hewlett-Packard led Rivas and Gobeli (2005) to conclude that freely distributed information, across multi-functional teams, where there were clearly identified roles, are crucial lessons for success. Recent research by Drechsler *et al.* (2013) showed that marketing as a distinct function contributing to the NPD processes were important for driving innovation success, and that distinct marketing capabilities, together with an influential status of marketing in the NPD process forge higher levels of marketing performance. So, there remains a strong case for multi-functional involvement in NPD to integrate technical and market knowledge to bring a successful innovation to market. Whilst there is significant validity in the view that successful NPD needs multi-functional perspectives to enhance success, there is also a large body of evidence, reviewed by Gerwin and Barrowman in 2002, to suggest that process concurrency enhances NPD performance. A more recent study by Ahmad *et al.* (2013), however, did not find evidence of an association between process concurrency on NPD performance.

The inclusion of third parties in the process

Another criticism of the 'traditional' process models is that they fail to show the importance of parties external to the firm who can have a decided impact on the success of NPD. Several studies have shown the importance of involving users in the NPD process to increase success rates (Von Hippel 1978; Thomke and Von Hippel 2002; Hillebrand and Biemans 2004). Equally, there is growing interest in the need for greater supplier involvement, in order to benefit from the advantages of supplier innovation and just-in-time policies. The role of suppliers is growing in the quest for speed to market. For example, Dell shifted much of its component design work – laptop screens, optical drives – to supplier partners, Dolan (2005). Similarly, when Whirlpool decided to invest in a range of products for domestic garages, it decided to outsource much of the manufacturing (Andrew and Sirkin 2003). A recent study of the involvement of suppliers in the car industry's product innovation suggested that supplier involvement in co-design with their customers has benefits with respect to knowledge sharing and product creation, but that there are also observable risks in terms of knowledge leakage (Jean *et al.* 2014). These observations call into focus the way the NPD process is organised, to account for multi-functional inputs, to allow iteration and to involve third parties. We will now look at these issues of organisation for NPD in more detail.

Organisational design for NPD

The process of developing successful new products essentially tries to match technological competence with market relevance. Based on our discussions thus far, numerous inputs are required to achieve these twin goals. Much research has been carried out into various aspects of 'co-ordination' and 'integration' of the perspectives of different disciplines in NPD. This research is confusing, however, not only because of the sheer number of aspects of functional co-ordination which have been investigated but also because of the variety of terms used to refer to what is called 'functional co-ordination'. Pinto and Pinto (1990: 203) make an informative summary of the different terms, which have been used. Whatever the precise definition, it is important for companies to institute NPD processes and design structures, which promote integration and co-ordination at the same time as preserving the efficiencies and expertise within functional speciality and, as the work by Jean *et al.* (2014) indicates, the need to build trust in preventing knowledge leakage where there are third parties contributing to the NPD process. Classic work by Olsen *et al.* (1995) identified seven types of new product structure, or co-ordination mechanisms, which they describe in terms of four structural attributes: complexity, distribution of authority, formalisation and unit autonomy. These are shown in Table 13.1.

The new types of product structure include:

- *Bureaucratic control* – This is the most formalised and centralised and the least participative mechanism, where a high-level general manager co-ordinates activities across functions and is the arbiter of conflicts between functions. Each functional development operates with relative autonomy within the constraints imposed by hierarchical directives and, therefore most information flows vertically within each department. In such a mechanism, the different functional activities work sequentially on the developing product.
- *Individual liaisons* – Individuals within one functional department have to communicate directly with their counterparts in other departments. Therefore, they supplement the vertical communication found in bureaucracies.
- *Integrating managers* – In this co-ordination structure, an additional manager is added to the functional structure, responsible for co-ordinating the efforts of the different functional departments, but without the authority to impose decisions on those departments. Thus, such integrating managers have to rely on persuasion and on their ability to encourage group decision-making and compromise to achieve successful results.
- *Matrix structures* – Whereas all the previous mechanisms maintain the primacy of the functional departmental structure, a matrix organisation structures activities not only according to product or market focus but also by function. Thus, individuals are responsible to both a functional manager and a new product manager.

According to this research, two newer structural forms have appeared in order to improve the timeliness and the effectiveness of the product development efforts within rapidly changing environments:

- *Design teams* – Like the matrix structure, design teams are composed of a set of functional specialists who work together on a specific NPD product. The difference is that such teams tend to be more self-governing and have greater authority to choose their own internal leader(s) who have more autonomy to establish their own operating procedures and resolve internal conflicts.
- *Design centres* – These centres have many of the same characteristics as a design team. However, such a centre is a permanent addition to an organisation's structure, and members of the centre are involved in multiple development projects over time.

As one moves from bureaucratic control towards more organic and participative structures, the structural complexity of the mechanisms increases. Authority becomes more decentralised, rules and procedures less formalised and less rigidly enforced and the individual units tend to have more autonomy. Consequently, members of relatively organic structures are more likely to share information across functional boundaries and to undertake interdependent tasks concurrently rather than sequentially.

In other words, as we move from left to right, structures become less 'mechanistic' and more 'organic' (Burns and Stalker 1961). Relatively organic mechanisms such as design teams have some important potential advantages for co-ordinating product development. Indeed, the participative decision-making, consensual conflict resolution and open communication processes of such

Table 13.1 Attributes of interfunctional co-ordination mechanisms

Structural and process variables	Bureaucratic control	Types of co-ordination mechanisms				Design teams	Design centres
		Individual liaisons	Temporary task forces	Integrating managers	Matrix structures		
Structural attributes							
Complexity	Simple structures				→	Complex structures	
Distribution of Authority	Centralised				→	Decentralised	
Formalisation	High: more reliance on rules and standard procedures				→	Low: fewer rules and standard procedures	
Unit autonomy	Low				→	High	

Source: Olsen *et al.* (1995), 'Organising for effective new product development. The moderating influence of product innovativeness', *Journal of Marketing*, 59: 48–62.

a structure can help reduce barriers between individuals and functional groups. Such participative structures can also create an atmosphere where innovative ideas are proposed, criticised and refined with a minimum of financial and social risk. Besides, by facilitating the open exchange of creative ideas across multiple functions, the likelihood of producing innovative products that successfully address the market desires as well as technical and operational requirements is increased.

Finally, reduced functional barriers help ensure that unanticipated problems that appear during the development process can be tackled directly by the people concerned. This reduces the possibility that vital information may be delayed, lost or altered.

On the other hand, more participative structures also have some potential disadvantages, especially in terms of costs and temporal efficiency. Creating and supporting several development teams can lead to overabundance in personnel and facilities. The main reason for this is that employees have less relevant experience when developing innovative product concepts and then depend more heavily on other functional specialists for the expertise, information and other resources needed to achieve a creative and successful product. Furthermore, these flows of information and resources are facilitated by less formal participative co-ordination structures. Thus, there is potential for stagnation in the process if the locus of control is unclear.

Structures used by industry

Many studies of innovation and product development give evidence of the 'structures' used to organise the process. Dyer *et al.* (1999) found that US firms which are 'first-to-market' tend to use project co-ordinators most often, followed by matrix and then dedicated team structures. They also found that dedicated teams are more successful, whilst project co-ordinators and matrix structures are rated to be less successful. Research by Markham and Lee (2013) investigated the use of different structures and concluded that the best performers in NPD used the following structures to a greater degree than the rest of the sample:

- a distinct division or venture group;
- NP department;
- project management/NP committee;
- formal partnership agreement.

At the risk of over-simplification, we can classify venture groups and new product departments as existing completely outside the normal functional lines, such as marketing, R&D or engineering.

- *Venture groups* tend to be a permanent 'maverick' group, with high status and separate budgets, reporting to the MD. Their responsibilities can vary, but include opportunity identification and feasibility studies through to management of the NPD. The advantages are that, freed from the 'humdrum' of current business, creativity can be encouraged, and the development has high-level support. On the other side, they can turn into acquisition hunters, may be prone to get into unrelated areas and can be seen as a waste of time if they acquire such information from inside the company, which might occur if they became involved with the development of existing products.
- *New product departments* have the same status as functional divisions and are essentially outside the 'mainstream' of business. They are usually staffed by a combination of functions from across the business. They may be used in different ways: as idea hunters, where ideas are passed

to the 'mainstream' for development, or as developers, who manage the new product from idea through to the market launch. In the latter instance, the 'handover' of the product will take place at the launch, which may engender feelings of 'not invented here'. However, the rationale for the complete segregation of new product activity is to encourage new ideas for products not contaminated by the vested interests of those managing the business. If, however, new product activity does need to draw on experience of current technologies in current markets, then some linkage with those managing the current business is clearly beneficial.

- *Project management, new products' committees, new product teams, product managers and new product managers* are all limited – some more directly than others – to the existing line structures. Indeed Page's (1993) study showed that the line functions most involved in NPD were marketing, R&D and engineering. The various teams, committees or individuals may be given 'part-time' responsibility for NPD.

There is an inevitable tension between the need for integration and existing authority and responsibility lines. Due to this tension, many firms will locate responsibility for NPD in one function, and bring others in as and when required. This, of course, raises problems in that development work may be in conflict with the management of current business. This would be manifested in time pressures, whereby development work is squeezed by existing product management, and in stifled creativity owing to procedures already being in place for existing products. Finally, fresh business perspectives may be lacking in people who are expert in managing the current business.

Alternatively, a post of 'new products manager' may be created in marketing or technical departments. The part-time option can suffer from time pressures and conflict of roles as besets many matrix structures and, worse, NPD can become something of a secondary goal. In addition, the individual new product manager tends not to be interdisciplinary, which forces negotiation with other departments, as opposed to collaboration. As a result, there tends to be a 'pass-the-parcel' approach to the development project, which is shunted around from one department to the next. Finally, this mechanism tends to be low level with little leverage for important resource decisions, leading to an incremental approach to NPD and a new product committee. This is made up of senior managers from salient functions and has the purpose of encouraging cross-functional co-operation at the appropriate senior level. However, these mechanisms may suffer from a remote perspective, as the line managers are not really carrying out the task.

Location of new product activity inside or outside existing functions requires a trade-off. Since autonomous structures are designed to allow the unfettered development of new ideas with greater levels of advantage without much reliance on the existing business, it follows logically that this type of development is precisely what they should carry out.

Once these autonomous units become involved with incremental product development, their inevitable reliance on those within the line function may cause a conflict. In any case, perhaps the efficiency of an autonomous unit to redevelop current lines is questionable. Indeed, the research by Olsen *et al.* (1995) showed that 'organic, decentralised participative co-ordination mechanisms *are* associated with better development performance . . . *but only* when used on projects involving innovative or new to the world concepts with which the company has little experience on which to draw' (Olsen *et al.* 1995: 61).

Looking at product development at Ciba Vision, a unit of the Swiss pharmaceutical company, Ciba-Geigy (now Novartis), provides an interesting example of the issues. Ciba Vision's management realised that radical new products were required to grow the company (and even to fend off decline) at the same time as continuing to make money from its more conventional portfolio of contact lens and eye care products. The decision was taken to launch six formal development projects aiming at revolutionary change, two in manufacturing processes and four in new products. Many smaller R&D projects, aimed at on-going product improvement were cancelled to release cash for the more ambitious R&D imperatives. Traditional business sections were still able to pursue incremental innovations of their own, but the R&D budget was dedicated to the development of real breakthroughs. These, however, were freed from the structures of the old organisation and instead autonomous units for the new projects were developed, each with its own R&D, finance and marketing functions.

This section has introduced some of the complexities involved in designing mechanisms, which provide the locus for integration of multi-functional views, which are capable of innovation on the one hand, and building on the expertise accumulated with regard to technologies and markets on the other. Although the success literature points to the need for cross-functional teams, the extent to which these should be autonomous will depend, amongst other things, on the type of NPD being pursued. Much of the research literature on NPD suggests that structures may exist either within or outside what might be termed 'existing line functions', although the study also noted that both engineering and marketing may drive (i.e. lead) successful product development. This suggests that the focus of responsibility for NPD will be contingent upon the industry, technology focus and competitive factors and that there is no one, right function wherein NPD leadership should be placed. What is important, however, is that focus is identified and maintained. This also has implications for how NPD is led in organisations, an observation which has fuelled research into top management involvement and leadership of NPD. Markham and Lee (2013) noted that senior managers in the high performing innovators in their study supported innovation significantly more than the rest of the sample (75.3 per cent vs. 53.8 per cent). Felekoglu and Moultrie (2014) have reviewed the literature on top management involvement (TMI) in new product development, concluding that whilst there is great variation in findings with respect to the roles and impact of top management in NPD, there is little understanding of why top management does or does not get involved with NPD projects, neither is there much insight into the nature and quality of TMI interactions with product development projects.

There is, in addition, a final set of issues which, impact upon the management of product and service innovation projects, namely, the extent to which this now takes place in networks that cross firms' traditional boundaries. This then calls into account skills for the management of relationships across firm boundaries, including capabilities such as alliancing, building trust, sharing resources and outcomes (Story *et al.* 2011). These issues are briefly considered below.

Managing networks for NPD

Research has highlighted the importance of 'inter-organisational collaboration', 'innovation networks' (e.g. Gnyawali and Madhavan 2001; Pyka 2002; Powell *et al.* 2005). Chesborough (2003) has long noted that within-firm competences are no longer sufficient for sustained innovative success through his examination of open innovation. Indeed, the successes of companies such as Wal-Mart and Microsoft have also been attributed to their system of networks (Iansiti and Levien 2004). Due to the emphasis on speed in the NPD process, together with the fact that it is a resource-hungry activity, firms will have to be engaged in learning races, requiring the capacity to work with specialised companies in their networks, so that all participants become better and faster (Powell 1998; Brown and Hagel 2005). In addition, due to the many different technologies involved in NPD, it will need networks to leverage the functional integration required for success. (Hakansson *et al.* 1999; Owen-Smith and Powell 2004).

Powell (1998) argues that in order to reduce the inherent uncertainties associated with new products or markets, inter-organisational learning in firm's networks plays a crucial role in creating a firm's competitive advantages. Eisenhardt and Martin (2000) define 'dynamic capability' as 'the firm's processes that use resources to integrate, reconfigure, gain and release resources – to match and even create market change . . . by which firms achieve new resource configurations' (Eisenhardt and Martin 2000: 1107). Dynamic capabilities consist of processes such as alliancing, i.e. product development by which managers combine varied skills and functional backgrounds through inter-firm collaboration. Moreover, 'dynamic capabilities', by achieving new resource configurations, turn the inter-organisational relationships in NPD networks into another important topic: 'the changing dynamics of competition and cooperation' (Wind and Mahajan 1997). Product innovation presents a set of challenges associated with uncertainty, both market and technological, which some firms seek to resolve by the formation of alliances. In the context of large firms, the goal may be to bring together complementary technologies to enhance product performance, as with BMW and Google, which have joint projects to develop automotive communication systems. In other cases, particularly for SMEs, relationships are formed in networks to access multiple resources than can be drawn upon, from technical expertise, to financial support, to legislative understanding. In such circumstances, firms share information, make non-retrievable investments and engage in collaboration of great intensity (Story *et al.* 2011). It is clear that there is significant adaptation by firms to the notion of collaboration, relationships and networks for NPD, with the CPAS study (Markham and Lee 2013) revealing that the use of open innovation activities ranges from 27 per cent to 56 per cent of the time for different activities throughout the NPD process. The study also reported, however, that expected open innovation activities such as promoting external collaboration and risk sharing were used at relatively low levels. Therefore, there is still much to be learned with respect to the nature and impact of open activities in order to help further the development of products with sustainable success.

Summary

This chapter has focused exclusively on how new products are developed. Starting with the proposition that it takes more than a good idea to make a successful new product, it has described the main activities needed to bring a new product to market successfully. In so doing, the main critical success factors for NPD, which have been revealed through research, have been woven into the discussion of the process models commonly exhorted as the blueprints for success. This discussion has, in turn, highlighted the importance of market information to the successful completion of new product development projects, but it has also shown that blind adherence to a model for NPD cannot be productive as the whole business needs to be characterised by flexibility and open to creativity from various sources within and outside companies. The argument has presented information as a central thread of successful NPD. The NPD process is one of uncertainty reduction, which requires information and the constant evaluation of options. In turn, these options require the integration of various functional perspectives, which also require the sharing of information. A review and critique of the current models is given, revealing their contribution to and constraints on the process of developing new products, and suggestions have been derived from recent research as to how they might be improved and managed.

References

Ahmad, S., Mallick, D. N. and Schroeder, R. G. (2013), 'New product development: Impact of project characteristics and development practices on performance', *Journal of Product Innovation Management*, 30(2): 331–348.
Andrew, J. P. and Sirkin, H. L. (2003), 'Innovating for cash', *Harvard Business Review*, (September): 76–83.
Barczak, G., Griffin, A. and Khan, K. B. (2009), 'Trends and drivers of success in NPD practices: Results of the 2003 PDMA Best Practices Study', *Journal of Product Innovation Management*, 26(3): 3–23.

Beerens, J., Van Boetzelaer, A., List, G., Mensing, P. and Veldhoen, S. (2004) *The Road Towards More Effective Product/Service Development*, New York: Booz Allen Hamilton.

Booz, E., Allen, J. and Hamilton, C. (1968), *Management of New Products*, Chicago, IL: Booz Allen & Hamilton.

Booz Allen Hamilton (1982), *New Products Management for the 1980s*, New York: Booz Allen Hamilton.

Brown, J. S. and Hagel, J. (2005), 'The next frontier of innovation', *McKinsey Quarterly*, 3: 82–91.

Burns, T. E. and Stalker, G. M. (1961), *The Management of Innovation*, Champaign, IL: University of Illinois at Urbana-Champaign's Academy for Entrepreneurial Leadership Historical Research Reference in Entrepreneurship.

Castellion, G. and Markham, S. K. (2013), 'Perspective: New product failure rates: Influence of argumentum and populum and self-interest', *Journal of Product Innovation Management*, 30(5): 976–979.

Chesborough, H. W. (2003), *Open Innovation: The New Imperative for Creating and Profiting from Technology*, Boston, MA: Harvard Business School Press.

Cooper, R. G. (1988), *Winning at New Products: Accelerating the Process from Idea to Launch*, Reading, MA: Addison-Wesley.

Cooper, R. G. (1990), 'Stage-gate systems: A new tool for managing new products', *Business Horizons*, 33(May/June): 44–54.

Cooper, R. G. (1993), *Winning at New Products; Accelerating the Process from Idea to Launch*, Reading, MA: Addison-Wesley.

Cooper, R. G., Edgett, S. and Kleinschmidt, E. (2004), 'Benchmarking best NPD practices-I', *Research Technology Management*, 47(1): 31–43.

Crawford, C. M. (1984), 'Protocol: New tool for product innovation', *Journal of Product Innovation Management*, 1(2): 85–91.

Dehoff, K. and Neely, D. (2004) *Innovation and Product Development: Clearing the New Performance Bar*, New York: Booz Allen Hamilton.

Dolan, K. (2005), 'Speed, the new X factor', *Forbes*, 176(13): 74.

Drechsler, W., Natter, M. and Leeflang, P. S. H. (2013), 'Improving marketing's contribution to new product development', *Journal of Product Innovation Management*, 30(2): 298–315.

Dyer, B., Gupta, A. K. and Wilemon, D. (1999), 'What first-to-market companies do differently', *Research-Technology Management* 42(2): 15–21.

Eisenhardt, K. and Martin, J. (2000), 'Dynamic capabilities: What are they?', *Strategic Management Journal*, 21(10/11): 1105–1121.

Eling, K., Langerak, F. and Griffin, A. (2013), 'A stage-wise approach to exploring performance effects of cycle time reduction', *The Journal of Product Innovation Management*, 30(4): 626–641.

Evanschitzky, H., Eisend, R., Calantone, J. and Jiang, Y. (2012), 'Success factors of product innovation: An updated meta-analysis', *Journal of Product Innovation Management*, 29(S1): 21–37.

Felekoglu, B. and Moultrie, J. (2014), 'Top management involvement in new product development: A review and synthesis', *The Journal of Product Innovation Management*, 31(1): 159–175.

Govindarajan, V. and Trimble, C. (2005), 'Building breakthrough businesses within established organization', *Harvard Business Review*, (May): 58–68.

Gnyawali, D. R. and Madhavan, R. (2001), 'Cooperative networks and competitive dynamics: A structural embeddedness perspective', *Academy of Management Review*, 26(3): 431–445.

Hakansson, H., Havila, V. and Pedersen, A.-C. (1999), 'Learning in networks', *Industrial Marketing Management*, 28(5): 443–452.

Hamel, G. and Prahalad, C. K. (2005), 'Strategic intent', *Harvard Business Review*, (July/August): 148–161.

Harmancioglu, N., Grinstein, A. and Goldman, A. (2010), 'Innovation and performance outcomes of market information collection efforts: The role of top management team involvement', *International Journal of Research in Marketing*, 27(1): 33–43.

Hart, S., Hultink, E. J., Tzokas, N. and Commandeur, H. R. (2003). 'Industrial companies' evaluation criteria in new product development gates', *Journal of Product Innovation Management*, 20(1): 22–36.

Hillebrand, B. and Biemans, W. (2004), 'Links between internal and external cooperation in product development: An exploratory study', *Journal of Product Innovation Management*, 21(2): 110.

Hultink, E. J. and Hart, S. (1998) 'The world's path to the better mousetrap: Myth or reality? An empirical investigation into the launch strategies of high and low advantage new products', *European Journal of Innovation Management*, 1(3): 106–122.

Iansiti, M. and Levien, R. (2004), 'Strategy as ecology', *Harvard Business Review*, 82(3): 68.

Jean, R-J. B., Sinkovics, R. R. and Heibaum, T. P. (2014), 'The effects of supplier involvement and knowledge protection in product innovation in customer-supplier relationships: A study of global automotive suppliers in China', *The Journal of Product Innovation Management*, 31(1): 98–113.

Katz, G. (2011), Available at http://ams-inc.com/, accessed 5 January 2016.

Kuester, S., Schumacher, M. C., Gast, B. and Worgul, A. (2013), 'Sectoral heterogeneity in new service development: An exploratory study of service types and success factors', *Journal of Product Innovation Management*, 30(3): 533–544.

Levitt, T. (1960), 'Marketing myopia', *Harvard Business Review*, (July/August): 45–56.

Maltz, E. (2000), 'Is all communication created equal?: An investigation into the effects of communication mode on perceived information quality', *Journal of Product Innovation Management*, 17(2): 110–127.

Markham, S. K. and Lee, H. (2013), 'Product Development and Management Association's 2012 comparative performance assessment study', *Journal of Product Innovation Management*, 30(3): 408–429.

Moenaert, R. K. and Souder, W. E. (1990), 'An information transfer model for integrating marketing and R&D personnel in NPD projects', *Journal of Product Innovation Management*, 7(2): 91–107.

Olsen, E. M., Walker, O. C. Jr and Ruekert, R. W. (1995), 'Organizing for effective new product development: The moderating influence of product innovativeness', *Journal of Marketing*, 59(1): 48–62.

Owen-Smith, J. and Powell, W. (2004), 'Knowledge networks as channel and conduits: The effects of spillovers in the Boston biotechnology community', *Organisational Science*, 15(1): 5–21.

Ozdemir, S., Tagg, S. and Hart, S. (2008), 'New product development vs. new service development? An analysis of similarities and differences between the anatomy of the innovation processes in services and products: Processes, stages and evaluation gates', *Product Development and Management Association (PDMA) Conference*, September, Orlando, FL.

Page, A. L. (1993), 'Assessing new product development practices and performance: establishing crucial norms', *Journal of Product Innovation Management*, 10(September): 273–290.

Page, A. L. and Schirr, G. R. (2008), 'Growth and development of a body of knowledge: 16 years of new product development research, 1989–2004', *Journal of Product Innovation Management* 25(3): 233–248.

Pinto, M. B. and Pinto, J. K. (1990), 'Project team communication and cross-functional co-operation in new product development', *Journal of Product Innovation Management*, 7(3): 200–212.

Powell, W. (1998), 'Learning from collaboration: Knowledge and networks in the biotechnology and pharmaceutical industries', *California Management Review*, 40(3): 228–240.

Powell, W., White, D. and Owen-Smith, J. (2005), 'Network dynamics and field evolution: the growth of inter-organizational collaboration in the life sciences', *The American Journal of Sociology*, 110(4): 1132–1205.

Pyka, A. (2002), 'Innovation networks in economics: from the incentive-based to the knowledge-based approaches', *European Journal of Innovation Management*, 5(3): 152–163.

Rivas, R. and Gobeli, D. H. (2005), 'Accelerating innovation at Hewlett-Packard: A case study identifies significant enablers as well as barriers to innovation, along with management lessons for speeding the process', *Research Technology Management*, 48(1): 32–39.

Story, V., O'Malley, L. and Hart, S. (2011), 'Roles, role performance, and radical innovation competences', *Industrial Marketing Management*, 40(6): 952–966.

Talay, M. B., Calantone, R. J. and Voorhees, C. M. (2014), 'Coevolutionary dynamics of automotive competition: Product innovation, change, marketplace survival', *Journal of Product Innovation Management*, 31(1): 61–78.

Talke, K and Snelders, D. (2013), 'Information in launch messages: Stimulating the adoption of new high-tech consumer products', *The Journal of Product Innovation Management*, 30(4): 732–749.

Thomke, S. and Von Hippel, E. (2002), 'Customers as innovators: A new way to create value', *Harvard Business Review*, 80(4): 74.

Tzokas, N. and Hart, S. (2001), Critical Information and the Quest for Customer Relevant NPD Processes, Unpublished report for the EU, University of Strathclyde.

Von Hippel, E. (1978), 'Successful industrial products from customer ideas: Presentation of a new customer-active paradigm with evidence and implications', *Journal of Marketing*, January: 39–49.

Wind, J. and Mahajan, V. (1997), 'Issues and opportunities in new product development', *Journal of Marketing Research* 34: 1–12.

14 Pricing

Mark Billige and David Smith

Introduction

Price is unique within the marketing mix insofar as it is the one marketing element that truly defines an organisation as a commercial entity: the ability and intention to make money. Whereas all other aspects of marketing concentrate on the creation of value, pricing is the only way in which the firm captures the counter value back from customers. Yet, incredibly, it remains one area of business that is often misunderstood, under resourced and generally lacks investment. This chapter will examine the impact of pricing on company profitability and set out a framework for considering pricing more broadly within the organisation. It will cover how to formulate a pricing strategy, alternative approaches to setting prices, how to implement prices in both B2C and B2B markets and, finally, it will discuss the infrastructure that a firm needs to be best-in-class in pricing and consider the legal framework within which pricing must operate.

The impact of price on profit

The basic economics of commercial organisations are incredibly simple: there are costs incurred to produce goods or services, and those goods or services are sold in a quantity and at a price. Thus, there are only three profit drivers in any business: cost, volume and price. Whereas cost and volume are measured almost religiously and managed on a daily basis, pricing is typically subject to far less internal and external scrutiny, has far fewer resources dedicated to it and is generally less reported, tracked and forecast.

This is surprising because, of the three profit drivers (cost, volume and price), price is by far the most powerful and has by far the greatest impact on the bottom line. To illustrate this let's consider the Profit and Loss (P&L) statement for a pizza restaurant called Pete's Pizza. Let's suppose that every pizza sold costs £6 to make and the fixed costs (rents, salaries, insurance, etc.) are £300,000 per year. Now imagine that Pete's sells 100,000 pizzas per year at a price of £10 per unit. Pete's P&L looks simple:

Revenue: £1,000,000
Unit variable cost: £600,000
Contribution: £400,000
Fixed cost: £300,000
Profit: £100,000

Now, let's suppose that Pete has the resources to focus only on one of the profit drivers in this equation and that he could improve that driver by 5 per cent. Figure 14.1 shows the impact (all else remaining equal) of a 5 per cent improvement in any one of the profit drivers. You can see that in this example, a 5 per cent improvement in price improves profits by 50 per cent. Similar improvements in volume, unit variable cost and fixed cost only drive improvements of 20 per cent, 30 per cent and 15 per cent respectively.

Whilst price is demonstrably the most effective profit driver, it works as the most powerful profit killer in equal but opposite fashion. Now imagining that each of Pete's profit drivers were worsened by 5 per cent, you will find that a 5 per cent decrease in price (all else remaining equal) leads to a 50 per cent fall in profits. Or, to put it another way, to return to the same level of profitability, Pete would need to increase volume by 14 per cent. It is hard to imagine increasing pizza sales by 14 per cent with just a 5 per cent (50p) discount and, practically speaking, meeting such a level of increased demand would place huge strain on the processes, infrastructure and production teams for Pete's business.

Given its power as a profit lever, price does not receive enough attention. Steve Balmer, former CEO of Microsoft, comments that:

> This thing called 'price' is really, really important. I still think that a lot of people under-think it through. You have a lot of companies that start and the only difference between the ones that succeed and fail is that one figured out how to make money, because they were deep-in thinking through the revenue, price, and business model. I think that's under-attended to generally.
>
> (Sawers 2014)[1]

Much of the blame for why pricing is under-thought is placed on factors external to the company. We often hear that companies do not invest in pricing because the, 'market sets the price', i.e. competitors have established a going rate and customers expect that. In our experience it is rarely this straightforward, and we see five more fundamental reasons why companies under-think pricing:

1   *Nobody really 'owns' pricing*

Pricing rarely has a clear and well-defined owner. Often responsibility for pricing is implicitly shared and managed between a combination of sales, finance and marketing managers. This is a natural consequence of the fact that pricing impacts so many aspects of a business. However, without clear ownership, pricing decisions are typically under-thought and deprioritised.

	Profit driver		Profit impact		
	Old	**New**	**Old**	**New**	
Price	£10 ▶	£10.50	£100,000 ▶	£150,000	50%
Unit variable cost	£6.00 ▶	£5.70	£100,000 ▶	£130,000	30%
Sales volume	100,000 ▶	105,000	£100,000 ▶	£120,000	20%
Fixed cost	£300,000 ▶	£285,000	£100,000 ▶	£115,000	15%

Figure 14.1 Price is the most powerful profit lever

2   *There are rarely enough resources in the team*

Whereas most firms have significant resources dedicated to tracking and working on costs, there are far fewer resources dedicated to pricing. Jeffrey Immelt, the ex-CEO of GE, speaks for many companies when he says:

> Not long ago, a guy here did an analysis of our pricing in appliances and found out that about $5 billion of it is discretionary. Given all the decisions that sales reps can make on their own, that's how much is in play. It was the most astounding number I'd ever heard—and that's just in appliances. Extrapolating across our businesses, there may be $50 billion that few people are tracking or accountable for. We would never allow something like that on the cost side. When it comes to the prices we pay, we study them, we map them, we work on them. But with the prices we charge, we're too sloppy.
>
> (Grant 2010)[2]

3   *Too few managers understand the fundamental economics*

Typically managers underestimate the strength of the relationship between volume, price and profit. In a recent study that we conducted with 2,700 managers and executives in 50 countries, we found that only one in five fully understood the impact of price on profit. Having shown them a simple P&L and asked them to tell us the volume they could afford to lose to remain profit neutral for a given price increase, 29 per cent could not answer, 38 per cent underestimated and only 21 per cent could answer correctly (Simon-Kucher, *Global Pricing Study 2012*).[3]

4   *It exposes conflicting management objectives*

Pricing inevitably requires some form of trade-off to be accepted. If prices increase, then volume is likely to fall as a result. Conversely, if prices are reduced then margins may be forgone. As such, one reason for pricing being under-managed is precisely because, in the absence of clearly agreed objectives, active price management leads to conflict. To illustrate this point, we posed a simple question to the senior management of a recent client in the Higher Education sector. We asked, 'If in one year's time you had higher profits but fewer students, would you consider that a success or a failure'. The answer: 48 per cent of senior management saw that as a success, 52 per cent as a failure. So in this case, whatever we proposed with pricing, we knew one-half of the management team would veto it given their own view of what pricing had to deliver: either profits or student numbers.

5   *Proving success is challenging*

Accurately isolating the impact of price changes is incredibly difficult. In the absence of being able to prove otherwise, price increases will often take the blame for declining volumes even if there are multiple factors at work, and they seldom take the credit for maintaining profits in an otherwise declining market. The key lies in estimating the right baseline, that is the expected sales volume had we not changed the price. This can be particularly challenging for volatile businesses or those for which demand is strongly influenced by external factors. Subsequently, many managers rely on their own judgement and 'gut feel', and pricing remains more of a theoretical tool. Pricing continues to be under-invested in versus the activities of sales and cost management, which are easier to measure and quantify.

A framework for optimising prices

So pricing is complex. And getting prices right is incredibly important for the long-term survival of a business. As such, companies need to make pricing decisions with a high degree of rigour, with control and precision, and in a structured and repeatable manner. In short, pricing needs to follow a process. But, unlike virtually all other business processes, the process for pricing centres on the determination of the *optimal* level of variation, as opposed to the *elimination* of variation. For example, the process that a manufacturer applies to the production line will be focused on making the exact same product with no variation every single time. On the other hand, when that same manufacturer comes to sell those identical units, it is unlikely having one single price will be optimal, so they look to get the best price in each deal and for each customer. The pricing process is illustrated below in Figure 14.2.

It is composed of three principal process steps. First, the determination of a **price strategy**. This answers how pricing supports the business's overall corporate strategy and how price positioning fits in the context of the competitive landscape. It is usually defined at a very senior level within the organisation, e.g. CEO or board. Second, **price setting** defines the optimal price level, structure and differentiation given a product's value proposition and customers' willingness to pay. This tends to be the principal task of product and pricing managers. Finally, there is a requirement for controlled **price implementation**. This deals with the way in which prices are taken to and communicated to the market, specifically looking to minimise price 'leakages'. Typically, the sales, commercial or trading teams are responsible for implementing prices. The pricing process is an ongoing, 'living' process and, as such, there is a constant feedback loop from price implementation back to price strategy: is execution in line with strategy, and how should we steer and correct the direction?

Underpinning this process is a **price infrastructure** comprising the organisational responsibility for pricing and the systems, data and tools required to make the process scalable and repeatable. The price infrastructure may well be delivered by a broad range of stakeholders, including IT, HR and business information teams. Outcomes from the pricing process are set within the context of the relevant **price environment**, that is to say the governing legal, regulatory and ethical framework. This will require input and guidance from a number of internal and external parties, including legal, risk management and compliance.

In our experience, having applied it in more than 5,000 projects, this process can deliver significant and long-lasting profit impacts. Simon *et al.* (2006) writing in *Manage for Profit Not for Market Share*[4] indicate that improved pricing processes typically deliver increases of 1 to 3 percentage points of profit. Moreover, the upside comes not from a 'magical fix' but from, 'straightforward, nose to the grindstone'

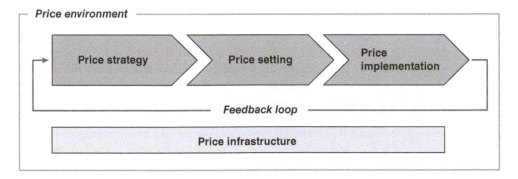

Figure 14.2 The pricing process

activities executed with diligence and focus. The rest of this chapter will examine the individual elements of the pricing process in more detail and provide a practical guide to its application.

Price strategy

A price strategy serves the critical purpose of translating a company's corporate targets and objectives into an appropriate market position for its products. Defining a price strategy is vitally important, but can be extremely difficult. It is vitally important because, without a pre-determined strategy, a company's price may be overly influenced by external developments in the market, be that the demands of customers or the actions of competitors. It can be extremely difficult, because it requires the company to undertake two different kinds of balancing act. First, in defining its price strategy a business must strike a balance between potentially conflicting corporate objectives (e.g. between the pursuit of market share or profitability). Second, the company has to strike the optimal balance between the value it creates and the price it charges. In the long term, healthy markets require companies to adopt balanced price strategies where prices charged are in line with value delivered. However, in the short term, imbalanced price strategies may be employed in the pursuit of specific corporate objectives (e.g. market penetration, new product launch, etc.), although this approach is not without risk and can have serious consequences.

Balancing corporate objectives

Within a single industry, one can observe different price strategies on the basis of differently balanced corporate objectives. Take for example, the very different strategies of General Motors (GM) and Porsche. Both manufacture cars, albeit with different target customer segments, and both work within the limitations of a strong competitive set and reasonably low levels of overall market growth. But their price strategies differ hugely. Throughout the early 2000s GM's focus was on market share. GM executives wore lapel pins bearing the number '29', which reflected their overall corporate objective of achieving market share of 29 per cent in North America (Simon *et al.* 2006).[5] Their pricing strategy was therefore formulated to support this market share goal. Richard Wagoner, the then CEO, stated, 'fixed costs are extremely high in our industry. We realized that in a crisis we fare better with low prices than by reducing volume. After all, in contrast to some competitors, we still make money with this strategy' (Simon 2009).[6]

In contrast to GM, Porsche prioritises a different corporate objective and, as such, employs a very different price strategy. Wendelin Wiedeking, the then Porsche CEO, said, 'We have a policy of keeping prices stable to protect our brand and to prevent a drop in prices for used cars. When demand goes down we reduce production but don't lower our prices' (Simon 2009).[7] Porsche's profit maximising objective means that it will trade-off volumes by proactively restricting supply in order to keep prices high. These two cases serve to illustrate that there is no such thing as a generically optimal price strategy, as what is right for one business may be wrong for another. The right price strategy is ultimately the one that aligns with and supports the overall corporate goal.

Balancing value and price

Dolan and Simon, writing in *Power Pricing*,[8] state that 'Price is the economic sacrifice a customer makes to acquire a product or a service. The customer always compares this sacrifice with his perception of the product's value. Price and value are the cornerstones of every economic transaction'. As such, price must be balanced with and aligned with value. In many markets, competing products and brands offer very distinct value propositions from low budget to premium. If we think of these options in the two dimensions of value and price, we can construct a 'value map'. Figure 14.3 shows a simple value map for London hotels with accommodation options ranging from a budget hotel, with limited home comforts, to a luxurious five star suite for several thousand pounds a night and all options in between.

The value map illustrates the big difference between *price* and *value for money*, terms which are too often used interchangeably. The fact that the Savoy charges many times the price of the Holiday Inn does not automatically imply that it provides worse value for money. So long as the value delivered balances with the price charged it is possible to be both very expensive and deliver very good value for money. Conversely, if the experience of a low price alternative is worse than expected, then even a very cheap hotel can be considered as poor value for money. As long as price and perceived value stay aligned, the market remains 'balanced' on the diagonal line across the value map.

In balanced markets competition tends to occur within value tiers, but not between them, as each tier is targeted at a distinct customer segment. Sometimes businesses will deliberately move off the 'balanced' line in pursuit of new customer segments or alternative objectives, either by stretching their brand to cover more value tiers or by repositioning it in a new tier entirely. Stretching a brand downwards into lower price tiers can be dangerous as it risks jeopardising the brand equity,

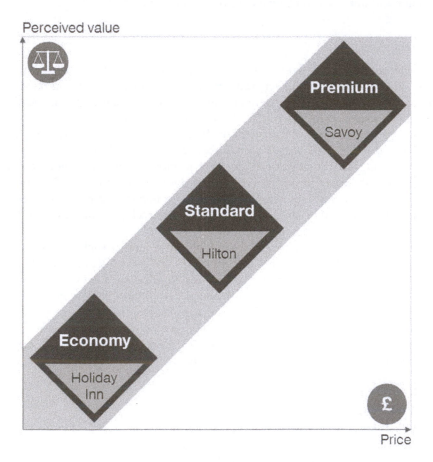

Figure 14.3 Conceptual value map showing 'balanced' pricing strategies

which enables it to command higher prices elsewhere. French fashion house, Pierre Cardin, serves as a well-documented example of how over-stretching a brand in this direction can go wrong. In the 1960s Pierre Cardin began extending out of their well-defined premium market into new categories to drive revenues and, by the late 1980s, were generating revenues of over $1 billion from licensing deals. The brand premium was eventually exhausted, and when the Pierre Cardin brand started appearing on completely unrelated, low value items (e.g. baseball caps and cigarettes), the margins collapsed.[9] The risk associated with stretching brands to cover more value tiers is typically greatest when moving downwards in price. However, moving up to higher price tiers can also carry risk when attempted without noticeable value improvements. Mulberry, the British fashion house, attempted to move its brand up-market to be more in line with established luxury brands such as Gucci and Louis Vuitton, by increasing the starting prices for its signature bags from £500 to £900. But the price move came without any significant change in quality and the result was an alienation of their core customer base, by essentially pricing them out of the brand. The result was a significant fall in sales and profits, with profit falling from £26m in 2013 to £14m in 2014, and only ended when the CEO was replaced and the strategy reversed.[10]

The pressure to move out of the balanced zone and around the value map can be driven to a certain degree by the nature of a product's lifecycle stage. In the early stages of development, the pressure to quickly grow sales may lead to purposeful 'under-pricing' of products. The 'freemium' strategy adopted by many online start-ups illustrates this well. Despite providing clear and substantial value to users, businesses such as Spotify, LinkedIn and Skype all offer a version of their core product for free. This extremely imbalanced price strategy is designed to quickly grow large user bases, which can then, in theory, be monetised at a later lifecycle stage. Conversely, in mature and declining lifecycle phases, products may well be purposefully 'over-priced' as they are retired and the focus switches to monetising what is left of the declining user base. Landline telephone connections are an example of a product in steady decline as customers migrate to mobile devices. Providers have been consistently increasing prices despite no additional value being offered, recognising that lower prices will not prevent the switch to mobile.

One way to access multiple value tiers with lower risk is to use a multi-brand strategy, making use of either sub-brands or entirely distinct brands to cater to different customer segments. Under one umbrella group, Volkswagen offers consumers the choice between a Skoda Fabia for £9,945[11] or a Bugatti Veyron for £1,410,000![12] Even within the more narrowly defined family hatchback market, they offer alternatives from SEAT, Skoda, Volkswagen and Audi, ranging from £9,995 to £34,950.[13, 14] Moreover, whilst these brands are seen as distinct in the eyes of the consumer, Volkswagen benefit from substantial economies of scale in production due to part sharing between brands. Using a multi-brand strategy, Volkswagen takes positions across the entire value map, delivering both high margins and volumes in parallel.

Balanced markets are characterised by brands with distinct customer propositions competing intelligently on both price and value. On the other hand, imbalanced markets over-emphasise price as a principal means of competition and run the constant risk of a price war in the pursuit of short-term market share gains. A price war is a period of fierce competition in which players engage in tit-for-tat price cuts in an attempt to increase their share of the market. To illustrate this, consider the price development of the three leading video games consoles between 2002 and 2003 in Figure 14.4. Having been launched at a price of €479 the price for Microsoft's Xbox was quickly 'slashed [to €299] . . . across the UK and Europe in an attempt to kick start sales'.[15] Nintendo responded by launching its Gamecube console €50 below the previously announced launch price of €249. Further simultaneous price cuts of the PS2 by Sony and Microsoft in September 2002 prompted further retaliation by Nintendo, who dropped the Gamecube price by another €30.

Similar stories have played out across the world in industries from cigarettes to breakfast cereals to airline flights. In almost all cases, the market share targeted by the aggressor fails to materialise as the *relative* price differential is maintained, leading to lower prices and lower profits for all players. In other words, the customer tends to be the only winner. As an example, at the end of the well-publicised price war between Dell and Compaq in the 1990s, Dell's ambition to use its cost advantage to drive Compaq out of the market ended with only a 4 per cent market share gain, but at a cost of $1bn in profits. Compaq, eventually bought by HP, remained in the market, but computer hardware prices never recovered.[16]

Clearly, the aggressive quest for market share carries with it the risk of price wars and, whilst all industries are at risk, there are certain conditions that create a 'tinderbox' setting. Dolan and Simon writing in *Power Pricing*[17] suggest 15 factors that heighten the risk. These include the underlying cost structure, levels of capacity utilisation, perishability, degree of brand loyalty, etc. But every price war requires a 'spark' to start it and it is often the case that this comes unwittingly. In Simon-Kucher's *Global Pricing Study*[18] we asked whether a company was engaged in a price war: 59 per cent of respondents confirmed that they were. We then asked those respondents to tell us who had started it. The answer is fascinating: 89 per cent believe it was the competitor. In other words, virtually every company caught up in a price war believes that somebody else started it. It's always the others!

Getting price strategy right is therefore important not only for the individual company but also for the sustainability of the whole market. Simon *et al.* (2006)[19] encourage managers to consider forms of more 'peaceful competition' defined as, 'the science of profitable differentiation'. In other words, trying to win market share through aggressive, price-driven competition almost inevitably leads to price wars, but competing on the basis of innovation and quality leads to better outcomes for all players. McKinsey, the management consultancy, recognises that for many businesses this requires a mindset change:

> What matters is not share of market, but share of scarce market profits . . . Market surplus will replace market share as the measure of success. Companies . . . will think not just about their own profits, but also about maximising both the total profits in their industry – the market surplus – and their companies' share of these profits.[20]

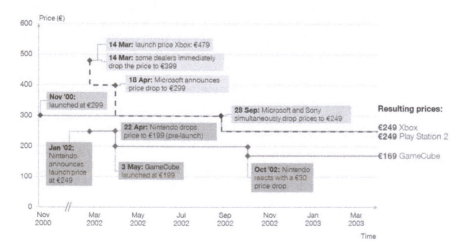

Figure 14.4 Price evolution in the game console market

Source: Prices taken from a leading online retailer.

Price setting

Price strategy is about the direction for pricing. At a market level it seeks to answer questions about how and where a company competes, what pricing success looks like (e.g. profit versus market share) and how to avoid damaging price competition (e.g. price wars). Price setting seeks to optimise prices within the context of this general direction.

Three price setting philosophies

As we have shown, small differences in price can deliver large differences in profitability. Logically it follows that the price setting process should be inherently quantitative and detailed, requiring analysis, tools and often specialist capability. Ultimately, price is a number. However, as we will see, this is not always the case, and some price setting methodologies are alarmingly simplistic. In general terms, there are three principal philosophies that a company can adopt to set prices: they can base their prices on their costs, they can base their prices on competitors' prices or they can base their prices on the value that customers perceive in their product or service.

Cost-based pricing

For many years, cost-based (or 'cost plus') pricing was the principal approach to price setting and, arguably, for straightforward businesses with transparent costs of production, it has inherent attractions as an approach. It is (on the face of it) relatively simple and, if price is higher than cost, it guarantees a profit margin per unit. However, there are a number of issues with pricing on the basis of costs, both in terms of its practical execution and the underlying principle.

First, costs are not always as simple to measure as first thought, and the allocation of fixed costs to products is often as much arbitrary as it is scientific. Consider a business that sells data to other businesses. The company has to employ a large team of analysts to write reports and build data models, which the sales team then sell to customers. The cost of production is almost entirely fixed and sunk in this case: when the sales team wins a new customer there is no or little additional incremental cost to serve that customer, and if a customer is lost, then the fixed cost of production does not go down as a result. In this case, the concept of a product cost or customer cost is highly arbitrary and, as such, is a bad starting point for price setting. In the service sector many firms have this issue as they tend to have far higher indirect costs than direct costs. On an even more fundamental level, the process of allocating fixed costs, by definition, requires an inherent assumption about the number of units to be sold. But, we know the number of units sold will be strongly influenced by the price charged, hence the exercise becomes circular.

Second, and most importantly, from a point of principle cost plus pricing is very unlikely to lead to optimal pricing outcomes. Customers do not know or care about the costs of production. They make purchase decisions based on the value they perceive in the product and the alternatives available to them. Following a cost plus approach is therefore sub-optimal in two ways, as illustrated below in Figure 14.5. If the cost plus the target margin is lower than the actual willingness to pay of the customer (i.e. the product appears cheap), then profit will be forgone. If the cost plus the target margin is higher than the willingness to pay (i.e. the product appears expensive), then sales are unlikely to develop as required. The profit *margin* on the units sold will be as expected, but the total *absolute* profit will be lower.

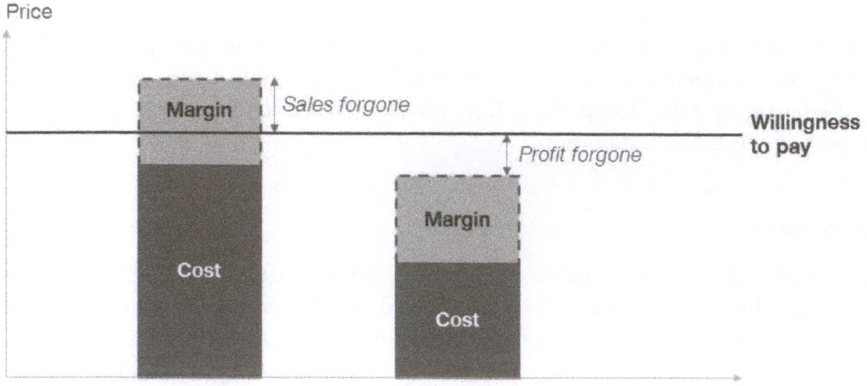

Figure 14.5 Sub-optimal outcomes from cost plus pricing

Competition-based pricing

The principal problem with cost-based pricing is that, as an approach, it is inherently inward look-ing, considering only a company's costs and its own ambitions for profit. Clearly, there is a need to consider what consumers are actually willing to pay, and this will be heavily impacted by the alternatives that they have available to them. It is therefore important to be mindful of competitors' prices, but using this information as the sole or primary pricing basis has its own very specific risks and disadvantages, again both in practice and in principle.

In practice, it is not always a simple task to benchmark competitors' prices. There is not always a directly comparable product, not every business has or publishes a price list and, even if there were a list price, any discounts given are rarely transparent. The problem is less acute in B2C markets, because prices tend to be published and not negotiated. However, the proliferation of promotions and special offers (such as buy-one-get-one-free or multi-buy offers) makes it harder to understand what customers perceive they are actually paying for a product. Technology can help, especially as more products are sold online, with tools such as screen-scrapers that are able to build intelligence on competitor product prices and promotions economically and at scale.

But whilst some of the practical challenges can be overcome, there remain significant issues with the principle of competitor-based pricing. First, basing prices on a competitor's price is an inherently reactive approach. A competitor may well have a very different cost base, margin aspi-ration, positioning strategy and growth goal for their product, which means that the price that is right for them may not necessarily be right for all of the other players in that market. Second, if two competitors in a market both adopt competitor-based pricing, then each is an input into the other one's pricing, which carries significant risk of a price war. Any change in price by one player will inevitably lead to a series of price changes as a response and, in the case of price decreases, this could lead to a downward spiral of prices. Remember the statistic we shared earlier: 89 per cent of companies in a price war believe it was started by the other side.

It is important to note that whilst companies are free to consider the prices of their com-petitors when setting their own price, it is illegal for competitors to *collude* on prices; that is for companies to jointly agree on their prices together. This is covered in more detail in the 'Pricing environment'.

Customer-based pricing

Price is the counter of value. That is to say, companies create value through product design, customer service, delivery, etc. and capture value back from the customer through price. So it stands to reason that the most important input to setting the right price is the value that the customer perceives in a product and their resultant willingness to pay. The challenge with basing prices on value-to-customer is that 'value' is an abstract concept that is very hard to quantify, and customers have strong incentives not to reveal their true willingness to pay when asked. Value-based pricing is therefore complicated as an approach as it requires the measurement and quantification of these challenging concepts, which partly explains why it is not the principal pricing approach for most companies.

Customer-based pricing can deliver significant upsides. We have already seen that basing prices solely on costs most likely leads to either sales or profits being forgone. Knowing the true willingness to pay means that these opportunity costs are minimised. In the case that prices are set higher than the true willingness to pay, sales (and profits) are forgone. When Disneyland opened their Paris resort in 1990, they based the pricing on their American theme parks. The resultant European prices were perceived to be too high and admissions fell far below expectations, pushing the park close to bankruptcy in 1995. It was only after a 20 per cent price cut that demand recovered and the park became profitable (Woodyard 1995).[21] If prices are set lower than the true willingness to pay, profits are again forgone. When Tesco launched its Hudl tablet computer, it positioned it as the cheapest tablet on the market. In hindsight, they may have been unprepared for just how popular it would be, running out of stock twice and reportedly selling 35,000 models in the first 48 hours.[22]

Even in industries that appear highly commoditised, customer-based pricing can yield substantial positive outcomes. For a good example, take a look at the price of pencils. Cheap, own-brand pencils can be purchased for as little as 8p per unit. However, two of the biggest players, Staedtler and Faber Castell, sell their pencils at between 50p and £2 each. Even with a premium of up to 25 times the own-brand price, they are each among the largest producers of pencils in the world. If prices had been set on the basis of cost alone, then the premiums would have been a fraction of that achieved.

Whilst the benefits of customer-based pricing are clear, in reality its application is challenging, because customers are seldom homogenous in terms of their willingness to pay. As such, we find that the demand for a product typically varies as the price changes, that is, at any given price, only a proportion of total customers find that price acceptable for some or all of their demand. For most products, as the price increases the quantity demanded falls, because the proportion of the total customer base that finds the price acceptable decreases and/or each customer is willing to purchase less volume at that price. This relationship is known as the 'price elasticity of demand (PED)' and understanding it is the key to optimal price setting.

Price Elasticity of Demand (PED)

PED is the observed percentage change in sales volume for a given percentage change in price. The formula for computing PED is:

$$\frac{\% \text{ change in sales volume}}{\% \text{ change in price}}$$

For the vast majority of products and services, PEDs are negative, that is as prices go up, volumes go down. The relationship between the two variables, and hence the degree of elasticity, is very important when setting prices. Where the volume change in percentage terms is less than the change in price, the demand for a product is said to be inelastic and the PED would be between 0 and −1. This means that if prices increase, the relative fall in volume would be lower, leading to higher revenues overall. Conversely, where the percentage change in volume is greater than the change in price, the demand for a product is said to be elastic. In this case the PED would be more negative than −1 (e.g. −3). For a product with elastic demand, a small price increase will lead to a relatively larger fall in volume and hence to lower revenues overall.

With an understanding of the PED, a company can compute the profit optimal price for a product. The first step is to plot the price response curve (also referred to as the demand curve), which shows the total quantity demanded at different prices. Once the price response curve is established, it is a simple task to compute the revenue at each price by multiplying the quantity by the price, giving us the revenue curve. Finally, the profit curve can be computed by subtracting the variable unit cost from the revenue at each price, and then taking away fixed costs. This is illustrated in Figure 14.6 below.

Once we have the profit curve, it is simple to read off the profit optimal price point. Note that fixed costs do not influence the optimal price as they are the same for all prices and sales volumes considered. As such, fixed costs are simply deducted from the total contribution to yield the profit figure, but do not change the shape of the profit curve. As observed by Dolan and Simon,[23] an understanding of the profit curve leads us to three clear conclusions:

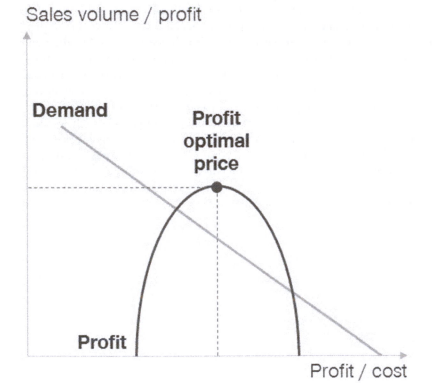

Figure 14.6 Deriving the profit optimal price point

1   There is *always* a profit maximising price.
2   The more one deviates from this price, the steeper the downward slope of the profit curve.
3   A price which is too high is just as bad as a price that is too low.

In reality, there are many factors that impact PED and the price response curve and, unlike our illustration, this curve is not always linear or stable; the curve and the PED change depending on the magnitude of the price change, whether price thresholds (e.g. £9.99) are crossed and whether prices are increasing or decreasing (i.e. PEDs can be asymmetric). Generally speaking though, the more commoditised a product, the more elastic its demand. Some of the factors that impact PED include:

- the availability of substitutes;
- the extent to which the product or service is a necessity;
- the extent to which the purchase can be put-off/delayed;
- the extent of any switching costs involved;
- the way in which the price change is communicated;
- the degree to which there is price transparency in the market;
- the amount of money involved in the purchase.

The fundamental requirement to calculate the PED is to understand how the demand for a product will vary at different price points. In our consulting engagements we typically use a combination of the following five methods to estimate the price response curve.

1   **Econometric analysis** – This involves analysing historic sales data to isolate the impact of past price changes on past volumes. Econometric analysis is therefore suitable where prices have changed in the past, it is possible to establish a baseline and if the historic context will continue to be relevant in the future. As such, this approach will not work in all situations and requires careful interpretation. One of the more challenging aspects of econometric analysis is identifying a baseline for measuring observed outcomes against which we can answer the question, 'What would have happened had we *not* changed the price?'. For stable businesses or those with regular seasonality this may be straightforward, but for less stable businesses or those where sales are strongly impacted by external factors (competitive offers, weather, etc.), this can be extremely challenging. In sectors with an abundance of sales data, such as retail, advanced regression techniques can overcome this problem to a degree by controlling for these other factors. Finally, the usefulness of econometric analysis is restricted by the context of the past price change. For example, PEDs derived from past observations cannot be reliably used in the future for radically different price strategies, crossing key price thresholds (such as £9.99), or reducing prices when prices have historically always increased.
2   **Price trials** – This involves changing prices in one part of a business whilst leaving prices unchanged in another (referred to as a 'control group'). For example, a retailer could change the price of a product in certain stores, but not in others, and then measure the incremental impact on volumes and profits. The key advantages of price trials compared to econometric analysis are that they overcome the issue of not having a baseline, and they are not limited by the historic business context. As such, price trials are typically one of the most reliable methods for estimating PEDs. However, price trials are difficult to implement for businesses with only a few products, customers, channels or markets and for businesses with a strong brand image

where the PR/customer backlash risk is high. Typically, businesses with a high proportion of online sales can quite easily implement price trials as they can randomly split their web traffic to show different prices for the same product.

3 **Conjoint** – This is an advanced market research technique which, unlike other forms of pricing research, looks to understand price sensitivity *indirectly* by forcing survey respondents to make trade-offs between different product options, which are described in terms of both their price and value-to-customer. In other words, just as in real life, a respondent has to make a choice between cheaper, inferior products, and more superior, but expensive options. In a conjoint study, a respondent is shown five to ten such trade-off scenarios and by analysing the choices made, the true sensitivity to price changes (and other feature changes) can be estimated. The outcome is an understanding of the relative importance of price versus other product features in the purchase decision, and how the demand for the product or service will vary at different price points and feature configurations. Advanced price research methodologies such as conjoint are extremely powerful, but can be complex and expensive to conduct. An example conjoint screen is shown in Figure 14.7.

4 **Other forms of pricing research** – Unlike conjoint, this involves asking potential customers direct questions about how they would respond to certain prices or price changes. There are a range of methodologies and approaches commonly used to infer price sensitivity in this way. One of the most commonly used is the Van Westendorp Price Sensitivity Meter.[24] In this case, respondents are asked to state which prices they see as 'fair', 'expensive', 'cheap' and 'too expensive' for a given product. The results can be analysed to identify a price range and any perceived 'price thresholds' where perceptions of price change dramatically. The advantages of such techniques over conjoint are their speed and flexibility. This kind of research can be fielded and analysed in a matter of days, and questions can be asked about a wide variety of scenarios. The disadvantage is that, given the direct nature of the questions, they are prone to over estimating price sensitivity.

5 **Expert judgement** – This involves harnessing the expertise that exists within a business in a systematic way, by having representatives from sales and marketing predict how volumes will react to future changes in price. This can be a very fast and cost-effective means of obtaining an estimate of PED and, in our experience, results are typically comparable to those gained from far more involved approaches. However, we would typically advocate using expert judgement as one of several inputs to estimating PEDs, validating with one or more of the other methods mentioned here.

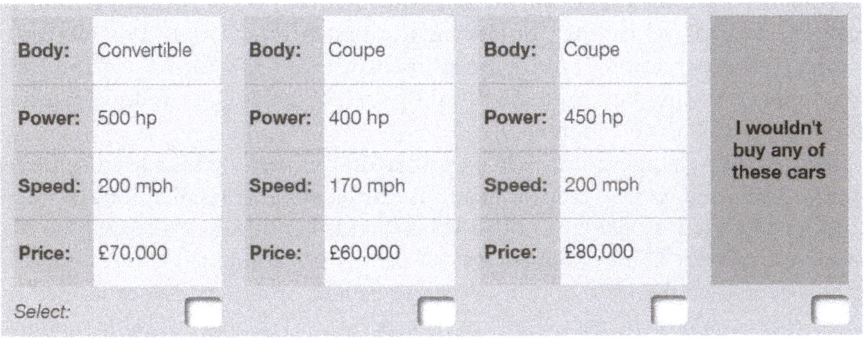

Figure 14.7 An example of a trade-off question in a conjoint experiment

Value-based price models

So far in this section we have focused exclusively on the optimisation of the price *level*, that is the price charged to a customer. However, the price level is just one of four elements of a complete price *model*. Beyond the actual price level, a complete price model deals with *how* a company prices: what exactly is the charging unit, how does the price develop as the number of units purchased develops and how does the price charged differ between buyers or channels. We refer to these as the price *metric*, the price *structure* and price *differentiation* respectively.

To bring this to life, consider two law firms. Both sell legal advice to clients in the same industry and both specialise in similar fields of law. When it comes to pricing, however, they operate different pricing models. Law firm A prices its services based on the number of hours it takes to deliver its legal advice. Law firm B prices its services based on a percentage of the money they save their clients as a result of their advice. In this example, the principal difference between the two firms is the unit of charging, or the price *metric*. Firm A uses time (in this case billable hours) as the price metric, whereas firm B uses the monetary value of the savings they generate for their clients.

Now imagine a third firm, firm C. Firm C also charges on the basis of billable hours but, whereas firm A charges a simple hourly rate, firm C charges their clients a fixed fee for the first 20 hours and an hourly rate thereafter. In other words, all of firm C's clients pay for at least 20 hours, even if they use less than this. In this case, the way the total price develops with the number of hours consumed differs. We call this the *price structure*.

Finally, imagine a fourth firm, firm D. Like firm A they also charge on a billable hour basis and each hour is charged for individually. However, firm D charges a different hourly rate depending on which region the lawyer is working in. As such, we say firm D is using *price differentiation*, i.e. for a given metric within a given structure the price differs on a predefined basis (in this case region).

Therefore, value pricing is about far more than just finding the optimal price level. In fact, the price model is fundamental to the maximisation of profits, because without understanding *how* a customer benefits from a product, one cannot understand *how* to structure the price. Thus, the price model should reflect as closely as possible the way in which benefits are delivered. Take aircraft engines as an example. The benefit to an airline of an engine is that they can get their planes from A to B and, in doing so, charge customers to travel on those planes. So the benefit of an aircraft engine to an airline only comes when the planes are flying. Rolls Royce understood this when they changed their pricing model from selling engines to airlines to selling them engine *thrust*.[25] In the new model airlines would not pay for the engine itself, but would actually pay for the thrust the engine generated. In this case, Rolls Royce used a radically new price metric – thrust per hour – to align far more closely with the value created by the product. When the aircraft is in the air earning money, then Rolls Royce charges the airline. When the aircraft is on the ground and idle, they do not.

As well as more closely aligning the prices charged with the value delivered, a different price model can make a product appear more or less attractive to consumers by changing the way in which prices are perceived. This is illustrated well by the German railway operator DeutscheBahn. In the 1990s DeutscheBahn was struggling to fill trains given a perceived price disadvantage versus travel by car. One of the key reasons for this was that, when considering driving, individuals focused only on the cost of petrol, which on a per kilometre basis was cheaper than the train. They failed to adequately take account of the fixed and sunk costs of car ownership such as depreciation, insurance, repairs, etc. The solution for DeutscheBahn was to change the price *structure* to make the comparison of prices between train and car more favourable. To do this DeutscheBahn launched the BahnCard, which, in exchange for an upfront payment today of €255 for second class and €515 for first class, entitled the holder to a 50 per cent discount off all rail travel in Germany. Thus, just like with car ownership, there was now a sunk and fixed cost plus a lower price per kilometre, the latter being all that customers tended to compare. Figure 14.8 below compares the pricing with and without the BahnCard.

The new price structure worked and the BahnCard was an immediate hit. Within four months, over 1 million cards had been sold, and the number continued to grow year by year to around 4 million by the year 2000. Importantly, although the BahnCard promised a discount of 50 per cent, in reality the actual discount realised was on average only 28 per cent. Given the upfront investment in the card, consumers only realised the savings after a certain distance was travelled and many BahnCard owners never reached that point.[26] Thus more sophisticated price structures can be a very powerful tool for proactively improving price *perceptions* and profits. This is illustrated below in Figure 14.9.

The final element of a comprehensive price model is the degree of price differentiation, which is the extent to which the price differs between customers for the same product. Price differentiation is a very powerful approach for simultaneously driving both volumes and profits. To illustrate how this is possible, if we take a product with a single price, P_1, and plot this against a demand curve we achieve a sales volume, V_1. All the customers with a willingness to pay P_1 or higher would buy the product. If, for simplicity, we assumed no variable cost then we would achieve contribution equal to $P_1 + V_1$, as illustrated by the square in Figure 14.10 below.

From a profit maximisation perspective this is unsatisfactory, as we cannot capture all the profits under the demand curve, represented by the two adjacent triangles. In triangle 1 there are customers with a willingness to pay greater than P_1 who would, therefore, have paid more. In triangle 2

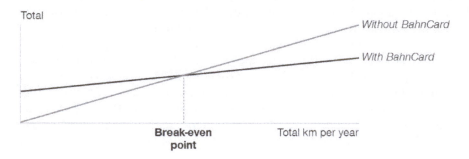

Figure 14.8 Total price with and without BahnCard.

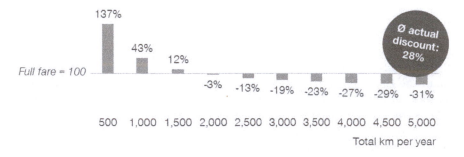

Figure 14.9 Actual discounts realised with BahnCard

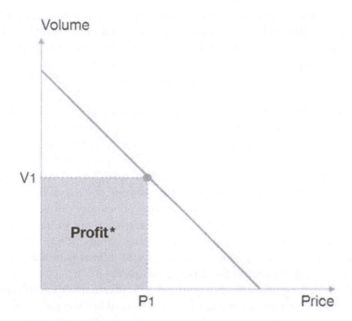

Figure 14.10 Contribution function with single price point

there are potential customers with a willingness to pay lower than P_1 who would have been willing to buy the product had it been available at a lower price. If we were now able to offer three price points (P_1, P_2 and P_3) rather than one, we would be able to extract some of the additional profits from these two previously unexploited profit pools. See Figure 14.11 below for an illustration.

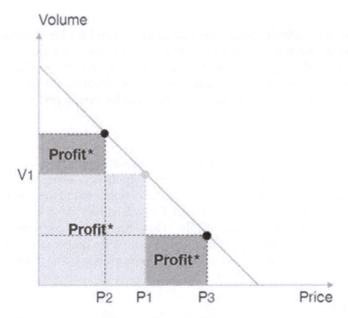

Figure 14.11 Contribution function with three price points

Thus a business will be able to extract more profit from the market by offering multiple prices than with a single price point. Ultimately, a different price point tailored to each individual customer's willingness to pay would yield the maximum profit, but, in reality, this is seldom feasible. Rather, businesses must find the optimal level of differentiation, carefully balancing the incremental profit gains from adding more price points with the additional cost and complexity this brings.

Of course, it is not enough to simply differentiate the price. If a company offers the exact same product to all customers at three different prices, we would not expect to sell anything at the two higher prices (sales would gravitate to the cheapest price, referred to as cannibalisation). In order to benefit from price differentiation, businesses must create 'fences' between their alternative offers. The cinema industry provides a good example of how to successfully fence multiple prices. Typically, the price for a cinema ticket varies by *customer* type (students, teens, senior citizens), by *day* of the week, by *time* of day, by *technology* (3D vs. 2D), by cinema *location* and by *seat* type. For a given film, one UK cinema chain uses approximately 150 prices every week. The price fences it has put in place mean that the lowest prices are only available to certain types of customer at certain times, thus minimising the risk of cannibalisation. It is important to note that not all forms of price differentiation are legal (or ethical). We will consider this in more detail later in the 'Pricing environment'.

So managers who are responsible for setting prices have to contend with considerable complexity. Not only is the approach to quantifying willingness to pay and PED complicated but also the development of value-based price models requires innovative approaches and creativity. However tempting it is, 'simple' pricing almost inevitably leaves money on the table. It is not by chance that industries with sophisticated pricing such as mobile telecoms and cinema have high profit margins even though they operate in mature and competitive markets.

Understandably, more complex pricing needs careful implementation. In the next section we consider how best to ensure that the prices that are set actually get achieved.

Price implementation

Having laid out the general direction for pricing given corporate objectives and market dynamics, and having developed optimal prices and price models to meet those objectives, the third stage in the pricing process is to implement those prices in the market. This may at first seem like an obvious and unnecessary stage, but in our experience there are multiple pricing 'leakages' that companies are either unaware of or neglect when it comes to actually implementing prices.

Price implementation in B2B markets

In B2B markets prices are usually implemented by a sales force who negotiate prices with customers on behalf of the company. As such, B2B price implementation is about developing the right guidelines, incentives and monitoring to ensure that sales reps act in the best interests of the business.

In most B2B sales environments the sales team is tasked to make judgements about each customer's willingness to pay and to negotiate prices accordingly. Thus, the price implementation framework needs to give sales reps enough authority to negotiate for the best outcome whilst at the same time preventing truly bad outcomes and providing control over margins. There are two principal tools to do this:

1   discount controls and escalations;
2   KPIs and incentives.

Discount controls and escalations

Many companies have a discount escalation structure whereby to offer bigger discounts, higher authority sign-off is required. Such controls certainly prevent major pricing mistakes, but do little to drive the best possible pricing outcomes. Indeed, a very common pricing leakage can be easily observed when looking at the frequency of average discounts by account. In one such case, we analysed the discount distribution of a random sample of deals for a B2B services business, shown in Figure 14.12 below. We found clear 'spikes' in discount frequency and, when we overlaid the escalation matrix, we saw immediately why this was the case. Sales reps interpreted the *maximum* discount allowed as a *suggested* discount, going as far as they could before having to obtain the next level of sign-off.

A more proactive approach would be to give sales reps guidance around what the optimal price or discount *should* be for certain deals and customers, as opposed to simply what it *could* be. One way of doing this would be to analyse the historic price distribution of groups of deals with shared characteristics (e.g. customer type and size) and then set a *target* price for subsequent comparable deals at the level that the top 25 per cent of sales reps are already achieving. In doing so, the price performance of the top quartile of a sales peer group provides the guidance for the rest, an approach we refer to as 'peer pricing'.

KPIs and incentives

The definition of KPIs, targets and incentive structures is incredibly important for successful price implementation in B2B markets. At the start of a project with a premium automotive manufacturer, the head of sales reflected:

> when we are honest with ourselves, it's clear that we just pay lip service to profit goals and targets. If our profit falls by 20 per cent, nothing happens. If our market share falls by even a fraction of a percentage point, heads roll. And everybody knows about it.
>
> (Simon *et al.* 2006)[27]

If the sales team – or indeed the whole company – believes that the most important KPI is volume or market share, then they will (or at least should) focus on selling higher volumes at lower prices

Figure 14.12 Deal distribution by discount

and are hence unlikely to support higher price targets. As such, the incentives and commission scheme for the sales team becomes a vital tool for price implementation.

Pricing in B2B organisations is therefore as much about the management of internal behaviour as it is about understanding customer willingness to pay. A lack of focus on price implementation can quickly undermine all efforts in price strategy and price setting.

Price implementation in B2C markets

In most B2C businesses the role of the sales organisation does not extend to negotiating prices with individual customers. Typically, B2C products have a published price, which all customers pay. Thus, price implementation in B2C settings strongly focuses on how prices are communicated to customers and how price is used as a lever to steer choice and behaviour.

Price communication

The way in which a price is perceived by consumers can be strongly influenced by the manner in which it is communicated. Careful choice of price communication can distort perceptions of expensiveness, for example, by pricing at £9.99 rather than £10.00 or by converting the price into a smaller increment such as 'car insurance from just 50p per day', instead of £182.50 for the year. Price perceptions have been aggressively managed for many years in the airline industry by low cost players such as Ryanair and Easyjet who created a low price image by stripping out costs such as taxes, booking fees and surcharges from the promoted price (however, various players have had to withdraw advertised prices when they failed to disclose certain unavoidable fees in the head-line price). A study of German consumers showed that when asked who had the cheaper flights: Ryanair or Lufthansa, respondents felt that Ryanair would be cheaper in 98 per cent of cases when in reality Lufthansa was cheaper on over 30 per cent of routes.[28]

The influence of price on consumer choice

Price acts as a strong signal to consumers about likely quality. Like it or not, we sub-consciously make assumptions about the quality of a product based on its price. This effect is most powerful where quality is difficult to quantify, or where there is a lack of knowledge about what constitutes 'good quality'. Whereas value is *subjective* (e.g. style, quality, taste), prices are inherently *objective* and therefore easy to rank. As such, consumers tend to over-rely on price when making quality judgements between alternatives. Wine is a perfect example of such a product, and many consumers take the price of a bottle of wine as an indicator of its relative quality versus other bottles.

Beyond being a signal of quality for a single product, price also leads to so-called 'context effects', that is to say pricing managers must consider the prices of surrounding products in addition to the price of the product itself. Two important examples of context effects are the *compromise effect* and *anchoring*. Both are very powerful drivers of behaviour and can be used by B2C businesses to steer consumer choice.

The compromise effect explains why consumers tend to choose the middle option of three choices more often than they should, because the middle options seems like a good compromise between alternatives.[29] Businesses can use this effect to their advantage by creating a three product line-up, often along the lines of 'good, better, best'.

Anchoring is the subliminal impact that other numbers or cues have on consumers' willingness to pay. In his fascinating book on this topic, *Predictably Irrational* (2008),[30] Dan Ariely shows how the simple act of reading the last two digits of one's social security number leads to higher or lower bids for an auction item. In an experiment participants were asked to write down the last two digits of their social security number. They were then all shown the same box of chocolates and asked the maximum they would pay. Those participants with digits in the range 0–19 on average stated they would pay $9.55. Those with digits in the range of 80–99 indicated an average willingness to pay of $20.64. Anchoring can therefore have powerful effects on consumer choice, and businesses need to consider this when positioning products and communicating options to consumers.

Price infrastructure

It takes a lot to deliver best-in-class pricing. Without the right price infrastructure to support and optimise ongoing pricing decision making, companies risk forgoing substantial profit potential. Price infrastructure can be thought of in two main dimensions: the 'Man' and the 'Machine'. The Man refers to the people required for pricing, both those taking decisions and those supporting. The Machine refers to the tools, data and systems that make pricing decisions more effective and more scalable.

Man: the people required for pricing

The experiences of the companies in our *Global Pricing Study 2012*[31] tell us that those who have a dedicated pricing function have a more positive profit outlook, they increase prices more often and they do so with far greater success. However, whilst the merits of having a pricing team may be clear, exactly where in the organisation that team should sit is far less clear cut.

The degree of (de)centralisation and the level of authority granted to the pricing team can vary widely between companies, even within the same industry, and there is no such thing as the 'perfect' structure. Broadly speaking, highly centralised pricing suits companies with a limited number of very important product lines, such as automotive or pharmaceutical companies, where overall price control and brand management are important. Conversely, highly diversified businesses selling into multiple markets and customer segments benefit from decentralisation in their pricing, given the need to be close to the customer and the market. Some companies have pricing represented at the very highest level in the organisation, as found by the consultancy Deloitte, who estimate that 8 per cent of companies have a chief pricing officer.[32] This makes sense where price image and brand management are key assets for a business. In the majority of cases, responsibility for price management occurs lower down in the organisational hierarchy, with the Deloitte study suggesting 82 per cent of pricing roles are to be found in middle management or at VP/director level. So, whilst there is no blueprint for where exactly a pricing team should fit within the organisation, there are clear benefits to having one.

Machine: the tools, data and systems required for pricing

In addition to the right people, it is also important that the right tools, data and systems are in place to enable the ongoing administration and management of pricing. At the most basic level, systems will provide the data, KPI dashboards and reports required to monitor pricing performance and the impact of price changes. For some businesses, systems play a much more active role in the actual setting of prices, for example, in the travel and tourism sector, where prices are optimised dynamically according to algorithms.

Given the importance of price in driving profits, frequent monitoring of actually achieved prices is vital in order to be able to steer the business and enable corrective action. But, more uniquely, much can be learned about the PED from measuring the impact of price changes on volumes and customer behaviours. As such, it is likely that various business systems and data sets will need to be interrogated for pricing purposes, capturing both internal data (net prices, average discounts, volumes, sales mix, etc.) and external data (competitor prices, customer satisfaction scores, market share changes, etc.).

In practice, measuring and tracking pricing performance can be very challenging for two principal reasons. First, the business needs to understand whether and how changes in price have led to changes in business outcomes. However, given the huge number of external factors at play, it can be very hard to isolate this impact (earlier in this chapter we set out the principles of econometric analysis that can help to deal with this issue). Second, the positive impact of a pricing decision is often hard to see because, rather than being a tangible outcome, it is an opportunity cost minimised. For instance, whilst it is easy to point to higher sales volumes as a positive outcome, it is far harder to point to the profits forgone in the pursuit of that volume. Of course, it is very hard to prove this kind of impact. In reality, no profit is actually *lost*, it is just not earned in the first place. As a result, the measurement of pricing remains a challenging concept for many businesses and continues to be under-invested in versus the much easier measurement of sales and costs.

Price environment

Pricing must be considered within the legal and regulatory context that the business operates in and, whilst the legal aspects of pricing are not the core focus of this chapter, it is important to consider the broad principles and how they constrain and impact the pricing process.

Broadly speaking, the laws governing pricing fall into two main topics: agreements between the players in a market and the abuse of market power. In both cases, the law seeks to stop activities that might prevent, restrict or distort competition within the market.

Agreements between the players in a market can be thought of along two dimensions: horizontal agreements and vertical agreements. Horizontal agreements are those between competitors in a market. Examples of illegal behaviour include:

- agreements between competitors to set prices;
- agreements between competitors to restrict supply (with the aim of ultimately driving prices up);
- agreements between competitors to sell in specific geographical areas, known as a 'market sharing cartel'.

Vertical agreements are those between suppliers and resellers, whereby suppliers attempt to influence the prices that resellers charge for their products (also known as 'resale price maintenance') or attempt to impose contractual terms on them. Examples of illegal behaviour include:

- contractually obliging downstream firms to resell a product or service at a set price;
- penalising downstream firms for not selling at the suggested resell price;
- blocking resale to certain companies;
- blocking resale to certain regions (to enforce a price differential between the two).

Other areas where illegal agreements could occur include discount levels, price differentials and credit terms. Forms of price communication and signalling between market players may also be illegal, depending on the situation and the manner in which they are conducted.

The second key topic is the abuse of market dominance, where a firm with some degree of market power uses this power to distort the market. Having a high market share can imply certain restrictions on what a firm can or cannot do (or even give the appearance of doing). Examples would include a firm with a high market share looking to leverage its position to block out competitors or to force them out of business entirely. Selling below cost (i.e. below the long run average variable cost) for example, may be deemed illegal under certain circumstances, particularly if a firm is a dominant player within a market. Indeed the fines can be substantial if a firm is found to be abusing a dominant position.

Price discrimination, i.e. charging different prices to different customers for the same product can be illegal where there is an intent to harm competitors (e.g. lower prices to block out other competitors). As such, this can be particularly important for dominant players in a market, and in that case, differences in price must be related to a cost-based saving (for example, volume discounts related to scale efficiencies). In most cases, it is not permissible to differentiate prices between consumers on the basis of sex, religion or race.

The simple advice is that, if in doubt about the legality of any aspect of pricing, consult with a lawyer.

Summary and future outlook for pricing

Price is unique within marketing as it is the only element of the marketing mix that defines an organisation as a commercial entity, i.e. the intention and the ability to make money. Given this fundamental role in shaping commercial outcomes, it is surprising how under-invested many firms are in the area of pricing and price management, especially when we consider how much more powerful pricing is in driving the bottom line than cost or volume (both of which typically receive far more management attention). Pricing therefore represents an area of significant opportunity for many businesses.

This chapter set out the five key elements that need to be considered as part of a holistic approach to price management:

1 **Price strategy**. Companies are not alone in the market, hence they need to develop a price strategy that makes sense given both their own corporate targets and objectives and which accounts for the market position for their products in a competitive environment. The price strategy has to carefully balance the price charged with the value-to-customer delivered and should avoid the aggressive pursuit of market share which carries with it the risk of price wars.

2 **Price setting**. Price is the counter of value. So it stands to reason that the most important input to setting the right price is the value that the customer perceives in a product and their resultant willingness to pay for it. Quantifying value-to-customer and how demand will change as the price changes (the PED) is not easy, but is vital to compute the profit maximising price. There are a number of approaches to quantifying PED including econometric analysis, price trials and customer research. Price setting becomes more complicated when the price model is considered, that is to say *how* a company prices, not just what they charge. Real customer-based pricing considers innovative ways to truly capture a share of the value they deliver to their customers.

3 **Price implementation**. This step in the process deals with the way in which prices are taken to and communicated to the market, specifically looking to minimise price 'leakages'. In most B2B companies, the principal focus of price implementation is the steering and controlling of the sales force. In B2C environments, price psychology and price communication become important concepts for influencing choice and price perceptions.

4   **Price infrastructure**. It is important to define who has responsibility for which parts of the pricing process. Importantly, there needs to be an infrastructure and systems in place to deliver the data and information required to make ongoing pricing decisions in a scalable and repeatable way.

5   **Price environment**. Every pricing decision needs to be made in the context of the governing legal, regulatory and ethical framework. There is specific legislation and regulation governing pricing and price setting, which differs between regions and industries that may require specialist input and guidance.

As with all aspects of marketing, the science of pricing is constantly developing, and technology in particular plays a key role in shaping how organisations think about and set their prices. Having access to more customer data and better software gives companies the power to 'personalise' pricing to a degree simply not possible even ten years ago. In reality, the future of pricing is not about higher or lower prices, but is about *more* prices and prices that change more often. Unlike most areas of business improvement, advances in pricing have not been focused on process simplification or variance reduction. Quite the opposite is true: pricing is the one area of business where variation pays, and where simplification leaves money on the table. Pricing therefore remains an area of massive opportunity for almost every business and, with technology as an enabler, more and more businesses will begin to benefit from a more scientific approach to price management.

Notes

1   Sawers, P. (2014), *Be All-In, or All-Out: Steve Ballmer's Advice for Startups*, accessed 10 September 2014, available at http://thenextweb.com/insider/2014/03/04/steve-ballmers-advice-startups/

2   Grant, R. (2010), *Contemporary Strategy Analysis: Text & Cases*, seventh edition, New York: Wiley.

3   Simon-Kucher & Partners (2012), *Global Pricing Study 2012 – Profits Jump When CEOs Take an Active Role in Pricing*, accessed 30 September 2014, available at http://www.simon-kucher.com/en-gb/content/pricing

4   Simon, H., Bilstein, F. and Luby, F. (2006), *Manage For Profit, Not For Market Share*, Boston, MA: Harvard Business School Press.

5   Simon, H., Bilstein, F. and Luby, F. (2006), *Manage For Profit, Not For Market Share*, Boston, MA: Harvard Business School Press.

6   Simon, H. (2009), *Beat the Crisis: 33 Quick Solutions for Your Company*, New York: Springer Science + Business Media.

7   Simon, H. (2009), *Beat the Crisis: 33 Quick Solutions for Your Company*, New York: Springer Science + Business Media.

8   Dolan, R. and Simon, H. (1996), *Power Pricing*, New York: The Free Press.

9   Reddy, M. and Terblanche, N. (2005), *How Not to Extend Your Luxury Brand*, accessed 30 September 2014, available at http://hbr.org/2005/12/how-not-to-extend-your-luxury-brand/ar/1

10 BBC News (2014) *Mulberry Targets Lower-Priced Handbags as Profits Fall*, accessed 30 September 2014, available at http://www.bbc.com/news/business-27809111

11 Skoda (2014), *Fabia Hatch – List Prices*, accessed 10 September 2014, available at http://www.skoda.co.uk/models/fabiahatch/prices

12 H. R. Owen (2014), *Veyron Grand Sport 16.4*, accessed 10 September 2014, available at http://www.hrowen.co.uk/bugatti/new-cars/veyron-grand-sport/

13 Seat (2014), *Ibiza SC Toca*, accessed 10 September 2010, available at http://www.seat.co.uk/content/uk/brand/en/models/special-offers/new-cars/ibiza-sc.html

14 Audi (2014), *A3 Sportback e-Tron*, accessed 10 September 2010, available at http://www.audi.co.uk/new-cars/a3/a3-sportback-etron.html

15 BBC News (2002) *Microsoft Drops Xbox Price*, accessed 10 September 2014, available at http://news.bbc.co.uk/2/hi/entertainment/1936791.stm

16 HP Press Release (2011) *Hewlett-Packard and Compaq Agree to Merge, Creating $87 Billion Global Technology Leader*, accessed 10 September 2014, available at http://www8.hp.com/us/en/hp-news/press-release.html?id=230610#.VBByLOLhlk5

17 Dolan, R. and Simon, H. (1996), *Power Pricing*, New York: The Free Press.

18 Simon-Kucher & Partners (2012), *Global Pricing Study 2012 – Profits Jump When CEOs Take an Active Role in Pricing*, accessed 30 September 2014, available at http://www.simon-kucher.com/en-gb/content/pricing

19 Simon, H., Bilstein, F. and Luby F. (2006), *Manage For Profit, Not For Market Share*, Boston, MA: Harvard Business School Press.

20 Court, D., Freeling, A. and George, M. (1994), *Marketers' Metamorphosis*, McKinsey Quarterly.

21 Woodyard, C. (1995), *Euro Disney Posts 1st Profit in 3 Years: Earnings: Debt Repurchase and 'Interest Moratorium' Play a Role in the Turnaround for the Operator of Disneyland Paris*, accessed 30 September 2014, available at http://articles.latimes.com/1995–07–26/business/fi-28076_1_euro-disney

22 http://www.dailymail.co.uk/sciencetech/article-2516790/Tescos-Hudl-sold-TWICE-run-Christmas-firm-struggles-demand-119-tablet.html#ixzz3EohurrJv

23 Dolan, R. and Simon, H. (1996), *Power Pricing*, New York: The Free Press.

24 Van Westendorp, P. (1976), *NSS-Price Sensitivity Meter (PSM)- A New Approach to Study Consumer Perception of Price*, proceedings of the ESOMAR Congress.

25 Rolls Royce (2014), *Rolls-Royce Celebrates 50th Anniversary of Power-by-the-Hour*, accessed 30 September 2014, available at http://www.rolls-royce.com/news/press_releases/2012/121030_the_Hour.jsp

26 Dolan, R. and Simon, H. (1996), *Power Pricing*, New York: The Free Press.

27 Simon, H., Bilstein, F. and Luby F. (2006), *Manage For Profit, Not For Market Share*, Boston, MA: Harvard Business School Press.

28 Research conducted by Simon-Kucher & Partners.

29 Cheng, Y. H. (2012), *The Impact of Purchase Quantity on the Compromise Effect: The Balance Heuristic*, accessed 30 September 2014, available at *journal.sjdm.org/11/11619/jdm11619.pdf*

30 Ariely, D. (2008), *Predictably Irrational: The Hidden Forces that Shape our Decisions*, London: HarperCollins Publishers.

31 Simon-Kucher & Partners (2012), *Global Pricing Study 2012 – Profits Jump When CEOs Take an Active Role in Pricing*, accessed 30 September 2014, available at http://www.simon-kucher.com/en-gb/content/pricing

32 Montan, L. and Simonetto, M. (2009), *Is There a Career in Pricing? An Insider's View of the Pricing Profession*, accessed 30 September 2014, available at http://webcache.googleusercontent.com/search?q=cache:6wkT_-HaNoJ:www.deloitte.com/assets/Dcom-UnitedStates/Localpercent2520Assets/Documents/us_ppm_IsThereACareerInPricing.pdf+&cd=4&hl=en&ct=clnk&gl=uk&client=firefox

15 Sales management

Spiros Gounaris

Introduction

Although it could be considered common knowledge, many tend to forget or chose to ignore the fact that one way or another almost everyone is making a living by selling something to someone at a profit. Ordinary people sell their labour and individual skills to corporations, professionals to their clients, companies to their customers. Even prime ministers and presidents sell to their international counterparts on behalf of their country's industries and interests. Since trade and money was invented, economic activity and societal prosperity have both been intrinsically related with the ability of individuals, societies and countries to sell. Thus, a reasonable expectation is that the sales profession would be among the most glorified of occupations and the potential to build a successful career in sales would be attractive to many. However, this is not reflected in the ranking a prospective career in sales receives in different classification lists. For instance, in a list released by *The Telegraph*,[1] a career in sales (sales rep) takes the 120th position among 200 alternative careers. An advertising sales rep ranks at number 135, while a retail sales person goes down another five places to number 140. Interestingly, though, in the same list market research analyst hits number 40 and management consultant number 48! So what drives this alienation between the society and sales as a profession?

There are certainly many reasons, but two are probably prevalent. The (bad) practices many salespeople would easily adopt, such as presenting what they offer as (unjustifiably) superior to competition, or promising to fit the prospective buyer's needs so eventually they can secure the sale; and the (mis)understanding that it takes merely a kind of charismatic personality and a talent for interpersonal relations to become successful in sales. With these qualities in hand and through years of experience and training that develop these inherited gifts further, success in sales is promised and open to anyone regardless of their background. This kind of negative predisposition has led even the management of the marketing department to draw a clear line of distinction between themselves and their colleagues in sales. As a result, when both coexist in the organisation, marketing is often seen to represent the important strategic arm leading the company's effort to achieve its market objectives. In contrast, sales are all too often considered to be the lower-ranked boots in the field who have the responsibility to implement the strategy marketing has developed and help achieve their objectives. Not surprisingly, when this is the case, friction and tension between the two can arise.

The first objective of this chapter is thus to discuss the relationship between marketing and sales and how both departments need to work together to achieve the company's market objectives. The second objective is to dislodge the myths around selling by demonstrating that: (1) selling is a demanding profession that requires a strong knowledge background and, as such, goes far beyond the art of persuasion; (2) managing the personal sales task in the corporate context is a major challenge, which requires a strong theoretical background drawn from across the different fields of management; and (3) selling and ethos are not two incompatible notions. To serve these objectives, the rest of this chapter is organised around the following sections. First, we will discuss the evolution of the marketing era and how companies (can) move from a short-sighted product dominant orientation to focus on the actual needs of the customer while slightly touching on the implications for the marketing and sales departments for companies that adopt a market orientation. Next, we will address the reasons why the relationship between the two departments may not always be as cordial as one might expect, and we will recommend potential remedies that could bring marketing and sales closer together. We will then move the discussion on to the actual challenges of managing the sales effort and close the chapter with a brief, yet important, note on ethics and their effect on the practice of sales.

From product to market orientation through the adoption of a sales orientation

Arguably, every business that has survived the early days and managed to grow in size achieved this because the product or service the company was offering as a start-up was successfully addressing a problem in the market, allowing it to meet the needs of a specific customer base better than its competitors. Not uncommonly, behind almost every start-up, one individual or a group of partners possessing a strong technical understanding of the product or the service the new organisation is going to deliver in the market can be traced. While still in its infancy, the management quickly realises the significance of marketing and sales for the newly founded company to survive. Often a partner will undertake the responsibility for these tasks or alternatively, depending on the nature of the product, the task of marketing and selling the company's product will be outsourced to some third party (e.g. a distributor or a forwarder), albeit negotiating with that agent will still be an issue for the management to handle. At some later stage as the company grows and more resources become available, the company may even consider hiring a marketing or a sales manager to carry on and expand the company's business model. Meanwhile, and as the company was growing, the management would have been investing in improving further the company's technical expertise and ability to excel in producing a product or delivering a service the company's customers would desire and which competitors will envy.

However, to sustain growth the management will sooner or later realise that the original product or service from which success was produced will no longer be enough. Many reasons can account for this: customers' preferences and expectations change over time, competitors eventually catch up or new technologies emerge that render the company's offering obsolete. Whatever the reason(s), at that point, the company is at a crossroad.

One route is grounded on the firm belief that the company's product (service) remains superior to any other alternative offered by competitors, which in fact it may well be from a technical perspective. Following from this belief, slowing down sales and eroding market share are considered temporary, and it will not be long before customers realise afresh this superiority and the company's sales rebound. Following on from this, the management of such companies will use the scarce resources, not to align the company's offering to the emergent market conditions but into diligent efforts to further improve the product (service) technically, so the company can get back on track sooner than later. We call this route *product orientation* (Atuahene-Gima 1995). Under product orientation the company concentrates its efforts on the product and its technical features. New and improved versions may appear as a result of the company's effort to regain the customers' preference through rigorous research and development projects that seek to bring into the market products (services) that are superior to those that competitors have developed and offer. Unfortunately, this is done at the expense of looking at the market and listening to customers' needs. As a result, such companies increasingly lose touch with their customers and not surprisingly their market performance never seriously recovers.

For companies who have made a futile attempt to get back on track based on their existing, strong technical skills and expertise, usually the next step is to adopt what has been described in the literature as a sales orientation (Hooley *et al.* 1990). Generally, sales orientation is acknowledged as following the production orientation in driving the efforts of the company (Keith 1960). Competitive forces, combined with unsatisfactory market performance, usually force the company to consider options that it has not seriously considered or practised before. For such organisations the most obvious option is to push their sales efforts harder. Once the transition from the product to the sales orientation is complete, the company concentrates on aggressively selling through all potential and available channels, using every promotional weapon, including price and discounts. Their intention is to regain market share lost to competition and/or to capture much needed new markets and customers. During this effort, sales and promotional budgets will increase dramatically in anticipation of an even stronger increase in the company's sales volumes. However, as a result of moving large resources towards the support of the selling effort, recognition of customers' needs continues to remain under nurtured and the company remains at a distance from the actual wants and expectations of the target market(s). Thus, differentiating from competition remains hard, and eventually heavy price discounts are required before the customers are persuaded to buy a product (service) that is little different from competition and does not match well enough with their needs. As a result, even if sales recover in the short or medium term, this is not a sustainable approach for the long term, as profitability suffers and the momentum in sales is heavily conditioned by the amount of resources the company can throw at supporting the sales task.

The alternative route the management could have pursed though, was to admit that the company's business model and the product or service upon which it was grounded can no longer sustain continuous growth. In such cases, the management will realise that the original product (service) requires radical redesign or significant support from new products (services) to jointly form a portfolio the company can offer to the market to cater for the needs of different customer segments. This realisation gears the company towards a different business model and away from a producer-led interpretation of consumer needs. Such companies invest in understanding the needs of the customer, which then drives the configuration of their offering to the market (Baker 2010: 12). This alternative route has been described in the literature as the adoption of a market orientation based on the company's efforts to understand what the customers want and competitors offer, make the entire organisation well aware of the prevalent market conditions, and design the company response in a manner that will allow the company to produce products (services) that respond to specific customers' needs and deliver them profitably (Kohli and Jaworski 1990). What is worth noting is that companies adopting this orientation go beyond the functional role and tasks that the marketing or the sales department (or both) may have. In such companies, customer centricity, customer responsiveness and customer value generation become the principles entwining the philosophy underlying the company's business model and drive success (Baker *et al.* 1988). In other words, the task of marketing and generating value for the customers becomes a responsibility for every organisational function.

This of course does not imply that the marketing and the sales department become redundant. On the contrary, both of them become the customers' ambassadors within the company. In addition to echoing the voice of the customer, both departments have to coordinate and jointly lead the company's efforts to understand what customers want, what competitors offer and how the company can better respond to the market conditions. The marketing department usually contributes through market intelligence collection and the analysis of market data the department generates from both market research and market studies. The sales department also contributes mainly through reporting back to the company the first hand experiences of the efforts to sell the company's product (service), how and why customers resist buying and what it would take to make customers actually purchase the company's product. Although all this information is clearly complementary in allowing the company to better respond to the needs of the customer, the different sources from which this information is derived and the different perspective of the market these different types of information capture can easily fuel contrasting views of how the company should respond to the conditions of the market most effectively. When this happens, the two departments may adopt quite divergent views, which in turn could fuel friction in the relationship between the two. The implication is that the two departments need to overcome such tensions and coordinate their efforts more closely if they are to deliver what is expected of them under the marketing philosophy. As we explain in the next section, this is not always an easy task.

The significance of bridging the gap between sales and marketing

The significance of ensuring a seamless interface between the marketing and the sales departments has been highlighted for quite some time now in the marketing literature (cf. Cespedes 1993). The complementarity of the roles the two departments play explains why a smooth, friendly interaction between the two is so important.

American Marketing Association describes marketing as the set of institutions, processes and activities for creating, communicating, delivering and exchanging offerings that have value for customers, clients, partners and society at large. Sales, on the other hand, are responsible for creating value (sales revenue and profits) for the firm at the point of contact with a customer (Rouziès *et al.* 2005). As such, the role of the two departments is clearly complimentary, oriented towards the market and focused on the customer (Shapiro 2002). Together, marketing and sales have a common goal of offering superior customer value; therefore, these two units most work closely and in harmony.

To better capture the nature and scope of this collaboration, academics have relied on organisational theory, behavioural science, the resource dependency theory and the contingency theory to identify the key elements of the relationship between the two departments that, when present, manifest a healthy on-going relationship:

- *collaborative climate*, capturing the degree to which the two departments share goals, resources and activities and have developed a mutual understanding of key organisational priorities and goals (Kahn and Mentzer 1998);
- *effective interaction*, capturing both the formal and informal communication processes and flow of information between the two (Guenzi and Troilo 2007);
- *harmony* of relationship, reflecting the degree to which communication, interaction and collegiality characterises the interaction between managers across the two departments (Song *et al.* 2000);
- *quality of cooperation*, defining the extent to which unity of effort characterises the collaboration between the marketing and the sales departments (Homburg and Jensen 2007);
- *coordination*, defining how well the two departments jointly perform in using the scarce organisational resources to create and deliver superior value for target customers (Narver and Slater 1990);

- *justice (or 'fairness')*, reflecting how do managers make decisions on the distribution of resources between the two departments, the fairness of the procedures and the quality of the interaction between those involved from the two departments (Hulland *et al.* 2012);
- *integration*, capturing the extent to which the activities carried out by the two departments are supportive of each other (Rouziès *et al.* 2005);
- *benevolent functional conflict*, which can be beneficial for the two departments and the organisation as a whole (cf. Menguc and Auh 2008), as long as such conflict allows them and the organisation as a whole to challenge existing practices and conducts in favour of innovative behaviours that better align the company with the realities of the market place. Such conflicts, to be productive, involve consultative interactions, mutual respect and mutually beneficial barter between the two departments when cascading strategic corporate objectives and priorities down to the practices each department employs (Massey and Dawes 2007).

Nevertheless, although academics have been highlighting the need for cordial and coordinated collaboration between marketing and sales, in practice the working relationship between the two is more than often characterised by tension, friction and frequently by a subtle hostility (Avlonitis *et al.* 2010). Sales personnel often tend to think that marketers, lacking a close proximity to the market itself, become detached from the customers' real needs and expectations. Marketers on the other hand accuse salespeople of myopically focusing on individual customers and the short-term sales volume at the expense of longer-term goals and performance (Kotler *et al.* 2006). As a result, the contribution one department makes in what should have been a common effort is underrated by the other and, consequently, it is no surprise that managers from both departments complain about the lack of understanding, disbelief and poor cooperation their counterparts from the other department demonstrate (Dewsnap and Jobber 2000, 2002; Rouziès *et al.* 2005; Le Meunier-FitzHugh and Piercy 2007). Thus, in practice, tension often grows between the two.

This tension haunts many companies and deters them from fulfilling their potential. The quality of the interface between the two departments impacts both the company's ability to generate value for the customer and effectively adapt to a rapidly changing environment and, at the same time, conditions the company's ability to achieve market-based objectives. As such, improving the business relationship between marketing and sales is a key antecedent for improving the company's performance across a number of different performance metrics (Guenzi and Troilo 2007). Clearly, then, the obvious question is, 'What can the managers from the two department do to build stronger bridges and improve their collaboration in serving what apparently are their common objectives?'.

Based on empirical findings, a recent study has attempted to address this question (Avlonitis *et al.* 2010). The findings from this study are quite enlightening and allow for some clear, straightforward priorities that the managers from both departments must address to improve the interdepartmental coordination (Lionakis *et al.* 2013). These include:

1   addressing the distribution of power between the two departments;
2   ensuring appropriate delegation of tasks between the two;
3   improving the strategic alignment between marketing and sales;
4   enhancing the market orientation as the prevalent philosophy driving both departments' plans and actions.

Power and how it is balanced between the two departments and across the organisation is a serious concern, mainly because of the implications perceived power has on a number of subjects. These include the availability and use of resources; the decision-making procedures and the criteria upon which decisions are made; the climate and the interpersonal relationships between employees and managers from sales and marketing, as well as with the other departments. Practice shows that when the two departments share an equal level of power, then conflict between the two decreases, and this has a direct positive benefit for organisational performance in the market. The challenge for the company's management is thus to ensure a balance of power between marketing and sales. One way to do this is by appropriately delegating the major responsibility for different marketing tasks that would appear to be more closely relating to the role sales and marketing respectively hold within the organisation. For instance, market research, managing existing product lines, setting the non-personal communication mix or shaping the positioning strategy of the product are clearly marketing tasks that the marketing department can and should lead, mainly because of the skills and knowledge that are typically available within the department. Likewise, sales are more suitable to maintaining the major responsibility for such activities as the recruitment of distributors, setting the most effective credit policy or putting together the company's personal communication strategy. At the same time, the two departments must closely collaborate when making decisions on certain elements of the company's market and customer strategy that would benefit from input from both departments. Customer segmentation and targeting, new product development or control of the commercial effort and performance are typical examples of such elements.

An additional benefit for both departments emerging from such an integrative collaboration is the opportunity to better understand each other's concerns, objectives, strategies and limitations to meet these objectives. As a result, the strategy each department deploys fits well with the strategy the other department pursues, and consequently the two departments and their individual strategies serve better the fulfilment of the overall organisational strategic objectives in the marketplace. Hence, strategic alignment between sales and marketing is facilitated. The latter is crucial if the organisation as a whole is to adopt an orientation geared towards the market, the satisfaction of the customers' needs and dominance over the competition. Compared to other departments, marketing and sales are the only two operating at the organisation's boundaries. As such they have both been identified as the ambassadors of the market orientation philosophy in the organisation since the 1990s (cf. Kohli and Jaworski 1990). When working together they become effective agents of change and can drive the company's efforts to become more attentive and more responsive to the specific needs of the defined customers the company has chosen to target. When tension, misunderstanding or lack of coordination prevails between the two departments, the company's ability to remain alert to market developments, or even better to lead them through commercially successful product and/or process innovations, contracts severely (Avlonitis *et al.* 2010). Such companies tend to adopt a sales or a product orientation, both of which usually translate into poorer performance compared to those companies with a strong market orientation (Avlonitis and Gounaris 1999; Rouziès *et al.* 2005; Le Meunier-FitzHugh and Piercy 2011). Interestingly enough, in such market-oriented companies, marketing is considered more as a set of organisational processes in which, at the end of the day, the entire company participates in an organisation-wide fashion and less as a separate functional unit, which is limited in a confined number of tasks (Moorman and Rust 1999).

Taking account of all factors, when discussing the effective management of the sales effort, clearly one has to start with the relationship between the marketing and the sales departments. No matter how paradoxical it may seem, the relationship between the two frequently suffers from a lack of understanding and frequently from compartmentalisation too. Such conditions may deter the company from realising its full market potential and undermine its utilisation of resources. Management can monitor certain signals and determine whether this is the case or not. When many of these signals change to amber, or worse to red, management needs to take action that will eliminate the stress and improve the working relationship between the two departments. The four actions discussed above can help management in this regard.

Knowledge-based design, organisation and management of the sales force

Understanding the sales task(s)

McMurray (1961) in a seminal piece of work clearly explained that not every sales person performs exactly the same tasks. The different tasks different salespeople perform warrant a classification system that allows academics and practitioners alike to understand the differences and the similarities of the different sales tasks. This will inform how they drive the management of the sales effort and sales personnel in the most effective fashion. Using creativity as the major ingredient different types of sales tasks require in various doses, McMurray described six different types of sales tasks:

1   those that require the salesperson simply to deliver the product, with selling responsibilities coming second in rank;
2   those that require the salesperson to predominantly act as an order taker, working either from the office or in the field;
3   those that seek to cultivate trust and goodwill between the customer and the company; selling per se is not expected or even not permitted;
4   those that require a great technical expertise around the product (such as an engineer seller);
5   those that require creatively selling a tangible consumer product;
6   those that require an even larger amount of creativity as they involve the selling of intangible services.

Conditioned upon the tasks the different sales people perform, McMurray suggested it is possible to classify the sales people and manage them accordingly.

Over the years since this first attempt, many academics have sought to improve or update the original classification McMurray had suggested. As a result, a large number of new classification systems and schemas have emerged. In fact, this large production of different systems to classify the sales task has arguably led to the investigation of the forces underlying the composition and the nature of the tasks sales people perform (Anderson 1996). This research stream produced a categorisation of the major forces that impact the nature of the selling task and, consequently, allow for new taxonomies of salespeople to emerge to facilitate the management of the sales effort: behavioural, technological and managerial. **Behavioural forces** include raising customer expectations, globalisation of markets and demassification of domestic markets. **Technological forces** include sales force automation, virtual offices and electronic channels of selling. **Managerially driven forces** include a shift to direct marketing alternatives, outsourcing of components of the sales function and a blending of the sales and marketing functions within a firm.

A recent study has employed a popular combination of statistical techniques (factor and cluster analysis) to produce what now seems to be the most contemporary and relevant classification of sales employees based on the sales tasks they perform (Moncrief *et al.* 2006). Using a sample of 1,500 companies and factor analysis, this study managed to identify 12 broader areas that summarise the 105 sales activities investigated in the research. The results are summarised in Table 15.1 and provide a very useful insight into how different sales tasks fall in together to form a smaller manageable set, ranging from relationship selling and promotional activities and sales service to channel support. Using these 12 main factors, it was then possible to classify the different salespeople based

Table 15.1 The different tasks salespersons perform in contemporary organisations

Relationship maintenance & selling
1 Build trust
2 Ask questions
3 Build rapport
4 Listen
5 Consult with customers
6 Adapt presentations
7 Sell value added
8 Overcome objections
9 Sell unique competencies
10 Close the sale
11 Work with key accounts
12 ID person in authority
13 Read body language
14 Plan selling activities
15 Call on multiple individuals
16 Correspond with customers
17 Help clients plan

Promotional activities and sales service
1 Point of purchase
2 Set up displays
3 Handle advertising
4 Demonstrate the product
5 Train customers with product
6 Use VCR to sell
7 Sell product accessories
8 Create newsletters
9 Check customer inventory
10 Work trade shows
11 Write up orders
12 Handle back orders
13 Introduce new products

Entertaining customers
1 Entertain with leisure
2 Take clients to dinner
3 Take clients for drinks
4 Play golf
5 Take clients to lunch
6 Throw parties

Prospecting and following leads
1 Call on potential accounts
2 Search out new leads
3 Respond to referrals
4 Submit bids
5 Make multiple calls

Computer usage
1 Use internet
2 Work on web
3 Check email
4 Learn software
5 Enter data on laptop
6 Collect database information
7 Presentation with laptop

Travel
1 Spend night on the road
2 Travel out of town

Recruiting and training
1 Train new sales reps
2 Mentor junior sales reps
3 Recruit sales reps
4 Ride with reps

Delivery
1 Deliver product samples
2 Deliver product
3 Stock shelves

Product service & support
1 Supervise installation
2 Modify the product
3 Perform maintenance
4 Take clients on site
5 Expedite orders

Educational activities
1 Attend sales meetings
2 Attend training sessions
3 Learn about products

Spend time at office
1 Fill out expense reports
2 Check voice mail

Channel support
1 Establish relationships with distributors
2 Train brokers/middlemen

Source: Adapted from Moncrief et al. (2006).

on which tasks they perform and how much they get involved with each of these tasks and which they tend to avoid. The results appear in Table 15.2.

In brief, the **consultative sellers** (representing 34.2 per cent of the participants) have the highest score on *relationship selling* (that is building and maintaining relationships with customers) as well as the highest score on *promotional activities and sales service* (0.408), with *product support* ranking the second highest (0.368). *Prospecting, channel support* and *delivery* were also tasks positively associated with this type of salesperson, but only just. Companies expect this category of salesperson to nurture existing clients (minimal prospecting) and spend a great deal of time in product support and promotional activities. Consultative sellers are found across any industry or sector, but have a particularly heavy representation in traditional B2B settings (machinery, electronic and metal products). This signals that consultative sellers have emerged as an evolution of the traditional *technical salesman* that earlier classification systems had identified in the past. Today's consultative sellers, based on the empirical findings, are less likely to be women. Also, this kind of seller is very often college-educated whose compensation relies heavily on commission from the sales they secure.

New business/channel development sellers accounting for around 25 per cent of the participants are the second group of sales people identified in the survey. They take on *computer usage, entertaining customers, prospecting, training/recruiting, educational activities* and *channel support*. The group is second among all groups in relationship selling (although much lower than the consultative sellers) and in travel. In addition, they are frequently involved with promotional activities and sales service. Like the consultative sellers, companies employ this group across different sectors of mainly consumer products. Again, female sales people are unlikely to fall within this group, which is not necessarily

Table 15.2 A six groups classification system of contemporary salespeople on the grounds of their most common sales tasks

Consultative seller (34%)		New business/channel development seller (25%)		Missionary seller (15%)	
Tasks	Rank	Tasks	Rank	Tasks	Rank
Relationship selling	1	Computer (5)	1	Training/recruiting	2
Promotion/service	1	Entertaining (3)	1	Travel	3
Product support	2	Training/recruiting (7)	1	Delivery	2
Prospecting	3	Travel (6)	2	Education	2
Channel support	4	Prospecting (4)	1	Promotion/service	2
Delivery	3	Channel support (12)	1	Relationship selling	3
		Education (10)	1		
		Relationship selling (1)	2		

Delivery seller (9%)		Sales support (9%)		Key account seller (8%)	
Tasks	Rank	Tasks	Rank	Tasks	Rank
Delivery	1	Office	2	Product support	1
Prospecting	2	Training/recruiting	3	Travel	1
		Channel support	3	Office	1
				Channel support	2
				Computer	2
				Entertaining	2

Source: Adapted from Moncrief *et al.* (2006).

the highest paid, but did have the fewest salespeople making under £46,000 per year. Compensation tends to be a mix of salary and commission. They are in the middle of the six groups in terms of the average number of accounts and average sales calls per week. A third of the companies in the sample have at least 30 per cent of their sales force in this category, signalling the popularity of this kind of salesperson in today's business world. As such, they appear to be the evolution of the trade salesperson earlier classifications had identified (cf. Newton 1973; Moncrief 1986).

Next comes the ***missionary seller*** accounting for 15 per cent of the total sample. They do very little prospecting and ranked fifth out of six in five groups of sales tasks, such as *channel support*, *computer usage*, *entertaining customers* or *product support*. On the other hand, the missionary seller was second in *training/recruiting*, *delivery*, *educational activities* and *promotional activities and sales service*; all typical missionary activities as identified by earlier studies. Nowadays, however, missionary sellers travel frequently and they also engage in a degree of *relationship selling*.

Again, consistent with typical missionary salespeople as defined by earlier classifications, missionary sellers are very much engaged with *delivering samples* to the customers, but not with delivering the product. As such, they would appear to be the modern version of the typical missionary salespeople identified in earlier classification systems that have taken on some additional activities as a result of the changes coming from managerial and environmental forces. This type of seller is (still) very popular among pharmaceutical and medical supply companies, whose salespeople traditionally leave samples for medical personnel. However, other organisations from printing and furniture have also started adopting this kind of sales personnel. Salespeople of this kind would appear to fall in older age groups and include more females than the previous two types of sellers. Moreover, they have the highest percentage of more highly paid personnel who are most frequently compensated by a combination of both straight salary and straight commission.

Delivery sellers, representing 9 per cent of the participants in the study, are the fourth type of sales people employed in the modern organisation. From Table 15.2 it is clear that this kind of seller has a well-specified, yet very narrow set of tasks. Their main responsibilities include delivery and prospecting. Corroborative evidence for differentiating the delivery seller from, say, the new business/channel development sellers can be found by examining several individual activities within the delivery factor of activities. For example, this factor exhibits the highest factor loading for stocking shelves and is third for checking inventory and for writing up orders. In addition, delivery sellers pose an interesting demographic compared to the rest. They are the youngest group, 25 per cent are females and they have the lowest percentage of college degrees. More than half (58 per cent) of the group has been on-the-job two years or less, and there is a high preponderance of lower-paid salespeople with 90 per cent getting less than £46,000 per annum, while more than 80 per cent of them maintain more than 100 accounts. Again, delivery sellers would appear to be an evolved version of the order taker identified in earlier systems (cf. McMurray 1961; Moncrief 1986). This can be explained to an extent by the influence and growth of telemarketing and the internet, which together may have replaced traditional order-taking in the bulk of applications (Rackham and DeVincentis 1999).

The fifth group of sellers is ***sales support***, representing roughly 9 per cent of the participants in this recent study. However, it would appear that sales personnel in this group do relatively little actual selling. These individuals are mainly involved in office functions and training/recruiting since they are mostly riding with reps and recruiting new reps. When involved with sales tasks, they usually engage in overcoming objections, checking back orders and planning selling activities, They are predominately (94 per cent) male and a third of the participants make more than £65,000 per annum, the highest income among all groups, whereas more than half of the individuals in this group have fewer than 20 accounts assigned to them. Based on these, it would appear that this group represents managers who are likely to sell as well as support the salespeople in their unit in various ways, and support staff who may also do some selling. This category is not mentioned in any of the previous taxonomies. Hence, this new group appears to be the outcome of developments and recent trends in the management of the sales effort. In the light of intensified competition and increasing demands from customers, more senior managers need to get more actively involved in the sales effort and at the same time more support is necessary for the rest of the salespeople.

The last cluster of sellers identified in this study are the *key account sellers* representing about 8 per cent of the participants. Key account sellers are substantially involved in product support, which subsumes a number of specific technical activities such as maintenance and installation. Key account sellers also had the highest score on travel and office and were second highest on channel support, computer and entertaining customers, all of which are typical activities of the key account manager as identified in the pertinent literature (cf. Weitz and Bradford 1999; Homburg *et al.* 2002). Usually this kind of seller represents only a small fraction of the total number of sales personnel employed in any of the companies that participated in the study, which again conforms to the pertinent literature. This category had the highest percentage of females (33 per cent) and the highest percentage of people on straight salary (57 per cent) with none on straight commission. Moreover, this group had the highest percentage of college graduates (82 per cent) and the highest level of selling experience. They do not make many calls to customers per week (65 per cent make fewer than 6 per week) and more than half of them have fewer than 20 accounts. This is another category not reported in the earlier classification taxonomies; rather, like the previous group, this too has emerged as a result of the emphasis modern companies place in managing their relationships with accounts that fit and benefit their own strategic goals and objectives over a period of three to five years (Gounaris and Tzempelikos 2013).

In summary, past research has reported that it is possible to classify salespeople in a meaningful taxonomy based on the different tasks the sales personnel perform. Such a classification allows management to draw useful insights into the similarities and differences of the overall job description and the tasks different salespeople have. Using these insights, management can then tailor specific policies and practices to fit the different characteristics of the different sales jobs resulting from the discrete tasks they entail. Having discussed the most recent effort to update such taxonomies, we will thus focus the following discussion on the most appropriate ones. However, many things have changed in the technological environment over the last ten years and customers' expectations have followed too. Consciously or not, companies have also adjusted their practices and the nature of the different sales tasks. As a result, past groups have evolved and new ones have emerged. Unfortunately, though, the extant literature has still not addressed the question of what are the most appropriate practices to manage the evolved and emerged types of sales jobs/tasks. Hence, in the following paragraphs, we shall rely on the characteristics of the six groups that have been recently identified in combination with what is already known regarding the effective management of the sales task to produce a useful discussion on how the sales force can be managed for effectiveness and success.

Design and management of the sales force

The effort of designing and managing the company's sales effort and force is summarised in Figure 15.1. In designing the sales force, management needs to decide on the specific objectives the sales force will need to achieve. Such objectives can and should not only relate to sales revenue. Rather they will need to harvest in full the potential of the sales personnel to make a contribution within the company's overall marketing strategy and objectives. Consequently, the next step in defining the sales strategy will also need to reflect and relate to the marketing strategy while serving the company's overall strategy. The structure to adopt is another important concern when designing the sales force since it needs to serve and at the same time facilitate the implementation of the sales force strategy. The size of the sales force will determine not only the cost associated with the sales efforts but also the effectiveness of the sales team and the ability to meet the objectives.

The compensation for the sales force has a similar role to play in the overall design and management effort. On the one hand, the compensation mix must motivate the sales people and gear them towards the realisation of those objectives the company is seeking to achieve, and at the same time it must be attractive enough for the kind of people and talent the company will seek to recruit. Finally, when it comes to the management of the sales team, recruitment, training, motivating, supervising and evaluating the salespeople are the main tasks for the sales manager. The following paragraphs offer an elaborated discussion of these facets of the design and management of the sales force. Moreover, to make the discussion useful and relevant for the practising managers as well, the management of the sales force will also consider the different types of salesperson identified in the Moncrief *et al.* 2006 taxonomy.

Designing an effective sales force

The discussion of the sales force management that follows should not lure the reader into assuming that it only fits the effort to design a sales force afresh. What follows applies equally to companies that, at some point, review their existing sales organisation. Many reasons from the external or internal environment can necessitate this review. In fact, it would be advisable for companies with established sales organisations to perform this exercise on a regular basis, say every five to seven years to ensure, if nothing else, that as things change their choices remain appropriate.

Sales force objectives

The first step in designing the sales organisation, either afresh or reviewing an existing organisation, is to decide on the specific objectives the organisation will pursue. In other words, what the

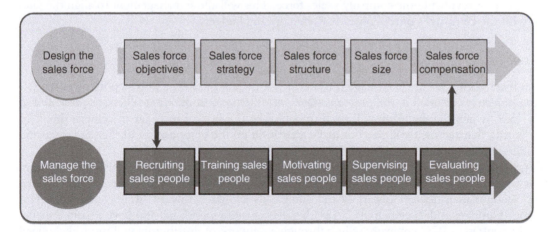

Figure 15.1 The process of sales force design and management

company's management expects to achieve through and from the sales force, not what individual sales people will need to perform.

Table 15.1 above summarised the key sales activities the salespeople can perform. The question thus for the company's management is how each of these activities fits with the company's overall business and marketing objectives. If product service is a key element of the company's offering, is the company willing to maintain the service in-house or is it going to opt for outsourcing? Moreover, if the choice is for in-house, should the sales personnel get involved and deliver the service or should specialised service personnel get involved? If salespeople deliver the service, then this probably means that they will have to spend more time with existing customers rather than prospecting for new customers. Is this desirable? Who is going to generate and follow sales leads to create new business?

Likewise, if the company is pursuing a key account management approach in dealing with customers of strategic importance, how does this affect the objectives the sales force must meet? Empirical evidence has shown that successful key account management potentially leads to a variety of benefits for the supplier that will go beyond profits and/or sales (Gounaris and Tzempelikos 2014). Therefore, if the company aims to improve its reference value and image, or to increase the opportunities for knowledge sharing with strategically important customers, relational selling is a key activity the sales force will need to perform.

In addition, the company's management will also have to consider the need to integrate the elements of the communication effort in one coherent communication strategy. Once again, this need will have an impact on the sales force and the objectives they must deliver. For instance, are trade shows and participation in exhibitions an integral element of the company's communication effort? How often and in how many events will the company need to participate? What are the implications of participation for the sales personnel? Likewise, if social media are part of the communication effort (as is the case with most companies today), how does this impact the sales personnel and consequently the expectations management has of the sales force in terms of tasks or time spent with computers. Moreover, what are the implications for coordinating the outgoing context through social media, the size of the sales force and so on and so forth?

In summary, investing time and effort to clearly consider and specify what the company's exact expectations from the sales force are, then looking at how these expectations translate into the specific objectives that the sales force will need to fulfil in the future, are the first necessary steps in designing or reviewing the company's sales force. This will allow management to align the sales force with the company's overall objectives, strategy and budgets.

Sales force strategy

Once objectives are set, the next stage is to decide on the sales strategy. This step involves matching the objectives decided in the previous stage with the types of different sellers, as presented in Table 15.2, which the company will need to deploy in the market in order to achieve them. In other words, management will need to make a decision on the composition of the sales force and the different roles required to achieve the sales force's objectives.

For instance, a B2B company will most likely need to recruit consultative sellers whose main task is to develop and nurture long-term oriented relationships with the company's customers. If key account management is part of the company's approach towards strategically important accounts (Gounaris and Tzempelikos 2013), then key account sellers will also have to join the sales force. In contrast, a B2C company selling through a network of distributors will most likely need to build the sales force with new business/channel development sellers who will mainly undertake the task of promoting the company's products while serving the needs of the distributors and, at the same time, prospecting for new business opportunities.

The company will also need to decide on whether missionary sellers are needed or not. While for pharmaceutical or printing and furniture companies this may well be the main approach towards personal selling, companies from other sectors could still find it beneficial to use this type of selling activity/approach to further strengthen their message to existing and potential customers. Likewise, management will need to consider if and how the other types of sellers presented in Table 15.2 could be part of the overall sales strategy. For instance, will (should) more senior managers get involved in the sales effort? Does meeting the company's sales objective require employing delivery sellers? Will the salespeople need significant support that would justify setting up a special group? Key parameters to consider in making these strategic decisions include (Blessington 1992; Lane and Piercy 2004):

- *The industry in which the company competes* – in most B2B sectors, for example, salespeople are mainly involved in consultative selling whereas in most B2C businesses salespeople are usually involved in developing business opportunities with members of the company's distribution channel.
- *The type of the company's offering* – when the value for the buyer is service driven, the seller has to ensure delivery of a high quality service in a competitive manner, which usually requires individual salespeople to spend more time with the company's existing customers, and this in turn may call for a separate sales force calling on new customers and prospecting for new business opportunities.
- *Competition* – the company will need to keep a close eye on what direct competitors do and ensure that competition does not outperform the company's effort to service existing customers, to call on new customers and so on.
- *Customers' expectations* – for instance, customers driven by a transaction-based purchasing orientation emphasising efficiencies and pricing will require the seller to adopt a less relational or consultative approach to selling, which, on the other hand, will be required if the customers mainly need to work closely with suppliers to explore new business models, ideas or innovations.
- *Marketing objectives/competitive advantage* – how does the sales force contribute to the company's competitiveness? For instance, if know-how and customer service are the bases upon which the company seeks to develop its competitive proposition for the customer, management may wish to mingle consultative sellers with a separate support task. Key account sellers may also be considered if, for instance, the company competes in the B2B context.
- *Sales revenue per exchange* – technology offers opportunities to reduce expenses (hence improving the profitability of infrequent buyers or smaller orders). The internet, for instance, has allowed many companies to develop an alternative direct sales channel that many companies employ to serve either infrequently buying customers or relatively smaller order placers, or both. This strategy calls for a force that will basically support the sales through this medium while at the same time allowing for a relatively smaller and thus more efficient force to focus on the company's alternative channels of distribution.

Sales force structure

The strategy of the sales force will have implications for the sales force structure. What must be clear though is that there is no perfect solution for structuring the sales force, since every approach comes with certain advantages as well as with disadvantages. For instance, one very common and popular approach is the **territorial** structuring of the sales force. One main advantage of this approach is the ease of managing and monitoring the performance of individual salespeople to whom a territory has been assigned. Also, territorial responsibility and assignment is easy to explain to salespeople. Further, programming and planning to improve the efficiency and effectiveness of covering a certain territory is possible through linear programming models, which seek to optimise routes given certain time constrains. On the other hand, though, it is not entirely possible to always come up with territorial designs that are comparable or equally attractive for the salespeople in terms of the potential both to generate sales revenue and service existing customers. Such situations can easily harm the sense of fairness among salespeople and eventually prove catastrophic for the team spirit the salespeople need to share. Likewise, if the company sells a significant number of products, or if the products the company sells are rather complex and require technical expertise to promote them effectively, or if the needs of the customers are quite dispersed, it is quite unlikely that a single salesperson can have all the skills and knowledge to meet all the different challenges that can emerge within their territory.

Under such situations the company may consider adopting a **product** or a **customer** structure for the sales force. A product structure means that different salespeople of the same company represent different products from the company's product portfolio, which allows them to have much more expertise on the technical characteristics of the products they represent. While this approach has clear benefits when the company's products are rather technical, and this technical expertise allows the salesperson to make an effective presentation of the product features and how these features translate to specific benefits for the customer, it can prove inefficient for such customers who need a larger array of the company's offerings. In such situations it is possible that different salespeople from the same company call to the same customer. The opposing perspective is that, if the needs of the customers are rather diverse, the company may find it beneficial to organise the sales force around individual customers and have the sales force become experts in understanding and serving a set of customers with a homogeneous set of needs and expectations. Such salespeople become experts in meeting the needs of specific customers, although again inefficiencies may emerge, particularly for relatively small customers and orders. Also, opportunities for cross-selling may well be wasted unless the salesperson is quite familiar with the full range of products the company offers. A way around the disadvantages the product and customer structures have is to consider adopting a more complex, **hybrid** or **matrix structure** that allocates both specific products and specific customers to specific salespeople. However, such structures are harder to manage and monitor while exchange transaction costs can rise unexpectedly.

Finally, many B2B companies who adopt the key account management profile adjust their structure accordingly. When successful, such companies have adopted a certain system of values, termed *key account orientation*, which promotes a long-term orientation towards the relationship with their key accounts (Tzempelikos and Gounaris 2013), and this is then reflected in the structuring of their key account management efforts. Such companies tend to adopt more decentralised and informal structures (Gounaris and Tzempelikos 2014), which entails more team selling and greater involvement of the company's top management in the formulation of the company's strategy at the individual key account level (Tzempelikos and Gounaris 2015).

Sales force size

Deciding on the size of the sales force is the next step in the design process. Again, this is a fundamental task, because it will affect both the costs associated with the sales effort and the income the company will generate from the sales force. Ultimately, the size of the sales force will be one of the three major parameters affecting the impact of sales on a company's profitability, the other two being the skills and resources the salespeople have (Cron *et al.* 2014).

In setting the size of the sales force, usually managers rely either on the *workload approach* or the *incremental sales approach*, both of which are discussed below. However, preceding this discussion a number of points are worth considering. Companies begin their lives as start-ups, then move on into growth, maturity and decline, albeit during this cycle they can regress back from maturity or decline into growth when, for instance, they enter a new market or introduce a significant innovation or new business model. The size of the sales force must appropriately reflect the life cycle of the company for the sales efforts to be effective (Zoltners *et al.* 2006). This is rarely the case and frequently the sales team is undersized for good reason. For instance, the pressure to maintain control over costs is arguably one good cause. Moreover, new salespeople, as they join the sales team are likely to underperform in sales income generation, because at the outset they may lack the experience with the company's products or markets, the selling cycles may be rather long or significant carry-over effects (sales accruing in the future as a result of present efforts), especially in B2B sections. However, many different studies have shown that undersized sales teams may do better in generating profits in the short run, but in the long run the larger sales teams deliver more cumulative profits. For instance, Zoltners *et al.* (2006) report that, on average, the size of the sales force that maximises the company's profits is 18 per cent larger than the sales force that maximises one-year profits. With this in mind, we can now discuss the two alternative approaches for establishing the appropriate size of sales force.

The *workload approach* requires the company to first identify and place existing and potential customers into meaningful groups based on the individual customer's annual sales potential. The company will also need to estimate the number of calls per customer per group that will be necessary in a year to sustain/develop business with the customers from each group. This information is not always readily available though and frequently can be inaccurate, especially for relatively new companies and/or when entering relatively new markets. A sound, detailed sales database of past sales activities and results records will help improve the accuracy of the estimation. The number of accounts in each group is then multiplied by the corresponding call frequency to arrive at the total workload in sales calls per year. Given the whole set of activities within the salespeople job description, including calling on customers, the maximum number of calls each seller can do per year is then estimated. Dividing the total workload by this number produces the required size of the sales force, given the specific accounts the company targets to keep and/or acquire.

The *incremental sales approach* is based on *marginal theory*, which, when adapted to the problem of determining the optimum size of the sales force, states that company net profits will increase when additional salespeople are added if the incremental sales revenue this additional salesperson produces exceeds the incremental cost associated with the extra salesperson. Table 15.3 offers a simple example for illustrative purposes.

In the example in Table 15.3 column (1) gives the total number of salespeople the company can employ. The next column shows how the company's total sales revenue increases each time a new salesperson joins the sales force. The total sales increase at a negative rate, because the impact of the additional salesperson is limited by such factors as the finite number of existing and potential customers, the pre-determined amount of orders each customer can make and so on. Column (3) shows the increment in sales revenue each individual salesperson contributes, which is thus diminishing. On the other hand, incremental cost in column (5) is the change in the total cost of the sales force resulting from adding the one extra seller required to produce the incremental sales revenue shown in column (3). This figure is increasing every time an additional salesperson joins the company, because of the fixed costs the additional salesperson will produce, such as salary or annual pension, the cost of insurance and fringe benefits and so on. As a result, incremental profits in column (6), which are calculated when subtracting column (5) from (3), would also keep decreasing. When at nil, the company has maximised its profits since, in this case, the addition of the eighth salesperson produces an incremental loss of £10k and, as a result, total profits go down from £360k to £350k. Clearly, this is still profit and not a loss. Hiring the eighth seller though will decrease the company's ROI performance, an index the financial markets and hence most of the chief executive officers cherish.

While this is just a simplified example, more elaboration is possible to improve the realism of the calculations and the decision. For instance, admittedly not all salespeople will have an equal capacity and the abilities to generate sales and their optimum performance may well vary. To reflect this, management may again consider classifying the salespeople in different sales groups. Such groups will comprise salespeople with similar profiles and skills in selling the company's products to accounts, who appreciate the skills the salespeople have and match with their profile. Through such a homogenisation, the unit of analysis becomes first the different sales groups and then, within each group, the salespeople comprising the group. Thus, the relevance of the analysis and the quality of the decisions improve.

The main disadvantages of this method are that the company must have historical data to allow for projections into the future, and the figures upon which the method relies are projected estimations and hence are subjective. Also, management needs to have a good grasp of the interplay between all parameters in the function that explain salespeople's ability to generate revenue and close a deal. Finally, the method assumes that the company's ability to recruit salespeople with the desirable profile, skills and abilities is unlimited.

On the other hand, this method revolves around profit actualisation and ROI performance. As such, it is a powerful aid when negotiating the size of the sales force with the company's top management. At the same time, the method helps the sales manager to maintain a profit orientation, which in turn allows for an improvement in the alignment of objectives between marketing (whose major priority is to nurture the company's profits through customer satisfaction) and sales. Finally, the method allows for scenario development and performing sensitivity analysis, which in turn give the sales manager the ability to explore different options and question the feasibility as well as the scope of each option, both strategically and critically.

Finally, it should be noted that other methods, such as the *all we can afford* or the *sales breakdown* approach do also exist. Although simple to employ, their unduly simplistic nature: (1) casts reasonable doubt on the reliability of the outcome each method can produce; and (2) enhances the false perception that the design and management of the sales effort is potentially effective even in the absence of a certain knowledge background and ability.

Table 15.3 Deciding on the sales force size using the incremental sales approach

(1)	(2)	(3)	(4)	(5)	(6)	(7)
No. of sellers	Total sales force revenue	Incremental sales force revenue	Total sales force cost	Incremental cost	Incremental profit/(loss)	Total profits
1	100,000	100,000	40,000	40,000	60,000	60,000
2	198,000	98,000	47,000	7,000	91,000	151,000
3	292,000	94,000	62,000	15,000	79,000	230,000
4	382,000	90,000	87,000	25,000	65,000	295,000
5	467,000	85,000	117,000	30,000	55,000	350,000
6	517,000	50,000	157,000	40,000	10,000	360,000
7	**560,000**	**43,000**	**200,000**	**43,000**	**0**	**360,000**
8	600,000	40,000	250,000	50,000	–10,000	350,000

Sales force compensation

The final step in designing the sales force is the decision regarding the compensation of the sales-people. A whole range of factors, one of which is the company's compensation plan, motivates sellers. We will address these factors later in the chapter. Meanwhile, we will focus on compensation since in addition to its motivating role, it has significant financial implications.

Sales personnel would like income regularity, extra reward for above average performance and a fair payment for experience and longevity as well as for the non-sales specific tasks they do as part of their job description, which reduce their selling opportunities. Management, on the other hand, would appear to primarily care for economy, simplicity (which produces further economies of the transaction cost) and control (over the sales expenditures). The meaning each side gives to these concepts is usually subjective. It is not always clear to approach and define fairness in a compensation plan or economy. As a result, the compensation plan can easily trigger tension, conflicts and eventually frustration if mismanaged. Such a negative climate will produce dissatisfaction among the salespeople. Before those who can leave (usually the most competitive ones) actually do so, their disappointment will directly impact their sales performance and the customers' level of satis-faction from the sales reps, as a plethora of studies have shown during the last 30 years (cf. Babakus *et al.* 1996; Netemeyer *et al.* 2010; Gounaris and Boukis 2013). Therefore getting the compensation scheme right is indeed crucial not just for the direct impact the plan will have on the company's budgets and financial performance.

The first issue to address is how much should the salesperson receive on average on an annual basis. This is an easy question to answer, because the labour market has already answered that. There is an on-going average income for certain employees with certain skills and abilities that management can either find out for themselves through different personal (e.g. trade shows and colleagues) and impersonal sources of information (trade press, internet), or by having a human resource consultant advise them. Unless management is willing to pay this money, it will be impossible to recruit the right salesperson for the job. In fact, management will often have to pay a premium to attract high calibre salespersons when, for instance, the company's reputation in the market is not strong enough.

The second issue, which represents a greater challenge, is to design the compensation plan in such a manner that the plan will allow both individual salespeople and the company to achieve their own interests. In practice, the components of the compensation plan fall into three major categories: a *fixed part*, usually salary; a *variable part*, usually commission and/or bonus; and a *benefits part*. The salary is provided to give a sense of economic stability through income security and to compensate for the time the salesperson will have to spend for the non-selling oriented tasks and supporting colleagues and/or serving existing customers. The variable part is incorporated in the plan to stimulate and reward performance, while the benefits (such as insurance expenses, car, cell phone accounts, dining or entertainment) help salespeople to cover the costs associated with the nature of the selling job. The challenge in putting together an effective compensation plan lies in the decision about the proportion each of the three elements should represent. As a rule of thumb, practice suggests that 70 per cent should be fixed and the remaining allocated between variable and benefits. Yet this is hardly general and many variations occur. Also, the nature of commission is different from that of bonus, so again many variations exist with regard to the relative importance the two have in the overall compensation plan. Unfortunately, because of significant variations in practice, a mathematical or econometric model for universal use has not yet been developed, if it is feasible to produce one at all. Management has to exercise their own judgement and expertise, but they can also benefit from the following points:

- Salary is usually *higher* when *sales cycles are longer* and *sales revenue per order is high.*
- Salary combined with *bonus* is usually preferred when closing a sales require *team effort*, as for instance in many B2B sectors or for high-tech products/services.
- Salary is also *higher* when *a lot of non-selling tasks* consume the salespersons' time.
- Commission is *higher* and preferred when the sale is the result of *individual effort.*
- Commission is also *preferred* when the sales follow a *short cyclical pattern*, as for instance with many consumer goods sold through distributors.

Finally, management must keep in mind that as the fixed part of the compensation becomes higher, the compensation plan becomes simpler to manage and the salespeople become more willing to perform non-selling tasks. Also, they will reduce any inclination to attempt overstocking customers, a bad practice for the relationship with customers in the short and medium term and which also impacts negatively on long-term sales income and profits. Salespeople's turnover also becomes lower as the proportion of fixed income in the compensation plan increases. But the cost of sales becomes less flexible and less reflective of market conditions and the company's actual sales levels. Moreover, the higher the role the fixed income plays in the compensation plan, the higher the need for monitoring and controlling sales personnel activities, which in turn increases the administrative cost of the sales effort. Finally, the motivational effect of such a plan that relies considerably on fixed income will tend to be modest, and the ability to use the variable part of the income to gear salespeople towards achieving specific strategic objectives will also be rather limited.

Managing the sales force

With the different elements of the sales force design in place, management can next concentrate on the actual management of the salespeople. The major tasks in the management of the sales force are *recruiting*, *training*, *motivating*, *supervising* and *evaluating* the salespeople. The following paragraphs will address each of them separately.

Recruiting

The success of recruitment efforts has a major impact on sales force effectiveness and costs. Recruitment includes all the activities managers engage in to develop a pool of candidates for the sales function who share the desirable skills and traits required for success in sales. Moreover, good recruitment practices are essential to ensure lower salespeople training costs (Salsbury 1982) and lower turnover (Darmon 2004), which causes disruption to the sales strategy and customer service along with further increasing the training costs. Recruitment is thus a fundamental aspect of successfully managing the sales force. The starting point for succeeding in recruitment is to have a clear understanding of what skills and traits the company should be looking for in the different candidates. Although many academic studies have sought to answer what makes a good salesperson, the answer remains elusive, probably because of the great variety of situations and tasks salespeople face.

Hence, a good starting point is to understand the traits salespeople should have by asking the company's customers to identify what they think a good salesperson looks like. *Honesty, reliability, knowledge* (of products/services and customer's needs) and *professionalism* are characteristics that frequently emerge, not surprisingly since these are the most commonly identified positive characteristics associated with salespeople (Lee *et al.* 2007). To populate the list further, management can also consider what characteristics the most successful salespeople have in the company and seek to enhance them through new recruits. Several studies in the past have also attempted to investigate the qualities of the top performing salesperson and thereby add to the list of traits that successful salespeople share: a strong sense of inner motivation to succeed, ego driven, empathy (Greenberg and Sweeney 2012), service motivation and conscientiousness (Greenberg 2003). Yet in addition to character traits, successful salespeople also need specific skills that are necessary for the job. Knowledge of the company's products/services and the company's policies are obviously significant. Salespeople will most probably acquire these through training, but if detailed knowledge of rather technical or complex, high-tech products is necessary the management may need to consider internal recruiting, as explained later on. Other sought after abilities may include prolific computer skills as well as skills in communication, planning and administration, managing business relationships and, of course, selling skills.

While this is certainly an extensive list of skills the company should be looking for in new recruits, clearly not all of them will be of equal importance. The type of salesperson the company seeks to employ (see Table 15.2) and the different sales tasks the new recruit will have to perform (see Table 15.1), will be a key determinant of the significance different skills will have in determining a good candidate. For instance, key account sellers as well as consultative sellers will be more likely to get involved in account planning when trying to coordinate the supplier's response to the customer's needs. For such salespersons, analytical thinking and planning would thus appear to be a lot more significant than for delivery sellers, for whom the ability to organise activities and deliveries and prospecting would probably be more valuable to possess or develop.

With a clear pool of qualities and skills required, the company can then decide the procedures and sources of recruitment. Regarding the procedures, the sales/marketing department(s) need to work closely with human resources (HR) in a collaborative manner, each contributing their expertise. HR, for instance, may be more involved in screening an initial pool of candidates and assessing them against the specific personal traits discussed above. The terms and the conditions of the employment contract will also require the involvement of the HR department at a later stage. Once the short list of candidates has been completed, the sales/marketing department(s) will need to make the final choice, ensuring that a job is offered to those candidates whose abilities and skills match the sales position they occupy.

Finally, there is a somewhat diverse variety of sources from which the company can seek to attract candidates to staff the sales force, including competition, soliciting names from existing salespersons, employment agencies and consultants, colleges and universities, job adverts, social media and frequently the company itself (internal transfers). Although a recruitment campaign covering all alternative sources may not be too expensive to generate an initial pool of candidates, studies monitoring best recruiting practices over the years (cf. Avlonitis *et al.* 1986; Tzokas *et al.* 2001; Khosla *et al.* 2009) would seem to converge on recommending specific sources depending on the type of sales job and on the type (B2C versus B2B) of customers. For instance, *key account sellers* are frequently recruited either from within and specifically from the sales department itself or from competition. *Consultative sellers* selling mainly to B2B customers would also most likely be recruited from within and particularly from the technical/production functions of the company so as to have a good understanding of the product/service features, which they will need to explain to the customer. On the contrary, *channel development sellers*, particularly when selling B2C products/services, or *delivery sellers* are more likely to come through external sources. Finally, it is worth noting that particularly in the UK directly attracting college or university graduates appears to be a declining practice since the prospect of developing a career in sales is hampered by many negative stereotypes among this group of the population (Lee *et al.* 2007).

Training

Following recruitment, many companies are still tempted to send their newly appointed salespeople into the field, supplying them with bulky sales and policy manuals as well as descriptions and guidelines regarding their territory, customers or products/services. Clearly this is a bad practice, because training is a valuable investment for the sales force, as today's demanding customers cannot put up with inept salespeople. The objectives of the training programme include:

- building knowledge of the company's products/services;
- fostering salesperson's identification with the company;
- understanding the company's sales strategy, policies and procedures;
- recognising and becoming aware of major competitors and their offerings;
- becoming effective in meeting the challenges of selling.

In-house training, hiring experts or a combination of both are the three options available for training the sales force to create this necessary knowledge background. Role playing, use of multimedia material and programmed learning are some of the techniques most frequently employed. More experienced top performing salespeople can also become engaged in the training of new recruits (on-the-job training) albeit this approach entails the risk of new salespeople picking up whatever bad habits their mentor may have and hence should be consciously employed. Besides, the development of sales automation technology and direct selling through the internet has allowed the freeing up of salespeople who can now spend more time in the field. As a result, sales forces in many companies have become more efficient yet smaller compared to in the past. Consequently, there are simply not enough salespeople available to undertake the training task, which has created an increasing demand for professional experts to become more involved in the training of the newly hired or existing sales people.

Once again, HR and the sales/marketing departments will need to collaborate in producing the company's approach towards the training of the sales employees. In doing so, they will need to clearly create and agree upon the objectives of the training effort and ensure they have the right measures for assessing the effectiveness of the time, effort and money invested in training the sales staff. Employees benefit from appropriately developed training programmes that match the needs of their job description (Gounaris 2006), because training facilitates their effort to achieve their job objectives, which in turn results in greater job satisfaction and self-confidence. The two combined have a strong positive effect on the success of the salesperson.

Motivating

Although salespeople are selected on the grounds of being self-motivated, coaching and driving them is another essential task of the overall managerial effort. This is because of the frustration the selling job frequently entails, the stimulation that people usually require to put all of their effort into a task or job and the personal issues and problems that salespeople, like anybody else, can occasionally be faced with. If, however, these issues or problems are allowed to disrupt the selling effort, this can have a significant impact on the company's performance. Besides, an appropriate motivation mix can help management focus the efforts of the sales force towards the company's strategic objectives and priorities. This is usually helpful and often crucial, especially when the company introduces objectives and strategies that require salespeople to move beyond their comfort zone.

For reasons of inertia, personal preferences or other factors, salespeople will not necessarily take such objectives on board easily, unless appropriately motivated to do so.

The literature on employee motivation is vast, and any attempt to present the theoretical principles behind the practices sales managers need to adopt in motivating their salespeople would certainly be incomplete within the contexts of this chapter. The following discussion therefore focuses on the practices that are most likely to optimise the motivational effect on the behaviour and performance of the salesperson.

Clearly, *money* is a motivational factor. Like all employees, salespersons do their job for a living. Therefore, financial rewards are likely to stimulate a salesperson to intensify the efforts they put into the job and thus improve their performance. Yet, unless money carries a symbolic nature for this specific salesperson, for instance, a measure of success or power, then following utility theory, the ability of financial rewards to motivate the salesperson will be declining (see Figure 15.2) once a certain level has been achieved, because of the (additional) sacrifices in say personal time this person will have to do to acquire this extra money. Consequently, the sales manager has to use a mix of motivators that include both financial rewards and what the literature describes as *higher order motivators*, including, for instance, recognition, liking, respect, career opportunities and promotion or a sense of accomplishment. Thus it is no surprise that financial motivators are stronger among early career salespersons who have not yet achieved the saturation level, whereas more senior and experienced ones, who already earn a considerable amount of money, are more motivated by such higher order drivers.

A strong instrument which may be used towards effectively motivating the sales personnel is sales quota and objectives. Again, the literature on setting objectives is huge and will not be discussed in this chapter. As an all rounder, objectives need to be specific of time for accomplishment and of size; additionally, objectives must also be realistic and achievable. In sales management, the latter qualities are really important; not to be ignored or purposefully breached. Many managers set objectives above what realistically the salesperson can achieve, given the resources and skills available. The idea is that this way the salesperson will eventually produce what the company would have really expected when some, unavoidable, degree of underperformance from the objectives set and agreed has also been considered. Nonetheless, if sales personnel see themselves as continually underperforming against what the company expects from them, they will eventually become frustrated and demotivated.

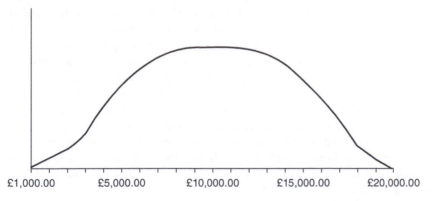

Figure 15.2 Monetary rewards: a generic representation of their motivational strength

Sales quota and targets need to therefore meet all these qualities (including realism), and the sales manager has to work closely with each individual salesperson in setting quotas in terms of sales volume, revenue and profits (all three are equally important for the contemporary sales force) for specific territories, products and/or customers, depending on the sales structure the company has adopted. In essence, this is a negotiation process between the sales manager and each individual salesperson. During this negotiation it is essential for the sales manager to remain professional. Professionalism means that the sales manager will seek an agreement with the salesperson that is satisfactory for the company and achievable by the salesperson. Some academics have advised in favour of setting quotas higher than what realism would suggest to motivate the salesperson (Kotler 1997: 700), but practising managers should be mindful of the consequences on the moral of the sales force such practice may have.

In addition to sales quota, sales managers can use a variety of supplementary tools to motivate the sales force. Meetings, for instance, provide an excellent opportunity to praise performance and achievements of individual sales people. Likewise, sales force contests that relate a specific award such as a company paid trip or a company gift for achieving a specific strategically important objective is another option many managers employ. Caution is needed though when running such contests to ensure that salespeople do not defer their sales for the contest period. Also, managers must be mindful that the motivational impact across the sales force of such contests will diminish if the perception is that only an exceptional few will be able to meet the challenge and claim the reward.

Supervising

Selling, like any other task, needs tracking and performance needs monitoring. Different salespeople will receive varying degrees of supervision depending on the nature of their task and how they are compensated. The general norm has been to closely supervise those whose annual income relies more on salary and less the ones who rely more on commission, the principle being that the latter will not get paid unless they produce sales and so compared to the former do not need very close supervision.

Intense competition and harsh pressure from top management for efficiency and effectiveness has made such norms of the past less relevant in today's conditions. It is of little difference if, for instance, a meeting is held weekly, biweekly, or more or less frequently. What is important is that supervision is increasingly becoming closer, a trend also facilitated by IT, which has allowed easier and faster integration of different pieces of internal information that helps improve the quality of monitoring and widen its scope. This is important because of the compelling evidence many years of academic research has produced demonstrating the close relationship between supervision and performance of the sales force (cf. Challagalla, and Shervani 1996). It is also important that the sales manager has developed a comprehensive process and appropriate tools to keep track of salespersons' performance. Also it is essential that the sales manager is not seen as a distant judge or assessor of salespeople, and the supervisory process is not regarded by the sales force as a threatening or unfair means of practising control. Quite the contrary. Both the process and the tools need to be fair and transparent, and the sales manager has to maintain the status of the coach of the sales force who genuinely and benevolently helps salespeople improve their performance using supervision as an additional mechanism that helps them in meeting their job targets and the company's expectations (Piercy *et al.* 2012).

To successfully supervise the sales team, the sales manager needs to have a clear plan for customer calls, prospecting calls and other tasks the salesperson will have to deliver on an annual basis, depending on the nature of the task and the type of sales team the manager supervises (see Tables 15.1 and 15.2). For instance, *key account sellers* as well as *consultative sellers* are expected to spend more time with existing customers solving their problems than prospecting for new accounts, a task that is more important primarily for *new business/channel development sellers*. These two types of salespersons will also have to spend some considerable time in-house to coordinate the company's response to the needs of their accounts. Likewise, *sales support* will also have to spend more time internally, providing support to the sales personnel who actually visit the existing and potential customers. Supervisory plans and performance benchmarks for customer and prospecting calls need to reflect such differences coming from the specific job description different salespeople have to deliver.

Another useful tool sales managers can employ in supervision is the *time and duty* (TnD) analysis, which allows sales personnel to record and review their daily activity against best practices. TnD reflects in detail the different tasks a salesperson could perform on a daily basis. These may include:

- *preparation*, capturing the effort the salesperson puts in making the necessary preparations that are required to meet with the existing or the new account and present the company's solution to the accounts needs;
- *waiting*, to meet with customers;
- *selling*, reflecting the actual time spent in presenting and selling the company's offering to the customer;
- *travelling*, from headquarters to the accounts' premises;
- *meetings*, internally to coordinate the company's response to customer requirements and expectations;
- *lunch and entertainment*, with existing or potential customers that are necessary to establish a professional rapport;
- *administration*, that is the time the salesperson will need to use for completing non-selling tasks internally but also to fill in sales reports, which feed the company's management information system;
- *miscellaneous*, including time invested in training and/or skills development, following market development and monitoring completion and so on.

All these tasks are important and the sales manager needs to make sure the salespersons are involved with each and every one; however, in practical terms this may sometimes be problematic since a typical working week is around 40 hours. Occasionally, and under special conditions, such as if a crisis emerged or an opportunity to make a major offer or bid came out, it may be possible to push this figure up, but these are extraordinary circumstances. Therefore, it is imperative that the sales manager works closely with the sales people to ensure that adequate time is allocated across the different tasks and the time-plan is realistic and followed.

Evaluating

Last but not least is the evaluation of the salesperson's performance. Like supervising, evaluation should also primarily be seen and practised as a means to improve the performance of the salesperson. When coupled with clear and unambiguous feedback for the salesperson, the outcome of the evaluation effort has a significant and positive effect on the actual sales performance (Pelham and Kravitz 2008). However, this is not necessarily an easy task, because of the various challenges associated with the evaluation task.

Arguably, one could ask why evaluating the performance of the salespersons should be a challenge? Their task is to sell, so either they have managed to sell according to the objectives or they have not. As we have explained, this is not entirely accurate because as Table 15.2 showed there are sales people who actually do very little if any selling themselves. Likewise, when it comes to key account sellers for instance, meeting the expectations of the key account and securing the sale is frequently a function of parameters that are not entirely under the control of the seller. Delays in production or delivery can harm the relationship between the two companies, yet the seller does not necessarily have hierarchical authority to resolve the causes of such problems. The opposite can also be true: when team selling is necessary, it is hard to say how much an individual member of the team did to influence a successful sale. Moreover, even when selling can be traced back to the efforts of an individual salesperson, once again it can be very unclear how such parameters, for instance, the features of the product, the competition or the macro economic environment, influenced the achievements of the individual salesperson. For example, consider the positive effect the recent 2014 Commonwealth Games had on the sales for a great variety of products. It is difficult to precisely calculate what the effects were, especially in a 12-month period. Also, the sales manager faces the challenge to decompose this effect from next year's goals against which the evaluation will take place.

Given the different challenges just described and many others that could also have been discussed, the fundamental question then is whether it is possible to produce a completely accurate, fair and totally unambiguous evaluation of the performance of individual salespeople. In a single word, no. But structuring appropriately the evaluation process will help the sales manager to closely approach the ideal system of evaluation. To do this, the sales manager must answer three questions, 'What do we need to evaluate?', 'How can we best evaluate what it has been deemed necessary to evaluate?' and, 'Where do we get the necessary information from?'.

To answer the first question, the manager has to bring together the company's overall strategic objectives and priorities with the different tasks individual salespeople perform. Earlier in the chapter the different tasks a seller can potentially perform were discussed. The sales manager needs to consider each task the salesperson performs in relation to the company's overall strategic objectives. For instance, if building market share in new markets is the company's priority, the different tasks will be considered and evaluated relative to this objective. In this case, building trust and selling unique product features in relational selling will be particularly important for relational salespeople and especially when serving or prospecting for new customers in the new markets in which the company is attempting to increase its market share. Likewise, while sales volumes and revenue will clearly be important, more emphasis on other factors will be necessary to improve figures from customers that better fit the overall objective of increasing market share in new markets. Other tasks different salespeople may perform, like for instance responding to referrals or handling back orders, will also have to be considered with regard to the contribution they make to the company's effort to increase market share in new markets.

Other strategic objectives may include improving profits and/or profitability, enhancing the efficiency of operations, reducing operational costs, improving customer satisfaction and so on. Most likely, the company will be pursuing a set of two or three strategic goals. Hence, the challenge the sales manager faces to meaningfully embed the corporate strategic objectives in the different tasks the salespeople perform.

Having clarified what needs to be evaluated, the next question is how to measure everything that has been deemed in need of measurement for the purposes of the evaluation process. Measurement can be either objective, subjective or both. Objective measures are usually quantitative in nature, and sales managers rely on performance indices, frequently referred to as *key performance indicators* to draw comparisons between different salespersons as well as between different periods for the same salesperson. The benefit of using such objective measures is that both the manager and the salesperson can calculate them individually and therefore come to the same conclusions, providing an overview of the salesperson's performance; hence the objectivity of the measures. Thus, to use them, the sales manager needs to put in place a clear and easy to understand system of indices and monitoring mechanisms the salespeople can understand, accept and agree as being fair. Unfortunately, though, the interpretation of the results as well as the identification of the causes behind the results unavoidably will remain open to subjective analysis and understanding, which can easily spark tension or spoil the climate between the manager and the salesperson. This is yet another reason why the process of producing such performance measures must be transparent and easy for the salesperson to understand.

There are various indices the sales manager may wish to consider (Panagopoulos 2011). Some are rather simple and straightforward to understand and produce including achieved sales (revenue and/or volume), goals achievement index, expenditures to sales ratio, average time for order processing and delivery, returns to total units delivered ratio and cancelled orders to total orders ratio. Management may also consider employing more complex indices that require combining different pieces of information.

Such indices may include the average share of wallet, which reflects the average sales each seller has achieved with each individual account as a percentage of the total purchases each customer makes, including purchases from competitors. Another more complex, but useful, index would be to calculate and monitor the average life-time value (LTV) of the salesperson's customers. To use this index the sales manager will first need to calculate the LTV in pounds for each individual account of the salesperson. The formula for this is:

$$\text{LTV} = \sum_{t=1}^{T} PM_t \left(\frac{1}{1+i} \right)^t$$

where *PM* is the company's *gross profit margin* from serving a specific customer, *i* is the *desired return rate* the company is aiming to achieve (must be the same for all customers and all salespeople, but can change from year to year), *t* is a *unit of time*, (a quarter, a semester or a year) and *T* is *the total number of time units* for which the LTV is calculated. Once the LTV has been calculated for all the customers in the salesperson's portfolio, the simple arithmetic mean will allow the average LTV of the salesperson's customer portfolio to be produced. The deviation of each individual customer in the portfolio from the average LTV is another useful calculation, because this information can help the sales manager and the salesperson to get a more strategic view of the different customers and consequently guide their future actions and plans accordingly.

The number of different indices the sales manager can produce is indeed large, and not all of them will be equally relevant for all companies. The degree of relevance depends on the salesperson's tasks and the company's strategic objectives. What the sales manager must take from this discussion is the actual need to use objective measures, because they are not disputable. Also, there should be a strong emphasis put on the importance of maintaining a strong sense of fairness when calculating the indicators the manager will use, because although objective themselves, they remain open to subjective interpretations of the causes that have produced them.

In addition to the use of objective measures, the sales manager will have to also rely on some subjective measures to evaluate the performance of the salesperson. Subjective measures are qualitative in nature and are useful to assess such dimensions of performance that are impossible or extremely difficult to quantify. Examples would include assessing the acceptance the sales person has gained among customers and/or colleagues, evaluating the salesperson's communication and presentation skills, their appearance and so on. Qualitative measures are also employed to evaluate the salesperson's knowledge of the company's products and selling policies, responsibilities or the company's competition.

In practice, the sales manager will usually combine both quantitative and qualitative measures to evaluate the performance of each individual salesperson across the different tasks the salespeople perform and in relation to the company's overall strategic objectives. Once the criteria have been set, the final challenge is to collect the information necessary for the evaluation.

Usually, the information required for producing the quantitative measures will come from the company's own records in its database. Securing this information is not necessarily an easy task. Information technology has certainly become very helpful in producing solutions that make it possible to meaningfully integrate the different pieces of information that different company activities generate, through software and systems supporting enterprise resource planning (ERP). Also, customer relationship management (CRM) systems are very helpful in generating information, which makes it more comprehensive to decipher and understand the interactions between the salespeople and their customers. From this information it is possible to produce many of the tracking indices that the sales manager is likely to need. However, maintaining the database is not always an easy or straightforward task. Moreover, many salespeople see the task relating to feeding the CRM system as unduly and unjustifiably time-consuming and bureaucratic. The challenge for the sales manager is thus to ensure that the company's databases are appropriately maintained and updated.

Sales automation has little to offer when it comes to the qualitative measures. The manager will need to become personally involved in producing this information through observation and interviewing. Therefore, from the manager's perspective, such measures will be more time-consuming to produce. Thus, it is a good idea to have a clear plan of procedures and a realistic timetable for producing these kinds of measures.

In conclusion, the evaluation of the salespersons' performance is crucial for two reasons. First, it helps management to keep track of their performance and consequently of the company's ability to meet its objectives. Second, if mismanaged, the evaluation process can have a negative impact on the team climate and esprit de corps within the sales team, which in turn will result in a vicious cycle of salesperson dissatisfaction, customer dissatisfaction, lost customers, salesperson under performance and increased turnover.

Ethical selling

Ethics has been termed the study and philosophy of human conduct, with an emphasis on the determination of right and wrong. For marketing and sales, ethics in the workplace would thus refer to rules (standards, principles) governing the conduct of organisational members and the consequences of marketing decisions (Ferrell 2005). Therefore, from a normative perspective approach, ethical conduct in marketing is defined as practices that emphasise transparent, trustworthy and responsible personal and organisational policies and actions that exhibit integrity as well as fairness to consumers and other stakeholders (Murphy *et al.* 2005). Marketing ethics focuses on principles and standards that define acceptable marketing conduct, as determined by *various stakeholders* and the organisation responsible for marketing activities. While many of the basic principles have been codified as laws and regulations to require marketers to conform to society's expectations of conduct, marketing ethics goes beyond legal and regulatory issues. Ethical marketing practices and principles are core building blocks in establishing trust, which help build long-term marketing relationships. Moreover, as societies progress towards more transparent and democratic values, the members of the society expect this kind of conduct from firms and the company's employees. Compliance with these expectations of society would enable the company and its employees to gain the emotional reward of recognition and generally a favourable status in society.

In a recent empirical study, Lee and his colleagues (2007) investigated what college and university students think of salespeople. Table 15.4 offers one aspect of their findings.

The picture is clearly not encouraging as apparently the negative opinions surpass the positive ones. Is this a well-rooted stereotype? If so, is it unjustified and unfair?

Many academics as well as practitioners describe the sales force as, 'the company's boots fighting for sales and achieving the company's objectives over competition'. As competition has intensified at a global level, it is becoming increasingly harder for the salesperson to achieve the goals in sales the company expects. Moreover, public corporations face the pressure from their shareholders for continuously improving revenue and profits. This pressure is eventually passed on to the sales force. Under such conditions, it is very likely that certain practices of a questionable ethos and some wrong-doings emerge. A sales person may in fact be more attentive to the goals of the company than to the needs of the customer. They may intentionally withhold information from the customer to secure the sale or they may be tempted to oversell the benefits of the company's product while underrating the competitors' offerings without just reasons. Also, the seller's individual character and system of inner drivers for success can possibly enhance the frequency and the intensity of such dubious practices.

Table 15.4 Most associated characteristics for salespeople (MACS)

Traits	
Negative	Positive
• Pushy	• Helpful
• Arrogant	• Professional
• Annoying	• Well-educated
• False	• Friendly
• Rude	• Knowledgeable about products
• Overpowering	• Customer-oriented
• Fast-talking	
• Persistent	
• Conniving	
• Unknowledgeable about products	
• Sales-oriented	
• A nuisance	
Emotions	
Negative	Positive
• Helpless	• Content
• Forced into purchase	• Happy
• Annoyed	

Source: Adapted from Lee *et al.* (2007).

Therefore, clearly, the picture presented by Lee *et al.* (2007) is not by chance and it is thus no surprise that, broadly speaking, sales and marketing alike have quite a negative image in society. Ethical business conduct and transparency are the behaviours that salespeople need to pick up and adopt if this perception is to reverse. At the company level, changing this perception is crucial for long-term success, because long-term sustainability requires that both the company and its salespeople be accepted within society, which holds a positive attitude towards both the company and the salespeople. Hence why it is significant to develop an ethos and demonstrate ethical behaviour.

Following on from the earlier brief discussion into the nature and scope of ethics at the beginning of this section, it would appear to be straightforward to embed a strong ethical code in the practice of (almost) every organisation. Unfortunately, this is not the case at all, because marketing as well as business in general deal with subjective moral choices that draw upon the moral codes of the society in which the business is being conducted. Consider, for example, the hypothetical firm XYZ Ltd doing business in the United Kingdom, but having manufacturing operations in Burundi in Africa. In the UK society has accepted the pursuit of profit as ethical and the different shareholders expect XYZ Ltd to deliver a good share of profits. At the same time, British society is clearly protective and concerned with the rights of children and other vulnerable members of society. As a result, company XYZ Ltd would likely refrain from hiring children and exploiting child labour. However, with annual salaries around $560, local households need children to work in order for the family to survive. Moreover, by paying the average annual salary, company XYZ Ltd generates the profit margins that are necessary to keep the shareholders at home happy. By doing so, however, the company contributes to keeping that society in poverty. Answering whether there is a deficit in morals or ethos in the practices of this hypothetical company is a tricky task.

What seems to be less of a problem though is narrowing down the concept of the various stakeholders to the ethical responsibility of sales to the company's customers. Following on from this, it is possible to define ethical marketing as 'the process through which companies generate customer interest in products/services, build strong customer interest/relationships, and create value . . . by incorporating social and environmental considerations in products and promotions' (adapted from Lexicon.ft.com 2014).[2] All aspects of marketing are considered, from sales techniques to business communication and business development. Following these guidelines, the salesperson who seeks to develop an ethical practice would refrain from pressuring customers to purchase, invading their privacy or attempting to deceive them by withholding information or passing them misleading and inaccurate information. Likewise, attempting to gain the customer's preference over competition with such means as very expensive gifts, extraordinary entertainment and customer treatment or prodigious rewards are all practices that the ethical approach to selling has to eliminate.

At the same time though, to be effective, an ethical campaign towards selling will require the sales manager to abide by the principles of ethical selling before it can be successful. In practice this translates into the sales manager refraining from placing undue pressure on the sales force to achieve unrealistic results, say through unrealistically high sales targets that could potentially draw the salesperson into adopting unethical sales behaviours.

Notes

1   http://www.telegraph.co.uk/finance/jobs/10012272/Revealed-the-best-jobs-to-pursue-as-a-career.html
2   http://lexicon.ft.com/Term?term=ethical-marketing

References

Anderson, R. E. (1996), 'Personal selling and sales management in the new millennium', *Journal of Personal Selling and Sales Management*, 16(4): 17–32.

Atuahene-Gima, K. (1995), 'An exploratory analysis of the impact of market orientation on new product performance', *Journal of Product Innovation Management*, 12(4): 275–293.

Avlonitis, G. and Gounaris, S. (1999), 'Marketing orientation and its determinants: An empirical analysis', *European Journal of Marketing*, 33(11/12): 1003–1037.

Avlonitis, G., Boyle, K. and Kouremenos, A. (1986), 'Matching salesmen to the selling job', *Industrial Marketing Management*, 15(1): 45–54.

Avlonitis, G., Lionakis, K. and Panagopoulos, N. (2010), 'Antecedents and consequences of the conflict between the marketing and sales departments', *Journal of Selling and Major Account Management* 10(1): 21–32.

Babakus, E., Cravens, D. W., Johnston, M. and Moncrief, W. C. (1996), 'Examining the role of organizational variables in the salesperson job satisfaction model', *Journal of Personal Selling and Sales Management*, 16(3): 33–46.

Baker, M. J. (2010), 'Marketing: Philosophy or function?', in Baker, M. J. and Saren, M. (eds) *Marketing Theory: A Student Text*, London: Sage Publications.

Baker, M. J., Black, C. D. and Hart, S. J. (1988), 'The competitiveness of British industry: What really makes the difference?', *European Journal of Marketing*, 22(2): 70–85.

Blessington, M. (1992), 'Designing a sales strategy with the customer in mind', *Compensation and Benefits Review*, 24(2): 30–41.

Cespedes, F. V. (1993), 'Coordinating sales and marketing in consumer goods firms', *Journal of Consumer Marketing*, 10(2): 37–55.

Challagalla, G. N. and Shervani, T. A. (1996), 'Dimensions and types of supervisory control: Effects on salesperson performance and satisfaction', *The Journal of Marketing*, 60(1): 89–105.

Cron, W. L., Baldauf, A., Leigh, T. W. and Grossenbacher, S. (2014), 'The strategic role of the sales force: Perceptions of senior sales executives', *Academy of Marketing Science Journal*, 42(5): 471–489.

Darmon, R. Y. (2004), 'Controlling sales force turnover costs through optimal recruiting and training policies', *European Journal of Operational Research*, 154(1): 291–303.

Dewsnap, B. and Jobber, D. (2000), 'The sales-marketing interface in consumer packaged-goods companies: A conceptual framework', *Journal of Personal Selling and Sales Management*, 20(2): 109–119.

Dewsnap, B. and Jobber, D. (2002), 'A social psychological model of relations between marketing and sales', *European Journal of Marketing*, 36(7/8): 874–894.

Ferrell, O. C. (2005), 'A framework for understanding organizational ethics', in Peterson, R. A. and Ferrell, O. C. (eds) *Business Ethics: New Challenges for Business Schools and Corporate Leaders*, Armonk, NY: M.E. Sharpe, pp. 3–17.

Gounaris, S. (2006), 'Internal-market orientation and its measurement', *Journal of Business Research*, 59(4): 432–448.

Gounaris, S. and Boukis, A. (2013), 'The role of employee job satisfaction in strengthening customer repurchase intentions', *Journal of Services Marketing*, 27(4): 322–333.

Gounaris, S. and Tzempelikos, N. (2013), 'Key account management orientation and its implications: A conceptual and empirical examination', *Journal of Business to Business Marketing*, 20(1): 33–50.

Gounaris, S. and Tzempelikos, N. (2014), 'Relational key account management: Building key account management effectiveness through structural reformations and relationship management skills', *Industrial Marketing Management*, 15 July 2014, available at ISSN 0019–8501, http://dx.doi.org/10.1016/j.indmarman.2014.06.001

Greenberg, H. (2003), *How to Hire and Develop Your Next Top Performer: The Five Qualities That Make Salespeople Great*, New York: McGraw-Hill Professional.

Greenberg, H. and Sweeney, P. (2012), *How to Hire and Develop Your Next Top Performer 2nd edition: The Qualities That Make Salespeople Great*, New York: McGraw-Hill Professional.

Guenzi, P. and Troilo, G. (2007), 'The joint contribution of marketing and sales to the creation of superior customer value', *Journal of Business Research*, 60: 98–107.

Homburg, C. and Jensen, O. (2007), 'The thought worlds of marketing and sales: Which differences make a difference?', *Journal of Marketing*, 71(3): 124–142.

Homburg, C., Workman, Jr, J. P. and Jensen, O. (2002), 'A configurational perspective on key account management', *Journal of Marketing*, 66(2): 38–60.

Hooley, G. J., Lynch, J. E. and Shepherd, J. (1990), 'The marketing concept: Putting the theory into practice', *European Journal of Marketing*, 24(9): 7–24.

Hulland J., Nenkov G. and Barclay D. (2012), 'Perceived marketing–sales relationship effectiveness: A matter of justice', *Journal of the Academy of Marketing Science*, 40(3): 450–467.

Kahn, K. B. and Mentzer, J. T. (1998), 'Marketing's integration with other departments', *Journal of Business Research*, 42(1): 53–62.

Keith, R. J. (1960), 'The marketing revolution', *The Journal of Marketing*, 24(3): 35–38.

Khosla, R., Goonesekera, T. and Chu, M. T. (2009), 'Separating the wheat from the chaff: An intelligent sales recruitment and benchmarking system', *Expert Systems with Applications*, 36(2): 3017–3027.

Kohli, A. K., and Jaworski, B. J. (1990), 'Market orientation: The construct, research propositions, and managerial implications', *The Journal of Marketing*, 54(2): 1–18.

Kotler, P. (1997), *Marketing Management: Analysis, Planning, Implementation and Control*, ninth edition, Englewood Cliffs, NJ: Prentice Hall.

Kotler, P., Rackham, N. and Krishnaswamy, S. (2006), 'Ending the war between sales and marketing', *Harvard Business Review*, 84(7): 68–78.

Lane, N. and Piercy, N. (2004), 'Strategic customer management: Designing a profitable future for your sales organization', *European Management Journal*, 22(6): 659–668.

Lee, N., Sandfield, A. and Dhaliwal, B. (2007), 'An empirical study of salesperson stereotypes amongst UK students and their implications for recruitment', *Journal of Marketing Management*, 23(7/8): 723–744.

Le Meunier-FitzHugh, K. and Piercy, N. F. (2007), 'Exploring collaboration between sales and marketing', *European Journal of Marketing*, 41(7/8): 939–955.

Le Meunier-FitzHugh, K. and Piercy, N. F. (2011), 'Exploring the relationship between market orientation and sales and marketing collaboration', *Journal of Personal Selling and Sales Management*, 31(3): 287–296.

Lionakis, K., Avlonitis, J. G. and Panagopoulos, N. (2013), *Relative Power of Marketing and Sales Departments: An Empirical Examination of its Consequences for the Organization*, Winter Marketing Educators Conference (AMA), Las Vegas.

Massey, G. R. and Dawes, P. L. (2007), 'The antecedents and consequence of functional and dysfunctional conflict between Marketing Managers and Sales Managers', *Industrial Marketing Management*, 36(8): 1118–1129.

McMurray, R. N. (1961), 'The mystique of super-salesmanship', *Harvard Business Review*, 39(2): 113–122.

Menguc, B. and Auh, S. (2008), 'Conflict, leadership, and market orientation', *International Journal of Research in Marketing*, 25(1): 34–45.

Moncrief, W. C. III (1986), 'Selling activity and sales position taxonomies for industrial salesforces', *Journal of Marketing Research*, 23: 261–270.

Moncrief, W. C. III, Marshall, G. W. and Lassk, F. G. (2006), 'A contemporary taxonomy of sales positions', *Journal of Personal Selling and Sales Management*, 26(1): 55–65.

Moorman, C. and Rust, T. R. (1999), 'The role of marketing', *Journal of Marketing*, 63(special issue): 180–197.

Murphy, P. E., Laczniak, G. R., Bowie, N. E. and Klein, T. A. (2005), *Ethical Marketing*, Upper Saddle River, NJ: Pearson Prentice Hall.

Narver, J. C. and Slater, S. F. (1990), 'The effect of a market orientation on business profitability', *Journal of Marketing*, 54(4): 20–35.

Netemeyer, R. G., Maxham, J. G. and Lichtenstein, D. R. (2010), 'Store manager performance and satisfaction: Effects on store employee performance and satisfaction, store customer satisfaction, and store customer spending growth', *Journal of Applied Psychology*, 95(3): 530–545.

Newton, D. A. (1973), *Sales Force Performance and Turnover*, Cambridge, MA: Marketing Science Institute, p. 3.

Panagopoulos, N. G. (2011), 'Customer relationship management (CRM) system implementation in sales organizations', in Guenzi, P. and Geiger, S. (eds) *Sales Management: A Multinational Perspective*, p. 116.

Pelham, A. M. and Kravitz, P. (2008), 'An exploratory study of the influence of sales training content and salesperson evaluation on salesperson adaptive selling, customer orientation, listening, and consulting behaviors', *Journal of Strategic Marketing*, 16(5): 413–435.

Piercy, N. F., Cravens, D. W. and Lane, N. (2012), 'Sales manager behavior-based control and salesperson performance: The effects of manager control competencies and organizational citizenship behavior', *The Journal of Marketing Theory and Practice*, 20(1): 7–22.

Rackham, N. and DeVincentis, J. (1999), *Rethinking the Sales Force*, New York: McGraw-Hill.

Rouziès, D., Anderson, E., Kohli, A., Michaels, R., Weitz, B. and Zoltners, A. (2005), 'Sales and marketing integration: A proposed framework', *Journal of Personal Selling and Sales Management*, 25(2): 113–122.

Salsbury, G. B. (1982), 'Properly recruit salespeople to reduce training cost', *Industrial Marketing Management*, 11(2): 143–146.

Shapiro, B. (2002), *Creating the Customer-Centric Team: Coordinating Sales and Marketing*, Boston, MA: Harvard Business School Publishing.

Song, X. M., Jinhong X., and Dyer, B. (2000), 'Antecedents and consequences of marketing managers' conflict-handling behaviors', *Journal of Marketing*, 64(1): 50–66.

Tzempelikos, N. and Gounaris, S. (2013), 'Approaching key account management from a long-term perspective', *Journal of Strategic Marketing*, 21(2): 179–198.

Tzempelikos, N. and Gounaris, S. (2015), 'Linking key account management practices to performance outcomes', *Industrial Marketing Management*, 45: 22–34.

Tzokas, N., Saren, M. and Kyziridis, P. (2001), 'Aligning sales management and relationship marketing in the services sector', *Service Industries Journal*, 21(1): 195–210.

Weitz, B. A. and Bradford, K. D. (1999), 'Personal selling and sales management: A relationship marketing perspective', *Journal of the Academy of Marketing Science*, 27(2): 241–254.

Zoltners, A. A., Sinha, P. and Lorimer, S. E. (2006), 'Match your sales force structure to your business life cycle', *Harvard Business Review*, 84(7/8): 80.

16 The roles of brands revisited

Francesca Dall'Olmo Riley

Introduction

In the 1990s commentators frequently reported on the sick health of brands, foreseeing their 'death' at the hands of price cutting and the 'commoditisation' of markets due to private labels, the growing power of retailers and the short-termism of brand managers (*The Economist* 1993, 1994, 1996; de Chernatony 1996; de Chernatony and Dall'Olmo Riley 1998a). Some of these threats still remain today: price discounting is still rife particularly in the grocery sector (*The Economist* 2014b), and in recent years many luxury brands have introduced lower priced ranges at the risk of pursuing short-term profit at the expense of brand exclusivity (Bokaie 2008; Buss 2013). Furthermore, once well-established brands like Woolworth (UK), Comet and Blockbusters have not been capable of adapting to technological, social or consumer behaviour changes and have disappeared from the market. At the same time, since the start of the twenty-first century, new brands and online retail brands such as Google and Amazon have entered the market and have quickly grown to dominate the Interbrand and BrandZ rankings of the top 100 global brands, having surpassed fast-moving consumer goods brands like Coca-Cola in terms of financial value. Having survived the trials of the 1990s and difficult global economic conditions, brands are considered to be the most valuable asset that companies own (*The Economist* 2014a). According to the brand consultancy, Millward Brown (2014), the combined value of the top 100 global brands in 2014 was US$2.9 trillion, up 12 per cent from the previous year. Google alone, the top ranking brand in 2014, was valued at US$158.8 billion.

However, new challenges to brands have arisen in recent years, for instance on the grounds of ethical, environmental and health-related corporate social responsibility issues. Food brands like McDonald's and Coca-Cola have been accused of being the culprit for increased rates of obesity, while fashion brands like Primark are criticised for their lack of concern for the welfare of workers employed by third-party manufacturers and for contributing to global warming with the high degree of waste caused by 'fast fashion' strategies. Anti-globalisation, anti-consumption and brand avoidance movements, as well as anti-brand websites and blogs challenge the very existence of brands in general and instigate consumers to boycott specific brands (e.g. Holt 2002; Krishnamurthy and Kucuk 2009; Lee *et al.* 2009).

At the forefront of these criticisms has been Klein's (2000a, 2000b) condemnation of the ubiquity and 'tyranny of the brands', leaving *no space* free of brands, *no choice* to consumers and ultimately *no jobs* for the workers. Not even schools are free from branded activities, such as the sponsoring of sport teams by Nike or Reebok, or voucher collections schemes like Tesco's Computers for Schools or Walkers Crisps Books for Schools. Retail chain brands dominate town centres and increasingly even small villages, inflating store rents and forcing independent retailers out of business; this leaves no real choice for consumers. Workers lose their jobs, because production is moved to countries where labour is cheaper. In such countries, workers are exploited and they work in overcrowded and dangerous conditions at the mercy of employers, with no contracts or just temporary ones, often drawn in bulk with employment agencies rather than with individuals. Even in Western, rich countries like the UK, workers employed by many major retailer brands are subjected to 'zero hour' or temporary contracts and are paid below the 'living wage' (KPMG 2014). These negative consequences of brands, Klein believes, stem from a change in their role since the mid-1980s, 'rather than serving as a guarantee of value on a product, the brand itself has increasingly become the product, a free standing idea pasted on to innumerable surfaces' (Klein 2000b: 25). According to Klein, this change has been brought about by the transformation of the role of organisations from manufacturers responsible for the production of quality products and for the welfare of the workers employed in their factories, to creators of the 'ideas', 'images' and 'lifestyle' personified by their brands.

On the other hand, supporters of brands maintain that the fundamental axioms of brands and their essential roles in consumers' lives have not changed. Brands not only help consumers make choices and buy efficiently among a myriad of almost undistinguishable alternatives but also protect consumers, who know where to complain if they have a problem with a product (*The Economist* 2001a). Furthermore, defenders of brands sustain that, through their purchase choices, it is consumers who dictate to companies and ultimately decide the fate of brands rather than the other way round (*The Economist* 2001b). The recent fall in sales of supermarket giants, Tesco and Sainsbury's, in favour of the cheaper alternatives, Aldi and Lidl, or the demise of the once sought after car brand, Hummer, support this view. Furthermore, through their actions and brand choices, consumers do have the opportunity to influence the behaviour of companies. Indeed, Nike started to report on the working conditions in the factories used to manufacture their products, as a result of mounting pressure from consumers. Increasing pressure from health and environmental campaigners has undoubtedly encouraged McDonald's not only to offer healthier menu options, but also to overhaul their supply chain and seek sources of sustainable beef (Sayon 2014a). In the words of the late Wally Olins, 'far from being evil, brands are becoming an effective weapon for holding even the largest global corporations to account. If we do not use them for that purpose we are lazy and indifferent and we deserve what we get' (cited in *The Economist* 2001b: 26).

Indeed, heightened consumer awareness of corporate social responsibility issues in production and marketing practices has actually encouraged the growth of brands positioned on ethical or environmental characteristics, such as the fashion brand, People Tree, or the detergent brand, Ecover. For other brands, such as Patagonia and Timberland, in the fashion industry, or for the food brand, Innocent, corporate social responsibility is an integral part of their identity. Therefore, the challenge from consumer movements has also created new opportunities for brands.

Another recent challenge to brands has arisen from internet technologies, which have made information about brand alternatives easily available to consumers, increasing their opportunity to switch brand loyalties (Simonson and Rosen 2014). On the other hand, Heskett (2014) notes that too much information may lead to increased consumer confusion, resulting in the greater use of brands in purchasing decisions as a 'route through the confusion', bringing about greater, rather than less, brand loyalty. Nonetheless, as the quality of technologies such as search and feedback mechanisms improves, the internet may become a means for consumers to delegate their purchase decisions to 'smart shopper' tools. For example, mysupermarket.com calculates the price of a basket of groceries from different retailers, enabling consumers to choose where to buy their groceries purely on the basis of the overall price of the goods sought in a specific purchase occasion, rather than by choosing a specific grocery retailer where to shop or specific brands.

The internet has also allowed consumers to exchange information and sometimes their passion (rather than their hate – see above) for brands online, for instance in virtual communities of brand lovers, such as the online brand community for the chocolate spread brand, Nutella, discussed by Cova and Pace (2006). Intensified engagement with brands and with other consumers online can be both a threat and an opportunity for organisations. It can be a threat in terms of loss of control: brand owners cannot control their message in the same way as with traditional forms of advertising and communication. Furthermore, the brand may be exposed and even be damaged by uncontrolled sharing of information online.

On the other hand, greater exchange of information between organisations and consumers offers opportunities for products' and services' co-creation shaping the future directions of brands, as illustrated by Hatch and Schultz (2010) with the LEGO case. But, while co-creation can be effective at engaging customers and other stakeholders with the brand, it can raise issues in terms of revenue sharing from co-created products and also competitive risk from too much transparency about business practices and new product development plans (Hatch and Schultz 2010).

Nonetheless, we should note that both the opportunities and the threats from enhanced consumer interest and engagement with brands appear to be small so far: evidence suggests that with few exceptions (e.g. for Sony PlayStation's social microsite called Greatness Awaits) the vast majority of consumers do not engage or create relationships with brands on social media in spite of the many opportunities to do so (Sayon 2014b). For instance, a recent report from Ogilvy (February 2014) highlights that brands on Facebook and Twitter reach only around 2 per cent of fans and followers, and less than 0.1 per cent of them interact with each post, on average (cited in Sayon 2014b).

In the light of the increasingly complex environment faced by brands, it is important to revisit the theoretical foundations of the different roles brands play for consumers as well as organisations, and to assess whether such roles have changed with changes in the social, economic and technological environment. To this end, the chapter revisits the roles of brands for consumers and for organisations also in relation to different perspectives of what a 'brand' is. Finally, the chapter discusses the concept of brand extensions as an illustration of the enduring importance of brands as exploitable assets for their owners and as quality guarantees to consumers even in the most disparate product categories.

The roles of brands for consumers

The roles of brands for consumers (and for organisations) closely relate to the essence of the brand concept itself and to what defines a 'brand' as a distinctive entity from a 'product'. In the following pages, the roles of brands are therefore discussed in the context of the different aspects and perspectives of the brand concept.

Brands as identifiers, guarantees, short hands and risk reducers

It is well known that brands were born as marks burnt on livestock (and even on slaves) to identify ownership and prevent theft. Indeed, 'brand' derives from the Old Norse term brandr, meaning to burn. From this original function of marks identifying ownership, brands and, eventually, brand names have evolved to become endorsements of authenticity, guaranteeing quality and consistency of performance (Duckworth 1991). This role has enabled consumers to simplify and structure their buying patterns and to gradually learn to associate brand names with sets of meanings.

Modern-day brands essentially fulfil the same role of providing information, acting as mental shorthands of functional and emotional benefits, hence enabling rapid recall of information in memory and speedier purchase decisions (McWilliam 1991). Brands enable consumers to identify products and services, which promise specific benefits (Crainer 1995), removing the need to shop around and analyse all available alternatives (Arnold 1992). Furthermore, according to Aaker (1991), a brand protects both the customer and the producer from competitors who attempt to provide products that appear to be identical, offering a 'route through the confusion' brought about by the 'commoditisation' of many markets (The *Economist* 1994: 12). As guarantees of consistent quality, brands also act as risk reducers, particularly for products and services where it is hard for consumers to assess performance before purchase (Dall'Olmo Riley and de Chernatony 2000).

The extent to which consumers consider brands as important devices for making risk-free choices and as a guarantee of quality is illustrated by the need for consumers to 'invent' brands in those circumstances when brands do not exist. For example, de Chernatony and Dall'Olmo Riley (1998a) report the story that in communist Russia people learnt to recognise the code-numbers identifying the factories where unbranded products were produced. Such numbers communicated to consumers the quality and characteristics to be expected from products originating from different factories, fulfilling one of the most important roles of brands. As Alba *et al.* (1997) note, 'a brand is a search attribute that assures consumers of a consistent level of product quality. It might be the only attribute available to assess some credence goods' (Alba *et al.* 1997: 49).

Alba *et al.*'s (1997) observation about the role of brand as a 'search attribute' applies not only to intangible goods such as professional services but also to any circumstance where it is not possible to physically evaluate the product before purchase. The roles of brands as identifiers, guarantees, shorthands and risk reducers are therefore still extremely relevant and important today, for instance for consumers shopping online. According to Citrin *et al.* (2003), brands play an important role in shifting consumers' perceptions away from experience attributes, such as tactility, to search attributes, such as reputation. Hence, brands are important risk relievers and facilitators of choice for online shoppers (Van den Poel and Leunis 1999). Consumers' tendency to shop online for goods with well-known brands and to shop from well-known retailers, even if they carry lesser-known brands (Kau *et al.* 2003; Lee and Tan 2003) does not seem to have changed significantly since the mid-2000s, even though shopping online has become almost as widespread and habitual behaviour as shopping in store. Well-known retailers now include online stores such as Amazon and Asos, which over time have gained the trust of shoppers, while many consumers do shop at sites operated by a traditional store or catalogue retailer or by a manufacturer they are already familiar with (Mintel 2014).

From a consumer psychology perspective, Janiszewski and Van Osselaer (2000) explain the processes by which brands function as not only associative cues for information retrieval but also as predictive cues about product performance. They compare two types of learning models: the 'spreading activation model' and the 'least mean squares (LMS) connectionist model'. The 'spreading activation model' is the framework traditionally employed by researchers to depict the mechanism by which brand knowledge is stored in memory (see, for instance, Keller 1993; Henderson *et al.* 1998). According to this model, brand knowledge is stored in memory nodes, connected by links, which vary in association strength; a process of concurrent activation allows associative links from a brand name to an outcome to be updated, while the degree of updating depends on the quality of processing. Janiszewski and van Osselaer (2000) remark that, consistent with multi-attribute utility models, any salient cues such as brand names and features could gain predictive value, while each cue is independent and additive. In contrast, 'LMS connectionist models' are consistent with an adaptive learning process mechanism, whereby the strength of the link from one node to another is not necessarily equal to the strength of the link in the reverse direction. A second assumption of adaptive learning models is that feedback is used to update the association strength between cues and outcomes. A further, important, assumption of this kind of model is that cues compete to predict outcomes; therefore the association strengths between each cue and an outcome depend on the association strengths between other cues and the same outcome. The impact of a brand name as a predictive cue and the relevant underlying mechanisms are investigated by Janiszewski and Van Osselaer (2000) in five studies concerning different branding strategies. The main finding is that an adaptive learning process mechanism, such as the one described by the LMS connectionist model, is best suited to situations where cues are used with a predictive value. On the other hand, learning to recall may best be described by spreading activation models.

The roles of brands for consumers discussed in this section relate to analogous definitions and interpretations of the brand concept. The role of the brand as identifier corresponds to the traditional definition put forward by the American Marketing Association (AMA) in 1960 of a *brand as a logo*, enabling consumers to recognise different brands at the point of purchase. The role of the brand as a guarantee of consistent quality reducing performance risk is related to the concept of the brand as a contract between the organisation and the consumer (Staveley 1987; Kapferer 1995). In its role as a memory shortcut facilitating choice, 'a brand name is nothing more or less than the sum of all the mental connections people have around it' (Brown 1992, cited in de Chernatony and Dall'Olmo Riley 1998b). Finally, as short hands of meanings:

> a brand is more than the label employed to differentiate among the manufacturers of a product. It is a complex symbol that represents a variety of ideas and attributes. It tells the consumers many things, not only by the way it sounds (and its literal meaning if it has one) but, more important, via the body of associations it has built and acquired as a public object over a period of time.
>
> (Gardner and Levy 1955: 35)

Though sixty years old, this interpretation of the brand concept is probably the most relevant in the context of the diverse and complex roles that brands have been assuming in recent years as self-expression devices for consumers and which are addressed in the next section.

Brands as self-expressive devices

Beyond the more 'utilitarian' roles of brands discussed in the previous section, brands are carriers of symbolic meanings (Levy 1959). A fundamental role of brands for consumers is to enable them to make sense and to create meanings for themselves in the social world of consumption (Escalas and Bettman 2003). For example, different brands of clothes, cars and accessories make visible statements about the user's style, modernity or wealth, enabling people to tell the world who they are (*The Economist* 1994); in the words of Belk (1988: 160), 'we are what we have'.

Stokburger-Sauer *et al.* (2012) remark that the extent to which brands have the ability to embody, inform and communicate desirable consumer identities has been the object of extensive research in recent years (e.g. Fournier 1998, 2009; Bhattacharya and Sen 2003; Escalas and Bettman 2003, 2009; Escalas 2004; Tsai 2005; Strizhakova *et al.* 2008; Lam *et al.* 2010). In particular, Stokburger-Sauer *et al.* (2012) note that a growing body of research has focused on what it means for consumers to identify with brands and the implications of such consumer–brand identification for both consumer behaviour and effective brand management (e.g. Escalas and Bettman 2003, 2009; Lam *et al.* 2010; Chernev *et al.* 2011).

Consistent with social identity (Tajfel and Turner 1979) and identity (Stryker 1968) theories, consumers' self-enhancement and self-definitional needs can be fulfilled by identifying with companies with certain characteristics (Bhattacharya *et al.* 1995; Bhattacharya and Sen 2003; Ahearne *et al.* 2005) or by bonding with brands whose identities are consonant with desirable reference groups and celebrity endorsers (Escalas and Bettman 2003, 2009).

Interestingly, Lee *et al.* (2009) note that while some consumers express themselves and construct their identities/self-concepts through the brands they use, others reject specific brands in order to avoid adding undesired meanings to their lives. Apart from avoiding brands due to past negative experiences or poor quality ('experiential avoidance'), consumers may avoid brands, which they consider as incompatible with their identity ('identity avoidance') or when brand management policies are perceived to have a negative impact on society ('moral avoidance'). For example, the fashion brand, Jack Wills, may be avoided by young consumers who do not identify with the 'private school', 'preppy' identity of the brand. On the other hand, examples of moral avoidance behaviour include pledges to avoid shopping from Amazon because of their poor record in paying tax in the countries where they sell their products or in paying living wage rates to their workers. Hence, brands can fulfil the role of self-expressive devices even when they are avoided or boycotted.

Finally, brands also enable consumers to fulfil interpersonal goals by participating in communities of individuals who identify themselves with similar brands (e.g. Schouten and McAlexander 1995; Muniz and O'Guinn 2001; McAlexander *et al.* 2002; O'Guinn and Muniz 2009). Cova and Pace (2006) discuss brand communities as new forms of sociality and customer empowerment, not based on interaction between peers but on personal self-exhibition in front of other consumers through the marks and rituals linked to the brand. Hatch and Schultz (2010: 592) go a step further and describe brand communities as 'contexts for co-creation', whereby consumers can engage with brands even to the extent of co-creating products, services and the overall direction of the brand.

The complex role of brands as self-expressive and self-enhancing devices relate to concepts of brands as a *company*, as *identity* and *value systems*, as a *personality*, as a *relationship* and as *adding value* (see de Chernatony and Dall'Olmo Riley 1998b). The concept of brand as a company is 'the projection of the amalgamated values of a corporation' (de Chernatony 2008: 308). Brand values, such as those related to the company's credentials in terms of social responsibilities, enable consumer-company identification (e.g. see Du *et al.* 2007) and the role of the corporate brand as a self-expressive device.

The definitions of brands as identity (e.g. Hatch and Schultz 2000; Kapferer 2012), value systems (e.g. Meenaghan 1995) and adding value (de Chernatony *et al.* 2011), transcend the mere functional characteristics of the branded product and focus instead on the essential vision and symbolic aspects of what makes a 'product' become a 'brand'. Consumer-brand identification occurs when the identity and values of the individual are matched by the values characterising the brand; hence, brands enable purchases, which satisfy specific consumer values and needs.

Similarly, since the 1990s, a considerable volume of research has defined brands as symbolic devices with personalities that users value beyond their functional utility (e.g. Alt and Griggs 1988; Aaker 1997; Aaker *et al.* 2001; Azoulay and Kapferer 2003). When choosing between competing brands, consumers can assess the fit between the personalities of the brand and the personality they wish to project (Zinkhan *et al.* 1996; Johar *et al.* 2005; Swaminathan *et al.* 2009; Malär *et al.* 2011).

The notion of a brand as a relationship is the logical extension of brand as a personality (Blackston 1992). If brands can be personified, then consumers would not just perceive them, but would also have relationships with them (Blackston 1993; Kapferer 2012). Indeed, brand–consumer relationships have been the subject of extensive research in recent years (e.g. Belk 1988; Fournier 1998;

Aggarwal 2004; Albert *et al.* 2008; Fetscherin and Heinrich 2014). The strength of the consumer-brand relationship (from strong to weak) and the valence (positive or negative) of a consumer's feelings towards a brand determine the role that a brand plays in the life of the consumer (Fetscherin and Heinrich 2014) and may even reflect the 'age' of the relationship (Reimann *et al.* 2012).

It follows from the above discussion that different definitions and interpretations of the brand concept closely match the multiple roles and the value of brands for consumers, not only with regard to their purchase behaviour but also in relation to their lifestyle and self-concept as individuals. Brands in the twenty-first century may be under threat and subject to criticism on various fronts, but they continue to fulfil fundamental and indispensable roles for consumers, as in the past.

To the roles of brands for consumers correspond equally important brand roles for organisations, which motivate firms to invest in brands.

Firms' motivations for branding and the roles of brands for the firm

Firms' motivations for branding relate to the numerous roles expected from brands by organisations and can be approached from either an economics, strategy, marketing or financial perspective. We look at the origin of these approaches in the following pages.

Economics motivations

The concept of 'branding' from the firm perspective finds its origins in the economics literature, in terms of the economies of scale and of scope that brands can bring to organisations. For example, Demsetz (1973) argued that brands with high sales enjoy *production* economies and that this asymmetry between sales and cost generates efficiency rents for low cost firms. A different source of asymmetry was discussed by Thomas (1989), in the form of lower *unit-marketing* costs for brands with high sales. Furthermore, brand names constitute a 'natural' barrier to entry due to the sunk costs of advertising, according to Demsetz (1982).

Firms benefit from economies of scope when they successfully create a brand in one market and extend it into another, due to accumulated market expertise (Watkins 1986). Similarly, Wernerfelt (1988) suggested that brands enable *reputational* economies of scope; for instance, a multi-product firm can use its reputation as a bond for quality, when extending an established brand name. Therefore 'umbrella' or 'banner' branding across a range of different products could be used to send a noise-free, credible signal about the quality of each product (for further details see later in the chapter on page 403).

In the economics literature, the brand is also considered a device to create a form of 'imperfect competition' through differentiation, enabling the brand owner to obtain some of the benefits, which accrue to a monopoly, particularly those benefits related to decreased price competition (Mercer 1992). The value a brand offers to consumers through differentiation, and the consequent price inelasticity, distinguish a brand from a commodity whose value has been discounted by parity competition and whose price is vulnerable to grinding down (Hanan and Karp 1991). Higher prices are a potential source of economic rents for brands (Thomas 1989). If a firm can establish brand loyalty for its brand and thereby render the demand inelastic, it can increase prices without suffering a large drop in demand (Watkins 1986).

Finally, Klein and Leffler (1981) contended that branding is a way for sellers to produce attributes that are difficult for third parties to verify. Accordingly, sellers should be more likely to brand when consumers find personal search and experimentation relatively unattractive (Png and Reitman 1995). When consumers pay a premium price for branded products, they are paying for an implicit guarantee of superior quality, consistent with information theory (Png and Reitman 1995). Consumers seeking to advertise their wealth are willing to pay a higher price for 'luxury' brands, even though such brands may not be intrinsically superior to lower priced brands (Bagwell and Bernheim 1996).

Strategy motivations

Porter (1985) identified two basic sources of competitive advantage for firms: low cost and differentiation. While Porter did not specifically mention 'brands', but talked about 'products', brands are the means by which low cost or differentiation strategies can be implemented. There are innumerable examples of organisations, which, through their branding strategies, pursue either strategy or, sometimes, both strategies with different brands in their portfolio. For instance, in the US diapers market, Procter & Gamble pursues a low cost strategy with the brand Luvs and at the same time a differentiation strategy with the Pampers brand, which is priced at a premium. In the UK grocery market, some retailers practise a low cost strategy (Aldi, Lidl, Tesco, Asda and Morrisons), others a differentiation strategy through their brands (Waitrose and Marks & Spencer), while others are 'stuck in the middle' (Sainsbury's).

In earlier work, Porter (1976) mentioned brands as competitive tools, explaining that developing a strong brand image is the manufacturer's prime strategy for differentiating its products. According to Porter, a strong brand image is also a bargaining weapon for manufacturers when dealing with retailers. A strong brand assures profits to retailers who stock it, but at the same time denies them the bargaining counter of refusing to sell it and less persuasion power is needed from the producer of the brand.

Fundamental to developing a strong brand image and gaining competitive advantage is the ability of a firm to select the brand central concept on either a functional, or symbolic or experiential positioning, according to Park *et al.* (1986). Their brand concept management (BCM) framework offers a structured pathway for the management and control of the brand's image throughout its life, from introduction, to elaboration and fortification. Within each stage, specific positioning strategies are recommended, depending on whether the brand concept is functional, symbolic or experiential. However, Henderson *et al.* (1998) disagree with this approach, arguing that understanding consumer perceptions and associations is more important than 'a priori managerial statements of intended brand strategies' (Henderson *et al.* 1998: 307) in developing a strong brand.

Nonetheless, whatever the perspective, there is broad agreement among scholars that organisations can derive a number of strategic advantages from developing strong brands. For instance, Aaker (1995) pointed out that a strategy based on strong brands is likely to be sustainable, due to the competitive barriers arising, for example, from restricted distribution channel access. Other barriers to entry identified by Porter (1980) arise from product differentiation, as a source of established brand identification and customer loyalty.

Incumbency is the central competitive advantage of long-established brands, according to Kay (1993). This is because of the sunk costs of achieving similar wide distribution and consumer recognition in the face of well-established incumbents. Kay (1993) identified a number of roles that brands serve: (1) they are a means by which the producer can establish the reputation of a product; (2) they provide assurance of consistency; (3) they may reflect a distinctive recipe; and (4) they may be a means through which consumers signal information of themselves to others.

Shifting the emphasis from positioning advantages to the sources for strategy, Hamel and Prahalad (1996) advocated the exploitation of the company's core competencies in order to build 'banner' brands, spanning multiple products and businesses. The main aim of banner brands is to pre-empt competition by helping consumers transfer the goodwill between the company's products. The 'warrant' created through a banner brand is a particularly important source of competitive advantage when trying to establish new competitive space through creating a new product category. Furthermore, banner brands facilitate the access of new products to existing distribution channels. The concept of 'banner' brands will be further discussed later in the chapter, in the context of brand extensions.

Marketing motivations

Consistent with the economics and strategy motivations for branding, marketing scholars have related the advantage of branding to the value added by brands to the core product or service (e.g. Jones 1986; Quelch and Harding 1996; de Chernatony *et al.* 2011). Keller (1993) explained that brands bring value or equity to firms, because favourable outcomes result from the marketing of a product or service due to its brand name. Aaker (1991) related the value of the brand to the levels of loyalty, awareness, perceived quality and other associations it has with it. More recently, Hoeffler and Keller (2003) summarised the marketing advantages that organisations can derive from building strong brands. Hoeffler and Keller (2003) discuss how brand strength (operationalised either as brand familiarity, brand knowledge or brand performance) can have differential effects on consumer behaviour. Strong brands are thought to enjoy several advantages over lesser-known brands in terms of memory encoding and storage and, consequently, of their likelihood of being included in consumers' consideration sets. Hoeffler and Keller (2003) also suggest a number of effects related to consumer responses to marketing activities. For instance, strong brands are able to extend more successfully and into more diverse product categories than lesser-known competitors, are more resistant to dilution, can weather product-harm crises better and command higher prices.

Besides helping the firm to grow, according to Kapferer (2012) brands can provide a haven of stability, evoking clear identities. Brands anchor the origins of products, clarify why they exist and show where they are going, thereby setting guidelines and helping focus the activities of employees and stakeholders. This is particularly important for people-based services such as financial or legal services, where brands can fulfil the role of internal cohesive devices, allowing employees to retain the flexibility to deal with different people and situations, while conforming to the brand concept (George 1990; Greene *et al.* 1994; de Chernatony and Dall'Olmo Riley 1999).

Finally, consistent with economics and strategy scholars, marketing scholars have noted that branding can also act as a form of protection against competition. Besides the legal protection afforded by patents and trademarks (Jones 1986), the differentiation achieved through branding constitutes a barrier to entry by making it difficult for competitors to emulate the company's offerings (Jones 1986; de Chernatony *et al.* 2011). Furthermore, the equity accumulated by a brand prevents market share erosion during price and promotional wars (Kamakura and Russell 1993). The longevity of brands such as Heinz in the baked beans market and their ability to sustain their market share at a price premium in the face of cut-price competition by supermarket brands is an example of this.

Financial motivations

The economics, strategic and marketing motivations for branding have a common outcome in the financial returns that accrue to organisations from their investment into brands. Interest in the brands as assets on the balance sheet and in the financial returns from selling brands has been sparked by a number of high profile mergers and acquisitions since the 1990s, such as the acquisition of Rowntree by Nestlé in 1990 and, more recently, of Gillette by Procter & Gamble, of Cadbury by Kraft and of Heinz by Warren Buffet. In all cases, a substantial price premium was paid over and above the brands' tangible assets. For instance, of US$57 billion paid by Procter & Gamble for the Gillette Company, US$24 billion were attributed to the value of the Gillette brand alone (*The Economist* 2014c). Overall, the value of brands is thought to account for 20 to 30 per cent of the global economy (Clifton 2013).

The financial benefits of brands or the financial value of brands for organisations are generally expressed in terms of the incremental cash flow or profit that can be attributed to a brand (Barwise *et al.* 1990; Simon and Sullivan 1993). However, there are substantial issues with regard to measuring the financial benefits of brands, with no agreed measures, nor methodologies. Various measures of a brand financial value have been proposed by academic researchers and by commercial consultancies. These measures vary from the residual approach proposed by Simon and Sullivan (1993), to the estimate of the brand equity component in the price paid for mergers and acquisitions (e.g. Rao *et al.* 1991; Mahajan *et al.* 1994), to the 'present value of future cash flows that accrue to a branded offering' (Bahadir *et al.* 2008: 49). The consultancy, Interbrand (2014), also takes a discounted cash flow approach, in combination with product-market measures. On the other hand, the consultancy, Millward Brown (2014), combines financial measures with their BrandZ customer mind-set measures. The discrepancies between Interbrand and Millward Brown in the financial value attributed to the same brands is a striking sign of the difficulties in achieving an objective estimate of a brand's financial return on investment (e.g. see Ritson 2006; *The Economist* 2014c). As Barwise (1993) and Barwise *et al.* (1990) discuss, brand valuation is inherently subjective for three reasons. First, 'value' is per se a subjective construct, as also illustrated by Bahadir *et al.* (2008) in the context of the financial value of brands in mergers and acquisitions. Second, it is difficult, if not impossible, to separate a brand's intangible value from the rest of the firm's assets. Third, brand valuation usually relies on some kind of forecasting, which again requires subjective, context specific assumptions.

In conclusion, as economic, strategic, marketing and financial tools, brands are valuable assets for organisations. As such, brands are nurtured and leveraged by firms often beyond their original product or service category. This is so in the case of brand extensions. The roles of the brand in brand extensions for organisations and for consumers are discussed next.

The roles of brands in brand extensions

Launching new products and services is necessary if organisations are to grow, remain competitive and address changing consumer needs. Using an existing brand when launching a new product or service, creating a sort of 'banner brand' that extends over the new product(s), has a number of advantages over the alternative of creating a new brand (Hamel and Prahalad 1996).

First, by extending a brand firms can reduce (although not eliminate – see below) the costs and the risks associated with launching a new product. According to Hamel and Prahalad (1996: 187), 'familiarity with a high quality banner brand creates a strong predisposition on the part of the customers to at least consider purchasing new products that bear the "maker's mark"'. By extending a brand, organisations help consumers transfer the goodwill that has been built up through the positive experience with one company's products to other products. A trusted brand is a warrant to consumers that the new product or service will perform to a high standard. This is consistent with Wernerfelt's (1988) suggestion that brands enable *reputational* economies of scope for the firm. Such reputational economies of scope are particularly important with innovative products, since customers are likely to require the security of a brand that has proven itself trustworthy in the past.

For example, through the years Apple has successfully introduced a series of entirely new product concepts capitalising on their brand associations for innovative, state-of-the-art technology and design. Furthermore, the predisposition of consumers to purchase a new product launched by a trusted brand increases retailers' willingness to stock the new product.

The use of an existing brand when launching a new product also warrants economies of scale. For instance, Braig and Tybout (2005) note that extending an established brand name to a new product generally reduces advertising costs since consumers are already aware of the brand's features and benefits. Such knowledge of the brand and its benefits can be automatically transferred to new products, which are perceived to be compatible with the parent brand. Furthermore, appropriate brand extensions can benefit the parent brand by reinforcing the standing and the image of the brand in the marketplace and may also reduce a firm's dependence on a single product flavour, form or category, which may become obsolete or fall out of favour with consumer tastes. Thus, every new successful introduction of a new product reinforces the image of the Apple parent brand and its standing as an innovative company at the forefront of technology. In contrast, Polaroid and Kodak are examples of organisations, which have failed to do so.

The discussion so far on firms' motivations for extending a brand and the advantages of brand extensions for both companies and consumers further highlights the role of brands as strategic tools for organisations and as facilitators of purchase decisions for consumers.

But, notwithstanding the many advantages of employing an existing brand when launching a new product, in practice failure rates of brand extensions are reported to be as high as 80 per cent (Ernst and Young and ACNielsen 1999; Marketing 2003). Importantly, failed extensions can tarnish the image of the parent brand, particularly if the failure is due to low quality. Furthermore, as Keller *et al.* (2012) point out, there are a number of risks associated with extending a brand. First, a plethora of extensions can confuse consumers about which version is the right one for them. This confusion may prompt consumers to switch to a brand with fewer, simpler options, or to the more mainstream 'all-purpose' brand. Second, too many flavours, forms or variants of the same product can encounter retailer resistance. Even in the largest stores shelf space is finite, given the vast number of available products and brands. Twining's range of teas is vast and new flavours or variants are introduced almost on a daily basis, but they can be displayed only in Twining's own shops, while retailers can stock only the most popular and/or profitable varieties. As a matter of fact, the inability to find an advertised new variety, if retailers are unable or unwilling to stock it, may frustrate customers.

Additionally, even successful extensions may have negative consequences if, for example, they cannibalise the sales of existing products. This risk is particularly relevant in the case of a 'vertical' extension, namely the introduction of a new product version at a lower price level. Brands positioned at the upper end of the quality/prestige spectrum run the greatest risk, because defining factors such as high exclusivity and desirability can be lost and their luxury appeal may become diluted by the introduction of lower priced products.

Finally, by introducing a new product as a brand extension, a company can forgo the opportunity to develop a new brand targeting a different customer segment or a new brand with higher margin potential than the extension.

Given this background, it is very important for managers to understand the roles of brands in consumers' evaluations of extensions, the mental processes by which consumers assess a brand extension and the effect of brand extensions on the way consumers perceive and make sense of brands. The rest of this chapter deals with these issues. The focus of the discussion is on line extensions, namely new product launches within the brand's current product category, rather than extensions into a new product category (category extensions). This is because, in practice, line extensions are almost four times more frequent than category extensions (*Les Échos* 2004). Keller (2008) estimates that, in any given year, typically 80 to 90 per cent of new products are line extensions. The general characteristics of line extensions are considered next, followed by a discussion of the factors influencing consumers' evaluations of brand extensions, including the role of different types of brands. Finally, the chapter outlines the mental processes governing how consumers make sense of brand extensions and of the brand's image after an extension.

Line extensions

Line extensions consist of the use of an existing brand name to introduce new products within the same product category. Line extensions comprise either vertical or horizontal extensions, depending on whether the new product is at a different price-quality level or not. Horizontal line extensions usually involve line stretching, with products that simply provide a new flavour or a new functional feature. For instance, the skin care brand, Dove, has introduced several different scents as horizontal extensions of the original body lotion. On the other hand, with vertical line extensions the brand extends into a new market segment through upscale (upward or step-up) or downscale (downward or step-down) changes in price and positioning. By means of upscale extensions, a superior version of the main product can target the premium sector of the market. For example, Dove has recently extended upward with the introduction of a new range of products called Dove DermaSeries, positioned at a considerably higher price than the existing Dove products and sold exclusively in upmarket stores like Selfridges, rather than via mass distribution channels. Alternatively, downscale extensions often entail both a lower quality level and a lower price point that suits the necessities of price conscious consumers, like in the case of the luxury fashion brand Giorgio Armani's extensions into lower priced products with the Emporio Armani and Armani Exchange ranges.

Although it would be logical to envisage a higher level of risk for extensions into an altogether different product category (category extensions) than for extensions within the same original product category, line extensions are not without risks. For example, in vertical downscale extensions there is a strong risk of brand image dilution, should consumers find a disparity between the quality of the parent brand and the quality of the extension. Not only could the core brand acquire low quality associations but the image of other products under the brand's umbrella could be tarnished. As Randall *et al.* (1998) noted, this risk is particularly serious for luxury brands. Maintaining brand associations of prestige and exclusivity can be an impossible task if the company launches vertical extensions targeting the low-end of the market, but which are not different enough from the original, more expensive products. Indeed, recent studies on vertical extensions of luxury brands have been particularly concerned with the effect of such extensions on core brand associations, with general agreement that downscale extensions can be damaging to the parent brand's associations with luxury (e.g. Magnoni and Roux 2012; Hennings *et al.* 2013).

Regarding upscale extensions, Munthree *et al.* (2006) suggest that this strategy may help revitalise a brand, whenever the positioning and the credibility of the new product are adequate and the extension is neither first-to-market nor late-to-market. However, although upscale extensions can build positive brand associations, consumers might be suspicious of formerly inexpensive brands that promise to deliver functional and emotional benefits in premium segments. Furthermore, retailers may be reluctant to stock upmarket versions of inexpensive brands, in competition with other premium-priced brands they already sell. These are potential problems for the newly introduced Dove DermaSeries upscale extension.

As the discussion so far suggests, the success of a brand extension depends on the transfer of positive associations from the parent brand to the new product. A large number of studies from the 1990s to the present day have shown that perception of 'fit' between the parent brand and the new product is essential for the positive transfer of associations to occur. The brand extension literature has consistently shown that the higher the fit, the higher the transference of positive associations from the brand to the extension, which improves both the extension attitude (Boush and Loken 1991; Klink and Smith 2001; Völckner and Sattler 2006) and the parent brand's image (Loken and John 1993; John *et al.* 1998). On the other hand, brands that stretch too widely can lead to the loss of brand meaning and may cannibalise the sales of other products in the brand portfolio (Kim and Lavack 1996; Liu 2002). Therefore, line extensions should develop a new identity that reduces the risk of cannibalisation and, in the case of vertical stretching, position the new product in the desirable price-quality level, while maintaining some degree of coherence with the higher or lower price-quality image of the parent brand (Michel and Salha 2005). For this reason, many companies resort to second brand names or descriptors as means to distinguish cheaper extensions (Farquhar *et al.* 1992), as in the case of Marriott Hotels launching the downscale extension Courtyard Inn by Marriott.

Many factors such as consumer characteristics, the type of brand, the company's strategy when launching an extension and competitors' activities can influence the process by which consumers evaluate a brand extension and its ultimate outcome in terms of success or failure. Given that the focus of this chapter is the role of brands, the next few pages will address more specifically the role of the type of brand in line extensions and relating consumers' mental processes, with implications for brand extension strategies.

The role of the type of brand in line extensions

Since the mid-1990s researchers have considered the type of brand to be extended as an important factor in line extensions, in particular the distinction between functional (e.g. Dove) and luxury (e.g. Dior) brands (see, for example, Park *et al.* 1991; McWilliam 1993; Sharp 1993; Broniarczyk and Alba 1994; Pitta and Katsanis 1995; Kim and Lavack 1996; Kirmani *et al.* 1999). Kim and Lavack (1996) provided empirical evidence for the potentially negative effects of vertical line extensions on the post-extension evaluation of the parent brand, showing that downscale extensions of luxury brands are more damaging to the brand than downscale extensions of functional brands. Kirmani *et al.* (1999) found both positive and negative evaluations of vertical extensions, depending on the type of consumer (user vs. non-user), on the extension's direction (upscale vs. downscale), and on the brand concept (functional vs. luxury). Their results showed that users of functional brands evaluate both upscale and downscale extensions more favourably than non-users. However, users of luxury brands evaluate upscale extensions more favourably, and downscale extensions less favourably than non-users, because of the users' desire to maintain brand exclusivity. Overall, introducing a vertical line extension with a 40 per cent discount on the initial price leads to more negative evaluations for the luxury brand than for the functional brand.

However, Broniarczyk and Alba (1994) noted that the distinction between functionality and prestige is too broad and that what counts is the relevance of brand specific associations in the extension context, since perceptions of incompatibility and confusion might arise if a brand positioned at one end of the price or status continuum were to launch an extension at the other end of the continuum (e.g. an 'economy' car brand launching a 'luxury' car). At the same time, the downscale extension of a brand whose core associations are status and high price may be problematic and may tarnish the image of the parent brand (Pitta and Katsanis 1995). Indeed, Kim *et al.* (2001) showed that regardless of the type of brand (functional or luxury) and regardless of the direction of extension (upscale or downscale), the introduction of vertical line extensions can have a negative impact on the parent brand. Kim *et al.* (2001) explained this negative impact by means of the 'bookkeeping' mental process model of categorisation theory (Weber and Crocker 1983), whereby consumers' beliefs change incrementally with any new piece of information, and any inconsistent information about a new brand extension (e.g. the reduction in price and quality) results in the dilution of the corresponding belief about the parent brand.

Kim *et al.* (2001) also noted that distancing techniques can be effective in reducing the dilution of the core brand image, particularly in the case of a downscale extension of a luxury brand (see below for more discussion on distancing techniques). However, the opposite result occurs with regard to the consumer evaluation of the downscale extension itself (whether luxury or functional brands, it does not matter), whereby distancing lowers the evaluation of the extension product. The trade-off of distancing in the case of downscale extensions suggests that use of this technique should depend upon the strategic goals of the company, i.e. whether maintenance of the core brand or the long-term success of the vertical extension is more important to the future profitability of the firm.

As highlighted in the discussion so far, researchers agree that differentiating or distancing the extension from the parent brand often helps to resolve consumer perceptions of inconsistencies between the vertical extension and the core brand and reduces or eliminates the risk of brand image dilution (e.g. Farquhar *et al.* 1992; Kim *et al.* 2001; Michel and Salha 2005). However, with regard to the effect of distancing techniques on consumers' evaluations of vertical line extensions, the results are less straightforward. For example, graphic or linguistic distancing techniques (e.g. the use of sub-branding) appear to have a negative effect on consumers' evaluations of downscale brand extensions, but a positive effect on upscale brand extensions evaluations (Kim *et al.* 2001).

The sub-typing (typicality) mental process model from categorisation theory (Weber and Crocker 1983; Sujan and Bettman 1989) helps to explain the dynamics of distancing strategies of various kinds. As Gürhan-Canli and Maheswaran (1998) explained:

> [t]he sub-typing model suggests that atypical instances generally are considered exceptions and categorized as sub-types, with separate sets of beliefs associated with each subtype. Thus, the formation of a subcategory limits the impact of extreme incongruent information on the schema.
>
> (Gürhan-Canli and Maheswaran 1998: 465)

In the instance of a vertical extension, increasing the distance between the extension and the core brand enhances the formation of a subcategory and limits the negative impact of incongruent information from the extension on the parent brand schema.

The sub-typing model explains the findings by Kim *et al.* (2001) and other researchers that graphical or linguistic distancing of the core brand from the extension reduces the negative impact on the core brand. However, there is the drawback that distancing a downscale line extension from the parent brand, hence reducing its typicality within the brand schema, may limit the transfer of positive associations from the core brand to the extension. Therefore, the evaluation of a downscale extension is less favourable when the extension is further away from the core brand and more favourable when the extension is closer (Kim *et al.* 2001). On the other hand, as Kim *et al.* (2001) showed, greater distancing (i.e. less typicality) may benefit the evaluation of an upscale extension, since it avoids the transfer of lesser quality perceptions from the core brand to the extension.

Finally, Michel and Salha (2005) suggested that a large price differential for the extension product may in itself be an effective distancing technique, helping to avoid the possible loss of coherence between the vertical extension and the quality-price perception of the core brand

and positioning the new product in an altogether different market segment. This suggestion is consistent with the sub-typing mental process model, whereby consumers will perceive an extension with a price considerably higher or lower than other products as less typical of the parent brand and will be less likely to make any inference from the extension to the brand (see also Loken and John 1993). Michel and Salha's (2005) suggestions are supported by recent evidence in the context of the vertical extensions of luxury brands showing that the magnitude of discount has a stronger impact on the post-extension brand image than on the evaluation of the downscale extensions themselves. A smaller price differential appears to have a more negative impact on brand image than the larger discount. Thus, price has a role to play as a distancing technique, creating a subcategory in consumers' minds, which helps to reduce the dilution of the post-extension brand image, particularly in the case of prestige brands in conspicuous product categories like cars. On the other hand, the magnitude of price discount does not appear to affect the extension evaluation (Dall'Olmo Riley *et al.* 2013).

Conclusion

This chapter has revisited the roles of brands for consumers and organisations, in the context of the challenges and opportunities faced by brands in the first two decades of the twenty-first century. A review of academic and practitioner perspectives indicates that the fundamental axioms of the roles of brands for consumers and for organisations have remained essentially the same notwithstanding the economic, social and technological changes in the environment.

For consumers, brands remain indispensable tools as identifiers, guarantees, shorthands and risk reducers whether purchasing in store or online. Besides these unchanged utilitarian roles, brands also enable consumers to create meanings for themselves in the social world of consumption. While the role of brands as self-expressive devices is not new, technological advances such as online brand communities have enhanced the opportunities for consumers to express themselves through the brands they use or, even, through the ones they reject.

For organisations, brands are extremely valuable assets, in terms of the economic, strategic, marketing and financial advantages they offer. As such, brands can be leveraged by organisations as a banner over a wide range of goods and services, enabling reputational economies of scope and economies of scale for the firm. This is so in the case of brand extensions, as demonstrated by their widespread use as a strategy for growth when introducing new products. Crucially, organisations can use brand extensions as a powerful, credible signal about the quality and overall characteristics of each new product they introduce, even though the clarity of such signal may actually depend on appropriate 'distancing' of the new product from the parent brand. At the same time, consumers can use brand extensions as a means to structure and categorise in their minds the relationship between the different products offered by a firm.

Finally, the chapter has provided research-based evidence of the complexities of introducing successful brand extensions in terms of achieving consumer acceptance of the new product, while retaining the core associations of the parent brand, particularly in the case of the downscale extensions of luxury brands. Hopefully, the suggestions offered by academic researchers on how to manage vertical line extensions successfully will be useful to readers.

References

Aaker, D. (1991), *Managing Brand Equity: Capitalising on the Value of a Brand Name*. New York: The Free Press.
Aaker, D. (1995), *Developing Business Strategies*, fourth edition, New York: John Wiley & Sons.

Aaker, J. L. (1997), 'Dimensions of brand personality', *Journal of Marketing Research*, 34(August): 342–352.

Aaker, J. L., Benet-Martinez, V. and Garolera, J. (2001), 'Consumption symbols as carriers of culture: A study of Japanese and Spanish brand personality constructs', *Journal of Personality and Psychology*, 81(3): 492–508.

Aggarwal, P. (2004), 'The effects of brand relationship norms on consumer attitudes and behavior', *Journal of Consumer Research*, 31(June): 87–101.

Ahearne, M., Bhattacharya, C. B. and Gruen, T. (2005), 'Antecedents and consequences of customer–company identification: Expanding the role of relationship marketing', *Journal of Applied Psychology*, 90(3): 574–585.

Alba, J., Lynch, J., Weitz, B., Janiszewski, C., Lutz, R., Sawyer, A. and Wood, S. (1997), 'Interactive home shopping: Consumer, retailer, and manufacturer incentives to participate in electronic marketplaces', *Journal of Marketing*, 61(July): 38–53.

Albert, N., Merunka, D. and Valette-Florence, P. (2008), 'When consumers love their brands: Exploring the concept and its dimensions', *Journal of Business Research*, 61: 1062–1075.

Alt, M. and Griggs, S. (1988), 'Can a brand be cheeky?', *Marketing Intelligence and Planning*, 6(4): 9–26.

AMA (1960), *Marketing Definitions: A Glossary or Marketing Terms*, Chicago, IL: AMA.

Arnold, D. (1992) *The Handbook of Brand Management*, London: Century Business, Economist Books.

Azoulay, A. and Kapferer, J. N. (2003), 'Do brand personality scales really measure brand personality?', *Journal of Brand Management*, 11(2): 143–155.

Bagwell, L. S. and Bernheim, B. D. (1996), 'Veblen effects in a theory of conspicuous consumption', *The American Economic Review*, 86: 349–373.

Bahadir, S. C., Bharadwaj, S. G. and Srivastava, R. K. (2008), 'Financial value of brands in mergers and acquisitions: Is value in the eye of the beholder', *Journal of Marketing*, 72(November): 49–64.

Barwise, T. P. (1993), 'Brand equity: Snark or boojum', *International Journal of Research in Marketing*, 10(1): 93–104.

Barwise, T. P., Higson, C., Likierman, A. and Marsh, P. (1990), 'Brands as "separable assets"', *Business Strategy Review*, 1(Summer): 43–59.

Belk, R. W. (1988), 'Possessions and the extended self', *Journal of Consumer Research*, 15(2): 139–168.

Bhattacharya, C. B. and Sen, S. (2003), 'Consumer–company identification: A framework for understanding consumers' relationships with companies', *Journal of Marketing*, 67(2): 76–88.

Bhattacharya, C. B., Rao, H. and Glynn, M. A. (1995), 'Understanding the bond of identification: An investigation of its correlates among art museum members', *Journal of Marketing*, 59(4): 46–57.

Blackston, M. (1992), 'Observations: Building brand equity by managing the brand's relationships', *Journal of Advertising Research*, 32 (May/June): 79–83.

Blackston, M. (1993), 'A brand with an attitude: A suitable case for treatment', *Journal of the Market Research Society*, 34(3): 231–241.

Bokaie, J. (2008), 'Profit at the expense of prestige', *Marketing*, 7 May: 18.

Boush, D. M. and Loken, B. (1991), 'A process-tracing study of brand extension evaluation', *Journal of Marketing Research*, 28 (February): 16–28.

Braig, B. M. and Tybout, A. M. (2005), 'Brand extensions', in Tybout, A. M. and Calkins, T. (eds) *Kellogg on Branding*, Hoboken, NJ, John Wiley & Sons.

Broniarczyk, S. M. and Alba, J. W. (1994), 'The importance of the brand in brand extension', *Journal of Marketing Research*, 31(May): 214–228.

Buss, D. (2013), 'Cadillac, Porsche emphasize accessible luxury as they lead industry sales surge', *brandchannel*, available at http://www.brandchannel.com/home/post/2013/09/03/Cadillac-Porsche-Accessibility-090313.aspx (accessed 11 September 2013).

Chernev, A., Hamilton, R. and Gal, D. (2011), 'Competing for consumer identity: Limits to self-expression and the perils of lifestyle branding', *Journal of Marketing*, 75(3): 66–82.

Citrin, A. V., Stern, D. E., Spangenberg, E. R. and Clark, M. J. (2003), 'Consumer need for tactile input. An internet retailing challenge', *Journal of Business Research*, 56: 915–922.

Clifton, R. (2013), *Brands, Capital and Crises*, The Brands Lecture, 18 September 2013, available at http://www.britishbrandsgroup.org.uk/the-brands-lecture

Cova, B. and Pace, S. (2006), 'Brand community of convenience products: New forms of customer empowerment: The case "my Nutella the Community"', *European Journal of Marketing*, 40(9/10): 1087–1105.

Crainer, S. (1995), *The Real Power of Brands. Making Brands Work for Competitive Advantage*, London: FT Pitman Publishing.

Dall'Olmo Riley, F. and de Chernatony, L. (2000), 'The service brand as relationship builder', *British Journal of Management*, 11(2): 137–150.

Dall'Olmo Riley, F., Pina, J. M. and Bravo, R. (2013), 'Downscale extensions: Consumer evaluation and feedback effects', *Journal of Business Research*, 62(2): 196–206.

De Chernatony, L. (1996), '2001: The brand management odyssey', *Journal of General Management*, 21(4): 15–30.

De Chernatony, L. (2008), 'Brand building', in Baker, M. and Hart, S. (eds) *The Marketing Book*, sixth edition. London: Routledge.

De Chernatony, L. and Dall'Olmo Riley, F. (1998a), 'Experts' views on roles of brands: Implications for marketing communications', *Journal of Marketing Communications*, 4: 87–100.

De Chernatony, L. and Dall'Olmo Riley, F. (1998b), 'Defining a "brand": Beyond the literature with experts' interpretations', *Journal of Marketing Management*, 14(5): 417–443.

De Chernatony, L. and Dall'Olmo Riley, F. (1999), 'Experts' views about defining services brands and the principles of services branding', *Journal of Business Research*, 46(2): 181–192.

De Chernatony, L., McDonald, M. and Wallace, E. (2011), *Creating Powerful Brands*, fourth edition, Oxford, UK: Butterworth-Heinemann.

Demsetz, H. (1973), 'Industry structure, market rivalry and public policy', *Journal of Law and Economics*, 16(1): 1–9.

Demsetz, H. (1982), 'Barrier to entry', *American Economic Review*, 72, 47–57.

Du, S., Bhattacharya, C. B. and Sen, S. (2007), 'Reaping relational rewards from corporate social responsibility: The role of competitive positioning', *International Journal of Research in Marketing*, 24(3): 224–241.

Duckworth, G. (1991), 'Brands and the role of advertising', in Cowley, D. (ed.) *Understanding Brands by 10 People Who Do*, London: Kogan Page.

Ernst & Young and ACNielsen (1999), *New Product Introduction: Successful Innovation/Failure: A Fragile Boundary*. Paris, France: Ernst & Young Global Client Consulting.

Escalas, J. E. (2004), 'Narrative processing: Building consumer connections to brands', *Journal of Consumer Psychology*, 14(1/2): 168–180.

Escalas, J. E. and Bettman, J. R. (2003), 'You are what they eat: The influence of reference groups on consumers' connections to brands', *Journal of Consumer Psychology*, 13(3): 339–348.

Escalas, J. E. and Bettman, J. R. (2009), 'Self-brand connections: The role of reference groups and celebrity endorsers in the creation of brand meaning', in MacInnis, D. J., Park, C. W. and Priester, J. R. (eds) *Handbook of Brand Relationships*, Armonk, NY: M.E. Sharpe, pp. 107–123.

Farquhar, P. H., Han, J. Y., Herr, P. M. and Ijiri, Y. (1992), 'Strategies for leveraging master brands', *Marketing Research*, 4(September): 32–43.

Fetscherin, M. and Heinrich, D. (2014), 'Consumer brand relationships: A research landscape', *Journal of Brand Management*, 21: 366–371.

Fournier, S. M. (1998), 'Consumers and their brands: Developing relationship theory in consumer research', *Journal of Consumer Research*, 24(4): 343–373.

Fournier, S. M. (2009), 'Lessons learned about consumers' relationships with their brands', in MacInnis, D. J., Park, C. W. and Priester, J. R. (eds) *Handbook of Brand Relationships*, Armonk, NY: M.E. Sharpe, pp. 5–23.

Gardner, B. B. and Levy, S. J. (1955), 'The product and the brand', *Harvard Business Review*, 33(March/April): 33–39.

George, W. R. (1990), 'Internal marketing and organisational behaviour: A partnership in developing consumer conscious employees at every level', *Journal of Business Research*, 20: 63–70.

Greene, W. E., Walls, G. D. and Schrest, L. J. (1994), 'Internal marketing: The key to external marketing success', *Journal of Services Marketing*, 8: 5–13.

Gürhan-Canli, Z. and Maheswaran, D. (1998), 'The effects of extensions on brand name dilution and enhancement', *Journal of Marketing Research*, 35(November): 464–473.

Hamel, G. and Prahalad, C. K. (1996), *Competing for the Future*, Boston, MA: Harvard Business School Press.

Hanan, M. and Karp, P. (1991), *Competing on Value*, New York: AMA.

Hatch, M. J. and Schultz, M. (2010), 'Toward a theory of brand co-creation with implications for brand governance', *Journal of Brand Management*, 17(July/August): 590–604.

Henderson, G. R., Iacobucci, D. and Calder, B. J. (1998), 'Brand diagnostics: mapping branding effects using consumer associative networks', *European Journal of Operational Research*, 111(2): 306–327.

Hennings, N., Wiedmann, K. P., Behrens, S., Klarmann, C. and Carduck, J. (2013), 'Brand extensions. A successful strategy in luxury fashion branding? Assessing consumers' implicit associations', *Journal of Fashion Marketing and Management*, 17(4): 390–402.

Heskett, J. (2014), 'Does internet technology threaten brand loyalty?', in *Harvard Business School Working Knowledge*, available at http://hbswk.hbs.edu/item/7546.html (accessed 25 November 2014).

Hoeffler, K. and Keller, K. L. (2003), 'The marketing advantages of a strong brand', *Journal of Brand Management*, 10(6): 421–445.

Holt, D. B. (2002), 'Why do brands cause trouble? A dialectic theory of consumer culture and branding', *Journal of Consumer Research*, 29(June): 70–90.

Interbrand (2014), *Best Global Brands*, available at http://www.bestglobalbrands.com/2014/ranking/ (accessed 2 December 2015).

Janiszewski, C. and van Osselaer, S. M. J. (2000), 'A connectionist model of brand-quality associations', *Journal of Marketing Research*, XXXVII(3): 331–350.

Johar, G. V., Sengupta, J. and Aaker, J. (2005), 'Two roads to updating brand personality impressions: Trait versus evaluative inferencing', *Journal of Marketing Research*, 42(4): 458–469.

John, R. D., Loken, B. and Joiner, C. (1998), 'The negative impact of extensions: Can flagship products be diluted', *Journal of Marketing*, 62(January): 19–32.

Jones, P. J. (1986). *What's in a name?* Aldershot, UK: Gower.

Kamakura, W. A. and Russell, G. J. (1993), 'Measuring brand value with scanner data', *International Journal of Research in Marketing*, 10: 9–22.

Kapferer, J. N. (1995), 'Stealing brand equity: Measuring perceptual confusion between national brands and "copycat" own labels', *Marketing and Research Today*, 23(May): 96–103.

Kapferer, J. N. (2012), *The New Strategic Brand Management*, fifth edition, London: Kogan Page.

Kau, A. K., Tang, Y. E. and Ghose, S. (2003), 'Typology of online shoppers', *Journal of Consumer Marketing*, 20(2): 139–156.

Kay, J. (1993), *Foundations of Corporate Success*, Oxford, UK: Oxford University Press.

Keller, K. L. (1993), 'Conceptualizing, measuring, and managing customer-based brand equity', *Journal of Marketing*, 57(1): 1–22.

Keller, K. L. (2008), *Strategic Brand Management: Building, Measuring and Managing Brand Equity*, Upper Saddle River, NJ: Prentice Hall.

Keller, K. L., Apéria, T. and Georgson, M. (2012), *Strategic Brand Management. A European Perspective*, Harlow, UK: Pearson Education Limited.

Kim, C. K. and Lavack, A. M. (1996), 'Vertical brand extensions: Current research and managerial implications', *Journal of Product and Brand Management*, 5(6): 24–37.

Kim, C. K., Lavack, A. M. and Smith, M. (2001), 'Consumer evaluation of vertical brand extensions and core brands', *Journal of Business Research*, 52(3): 211–222.

Kirmani, A., Sood, S. and Bridges, S. (1999), 'The ownership effect in consumer responses to brand line stretches', *Journal of Marketing*, 63(January): 88–101.

Klein, B. and Leffler, K. B. (1981), 'The role of market forces in assuring contractual performance', *Journal of Political Economy*, 89: 615–641.

Klein, N. (2000a), *No Logo*, London: Flamingo.

Klein, N. (2000b), 'The tyranny of the brands', *New Statesman*, 24 January 2000: 25–28.

Klink, R. R. and Smith, D. C. (2001), 'Threats to the external validity of brand extension research', *Journal of Marketing Research*, 38(August): 326–335.

KPMG (2014), *The Living Wage*, available at http://www.kpmg.com/uk/en/issuesandinsights/articlespublications/pages/living-wage.aspx (accessed 3 December 2014).

Krishnamurthy, S. and Kucuk, S. U. (2009), 'Anti-branding on the internet', *Journal of Business Research*, 62(11): 1119–1126.

Lam, S. K., Ahearne, M., Hu, Y. and Schillewaert, N. (2010), 'Resistance to brand switching when a radically new brand is introduced: A social identity theory perspective', *Journal of Marketing*, 74(6): 128–146.

Lee, M. S. W., Motion, J. and Conroy, D. (2009), 'Anti-consumption and brand avoidance', *Journal of Business Research*, 62: 169–180.

Lee, K. S. and Tan, S. J. (2003), 'E-retailing versus physical retailing: A theoretical model and empirical test of consumer choice', *Journal of Business Research*, 56, 877–886.

Les Échos (2004), 'Étendre sa marque, un pari souvent gagnat N 19301', 7 December, p. 15, available at http://archives.lesechos.fr/archives/2004/LesEchos/19301-50-ECH.htm (accessed 4 August 2008).

Levy, S. J. (1959), 'Symbols for sale', *Harvard Business Review*, 37(4): 117–124.

Liu, C. M. (2002), 'The effects of promotional activities on brand decision in the cellular telephone industry', *Journal of Product and Brand Management*, 11(1): 42–51.

Loken, B. and John, R. D. (1993), 'Diluting brand beliefs: When do brand extensions have a negative impact?', *Journal of Marketing*, 57(July): 71–84.

Magnoni, F. and Roux, E. (2012), 'The impact of step-down line extension on consumer-brand relationships: A risky strategy for luxury brands', *Journal of Brand Management*, 19(7): 595–608.

Mahajan, V., Rao, V. R. and Srivastava, R. K. (1994), 'An approach to assess the importance of brand equity in acquisition decisions', *Journal of Product Innovation Management*, 11(3): 221–235.

Malär, L., Krohmer, H., Hoyer, W. D. and Nyffenegger, B. (2011), 'Emotional brand attachment and brand personality: The relative importance of the actual and the ideal self', *Journal of Marketing*, 75(July): 35–52.

Marketing (UK) (2003), 'Premium extensions are proving to be the most promising FMCG launches, as manufacturers look to counteract retailers' price cuts', 28 August: 25.

McAlexander, J. H., Schouten, J. W. and Koenig, H. F. (2002), 'Building brand community', *Journal of Marketing*, 66(1): 38–54.

McWilliam, G. (1991), 'Managing the brand manager', in Murphy, J. (ed.) *Brand Valuation*, London: Business Books Limited, pp. 154–166.

McWilliam, G. (1993), 'The effect of brand typology on brand extension fit: Commercial and academic research findings', *European Advances in Consumer Research*, 1: 485–491.

Meenaghan, T. (1995), 'The role of advertising in brand image development', *Journal of Product and Brand Management*, 4(4): 23–34.

Mercer, D. (1992), *Marketing Management*, Oxford, UK: Blackwell.

Michel, G. and Salha, B. (2005), 'L'extension de gamme verticale: Clarification du concept', *Recherche et Applications en Marketing*, 20(1): 65–78 (in French).

Millward Brown (2014), *Top 100 Global Brands*, available at http://www.millwardbrown.com/mb-global/brand-strategy/brand-equity/brandz (accessed 2 December 2015).

Mintel (2014), *Fashion Online UK*, August, London: Mintel International Group Limited.

Muniz, A. M. Jr. and O'Guinn, T. C. (2001), 'Brand community', *Journal of Consumer Research*, 27(4): 412–432.

Munthree, S., Bick, G. R. and Abratt, R. (2006), 'A framework for brand revitalization through an upscale line extension', *Journal of Product and Brand Management*, 15(3): 157–167.

O'Guinn, T. C. and Muniz, A. M. Jr. (2009), 'Collective brand relationships', in MacInnis, D. J., Park, C. W. and Priester, J. R. (eds) *Handbook of Brand Relationships*, Armonk, NY: M.E. Sharpe, pp. 173–194.

Park, C. W., Jaworski, B. J. and MacInnis, D. J. (1986), 'Strategic brand concept-image management', *Journal of Marketing*, 50(4): 135–145.

Park, C. W., Milberg, S. and Lawson, R. (1991), 'Evaluations of brand extensions: The role of product feature similarity and brand concept consistency', *Journal of Consumer Research*, 18(September): 185–193.

Pitta, D. A. and Katsanis, L. P. (1995), 'Understanding brand equity for successful brand extension', *Journal of Consumer Marketing*, 12(4): 51–64.

Png, I. P. and Reitman, D. (1995), 'Why are some products branded and others not?', *Journal of Law and Economics*, 38: 207–224.

Porter, M. E. (1976), *Interbrand Choice, Strategy, and Bilateral Market Power*, Cambridge, MA: Harvard University Press.

Porter, M. E. (1980), *Competitive Strategy*, New York: The Free Press.

Porter, M. E. (1985), *Competitive Advantage*, New York: The Free Press.

Quelch, J. A. and Harding, D. (1996), 'Brands versus private labels: Fighting to win', *Harvard Business Review*, 77(January/February): 99–109.

Randall, T., Ulrich, K. and Reibstein, D. (1998), 'Brand equity and vertical product line extent', *Marketing Science*, 17(4): 356–379.

Rao, V. R., Mahajan, V. and Baraya, N. P. (1991), 'A balance model for evaluating firms for acquisition', *Management Science*, 37(3): 331–349.

Reimann, M., Castaño, R., Zaichkowsky, J. and Bechara, A. (2012), 'How we relate to brands: Psychological and neurophysiological insights into consumer-brand relationship', *Journal of Consumer Psychology*, 22: 128–142.

Ritson, M. (2006), 'Strength in numbers', *Marketing*, April 5: 16.

Sayon, S. (2014a), 'McDonald's is the latest brand to embrace collaborative sustainability', in *brandchannel*, available at http://www.brandchannel.com/home/post/2014/05/02/140502-Corporate-Responsibility-Collaboration.aspx (accessed 25 November 2014).

Sayon, S. (2014b), 'Brands on Facebook and Twitter take note: Your reach is waning', in *brandchannel*, available at http://www.brandchannel.com/home/post/2014/11/21/141121-Social-Relationship-Strategies.aspx?utm_campaign=141121-Social-Relationship-Strategiesandutm_source=newsletterandutm_medium=email (accessed 25 November 2014).

Schouten, J. W. and McAlexander, J. H. (1995), 'Subcultures of consumption: An ethnography of the new bikers', *Journal of Consumer Research*, 22(1): 43–61.

Sharp, B. M. (1993), 'Managing brand extensions', *Journal of Consumer Marketing*, 10(3): 11–17.

Simon, C. J. and Sullivan, M. W. (1993), 'The measurements and determinants of brand equity: A financial approach', *Marketing Science*, 12(Winter): 28–52.

Simonson, I. and Rosen, E. (2014), *Absolute Value: What Really Influences Customers in the Age of (Nearly) Perfect Information*, New York: Harper Business.

Staveley, N. (1987), 'Advertising, marketing and brands', *Admap*, 23: 31–35.

Stokburger-Sauer, N., Ratneshwar, S. and Sen, S. (2012), 'Drivers of consumer-brand identification', *International Journal of Research in Marketing*, 29: 406–418.

Strizhakova, Y., Coulter, R. A. and Price, L. L. (2008), 'The meanings of branded products: A cross-national scale development and meaning assessment', *International Journal of Research in Marketing*, 25(2): 82–93.

Stryker, S. (1968), 'Identity salience and role performance: The relevance of symbolic interaction theory for family research', *Journal of Marriage and Family*, 30(4): 558–564.

Sujan, M. and Bettman, J. R. (1989), 'The effects of brand positioning strategies on consumers' brand and category perceptions: Some insights from schema research', *Journal of Marketing Research*, 26(November): 454–468.

Swaminathan, V., Stilley, K. M. and Ahluwalia, R. (2009), 'When brand personality matters: The moderating role of attachment styles', *Journal of Consumer Research*, 35(April): 985–1002.

Tajfel, H. and Turner, J. C. (1979), 'The social identity theory of intergroup behavior', in Worchel, S. and Austin, W. G. (eds) *Psychology of Intergroup Relations*, Chicago, IL: Nelson-Hall, pp. 33–47.

The Economist (1993), Shoot out at the check-out, 5 June: 81–82.

The Economist (1994), Don't get left on the shelf, 2 July: 11–12.

The Economist (1996), Cereal thriller, 15 June: 91–92.

The Economist (2001a), The case for brands, 8 September: 9.

The Economist (2001b), Who's wearing the trousers?, 8 September: 27–29.

The Economist (2014a), What are brands for?, 30 August: 53–54.

The Economist (2014b), Trolley wars, 14 October.

The Economist (2014c), Untouchable intangibles, 30 August: 54.

Thomas, L. G. (1989), 'Advertising in consumer goods industries: Durability, economies of scale and heterogeneity', *Journal of Law and Economics*, 32: 163–193.

Tsai, S. (2005), 'Utility, cultural symbolism and emotion: A comprehensive model of brand purchase value', *International Journal of Research in Marketing*, 22(3): 277–291.

Van den Poel, D. and Leunis, J. (1999), 'Consumer acceptance of the Internet as a channel of distribution', *Journal of Business Research*, 45: 249–256.

Völckner, F. and Sattler, H. (2006), 'Drivers of brand extension success', *Journal of Marketing*, 70(2): 18–34.

Watkins, T. (1986), *The Economics of the Brand*, London: McGraw-Hill.

Weber, R. and Crocker, J. (1983), 'Cognitive processes in the revision of stereotypic beliefs', *Journal of Personality and Social Psychology*, 45(November): 961–977.

Wernerfelt, B. (1988), 'Umbrella branding as a signal of new product quality: An example of signalling by posting a bond', *RAND Journal of Economics*, 19(30): 458–466.

Zinkhan, G., Haytko, D. and Ward, A. (1996), 'Self-concept theory', *Journal of Marketing Communication*, 2(1): 1–19.

17 The end of marketing as usual

'Be social: be digital'

Jim Hamill

Introduction

In two journal articles published in the late 1990s, the author argued that the study and practice of marketing would be revolutionised by the rapid growth of the internet and world wide web (the most commonly used descriptor at the time). The web, even then, represented a fundamentally different environment compared to offline marketing, and new marketing paradigms would need to be developed for the emerging electronic age (Hamill 1997; Hamill and Gregory 1997). Fast forward to the mid-2010s and there can be little doubt that the internet has had a profound impact on all aspects of business, and marketing in particular, since publication of the two papers.

The proposition advanced in this chapter is that we have entered a new and even more revolutionary phase in the development of the internet and digital technology more generally; an era characterised by disruptive digital-led change, the growing empowerment of constantly connected customers (Generation C), social media, mobile connectivity, the cloud, big data, the 'internet of customers' and the 'internet of things'. The chapter argues that, as a consequence of digital disruption, marketing as we know it is in danger of becoming obsolete. Does the marketing profession need to 'adapt or die'?

The chapter is divided into six main sections. The section to follow discusses the revolutionary impact of disruptive technologies on marketing based on a review of leading authors in this area. Given the target audience of the book, undergraduates coming to the subject for the first time, non-marketers pursuing masters' degrees with a marketing content, practitioners and academics, the chapter then discusses the potential impact of social media and digital disruption in four highly pertinent areas:

1   The study of marketing – especially in the two related areas of content and pedagogy (what we teach and how we teach it). Is the content of our courses and the way they are delivered 'fit for purpose' in a digital age? Are our undergraduate and masters' programmes equipping our young people and managers with the skills and knowledge essential for success in an increasingly digital world? Is marketing education as we know it becoming obsolete? These are important questions to address given the strong evidence of an emerging digital skills crisis.

2   Academic research – in a similar vein, is the academic research that we undertake, the research that should power our course content, becoming obsolete? Is there evidence of research leadership covering the impact of social and digital technologies on the study and practice of marketing? Or are we stuck in a time warp producing academic research that delivers little value in a digital world. A review of recent academic publications would suggest that there is much scope for improvement. In one area in particular, small and medium

sized enterprise (SME) internationalisation, academic research and associated public sector support to SME exporters appears to be stuck in a 30-year time warp.

3   Practitioners – given the 'new rules of marketing, PR and sales' that have emerged as a consequence of the social and digital revolutions (Scott 2007, 2013, 2014), this section provides highly practical advice covering the development, implementation and management of effective social media and digital marketing strategies to achieve agreed business goals and objectives, including new approaches to social/digital marketing performance measurement.

4   Personal branding – in the same way that disruptive technologies are having a major impact on the traditional approach to brand management, the career paths of our young people will also be radically different in a digital era. This section provides brief advice on building personal brands online.

The final section presents a synthesis and conclusion. The title of the chapter has been adapted from the excellent book by Brian Solis (2012) *The End of Business as Usual: Rewiring the Way you Work in an Era of Constantly Connected Customers*, discussed in more detail later.

The social media and digital revolutions

Little purpose would be served presenting detailed statistics in this section covering the rapid growth of social media and other disruptive technologies. Due to the dynamic pace of change taking place, any statistics presented would become dated very quickly and would almost certainly be out-of-date given the time lag between manuscript preparation (September 2014) and book publication. The excellent #Socialnomics video by Eric Qualman (2014) is highly recommended for readers requiring a quick overview of the social media and digital revolutions.

Figure 17.1 presents a brief summary of the main disruptive technologies having a profound impact on the study and practice of marketing. There can be little doubt that the use and spread of these technologies has become ubiquitous – the mobile revolution, 5 billion smartphones by 2017; the connected revolution, 75 billion connected products by 2020; the social revolution 2.3 billon social network users by 2017; the data revolution 1.5 billion terabytes of data being generated by business every year; the app revolution, 40 billion mobile app downloads (Salesforce 2014).

Rather than dwelling too much on the statistics of rapid change, the main aim of this section is to discuss the impact of disruptive social and digital technologies on marketing as we know it. The way it has been taught and practised for decades. Five key challenges are presented below based on the work of leading authors in this area.

It's a revolution

> *Social media and disruptive technologies represent a fundamental and revolutionary change in the way we communicate and interact, in online behaviour, expectations and the online customer experience. It represents the end of the 'read only' Internet. Customers now expect to be heard and to have their social comments/complaints responded to in a timely, professional manner.*

Don Tapscott, in his early work in this area, was one of the first authors to identify the revolutionary business impact of emerging technologies. In his 1997 book *The Digital Economy*, he discussed how the internet would fundamentally reinvent a diverse range of industries (Tapscott 1997). At a time when the majority of the population were either not connected to the internet or connected through a slow 26k or 56k modem (the *world web wait*), Tapscott confidently predicted that in a few

Technology	Summary
Social media	The social interaction that takes place among people across a range of online platforms including blogs, Twitter, Linkedin, Facebook, YouTube, Pinterest and other online communities of interest.
Enterprise social	The use of social technologies within an organisation to improve business processes and systems; improve the efficiency and effectiveness of internal communications, knowledge sharing and collaboration.
Mobile	Technology that allows internet connectivity 'on the move', e.g. smartphones, tablets, laptops.
The cloud	A generally used term to describe the delivery of hosted services over the internet including: Infrastructure-as-a-Service (IaaS); Platform-as-a-Service (PaaS) and Software-as-a-Service (SaaS).
Big data	An all-encompassing term for large and complex data sets difficult to process using traditional data processing applications. The rapid growth of social media, the Internet of Things, etc. has led to an explosion in Big Data.
The internet of customers	Most often used to describe the way in which new technology is leading to a major power shift from suppliers to customers – the growing empowerment of customers.
The internet of things	A situation where everyday objects have network connectivity, allowing them to send and receive data. Generally expected to be the 'next big thing' on the internet with 75m connected products by 2020.
Wearable technologies	Any wearable device supporting internet connectivity, e.g. Google Glasses, Apple iwatches, etc.
Marketing automation	Software platforms and technologies that allow marketing departments to be more effective across multiple channels online through automating repetitive tasks.

Figure 17.1 Disruptive technologies

Source: The author.

years' time we would stop buying newspapers and be streaming our music online. There can be little doubt that both of these industries, and many others, have been totally transformed by technology.

The author's early ideas were more fully developed in two more recent books *Wikinomics* (Tapscott and Williams 2006) and *MacroWikinomics* (Tapscott and Williams 2010); the latter contains an excellent chapter on the future of higher education in a digital age (see later). According to Tapscott (1997), the social web represents a phase in the development of the internet characterised by information 'pull' rather than 'push', user generated content, openness, sharing, collaboration, interaction, communities and social networking. New generation web-based communities and hosted applications, such as social network and social content websites, blogs, wikis, podcasts and vodcasts, virtual realities, mash ups, RSS feeds and mobile applications, were already (in 2006) beginning to have a major impact on customer behaviour across a diverse range of industries, both B2C and B2B. Especially among 'born digitals', Tapscott and Williams (2010) argue that there is growing cynicism and resistance to supplier-led brand messages, with the collective knowledge and feedback of the network beginning to have a more important impact on purchasing decisions.

From a marketing perspective, the most distinctive feature is not the technology involved but rather the growth of a new global culture – a 'net generation' culture based on decentralised authority rather than hierarchy and control, online socialising and collaboration, user generated and distributed content, open communications, peer-to-peer sharing and global participation. The new web empowers people, 'tribes', communities and networks. The author presents a strong argument that success in this new online environment, characterised by people and network empowerment, requires new 'mindsets' and innovative new approaches to marketing, customer and network relationships.

Crowdsourcing, co-creation, customer/tribe engagement and e-word-of-mouth have become the new buzz terms for online marketing success.

It's social

> Social media is called social media because it is meant to be social – a fact that seems to have escape most companies who continue to use it as a traditional marketing communications channel for broadcasting PR and sales messages AT customers. Social media redefines marketing as a two-way conversation with customers rather than a one way broadcast. The starting point is to 'shut up and listen'.

The social nature of the new web has been most enthusiastically discussed by Brian Solis. In two recent books, *The End of Business as Usual* (Solis 2012) and *What's the Future of Business* (Solis 2013) and in a series of articles on the Brian Solis blog (www.briansolis.com), the author presents his thoughts on the wide ranging business impact of social media and other disruptive technologies. Two concepts central to his argument are Generation C and Digital Darwinism.

According to Solis, management models and marketing practices that have been taught for generations are being severely tested as a consequence of the widespread permeation of technology in society. Digital devices, services, networks and apps have created a new generation of consumer – Generation C – the constantly connected generation. Generation C is not age specific. It is anyone who lives a digital lifestyle (social, mobile, real time) supported by smartphones, tablets or any other digital device; in other words, most of us.

Solis argues that it is time to rethink the value proposition of marketing and communications. To reach Generation C requires a radically different organisational vision and philosophy, where the emphasis is very much on two-way engagement and delivering exceptional online experiences rather than one-way broadcasting (see discussion of 'Ultimate Moment of Truth (UMOT)' in the next section).

The major challenge for organisations, according to Solis, is that most executives and decision-makers see the world as they know it, rather than seeing it for what it is or what it is becoming. Most organisations are reacting to the social and digital revolutions with 'terminal scepticism' or at best, half-baked attempts to embrace new technologies and opportunities. Traditional management and marketing practices and the structures that support them are not only aging, they have become liabilities and competitive disadvantages. Organisations that fail to adapt run the risk of becoming digital dinosaurs as a consequence of Digital Darwinism – a phenomena where technology and society evolve faster than an organisation's ability to adapt (Solis 2014).

There is a growing list of companies and brands who have become, or are becoming, digital dinosaurs due to their failure to adapt to new technologies – newspapers, the music industry, Kodak, HMV, Nokia, Blackberry and others. According to some authors, higher education may be about to join this list.

To avoid being a victim of Digital Darwinism, Solis argues that organisations need to reinvent processes, systems and products to align with the expectations and behaviour of Generation C; consistently delivering exceptional customer experiences, across multiple digital touch points and at key moments of truth in the customer journey.

It is worth pointing out at this stage that digital natives will account for 70 per cent of the global workforce by the year 2025. This will have a major impact on the internal operations and organisational structure of most companies. Enterprise social, the internal use of social technologies within organisations to improve communications and achieve operational efficiencies, has already become a major growth area.

Power shift

> *Social media empowers customers, it empowers the network. In a social era, the brand becomes the customer experience of the brand – experiences that are widely shared online. Social is 'word-of-mouth' on steroids. Positive word-of-mouth spreads quickly; negative word-of-mouth spreads even more quickly.*

As a consequence of the social and digital revolutions, the future of brands lies with the proactive management of the customer experience of the brand across diverse digital channels and at key moments of truth in the customer relationship with the brand.

This is illustrated in the UMOT diagram shown in Figure 17.2. The UMOT, according to Solis, is where people convert a brand experience into discoverable content posted on any one of countless social platforms, e.g. a TripAdvisor review, Facebook image, course review, LinkedIn recommendation, etc. In a highly connected world, these UMOTs are becoming the next person's Zero Moment of Truth (first impression of the brand); and as we know, especially online, first impressions count. Online peer recommendations (positive or negative) now have a major influence on future purchasing behaviour.

UMOT has a major impact on brand management. In a social/digital world, the brand is no longer what marketers say it is. The brand has become the customer experience of the brand; experiences that are widely shared online. As a consequence, marketers should spend less time telling people how good the brand is and more time proving it through delivering exceptional customer experiences at all stages of the customer journey with the brand. These experiences are increasingly taking place online. Proactive management of the online customer experience has become the new brand management, according to Solis (2014).

Declining effectiveness of traditional approaches to sales and marketing

> *As a consequence of the power shift that is taking place, customers are no longer passive recipients of brand messages. Traditional approaches to sales and marketing are declining in effectiveness, being replaced by a*

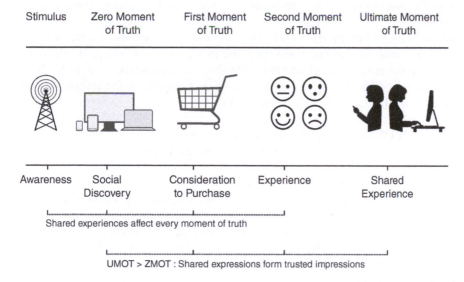

Figure 17.2 The ultimate moment of truth

Source: Solis (2013).

new approach based on the principles of Inbound and Content Marketing. Delivering online content that adds value to customers is now critical to business growth and competitiveness.

In a Harvard Business School blog post entitled *Marketing is Dead*, Lee (2012) states that traditional marketing – including advertising, public relations, branding and corporate communications – is dead. According to the author, many people in traditional marketing roles and organisations do not realise that they are operating within a dead paradigm, but they are. His argument can be summarised in three key points:

1   Buyers are no longer paying attention to traditional marketing communications. They check out product and service information in their own way, often through the internet, and often from sources outside the firm including word-of-mouth and customer reviews.
2   CEOs are losing patience with the declining effectiveness of traditional marketing.
3   In today's increasingly social media–infused environment, traditional marketing no longer makes sense. Traditional marketing logic will not work in the world of social media.

The declining effectiveness of traditional approaches to marketing communications has been discussed by many other writers, most notably David Meerman Scott in his two recent best-selling books *The New Rules of Marketing and PR* (Scott 2007, 2013) and *The New Rules of Sales and Service* (Scott 2014). According to the author, the 'new rules of marketing & PR' on the web are vastly different from marketing and public relations using mainstream media. The 'old rules' of mainstream media are about controlling the message. The only way to get the message into the public domain is by using mainstream media, either by buying expensive advertising or begging the media to write about you. These methods do not work on the web. The rules of marketing, PR and sales have changed. Instead of buying or begging your way in, the author argues that brands can earn attention by 'publishing their way in' using the various tools made available by social media such as blogs, podcasts, online news releases, online video, viral marketing and so on. Marketers will gain the best return on their investment by focusing on content creation rather than traditional advertising.

Based on the work of Scott and many others, the last few years have witnessed a tremendous growth of interest in a new inbound, content-based approach to sales and marketing. While many authors have commented in this area, the work of Michael Stelzner is of particular note. In his 2011 book entitled *Launch: How to Quickly Propel your Business beyond the Competition*, the author presents his simple new formula for marketing success (Stelzner 2011a):

Great Content **PLUS** Other People (the strength of your online network)
MINUS Marketing Messages **EQUALS** Business Growth

This is illustrated in the 'elevation principle' shown in Figure 17.3.

At the risk of over-simplification, old/outbound marketing is considered by Stelzner to be:

- propaganda marketing – 'this is how great our product/service is, now buy it';
- interruption marketing – direct mail, advertising;
- one-way shouting AT customers;
- short-term sales/campaign driven;
- using channels such as print ads; TV/Radio ads; cold calling; email blasts; online advertising; websites that talk AT customers.

Figure 17.3 The elevation principle

Source: Stelzner (2011).

As customers are no longer passive recipients of brand messages, traditional outbound marketing is declining in effectiveness. It is being replaced with a new approach based on the principles of inbound and content marketing where the emphasis is as follows:

- Content is king! – but content is only 'great' if it adds value to the customer so the . . .
- Customer is king! Adopt a customer-led approach.
- Produce great content that is 'customer-led'; authentic; compelling; entertaining; surprising; valuable; interesting.
- Establish your company as a 'thought leader' – a 'trusted resource'.
- Produce great content and your customer will come to you. Produce really great content and they will share it.
- Key channels are social media, blogs, online white papers, online videos, infographics, etc.
- The overall objective is to ignite or elevate your business through great content. To 'sell without selling'.
- Build a quality online network; a quality customer base through high value content and engagement.
- Great content drives the conversation. The conversation drives engagement. Engagement drives sales.
- Great, customer-led content is a competitive advantage.
- The bottom line is to create music not noise.

Stelzner expanded on these issues in a blog article entitled *Rest in Peace Marketing: I Never Really Liked You Anyway* (Stelzner 2011b). He criticises the American Marketing Association's definition of marketing, 'Marketing is the activity, set of institutions, and processes for creating, communicating, delivering, and exchanging offerings that have value for customers, clients, partners, and society at large.'

According to Stelzner, the focus on 'exchange offerings' has led most of us to have been taught that marketing is about making an offer that attracts people. We have been trained to focus on crafting the right arrangement of words and delivering them in the right place, at the right time, using the right medium. The brand makes the offer and the customer is compelled to comply. The problem with this approach is that empowered customers are no longer passive sheep waiting to be driven to your offer (Hamill 2011a, 2011b). Stelzner himself uses a fish analogy:

> Here's the problem . . . We're treating people like fish. If we just create a better lure than our competitors, silently climb into a boat, and simply cast that bait right on top of our customers, they'll bite. Or so the theory goes.

A key point summary of his article is presented below:

- Social and selling just don't mix – the last thing anyone wants in a social context is a commercial or to be sold to.
- It's time for change – marketing needs to transform itself from 'promoting' products and services to more of a relationship-based approach. Marketing should no longer be about making an offer that attracts people by delivering the right message to the right people at the right time using the right channel. People should be treated like humans not fish.
- People are tuning out – due to channel overload, people are 'tuning out'. Fewer than one in three people trust marketing messages, yet building trust is more important than delivering great products and services. Do your prospects and customers trust you?
- Focus on people – if great products alone won't gain the trust of consumers, what will? If no one is paying attention to sales messages, what can your business do to gain the attention and respect of people? The answer is to connect and engage with customers. Focus on people, meet their needs, solve their problems and provide insight that delivers real customer value.
- Content as the enabler – engaging content is the key to achieving rapid growth as explained in the Elevation Principle above.
- Change the question from 'What can we sell you?' to 'How can we help you?' Instead of investing in advertising, invest in creating content, experiences, gathering places and communities where people who need help can find it. Instead of relying on traditional marketing channels, become the centre of your industry, niche or local market. When that happens, according to the author, you launch an unstoppable growth trajectory.

New 'mindsets' required

New business approaches and new performance measures are required. Social is NOT a broadcast medium. It's about listening to and engaging with customers. There will be 'winners' and 'losers' in social media. 'Winners' will be those organisations who fully utilise the interactive power of social for engaging with and energising customer and network relationships. New performance measures are required based on the quality of your online network; the strength of the relationship you have with that network; and your ability to leverage that relationship.

In a three-part series of blog posts, Hamill (2014a) shows the way in which a '6Is' approach can be used to measure digital/social media performance measurement and business impact, as shown in Figure 17.4. The '6Is' are:

- involvement – network/community numbers/quality, time spent, frequency, geography;
- interaction – actions they take – read, post, comment, reviews, recommendations;
- intimacy – affection/aversion to the brand; community sentiments, opinions expressed, etc.;
- influence – advocacy, viral forwards, referrals and recommendations, social bookmarking;
- insight – customer insight;
- impact – business impact.

The '6Is' approach to performance evaluation can be applied at four main levels – see Hamill (2014a) for a more detailed explanation.

1 the performance of individual social media channels;
2 overall 'brand buzz';
3 internal social business performance;
4 overall business impact.

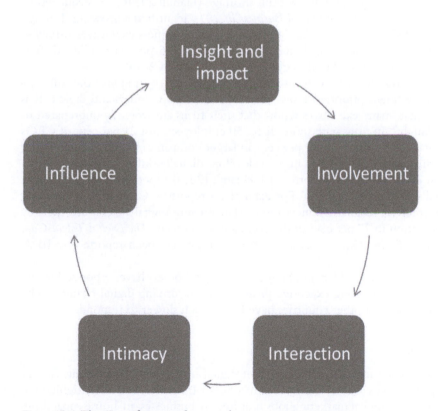

Figure 17.4 The 6Is performance framework

Source: The author.

In the remaining sections of this chapter, we examine the potential impact of social media and other disruptive technologies in four main areas: the study of marketing, academic research, digital marketing strategy and management and online personal branding.

The study of marketing

Given the impact of disruptive technologies as outlined above, do we as marketing professionals and marketing academics need to reassess the content of what we teach and how we teach it? Is the content of our marketing courses 'fit for purpose' in a digital world – a world where digital marketing should lead offline marketing? At undergraduate level, are we equipping our young people with the skills and knowledge required for developing successful careers in digital marketing? At executive level, are we developing future digital leaders? In an era where almost all of our customers (students) are digital natives, do we need to change teaching and delivery modes? Has the traditional 'sage on the stage' lecture become redundant?

The evidence would suggest that significant improvements can be made in all of these areas, especially in digital skills development and pedagogy.

Digital leaders urgently required

There is growing evidence of an emerging digital skills shortage (Hamill 2014b). A recent report by Forrester Research (2014), *The State of Digital Business in 2014* identified a growing shortage of digital business leaders (defined later). While 74 per cent of the business executives surveyed claimed to have a strategy for dealing with digital disruption, only 15 per cent believed their company had the capability to execute the strategy (Forrester Research 2014).

Successful digital business transformation, according to Forrester (2014), requires the full support of CEOs to drive investment priorities. However, few CEOs fully understand digital. It is not surprising, therefore, that 'many executives report that their firms are woefully unprepared to deal with the digital onslaught'. In firms with more than 250 employees, just 21 per cent of CEOs set a clear vision for digital. This falls to just 17 per cent in larger companies with 1,000 to 10,000 employees. To correct this, companies need to hire, or develop, digitally skilled employees.

The digital execution crisis identified by Forrester Research (2014) supports previous research highlighting a major skills shortage in this area. For example, a report by Capgemini Consulting (2013) and the MIT Center for Digital Business found that missing digital skills were the key hurdle to digital transformation in 77 per cent of the companies surveyed (*The Digital Talent Gap: Developing Skills for Today's Digital Organizations*). Similar findings have been reported by IBM, Accenture and others.

Leading US business schools such as Harvard, Stanford, MIT and others have responded to the digital business skills shortage by offering executive programmes in 'driving digital change'. The majority of business schools in most other countries have been much slower to respond.

Digital marketing management

Similar skills shortages have been identified in the area of digital marketing management. A very interesting infographic produced by Dave Chaffey's team at Smart Insights in late 2013 highlighted the growing talent gap between digital marketing jobs required by businesses, in-house capabilities and hiring barriers (Chaffey 2013). The evidence is US based, but there is no reason to think that the picture will be any different in other countries. Key headline findings were as follows:

- 78 per cent of companies report in-house skills shortages in at least one key area of digital marketing.
- Two-thirds stated that on-demand classes, customised e-learning or in-person workshops would be extremely valuable to their organisation.
- The biggest in-house skills gaps were reported as being analytics (37 per cent), mobile (29 per cent), content marketing, social media and email marketing (each at 27 per cent) and marketing automation (24 per cent). There was less of a skills' shortage in more traditional digital marketing areas such as search engine optimisation (19 per cent) and digital advertising (12 per cent).
- 34 per cent of hiring managers reported that a 'lack of previous work experience' was a major barrier to recruitment, with 30 per cent reporting that they were unable to find capable digital talent.

Similar digital marketing skills shortages have been reported in other studies.

Developing next generation marketers

While there is a growing recognition of the need for digital transformation, industry leaders (with a few exceptions) lack the digital knowledge, understanding and confidence to drive change. Younger managers (digital natives) may have the technology skills and confidence required, but will lack the high-level strategic understanding of how to fully align digital technology to support core business goals and objectives.

A new breed of senior executive is required – digital business leaders – executives who can combine high-level business knowledge, experience and understanding with the ability to develop digital transformation strategies fully aligned with and supportive of agreed business goals and objectives, i.e. executives with the personal skills and confidence to drive organisational change.

A major question arises here over who should fill this gap? Should future digital leaders come with an information technology or business/marketing background? The consensus seems to be that a new breed of chief information officer (CIO) rather than chief marketing officer (CMO) is required. Indeed, the Forrester Research Report (2014) argues that the marketing profession has actually become a hindrance rather than a driver of digital change. The fact that marketing tends to dominate digital responsibilities in most organisations, according to Forrester Research (2014), is a major barrier to digital transformation. While marketing teams may be expert in areas such as social media, social CRM, customer analytics and so on, they pay little attention to how digital can transform internal business operations.

In the view of the present author, the above raises serious challenges for marketing. Has the marketing profession really become a hindrance to digital transformation or can the profession emerge as a major driver of change? Given that digital transformation is really about building two-way engagement with customers, and internally with staff, its natural home should be marketing not IT. However, this will require the training of a new generation of marketers with hybrid skills including analytical, creative and technology, as well as core marketing skills. Next generation marketers will have the skills and knowledge to deliver services across a wide range of digital platforms including search, mobile, social, content, analytics, web, PR and email marketing. They will also require the skills and experience to drive internal change built around the innovative use of enterprise social technologies.

This begs the questions, 'Are we currently educating the next generation of marketers with the skills and knowledge required?', 'Are our business schools delivering?' and 'Are we educating the digital leaders of the future?'

If marketing is ready for the challenge of digital leadership, we need to ensure that our graduates are equipped with the knowledge and skills to deliver change. This will require more than the odd social media/digital marketing elective class on our programmes, often thrown in as an afterthought. It will require a fundamental reinvention of the marketing curriculum.

To assist the debate in this area, Figure 17.5 presents a detailed list of the hybrid skills, knowledge and experience required by next generation marketers covering three main areas – digital strategy, digital management and digital marketing. How well are our current programmes delivering in these areas?

Digital strategy

- Research and listening skills – the ability to use digital technologies for developing actionable customer and market insights derived from social media listening ensuring speed of response to rapidly changing marketing conditions.
- Excellent knowledge of the whole digital marketing mix – websites, SEO, social, mobile, etc.
- A clear understanding of the unique attitudes and behaviour of digital customers, both B2B and B2C; digital natives.
- Strategy development – the ability to develop digital marketing and social media strategies fully aligned with and supportive of agreed business goals and objectives with agreed KPIs and targets.
- An understanding of how digital and social impacts on all value chain activities, not just marketing.
- An understanding of (enterprise social) – the way in which digital and social technologies can be used internally to improve communications flows, knowledge sharing, collaboration and operational efficiency.

Digital management

- Project management skills – the ability to deliver on time, within budget, ensuring that key project objectives are achieved.
- Client/key account and agency management skills.
- Change management skills.
- General management and leadership skills – the ability to manage cross-functional teams, build relationships with key internal partners especially IT.
- Data analysis skills.

Digital marketing

- Content strategy – the ability to develop a clear content strategy to support agreed objectives.
- Content management – the skills and experience to set up and effectively manage a content development team and content management system; copywriting skills; video and Photoshop editing, etc.
- Channel specific skills – the ability to successfully integrate and manage multiple online channels including websites; SEO; e-marketing; e-newsletters; social media channels including blogs, Twitter, Linkedin, Facebook, YouTube and others.
- Analytics and performance measurement – the ability to work with web analytics, big data and social media performance measurement tools to deliver up-to-date progress reports to senior executives, providing actionable insights from the data generated.
- A clear understanding of the growing importance of and ability to provide exceptional social customer service and online customer experiences.

Others

- Software skills – the ability to work with a wide range of software packages, e.g. content management systems, Hootsuite, Buffer App, Feedly, Conversocial and others.
- Finance budgeting and ROI.
- Negotiating and presentation skills.

Figure 17.5 Next generation marketing skills

Source: The author.

Pedagogy

In addition to reinventing our courses to educate the new generation of digital marketing leaders, should we, as marketing educators, also be asking questions about teaching and delivery modes? In an era where almost all of our students will be digital natives, has the traditional 'sage on the stage' lecture become redundant?

Tapscott and Williams (2010) certainly think so. In Chapter 8 of *Macrowikinomics*, entitled 'Rethinking the university: Collaborative learning', the authors present a thought provoking analysis of the future of higher education in a digital world. In the absence of profound change, higher education may be on the road to becoming the next digital dinosaur (please also see Clayton Christensen's (2013) prediction that half of all US universities will be bankrupt within 15 years).

According to both authors, higher education is facing a number of major challenges, which threaten its very existence. These include high drop-out rates; the high cost of attending; escalating student debt which, in turn, is leading to a change in 'mindset' among young people regarding the benefits of having a university degree and whether it is worth it; declining public sector funding support; the growth of online alternatives, especially massively open online courses (MOOCs); the market for new graduates and whether higher education is producing graduates with the right skills; high non-attendance rates for lectures; and even when they do attend, short attention spans which, in turn, are a consequence of digital technology.

In most cases the response to these challenges has been to cut costs. However, according to the authors, more revolutionary change is required. There is a fundamental need to reinvent the university especially in two main areas – pedagogy and 'modus operandi'.

In terms of the former, Tapscott and Williams (2010) argue that it is time to toss out the old pedagogy, replacing it with a new model based on collaboration. The current model is built around a pedagogy of absorbing content and recalling it in exams. The teacher is essentially a broadcaster; a 'sage on the stage', a transmitter of knowledge to an inert audience in a one-way linear fashion. In a digital age, this is anachronistic – 'yesterday you graduated today your knowledge is obsolete'. Because of digital technology, what really matters is the capacity for life-long learning. We need to focus less on what we learn and more on how we learn – the ability to think, research, find information, analyse, synthesise, contextualise and critically evaluate; to apply research to solving problems; to collaborate and communicate.

This, according to the authors, requires new collaborative social media models of learning that change the actual pedagogy in fundamental ways, involving the active participation of students in content development and delivery supported by digital technology. We should all spend less time lecturing and more time collaborating with our students online. Replace teaching with more collaborative approaches to knowledge development, including the shift from mass production to mass customisation – not one lecture but 60 lectures of one. A key premise of their argument is that the collective knowledge of the network (the crowd) will always exceed that of the 'expert on the stage'. Students have at their fingertips the most powerful tool ever for discovery, constructing knowledge and learning.

Tapscott and Williams (2010) also raise serious questions concerning the 'modus operandi' of higher education. The existing 'textbook' mode is slow and expensive; entirely new ways of operating are required, especially in terms of how higher education content is produced. Universities, professors and research staff should contribute to an open platform of world-class educational resources that students anywhere can access anytime during their life time. In a highly connected world, universities still operate as largely autonomous islands of scholarship and learning. There has been a failure to seize the opportunities provided by the internet for breaking down the walls that divide institutions, professors and students. The twenty-first century university should be a network and an eco-system rather than an ivory tower. Enormous opportunities exist to create excellent student experiences by assembling the world's best learning resources online, allowing students to select a customised learning path with support from a global network of instructors and facilitators. However, this will require deep structural changes and a new 'mindset'; a 'meta university' – a communally constructed framework of open materials and platforms. The web provides the communications infrastructure to support this. A global open access library of course materials is required to provide the content. The rapid growth of MOOCs in recent years could be seen as a move in this direction.

The need for radical change in higher education has been extensively discussed by other authors. Indeed, a special edition of *The Economist* magazine has recently been devoted to the topic. Entitled *Terminal Degrees*, it contains the following hard-hitting statement:

> If universities were to face the same conditions over the next 10 to 20 years that daily newspapers faced over the last 10 to 20, then revenues would fall by more than half, employment in the industry would drop by nearly 30% and more than 700 institutions would shut their doors.
> (*The Economist* 2014)

In the view of the present author, it is now time to accelerate the debate concerning the future of higher education in an increasingly online world. To assist in this debate, a recent blog post pulled together a list of relevant articles published in the early part of 2014 covering the future of higher education in an online world and the critically important role of digital technology in enhancing the student learning experience. Hyperlinked references to all of the articles can be found on the original blog post (Hamill 2014c). These include the following:

- **Higher education**: **Creative destruction** – from *The Economist*; a cost crisis, changing labour markets and new technology will turn an old institution on its head.
- **The future of universities**: **The digital degree** – also from *The Economist*; the staid higher-education business is about to experience a welcome earthquake.
- **Do MOOCs upend traditional business education?** – interesting research results from Knowledge@Wharton; free Massively Open Online Courses do not undermine traditional Business Schools. They can complement existing programmes by reaching new audiences, enriching the student experience while providing an opportunity to engage with a wider and more diverse student population.
- **Teaching business in the digital age** – from Emory News Centre; business education is in the throes of a historic transformation. Changes driven by technological advances and the corresponding demands of business are affecting how students learn, how professors teach and how schools both organise and market themselves.
- **How innovation and the 'reimagined' classroom will change learning** – from Knowledge@Wharton; higher education is undergoing a revolution. New technologies and new approaches to learning are altering the way educational programmes are delivered and are changing the way we learn. But there is no silver bullet. No single innovative teaching method has become widely promoted or adopted; the traditional lecture hall is still the norm.
- **The unfulfilled promise of educational technology** – from Harvard; with 50 million public school students in America, technology holds much potential to transform schools. So why isn't it happening?

- **Social media and alumni**: **how higher education can always be socializing** – from Hootsuite; maintaining post-graduation relationships with students has never been easier, but there does need to be a strategy.
- **$60,000 online degree**: **a lesson in digital business** – from *Information Week*; the title says it all.
- **MBA grads may still need to learn the rules of social media** – from Mashable; congratulations class of 2014! You navigated your way through accounting and calculus, macroeconomics and marketing — but have you mastered the algorithm necessary to be a 'social professional?' Social professional may sound like an ironic hashtag, but it has come to describe a serious business requirement.

Academic research

In a similar vein to the previous section, is the academic research that we undertake, the research that should power our course content, becoming obsolete? Is there evidence of leading-edge academic research being undertaken covering the impact of social and digital technologies on the study and practice of marketing; or, are we stuck in a time warp producing research of little value in a digital world? A review of recently published academic papers would suggest that there is much scope for improvement.

Using Google Scholar, a list of the 300 most recently published academic papers was examined – 100 publications for each of the following keywords 'marketing', 'digital marketing' and 'social media marketing' – covering the period January to end September 2014. The results provided some very interesting pointers to the direction that academic research is taking in this area.

Using the key word 'marketing', only 4 of the 100 articles returned mentioned digital, social or other disruptive technologies in their title or abstract. A much larger number of publications were obviously returned using the other two search terms. These included interesting papers covering a range of social/digital topics such as the impact of digital on specific industries (e.g. tourism, advertising, etc.); the impact on B2C and B2B buying behaviour; SMEs and their use of social/digital technologies; crowdfunding; mobile marketing; social media and branding and so on.

While it is good to see the emergence of a growing body of academic literature in this area, very few studies have yet been published addressing the more fundamental question of whether new approaches to marketing and new marketing paradigms need to be developed for the digital era. The following publications are worthy of note in this respect (Aiossa 2014; Atwong 2014; Benson *et al.* 2014; Leeflang *et al.* 2014; Ng 2014; Rao and Prabhala 2014; Royle and Laing 2014; Stone and Woodcock 2014; Wind 2014).

Based on the above, it would appear that authors from a non-academic background are leading the field when it comes to the new paradigms required, as discussed in the early sections of this chapter.

SME internationalisation

It is the view of the present author that there is one area in particular where academic research and publication seem to be stuck in a 30-year digital time warp, namely, the body of literature on SME internationalisation. The promotion of SME expansion into international markets has been a major policy objective of most governments for the last 50 years or so. The underlying rationale has been based on three key propositions:

- Having a strong base of SMEs competing in international markets is critical to national economic prosperity and job creation – especially in an increasingly global and inter-connected world.
- SMEs face a range of internal and external barriers when trying to expand abroad (e.g. lack of resources, time, knowledge; fear of the unknown; product/service suitability for foreign markets; export paperwork and documentation; risks; tariffs and non-tariff barriers to trade etc.).
- As a consequence, public sector support is required to help overcome these barriers with most nation-states having implemented a range of export support programmes aimed specifically at SMEs.

Given the importance of this topic, it is not surprising that a large volume of academic literature exists on SME internationalisation. A popular textbook summarised the state of the literature in the 1980s (Young *et al.* 1989). Since then, numerous further studies have been undertaken identifying the main barriers and challenges facing SMEs when going international. There have even been research papers researching the research papers.

Having looked at the recent literature in this area, the author would argue that academic research on SME internationalisation, and the export support programmes that derive from this research, are stuck in a pre-digital, pre-social media time warp. Used effectively, digital technology and social media can help to overcome many of the traditional barriers to SME exporting, leading to the more rapid internationalisation of the sector. Despite the opportunities presented, however, the role of digital technology in improving the export competitiveness of SMEs is an issue that has been almost completely overlooked in recent research in this area. At best, lip service is being paid to the new opportunities and threats presented by the digital and social media revolutions.

Given that very few SMEs are exploiting the full potential of social media and digital technology for 'going global', there is an urgent need to digitise and socialise academic research in this area and related export support programmes to equip SMEs with the digital/social media knowledge, skills and confidence for using emerging technologies to support global expansion.

Rather than promoting the slow, incremental approach to international growth, a natural outcome from most of the research in this area, a new approach to export support is required – an approach that leverages the full potential of digital and social technologies for supporting SME internationalisation. This would comprise at least ten key features:

1   use of digital and social media for export knowledge and export market research;
2   the importance of setting up a social media listening system to support export growth;
3   using 'hub' communities (knowledge- and relationship-based);
4   e-marketplaces for direct online selling in international markets;
5   use of digital and social media for supporting trade missions: making the right connections before you go;
6   proactively developing and implementing a digital/social media supported export strategy (website, website marketing, social media channels etc.);
7   implementing a content marketing plan for international markets (inbound marketing);
8   internal use of social technology to improve business processes, productivity and export competitiveness;
9   digital/social collaboration with overseas partners;
10 strategy and performance measurement.

It is time for a major rethink of our approach to SME export support. We need export support policies and SME export strategies which are 'fit for purpose' in a constantly connected world.

Research dissemination

Although there is a growing body of literature on digital and social media marketing, it has always been a source of surprise to the present author that so few of my academic colleagues are actively using social media to disseminate their research findings or to support the student learning experience.

Recent research from Michigan State University (2014) suggests that many academics are stuck in an ivory tower when it comes to their own use of social media to disseminate research findings. Scholars are largely resisting the use of social media to circulate their scientific findings or to engage with their tech-savvy students. In a survey of 1,600 researchers, only 15 per cent used Twitter for professional purposes. For YouTube and Facebook, this increased to 28 per cent and 39 per cent respectively, but still very much the minority. Even for those actively involved, most use social media to find collaborators and disseminate their work rather than to support teaching activities.

This leads Christine Greenhow (Assistant Professor in MSU's College of Education), one of the co-authors of the paper (Michigan State University 2014), to conclude that social media has failed to take hold in academia's ivory towers.

> Academia is not serving as a model of social media use or preparing future faculty to do this . . . This is troubling given that universities in the United States and Europe are trying to increase access to publicly funded research . . . Only a minority of university researchers are using free and widely available social media to get their results and published insights out and into the hands of the public, even though the mission of public universities is to create knowledge that makes a difference in people's lives. Simply put, there's not much tweeting from Ivory Towers . . . This issue is at the heart of larger discussions regarding accessibility, equal rights to higher education, transparency and accountability.

Practitioners

Given the, 'new rules of marketing, PR and sales' that have emerged as a consequence of the social and digital revolutions (Scott 2007, 2013, 2014), this section provides highly practical advice covering the development, implementation and management of effective digital marketing and social media strategies for achieving agreed business goals and objectives.

A key theme running through this chapter has been the need for radical change in our approach to business strategy and marketing as a consequence of the digital and social revolutions. What is not being advocated, however, is the adoption of a technology-led approach. It has always been the case that, 'strategy should determine tactics – never the other way round'. This is especially true in digital where there is a real danger of being seduced by the latest technology – setting up social media channels because everyone else is doing it.

Most senior executives are beginning to understand the profound impact that digital is having on their business and the need for change. What is lacking is a roadmap for 'getting there'. To assist in this area, the section below presents a framework for digital marketing/social media strategy development based on a simplified balanced scorecard (BSC) approach. The key word here is 'simplified'. The aim is to present a coordinated framework for guiding strategic thinking in this area. 'Paralysis by analysis' is not being recommended. Keep it simple, but not too simple. The key premise being advanced is that 'digital marketing/social media planning pays'. In other words, planning will not guarantee success; however, done properly, it will significantly reduce the likelihood of failure.

The scorecard approach

Since its original incarnation in the early 1990s, the balanced scorecard (BSC) has emerged as one of the most widely used frameworks for strategy development, implementation and performance measurement (Kaplan and Norton 1996). A simplified BSC approach to digital marketing/social media strategy planning will ensure that:

- The digital marketing/social media actions and initiatives implemented are fully aligned with and supportive of overall business goals and objectives.
- KPIs and targets are agreed for monitoring and evaluating digital marketing/social media performance, business impact and ROI.
- All key success factors are considered, especially the organisation, people and resource aspects critical to successful strategy implementation.
- The organisation does not suffer from 'paralysis by analysis'. By providing an agreed framework to follow, the Balanced Scorecard considerably speeds up, rather than slows down, the strategy development and implementation process.

A BSC approach can also be very useful for internal and external communications – a simple framework to present digital/social media business goals, objectives, key actions and initiatives to colleagues, partners and other stakeholders. The implementation of a BSC approach to digital/social strategy development should cover the five main issues listed in Figure 17.6 and explained in more detail below. These are best addressed in a senior executive/staff 'brainstorming' session.

Vision	What is the overall digital/social media vision for the organisation?
Objectives	What are the key objectives and targets to be achieved? Are these fully aligned with and supportive of overall business goals and objectives? What KPIs will be used to measure ongoing performance and business impact?
Customers	Who are the main customers for the digital/social media strategy? In particular, who are the 'most valuable' and 'most growable customers'? (Note: a broad definition of customers should be used to include existing customers, potential customers, internal customers (staff) and business partners).
Actions and initiatives	What digital marketing/social media actions and initiatives should be implemented to achieve the objectives agreed above? What generic digital/social strategy should be followed in terms of the number of channels used and depth of engagement in each channel? What is the appropriate balance between 'external' social media and 'internal' social business initiatives?
	Once priority actions and initiatives have been agreed, the BSC approach can be cascaded to develop an agreed strategy for each social media channel.
	For each priority channel, the following decisions need to be made:
	• What are the core objectives to be achieved from that channel?
	• What KPIs will be used for measuring ongoing channel performance?
	• What are your targets for each KPI?
	• What key tasks are needed to achieve these targets?
	The strategy and action plan for each digital/social media channel should always be fully aligned with and supportive of the overall business goals and objectives agreed previously.
Organisation, resource, people issues	Organisation, resource and people issues are critical to the successful implementation of a SM/SB Strategy. A wide range of decisions need to be made in this area covering roles and responsibilities, costs and so on.

Figure 17.6 Key scorecard questions

Source: The author.

Vision: The purpose of developing a digital/social media vision statement is to communicate to all stakeholders: why the organisation is becoming 'more digital, more social', the associated business benefits and the new organisational culture required. The aim is to communicate a shared vision and set of realistic objectives, winning the support and enthusiasm of key stakeholders. It should capture in a very clear no-nonsense manner what the organisation is planning to do and why.

Objectives, KPIs and targets: Used effectively, digital technology and social media can deliver a wide range of business benefits across the full spectrum of value chain activities, including marketing and sales. The starting point in developing an effective social media strategy is to be very clear on the business objectives to be achieved and the KPIs to be used in measuring ongoing performance and business impact. Too many companies launch digital and social media initiatives without any clear appreciation of why they are doing it or how they are going to measure impact and ROI. In the rush to become 'cool and funky', many organisations have set up social media platforms without thinking strategically. A key question that needs to be addressed is how will social media help to achieve agreed business goals and objectives? The BSC framework is particularly useful in helping to clarify goals and objectives, especially in the distinction it makes between 'lag' and 'lead' measures as summarised in Figure 17.7.

- 'Lag' measures – your ultimate business goals, e.g. increase sales, reduce costs, build a strong base of high value, high growth potential customers.
- 'Lead' measures are the main digital and social media drivers that help to achieve agreed business goals and objectives. They are not business goals in their own right. Rather, they are the main drivers that help to achieve ultimate business objectives.

Customers: Business goals and objectives will be achieved through building strong 'one-to-one' customer relationships, especially with high growth potential, high margin customers. Undertaking a

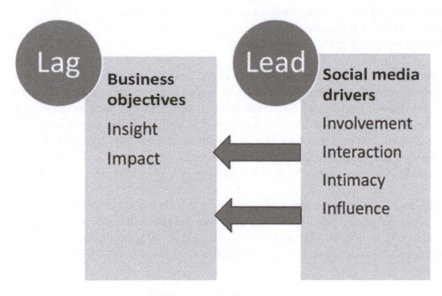

Figure 17.7 Balanced scorecard: 'lag' and 'lead' measures

Source: The author.

detailed customer mapping and segmentation analysis is a critical element in developing a digital/social media strategy, as it will have a big impact on the subsequent channels to be used and the supporting content plan. There are three main stages involved:

1   Segment your customers into groups with 'common interests' and with similar 'needs and wants'.
2   Agree priority customer segments, i.e. customers segments who will best help you to achieve your overall business goals and objectives.
3   Develop 'personas' for your high priority customers.

Following the above approach will ensure that:

- future social media efforts are focused on 'high value, high growth' potential customers resulting in a more efficient allocation of scarce resources. The '80/20 rule' applies here, i.e. 20 per cent of customers generate 80 per cent of sales/profits. Companies should develop digital and social media strategies aimed at 'identifying, acquiring, retaining and growing 'most valuable' and 'most growable' customers;
- the content you post on various social media channels is relevant and adds value, especially to high priority customers. A content plan should be developed targeted at key customer segments.

Failure to follow this approach will result in resources, time and effort being wasted on low value customers. Content will deliver little value to your customers.

Key actions and initiatives: Once core business objectives and priority customer groups have been agreed, the focus then shifts to agreeing the key digital/social media actions and initiatives for 'getting there'. Some of the key decisions that need to be made are:

- the number and range of channels to be developed;
- the balance between external facing social media and internal social business;
- the depth of engagement in each channel;
- channel success factors and performance measurement.

An implementation plan for each priority channel should then be agreed. This will involve cascading the BSC approach to cover each priority channel with decisions being made covering the core business objectives to be achieved from the channel; the KPIs and targets to be used in measuring ongoing channel performance; the key channel actions required to achieve these targets; organisation, people and resource issues. It is critical to ensure that channel strategy is fully aligned with and supportive of overall business goals and objectives as agreed previously. Agreeing a well-developed, integrated and coordinated content management plan is critical to successful channel management.

Organisation, people and resource issues: Organisational, resource and people issues sit at the bottom of the digital/social media BSC NOT because they are the least important issues to address. In fact, the exact opposite is true. The success of digital and social media initiatives is very much dependent upon appropriate decisions being made in the areas listed below. The following questions should be addressed:

- Does the organisation have the right 'culture' and 'mindset' for becoming digital/becoming social?
- Is the right organisational and decision-making structure in place?

- Has agreement been reached on resource allocation?
- Who will be responsible for digital and social media activities?
- What balance has been agreed between internal and external roles and responsibilities?
- Who is the digital/ social media champion?
- Does the organisation have agreed social media policies and guidelines in place covering 'proper use', 'content management', 'customer response times/quality', 'legal' aspects and so on?

Performance measurement: Finally, to ensure that your digital/social media strategy delivers a return on investment, it is important to monitor and evaluate ongoing performance benchmarked against agreed objectives, KPIs and targets.

The '6Is' approach to measuring digital and social media performance was discussed in a previous section of this chapter. It is important to note that the '6Is' listed previously are not abstract, difficult to measure concepts. Rather, they can be measured to a very high degree of accuracy; a level of accuracy not available in offline marketing. Each social media channel provides detailed statistics that can be used for measuring involvement, interaction, intimacy and influence, e.g. Facebook Insights, YouTube stats, LinkedIn Connections etc. In addition, there are a large number of tools available for measuring overall 'brand buzz' across different social media channels. These range from completely free to very expensive tools costing several thousand of pounds per month for a single user licence.

Online personal branding

In the same way that disruptive technologies are having a major impact on the traditional approach to brand management, the career paths of our young people will be radically different in a digital world. This section provides some brief advice on the important topic of online personal branding.

Especially for our young graduates, but also for practising marketing managers, effective personal use of social media has become critical to career development. Employers are increasingly using social media channels at some point in the recruitment process – either by proactively targeting those with high social media 'clout' or, at the very least, checking your social profile before making an offer.

It is critical, therefore, to differentiate your online personal brand, to stand out from the crowd, through the innovative use of social media. A new approach to recruitment and career development is emerging – an approach based on developing online relationships and online networking. This improves the efficiency and effectiveness of job efforts through 'attraction-based' marketing compared to the more traditional route of applying for jobs. This is illustrated clearly in Figure 17.8, which compares the new social approach to the more traditional one.

Some of the key channels to consider are:

- personal blog for 'telling your story';
- Twitter for conversations;
- LinkedIn for professional networking;
- Facebook for personal stuff (but be careful, very careful);
- Google + – the 'new kid on the block';
- develop a Youtube channel including your own video, e.g. presentations;
- your resume/CV as an infographic;
- actively engage/network/build relationships.

Traditional approach	New approach
• Develop a resume/CV and covering letter • Search/find vacancies • Submit CV/covering letter for available job or 'on spec' • Wait for the phone call/email that never comes, because the job market is becoming increasingly competitive • Same as above, but go through an agency/online job site	**Use social media to:** • Search/listen/keep an ear to the ground • Build your personal brand, differentiate, stand out from the crowd • Identify, join, lurk, participate in relevant forums, groups • Actively engage/network – build relationships • Leverage 'attraction' based marketing • Monitor performance and 'buzz'

Figure 17.8 Career development in a digital/social era

Source: The author.

At all stages, it is critical to follow accepted 'best practice' and 'netiquette':

- always try to add value;
- don't SHOUT;
- talk WITH rather than AT;
- listen first;
- don't be a show off;
- don't get angry or respond in an aggressive way;
- be careful of your 'digital footprint';
- don't spam or over post;
- don't underestimate the power of the network;
- hang out in the right places with the right people.

Summary and conclusions

This chapter has discussed a wide range of issues relating to the impact of the digital and social media revolutions on the study and practice of marketing as we know it. The question is no longer whether organisations should 'be social: be digital'. The only legitimate question now is how – what is the best way to 'get there'? To paraphrase Bob Dylan (1964):

> *Your old road is*
> *Rapidly agin'*
> *Then you better start swimmin'*
> *Or you'll sink like a stone*
> *For the times they are a-changin'*

Further reading

Baer, J. (2013), *Youtility: Why Smart Marketing Is about Help Not Hype*, Harlow, UK: Penguin.

Bradley, A. J. and McDonald, M. P. (2011), *The Social Organization: How to Use Social Media to Tap the Collective Genius of Your Customers and Employees*, Boston, MA: Harvard Business School Publishing.

Eliason, F. (2012), *At Your Service: How to Attract New Customers, Increase Sales, and Grow Your Business Using Simple Customer Service*, Chichester, UK: John Wiley & Sons.

Fidelman, M. (2012), *Socialized!: How the Most Successful Businesses Harness the Power of Social*, Boston, MA: Bibliomotion.

Frank, M., Roehrig, P. and Pring, B. (2014), *Code Halos: How the Digital Lives of People, Things, and Organizations are Changing the Rules of Business*, Chichester, UK: John Wiley & Sons.

Handley, A. and Chapman, C. C. (2012), *Content Rules: How to Create Killer Blogs, Podcasts, Videos, Ebooks, Webinars (and More) That Engage Customers*, Chichester, UK: John Wiley & Sons.

Li, C. and Bernoff, J. (2011), *Groundswell, Expanded and Revised Edition: Winning in a World Transformed by Social Technologies*, Boston, MA: Harvard Business Review Press: Forrester Research.

Mayer-Schonberger, V. and Cukier, K. (2013), *Big Data: A Revolution That Will Transform How We Live, Work and Think*, London: John Murray Publishers.

Pulizzi, J. (2013), *Epic Content Marketing: How to Tell a Different Story, Break through the Clutter, and Win More Customers by Marketing Less*, Maidenhead, UK: McGraw-Hill.

Vaynerchuk, G. (2011), *The Thank You Economy*, London: HarperCollins.

References

Aiossa, E. (2014), '21st century digital marketing', *Journal of Digital & Social Media Marketing*, 1(4): 319–323.

Atwong, A. T. (2014), 'An action learning approach to social media marketing and analytics', *Marketing Educators Annual Conference Proceedings*.

Benson, V., Morgan, S. and Filippaios, F. (2014), 'Social career management: Social media and employability skills gap', *Computers in Human Behavior*, 30: 519–525.

Capgemini Consulting (2013), *The Digital Talent Gap: Developing Skills for Today's Digital Organizations*, available at http://www.capgemini.com/resources/the-digital-talent-gap-developing-skills-for-todays-digital-organizations (accessed 2 December 2015).

Chaffey, D. (2013), *Digital Marketing Careers* [infographic], available at http://www.smartinsights.com/managing-digital-marketing/resourcing-digital-marketing/popular-digital-marketing-jobs/ (accessed 2 December 2015).

Christensen, C. (2013), *In 15 years from now Half of US Universities May be Bankrupt*, available at http://www.bothsidesofthetable.com/2013/03/03/in-15-years-from-now-half-of-us-universities-may-be-in-bankruptcy-my-surprise-discussion-with-claychristensen/ (accessed 2 December 2015).

Forrester Research (2014), 'Businesses having trouble getting with the digital times', *InfoWorld Tech Watch*, available at www.infoworld.com/article/2608153/it-strategy/forrester–businesses-having-trouble-getting-with-the-digital-times.html (accessed 2 December 2015).

Hamill, J. (1997), 'The internet and international marketing', *International Marketing Review*, 14(5): 300–323.

Hamill, J. (2011a), 'Are you a fish or a sheep?', *Energise Blog*, available at http://energise2-0.com/2011/07/12/are-you-a-fish-or-a-sheep/ (accessed 2 December 2015).

Hamill, J. (2011b), 'I am not a suspect', *Energise Blog*, available at http://energise2-0.com/2011/06/18/i-am-not-a-suspect/2011 (accessed 2 December 2015).

Hamill, J. (2014a), 'Three part series on social media performance measurement', *Energise Blog*, available at www.energise2-0.com/category/social-media-performance/ (accessed 2 December 2015).

Hamill, J. (2014b), 'Digital business leaders urgently required', *Energise Blog*, available at www.energise2-0.com/2014/05/07/digital-business-leaders-urgently-required/ (accessed 2 December 2015).

Hamill, J. (2014c), 'The future of higher education in a digital world', *Energise Blog*, available at www.energise2-0.com/2014/07/03/the-future-of-higher-education-in-a-digital-world-12-useful-articles/ (accessed 2 December 2015).

Hamill, J. and Gregory, K. (1997), 'Internet marketing in the internationalisation of UK SMEs, Special Edition', *Journal of Marketing Management*, 13(1/3): 9–28.

Kaplan, R. S. and Norton, D. P. (1996), *The Balanced Scorecard: Translating Strategy into Action*, Boston, MA: Harvard Business School Press.

Lee, B. (2012), 'Marketing is dead', *Harvard Business Review Blog*, available at www.blogs.hbr.org/2012/08/marketing-is-dead/ (accessed 2 December 2015).

Leeflang, P. S. H., Verhoef, P. C. and Dahlstrom, P. (2014), 'Challenges and solutions for marketing in a digital era', *European Management Journal*, 32(1): 1–12.

Michigan State University (2014), '"Ivory Tower" bucking social media', *MSU Today*, available at http://msutoday. msu.edu/news/2014/ivory-tower-bucking-social-media/ (accessed 2 December 2015).

Ng, I. C. L. (2014), 'New business and economic models in the connected digital economy', *Journal of Revenue and Pricing Management*, 13(2): 149–155.

Qualman, E. (2014), #Socialnomics, available at http://www.youtube.com/watch?v=zxpa4dNVd3c&feature=yo utube (accessed 2 December 2015).

Rao, T. U. and Prabhala, K. (2014), 'New technology paradigm shift in marketing: Digitalization', *International Journal of Logistics and Supply Chain Management Perspectives*.

Royle, J. and Laing, A. (2014), 'The digital marketing skills gap: Developing a digital marketer model for the communication industries', *International Journal of Information Management*, 34(2): 65–73.

Salesforce (2014), 'The future of marketing revealed', *Salesforce Blog*, available at http://blogs.salesforce.com/ company/2014/09/the-future-of-marketing-revealed-at-connections-2014.html (accessed 2 December 2015).

Scott, D. M. (2007), *The New Rules of Marketing & PR: How to Use Social Media, Online Video, Mobile Applications, Blogs, News Releases, and Viral Marketing to Reach Buyers Directly*, Hoboken, NJ: John Wiley & Sons.

Scott, D. M. (2013), *The New Rules of Marketing & PR: How to Use Social Media, Online Video, Mobile Applications, Blogs, News Releases, and Viral Marketing to Reach Buyers Directly*, Hoboken, NJ: John Wiley & Sons.

Scott, D. M. (2014), *The New Rules of Sales and Service: How to Use Agile Selling, Real-Time Customer Engagement, Big Data, Content, and Storytelling to Grow Your Business*, Hoboken, NJ: John Wiley & Sons.

Solis, B. (2012), *The End of Business As Usual: Rewire the Way You Work to Succeed in the Consumer Revolution*, Hoboken, NJ: John Wiley & Sons.

Solis, B. (2013), *What's the Future of Business: Changing the Way Businesses Create Experiences*, Hoboken, NJ: John Wiley & Sons.

Solis, B. (2014), 'Digital transformation and the race against digital Darwinism', *Brian Solis Blog*, available at http:// www.briansolis.com/2014/09/digital-transformation-race-digital-darwinism/ (accessed 2 December 2015).

Stelzner, M. A. (2011a), *Launch: How to Quickly Propel Your Business Beyond the Competition*, Hoboken, NJ: John Wiley & Sons.

Stelzner, M. A. (2011b), 'Rest in peace marketing: I never really liked you anyway', available at http://www.brian solis.com/2011/06/rest-in-peace-marketing-i-never-really-liked-you-anyway/ (accessed 2 December 2015).

Stone, M. D. and Woodcock, N. D. (2014), 'Interactive, direct and digital marketing: A future that depends on better use of business intelligence', *Journal of Research in Interactive Marketing*, 8(1): 4–17.

Tapscott, D. (1997), *The Digital Economy: Promise and Peril in the Age of Networked Intelligence*, Maidenhead, UK: McGraw-Hill.

Tapscott, D. and Williams, A. (2006), *Wikinomics: How Mass Collaboration Changes Everything*, London: Atlantic Books.

Tapscott, D. and Williams, A. (2010), *MacroWikinomics: New Solutions for a Connected Planet*, Harlow, UK: Penguin.

The Economist (2014), *Higher Education: Terminal Degrees*, available at www.economist.com/blogs/freeexchange/2014/07/ higher-education?zid 316&ah=2f6fb672faf113fdd3b11cd1b1bf8a77 (accessed 2 December 2015).

Wind, Y. J. (2014), 'Toward a new marketing paradigm', *Routledge Companion to the Future of Marketing*, Oxford, UK: Routledge.

Young, S., Hamill, J., Wheeler, C. and Davies, J. R. (1989), *International Market Entry and Development: Strategies and Management*, Harlow, UK: Harvester Wheatsheaf.

18 Customer relationship management

Strategy and implementation

Adrian Payne and Pennie Frow

Introduction

Customer relationship management, or CRM, is a management approach that seeks to create, develop and enhance relationships with carefully targeted customers in order to maximise customer value, corporate profitability and thus shareholder value. CRM also involves utilising information technology (IT) to implement relationship marketing strategies.

The market for CRM services is expanding, representing a significant growth sector. This is evident in both the take-up of CRM and the investment in CRM tools and techniques. The increased interest in CRM as a strategic business approach is a consequence of a number of trends. These include:

- the shift in business focus from transactional marketing to relationship marketing;
- the transition in organisational structures from functions to processes;
- the recognition of the benefits of using information proactively rather than solely reactively;
- the greater utilisation of technology in managing and maximising customer insight;
- the increasing importance of digital marketing and social media.

However, there remains considerable confusion about what exactly is CRM. Confusion surrounding the definition and role of CRM may be explained by: its relatively recent arrival; the lack of a widely accepted and clear definition of its scope; an emphasis on IT aspects rather than its benefits in terms of building relationships with customers; and its associations with specific tools sold by IT vendors.

In this chapter we outline a strategic framework for addressing CRM. This framework has been developed to clarify CRM's function and 'fit' within the organisation, and to help optimise its use as a strategic management approach. This framework comprises five interrelated cross-functional processes:

1   the strategy development process;
2   the value creation process;
3   the multi-channel integration process;
4   the information management process;
5   the performance assessment process.

While these processes have universal application in all organisations, the extent to which they need to be emphasised will vary according to each organisation's unique situation.

This chapter provides a framework for understanding and implementing CRM as a means of ensuring that the overall business strategy delivers increased shareholder results. The structure of the chapter is as follows: first, we briefly review the nature of CRM and provide a definition. Second, a framework for understanding CRM at strategic level is outlined. Third, five cross-functional processes that enable CRM to be adopted and implemented effectively are each examined in turn. Finally, we address four critical areas that need to be addressed for successful CRM implementation.

Defining CRM

The term CRM emerged within the IT vendor community and practitioner community in the mid 1990s. It is typically used to describe technology-based customer solutions such as sales force automation. Within the academic community, the two terms relationship marketing and CRM are often used interchangeably. However, they should be considered as being distinct, but interrelated (Mitussis *et al.* 2005; Shukla 2010; Payne and Frow 2013). However, CRM is more commonly used in the context of technology solutions and has been described as, 'information-enabled relationship marketing'.

A significant problem faced by many organisations deciding to adopt CRM stems from the fact that there is still a great deal of confusion about what constitutes CRM. In interviews with executives, which formed part of our research, we found a wide range of views regarding what is meant by CRM. To some it meant direct mail, a loyalty card scheme or a database, while others viewed it as a help desk or a call centre. Some said it was about populating a data warehouse or undertaking data mining, others saw CRM as an e-commerce solution such as the use of a person-alisation engine on the internet, a relational database for sales force automation; or a social media application. The lack of a widely accepted and appropriate definition of CRM can contribute to the failure of a CRM project where an organisation views CRM from a limited technology per-spective or undertakes CRM on a fragmented basis.

We believe that how CRM is defined is not merely a question of semantics. Its definition can have a significant impact on how CRM is accepted and practiced by the entire organisation. From a strategic standpoint, CRM is not simply an IT solution to acquiring and growing a customer base: rather it involves a profound synthesis of strategic vision; a corporate understanding of the nature of customer value within a multi-channel environment; the utilisation of the appropri-ate information management and CRM applications; and high quality operations, fulfilment and service. Thus CRM, in any organisation, should be viewed in a broad strategic context. We define CRM as follows:

> CRM is a cross-functional strategic approach concerned with creating improved shareholder value through the development of appropriate relationships with key customers and customer segments. It typically involves identifying appropriate business and customer strategies, the acquisition and diffusion of customer knowledge, deciding appropriate segment granularity, managing the co-creation of customer value, developing integrated channel strategies, and the intelligent use of data and technology solutions to create superior customer experiences.
>
> (Payne and Frow 2013)

This definition provided guidance for the development of the strategic framework we now outline.[1]

A strategic framework for CRM

Organisations large and small, across a variety of sectors, have embraced CRM as a major element of corporate strategy for two important reasons: new technologies now enable companies to target chosen market segments, micro-segments or individual customers more precisely; and new marketing thinking has recognised the limitations of tradtional marketing and the potential of more customer-focused, process-oriented and co-creative perspectives.

However, CRM's recognised potential to deliver commercial improvement remains curtailed by a lack of clear guidance on: what CRM is; what its component parts are; and how the component parts can be integrated successfully within the organisation. When an organisation views CRM narrowly as a direct mail initiative, a loyalty card scheme, or a call centre, it is likely to develop its CRM activities on a piecemeal and fragmented basis.

In this chapter we position CRM as a strategic set of activities that commence with a detailed review of an organisation's strategy and conclude with an improvement in shareholder value. The notion that competitive advantage stems from the creation of value for the customer *and* for the company is key to the success of CRM, which demands that responsibility for value delivery is shared across functions and hierarchies. Because CRM is a cross-functional activity, and in large companies seeks to focus on potentially millions of individual customer relationships simultaneously, it can be unwieldy to implement and impossible to get right without a purposeful and systematic approach.

The strategic framework for CRM, outlined in Figure 18.1, is based on the interaction of five cross-functional business processes that comprise: *strategy development, value creation, multi-channel integration, information management* and *performance assessment*. These processes make a greater contribution to organisational prosperity collectively than they can individually, and must therefore be treated as an integrated and iterative set of activities. A detailed consideration of each of the processes will help managers realised the benefits of CRM.

The framework is based on the premise that all five processes are critical to the business and that they need to be closely integrated with each other. The way in which the framework can be best considered is as a progression through each of the processes, approaching them essentially from left to right. It should start with a review of the organisation's strategic context and conclude with improvement in shareholder value. The framework, as the arrows in both directions in Figure 18.1 suggest, is iterative and interactive. A review of a later process is likely to require a reconsideration of elements within processes examined earlier. Rather than be seen as a one-way linear progression the framework should be viewed as an iterative feedback-driven progression aimed at continually enhancing the benefits of CRM. To understand what these benefits are and how they are manifested, it is necessary to consider each of the processes in turn.

The strategy development process

Where are we and what do we want to achieve?

Who are the customers that we want and how should we segment them?

Most companies today recognise that their future depends on the strength of their business relationships and, most crucially, their relationships with customers. In an effort to effect better CRM, many organisations are introducing technology solutions in an effort to break the bonds of antiquated IT legacy systems – often with disappointing outcomes. CRM, however, is not simply an

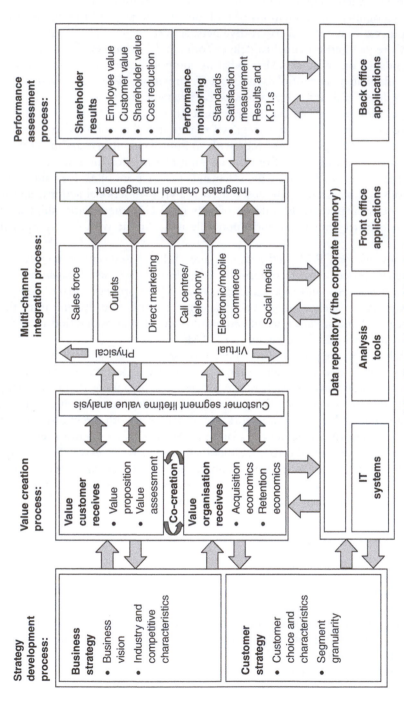

Figure 18.1 The strategic framework for CRM

Source: Based on Payne and Frow (2013).

IT solution to the problem of getting the right customer base and growing it. CRM is much more than that.

Rather than immediately turning to such technology solutions, managers need to first consider CRM in the context of overall business strategy. CRM must actively reflect and reinforce the wider goals of the business if it is to be successful. The strategy development process requires a dual focus on the organisation's *business strategy* and its *customer strategy*: how well the two interrelate will fundamentally affect the success of the CRM strategy.

Business strategy

A comprehensive review of the business strategy will provide a realistic platform on which to construct the CRM strategy, as well as generate recommendations for general improvement. The area of business strategy is well known, so it requires little commentary here. An examination of both industry and competitive characteristics (e.g. Porter 2008) need to be considered in terms of future possible structural change, including creating challenges to traditional business models.

Business vision and competitive characteristics

The organisation needs to fully understand its own competencies within a competitive context in order to be able to transfer them to the customer as customer value. It is also vital that everyone in the organisation is pulling in the same, strategic direction and that they are alert to changes, which might signal opportunity or disaster. This is especially important where the organisation is in transition from a product orientation to customer orientation. Consideration of the following key business issues, present and future, will serve to re-affirm the appropriate course and direction for the organisation:

- **Stage of industry evolution**: What is the current state of your industry structure? What are the likely and possible future changes?
- **Competitors' profiles**: What is the nature of your competitors? How do they compete? How will new competitors evolve in the future? Are there new entrants on the horizon that are not hindered by the same legacy architecture? Are there new strategic alliances that may disrupt the value market?
- **Your company's profile**: Where does your company fit within the industry structure? What are your organisation's resources and competencies?
- **Business definition**: What is your strategic intent? In the light of industry evolution and the competitive environment, how should you define your business scope? Have you developed a statement of business purpose or a mission statement that clearly communicates this to relevant stakeholders?
- **Channels of distribution**: What is the current and future role of different distribution channels? What opportunities exist for disintermediation or reintermediation? What opportunities exist for new forms of distribution and delivery in terms of electronic commerce and mobile commerce?
- **Information technology platform**: What are the appropriate IT platforms for serving present and future customers, corporate needs and engaging with customers and other stakeholders in social media?

The value of such a review is that it will provide a realistic platform on which to construct the business's CRM strategy. A company needs to fully understand its own competencies in order to be able to transfer them to the customer as customer value. It is also vital that everyone within the organisation is clear on the business's overall purpose and intent so that they can pull in the same strategic direction.

A greater understanding of the external environment will also benefit the company's understanding of customers, of the opportunities and also the threats they face in the market place. The purpose of addressing business strategy, as part of the CRM strategy development process, is to determine how the organisation's customer strategy should be developed and how it will evolve in the future.

Customer strategy

The other half of the strategy equation is deciding which customers the business wants most to attract and to keep, and which customers it would prefer to be without. No firm can successfully be 'all things to all people', and thus finding the best potential customers and retaining them is vital.

Customer choice and customer characteristics

The prior review of business strategy will be instrumental in reaching a judgement on broad customer focus. A consideration of the following issues will assist the organisation to determine more specifically its choice of customers and their characteristics when defining the role of CRM in the organisation:

- **Nature of customer strategy**: Do you have one? Is it flexible enough to withstand change in the competitive environment, and strong enough to lead constructive change within the organisation? What is the current nature of your dealings with customers? Are they basic transactions or more formalised relationships? Do you specialise in serving an elite clientele or is your focus more 'mass market'?
- **Status of customer strategy**: Is your customer strategy considered important within the organisation? Does the management of customers receive sufficient and appropriate support in terms of resource, recognition and real commitment? Is it working? If not, why not?
- **Customer segments**: Who are your existing and potential customers? Which forms of segmentation are most appropriate rather than easiest to achieve? What are the major segments? What are the opportunities for micro-segmentation, one-to-one marketing and mass customisation?
- **Knowledge of customer base**: Can you describe in detail the profile(s) of your customers? Can you identify patterns in their motivations and behaviours? If so, in a refined, or basic, manner? Do you actively and proactively seek to build your customer 'intelligence'? Do you fully exploit the customer intelligence you have?
- **Product/service involvement and complexity of purchasing behaviour**: Who constitutes the decision-making unit in your customers? How are your products/services purchased? How important are they to your customers? Is your average level of customer service quality exceptional/adequate/poor? Are you working to improve/maintain it?
- **Customer relationships**: What kinds of relationship do you have or want to have with your customers? How retainable are your customers? How do you 'remember' and 'reward' your customers? Do you feed customer communication back into the business so you can relate to customers on a one-to-one basis?

- **Value of customer base**: Do you formally quantify the value your customers? In what terms (loyalty, customer lifetime value revenue, referrals, etc.)? Do you actively seek to select the most valuable customers and deselect the less or least valuable customers?

The organisation will need to determine the amount and kind of customer information it requires as well as how closely and through what channels it should interact with its customer base both now and in the future. Furthermore, while the ability to satisfy customers' existing needs is paramount, companies must also strive to pre-empt their future, often unexpressed, needs.

It is important to recognise that customers differ and thus relationships with customers will have to be managed differently if they are to be successful. This is a key principle of CRM. The aim of CRM is to build relationship strategies that refine relationships and in this way increase their value. Creating competitive advantage through the skilful management of customer relationships will normally require a reappraisal of the way in which customers are approached and segmented, and the way in which resources are allocated and used. To achieve this level of refinement requires a careful choice of the levels at which segmentation is undertaken (McDonald and Dunbar 2010).

Segment granularity

Creating competitive advantage through the skilful management of customer relationships will normally require a reappraisal of the way in which customers are approached and segmented, and the way in which resources are allocated and used. Customer strategy involves determining the appropriate level of *segmentation granularity* (including whether a macro-segmentation, micro-segmentation or one-to-one is appropriate), identifying key customer segments and building strategies to address these customers. If a company operates in an intermediated market, it will have a number of customer groups and each of them needs to be fully considered in terms of segmentation approach and granularity.

Decisions regarding segmentation need to be taken in the context of a number of considerations. These include the existing and potential profitability of different customer types; the information on customers that is available and that can be collected at a justifiable cost; the level of competition; and the existing and likely future use of channels. Considerable attention has been directed at the potential for shifting from a mass market to a 'one-to-one' marketing environment (Peppers and Rogers 1993, 2004). Exploiting e-commerce opportunities and understanding the fundamental economic characteristics of the internet and social media can enable a much deeper level of segmentation granularity than is usually provided by other channels.

However, segment granularity needs to be examined in the company and industry context in which it is being considered. In some cases, especially in an e-commerce environment, an immediate migration to a 'one-to-one' or a 'one-to-few' may be undertaken. However, in more traditional businesses, more 'macro' forms of segmentation will be relevant. It is worth making the point that many business to business enterprises have for a long time adopted one-to-one marketing through a key account management system, although it was not referred to as such.

A further important point is that 'one-to-one' marketing does not imply adopting a 'one-to-one' approach with every single customer. Rather, it suggests understanding customers in terms of their economic importance and then adjusting the marketing approach to reflect the importance of different customer groups according to their existing and potential profitability. However, this point is sometimes disregarded when a discussion of one-to-one marketing is undertaken.

Thus, clear segmentation of the customer base and adopting the correct level of segment granularity is an important element of customer strategy. It is also a necessary pre-condition before considering *the value creation process*, as segmentation is crucial to this process.

The value creation process

How should we deliver value to our customers?

How should we maximise the lifetime value of the customers we want?

The value creation process is concerned with transforming the outputs of the strategy development process into programmes to deliver value to both the customer and the supplier organisation. The *value creation process* consists of four key elements: determining what value the company can provide to its customers (the 'value customer receives'); determining the value that the organisation receives from its customers (the 'value organisation receives'); engaging more actively in co-creation of value; and, by successfully managing this value exchange, the organisation then aims to maximise the lifetime value of desirable customer segments.

However, the emphasis in many companies is on the second element of value. To these companies, customer value means:

- How much money can we extract from customers?
- How we can sell them more of the existing products and services they are buying?
- How we can cross-sell them new products and services?

Most companies do not consider, in sufficient detail, the value the company seeks to deliver to customers in clearly identified customer segments and micro-segments, and *how* they are going to achieve this. Where both sides of the value exchange are not addressed in an integrated manner, it is not surprising that a supplier's offering to customers does not have a strong impact on key customer segments. Operating with a detailed understanding of the increased value a company can deliver to its customer is likely to significantly increase the value the organisation subsequently receives from its key customer segments.

The value the customer receives

The value the customer receives from the supplier organisation can be determined by developing value propositions and undertaking a value assessment. Here, customer value is seen as an inherent part of the product and one that can be managed actively by a company to benefit the customer. In fact, customers are not buying goods or services – they really buy specific benefits, which solve problems. The value they attach to the offer is in proportion to the perceived ability of the offer to solve their problem. Product augmentation is a means of creating product differentiation and thus added value from the customer perspective.

For managers wishing to review the existing 'offer' to customers and consider the potential for increasing the value they provide to their customers, some structured framework or methodology to do this is desirable. One useful approach is the value proposition concept.

The value proposition

In recent years, managers have started to use the term *value proposition* increasingly frequently. All businesses exist to deliver some form of value proposition, which may be implicit or explicit. A company should aim to create a value proposition that is superior to and more profitable than those of its competitors. However, our discussions with many organisations suggest that they rarely develop a value proposition and, where they do, it is not usually underpinned by an analytical process.

The term value proposition is used by organisations in two ways. In general terms, it is used to describe the notion of creating customer value in a very broad sense. In more specific terms, it is used to describe a particular approach to creating customer value, which was first developed at consulting firm, McKinsey & Co. Here, the term value proposition is used to describe an approach that formally defines:

- the target customers;
- the benefits offered to these customers;
- the price charged relative to the competition.

Value propositions provide an explanation of the relationship between the performance attributes of a product or service, the fulfilment of needs across multiple customer roles (e.g. acquiring, using and disposing of products) and the total cost. Thus, they should be based on an understanding of the total customer relationship life cycle.

Value assessment

Having developed a value proposition, the next step should be to undertake a value assessment. A value assessment seeks to determine if the value proposition that has been developed is likely to result in superior customer experience. Value assessment may be undertaken in a number of ways.

A frequent method is for a company to make an assessment based on subjective judgements about the attributes and benefits, which are important to the customer. A frequent mistake made by companies is in assuming that customers attach the same importance to these attributes as does the supplier company. Experience suggests companies often do not identify all the relevant attributes; and, even when a company correctly identifies those attributes, which are most relevant to the customer, the ranking of these by the customer and the supplier may vary significantly.

The first step should be to identify the attributes of importance to given customer segments *from the perspective of the customer*. Once these attributes are defined, we can seek to identify the relative importance of each and the company's perceived performance on these attributes relative to the competition. There are various ways of discovering the importance that the customer attaches to each attribute. One method is to ask a representative sample of customers to rank them in importance of a five-point scale. However, this is impractical when there are a large number of attributes, as this gives little insight into their relative importance. Alternatively, rankings could be made on the attributes and a weight placed on them. A more sophisticated solution is to adopt an innovation developed in customer market research: the use of conjoint analysis (e.g. Aaker *et al.* 2010). Conjoint analysis is based on the concept of successively trading off one of these attributes against another. Also known as trade-off analysis, it is now used more regularly by consulting firms, market research firms and advertising agencies.

Recognising the differences between customer segments is critical. Trade-off analysis can also be used to identify customers who share common preferences in terms of attributes. Experience of researchers and consultants working in this area suggest that this form of analysis may often reveal substantial market segments with service needs that are not fully catered for by existing offers.

The value the organisation receives

As indicated above, the value the company receives from the customer has the greatest association with customer value for most organisations. Customer value from this perspective of value is an output of, rather than an input to, value creation. As such, it focuses not on the creation of value for the customer but on the value outcome derived from providing and delivering superior customer value. Fundamental to the concept of customer value in this context is understanding the economics of customer acquisition and customer retention.

Customer acquisition and its economics

The importance of customer acquisition varies considerably according to a company's specific situation. For example, a new entrant will primarily be concerned with customer acquisition, while an established company operating in a mature market may be more concerned with customer retention. The customer acquisition process is typically concerned with:

- acquiring customers at a lower cost;
- acquiring more customers;
- acquiring more attractive customers.

The starting point in understanding customer value is to determine the existing customer acquisition costs within the existing channels that are utilised and to determine how these vary across different segments or micro-segments. The next step is to consider how acquisition costs may vary across different channels. The internet has allowed many companies to create websites, which have enabled customers to be acquired at a fraction of the costs of other more traditional channels.

Once a company has an understanding of how acquisition costs vary, at both the segment and channel levels, they can then start to explore the issue of acquiring more customers and more attractive customers. For most marketing managers, acquiring more customers, within a given segment and channel, usually means using a better promotional approach in terms of more targeted direct mail, more effective advertising, or an improved website. However, the opportunity of using existing customers to attract new customers should also be considered. This means creating 'advocacy' amongst your existing customers through delivering a superior value proposition that results in much better service than that of the competition. The engagement of existing customers in social media has an important role to play in this task.

In many instances, customer acquisition can be improved through insights from the analysis undertaken in developing the value proposition and value assessment outlined above. This should result in a better focus on key customer segments, adopting the appropriate level of segment granularity and creating propositions attractive to those target customers.

Customer retention and its economics

Researchers have found that it costs around five times more to get a new customer than it does to keep an existing one. Despite this finding, many companies focus their marketing activity on acquiring new customers, rather than retaining existing customers. This may be partly due to the historical convention in many companies that rewards customer acquisition to a much greater extent than customer retention.

While most companies recognise that customer retention is important, relatively few of them understand the economics of customer retention within their own firm. Until the early 1990s, there was little research that critically evaluated the relative financial benefits of customer acquisition versus customer retention. In 1990 a partner at consulting firm, Bain & Co, and a professor at the Harvard Business School published some revealing research findings, which demonstrated the financial impact of customer retention (Reichheld and Sasser 1990). They found that even a small increase in customer retention produced a dramatic and positive effect on profitability. Their research showed that a 5 per cent increase in customer retention yielded a very high improvement in profitability in net present value (NPV) terms. Increasing the customer retention rate from, say, 85 per cent to 90 per cent represented an NPV profit increase from 35 per cent to 95 per cent amongst the businesses they examined.

Given these dramatic findings about the impact of improvement in customer retention and the explanations for them, there is a strong imperative for companies to examine the economics of customer retention in their own businesses. However, our research suggests that managers are slow at implementing changes in marketing activities that emphasise customer retention.

Co-creation

The third element that forms part of the value creation process is the co-creation of value. It is now more widely acknowledged that, 'the customer is always a co-creator of value'. (Vargo and Lusch 2004). Traditionally, suppliers produced goods and services, and customers purchased goods and services. Today, customers engage in dialogue with suppliers much more readily during each stage of product design and delivery. Together, supplier and customer have the opportunity to create greater value through customised, co-produced offerings. The co-creation of value is a desirable goal as it can assist firms in highlighting the customer's point of view and in improving the process of identifying customers' needs and wants (Payne *et al.* 2008).

The customer's value creation processes include activities performed by the customer to achieve a particular goal. The importance of recognising customer processes rests with the need to develop a full understanding of where a supplier's offering fits within the customer's over-all activities. For example, a leading international airline 'mapped' how the travel experience on their aircraft fitted within the total consumption system of their first class and business class passengers. The airline used a 'shadowing' technique where, with the customer's prior permis-sion, highly personable employees of the airline arrived at the customer's home as they were preparing to travel. The airline employee then accompanied the business customer to the airport, travelled with them to their destination, remained with them throughout the day, flew back with them and returned with them to their home. The insights gained were used to inform future service development. Value co-creation demands a change in planning processes from 'making, selling and servicing' to 'listening, customising and co-creating'.

Customer segment lifetime value analysis

A balance is needed between the marketing efforts directed towards existing and new customers. This balance will vary greatly depending on whether the business is a 'dotcom' startup or a mature 'bricks and mortar' company. However, in general, marketing expenditure is unbalanced, with too much attention being directed at customer acquisition.

To enable a decision on the relative amount of emphasis that needs to be placed on them, an understanding of both acquisition and retention economics at the segment level is critical. To calculate a customer's real value, a company must look at the projected profit over the life of the account. This represents the expected profit flow over a customer's lifetime. The key metric used here is customer lifetime value (CLV), which is defined as the NPV of the future profit flow over a customer's lifetime.

It should not be assumed that companies would wish to retain *all* their customers. Some customers may cost too much money to service, or have such high acquisition costs in relation to their profitability, that they will never prove to be worthwhile and profitable. Clearly, it would be inadvisable to invest further in such customer segments. It is likely that within a given portfolio of customers, there may be some segments that are profitable, some that are at break-even point and some that are unprofitable. Thus, increasing customer retention does not always yield increases in customer profitability. In some instances, increasing the retention of such unprofitable customers will decrease profitability. It should be recognised, however, that unprofitable customers may be valuable in their contribution towards fixed costs and considerable caution needs to be placed in the allocation of fixed and variable costs to ensure that customers who make a contribution to fixed costs are not simple discarded.

Advanced analytical models can help organisations determine customer value in terms of CLV. However, thoroughly understanding existing acquisition economics and retention economics at the segment and micro-segment levels is a stage relatively few organisations have achieved. Once this stage has been reached, the organisation should move to modelling *future profit potential* for each market segment. Modelling of future profit potential takes into account that individual consumers may be persuaded to buy other products, or more of an existing product, over time. Further, future profit potential may be significantly enhanced through creatively exploiting *alternative channel structures*, which we now consider.

The multi-channel integration process

What are the best ways for us to get to customers and for customers to get to us?

What does a 'perfect' or outstanding customer experience, deliverable at an affordable cost, look like?

The multi-channel integration process involves making decisions about the most appropriate combination of channels through which to interact with your customer base; how to ensure the customer experiences highly positive interactions within those channels; and, where customers interact with more than one channel, how to create a 'single unified view' of the customer experience. To determine the nature of the business's customer interface, it is necessary to consider the key issues underlying channel selection; the purpose of multi-channel integration; the channel options available; and the importance of integrated channel management in delivering an outstanding customer experience.

Issues in channel selection

Selecting the company's route to market (i.e. how to make its products or services available to the end consumer) involves considering a number of issues, which may be summarised under the headings of channel suitability and channel structure.

Channel suitability

The most appropriate choice of channel (or channels) for any company will be the one that is most attractive to the end consumers in the target market segment. The level of attractiveness will be determined by the company's ability to create customer value relevant to those customers' needs.

Thus, when developing channel strategy, a company must be equipped with an understanding of the benefits sought by the end consumer at the different stages of the buying process, from the customer's initial point of enquiry through to their ownership and use of the product or service.

Depending on the offer made, inherent benefits to the customer might include the ability to obtain information quickly; access the channel easily; communicate with the supplier effectively; physically inspect the product prior to purchase; have the product customised; and obtain service and support during the course of ownership. By identifying which benefits the customer seeks and the relative importance attributed to them, the company can evaluate channel suitability and determine which channel option would deliver these benefits to the greatest degree for the lowest cost. This emphasises the point that creating a value proposition, which will attract target customers, does not simply rest with the design of the product or service: it also relies on how the offer is made available to the end consumer in terms of route, presentation and sales support.

Channel structure

In addition to channel suitability, the way in which the channel is organised can seriously influence the success or failure of the channel. Besides considering target customers' current buying behaviours and motivations, the company should also consider how these might change over time, particularly with respect to the impact of developing technology. Over the last decade, the traditional channel structures of many industries have been dismantled and reconfigured in response to new technologies that have opened up new paths to market. Managers responsible for channel strategy need to understand both the nature of their industry channel structure now and how it is likely to alter in the future. Valuable insights into emerging trends within channel structures can be gained from examining the experiences of other sectors or other industries on a global basis. Two types of structural behaviour are important:

- *disintermediation* where changes in the current business model or advances in technology mean that a company ceases to need to use intermediaries to create the value sought by end consumers;
- *reintermediation* where changes in the current business model or advances in technology result in the emergence of new types of intermediary that can create more value than was possible in the previous channel structure.

Examples of *disintermediation* can be found in businesses that have adopted call centre technology and computer telephony integration (CTI) rather than utilising traditional branch-based intermediaries. The UK insurance company, Direct Line, for example, was able to create additional customer value by offering customers the opportunity to deal directly, and thus more cost-effectively, through the use of advances in call centre and web technology. A good example of *reintermediation* exists on the web in the form of so-called 'infomediaries', or web-enabled information agents. Rather than the consumer having to spend considerable time researching the alternatives available when considering purchasing a type of product, the infomediary performs that function on their behalf, e.g. Autobytel and CarsDirect.com.

Once macro-level decisions have been made regarding the most appropriate routes to market, the extent to which intermediaries are to be used and how these may change over time, the organisation then needs to consider multi-channel options and their combination in greater detail.

Multi-channel integration

Faced with the necessity of offering consumers different channel types to meet their changing needs during the sales cycle (pre sale, sale and post sale), it is increasingly imperative to integrate the activities in those different channels to produce the most positive customer experience and to create the maximum value. Competitive advantage today is not just about selling products and services to customers; it is about building long-term and profitable relationships with customers, which are founded on mutual benefit and trust. To succeed, therefore, the company must consistently seek to offer an individualised relationship in every customer interaction through whatever channel is being used. This will inevitably lead the company to undertake an ongoing review of *all* the possible means of interacting with customers. While some businesses may choose a single channel strategy, many more will benefit from a strategy based on the integration of multiple channels.

Discussions on channels are usually dominated by those that are involved in making the sale. However, for strategic CRM, the channels need to be considered in the context of the whole interaction over the life cycle of the customer relationship, not just in terms of the specific sales activity. The stages of a customer relationship can be considered under the three broad headings: acquisition, consolidation and enhancement.

Within these typical stages, a great number of interactions occur between the customer and the organisation across different channels. Understanding the nature of different customer encounters within a multi-channel environment is essential if the organisation's CRM activities are to be fully effective. Further, customers' needs during the customer relationship life cycle phases will vary according to the segment to which they belong and the product or service involved. Thus, determining the most appropriate forms of channel options for specific customer segments is also critical.

Channel options

The multi-channel integration process involves a consideration of channel options. These options fall into six main channel categories as shown in the strategic framework for CRM in Figure 18.1:

- sales force/personal representation;
- outlets;
- call centres/telephony;
- direct mail;
- electronic/mobile commerce;
- social media.

Although there are many individual channel options, we have found it convenient to group them into these six categories. Thus, options such as retail branches and kiosks are included within 'outlets' and telephone contact and fax within call 'centres/telephony'; and the internet and digital TV within 'electronic/mobile commerce'.

These channel categories can be represented as a continuum of forms of customer contact ranging from the physical (such as a face-to-face encounter with a company representative) to the virtual (such as a mobile commerce transaction or social media). Clearly, employing a combination of the channels most appropriate to the target customer base and enterprise structure will provide the greatest commercial exposure and return. Over time, more and more of these channels will be used concurrently by enterprises.

Adopting social media gives marketers an opportunity to avoid any marketing mistakes preciously made when implementing other channels. Most successful adoptions of the social media channel start by 'listening' rather than 'broadcasting'. Typical 'listening' applications begin with monitoring and analysing brand-focused conversations. This provides marketers with new insights into brand-focused perceptions, based on the customer's own words and value analysis.

Further analysis can highlight recurring conversations. The first steps are to identify key influencers that can be exploited during future campaigns and product launches. For success, an integrated approach is needed to establish a social media presence across all the social media channels as well as the existing legacy channels.

Integrated channel management

Integrated channel management involves understanding what defines an outstanding customer experience and being able to deliver it at an affordable cost to the organisation. This raises two questions: what does an outstanding customer experience look like *within a given channel*; and, where customers may interact with more than one channel, how do we create the appropriate look, touch and feel *across different channels*, bearing in mind the inherent differences in the nature of these channels?

In tackling these issues, the enterprise needs first to consider what constitutes an outstanding customer experience for different customer segments in each of the channels being used (or considered), and to determine how such an experience might be delivered in a consistent manner and at an affordable cost within each channel.

Having established a set of standards for each channel, the enterprise can then work to integrate the channels, trying to optimise but not compromise the accepted channel standards. Achieving integration across the different channels will require attending to a myriad of areas in order to ensure that the multi-channel service matches the individual needs of customers in different segments. A major objective will be to achieve brand consistency across these channels and this will require skilful channel management.

Modern customers expect to be served through a multitude of channels. At the same time, these customers are individuals who make their purchasing decisions according to the unique factors of each given situation. Therefore, customers may belong to a number of different customer segments, simultaneously. Taken together, these two aspects of customer nature present a considerable challenge: how to provide a high quality, multi-channel service that satisfies the individual and the changing needs of increasingly empowered customers.

Providing services in both traditional and contemporary channels is a priority for companies that are seeking to meet or, indeed, exceed the expectations of discriminating customers. However, many companies do not seem to recognise the need to maintain equally high standards of service *across* multiple channels. Because the quality of a company's service provision is only as good as the weakest link in their multi-channel service mix, successful channel integration demands that a company uphold the same high standard of service their customers have come to expect from the company in all of the channels being used. To succeed in integrated channel management, the company must be able to collect, analyse and utilise a wide range of customer information available from different channels as well as other sources. This is the role of *the information management process*.

The information management process

> *How should we organise information on customers?*
>
> *How can we 'replicate' the mind of the customer?*

The information management process is concerned with two key activities: the collection and collation of customer information from all customer contact points; and the utilisation of this information to construct complete and current customer profiles, which can be used to enhance the quality of the customer experience. As companies grow and interact with an increasing number of customers through an increasing diversity of channels, the need for a systematic approach to organising and employing information becomes ever greater. Where customer information is spread across disparate functions and departments, interactions with the customer may be based on partial or no knowledge of the customer, even though the customer may have been with the organisation for years. This fragmentation of customer knowledge creates two major problems for the company. First, the customer is treated in an impersonal way, which may lead to dissatisfaction and defection. Second, there is no single unified view of the customer upon which to act and to plan.

A key role of the information management process is to 'replicate the mind of the customer'. Thus, the emphasis in this process needs to be on how we can use this information in a proactive way to develop enhanced relationships with the customer, rather than on the elegance and sophistication of the technology solution.

In an effort to keep pace with escalating volumes of data, the tendency is for organisations to create more or bigger databases within functions or departments, leading to a wealth of disparate silos of customer information. Companies are thus left with a fragmented and often unwieldy body of information upon which to make crucial management decisions. The elevation of CRM from the level of a specific application such as a call centre, to the level of a pan-company strategy requires the integration of customer interactions across all communication channels, front- and back-office applications and business functions. What is required to manage this integration on an ongoing basis is a purposefully designed process that brings together data, computers, procedure and people. The key material elements of the information management process consist of: *the data repository, IT systems, analytical processes,* and *front-office and back-office systems.*

Data repository

To make an enterprise customer-focused, it is not sufficient simply to collect data about customers, or even to generate management information from individual databases, because they normally provide only a partial view of the customer. To understand and manage customers as complete and unique entities, it is necessary to have a powerful corporate memory of customers; an integrated enterprise-wide data store, which can provide the data analyses needed to inform strategic and tactical decision-making processes. The approach best suited to providing such a resource is the use of a data repository, together with appropriate analytical tools. In most cases, integration of information from different databases and departments will also be required.

The role of the data repository is to collect, hold and integrate customer information, and thus enable the company to develop and manage customer relationships effectively. In simple terms, the data repository comprises two main parts: *databases* and the *data warehouse*, as shown in Figure 18.2.

Databases comprise a set of computer programs and software packages for storing data gathered from a source such as a call centre, the sales force, customer and market surveys, electronic points of sale and so on. Each database usually operates separately and is constructed to be user-specific, storing only that which is relevant to the tasks of its main users. Management and planning information drawn from a single database is therefore limited in value, because it provides an incomplete view of customer-related activity.

The *data warehouse* is a collection of related databases that have been brought together so that the maximum value can be extracted from them. The basic idea of data warehousing is to gather as much data as possible in the hope that a meaningful picture will emerge.

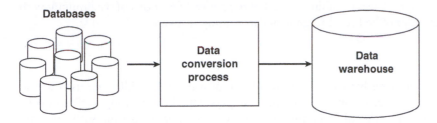

Figure 18.2 The data repository

An *enterprise data model* is used to manage this data conversion process model in order to minimise data duplication and to resolve any inconsistencies between databases. As well as connecting to internal systems, the data warehouse also often takes feeds from external sources. The data warehouse is organised to support the kinds of analyses performed at customer management and strategic planning levels. Analytical tools such as data mining can be used to reveal patterns in customer data, such as buying habits, which form the basis of improved customer understanding relationship building. End-users can access the data warehouse using online analytical processing tools.

Using a data warehouse has two key advantages. First, it stops complex data analysis from interfering with normal business activity by removing a heavy demand on the databases. Second, the data in a data warehouse changes only periodically (e.g. every 24 hours), allowing meaningful comparisons to be made on stable sets of data, which exist in between updates of the data warehouse. If databases were used for analysis, analyses made at different times would produce different results, making it impossible to compare, for example, the sale of different products or the volume of sales in different regions.

Through the effective use of data analysis tools, the data warehouse can help to answer questions about customers' behaviours and preferences, and the value they provide to the enterprise. The data warehouse is therefore instrumental in the CRM task of identifying the enterprise's best customers, and identifying ways to retain them and enhance their value. More importantly, once firmly established, the data warehouse supports the monitoring of customers and provides a mechanism for testing and refining customer strategy.

Analytical tools

The analytical tools that enable effective use of the data warehouse can be found in general data mining packages and in specific software application packages. Data mining packages enable the analysis of large quantities of data to discover meaningful patterns and relationships. Each pattern and relationship explains something about customer behaviour and provides indications of how customer relationships can be improved. More specific software application packages include analytical tools that focus on such tasks as:

- campaign management analysis;
- churn management;
- credit scoring;
- customer profiling;
- market segmentation analysis;
- profitability analysis.

These task-specific software packages combine several of the general functions of data mining with support for the task that will not be found in general data mining software.

IT systems

IT systems consist of the computer hardware and the related software and middleware used within the organisation. Normally, organisations' IT structures are developed over a long period of time and thus different, and often incompatible, computing systems – both hardware and software – are utilised in different parts of the business. Frequently, there is insufficient integration of these different systems, and therefore technology integration is required before databases can be integrated into a data warehouse and user access can be provided across the company.

The driving consideration should be how to configure the organisation's IT systems so that they deliver the information that we need on customers both now and in the foreseeable future, as well as the other administrative systems that are required. In particular, as the number of customers and customer transactions escalate, how to scale existing systems or plan for the migration to larger systems without disrupting business operations is critical.

Front- and back-office applications

Front-office applications are the technologies used to support customer-facing activities and are ones where a great deal of current CRM emphasis has been placed. They encompass all those activities that involve direct interface with customers and include sales force automation, call centre management, product configuration tools, and sales force and marketing automation. These applications are used to increase revenues by improving customer retention and raising sales closure rates. *Back-office applications* support internal administration activities and supplier relationships, involving human resources, procurement, warehouse management, logistics software and some financial processes.

The main concern about front- and back-office applications is ensuring that they are sufficiently coordinated and connected to optimise customer relations and workflow. They can represent a fault-line in the company's ability to provide consistent customer value where communication and information functions are not integrated seamlessly. For instance, dozens of applications may be spread throughout an organisation; or departments may be organised around products and services or business functions, rather than processes, which support the customer relationship. For this reason, it is useful to review existing applications from the perspective of customer interaction, so that customer needs drive technology solutions, rather than the other way around.

Clearly, the information management process plays an increasingly important role in CRM, supporting the collection and analysis of enormous volumes of complex customer data. Like other resources, data has a value in use, as well as a limited shelf life. It is therefore crucial that customer data is accumulated and deployed in an organised and integrated fashion to provide a comprehensive and current perspective of customers. Selecting appropriate IT hardware and software is a challenging task owing to the constraints of legacy systems and the enormous range of technology options. To ensure that technology solutions support CRM, it is important to conduct IT planning from the perspective of providing a seamless customer service, rather than planning for functional or product-centred departments and activities. Such a customer-centred approach to IT planning will ensure that customer information is used effectively to maximise customer value and the profitability of each customer. Furthermore, data analysis tools, such as those outlined above, make it possible to measure business activities to determine whether new ways of managing customer relationships might be advantageous in increasing shareholder value. This kind of analysis provides the basis for *the performance assessment process.*

The performance assessment process

How can we create increased profits and shareholder value?

How should we set standards, develop metrics, measure our results and improve our performance?

The performance assessment process involves an evaluation of the success of CRM. It is this process, which ensures that the organisation's strategic aims, in terms of CRM, are being delivered to an appropriate and acceptable standard and a basis for future improvement is established. The key actions involve understanding the drivers of shareholder value, identifying the appropriate metrics against which the various CRM activities can be measured, and establishing an effective performance monitoring system to apply these measures on an ongoing basis. The shareholder results element and performance monitoring element of this process have some overlap between them. However, the former involves a more 'macro' view of overall relationships, which drive performance, while the latter is concerned with a much more detailed 'micro' view of metrics and key performance indicators (KPIs).

Shareholder results

The ultimate objective of CRM for commercial organisations is to deliver shareholder results through an increase in shareholder value. Before a review of performance monitoring takes place, the enterprise should understand the specific drivers of shareholder results that ultimately determine CRM success. These drivers need to be considered in the context of the business strategy and the customer strategy set out in the strategy development process. These are four key drivers that impact shareholder results: building employee value; building customer value; building shareholder value; and reducing costs. The first three represent the main stakeholder groups from which shareholder results are obtained, while the latter impacts positively on shareholder results by lowering costs to improve profit margins.

Employee value, customer value and shareholder value

Many organisations acknowledge the importance of three key groups of stakeholders: employees, customers and shareholders, who are critical to organisational success. These three groups clearly have a relationship with each other. However, the precise nature of the relationship between them has only recently been closely examined. This has led to the recognition of a need to adopt a more integrated approach across these groups and understand more deeply the linkages between them.

Managers readily agree that there is linkage, as shown in the performance 'linkage model' in Figure 18.3, between good leadership and management behaviour, improved employee attitudes, customer satisfaction and increased sales, profits and shareholder results. However, most managers have no idea how much a quantified improvement in one variable in this linkage will lead to a measurable increase in another.

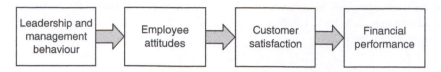

Figure 18.3 The performance linkage model

Enterprises are using such linkage models to explore these relationships more explicitly. The best known of these is the 'service profit chain model' (e.g. Heskett and Sasser 2010), which illustrates the 'knock-on' effect between good leadership, strong and appropriate management, happy employees, satisfied customers and improved financial performance. This work provides, amongst other findings, strong evidence that profit is linked to customer loyalty, which is linked to consistent customer satisfaction. However, while few would argue with the logic of such a linkage model, only recently has any serious effort been made to investigate and identify quantitative relationships between variables in the model.

For example, Sears Roebuck and Co, the large US department store chain, has been highly innovative in its efforts in this area. In addition to addressing the more common elements of CRM, such as streamlining their information systems – which previously involved 18 separate legacy databases – into a single, integrated data warehouse, they also developed a linkage model to help manage shareholder results. They used a modified version of the service profit chain model to predict revenue growth and profitability. Using sophisticated causal pathway analysis, the company was able to identify 20 customer measures, 25 employee measures and 19 financial measures that together provided profit indicators. This illustrates how the specific metrics and KPIs can be derived from this more macro investigation of the drivers of shareholder value. For example, by applying these metrics in the evaluation of performance, the company discovered that a 5-unit increase in employee attitude drives a 1.3 unit increase in customer impression, a 0.5 increase in revenue growth and a quantifiable increase in profitability (Rucci *et al.* 1998). With this knowledge and understanding, the company was able to effect a great improvement in performance and overall growth.

The development of linkage models, such as the service profit chain, has been a welcome development in enabling companies to evaluate the effectiveness of CRM at a strategic level in terms of improving shareholder results. More companies are now starting to recognise the value of addressing these higher-level drivers before determining standards, metrics and KPIs.

Cost reduction

The improvement of shareholder results through cost reduction is probably the area most often associated with managers' efforts to improve profitability. Cost reduction can be achieved many ways. However, two ways are of special interest in the context of CRM: deploying electronic systems, such as automated telephony services that lower costs by enabling reductions in terms of staff number and overheads; and by utilising new channels, such as online self-service facilities, which can lower the costs of customer acquisition, transaction and servicing.

The savings from automation and adoption of automated services and alternative channels are well documented. For example, replacing customer contact with branch-based employees with a centralised call centre; or replacing a branch-based customer transaction with an internet banking transaction that is many times cheaper. However, an over-concentration on cost reduction as a means of delivering shareholder results can be counterproductive if it decreases customer value. Companies need to determine what effect cost reduction will have on their customer base. For example, many individuals have had an increasing number of negative experiences with their bank as it continually seeks ways to implement cost reduction. Creating a central call centre will reduce costs, but is also likely to disenfranchise customers who can no longer telephone their branches and have personalised contact with bank employees whom they know. Banks may lose many of their best customers as a result.

Achieving a productive balance between fiscal efficiency and profitability means understanding that customer value may be destroyed or enhanced as a result of such changes. Avoiding customer value destruction when reducing costs is a key element of successful CRM.

Performance monitoring

Despite the increasing focus on customer-facing activities, there is growing concern that metrics generally used by companies for CRM are not nearly as advanced as they should be. In particular, more detailed standards, measures and KPIs are needed to ensure CRM activities are planned and practised effectively, and that a feedback loop exists to maximise performance improvement and organisational learning.

Standards

A set of CRM standards against which best practice is measured is needed so companies can measure their performance against that of others. As yet, there is no such internationally recognised set of standards for CRM. However, a number of initiatives are underway in this area. Some, such as the COPC Standard (COPC 2004), focus on specific aspects of CRM such as call centres. Others, such as a standards initiative at BT (British Telecom), are concerned with identifying key areas in which standards should be set across all the major areas of CRM.

In terms of CRM standards set in a specific context, the COPC-2000® Standard is a good example. The standard was developed by a core group of users of call centre services and associated distribution fulfilment operations, including American Express, Dell, Microsoft and L.L. Bean (COPC 2004). The standard describes the performance measurement approaches that a customer service provider must establish and it defines the metrics it must use to evaluate the effectiveness and efficiency of its approaches. The Malcolm Baldrige National Quality Award criteria and framework were used as the basis for the standard. While COPC does not set specific performance objectives, such as a particular service level that every call centre must meet, it does require that all performance metrics be tracked, linked to drivers of customer satisfaction and used to improve overall call centre performance.

In terms of more universal CRM standards, UK telecommunications company, BT, developed a set of standards, based on the concept of the COPC Standard, against which to measure best practice in the following areas (Chidley 2000):

1   Does my organisation demonstrate leadership in CRM? How do I compare with other organisations?
2   How satisfied are my customers with the products and services offered by my organisation?
3   What is the lifetime value of my customers? How can I be more cost effective in delivering customer service to them?
4   How effective and integrated is the access that my customers use to reach my organisation?

5   How effective are the customer solutions and applications that enable my customers to obtain my products and services?
6   How do I manage the customer information used and generated at each customer contact to deliver the maximum value from my customers?
7   Do I have the skilled and motivated people to deliver my products and services to customers?
8   Does my organisation have the appropriate customer-related processes to deliver quality products and services?
9   Does my organisation have the appropriate performance and reporting procedures to measure the impact of CRM strategy and operations on the organisation?

Each of these questions translates into a set of standards that can be used by an organisation to assess their CRM capabilities. Companies should consider developing a set of customer-related standards in all the major areas of the CRM framework and putting metrics and KPIs in place that permit a rigorous performance assessment to be undertaken.

Metrics, KPIs and results

Two main questions need to be addressed if CRM performance is to be measured and monitored successfully:

1   What metrics and KPIs should be used that adequately reflect the performance standards across the five major CRM processes?
2   How are these metrics and KPIs linked, and what opportunity do these linkages provide for improved results through better management of CRM across the organisation?

The performance measurement systems adopted by organisations in the past have tended to be functionally driven. Thus financial measures were mainly the concern of the finance department and the board; marketing measures the domain of the marketing department; and people measures the responsibility of the HR department. Such a functional separation of performance measures is clearly inappropriate for CRM that is a cross-functional and holistic management approach. Therefore the measures used to appraise CRM performance must be selected on the basis that they interrelate and are applied together to give a complete view of the entire organisation.

One of the most popular attempts to provide cross-functional measures is the 'balanced scorecard' developed by Kaplan and Norton (1996, 2004). This scorecard works by providing a cumulative view of several perspectives of the business: the customer perspective; the internal perspective, including internal performance measures; the growth perspective, including measures reflecting knowledge creation, innovation and learning; and the financial perspective, which considers the shareholders' view of the organisation. At a strategic level, it is concerned with issues relating to the shareholder results described above. At an implementation level, it is concerned with identifying appropriate metrics and KPIs. However, a drawback to using the balanced scorecard approach is that there is no universally successful list of measures to use, as each organisation's measurement criteria will require a different emphasis and mix of measures. The balanced scorecard is, however, a significant development in focusing on the importance of non-financial measures that previously had largely been ignored in performance measurement systems.

The challenge for companies in evaluating and enhancing their CRM performance is therefore to identify the measures appropriate to the organisation and to understand the linkages between them. As CRM has become increasingly critical to overall competitive performance, there is a great need to develop robust categories of metrics for measuring, monitoring and benchmarking good CRM practice. Payne and Frow (2013) provide a detailed review of five key categories for consideration: *customer metrics*; *people and process metrics*; *strategic metrics*; *output and operational metrics*; and *special metrics* (including e-metrics and special metrics for social media and social influence marketing).

Inevitably, it is much easier to select which metrics to use than it is to determine how to monitor them in an integrated manner. It is therefore important not only to identify the appropriate standards of measurement but also to understand the relationship between the metrics so that the CRM processes can be refined, individually and collectively, to maximum effect.

Overall, the test of the performance assessment process lies in the organisation's ability to respond confidently to the following fundamental questions:

1   Have we selected the most appropriate CRM performance standards? Do we benchmark our standards against 'best in class'?
2   Have we determined appropriate metrics and KPIs? Do we understand where these performance metrics are linked?
3   Can we determine the impact of each metric, individually and cumulatively, on our results?
4   Do we have appropriate feedback built into our CRM monitoring process so that there is continual improvement?

Organising for CRM implementation

In the previous sections of this chapter we examined five key processes that comprise the strategic framework for CRM. In this section we examine the key issues involved in organising for implementation of a CRM programme. The effective management of customer relationships involves many different and interlinked aspects. However, simply addressing the processes is not enough to ensure CRM is effectively implemented. Firms have to *organise* appropriately to ensure that they achieve satisfactory results from their CRM programmes.

Our research has identified four critical elements for successful CRM implementation. These include: CRM readiness assessment; CRM change management; CRM project management; and employee engagement. These four implementation elements are shown in Figure 18.4 in relation to the five strategic processes of CRM.

We now consider how the four implementation elements in Figure 18.4 come together to support the organisation of a CRM strategy.

CRM readiness assessment

A CRM readiness assessment can help managers assess the overall position in terms of readiness to progress with CRM implementation and to identify how well developed their organisation is relative to other companies. Research by Ryals and Payne (2001) shows that there are identifiable stages of maturity in CRM development: pre-CRM planning; building a data repository; moderately developed; well developed; and highly advanced. Each of these stages represents a level of CRM maturity characterised by the extent to which customer information is used to enhance the customer experience and customer-generated cash flows.

If an organisation is in the early stages of CRM development, it is useful to start with *an overview audit* of the five key CRM processes to help secure senior management understanding and buy-in at an early stage. The overview form of readiness audit can be used to rapidly form an initial view of the key CRM priorities, to define the relative importance of these priorities and to determine

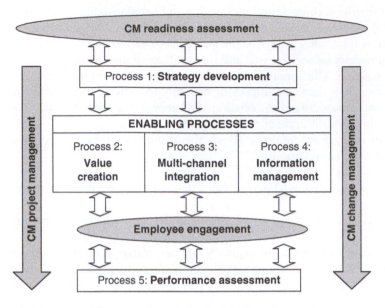

Figure 18.4 Key elements in organising for CRM implementation

where effort needs to be applied. Figure 18.5 shows the output of such an exercise for a major European bank. In the case of this bank, changes were considered to be necessary in all processes, with the greatest improvement needed in the value creation and performance assessment processes, as shown in Figure 18.5. A number of important new CRM initiatives were identified and project teams were formed to implement them. Other organisations have found this overview audit

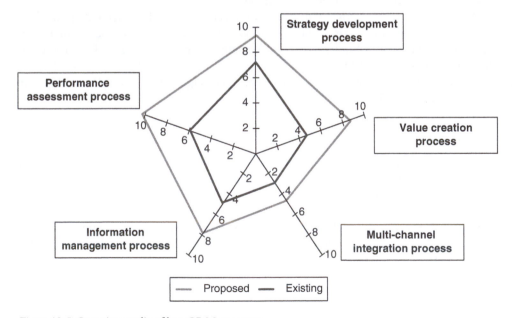

Figure 18.5 Overview audit of key CRM processes

extremely helpful in identifying progress and challenges in their CRM initiatives. Such organisations typically found significant differences in the gap between the current position and the desired position and in the relative emphasis on each process.

Although simple in concept, we found the completion of an overview audit and a structured discussion with a company's managers around the scorings was extremely valuable in highlighting areas an organisation should concentrate on in order to improve its CRM performance. To extend the range of executives' views it is possible to develop a simple web-based programme to collect and aggregate information from around the company.

Firms that are more advanced, or ones that wish to go into greater detail, can undertake a more comprehensive CRM audit. A number of CRM audit tools have also been developed, mainly by consulting firms. These audits vary greatly in detail and quality. Some are little more than a quiz and others show little evidence of understanding the strategic issues relevant to CRM. Two audits that are more robust are the CMAT assessment tool (QCI 2004) and a detailed 100-item comprehensive CRM process audit developed by Payne and Frow (2013).

CRM change management

To implement a large-scale and complex CRM initiative, companies will typically have to undergo substantial organisational and cultural change. A critical dimension of any large CRM programme, therefore, is an effective change management programme. (We make a distinction here between *change management*, which is concerned with strategic organisational change and *employee engagement*, which was seen as a more operationally oriented set of activities. These activities are, however, closely entwined.)

Because CRM is potentially so wide-ranging in terms of the organisational ramifications, a robust analytical framework is needed to help assist CRM leaders in identifying the organisational change management issues in relation to a particular CRM programme. One well known change management framework, the 'Seven S' framework (Peters 1984), is a useful tool to help the organisation identify those issues relevant to their business. This framework provides a means of viewing organisations as packages of key skills, or skill gaps. Hence, it can be used as a tool for analysing organisational deficiencies, building on positive skills and identifying any new skills required.

CRM project management

CRM project management has increasing importance as the size and complexity of CRM initiatives increase. There are two main types of CRM projects: first, where a team of specialists is brought together on a temporary basis to address a particular project with a finite completion date; second, where a cross-functional team is assembled with a remit of ongoing management of part of the enterprise's CRM initiative. Successful CRM projects deliver against the CRM objectives derived from the corporate objectives and support the overall business strategy. Our research identified that CRM projects that overrun budgets and timescales create considerable damage to CRM credibility, hence effective CRM project management is essential.

Some organisations adopt a large-scale and very comprehensive approach to CRM implementation. However, others had found that an incremental and modular approach to CRM development, or enhancement, was more appropriate. These latter companies typically engaged in a series of smaller individual CRM projects, undertaken in an appropriate sequence, each with clearly defined objectives and return on investment outcomes. These projects varied in the emphasis placed on analytical CRM, operational CRM and collaborative CRM.

As the CRM project plan is implemented, two further issues should be considered: *creep in project scope* and *understanding the implications of scale*. Ebner *et al.* (2002) point out that as a project grows in scope, the system's development can take on a life of its own, incorporating new features that do not support business objectives, but which add considerable complexity and cost. IT professionals have learnt that the bigger the project, the harder it is to integrate and the more likely it is to miss its deadlines or be scrapped altogether. The business objectives that the CRM system was intended to achieve must be kept under constant scrutiny and any efforts to increase the scope of the project must be evaluated very carefully. Further, as a project is planned, it is critical that the implications of scale increase are understood. Point estimates of future demand should be replaced with estimates based on three levels of potential future demand: optimistic, most likely and pessimistic. As the number of users and customers grows, the system must be robust enough to accept higher possible increases in volume.

Employee engagement

The final of the four implementation elements is the engagement of employees to support the various initiatives that comprise the overall CRM programme. Employees have a crucial role to play within the CRM processes and implementation activities outlined in this chapter. An organisation cannot develop and operate appropriate customer-focused systems and processes without motivated and trained employees.

Change management and project management are particularly dependent on engagement of employees for their success. Ensuring the delivery of a superior customer experience during times of unexpectedly high demand requires the active engagement and commitment of all customer-facing staff and is a hallmark of a well-planned CRM implementation. Increasingly, organisations are recognising the significant value their employees contribute to the business, which extends well beyond the basic fulfilment of core duties. Employees are instrumental in implementing processes, including customer service, improving efficiencies and nurturing consumer confidence and repeat purchase. The role of senior executives in facilitating employee engagement is also vital. However, at board level, issues such as governance, finance, acquisitions and cost reduction may predominate over issues of customer management, marketing and employees.

Summary

The strategic framework for CRM outlined in this chapter is a formal response to the confusion and frustration many companies experience in their efforts to adopt CRM. Its purpose is to provide a comprehensive framework for the development of CRM strategy. By breaking CRM down into its key cross-functional processes, it is possible to communicate the underlying principles of CRM strategy, demonstrate the interdependence of CRM activities and plan CRM activity on a strategic and well-integrated basis.

The framework positions CRM as a strategic set of activities that commence with a detailed review of an organisation's strategy (the strategy development process) and conclude with an improvement in business results and increased shareholder value (the performance assessment process). It is based on the proposition that creation of value for the customer *and* for the company (the value creation process) is the key to the success of relationships. CRM involves collecting, and intelligently utilising, customer and other relevant data to generate customer insight (the information management process) in order to build a superior customer experience at each touch-point where the customer and supplier interact (the multi-channel integration process).

Organising for CRM implementation involves four elements that are critical to a successful CRM programme: CRM readiness assessment, CRM change management, CRM project management and employee engagement. Implementing CRM represents a considerable challenge in most enterprises. Any successful CRM implementation should be preceded by the development of a clear, relevant and well-communicated CRM strategy. Organisations also need to adopt a strategic definition of CRM that focuses on business issues rather than emphasising IT issues.

Successful CRM demands coordination and collaboration and, most of all, integration: integration of information and information systems to provide business intelligence; integration of channels to enable the development and delivery of a single unified view of the customer; integration of resources, functions and processes to ensure a productive, customer-oriented working environment and competitive organisational performance. CRM is a complex task, but by adopting a strategic approach, as outlined in this chapter, organisations should be able to realise the substantial benefits of effective CRM and make progress on the journey towards achieving excellence in customer management.

Further reading

Christopher, M., Payne, A. and Ballantyne, D. (2002), *Relationship Marketing*, second edition, Oxford, UK: Butterworth-Heinemann.
This book focuses on the creation of stakeholder value and emphasises how quality and customer service are critical foundations for long-term customer relationships.
Friedman, L. G. and Furey, T. R. (1999), *The Channel Advantage: Going to Market with Multiple Sales Channels to Reach More Customers, Sell More Products, Make More Profit*, Oxford, UK: Butterworth-Heinemann; and Wilson, H., Street, R. and Bruce, L. (2008), *The Multichannel Challenge: Integrating Customer Experiences for Profit*, Oxford, UK: Butterworth-Heinemann.
Good treatments of issues relating to multi-channel integration.
Gentle, M. (2002), *The CRM Project Management Handbook*, London: Kogan Page; and, Siragher, N. (2001), *Carving Jelly: A Managers Reference to Implementing CRM*, High Wycombe, UK: Chiltern Publishing International Ltd.
Useful explorations of CRM implementation from experienced practitioners.
Golfarelli, M. and Rizzi, S. (2009), *Data Warehouse Design. Modern Principles and Methodologies*, New York: McGraw-Hill; Laberge, R. (2011), *The Data Warehouse Mentor: Practical Data Warehouse and Business Intelligence Insights*, New York: McGraw-Hill; Han, J., Kamber, M. and Pei, J. (2012), *Data Mining: Concepts and Techniques*, third edition, Burlington, MA: Morgan Kaufmann Publishers; and Tsiptsis, K. and Chorianopoulos, A. (2010), *Data Mining Techniques in CRM: Inside Customer Segmentation*, Chichester, UK: John Wiley & Sons.
Detailed insights into data warehousing and data mining.
Lovett, J. (2011), *Social Media Metrics Secrets*, Chichester, UK: John Wiley & Sons; Sterne, J. (2010), *Social Media Metrics: How to Measure and Optimize Your Marketing Investment*, Chichester, UK: John Wiley & Sons; and Sponder, M. (2012), *Social Media Analytics: Effective Tools for Building, Interpreting, and Using Metrics*, New York: McGraw-Hill.
Detailed exploration of social media metrics to support CRM.

Note

1   This chapter draws on material from: Payne, A. and Frow, P. (2005), 'A strategic framework for CRM', *Journal of Marketing*, 69(4): 167–176; Payne, A. and Frow, P. (2006), 'Customer relationship management: From strategy to implementation', *Journal of Marketing Management*, 22(1/2): 135–168; Payne, A. (2006), *The Handbook of CRM: Achieving Excellence in Customer Management*, Oxford, UK: Elsevier Butterworth-Heinemann; and Payne, A. and Frow, P. (2013), *Strategic Customer Management: Integrating CRM and Relationship Marketing*, Cambridge, UK: Cambridge University Press.

References

Aaker, D. A., Kumar, V., Day, G. S. and Leone, R. P. (2010), *Marketing Research*, tenth edition, New York: John Wiley & Sons.

Chidley, J. (2000), *Setting Customer-Based Standards for CRM*, BT internal document.

COPC (2004). Available at www.copc.com

Ebner, M., Hu, A., Levitt, D. and McCory, J. (2002), 'How to rescue CRM', *McKinsey Quarterly*, Special Edition: Technology, pp. 49–57.

Heskett, J. L., Sasser, W. E. (2010), 'The service profit chain: From satisfaction to ownership', in Maglio, P., Kieliszewski, C. and Spohrer, J. (eds) *Handbook of Service Science, Service Science: Research and Innovations in the Service Economy*, part 1, pp. 19–29.

Kaplan, R. S. and Norton D. P. (1996), *The Balanced Scorecard*, Boston, MA: Harvard Business School Press.

Kaplan, R. S. and Norton, D. P. (2004), *Strategy Maps: Converting Intangible Assets into Tangible Outcomes*, Boston, MA: Harvard Business School Press.

McDonald, M. and Dunbar, I. (2010), *Market Segmentation: How to Do It, How to Profit from It*, Oxford, UK: Goodfellow Publishing.

Mitussis, D., O'Malley, L. and Patterson, M. (2005), 'Mapping the reengagement of CRM with relationship marketing', *European Journal of Marketing*, 40(5/6): 572–589.

Payne, A. (2006), *The Handbook of CRM: Achieving Excellence in Customer Management*, Oxford, UK: Elsevier Butterworth-Heinemann.

Payne, A. and Frow, P. (2005), 'A strategic framework for CRM', *Journal of Marketing*, 69(4): 167–176.

Payne, A. and Frow, P. (2006), 'Customer relationship management: From strategy to implementation', *Journal of Marketing Management*, 22(1/2): 135–168.

Payne, A. and Frow, P. (2013), *Strategic Customer Management: Integrating CRM and Relationship Marketing*, Cambridge, UK: Cambridge University Press.

Payne, A., Storbacka, K. and Frow, P. (2008), 'Managing the co-creation of value', *Journal of the Academy of Marketing Science*, 36(1): 83–96.

Peppers, D. and Rogers, M. (1993), *The One-to-one Future: Building Business Relationships One Customer at a Time*, London: Piatkus Books.

Peppers, D. and Rogers, M. (2004), *Managing Customer Relationships: A Strategic Framework*, Chichester, UK: John Wiley & Sons.

Peters, T. (1984), 'Strategy follows structure: Developing distinctive skills', *California Management Review*, 26(3): 111–125.

Porter, M. E. (2008), 'The five competitive forces that shape strategy', *Harvard Business Review*, 86(1): 25–40.

QCI (2004), 'CMAT', available at www.qci.co.uk

Reichheld, F. F. and Sasser, W. E. (1990), 'Zero defections: Quality comes to services', *Harvard Business Review*, 68(5): 105–111.

Rucci, A. J., Kirn, S. P. and Quinn, R. T. (1998), 'The employee-customer-profit chain at Sears', *Harvard Business Review*, January-February: 83–97.

Ryals, L. and Payne, A. (2001), 'Customer relationship management in financial services: Towards information-enabled relationship marketing', *Journal of Strategic Marketing*, 9(1): 3–27.

Shukla, P. (2010), Relationship marketing and CRM, in Bidgoli, H. (ed.) *The Handbook of Technology Management, Volume 2: Supply Chain Management, Marketing and Advertising, and Global Management*, Hoboken, NJ: Wiley, pp. 462–472.

Vargo, S. L. and Lusch, R. F. (2004), 'Evolving to a new dominant logic for marketing', *Journal of Marketing*, 68(1): 1–17.

Part IV

Marketing applications and contexts of marketing

19 Services marketing

Toni Hilton

Introduction

It is difficult to overstate the importance of services given the way in which economies develop. Comprising three sectors (agriculture, industry and services), developing economies shift from reliance upon agriculture through industrialisation to post industrialisation, which is evidenced by an increasing reliance upon the service sector. Pine and Gilmore (1999) use the coffee bean to illustrate how economies develop and claim that even the service economy is being replaced by the 'experience economy'. Those that grow, harvest and sell the coffee beans receive very little for the 'commodity' compared with the price achieved per cup of coffee served in a five-star restaurant, or in one of the illustrious cafes in St. Mark's Square in Venice. They argue that customers are happy to pay this price for the experience of which the cup of coffee is a part.

The World Bank estimates that services account for only 35 per cent of the GDP in low income economies, compared with around 78 per cent of the UK GDP, which has a particularly strong reliance upon the financial services sector. Over 1.5 million people are employed within the UK NHS (National Health Service). It was the services sector that led both the UK and the US out of the recent recession.

Most organisations are involved in service provision in some way or another, whether they operate in the private, public, charity or business-to-business sectors. For many, their core business is a service such as healthcare, education, travel, delivery, maintenance or recruitment services. For others, service is part of their business and often revolves around ongoing customer support. Organisations can use service provision to gain a competitive advantage perhaps through more knowledgeable employees, faster delivery services or greater customisation, no matter what the core business is.

Services marketing theory is relatively young, because it took some time for the marketing discipline to accept the need for a distinct body of theory. Lyn Shostack, in her influential article (1977) argued that traditional marketing theory was myopic and had failed to create theories that were useful to practitioners in service-driven organisations, such as banking. This led to a dramatic increase in the quantity of academic articles published about services marketing.

Research and theory development since the 1980s focused upon identifying, understanding and resolving management problems associated with the characteristics and nature of service provision, particularly those arising from the reliance upon people-to-people interactions. Much of this research requires a cross-disciplinary approach. Managing employees involves HR management and service design, and delivery draws upon operations management. Indeed, the effective management of service organisations is an area where these three management disciplines combine to develop knowledge very happily for the benefit of practitioners. The recent rise in *technology-based self-service* (TBSS) illustrates how this inter-disciplinary approach has extended to encompass IT and engineering perspectives. Phrases such as 'service system' and 'service science' have emerged. Service science, management and engineering (SSME) was acknowledged as an emerging field of study by a symposium held at Cambridge University in July 2007.

Booms and Bitner (1981) extended the 'four Ps' (McCarthy 1960) of the marketing mix to include *people*, *process* and *physical evidence* to take account of four characteristics that differenti-ate services from products: *intangibility*, *inseparability*, *heterogeneity* and *perishability*. This chapter discusses the managerial implications of these characteristics as well as providing an alternative perspective. The extended marketing mix remains a useful way to analyse and manage the provi-sion of services. People and the physical evidence comprise the *tangible* or *visible* elements of the service. Although less visible, the process is crucial to the service experience. This section is impor-tant, because it introduces most of the management challenges associated with the provision of services, which are addressed throughout the rest of the chapter.

We then turn to the adoption of *theatre* and *factory metaphors* by services marketers, and look at how these enable service providers to address the operational and experiential imperatives. *Blue-printing* and *service mapping* are introduced as useful tools for designing and enhancing the service process. Discussion of the *servicescape* stresses the importance of ensuring that the physical environ-ment, including online, in which the service provision takes place is consistent with the positioning of the service.

A key aspect of managing service organisations is that of *service quality* and this has been the focus of considerable research since Zeithaml *et al.* published their pioneering 'gaps model' of service quality in 1985. Although this model has been critiqued over the years, it remains a benchmark against which other models are evaluated and is popular with practitioners. The importance of *per-ceived service quality* is discussed before identifying the dimensions of service quality and summarising the SERVQUAL measurement instrument.

The section on service *profitability* addresses the need to balance quality and productivity. Research identifying the role that customer *satisfaction* as well as customer and employee *loyalty* might play in achieving profitability is also considered.

Arguably, the most significant current influence within the services sector is the rapid growth of TBSS or *self-service technologies* (SST). These are technologies provided by an organisation to facilitate self-service by customers. In many cases, this will involve customers performing tasks previously done by employees (Hilton and Hughes 2013). This chapter ends with an overview of the management challenges inherent within TBSS.

A fundamental challenge to the way in which marketing had positioned services marketing as a sub-discipline arose in 2004 with the publication of what has proved to be a very influential arti-cle by Vargo and Lusch in the *Journal of Marketing*. They remind us that the fundamental concern of marketing is the process of exchange. Their thesis is that the basis for all exchange is service. Although a more emphatic argument than those made by services marketers, they distinguish *services* (plural), defined as outputs, from *service* (singular) defined as using one's resources for the benefit of another person or entity. Vargo and Lusch (2004) assert that manufactured goods exist only to facilitate service provision. So, we buy washing machines to perform a laundry service at home, and cars facilitate our personal transportation needs. Put in this light it appears that manufac-tured goods have facilitated self-service for decades and TBSS is not a new phenomena at all! The service-dominant logic (S-DL) thesis has become such a controversial contribution to marketing theory that it is appropriate to summarise much of the debate before discussing services marketing theories in greater depth.

Service-Dominant Logic (S-DL)

In summary, S-DL is concerned with how parties to an exchange integrate their resources to co-create value. Each aspect of this requires discussion.

First, the basis for all exchange is service. Service is the process of using one's resources for the benefit of another, and therefore goods only exist to facilitate service, or self-service. Product attributes refine the service performance. Washing machines vary in terms of load capacity, spin speeds and fabrics that can be laundered. Some cars provide a safer, faster or a more economical drive than others. In the business-to-business context there is an amazing array of photocopying machines available depending upon the service needs.

S-DL has done a terrific job in drawing attention to the broad range of resources that actors possess. Vargo and Lusch (2004) distinguish between two types of resources that both have the potential to create value when integrated with other resources. Operand resources, such as raw materials, are 'resources on which an operation or act is performed to produce an effect' (Vargo and Lusch 2004: 2). These are usually tangible, inert and passive, and require input from an active agent to realise value potential (Arnould *et al.* 2006). Operant resources are those employed to act on operand resources and on other operant resources to create value. These are usually intangible, such as knowledge, skills and labour (Arnould *et al.* 2006; Vargo and Lusch 2004). Vargo and Lusch (2004) emphasise the competitive advantage inherent within operant resources. Operant resources include the tacit knowledge of all actors.

S-DL requires the integration of actors' resources for co-creation to take place. There has been some debate in the S-DL literature over the terminology here. Co-production and co-creation have been used interchangeably by some authors, although Vargo and Lusch (2004) clearly identify two concepts. They associate co-creation with value and co-production with task performance to achieve the service provision. One outcome of resource integration processes is likely to be modified resources of the original actors (Hilton *et al.* 2012). In many cases, this is the purpose of the resource integration: education would be a good example.

Central to S-DL is an active, participatory role for customers as well as organisations. While economic theory views customers as passive consumers of value that is created and delivered by organisations, S-DL argues that value occurs at the time of use, consumption or experience of the product or service, i.e. 'value-in-use'. Consistent with this position is the notion that organisations offer *value propositions* to attract the resources of other actors. '*Actor*' is the preferred title for all participants in value creation and moves customers further away from the passive consumption role. It is the intended integration of resources by actors, which, Vargo and Lusch (2004) assert, results in value co-creation. This assertion is not universally accepted and attention has been drawn to the ontological inconsistency between this position and the S-DL claim that value is always, and uniquely, determined by the beneficiary, which is central to 'value-in-use'.

Hilton *et al.* (2012) argue that, while service can indeed be co-created (through resource integration), value cannot. They conceptualise service co-creation as a process comprising value potential, value propositions, resource integration and resource modification (see Figure 19.1). They assert that, because value is a personal evaluative judgement, it cannot be co-created. Value is realised by actors as an outcome of the service co-creation process, which they define as planned resource integration behaviours by actors intending to realise a value proposition.

This debate has some way to go; however, the concept of value propositions is currently gaining considerable attention from academic researchers (e.g. Frow *et al.* 2014) as it appears to offer a useful framework for practitioners to analyse the value potential of their resources and

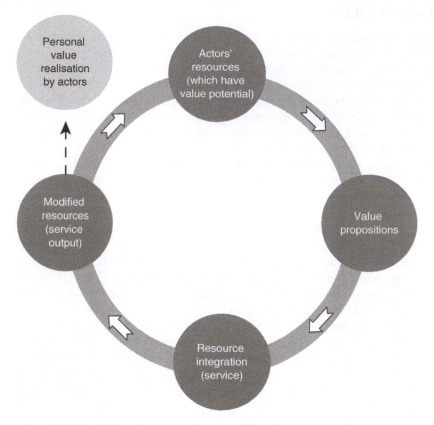

Figure 19.1 Model of service co-creation

Source: Hilton *et al.* (2012).

those of their customers. This will help to determine the knowledge and skills that customers might need to co-create the service, particularly if that service comprises an element of self-service. If customers do not have those operant resources, then the organisation will need to provide up-skilling opportunities. Value propositions are also a way for organisations to identify potential collaborators if they do not possess all of the required resources to achieve the value proposition alone.

The rest of this chapter draws upon the terminology and conceptualisation of S-DL where appropriate.

Characteristics of services

The characteristics that have become associated with services arise from the time when services marketing pioneers sought to establish how services differed from products to justify the need for new theory development. As a result, the four characteristics are essentially a list of ways in which services are 'not products'. However, they are a useful place to start to understand services and the managerial implications that arise.

Intangibility

The intangible nature of services raises risks for purchasers. Some are riskier than others depending upon whether they are high in:

- search factors;
- experience factors;
- credence factors.

Services high in search factors enable customers to identify information that influences perceptions of the risks involved prior to purchase. Performance claims by service providers are useful here. Food delivery services frequently provide a guaranteed delivery time or they provide the food free of charge.

A service that has to be experienced before customers can evaluate the value for money is said to be high in experience factors. Vacations are a good example: the experience of a holiday goes far beyond what you might see in a brochure.

Services that are high in credence factors are difficult to evaluate even after the experience. Professional services generally fall into this category. Most of us find it difficult to evaluate whether the services we receive from our doctors, lawyers, accountants, surveyors, car mechanics, vets, plumbers or electricians are value for money, because we do not have the professional knowledge to do so. These services are therefore perceived to be more risky and customers frequently seek high levels of reassurance from the service providers, or other users, before they are comfortable investing in the service provider.

Service organisations attempt to manage intangibility by adding as many tangible elements as possible. The additional marketing mix 'P' of *physical evidence* demonstrates the importance of the tangible elements of the service provision. Customers, or clients, frequently rely on the tangible elements when evaluating the provision, because they provide a more objective, or rational, basis than the subjective feelings they might have about their experiences. The physical environment in which the provision takes place is important, including the sights, sounds and smells. Iconic buildings in expensive parts of the city may lead clients to question the value for money they are getting, or it may raise their expectations regarding the performance outcomes. The opposite is also true. The service organisation should ensure that the physical surroundings as well as the image projected by the service providers are consistent with the service performance levels they aspire to deliver (market positioning).

Professional services firms provide brochures, and everyone has a website today. These frequently provide photographs of the service providers and a 'biopic' with information about the services they provide. Testimonials from previous clients are an opportunity to provide word-of-mouth advocacy for the organisation. Check lists 'evidence' the tasks that have been carried out during a car service and justify the bill. All of this helps to reduce the risk perceived by potential clients.

Heterogeneity

No two service providers perform a given service in exactly the same way and no two customers perceive the service provision in the same way. The performance of service providers will be influenced by the knowledge they have of the services they are providing, how they are feeling, what else is on their mind and their workload. Customers differ in terms of their expectations of service provision and this can affect their evaluations as well as how they are feeling. Previous good experiences of a given service can raise the bar for a new service provider, and poor previous experiences can result in a perception that another provider has gone the extra mile.

People are not machines and cannot be programmed to repeat perform at a prescribed quality standard. Technology-based service provision does seek to achieve this, but there remains the heterogeneity of customer evaluations.

Service providers seek to reduce performance variability through *service design* and establishing explicit service performance standards against which they measure their employees. Some service designs can be overly restrictive and there is a need to empower front-line staff to use their knowledge, expertise and judgement to adapt performance to meet the expectations and requirements of individual clients where possible. Maintaining service performance standards and getting the balance right between standardisation and flexibility is difficult and, unfortunately, *service failures* are inevitable. It is therefore important to design in *service recovery* processes.

The heterogeneity and inseparability (below) characteristics give rise to the additional 'P' of *people*. The growth in self-service and particularly those that are technology-driven, result in the acknowledgement of customers as *partial employees* and S-DL's reference to *actors* reminds managers that customers are active participants whose contribution needs to be managed as well as employees.

Inseparability

In many service operations production and consumption of the service are contemporaneous and it is not possible to separate the provider from the customer or beneficiary of the service. In addition to the additional marketing mix element of *people*, *process* also becomes relevant, because it is by engaging in the service process that customers experience the service provision. Inseparability of the customer from the service provision frequently requires the management of customer-to-customer interactions and the management of one customer's behaviour upon another. Prompt attendance is a universal expectation for appointment-driven services, such as healthcare, because of the impact upon other patients. Refraining from smoking and maintaining the cleanliness of facilities are other examples and most people know how they should behave in the theatre or cinema.

Although service providers may prepare in advance, actual service provision generally takes place in the presence of the beneficiary. This is true of personal services, such as medical services, hairdressing and beauty treatments. However, this is not always the case in professional services such as car servicing and many aspects of legal and accounting services and medical testing services. In these cases, it remains true that the service provider is inseparable from the service provision.

Waiting times and how customers are treated during the service all alter the experience on any given occasion. The experience of the daily train journey to work will be different for those who are standing in corridors from those sitting comfortably in seats. Waiting for a table at a busy restaurant can involve a tedious wait standing around at the restaurant entrance, or it could involve a relaxing drink in a purpose-designed bar area.

In self-service, it is the customer who is more likely to be inseparable from the service, because they are the ones performing it. Managing customers as *partial employees* is a growing challenge for many service organisations. They need to ensure that customers have the requisite knowledge and skills to perform the tasks, and are well supported while they do so. This has led to additional new employee roles, which are unlikely to reduce even when customers have gained the skills required, because they are needed for service recovery tasks. This also changes the relationship between the customer and the customer-facing employee and presents another challenge for service organisations, as they need to deal with the frustrations of exasperated customers who may feel that they are paying for the privilege of performing the service themselves!

Perishability

Unlike goods, services cannot be inventoried or stored. The empty seat on the plane from London to Singapore cannot be replaced by the airline with the consequential revenue implications. Perishability problems are compounded by the challenges of distinct peaks and troughs, which are inherent in many services. Ensuring sufficient trains during rush hour is challenging when expensive rolling stock will be underutilised for the rest of the day. Perishability requires careful demand forecasting, along with differential pricing and promotion strategies to even out demand where possible. Creative employment contracts may also contribute. These issues draw attention to the importance of managing the *process*.

When demand exceeds supply, customers have to wait, and waiting is a major source of dissatisfaction for customers. Managers can reduce *actual* waiting times, or reduce *perceptions* of waiting times or manage the *impact* of delays (Sarel and Marmorstein 1998). Reducing actual waiting times can be achieved through demand forecasting and employee allocation strategies. SST may also play a role. Splitting the service into multiple elements may result in customers experiencing multiple encounters with various employees. Disney theme parks offer a good illustration of impression management that reduces the perceptions of waiting times. Lines constantly move, even though they may be long, and there are frequently shows to watch that manage expectations and behaviours in preparation for the ride. During peak usage times, delays are probably unavoidable so employees should show empathy and understanding for the plight of the customer. The extent to which customers perceive the staff genuinely care for them is likely to influence their reaction to the wait.

Critique of this traditional approach

Inseparability and perishability are two areas where the traditional four characteristics model can be justifiably critiqued on the basis of contrivance, because it results from a goods-oriented or manufacturing-oriented mindset. Hence, the characteristics are no more than a list of ways in which services are 'not goods'. Beaven and Scotti (1990) made this assertion and devised a set of characteristics from a 'service-oriented' perspective. These are useful in highlighting the importance of the active role of the customer, the personal evaluation of service experiences, which leave 'concrete impressions' and the non-perishable nature of many service outcomes. It is quite clear that many legal services, such as a property conveyance or a divorce, have outcomes and impressions that are quite easy to recall and are certainly not perishable in the way that service characteristics are traditionally described (see Figure 19.2).

Beaven and Scotti (1990) propose the need to consider the following aspects of service provision within their SOAR model:

- **S**cripts: the understanding and expectations of the service process. The roles played by the customer and the service provider.
- **O**utlay: all financial and non-financial costs incurred by customers when accessing, participating in and consuming services, many of which are in addition to the price paid to the service provider for the service. These include costs of travel, time involved and psychological costs.

Manufacturing-oriented thinking	Service-oriented thinking
1 Services are abstract and intangible products.	1 Services are processes with outcomes that can be perceived directly and indirectly, leaving concrete impressions.
2 Services are non-standardised heterogeneous outputs.	
3 Services are instantly perishable and cannot be produced in advance or stored for future sale.	2 Services are personal experiences that can be uniquely tailored to meet individual needs and expectations.
4 Services are simultaneously produced and consumed; customer involvement often interrupts operations and interferes with efficiency.	3 Services are processes that are created and experienced, with outcomes that are often distinct, direct and imperishable.
	4 Services are encounters that afford opportunities for greater satisfaction through participation, shared responsibility and timely feedback.

Figure 19.2 Manufacturing vs. service oriented thinking

Source: Adapted from Beaven and Scotti (1990).

- **A**ccommodation: availability of the service and ease of use for the customer, including the ease of physical access (public transport, car parking, physical disability issues) and opening hours as well as the physical environment within which the service takes place; the need to provide the service in the most convenient way, to reduce customer outlay and to encourage participation.
- **R**epresentation: the promises made regarding the way in which the service will be performed and the service quality specifications. These include implicit as well as explicit promises and representations in organisational brochures or advertisements.

Service goals

Services marketers adopt two metaphors depending upon the goal: the factory and the theatre.

The theatre metaphor

Grove and Fisk (1983) conceptualise services as a dramatic performance similar to a theatrical production. The goal of the theatre metaphor is 'rave reviews' from the audience (customers). The key components of the service experience are the setting, the actors, the audience and the performance. Management attention is directed to the content of the service and particularly the interactions between the 'actors' who are the contact personnel and the audience who are the customers. The *roles* and *scripts* of the actors and audience become important, as does the design of the service setting, the physical environment. Customers are likened to an audience that are stimulated into the 'experience' by cues that are stage-managed. The service is likened to a stage play that incorporates the hedonistic elements of experiential service consumption, with attention drawn to the service *performance* rather than the process. The visible elements of the performance are referred to as *front-stage* with the invisible elements being *back-stage*.

This metaphor is a reminder of the important role that contact employees and customers have, as well as the impact that one customer might have on another (*co-consumption*). It is useful to consider how encounters might be enhanced through scripts and stage-management. However, there is still a need for actors to ad lib when lines are forgotten and to demonstrate initiative to respond to *critical incidents*, such as the sickness of an actor or the ceiling falling onto the audience.

The factory metaphor

If the goal is *efficiency*, then the service can be likened to a factory. This focuses management attention on the efficient processing of customers by reducing waiting bottlenecks and acknowledging the importance of quality control. The factory metaphor views service as a system and has led to a number of helpful structural models to describe service provision. The first of these is the 'servuction system' model presented by Bateson (1992), but originally developed by Eric Langeard and Pierre Eiglier. This model identifies the bundle of benefits that a customer receives from each service experience as a direct result of their interaction with the visible elements of the service system. Lovelock (1992) proposed the services marketing system, which conceptualises service businesses as comprising three overlapping systems and requiring the integration of the functional areas of marketing, operations and human resources:

1   the service operations system;
2   the service delivery system;
3   the service marketing system.

The *service operations system* generally comprises the *invisible* elements of the service, such as stock control and IT training for staff, although there are some operational aspects that customers are exposed to. Customers might see cleaning taking place or replacement shelf filling or they might even be asked to participate in staff training exercises. Some organisations make a feature of exposing elements of their operations as part of the service experience. Restaurants might expose their chefs to evidence their expertise and influence customer perceptions of the quality of the service. However, it can be argued that this moves the preparation of the food to the service delivery system, because it becomes a visible part of the customer experience.

The *service delivery system* comprises the *visible* elements of the service operating system, employees and the physical facilities, including relevant equipment, as well as exposure to other customers. Service providers frequently benefit from interactions between their customers and they do need to manage these effectively, as these interaction opportunities do give rise to *critical incidents*. Waiting times need to be managed well and, where it can be observed, consistent treatment of customers needs to occur. The physical facilities should be consistent with the image that the service business creates. Bitner (1992) coined the term, *servicescape* to describe the physical environment.

The *service marketing system* comprises elements of the service experience that may contribute to customer evaluations of the experience and the organisation, but which are not specifically part of the delivery system. Some of these are within the control of the organisation, such as advertising, and others, such as word-of-mouth, are not. Understanding that the organisation cannot control messages regarding its service performance is increasingly important in today's technologically enhanced climate, where the ability to communicate to large audiences immediately is pervasive. *Service failures* can be instantly broadcast to millions globally via social media (e.g. Twitter, Facebook or Sina Weibo), so it is imperative to identify *critical incidents* within the service design and to *empower employees* to exercise judgement and initiative to manage *service recovery* processes. It is imperative to track what is going on in the 'cyber world' and respond where appropriate.

Balancing marketing effectiveness and operational efficiency

There is greater opportunity for personalisation of service provision than within product manufacture. However, the greater the personalisation the less opportunity there is for cross-utilisation of resources and, therefore, operational efficiencies are lost. Smaller organisations can overlook the need to identify the true operational costs of personalisation and fail to price their services appropriately.

Service organisations may also overlook the effort that customers put into the service. This is not limited to the resources that they put into achieving the service itself (see S-DL discussion above). A big difference between products and services is that product manufacturers put a lot of effort into getting their products into the right place for the customer to buy. Food manufacturers ensure that their products are on the supermarket shelves and are well aware of the negative impact that 'out of stock' situations have on their business. Customers frequently have to travel to a specified location to access the service, which will add both time and money to the cost of the service to them. They will have planned the visit into their day, maybe taken time off work to attend. This is especially true of personal and professional services. Some services, such as medical, dental and legal services, are entered into with reluctance and trepidation. Beaven and Scotti (1990) use *outlay* to refer to the financial and non-financial costs incurred by customers when accessing, participating in and consuming services, many of which are in addition to the price paid to the service provider. These include costs of travel, time involved and psychological costs. They urge service providers to consider *accommodation*, by which they mean the need to provide the service in the most convenient way, to reduce customer outlay and encourage participation. Both concepts are relevant when considering capacity management and growing service businesses.

Capacity management

Our 24/7 world, where customers expect to access services at a time of their choosing, is challenging for service providers. They need to understand the cost of provision across the day, week or year depending on the service business. A 24-hour supermarket will need to provide an appropriate level of services to ensure that the customer experience of accessing the service at both peak and trough periods is satisfactory while managing their costs, particularly when customer 'footfall' is low. Providers of personal services such as beauty treatments and hairdressers frequently close on Mondays, while operating extended hours on Fridays and Saturdays. Restaurants might offer 'two meals for the price of one' before 7 p.m. and bars might offer price reductions on drinks during 'happy hour'. Train companies provide a range of prices depending on the time of day and day of the week. Travel companies and tourist attractions vary their prices across the year.

At peak times, customers can experience very different service provision, which can create frustration and dissatisfaction. Peak hour rail travel into and out of London, England evidences this differential provision well. Commuter trains are crammed full and many passengers have to stand, even though they pay the same price as those with a seat. Theme parks usually manage queues for their most popular rides well, providing activities to maintain interest and update likely wait times to manage expectations.

Growing service businesses

The growth potential for service businesses ultimately depends upon people: the service providers and the customers that can access the service. The fixed location of a service business can be a major competitive advantage. Good locations that attract a high level of customers, because they are easily accessed by public transport or have good parking facilities, facilitate growth. It is now common-place to find smaller service businesses, such as dry cleaners and travel agents, renting space within larger supermarkets. They aim to attract more customers by providing multiple reasons to visit the one location. UK supermarkets provide free bus services to draw more customers to their site.

Conversely, the more specialised the service provided by an individual, the less likely that business can grow by increasing the number of customers. A fabulous hairdresser can only manage so many haircuts a week no matter how well sought after they might be. Such an expert might grow business revenue through increasing the price of each haircut. Alternatively, expertise-based businesses can increase the number of experts able to deliver the services. This frequently happens with professional services firms, such as legal and financial services.

The internet offers a way for service providers to reach a wider audience. This can be useful for fixed location businesses that do not require customers to be present while they perform the service. Travel services and some professional services can be delivered in this way.

The internet can also establish a new service industry beyond national boundaries. Cosmetic surgery tourism is a rapidly growing global service industry that has prospered largely because of the internet.

The internet provides a mechanism for emerging economies to develop too. Within emerging economies, such as Africa, adoption of mobile technology has resulted in increased access to financial services. According to Kathleen Caulderwood (2014), 68 per cent of Kenyans with mobile phones use them for mobile payments, compared with around 8 per cent outside of sub-Saharan Africa. There is also high access (approximately 70 per cent) to social networking sites such as Facebook and Twitter. Due to the very high number of people living in developing economies, key countries such as China, India and Brazil have significantly more internet users than developed economies, although in percentage terms penetration of the population within those countries remains much lower (see Figure 19.3).

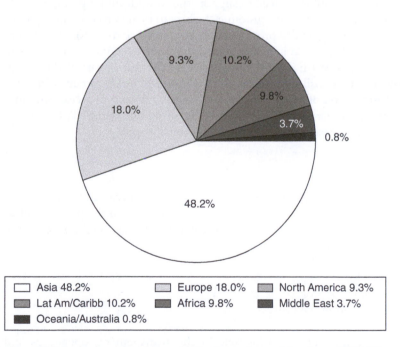

Figure 19.3 Internet users in the world distributon by world regions – 2012 Q2

Reproduced with permission from Internet World Stats available at: http://www.internetworldstats.com/stats.htm

Table 19.1 World internet usage statistics

World Regions	Population (2015 Est.)	Population % of World	Internet Users 30 Nov 2015	Penetration (% Population)	Growth 2000–2015	Users % of Table
World Internet Usage and Population Statistics November 30, 2015						
Africa	1,158,355,663	16.0 %	330,965,359	28.6 %	7,231.3 %	9.8 %
Asia	4,032,466,882	55.5 %	1,622,084,293	40.2 %	1,319.1 %	48.2 %
Europe	821,555,904	11.3 %	604,147,280	73.5 %	474.9 %	18.0 %
Middle East	236,137,235	3.3 %	123,172,132	52.2 %	3,649.8 %	3.7 %
North America	357,178,284	4.9 %	313,867,363	87.9 %	190.4 %	9.3 %
Latin America/ Caribbean	617,049,712	8.5 %	344,824,199	55.9 %	1,808.4 %	10.2 %
Oceania/Australia	37,158,563	0.5 %	27,200,530	73.2 %	256.9 %	0.8 %
WORLD TOTAL	7,259,902,243	100.0 %	3,366,261,156	46.4 %	832.5 %	100.0 %

Service design

Service design covers both the process and the physical environment. Services comprise visible and invisible elements. The visible elements are the people and the physical evidence elements of the extended marketing mix (see above). The process elements can be both visible and invisible and can involve employees and fellow customers (co-customers). Elements of the service operations system may not be seen by customers, but they need to support the smooth running of the visible elements of the service, which are evaluated by the customer. Failure to maintain computer systems results in the inability of customer-facing staff to provide a consistent service to customers. Where customers access computer systems directly, as in TBSS, such failures are even more critical. Most services will have a website, and it is worth determining a strategy for that as part of the design process. Understanding how customers will want to use the website will be important. If it is for self-service purposes, then consideration of which services customers will want to access, and how much knowledge and skill (*operant resources*) they will need to do so will be required. Two techniques are frequently used for service design: blueprinting and service mapping.

Blueprinting

Much like the plans of an architect, blueprinting provides a comprehensive visual model of a service process. This enables management to identify strong and weak links in the process and to discuss the efficiency and effectiveness impact that potential structural changes might have on the process and organisation. Normally, a blueprint would:

1   break down the process into logical steps;
2   recognise the variability within the process;
3   identify the *invisible* elements within the process.

Blueprinting provides an opportunity for discussion within the management, operations and service delivery teams as they identify and agree on the logical steps, points of variability and

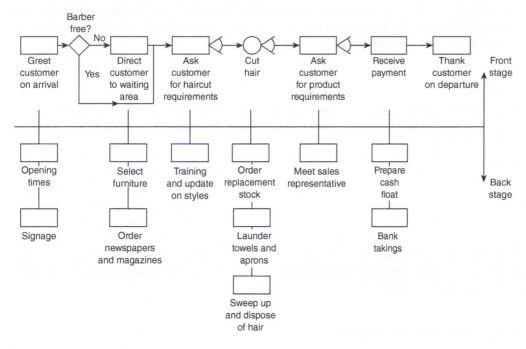

Figure 19.4 Blueprint for a one man gent's barber

Source: Baron *et al.* (2009), *Services Marketing: Text and Cases*, third edition, Basingstoke, UK: Palgrave Macmillan, reproduced with permission of Palgrave Macmillan. The full, published version of this publication is available at http://www.palgrave.com/products/title.aspx?pid=278695

potential 'weak links' – the *service failure* points. Figure 19.4 provides an example of a blueprint for a one-man gent's barber. The blueprint identifies visible and invisible elements using the theatre terminology of front-stage and back-stage. The fan symbol indicates variability within the process. Variability can be either:

- planned and controlled by the service provider drawn from a range of potential actions;
- unplanned, as a result of potential events that might occur.

So, the first fan indicates variability that is planned by the barber as a result of the type of haircut required by the customer. This will be drawn from a limited range of options. The second fan, following a circle, indicates unplanned variability as no two haircuts are truly identical. Individual head shapes and hair properties, as well as the barber's ability to tackle these, will result in variable outcomes. There are tolerance levels built into different cuts, such as 'short-back-and-sides' or 'trim' or 'square-neck'. A trim that resembles a 'short-back-and-sides' is likely to breach that tolerance, become a quality issue and result in a *service failure*.

Blueprinting can be a very useful tool particularly when seeking to provide many employees with an overview of a highly complex organisation in which they might perform a small part of the service, and is particularly useful for those involved in back-stage activities to understand how they support high-quality front-stage service provision. However, blueprinting is acknowledged to be a very difficult thing to do, in part because it should be done from the customer perspective and, in practice, this rarely happens.

Service mapping

Building on the blueprinting approach, service maps add two features. First, they pay greater attention to customer interactions with the service organisation, distinguishing customer actions from service contact employees.

Second, they add vertical layers to separate invisible elements performed by front-line employees, support staff and management services. The *line of interaction* distinguishes customer and front-line employee roles within the service encounter. The *line of visibility* identifies which tasks performed by front-line employees will be visible or invisible to the customer. The *line of internal interaction* identifies elements of the service operation system that support the service delivery system and distinguishes back-stage activities that support the service delivery system from those that support the business as a whole. The *line of implementation* identifies management services that support the business, which might include production of sales reports or costing data and the monthly accounts.

Using blueprinting and service mapping

There are five main benefits of adopting diagrammatic approaches for service design.

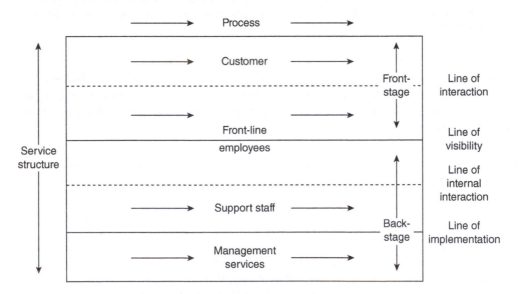

Figure 19.5 The layers and features of the service map

1   *Identify service failures and implement 'fail-safeing'*

Designing services is challenging, because the involvement of people as service providers as well as customers renders successful service provision complex. It is impossible to standardise the experience, and evaluation of that experience, in the same way that is possible to manufacture products to a set quality standard. No two people share exactly the same service experience. Some may wait longer; some may be seated while others stand. Individual tolerances differ between people so a 15-minute wait may be fine for one, but totally unacceptable for another person. Each point of contact with the service provision provides an opportunity for customer evaluation. Evaluations that are either satisfying or dissatisfying are considered *critical incidents*. Given the reliance on individual subjectivities, it is inevitable that things will go wrong, *critical incidents* will result in dissatisfaction and *service failure* will occur. It is therefore important to design *service recovery* strategies into the service process.

Diagrammatic approaches facilitate the identification of points within the service process that have greater opportunity to result in a *service failure*. Once identified, *fail-safes* can be designed into the process to reduce the risk of human error resulting in service failure. Dental surgeries, hospitals and hairdressers frequently text appointment reminders. Plumbing, broadband providers and energy companies have started to do the same to ensure that they do not have to bear the cost of turning up to an empty home.

2   *Ensuring safety*

Service providers, such as schools, hospitals, theme parks and airlines, are charged with ensuring the health and safety of their customers when on their premises. Restaurants are frequently monitored for cleanliness and adherence to the hygienic preparation of food. A study of butchers' shops within the UK (Worsfold 2001) discovered that hand washing did not generally occur between handling money and handling meat. Such practices clearly have safety implications. Diagrammatic attention to all elements of the service process frequently identifies back-stage activities that are missing.

3   *Identify complexity and divergence and address service positioning*

Complexity relates to the number of steps and sequences and the interrelationships between them. Divergence relates to the degree of planned scope or latitude that contact employees have. A business that seeks to focus on efficiency might use the diagrams to identify opportunities to reduce complexity and divergence in order to reduce costs within the service process. The barber may choose not to sell any hair products. This would reduce the time and effort spent liaising with suppliers and increase the time spent cutting hair. Conversely, they might reposition their business by increasing the range of products they sell, adding massage chairs or rent out a chair to another barber thereby increasing complexity.

4   *Stimulate creativity*

Service process diagrams can stimulate innovation and discussion, particularly around complexity and divergence of the offering, which will influence market positioning. They are especially helpful for new businesses, or for those businesses that have reached a significant point in their development.

5   *Ensure responsiveness, fulfilment and delivery to support self-service*

These diagrammatic techniques are very useful in identifying the invisible elements of self-service, where the customer is also invisible. This places particular demands on the fulfilment elements of the business. In the early days of the internet, service businesses that had performance standards for face-to-face service frequently overlooked the need to put in place appropriate standards for responding to and fulfilling the self-service orders.

Designing the physical environment: the servicescape

Servicescape (Bitner 1992) refers to the manmade, physical surroundings in which services are delivered and is important in conveying an image consistent with the market position of that business. Professional service providers seek environments consistent with a professional image and one that is consistent with the fees that they charge. Dentists might hang mobiles from the ceiling to provide a relaxing distraction for their patients. Supermarkets might pump the aroma of freshly baked bread through the store. Teaching institutions experiment with colours to create conducive learning environments. Customers should feel at ease in a service environment, so the servicescape includes air quality and temperature as well as the lighting, sounds and aromas. Customers expect to be able to regulate the temperature of their hotel room. The level of noise created by background music can put off some restaurant customers.

The physical environment can influence the behaviours of customers and employees, so it needs to be consistent with the nature of the business, the time that the customer spends on site and the expectations created by the market position. A dry cleaner could take a utilitarian approach, which would not be acceptable for a premium fashion store. Many premium service businesses, who seek to provide an enhanced customer experience, design their physical environment to provide a more hedonistic experience. Customers paying for premium-priced hotels expect larger beds with better quality mattresses, pillows and fluffier towels than at cheaper hotels. It is interesting to compare Changi airport with Heathrow. Heathrow has adopted a functional and utilitarian approach to the physical environment, whereas Changi has incorporated, among other things, a themed indoor orchid garden complete with streams, bridges, seats and tropical fish. There is, of course, a balance to be struck and the environment still needs to be operationally efficient. As a guide, the longer a customer spends on site, the more likely it is that the purpose of the visit is hedonic, and therefore the servicescape should be designed to encourage affective responses. Conversely, short visits suggest utilitarian purposes, so the servicescape should be designed for efficient throughput.

E-scapes: online and SST

The term 'e-scapes' originally referred to online environments. However, it is probably useful to broaden usage to include self-service provision accessed electronically, whether remotely through the internet or in situ at the point of service. Indeed, there is a trend towards both environments operating together as in online check-in for air travel. Customers now travel to airports with boarding passes printed at home or sent to their mobile to 'drop' their bags and proceed to the plane.

Websites are frequently the first point of contact with contemporary service businesses from universities to premium hotels. Website design needs to consider how customers will navigate the site to ensure that it is both functional (efficient) and enjoyable (effective). Customers expect websites to do more than provide information, and their expectations regarding response times can create service quality issues for service providers.

Organisations adopting SST in situ as well as online will need to design the self-service technologies to accommodate diversity in physical operant resources available to customers, such as eyesight and dexterity, as well as cognitive resources, such as familiarity with technology and material resources, including computer/broadband access, credit cards and bank accounts. It should be as intuitive to use to the broadest range of people as possible and free from jargon and technical terminology. Hilton *et al.* (2013) point out that, 'the tacit knowledge held by employees must be codified into the SST to overcome consumer suspicions around the difficulty of achieving the "best price" or gaining access to the most useful information' (Hilton *et al.* 2013: 8). Their study revealed that people frequently question the ability of SST to take account of discounts, such as pensioner travel rates, which results in a preference for interacting with employees.

Service quality

Service quality has attracted significant attention from academic researchers as well as practitioners and remains one of the most researched areas of services marketing. High service quality standards can create a competitive advantage and therefore is frequently a strategic imperative. Organisations with a 24-hour helpline will be able to help more customers than one that operates only 8 a.m. to 6 p.m. Service quality is considered to be a customer-driven judgement or evaluation and is therefore identified and measured as a customer perception.

Perceived service quality is the gap between customer perceptions and their expectations of a service. Parasuraman, Zeithaml and Berry (PZB) identified four factors that might influence customer expectations.

1 word-of-mouth communications. Today this would include social media. These are not managed by the organisation so differ from point 4 below;
2 personal needs and preferences;
3 past experience of a particular service provider or others in the same service sector;
4 external communications such as advertising or other representations that are managed by the organisation.

Perceived service quality

Defining, measuring and monitoring quality is more challenging for services than it is for physical goods. Fresh produce can be graded on size, shape and colour, and manufactured products are rejected based upon strict adherence to manufacturing tolerances. Such standardisation is impossible when services are performed, and evaluated, by a diverse range of people. Additionally, the evaluation of physical goods relates to the final outcome: the tangible product. Much customer evaluation of services relates to the service delivery process (the performance) as well as the final outcome. In credence-based services, such as medical and legal services, customers are only able to judge the service delivery process and make assumptions regarding the outcome, based upon the fact that things, 'seem to be ok'.

Distinctions have been drawn between objective measures of quality and subjective customer perceptions. Grönroos (1983) identifies two quality dimensions:

1 technical quality: the relatively quantifiable aspects which are frequently referred to as *what* is being done;
2 functional quality: *how* the technical quality is performed or delivered.

Dimensions of service quality

PZB pioneered research into the dimensions of service quality. Originally a list of ten, a model comprising five factors, or determinants, emerged, which are known as RATER:

1 reliability: dependability of the service provider and accuracy of performance;
2 assurance: knowledge and courtesy of employees and their ability to inspire trust and confidence;

3   tangibles: including the physical environment (servicescapes);
4   empathy: caring, individual attention provided;
5   responsiveness: promptness and helpfulness.

Using the RATER variables, PZB proposed a conceptual framework known as the *Gaps Model*, which identifies possible causes of service quality shortfalls and a measurement instrument: SERVQUAL. Both have been widely adopted by academic researchers and practitioners.

PZB label the gap between customer expectations and perceptions as Gap 5. They then identify four potential causes of shortfalls in perceived service quality.

• Gap 1: the gap between customers' expectations and how management perceive customer expectations;
• Gap 2: the gap between management perception of customers' expectations and service quality specifications;
• Gap 3: the gap between service quality specifications and actual service delivery;
• Gap 4: the gap between service delivery and external communications – how the service performance is represented that gives rise to expectations. This is also known as the *promises gap*.

Gap 1 occurs when management are unaware of customer expectations; Gap 2 when management are aware of customer expectations, but set specific service performance standards that do not achieve them. Alternatively, correct service quality specifications are mandated, but not achieved by employees who may not have the resources (operant or operand) to perform to those standards. They may not have the correct training or the specifications may not have been communicated effectively. These situations give rise to Gap 3. Gap 4 occurs where the organisation over promises and under delivers, maybe due to poor internal communications. Beaven and Scotti (1990) specifically address this situation within the 'representation' element of SOAR.

The SERVQUAL research instrument

SERVQUAL comprises 22 quality-related measurement items drawn from the 5 RATER service quality dimensions. The original instrument was designed for use in a banking context, so researchers often modify the items. SERVQUAL remains popular, because it is easy to administer, is a useful starting point to understand the academic approach to measuring service quality and provides clear direction for organisations seeking to measure and improve service quality. Customers rate the importance of each of the dimensions for the ideal or excellent service organisation (expectations) and then rate the performance of the researched organisation (quality perception) on the same dimensions. The gap between the two scores provides the perceived service quality gap.

Although there have been a number of criticisms of SERVQUAL, of which the following three are the most enduring and persuasive, researchers still use SERVQUAL.

1   The SERVQUAL dimensions are not generic and therefore need to be modified to the researched context (see paragraph above).
2   The timing of the expectations measurement is significant. Ideally, the expectations element should be completed before the service has been experienced and, because this is not always practical, the majority of SERVQUAL research involves customers completing both elements at the same time. Clow and Vorhies (1993) found that the consumption experience influences the measurement of expectations.

3   Teas (1993) argues that it is difficult to use perceptions–expectations (P-E) scores to indicate comparative quality of services. A customer may perceive the quality experience to be
equivalent to their expectations and their expectations might be very high, so they score
both at 6 out of the possible 7. In that case, the P-E score would be 0. If another customer is
pessimistic about the experience, they might give an expectation score of 1. If they were to
provide a perception score of 3, then the P-E score will be 2 indicating a performance that
exceeds expectations.

Service profitability

Costing service provision is challenging. It would be foolhardy to prioritise the achievement of
customer satisfaction without regard to resource allocation priorities and the overall cost of the
service. It is claimed that satisfied customers will increase long-term revenues and profitability.
So prioritising customer satisfaction is said to be a *revenue emphasis*. Accountants and operations
management tend to emphasise the financial benefits of operational improvements that increase
efficiency and reduce costs. Total quality management (TQM), Six Sigma and statistical process
control (SPC) are all examples of quality programmes that adopt this *cost emphasis*. The *dual emphasis*
combines the two approaches, arguing that the greatest financial benefits will accrue to organisations that are able to reduce costs through efficiency while also improving customer satisfaction to
increase revenue. Research findings are mixed and appear to suggest a difference between those
organisations *trying* to achieve a dual emphasis and those that *achieve* it. It appears that the process
of achievement may increase short-term costs (Baron *et al.* 2009).

Profit impact of marketing strategies (PIMS) project

The PIMS project continues to provide persuasive support for a positive relationship between
perceived quality and return on investment (ROI). Gale (1994) summarises the key findings from
PIMS as:

1   superior quality leads to higher selling prices;
2   achieving superior quality does not mean higher costs;
3   superior quality drives profitability.

Such findings are extremely appealing, but caution should be exercised for a number of reasons:

1   Measuring quality is challenging and PIMS adopts a particular measurement approach that
results in classifying businesses into one of five categories:

   a   inferior quality;
   b   somewhat worse quality;
   c   about the same quality;
   d   somewhat better quality;
   e   superior quality.

2   The relationship between quality measures and specific financial indicators differ between
industries and business sectors.
3   Some of the earlier measures within the PIMS database were arrived at through their assessment of customers' perceptions and were not drawn directly from customers.

4   PIMS does not explicitly explore the causal processes by which quality influences profitability.
5   The PIMS database comprises large organisations, so findings may not be generalisable to the smaller organisations that tend to characterise the services sectors.

Quality, productivity and profitability programme

Evert Gummesson (1992) and his colleagues in Sweden use actual company case studies to examine the interactions between the 'triplets' of quality, productivity and profitability. They suggest that each of the triplets has a 'tribal' following that is primarily concerned with particular aspects of the business.

- The 'productivity tribe' is concerned with cost reduction.
- The 'quality tribe' is concerned with revenue generation.
- The 'profitability tribe' is concerned with cost reduction and revenue generation and therefore seek to balance the concerns of the other two tribes.

However, once again, there are difficulties in measuring the relationships between the three triplets, because they are not easy to define and so they are unable to endorse their original findings that appeared to support the following hypotheses that:

1   Productivity improvements increase profits.
2   Quality improvements increase productivity.
3   Quality improvements increase profits.

As a result, their model remains conceptual and without firm empirical support.

The customer pyramid

Not all customers are equally profitable to the organisation. The Pareto principle (the 80:20 rule) holds that disproportionate value is contributed by a minority of customers. Organisations from banks to airlines categorise their customers according to the value they contribute in both one-off transactions and over a period of time. Airline passengers receive differential service levels depending upon the price they pay (first, business or economy class) and their contribution over time is rewarded through frequent flyer point schemes as well as the annual categorisation into, for instance, the 'gold', 'silver' or 'bronze' tiers of Singapore Airlines.

Zeithaml *et al.* (2001) propose categorising customers into one of four tiers depending upon the amount they spend, the cost of servicing them and their potential to spread positive word-of-mouth. They say the pyramid approach facilitates well-informed decisions regarding resource allocation and ensures that the best customers are not underserved. It is also possible to increase profitability by managing customers between tiers by encouraging customers to increase their spend in order to achieve higher service levels. Airlines manage the frequent flyer tiers annually, which can lead to customer disappointment at, for instance, being sent out a silver card instead of a gold card.

Satisfaction, loyalty and profitability

Influential articles published in the *Harvard Business Review* in the late 1990s drew considerable attention to the effects of customer and employee loyalty on profitability. Reichheld and

Sasser (1990) published results of customer defections over a range of service sectors, concluding that defections 'have a surprisingly powerful impact on the bottom line'. Their findings suggest that:

- a loyal customer generates more profit over time;
- a reduction in customer defections of five per cent can boost profits by 25 per cent to 85 per cent.

They rationalise that customers become more profitable over time because of:

- a reduction in operating costs per customer, because first-time customers frequently incur one-off costs;
- a 'trading up' of customers over time as they become more familiar with and confident in the service;
- the free advertising they provide through advocacy and positive word-of-mouth.

These findings inspired researchers to examine the relationship between customer satisfaction, service quality and customer loyalty and led to the development of the satisfaction-profit chain (Anderson and Mittal 2000) and the service-profit chain (Heskett *et al.* 1994). The key difference between these two models is that the satisfaction-profit chain focuses entirely on the customers, while the service-profit chain also models the influence of employees and internal service quality on customer satisfaction. The links between the variables in the satisfaction-profit chain are said to be asymmetric and nonlinear (Anderson and Mittal 2000), which means that the impact of increases and decreases may not be of the same magnitude. Anderson and Mittal (2000) claim that decreases in customer satisfaction are more detrimental than the benefits gained from an equivalent increase in satisfaction.

Employee loyalty

Although there are no definitive studies of the impact of employee loyalty on customer satisfaction, Schlesinger and Heskett (1991) warn service organisations against the 'cycle of failure'. Cutting costs to achieve short-term goals, which increases employee turnover and results in fewer, less knowledgeable contact personnel, may negatively impact on the service experience of customers. Dissatisfied customers who complain or exhibit negative feelings towards employees may demotivate remaining staff, leading to further employee turnover with its consequent impact on customer service.

Reichheld (1993) proposed a loyalty-based system chain with direct links between increasing employee pay, employee satisfaction and customer loyalty, which then provides a competitive advantage. Although the model has intuitive appeal, it requires empirical substantiation.

TBSS: management challenges

Managing services involves managing the customer experience of the service process and, particularly, the service encounters. Historically, service encounters were face-to-face with customer-contact employees delivering or performing the service for the customer. Today, many encounters have become customer-to-machine encounters, with customers performing tasks previously performed by employees. Technology and the 24/7 mentality are driving an explosion in self-service provision.

Self-service fundamentally changes the co-creation roles of the service organisation and the customer, which creates several significant management challenges (Hilton 2008).

1   *A need to maintain focus on customer-perceived quality*

There is a risk that the service organisation's contribution to service co-creation centres on the provision of technology and back-stage fulfilment activities, such as logistics and transportation. There is a danger that self-service may be conceptualised as an integration of IT, engineering and operations management and overlooks established customer experience knowledge. It is imperative that service organisations focus on customer-perceived quality as well as paying close attention to the design of the self-service interface (e-servicescape) and the self-service process. Learning from the theatre metaphor should not be overlooked in the desire to improve overall efficiency.

2   *Market segmentation and differentiation opportunities*

The provision of face-to-face service as well as self-service may enable a service provider to differentiate service quality levels to leverage the customer pyramid approach to profitability. Face-to-face provision may facilitate a premium market position.

3   *Customers as a source of competitive advantage*

S-DL claims that *operant resources* are the fundamental source of competitive advantage, so increasing reliance upon customers presents a strategic challenge. Customer motivations are likely to differ from employee motivations. They may choose self-service for 'experiential' outcomes, such as convenience, greater control or more fun. Customers cannot be incentivised to perform in the same way as employees; neither can they be required to leave! Organisations need to consider how to attract key customers to self-service and whether the use of self-service disadvantages or discriminates against some customer groups.

Customers who are unable or unwilling to engage in self-service might become disadvantaged. The technology itself should not unwittingly create disadvantage by failing to take account of age-related factors, such as the size of the writing and amount of dexterity required to operate them. Similar issues arise with customers with hearing and sight impairments. The rise of the global consumer has led to a need for multi-language provision. Consumers without internet access, bank accounts and credit cards may also need special considerations.

4   *Integrating the operant resources of customers: design considerations*

Self-service moves the operant resource input from service employees to customers. While this may reduce servicing costs and improve organisational productivity along the lines of the factory approach, there is no need to ignore the theatre approach or substitute customer resource for employee resource entirely. Collaborative integration of customers and employee resources to co-create the service may enhance the customer experience. Customers may be more willing to co-create where they perceive a benefit to themselves. Consideration of both approaches would determine which elements should be efficiency-driven and which might earn the 'rave review' from hedonistic elements, which can be designed into the process.

5   *Customers as partial employees*

Reliance on customer resources means they become *partial employees*, so it is worth remembering that they are not as easy to manage as employees. Employees are recruited for their knowledge, skills, capabilities and experiences. They are inducted into the organisation and receive training to enhance their operant resources. Service organisations need to articulate exactly what knowledge, skills and capabilities customers require, how they will acquire them and what the associated learning curve will involve. Organisations will need to factor in the time and cost of the learning curve, as well as the impact of customer churn, the equivalent to employee turnover, in the same way that they do for employees. Self-service may cost service organisations more than maintaining employees where there is high customer churn, where the number of 'novice' (Bateson 2002) or new customers, outweigh returning or 'expert' (Bateson 2002) customers, and where a large number of service employees are required to develop the operant resources of those novices.

6   *Capacity management*

Customer-driven resources will be less visible to the organisation, so capacity management needs greater attention. The organisation may need to provide greater *back-stage* support for customers who will access the systems less frequently than employees would. Customers may want to access order fulfilment systems to track orders. *Blueprinting* and *service mapping* would identify all relevant tracking points within the process.

7   *New employee roles require new skills*

In face-to-face delivery, contact employees deliver the service. Self-service changes the timing and nature of the service encounter with service employees. Employees still deliver a service, but move into a *service recovery* role. A problem occurs, creating a *critical incident*. The service delivery employee becomes a *service recovery* employee and this may require different interpersonal skills and knowledge of the organisational systems. Alternatively, and particularly when self-service co-exists in situ with face-to-face provision (e.g. retail self-scanning), the service employee becomes a trainer responsible for ensuring the customer gains the required knowledge and skills.

Summary

This chapter acknowledges the economic importance of services and the potential of the internet to advance the services sector in developing economies. Whether viewed from a 'manufacturing-oriented' or a 'service-oriented' perspective, the nature and characteristics (*intangibility*, *heterogeneity*, *inseparability and perishability*) of services requires the development of a specific body of knowledge. This leads to a better understanding of the management challenges inherent when people are so involved in service provision as both providers and beneficiaries.

It is the nature and characteristics of services, as distinct from products and goods, that led to the addition of *people, process* and *physical evidence* to the '4Ps' of the marketing mix and which comprise the *extended marketing mix*. The SOAR (scripts, outlay, accommodation and representation) approach provides an additional set of considerations for managers.

Two metaphors (*factory* and *theatre*) help draw attention to the two key goals of service: efficiency and effectiveness as measured by 'rave reviews'. Both are important considerations when designing a service and two tools were introduced (*blueprinting* and *service mapping*) to assist with service process design, particularly identifying *complexity* and *divergence*. *Servicescape* and *e-servicescape* remind managers of the importance of the physical environment in which service and self-service takes place. In part, this is a market segmentation and positioning consideration, but, particularly with reference to self-service, there may be a need to consider which customer groups might be disadvantaged.

Service quality is arguably the most researched aspect of service provision and the PZB *'gaps model'* along with their SERVQUAL measurement instrument remain the most popular theoretical approaches, although not without critique.

The *profitability* of services remains an under-researched area. The link between *quality*, *productivity* and *profitability* is explored, as is the role of customer and employee *satisfaction* and *loyalty*. The *customer pyramid* has a number of practical applications for service managers.

Much of the chapter focuses on the rise of *self-service* and the introduction and development of the SD-L thesis, because these are the most current trends and are set to continue. S–DL is likely to draw further academic attention to develop greater clarity around the terminology and evidence the logic in practice through research studies. Currently, the hot research and discussion topics are (value) co-creation and value propositions. It may be no coincidence that S-DL kick-started intensive dialogue around the participatory role of customers as active actors, rather than passive consumers, around the same time that self-service began to boom. Most organisations recognise the importance of the customer, but, 'putting the customer at the centre' of the organisation is frequently poorly implemented, perhaps because 'the customer' is simply too vague. S-DL's focus on customer resources is therefore very helpful. Self-service does not necessarily mean shifting all service tasks from employees to customers, but rather considering what resources are required to perform the service and how best to integrate the resources contributed by each actor to achieve the task, not forgetting the support needs of all actors. Self-service may not actually reduce service costs for the organisation, because of the need to manage the customer resource integration process, including support needs. This may require new and additional employee roles and will change the nature of the customer-employee interaction, which has always been central to services marketing.

Further reading

Baron, S., Harris, K. and Hilton, T. (2009), *Services Marketing Text and Cases*, Basingstoke, UK: Palgrave Macmillan.
Lusch, R. F. and Vargo, S. L. (2006), *The Service Dominant Logic of Marketing: Dialog, Debate and Directions*, Armonk, NY: M.E. Sharpe.
Lusch, R. F. and Vargo, S. L. (2014), *Service-Dominant Logic: Premises, Perspectives, Possibilities*, Cambridge, UK: Cambridge University Press.
Vargo, S. L. and Lusch, R. F. (2008), 'Service-dominant logic: Continuing the evolution', *Journal of the Academy of Marketing Science*, 36(1): 1–10.

References

Anderson, E. W. and Mittal, V. (2000), 'Strengthening the satisfaction-profit chain', *Journal of Service Research*, 3(2): 107–120.
Arnould, E. J., Price, L. L. and Malshe, A. (2006), 'Toward a cultural resource-based theory of the customer', in Lusch, R. F. and Vargo, S. L. (eds) *The Service-Dominant Logic of Marketing: Dialog, Debate and Directions*, Armonk, NY: M.E. Sharpe, pp. 320–333.
Baron, S., Harris, K. and Hilton, T. (2009), *Services Marketing Text and Cases*, Basingstoke, UK: Palgrave Macmillan.
Bateson, J. E. G. (1992), *Managing Services Marketing: Text and Readings*, second edition, Oak Brook, IL: The Dryden Press.
Bateson, J. (2002), 'Are your customers good enough for your service business?', *Academy of Management Executive*, 16(4): 110–120.
Beaven, M. H. and Scotti, D. J. (1990), 'Service-oriented thinking and its implications for the marketing mix', *Journal of Services Marketing*, 4(4): 5–19.
Bitner, M. J. (1992), 'Servicescapes: The impact of physical surroundings on customers and employees', *Journal of Marketing*, 56: 57–71.
Booms, B. H. and Bitner, M. J. (1981), 'Marketing strategies and organisational structures for service firms', in Donnelly, J. and W. R. George, (eds) *Marketing of Services*, Chicago, IL: AMA, pp. 51–67.
Caulderwood, K. (2014), 'More than 70 per cent of emerging market internet users are on Facebook (FB) and Twitter (TWTR)', *International Business Times*, available at http://www.ibtimes.com/more-70-emerging-market-internet-users-are-facebook-fb-twitter-twtr-1555333 (accessed 21 May 2014).
Clow, K. E. and Vorhies, D. W. (1993), 'Building a competitive advantage for service firms', *Journal of Services Marketing*, 7(1): 22–32.

Frow, P., McColl-Kennedy, J. R., Hilton, T., Davidson, A., Payne, A. and Brozovic, D. (2014), 'Value proposi-tions: A service ecosystem perspective', *Marketing Theory*, 14(3): 327–351.

Gale, B. T. (1994), 'Customer satisfaction – Relative to competitors: Is where it's at (strong evidence that superior quality drives the bottom line and shareholder value)', *Marketing and Research Today*, 22(1): 39–53.

Grönroos, C. (1983), 'Innovative marketing strategies and organizational structures for service firms', in Berry, L. L., Shostack, G. L. and Upah, G. D. (eds) *Emerging Perspectives on Services Marketing*, Chicago, IL: AMA, pp. 9–21.

Grove, S. J. and Fisk, R. P. (1983), 'The dramaturgy of services exchange: An analytical framework for services marketing', in Berr, L. L., Shostack, G. L. and Upah, G. D. (eds) *Emerging Perspectives on Services Marketing*, Chicago, IL: AMA.

Gummesson, E. (1992), 'Service productivity: A blasphemous approach', *Proceedings of 2nd International Research Seminar in Service Management*, La-Londe-les-Maures, France, June.

Heskett, J. L., Jones, T. O., Loveman, G. W., Sasser, W. E. Jr and Schlesinger, L. A. (1994), 'Putting the service-profit chain to work', *Harvard Business Review*, 72(2): 164–174.

Hilton, T. (2008), 'Leveraging operant resources of consumers: Improving consumer experiences or productivity?', *The Marketing Review*, 8(4): 359–365.

Hilton, T. and Hughes, T. (2013), 'Co-production and self-service: The application of service-dominant logic', *Journal of Marketing Management*, 29(7/8): 861–881.

Hilton, T., Hughes, T. and Chalcraft, D. (2012), 'Service co-creation: Resource integration and value realisation', *Journal of Marketing Management*, 28(13/14): 1504–1519.

Hilton, T., Hughes, T., Little, E. and Marandi, E. (2013), 'Adopting self-service technology to do more with less', *Journal of Services Marketing*, 27(1): 3–12.

Lovelock, C. H. (1992), *Managing Services Marketing, Operations and Human Resources*, second edition, Englewood Cliffs, NJ: Prentice Hall International.

McCarthy, J. E. (1960), *Basic Marketing: A Management Approach*, Homewood, IL: Irwin.

Parasuraman, A., Zeithaml, V. A. and Berry, L. L. (1985), 'A conceptual model of service quality and its implica-tions for future research', *Journal of Marketing*, 49(4): 41–50.

Parasuraman, A., Zeithaml, V. A. and Berry, L. L. (1988), 'SERVQUAL: A multiple-item scale for measuring consumer perceptions of service quality', *Journal of Retailing*, 64(1): 12–40.

Parasuraman, A., Berry, L. L. and Zeithaml, V. A. (1991), 'Refinement and reassessment of the SERVQUAL scale', *Journal of Retailing*, 67(4): 420–450.

Pine, J. B. II and Gilmore, J. H. (1999), *The Experience Economy: Work is Theatre and Every Business a Stage*, Boston, MA: Harvard Business School Press.

Reichheld, F. F. (1993), 'Loyalty-based management', *Harvard Business Review*, March/April: 64–73.

Reichheld, F. F. and Sasser, W. E. Jr (1990), 'Zero defections: Quality comes to services', *Harvard Business Review*, 68(5): 105–111.

Sarel, D. and Marmorstein, H. (1998), 'Managing the delayed service encounter: The role of employee action and customer prior experience', *Journal of Services Marketing*, 12(3): 195–208.

Schlesinger, L. A. and Heskett, J. L. (1991), 'The service-driven service company', *Harvard Business Review*, 69(5): 71–81.

Shostack, G. L. (1977), 'Breaking free from product marketing', *Journal of Marketing*, 41(2): 73–80.

Teas, R. K. (1993), 'Expectation, performance evaluation and consumers' perceptions of quality', *Journal of Marketing*, 57(October): 18–34.

Vargo, S. L. and Lusch, R. F. (2004), 'Evolving to a new dominant logic for marketing', *The Journal of Marketing*, 68(1): 1–17.

Worsfold, D. (2001), 'Food safety behaviour in butchers' shops', *Nutrition and Food Science*, 31(1): 13–19.

Zeithaml, V. A., Berry, L. L. and Parasuraman, A. (1985), 'A conceptual model of service quality and its implica-tions for future research', *The Journal of Marketing*, 49(4): 41–50.

Zeithaml, V. A., Berry, L. L. and Parasuraman, A. (1993), 'The nature and determinants of customer expectations of service', *Journal of the Academy of Marketing Science*, 21(1): 1–12.

Zeithaml, V. A., Rust, R. T. and Lemon, K. N. (2001), 'The customer pyramid: Creating and service profitable customers', *California Management Review*, 43(4): 118–142.

20 International marketing

Anne Marie Doherty

Introduction

This chapter considers the motivations underlying a firm's move into international markets, the theories that underpin the internationalisation of the firm, the market selection process and market entry methods available to firms when considering the move abroad and the marketing strategies to be considered when operating in international markets. The chapter concludes with a discussion on international divestment, a crucial but sometimes overlooked area of international marketing strategy.

Motivations for internationalisation

Why do firms internationalise? The fundamental basic reason firms internationalise is to grow and increase profits. However, that said, there are usually myriad reasons, which ultimately account for a move outside the home market. The reasons for internationalisation or motives for internationalisation have variously been described as reactive and proactive motives, or 'push and pull' factors, which either encourage the firm to expand outside the domestic market, or proactively pull the firm into international markets.

Different sectors, size of firm, and home and host market characteristics can account for a range of different reasons why firms internationalise. For example, Evers (2011: 19–23) reviews the considerable research that has been carried out on the reasons why SMEs and international new ventures (INVs) consider the move outside the home market, revealing a range of motives:

- client following abroad (Bell 1995);
- international orientation of management/global vision (Moen 2002; Hutchinson *et al.* 2007);
- strong international business networks (Coviello and Munro 1995; Oviatt and McDougall 1995; Knight and Cavusgil 1996);
- limited domestic demand/end of lifecycle (Coviello and Munro 1995; Oviatt and McDougall 1995; Madsen and Servais 1997);
- exploiting an international niche (Knight and Cavusgil 1996).

In certain sectors, such as retailing for example, considerable research effort has been dedicated to addressing the specific question as to why retail firms internationalise (Alexander 1990; Williams

1992; Hutchinson *et al.* 2007). The following highlights some of the major reasons retailers move beyond their domestic borders:

- niche opportunities in the new market;
- size of the new market;
- level of economic prosperity;
- the retailer's operating format;
- underdeveloped nature of retailing in the new market highlighting opportunities for growth;
- favourable exchange rates;
- favourable operating environment, for example, due to regulation;
- saturation of the home market;
- real estate investment potential;
- favourable labour climate.

(Alexander (1990) in Alexander and Doherty 2009: 222)

More recently, specific research has focused on larger firms from emerging markets and their specific motivations for internationalisation (Gaffney *et al.* 2013). For these firms, internationalisation is, 'a process to acquire and maintain resources necessary to become globally competitive' (Gaffney *et al.* 2013: 109). According to these authors, emerging market multinational enterprises' (EMNEs') motivations to internationalise exist on a continuum of asset exploitation and asset augmentation whereby these firms internationalise to exploit their existing firm specific advantages and to acquire new capabilities.

Therefore, it can be seen that motivations are myriad and complex. In most cases it is not one specific factor, which is responsible for the move outside the home market, but rather a range of interconnected reasons, which coincide at a point in time to either draw the firm into the international marketplace in a proactive fashion or push the firm out of the domestic market as a reaction to less than favourable conditions at home.

Theories of the international firm

Theories of the international firm can be delineated into two main approaches:

1 the economics-based or efficiency-based theories of the international firm;
2 the behavioural or process theories of internationalisation.

The key economics-based or efficiency-based theories are transaction cost economics and internalisation theory, which undergird the reason for the existence of the multinational enterprise (Buckley and Casson 1976) and Dunning's eclectic paradigm (Dunning 1977). To a lesser extent, agency theory (Combs *et al.* 2011) also fits within this perspective, but its remit is narrower given it is largely associated with helping to explain how and why firms employ one particular entry method, namely franchising, in international markets (Doherty and Quinn 1999; Doherty *et al.* 2014). Theories aligned with more behavioural or process perspectives are: the stages theory of internationalisation and the related psychic distance concept (Johanson and Vahlne 1974, 1977; Johanson and Wiedersheim-Paul 1975) and 'born globals' (Oviatt and McDougall 1994; Cavusgil and Knight 2015). We will now discuss each of these theories in turn.

Economics/efficiency-based theories

Transaction costs and internalisation theory

Internalisation theory, and the transaction costs associated with it, has its roots in the seminal work of Coase (1937), although it is probably most associated with the later work of Williamson (1975, 1981). Originally devised as a theory to explain why firms exist – as opposed to why international firms exist – Coase (1937) posited that firms exist, because there are transaction costs associated with using the market, i.e. the price mechanism. These costs can be described as ex-ante and ex-post costs. Ex-ante costs are those associated with searching and contracting, while ex-post costs are those involved with the monitoring and enforcement of agreements and contracts. The assumption is that the firm will aim to minimise these costs when making decisions about how to best undertake transactions (Williamson 1975). The result is that the firm will either internalise, that is, vertically integrate, or externalise, operations to manage potential costs.

This logic of why the firm exists was subsequently extended by Buckley and Casson (1976), Hennart (1977) and others to explain why the multinational enterprise (MNE) exists and why foreign direct investment (FDI) occurs. The key issue the firm must consider is how its knowledge is embedded and therefore protected, that is, the focus is on intangible assets in the form of technology, goodwill and knowledge. If the firm's knowledge is tacit knowledge, that is, it is potentially easily copied and therefore prone to opportunistic behaviour on the open market due to high transaction costs, then internalisation theory would predict that the firm will internalise its knowledge, creating its own internal market via FDI. If, however, a firm's knowledge is protected in law, through for example, a patent or trademark, then a contractual mode such as licensing may be a better and certainly a less expensive route to the international market place.

Essentially, internalisation theory offers an economics-based approach to the market entry decision process for the firm considering the move into international markets. The firm therefore must decide if it is more efficient for it to internationalise through owning its own operations abroad, i.e. internalising its assets, or whether it is best to enter into some form of contractual arrangement thereby externalising its assets, for example, franchising, licensing and so on.

Various authors have employed the transaction cost economics of internalisation theory to try to explain the market entry mode choice decision of manufacturing firms, beginning with the seminal paper by Anderson and Gatignon (1986). Seggie (2012) provides a more up-to-date account of how transaction costs have been applied in the international marketing domain.

Dunning's eclectic paradigm

Dunning's eclectic paradigm (Dunning 1977, 1983, 1988, 1989) has the intention of providing a more holistic framework to explain the different sets of advantages that a firm should have in place before it would consider production outside the home market. Sometimes referred to the OLI framework, Dunning identifies ownership, location and internalisation advantages that a firm should have in place in order to compete against indigenous firms in the market in which it intends to internationalise. According to Dunning, a firm should move through a series of decisions based on the presence of the three named advantages in order to decide whether and how to internationalise. Welch *et al.* (2007) provide an excellent step-by-step guide to the process a firm should go through when applying OLI logic to its decision to internationalise and which entry method it may pursue in the international market.

In the first instance, the firm needs to possess some form of ownership (O) advantage over indigenous firms in the foreign market before deciding whether or not internationalisation is possible for the firm, that is, if the firm does not possess ownership advantages over indigenous firms then it should not internationalise and should remain in the domestic market. If, on the other hand, it does possess assets, which give it a competitive advantage over indigenous firms in the foreign market, it should move to consider the 'L' element of the OLI framework – location. The question now is whether the firm can derive locational advantages by locating production outside the home market. Again, if the answer to this question is 'no', then the framework recommends the firm does not internationalise production and continues to produce at home, employing exporting as a route to the international marketplace. That said, if it is deemed that locational advantages can be derived from a move abroad to a specific market, the subsequent question is whether the firm should internalise (I) its assets through owning its production facilities abroad or, alternatively, contract them out via a contractual entry mode such as franchising or licensing. The transaction cost logic, as highlighted above regarding costs, comes into play here with regard to the internalisation or externalisation decision.

While Dunning's eclectic paradigm has enjoyed significant traction in the international marketing and international business literatures, this has not happened without criticism. The framework has been deemed to be too static, the myriad variables included make its predictive value limited and its application to the manufacturing sector has made it less relevant, as the balance has shifted over recent decades to the internationalisation of services. More recently Eden and Dai (2010) highlighted what they call 'the big tent' nature of the paradigm: in many ways its main advantage, i.e. the attempt to provide a holistic framework, is also its major limitation as it is simply trying to achieve too much. That said, Dunning added and modified his thinking throughout his lifetime (see, for example, Dunning 1988; Dunning and Lundan 2010; Narula and Dunning 2010) and has left a legacy in international business equalled by very few.

Behavioural/process theories of internationalisation

While internalisation theory and Dunning's eclectic paradigm have their bases in international economics and are largely focused on the market entry mode decision, the stages model of internationalisation and 'born globals' emanate from a more behavioural, process-oriented approach to internationalisation, where organisational learning and the evolution of firm knowledge dominate the argument.

The stages model of internationalisation

Sometimes known as the Uppsala Stages Model due to the home institution of the academics publishing the work at the University of Uppsala, the stages model of internationalisation is an incremental process of development from the home market to the international market through increasing levels of market commitment and experiential knowledge and learning (Johanson and Vahlne 1974, 1977, 1990). Over time, firms move to more psychically distant (Johanson and Wiedersheim-Paul 1975) markets through a sequential process of increasing mode commitment.

The initial work of Johanson and Wiedersheim-Paul (1975) focuses on the process of internationalisation followed by four Swedish firms – Sandvik, Atlas Copco, Facit and Volvo. Starting with the basic assumption that firms begin their development in the domestic market before considering internationalisation, Johanson and Wiedersheim-Paul (1975: 307) present four stages in the internationalisation process of these firms:

1   no regular export activities;
2   export via independent representatives (agent);
3   sales subsidiary;
4   production/manufacturing.

These four sequential stages are called *the establishment chain* (Johanson and Wiedersheim-Paul 1975), which sometimes gives rise to the model being called the establishment chain model of internationalisation. Each stage represents increasing commitment by the firm in the international market. Interestingly, one of the main subsequent criticisms of the model has been that all firms do not necessarily pass through each of these stages, and firms may skip stages. A close inspection of the original work highlights that Johanson and Wiedersheim-Paul (1975) were acutely aware that this was indeed the case:

> Of course we do not expect the development always to follow the whole chain. First, several markets are not large enough for the resource demanding stages. Second, we could expect jumps in the establishment chain in firms with extensive experience from other foreign markets.
>
> Johanson and Wiedersheim-Paul (1975: 307)

The establishment chain was complemented by the addition of the concept of psychic distance, that is, firms will first internationalise to those markets, which are deemed to be psychically and culturally close to the home market before moving to more distant markets when they become more experienced internationalists (Vahlne and Wiedersheim-Paul 1973; Johanson and Wiedersheim-Paul 1975). Johanson and Vahlne (1977) further built on this initial conceptualisation by emphasising state and change aspects, which impact on the process of internationalisation. State aspects are market commitments in terms of resources and knowledge about the foreign market. Changes aspects are the decisions to commit resources and the performance of current business activities. Subsequent reaction to this process model resulted in a raft of internationalisation process models from US-based academics (Bilkey and Tesar 1977; Cavusgil 1980; Czinkota 1982; and see Alexander and Doherty 2009: 46, for diagrammatic integration of these models).

In later work, Johanson and Vahlne (1990) return to the state and change aspects, bringing their model more in line with the developments in the contemporary world of internationalisation, focusing on dynamic capabilities, network position and the inter-organisational processes of learning, creating and trust building. They also return to a case study of Volvo trucks (Vahlne *et al.* 2011), one of the original four firms from the work of Johanson and Wiedersheim-Paul (1975), adapting the process model to explain how the globalisation process of the firm has evolved.

Hence, they attempt to address their critics who considered the early model too deterministic (Reid 1983) and not relevant for services (Engwall and Wallenstal 1988). Moreover, the concept of psychic distance was called into question, as markets became increasingly homogeneous (Nordstrom 1990). It is precisely this potential for the globalisation of markets (Levitt 1983) that provides the backdrop for the most recent 'theory' of the global firm, that of 'born globals' (Oviatt and McDougall 1994; Chetty and Campbell-Hunt 2004).

Born globals

The concept of 'born globals' focused attention on an increasingly prevalent small firm type: those firms that do not follow a sequential establishment chain on the road to internationalisation and are deemed to operate globally virtually from inception (Oviatt and McDougall 1994; Chetty and Campbell-Hunt 2004). Characterised as 'international new ventures' by Oviatt and McDougall (1994: 49) they define these firms as 'a business organization that, from inception, seeks to derive significant competitive advantage from the use of resources and the sale of outputs in multiple countries'. The focus for these authors is the age of the firms in question when they become international, rather than firm size, which had dominated much of the discussion in the literature to that point. Four types of INV are identified: new international market makers, which comprise the export/import start up and multinational traders; geographically focused start-ups; and global start-ups. These firms are international from inception because 'competitive forces preclude a successful domestic focus. Their emphasis on controlling rather than owning assets is due to resource scarcity that is common among new organisations' (Oviatt and McDougall 1994: 60).

Chetty and Campbell-Hunt (2004: 66) further emphasise key elements of the 'born global' firm, which distinguishes it from the traditional stages model view:

- the domestic market is largely irrelevant;
- the founder has significant internationalisation experience;
- simultaneous and rapid pace and extent of development of international markets;
- psychic distance is not relevant;
- as a result of superior knowledge of the international market place knowledge is assimilated and applied more quickly;
- product/market is very focused;
- information technology is employed as an enabler of learning and global market reach;
- network of partners crucial to development;
- internationalisation takes place within two years of inception.

The importance of 'born globals' to the development of international marketing theory is noted most recently by Cavusgil and Knight (2015) and Coviello (2015), both of whom highlight the continued importance and proliferation of the 'born global' firm.

Market selection

Once the decision to internationalise has been taken, the next decision a firm must make is which market or markets to enter. Selecting a market or markets can be achieved through a logical process of assessing risks and opportunities. It should also be noted at this juncture that market selection may go hand-in-hand with entry mode selection when a firm internationalises through an opportunistic approach by a prospective partner (Doherty 2009).

The market selection process typically consists of two key stages: market scanning and market research. With over 200 potential country markets to choose from, the scanning process takes an overarching view of the global marketplace, scanning across markets to screen out the least desirable ones with the aim of focusing the firm on those markets where investment in more detailed market research is worthwhile. Market scanning, therefore, consists of exploration of a series of macroindicators, such as the economic, political/legal and socio-cultural environment. Adverse economic conditions, strict regulations on incoming foreign firms, significant differences in psychic distance and potentially difficulties in overcoming cultural barriers are all examples of reasons why a market may not be suitable. For further detailed discussion of each element of the screening process, see Hollensen (2013).

The market scanning process should result in a shortlist of potential markets where the firm could potentially operate. While the market scanning process is characterised by the use of secondary sources primarily undertaken through desk research, the market research process involves a more detailed, fine grained approach to determine realistic possibilities of successful market entry. For example, a retail firm considering international markets will need a detailed analysis of indigenous and international competitors and an in-depth understanding of consumer behaviour, retail infrastructure in terms of the travel network, information technology advancement, employment and property law and so on. In some markets, such as India for example, specific regulation exists with regard to incoming international retailers. Regulations differ in terms of multi-brand and single brand retailers aiming to enter the market and how this may or may not be possible. Certain firms may spend years carrying out this type of detailed market research, particularly if considering entry to markets such as Japan where the prospect of divestment and re-entry at a later date is not an option. While it may seem an obvious statement, detailed market analysis and the time and financial commitment this entails is crucial to success in the market. As we will return to later when we discuss divestment, poor market research, which results in a lack of understanding of the consumer, for example, can lead to subsequent market exit. Therefore underestimating the importance of deep market analysis at the market selection stage of the internationalisation process can be fatal for a firm.

While market selection is a key practical element of international marketing, it is also an area that has garnered a developed body of academic work (Papadopoulos and Martin Martin 2011). For example, while Hofstede's work on culture and its impact on the market selection decision is central to this aspect of international marketing strategy, it is not universally accepted and continues to attract constructive criticism and debate (McSweeney 2013; Veniak and Brewer 2013). Papadopoulos and Martin Martin (2011) highlight the complexity of international market selection and acknowledge it is inherently difficult in practice. As such, it remains a ripe area for academic research.

The market entry mode/method decision and process

The ways in which firms enter international markets has been a mainstay of international marketing research for decades. The classic and much referenced definition of an international market entry mode is offered by Root (1994: 5): 'An international market entry mode is an institutional arrangement that makes possible the entry of a company's products, technology, human skills, management, or other resources into a foreign *country*'.

Entry modes are often classified into export modes, contractual entry modes and investment modes (Root 1994; Benito *et al.* 2007). Using both of these sources, the major modes available to firms when considering the move outside the home market are thus:

- Export modes:

    a   indirect exporting;
    b   direct exporting;
    c   own sales office or sales subsidiary.

- Contractual entry modes:

    a   franchising;
    b   licensing;
    c   management contracts;
    d   contract manufacture;
    e   alliances.

- Investment modes:

    a   acquisition;
    b   wholly-owned subsidiary (WOS);
    c   joint venture (minor/equal/majority ownership).

Two excellent textbooks specifically on entry modes offer very detailed discussion on each of these options, that is, Root (1994) and Welch *et al.* (2007). Hollensen (2013) also provides excellent detailed coverage of the entry modes available in the international marketplace.

Entry modes have tended to be categorised on a risk/control continuum, with the entry methods offering higher control also being those with the higher financial risk and limited flexibility, for example, WOS or acquisition. Contractual modes such as franchising and licensing fall midway within the continuum offering ways to market that have relatively limited financial risk at the expense of levels of control. Exporting modes are deemed to offer the least control, but also incur the least risk. If we link back to the theories of the firm, particularly internalisation theory and the associated transaction cost economics associated with it, export modes are seen to be externalising modes and investment modes are internalising modes.

Often linked to the theories of the international firm, market entry choice is predominately viewed as a list of potential discrete options a firm can choose between, when in reality the entry mode decision can be somewhat opportunistic and reactive rather than strategic and intentional (Doherty 2009). It is also important to note that much research focuses on the *initial* market entry mode decision, whereas in reality a firm will probably move through a range of operational modes once it has entered a market (Benito *et al.* 2009). Indeed, firms will operate a range of methods both within the same international market and across markets. For example, while Zara's preferred method of operating is through owned operations in international markets, in some countries it operates through franchising due to a variety of reasons including market size, regulation and potential risk factors (Alexander and Doherty 2009). A host of reasons need to be taken into account when firms choose ways of operating in the international marketplace. These include:

- financial considerations;
- political and economic risk;
- regulation;
- the specifics of the product/service/brand being internationalised and the nature of knowledge being transferred;
- psychic distance;
- market size.

Assuming that the entry mode decision for firms is a discrete, linear process would be to underestimate the complexity and indeed potential opportunism that characterises the decision and process in practice. Indeed, Shaver (2013) advocates that we should try to understand the interdependence issue in more depth in entry mode studies. Understanding the reasons behind why a firm chooses an initial entry mode decision is important, but it is equally important to recognise that once in the market, operational modes change over time and indeed across markets. They are also sector specific, that is, entry methods that will work for a retailer will be different for a manufacturer and another service provider such as a hotel. Assuming that the theories of the firm can be applied equally to all sectors to help guide the entry mode decision would again be to underestimate the complexity therein.

Global and multinational strategies for international markets

Designing the international marketing mix is the next key decision for the internationalising firm. Detailed discussions on the elements of the marketing mix – product, price, place and promotion – are provided elsewhere in this book and it is not the purpose of this chapter to reiterate these analyses. In the international marketing context, the challenge for the firm is whether to adopt a global approach to marketing strategy or a multinational approach, that is, does the firm adapt or standardise its offer?

The standardisation/adaptation debate has been ongoing since the 1960s, acknowledged most recently in the work of Schmid and Kotulla (2011). Their literature review of over 300 articles on the subject concludes that:

> [a] high degree of international product standardization is likely to enhance foreign product profit, as compared to all alternative strategies, if there is (1) a high cross-national homogeneity of demand, (2) a high potential for cross-national economies of scale, (3) a high cost of modification, (4) a high foreign price elasticity of demand, (5) a small perceptual error of the managers, and (6) a high quality of strategy execution.
>
> (Schmid and Kotulla 2011: 491)

In attempting to show how a firm may make the decision to adapt or standardise, Hollensen (2004: 447) identifies the key factors to consider – see Table 20.1.

In a comprehensive review of the evidence from the literature, Birnik and Bowman (2007) provide some very insightful conclusions on the practice of standardisation across the elements of the international marketing mix. They conclude that:

- pricing is the least, or one of the least, standardised elements;
- brand and product are the most standardised;
- packaging is standardised to a medium degree;
- advertising is also standardised to a medium degree;
- the lowest levels of standardisation are found in sales, distribution and promotion.

Interestingly, their review of the literature highlights inconclusive and conflicting results regarding the performance outcomes of standardisation, that is, it is not clear whether standardisation or adaptation offers the best strategy for improving performance. That said, only 5 per cent of the articles on the issue adopted a qualitative approach. Trying to find generalisable answers to context specific questions may be the issue here. It is probably fair to say that

Table 20.1 How to make the decision to standardise or adapt

Factors favouring standardisation	Factors favouring adaptation
Economies of scale in R&D, production and marketing	Local environment-induced adaptation: government and regulatory influences
Global competition	Local competition
Convergence of tastes and consumer needs	Variation in consumer needs
Centralised management of international operations	Fragmented and decentralised management with independent country subsidiaries
A standardised concept is used by competitors	An adapted concept is used by competitors

Source: Hollensen (2004: 447).

for most international firms, some elements of the marketing mix will be standardised and others will have some level of adaptation depending on context. Even those firms held up as the epitomy of globalisation, such as McDonald's, incorporate elements of adaptation where necessary. The standardisation/adaptation challenge is one that is unique to each firm; therefore more qualitative studies of the phenomenon may reveal much greater insight than that provided by the vast majority of studies in this area, which have adopted a quantitative approach.

Divesting from international markets

As has been a persistent theme in this chapter, the process of internationalisation for the firm is not always a simple, logical, linear process; in most instances it is iterative, recursive and, in many cases, opportunistic and reactive. Few firms enter international markets with the potential of divesting from the market being a consideration; yet international divestment is increasingly prevalent. Tesco's announcement of its decision to exit the US market in April 2013, having only operated there since 2007, is a pertinent case in point. While the issue of divestment within a domestic context is well discussed in the literature, international divestment has received relatively less attention. Decker and Mellewigt (2007) and Brauer (2006) provide excellent reviews of this broader divestment literature.

A host of terms have been used to describe what is termed here as divestment (see Alexander and Doherty 2009: 327 for further details). Divestment, divestiture, market exit, business exit, deinternationalisation, decommitment, failure and business restructuring (Alexander and Doherty 2009: 327), have all been employed to discuss the issue. For ease of understanding, divestment is taken to be 'company actions resulting in a reduced presence in an international market' (Alexander *et al.* 2005: 8). As these authors correctly note, 'divestment may or may not involve market exit' (Alexander *et al.* 2005: 8). This is crucially important, as divestment is sometimes wrongly only seen as a negative action by a firm and therefore considered a 'failure' (Burt *et al.* 2003). The portfolio restructuring argument and indeed 'company renewal', as posited by Decker and Mellewigt (2007), provides a more rounded approach to the discussion of divestment than a perspective based on failure alone would allow us to achieve. Indeed, there is considerable research evidence, which concludes that the announcement of divestment is received very positively by the market, signalling a firm with a strong strategic direction that is prepared to make difficult decisions.

Essentially, there are myriad reasons why firms decide or reduce their presence in an international market. Benito and Welch (1997) provide a very insightful view of the theoretical perspectives, which can be employed to understand the reasons for international divestment. The economic perspective highlights unsatisfactory profit levels, changes in entry mode from a higher to a lower investment mode, e.g. from internalised operations to contractual modes, and lack of interrelatedness between businesses as reasons for divestment. The strategic management perspective emphasises the firm as a portfolio of interrelated businesses. If some business units are not performing well or lack interrelatedness with the rest of the business, then divestment may occur. Finally, Benito and Welch (1997) discuss what they term 'internationalisation-management', and related reasons for international divestment include refocusing on core business, changes in leadership, poor performance in the international market, reduction in commitment to the international venture by senior management and divestment as a by-product of merger and acquisition activity.

Following the initial work of Benito (1997) and Benito and Welch (2007), the past decade has witnessed a particular focus of research on international divestment in the retail sector, beginning with the work of Alexander and Quinn (2002) on the Arcadia Group and Marks & Spencer. Subsequent research provides interesting accounts of the divestment activities of Home Depot (Bianchi and Arnold 2004), Tesco (Palmer 2004, 2005), Boots (Burt *et al.* 2005) and Ahold (Wrigley and Currah 2003; Palmer and Quinn 2007). According to Alexander and Doherty (2009), a range of reasons can account for divestment from the international marketplace:

- *Lack of market research.* It may be somewhat surprising to many that one of the reasons offered for international divestment is that the investing firm did not carry out sufficient and detailed market research in order to ensure the business would be successful. The case of Wal-Mart in Germany is a case in point, whereby the firm underestimated the fact that German consumers were well acquainted with discounters in the form of, for example, Aldi, Lidl and others, and that therefore Wal-Mart's offer was certainly not unique. Often firms seem to not invest sufficient time and effort pre-entry in understanding consumer behaviour in the international market. Home Depot's experience in Chile (Bianchi and Arnold 2004) and Tesco's early foray into Ireland in the 1970s (Palmer 2004) are only some examples of this trend.
- *Links between entry modes and divestment.* Firms that internationalise via high investment modes such as owned operations and acquisition in the international market place are more likely to divest than those firms internationalising through other entry methods. It is also of course the case that these high investment modes will attract more attention when a divestment decision is announced, as in the case of Tesco's recent announcement concerning its owned operations in the US, as compared to the divestment of an international franchise or the closure of an export account where limited resources have been committed in the international market by the focal firm.
- *Poor international market performance.* At the negative end of the scale, poor market performance through, for example, increased competition and/or changes in regulation can lead to divestment. However, a more positive, portfolio restructuring perspective can be applied to those firms who seek to be a market leader in an international market, i.e. number one or two in the market, but do not achieve this ambition and as a result divest. Tesco's divestment from Taiwan in 2005 was done on this basis.
- *Refocus on core business.* Rather than poor market performance in the international market being the main reason for divestment, poor performance at home can often lead to the decision to divest internationally, thereby allowing the firm to focus its resources on its core business in the domestic market. Marks & Spencer's divestment programme in the early 2000s is a case in point here – its poor performance in the UK was a key factor in the decision to divest operations in the US, Canada and Europe.
- *Change in leadership and a response to escalation of commitment.* A change in top leadership can be the tipping point that allows a firm to take the decision to divest (Matthyssens and Pauwels 2000). Research has shown that leaders become increasingly committed to those operations where they have made the decision to invest, even when it becomes clear that divestment is a better strategic option for the firm. In some cases it is only with a change in leadership, whereby the new leader is not the person who made the investment decision, that the divestment decision is made. Certainly, Marks & Spencer's divestment programme in the early 2000s and more recently Tesco's announcement of its US divestment can be linked to changes in CEO.

In the above discussion, it is clear that there is a host of reasons why firms will divest an international operation. However, it is important to remember that while 'failure' in the international market may well be the key factor behind the divestment decision, portfolio restructuring and good strategic management may also lie behind these decisions, with the result that they are received positively by the market and ultimately may reflect well on the firm going forward.

Conclusion

This chapter has highlighted the key issues of international marketing strategy faced by a firm considering a move outside its domestic borders. While these fundamental issues have dominated research on international marketing and helped to describe the internationalisation process, future research themes are more likely to address, for example, the increasing influence of social media in the early stages of marketing the firm in the international marketplace; new forms of market entry that may involve less financial commitment due to the power of social media; the internet as a market entry method; and the growing acculturation of the global consumer. How firms anticipate and manage these changing dynamics will be crucial to success. Ultimately, and regardless of sector or firm size, a company with a strong brand offering underpinned by innovation, finance and strong, decisive management can become an international player no matter how large or limited their international aspirations may be.

References

Alexander, N. (1990), 'Retailers and international markets: Motives for expansion', *International Marketing Review*, 7(4): 75–85.

Alexander, N. and Quinn, B. (2002), 'International retail divestment', *International Journal of Retail and Distribution Management*, 30(2): 112–125.

Alexander, N. and Doherty, A. M. (2009), *International Retailing*, Oxford, UK: Oxford University Press.

Alexander, N., Quinn, B. and Cairns, P. (2005), 'International retail divestment activity', *International Journal of Retail and Distribution Management*, 33(1): 5–22.

Anderson, E. and Gatignon, H. (1986), 'Modes of foreign entry: A transaction cost analysis and propositions', *Journal of International Business Studies*, 17(3): 1–26.

Bell, J. (1995), 'The internationalisation of small computer software firms: A further challenge to "stage" theories', *European Journal of Marketing*, 29(8): 60–75.

Benito, G. R. G. (1997), 'Divestment of foreign production operations', *Applied Economics*, 29(10): 1365–1378.

Benito, G. R. G. and Welch, L. S. (1997), 'De-internationalization', *Management International Review*, 37(2): 7–25.

Benito, G. R. G. and Welch, L. S. (2007),

Benito, G. R. G., *et al.* (2007),

Benito, G. R. G., Petersen, B. and Welch, L. S. (2009), 'Towards more realistic conceptualisations of foreign operation modes', *Journal of International Business Studies*, 40(9): 1455–1470.

Bianchi, C. and Arnold, S. J. (2004), 'An institutional perspective in retail internationalization success: Home depot in Chile', *International Review of Retail, Distribution and Consumer Research*, 14(2): 149–169.

Bilkey, W. J. and Tesar, G. (1977), 'The export behaviour of smaller Wisconsin manufacturing firms', *Journal of International Business Studies*, 8(1): 93–98.

Birnik, A. and Bowman, C. (2007), 'Marketing mix standardization in multinational corporation: A review of the evidence', *International Journal of Management Reviews*, 9(4): 303–324.

Brauer, M. (2006), 'What have we acquired and what should we acquire in divestiture research? A review and research agenda', *Journal of Management*, 32(6): 751–785.

Buckley, P. and Casson, M. (1976), *The Future of the Multinational Enterprise*, London: Macmillan.

Burt, S., Dawson, J. and Sparks, L. (2003), 'Failure in international retailing: Research propositions', *International Review of Retail, Distribution and Consumer Research*, 13(4): 355–373.

Burt, S., Davies, K., McAuley, A. and Sparks, L. (2005), 'Retail internationalisation: From formats to implants', *European Management Journal*, 23(2): 195–202.

Cavusgil, S. T. (1980), 'On the internationalisation process of firms', *European Research*, 8(6): 273–281.

Cavusgil, S. T. and Knight, G. (2015), 'Retrospective: The born global firm: An entrepreneurial and capabilities perspective on early and rapid internationalization', *Journal of International Business Studies*, 46(1): 3–16.

Chetty, S. and Campbell-Hunt, C. (2004), 'A strategic approach to internationalization: A traditional versus a "born-global" approach', *Journal of International Marketing*, 12(1): 57–81.

Coase, R. H. (1937), 'The nature of the firm', *Economica*, 4(16): 386–405.

Combs, J. G., Ketchen, D. J., Shook, C. L. and Short, J. C. (2011), 'Antecedents and consequences of franchising: Past accomplishments and future challenges', *Journal of Management*, 37(1): 99–126.

Coviello, N. (2015), 'Rethinking research on born globals', *Journal of International Business Studies*, 46(1): 17–26.

Coviello, N. and Munro, H. (1995), 'Growing the entrepreneurial firm: Networking for international market development', *European Journal of Marketing*, 29(7): 49–62.

Czinkota, M. R. (1982), *Export Development Policies: U.S. Promotion Policy*, New York: Praeger.

Decker, C. and Mellewigt, T. (2007), 'Thirty years after Michael E. Porter: What do we know about business exit?', *Academy of Management Perspectives*, 21(2): 41–54.

Doherty, A. M. (2009), 'Market and partner selection processes in international retail franchising', *Journal of Business Research*, 62(5): 528–534.

Doherty, A. M. and Quinn, B. (1999), 'International retail franchising: An agency theory perspective', *International Journal of Retail and Distribution Management*, 27(6): 224–266.

Doherty, A. M., Chen, X. and Alexander, N. (2014), 'Exploring the franchise relationship in China: Agency and institutional theory perspectives', *European Journal of Marketing*, 48(9/10): 1664–1689.

Dunning, J. H. (1977), 'Trade, location of economic activity and the MNE: A search for and eclectic approach', in Ohlin, B., Hesselborn, P. O. and Wiskman, P. J. (eds) *The International Allocation of Economic Activity*, London: Macmillan, pp. 395–418.

Dunning, J. H. (1983), 'Market power of the firm and the international transfer of technology', *International Journal of Industrial Organisation*, 1(4): 333–351.

Dunning, J. H. (1988), 'The eclectic paradigm of international production: A restatement and some possible extensions', *Journal of International Business Studies*, 19(1): 1–31.

Dunning, J. H. (1989), 'The study of international business: A plea for a more interdisciplinary approach', *Journal of International Business Studies*, 20(3): 411–436.

Dunning, J. H. and Lundan, S. M. (2010), 'The institutional origins of dynamic capabilities in multinational enterprises', *Industrial and Corporate Change*, 19(4): 1225–1246.

Eden, L. and Dai, L. (2010), 'Rethinking the "O" in Dunning's OLI/eclectic paradigm', *Multinational Business Review*, 18(2): 13–34.

Engwall, L. and Wallenstal, M. (1988), 'Tit for tat in small steps: The internationalisation of Swedish banks', *Scandinavian Journal of Management*, 4(3/4): 147–155.

Evers, N. (2011), 'Why do new ventures internationalise? A review of the literature of factors that influence new venture internationalisation', *Irish Journal of Management*, 30(2): 17–46/

Gaffney, N., Kedia, B. and Clampit, J. (2013), 'A resource dependence perspective of EMNE FDI strategy', *International Business Review*, 22(6): 1092–1100.

Hennart, J-F. (1977), *A Theory of Foreign Direct Investment*, PhD Dissertation, University of Maryland.

Hofstede, (XXXX)

Hollensen S. (2004), *Global Marketing: A Decision-Oriented Approach*, third edition, Englewood Cliffs, NJ: FT Prentice Hall.

Hollensen, S. (2013), *Global Marketing*, sixth edition, London: Pearson.

Hutchinson, K., Alexander, N., Quinn, B. and Doherty, A. M. (2007), 'Internationalization motives and facilitating factors: Qualitative evidence from smaller specialist retailers', *Journal of International Marketing*, 15(3): 96–122.

Johanson, J. and Vahlne, J.-E. (1974), *The Internationalisation Process of the Firm*, Working Paper, Department of Business Administration, University of Uppsala, Sweden.

Johanson, J. and Wiedersheim-Paul, J. (1975), 'The internationalisation of the firm: Four Swedish cases', *Journal of Management Studies*, 12(3): 305–322.

Johanson, J. and Vahlne, J.-E. (1977), 'The internationalisation process of the firm: A model of development and increasing foreign market commitment', *Journal of International Business Studies*, 8(1): 23–32.

Johanson, J. and Vahlne, J.-E. (1990), 'The mechanisms of internationalisation', *International Marketing Review*, 7(4): 11–24.

Knight, G. and Cavusgil, S. T. (1996), 'The born global firm: A challenge to traditional internationalization theory', in Cavusgil, S. T. and Madsen, T. (eds) *Advances in International Marketing*, 8: 11–26, Greenwich, CT: JAI Press.

Levitt, T. (1983), 'The globalisation of markets', *Harvard Business Review*, 61(3): 92–102.

Madsen, T. K. and Servais, P. (1997), 'The internationalization of born globals: An evolutionary process?', *International Business Review*, 6(6): 561–583.

Matthyssens, and Pauwels, (2000),

McSweeney, B. (2013), 'Fashion founded on a flaw: The ecological mono-deterministic fallacy of Hofstede, GLOBE and followers', *International Marketing Review*, 30(5): 483–504.

Moen, O. (2002), 'The born globals: A new generation of small European exporters', *International Marketing Review*, 19(2): 156–175.

Narula, R. and Dunning, J. H. (2010), 'Multinational enterprises, development and globalization: Some clarifications and a research agenda', *Oxford Development Studies*, 38(3): 263–287.

Nordstrom, K. A. (1990), *The Internationalisation Process of the Firm – Searching for New Patterns and Explanations*, Institute of International Business, Stockholm University of Economics, Sweden.

Oviatt, B. M. and McDougall, P. P. (1994), 'Toward a theory of international new ventures', *Journal of International Business Studies*, 25(1): 45–64.

Oviatt, B. M. and McDougall, P. P. (1995), 'Global start-ups: Entrepreneurs on a worldwide stage', *Academy of Management Executive*, 9(2): 30–43.

Papadopoulos, N. and Martin Martin, O. (2011), 'International market selection and segmentation: Perspectives and challenges', *International Marketing Review*, 28(2): 132–149.

Palmer, M. (2004), 'International retail restructuring and divestment: The experience of Tesco', *Journal of Marketing Management*, 20(10): 1075–1105.

Palmer, M. (2005), 'Retail multinational learning: A case study of Tesco', *International Journal of Retail and Distribution Management*, 33(1): 23–48.

Palmer, M. and Quinn, B. (2007), 'The nature of international retail divestment: Insights from Ahold', *International Marketing Review*, 24(1): 26–44.

Reid, S. (1983), 'Firm internationalization, transaction costs and strategic choice', *International Marketing Review*, 1(2): 45–55.

Root, F. R. (1994), *Entry Strategies for International Markets*, San Francisco, CA: Jossey-Bass.

Schmid, S. and Kotulla, T. (2011), '50 years of research on international standardization and adaptation: From a systematic literature analysis to a theoretical framework', *International Business Review*, 20(5): 491–507.

Seggie, S. H. (2012), 'Transaction cost economics in international marketing: A review and suggestions for future research', *Journal of International Marketing*, 20(2): 49–71.

Shaver, J. M. (2013), 'Do we really need more entry mode studies?', *Journal of International Business Studies*, 44(1): 23–27.

Vahlne, J.-E. and Wiedersheim-Paul, F. (1973), 'Economic distance: Model and empirical investigation', in Hornell, E., Vahlne, J-E., and Wiedersheim-Paul, F. (Eds) *Export and Foreign Establishments*, Uppsala, Sweden, pp. 81–159.

Vahlne, J.-E., Ivarsson, I. and Johanson, J. (2011), 'The tortuous road to globalization for Volvo's heavy truck business extending the scope of the Uppsala model', *International Business Review*, 20(1): 1–14.

Veniak, S. and Brewer, P. (2013), 'Critical issues in the Hofstede and GLOBE national culture models', *International Marketing Review*, 30(5): 469–482.

Welch, L. S., Benito, G. R. G. and Petersen, B. (2007), *Foreign Operation Modes: Theory, Methods and Analysis*, Cheltenham, UK: Edward Elgar.

Williams, D. (1992), 'Motives for retailer internationalization: Their impact, structure, and implications', *Journal of Marketing Management*, 8(3): 269–285.

Williamson, O. E. (1975), *Markets and Hierarchies: Analysis and Anti-trust Implication*, New York: The Free Press.

Williamson, O. E. (1981), 'The economics of organisation: The transaction cost approach', *American Journal of Sociology*, 87(3): 548–577.

Wrigley, N. and Currah, A. (2003), 'The "stresses" of retail internationalisation: Lessons from Royal Ahold's experience in Latin America', *International Review of Retail, Distribution and Consumer Research*, 13(3): 221–243.

21 Social marketing

Rebekah Russell-Bennett

Introduction

Social marketing is a behaviour change strategy that is used by governments and non-profits around the world to address social problems such as over-consumption of alcohol, poor eating habits, poverty, conservation of natural resources and violation of human rights. Social marketing is a distinct sub-discipline of marketing that began formally in 1971, when scholars promoted the idea that marketing could accomplish more than just selling soft drinks. Social marketing has flourished due to the effectiveness of interventions and campaigns in improving quality of life for societies and individuals around the globe. This chapter outlines the historical development of social marketing, the key issues and challenges in applying marketing thinking to social problems and demonstrates the application and effectiveness of marketing actions to change behaviour.

What is social marketing?

Social marketing is the application of commercial principles to social problems such alcohol consumption, smoking, obesity, road safety, water usage, environmental protection and fire safety. Social marketing commenced as a sub-discipline of marketing in the early 1970s when Kotler and Zaltman (1971) published the first social marketing article in the *Journal of Marketing*. They proposed that social marketing was a natural extension of commercial marketing, with the aim of marketing socially beneficial behaviours. Social marketing thus involves the same processes as commercial marketing, including the strategic planning process, consumer research, segmentation and the development of a marketing mix. The difference between commercial and social marketing is the nature of the product and the recipient of the benefits, as is shown in Table 21.1. Examples of socially beneficial influences are shown in Figures 21.1 to 21.3. These differences will be discussed in more detail throughout this chapter.

Defining social marketing

Since 1971, when social marketing was first described, there has been a myriad of social marketing definitions, with one recent article identifying 45 definitions (Dann 2010). Dann (2010) posed three reasons for the changes to the definition: (1) the alignment with changes in the definition of marketing by marketing associations; (2) changes in the practice of commercial marketing; and (3) historical development within the field of social marketing. In this chapter we choose selected definitions from each decade to show the evolution of the definition.

Table 21.1 Differences between commercial vs social marketing

	Commercial marketing	Social marketing
Goal	Profit	Social good
Organization	For profit and non-profit	Government and non-profit
Example success metrics	Satisfaction, loyalty, revenue, sales, market share	Lives saved, water conserved, waste reduced
Benefit timeframe	Immediately	Delayed
Budget	Typically larger budget for large enterprises	Typically lower
Responsiveness	Typically more adaptive and responsive to changes in the environment	Typically less adaptive and responsive to changes in the environment
Stakeholder focus	Less inclusive of partners	More inclusive of partners (partly for ease of access and budget maximization)

Figure 21.1 Socially beneficial influences – healthy eating

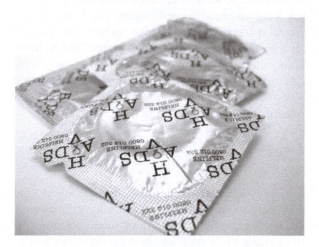

Figure 21.2 Socially beneficial influences – safe sex

Figure 21.3 Socially beneficial influences – recycling

1970s

In the 1970s the presence of social advertising (advertising that was aimed at communicating messages of social benefit) within the US was widely accepted. One problem of this widespread acceptance was the inflation of the ability of social advertising to influence the necessary behaviours to bring about social change (Kotler and Zaltman 1971). While social advertising is a highly influential communication medium, on its own it cannot address the complex motivations and barriers to undertaking socially beneficial behaviours, such as reduced drinking, eating healthily, recycling and conserving energy. Thus there emerged a need to distinguish between social advertising, and the broader approach of social marketing. This resulted in the first definition of social marketing: 'The design, implementation, and control of programs calculated to influence the acceptability of social ideas and involving considerations of product planning, pricing, communication, distribution, and marketing research' (Kotler and Zaltman 1971: 5). This definition has a specific focus on the 4P marketing mix to demonstrate that social marketing is distinct from social advertising. Interestingly, in this definition, there is no explicit mention of behavioural outcomes (a feature of later definitions).

1980s

The 1980s was a boom time for the discipline of marketing, with business schools around the world introducing marketing subjects and majors to a new generation of undergraduate students. Social marketing as a sub-discipline grew beyond a campaign focus to a broader program emphasis and replaced the specific mention of the 4P marketing mix with an emphasis on the social product (idea of practice). This led to the adapted definition of, 'a social-change management technology involving the design, implementation and control of programs aimed at increasing the acceptability of a social idea or practice' (Kotler and Roberto 1989: 24).

1990s

In the 1990s Alan Andreasen entered the field and left an indelible mark with his view of social marketing and its constituent parts (Andreasen 1994). A notable contribution was the seminal paper on benchmark criteria (discussed later in this chapter). The 1990s was a time that saw the establishment of the first journal of social marketing *Social Marketing Quarterly*, and dedicated social marketing conferences and centres around the world. A change in the definition was the introduction of the terms 'voluntary' and 'behaviour': 'Social marketing is the adaptation of commercial marketing technologies to programs designed to influence the voluntary behavior of target audiences to improve their personal welfare and that of society in which they are a part' (Andreasen 1994: 110). Commercial marketing by its nature is voluntary, as the organizations that conduct commercial marketing are profit enterprises and cannot force people to buy their products. The freedom to choose, or consumer sovereignty, is a central tenet in marketing and by extension so too in social marketing (Dann and Dann 1998). Social marketing, however, is typically conducted by governments, whereby law and policy are often associated with the behaviour change. Distinguishing social marketing as a strategy separate from legislation was necessary, as a central tenet of marketing is persuasion rather than coercion.

2000s

The 2000s was a time of momentum as social marketing took off as a genuine social change strategy within governments around the world and as a research area of interest within universities. A significant event was the establishment in the UK of the National Social Marketing Centre (NSMC), which was a joint venture between the UK Department of Health and a consumer lobby group. This centre, headed by Professor Jeff French, saw the documentation of evidence of social marketing effectiveness through case studies and a new set of benchmark criteria. During this era, the 4P marketing mix was critiqued with a variety of options offered (discussed further in this chapter). The result of both the centre and the critique of the 4Ps led to a new definition by Professor French and colleague, Dr Clive Blair-Stevens, as, 'the systematic application of marketing concepts and techniques to achieve specific behavioural goals relevant to a social good' (French and Blair-Stevens 2005: 31).

This was the first definition to specifically state the behavioural emphasis of social marketing, distinguishing it from social advertising's goal of attitudinal change.

Interestingly, the commercial marketing definition altered in the 2000s to recognize the application of marketing to the non-commercial sectors, and in 2008 the American Marketing Association (AMA) included for the first time the notion of societal benefit in their definition of marketing. This was formal acknowledgement of the expansion of the domain of marketing to government and the nonprofit sectors (AMA 2008).

A ground-breaking analysis of all previous definitions by Dr Stephen Dann of Australia investigated the core components of 45 definitions of social marketing to develop a consolidated definition of, 'the adaptation and adoption of commercial marketing activities, institutions and processes as a means to induce behavioural change in a targeted audience on a temporary or permanent basis to achieve a social goal' (Dann 2010: 151). This definition emphasized commercial marketing as the base for social marketing, the focus on behaviour change and the social goal.

2010s

The next decade of the 2000s saw an explosion in the number of scholarly articles in the field of social marketing, with the social marketing track at major marketing conferences attracting a large proportion of submissions. Since 1971, there have been 93 doctoral theses awarded in the area of social marketing, with 80 per cent of these occurring since 2001 (Truong *et al.* 2014). In 2011 the second scholarly journal was developed, the *Journal of Social Marketing*, and three social marketing associations were formed, with the first being the Australian Association of Social Marketing (www.aasm.org.au) (AASM) in 2009, the International Social Marketing Association in 2011 (www.i-socialmarketing.org) and the European Association of Social Marketing (www.european socialmarketing.org) in 2012. These three associations represent both practitioners and scholars of social marketing around the world, and were able to achieve a world first, global consensus on the definition of social marketing. This was the result of a concerted effort by international scholars and practitioners to answer the question, 'What is social marketing?', leading to a consensus definition adopted by the three formal social marketing associations above. This definition is, 'social marketing seeks to develop and integrate marketing concepts with other approaches to influence behaviour that benefits individuals and communities for the greater social good' (AASM 2013). For the purposes of this chapter, we adopt this definition.

Evolution of definition of social marketing

1971 Kotler and Zaltman

The design, implementation, and control of programmes calculated to influence the acceptability of social ideas and involving considerations of product planning, pricing, communication, distribution and marketing research

1989 Kotler and Roberto

A social-change management technology involving the design, implementation and control of programmes aimed at increasing the acceptability of a social idea or practice

1994 Andreasen

Social marketing is the adaptation of commercial marketing technologies to programmes designed to influence the voluntary behaviour of target audiences to improve their personal welfare and that of society of which they are a part

2006 French and Blair-Stevens

The systematic application of marketing concepts and techniques to achieve specific behavioral goals relevant to a social good

2010 Dann

The adaptation and adoption of commercial marketing activities, institutions and processes as a means to induce behavioural change in a targeted audience on a temporary or permanent basis to achieve a social goal

---

> **2013 International Social Marketing Association**
>
> Social marketing seeks to develop and integrate marketing concepts with other approaches to influence behaviour that benefits individuals and communities for the greater social good

So why is an understanding of the definition of social marketing important? There are three answers to this question:

1   A definition scopes the essential elements and processes and determines what is within and outside the scope of social marketing. This overcomes confusion with other social change approaches such as social advertising or health promotion.
2   Once a program can be identified as social marketing, benchmarking can occur to identify what the approach is capable of achieving in terms of social behaviours and what it cannot.
3   A definition leads to a set of benchmarks and criteria that assist practitioners in designing social marketing interventions that have a higher level of success and effectiveness.

Myths about social marketing

There are two key myths about social marketing; the first relates to social advertising and the second relates to social media marketing. Social marketing has its origins in social advertising (the use of information and messages to influence public attitudes and behaviours). It began when government agencies and nonprofit agencies realized the benefits of applying commercial advertising principles to social issues, such as sexual health and energy use (Fox and Kotler 1980). However, the limitations of a social advertising approach became quickly apparent with the realization that knowledge alone couldn't influence behaviour. Take, for instance, advertising campaigns to people about the importance of using a condom to prevent pregnancy; increasing awareness about the benefits of a condom is not useful for people who cannot afford a condom or whose cultural/social beliefs prevent them from using a contraceptive device. Back in the 1980s social marketing researchers were observing that 'mass communications have much less direct influence on behaviour than has been thought, and much of their influence is mediated through the opinion leadership of other people' (Fox and Kotler 1980: 25). As these limitations became better understood, the social marketing paradigm began to replace social advertising/communication as an approach for generating social change, with the addition of the marketing research (consumer insight), product development, incentives and access/convenience (Fox and Kotler 1980).

Despite the observations of Fox and Kotler (1980), in the mid-2010s there is still confusion about social marketing and social advertising, with many government agencies confusing the two and equating a media campaign as social marketing. The danger of this confusion is more than semantics; significant investment in a communication-only strategy may create awareness, but does little else to influence a consumer's approach to behaviour change and maintaining positive behaviours. For example, shocking advertisements about topics such as sex trafficking raise awareness of the problem, but if they don't offer a mechanism to prevent sex trafficking then the net result is a lot of conversation about the issue, but no change.

The second myth is that social marketing is the same as social media marketing. Social media marketing involves the use of social media, such as Facebook, Snapchat, Twitter, Tumblr, YouTube and countless other sites, in a marketing mix. This is clearly different to broad marketing strategies aimed at generating social benefit. While social marketing may use social media as part of the intervention mix, they are not the same thing. So why has this confusion occurred? In short, it's a case of better brand awareness (Wood 2011). Social marketing is a term for the insiders; for market-ers to use within their profession to describe a particular social change approach. Social media is a service that is used globally by consumers in their everyday lives, so it is not surprising that when more people are aware of the term 'social media' when they encounter the term 'social marketing', they assume they are the same.

Vignette 1: Does social marketing work? Snake condoms

Figure 21.4 Snake condoms

Image source: http://www.snakecondoms.org.au/shop/snake-condoms

Problem: In 2003 teen pregnancy and sexually transmitted disease were identified as problems within the indigenous community in regional Victoria. Condoms were identified as a key solution to this problem; however, uptake was not at suitable rates despite being free from local health services. Reasons for the lack of condom use were identified as lack of cultural relevance to Aboriginal youth, too expensive, not available when needed.

Objective: To increase condom use by indigenous youth.

Consumer insight: Buying condoms from local services was perceived as embarrassing and more relevant to white people.

Social marketing mix: A new brand of condom was developed called 'Snake Condoms' featuring the colours of the Aboriginal flag (red, black and yellow) that were distributed by local youth trained to sell (called snake charmers). The price was just over 20c each, which is significantly cheaper than commercial brands that average 45c each. Promotion included music festival launch, narrowcast and broadcast mediums and merchandise.

Results: A year after launch there was an increase in the number of people indicating they used a condom (from 50 per cent to 80 per cent of people), over 15,000 condoms were sold and there was an increase in concern about having unprotected sex (from 21 per cent to 46 per cent).

Sources: Molloy *et al.* (2004); www.snakecondoms.org.au

For more information watch the video: https://www.youtube.com/watch?v=f_HvyndyzbE

Source: http://www.snakecondoms.org.au/about-snake/snake-history

Benchmark criteria of social marketing

To address the confusion in the marketplace amongst both marketers and government/nonprofit agencies about the nature of a social marketing program and to distinguish social marketing from other approaches to social change, benchmark criteria were developed. The purpose of these criteria was to state the scope of social marketing and to determine which programs were true to the definition of social marketing and which ones simply adopted the label of social marketing. At this stage you might be asking yourself, why would an organization adopt the label of social marketing falsely? The answer to this is threefold. The first is that the organization may believe they are doing social marketing, but in reality there is a lack of understanding of the specific components of social marketing – more typically an overreliance on communication and advertising rather than a full marketing mix. The second is that social marketing has become a buzz word and many practitioners and scholars want to be associated with a hot topic that will yield research or financial success. The desire to 'jump on the band-wagon' can result in people without the necessary knowledge or experience claiming to be social marketers. The third is that many of the practitioners of social marketing are 'part-time', who have a background in a non-marketing field such as health or environment and end up having social marketing 'tacked' onto their job (Tapp and Spotswood 2013).

Andreasen (2002) originally identified six benchmark criteria for identifying social marketing, which define it as distinct from commercial marketing. These criteria are: (1) a focus on behaviour change; (2) the use of consumer research to understand the target market segment; (3) the use of segmentation and targeting; (4) the creation of attractive and motivational exchanges; (5) the use of a methods mix; and (6) having an understanding of the competition (Andreasen 2002). These benchmark criteria were later expanded upon by the NSMC in the UK to include two additional criteria (see Table 21.2). The first is the inclusion of a customer orientation, which seeks to understand fully participants' lives, behaviours and the issues surrounding them through a mix of data sources and research methods. The second is the use of theory to understand behaviour and inform the intervention (NSMC 2010).

Table 21.2 Comparing the benchmark criteria

NSMC criteria (French and Blair-Stevens 2006)	Andreason 2002
1 **Customer orientation**. 'Customer in the round'. Develops a robust understanding of the audience, based on good market and consumer research, combining data from different sources.	–
2 **Behavioural goal**	Behaviour-change
3 **Theory**. Is behavioural theory-based and informed. Drawing from an integrated theory framework.	–
4 **Insight**. Based on developing a deeper 'insight' approach focusing on what 'moves and motivates'.	Research
5 **Exchange**. Incorporates an 'exchange' analysis. Understanding what the person has to give to get the benefits proposed.	Exchange
6 **Competition**. Incorporates a 'competition' analysis to understand what competes for the time and attention of the audience.	Competition
7 **Segmentation**. Uses a developed segmentation approach (not just targeting). Avoids blanket approaches.	Segmentation
8 **Methods mix**. Identifies an appropriate 'mix of methods'.	Marketing mix

What is the social marketing mix?

The original marketing mix was the 4P framework: product, price, promotion and place, and was the main framework for almost every marketing textbook until the 1990s. Services marketing emerged in the 1990s and added three more Ps (people, processes and physical evidence) to the marketing mix to reflect the intangible nature of services rather than the characteristics of manufactured goods. The rise of services thinking combined with the rise in social marketing meant that the term 'product' took on a more generic meaning to include goods (e.g. soft drink, motor vehicle, house), services (e.g. hairdressing, education, entertainment) or ideas (e.g. political parties, causes, behaviours). In social marketing, there grew divergent schools of thought about what to call the marketing mix, with some scholars advocating the 4P approach (namely Kotler and various colleagues), some social marketers using a services marketing framework adapting the 7Ps (Russell-Bennett *et al.* 2013), with others seeking to dismiss the Ps completely (Peattie and Peattie 2003; Donovan 2011; Gordon 2013; Tapp and Spotswood 2013).

Social marketing solutions often involve the delivery of a service, whether this be a cancer screening health service or park rangers patrolling the environment. Social marketing solutions can also involve manufactured goods, such as condoms or pedometers. So where then is the marketing mix framework to be used? An approach to marketing proposed in the mid-2000s poses that service and goods are not necessarily separate, but can be intertwined. Terming this idea *service-dominant logic*, Vargo and Lusch (2004) indicate that all goods include a service and that all services involve goods. To illustrate this point, let's consider the examples of a table and a hairdresser. Nobody buys a table just to buy a table, they buy the table for the service it provides: a functional service of holding plates and food or an emotional service of looking nice. So a table is both a manufactured good and provides a service. Likewise a hairdresser provides both the service of hair styling and uses goods such as shampoo and colour to deliver this service. So given that all products include a service aspect in some way, we adopt the social marketing service mix of 7Ps as recommended by Russell-Bennett *et al.* (2013) in the *Journal of Social Marketing*:

1   social product;
2   social price;
3   social place;
4   social promotion;
5   people;
6   processes;
7   physical evidence.

Social product

In social marketing, the product element is termed, 'the social product' and includes ideas, behaviours, goods and services (see Figure 21.5). This concept builds on Kotler and Roberto's (1989) definition of the social product as ideas, practices and tangible objects. Let's apply this definition to the example of a social marketing program related to reducing alcohol consumption. The social idea can be an attitude, a belief or a value such as 'drinking in moderation is desirable and good for a person's health'. The behaviour associated with this idea of moderate drinking may be 'drinking less than four drinks per night', or 'making every second drink a glass of water'. The goods associated with both the idea and behaviour may be bottles of water or non-alcoholic drinks being available, and a service may be an e-service such as a smartphone app that counts the number of drinks that have been consumed.

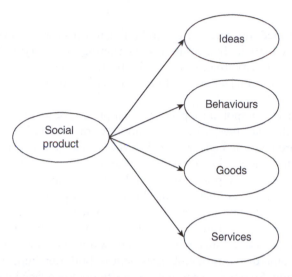

Figure 21.5 The social product

Not every social product needs to involve all four aspects; however, given that the intention of social marketing is to gain action (behaviour change or maintenance), the social product must have at least the idea and behaviour components. An example of a social product in breastfeeding is the MumBubConnect (MBC) (Figure 21.6) SMS service for new mothers in Australia (Russell-Bennett *et al.* 2012). Developed in 2010 by the Australian Breastfeeding Association (ABA) and researchers from Queensland University of Technology and University of Queensland, MBC developed a social product consisting of the following components:

1   Social idea: Any breastmilk is doing your baby good.
2   Behaviour: Give your baby breastmilk every day.
3   Goods: There were no goods specifically associated with the MBC program, however, the ABA offers a range of maternity wear and baby feeding items from their online Mothers Direct.
4   Services: An automated two-way SMS program that provides positive reinforcement and normalizes breastfeeding problems. For women who sent a text indicating problems, an outbound phone call from the ABA Helpline Service was made.

Figure 21.6 MumBub Connect

Price

In social marketing, the price element is termed 'the social price' and refers to the cost of undertaking a particular behaviour by the target market. In commercial marketing cost is typically considered to be financial; however, in social marketing, costs can be both financial and non-financial (see Table 21.3 for examples). Non-financial costs include time, effort, psychological, physical and emotional.

The marketing concept of exchange is a very important aspect of social price. For a consumer to be willing to adopt the social product, the exchange needs to be positive; that is the benefits associated with the product need to be more than the benefit gained. If the exchange is negative, that is the benefits are less than the costs, then the product offers less value to the consumer than the alternatives and they are unlikely to pay the social price. An example of this is in the area of sexual health. A study undertaken in the UK indicated that the social price of using a condom to prevent sexually transmitted diseases was deemed to be a negative exchange, whereas the benefits of using a condom were less than the cost of using one (Bird 2010). In this example, the benefits of protection from infection, preventing regret, or compliance with a partner wanting to use a condom were not motivating enough to overcome the costs of embarrassment of both obtaining and using a condom, or perceived lack of sensation. So what is a social marketer to do when faced with a negative exchange? According to Kotler and Lee (2008), there are six social pricing strategies:

1   increase financial benefits for the desired behaviour;
2   decrease financial costs for the desired behaviour;
3   increase non-financial benefits for the desired behaviour;
4   decrease non-financial costs for the desired behaviour;
5   increase financial costs for the competing behaviour;
6   increase nonmonetary costs for the competing behaviour.

So taking the example of condom use, let's examine the six social pricing options, with condom use being the desired behaviour and unprotected sex being the competing behaviour (see Table 21.4). Of these six pricing strategies, some are more practical (and ethical) than others. For instance, it is not possible to introduce fines for unprotected sex – how would you monitor and police this? Likewise, paying people to use a condom rather than having unprotected sex would be difficult to monitor and, from an ethics point of view, is this something on which a government or nonprofit agency would be spending money?

Table 21.3 Examples of costs for social products

Social product	Financial cost	Non-financial costs
Drinking moderately	Purchasing water or non-alcoholic drinks	Feeling left out of the friendship group if they drink
		Being perceived as uncool
Recycling	Purchasing a new wheelie bin to separate rubbish	Effort in separating rubbish or walking to a recycling bin
	Cost of petrol to drive to recycling centre	Feeling embarrassed in front of peers
Donating blood	Cost of transport to blood donation centre	Fear of needles
		Loss of work time and productivity if done during work hours

Table 21.4 Social pricing strategies for condom use

Social pricing strategies	Application for condom use
1 Increase financial benefits for the desired behaviour.	Provide financial incentive (paying people) or price adjustments for the use of condoms (discounts off another item if they also buy a condom).
2 Decrease the financial costs for the desired behaviour.	Reduce the monetary price of condoms by either offering a cheaper product or providing a discount voucher.
3 Increase nonfinancial benefits for the desired behaviour.	Provide recognition for people who have used a condom, encourage sexual partners to praise their partner for using a condom.
4 Decrease nonfinancial costs for the desired behaviour.	Reduce the embarrassment of using a condom by influencing positive social norms.
	Promote or sell a condom that increases the sensation/stimulation experienced when using one.
5 Increase the financial costs for the competing behaviour.	Introduce fines for unprotected sex.
6 Increase the nonmonetary costs for the competing behaviour.	Create a social norm that discourages and disapproves of unprotected sex.

Social place

In commercial marketing 'place' refers to the distribution channel of a good and the delivery of a service. 'Social place' refers to where and when the target market undertakes the social product and typically involves ease of access and convenience. As a social marketer, we want to reduce the costs of undertaking a behaviour, and this can be achieved in conjunction with the place element of the marketing mix. For example, we can alter physical locations where a behaviour occurs, such as place healthier food options in a cafeteria in an eye-catching location, or provide convenient access to a help-service that is 24 hours a day and seven days a week. A good example of the use of social place is the change of location for breastscreening services from a hospital to a retail centre. By changing the location of the service, there is a decoupling of the service image from one associated with medical treatment to that of prevention (thus reducing psychological costs of anxiety and fear). Undertaking the behaviour of cancer screening doesn't require a special trip, it can be combined with an everyday activity such as shopping. In Australia, Queensland Health recognized the need to overcome the time cost associated with having a breastscreen and introduced a screening service called 'The Rose Clinic' in local department stores near the women's clothing and lingerie (Figure 21.7) (Queensland Health 2014).

Partnerships are a necessary part of most social marketing interventions. These partnerships bring together the multiple stakeholders needed for a social change to occur and are part of the 'place' element of the marketing mix. Examples of partners include local authorities, community groups, media, schools, local businesses or lobby groups.

Social promotion (communication)

Similar to commercial marketing, promotion involves the communication of messages to educate and inform target audiences. This involves a variety of media channels and approaches, and needs to promote the benefits of the target behaviour as well as persuade consumers to view the marketing exchange as positive (social price). The communication may also inform consumers about the

Figure 21.7 Reception desk at the Rose Clinic

behaviour (create knowledge or correct myths) and inform about locations and ways to access goods and services or perform the behaviour (social place). This is the element of the marketing mix most associated with social marketing, as social marketing grew out of social advertising in the 1970s.

Promotion plays different roles in social marketing programs and depends largely on how informed the target market is about the behaviour. When consumers lack knowledge about a behaviour (benefits and how to do the behaviour) there will be a stronger emphasis on communication to inform and educate. In situations where consumers may be well-informed, but for certain reasons may not undertake the behaviour, the emphasis will be on providing ways to help them undertake the behaviour. For example, take the case of breastfeeding in Western countries. There is a segment of the population who are middle-class women, reasonably well-educated who are knowledgeable about the benefits of breastfeeding their baby (see Parkinson *et al.* 2012). Given this segment already knows about the benefits of the social product (breastfeeding), if they are not intending to breastfeed and the reason for this was because of return to work, a social marketing intervention may emphasize the service of the Breastfeeding Friendly Workplace Initiative in the social product (ensuring that workplaces meet legislative requirements to provide safe clean areas for mothers to breastfeed or express milk), and use promotion to communicate this initiative to mothers (Figure 21.8).

People

The 'people' element of the services marketing mix involves managing the people who are involved in the delivery of the social marketing service. This includes recruitment, training and developing staff to deliver a service that meets the needs of the target market. The role of people in the social marketing mix depends largely on the type of service. If the service is a people-processing service (services aimed at the body), then the role of people plays a critical role, unlike a possession-processing service (services aimed at possessions). In commercial marketing, any person hired to

Figure 21.8 Australian Breastfeeding Association

deliver a service would know that customer service is part of their role and dissatisfied customers who do not return affects the bottom line of profit. In social marketing, the people hired to deliver a service are more likely to be unaware of their role in customer service and may therefore act in ways that do not encourage consumers to return. Take, for instance, breastscreening, which involves radiographers as the key people delivering the mammography service. In a study on Breastscreen Queensland, the structural separation of health promotion staff from service delivery staff was preventing the achievement of a 'whole of service' approach and compartmentalizing the functions of social marketing to the health promotion officers (not the service delivery staff – the radiographers) (Russell-Bennett *et al.* 2013). So if service delivery staff do not adopt notions of customer orientation, it is unlikely that the target market will receive the service that encourages them to either maintain a desired behaviour or to change their behaviour.

Processes

The process element of the services marketing mix involves designing the service to be efficient, cost-effective and valuable to the target market. In commercial organizations this occurs to generate profit and in social marketing this occurs to influence a desired behaviour (either change or maintenance). However, given that social marketing services are typically delivered by government agencies, the idea of designing that service based on the needs of the target market is not necessarily a foundation principle. A focus on the needs of consumers requires a marketing orientation and this is something that is lacking in many government agencies. Indeed, a recent report (Dann and Dann 2005) identified government distaste for all things marketing, and while progress has been made in terms of improving government attitudes towards marketing, not all government employees share this.

One particular aspect of government that makes it difficult to effectively implement a social marketing services mix is the structural barriers within government. Typically, government separates the marketing functions; for instance, there is often a department called marketing communication that may have responsibility for social marketing; however, it does not control the service delivery, pricing or place elements (Russell-Bennett *et al.* 2013). This functional separation means that the service processes may not be as efficient as they might be, given a more coordinated customer-oriented approach.

Vignette 2: Does social marketing work? Project Bernie

Figure 21.9 Grass is green fire is mean

Image source: http://www.bernie.uk.com/

Problem: In South West Wales, 95 per cent of grass fires were deliberately lit creating an unnecessary burden on the local fire departments as well as endangering life and property. These fires cost an estimated £7m to the public purse, money that could be spent elsewhere. Previous campaigns on fire safety messages had been largely ineffective with incidences not reducing.

Objective: Reduce the incidence of deliberate grass fires in the Tonypandy target area by 15 per cent during the fortnight's Easter vacation period (26 March–12 April 2010).

Consumer insight: Fires were being lit by mainly teen males from varied educational backgrounds, to alleviate boredom and for experimentation. Seeing a fire truck arrive was an added bonus.

Social marketing mix: A holiday programme (service) with exciting activities as a diversion from fire-lighting that involved local firefighters, development of the Bernie brand (a sheep that didn't like her grass being set on fire). The promotions consisted of supermarket flyers, competitions, prizes, merchandise and social media.

Results: After the Easter period, there were 46 per cent fewer fires in the area and after Easter there was a reduction of 74 per cent.

Sources: Peattie *et al.* (2012); www.bernie.uk.com

Physical evidence

The last of the social marketing service mix elements is physical evidence. A service has intangible elements that increase the risk associated with using that service. One way of reducing the risk and providing quality cues is physical evidence. This evidence can be in the form of third-party endorsements (such as the heart foundation tick on food products), uniforms (such as a white lab coat for medical staff), certificates, awards and qualifications, or the service environment's physical features (such as layout of the building, smell, colour, light). The physical evidence communicates information to the consumer about the service quality, which in turn can influence the consumer's repeated use of the service. A study on blood donation found that physical cues, such as the medi-calized layout of a blood donor van and the colour red was very off-putting to younger people and deterred them from donating blood (Russell-Bennett *et al.* 2013).

Who does social marketing?

So who then can 'do' social marketing? While it has long been the domain of governments and non-profits, the advent of cause-related marketing and socially responsible marketing has led to commercial organizations seeking to leverage social marketing. While commercial organizations should be considered part of the solution to any social issue, and indeed may offer the very goods and services needed to help people achieve the goals of social marketing, the bottom line for a commercial organization is profit (Donovan 2011). This bottom line therefore precludes commercial organizations from being able to lead a social marketing intervention. The goal of social marketing is social good not profit and when these two goals come into conflict, for a commercial organization the profit goal comes up trumps (Hastings and Angus 2011).

However, despite this very obvious competition in goals, the popularity of social marketing as a social change approach, and the funding that is therefore available, attracts many commercial organizations to dabble in the waters. The term 'corporate social marketing' was first introduced by Kotler and Lee (2004) and is a contested term. Advocates claim that commercial organizations can 'improve society while at the same time building markets for products or services' (Kotler and Lee 2004: 14), whereas opponents argue that when conflict arises between the social and profit goals, the profit goal will dominate for a commercial organization (Donovan 2011). Two industries that have attempted to co-op social marketing under the label of social responsibility are the tobacco and alcohol industries (Hastings and Angus 2011).

Tobacco

The tobacco industry has attempted to demonstrate social responsibility by channeling funds into smoking prevention campaigns. However, research has shown that the opposite effect is achieved with consumers becoming more favourable towards tobacco than against (see Henriksen *et al.* 2006; Wakefield *et al.* 2006).

Alcohol

When alcohol companies include messages on the labels such as 'drink responsibly' or 'alcohol consumption can harm unborn children', instead of turning consumers off, this can actually create a favourable image of the company for appearing to 'be concerned' (Christie *et al.* 2001). There is also a lighter focus on the harmful effects of the product, with any significant health consequences often omitted.

So what then is the role of industry in the social marketing process? Well, it depends on who you ask. A person with a cynical view about the ability of industry to adequately serve the needs of society would say that industry has little role to play and should be regulated to ensure that their activities are socially responsible. Alternatively, a person with a more market-driven view may say that when consumers demand that industry provide socially responsible products, then industry supply of these products will follow. Given that the budgets of industry well exceed the budgets of governments and non-profits, it would seem logical that involving industry in some capacity to be part of a solution would be appropriate.

Applying strategic thinking to social change

Strategic thinking for social change focuses on finding a balance between analysis (understanding the social problem) and action (tactics that provide solutions to the problem). In common managerial terms this is the balance between strategy formulation and strategic implementation to realize the overall goal of any social marketing program. To achieve these ends, Lagarde (2011) notes that social marketers will have a better chance of influencing people to adopt a behaviour (behaviour focus) if:

1   they have detailed knowledge about a target market's lifestyle, thoughts and feelings (consumer orientation);
2   recognize that not all people are prepared to change (segmentation);
3   consider how other behaviours and existing preferences will compete with the social change proposition (competition);
4   make it desirable and easy for people (value exchange, marketing mix);
5   partner with influential people (place);
6   communicate effectively (promotion);
7   are in it for the long run (sustainability).

These seven elements of social marketing are the building blocks on which social marketers rely to effect social change. Yet to achieve the grander enterprise of effecting change in wider society, and to create and achieve positive social goals, it is important to consider how social marketing works at multiple levels: the 'downstream' individual-level, the 'midstream' organizational level and 'upstream' policy/institutional level.

Downstream level

The 'upstream' and 'downstream' metaphor is widely used in social marketing to describe the intervention level of a social marketing program and campaigns. The downstream-dominant approach targets individuals and uses marketing-like tactics to create an 'exchange of value', based on the target market giving up risky behaviours for a more socially desirable solution. For example, in developed countries such as Australia, the UK and the US, wide-ranging social marketing campaigns have been implemented to encourage people to change their eating habits and increase their physical activity as a preventative health approach to reducing the heart risks associated with obesity. These campaigns draw on individual-level social marketing messages such as 'go for 2 and 5', which encourages target audiences to 'eat two fruit and five serves of vegetables' daily as the foundation to a balanced diet. This message is supported with marketing collateral – cook books, promotional cooking programs and celebrity endorsements – to motivate consumers to more regularly cook balanced nutritional meals at home, rather than buying calorie-dense fast food options. The foundation of the downstream approach is an emphasis on personal responsibility and positioning of behaviour change as voluntary.

Upstream level

'Upstream' social marketing contrasts this approach by focusing on policy and regulation. These tools become the marketing-like activities used to effect the structural change needed to support or encourage individuals and groups in society to participate in social change programs and sustain positive behaviours. This is a hotly contested strategy in social marketing, particularly for social marketers who stress the importance of voluntary behaviour (e.g. Dann and Dann 1998), and for those who argue that social marketing programs can involve coercion or legislation that enforces people to change (Donovan 2011). In recent times, many social marketers have argued that the heavy reliance on individual voluntary behaviour change is outdated and have embraced applying social marketing activities to influence other change factors that leverage cultural and social-ecological levels of the environment (Tapp and Spotswood 2013). For example, activities such as supporting needle exchange programs for drug users; testifying before government decision-makers for the purpose of increasing funding to research; and condom availability or free testing facilities for HIV/AIDS, are proposed upstream approaches that can be effective motivation and persuasion activities that impact societal change for good. Social marketers who think strategically about upstream strategy are concentrating on changing the conditions in which people make decisions and are focused on making it 'easier' for consumers to make the right lifestyle choices for themselves and their society (Eagle *et al.* 2013).

Midstream level

'Midstream' social marketing strategy focuses the social marketer's attention on the organizational and community resources available in society that can be leveraged to effect and sustain a social change program. Russell-Bennett *et al.* (2013) point out that services marketing thinking directs social marketers to engage service elements (e.g. service process, employees and decision-makers), which can be coordinated to impact a target market's abilities to initiate and sustain behaviour change goals. At the same time, there are also resources available in the community that can be leveraged to facilitate social change. Thus, midstream strategies also involve building partnerships to create a system of connections between existing and potentially new organizations for the purpose of providing resources (e.g. professional expertise or skills) to support wider community adoption of a social marketing campaign. Because social marketing strategy is typically confronted with restricted budget options, partnerships offer additional value to a social change strategy through collaborative relationships in which partners can work together to achieve agreed behaviour change goals, sharing risks and responsibilities, as well as competencies that create value for both partners and recipients of the partners' activity (Eagle *et al.* 2013).

Strategic social marketing and a multi-level approach

Figure 21.10 illustrates the social change continuum and conceptualizes the interrelationships between the 'streams' of social marketing thinking and operational activities needed to support and create change that benefits and improves society.

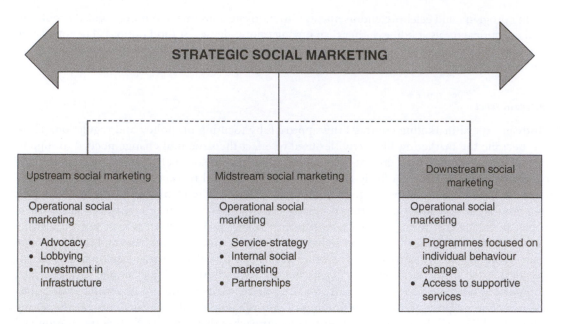

Figure 21.10 Strategic levels of social marketing thinking

Table 21.5 provides an example of social marketing strategies employed along the social change intervention continuum for the social issue of energy use. Social problems are complex and are rarely solvable by single-level interventions. Focusing on the downstream level leads to an overemphasis on individuals being accountable for rectifying the situation, when in reality the problem can only be solved through the coordinated efforts of all parties involved (government, industry and consumers). Likewise, focusing on the upstream level leads to an overemphasis on regulation and policy, which aims to control industry and consumers, and can stifle innovation and override the rights of the individual to choose. As suggested in Figure 21.10, a multi-level approach offers a holistic solution that is inclusive of all stakeholders committed to a common goal with shared responsibility.

Social marketing planning process

Applying the social marketing approach to behaviour change starts from an understanding that there are a range of interventional options – downstream, midstream and upstream – that can be deployed to achieve particular behavioural goals with different stakeholder groups. In social marketing it is widely acknowledged that single interventions are less effective than multi-level interventions, therefore the key to planning a sound strategy is making a reasoned judgement about the balance or mix of interventions to be implemented and how they will be evaluated. There is no single correct approach to developing social marketing interventions; however, in 'theory' there is a shared logical process to follow when considering how to use marketing resources to achieved objectives and goals.

There are a multitude of frameworks for planning social marketing activities, including the STELa planning process. Developed by Professor Jeff French, this model contains four steps: scope, test, enact, learn/act. For more details, visit http://www.stelamodel.com/ or https://www.you tube.com/watch?v=z2YnsTfbS-s

Table 21.5 Social marketing strategies for the social change continuum

Marketing function	Strategy		
	Upstream policymakers	Midstream energy providers will:	Downstream consumers will:
Product	Idea: Believe that a conducive environment/infrastructure is needed to incentivize innovation and support for efficient energy use	Idea: Believe that conserving energy and using renewable energy sources is a profitable business model	Idea: Believe that energy should be conserved and renewable energy is preferable
	Behaviour: Collaborate with industry and consult with consumers to provide affordable efficient energy solutions	Behaviour: Design affordable energy affordable efficient services for consumers	Behaviour: Switch off unnecessary appliances and wash in cold water
	Good: If government owns infrastructure, efficient infrastructure needs to be developed and maintained	Good: Provide reliable energy efficient products	Good: Home electricity monitors
	Service: Support services to help industry and consumers to engage in reducing energy use	Service: Flexible and responsive services to meet customer needs for conserving energy use	Service: In home electricity check/smartphone app to monitor usage
Price	Increase financial benefits for desired behaviour (e.g., incentivize energy providers offering energy efficient goods and services)	Decrease the financial costs for the desired behaviour (e.g. reduce the cost of producing renewable energy)	Decrease the financial costs for the desired behaviour (e.g. reduce the cost of energy for consumers)
	Increase the financial costs for the competing behaviour (e.g. offering nonrenewable sources of energy)		
Place	Making access to energy use data easy and convenient through infrastructure technology such as smart-meters	Provide convenient services that diagnose, monitor and improve energy use (in-person or electronic)	Use the services to monitor consumption and identify opportunities to reduce energy use. Easily access solutions

(continued)

Table 21.5 (continued)

Marketing function	Strategy		
	Upstream policymakers	*Midstream energy providers will:*	*Downstream consumers will:*
Promotion	Provide advice and advocate for alternative service solutions that support consumers in conserving energy and using renewable sources	Conduct a community event that involves energy providers and consumers	Exciting promotional tactics that entertain and persuade energy users
People	Develop an understanding across key stakeholders of a service orientation and the need for consumer evaluation	Ensure that front-line service staff adopt a market orientation and are sensitive to consumer needs	Provide well-trained, efficient staff to assist consumers
Processes	Reduce government red tape	Transparency around pricing	Processes for conserving energy and using renewable sources need to be consumer friendly and easy to understand and implement
Physical evidence	Provide accreditation and certification, green schemes	Seek third-party endorsement and seek accreditation by meeting green standards. Provide easier to understand evidence on energy bills	Use services and products from accredited suppliers. Increase energy literacy

The UK's NSMC's total process (see Figure 21.11) planning framework embraces the key steps social marketers typically employ when approaching the design, implementation and evaluation of social marketing programs and campaigns. A key aspect of this planning framework is that it is *process* oriented, which makes an important point about the need to adjust and tailor planning tasks and marketing activities to the expectations, contexts and resources available, and that these need to be frequently assessed during the program's lifecycle (Ong and Blair-Stevens 2010).

- **Scoping the problem** is a crucial first step in the process and involves considerable background and desk research, and the multitude of other information an organization has to inform the social marketing approach. Critically, this scoping stage is about understanding the behaviour (include the target audience, employees, community members, etc.) and what resources an organization has to deliver on the planned objectives and goals set for the social marketing program.

  Deliverables: scoping report and decision on interventions to carry forward into the development step.

- **Developing the intervention** involves a range of techniques, which are designed in response to the social issues/challenges and problems identified during scoping. At the development stage, the social marketer chooses a mix of techniques and marketing-like activities to address the multiple levels of influence, to be coordinated with a clear focus on achieving program objectives and goals.

  Deliverables: strategy document and marketing plan.

- **Implementing the strategy** is about launching the program and when the marketing activities 'go live'. A critical element in this step is about the social marketer being responsive to the intervention mix and techniques that have been stipulated during scoping and development. Important processes include live tracking, which is a focus on looking for opportunities (e.g. media reports generate additional interest and social media users promote the program) or risks (e.g. if the campaign message gets high jacked by an inappropriate audience, or potential threats that could undermine the interventions).

  Deliverables: monitoring and tracking results on interventions and marketing activities.

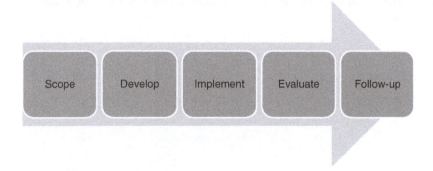

Figure 21.11 NSMC's total process

- **Evaluating the interventions** and marketing activities involves the social marketer and other organizational members reviewing the original aims and objectives and using the data and views collated to assess the success metrics. These will include measures such as impact and cost-effectiveness.

Deliverables: evaluation reports.

- **Follow-up** involves social marketers working with other organizational members to review reports and other commissioned research. This may include considerations of the role of stakeholders and the return on marketing investment in the social marketing program.

Deliverables: recommendations and proposals for future marketing activities.

Future directions for social marketing

So four decades after the first published definition, the discipline and practice of social marketing is used in many countries to address a myriad of social issues and to effect positive social change. Drawing on current thinking, including reflections on social marketing by practitioners and scholars at the 2nd World Social Marketing Conference held in Dublin, Beall *et al.* (2012) indicate three areas for the future of social marketing:

1   Branding of social marketing: The need to more assertively publicize the scope and contribution of social marketing for social change (Wood 2011; Beall *et al.* 2012).
2   An evidence base:

- The need to learn from both the success and failure of social marketing. This is a challenge for organizations to make failure public, particularly given the political implications for government agencies.
- Social marketers need to continue adhering to strong practice standards and ensure that evaluation of social marketing programs are both rigorous and relevant (Beall *et al.* 2012).

3   Working collaboratively:

- At a strategic level social marketing needs to work seamlessly with other organizations and individuals who use different approaches to achieve the social goal (Beall *et al.* 2012).
- Be open to a cooperative view (working together) rather than competitive view of industry (us vs. them) to work with suppliers of services and goods that can assist consumers to enact behaviour change.

References

AASM (2013), Available at www.aasm.org.au

AMA (2008) 'Definition of marketing', *Marketing News*, 15 January: 28–29.

Andreasen, A. R. (1994), 'Social marketing: Its definition and domain', *Journal of Public Policy and Marketing*, 13(1): 108–114.

Andreasen, A. R. (2002), 'Marketing social marketing in the social change marketplace', *Journal of Public Policy and Marketing*, 21(1): 3–13.

Beall, T., Wayman, J., D'Agostino, H., Liang, A. and Perellis, C. (2012), 'Social marketing at a critical turning point', *Journal of Social Marketing*, 2(2): 103–117.

Bird, S. (2010), 'Passionate escapism versus rational thought', paper presented at the *International Nonprofit and Social Marketing Conference* 15–16 July, Brisbane, Australia.

Christie, J., Fisher, D., Kozup, J. C., Smith, S., Burton, S. and Creyer, E. H. (2001), 'The effects of bar-sponsored alcohol beverage promotions across binge and nonbinge drinkers', *Journal of Public Policy & Marketing*, 20(2): 240–253.

Dann, S. (2010), 'Redefining social marketing with contemporary commercial marketing definitions', *Journal of Business Research*, 63(2): 147–153.

Dann, S. and Dann, S. (1998), 'Cybercommuning: Global village halls', in Alba, J. W. and Hutchinson, J. W. (eds) *Advances in Consumer Research Volume 25*, Provo, UT: Association for Consumer Research.

Dann, S and Dann, S (2005), *Insight and Overview of Social Marketing*, Premiers Department, Queensland Government, available at http://www.premiers.qld.gov.au/publications/categories/reports/assets/social-marketing-final-report.pdf (accessed 20 October 2014).

Donovan, R. (2011), 'Social marketing's mythunderstandings', *Journal of Social Marketing*, 1(1): 8–16.

Eagle, L., Dahl, S., Hill, S., Bird, S., Spotswood, F. and Tapp, A. (2013), *Social Marketing*, Sydney, Australia: Pearson.

Fox, K. F. A and Kotler, P. (1980), 'The marketing of social causes: The first 10 years', *Journal of Marketing*, 44(4): 24–33.

French, J. and Blair-Stevens, C. (2005), 'Social marketing pocket guide', first edition, *National Social Marketing Centre for Excellence*, London: Department of Health, National Consumer Council.

French, J. and Blair-Stevens, C. (2006), 'From snake oil salesmen to trusted policy advisors: The development of a strategic approach to the application of social marketing in England', *Social Marketing Quarterly*, vol. 12, no. 3, pp. 29–40.

Gordon, R. (2013), 'Unlocking the potential of upstream social marketing', *European Journal of Marketing*, 47(9): 1525–1547.

Hastings, G. and Angus, K. (2011), 'When is social marketing not social marketing?', *Journal of Social Marketing*, 1(1): 45–53.

Henriksen, L., Dauphinee, A. L., Wang, Y. and Fortmann, S. P. (2006), 'Industry sponsored anti-smoking ads and adolescent reactance: Test of a boomerang effect', *Tobacco Control*, 15(1): 13–18.

Kotler P. and Zaltman, G. (1971), 'Social marketing: An approach to planned social change', *Journal of Marketing*, 35(3): 3–12.

Kotler, P. and Roberto, E. L. (1989), *Social Marketing*, London: Macmillan Publishing.

Kotler, P. and Lee, N. (2004), 'Best of breed: When it comes to gaining a market edge while supporting a social cause "corporate social marketing" leads the pack', *Stanford Social Innovation Review*, Spring: 14–23.

Kotler, P. and Lee, N. (2008), *Social Marketing*, Thousand Oaks, CA: Sage Publications.

Lagarde, F. (2011), 'Insightful social marketing leadership', *Social Marketing Quarterly*, 18(1): 77–81.

Molloy, R., Greet, B. and Knight, K. (2004), 'Don't let your community get bitten. Ask for a snake', *Aboriginal and Islander Health Worker Journal*, 28(6): 14–16.

NSMC (2010), *Social Marketing Benchmark Criteria*, available at http://www.nsmcentre.org.uk/sites/default/files/benchmark-criteria-090910.pdf (accessed 20 November 2014).

Ong, D. and Blair-Stevens, C. (2010), 'The total process planning (TPP) framework', in French, J., Blair-Stevens, C., McVey, D. and Merritt, R. (eds) *Social Marketing and Public Health*, Oxford, UK: Oxford University Press, pp. 151–160.

Parkinson, J., Russell-Bennett, R. and Previte, J. (2012), 'Mum or bub? Which influences breastfeeding loyalty', *Australasian Marketing Journal*, 20(1): 16–23.

Peattie, S. and Peattie, K. (2003), 'Ready to fly solo? Reducing social marketing's dependence on commercial marketing theory', *Marketing Theory*, 3(3): 365–385.

Peattie, S., Peattie, K. and Thomas, R. (2012), 'Social marketing as transformational marketing in public services', *Public Management Review*, 14(7): 987–1010.

Queensland Health (2014), *New Service at David Jones*, available at http://www.health.qld.gov.au/breastscreen/david-jones.asp (accessed 31 October 2014).

Russell-Bennett, R., Gallegos, D., and Previte, J. (2012), 'Overcoming barriers through new technology: Support via text messaging', in Thorley, V. and Vickers, M. (eds) *Mother Support: The 10th Step*, Amarillo, TX: Hale Publishing.

Russell-Bennett, R., Wood, M. and Previte, J. (2013), 'Fresh ideas: Services thinking for social marketing', *Journal of Social Marketing*, 3(3): 223–238.

Tapp, A. and Spotswood, F. (2013), 'From the 4Ps to COM-SM: Reconfiguring the social marketing mix', *Journal of Social Marketing*, 3(3): 206–222.

Truong, V. D., Garry, T. and Hall, M. (2014), 'Social marketing as the subject of doctoral dissertations', *Social Marketing Quarterly*, 20(4): 1–20.

Vargo, S. L. and Lusch, R. F. (2004), 'Evolving to a new dominant logic for marketing', *Journal of Marketing*, 68(1): 1–17.

Wakefield, M., McLeod, K. and Perry, C. L. (2006), 'Stay away from them until you're old enough to make a decision: Tobacco company testimony about youth smoking initiation', *Tobacco Control*, 15(4): iv44–iv53 (supplement).

Wood, M. (2011), 'Marketing social marketing', *Journal of Social Marketing*, 2(2): 94–102.

22 Marketing for nonprofit organisations

Adrian Sargeant and Ian MacQuillin

Introduction

Although historians have now taught us that the idea of applying marketing ideas to key nonprofit contexts such as fundraising has a tradition spanning centuries (Mullin 1995), it was not until the late 1960s that academic interest in the topic first began to emerge. Kotler and Levy (1969) are credited with opening the academic debate on this issue, arguing that marketing had been regarded for too long as a narrow business function and rebuking both academics and practitioners for ignoring the broader relevance of our ideas. At the time, their perspective gave rise to much discussion, particularly in the early 1970s (see for example Luck 1969; Ferber 1970; Lavidge 1970). Lovelock and Weinberg (1990) argued that this early debate 'fizzled-out' in the latter part of that decade as marketers became more concerned with other variants of their discipline and, in particular, turned their attention to the issue of whether service marketing might be any different from the marketing of products. By the end of the 1970s, Kotler and Levy's revised definition of marketing as 'serving human needs and wants sensitively' (Kotler and Levy 1969: 15) was no longer controversial.

A number of landmarks have been passed since then. In 1971 the *Journal of Marketing* provided an entire issue devoted to marketing's social/environmental role, and the first empirical studies then followed (see e.g. Meade 1974; Miller 1974). In the early 1980s the first generic nonprofit marketing textbooks appeared, with work by Rados (1981), Kotler and Andreasen (1982) and Lovelock and Weinberg (1989) being particularly noteworthy. Textbooks also began to appear in the specific fields of healthcare (Cooper 1979; Frederiksen *et al.* 1984; Kotler and Clarke 1986), education (Kotler and Fox 1985), the arts (Mokwa *et al.* 1980), the marketing of ideas (Fine 1981), social marketing (Manoff 1985; Kotler and Roberto 1989), and, most recently, fundraising (Sargeant and Jay 2004; Sargeant and Shang 2010).

The 1980s and early 1990s saw the introduction of a number of scholarly journals, including the generic *Journal of Nonprofit and Public Sector Marketing* and the *International Journal of Nonprofit and Voluntary Sector Marketing*. Sector specific journals also emerged including *New Directions in Philanthropic Fundraising*, the *Journal of Educational Advancement*, *Health Marketing Quarterly*, the *Journal of Health Care Marketing*, the *Journal of Marketing for Higher Education* and the *Social Marketing Quarterly*. It was also not unusual to find journals from other disciplines printing studies from the field of nonprofit marketing. Andreasen and Kotler (2004) note studies in fields as diverse as library science, art history and hospital management.

It would be impossible to do justice to the full range of this scholarly enterprise in this brief chapter, but neither is it necessary to do so in a volume comprising the best of current marketing thought. Many marketing ideas, models and frameworks have as much relevance to the nonprofit as the for-profit domain. Indeed, the eminent marketing scholar, Shelby Hunt (1977), argued that a profit/nonprofit dichotomy would only be valuable until:

1   the broadening of the marketing concept was no longer regarded as controversial;
2   the nonprofit sector and the issues that must be addressed therein were completely integrated into all marketing courses and not treated as a separate subject;
3   nonprofit managers perceived their organisations as having marketing problems;
4   nonprofits established marketing departments (where appropriate) and employed marketing personnel.

Since the adoption of marketing ideas in the nonprofit arena is no longer controversial and many nonprofits now employ marketing personnel to address marketing issues, the second of Hunt's (1977) tests seems the only area of difficulty. Nonprofit marketing has yet to be properly integrated into 'mainstream' marketing courses, quite possibly because it is seen as being of less interest to the majority of marketing students and/or employers. Whilst this may seem intuitive, it fails to reflect the pattern of the majority of modern careers, where many individuals will now work for a variety of employers and quite possibly in a variety of contexts. The need for a broader perspective on the subject has therefore never been greater.

That is not to say, however, that we should necessarily agree with Shelby Hunt that it is desirable that nonprofit and for-profit marketing be merged, should this latter criterion be met. Whilst greater coverage of nonprofit marketing in generic marketing modules would be applauded, the body of knowledge that comprises nonprofit marketing is beginning to develop to a point where it would be difficult to do more than merely scratch the surface of the topic in any generic course. The bodies of knowledge, in particular, for fundraising/volunteering and social marketing are now very well developed, as is the evidence that simply applying for-profit ideas to these contexts would be inappropriate. Nonprofit organisations share a number of characteristics that make the adaptation of marketing thought essential, and in this chapter we will therefore conduct a review of these factors and suggest how marketing tools and ideas may be adapted to make them more suitable for the nonprofit context.

How is nonprofit marketing really different?

Over the years, many scholars have discussed this issue and there is considerable debate about whether any differences are as real as they might at first appear (Sargeant 1999). Nevertheless, the following eight characteristics of nonprofits may help to explain some of the complexities that the marketing function in a typical organisation may encounter.

1   two distinct markets;
2   multiple constituencies;
3   need for societal not market orientation;
4   non-financial objectives;
5   services and social behaviours rather than physical goods;
6   collaboration not competition;
7   public scrutiny/non-market pressures;
8   higher ethical standards.

We will consider each in turn.

Two distinct markets

In a for-profit context the marketing function is concerned with developing goods and services, which will then be sold to customers. This will generate revenue, which can in turn be used to purchase the raw materials necessary to produce the next generation of goods and services and so on. In short, there is only one primary constituency that needs to be addressed by the marketing function, namely the customers of the organisation. In many nonprofits, however, there are two constituencies, since the funders of the organisation are frequently not its service users. Funders merely pay for, or subsidise, the provision of benefits for others. Many nonprofits therefore have to employ marketing ideas in two distinct contexts, the market for resource attraction and the market for resource allocation.

Of course, one might argue that this difference between the two sectors is illusory. Some businesses draw income from a variety of sources, not necessarily just their primary customer group(s). Some may even attract significant government funding or seek occasionally to raise funds from a new issue of shares. Thus, marketers in business organisations can find themselves dealing with multiple constituencies too. It does seem safe to conclude, however, that the division between resource attraction and resource allocation is rarely so clear-cut as it is in the majority of nonprofit organisations.

This difference is highly significant for three reasons. First, nonprofit managers have to balance their desire to provide mission-related products and services with their ability to sustain the income necessary to support them. Sadly, some activities may be highly relevant to the organisation's mission, but they may be more difficult to fund than others that are perhaps more tangential. This makes the management of an appropriate portfolio of activities much more complex than would be the case in the for-profit environment.

Second, the majority of scholarly marketing thought has been focused on the exchange of tangible goods or services. This tends to form the core of marketing thought taught in our business schools and reported in our textbooks. Whilst understandable, it neglects the growing body of work conducted into the market for resource attraction, much of which delivers real practical value for nonprofit managers, enhancing their understanding of the operation of this market and the manner in which it could best be approached.

Third, the marketing function in nonprofit organisations tends to be split between the fundraising department, which takes responsibility for marketing to donors to secure income, and the campaigning, service delivery and communications functions that assume the role of marketing products and services to beneficiaries and conducting any social marketing, lobbying or campaigning. There are therefore multiple marketing roles. We will examine each of these issues in turn.

Nonprofit portfolio management

Whilst a variety of portfolio models have been employed over the years, these have largely been developed in the business context and are thus difficult to apply to the context of nonprofit marketing. In particular, nonprofit marketers should studiously avoid any portfolio model that has as its base the concept of market share (e.g. the Boston Box), since this notion cannot be meaningfully applied to the nonprofit context. This is the case for three reasons:

1   The sheer scale of the nonprofit sector and the fact that service and/or fundraising performance is usually reported in aggregate terms only means that it would be impossible to meaningfully quantify market share for most organisations.

2   Portfolio models employing market share assume that the performance of a product or service is related to market share (i.e. that there are economies of scale). This is simply not the case in most nonprofit contexts.

3   Market share is employed in many portfolio models, because it indicates the position of each competitor in a given market. Since many nonprofits do not compete, the use of such models is again problematic.

For these reasons, the portfolio model in Figure 22.1 is to be preferred. Its adoption would provide nonprofit managers with a clearer perspective on the overall health of their portfolio and offer general guidance in respect of where future investment and effort may be targeted.

To utilise the model it is necessary to begin by examining in detail the components of the two axes, namely external attractiveness and internal appropriateness. If we consider first the question of external attractiveness, this relates to a particular organisation's ability to attract resources. Not all of an organisation's services will be equally attractive to potential funders and, whilst most charities would not exclude the provision of a service simply because it was perceived by donors as unsavoury, few would argue that the ability to raise funds was not an issue. Whilst the specific factors will undoubtedly vary from one organisation to another, the degree of support donors are willing to give a particular activity is likely to depend on:

- the level of general public concern;
- likely trends in public concern;
- numbers of people aided;
- immediacy of impact on beneficiary group.

It is important to recognise that this list is not exhaustive, and the beauty of this model is that organisations can utilise whatever factors they perceive as being relevant to their own environment and circumstances.

Turning now to the question of internal appropriateness, this relates to the extent to which the service 'fits' the profile of the organisation providing it. In other words, is provision appropriate given the skills, expertise and resources available within the organisation? Relevant factors here might include:

- the level of previous experience with the activity;
- the perceived importance of the activity;

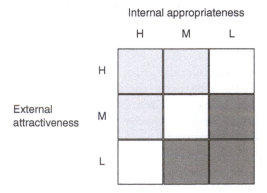

Figure 22.1 Non-profit portfolio analysis

- the extent to which the activity is compatible with the organisation's mission;
- the extent to which the organisation has unique expertise to offer.

Once again, this list can be expected to vary from context to context and an organisation would look to identify those factors that are most pertinent to its particular circumstances.

Having now defined the components of internal appropriateness and external attractiveness, the reader will appreciate that not all the factors identified could be seen as having equal importance to a given organisation. For this reason, it is important to weight the factors according to their relative importance. This is illustrated in Table 22.1. The reader will note that the weights for the components of each axis should all add up to 1. In the example given, the number of people the organisation can aid is seen as being a more important determinant of external attractiveness than the question of how immediately the assistance can be provided. Donors to this organisation do not appear to have any difficulty in taking a long-term view of the impact of their support.

The next step is to take each activity in which the organisation is engaged and give it a score from 1 (very poor) to 10 (excellent) in terms of how it measures up against each of the components listed. To make this process clear, a fictional example (let us call it Activity A) has been worked through in Tables 22.1 and 22.2. Considering first the question of how externally attractive this activity might be, it is clear that public support for it looks set to decline in the future and it is for this reason that a relatively low rating of 3 has been awarded against this factor. The activity does have the merit, however, of having an immediate and beneficial impact on a large number of people and somewhat higher ratings are therefore awarded for these factors. Multiplying the weights by the ratings assigned produces a value for each factor. Summing these values gives an overall score for (in this case) the external attractiveness axis of 5.8.

Similarly, in the case of the internal attractiveness axis, each factor is assigned a weight. Each activity in which the organisation is engaged is given a rating according to its performance in respect of each factor. Once again 1 = very poor 10 = excellent. Returning to our analysis of Activity A, Table 22.2 makes it clear that the charity has only moderate experience to offer and does not view its provision as being particularly important (even though it would appear to

Table 22.1 External attractiveness

Factor	Weight	Rating	Value
The general level of public concern	0.2	5	1.0
Likely trends in public concern	0.3	3	0.9
Numbers of people aided	0.4	8	3.2
Immediacy of impact on the beneficiary group	0.1	7	0.7
Total	1.0		5.8

Table 22.2 Internal appropriateness

Factor	Weight	Rating	Value
Level of previous experience with the activity	0.1	5	0.5
Perceived importance of the activity	0.2	2	0.4
Extent to which the activity is compatible with the organisation's mission	0.5	6	3.0
Extent to which the organisation has unique expertise to offer	0.2	7	1.4
Total	1		5.3

come within the organisation's mission). The charity does, however, have fairly unique expertise, which it could offer to recipients. The result is an aggregate score of 5.3 on the internal appropriateness axis.

These figures can now be plotted on the matrix in Figure 22.2, where the position of Activity A has been clearly indicated. If it is conceptually useful, some organisations choose to progress the analysis one stage further and draw a circle around the plotted position, the diameter of which is directly proportional to the percentage of overall expenditure that is allocated to each activity. In this way, managers can see at a glance how funds are allocated between each of the services in the portfolio. Of course, for this to happen, all the services that a particular organisation provides would be plotted in this way and then an analysis undertaken of the health (and balance) of the portfolio as a whole. Depending on the location of each activity within the matrix, the organisation can then look either to invest further in its development, or divest the activity and use the resources elsewhere, or subject the activity to further evaluation if the position still remains unclear.

Activities falling in the top left hand corner of the matrix are clearly those that are perceived as fulfilling an important need in society and the attraction of funding is unproblematic. The organisation also appears well placed to provide these services, as it has the necessary expertise and/or experience in-house. The activities are also more likely to be seen as being compatible with the organisation's mission and are hence excellent candidates for continuing investment.

Activities falling in the bottom right hand corner, however, are clearly activities that could be causing an unnecessary drain on resources. They are not seen as being important by society and are not compatible with the organisation's mission. Indeed, there may be other potential providers who could supply a much higher quality of service. Activities in this area of the matrix should then be scrutinised with a view to divestment. After all, if the activity is difficult to raise funds for, and the organisation is not good at providing the service anyway, what could the rationale possibly be for continuing? Of course, this is only a model and the activity would have to be scrutinised very carefully before a divestment decision was taken, but the analysis has at least yielded considerable insight into the potential for valuable resources to be conserved and perhaps put to other, more appropriate uses.

This leaves the question of activities falling within the central diagonal, such as those in our fictional example. These should be carefully evaluated as they are only moderately appropriate for the organisation to provide and they have only limited external attractiveness. It may be that there are very good strategic reasons for continuing to offer these services, or it may equally be that they

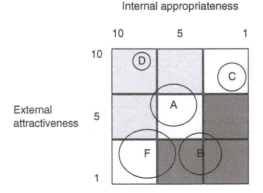

Figure 22.2 Example portfolio analysis

could comfortably be left to another better qualified organisation to supply. Further analysis would clearly be warranted.

Understanding donor markets

Nonprofits typically derive their voluntary income from one or more of the following sources:

- individual donors;
- corporate donors;
- trusts/foundations.

Government funds also form a significant source of income for the sector, but this is frequently in the form of a contractual relationship for the provision of specific goods or services and therefore not regarded as a 'voluntary' contribution. Gifts from living individuals form the majority of a typical organisation's voluntary income. In the US, for example, total giving to the nonprofit sector in 2013 stood at US$335.17 billion. Over 80 per cent of Americans offered donations to nonprofits with people giving on average two per cent of their income and contributing 72 per cent of the total income accruing to the sector (the balance coming from corporations, foundations and bequests) (Giving USA Foundation 2014).

Gift giving by individuals has therefore been the focus of much research, with contributions emerging from the fields of economics, clinical psychology, social psychology, anthropology and sociology. A key contribution from the discipline of nonprofit marketing has been the development of composite models of helping behaviour, whose goal has been to explain the donation of money, time and even body parts (Burnett and Wood 1988; Guy and Patton 1989; Bendapudi *et al.* 1996; Sargeant 1999; Sargeant and Woodliffe 2007).

Focusing specifically on the motives for individual giving, Sargeant and Jay (2014) conceptualise donations as offering a range of different classes of utility to donors:

- Emotional utility: in the sense of the warm glow considered by the economist, Andreoni, and others. Donors will be more likely to give to organisations where the sense of having done the right thing, accomplishment or self-worth will be highest.
- Familial utility: donors may also prioritise organisations that they or their family and friends might benefit from (or might in the future). They may also elect to give in memory of a loved one.
- Demonstrable utility: donors may also give where they can see the biggest impact for their gift. From this perspective, donors can rationally decide between competing organisations to see where they believe their donation would deliver the greatest impact on the cause.
- Practical utility: where donors may give simply because they want the practical benefits that accrue to them from giving. They might thus join the National Trust to gain discounted access to the properties they wish to visit and/or to enjoy a variety of the other membership benefits the nonprofit is able to offer.
- Spiritual utility: where donors select a nonprofit because it has the strongest fit with their spiritual needs and identity.

Similarly, Bekkers and Wiepking (2011) identify eight mechanisms as the most important forces that drive charitable giving: (1) awareness of need; (2) solicitation; (3) costs and benefits; (4) altruism; (5) reputation; (6) psychological benefits; (7) values; and (8) efficacy. In their view, these mechanisms can provide a basic theoretical framework for future research explaining individual giving.

Business giving too, has been the focus of much research, particularly in relation to the issue of their motives for the support of nonprofits. The literature suggests that there are broadly three categories of such motives, namely dual agenda motives, altruistic motives and the influence of the personal motives of the managers involved.

In respect of the former, Friedman (1970) argued that the business of business was to make a profit and that senior managers should leave the issue of how to disperse their earnings to the shareholders. Managers should simply serve the interests of business owners by making more money, whilst playing by the basic rules of society. Corporate giving from this perspective should be viewed as instrumental, in that it should be undertaken only to achieve specific business benefits. Inevitably, there has been considerable academic interest in delineating what these might be and extant work has highlighted variables as diverse as brand differentiation; enhanced brand image; improved employee recruitment, morale and retention; enhanced government relations; and the ability to reach new customer segments (e.g. Andreasen 1996; Drumwright 1996; Sagawa 2001; Porter and Kramer 2002; Wymer and Samu 2003). Ricks (2005) also highlights increasing visibility, enhancing corporate image and thwarting negative publicity as important marketing reasons for corporate philanthropy.

More recently, writers such as Porter and Kramer (2011) have argued that corporate philanthropy should be more deeply integrated with the corporate strategy of the originating organisation. The authors thus champion the notion of corporate shared value (CSV), where organisations adopt policies and practices that enhance the competitiveness of a company whilst *simultaneously* advancing economic and social conditions in the communities in which it operates. From this perspective, philanthropy becomes a route to competitive advantage and ultimately to profit maximisation. Customers will buy products and services, because of the ties the organisation has to the communities in which it operates and the social good it can simultaneously deliver. It seems likely, however, that these ideas are more easily applied to the philanthropy of large multinational organisations, since few smaller enterprises are likely to have the economic or social muscle to have a genuinely systemic impact on society's ills.

Division of the marketing function

As noted above, nonprofits serve two distinct markets, because they have a dual role – delivering services to beneficiaries/users and generating the income needed to deliver those services. For many nonprofits, this entails running two entirely separate marketing operations – one that is focused on providing services and the other on generating income.

The picture is further complicated by the nature of service provision, in that some nonprofits engage in multiple forms of service marketing, including corporate marketing, promoting the brand or image of the organisation and campaigning, lobbying, advocacy and social marketing. Many of these functions may employ specialist teams who must then compete with other marketers in the organisation for power, influence and the budgets that are garnered as a consequence. There can also be friction generated by the, sometimes, competing goals and objectives of these various teams.

As an example, a report into aftermath of the Ethiopian famine in 1984 highlighted a conflict of interest between those fundraisers who considered it acceptable to portray victims of the famine in a negative light, because such images had been proven to generate more voluntary income, and those in service delivery and campaigning staff who preferred to present messages of 'justice and equality' (Van Der Gaag and Nash 1987). The authors of this report – a joint project by the UN's Food and Agriculture Committee and European and African NGOs – concluded that the overall impression was one of a 'mass of contradictions, arising from the different and even opposing aims of different departments' (Van Der Gaag and Nash 1987: 76).

Multiple constituencies

The second key difference between for-profits and nonprofits follows from the first. Although there are typically two primary markets to be addressed by nonprofit marketers, there is a much wider set of constituencies or 'publics' that a typical nonprofit must take account of in the design of strategy. Kotler and Andreasen (1991: 89) use the term 'publics' to refer to 'a distinct group of people, organisations, or both, whose actual or potential needs must in some sense be served'.

The term 'publics' is therefore more general in its meaning than the concept of 'customer' and embraces every group whose needs must be taken account of by the focal organisation. For a charity, this might typically include individual donors, corporate donors, trusts/foundations, legislators, the local community, the general public, local and national media, recipients of goods and services, the organisation's own staff, volunteers, etc. Whilst businesses, too, may serve a number of different publics, the power and relative significance of each is rarely so diffuse as it is in the nonprofit context. At a very practical level, the views of a much wider number of audiences must continually be addressed.

Societal not market orientation

A further key difference relates to the nature of some nonprofit missions. Many nonprofit organisations are compelled by their mission to take a long-term view of their relationships with their target markets. Health and welfare groups in the developing world, for example, may be promoting the use of contraception in direct conflict with the established patterns of local belief and culture. Similarly, many theatres and arts centres have a mission to explore a wide range of art forms, not just to provide those forms of entertainment that they know will be well patronised by their local community. There is therefore a tension between the satisfaction of current customer needs and the fulfilment of a particular organisation's mission. Short-term customer satisfaction may often have to be sacrificed by nonprofits as they take a longer-term view of the benefit they can offer to society as a whole. This matters because it reveals a deep philosophical difference between the application of marketing in the for-profit context and the application of marketing in nonprofit organisations.

Since the 1950s, practitioners and academics have sought to explain what it means for an organisation to fully grasp and implement the marketing concept. More recently, firms that successfully operationalise the marketing concept have come to be labelled 'market oriented' (Kohli and Jaworski 1990; Narver and Slater 1990). Whilst perspectives on what this means in practice do vary, a number of common themes have now emerged, including a focus on customers, a focus on competitors and the development of a culture that facilitates the sharing of market information around the organisation to ensure it has the maximum possible influence on strategy. The level of market orientation attained matters, because numerous studies have linked this with the level of performance (e.g. market share, performance, customer loyalty) that an organisation is able to achieve (see e.g. Jaworski and Kohli 1993).

One might therefore be tempted into arguing that the achievement of a market orientation would be a good thing for nonprofits and for-profits alike and, indeed, many studies have now explored market orientation in the nonprofit context (e.g. Bennett 1998; Caruana *et al.* 1998). There are, however, a number of good reasons why this assumption should be questioned.

First, the market orientation construct was an attempt to operationalise for-profit definitions of marketing that were developed in large commercial organisations in the mid-1960s. Very different definitions of marketing have been developed in the nonprofit context, and attempting to operationalise Kotler and Levy's (1969) 'sensitively serving and satisfying human need', for example, is likely to have a very different outcome from operationalising the definition of marketing provided by the Chartered Institute of Marketing.

Similarly, some of the terminology used in the for-profit context does not transfer well to the nonprofit arena. The very term market orientation implies an orientation towards markets. Even though it has already been argued that nonprofits have a market for resource acquisition and a market for resource allocation, these are often not markets in the economic sense of the term. In fact as Hansmann (1980) notes, nonprofits can often be seen as a response to a very particular form of market failure.

The second key argument for revising the terminology in this context is that the notion of 'market' implies some form of exchange will take place between the supplier and the recipient of goods and services. There are is a plethora of occasions when nonprofit organisations do exchange monetary value with the recipients of their goods or services (or even a warm feeling in return for donations). However, there are also many occasions when the notion of exchange has little meaning. The recipients of international aid exchange nothing except their need and gratitude with their supplying organisation.

The components of market orientation are also problematic in the nonprofit context. Whilst a focus on customers is still important, in the nonprofit context (as was explained earlier) organisations are often less concerned with customer satisfaction per se than they are with the notion of longer-term benefit to society. It is thus necessary to broaden the focus on customers to address the needs of a wider range of stakeholders and perhaps even society as a whole.

Competition is also different in the nonprofit arena. Demand for nonprofit goods and services is often so insatiable that to regard other organisations as direct competitors would be ludicrous (Bruce 1995). Naturally, there are occasions when competition is of significance, as when, for example, organisations compete for funds, but it is often the case in relation to service delivery that potential collaboration between organisations is more of an issue than competition per se.

It has also been argued that to sensitively serve the needs of society, nonprofits must be responsive to such needs. Whilst businesses too must be responsive, in the nonprofit context it is the rapidity of this response that defines many organisations. This is accomplished because there is no requirement to consider either the political consequences of action or the financial returns that might accrue to shareholders. Nonprofits have the necessary freedom, flexibility and moral imperative to respond quickly to the dictates of social need and must ensure that they do so if the maximum benefit to society is to accrue (Jordan 1964; Dahrendorf 1997).

In recognition of these difficulties, Sargeant *et al.* (2002) propose the alternative framework of 'societal orientation' illustrated in Figure 22.3. The model is offered as an attempt to operationalise the Kotler and Levy (1969) definition of marketing referred to earlier. In this case, the authors have delineated the societal orientation construct itself and included what they regarded as the antecedents of a societal orientation and the benefits and consequences thereof.

Considering first the antecedents, the authors argue that nonprofits will only be able to achieve a societal orientation if they have a strong, clear mission that reflects the goals of the organisation's key stakeholder groups. Similarly, these goals should be common (i.e. shared) across all the stakeholder groups and the nonprofit must have established appropriate systems and structures to ensure that they are in a position to be achieved.

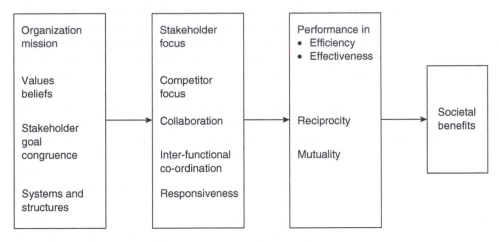

Figure 22.3 Societal orientation

In respect of consequences, the authors posit that societally-oriented organisations will achieve significantly higher performance than those without such an orientation. In the nonprofit context this means that nonprofits would be: (a) more effective in achieving their mission; and (b) make a more efficient use of resources in doing so.

According to the authors, however, these should not be viewed as the only outcomes from the successful attainment of a societal orientation. An additional dimension derives from the division between resource acquisition and resource allocation. Those individuals that supply an organisation's funding are not necessarily those that will derive the primary benefit. One of the primary outcomes from the attainment of a societal orientation can therefore be the bringing together of these two groups, resulting in a mutual exchange of values, ideas and a shared sense of identity. The authors refer to this as reciprocity and mutuality.

Non-financial objectives

Nonprofits also differ from their for-profit counterparts in that the derivation of appropriate organisational and thus marketing objectives is markedly more difficult. As Drucker (1990: 107) notes, 'performance is the ultimate test of any institution. Every non-profit institution exists for the sake of performance in changing people and society. Yet, performance is also one of the truly difficult areas for the executive in the non-profit institution'.

Setting objectives, which can then be used to monitor nonprofit performance, is problematic because of the intangible nature of much of the service provided. It is also a problem, because, as Drucker goes on to note, the results of a nonprofit institution are always outside the organisation, not inside. Traditional internal measures such as return on investment and profit have no meaning in this context. Their results are therefore inherently more difficult to measure. This is not to suggest, however, that nonprofit organisations should not at least try to set targets. As Drucker (1990: 107) makes clear:

> In a non-profit organisation there is no such [thing as a] bottom line. But there is also a temptation to downplay results. There is the temptation to say: We are serving a good cause. We are doing the Lord's work. Or we are doing something to make life a little better for people

and that's a result in itself. That is not enough. If a business wastes its resources on non-results, by and large it loses its own money. In a non-profit institution though, it's somebody else's money – the donor's money. Service organisations are accountable to donors, accountable for putting the money where the results are, and for performance. So, this is an area that needs special emphasis for non-profit executives. Good intentions only pave the way to Hell!

Objective setting is also difficult because a nonprofit can have amorphous goals (Newman and Wallender 1978). What Dahrendorf (1997) refers to as the creative chaos of the voluntary sector may well be a strength, but this feature complicates the delineation of appropriate measures of performance. Indeed, authors such as Weick (1977) have cautioned against the use of performance measures adopted from business, since if efficiency and production measures predominate, then the random 'deviant' behaviours that enhance an organisation's ability to develop creative responses may be lost.

Work in this field has therefore suggested employing multiple measures of performance, considering both effectiveness and efficiency. An assessment of the former might begin with an analysis of 'mission directedness' or the extent to which an organisation might be said to be fulfilling its mission (Sheehan 1996). Effectiveness could also be assessed by the extent to which specific operational objectives have been met or exceeded (Hall 1978). These may be written in terms of maximising inputs and outputs, but in respect of service delivery they may also be couched in terms of the quality of intervention achieved. Both are important. Whilst a drug rehabilitation centre may have an objective to increase the throughput of clients, it will be at least, if not more, concerned with the quality of care it is able to supply to these individuals. Increasing throughput at the expense of the quality of the intervention would ultimately be self-defeating.

Nonprofit efficiency is also very much an issue. Fundraising and administrative efficiency have generated a lot of interest, certainly in the popular press. Donors now appear to have a clear idea of what represents an acceptable percentage of income that may be applied to both administration and fundraising costs, and organisations exceed these at their peril. Warwick (1994) identified that donors expect the ratio between administration/fundraising costs and so-called charitable expenditure would be 20:80. It is interesting to note that, despite this expectation, most donors believe that the actual ratio is closer to 50:50. For example, Bennett and Savani's (2003) research shows that respondents perceived that only 46 per cent of the focal charities' expenditures reached beneficiaries, when in reality the average figure was 82 per cent. This matters, because research has consistently shown a link between such perceptions, the longevity of the donor–nonprofit relationship, and the percentage of an individual's charitable pot that they may be willing to give to a certain organisation. In objective writing, organisations may therefore want to concern themselves as much with perceptions of their performance as with the reality thereof. These concerns seem peculiar to the nonprofit context. Consumers in the commercial world rarely concern themselves with how well they perceive a manufacturer to be managed, or with issues such as the salaries of senior staff.

Services and social behaviours rather than physical goods

The majority of nonprofits produce services rather than physical goods. Day-to-day nonprofit marketing therefore has much more in common with the marketing of services than the marketing of consumer products. Nonprofit marketers therefore have to deal with the added complexities envisaged by Zeithaml (1996) including:

- **Intangibility**: When a customer purchases a physical item or service they can assess it by its appearance, taste, smell, etc. They can therefore 'confirm' their expectations about the properties of the product they are going to receive. With a service, however, the consumer has no way of verifying the claims of the producer until the service has actually been purchased. This is all the more problematic in the nonprofit context, because funders may well be purchasing services that will be consumed by an entirely different societal group.

- **Inseparability**: Physical goods are produced and then purchased by the customer. With services, the process is the other way around. Services are sold first and then produced at the time of consumption by the customer. In this sense, production and consumption are said to be inseparable. This means that producer and consumer have to interact to produce the service. Marketing a service therefore involves not only facilitating an exchange process but also facilitating an often quite complex producer/consumer interaction.

- **Heterogeneity**: Allied to the previous point, since production and consumption are inseparable, there are few chances for a service supplier to carry out pre-inspection or quality control in the same way that one can with physical goods. Indeed, monitoring and control processes are of necessity considerably more complex in the context of services.

- **Perishability**: Services cannot be stored in the same way that one can store food or electrical items in a retail outlet. If a theatrical performance begins with a half empty house, or there are last minute cancellations of a physician's appointments, those services have been lost forever. Marketers, therefore, have a more complex balancing operation to perform to ensure that their services remain as optimally utilised as possible.

Some nonprofits do not even produce a service that one could clearly define. They exist to attempt to alter some form of social behaviour through either direct communication with the target group, or indirectly through the lobbying of government. When it was first recognised in the 1970s that marketing tools could be applied equally well to the marketing of social ideas (Kotler and Zaltman 1971), a new discipline of 'social marketing' was born.

Since then Andreasen (1995) notes that social marketing has tended to be employed where individual members of the public engage in unsafe, resistant behaviours and where, as a consequence, behaviour change would improve their personal welfare and that of wider society. Much of the early research in this field focused on the promotion of products associated with such behaviour change and, thus, on the marketing of pharmaceuticals, condoms, oral rehydration tablets, etc. (Andreasen 2002). More recently, work has focused on specific issues such as HIV infection and sexual responsibility (e.g. Moore *et al.* 2002; Wakhisi *et al.* 2011; Kavle *et al.* 2012), smoking (e.g. McKenna *et al.* 2000; Zucker *et al.* 2000), drink driving (e.g., Cismaru *et al.* 2009), obesity (Gracia-Marco *et al.* 2011), recycling/energy conservation (McKenzie-Mohr 1994), breast feeding (Lowry *et al.* 2011), skin cancer prevention (Peattie *et al.* 2001), drug, solvent or alcohol abuse (e.g. Stanton *et al.* 2000; Gallopel-Morvan *et al.* 2011) and even ocean sustainability (Bates 2010).

Other more generic work has focused on the development of frameworks and approaches drawn from successful professional practice (Goldberg 1997; Rothschild 1999), alternative consumer behaviour models (Hornik 2001), the use of specific forms of message, e.g. fear (Rossiter and Jones 2004) and differing perspectives on social marketing channels that suggest new target audiences. Authors such as Gordon (2013), for example, have posited that influencing policy makers, regulators and educators can help address societal problems 'upstream'. They therefore recommend techniques such as advocacy, stakeholder engagement and, through peer influence, direct involvement in evidence-based policy-making.

Collaboration not competition

The fifth key difference between for-profit and nonprofit marketing has already been alluded to above. Competition is a key strategic issue for many nonprofits, but collaboration is an equally important facet of their relationship with other organisations. Many developing world agencies, for example, will share transportation channels to maximise the distribution and impact of aid, whilst minimising cost. Indeed, in addition to other similar organisations, nonprofits may be able to identify suitable opportunities for collaboration with both public and private sector bodies (Andreasen and Kotler 2004). In the fundraising context, it is also commonplace for nonprofits to share lists of lower value donors with other organisations, in the hope that every participant in the exchange will benefit from the sharing of these resources (Sargeant and Jay 2004).

Thus, in conducting a fundraising or marketing audit, it is instructive to consider examples of where organisations have collaborated successfully in the past and the factors that led to that success. The nonprofit should look to see what it could learn from these collaborations and whether there might be any way in which it could work in partnership with others. If this is felt to be desirable, it will be instructive to conduct background research into potential partners and to explore how such relationships might develop. An approach to one or more partners could then be included in the marketing strategy/tactics.

The content of a competitor analysis would also vary in the nonprofit context. When conducting an assessment of competitors, there are essentially three categories of organisations who are worthy of investigation.

- **Competitors for resources**: that is, other nonprofit organisations that seek to attract resources from the same sources as the nonprofit in question. Typically, nonprofits might look both at the fundraising undertaken by other organisations of a similar size *and* by organisations working with the same issue or cause.
- **Competitors for provision of nonprofit services**: nonprofits may encounter competition from other organisations that seek to provide the same services as themselves. Increasingly, this competition may come from for-profit organisations that may decide to compete, for example, for government service contracts.
- **Organisations with competing missions**: many nonprofits now exist whose primary goal is to persuade society to adopt new forms of purchasing, smoking or sexual behaviours. Such nonprofits typically encounter opposition from other organisations that exist to further exactly the opposite forms of behaviour. In the US, for example, the campaigning organisation, Planned Parenthood, frequently finds itself in competition for a share of the media voice with the Catholic church or 'pro-life' bodies opposed to its stance on abortion. In such circumstances, these organisations should clearly be regarded as competitors and subject to an equally detailed level of analysis.

Public scrutiny/non-market pressures

Certain categories of organisation within the nonprofit sector are open to intense levels of public scrutiny. The emergency services, local authorities, hospitals and even universities are subject to regular public scrutiny. UK universities, for example, are comprehensively audited on the quality of their teaching and research every few years. In the healthcare sector the Audit Commission has responsibility for ensuring that the National Health Service continues to provide 'value for money'.

The charity sector is also subject to enhanced scrutiny. In the UK fundraisers must abide by the Code of Fundraising Practice laid down by the Institute of Fundraising, and individual members of the public who are dissatisfied with a fundraising solicitation may now complain to a new Fundraising Standards Board, a self-regulatory body established by the industry in an attempt to bolster public trust and confidence in the profession. Fundraising is therefore one of the few forms of marketing to be singled out for enhanced public scrutiny.

It is interesting to note that the Fundraising Standards Board has felt it necessary to move beyond the baseline laid down by the Code of Fundraising Practice and to offer donors a 'Fundraising Promise', providing a number of enhanced rights, such as not to be subject to 'undue pressure' at the point of solicitation. This move has brought the UK closer to the model adopted in the US, where the Association of Fundraising Professionals has long committed to a Donor Bill of Rights

Nonprofits also have to contend with a variety of other non-market pressures. Whilst no-one would claim for a moment that it is easy for a business organisation to be able to forecast demand for its products, demand for the services of a nonprofit can fall away to nothing or literally double overnight. The nature of Oxfam's work overseas with developing countries can change radically from year to year depending on political, economic and climatic conditions. The very nature of a focus on the disadvantaged makes it almost impossible to know where future priorities might lie.

The instability of the environment in which many nonprofits operate thus contributes to the fact that such organisations often have less control over their own destiny than their counterparts in the for-profit sector. Marketers in nonprofits therefore have a much more complex role to perform.

Higher ethical standards

The final difference between the two sectors lies in the standards of professional behaviour that society has a right to expect. Whilst it is undoubtedly true that ethical considerations are becoming increasingly important for business, the very nature of nonprofit organisations imposes additional moral responsibilities. Indeed, one of the distinguishing characteristics for many nonprofit organisations is the ethical nature of their operations. Since they do not have to seek to maximise profit they can (and perhaps should) take decisions that seek to maximise the benefit that accrues to society as a whole. In other words, they are freed up to 'do the right thing' or take 'the right decision'. Of course, it is then necessary to decide what exactly the 'right' decision might be. For many nonprofits this is a matter of balance.

Research by the Advertising Standards Authority (ASA) in the UK in 2012, for example, reported widespread public concern about 'hard-hitting' social marketing adverts (e.g. anti-smoking) and 'shocking content' in charity advertisements that made people feel guilty in a way they considered inappropriate, often because they portrayed violence and mistreatment. The trend was considered particularly troubling since the study also revealed that most children who participated could spontaneously recall a charity advert that had upset them (ASA 2012). Nonprofits thus need to strike a balance between generating communications that are effective at inculcating or changing a focal behaviour whilst not causing unnecessary distress to those not in the target audience, or perhaps even harming the very societal groups they set out to serve.

The picture is further complicated in the nonprofit domain by the fact that what is considered 'right' by one marketing team may not be considered 'right' by another. We have already seen how the Images for Africa investigation reported a conflict between how fundraisers and service/delivery campaigning staff wished to portray victims of the Ethiopian famine (Van Der Gaag and Nash 1987).

This becomes an ethical issue, deciding how beneficiaries 'ought' to be portrayed in a nonprofit's marketing materials. For fundraisers, images 'ought' to be used that are proven to raise sufficient money to alleviate the plight of beneficiaries; for service delivery staff, images 'ought' to be used that maintain beneficiaries' dignity.

The contrast here is one of consequentialist and deontological approaches to ethics (LaFollette 1997: 8–10).

Deontology is duty-based ethics – very simply, is this the right thing to do, as a matter of principle, irrespective of the consequences? An example of duty-based ethics is Kant's (2009) injunction against lying.

Consequentialism explores whether some action is ethical based on the effect it has (for example, utilitarianism aims to deliver the greatest good to the greatest number).

Both fundraisers and service delivery/campaigning teams have the best interests of the beneficiaries at heart. Fundraisers believe they can best serve their interests by using images that generate the most income (consequentialism). Service delivery staff may believe beneficiaries' best interests are served by dignified portrayals that convey messages of justice (deontology).

The conflict identified in Images for Africa resulted in several new codes of practice on the use of images by nonprofits (Van Der Gaag 2007) and similar consequentialist/deontological divisions are evident in other forms of nonprofit marketing. For example, the Code of Fundraising Practice set by the Institute of Fundraising in the UK prohibits the inclusion in direct mail packs of any gift that aims to induce a sense of 'financial guilt' in the recipient (deontology), even though including such gifts is proven to increase response (consequentialism).

Fundraising bodies in both the US and the UK have attempted to address ethical issues not just through their codes of practice but also in the ethical promises they have made to donors. The Association of Fundraising Professionals in their Donor Bill of Rights sets out donors' rights and fundraisers' duties and responsibilities to their donors, which is available in English, Spanish and French. Among its key provisions are the right:

- to be informed of the organisation's mission, of the way the organisation intends to use donated resources, and of its capacity to use donations effectively for their intended purposes;
- to receive appropriate acknowledgement and recognition;
- to expect that all relationships with individuals representing organisations of interest to the donor will be professional in nature;
- to be assured that information about their donation is handled with respect and with confidentiality to the extent provided by law.

The UK's Fundraising Standards Board operates a similar document – the Fundraising Promise. There is also the International Statement on Ethical Principles in Fundraising, jointly developed by a number of fundraising umbrella bodies around the world. The International Statement requires fundraisers to, among other things, respect their beneficiaries' dignity and self-respect by not using fundraising materials or techniques that undermine this dignity. It says nothing, however, about fundraisers' duties to maximise income to alleviate the plight of those beneficiaries. It also stipulates that fundraisers are 'strictly answerable' to all stakeholders, including donors, beneficiaries and employers (Association of Fundraising Professionals 2006). This has the potential to put fundraisers in an ethical quandary, because it makes them answerable to both of the nonprofits' core markets, whilst directly serving just one of them. There is very little published guidance to help nonprofit marketers resolve ethical quandaries, such as balancing a graphic image that will maximise income with the preservation of their beneficiaries' dignity; or the level at which public irritation at using interruption marketing techniques such as street fundraising outweighs (if in fact it ever does) the benefits this extra income delivers to beneficiaries.

Work to develop a 'marketing' orientation that is bespoke to the nonprofit sector, such as societal organisation (above), may help resolve this by removing or weakening the schism of the marketing function between fundraising and the rest of the organisation, by more clearly outlining fundraisers' duties to their beneficiaries as well as their donors.

Any readers interested in a further exploration of the topic of ethics in nonprofit management are advised to consult Anderson (1996) for a consideration of ethics in fundraising, Malaro (1994) for ethics in arts management and the Humanitarian Studies Unit (2001) for ethics in aid and development. The ethical literature in relation to healthcare and education are perhaps the most well developed (see, for example, Weber 2001; Nash 2002).

Conclusions

In this brief review we have focused on the key differences between for-profit and nonprofit marketing and used these as a vehicle for exploring the wider nonprofit literature. As the reader will by now be aware, the discipline of nonprofit marketing embraces a diverse range of contexts and categories of organisation. Since its inception at the end of the 1960s, nonprofit marketing has come a long way. It has gained widespread acceptance as a distinctive sphere of marketing practice, and the relevance of marketing ideas to the nonprofit domain is no longer in dispute. The critical issue that remains to be addressed is the dissemination of this body of knowledge to the professionals who may benefit. Whilst for-profit marketing classes are commonplace at almost every university, nonprofit marketing classes are not. This is particularly problematic since, as this brief review has shown, there remain many differences between for-profit and nonprofit marketing in the way that the function is typically structured, and the key issues that will typically be encountered by its practitioners.

Further reading

Fundraising

Burnett, K. (2002), *Relationship Fundraising: A Donor Based Approach to the Business of Raising Money*, San Francisco, CA: Jossey-Bass.

Klein, K. (2011), *Fundraising for Social Change*, sixth edition, San Francisco, CA: Jossey-Bass.

Sargeant, A. and Jay, E. (2014), *Fundraising Management: Analysis, Planning and Practice*, third edition, London: Routledge.

Smith, G. (1996), *Asking Properly*, London: White Lion Press.

Warwick, M. (2004), *Revolution in the Mailbox: Your Guide to Successful Direct Mail Fundraising*, San Francisco, CA: Jossey-Bass.

Arts marketing

Bernstein, J. S. and Kotler, P. (2006), *Arts Marketing Insights: The Dynamics of Building and Retaining Performing Arts Audiences*, San Francisco, CA: Jossey-Bass.

Colbert, F., Nantel, J., Bilodeau, S. and Rich, J. D. (2001), *Marketing Culture and the Arts*, Concord, MA: Paul and Co Publishing Consortium.

Kerrigan, F., Fraser, P. and Ozbilgin, M. (2004), *Arts Marketing*, London: Butterworth-Heinemann.

Kotler, P. and Bernstein J. S. (2001), *Standing Room Only: Strategies for Marketing The Performing Arts*, Boston, MA: Harvard Business School Press.

O'Reilly, D. and Kerrigan, F. (2010), *Marketing the Arts: A Fresh Approach*, London: Routledge.

Education marketing

Foster, B. (2011), *School Marketing for the Digital Age*, third edition, Benowa, QLD, Australia: Great Developments PTY.

Foster, R. S. and Sauser, W. I. (1994), M*arketing University Outreach Programs*, Binghamton, NY: Haworth Press.

Hayes, T. J. (2002), *New Strategies in Higher Education Marketing*, Binghamton, NY: Haworth Press.

Kirp, D. L., Berman, E. P., Homan, J. T. and Roberts, P. (2004), *Shakespeare, and the Bottom Line: The Marketing of Higher Education*, Boston, MA: Harvard University Press.

Kotler, P. and Fox, K. F. A. (1995), *Strategic Marketing for Educational Institutions*, Englewood Cliffs, NJ: Prentice Hall.

Maringe, F. and Gibbs, P. (2008), *Marketing Higher Education: Theory and Practice*, Milton Keynes, UK: Open University Press.

Healthcare marketing

Berkowitz, E. N. (2010), *Essentials of Health Care Marketing*, third edition, Boston, MA: Jones and Bartlett Publishers International.

Fortenberry, J. L. (2005), *Marketing Tools for Healthcare Executives*, second edition, Oxford, UK: Oxford Crest.

Ginter, P. M., Duncan, W. J., Sappington, A. A. and Swayne, L. (2004), *Strategic Management of Health Care Organizations*, Boston, MA: Blackwell Publishing.

Hillestad, S. G. and Berkowitz, E. N. (2012), *Health Care Market Strategy*, fourth edition, Boston, MA: Jones and Bartlett Publishers International.

Public sector marketing

Bean, J. and Hussey, L. (2012), *Marketing Public Sector Services (Essential Skills for the Public Sector)*, second edition, London: H. B. Publications.

Chapman, D. and Cowdell, T. (1997), *New Public Sector Marketing*, London: Pitman Publishing.

Coffman, L. L. (1986), *Public Sector Marketing: A Guide for Practitioners*, Chichester, UK: John Wiley.

Kotler, P. and Lee, N. (2006), *Marketing in the Public Sector: A Roadmap for Improved Performance*, Philadelphia, PA: Wharton School Publishing.

Pasquier, L. G. and Villeneuve, J. P. (2012), *Marketing Management and Communications in the Public Sector*, London: Routledge.

Titman, L. G. (1995), *Marketing in the New Public Sector*, London: FT and Prentice Hall.

Social marketing

Andreasen, A. R. (1995), *Marketing Social Change: Changing Behavior to Promote Health, Service Development and the Environment*, San Francisco, CA: Jossey-Bass.

Andreasen A. R. (2001), *Ethics in Social Marketing*, Washington, DC: Georgetown University Press.

Andreasen, A. R. (2005), *Social Marketing in the 21st Century*, Thousand Oaks, CA: Sage Publications.

Basil D. Z. (2007), *Social Marketing: Advances in Research and Theory*, Binghamton, NY: Haworth Press.

French, J., Blair-Stevens, C., McVey, D. and Merritt, R. (2009), *Social Marketing and Public Health: Theory and Practice*, Oxford, UK: Oxford University Press.

Kotler, P., Roberto, N. and Lee, N. R. (2002), *Social Marketing: Improving the Quality of Life*, Thousand Oaks, CA: Sage Publications.

Lee, N. R and Kotler, P. A. (2011), *Social Marketing: Influencing Behaviors for Good*, Thousand Oaks, CA: Sage Publications.

References

Anderson, A. (1996), *Ethics for Fundraisers*, Indianapolis, IN: Indiana University Press.

Andreasen, A. R. (1995), *Marketing Social Change*, San Francisco, CA: Jossey-Bass.

Andreasen, A. R. (1996), 'Profits for nonprofits: Find a corporate partner', *Harvard Business Review*, 74(6): 47–59.

Andreasen, A. R. (2002), 'Marketing social marketing in the social change marketplace', *Journal of Public Policy and Marketing*, 21(1): 3–13.

Andreasen, A. R. and Kotler, P. (2004), *Strategic Marketing for Nonprofit Organizations*, sixth edition, Englewood Cliffs, NJ: Prentice Hall.

ASA (2012), *Public Perception of Harm and Offence in UK Advertising*, London: ASA.

Association of Fundraising Professionals (2006), *International Statement of Ethical Principles in Fundraising*, available at http://www.afpnet.org/Ethics/IntlArticleDetail.cfm?ItemNumber=3681 (accessed 1 August 2014).

Bates, C. H. (2010), 'Use of social marketing concepts to evaluate ocean sustainability campaigns', *Social Marketing Quarterly*, 16(1): 71–96.

Bekkers, R. and Wiepking, P. (2011), 'A literature review of empirical studies of philanthropy: Eight mechanisms that drive charitable giving', *Nonprofit and Voluntary Sector Quarterly*, 40(5): 924–973.

Bendapudi, N., Singh, S. N. and Bendapudi, V. (1996), 'Enhancing helping behavior: An integrative framework for promotion planning', *Journal of Marketing*, 60(3): 33–54.

Bennett, R. (1998), 'Market orientation among small to medium sized uk charitable organisations: Implications for fund-raising performance', *Journal of Nonprofit and Public Sector Marketing*, 6(1): 31–45.

Bennett, R. and Savani, S. (2003), 'Predicting the accuracy of public perceptions of charity performance', *Journal of Targeting, Measurement and Analysis for Marketing*, 11(4): 326–342.

Bruce, I. (1995), 'Do not-for-profits value their customers and their needs?', *International Marketing Review*, 12(4): 77–84.

Burnett, J. J. and Wood, V. R. (1988), 'A proposed model of the donation decision process', *Research in Consumer Behavior*, 3: 1–47.

Caruana, A., Ramaseshan, B. and Ewing, M. T. (1998), 'The marketing orientation–performance link: Some evidence from the public sector and universities', *Journal of Nonprofit and Public Sector Marketing*, 6(1): 63–82.

Cismaru, M., Lavack, A. M. and Markewich, E. (2009), 'Social marketing campaigns aimed at preventing drunk driving: A review and recommendations', *International Marketing Review*, 26(3): 292–311.

Cooper P. D. (1979), *Healthcare Marketing: Issues and Trends*, Germantown, MD: Aspen Systems Corporation.

Dahrendorf, R. (1997), *Keynote Address to Charities Aid Foundation Conference*, QEII Conference Centre, October, London.

Drucker, P. (1990), *Managing The Non-Profit Organization*, Oxford, UK: Butterworth-Heinemann.

Drumwright, M. E. (1996), 'Company advertising with a social dimension: The role of noneconomic criteria', *Journal of Marketing*, 60(4): 71–87.

Ferber, R. (1970), 'The expanding role of marketing in the 1970s', *Journal of Marketing*, 34(1): 29–30.

Fine, S. F. (1981), *The Marketing of Ideas and Social Issues*, New York: Praeger.

Frederiksen, L. W., Solomon, L. J. and Brehony, K. A. (1984), *Marketing Health Behavior*, New York: Plenum.

Friedman, M. (1970), 'The social responsibility of business is to increase its profits', *New York Times Magazine*, pp. 122–126.

Gallopel-Morvan, K., Gabriel, P., Le Gall-Ely, M., Rieunier, S. and Urien, B. (2011), 'The use of visual warnings in social marketing: The case of tobacco', *Journal of Business Research*, 64(1): 7–11.

Giving USA Foundation (2014), Giving USA 2014, Giving USA Foundation, Indianapolis, IN.

Goldberg, M. (1997), 'Social marketing: Are we fiddling whilst Rome burns?', *Journal of Consumer Psychology*, 4(4): 347–370.

Gordon, R. (2013), 'Unlocking the potential of upstream social marketing', *European Journal of Marketing*, 47(9): 1525–1547.

Gracia-Marco, L., Vicente-Rodriquez, G., Borys, J. M., Le Bodo, Y., Pettigrew, S. and Moreno, L. A. (2011), 'Contribution of social marketing strategies to community-based obesity prevention programmes in children', *International Journal of Obesity*, 35(4): 472–479.

Guy, B. S. and Patton, W. E. (1989), 'The marketing of altruistic causes: Understanding why people help', *Journal of Services Marketing*, 2(1): 5–16.

Hall, R. P. (1978), *Conceptual, Methodological and Moral Issues in the Study of Organizational Effectiveness*, Working Paper, Albany, NY: SUNY, Department of Sociology.

Hansmann H. B. (1980), 'The role of nonprofit enterprise', *The Yale Law Journal*, 89(5): 835–901.

Hornik, R. (2001), *Remarks on the Occasion of the Andreasen Fellowship Lecture*, Paper presented at the Social Marketing and Health Conference, Clearwater, FL, 22 June.

Humanitarian Studies Unit (2001), *Reflections on Humanitarian Action: Principles, Ethics and Contradictions*, London: Pluto Press.

Hunt, S. D. (1977), 'The three dichotomies model of marketing: An elaboration of issues', in Slater, C. C. (ed.) *Macro-Marketing: Distributive Processes From A Societal Perspective*, Boulder, CO: University of Colorado, pp. 52–56.

Jaworski, B. J. and Kohli, A. K. (1993), 'Marketing orientation: Antecedents and consequences', *Journal of Marketing*, 57(3): 53–70.

Jordan, W. K. (1964), *Philanthropy in England 1480–1660*, London: George Allen and Unwin.

Kant, I. (2009), *Fundamental Principles of the Metaphysic of Morals*, Dublin, Ireland: Merchant Books.

Kavle, J., Eber, M. and Lundgren, R. (2012), 'The potential for social marketing: A knowledge-based family planning method', *Social Marketing Quarterly*, 18(2): 152–166.

Kohli, A. K. and Jaworski, B. J. (1990), 'Market orientation: The construct, research propositions and managerial implications', *Journal of Marketing*, 54(2): 1–18.

Kotler, P and Levy, S. J. (1969), 'Broadening the concept of marketing', *Journal of Marketing*, 33(2): 10–15.

Kotler, P. and Zaltman, G. (1971), 'Social marketing: An approach to planned social change', *Journal of Marketing*, 44(Fall): 24–33.

Kotler, P. and Andreasen, A. (1982), *Strategic Marketing for Nonprofit Organizations*, Englewood Cliffs, NJ: Prentice Hall.

Kotler, P. and Fox, K. F. A. (1985), *Strategic Marketing for Educational Institutions*, Englewood Cliffs, NJ: Prentice Hall.

Kotler, P. and Clarke, R. N. (1986), *Marketing for Health Care Organizations*, Englewood Cliffs, NJ: Prentice Hall.

Kotler, P. and Roberto, E. L. (1989), *Social Marketing: Strategies for Changing Public Behavior*, New York: The Free Press.

Kotler, P. and Andreasen, A. (1991), *Strategic Marketing for Nonprofit Organizations*, fourth edition, Englewood Cliffs, NJ: Prentice Hall.

LaFollette, H. (1997), *Ethics in Practice*, London: Blackwell.

Lavidge, R. J. (1970), 'The growing responsibilities of marketing', *Journal of Marketing*, 34(1): 25–28.

Lovelock, C. H. and Weinberg, C. B. (1989), *Marketing for Public and Nonprofit Managers*, second edition, Redwood City, CA: The Scientific Press.

Lovelock, C. H. and Weinberg, C. B. (1990), *Public and Nonprofit Marketing: Readings and Cases*, Redwood City, CA: The Scientific Press.

Lowry, R., Austin, J. and Patterson, M. (2011), 'Using social marketing to improve breast-feeding rates in a low socioeconomic area', *Social Marketing Quarterly*, 17(2): 64–75.

Luck, D. J. (1969), 'Broadening the concept of marketing too far', *Journal of Marketing*, 33(2): 53–55.

Malaro, M. C. (1994), *Museum Governance: Mission, Ethics, Policy*, Englewood Cliffs, NJ: Prentice Hall.

Manoff, R. K. (1985), *Social Marketing*, New York: Praeger.

McKenna, J., Gutierez, K. and McCall, K. (2000), 'Strategies for effective youth countermarketing program: Recommendations from commercial marketing experts', *Journal of Public Health Management Practice*, 6(3): 7–13.

McKenzie-Mohr, D. (1994), 'Social marketing for sustainability: The case of residential energy conservation', *Futures*, 26(2): 224–233.

Meade, J. (1974), 'A mathematical model for deriving hospital service areas', *International Journal of Health Services*, 4(2): 353–357.

Miller, S. J. (1974), *Market Segmentation and Forecasting for a Charitable Health Organization*, Paper presented to the Southern Marketing Association Conference, Atlanta, GA.

Mokwa, M. P., Dawson, W. M. and Prieve, E. A. (eds) (1980), *Marketing The Arts*, volume xvi, New York: Praeger Publishers Inc.

Moore, J. N., Raymond, M. A., Mittelstaedt, J. D. and Tanner, J. F. (2002), 'Age and consumer socialisation agent influences on adolescents' sexual knowledge, attitudes and behaviour: Implications for social marketing initiatives and public policy', *Journal of Public Policy and Marketing*, 21(1): 37–52.

Mullin, R. (1995), *Foundations for Fundraising*, London: ICSA Publishing.

Narver, J. C. and Slater, S. F. (1990), 'The effect of a market orientation on business profitability', *Journal of Marketing*, 54(4): 20–35.

Nash, R. J. (2002), *Real World Ethics: Frameworks for Educators and Human Service Professionals*, Boston, MA: Teachers College Press.

Newman, W. H. and Wallender, H. W. (1978), 'Managing for Nonprofit Enterprises', *Academy of Management Review*, 3(1): 24–32.

Peattie, K., Peattie, S. and Clarke, P. (2001), 'Skin cancer prevention: Re-evaluating the public policy implications', *Journal of Public Policy and Marketing*, 20(2): 268–279.

Porter, M. E. and Kramer, M. R. (2002), 'The competitive advantage of corporate philanthropy', *Harvard Business Review*, 80(12): 56–61.

Porter, M. E. and Kramer, M. R. (2011), 'Creating shared value', *Harvard Business Review*, 89(1): 2–17.

Rados, D. L. (1981), *Marketing for Non-Profit Organizations*, Dover, MA: Auburn House.

Ricks, J. M. Jr (2005), 'An assessment of strategic corporate philanthropy on perceptions of brand equity variables', *Journal of Consumer Marketing*, 22(3): 121–134.

Rothschild, M. L. (1999), 'Carrots, sticks and promises: A conceptual framework for the management of public health and social issues behaviours', *Journal of Marketing*, 63(4): 24–37.

Rossiter, J. R. and Jones, S. (2004), 'Special issue editorial: Fear appeals in social marketing campaigns', *Psychology & Marketing*, 21(11): 885–887.

Sagawa, S. (2001), 'New value partnerships: The lessons of Denny's/Save the Children partnership for building high-yielding cross-sector alliances', *International Journal of Nonprofit & Voluntary Sector Marketing*, 6(3): 199–214.

Sargeant, A. (1999), *Marketing Management for Nonprofit Organisations*, Oxford, UK: Oxford University Press.

Sargeant, A. and Jay, E. (2004), *Fundraising Management: Analysis, Planning and Practice*, London: Routledge.

Sargeant, A. and Woodliffe, L. (2007), A Review of the Gift-Giving Literature, in Sargeant, A. and Wymer, W. (eds) *The Nonprofit Marketing Companion*, London: Routledge.

Sargeant, A. and Shang, J. (2010), *Fundraising Principles and Practice*, San Francisco, CA: Jossey-Bass.

Sargeant, A. and Jay, E. (2014), *Fundraising Management*, third edition, London: Routledge.

Sargeant, A., Foreman, S. and Liao, M. (2002), 'Operationalising the marketing concept in the nonprofit sector', *Journal of Nonprofit and Public Sector Marketing*, 10(2): 41–65.

Sheehan, R. (1996), 'Mission accomplishment as philanthropic organizational effectiveness: Key findings from the excellence in philanthropy project', *Nonprofit and Voluntary Sector Quarterly*, 25(1): 110–123.

Stanton, A., Kennedy, M., Springarn, R. and Rotheram-Borus, M. J. (2000), 'Developing services for substance-abusing HIV positive youth with mental health disorders', *Journal of Behavioral Health Services Research*, 27(4): 380–389.

Van Der Gaag, N. (2007), 'Images in fundraising', in Mordaunt, J. and Paton, R. (eds) *Thoughtful Fundraising*, London: Routledge.

Van Der Gaag, N. and Nash, C. (1987), *Images for Africa*, available at http://www.imaging-famine.org/images_africa.htm (accessed 3 May 2014).

Wakhisi, A. S., Allotey, P., Dhillon, N. and Reidpath, D. D. (2011), 'The effectiveness of social marketing in reduction of teenage pregnancies: A review of studies in developed countries', *Social Marketing Quarterly*, 17(1): 56–90.

Warwick, M. (1994), *Raising Money by Mail: Strategies For Growth and Financial Stability*, Berkeley, CA: Strathmoor Press.

Weber, L. (2001), *Business Ethics In Healthcare: Beyond Compliance*, Indianapolis, IN: Indiana University Press.

Weick, K. E. (1977), 'Re-punctuating the problem', in Goodman, P. S. and Pennings, J. (eds) *New Perspectives on Organizational Effectiveness*, San Francisco, CA: Jossey-Bass, pp. 63–95.

Wymer, W. W. Jr and Samu, S. (2003), 'Dimensions of business and nonprofit collaborative relationships', *Journal of Nonprofit & Public Sector Marketing*, 11(1): 3–23.

Zeithaml, V. (1996), *Services Marketing*, Maidenhead, UK: McGraw-Hill.

Zucker, D., Hopkins, R. S., Sly, D. F., Urich, J., Kershaw, J. M. and Solari, S. (2000), 'Florida's truth campaign: A countermarketing anti-tobacco media campaign', *Journal of Public Health Management Practice*, 6(3): 1–6.

23 Marketing ethics

Andrea Prothero

Introduction

> We are not proposing that marketers take the moral high ground on every issue. But when marketers are considered about as trustworthy as used-car salespeople, it would be a major step for marketers to lead the revolt against immoral practices and the cynical misuse of ethical policies. This way, the standing of the profession as a whole can be increased and we can work towards a fairer, more decent society – whilst still ensuring that the economy thrives.
>
> (Chartered Institute of Marketing 2004, cited in Baker and Hart 2008)

The most startling aspect of the above quote is not the quote itself, but rather its source – the Chartered Institute of Marketing, the professional body for marketers in the UK. In the twenty-first century marketers themselves have recognized the importance of ethics to marketing practice. Consequently, the study of marketing ethics is important, as society, business and marketers begin to reflect further on ethical issues of importance – be they global concerns over the warming of the earth and humans' responsibility for the destruction of our natural environment, or more micro, firm-based issues, which focus on unethical business and marketing practices. Trust for both business and marketing activities is declining, particularly following large corporate scandals such as the Arthur Andersen, Enron and WorldCom affairs, and the collapse of the global financial sector in the mid-2000s, with large financial institutions such as the investment bank, Lehman Brothers, becoming bankrupt, and many banks, such as Northern Rock and Royal Bank of Scotland and Lloyds Banking Group in the UK, requiring enormous bailouts from governments. Even the ethical bank, The Co-operative, required significant financial assistance in 2013, and its non-executive chairman, Paul Flowers, resigned his post following a number of scandals. It seems imperative then that a text such as *The Marketing Book* focuses on the subject of marketing ethics. Indeed, marketing ethics is not a new topic and has been debated, contested and explored in detail since the 1950s in academic texts and articles (see, for example, Adler *et al.* 1981; Tsalikis and Fritzsche 1989; Jacobsen and Mazur 1995; Davidson 2003; Laczniak and Murphy 2006), as well as in more mainstream texts such as Vance Packard's (1957) critique of advertising, *The Hidden Persuaders* and critiques of consumer society (Fromm 1955; Marcuse 1964; Debord 1977).

Before exploring marketing ethics and its implications for our understanding of both the theory and practice of marketing, it is first important to place it into a wider ethical context; as such it is necessary to briefly explore ethics generally and more specifically business ethics.

Ethics

The study of ethics has a deep, varied and rich history and focuses on questions of good and bad; right and wrong; and what it means to have or take responsibility, or promote human flourishing. Famous and influential philosophers, such as Plato, Aristotle, Immanuel Kant, and John Stuart Mill all considered ethical questions were central to human life and human interactions, including public life. There are various ethical theories, which have been developed over a long period of time ranging from absolutist theories – that focus on universal ethical principles regarding what everyone should do in all situations – to relativist theories focusing upon subjective concerns in particular contexts and particular moments. Consequential ethical theories are concerned with the intended outcomes of actions and include utilitarian ethics that focus in various ways on the greatest good for the greatest number of people. Non-consequential theories consider the decision makers' motives and include deontological ethics' concern with one's 'duty' and the ethics of rights and justice. Consequently, if you view ethics from a deontological perspective, your primary focus is on one's actions (and whether they are right or wrong; or good or bad). If you focus on consequential ethics you recognize that whether or not actions are right or wrong; or good or bad, will depend on the consequences of those actions. Take, for example, a manufacturing firm choosing to close down its production facilities in a country in which it has been operating for over 100 years, and move to another location where operating and employment costs would be cheaper. Adopting a utilitarian perspective, the company will chose to move locations or not based on the greatest good for the greatest number of people involved, and is likely to conduct a cost/benefit analysis to reach its conclusions. If it operates from a deontological, duties-based perspective, it is likely to remain in its current location, as the company will have a sense of duty to its workforce of longstanding and the community in which it operates.

There are various ethical theories and principles attached to the world's many religions, as well as contemporary ethical theories such as environmental ethics and feminist ethics, invoking values and concerns often ignored or left out of longstanding traditional views. Which perspective you decide to explore ethics from and what types of concerns you consider important, impact the way you view the study and implementation of business ethics generally and marketing ethics specifically.

When considering ethics and how we view whether or not an act is deemed ethical or not, we will consider not only our ideological perspective on how we view ethics (e.g. from a duty or a consequential perspective) but also on what the context of the situation is and similarly what the context is for the individual and/or organization involved with the ethical issue under investigation. If we consider the whole gamut of issues under investigation, we can say that to garner a full understanding of ethical decision-making we must consider the ethical issue, the motivations involved in choosing one course of action over another, the action itself and the outcome(s) of that action. In today's world we tend to consider both the action and the consequences of that action when making ethical choices and thus, all of these factors combined will help us in trying to garner a full picture of how ethical decisions are made. These motivations, actions and outcomes will also be impacted by the norms and values of society, the legal and regulatory framework, and the characteristics of the individual making the decision (e.g. an individual's values, beliefs, religion, culture, age, gender and moral character are all said to impact on one's ethical choices). Similarly, at the organizational level, the norms and values of firms, professions, industries and the codes of conduct developed therein, as well as legal and regulatory requirements, will impact the ethical choices made within an organizational context.

Business ethics

A recurring joke among students, at all levels, when taught business ethics has been 'Business ethics: I didn't know there were any'. It is accepted, however, that the ethical practices of business are under scrutiny now more than ever and ethical business practices are a way of thinking for all businesses in the twenty-first century. Consequently, it is fair to suggest that business and ethics are intrinsically linked, and will remain so, well into the next century and, as such, the manner in which organizations conduct their activities will continue to play an important role in society. This is not least because it has been well documented both academically and in the popular press that doing 'bad' is 'bad' for business. Nike's share price, for example, plummeted after it admitted unethical behaviour at its Indonesian plants in 2001. Newspapers themselves like nothing better than to criticize poor behaviour, as evidenced in the coverage of the unethical practices of individuals such as Martha Stewart, and Kenneth Lay and Jeffrey Skilling of Enron, as well as being critical of organizations and the key individuals within these same companies who market themselves as ethical and/or socially responsible. For instance, criticisms of the Body Shop and its founder, Anita Roddick, were intense during the 1980s and early 1990s at a time when it was generally recognized that the Body Shop's ethical and environmental actions were far superior to others in the cosmetics industry on a number of fronts. As well as popular press criticism of unethical practices, there are a number of anti-corporation best sellers such as Naomi Klein's *No Logo*, which depict business in a bad light. Similarly, there has been a plethora of successful film documentaries criticizing business activity – see, for example, *Exit Through the Gift Shop, The Greatest Movie Ever Sold, Capitalism: A Love Story, Super Size Me, The Corporation, Enron: The Smartest Guys in the Room, Wal-Mart: The High Cost of Low Price* and *An Inconvenient Truth*. Movies themselves (both those based on factual events and fictional pieces) have also raised important issues about various ethical practices – recent examples include *The Wolf of Wall Street, The Social Network* and *Thank You for Smoking*. Students can learn much about business ethics by watching documentaries and movies around the subject. Similarly, there are some excellent non-fiction business books ranging from Dale Carnegie's *How to Win Friends and Influence People* in 1936, to more recent tomes such as Nick Bilton's (2013) excellent *Hatching Twitter: A True Story of Money, Power, Friendship and Betrayal*, Seth Godin's (2005) *All Marketers are Liars*, and the wonderful *Barbarians at the Gate* by Bryan Burrough and John Helyar (1990), all provide an excellent insight into the role of ethics in business organizations. We can learn a lot from novels too – some excellent suggestions for further reading include – George Orwell's 1937 classic *The Road to Wigan Pier*, Ayn Rand's (1943) *The Fountainhead*, and Philip Roth's (1997) masterpiece, *American Pastoral*.

Companies are targeted by pressure groups and NGOs, consumers, lawyers and their employees who question the ethics of business strategies and practices. All of this public scrutiny has led to organizations continually redressing their impact on society and its stakeholders, at a time when ethical problems are becoming more complex. Thus, all business activities can be subjected to public scrutiny be they related to workplace, community, environmental or marketplace issues. Consequently, these issues have significant implications for marketing activities, an area of business, which has been seen to be responsible for significant unethical practices. In their student text Steiner and Steiner (2011: 197) define business ethics simply as 'The study of good and evil, right and wrong, and just and unjust actions in business'.

It is these issues of good and evil, and right and wrong which have their roots in our understanding of the various ethical theories briefly discussed above, which then transcend into our assessment of marketing ethics by focusing on issues of right and wrong in relation to marketing as a philosophy, discipline and practice. What is very clear from this definition is that the study of business ethics (and indeed ethics generally, or marketing ethics more specifically) is not rocket science! The problem arises when we try to determine what is good versus evil or right versus wrong, what ethical lens we use to consider these issues, and who gets to decide what is good or evil and/or right or wrong. Consequently, because ethics is ultimately subjective, it will always be a quagmire, and it is this quagmire, which has led to humans disagreeing over ethics for thousands of years. As well as considering right and wrong and good versus evil we must also consider the context within which ethical decision-making is being framed – for instance, is there a significant difference between an individual in an organization taking a small bribe (e.g. a free meal), versus the widespread payment of bribes by an organization's employees to various stakeholders (e.g. planners, developers, politicians, lawyers)? Businesses, themselves, will develop, implement and act on their own moral and ethical codes, and these will be framed within wider societal and industry contexts.

Marketing ethics

Although in recent years many of the major ethical controversies in business have been related to the accountancy and finance areas, marketing has very often been the business function most associated with unethical behaviour (Tsalikis and Fritzsche 1989; Armstrong and Sweeney 1994; Nantel and Weeks 1996), and it has been argued that elements of the recent global financial crisis can also be attributed to marketing activities (Murphy *et al.* 2012). It is therefore imperative that a book such as this devotes attention to the study of marketing ethics. There were a number of attempts to develop ethical marketing theories in the 1980s (Ferrell and Gresham 1985; Hunt and Vitell 1986; Dubinsky and Loken 1989) and 1990s (Laczniak and Murphy 1993) and more recently in the 2000s with an update of Hunt and Vitell's general theory of marketing ethics (Hunt and Vitell 2006) and a normative offering from Laczniak and Murphy (2006). These theories explore marketing ethics from different theoretical perspectives and as such are dependent on how one views and examines ethics generally, as discussed in the ethics section above. In recent years there has been a number of texts and case studies focusing specifically on ethical marketing issues (Laczniak and Murphy 2006; Murphy *et al.* 2012) and articles which consider ethical marketing within particular contexts (Martin *et al.* 2011; Williams and Aitken 2011) across cultures (Nill and Schultz 1997) and the influence of ethical issues upon marketing students (Singhapakdi 2004; Nill and Schibrowsky 2005). Regardless of how one decides to explore ethics and which perspective is adopted, from a practical viewpoint all exchanges have an impact on society and, as such, every transaction can be considered through an ethical lens (Laczniak and Murphy 2006). Consequently, when one is exploring the various marketing strategies and practices detailed throughout this book, it is vital that we explore and assess these from an ethical perspective.

Murphy *et al.* (2012: 4) provide the following normative definition: 'Ethical marketing refers to practices that emphasize transparent, trustworthy, and responsible personal and/or organizational marketing policies and actions that exhibit integrity as well as fairness to consumers and other stakeholders'.

What this definition emphasizes is a prescriptive account of 'what marketing and marketers should aspire to' (Murphy *et al.* 2012: 4). Such a definition means that as students studying marketing from an ethical perspective we must consider the ethical implications for our understanding of what marketing is and how marketing is applied in practice. This has consequences for the organizational policies of companies, the practices of marketing managers and ultimately the implications of these policies and practices for wider society. We will explore each of these issues below.

Macromarketing: examining the interactions among markets, marketing and society

When exploring marketing ethics one can begin by asking two basic questions. First, 'What impact does marketing have on society?'; and second, 'What impact does society have on marketing?' By doing so we are able to explore marketing from a macro, societal, rather than a micro, firm level. As such, we will then want to consider not only the ethical practices of marketers at a firm level but also explore marketing activities on a much wider, societal level. In this context, we can examine marketing from a macromarketing perspective. Here we argue that marketing is not only a set of managerial practices or indeed an organizational philosophy but also a social institution. Macromarketing itself is a discipline that predates the term and has been a topic of investigation for as far back in time as the Greek philosophers, Plato and Socrates. Terms such as, 'marketing in/and society' are used regularly by academics and, in essence, we can substitute this term for macromarketing. When focusing on macromarketing, one is exploring issues relating to 'ethics, marketing systems, public policy, and social responsibility' (Hunt and Vitell 2006). Examining the interactions among markets, marketing and society allows us to begin to explore and ask questions concerning what marketing's impacts are on society and what the ethical implications are of this? With a macro focus we can ask questions such as 'is marketing inherently bad?', before focusing more specifically on the unethical strategies and practices of marketing departments and managers themselves. This allows us to consider marketing activities from both an absolutist and a relativist perspective. It also allows us to explore the norms and values of society and consider how these impact on marketing decision-making at the organizational level. In short, we can have philosophical debates about marketing as a social institution.

Macromarketing: ethical debates

The use of marketing by businesses, and indeed governments and NGOs, has been severely criticized by many in society for many decades now. Some key arguments, which focus on the notion that marketing is somehow inherently bad and/or has deleterious consequences for society, are considered further below:

- **Marketing purports to the pursuit of happiness via consumption**: It is well documented in the literature that marketing is concerned with creating value, exchange relationships and the satisfaction of consumers; it is these goals that marketers attempt to achieve for their organization. However, there have been critical assessments of pursuing the notion of satisfying consumers, most notably as a result of such activities not necessarily leading to satisfied and happy consumers. It is argued that the pursuit of happiness via consumption ultimately leads to perpetual dissatisfaction, where consumers' needs are never fully met as there are always more goods to buy, or more services to be experienced. As Blackburn commented in 2004, 'At a time when materially "we've never had it so good", we feel more anxious and unhappy than ever', where it is suggested that the generation born in the 1970s are the unhappiest ever. Many of these criticisms are indeed not only a criticism of marketing per se but of business generally and specifically the pursuit of market capitalism. As such, when engaging in a critique of marketing principles and practices, very often this also leads to a debate of the role of capitalism in society and the role marketing plays therein.
- **Marketing leads to the pursuit of the ideal self via consumption, and this ideal self is promoted through marketing communications campaigns**: Recently there has

been much debate surrounding the ideal self and how marketers use notions of this ideal self to tempt consumers into buying more goods and services. This ideal self is then promoted through various marketing communications campaigns, which suggest 'buy this product and you will look/be like me', thus leading to much consumer dissonance when the ideal self is not achieved. Similarly, authors have questioned who determines what the 'ideal self' should look like, thus forming another contentious issue. It is argued that marketing communications lead to an idealized notion of what a 'good life' should be, while at the same time also reinforcing social stereotypes.

- **By the use of various marketing activities, marketing stereotypes consumers**: Connected to the discussion above, many have argued that marketers stereotype consumers in particular ways. For instance, in their advertising campaigns companies have been criticized for various stereotyping actions – for example, an over-reliance on white middle-class families; only using the 'traditional' family in ads; not using enough older consumers in ads; only showing beautiful, thin, 'perfect' consumers in ads. Such stereotyping, it is argued, leads to dissatisfaction and isolation for those in society who do not conform to particular stereotypes.
- **Marketing targets vulnerable groups in society**: Companies have been criticized in many diverse product ranges for targeting vulnerable groups – for instance, by promoting smoking or encouraging the use of formula rather than breast milk in developing nations. In developed nations unscrupulous companies have been criticized for targeting vulnerable groups – for instance, the use of door-to-door salespeople to encourage elderly people to buy expensive home security systems. Marketers have also been subject to condemnation over its marketing campaigns to children and teenagers, for instance, in the promotion of foods high in fat, salt and sugar.
- **Marketing actively excludes potential customers from the marketplace**: In many situations, companies wish to maintain an exclusivity about their products and as such actively discourage some groups from buying their products. An obvious way to do this is to price goods at a significantly high level to allow companies to maintain such exclusivity.

Micromarketing: unethical marketing at the level of the firm

At a firm micro level, companies have been criticized for many unscrupulous marketing activities, both at a strategic and a tactical level. Activities at a micro level can have long-term implications for society. Macro criticisms can be considered at the micro, firm level, and it is important to see the two as interrelated. At a micro level the organizational strategies and marketing practices applied by companies will depend in part on the values and norms of the firm in question and the profession and/or industry to which that firm belongs. Some have argued, for instance, that some industries are more unscrupulous than others; some industries may also have more stringent rules and regulations than others. By evaluating ethical activities at a firm level, we can explore the applied marketing strategies and practices put in place by firms and provide examples of various unethical activities. At this juncture it is important to remember from our earlier discussions, that what is deemed ethical or not will depend on the lens through which we view ethics, the motivations, actions and outcomes as a result of the act in question, and our subjective opinions, which will be based on many different factors.

Marketing in practice

In order to create value, firms will engage in pursuing a number of different marketing strategies. They will make attempts to understand the market they are operating in, as well as understand their current (and potential) consumer base. Strategies will be put in place to develop a successful relationship (via customer relationship management (CRM) policies) with customers. The product/service being offered to the marketplace will take centre stage, and organizations will attempt to develop successful brands. At the same time, organizations will aim to develop successful pricing strategies and manage their distribution channels effectively. Communications strategies will be developed to convey a successful brand story. Each of these marketing activities could lead to unethical marketing practices, and we will explore some examples of unethical practices below.

- **Segmentation and targeting**: One area of constant worry is how firms utilize marketing strategies to target vulnerable groups; as discussed above, this can include children, the elderly and the poor.
- **Marketing research, direct marketing and data analytics**: The use of database and direct marketing has increased exponentially in recent years and, along with it, so have the number of complaints about the use of these particular marketing strategies. Environmentalists, for example, complain about the waste of paper following direct market campaigns, while consumers complain about intrusion into their everyday lives by marketing activities – be this via cold calling on the telephone, or via the use of spam emails selling various goods and services. There have been revolutionary changes in the media landscape and in our use of the internet, and in particular our use of social media in what has been termed the Digital Age. This has had an enormous impact on how companies interact with their consumers and with the marketplace more generally. Ethical issues here abound, and none more so than in the use of our personal data collected online and then utilized by organizations to understand its consumers better and ultimately develop strategies aimed at the identified target group. Issues of intrusion and privacy are central concerns. Every time consumers buy something they give away information about themselves (e.g. gender, age) and their shopping habits, which retailers can utilize to build up a profile of their consumers. Recently in the US, *Forbes* magazine (Hill 2012) detailed how the retailer, Target, utilized its database to build up a 'pregnancy prediction' score for its consumers and then used this information to send coupons, etc. to potential new parents, so much so that the store was able to determine a teenager's pregnancy before this information was disclosed to her parents.
- **Marketing mix**: The marketing mix is a mainstay for discussing marketing in the classroom, and while it is not without its critics (see, for example, O'Malley and Patterson 1998) it does provide a useful means by which to explore various marketing activities, and we can equally apply this to an evaluation of ethical marketing activities.
- **Product issues**: From a product perspective, companies have been disparaged for selling **dangerous products** ranging from cigarettes (and in recent times e-cigarettes) and alcohol, to the sale of weapons of mass destruction. There are also concerns over the sale of **unsafe products**. In the EU **product recalls** have increased significantly recently and it has been suggested this is due to new legislation governing unsafe products. An average of two product recalls a day are listed on the European Commission website, with the main offenders being children's toys and electrical goods. Details of product recalls in the UK are updated regularly on the Trading Standards website (http://www.tradingstandards.gov.uk/). A very visible recall in 2006 was the withdrawal of one million bars of chocolate by Cadbury's following a salmonella scare. Reports suggest the recall cost the company between £20 million and £30 million, as well as a temporary removal of the company's sponsorship of Coronation Street, the removal of other marketing communications activities and a temporary hold on the launch of new products within the company. Following the reintroduction of marketing communications, the company increased its advertising spend by £7 million. Subsequent to the product recall there was an initial decrease

in sales of Cadbury's products, but suppliers were soon reporting sales back to their pre-recall levels. The company pleaded guilty to nine charges brought against them by the Food Standards Agency and were fined £1 million. In 2008 Cadbury's was faced with recalling 11 products in its Asia and Pacific markets, following contamination in its manufacturing plants. **Planned obsolescence** is another criticism aimed at organizations. Here firms deliberately make products, ranging from electronics and video games to student textbooks to have a limited life span, and they have been criticized for both the environmental waste of such actions and for exploiting customers by forcing them to buy new products. Counter arguments suggest that the introduction of new and innovative designs is a result of the free market working effectively and customers demanding new product ranges.

- **Pricing issues**: Pricing irregularities are a common occurrence in business and many companies have been criticized for their pricing strategies. In 2012 British Airways were fined £58.5 million for **price fixing** on its fuel surcharge, in a collusion with Virgin. Virgin struck a deal with the Office of Fair Trading and was not fined. **Deceptive pricing** is another ethical pricing concern, and a number of deceptive pricing strategies exist. In essence firms attempt to persuade consumers they are receiving a bargain price, when in fact they are not. One example is **bait and switch** pricing – here a company uses a particular pricing deal to tempt consumers into the store (bait), but then utilizes a number of possible strategies (e.g. not having the bait item in stock) to persuade them to purchase a different item (switch). **Predatory pricing** is another example of unethical pricing strategies; in this case a company sets a price at a very low level with the ultimate aim of forcing competitors out of the market. In 2009 the European Court of Justice upheld a €10.35 million fine against France Telecom/Wanadoo for predatory pricing activities in the broadband market. While there is legislation to tackle illegal pricing strategies and strict competition laws, examples of pricing irregularities are not uncommon. **Price wars** provide another illustration of ethical concerns. In this instance, consumers benefit from a reduction in prices, but a more in-depth analysis shows us that price wars tend to be short-lived and consumers are charged more for items in the longer term, and there are concerns regarding the impact of price wars on suppliers. Farmers, for example, have been protesting in recent years over the impact of supermarket price wars on their livelihoods. In 2013 a group of Irish farmers protested outside supermarkets to highlight the cost to them of a supermarket price war on the sales of fruit and vegetables. In 2008 the British charity *Action Aid* published a short video, 'Who pays the real cost of supermarket price wars?', highlighting the implications of such pricing strategies for employees in developing nations.

- **Marketing communications**: Marketing communications is the one arena in which we are probably most familiar with ethical complaints. There are ethical concerns involving the marketing message being communicated, the manner in which the message is communicated and the medium through which this message takes place. Each is explored further below:

1   **Misleading consumers as to the benefits of their products** – Companies have long been said to exaggerate the benefits of their products to consumers, often referred to as **puffery**. Puffery is legally allowed, but **false** and **deceptive** advertising are not. The problem lies when the puffery case of exaggeration exceeds what is considered acceptable. This may be in a very suggestive way, by perhaps alluding that using a particular product will make you more attractive, or more beautiful in some way for instance; or a company can make unsubstantiated claims about their products, by suggesting that a diet product will make you thinner for example, without emphasizing that this has to be in conjunction with a change in diet and regular exercise.

2 **Adopting dubious marketing communications strategies** – One of the biggest criticisms of marketing activities is in the use of company marketing communication strategies. These range from **deception** and **negative** advertising to the use of **misleading** advertising claims. Companies can be criticized by both the general public and by its competitors. Examples of recent controversies include:

a In 2010 Largo Foods, the manufacturer of Hunky-Dory crisps in Ireland, had to withdraw a number of advertisements following complaints by consumers and a decision by the Advertising Standards Authority of Ireland that the ads broke the ASAIs code of conduct. The ads showed women playing rugby, but wearing provocative clothing rather than sportswear. Taglines to go along with the ads included comments such as 'Are you staring at my crisps?', 'Tackle these' and 'Others haka, we hunky'. The ads were widely condemned for their objectification of women and were discussed not only in Ireland but also internationally.

b Kellogg's social media campaign, 'Give a child a breakfast', was publically condemned in 2013. Via Twitter, Kellogg's asked consumers to 'RT [retweet] this to give a vulnerable child breakfast'. Following widespread condemnation on Twitter the company withdrew the tweet, but criticism of its social media campaign to provide food to the vulnerable remained, with many unhappy at what was considered to be cynical marketing practice by the company.

c Pizza company, DiGiornio, was involved in a social media controversy in the US after trying to make light of an ongoing social media conversation concerning domestic violence under the hashtag #WhyIStayed; the company posted '#WhyIStayed you had pizza'. The tweet was removed very quickly and the company followed up by emphasizing that it wasn't aware of the domestic violence context of the hashtag and stated, 'A million apologies. Did not read what the hashtag was about before posting'.

d Ikea was criticized for the removal of women from its catalogue in Saudi Arabia; women were air-brushed from the magazine and this led to criticism from the public and governments. A company spokesperson later stressed, 'We should have reacted and realised that excluding women from the Saudi Arabian version of the catalogue is in conflict with Ikea group values' (Paterson 2012).

e Complaints were received by Ofcom in 2012 over posters used by Channel 4 to promote its series *My Big Fat Gypsy Wedding*. It was argued that the ads were racist, and the use of the word 'gypsier' in the tagline, 'Bigger. Fatter. Gypsier' was unacceptable. Ofcom rejected the complaints and accepted the arguments put forward by Channel 4 that the use of the term 'gypsier' was not negative. A spokesperson for the traveller community responded to the outcome by stating, 'We wonder if Channel 4 would have been so ready to use adverts with similarly compromising images phrasing for other ethnic groups: "Jewisher" or "more Asian" or "Blacker"?' (Crookes 2012).

3 **Sponsorship** – Sponsorship is big business, a multi-billion pound global industry, and one of the biggest expenditure items in firms' marketing communications budgets. In recent years both the effectiveness and ethical nature of sponsorship activities have been called into question. Sporting events and sporting clubs have faced criticism over what many deem inappropriate sponsors, in particular by alcohol and gambling companies. The payday loan company, Wonga, is currently sponsor to Newcastle United Football Club, and the club faced heavy criticism from many different quarters over allowing sponsorship of

the club by a company facing considerable criticism over its business model. One of the club's players, Papiss Cissé, initially refused to wear the name on his shirt, and the Church of England called the company 'morally wrong'.

a   **Celebrity endorsement** – In attempting to build the reputation of their brand firms often do this by seeking the endorsement of actors and sports figures for their products. Like sponsorship, celebrity endorsements are big business; Rory McIlroy, for example, signed a deal said to be worth £155 million over ten years with Nike in 2013. What happens though when the celebrity behaves unethically – does this have a negative impact on the brand they endorse? One of the best examples of this is the Livestrong clothing brand of the Nike Corporation, directly linked to the Livestrong foundation of Lance Armstrong. A collaboration between Nike and the foundation led to a lucrative relationship for both organizations. Following the revelations about his use of performing enhancing drugs, Nike ceased to sponsor Lance Armstrong in 2012, the Livestrong brand of clothing and apparel was, however, a very successful brand for the company, and severing the relationship was announced later in 2013. In this case the reputational damage caused by Mr Armstrong led to Nike dropping an entire brand from its product range. Sticking with the golf theme, the fall from grace of Tiger Woods, following details of his personal life, meant many of his sponsors, including AT&T, Gatorade and Gillette severed their business relationship with him. Some companies however stood by their man and continued to provide sponsorship, including Nike and Rolex. The issue of celebrity endorsements raises an interesting question. In the Tiger Woods case it was argued that his personal life should have no bearing on his sponsorship deals, which were directly related to Mr Woods' golfing capabilities; whereas others argued that Tiger Woods was a role model and his indiscretions would damage the reputation of the endorser. An interesting ethical conversation is to consider if both Lance Armstrong and Tiger Woods' endorsements were severed for ethical reasons and/or business ones.

4   **Packaging** – The packaging of products has come under scrutiny for various reasons. **Excess packaging**, and the implications of this from a sustainability perspective provides one illustration, the use of **on-pack advertising** another. Recently, for example, the Australian government has banned the use of logos and branding on cigarette packaging. One area of recent concern is the use of **labelling** and, in particular, the possibility of misleading and/or confusing consumers with information provided on labels. In the food industry companies have been criticized for using terms such as 'fresh', 'natural', 'organic' and 'pure' inaccurately, as well as for the use of confusing labels highlighting a product's fat, sugar and salt contents. The Food Standards Agency has introduced a voluntary traffic light system for the labelling of foods and a number of high profile retailers, such as the Co-op, Marks & Spencer, Sainsbury's and Waitrose have introduced the system. Other companies though have not followed suit, and NGOs argue that confusion surrounding what is healthy remains, and indeed that companies play a role in contributing to this confusion.

•   **Marketing channels**: Ethical issues which occur within the distribution channel include **bribery**, **coercion** and misuse of **power**, and can oftentimes be exacerbated when occurring on a global scale and cultural differences come into play. What is deemed unethical in one country, for example, may be normal business practice in another. As we discussed earlier, marketers must therefore be aware not only of the ethical issues but also the context in which it is occurring. Examples of unethical marketing practices include limiting a product's availability in certain locations (e.g. pharmaceutical products in developing nations); increasing a product's availability in certain locations (e.g. providing unhealthy products in school vending machines); utilizing power to pass on the cost of price reductions to consumers (see the pricing examples above). Bribery and corruption are key areas of concern in the global marketplace and there are many examples in these areas. Recently, the medical nutrition company, *Nutricia*, was accused of bribing doctors in Beijing, and in another medical case, a senior marketing manager for the company, DePuy (a subsidiary of Johnson and Johnson), was sentenced to a year in prison for bribing Greek surgeons, although the sentence was later overturned, with the court citing the co-operation of the manager in exposing the considerable corruption in the industry.

Marketing's response: ethical and legal requirements, codes of conduct

The reaction of businesses and marketers to their critics is that their activities are subject to both stringent professional codes of conduct and legislative requirements (at supra, national and local levels). There are many professional marketing associations and most will have their own codes of conduct, some of which will be subject to legislative requirements and others that are stipulated as best practice for marketers to follow. In the UK the Chartered Institute of Marketing has a professional code for its members. Many individual organizations have a company-wide corporate social responsibility (CSR) policy, which will include ethical marketing policies. Consequently, many of the unethical activities, such as direct marketing and misleading advertising discussed above, are covered by codes of conduct and legal requirements. Marketers' response to ethical criticisms are that it is only a small minority who do not follow codes and/or legal requirements, and if they continue these practices they will be punished by the market in the longer term.

Legislative acts enforced by trading standards officers, which marketers are affected by include:

- Consumer Credit Act 2006;
- Consumer Protection Act 1987;
- Food Safety Act 1990;
- Prices Act 1974 and 1975;
- Trade Descriptions Act 1968.

Examples of marketing communications codes include the UK Code of Advertising, Sales Promotion and Direct Marketing and the UK Code of Broadcast Advertising. There are independent bodies and watchdogs that regulate very specific business practices – for example, PhonePayPlus (formerly known as the Independent Committee for the Supervision of Standards of the Telephone Information Services (ICSTIS)) is responsible for premium rate telephone communication services. The watchdog investigated the overcharging for premium rate calls by a number of different television channels, including popular television programmes such as *ITVs X Factor* and *Big Brother* and the *Richard and Judy* show on *Channel 4*. Consequently, marketers argue that with government legislation, self-imposed regulatory bodies and individual company codes of conduct it is only a small minority who damage marketing's reputation. Critics would counter that both legislation and self-imposed regulations do not always go far enough to protect consumers, animals and/or the environment.

Consumer responses to unethical marketing

Consumers have responded to the unethical practices of business and marketers in many different ways. Perhaps the most significant, has been the actions by some to opt out of the marketplace, as a recognition that consuming goods and services does not necessarily lead to happiness. There is much talk, for example, of consumer downsizing and voluntary simplicity in developed nations, as well as alternative consumer societies setting up (see, for example, McDonald *et al.* 2006). Other examples of consumer resistance to the marketplace include groups who continue to work and live within society, but who opt out of the market in particular ways, for instance, consumers who engage in activities such as *Buy Nothing Day* or perhaps boycott particular products as a result of company activities.

Consumer boycotts

One very visible method in which consumers can apply ethical principles to their everyday behaviour is to boycott the purchase of goods from particular companies, industries and/or countries. This option has been available to consumers for hundreds of years and one of the first campaigns was organized by the National Negro Convention in the 1800s: the campaign called for the boycott of slave-produced goods.

Consumer boycotts can range from small-scale local boycotts of a company's products to much larger international boycotts; indeed motivations for boycotts vary enormously. In 2011 *consumer outrage* was listed as one of *Time Magazine*'s hot trends, and in 2007 it was estimated that boycotts cost UK firms £3.2 billion, up £600 million on 2003 estimates (Hickman 2005). In some instances the boycott can be where the company itself has not behaved unethically, but is caught up in wider geo-political events. Sales of dairy products made by the Arla Foods company of Denmark in the Middle East, for example, plummeted as a result of the boycotting of Danish products by Muslims, following the publishing of cartoons featuring Mohammed in a Danish newspaper. Other recent boycotts of particular countries include the *Boycott Japan* campaign as a result of the country's policy on the killing of whales and a boycotting of French products in the US because of the country's stance on the Iraq war.

Recent boycotts in the UK as a result of unethical company activities include boycotts of Amazon and Starbucks (tax avoidance) SodaStream (Israel/Palestine conflict) and Superdrug (based on the tar sands activities of sister company, Husky Energy, in Canada) (see http://www.ethicalconsumer.org/boycotts/boycotts_list.htm for details of individual campaigns). Boycotts themselves have mixed results, and drops in sales are usually short-lived. There have though been some very notable successes, including the boycotting of various companies such as Barclays Bank in the 1980s, due to its dealings in the then apartheid South Africa, and Shell's decision not to proceed with the sinking of its Brent Spar platform. In 2009 the largest ever student led boycott in the US led to the Fruit of the Loom company reinstating the jobs of over 1,000 employees in its Honduran factory; the factory was initially closed after the employees became unionized.

As ethical issues continue to maintain a high prominence in society, one can expect boycotts to remain a visible and easy tactic for consumers and pressure groups to target unethical business practices. The use of social media platforms is also changing the landscape for consumers and provides NGOs and pressure groups with another platform to garner support for boycotts and bring unethical behaviour to the attention of society. Greenpeace's *Detox* campaign, calling for the fashion industry to stop polluting water with hazardous chemicals, was very successful in various social media platforms, including Facebook and Twitter, and led to major fashion companies (including Adidas, H&M, Marks & Spencer, Nike and Primark) committing to the *Detox Fashion Manifesto*.

Ethical consumers

An alternative to consumer boycotts is the purchase of ethical and fairly-traded products; both categories are increasing in significance in developed nations. According to the Ethical Consumer Organization (ethicalconsumer.org), the ethical market in the UK was worth £354 billion in 2012, up from £29.3 billion in 2005 and approximately £8 billion in 1999, with more money spent on ethical products in 2012 than was spent on both tobacco and alcohol. The report suggests the ethical market grew by 12 per cent in 2012, against a backdrop of a 0.2 per cent growth for the UK economy as a whole. In 2013 the fair trade market was said to have a retail value of £17.8 billion (fairtrade.org.uk/), an increase of 14 per cent on figures for 2012, and compared to £140 million in 2005 (Moore *et al.* 2006) and, as with ethical products, this market is expected to continue to grow in the longer term. There are many who support such products, but they have also received criticism from some who suggest that many companies are jumping on the ethical bandwagon without substantially changing their activities. If implemented properly, however, many agree that the sales of ethical and fairly-traded products will increase in the future and will be good for both business and the consumer. Ethical product ranges are diverse and range from banking and ethical investment products and services to beauty and cosmetics product ranges. While ethical and fair trade spending is still comparatively low, many expect these niche markets to continue to grow as consumers become ever more conscious about what they spend their money on and also critical of companies who only pay lip-service to ethical issues, rather than embrace the concept into all business activities.

As with ethical activities, however, what it means to be an ethical consumer is contested. What is ethical consumption to one consumer may indeed be unethical to another. For example, one person may consider their consumption to be ethical, because they recycle their products, whereas another consumer may question the need for the recycled products in the first instance. Does 'to buy ethical' mean, for example, to buy local; to buy organic; to buy fair trade; or to buy all of these? What then of conflicts? For instance, is a consumer being more ethical by buying only locally produced products and thus reducing transportation and environmental costs as a consequence, or by buying a fairly-traded product from a developing nation? Barnett *et al.* (2005) suggest that, 'ethical consumption, then, involves both a governing of consumption and a governing of the consuming self', and this is perhaps a good definition to help us to begin to explore the complexities involved when attempting to understand what one means by ethical consumption.

As well as ethical products, companies have been successful in redefining their product ranges in other ethical ways. By far the biggest success in this category was the relaunch of Dove skin care products in 2004. Rather than change their products significantly, Dove took a risk and significantly changed the way in which beauty products for women were advertised. The company broke the mould in the cosmetics industry by using what it labelled 'real' women in their marketing communications campaigns (rather than rely on female models) and by doing so challenged the stereotypical view of the 'perfect' woman utilized by advertisers. As a result, they reignited an international debate on beauty. The company defined its beauty theory as:

> Dove makes it clear it sees beauty in imperfections and doesn't worship stereotypes. Dove's beauty is self-defined, beauty with brains, democratic. Dove recognizes not only the exterior,

but also the woman within. There is a depth of character behind the eyes, a strength of vitality and personality showing through.

(Johnson 2005)

The initial campaign, and subsequent ones which have followed, have been hugely successful for the company and have seen significant increases in the sales of its products; its cleansing brand became brand leader in the market place and global sales of the product increased from 13 per cent to 25 per cent (Kolstad 2007). The companies *Campaign for Real Beauty* was a universal success and illustrated how companies and consumers could work together in changing people's perceptions of what beauty means. Dove, owned by large multi-national Unilever, made a number of other commitments by creating the Dove Self-Esteem Fund, a charity which helps various women's causes; the company even advertised the Fund rather than the product range during the 2005 Super Bowl final, one of the most expensive global advertising slots. In 2010 the campaign was overhauled and rebranded as *The Dove Movement for Self-Esteem*, and there have been some claims that Dove products contribute to women's poor self-esteem when it comes to body image. At the same time Unilever has been criticized for unethical behaviour in its other product ranges – the objectification of women in its advertisements for Lynx providing one example. Indeed, some of the Lynx adverts were banned by the Advertising Standards Authority in 2011 for their objectification of women. While the company has received criticism for ultimately selling beauty products, which some consider unnecessary and/or contributing to negative perceptions of one's body, by and large the publicity for its efforts was positive, with many believing the company successfully managed the relationship between a particular cause, in this case perceptions of beauty, and selling products. Now in its tenth year it will be interesting to see how the campaign develops in the future and what role beauty companies will play in conversations around body image and self-concept.

Unethical consumers

While considering marketing's impact on society it is equally important to recognize that consumers also behave unethically in the marketplace. Consumer theft is a major issue for companies large and small, and such theft can occur on small or grand scales. Consumer frauds, such as internet cons and telemarketing scams are a major worry for consumers and companies alike and will ultimately have an impact on all consumers in the forms of higher prices to offset company losses. Whether consumer theft involves an individual stealing from a supermarket or a large-scale consumer fraud, ultimately all agree that it is the consumer who pays the price for the illegal activities of others. The increased use of online shopping and the use of the internet for various exchange activities such as online banking has led to new ways in which consumers can be caught out by the actions of others – phishing, via the use of misleading email and websites, allows illegal access to online bank accounts and is the fastest growing form of consumer theft in the US and such trends are set to continue.

The 'black' or 'underground' market is another example of unethical and illegal consumer activities. The selling of illegally acquired products or the counterfeiting of other companies' products is a very lucrative business, particularly in developing nations. According to the International AntiCounterfeiting Coalition (IACC), the projected global counterfeit and pirated physical goods market will likely be worth US$1.77 trillion dollars in 2015 (see http://www.iacc.org/). Markets range from the selling of illegal drugs and prostitution through to the use of copyrighted media, such as music, movies and video games, and the piracy of products, including prescription medicines and fashion apparel. Questions of ethics become important here, as do people's perceptions of what is ethical and what is not. For instance, many consumers will not think they are doing anything wrong when illegally downloading movies, music or software on their mobile device, computer or tablet, even though their actions are in fact illegal; and a significant number of British teenagers drink alcohol before the age of 18. It is when exploring areas such as consumer theft and underground markets that we can engage in interesting debates about ethics and 'right' versus 'wrong'. Very often, individual opinion does not follow legislative requirements and vice versa and thus discussions can very quickly become both complex and controversial. For example, an individual might think that the use of cannabis is an illegal activity, but would make an exception for someone who is using the drug to help with a debilitating medical illness, even though this individual would be deemed in law to be acting illegally.

Consumers can behave unethically in their everyday dealings with companies. The old adage 'the customer is always right' has brought with it ramifications for how some consumers interact with company employees – be this via rudeness to staff in a restaurant or becoming verbally abusive to a customer careline. While stories of poor customer service are plentiful, and CRM has become a core business strategy of customer-facing industries, the behaviour of customers themselves has been called into question. In 2007, for example, the telephone company, Sprint, terminated its contract with a small number of customers who made 'excessive' calls to Sprint's customer service teams. Indeed, how to deal with difficult customers is a central component of employee training programmes.

Conclusions

In summary, this chapter has explored key issues of importance in our understanding of ethical issues within marketing. It has provided a brief summary of the different ways in which we can explore ethics and has considered the issue of business ethics before exploring marketing ethics in detail. When considering ethical marketing, one can examine philosophical debates surrounding marketing, and in particular its interactions with society. Examples of macromarketing ethical concerns are considered. Ethical issues at the level of the firm are examined next, and contemporary examples of unethical marketing activities are provided. The chapter next assesses the response of marketers in the form of legislative and regulatory provisions to tackle unethical practices. Finally, the chapter explores the role of consumers, both in terms of their unethical practices and their ethical responses in the marketplace.

There is no doubt that in today's business world issues of ethics are core components for all companies, small or large. While there is much debate and public controversy surrounding how specific responsibilities are defined and played out in the marketplace, there is no doubting their importance. While it is true to say that different companies will be affected in different ways, it is also true that no company will be immune to issues of ethical importance. Documentation for *Business in the Community, Ireland* sum up the importance of responsible business as 'The constantly challenging goal is to ensure that responsible business is integrated and embedded in the decision-making culture rather than confined to a progressive individual, area or division'.

Such a shift in business culture will have a profound effect on the marketing strategies and practices of all businesses. Philosophical debates surrounding what is right and wrong will continue, firms will engage in unethical practices, consumers, organizations and legislative bodies will respond accordingly, and marketing ethics will remain an important topic of conversation in the classroom.

Further reading

Journals

There are a number of journals that focus specifically on issues relating to marketing ethics – the two most important are the *Journal of Macromarketing* and the *Journal of Public Policy and Marketing*. Both journals are a must for anyone wishing to get an up-to-date angle on marketing ethics topics. There was a special issue of the *Journal of Macromarketing* on marketing ethics published in 2008. The *Journal of Business Ethics* has many articles with a marketing focus. There was also a special issue of the *Journal of Strategic Marketing* in 2006 focusing on fair trade – McDonagh, P. and Strong, C. (2006), 'Liberté, equalité, fraternité: Reflections on the genesis and growth of fair trade for business strategy', *Journal of Strategic Marketing*, 14(4).

Books and journal articles

Crane, A. and Matten, D. (2010), *Business Ethics: Managing Corporate Citizenship and Sustainability in the Age of Globalisation*, Oxford, UK: Oxford University Press – An excellent introductory student text to core business ethics issues.

Green, G. (2004), *Eight Theories of Ethics*, London: Routledge – An introduction to different ethical theories for those who wish to explore ethical theories in more detail.

Murphy, P. M., Laczniak, G. R., Bowie, N. E. and Klein, T. A. (2005), *Ethical Marketing*, Upper Saddle River, NJ: Pearson Prentice Hall – Excellent introductory text, which examines the many in-depth marketing ethics issues.

Robinson, D. (2012), *Introducing Ethics for Everyday Life: A Practical Guide*, Royston, UK: Icon Books Ltd – Part of the excellent *Introducing* series of Icon Books; offers an illustrative introduction to key ethical issues.

Websites

adbusters.org/home/ – Website for the activist networking group, Adbusters Media Foundation.
asa.org.uk – Website for the independent regulator for advertising, sales promotion and direct marketing.
campaignforrealbeauty.com – Dove's international campaign focusing on various beauty related issues.
ethicalconsumer.org – Website for the charitable organization 'The Ethical Consumer'.
fairtrade.org.uk – Website for the Fairtrade Foundation.
iacc.org – The International AntiCounterfeiting Coalition.
tradingstandards.gov.uk – Government-based website for the Trading Standards Institute, which provides information on a variety of consumer protection and safety issues.
which.co.uk – Independent consumers' association in the UK.

References

Adler, R. D., Robinson, L. M. and Carlson, J. E. (1981), *Marketing and Society: Cases and Commentaries*, Englewood Cliffs, NJ: Prentice Hall.

Armstrong, R. and Sweeney, J. (1994), 'Industry type, culture, mode of entry and perceptions of international marketing ethics: A cross-cultural comparison', *Journal of Business Ethics*, 13(4): 775–785.

Baker, M. J. and Hart, S. (eds) (2008), *The Marketing Book*, sixth edition, Oxford, UK: Butterworth-Heinemann.

Barnett, C., Cloke, P., Clarke, N. and Malpass, A. (2005), 'Consuming ethics: Articulating the subjects and spaces of ethical consumption', *Antipode*, 37(1): 23–45.

Bilton, N. (2013), *Hatching Twitter: A True Story of Money, Power, Friendship, and Betrayal*, London: Penguin.

Blackburn, D. (2004), 'Dealing with the decade of anxiety', Market Research Society Annual Conference, 2004.

Burrough, B. and Helyar, J. (2010), *Barbarians at the Gate: The Fall of RJR Nabisco*. London: Random House.

Crookes, D. (2012), 'Big fat gypsy wedding advert cleared after complaints', *BBC Newsbeat*, available at http://www.bbc.co.uk/newsbeat/17442056, accessed 4 December 2015.

Davidson, K. (2003), *Selling Sin: The Marketing of Socially Unacceptable Products*, second edition, Westport, CT: Quorum Books.

Debord, G. (1977), *Society of the Spectacle*, Detroit, MI: Black and Red.

Dubinsky, A. J. and Loken, B. (1989), 'Analysing ethical decision making in marketing', *Journal of Business Research*, 19(2): 83–107.

Ferrell, O. C. and Gresham, L. G. (1985), 'A contingency framework for understanding ethical decision making in marketing', *Journal of Marketing*, 49(3): 87–96.

Fromm, E. (1976), *To Have or To Be*, London: Routledge and Keegan Paul.

Godin, S. (2005), *All Marketers Are Liars: The Power of Telling Authentic Stories in a Low-Trust World*, London: Portfolio.

Hickman, L. (2005), 'Should I . . . support a consumer boycott?', *The Guardian*, 4 October, available at http://www.theguardian.com/money/2005/oct/04/ethicalmoney.shopping, accessed 16 December 2015.

Hill, K. (2012), 'How Target figured out a teen girl was pregnant before her father did', *Forbes*, available at http://www.forbes.com/sites/kashmirhill/2012/02/16/how-target-figured-out-a-teen-girl-was-pregnant-before-her-father-did/, accessed 4 December 2015.

Hunt, S. D. and Vitell, S. J. (1986), 'A general theory of marketing ethics', *Journal of Macromarketing*, 8(spring): 5–16.

Hunt, S. D. and Vitell, S. J. (2006), 'The general theory of marketing ethics: A revision and three questions', *Journal of Macromarketing*, 26(2): 143–153.

Jacobsen, M. F. and Mazur, L. A. (1995), *Marketing Madness*, Boulder, CO: Westview Press.

Johnson, O. (2005), 'How Dove changed the rules of the beauty game', *Market Leader*, 31(winter): 43–46.

Kolstad, J. (2007), 'Unilever PLC: Campaign for real beauty campaign', *Encyclopedia of Major Marketing Campaigns*, 2: 1679–1686.

Laczniak, G. and Murphy, P. (1993), *Ethical Marketing Decisions*, Toronto, Canada: Allyn & Bacon.

Laczniak, G. and Murphy, P. (2006), 'Normative perspectives for ethical and socially responsible marketing', *Journal of Macromarketing*, 26(2): 154–177.

Marcuse, H. (1964), *One Dimensional Man*, Boston, MA: Beacon.

Martin, K. D., Johnson, J. L. and French, J. J. (2011), 'Institutional pressures and marketing ethics initiatives: The focal role of organizational identity', *Journal of the Academy of Marketing Science*, 39(4): 574–591.

McDonald, S., Oates, C. J., Young, C. W. and Hwang, K. (2006), 'Towards sustainable consumption: Researching voluntary simplifiers', *Psychology and Marketing*, 23(6): 515–534.

Moore, G., Gibbon, J. and Slack, R. (2006), 'The mainstreaming of fair trade: A macromarketing perspective', *Journal of Strategic Marketing*, 14(4): 329–353.

Murphy, P. M., Laczniak, G. R. and Prothero, A. (2012), *Ethics in Marketing: International Cases and Perspectives*, London: Routledge.

Nantel, J. and Weeks, W. A. (1996), 'Marketing ethics: Is there more to it than the utilitarian approach?', *European Journal of Marketing*, 30(5): 9–20.

Naomi, K. (2001), *No Logo*, London: Flamingo.

Nill, A. and Schultz, C. II (1997), 'Marketing ethics across cultures: Decision-making guidelines and the emergence of dialogic idealism', *Journal of Macromarketing*, 17(4): 4–19.

Nill, A. and Schibrowsky, J. A. (2005), 'The impact of corporate culture, the reward system, and perceived moral intensity on marketing students' ethical decision making', *Journal of Marketing Education*, 27(1): 68–80.

O'Malley, L. and Patterson, M. (1998), 'Vanishing point: The mix management paradigm re-viewed', *Journal of Marketing Management*, 14(8): 829–851.

Orwell, G. (1937), *The Road to Wigan Pier*, London: Victor Gollancz.

Packard, V. (1957), *The Hidden Persuaders*, New York: David McKay.

Paterson, T. (2012), 'Swedish furniture giant criticised for removing images in bid not to upset Arab customers', *The Independent*, available at http://www.independent.co.uk/news/world/middle-east/ikea-airbrushes-women-from-its-saudi-catalogue-8193204.html, accessed 4 December 2015.

Rand, A. (1943), *The Fountainhead*, Indianapolis, IN: Bobbs-Merrill Company.

Roth, P. (1997), *American Pastoral*, London: Jonathan Cape.

Singhapakdi, A. (2004), 'Important factors underlying ethical intentions of students: Implications for marketing education', *Journal of Marketing Education*, 26(3): 261–270.

Steiner, J. and Steiner, G. (2011), *Business, Government, and Society: A Managerial Perspective, Text and Cases*, thirteenth edition, New York: McGraw-Hill.

Tsalikis, J. and Fritzsche, D. J. (1989), 'Business ethics: A literature review with a focus on marketing ethics', *Journal of Business Ethics*, 8(9): 695–743.

Williams, J. and Aitken, R. (2011), 'The service-dominant logic of marketing and marketing ethics', *Journal of Business Ethics*, 102(3): 439–454.

24 Green marketing

Ken Peattie

Introduction

It is over 25 years since the Brundtland Report, *Our Common Future* (WCED 1987), brought the concept of 'sustainable development' into the mainstream of business and political debate. It put forward a convincing case that the economic growth of the late twentieth century was not sustainable in environmental, social and, ultimately, economic terms. It put forward the need for development that 'meets the needs of the present without compromising the ability of future generations to meet their own needs' (WCED 1987: 43). Following the Earth Summits in 1992, 2002 and 2012, governments and major corporations alike have generally adopted the pursuit of sustainability as a strategic goal. Sustainability reporting has increasingly become the norm for public companies and, by 2014, has been adopted by 93 per cent of Fortune 500 firms (Ceres 2014). Business sustainability is often framed in terms of a *triple bottom line* strategy (Elkington 1997) that seeks to balance economic prosperity (profit) with social justice (people) and environmental quality (planet). The challenge lies in turning these good intentions into meaningful progress in the face of powerful vested interests, an entrenched and environmentally hostile dominant social (and management) paradigm (DSP), and a global economy with tremendous momentum on a trajectory that pursues conventional economic growth.

Although there is consensus on the need to move our economies and societies towards sustainability, what that means and how it can be achieved and measured, has proved more controversial. Across different academic disciplines and national contexts, ideas about what constitutes sustainability vary considerably (and both geologists and physicists will argue there is no such thing, since nothing lasts forever). Within 5 years of the Brundtland Report, around 70 definitions of 'sustainable development' had emerged (Holmberg and Sandbrook 1992), and the term 'sustainable' has proved to be susceptible to misuse and 'hijacking' (Robinson 2004). A useful way to understand business sustainability comes from Hopwood *et al.* (2005). They propose that a sustainability initiative is one that goes beyond the existing status quo by contributing demonstrably to either greater social equity (in the sense of the distribution of benefits, burdens and risks linked to economic activity) or the protection of environmental quality (or both). Such contributions can be limited to those seeking to sustain our current business systems by ensuring that environmental and social limits are not breached ('soft' sustainability), or more radical changes that seek to sustain and even improve long-term environmental quality and the quality of life ('hard' sustainability). In understanding sustainability issues it is worth stressing that the division between environmental and social is often artificial and unhelpful, because the two are so intertwined. This is most notable in relatively poor countries where there is greatest direct reliance on the environment to meet peoples' needs and where environmental degradation and poverty frequently reinforce one another.

For marketing, a range of suffixes is used to indicate a sustainability orientation, including environmental, eco and sustainable amongst others. This chapter will use the term 'green', as it is used in politics, to indicate a combined social and environmental orientation. The focus here also follows the majority of academic writing on sustainability and marketing, by concentrating on its environmental aspects, partly because the chapter considering marketing ethics (Chapter 23) deals with key social and societal challenges.

The pursuit of business sustainability is often framed in terms of corporate social responsibility (CSR) and therefore as relevant across all business functions. This is true, yet marketing has a unique position, partly through taking a significant share of the blame for the current unsustainability of business, particularly from critics who accuse it of driving over-consumption (Van Dam and Apeldoorn 1996). However, as a key interface between a company and its external stakeholders, and particularly customers, marketing is well positioned to tackle sustainability challenges. Many of the key environmental impacts within global supply chains reflect marketing decisions related to product specifications, the resources consumed for packaging, or the energy and emissions linked to product distribution. As Crane (2000) notes:

> [m]arketing activities can be seen to have further contributed to environmental deterioration through its reliance on enormous quantities of packaging, the creation of out-of-town shopping centres and the resource-sapping movement of consumer goods across the globe. The demands of the grocery and fast food industries for standardization and predictability in food products in the name of customer satisfaction have also led to myriad ecological problems associated with the use of agrochemicals, industrial pesticides and genetically modified crops.
>
> Crane (2000: 13)

It is perhaps telling that for the 75th anniversary edition of the *Journal of Marketing* in 2011, Professor Philip Kotler's contribution was entitled, 'Reinventing marketing to manage the environmental imperative'. In it he argued that:

> With regard to marketing, companies and their marketers have operated on the assumption of an endless supply of resources and, furthermore, that production, distribution, and consumption do not add to pollution, water shortage, and other costs, or at least that companies do not have to bear these costs. Once we begin to acknowledge resource limitations and externality costs, marketing will have to reinvent its practices to be environmentally responsible.
>
> (Kotler 2011: 132)

Evidence that companies and their marketers are increasingly engaged with the sustainability agenda is all around us. The ubiquity of Fairtrade coffee or recycled and recyclable packaging on the high street; the prevalence of low-energy lightbulbs and concentrated detergents in our homes; the emphasis on environmental performance in the promotion of domestic appliances in the media; and the growing number of hybrid and other low-emission vehicles on our roads all suggest that sustainability is influencing the behaviour of consumers and marketers. Sustainability issues are also relevant to a number of different branches of marketing practice and scholarship. Consumer marketing has been the primary focus of attention, and this chapter largely follows that convention. However, sustainability issues are increasingly influential in business-to-business marketing as companies seek to understand and manage their socio-environmental impacts and risks back down their supply chains (see, for example, Sharma *et al.* 2010). In public markets, governmental purchasing criteria have also evolved so that sustainability policy goals are reflected in the purchasing behaviour of public bodies at many levels, subject of course to the inevitable pressures on budgets (Walker and Brammer 2009). Within social marketing, a field originally dominated by the application of marketing techniques to influence health behaviours is increasingly focusing on behaviours linked to environmental sustainability (Peattie and Peattie 2012). For some specific industries, such as tourism, sustainability issues are particularly visible within marketing practice and scholarship. In the case of tourism, this reflects partly the pressing need to maintain the environmental quality and cultural attractiveness of a destination and avoiding this being eroded by its success in attracting visitors (Medway *et al.* 2010), and partly the very real long-term challenges that climate change and water shortages could pose to particular destinations and activities.

There are generally three key starting points from which marketers become motivated to engage with sustainability. Within the competitive environment, changing demands from customers relating to the socio-environmental performance of the products they use and the companies they patronise may directly influence marketing strategies. Within the macroenvironment, changes to regulations or the socio-cultural zeitgeist can require adjustments to elements of marketing strategy such as product development, communications campaigns or pricing. Finally, priorities within the corporate environment may change to reflect CSR strategies that address the interests of a wider range of stakeholders than the conventional focus on shareholders and customers.

Since no business is entirely free of socio-environmental impacts, sustainability is relevant to all companies, even if they vary in the extent to which they face direct, significant and immediate opportunities and challenges. At its simplest, engagement with sustainability can be a purely tactical or operational response to the opportunities and pressures that the sustainability agenda creates. Examples would include the pursuit of differentiation by developing a cause-related marketing strategy linking the promotion of a particular brand to a social or environmental charity; advertising that highlights the pre-existing environmental benefits of a product; or a switch to recycled packaging. Further engagement can move a company towards a more strategic perspective with socio-environmental issues becoming a basis for competitive strategy and the development and positioning of new products. At its most profound, engagement with sustainability can become transformational and the basis for new business models, new ways to address consumer needs and new forms of strategic relationship. The transformational nature of sustainability also applies to marketing theory, since it challenges a great deal of conventional marketing thinking and wisdom.

Green marketing represents a specific 'type' of marketing and is therefore worthy of a separate chapter within this collection, and arguably represents a further step in the evolution of marketing theory and practice. This chapter aims to illustrate how the 'green challenge' is exerting a growing influence on marketing practice and how its implications will eventually require a more profound shift in the marketing mindset, if marketers are to continue delivering customer satisfaction at a profit into the twenty-second century.

The evolution of green marketing

Marketing as both commercial activity and academic discipline has continually evolved. New technologies, information sources and ideas from other disciplines have enriched and extended what marketers are able to do, and changes in society and the marketing environment have constantly created new opportunities and challenges for marketers and marketing to respond to.

At the time when the, 'modern managerialist marketing paradigm' matured in the 1960s, many of the socio-environmental impacts involved in making, using and disposing of the products we consume were treated as 'externalities'. The assumption was that these would be addressed by governments, with their costs met (at least theoretically) through taxation. Such impacts were not reflected in the prices consumers paid nor given much consideration within the marketing agenda.

During the 1970s, this situation began to change as the socio-environmental implications of consumption and production activities increasingly became recognised as marketing issues (Fisk 1974). This was reflected in the rise of societal marketing (which is dealt with in Chapter 23) and also the emergence of macromarketing as an explicit discipline dealing with the collective consequences of marketing activity and the relationship between the discipline and society. The 1970s also represented the first of three stages in the evolution of the green marketing agenda (Peattie 2001).

1970s ecological marketing

In the 1970s a wave of environmental concern linked to the oil 'shocks' of the period, several major pollution incidents and evidence of the human and environmental impacts of chemicals such as DDT and pollutants such as air-borne lead, spawned the concept of 'ecological marketing' (Henion and Kinnear 1976). This was largely concerned with those industries with the severest environmental impacts (including oil, cars and chemicals) and tended to focus on technical solutions to alleviate particular environmental problems. Marketing scholarship at this time was mostly limited to issues such as energy conservation, recycling and consumer attitudes to pollution, along with broader consideration of the environmental challenge to marketing and early attempts to identify ecologically concerned consumers (Kilbourne and Beckmann 1998). Most business responses focused on production or waste system improvements, but there were examples of environmentally inspired new product introductions (such as smaller-engine, fuel-efficient cars) or the repositioning of existing products (such as a 'back to nature' repositioning of granola-style breakfast cereals). By the end of the 1970s, however, companies like *Body Shop* and *Ben and Jerry's*, that would go on to become iconic green brands, had been founded by environmentally concerned entrepreneurs.

1980s environmental marketing

During the 1980s, concern about the environmental impacts of business resurfaced following further incidents such as the Exxon-Valdez oil spill, the chemical plant explosion at Bhopal and mounting scientific evidence of man-made stress in global environmental systems (including evidence of rainforest depletion, global warming and a hole in the stratospheric ozone layer). This concern led to a mainstreaming of environmental concern within society, resulting in consumer boycotts, new environmental legislation and a growing demand for 'green' products, such as recycled paper, unleaded fuel, energy efficient appliances and organic food. The range of industries affected broadened further, even to service industries such as tourism and banking. In relation to business practice there was also widespread discussion about the implications of environmental concern for marketing (and vice versa) using labels including 'green marketing', 'greener marketing' and 'environmental marketing'. Marketing scholarship at this time was still relatively sparse, and mostly narrowly focused on deepening the understanding of consumer response to environmental issues.

The environmental marketing of the 1980s was largely an extension of the societal marketing concept, with a focus on the responsibilities of marketers and the need to constrain and ameliorate the environmental impacts of marketing activities through product innovations and adapted production processes. The previous 1970s focus on 'end-of-pipe' process improvement evolved into the 'cleaner production' movement that emphasised product and process redesign to reduce energy and resource use, toxic materials, pollution and waste (and their associated costs). The growing consumer interest in sustainability issues was reflected in the success of the first *Green Consumer Guide* (Elkington and Hailes 1988), which spent over 40 weeks in the UK best-sellers list and went on to sell over 1 million copies across more than 20 countries. This was also reflected in leading companies in markets including grocery retail, cars, batteries, detergents and domestic appliances being seen to vie with one another to demonstrate their socio-environmental credentials.

1990s onwards – towards sustainable marketing

During the 1990s, the mainstreaming of the concept of sustainable development prompted many major companies to develop sustainability or CSR strategies that sought to integrate and better balance their environmental, social and economic responsibilities. There was also an increasing focus on the potential of superior socio-environmental performance to appeal to consumers and generate 'win-win' competitive advantage (Porter and van der Linde 1995). This in part led to a proliferation in sustainability orientated product introductions, claims and advertising messages, along with rapid growth in specific market segments, such as Fairtrade and organic produce, and ecotourism.

In green marketing scholarship, there was a rapid expansion into areas including environmental advertising, new product development, labelling and packaging, as well as a deepening of the green consumer research agenda (Kilbourne and Beckmann 1998). Marketing academics also began to seriously discuss the physical implications and sustainability of marketing (e.g. Van Dam and Apeldoorn 1996) and to consider the environmental, social and economic dimensions of marketing in a more integrated way. The established managerialist stream of research discussing how sustainability issues could be integrated into marketing practice was complemented by new, more critical and challenging work questioning some of the more fundamental assumptions about marketing (Kilbourne and Beckmann 1998).

Moving towards and into the new millennium, far more radical ideas about the integration of marketing and sustainability began to emerge. Fuller's (1999) concept of 'sustainable marketing' adopted the physical systems perspective of industrial ecology and set out a practical approach to marketing as a waste-free, closed-loop system that does not degrade or over-burden natural systems or resources. Authors such as Belz and Peattie (2012) and Martin and Schouten (2011) also put forward detailed explorations of what sustainability orientated marketing might look like in practice. The fundamental difference between such visions of marketing and the conventional mainstream, is that they do not think in terms of social and environmental 'issues' that must be audited, understood and accommodated within marketing processes. Instead, they acknowledge sustainability as an alternative approach to thinking about the economy, business, marketing, consumption and production. The key differences between such sustainability orientated concepts of green marketing and the existing societal marketing concept lie in:

- an emphasis on the ultimate physical sustainability of the marketing process, as well as its social acceptability;
- a more holistic and interdependent view of the relationship between the economy, society and the environment;
- an open-ended and multi-generational, rather than a long-term, perspective;
- the treatment of the environment as something with intrinsic value over and above its usefulness to society;

- a focus on global concerns, rather than those of particular societies;
- an emphasis on socio-environmental issues as a potential source of innovation and opportunity for marketers, rather than just as a set of constraints and potential costs.

The reinvention of marketing to become environmentally (and socially) responsible represents the most significant challenge facing the discipline over the next 75 years (and beyond). It can best be understood from three interconnected perspectives that the rest of this chapter explores:

1   a socio-environmental perspective that considers markets holistically as production and consumption systems, and seeks to understand and manage the interrelationships between marketing activities, consumption and socio-environmental issues;
2   a managerial perspective that integrates sustainability principles into the marketing strategy process and the marketing mix;
3   a critical perspective that challenges existing marketing assumptions, theory and practice to allow the discipline to further evolve in order to embrace sustainability.

Green marketing: a socio-environmental perspective

In 1974 Fisk highlighted that consumption and over-consumption were contributing to emerging environmental problems, making the physical environment a marketing issue. Despite this, conventional marketing thinking has not made strong connections between marketing activities and the physical environmental and social systems within which they take place. This may partly be explained by the dominance of ideas derived from economics, a discipline notorious for abstraction, and psychology, a discipline focused on the individual. The emergence of macromarketing as a sub-discipline partly sought to address these shortcomings but, as Kotler's (2011) call to reinvent marketing illustrates, the discipline has yet to fully come back 'down to earth'.

Key sustainability challenges

The importance of particular sustainability issues for marketers will vary between industries, presenting operational and reputational risks to some, and opportunities to contribute to solutions for others. Some of the key environmental sustainability issues include climate change; water shortages in many regions; deforestation; soil erosion and impoverishment; loss of biodiversity; and over-exploitation of non-renewable resources. Many of the social sustainability challenges linked to notions of quality of life are connected to the issue of poverty and income inequality. Other issues like hunger and malnutrition, access to clean water, literacy and education are strongly bound up with poverty. Two key social sustainability challenges with very direct marketing implications relate to health and cultural diversity. Although health issues might not seem relevant to marketers, other than those seeking to market health treatments or promote healthy behaviours, it is worth noting that the 2000 World Health Organization (WHO) Report *Obesity: Preventing and Managing the Global Epidemic* concluded that in an increasing number of countries the consumption-related condition of obesity was replacing more traditional factors like infectious diseases as the prime cause of ill-health (WHO 2000). The contribution of marketing activities, particularly the promotion of unhealthy food to children, to the growth in obesity has been a key focus for criticism (e.g. Harris *et al.* 2009.). The growing concern about the erosion of cultural diversity partly relates to the globalisation of consumer culture and the media, and the tendency to create a homogenised culture of global brands, icons, values and cultural phenomena (Ritzer 2004). It also partly relates to the threat to ethnic minorities and the lifestyles of indigenous peoples from the destructive impact of mineral resource exploitation, tourism and the spread of standardised agricultural technologies (Blench 2001).

A final sustainability issue, which links the social and environmental and has implications for marketing, is population growth. Our natural resource systems, which are already being unsustainably exploited, must accommodate another 75 million people every year. Added to this, an increasing middle class within populous nations such as China, India and Brazil is increasing demand for environmentally impactful products such as cars, tourism, meat and dairy produce. OECD projections forecast that India and China's share of global middle-class consumer spending will rise from just over 5 per cent in 2009 to 41 per cent by 2030.

Collectively, these issues represent a long-term threat to the stability of the economic system (which sits within, and depends upon, the social and environmental systems). The best scientific evidence available highlights the unsustainability of the current situation. The results of global ecological footprint analysis determined that it was 14 August 2014 that represented 2014's *Earth Overshoot Day* (GFN 2014). This is the point in the year by which humankind has consumed the resources that can be sustained as 'income' from natural systems. The rest of the year is spent effectively consuming natural capital, reducing the productivity of ecosystems and bringing forward a little the overshoot day for the following year. The UN's *Millennium Ecosystem Assessment* (WRI 2005) concluded that unparalleled economic growth during the second half of the twentieth century had resulted in 'a substantial and largely irreversible loss in the diversity of life on Earth' and that:

> [g]ains in human well-being and economic development have been achieved at growing costs in the form of the degradation of many ecosystem services . . . and the exacerbation of poverty for some groups of people. These problems, unless addressed, will substantially diminish the benefits that future generations obtain from ecosystems.

The greatest long-term threat to global environmental, social and economic stability is climate change driven by greenhouse gases such as CO_2. The Intergovernmental Panel on Climate Change (IPCC 2014) concluded that it would require 'aggressive' mitigation policies to halve global emissions by 2050 to keep average global temperature rise by the end of the century to below a (still significantly disruptive) 2°C. The panel noted that for businesses the choice is between significant impacts sooner due to efforts to mitigate change, or even more significant impacts later due to changes to the climate.

A production–consumption systems perspective

Fully understanding the significance of such socio-environmental issues for companies and marketers requires the adoption of a sustainable production and consumption system (SPC) perspective. An SPC is defined as a system that links goods and services, individuals, households and organisations through linkages in which energy and materials are transformed, utility is derived and relationships (particularly marketing relationships) take place (Lebel and Lorek 2008). An SPC perspective considers the impacts of a product back through the supply chain and also takes in those associated with product use and disposal. Understanding a company's socio-environmental impacts requires a physical product lifecycle perspective to complement the sales-related economic product lifecycle familiar to marketers. Lifecycle analysis can be used to analyse and quantify the full range of 'cradle to grave' impacts related to each stage in production and consumption. Procter & Gamble's lifecycle analysis revealed the extent to which impacts for some key brands were linked to consumption activities, prompting the company to develop its *future friendly* multi-brand campaign to promote more sustainable consumption practices and a product line aimed at reducing impacts. Similarly, Puma used natural capital accounting to develop an *environmental profit and loss account* for the firm that revealed the 'full' costs of doing business and helped to identify supply chain vulnerabilities and future resource-related risks.

In a comprehensive review of research focusing on an SPC perspective, Lebel and Lorek (2008) explored 11 key 'enabling mechanisms' with the potential to promote progress towards more sustainable SPC systems. Table 24.1 presents a slightly adapted version of their summary of these mechanisms and the challenges involved in pursuing each. The mechanisms cover production, marketing and consumption (including waste disposal) and it is worth noting that only the first two operate entirely 'upstream' of the consumer, within the company and its supply chain. All the others involve consumers to some extent, and their success will depend very substantially on developing effective sustainable marketing relationships.

The greening of supply chains is usually considered from a supply chain management perspective; however, the greening of each link also represents the interactions within a business-to-business marketing relationship (Sharma *et al.* 2010). The greening of production processes and supply chains can yield benefits in terms of cost reduction through eco-efficiency strategies linked to material, energy and waste reductions (Porter and van der Linde 1995). Production methods may also be the basis for environmental performance-based appeals to the consumer to encourage responsible consumption, with examples including organic or non-GM food, recycled paper, free-range eggs, remanufactured printer cartridges or cruelty-free cosmetics. There are circumstances in which improved environmental performance in production is not communicated to consumers, particularly because they sometimes make assumptions about a reduced level of technical performance from environmentally superior products (Luchs *et al.* 2010).

Regulation and extended producer responsibility

Regulation can influence marketing strategies directly by mandating or prohibiting the use of particular materials or technologies on environmental grounds. The mandating of catalytic converters in cars or the banning of incandescent lightbulbs has impacted consumers and the designers and manufacturers of the relevant products across Europe. Extended producer responsibility (EPR) is being enshrined in regulations governing a number of key markets for products including vehicles, electronics, packaging and batteries. In Europe the *End of Life Vehicles (ELV) Directive* and the *Waste Electronic and Electrical Equipment (WEEE) Directive* both require manufacturers to resume responsibility for old products when the consumer disposes of them. Although this can be covered by taking financial responsibility to fund appropriate disposal and recycling arrangements, for manufacturers in markets such as cars there can be strategic value in taking physical responsibility for old products in order to recycle/remanufacture them. Although developing reverse logistics systems to access and recover old products is normally presented as an operations management challenge, it also represents a considerable marketing challenge in maintaining a long-term relationship with customers and motivating them to return old products appropriately into the reverse logistics system (Seitz and Peattie 2004). It also represents a significant shift in the presumed responsibilities of the marketer, which were previously assumed to end at the moment of purchase and the legal transfer of ownership of a product to the consumer. There were forecasts that meeting the requirements or EPR regulation would stimulate innovation amongst product designers to design for disassembly, recycling and remanufacture, but there is little evidence yet of such a change (Seitz and Peattie 2004; Lebel and Lorek 2008).

Table 24.1 Enabling mechanisms for sustainable production-consumption systems

Enabling mechanism	Short description	Concerns, constraints or challenges
Produce with less	Innovations in production processes reduce the environmental impact per unit made.	Rebound effects occur through which gains are wiped out by increases in the number of units or how they are used.
Green supply chains	Firms with leverage in a chain impose standards on their suppliers to improve environmental performance.	There may be unfair pressures on small producers.
Co-design	Consumers are involved in the design of products and services to fulfil needs with less environmental impact.	Incentives are not adequate to involve consumers.
Producer responsibly	Producers are made responsible for waste from product disposal at end-of-life.	Incentives for compliance without regulation may be too low for many types of products.
Service rather than sell	Producers provide service rather than sell or transfer ownership of assets, which reduces the number of units made while still providing functions needed.	This is a difficult transition for firms and consumers to make as it requires new business models, behaviours and values.
Certify and label	Consumers preferentially buy labelled goods. Labels are based on independent certification and producers with good practices increase their market share.	Consumers are easily confused with too much information or with a lack of transparency and credibility of competing schemes.
Trade fairly	Through minimum price agreements and other investments or benefits for producers. Consumers prefer to buy products labelled as or sold through fair trade channels so producers get a better deal.	Mainstream trade still dominates. It is hard to maintain fair trade benefits for producers when a product becomes mainstream.
Market ethically	Reducing unethical practices in marketing and advertising would reduce wasteful and overconsumption practices.	There is a reluctance by policy-makers to tackle very powerful private sector interests with regulation.
Consume responsibly	Campaigns educate consumers about impacts of individual products, classes of products and consumption patterns, resulting in overall behaviour changes.	Converting intentions and values into actions in everyday life is often difficult for consumers. Issues of convenience, flexibility and function still matter a lot.
Use less	Consumption may be reduced for a variety of reasons, for example, as a consequence of working less. There are many potential environmental gains from less overall consumption.	There is a dominant perception that using less means sacrifice. Less income and consumption may not automatically translate into better consumption impacts. Growth is still a priority.
Increase wisely	Increasing the consumption of underconsumers to alleviate poverty can be effected in ways that minimise environmental impacts as economic activity expands.	Wealthy developed countries need incentives and goodwill to assist the poor and those in developing countries, for example, by leaving adequate space and natural resources for them to develop.

Source: Adapted from Lebel and Lorek (2008).

Product–service systems (PSS)

Product–service substitutions are one of the core strategies proposed for the greening of markets and have significant implications for marketers and consumers. They involve the dematerialisation of market transactions by offering the customer a PSS based around the use of a product, rather than through its ownership. It is more commonly used in business-to-business markets where companies pay for a service that includes the use of products ranging from cars and photocopiers to carpets or jet engines. PSS solutions for consumers are usually marketed on the basis of convenience and flexibility and, where applicable, savings from a pay-to-use pricing system.

PSS can be difficult to market to consumers for a number of reasons, including a lack of familiarity with ownership-less consumption, the symbolic value of product ownership and the importance of transaction costs linked to perceived control, convenience and uncertainty (Lebel and Lorek 2008). From the marketer's perspective, a move towards PSS provides a dual challenge in terms of persuading the consumer to adopt a significantly different mode of consumption and transforming their own business models, marketing perspective and capabilities away from product-based towards service-based marketing (Baines *et al.* 2007).

Co-design

Another mechanism to promote an SPC perspective that can help in greening marketing offerings, including moving consumers away from expecting product ownership and towards accepting service use as a substitute, is the application of co-design. Co-design takes the process of understanding consumer needs beyond arms-length marketing research to involve consumers in the design process. In low-energy housing developments in Finland, Heiskanen and Lovio (2010) observed that user involvement in the design process, and good communication and knowledge sharing between them and marketers, aided both the process of innovation and the ultimate adoption and use of the energy-saving innovations by consumers.

The green consumer

Although marketers may have to respond to environmentally related developments in the corporate environment, the legal environment or through the supply chain, it is when the socio-environmental impacts of consumption and production generate interest amongst consumers that they are most likely to respond. Most of the mechanisms aiming to promote the SPC perspective depend upon the preferences, decisions and behaviours of consumers, particularly in terms of *consuming responsibly*. A range of sources may first alert consumers to the socio-environmental implications of particular products or consumption behaviours. Media coverage of scientific research, pressure group campaigns, government information campaigns or corporate social and environmental reporting may all highlight particular issues. Marketing communication efforts, such as product labelling (D'Souza *et al.* 2006) can also be important in informing and educating consumers about sustainability issues and in promoting greener consumption. New media and online communities are also becoming increasingly influential in highlighting and debating sustainability issues and their relationship to consumption. Care2 is perhaps the largest such online community, claiming a membership of over 27 million people interested in campaigns about health, ethics and sustainability.

Sustainability related consumer responses can be negative, particularly through the boycotting of particular products, technologies or companies (a topic dealt with in Chapter 23). They can also be positive in expressing a demand for products that are perceived as contributing to greater social justice or reduced environmental burdens. Such reactions have led to the notion of the 'green consumer' who will differentiate in favour of those products with a superior socio-environmental performance.

Understanding green consumers and their behaviour

Academic researchers, market research agencies and arms of government have all striven to define and understand the relationship between peoples' socio-environmental concerns and their behaviour as consumers. Sustainability orientated consumer research uses a variety of labels for consumers and their behaviour in this respect including green, greener, pro-sustainability, pro-environmental, pro-social, environmentally conscious, altruistic, ecological, ethical or alternative (see Jackson 2005). Much of this research has attempted to profile consumers by their sustainability concerns to enable markets to be meaningfully segmented and targeted (Straughan and Roberts 1999). Other research has sought to profile consumer types to understand how each might be motivated to consume more sustainably (Jackson 2005), or to test the acceptability of price premiums for more sustainable products (Laroche *et al.* 2001). This last stream of research is notable for its embedded assumption and message to the research's subjects and audience that environmentally superior products will be more expensive. This may be true in cases where external environmental costs are being internalised and therefore reflected in the prices charged to consumers. However, green products that focus on energy, resource and waste reduction may be less costly and therefore cost competitive. Instead of research that asks consumers about the acceptability of paying 5 per cent more for 'environmentally superior products', questions could as easily be framed as to whether they find it acceptable for companies to continue to market products that are artificially cheap, because they impoverish the environment and people in other countries.

Many factors have been proposed as influences on green consumer behaviour, including changing consumer values and attitudes, demographic factors, consumer goals, knowledge of environmental problems and alternative products, perceived personal relevance, perceived consumer effectiveness, social identity, emotional response and a range of circumstantial factors (Jackson 2005; Wells *et al.* 2011). Early segmentation attempts were strongly orientated towards socio-demographic factors (Straughan and Roberts 1999), whilst later efforts have focused more on environmental attitudes, environmental knowledge, social consciousness or related behaviours to categorise consumers. The observation of Kilbourne and Beckmann (1998) that attempts to generate definitive segmentations of green consumers have been 'frequently inconclusive and sometimes contradictory' has continued to hold true.

The difficulties in isolating green consumers reflect several factors, not least that consumer behaviour is complex and challenging to understand even before an additional layer of social and environmental concern is added. There are other important considerations.

- They overlook the point made by Kardash (1976) that all consumers (barring a few who enjoy contrariness for its own sake) are 'green consumers' in that, faced with a choice between two products that are identical in all respects except for their eco-performance, they would differentiate in terms of the environmentally superior product.
- By attempting to relate a consumer's environmental concern to purchases, marketing researchers may be looking in the wrong place. Many significant pro-environmental contributions that consumers can make relate to product use, maintenance and disposal, or in delaying or avoiding a purchase through sharing products or adopting a 'make do and mend' mentality.
- Environmental improvements in products are often entangled with other social, economic or technical benefits. Energy-saving products provide economic and environmental benefits, and people may choose organic food for reasons of environmental concern, personal health concern or simply for the taste benefits.

- General environmental concern amongst consumers is not matched by good levels of 'environmental literacy' or a clear understanding of how specific consumption decisions relate to particular environmental or social problems.

These factors may help to explain two widely observed phenomena relating to green consumer behaviour. The first is the gap that exists between consumers' sustainability orientated attitudes and values, and their actual behaviours in action (Jackson 2005). The second is the degree of inconsistency that exists within the range of behaviours that consumers engage in. This can vary across types of behaviour, with McDonald *et al.* (2012) noting that even consumers with strong sustainability concerns treated some types of consumption as 'exceptions'. Such exceptions are viewed as 'non-negotiable' and may be strongly tied to other aspects of the consumer's sense of identity, including owning the latest electronic technologies, private car use, foreign holidays and meat consumption. Behaviour can also vary with consumption context, with consumers who exhibit strong sustainability orientated behaviours when at home not maintaining those same behaviours when on holiday.

One approach to understanding green consumer behaviour expressed as purchasing, may lie in considering the purchase rather than the purchaser. If we accept Kardash's (1976) proposal that, all other things being equal, most customers would differentiate in favour of greener products, then understanding green purchasing behaviour (and often the lack of it), is explained by the extent to which other things are not perceived as 'equal'. Many green purchases involve a compromise over conventional purchases in the form of a 'green premium', a need to accept a lower level of technical performance in exchange for improved eco-performance (e.g. rechargeable batteries provide less long-lasting power and require greater effort from the consumer in their management, but are ultimately more cost-effective and greener), some form of inconvenience such as travelling to non-standard distribution outlets, or psychological discomfort in moving away from a conventional product.

Where there is a compromise involved in making a greener purchase, a key factor, which will determine its acceptability to consumers, is the confidence they have in the socio-environmental benefits involved. Customers will need to be confident that the issue(s) involved are real problems; that a company's market offering has improved eco-performance compared to competitor or previous offerings; and that purchasing the product will make a material difference (perceived self-efficacy). The use of marketing communications tools such as third-party certified standards labels can be very important for building consumer confidence in the solutions they are offered (Lebel and Lorek 2008).

Understanding green consumer behaviour has proved challenging for companies, scholars and governments. There has been a tendency for it to be understood by grafting social and environmental concerns onto conventional models of consumer behaviour such as the theory of planned behaviour. In his thorough review of the challenge of promoting sustainable consumer behaviour, Jackson (2005) discusses the limitations of such an approach and the need to move beyond models and theories that concentrate on consumers as individuals and consumption as a very rational and conscious process of satisfying individual wants. Jackson's analysis demonstrates the importance of the social aspects of consumption, including the influence of families and households, of lifestyles, of the social meanings of products, of a view of sustainable behaviours as 'normal', and of habit on consumers' behaviours.

From consumer purchase to sustainable lifestyles

A limitation of conventional marketing approaches when understanding the environmental impacts of consumers from an SPC perspective is that they tend to focus on individual purchases (and the motivations behind them) as a consumption activity, rather than consumption as a total process and the consequences linked to it. Therefore, a highly environmentally orientated consumer who expresses their concerns by driving a Toyota Prius, drinking Fairtrade coffee, taking ecotourism vacations, investing ethically and recycling would register as an archetypal 'green consumer'. However, their lifestyle would have a far greater environmental impact than that of the environmentally disinterested climate sceptic who neither travels nor consumes much for reasons of poverty, poor health or disinterest. Similarly, the consumption choices of an individual will often have less influence on their overall environmental impacts than whether they live alone or share their household with others. A lifestyle perspective on consumption has helped us to understand that many key behaviours, particularly around household management, are not simply conscious choices, but are strongly influenced by household structure, habits, routines, shared routines and circumstantial factors such as location (particularly rural versus urban) or infrastructure for travel or waste management. This has led to a growing interest in understanding sustainable consumption from a social practices perspective as a complement to the conventional consumer behaviour perspective (Warde 2005).

Such insights have led to growing interest in the notion of sustainable lifestyles. This offers several benefits, including the ability to understand connections between behaviours and to help understand inconsistencies amongst different pro-sustainability behaviours. It also highlights that the benefits linked to some behaviours, part-motivated by financial gain (such as energy savings), may be offset by a 'rebound effect' if the savings are spent on other environmentally damaging purchases (such as a cheap flight somewhere). Another advantage is that it can help to focus attention on those elements of consumption with the greatest environmental impacts. The European *Environmental Impact of Products* (EIPRO) project applied an input-output-based methodology to assess 255 key elements of domestic consumption against a range of impacts including pollution, human and environmental health risks, and greenhouse gas emissions (Tukker and Jansen 2006). It concluded that 70 to 80 per cent of total impacts from domestic consumption relate to:

- food and drink: including production, distribution, storage, preparation and waste;
- housing: including construction and maintenance impacts, and domestic energy use;
- transport: including commuting, shopping, leisure and holiday travel.

The remaining impacts mostly concerned water use, domestic equipment (appliances, computers and home entertainment), furniture, clothing and shoes. This provides a relatively focused consumption agenda for both the development of sustainable lifestyles and the focusing of green marketing efforts.

It is notable that commercial marketers are increasingly seeking to engage with consumers on the sustainability agenda with a lifestyle approach, and are seeking to influence behaviours beyond purchase choices at the supermarket checkout. This has been notable in campaigns such as Procter & Gamble's *Turn to 30* campaign, and *Think Climate* from Marks & Spencer, which both sought to encourage consumers to wash clothes at lower temperatures. These were highly influential in increasing the proportion of UK households washing at 30°C from 2 per cent in 2002 to 17 per cent in 2007 and then to 38 per cent by 2011. A more systematic approach to influencing consumer lifestyles towards sustainability comes from Unilever's *Sustainable Living Plan*, which addresses a range of consumer lifestyle elements that intersect with the consumption of their products.

Evidence of growing commercial interest in promoting sustainable lifestyles came from a survey of managers by BSR/Futerra (2013) within companies responsible for 54 of the world's leading consumer brands. This revealed that although only 40 per cent of companies were actively involved in actions to promote sustainable consumer lifestyles, double that number were planning such actions in the next 5 years. Interestingly, although existing actions were mostly driven by a reactive agenda revolving around regulation, risk and reputation management, the majority of companies envisaged that by 2018 strong growth in consumer interest in sustainable lifestyles would become a key driver of future sales, market share and business innovation.

One consequence of the growing interest in sustainability has been the emergence of particular types of lifestyle reflecting consumers' socio-environmental concerns, including *lifestyles of health and sustainability* and *lifestyles of voluntary simplicity*. Consumers interested in the former have been identified as a particular target for greener products and services estimated as a growing market of 41 million people worth US$209 billion in the US alone (Kotler 2011). The latter addresses the SPC promoting mechanism of 'use less'. Although this runs against the prevailing consumer culture, there is increasing interest in notions of 'downshifting' and the pursuit of quality of life through a reduced emphasis on the work-earn-spend-consume lifestyle.

International dimensions

The majority of discussions about green marketing and consumption to date have related to industrialised economies. However, it is worth noting that these are global phenomena and that consumers in developing economies are also concerned with environmental quality. The 2014 National Geographic/Globescan GreenDex Survey covering 18,000 consumers across 18 countries, showed that the statement, 'I am very concerned about environmental problems' generated a stronger response amongst Indian, Chinese, Korean and Mexican consumers than their German, Swedish, Canadian or British counterparts. Consumers from those poorer countries were also more concerned about trying to reduce their own environmental impacts. Across a set of 65 aspects of consumption (covering food, housing, transport and goods), the consumers showing the greatest improvement in reducing their environmental impacts between 2012 and 2014 were those from India, followed by South Korea, Argentina, Mexico, Sweden and Australia.

Consuming less in material terms within industrialised economies will be an inevitable consequence of the need to pursue more sustainable consumption and production strategies. Greater material efficiency within both production and consumption can make a given market more sustainable, but gains here are frequently offset by growth in consumption volumes. Given population growth and the rapid expansion of the consuming class within populous countries such as China and India, it is difficult to escape the conclusion that some consumption reduction in economic terms is also required amongst industrialised economies. This, however, runs highly contrary to the DSP and explains why almost all the discourse about sustainability and marketing to date focuses on consuming differently (in terms of substitutions) rather than consuming less (Mont and Plepys 2008).

Within poorer countries, mass poverty and under-consumption also poses a considerable threat to environmental quality and sustainability. There are almost three billion people globally existing on less than $2 per day, who are therefore effectively excluded from the consumer economy. Ironically, poorer consumers often face price disadvantages due to their low volume purchasing or the perceived risks in serving them (Prahalad and Hammond 2002). Most of the measures aimed at stimulating consumption and growth where it is most needed fall outside the remit of marketing. One targeted growth strategy that has strong marketing relevance and implications is the emerging concept of *Bottom of the Pyramid* markets (Prahalad and Hammond 2002). This seeks to engage the poorest citizens of the world in the economy as consumers and entrepreneurs. One approach is to design consumable products, such as toiletries, in small and affordable quantities so that poorer consumers can access them. However, since such an approach effectively increases the volume of packaging material used per unit of product, there are inevitably environmental tradeoffs involved in the marketing of such products. For durable products, these can be made affordable through new business models that make them available on a shared community basis (Kirchgeorg and Winn 2006). With poorer consumers representing a heterogeneous and poorly understood market, serving them represents a considerable challenge that can require innovative approaches to developing and implementing marketing strategies from marketers (Prahalad and Hammond 2002; Kirchgeorg and Winn 2006).

The ultimate expression of an SPC perspective in marketing would be to see the discussion of socio-environmental issues evolving from being viewed as a potential constraint on marketing activities generated in the marketing environment, towards being considered as an integral component and starting point of marketing strategy processes, alongside consumer needs (Belz and Peattie 2012).

Green marketing: a managerial perspective

The majority of scholarship relating to the intersection between marketing and sustainability comes from a managerial perspective, focusing on the implications of sustainability issues for developing marketing strategies and their implementation through elements of the marketing mix (Kilbourne and Beckmann 1998).

Green marketing strategies

From a marketing strategy perspective, reactive and defensive strategies based on legislative compliance and bolting on 'end-of-pipe' technologies to alleviate pollution problems have gradually given way to more proactive and opportunity-driven strategies, with new products being developed and positioned as 'solutions' to socio-environmental problems. During the 1990s the argument that greening can act as a source of competitive advantage emerged from authors such as Elkington (1997) and Porter and van der Linde (1995). Porter and van der Linde's argument is that the search for environmentally superior solutions leads to innovation and the creation of more efficient and effective technologies. Their logic is that tough environmental legislation (often vigorously opposed by companies) creates new challenges for companies, which prompts them to innovate and secure improvements in competitive as well as environmental performance.

Although most marketing strategy writing focuses on the potential of superior environmental performance to act as a source of differentiation, Porter and van der Linde also suggest it as a source of low-cost competitive strategies if investments in clean technologies can reduce material and energy inputs, and cut inefficient pollution and waste. Amongst 181 waste reduction projects within 29 chemical industry plants they studied, only 1 led to a net cost increase and the average annual savings (on the projects where this could be meaningfully measured) was US$3.49 per dollar spent.

Many of the key green marketing success stories have involved greener products such as organic food and cruelty-free cosmetics that have succeeded within market niches comprising the most environmentally aware consumers. There is, however, a danger that the success of green niche products could effectively hold back the greening of markets. This could occur if by satisfying the most environmentally aware consumers, pressure to green the broader market becomes diluted and the momentum of change falters. In many industries it will require the greening of the mass market to make a substantive contribution to sustainability (Belz 2006).

Whether competitive and financial outperformance can be generated and sustained through sustainability strategies is a contentious subject, and the debate has mostly focused on corporate rather than marketing strategies. There is growing evidence that strong sustainability performance goes hand-in-hand with long-term financial outperformance (Eccles *et al.* 2014), but there are many anecdotal examples of well-intentioned sustainability strategies that have failed (Ottman *et al.* 2006). Often, in practice, sustainability issues have proved complex and costly to address, with customers being difficult to convince and greener product offerings sometimes struggling to compete on technical merits against conventional products. Furthermore, the media has often proved to be more critical of those attempting to improve their eco-performance and capitalise on it than they are of the most polluting and wasteful companies. Ottman *et al.* (2006) also warn of a new form of 'marketing myopia' in which the enthusiasm for a product's environmental credentials may lead the company to lose sight of its match with basic consumer needs and perceptions.

Green brands

With the emergence of strategies seeking to generate competitive advantage from superior eco-performance, there has been a growing interest in the creation of green or sustainable brands. Many of the iconic green brands were established by environmental entrepreneurs as 'alternative' businesses. It is notable how many of them have since been bought out by the larger and more mainstream firms they were originally established to challenge. Examples include Body Shop (L'Oréal), Ben & Jerry's (Unilever), Green & Blacks (Cadbury) and Ethos Water (Coca-Cola). Whether this indicates that the major brands are neutralising a perceived threat by absorbing it, or is symptomatic of the larger companies following the lead of the green pioneers, is open to interpretation. It is also notable that existing global companies have increasingly sought to link their brands (both product and corporate) to sustainability. Coca-Cola, Nike and Starbucks are amongst the global brands that have previously faced criticism linked to sustainability issues, but were amongst the leaders in sustainability reporting and initiatives highlighted in the Ceres (2014) survey of Fortune 500 firms. There is, however, perhaps an irony that the top four green brands in Interbrand's 2014 *Best Global Green Brand* survey, according to companies' efforts to improve their environmental sustainability performance, were all car manufacturers.

Marketing mix

The notion of a *marketing mix* of key variables that the marketer has at their disposal to implement their strategy and meet their customers' needs and expectations, dates back to the 1950s and was crystallised in 1960 in McCarthy's *Four Ps* of product, price, place (referring to distribution) and promotion (see Chapter 12). This mix model has endured despite considerable criticism, including that it is essentially producer rather than customer orientated (Shaw and Jones 2005), since it refers to what is produced and how it is priced, distributed and promoted by the producer. A large proportion of green marketing practice and research has focused on the greening of the mix variables, including green new product development (e.g. Pujari *et al.* 2003); pricing, particularly in terms of consumer acceptance of green premiums (e.g. Laroche *et al.* 2001); and communications, with an emphasis on green advertising, its suitability as a medium for green messages and how consumers respond to it (e.g. Zinkhan and Carlson 1995; Ottman *et al.* 2006).

The management of the mix for green products could be viewed as simply a particular formulation of the conventional mix, with socio-environmental performance providing a basis for differentiation. However, Kotler (2011) argues that sustainability issues introduce new and challenging questions for marketers into mix management. Belz and Peattie (2012) take this further by calling for a reformulation of the mix in order to make it both more customer orientated and more conducive to integrating sustainability issues into marketing strategy, based around 'four Cs':

- **Customer solutions**: As part of the more general shift in marketing away from a product and transaction focus, and towards a service and relationship focus, it can be helpful to consider green products and services as 'solutions' to consumer needs. This shift both aligns better with the marketing philosophy and fits better with a PSS perspective where the tangible product is only part of the solution on offer.
- **Cost**: Although everything purchased by consumers has a price, there may be other transaction costs involved including psychological costs linked to time, effort or worry expended. Some of the key purchases from a sustainability perspective, including homes, cars and energy using devices, have significant costs linked to use and maintenance rather than purchase. A switch in focus from purchase price to the lifetime cost of durable goods can create opportunities for different types of customer solution. One market that has witnessed a widespread shift of emphasis from price to cost is in the marketing of low-energy light bulbs. Energy efficient compact fluorescent and LED bulbs are relatively expensive to purchase, but over their lifespan save consumers money through reduced energy costs. For example the LED *Lifebulb* manufactured by Zeta uses just 8W to produce the equivalent light output of a 60W incandescent bulb (or an 11–13W compact fluorescent) and has a forecast lifespan of up to 20 years. Although the product's launch cost of £20 seemed expensive for a single bulb, at 2012 energy prices this would be recovered in only two years for each incandescent bulb replaced.
- **Convenience**: The notion of 'place' tends to over-emphasise the physical distribution of products, the organisation of distribution channels and the management of the relationships between producers and the intermediaries within them. Although these represent important operational elements of marketing management, for the consumer, providing a channel works as intended, they are of little interest. The emphasis on the point of exchange (or the service encounter), like the emphasis on prices, tends to focus attention on purchase as an activity more than consumption as a total process encompassing the use and disposal stages. The conventional concept of a physical place in many markets is also becoming increasingly irrelevant as more elements of the consumption and production process move into an online environment. The consumer benefit that underpins 'place' issues is convenience. Whether delivering goods and services to consumers in stores, online or directly to their homes, the efforts of marketers are geared towards making their offerings widely available, easily accessible and convenient to access and use. Convenience is highly valued by consumers, particularly amongst the cash rich/time poor, and strongly influences behaviour and satisfaction. Convenience also provides a challenge for marketing sustainable solutions, since historically there has often been a trade-off between convenience and environmental performance (e.g. in the use of rechargeable batteries). Some commentators argue that developing markets for sustainable solutions will depend upon matching conventional products for convenience (Ottman *et al.* 2006), whilst others argue that our devotion to, and notion of, convenience may have to change (Shove 2003). For some key elements of green marketing, such as getting customers to return old products and packaging into the value system through product take-back, making reverse logistics and recycling systems convenient to use will be important to engage consumer participation.

- **Communications**: For many years the unidirectional notion of 'promotion' has been super-seded by the more interactive concept of communication within mainstream marketing (see Chapter 12). For marketers of sustainable solutions, effective communications with consum-ers is vital, because such solutions may require people to consume in different ways, to consider different types of product and service, and to take a longer-term and more multi-dimensional perspective in assessing their value. Effective communication to maintain long-term relationships with consumers (that continue through use and post-use of the product) will be important to ensure that a whole lifecycle approach is taken to managing sustainable solutions. The manage-ment issues involved in green communication are similar to those of mainstream marketing in terms of developing a message and choosing an appropriate medium. There are, however, fur-ther challenges involved, because sustainability messages often involve complex issues that can be difficult to encapsulate in a short advertisement or label space. Some of the most common media used in conventional marketing may also not work as well in green markets. Direct mail's reputa-tion as 'junk mail' or sales promotions based on 'buy-one-get-one-free' will not easily reflect a message of avoiding waste and over-consumption.

The major challenge in green communications management is the avoidance of actual or perceived 'greenwashing'. In the 2010 report *The Seven Sins of Greenwashing*, US consultants, TerraChoice, investigated 12,061 environmental claims made by over 5,000 commonly available US or Canadian consumer products (TerraChoice 2010). The number being explicitly marketed as 'green' had grown by 73 per cent compared to the previous year, and of the claims checked, only 4.5 per cent avoided all forms of false, vague, irrelevant or misleading claims.

A good example of an integrated green marketing mix comes from Mobility Car Sharing, a company providing mobility solutions through a fleet of 2,650 cars at 1,395 locations across Switzerland. Pricing reflects which amongst ten vehicle models is chosen along with rental time and distance covered, and is competitive compared to the total costs of owning and running a car. Booking vehicles is made convenient through online and smartphone media linked to Google mapping that allows for immediate locating and booking of vehicles. A smart card for registered users provides easy access to cars and their on-board computers and can give added access to public transport to provide an integrated transport solution for a journey. Communication involves a mix of media, including publishing *Mobility Journal* with news and offers for users, but with a particular emphasis on online communication including initiatives like Mobility@campus targeting student users. By 2012 the company had signed up over 100,000 users representing 1 in 60 of the adult population, effectively sharing each car amongst 40 users at a significant environmental benefit compared to an ownership model.

One way in which green marketers have sought to overcome some of the limitations of conventional communications media is by embracing the possibilities that the digital world and new media represent. Online communication can avoid the negative associations of waste attached to direct mail, of visual pollution for outdoor media or of superficiality or greenwash-ing for conventional mass media advertising. An online environment allows the communication of the full range of socio-environmental issues and data associated with a product and its entire supply chain to interested consumers and other stakeholders in a way that is impossible using advertising or on-pack media. In frozen foods, for example, Iglo group, the European market leader and company behind the BirdsEye brand, complement ingredient and nutrition infor-mation with online details on where products come from and how they are processed, along with details of the company's *Forever Food* sustainability strategy. Online media also allows smaller firms with limited communications budgets to build a profile based on sustainability performance. Followfish, a niche player in the frozen fish market, uses on-pack tracking codes that allow consumers to see online where and how fish were cultivated (e.g. organic aquaculture in Vietnam) and how it was transported, with results presented using Google maps. Two of the most sophisticated proponents of online green marketing communications are the iconic green clothing brands, Patagonia and Timberland. Both companies provide full lifecycle information and broader sustainability reporting online, but also seek to engage customers through blogs, stories, videos, promotions and opportunities to comment in order to build a sense of online community that brings together consumers and members of the company. Timberland even developed a Facebook 'Virtual Forest' application, in which users can plant and manage their own online virtual forest, which is then linked to Timberland's real tree planting scheme in Haiti as a form of cause-related marketing.

Green marketing: a critical perspective

The notion of 'critical marketing' which, in the tradition of critical social theory, challenges the accepted assumptions, wisdom, aims, boundaries and methodologies that underpin the development of knowledge in marketing, has become an increasing focus of debate amongst scholars, albeit more at the margins of the discipline than within the mainstream. Most marketing scholarship seeks to create more effective and/or efficient marketing practice and therefore the generation of customer satisfaction at a profit. Critical marketing takes a step back and reflects upon the value and validity of the whole process (for example, see the edited collection by Maclaran *et al.* 2007). Unlike conventional marketing, critical marketing does not simply take for granted a DSP in industrialised economies in which economic growth and consumption are accepted as the determinants of quality of life, or where faith is placed in technology to solve environmental crises, or in liberal democracy to deliver social justice, or in private property ownership, free markets and limited government intervention to allocate resources (Kilbourne *et al.* 1997). If green marketing is viewed as the process of responding to socio-environmental concerns in the marketing environment, and producing products with superior eco-performance to meet customers' needs and to generate competitive advantage, it simply represents a variant of existing marketing thinking and practice. Answering Kotler's (2011) call for marketing to embrace the environmental challenge and integrate sustainability fully into marketing thinking and practice, will require more than an emphasis on the development of new greener products and cleaner production processes. It will require a re-evaluation of some fundamental marketing assumptions and concepts (Kilbourne *et al.* 1997; Varey 2010) including:

- *Marketing's legitimacy.* Within consumer economies marketing's role in driving forward growth by stimulating demand, and its perceived role in satisfying customer wants, have always provided legitimacy. The benefits of ever-increasing consumer choice, product innovation and economic growth have therefore gone largely unquestioned until recently. A sustainability perspective raises questions about the legitimacy and ethics of marketing as it is currently practised and its impact on non-consumers in particular. Conventional marketing has a focus on the wants and needs of the current generation of consumers, with little consideration of the impact of their consumption activities on the consumption and quality of life opportunities of future generations of consumers. Neither does it address the majority of the world's population who lack disposable income and therefore exist outside the consumer economy, yet who still depend for their survival upon an environment increasingly impacted by commercial production and consumption activities.

- *Customer satisfaction.* Conventionally, customer satisfaction has been judged in terms of the performance of a product at the moment (or during the period) of consumption. A green consumer may reject a product, because they become aware of the environmental harm that the product causes in production or disposal. They may also avoid a product, because they disapprove of the activities of the producer, its suppliers or investors. Even the concept that genuine satisfaction is derived from increasing levels of material consumption is being challenged. Ironically, marketing assumes that consuming products produces satisfaction, yet economics, a discipline that underpins marketing, assumes that human needs are insatiable. Critics of consumer culture, such as Hamilton (2003), argue that it is actually unhappiness and the generation of discontent (by marketers) that sustains economic growth and the process of change within markets. Research from psychology has demonstrated a complex and loose relationship between material consumption and happiness, and that beyond a certain level we derive little additional satisfaction from further consumption. Robert Lane (2000) in his book *The Loss of Happiness in Market Economies* outlines the risk that societal pressures to maintain high levels of material consumption (including commercial marketing) actually keep us away from more intrinsically satisfying activities, such as spending time with friends and family.
- *The product concept.* If customer satisfaction is increasingly dependent upon on all of the activities within a company's value chain, we are approaching the situation where the company itself (including its supply chain) is effectively becoming the product consumed. Drucker's (1973: 325) famous concept that 'Marketing is the whole business seen from its final result, that is from the customers' point of view', increasingly resonates as customers (or those who influence them) take a more active interest in all aspects of the companies they patronise.
- *Producer responsibility.* The responsibilities of the producer were conventionally seen in terms of ensuring that products were fit for purpose, fairly represented, safe and not priced or promoted in a way that exploited customers. Environmental concern has added a new layer of responsibility concerned with the fate of the product at the end of its lifespan (and increasingly enshrined in EPR legislation such as the European ELV and WEEE Directives). This is an issue, which was previously irrelevant to marketers beyond signalling the possibility of a new purchase. For consumer durables, such as cars, white goods and consumer electronics, these new responsibilities will have considerable impacts on product design and supply chain management.
- *Consumer responsibility.* Marketing is founded on the principle of consumer sovereignty, and conventional marketing thinking recognises consumer rights, but not responsibilities. An emerging notion of 'consumer social responsibility' as a complement to corporate social responsibility is becoming evident in relation to issues such as climate change. Consumers are increasingly recognising that they are responsible for contributing to climate change problems and therefore, along with companies and governments, have a legitimate responsibility to contribute to solutions (Wells *et al.* 2011).
- *Demarketing.* As noted earlier, consuming less may become unavoidable in many markets, and achieving this may require demarketing (either voluntarily or forcibly) to reduce consumption (Kotler 2011). Consumption reduction was explored by Fisk (1973) in his *Theory of Responsible Consumption*, but it is a concept that most politicians, economists and business practitioners would prefer not to contemplate. However, in tourism and energy markets, changes in pricing or access to products have been used to try to reduce levels of consumption.
- *Market structures and roles.* The terms 'supply chain' and 'value chain' indicate a view of markets as linear structures that produce value for consumers through a process that begins with material extraction from the environment and ends with the disposal of waste. Sustainability

requires a shift from such linear systems towards cyclical service-and-flow processes (including recycling and remanufacture), which mimic the circular material economies that prevail in nature (Capra 2002). The creation of more circular market structures will not only require some of the more basic models within marketing text books to be redrawn but also for the roles of actors within the system to be reconsidered. For example, as recycling becomes more prevalent within a particular market, the consumer gains an additional role as a 'resupplier of value' back into the system.

Conclusions: towards transformation

The relationship between marketing and the sustainability agenda is an intriguing one. For many people, marketing, and some of its key tools such as advertising, symbolise the unsustainability of our current economies and societies, because of their role in driving consumer demand and consumption. Yet marketing clearly has a key role to play in addressing the sustainability crisis. Some of the key steps needed to make our production and consumption systems more sustainable will involve product innovations, reducing the environmental burdens linked to packaging and distribution, factoring into prices the socio-environmental costs previously treated as externalities and changing how consumers seek to meet particular needs.

The debate about marketing and sustainability is beginning to shift beyond questions of how to 'green' marketing practices, to questions about how we can transform markets and marketing to become more sustainable as part of transforming society and moving beyond the current DSP that constrains marketing practices and discourse. Polonsky (2012), for example, argues for a transformation in and through the way that marketers calculate and communicate value; how they discuss the environment and the costs of action and inaction; and in refocusing marketing away from want satisfaction and the acquisition of goods towards the creation of value. Varey (2010) similarly argues for a transformation in marketing and its values towards a welfare-based model that pursues 'better' rather than 'more'.

Marketing as a management discipline is a reflection of the society in which it exists, and a transformation of marketing into something substantively more sustainable cannot happen without radical social changes in terms of the type of progress we seek to achieve and the means by which we pursue and measure it. However, marketing also has a potential role to play in that process of transformation towards a more sustainable society. Belz and Peattie (2012) argue that the conventional view of marketing organisations as relatively passive and influenced by the marketing environment, underplays the opportunities for them to influence stakeholders within that environment. Pioneering green companies have regularly lobbied to improve environmental standards within their industries and, as increasing numbers of companies develop a sustainability strategy, there is increasing pressure being applied down the supply chains of the most powerful companies, such as Walmart, to improve sustainability performance and reduce socio-environmental risks.

Perhaps one of the most important contributions that marketing can make to progress towards sustainability is the marketing of sustainability itself. As a complex and contested concept that runs contrary to the DSP and many of the messages that marketing has drummed into consumers for decades, changing and reducing material consumption for sustainability is not an easy sell. However, it is a challenge to which marketers are increasingly rising. This can be seen in the strategies to promote more sustainable lifestyles from companies such as Unilever, Procter & Gamble and Marks & Spencer. It is also increasingly in evidence in the social marketing efforts backed by governments seeking to promote more sustainable forms of consumption (Peattie and Peattie 2012). Whatever blame marketers may deserve for both pressing and emerging sustainability problems, the success of the marketing discipline and profession in rising to the challenges of marketing sustainability and making marketing more sustainable, will be crucial to the welfare of global society for generations to come.

Further reading

Belz, F.-M. and Peattie, K. (2012), *Sustainability Marketing: A Global Perspective*, Chichester, UK: John Wiley & Sons.

Aimed primarily as a teaching text, this book reconsiders marketing theory and practice from a sustainability perspective, with a strong emphasis on developing long-term relationships with customers based around sustainable value. It examines how social, ethical and environmental values can be integrated into marketing strategy formulation, and provides alternative perspectives on mix management and the role of marketing in society. It uses case studies drawn from a wide range of countries to illustrate key challenges and the innovative solutions being generated by companies at the forefront of the greening of marketing.

Jackson, T. (2005) *Motivating Sustainable Consumption: A Review of Evidence on Consumer Behavior and Behavioural Change*, London: Policy Studies Institute.

A tour de force covering the history of attempts to market to consumers on social, environmental and ethical grounds and exploring the different research traditions in green consumer behaviour research. It develops an integrated approach to understanding consumption and sustainability, combining conventional marketing research with insights from sociology and psychology and sets out the challenges involved in motivating behavioural change for policy-makers and businesses.

Jackson, T. (2011), *Prosperity without Growth: Economics for a Finite Planet*, London: Routledge.

Provides a thorough and well-argued case as to why the current economic system and DSP are unsustainable, and provides a coherent blueprint for a society that pursues prosperity for the benefit of its citizens instead of ever-increasing economic growth to their detriment. Strongly rooted in research into alternative economics from around the world, this should be required reading for every politician on Earth. Not a marketing text per se, but it answers all those questions about how we could contemplate a world not geared towards ever-expanding consumption.

'Special issue on contemporary issues in green marketing', *Journal of Marketing Management* (1998), 14(6).

This issue pulled together eight papers from leading experts in the field of green marketing covering theoretical contributions, a critical review of research in the field and papers relating to product development, recycling, sustainable communications and green alliances. An invaluable starting point for anyone seeking to understand green marketing from an academic perspective.

'Special issue: Revisiting contemporary issues in green/ethical marketing', *Journal of Marketing Management* (2012), 28(3/4).

A further collection of a dozen papers charting academic progress in the field of green marketing since the original collection in 1998. The papers have a strong focus on consumer response and consider a wide range of influences on consumer behaviour. A common theme is the complexity of green consumer behaviour and the need to understand consumption behaviours more holistically. This collection also covers some of the key markets for sustainability including food, cars and clothing.

Ottman, J. A., Stafford, E. R. and Hartman, C. L. (2006), 'Green marketing myopia', *Environment*, 48(5): 22–36.

A useful article that uses numerous examples to show how some green marketing initiatives failed, because they did not strike the right balance between environmental concern and customer focus. Explores the inescapable nature of a greener and more materially efficient future for marketing and the steps to successfully integrate environmental product attributes with perceived consumer value.

Ottman, J. A. (2010), *The New Rules of Green Marketing*, Sheffield, UK: Greenleaf.

This book aims to help practising managers to engage with, and succeed in, green marketing. It has a strong emphasis on mainstreaming green marketing offerings to take them beyond niche markets, with a focus on generating value. It uses a range of examples from well-known companies to illustrate how to succeed in developing effective green marketing strategies for managers by following 20 rules.

Websites

Centre for Sustainable Design

http://cfsd.org.uk

A longstanding research centre with an emphasis on innovation and product design for sustainability. Includes a range of reports, journal articles and other resources dedicated to innovation in sustainable business models, products, packaging and marketing strategies.

Ceres

http://www.ceres.org

Ceres is a long-established NGO with a mission to promote sustainable business leadership and investment. Although the website has a strong US orientation, it contains a wealth of reports and other resources, including sector-specific reports covering key sustainability sectors such as food, energy, and apparel and issues such as supply chain management.

futerra

http://www.futerra.co.uk/

futerra is a specialist marketing communications agency dedicated to sustainability, and with a particular emphasis on positioning green consumption as normal and desirable. Their website contains a wide range of valuable resources concerning issues such as green branding, effective messaging and how to avoid greenwashing.

Greenbiz

http://www.greenbiz.com

This has a vast collection of news stories and articles on a wide range of business sustainability issues. As well as sections dedicated to key sustainability sectors, there are resources dedicated specifically to cities, supply chain management and design. Although US orientated, many of the stories concern global companies.

National Geographic/Globescan GreenDex Survey

http://environment.nationalgeographic.com/environment/greendex/

A global green consumer lifestyle survey that has run since 2008 and now covers 18 countries, including mature industrial consumer economies and rapidly developing nations such as China, India and Brazil. The survey focuses on behaviours such as energy use and conservation, transportation choices, food sources, the relative use of green products versus conventional products, along with environment and sustainability attitudes and knowledge. Includes an online calculator to determine your personal GreenDex score.

Network for Business Sustainability

http://nbs.net/

NBS is a network of sustainability orientated business leaders and academic experts. They produce a range of resources including digests of recent sustainability research and systematic reviews across particular business fields. Topic areas include socially conscious consumerism (which includes a systematic review of research), strategy making, innovation and supply chain management, and there is a functional section dedicated to marketing.

References

Baines, T., Lightfoot, H., Evans, S., Neely, A. and Greenough, R. (2007), 'State-of-the-art in product-service systems', *Proceedings of the Institute of Mechanical Engineers*, 221(10): 1543–1552.

Belz, F.-M. (2006), 'Marketing in the 21st century', *Business Strategy and the Environment*, 15(2): 139–144.

Belz, F.-M. and Peattie, K. (2012), *Sustainability Marketing: A Global Perspective*, second edition, Chichester, UK: John Wiley & Sons.

Blench, R. (2001), 'Globalisation and policies towards cultural diversity', *Natural Resources Perspectives*, Number 70, London: Overseas Development Institute.

BSR/Futerra (2013), *Value-Gap: The Business Value of Changing Consumer Behaviors*, London: Report by the Sustainable Lifestyles Frontier Group.

Capra, F. (2002), *The Hidden Connections*, London: HarperCollins.

Ceres (2014), *Gaining Ground: Corporate Progress on the Ceres Roadmap for Sustainability*, Boston, MA: Ceres/Sustainalytics.

Crane, A. (2000), *Marketing, Morality and the Natural Environment*, London: Routledge.

Drucker, P. F. (1973), *Management: Tasks, Responsibilities, Practices*, New York: Harper & Row.

D'Souza, C., Taghian, M. and Lamb, P. (2006), 'An empirical study on influence of environmental labels on consumers', *Corporate Communications*, 11(2): 162–173.

Eccles, R. G., Ioannou, I. and Serafeim, G. (2014), 'The impact of corporate sustainability on organizational processes and performance', *Management Science*, 60(11): 2835–2857.

Elkington, J. (1997), *Cannibals with Forks: The Triple Bottom Line of 21st Century Business*, Oxford, UK: Capstone Publishing.

Elkington, J. and Hailes, J. (1988), *The Green Consumer Guide*, Victor-Gollanz, London.

Fisk G. (1973), 'Criteria for a theory of responsible consumption', *Journal of Marketing*, 37(2): 24–31.

Fisk, G. (1974), *Marketing and the Ecological Crisis*, New York: Harper & Row.

Fuller, D. A. (1999), *Sustainable Marketing: Managerial-Ecological Issues*, Thousand Oaks, CA: Sage Publications.

GFN (2014), *Earth Overshoot Day 2014*, Global Footprint Network, available at http://www.footprintnetwork.org/en/index.php/GFN/page/earth_overshoot_day/ (accessed 31 October 2014).

Hamilton, C. (2003) *Growth Fetish*, Crows Nest, NSW: Allen & Unwin.

Harris, J. L., Pomeranz, J. L., Lobstein, T. and Brownell, K. D. (2009), 'A crisis in the marketplace: How food marketing contributes to childhood obesity and what can be done', *Annual Review of Public Health*, 30: 211–225.

Heiskanen, E. and Lovio, R. (2010), 'User-producer interaction in housing energy innovations: Energy innovation as a communication challenge', *Journal of Industrial Ecology*, 14(1): 91–102.

Henion, K. E. and Kinnear, T. C. (1976), *Ecological Marketing*, Chicago, IL: AMA.

Holmberg, J. and Sandbrook, R. (1992) 'Sustainable development: What is to be done?', in Holmberg, J. (ed.) *Policies for a Small Planet*, London: Earthscan, pp. 19–38.

Hopwood, B., Mellor, M. and O'Brien, G. (2005), 'Sustainable development: Mapping different approaches', *Sustainable Development*, 13(1): 38–52.

IPCC (2014), *Climate Change 2014: Impacts, Adaptation, and Vulnerability*, Fifth Assessment Report, Geneva, Switzerland: Intergovernmental Panel on Climate Change.

Jackson, T. (2005), *Motivating Sustainable Consumption: A Review of Evidence on Consumer Behavior and Behavioural Change*, London: Policy Studies Institute.

Kardash, W. J. (1976), 'Corporate responsibility and the quality of life: Developing the ecologically concerned consumer', in Henion, K. E. and Kinnear T. C. (eds) *Ecological Marketing*, Chicago, IL: AMA.

Kilbourne, W. E. and Beckmann, S. C. (1998), 'Review and critical assessment of research on marketing and the environment', *Journal of Marketing Management*, 14(6): 513–532.

Kilbourne, W. E., McDonagh, P. and Prothero, A. (1997), 'Sustainable consumption and the quality of life: A macromarketing challenge to the dominant social paradigm', *Journal of Macromarketing*, 17(1): 4–24.

Kirchgeorg, M. and Winn, M. I. (2006), 'Sustainability marketing for the poorest of the poor', *Business Strategy and the Environment*, 15(3): 171–184.

Kotler, P. (2011), 'Reinventing marketing to manage the environmental imperative', *Journal of Marketing*, 75(4): 132–135.

Laroche, M., Bergeron, J. and Barbaro-Forleo, G. (2001), 'Targeting consumers who are willing to pay more for environmentally friendly products', *The Journal of Consumer Marketing*, 18(6): 503–521.

Lane, R. (2000), *The Loss of Happiness in Market Economies*, Yale, CT: Yale University Press.

Lebel, L. and Lorek, S. (2008), 'Enabling sustainable production-consumption systems', *Annual Review of Environment and Resources*, 33: 241–225.

Luchs, M. G., Naylor, R. W., Irwin, J. R. and Raghunathan, R. (2010), 'The sustainability liability: Potential negative effects of ethicality on product preference', *Journal of Marketing*, 74(5): 18–31.

Maclaran, P., Saren, M., Goulding, C., Elliott, R. and Caterall, M. (2007), *Critical Marketing: Defining the Field*, London: Routledge.

Martin, D. and Schouten, J. (2011), *Sustainable Marketing*, Upper Saddle River, NJ: Prentice-Hall/Pearson.

McCarthy, E. J. (1960), *Basic Marketing, A Managerial Approach*, Homewood, IL: Richard D. Irwin.

McDonald, S., Oates, C. J., Alevizou, P. J., Young, C. W. and Hwang, K. (2012), 'Individual strategies for sustainable consumption', *Journal of Marketing Management*, 28(3/4): 445–468.

Medway, D., Warnaby, G. and Dharni, S. (2010), 'Demarketing places: Rationales and strategies', *Journal of Marketing Management*, 27(1/2): 124–142.

Mont, O. and Plepys, A. (2008), 'Sustainable consumption progress: Should we be proud or alarmed?', *Journal of Cleaner Production*, 16(4): 531–537.

National Geographic/Globescan (2014), *GreenDex 2014: Consumer Choice and the Environment*, available at: http://environment.nationalgeographic.com/environment/greendex/ (accessed 4 December 2015).

Ottman, J. A., Stafford, E. R. and Hartman, C. L. (2006), 'Green marketing myopia', *Environment*, 48(5): 22–36.

Peattie, K. (2001), 'Towards sustainability: The third age of green marketing', *The Marketing Review*, 2(2): 129–146.

Peattie, S. and Peattie, K. (2012), 'Social marketing for a sustainable environment', in Hastings, G., Angus, K. and Bryant, C. (eds), *The SAGE Handbook of Social Marketing*, London: Sage Publications, pp. 343–358.

Polonsky, M. J. (2012), 'Transformative green marketing: Impediments and opportunities', *Journal of Business Research*, 64(12): 1311–1319.

Porter, M. E. and van der Linde, C. (1995), 'Green and competitive: Ending the stalemate', *Harvard Business Review*, 73(5): 120–133.

Prahalad, C. K. and Hammond, A. (2002), 'Serving the world's poor, profitably', *Harvard Business Review*, 80(9): 1–11.

Pujari, D., Wright, G. and Peattie, K. (2003), 'Green and competitive: Influences on environmental new product development performance', *Journal of Business Research*, 56(8): 657–671.

Ritzer, G. (2004), *The McDonaldization of Society: Revised New Century Edition*, Newbury Park, CA: Pine Forge Press.

Robinson, J. (2004), 'Squaring the circle? Some thoughts on the idea of sustainable development', *Ecological Economics*, 48(4): 369–384.

Seitz, M. A. and Peattie, K. (2004), 'Meeting the closed-loop challenge: The case of remanufacturing', *California Management Review*, 43(3): 16–25.

Sharma, A., Iyer, G. R., Mehrota, A. and Krishnan, R. (2010), 'Sustainability and business-to-business marketing: A framework and implications', *Industrial Marketing Management*, 39(2): 330–341.

Shaw, E. and Jones, D. G. B. (2005), 'A history of schools of marketing thought', *Marketing Theory*, 5(3): 239–281.

Shove, E. (2003), 'Converging conventions of comfort, cleanliness and convenience', *Journal of Consumer Policy*, 26(4): 395–418.

Straughan, R. D. and Roberts, J. A. (1999), 'Environmental segmentation alternatives: A look at green consumer behaviour in the new millennium', *Journal of Consumer Marketing*, 16(6): 558–575.

TerraChoice (2010), *The Seven Sins of Greenwashing: Environmental Claims in Consumer Markets*, Ottawa, ON: TerraChoice Environmental Marketing.

Tukker, A. and Jansen, B. (2006), 'Environmental impacts of products: A detailed review of studies', *Journal of Industrial Ecology*, 10(3): 159–182.

Van Dam, Y. K. and Apeldoorn, P. A. C. (1996), 'Sustainable marketing', *Journal of Macromarketing*, 16(2): 45–56.

Varey, R. (2010), 'Marketing means and ends for a sustainable society: A welfare agenda for transformative change', *Journal of Macromarketing*, 30(2): 112–126.

Walker, H. and Brammer, S. (2009), 'Sustainable procurement in the United Kingdom public sector', *Supply Chain Management: An International Journal*, 14(2): 128–137.

Warde, A. (2005), 'Consumption and theories of practice', *Journal of Consumer Culture*, 5(2): 131–153.

WCED (1987), *Our Common Future (The Brundtland Report)*, World Commission on Environment and Development, Oxford, UK: Oxford University Press.

Wells, V., Ponting, C. and Peattie, K. (2011), 'Behaviour and climate change: Consumer perceptions of responsibility', *Journal of Marketing Management*, 27(7/8): 803–833.

WHO (2000), *Obesity: Preventing and Managing the Global Epidemic*, WHO Technical Report Series 894, Geneva, Switzerland: WHO.

WRI (2005), *Ecosystems and Human Well-being: Synthesis Report (Millennium Ecosystem Assessment)*, World Resource Institute, Washington, DC: Island Press.

Zinkhan, G. M. and Carlson, L. (1995), 'Green advertising and the reluctant consumer', *Journal of Advertising*, 24(2): 1–6.

25 Retailing

Leigh Sparks

Introduction

> The retail industry has huge economic and social significance. It improves the standard of living and increases employment, it invests, it innovates, is responsible for anchoring urban regeneration in many parts of the country and – of huge importance – embodies the spirit of competition.
>
> (Tony DeNunzio, then CEO of Asda-Wal-Mart, in Department of Trade and Industry 2004)

Retailing (traditionally defined as the sale of articles, either individually or in small numbers, directly to the consumer) is a distinct, diverse and dynamic sector of many economies. However, for a long time, the ubiquitous presence and nature of the organisational structure of many retail outlets – large numbers of small, local, independent shops – has blinded many to the challenges and opportunities in retailing. With the emergence of modern techniques of retailing and retail marketing and the emergence of huge international retail corporations, involving new retail forms and formats including online and mobile shopping, retailing has become much more visible and central to consumers' and governments' concerns. Reflecting as it does cultures and consumers, retailing is the primary conduit for production and consumption linkages in economies. Virtually everyone experiences retailing, as virtually everyone shops! The closeness of these retailer and consumer linkages demands retail engagement in marketing. Indeed, many retailers could be judged to be consummate marketers, often at the forefront of the discipline.

Retailing is a huge component of many economies. Perhaps 25 per cent of all enterprises in the EU are involved in retailing. Almost 19 million people in the EU are engaged in retailing. There are over 3.5 million shops in the EU and a large retail presence on the internet in many EU countries. In the UK the retail sector constitutes an important part of the economy, contributing *c*.16 per cent of GDP and is worth *c*.£150 billion. It employs around three million people or one in nine of the workforce and involves over half a million retail premises. Despite the banking crisis and recession since 2008, retail property still dominates UK institutional investment, accounting for over half of the capital value of direct property assets held by institutions and property companies.

UK retailers are involved in global sourcing and global retailing activities. The global success of UK retailers is enhanced by a positive retail environment within the UK, with non-UK-based retailers being strongly represented in the country, especially in the major retail centre of London. The UK Government states that:

The UK retail sector is a leader in innovation. E-commerce and self-service are reshaping the shopping experience across the world and have put the UK at the vanguard of multi-channel shopping. UK retail accounts for 11 per cent of global internet retail sales and the UK has the highest spend per head for e-commerce of any country.

(UK Trade and Investment 2014)

The retail sector is thus enormous and influential. However, it contains massive contrasts. Retailing is operated through many single shop entrepreneurial businesses, but the sector also contains some of the world's largest companies. There are large and small fixed shops, as well as mobile, pop-up and virtual shops. Retailing is a local affair with local demands, but many retailers are increasingly international. Indeed, 'global retail brands' such as IKEA, Zara or H&M are significant. Although in many Western economies the banking crisis and recession has had an adverse impact on sales and many companies, in Asian economies retail sales are increasing. The number of shops is falling in many countries, however, and their format is changing. Minimum wage and low employee pay characterises much of the retail sector, but managerial pay is above average. Executive rewards can be considerable. Despite having a stagnant and then declining UK market share since 2007, spectacular failures in some overseas ventures, profit warnings and the loss of senior executives, the two executive directors of Tesco in 2013/14 were paid over £1.5m each.

For some consumers, the development of large retail outlets and large retail businesses simply provides a more convenient and recognisable place and way in which to shop. For others, the rise of the retail corporation has sanitised and standardised retailing, making towns clones or 'bland identikits dominated by a few retail behemoths' (Simms *et al.* 2005). The until recently seemingly irresistible rise of Wal-Mart in the US (Brunn 2006) and Tesco in the UK (Burt and Sparks 2003), has provoked reactions over the use of retail power and the practices 'imposed' by such retailers on farmers, suppliers, distributors and consumers. In the UK this concern has led to various investigations of the grocery sector (see House of Commons Library 2012) and the creation of a Groceries Code Adjudicator (supermarket ombudsman) in 2013. The horsemeat scandal of 2013 and the collapse of Rana Plaza in Dhaka, Bangladesh in the same year, seemed to signify that some retailers (or at least retailer supply chains) could be cutting too many corners in pursuit of profit and the desire for ever cheaper prices. But, whilst there is a wave of sentiment against some retailers in some of the media and in local opposition groups, consumers continue to spend on a wide range of product and services at corporate retailers, as well as local and independent stores. Retailing is centre stage in the consideration of economies, societies and the patterns of how we want to live our lives. We all need food and clothing and, for some, the latest iPhone. The question is how best to organise the distribution of the products that are demanded.

The changing retail sector in many countries has been the subject of much concern, especially since 2008 and the onset of the banking and credit crisis and the global recession. In the UK a wave of retail collapses, bankruptcies and poor performance has left many shops vacant and many high streets 'derelict'. The crisis of the high street in the UK (Portas 2011; Grimsey 2012, 2013) and the wider recognition of the parlous state of many of our town centres (Fraser 2013) has prompted questioning over retailing and place (see Findlay and Sparks 2013). This 'crisis' is a symbol of a wider truth: retailing has been undergoing a structural revolution brought on by internet retailing and online shopping and by the over-development of much retail space. The recession since 2008 has exacerbated and exaggerated the pace and consequences of change. Some countries, e.g. the UK and the US, have too many shops, of the wrong sort in the wrong places: retailing itself is being rethought.

This chapter examines the key components of the practice of retailing and seeks to investigate the distinctive and changing nature of the retail sector. As befits a chapter in a book on marketing, it begins with the cultural and consumer aspects of the retail environment. It then moves to the places and locations where retailing occurs. Interrelationships linking retail businesses with other organisations are examined, before a consideration of the internal operations of retailers themselves is presented. The people who take on the running of retail businesses and individual shops, the nature of the selling and retailing processes, and the supply and sale of goods, are introduced and discussed. The chapter concludes by summarising the state of the retail industry today and considers briefly some of the challenges for the future.

Culture and retail consumers

Any consideration of retailing should begin with the country, local environments and consumers with which it interacts. The very specific relationships retailing has with culture and consumers are crucial to the distinctiveness and operation of the sector (Dawson 2001). Retailing must be responsive to the culture within which it operates. Internationally, this creates a great diversity in terms of regulatory and shopping environments, service standards and store formats and layouts. For example, Japanese culture and societal behaviours are fundamentally different to the cultural norms and values of, for example, Saudi Arabia or the southern US. Some aspects of a global culture are emerging, however, and there will be similarities in some of the retailing across locations. Generally, however, retailing mainly adapts to the local or national situation and norms. Considerable differences in approaches and operations may thus be found, though the core process – making products available for consumers to buy – is the same.

These cultural norms are derived from societal and economic situations. Retailing is an economic transaction, but also in many cases is fundamentally a social interaction. The norms of economic and social behaviour permeate, inform and on occasions, constrain, retail operations. Restrictive German or French shop opening hours are a legal recognition of cultural dimensions to the organisation of society and have long-standing roots. The limitation of alcohol sales to government-owned shops in Sweden and parts of Canada reflects societal concerns over the use and abuse of alcohol. The persistence of fresh produce markets in Mediterranean Europe and wet markets in South-East Asia derives from traditional patterns of food preparation and consumption. The advertising of retail products through weekly newspaper 'fliers' or inserts in Denmark and the US have different origins and obligations, but nonetheless inform and constrain the retailer and retail practice. Such advertising and promotional offers would be deemed wasteful, inappropriate or ineffective in some other societies and economies. Limits on what can be advertised or sold in Islamic societies, or what advertisements or catalogues can contain, reflect cultural and religious norms.

It is tempting to use these examples to suggest that there are uniform national cultures and thus retailers' responses to culture work best on the national level. But, culture is a complex, multi-dimensional concept that derives from a range of personal and group values and attitudes. Culture, as a social phenomenon, may be learned and can be passed from generation to generation. The notion of culture suggests behaviours, desires and needs that can be stated. It is also adaptive in that culture can change to meet circumstances or outside stimuli. As the world becomes more interconnected and perhaps standardised, so perhaps the cultural influences from outside, e.g. American influences, come to play a bigger role. This, however, can be overstated. Local differences in taste, demands, brands and behaviours and attitudes still persist and 'force' retailers to work with the local cultures rather than against them. Some retailers are very much from a specific place.

For retailers, there are a number of implications of culture and its component aspects. First, as culture is absorbed, learned and transmitted from generation to generation, certain aspects of culture may become deep-rooted and thus hard to change. There are therefore boundaries on what, how or when products can be promoted or retailed. What is acceptable within societies varies.

Second, a shared culture binds some groups together and thus can provide the basis for identifying markets or market segments. The presence of different communities and particular consumer behaviour patterns in large cities across the world demonstrate the potential for group or local segmentation. Little Italy in Toronto and the various Chinatowns globally illustrate this point, but there are many smaller enclaves and groups based around a number of nationalities. In response to the increasing presence and role of a Hispanic population in southern Florida, food retailers have begun to develop more Spanish or Mexican themed, designed and run stores. Publix, a leading Florida-based supermarket chain has developed Publix Sabor a supermarket with major Hispanic influences. It is not only ethnicity, however, that can form a cultural segmentation. Aspects of 'youth culture' have proved attractive to retailers trying to target the young market. Top Shop would be a UK example, Abercrombie & Fitch a US model, but so too is Legit, a South African black urban fashion focused discount retail chain that is highly adapted to its target market.

Third, however, whilst retailing operates mainly within cultural norms and thus reflects these, retailers can also shape these cultural norms. Retail stores, operations and environments are not neutral entities, but rather can condition and structure consumer moods and behaviours and in some cases over the long-term influence cultural norms. The approaches of some stores 'develop' consumers by requiring them, implicitly or explicitly, to rethink aspects of their beliefs and attitudes. The replacement of wet markets by supermarkets in parts of Asia and the changes this signifies in consumer behaviour is one example. What was once probably unthinkable can become commonplace, as for example the presence of Ann Summers stores in high streets and shopping centres, or lovehoney.com as a 'respected' online retailer. Such operations, however, would still be seen as an outrage in many other countries.

Further examples of this in the UK include the design revolution sparked by Terence Conran's Habitat stores from the 1960s, the critical, unique and long-term importance of Marks & Spencer to British clothing manufacturing and retailing and the campaigning and ethical sensibilities overtly used by Anita Roddick and The Body Shop. These three retailers changed British society and aspects of British consumer and retail culture. IKEA, Louis Vuitton, McDonald's, 7-Eleven, Starbucks, Wal-Mart, Tesco, Zara and H&M are doing the same thing today, albeit in different ways and sectors and on an international basis. Tesco revolutionised the way in which food retailers are thought of and defined in the UK and the products and services that can be offered. By extending its brand into financial services, Tesco altered the perceptions of insurance and other financial and service products and the ways in which they could be priced and sold.

This emphasis on culture demands that retailers be embedded in the culture of the economy and society in which they operate. This may be best achieved by being part of that economy and society, or at least understanding it, and is thus mainly accomplished through an understanding of local consumers. Knowledge of what drives local consumers and what they need and want (in product and service terms) is fundamental to the operation of retailing. This embeddedness may be derived from the local operations, companies or managers or may be achieved by a thoroughly researched knowledge of the local consumer base. Whichever, there is a radical difference in retailing when compared to most other management activities and industrial sectors. In retailing the issues of consumer knowledge intrude directly into the business day in and day out. Retailing is dependent on people, both because it employs a lot of them to serve customers in stores or in fulfilment centres for online sales but also because an understanding of consumer' behaviours, attitudes and psychology are critical in most retail businesses. Failure to understand consumers and the local market means failure, full stop.

One basic constraint on the development of retailing is the demographic structure of any market. At its most simple, demographic change relates to features such as the number, age structure and location of individuals and households. For retailers, changes in these dimensions are fundamental as they affect the size and the location of their target markets. An examination of some demographic issues in Europe immediately identifies far-reaching changes in recent decades, which have major implications for the development of retailing.

First, whilst growth continues in the number of people in most countries, the rate of growth has reduced substantially since the 1960s. This can be attributed to lower birth rates, fertility levels and socio-economic changes, such as the full participation of women in the paid labour force. For retailers it means that they can no longer rely on previous assumptions of 'natural' population growth to increase market size. The battle for market share is thus much harder now as natural growth is that much slower. Where there is population growth, this may be of particular demographic origins, e.g. immigration, and the consumer behaviour patterns may be very different to the local population and require different solutions.

Second, whilst the population may still be growing, there has been a fundamental shift in its age composition. The decline in the birth rate, coupled with a reduction in child mortality, longer life expectancy and improved medical care have resulted in a much more 'elderly' population structure than before. Even though large numbers of this elderly population are more affluent and active than previous generations, retailers still have to consider how they respond to this and other population segments. The retail offer has to be adjusted to meet the changing numbers in different target markets. These different age segments have, of course, very different attitudes. Retailers have to understand these generations and their behaviours and attitudes and adjust their retail formats, locations, products and offers accordingly.

Third, consumer change can be considered at the household as well as the individual level. Demographic changes have been allied with socio-economic and lifestyle changes, such as later age of marriage and higher divorce rates, to radically restructure both the number and structure of households in most countries. There are now far more households in Europe than before, but there are fewer people (often only one person) in each of them. For retailers, this can provide selected opportunities and market growth, e.g. in furnishings, but also requires other retailers to adapt their product sizes and ranges, e.g. introduce package sizes suitable for individual consumption.

These basic demographic changes are combined with further changes in socio-economic status and lifestyle. How people live their lives has changed dramatically. Hopefully, teenage behaviour bears little resemblance to many activities carried out by previous generations of teenagers. For many groups of all ages, there are more opportunities, more choices and in some cases more affluence to enable satisfaction of needs. These needs themselves have of course altered fundamentally, and the use of technology to help satisfy these needs has been fundamental.

Examples of some of these changes include the different occupational structure of economies, together with an altered gender balance of the workforce. The distribution of income has changed both generally and between the sexes. More women are in paid employment than before and many have much greater economic power and freedom. Consumers are more educated and informed and have access to more data on choices and in real-time than ever before, especially via the internet. Of course, these changing situational factors have implications for attitudes and values and affect lifecycles and stages. The UK traditional caricature of marriage by 21, children by 25, the housewife staying at home whilst the male breadwinner works, has gone. Holidays are more likely to be in Spain or Florida than Blackpool. Curry is more commonly eaten than fish and chips. Such behaviours reflect the changed realities of living in the twenty-first century.

One particular certainty that has disappeared is the idea that whole swathes of the country would be doing the same things at the same times. Meal times previously were common. Television programmes (on three channels) were watched in huge numbers. People all dressed basically the same, often from Marks & Spencer, or worse C&A. Football matches took place at 3 p.m. on a Saturday. Telephone calls were made from home or a public phone box (for which you queued). Holidays were taken at the same time and often to the same place (Glasgow Fair Fortnight in Blackpool). Now, families eat together far less often. Digital TV and online availability has multiplied the choice of programmes to watch, and digital catch-up systems place the consumer in charge of the watching schedule and content. Other media bombard the marketplace with choice and options. Football occurs anytime, any day from across the world and is broadcast and narrowcast live and repackaged for consumption at the time and in the format the consumer decides. Mobile phones ring on trains and in lectures, and Twitter and other social media provide a running and shared commentary on activities and life. Countries may be fragmented, sectionalised and highly differentiated, but they increasingly contain a mobile, but connected society, though the connections are very different of those of previous generations. Retailers have to work much harder to identify the group commonalities that may exist and to react quickly to changing patterns, which themselves may be more diffuse and transient. They need to be able to respond to this massive change of content, control and pace.

Consumers are a dynamic grouping. Consumers change, and consumer behaviour develops over time. Norms of consumer behaviour that were once thought to be inviolate or immutable have altered considerably. As economies and societies have grown, so have consumer desires. What is important to the society or to groups of consumers has evolved. Consumers' needs and their ability to satisfy these needs, have altered dramatically giving rise to retailing concepts such as organic superstores, lifestyle shopping, farmers' markets, outlet malls, convenience stores, discounters, fast food and, of course, online retailing. At the product level, changing attitudes towards vegetarianism, meat consumption, ready meals or the acceptability of fur or products based on animal testing, are equivalent examples. More recently, as environmental concerns have continued to develop, some consumers expect retailers to act in a socially responsible and preferably sustainable way. For some, ethical retailing can be found only in small-scale local retail operations utilising local sourcing and products, but for others Fairtrade and other labels or marks are acceptable compromises.

A range of implications for retailers can be identified from these various cultural and consumer changes (see also Miller *et al.* 1998).

First, there are trends in consumption, i.e. the general structure of demand and the amount of specific goods consumed. A good example is the modern supermarket. Here, the increased product ranges in areas of ready meals and prepared foods reflect changing demand patterns. The segmentation of products by price or by other attributes, e.g. organic, gluten-free, healthy living or children's meals is a reaction to wider trends in the market. The extension of retailing into banking, insurance, health care and services, such as internet provision, mobile phone plans and top-up phone cards, also illustrates the shift in consumption towards services.

There are then implications for consumer behaviour, i.e. consumer decisions as to which of their wants they wish to satisfy and how, when and where they are going to obtain satisfaction. The most obvious change for retailers in this area has been the increasing demand for convenience. Convenience in terms of time and location has become increasingly important, giving rise to 24-hour trading, petrol station convenience stores, home and workplace delivery and small supermarkets at railway stations amongst a range of reactions. Convenience, however, also requires retailers to make it easier and simpler for consumers to obtain what they want, and it is here that the internet is having most success. Online and mobile computing has transformed the shopping experience for many consumers, raising questions over how consumers both buy and then receive products. Next-day or even next-hour delivery solutions are increasingly common, as are collection points in stores, at work, and at train stations. Convenience has become ever more demanding for the retailer to satisfy.

Third, there are changes in shopping behaviour, i.e. the consumer process during the shopping activity itself. As consumers have changed, so the elements of the retail offer that attracts them and encourages them to purchase or consume have changed. Much more attention has had to be paid by retailers to elements of store design, ambience and atmospherics generally, as well as issues to do with the balance between price, service and quality. For many, going shopping on occasions has become more of a leisure activity. Consumers expect to be more in control of the trip and, on occasions, to be entertained. The development of cafes in bookshops such as Waterstones, the redesign of the selling of a product as in Sephora, the experiential approach of Nike Town or involvement in production as in Build-A-Bear are illustrations that shopping behaviours are not solely functional activities. A similar set of concerns online have developed with consumers wanting ease of design, use, content and communication. Failure to deliver this, as in 2014 when Marks & Spencer renewed their website with disastrous outcomes, sees consumers opting to take their sales elsewhere online.

Combining these various strands of consumer change, there are now different reasons behind different shopping events and that consumers satisfy their desires in different ways and at different times (see Table 25.1). At some times, consumers need to replenish basic items and the shopping event is a highly functional one. At other times, similar items may be purchased using a different format, e.g. the same consumer might buy the same goods from a Tesco superstore, a Tesco Metro or Tesco.com, but at different times. Other shopping events are focused on the visit itself more

Table 25.1 Types of shopping events

Purpose	Reason	Product example	Format and retailer example
Essential	Replenishment of stock items; regular purchases	Food and regular household items	Food superstore (Tesco) or online grocery (Ocado)
Purposive	Major item purchase; clear purpose for event	Electrical items, major household items	Retail park (B&Q, SCS, etc.); shopping centre with department stores (House of Fraser, Argos)
Leisure (or fun)	Social activity, occasionally ancillary to visit to location	General purchases, gifts, services, tickets	Town centre; shopping centre or mall (e.g. Bluewater); leisure activity focus (museum shop, Forever 21, Manchester United Superstore, ticketmaster.com)
Convenience	Time constrained, top-up trip, everyday purchases	Ready meals, milk, bread	Convenience store (Spar); petrol station store (Shell Select); transport node store (Marks & Spencer Simply Food)
Special items	Unusual product or specialist	Local or specialist produce	Farm shop, farmers' markets, creative collective gallery (Made in Stirling)

than the shopping. Leisure in its broadest sense is critical to the experience of the event and of the shopping. Table 25.1 suggests that retailers have to be able to focus on consumers and their changing behaviours in order to continue to develop their businesses. This is much more complex than it has been in the past, as the direction, pace and dimensions of change have fragmented. It is also the case that more such shopping events have moved online, rendering the concept of a shopping trip a little ambiguous in some cases.

Retail locations and outlets

This emphasis on culture and consumers is reflected in the importance that is afforded by retailers to the places where retailing takes place – the locations of retailing. Despite the growth of online retailing, the physical shop remains a cornerstone of the sector. Chains of shops are in themselves a distinctive dimension of the retail industry, as few industries involve managing and operating such a diverse and dispersed outlet network. There are, for example, over 53,500 7-Eleven convenience stores across the world (end June 2014), with over 16,600 in Japan alone. The Body Shop operates over 2,500 outlets in 60 countries. Inditex (the parent company for Zara) has over 6,460 stores in 88 countries and employs over 128,000 people. It is hard to conceive of other businesses outside retailing having to organise and control such extensive branch networks. Whilst the old adage 'location, location, location' has probably been overplayed, it has some truth and, above all, it is an identifying characteristic of the retail trade. Retailers must understand the spaces within which consumers operate (and this includes virtual spaces) and try to match these in terms of their locational and operational decisions. Retailers thus manage the macro-location (the country, region or city), the micro-location (the store location and internal environment) and the virtual location (online, possibly internationally). In this section the macro-locational issues are considered, leaving store design and other internal store-based issues to later.

Retailing not only has a distinctive locational dimension but is also further distinguished by the diversity and dynamism of retail location. Some shop locations seem fixed in the most visible of ways as with Harrods in London, Galeries Lafayette and Printemps in Paris or Bloomingdales in New York. Others are more transient, such as street, wet or night markets, car-boot sales, farmers markets, pop-up stores and other similar activities. Whilst some street locations clearly have a retail premium, such as Ginza in Tokyo, Oxford Street in London or 5th Avenue in New York, others come and go from retail activity. Town centres and city centres are for many economies the main place of concentration of retailing and the centre of this economic and social interaction. Market spaces in British historic cities, such as Carlisle and York, or Nice and many other towns and cities in France, illustrate this well. In some economies, most notably the US, this town centre and central emphasis has been disturbed by the decentralisation of most retail activity (e.g. Longstreth 1997, 1999), driven by the introduction of the car as the main mode of shopping transport.

The most developed car-borne and thus decentralised retail economy is the US. In many town and city centres, particularly in the southern part of the US, the central area (the downtown) is a desolate, retail-free zone. The retail activity mainly occurs in regional and suburban malls and strip and power centres along important highways or at key road intersections. The historical location for retailing has thus been (often totally) replaced over time by locations that better reflect transport movements, modes and patterns, consumer preferences and retailer formats and cost structures. This locational shift has had important implications for the form of much of the retail infrastructure. Large hypermarkets, power centres, strip malls and covered shopping centres with huge car parks are a result of this process (Kowinski 2002). The internalisation and privatisation of retail space, as in a shopping mall, is a further outcome of this transformation of previously public retail space.

In the UK this process of locational decentralisation is seen quite clearly, though it is not as extensive as in the US, primarily due to more restrictive controls on retail development and a different attitude to the use of a more scarce resource, land. Retailing was for a long time a city or town centre activity, but since the Second World War, and the latter part of the twentieth century in particular, it has become more decentralised. This decentralisation is often portrayed as a series of 'waves' of types of retailing moving out-of-town (Schiller 1987; Hallsworth 1994; Fernie 1998; Thomas 2006). When people 'go shopping' now, they are as likely to be thinking of an off-centre superstore, a retail warehouse park, a regional shopping centre or a factory outlet centre as they are of the high street in the local town.

This movement away from central locations has been encouraged by a number of factors, including:

- the growth of an affluent and mobile population in suburban areas in contrast to a declining less affluent and less mobile town and city centre population;
- the development of strong corporate chains with fewer ties to a locality and more willingness and need to move shops to areas of demand and opportunity;
- changes in the methods of selling, which have seen a demand for larger stores and associated parking. Such stores are harder to accommodate in built-up areas as unit sizes and shapes have become less appropriate. It has been cheaper to build and easier to operate shops in decentralised purpose-built locations;
- the decentralisation of many non-retail activities, such as housing, offices, hotels, cinemas, leisure facilities and sports centres and schools, all of which remove footfall from the high streets and town centres, making them comparatively less desirable.

This decentralisation has been controversial as it utilises green field land in many instances, often has an adverse aesthetic impact and expands the reliance on private transport. Many consumers have embraced it, however. As a consequence, some locations, including both urban and rural situations, have seen a huge reduction in retail outlets and subsequent problems of accessibility and choice for consumers who are not mobile (economically or physically). Therefore, land-use planners have been increasingly concerned to integrate retail development within existing towns and cities. Nonetheless, the planning policies of the 1980s and 1990s resulted in large numbers of decentralised food and non-food superstores and some regional shopping centres. More recently policy has sought to control and limit out-of-town development and focus new retail space into town centres (Guy 2006; Findlay and Sparks 2014), but the rapid structural change in the sector (e.g. internet shopping) and the recession have made this problematic in some places.

There is a distinction between managed and unmanaged shopping locations. Individual shops are obviously managed. A shopping street, however, is basically a loose unmanaged collection of individual stores and thus provides a general node for shopping. Town centres are unmanaged amalgams of several such streets. However, there are also managed shopping environments. Some of these, e.g. arcades in city centres or town markets are long-standing, albeit relatively small components of the shopping panorama. Others, however, e.g. regional shopping centres and particularly those built more recently, are major retail destinations in their own right. As with other retail formats, shopping centres or malls have been getting larger. Nine of the ten largest shopping centres in the world are in Asia, with particular recent expansion in China. However, scale is no protection against market changes and some very large shopping centres have closed, particularly in the US (see www.deadmalls.org; www.mallofmemphis.org and the photo essay of Lawless 2014).

Many cities have various forms of planned shopping centres within their boundaries (see Table 25.2). For example, Buchanan Galleries in the centre of Glasgow is a major retail attraction. But, there are also decentralised locations containing shopping centres, which can draw people from large distances, and other planned environments serving a variety of functions. Gateshead's Metro Centre is an early UK off-centre regional shopping centre. The Mall at Cribbs Causeway in Bristol and Cheshire Oaks Designer Outlet Centre in the North-West of England are other examples of planned decentralised retail environments. These centres are designed, planned, branded, marketed and managed as distinctive retail locations (e.g. Bluewater in Kent, Silverburn in Glasgow). Given the recent restrictions via planning policy on out-of-town developments, however, some of the most modern planned shopping centres are in major city centres, such as The Bull Ring in Birmingham.

Across many Western countries, the twin processes of decentralisation and managed environments have transformed the retail landscape. The impact on existing locations has been considerable. As a consequence of this, there is increasing interest in whether management techniques from planned shopping centres can be applied to unplanned town centres. A number of UK towns now have town centre managers who engage in active place marketing to attract and retain consumers. Town centre management aims to market the whole of a town as a destination, including its competing retailers. Business improvements districts (BIDs) have become a more common approach in recent years, whereby existing businesses in an area collectively agree to pay an additional levy to promote and develop that area (see Donaghy *et al.* 2013). Locations rather than individual shops are thus also in competition.

Some retailers have become clear destinations in their own right and, as a result, have transformed the locational landscape wherever they develop. For example, in the UK, it used to be the case that towns fought hard to get a Marks & Spencer store, because of the spin-off benefit in increased consumer visits and prestige it brought. Marks & Spencer would receive favourable rental agreements to participate in a shopping centre scheme, whilst other retailers would then pay higher rents to locate next to the Marks & Spencer store. IKEA's arrival has the same impact in many countries. Wal-Mart Supercenters became destination stores in the US. The company has such a

Table 25.2 Types of shopping centre development

Type of shopping centre	Provision	Example (all Glasgow)
Major city-centre renewal schemes	Provide a wide range of shopping facilities adding to the provision of the existing town or city centre	Buchanan Galleries
Small in-town schemes	Usually provide specialist shopping facilities	Princes Square
Non-central-city centres (district and neighbourhood centres)	Comprise several stores and sometimes a superstore or hypermarket targeted at everyday consumption needs	Clydebank Shopping Centre
Edge-of-town and out-of-town centres (retail parks, factory outlet centres)	Typically based around one or two large superstores and containing retailers in a variety of product areas	The Forge, Glasgow Fort
Large out-of-town regional shopping centres	Create the equivalent of a new town centre outside the city	Braehead Shopping Centre, Silverburn
Centres associated with transport nodes	Built, for example, at sites such as railway stations (often within the urban area) and airports (outside it)	Central Station Concourse; Glasgow Airport

reputation that consumers will travel to it almost no matter where in a town or city it is located. The store becomes a desired destination and, if it moves, then customers follow. The hundreds of Wal-Mart stores in the US that have been closed as the company's locational and format demand has evolved, bear silent witness to their extensive construction and deconstruction of locational landscapes. These closed stores illustrate the volatility of retail demand and supply, but also the way in which some retailers can manipulate demand and consumer decision-making. They also demonstrate the difference between the US and Europe in that in the former, land is treated as a disposable asset.

Whilst location remains a key criterion of retail success, the technological revolution in shopping and retailing has begun to transform how we think about retail stores and places. As online retailing has expanded, so the virtual presence online has become a key component of retail location and the store has, in some cases, become less important, certainly in some locations. This structural revolution has questioned the number, size and location of physical stores that are needed both in absolute terms but also for every individual retailer.

We see this in a number of ways, including the strengthening of the role of the flagship fashion store, the decline in hypermarkets and the reconsideration of chain numbers by companies as diverse as Top Shop and B&Q. This process has been exacerbated and accelerated by the credit crunch/recession from 2008, which has led to many retail failures and considerable downsizing.

In the UK the visible evidence of these changing patterns is seen on many high streets, town centres and increasingly shopping centres. There are many vacancies, and we talk about the 'crisis of the high street' (Grimsey 2012), though not all places are affected equally (Wrigley and Dolega 2011). Retailers need footfall and so more accurately there is a crisis of behaviour and place, one consequence of which is to question the need for retail space and retail locations. What shops do we need to meet the changed consumer demand? What opportunities do these changes open up for new and local retailers?

In other parts of the world, however, such concerns are less prevalent and in some economies shopping mall development and retail space struggles to keep up with demand, as, for example, in Singapore and some other major Asian cities and countries. This again shows the local nature of places on which retailing depends.

Shopkeepers and retail managers

The nature of retail business is also distinctive and diverse in terms of those who take on the management and operation of retail businesses – shopkeepers and retail managers. The method of business organisation and firm type chosen has implications for resources, the scope of operations and decision-making roles and capabilities. Retailing remains numerically dominated in almost every country by independent retailers, i.e. retailers who operate single stores, with shopkeepers who are the owner and/or manager. This local form of retailing has been central to retail operations throughout history. Retailing has low entry and exit barriers. However, the independent retailer is but one form of business organisation in retailing. Five forms are generally identified (Table 25.3). The local shop run as an independent business is the mainstay in numerical terms of most retail sectors. They are located everywhere and could retail almost anything. Some are generalist shops, e.g. the corner store, whereas others are very specialist, e.g. second-hand wedding dresses.

In some countries, the government has been a major retailer controlling and operating many stores (e.g. as in the past in communist Poland), or reserving control for particular product lines (e.g. quasi-government liquor stores – the LCBO – in Ontario, Canada). Generally, however, such direct government involvement in the running of shops is rare.

Table 25.3 Retail organisational types

Type	Examples
Independent retailing	Single local shop
Government shops	LCBO (Liquor Control Board of Ontario Stores)
Corporate retailers	Marks & Spencer (public)
	Aldi (private)
Co-operatives	Co-operative Group, John Lewis Partnership
Contractual chains	Body Shop (franchise)
	Spar (affiliated group)
	NISA (buying group)

More commonly, there are corporate or multiple retailers. These are businesses operating several (or 'multiple') shops as a company entity, and thus gain from economies of scale, scope and replication. Such companies dominate the trading component of retailing in many countries and can be enormous businesses (e.g. Wal-Mart), sometimes with operations in many countries across the globe (e.g. Inditex, Carrefour or IKEA). Corporate retailers can be found operating large retail outlets, such as superstores, small stores in town centres and shopping malls and even concessions within department stores. They may be focused on particular lines of trade, e.g. JD Sports or New Look.

Historically, co-operatives have been strong in many countries and still remain important in some countries today (e.g. Finland, Denmark, Switzerland and Japan). These businesses are owned by members (often, but not always, the consumers) and typically are run for mutual benefit not shareholder profit. The Co-operative Group, with thousands of shops, dominates the co-operative movement in the UK (Wilson *et al.* 2013), although some smaller single shop societies do still exist (e.g. Grosmont in Yorkshire). The John Lewis Partnership is an example of a mutual business (Cox 2010). In some local communities, often as a response to the lack of retail facilities in an area, residents have grouped together to run a community-based shop, which may obtain logistical and other support from larger co-operatives.

Finally, many previously independent retailers have given up some degree of independence by becoming part of a contractual chain or a franchise, i.e. they are independent businesses but are supplied by, or legally linked to, a larger 'umbrella' organisation. The contractual forms vary from operation to operation (e.g. Spar, 7-Eleven Japan, Body Shop, Musgraves). All attempt to collectively maximise buying, marketing and other activities to improve overall performance, in the belief that working together, combined with independent shop ownership and its local community knowledge, enhances their competitive position. In essence, they seek the organisational benefits of the larger corporate chains, alongside the flexibility and entrepreneurial flair of the independent trader.

The convenience store sector in the UK, which has been growing rapidly and successfully in recent years, is a good example where retailers operating as part of a symbol group (e.g. Spar, Premier, Nisa) outperform the single unaffiliated independent operator (ACS 2014). In Ireland, Musgraves, a wholesaler, has used a franchise system with two formats (SuperValu and Centra) to expand significantly and to become the market leader in food retailing.

The balance of power amongst these business organisational forms varies from country to country and has altered over time. As a general rule, centrally controlled large organisations (running chains of large and small stores) have gained power and market share from other forms and particularly from independent and co-operative retailers. Corporate retailers have become the dominant commercial form in many countries. This power has been gained because of the cost and efficiency advantages of operating larger businesses under central control, e.g. in advertising, branding and operational consistency (Clarke *et al.* 2002). This illustrates the economies of scale and scope available to retailers but also suggests more distancing of the business from the local situation. The role and function of store management in a chain organisation has consequently become more critical over time, though the boundaries of central versus local control remain flexible and variable amongst multiple retailers. Independent local retailers with local knowledge and an ability to satisfy local needs and wants can be successful over a long period, and many independent retailers provide that point of difference in a high street or place. However, succession can be a problem for such retailers.

The scale of some of the leading corporate retailers is now almost hard to comprehend. Wal-Mart is the world's largest retailer. It had sales in 2013 (i.e. financial year ending 31 January 2014) of US$476 billion, operated over 6,100 stores in 26 countries, employed over 2.2 million associates, and achieved over US$26.8bn operating profit and US$16.6bn net profit. Wal-Mart reached the landmark of US$1bn annual sales in 1979, then achieved US$1bn sales in a week in 1993, before taking US$1bn in sales in a day in 2001. Given these sales figures, Wal-Mart must be doing things right in the eyes of its customers. Nonetheless, Wal-Mart as a retailer polarises opinion (Brunn 2006), with its detractors accusing it of many poor business practices and behaviours, which permit its low prices. Others believe it has been a driving force in the productivity growth in the US since the mid-1990s and has allowed lower income American consumers in particular to improve their standards of living. Notwithstanding this, there is evidence of a recent slowdown in its growth and changes in consumer reactions and patterns.

In the UK the largest and most successful retailer in recent times has been Tesco, which has achieved group sales of £71bn and pre-tax profits of more than £2.3bn. Its remarkable growth since the 1970s has seen it take over as the number one retailer in the country and in food retailing extend its market share lead over its rivals to an unprecedented extent (Seth and Randall 1999, 2005; Ryle 2013). In recent years, this growth has come at the cost of a backlash against the company, however. Its critics see it as too dominant in the country, stifling competition and forcing farmers and suppliers out of business, as Tesco use their power to extract extra margin and to make unreasonable demands. They also believe that the company drives local retailers out of business and makes retailing a standardised homogeneous experience (www.tescopoly.org). However, the company continued to expand its reach. This is mainly due to the willingness of consumers to continue to use the company and to expand their purchases with them, e.g. into non-food items and services. The last two years especially, however, coming after stagnant market share in the UK since 2007, failed internationalisation in Japan, the US and to a degree China, have been torrid and seen the company lose market share in the UK (though still at 28 per cent!), issue profit warnings and sack its CEO. The market is changing here, as elsewhere.

It should be clear from the discussion thus far that retailing is big business. This retail transformation necessarily extends to the management of retail businesses. As the scale of the retail store has increased and the scale of the retail business has grown, so too has the need for professional, well-trained management expanded. The types of skills and demands that a store manager in any organisational type has to exhibit are now very different to the shopkeepers of old. Independent shopkeepers compete in a massively competitive industry, where store management and business control principles and techniques have developed strongly in corporate and other chain businesses. Retail management skills are thus critical for success at all levels. At the very local level, independent retailers need also to hone their community engagement and local involvement skills. Their key differentiation lies in this local knowledge and embeddedness and in the difference they create versus the more standardised chains.

At the large scale end of the spectrum, a large food superstore or hypermarket could take well over £100 million in a year in sales. The store could be open 24 hours a day, 7 days a week. There might be over 600 employees on the site working a variety of shift patterns and at many different grades. The amount of product and consumers passing in and out of the store in a day is huge. The technology in the store is highly advanced and sophisticated. Yet this store is only one part of a business that could have £70bn worth of sales in a year and employ over half a million people. Its shops, marketing, buying and logistics operations are all professional and dynamic environments.

It is one of the facets of retailing, however, that the picture painted above of corporate management is but one aspect of the business. At the same time, others find their role in retailing by setting up companies, running small specialist stores or small chains and thus satisfying their own entrepreneurial and personal drive. In the UK companies such as Sock Shop, Body Shop, Evans Cycles, Cath Kidston, Cotton Traders, Hotel Chocolat, Lush, Jones the Bootmaker and Sweaty Betty have come from personal ambitions and drive to produce a better retail offer in a field that interests them. Retailing is one of the few sectors that can accommodate, and indeed needs, a variety of forms of operation and where a specialist can make a difference. Such businesses and all independent retailers, however, still require a variety of retail skills to succeed, as the retail process includes management, marketing, buying and operations.

Product sourcing, branding and distribution

> The challenge in retailing is that your customers experience your product directly . . . What they experience in the store is the brand. So stores have to be both internally and externally coherent. The way the brand is projected and advertised reflects the way it lives and works internally.
>
> (Norman 1999: 29)

The growth of large retail companies also illustrates another fundamental difference between retailing and other forms of business. To a much greater extent than, for example, manufacturing, retailers have to construct strategies for developing and managing multi-plant operations with much greater variety and variability in concepts and transactions (Reynolds and Cuthbertson 2004). Retail management at the highest level is very different to other production-based businesses and, at the local level, is much more open to local demand vicissitudes. The role of computer technology and systems in data capture and transmission and in chain control has therefore increased substantially.

The business of retailing involves the selection and assembly of goods for sale to customers, i.e. the process of product sourcing and distribution. This process is also one dominated by variety – of types of good, sourcing strategy and product mix. Retailers sell a wide variety of items. Some are concentrated in a narrow line of business (specialist stores, e.g. Lush) or a sector (e.g. Cath Kidston, Hollister, Oliver Bonas), whereas others are much wider in their scope (general stores, e.g. Asda/Wal-Mart, Debenhams). In any event, retailers have to source products for their product range. This involves dealing with particular suppliers (perhaps local suppliers), with wholesalers or other forms of intermediary.

The products that are sourced have changed over time. Whilst there always has been a market for exotic and non-local products, the expectations of many consumers and the abilities of many retailers have transformed the supply position. A reliance on local (i.e. immediate area) sourcing is now not the normal relationship. For many retailers, products from around the world are standard elements to be included in the product mix. Some would question the economic, cultural and environmental impacts of this to both the origin and the destination countries (e.g. Klein 1999), and there is rising concern over the desirability and sustainability of such practices. The concept of 'food miles' (the mileage of food before it reaches the consumer or the plate) has become synonymous with unsuitable and out-of-season sourcing of food and environmentally unsustainable practices. Retail opportunities focused on local food arise as a consequence of this, e.g. farmers' markets, independent local operations such as Weetons (www.weetons.com) and places like Todmorden reviving their community through local food (Warhurst and Dobson 2014). However, as yet there is only limited evidence of mass consumers factoring such issues into their purchasing patterns, though this is changing. The continued rise of farmers' and other markets, direct farm supply to consumers, and a general rising concern over traceability and authenticity, encouraged by events such as the horse-meat scandal of 2013, point to this expanding interest.

As retailers have become larger, and as their abilities have increased, they have been better able to exploit international product sourcing and buying opportunities. For many non-food products, the costs of production are much lower in countries outside the developed world, and it therefore makes economic sense to manufacture abroad (e.g. in Bangladesh, Laos, Vietnam and, of course, China) and transport the product long distances to stores. Thus, many clothing manufacturers in many countries have relocated factories to Asia or elsewhere, to meet the needs of consumers and retailers for cheap products. The management and logistics problems this creates are resolvable by retailers, but there has been consumer concern over exploitation of cheap labour in some locations and the loss of indigenous jobs, as well as recently over environmental issues. Concerns arise mainly over the conditions in which products are manufactured, and the use of, for example, child labour in 'sweat shops'.

In 2013 there was a collapse of a garment manufacturing plant (in Rana Plaza) in Dhaka, Bangladesh, with over 1,100 deaths. The standards and safety of this plant, producing clothes for Western retailers, were sharply criticised, as was the lack of oversight or concern of these Western retailers. Whilst a massive tragedy for the families involved, and some hand wringing from retailers, there is little evidence that mass consumption was at all affected. This is clearly not a desirable or a sustainable situation. Environmental and social rising concerns may in due course spark a wider re-evaluation by consumers of what they value, but this would require in most cases a need to look beyond obtaining products at the lowest price. Retailers, therefore, are under pressure both to make sure they act appropriately and to remain aware of changing consumer feelings on these issues, but at the same time to keep prices at a level their customers accept.

Whilst clothing production is an obvious example of products being sourced from far afield, the same is also true of food. Any British supermarket contains many non-UK or non-EU products. Control of the supply chain is thus vital to get products to the stores in good condition. This process of retailer control of supply systems and the use of computer technology for control of central distribution have been key features of recent years. In this respect, British logistics systems are amongst the most economically efficient in the world (Fernie and Sparks 2014).

In addition to control over the range and location of products, retailers have extended their influence over the contents of the product. Claims for organic production, sustainable forests and Fairtrade origins require control, often extending to audited codes of conduct for supplier inputs and methods of production. As societal and consumer concerns change, the retailer needs to source, manage and guarantee products, which meet these needs. There is now evidence that organic products have become more 'mainstream' in retailing, as consumer demand has expanded. Specialist retailers such as Whole Foods have had tremendous success, mainly in the US, even forcing retailers such as Wal-Mart to develop its organic range. In the UK and the rest of Europe organic and Fair Trade products have grown strongly and become a standard part of the food retailer's range. There remain issues, however, over the use of such products as a marketing message by some retailers, particularly when the products are imported or travel long distances rather than being locally produced and sourced.

In obtaining products, retailers have choices to make over what products to sell but also under what name to sell them. Many products carry the manufacturer's name or brand. Retailers, however, have become increasingly aware of the potential in supplying products produced under their own control and specification. The approach to retailer branding varies across the globe, but many retailers are becoming much more involved in managing and marketing their own retail names or brands (Burt and Sparks forthcoming). For a retailer, the name used on the product could have limited direct meaning, but increasingly retailers sell products that carry their own name (e.g. Asda, Marks & Spencer) or a brand they own and have developed (e.g. George, Per Una), recognising the potential for promotion, advertising and market positioning. Retail branding is extensive in clothing. Next, Mango, Gap, Zara, Benetton and H&M retail brands are well known. Retail branding is now becoming more extensive in other retail product sectors and some retail businesses are effectively collections of brands.

Retail branding in the UK is generally recognised to be more extensive than in many other countries and to take a larger share of sales (Burt 2000; Ailawadi and Keller 2004; Burt and Davies 2010; Burt and Sparks forthcoming). In food retailing a core product branding strategy has emerged that involves the development of three price and quality points. As Table 25.4 shows, all the leading food retailers have followed this approach. Initially, retail product branding was low quality, sometimes even generic product, designed to capture the attention of very price conscious consumers (though quality design was still a feature in, for example, Sainsbury – see Trunk 2011). This was followed by a movement slightly upmarket to target the leading manufacturer brands with a product of almost similar quality, priced just below the manufacturer's prices. In time, retail product developers began to copy the leading brands a little too closely, but by then retailers had also become aware that consumers were reacting well to their own branded products. It is from this base that the tri-position (good, better, best in the words of the retailers!) brand strategy has emerged. As Table 25.4 shows, products are priced and positioned at three levels to attract the economy consumer (e.g. 'Value' lines), the mainstream consumer (e.g. Tesco) and the 'luxury' or high quality consumer (e.g. 'Finest'). This tri-position brand strategy has also been extended into non-food and service lines, e.g. Finest credit card and Value mobile phone plan. Most of these retailers have also added to this brand approach by segmenting markets on dimensions other than price. Examples in Tesco include healthy living, organic, ingredients, free from, etc.

Retailers have also learned that as consumers have recognised and trusted their product branding, so there is an opportunity to extend the brand in other different ways. This is seen most clearly in the developments in financial and other services. Retailers have thus become banks, investment houses, lifestyle helpers, telecoms and internet solution providers and so on. At the store level, some retailers have segmented the market and adjusted store sizes and locations to meet perceived shopping needs. In Tesco's case, the store portfolio is branded under the core brand of Tesco and

Table 25.4 Retailers product brand segmentation strategies in the UK food sector

	Premium	*Core*	*Value*
Tesco	Finest	Tesco	Everyday Value
Morrisons	Signature	Morrisons	Morrisons Savers
Sainsbury	Taste the Difference	by Sainsbury's	Basics
Asda	Extra Special	Asda Chosen by You	Smart Price

attempts to live up to its strapline 'every little helps', through formats such as Extra, Express and Metro. In essence, this business and others like it are attempting to move away from thinking about product branding to thinking about corporate branding (Burt and Sparks 2002, forthcoming).

The importance of the perception of quality in the eyes of the British consumer in terms of retail product brands should not be underestimated. There has been phenomenal growth in the retail brand products. To some extent, this has always been the case, with the prime example being the St Michael brand from Marks & Spencer. However, after the problems of Marks & Spencer in the late 1990s, the company quietly dropped St Michael as the only brand in the store and instead are using a segmentation strategy based around the name Marks & Spencer and other specialist inhouse brands, such as Per Una. In a different way, the experience in the UK of Aldi, the German discount retailer, makes the same point. Aldi's strategy has been based around inhouse brands and product names with limited if any co-ordination. The packaging and approach, including perhaps of quality, reflected the hard discount emphasis. For UK consumers there was considerable resistance to purchasing products with unknown and often foreign sounding names. In 2006 Aldi introduced a co-ordinated and well-designed brand position across parts of their range, using a colour scheme that mimics Tesco's Finest and other retailers, and entitled 'Specially Selected'. This has received strong consumer acceptance and, partly due to this and the adjustment in consumer perceptions and also the onset of the recession in 2008, Aldi (and other discounters, such as Lidl, and non-food, Poundland) has done very well in recent years.

Business relationships and loyalty

> Sainsbury, which has tried loyalty cards to attract customers to new stores, yesterday dismissed them as 'electronic Green Shield stamps' that represented poor value for money. It has no plans to introduce them nationally, it said.
>
> (*The Independent*, 11 February 1995: 6)

As has been suggested, the process of retailing involves relationships with other businesses and groups. These too have their own distinctive characteristics arising from the nature of retailing. The requirement to source products, combined with issues over branding, inevitably means that retailers are concerned with relationships with business partners, as well as relationships with employees and consumers. These business relationships can take many forms and many variants, but essentially retailers can choose to have either collaborative or transactional (sometimes conflictual) relationships. In short, either retailers can work with partners to achieve shared objectives, or they can use their position alone to operate their business to achieve their own ends.

For example, product sourcing involves a number of elements, but retailers are attempting to purchase and obtain product at a given price and quality position. For some retailers price is the overriding concern and retailers will always seek the lowest price for products they know their customers will purchase. This means that the relationships they have with individual suppliers are often transient and focus on transactional price components alone. The relationship in that sense is straightforward, but often comes down to a conflict about price.

More complex, but of importance to many retailers, is the notion of a collaborative relationship with suppliers, which involves all parties in something rather more than simply a transaction based on price. The relationship might be to secure a source of supply or to obtain a given quality and quantity of a product. It might be to develop a product line, to ensure product consistency and quality, to enable flexibility of supply, or to allow access to a unique product. If a retailer is branding the product, then the collaborative arrangement may be about ensuring certain quality standards. For many retailers, therefore, whilst price will be very important, there could well be other aspects of the business relationship, which need to be in place. Some of these relationships or partnerships are long-standing and have involved extensive product development and resulted in the consequent growth of both partners.

Retailers, of course, have business relationships beyond product sourcing. Relationships exist with an array of service providers. Finance is one example, with independent retailers seeking bank finance and multiple or corporate retailers searching for institutional finance to enable them to develop their store portfolios. With retail sites being highly expensive to rent, buy or develop, retailers need to secure such institutional funding. One of the most important relationships occurs in the physical supply of products to the retailer. Product sourcing in a transactional sense has been identified above, but products have to be delivered to the retail store to be available for merchandising and for sale. Logistics systems and logistics providers, therefore, may be key components of another set of business relationships (Fernie and Sparks 2014). As might be imagined, with product sourcing complexities, expansion in the number of stores and spatial breadth in many companies and the increased expectations of consumers with respect to product quality and availability, supply chain management has become more and more important. For many retailers, being in retailing is sufficient, and logistics systems are often outsourced to these logistics services providers. Whilst many vehicles are seen on roads carrying retailer logos and livery, most of them are owned and operated by contractual logistics services partners.

These relationships in the supply chain can be critical to the nature of the retail performance. In recent years companies such as Zara and H&M, and in different ways Asos.com and Primark, have redefined the parameters of the fashion supply chain. The advent of 'fast fashion', with an emphasis on speed through the supply chain from design to production to purchase, has forced relationships and competitors to change (Bhardwaj and Fairhurst 2010). When Zara's supply chain is measured in days and weeks, other retailers with slower chains, e.g. months and years, will inevitably fall behind in consumer popularity.

Customer relationships have become increasingly important to retailers. Historically, whilst retailers were in competition with each other on a local level, customers were less mobile and less volatile or promiscuous in their patronage. As a result, there was a degree of certainty or relationship with the local store or local co-operative. As consumers changed behaviours and utilised their increased mobility and choice (including most recently via online shopping), so retailers have been less able to depend on certainty of demand. In such circumstances, large retailers have tried to identify, brand and get to know their customers.

One of the main mechanisms for the development of this relationship has been the 'loyalty' scheme or card. These have been enormously popular with some retailers and attempt to build a relationship with individual customers. The depth of this relationship may often be exaggerated, but retailers hope that by being a member of a company loyalty scheme, the customer will behave more loyally and shop around less. In turn, the retailer gains data on which to base strategic and tactical decision-making. For this knowledge and potential change in behaviour, retailers give customers some reward, usually a small dividend on purchase volume, but occasionally rights to buy products from a catalogue or to use their points in other ways. The modern loyalty card is a product both of consumer change and technology development. In essence, large retailers are using systems to identify customers. This is a practice or advantage that the best local retailers have almost instinctively. But, the advent of cheap but large computer systems has enabled large retailers to replicate these advantages.

There are many large loyalty card schemes across the world. In the UK Boots the Chemist's Advantage Card has almost 18 million active cardholders and is used in 60 per cent of sales transactions in the company. The Tesco Clubcard scheme (Humby *et al.* 2003) has probably 15 million members in the UK (it also operates in some other countries) and has been credited with helping the retailer attain a dominant market position. The information received on purchase patterns has been vital in adjusting the product, store and other offers and in targeted and micro-marketing activities. The data to some extent is the heart of the business strategy.

Other retailers have not been so convinced by the idea or practice of loyalty cards. Their argument is that it is an expensive way to learn about consumer behaviour, provides only partial data and does not really engender loyalty per se. Businesses such as Sainsbury, Asda, Morrisons and the Co-operative Group have at different times switched their views on the value of such schemes. The evidence, however, would seem to point to loyalty schemes being successful when managed and integrated fully with the business.

The consumer focus that a loyalty scheme can bring allows retailers to track mobile consumers as they shop in different ways across the company. Thus, for example, as Tesco has developed their various formats and channels (e.g. Metro, Express, Extra, Direct, Homeplus, Telecoms, etc.) so the Clubcard can be used as the connective mechanism to track consumers and their patterns of shopping. Such data, whilst somewhat problematic in both privacy and practical terms at the individual level (e.g. see Smith and Sparks 2004), does allow a strong degree of segmentation and a fuller understanding of actual and potential behaviours (Humby *et al.* 2003).

This loyalty relationship has been challenged in the last few years as consumers have become more volatile in their behaviours, driven by a combination of technology change, consumer priorities and the recession. So mobile shopping demands more from retailers and makes obtaining data about all patterns of behaviour more problematic (though retailers and others are catching up to this). The renewed and enhanced focus on price, as seen in the rise of discounters and retailers such as Poundland and Aldi, has provided a more fundamental test of loyalty behaviour.

Merchandising and selling

For many outside retailing, selling is often viewed as the same as retailing; selling is, however, one component of the retail operation. Selling itself varies of course, with the move to self-service in many product categories and retailers reducing the role of direct sales personnel in the store. In other retailers, the product knowledge and sales skills of the staff are critical in the delivery of customer service and the repeat patronage of consumers. The art and science of selling and the quality of the sales staff are of fundamental importance for much business success. In other situations, the lack of quality or knowledge of the staff acts as a negative influence on consumers. Online, the nature of selling is different again, reflecting visual and other descriptors, availability and the delivery of service promises.

Store and selling design varies enormously by situation (Underhill 1999). The emphasis on design, staff knowledge and staff competency may be vital in some situations, but of no consequence in others. The retail offer has become more disparate overall, as retailers have attempted to match their offer to the demands of the customer. Some stores are dramatic (e.g. Abercrombie & Fitch, Girl Heaven), some are functional (e.g. Aldi or Lidl), others playful (e.g. Build-A-Bear, Disney or REI). Some have many staff selling; others simply have takers of money. All, however, are based on retailers' understanding of what works with their customers.

Store-based selling has its own distinctive characteristics. How the product is merchandised and the ways in which design and display interact are important to attracting consumers and obtaining their custom. As a result, much effort is expended in laying out the store and in ensuring that products are presented appropriately. This presentation includes aspects of visual display, as well as essential product information. Depending on the product lines involved and the approach of the retailer, such merchandising may be of lesser or greater importance. Even in supposedly simple retailer situations, e.g. markets, product display can be sophisticated and help consumers make choices amongst 'stores' and products. Online retailers have similar selling objectives, but a different set of tasks and expectations to manage, with technological developments enhancing the potential interaction on the screen. Increasingly, these online attributes of enhanced visuality and interaction are being introduced into stores with plasma screens, touch panels, iPad displays, beacon guidance, real-time information, etc.

Store merchandising and display techniques condition the retail environment in every store. Some of the techniques are rather obvious and relatively easy to identify, whereas others are far more subtle and difficult to discern (Underhill 1999). Visual merchandising and design direct attention and movement by leading customers around and through the merchandise. 'Hot spots' in the store are created to 'drag' people through the shop and grab their attention. Lighting, music and visual effects are used in some stores to alter the mood of sections of shops. Colour is used to create an environment or an image. Touch is encouraged to exploit the tactile senses. Even smells are used to evoke responses, whether perfume, cosmetics or coffee and fresh bread. Some designs and displays may be organised to recreate remembered activities or past situations and provoke positive responses. In short, stores are not abstract collections of products, but rather managed selling environments designed to stimulate customer reactions and purchase. Fashion chains are often very good at this, e.g. Hollister. Possibly some of the most managed, yet involving, retail environments are found in flagship stores (Kozinets *et al.* 2002; Borghini *et al.* 2009; Kent and Brown 2009), especially of the fashion houses. For example, in Nike Town all aspects of the environment are managed to create a mix of a store, museum and interactive play zone (Sherry 1998; Peñaloza 1999). To fit with such an approach, employees and design have to support the brand marketing at every stage.

The state of the retail world

The description so far of the process of retailing has pointed to both the major functional areas of retail business activity and to some of the changes that have been taking place in the sector, and their implications for consumers (see also Clarke 2000; Clarke *et al.* 2006; Jackson *et al.* 2006). These can be summarised into a number of key issues.

First, recent decades have seen an enormous change in the location of retailing. Retailing takes place now in very different locations than previously. There has been a broad trend of decentralisation of retail locations and the rise of superstores and shopping centres. Other emerging retail locations include sports stadia (e.g. Manchester United Superstore), hospitals, airports (e.g. Heathrow) and museums or heritage sites (e.g. Britannia shop at Ocean Terminal, Leith). Less planned activities occur in open-air markets, car-boot sales, farmers markets, some charity shops and other, sometimes transient, events, e.g. pop-up shops. Retailing locations today have been transformed away from the high street and even the shopping centre.

Second, there has been an alteration in the formats through which retailing takes place. Shops and shopping today are not like the shops and shopping of previous times (e.g. Walsh 2011), and retailer strategies have become more segmented. Sainsbury, amongst others, has reacted to consumer change by developing and operating a range of format/locational store types. They differ in scale, design, technique and approach. Halfords has three store formats and sizes (Super, High St, Metro) to capture different consumers and/or different shopping patterns. Much effort has been expanded by large retailers to develop and transform the small shop as part of their corporate approach to retailing, as, for example, in Tesco. Even in catalogue retailing this format change has occurred, with the decline of the huge, agency, Grattans-style catalogue and its replacement by narrowly targeted 'specialogues', e.g. Artigiano, Toast, Cotton Traders or retailer brand channels, e.g. Next Directory. The online channel adds another dimension to shopping and the idea of what a shop is.

Third, retailers have increased in scale and power. They have grown enormously in size, often being larger than the manufacturers who supply them. Even in a short span of time, the scale of growth is remarkable (Table 25.5). UK retailing is dominated by these large and often food-based businesses. Through their scale, they can reorganise various relationships to suit themselves. This scale of operation brings practical and financial benefits to the business. The scale has increased

Table 25.5 The UK's largest retailers 1990/1 and 2013

(a) 2013

Rank	Name	UK sales (billion pounds)	UK stores (number)	UK sales area (million sq. ft)
1	Tesco	64.82	2,948	37.59
2	J. Sainsbury	23.30	1,106	20.34
3	ASDA*	22.80	565	20.96
4	Morrisons	18.11	498	13.42
5	Kingfisher Group	10.57	1,025	59.85
6	Marks & Spencer	10.02	1,253	22.48
7	Co-operative Group	7.44	2,816	10.78
8	Alliance Boots	6.54	2,476	8.54
9	Home Retail Group	5.47	748	2.74
10	John Lewis Partnership	3.04	40	4.58

* Owned by Wal-Mart

(b) 1990/1

Rank	Name	UK sales (billion pounds)	UK stores	UK sales area (million sq. ft)
1	J. Sainsbury	6.84	369	10.06
2	Tesco	6.35	384	9.66
3	Marks & Spencer	4.89	288	9.47
4	Argyll Group*	4.49	1,113	8.37
5	ASDA	4.34	365	10.27
6	Isosceles**	3.11	758	7.31
7	Kingfisher	3.11	2,095	19.20
8	Boots the Chemist	2.98	2,266	N/A
9	John Lewis Partnership	1.97	116	3.51
10	Sears	1.87	3,432	N/A

Notes: * Argyll Group became Safeway, which merged with Morrisons; ** Isosceles became Somerfield, which was taken over by The Co-operative Group.

Source: 1990/1 from Retail Intelligence/Mintel The UK Retail Rankings, 1992. Data for 2013 downloaded from www.retaileconomics.co.uk/top10-retailers.asp on the 8 October 2014.

to another level, with major mergers or takeovers on the international stage, e.g. Wal-Mart of Woolco in Canada and Asda in the UK; the merger of Carrefour and Promodes in France; and the expansion of other retailers across the world.

The world's leading retailers are now amongst some of the biggest organisations around and have an increasingly international approach (Dawson *et al.* 2003, 2006; Dawson and Mukoyama 2014). It is not just the scale of these retail organisations that is remarkable but the breadth of their business in spatial terms. This is shown in Table 25.6 which lists the largest retailers in the world in 2012 (the latest date for comparable data), the fastest growing over the last five years and the top e-retailers. The scale of Wal-Mart is immediately notable, as is the dominance of US-based retailers in the listing of largest retailers. This reflects the size of their national market. Table 25.6 also shows the different approach to internationalisation adopted by US and European firms. The listing of fastest growing retailers is more diverse than the largest ten, with retailers from many countries, although again the US is prevalent. This listing shows also that convenience and food chains have been developing rapidly, although probably the most notable companies are Apple and Amazon, neither of which would have been seen as a retailer even a few years ago. Amazon also appears in the final part of Table 25.6, which lists the largest e-retailers in the world. Table 25.6 again highlights the scale from the US but also the presence of traditional as well as new retailers. Three of the companies are pure-play online retailers, whereas others are multi-channel.

The first and third parts of Table 25.6 also draw attention to internationalisation. Traditional store-based internationalisation has increasingly been supplemented and/or replaced by online international retailing, with country specific sites or the ability to purchase and ship internationally. This adds other dimensions to competition and scale as well as to the operational practicalities.

It needs to be noted, however, that internationalisation is not always easy and successful. Indeed, failures and market exits are surprisingly common (Burt *et al.* 2004), even with high profile businesses. In 2006 Wal-Mart, for example, pulled out of Korea and Germany. Marks & Spencer endured a torrid exit from various markets in the early 2000s (Burt *et al.* 2002). Ahold, once one of the major 'stars' of grocery retailing internationalisation, has been forced to divest several markets (Wrigley and Currah 2003). Tesco has retrenched from the US, Japan and to an extent China in recent years. Various reasons behind these failures and exits can be put forward, but common themes include consumer acceptance of the transferability of store image across national boundaries and the required degree of format and product standardisation or adaptation (Salmon and Tordjman 1989). Conversely, companies that are seen to be locally embedded (Coe and Lee 2006, 2013; Wood *et al.* 2014) have a stronger chance of success.

Finally, there are obviously impacts of these trends. These impacts are felt at different levels. International activity affects the retail landscape at the local level. The nature of competition and availability is such that all elements of the retail sector interact and affect consumers everywhere. Who gains and loses from this local, national and international reconstruction of the retail landscape? There has to be concern about the quality of products available for people to buy, both in terms of what is available to them but also in terms of where it is made and under what conditions. What future is there for the local, indigenous retailers and should they be protected from multinational retail entries? Retailing has changed and, whilst there have been major benefits of the new system there are dangers and problems as well (see the Special Issue edited by Coe (2014) for examples).

Table 25.6 World's largest and fastest growing retailers

(a) Largest in 2012

Rank	Company	Country of origin	Retail sales (US$ billion in 2012)	Number of countries with stores	% revenue from foreign operations
1	Wal-Mart	USA	469.162	28	29
2	Tesco	UK	101.269	13	34
3	Costco	USA	99.137	9	28
4	Carrefour	France	98.757	31	54
5	Kroger	USA	96.751	1	0
6	Schwarz	Germany	87.236 e	26	58
7	Metro	Germany	85.832	32	62
8	Home Depot	USA	74.754	5	11
9	Aldi	Germany	73.035 e	17	59
10	Target	USA	71.960	1	0

(b) Fastest growing 2007–2012

Rank	Company	Country of origin	Retail sales (US$ billion in 2012)	Dominant format	Top 250 rank
1	Jumbo	Netherlands	8.950	Supermarket	114
2	Chongqing	China	4.340	Department store	209
3	Steinhoff	South Africa	7.952	Other speciality	125
4	Apple	USA	18.828	Electronics speciality	50
5	Amazon	USA	58.570	Non-store	16
6	OJSC Dixy	Russia	4.752	Supermarket	192
7	OJSC Magnit	Russia	14.424	Convenience/ forecourt	65
8	Bi-Lo	USA	9.870	Supermarket	102
9	BiM	Turkey	5.506	Discount store	167
10	China Resources Enterprise	Hong Kong	10.754	Hypermarket/ superstore	93

(c) Top e-retailers 2012

Rank	Company	Country of origin	e-commerce sales (US$ billion in 2012)	e-commerce sales as % of total sales	Top 250 rank
1	Amazon	USA	51.733	100%	16
2	Apple	USA	8.600	31.4%	50
3	Wal-Mart	USA	7.500	1.6%	1
4	Otto	Germany	7.410	57.1%	75
5	Beijing Jingdong	China	6.663	100%	142
6	Tesco	UK	4.761	4.7%	2
7	Liberty	USA	4.397	43.9%	99
8	Dell	USA	4.370	100%	207
9	Groupe Casino	France	3.422	6.4%	20
10	Jia.com	China	3.204	100%	n/a

Source: Deloitte (2014), Global Powers of Retailing 2014: Retail Beyond Begins.

Future retailing

The increasing scale of leading retailers is a good place to start any consideration of the future of retailing (Dawson 2000; Krafft and Mantrala 2006). Scale provides big benefits to retailers – if it is managed correctly. There are, however, dangers to huge scale. In particular, the management of retailing across continents and businesses is not a simple task. The pursuit of scale in retailing is likely to continue, but, as noted above, management has to be careful of how the organisation operates and relates to local consumers, as well as to consumer reactions.

Retailing in many countries may also be challenged by an oversupply of retail floor space and by turbulence in the environment. Retailing has gone through a period of major change. This process is not complete, and competition and volatility are ever-present in the market. For retailers, this is a major challenge. It is not helped by the tendency in recent decades to build more and more new stores in new locations. The retailing this 'replaces' remains to some degree. Some of the new developments were not well sited and/or were speculative development. Some of the 'old' space is simply left derelict. There is thus too much retail space, though conversely not enough high quality locations. Being in the right place at the right cost is a management headache.

In Western countries it has come to be realised that the changing patterns mean that some retailers need far fewer stores to meet demands. The growth of the internet and changing consumer behaviours make fewer stores more sensible for some retailers, e.g. Top Shop, B&Q. In some locations this has led to a cascading removal of chain stores from high streets; the process of adjustment to this is only now getting underway. Many companies have downsized their store portfolios and are seeking to link multi-channel operations to their activities. This is proving a challenge for those involved in town centre management, high streets and other place-based activities (Dobson 2015).

Retail management and marketing is also concerned with the activities the company undertakes. The impact of these activities is now becoming a major consumer and governmental concern. Retailers are under pressure to improve their environmental and social awareness activities and to minimise adverse effects of their business. Concerns about global production and sourcing, labour practices and the need for adaptation to local situations are increasing. Ethical and environmental concerns are increasing and in some cases have resulted in legislation, e.g. carrier bag charges. Some environmental actions are clearly beneficial for retailers, e.g. energy reduction, with companies striving to build the most energy-efficient stores. Other actions, e.g. reduction of food miles, traffic light labelling of 'unhealthy' food, 'Western' wages in 'Eastern' factories, tobacco display control, alcohol selling hours, are more problematic. One thing is clear: the environmental issues of retailing and consumers' use of retailers is going to remain high on the future retail agenda.

Any discussion of the future of retailing has to consider the issue of the continued impact of e-retailing or internet shopping. In the run-up to 2000, there was both spectacular hype and then the equally spectacular fall of many internet operations. Both the hype and the fall were probably overdone. Profitable internet retailers exist and the sector continues to develop strongly as the data in Table 25.6 show. Two of the most visited UK retail internet sites are Tesco and Argos, both of whom have added e-retailing to their existing channels of operations, enabling them to increase their product and customer range. Amazon and eBay are major retail players in the UK. Some specialist operators, including quite small and local businesses, are doing well. Many retailers would now describe themselves as multi-channel or even omni-channel. Whilst there seems to be an appetite in the UK and elsewhere for the internet as a shopping medium, the true extent to which it will eventually challenge, complement or replace existing retailing remains open to question. Though, as Figure 25.1 shows, there has been a relentless rise thus far in the UK, and many businesses are predicting 20 per cent of sales via the internet by 2020.

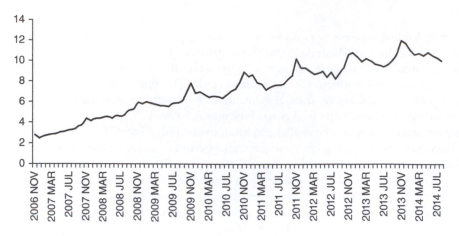

Figure 25.1 UK internet retail sales as a percentage of total retail sales

Source: ONS retail sales data.

One of the reasons why the full impact of e-retailing is as yet undecided is that there remain issues about the form and functions that need to be performed and the costs of these. Some have developed pure internet-based operations, e.g. amazon.co.uk. Others initially developed an internet operation on the back of existing activity, but with specialist picking facilities, e.g. Sainsbury. Tesco chose to add the internet channel to their existing store-based operation and to initially focus picking of orders and delivery from local stores. With the expanded ranges now provided online, they now also use their distribution network for picking and delivery of non-store carried products. Where volumes have proved to be too high for local stores to cope with, e.g. in highly dense urban networks, some so-called 'dark stores' have been opened. These focus on picking for internet delivery only and do not serve 'real' customers in the store. Click and Collect has proved a huge success for many retailers, linking online with the physical store network, or with collection lockers. These different models may be suitable in different circumstances, though concern in all cases remains about the mechanics (and profitability) of picking and delivery.

A good example of the ways in which retailers are having to think more about how they service customers via the internet comes from the citation for Asos when they won the Grand Prix Prize at the Hermes Retail Week Supply Chain Awards 2014:

> Asos has pushed back the next-day delivery cut-off from 9pm to 10pm; extended its evening next-day delivery service to service 99 per cent of customers seven days a week; offered a next-day delivery to Collect+ stores option if ordered by 6pm; and become an early adopter of DPD's Follow My Parcel 15 minute delivery window.

The judges commented that '(Asos) has delivered record-breaking peak volumes and customer experiences in both fulfilment and returns, not to mention pioneering market-leading delivery propositions all over the world' (*Retail Week* 10 October 2014: 43).

The internet has become an important factor in shopping and retailing in the UK and elsewhere. Whilst much depends on what is included in retail sales over the internet, the increase has been sustained and remarkable, both for individual retailers and overall (Figure 25.1). Individual retailers see most of their growth coming from the internet and have worked hard to seamlessly integrate their systems and activities. Internet sales are, however, but one component of this shifting arena; social media has become a major space for discussions, interactions, complaints, marketing, branding, launches, shows and so on. Increasingly, retailers are expected to be engaged in real and virtual activities.

However, this is not without concern for retailers. As retailers are challenged more across platforms and as volatile, restless and demanding consumers seek out what satisfies them, so too the control and power in the situation inexorably moves more towards the consumer and the range of services and options has to more closely fit individual consumer's needs. Consumers are perhaps more in control of the retail channel than ever before.

Summary

This chapter set out to introduce the subject and context of retailing. Retailing has undergone major change in form and to some extent function in recent decades. Components of this include:

- growth of particular organisational types;
- dominance of the market by major multiple retailers who continue to grow in scale;
- increasing internationalisation of retailing activity;
- a variety of responses to the changing consumer patterns of demand;
- an increasing professionalisation of management, including marketing, in many retail businesses;
- growing integration of internet retailing and shopping activities.

Retailing is a major component of the economies of many countries. Individuals experience retailing every day through their shopping activity. It has come to hold a higher place in people's minds, as it has been transformed from a functional sector providing necessities to one that provides a range of experiences and opportunities. With its close understanding of consumers, retailing continues to change and fascinate in equal measure. Retailers' practice of marketing has similarly to adapt to these new realities.

References

ACS (2014), *The Local Shop Report 2014*, Farnborough, UK: ACS.

Ailawadi, K. L. and Keller, K. L. (2004), 'Understanding retail branding: conceptual insights and research priorities', *Journal of Retailing*, 80(4): 331–342.

Bhardwaj, V. and Fairhurst, A. (2010), 'Fast fashion: Response to changes in the fashion industry', *The International Review of Retail, Distribution and Consumer Research*, 20(1): 165–173.

Borghini, S., Diamond, N., Kozinets, R. V., McGrath, M. A., Muniz, A. M. and Sherry, J. F. Jr (2009), 'Why are themed brandstores so powerful? Retail brand ideology at American Girl Place', *Journal of Retailing*, 85(3): 363–375.

Brunn, S. (ed.) (2006), *Wal-Mart World: The World's Biggest Corporation in the Global Economy*, New York: Routledge.

Burt, S. L. (2000), 'The strategic role of retail brands in British grocery retailing', *European Journal of Marketing*, 34(8): 875–890.

Burt, S. L. and Sparks, L. (2002), 'Corporate branding, retailing and retail internationalisation', *Corporate Reputation Review*, 5(2/3): 194–212.

Burt, S. L. and Sparks, L. (2003), 'Power and competition in the UK retail grocery market', *British Journal of Management*, 14(3): 237–254.

Burt, S. L. and Davies, K. (2010), 'From the retail brand to the retail-er as a brand: Themes and issues in retail branding research', *International Journal of Retail and Distribution Management*, 38(11/12): 865–878.

Burt, S. L. and Sparks, L. (forthcoming), 'Retail branding', in Dall'Olmo Riley, F., Singh, J. and Blankson, C. (eds) *The Routledge Companion to Brand Management*, London: Routledge.

Burt, S. L., Dawson, J. A. and Sparks, L. (2004), 'The international divestment activities of European grocery retailers', *European Management Journal*, 22(5): 483–492.

Burt, S. L., Mellahi, K., Jackson, T. P. and Sparks, L. (2002), 'Retail internationalisation and retail failure: Issues from the case of Marks & Spencer', *International Review of Retail, Distribution and Consumer Research*, 12: 191–219.

Clarke, I. (2000), 'Retail power, competition and local consumer choice in the UK grocery sector', *European Journal of Marketing*, 34(8): 975–1002.

Clarke, I., Hallsworth, A., Jackson, P., de Kervenoael, R., Perez del Aguila, R. and Kirkup, M. (2006), 'Retail restructuring and consumer choice 1: Long term changes in consumer behaviour: Portsmouth 1980–2002', *Environment and Planning A*, 38(1): 25–46.

Clarke, R., Davies, S., Dobson, P. and Waterson, M. (2002), *Buyer Power and Competition in European Food Retailing*, Cheltenham, UK: Edward Elgar.

Coe, N. M. (2014), 'Retail transitions in South East Asia', *The International Review of Retail, Distribution and Consumer Research*, 24(5): 479–499.

Coe, N. M. and Lee, Y. S. (2006), 'The strategic localization of transnational retailers: The case of Samsung-Tesco in South Korea', *Economic Geography*, 82(1): 61–88.

Coe, N. M. and Lee, Y. S. (2013), '"We've learnt to be local": The deepening territorial embeddedness of Samsung-Tesco in South Korea', *Journal of Economic Geography*, 13(2): 327–356.

Cox, P. (2010), *Spedan's Partnership: The Story of John Lewis and Waitrose*, Cambridge, UK: Labatie Books.

Dawson, J. A. (2000), 'Retailing at century end: Some challenges for management and research', *International Review of Retail, Distribution and Consumer Research*, 10(2): 119–148.

Dawson, J. A. (2001), 'Is there a new commerce in Europe?', *International Review of Retail, Distribution and Consumer Research*, 11(3): 287–299.

Dawson, J. A. and Mukoyama, M. (eds) (2014), *Global Strategies in Retailing: Asian and European Experiences*, London: Routledge.

Dawson, J. A., Larke, R. and Mukoyama, M. (eds) (2006), *Strategic Issues in International Retailing*, London: Routledge Curzon.

Dawson, J. A., Mukoyama, M., Choi, S. C. and Larke, R. (eds) (2003), *The Internationalisation of Retailing in Asia*, London: Routledge Curzon.

Deloitte (2014), *Global Powers of Retailing 2014: Retail Beyond Begins*, available at http://www2.deloitte.com/content/dam/Deloitte/global/Documents/Consumer-Business/dttl-CB-GPR14STORES.pdf (accessed 4 December 2015).

Dobson, J. (2015), *How To Save Our Town Centres*, Bristol, UK: Policy Press.

Donaghy, M., Findlay, A. M. and Sparks, L. (2013), 'The evaluation of Business improvement districts: Questions and issues from the Scottish experience', *Local Economy* 28(5): 471–487.

DTI (2004), *The Retail Strategy Group – Driving Change*, London: DTI.

Fernie, J. (1998), 'The breaking of the fourth wave', *International Review of Retail Distribution and Consumer Research*, 8(3): 303–317.

Fernie, J. and Sparks, L. (eds) (2014), *Logistics and Retail Management*, fourth edition, London: Kogan Page.

Findlay, A. M. and Sparks, L. (2013), 'Reviewing high streets and town centres', *Town and Country Planning Journal*, 82(11): 456A–G, available at www.stirlingretail.com (accessed 4 December 2015).

Findlay, A. M. and Sparks, L. (2014), 'Town centre first, second or not at all?', *Town and Country Planning Journal*, 83(4): 158–160, available at www.stirlingretail.com (accessed 4 December 2015).

Fraser, M. (2013), *Community and Enterprise in Scotland's Town Centres*, National Review of Town Centres External Advisory Group Report, Scottish Government, available at www.scotland.gov.uk/Topics/Built-Environment/regeneration/town-centres/review (accessed 4 December 2015).

Grimsey, B. (2012), *Sold Out*. Croydon, UK: Filament Publishing.

Grimsey, B. (2013), *The Grimsey Review: An Alternative for the High Street*, available at www.vanishinghighstreet. com/the-grimseyreview/ (accessed 4 December 2015).

Guy, C. (2006), *Planning for Retail Development*, London: Routledge.

Hallsworth, A. (1994), 'The decentralization of retailing in Britain: The breaking of the third wave', *Professional Geographer*, 46(3): 296–307.

House of Commons Library (2012), 'Supermarkets: Competition inquiries into the groceries market', *Commons Library Standard Note* SN03653, available at http://www.parliament.uk/search/results/?q=SN03653 (accessed 4 December 2015).

Humby, C., Hunt, H. and Phillips, T. (2003), *Scoring Points: How Tesco is Winning Customer Loyalty*, London: Kogan Page.

Jackson, P., Perez del Aguila, R., Clarke, I., Hallsworth, A., De Kervenoael, R. and Kirkup, M. (2006), 'Retail restructuring and consumer choice 2: Understanding consumer choice at the household level', *Environment and Planning A*, 38(1): 47–67.

Kent, T and Brown, R (eds) (2009), *Flagship Marketing: concepts and places*, London: Routledge.

Klein, N. (1999), *No Logo*, New York: Picador.

Kowinski, W. S. (2002), *The Malling of America*, updated second edition, Philadelphia, PA: Xlibris Corporation.

Kozinets, R. V., Sherry, J. F., Deberry-Spence, B., Duhachek, A., Nuttavuthisit, K. and Storm, D. (2002), 'Themed flagship brand stores in the new millennium: Theory, practice, prospects', *Journal of Retailing*, 78(1): 17–29.

Krafft, M. and Mantrala, M. K. (2006), *Retailing in the 21st Century*, Berlin, Germany: Springer Verlag.

Lawless S. (2014) *Black Friday – The Collapse of the American Shopping Mall*, available at www.sephlawless.com (accessed 4 December 2015).

Longstreth, R. (1997), *City Center to Regional Mall*, Cambridge, MA: MIT Press.

Longstreth, R. (1999), *The Drive-In, the Supermarket and the Transformation of Commercial Space in Los Angeles 1914–1941*, Cambridge, MA: MIT Press.

Miller, D., Jackson, P., Thrift, N., Holbrook, B. and Rowlands, M. (1998), *Shopping, Place and Identity*, London: Routledge.

Norman, A. (1999), 'Asda: The accelerated repositioning of a brand', in Gilmore, F. (ed.) *Brand Warriors*, London: Harper Collins, pp. 25–35.

Peñaloza, L. (1999), 'Just doing it: A visual ethnographic study of spectacular consumption behaviour at Nike Town', *Consumption, Markets and Culture*, 2(4): 337–400.

Portas, M. (2011), *The Portas Review: An Independent Review into the Future of our High Streets*, Department for Business, Innovation and Skills, available at www.gov.uk/government/uploads/system/uploads/attachment_data/file/6292/2081646.pdf (accessed 4 December 2015).

Reynolds, J. and Cuthbertson, C. (eds) (2004), *Retail Strategy: The View from the Bridge*, Oxford, UK: Elsevier.

Ryle, S. (2013), *The Making of Tesco*, London: Bantam Press.

Salmon, W. J. and Tordjman, A. (1989), 'The internationalization of retailing', *International Journal of Retailing*, 4(2): 3–16.

Schiller, R. (1987), 'Out of town exodus', in McFadyen, E. (ed.) *The Changing Face of British Retailing*, London: Newman Books, pp. 64–73.

Seth, A. and Randall, G. (1999), *The Grocers: the Rise and Rise of the Supermarket Chains*, London: Kogan Page.

Seth, A. and Randall, G. (2005), *Supermarket Wars: Global Strategies for Food Retailers*, Basingstoke, UK: Palgrave Macmillan.

Sherry, J. F. (1998), 'The soul of the company store, Nike Town, Chicago and the emplaced landscape', in Sherry, J. F. (ed.) *Servicescapes: The Concept of Place in Contemporary Markets*, Lincolnwood, IL: NTC Business Books, pp. 109–146.

Simms, A., Kjell, P. and Potts, R. (2005), *Clone Town Britain: The Survey Results on the Bland State of the Nation*, London: New Economics Foundation.

Smith, A. P. and Sparks, L. (2004), 'All about Eve?', *Journal of Marketing Management*, 20(3/4): 363–385.

The Independent (1995), 'Tesco offers loyalty bonus with discount card', 11 February: 6.

Thomas, C. J. (2006), 'New "high streets" in the suburbs? The growing competitive impact of evolving retail parks', *International Review of Retail Distribution and Consumer Research*, 16(1): 43–68.

Trunk, J. (2011), *Own Label: Sainsbury's Design Studio 1962–1977*, London: Fuel.

Underhill, P. (1999), *Why We Buy: The Science of Shopping*, London: Orion.

UK Trade and Investment (2014), *UK Retail Industry: International Action Plan*, available at https://www.gov.uk/government/publications/uk-retail-industry-international-action-plan/uk-retail-industry-international-action-plan (accessed 8 October 2014).

Walsh, B. (2011), *When the Shopping was Good*, Dublin, Ireland: Irish Academic Press.

Warhurst, P. and Dobson, J. (2014), *Incredible! Plant Veg, Grow a Revolution*, Leicestershire: Matador Press.

Wilson, J., Webster, A. and Vorberg-Rugh, R. (2013), *Building Co-operation: A Business History of The Co-operative Group, 1863–2013*, Oxford, UK: Oxford University Press.

Wood, S., Coe, N. M. and Wrigley, N. (2014), 'Multi-scalar localization and capability transference: Exploring embeddedness in the Asian retail expansion of Tesco', *Regional Studies*, available at http://www.tandfonline.com/doi/abs/10.1080/00343404.2014.926317?journalCode=cres20 (accessed 4 December 2015).

Wrigley, N. and Currah, A. (2003), 'The "stresses" of retail internationalisation: Lessons from Royal Ahold's experience in Latin America', *International Review of Retail, Distribution and Consumer Research*, 13(3): 221–243.

Wrigley, N. and Dolega, L. (2011), 'Resilience, fragility, and adaptation: New evidence on the performance of UK high streets during global economic crisis and its policy implications', *Environment and Planning A*, 43(10): 2337–2363.

Index